Lecture Notes in Computer Science 4981

Magnus Egerstedt Bud Mishra (Eds.)

Hybrid Systems: Computation and Control

11th International Workshop, HSCC 2008
St. Louis, MO, USA, April 22-24, 2008
Proceedings

Springer

Volume Editors

Magnus Egerstedt
Georgia Institute of Technology
School of Electrical and Computer Engineering
Atlanta, GA 30332, USA
E-mail: magnus@ece.gatech.edu

Bud Mishra
Courant Institute of Mathematical Sciences
New York, NY 10012, USA
E-mail: mishra@nyu.edu

Library of Congress Control Number: 2008924197

CR Subject Classification (1998): C.3, C.1.3, F.3, D.2, F.1.2, J.2, I.6

LNCS Sublibrary: SL 1 – Theoretical Computer Science and General Issues

ISSN	0302-9743
ISBN-10	3-540-78928-6 Springer Berlin Heidelberg New York
ISBN-13	978-3-540-78928-4 Springer Berlin Heidelberg New York

Springer is a part of Springer Science+Business Media

springer.com

Printed in Germany

Typesetting: Camera-ready by author, data conversion by Scientific Publishing Services, Chennai, India
Printed on acid-free paper SPIN: 12250455 06/3180 5 4 3 2 1 0

Preface

This volume contains the proceedings of the 11th Workshop on Hybrid Systems: Computation and Control (HSCC 2008) held in St. Louis, Missouri during April 22–24, 2008. The annual workshop on hybrid systems focuses on research in embedded, reactive systems involving the interplay between symbolic/switching and continuous dynamical behaviors. HSCC attracts academic as well as industrial researchers to exchange information on the latest developments of applications and theoretical advancements in the design, analysis, control, optimization, and implementation of hybrid systems, with particular attention to embedded and networked control systems.

New for this year was that HSCC was part of the inaugural CPSWEEK (Cyber-Physical Systems Week) – a co-located cluster of three conferences: HSCC, RTAS (Real-Time and Embedded Technology and Applications Symposium), and IPSN (International Conference on Information Processing in Sensor Networks).

The previous workshops in the series of HSCC were held in Berkeley, USA (1998), Nijmegen, The Netherlands (1999), Pittsburgh, USA (2000), Rome, Italy (2001), Palo Alto, USA (2002), Prague, Czech Republic (2003), Philadelphia, USA (2004), Zurich, Switzerland (2005) , Santa Barbara, USA (2006), and Pisa, Italy (2007).

We would like to thank the Program Committee members and the reviewers for an excellent job of evaluating the submissions and participating in the online Program Committee discussions. We are grateful to the Steering Committee for their helpful guidance and support. We would also like to thank Patrick Martin for putting together these proceedings, and Jiuguang Wang for developing and maintaining the HSCC 2008 website.

January 2008

Magnus Egerstedt
Bud Mishra

Organization

HSCC 2008 was technically co-sponsored by the IEEE Control Systems Society and organized in cooperation with ACM/SIGBED.

General Chairs

Magnus Egerstedt (Georgia Tech, USA)
Bud Mishra (NYU, USA)

Steering Committee

Rajeev Alur (University of Pennsylvania, USA)
Bruce Krogh (Carnegie Mellon University, USA)
Oded Maler (VERIMAG, France)
Manfred Morari (ETH, Switzerland)
George Pappas (University Pennsylvania, USA)
John Rushby (SRI Int., USA)

Program Committee

Karl-Erik Arzen (Lund University, Sweden)
Shun-ichi Azuma (Kyoto University, Japan)
Alexandre Bayen (University of California Berkeley, USA)
Calin Belta (Boston University, USA)
Alberto Bemporad (University of Siena, Italy)
Michael Branicky (Case Western Reserve University, USA)
Jen Davoren (University of Melbourne, Australia)
Bart De Schutter (Delft University, The Netherlands)
Emilio Frazzoli (MIT, USA)
Antoine Girard (University of Grenoble, France)
Alessandro Giua (Università di Cagliari, Italy)
Radu Grosu (S.U.N.Y. at Stony Brook, USA)
Maurice Heemels (Technical University of Eindhoven, The Netherlands)
Joao Hespanha (University of California Santa Barbara, USA)
Jun-ichi Imura (Tokyo Inst. of Technology, Japan)
Karl Henrik Johansson (Royal Inst. of Technology, Sweden)
Eric Klavins (University of Washington, USA)
Daniel Liberzon (University of Illinois Urbana Champaign, USA)
John Lygeros (ETH, Switzerland)
Rupak Majumdar (UCLA, USA)
Ian Mitchell (University of British Columbia, Canada)

Todd Murphey (University of Colorado Boulder, USA)
Carla Piazza (Università degli Studi di Udine, Italy)
Maria Prandini (Politecnico di Milano, Italy)
Jacob Roll (Linkoping University, Sweden)
Olaf Stursberg (Technical University of Munich, Germany)
Paulo Tabuada (UCLA, USA)
Claire Tomlin (University of California Berkeley, USA)
Yorai Wardi (Georgia Tech, USA)

Referees

A. Abate
A. Alessio
M. Althoff
S. Amin
A. Anta
M. Antoniotti
A. Arsie
K.E. Arzen
J. van Ast
S. Azuma
G. Batt
A. Bayen
C. Belta
A. Bemporad
M. Bernadsky
D. Bernardini
A. Bhatia
J. Bishop
M. Boccadoro
L. Bortolussi
M. Branicky
D. Bresolin
B. Brogliatio
M. Bujorianu
M.P. Cabasino
M. Capiluppi
A. Casagrande
G. Chaloulos
D. Chaterjee
E. Cinquemani
P. Collins
J. Davoren
E. De Santis
B. De Schutter
B. Djeridane
J. Enright
G. Fainekos
P. Fiorini
M. Franceschelli
E. Frazzoli
A. Girard
A. Giua
R. Goebel
R. Grosu
J. Habibi
M. Heemels
H. Herencia-Zapana
J. Hespanha
M. Hofbaur
J. Imura
K.H. Johansson
A. Julius
S. Karaman
E. Klavins
I. Klein
M. Kloetzer
K. Kobayshi
M. Lazar
C. Le Guernic
D. Liberzon
J. Lofberg
J. Lygeros
I. Lymperopoulos
C. Lyzell
C. Mahulea
R. Majumdar
M. Mazo
A. Mesquita
A. Milias-Argeitis
I. Mitchell
T. Murphey
N. Napp
H. Ohlsson
M. Pavone
S. Perk
C. Piazza
G. Pola
M. Prandini
G. Puppis
J. Richter
O. Riganelli
J. Roll
A. Rondepierre
S. Samii
R. Sanfelice
C. Seatzu
Y. Sharon
A. Singh
M. Sobotka
O. Stursberg
P. Tabuada
A. Tanwani
Y. Tazaki
D. Thorsley
C. Tomlin
R. Vidal
Y. Wardi
P. Ye
B. Yordanov

Sponsoring Institutions

Georgia Institute of Technology
US National Science Foundation

Table of Contents

Regular Papers

Markov Set-Chains as Abstractions of Stochastic Hybrid Systems 1
Alessandro Abate, Alessandro D'Innocenzo, Maria D. Di Benedetto, and Shankar S. Sastry

Co-simulation Tools for Networked Control Systems 16
Ahmad T. Al-Hammouri, Michael S. Branicky, and Vincenzo Liberatore

On the Maximum Principle for Impulsive Hybrid Systems 30
Vadim Azhmyakov, Sid Ahmed Attia, and Jörg Raisch

Algebraic Identification of MIMO SARX Models 43
Laurent Bako and René Vidal

Contract-Based Design for Computation and Verification of a Closed-Loop Hybrid System 58
L. Benvenuti, A. Ferrari, E. Mazzi, and A.L. Sangiovanni Vincentelli

Controller Synthesis with Budget Constraints 72
Krishnendu Chatterjee, Rupak Majumdar, and Thomas A. Henzinger

Trading Infinite Memory for Uniform Randomness in Timed Games ... 87
Krishnendu Chatterjee, Thomas A. Henzinger, and Vinayak S. Prabhu

Solutions to Switched Hamilton-Jacobi Equations and Conservation Laws Using Hybrid Components 101
Christian G. Claudel and Alexandre M. Bayen

Lost in Translation: Hybrid-Time Flows vs. Real-Time Transitions 116
P.J.L. Cuijpers and M.A. Reniers

A Control Lyapunov Approach to Predictive Control of Hybrid Systems 130
S. Di Cairano, M. Lazar, A. Bemporad, and W.P.M.H. Heemels

Discrete and Hybrid Stochastic State Estimation Algorithms for Networked Control Systems 144
S. Di Cairano, K.H. Johansson, A. Bemporad, and R.M. Murray

Anytime Control Algorithms for Embedded Real-Time Systems 158
Daniele Fontanelli, Luca Greco, and Antonio Bicchi

Stochastic Satisfiability Modulo Theory: A Novel Technique for the Analysis of Probabilistic Hybrid Systems ... 172
Martin Fränzle, Holger Hermanns, and Tino Teige

A Counterexample-Guided Approach to Parameter Synthesis for Linear Hybrid Automata ... 187
Goran Frehse, Sumit Kumar Jha, and Bruce H. Krogh

Approximately Bisimilar Symbolic Models for Incrementally Stable Switched Systems ... 201
Antoine Girard, Giordano Pola, and Paulo Tabuada

Zonotope/Hyperplane Intersection for Hybrid Systems Reachability Analysis ... 215
Antoine Girard and Colas Le Guernic

Learning and Detecting Emergent Behavior in Networks of Cardiac Myocytes ... 229
R. Grosu, E. Bartocci, F. Corradini, E. Entcheva, S.A. Smolka, and A. Wasilewska

Compositional Modeling and Minimization of Time-Inhomogeneous Markov Chains ... 244
Tingting Han, Joost-Pieter Katoen, and Alexandru Mereacre

Observer-Based Control of Linear Complementarity Systems ... 259
W.P.M.H. Heemels, M.K. Camlibel, B. Brogliato, and J.M. Schumacher

Complementarity Systems in Constrained Steady-State Optimal Control ... 273
A. Jokic, M. Lazar, and P.P.J. van den Bosch

Dealing with Nondeterminism in Symbolic Control ... 287
Marius Kloetzer and Calin Belta

Safety and Liveness in Intelligent Intersections ... 301
Hemant Kowshik, Derek Caveney, and P.R. Kumar

LTLC: Linear Temporal Logic for Control ... 316
YoungMin Kwon and Gul Agha

Switched and PieceWise Nonlinear Hybrid System Identification ... 330
Fabien Lauer and Gérard Bloch

Verification of Supervisory Control Software Using State Proximity and Merging ... 344
Flavio Lerda, James Kapinski, Edmund M. Clarke, and Bruce H. Krogh

Optimotaxis: A Stochastic Multi-agent Optimization Procedure with Point Measurements 358
Alexandre R. Mesquita, João P. Hespanha, and Karl Åström

Noncausal Optimal Tracking of Linear Switched Systems 372
Gou Nakura

Realization Theory for Discrete-Time Semi-algebraic Hybrid Systems ... 386
Mihály Petreczky and René Vidal

A Decidable Class of Planar Linear Hybrid Systems 401
Pavithra Prabhakar, Vladimeros Vladimerou, Mahesh Viswanathan, and Geir E. Dullerud

Reachability of Uncertain Nonlinear Systems Using a Nonlinear Hybridization 415
Nacim Ramdani, Nacim Meslem, and Yves Candau

Modeling and Simulation of Biochemical Processes Using Stochastic Hybrid Systems: The Sugar Cataract Development Process 429
Derek Riley, Xenofon Koutsoukos, and Kasandra Riley

Distributed Lyapunov Functions in Analysis of Graph Models of Software 443
Mardavij Roozbehani, Alexandre Megretski, Emilio Frazzoli, and Eric Feron

On the Optimality of Dubins Paths across Heterogeneous Terrain 457
Ricardo G. Sanfelice and Emilio Frazzoli

Switching Surface Design for Periodically Operated Discretely Controlled Continuous Systems 471
Axel Schild and Jan Lunze

Discrete Dynamics of Two-Dimensional Nonlinear Hybrid Automata ... 486
Lorenzo Sella and Pieter Collins

Input-to-State Stabilization with Quantized Output Feedback 500
Yoav Sharon and Daniel Liberzon

Bisimilar Finite Abstractions of Interconnected Systems 514
Yuichi Tazaki and Jun-ichi Imura

On Controllability of Timed Continuous Petri Nets 528
C. Renato Vázquez, Antonio Ramírez, Laura Recalde, and Manuel Silva

Parameter Synthesis for Piecewise Affine Systems from Temporal Logic Specifications 542
Boyan Yordanov and Calin Belta

Necessary Conditions for the Impulsive Time-Optimal Control of Finite-Dimensional Lagrangian Systems 556
Kerim Yunt

Composition of Motion Description Languages 570
Wenqi Zhang and Herbert G. Tanner

On Optimal Quadratic Regulation for Discrete-Time Switched Linear Systems 584
Wei Zhang and Jianghai Hu

Short Papers

Approximation of General Stochastic Hybrid Systems by Switching Diffusions with Random Hybrid Jumps 598
Alessandro Abate, Maria Prandini, John Lygeros, and Shankar Sastry

On Stability of Switched Linear Hyperbolic Conservation Laws with Reflecting Boundaries 602
Saurabh Amin, Falk M. Hante, and Alexandre M. Bayen

Sampling-Based Resolution-Complete Algorithms for Safety Falsification of Linear Systems 606
Amit Bhatia and Emilio Frazzoli

Reachability Analysis of Stochastic Hybrid Systems by Optimal Control 610
Manuela L. Bujorianu, John Lygeros, and Rom Langerak

An Integrated Approach to Parametric and Discrete Fault Diagnosis in Hybrid Systems 614
Matthew Daigle, Xenofon Koutsoukos, and Gautam Biswas

d-IRA: A Distributed Reachability Algorithm for Analysis of Linear Hybrid Automata 618
Sumit Kumar Jha

Sufficient Conditions for Zeno Behavior in Lagrangian Hybrid Systems 622
Andrew Lamperski and Aaron D. Ames

Separation in Stability Analysis of Piecewise Linear Systems in Discrete Time 626
Ji-Woong Lee

Level Set Methods for Computing Reachable Sets of Hybrid Systems with Differential Algebraic Equation Dynamics 630
Ian M. Mitchell and Yoshihiko Susuki

Approximate Control Design for Solar Driven Sensor Nodes 634
Clemens Moser, Lothar Thiele, Davide Brunelli, and Luca Benini

Modular Development of Hybrid Systems for Verification in *Coq* 638
Milad Niqui and Olga Tveretina

Steering a Leader-Follower Team Via Linear Consensus 642
Fabio Pasqualetti, Simone Martini, and Antonio Bicchi

Logical Verification and Systematic Parametric Analysis in Train Control 646
André Platzer and Jan-David Quesel

Information Theoretical Approach to Identification of Hybrid Systems 650
Li Pu, Jinchun Hu, and Badong Chen

A Policy Iteration Technique for Time Elapse over Template Polyhedra (Extended Abstract) 654
Sriram Sankaranarayanan, Thao Dang, and Franjo Ivančić

Generating Box Invariants 658
Ashish Tiwari

Qualitative Stability Patterns for Lotka-Volterra Systems on Rectangles 662
Laurent Tournier and Jean-Luc Gouzé

Sampled-Data Event Control of Hybrid Systems for Control Specifications Given by Predicates 666
Yoshiyuki Tsuchie and Toshimitsu Ushio

On the Timing of Discrete Events in Event-Driven Control Systems 670
Manel Velasco, Pau Martí, and Camilo Lozoya

Decentralized Event-Triggered Broadcasts over Networked Control Systems 674
Xiaofeng Wang and Michael D. Lemmon

Author Index 679

Markov Set-Chains as Abstractions of Stochastic Hybrid Systems*

Alessandro Abate[1], Alessandro D'Innocenzo[2], Maria D. Di Benedetto[2], and Shankar S. Sastry[3]

[1] Department of Aeronautics and Astronautics, Stanford University - USA
aabate@stanford.edu
[2] Department of Electrical Engineering and Computer Science, Center of Excellence DEWS, University of L'Aquila - Italy
{adinnoce,dibenede}@ing.univaq.it
[3] Department of Electrical Engineering and Computer Sciences, University of California, Berkeley - USA
sastry@eecs.berkeley.edu

Abstract. The objective of this study is to introduce an abstraction procedure that applies to a general class of dynamical systems, that is to discrete-time stochastic hybrid systems (dt-SHS). The procedure abstracts the original dt-SHS into a Markov set-chain (MSC) in two steps. First, a Markov chain (MC) is obtained by partitioning the hybrid state space, according to a controllable parameter, into non-overlapping domains and computing transition probabilities for these domains according to the dynamics of the dt-SHS. Second, explicit error bounds for the abstraction that depend on the above parameter are derived, and are associated to the computed transition probabilities of the MC, thus obtaining a MSC. We show that one can arbitrarily increase the accuracy of the abstraction by tuning the controllable parameter, albeit at an increase of the cardinality of the MSC. Resorting to a number of results from the MSC literature allows the analysis of the dynamics of the original dt-SHS. In the present work, the asymptotic behavior of the dt-SHS dynamics is assessed within the abstracted framework.

1 Introduction and Objectives

Hybrid Systems (HS) are dynamical systems with interleaved continuous and discrete behaviors. Their great expressive power is offset by two main issues. The first is the subtlety of their theoretical investigation: much research has been directed to further the understanding of their system-theoretical properties. The second is the problem of scalability, in particular with respect to computational complexity. For instance, the formal verification of properties of the system (e.g. *model checking* techniques [4]) is complicated by the continuity of the state-space and by the interaction between continuous and discrete dynamics.

* This work was partially supported by European Commission under Project IST NoE HYCON contract n. 511368, STREP project n. TREN/07/FP6AE/S07.71574/037180 IFLY, and by the NSF grant CCR-0225610.

M. Egerstedt and B. Mishra (Eds.): HSCC 2008, LNCS 4981, pp. 1–15, 2008.

A technique which is often employed to cope with system complexity and dimensionality is *abstraction*. According to this approach, a system with a smaller state space (possibly finite) is obtained, which is equivalent to the system under study. Systems equivalence is usually defined via the notions of language equivalence and bisimulation [2]. Recently, *approximate* notions of system equivalence [7] have been developed, where a metric is introduced to quantify the distance between the original system and the abstraction. The contribution in [6] proposes an algorithm to construct an approximate abstraction of a HS by means of a timed automaton. In [9] a notion of approximate bisimilarity is proposed for a class of Stochastic Hybrid Systems (SHS), that is HS which are endowed with probabilistic terms.

The present contribution introduces a formal abstraction procedure for a general class of SHS. This work refers to a discrete time framework and introduces the explicit presence of spatial guards in a class of SHS (named dt-SHS), and shows that it is possible to express the transition probability function in a compact way by employing the concept of probabilistic reachability. After introducing a partitioning procedure on the hybrid state space, the transition probabilities between these partitions are approximately computed, thus generating a Markov chain (MC). By raising some continuity assumptions on the entities that characterize the dynamics of the dt-SHS, explicit error bounds are associated to the transition probabilities. These error bounds depend on the diameter of the introduced partitions and can then be refined by this parameter. This allows to formally set up a Markov set-chain (MSC) associated to the partitioning procedure. The asymptotic behavior of the MSC is then related to that of the dt-SHS.

The present technique is analogous to the line of work presented in [10], which proposes a discretization of the continuous dynamics of a Markov process into that of a MC, defined on a grid on the state-space. The contribution shows weak convergence of the MC process to the original one, but no error bounds are explicitly derived. Both this work and [10] approximate the original process with a probabilistic discrete structure. This provides a connection to *model checking* of stochastic timed automata (which is a subclass of SHS), that has been investigated in [3]. A general understanding of the area of probabilistic model checking for SHS is however still far. As a first result towards this goal, we have shown the ability to construct a finite state abstraction that possibly allows us to efficiently compute the steady state of the original system with arbitrary precision.

2 The dt-SHS Model

This section formalizes the dt-SHS model first mentioned in section 1. The mathematical framework is inspired by that in [1], but we model the presence of a physical forcing guard set rather than introducing state-dependent transition probabilities. The use of a discrete time framework is motivated by the simplicity in dealing with measurability issues for events on the underlying probability space, as well as by the direct computability of transition probabilities.

Definition 1 (dt-SHS). *A discrete time stochastic hybrid system is a tuple* $\mathcal{H} = (\mathcal{Q}, \mathcal{S}^*, \mathcal{G}, T, R)$, *where*

- $\mathcal{Q} := \{q_1, q_2, \ldots, q_m\}$, *for some finite* $m \in \mathbb{N}$, *is the discrete component of the state space;*
- $\mathcal{S}^* := \cup_{i \in \mathcal{Q}} \{i\} \times \mathcal{D}_i^*$, *is the hybrid state space, made up by a set of continuous "domains" for each mode* $i \in \mathcal{Q}$, *each of which is defined to be a compact subset* $\mathcal{D}_i^* \subset \mathbb{R}^{n(i)}$. *The function* $n : \mathcal{Q} \to \mathbb{N}$ *assigns to each* $i \in \mathcal{Q}$ *the dimension of the continuous state space* $\mathbb{R}^{n(i)}$;
- $\mathcal{G} := \cup_{i \in \mathcal{Q}} \{i\} \times \mathcal{G}_i, \mathcal{G}_i = \{g_{ij}; j \in \mathcal{Q}, j \neq i, g_{ij} \subseteq \mathcal{D}_i^*\}$ *is the set of spatial guards. We assume that* $\forall i, j, k \in \mathcal{Q}, i \neq j \neq k, g_{ij} \cap g_{ik} = \emptyset$, *and that the guards have non-trivial volume:* $\mathcal{L}(g_{ij}) \neq 0, \forall i, j \in \mathcal{Q}, j \neq i$, *where* $\mathcal{L}(A)$ *denotes the Lebesgue measure associated to any Borel subset* $A \subset \mathcal{B}(\mathcal{D}_i^*)$. *Let us further introduce the set* $\mathcal{D}_i := \mathcal{D}_i^* \backslash \left\{ \cup_{j \in \mathcal{Q}, j \neq i} g_{ij} \right\}$, *the "invariant" of mode* i, *and* $\mathcal{S} := \cup_{i \in \mathcal{Q}} \{i\} \times \mathcal{D}_i$;
- $T : \mathcal{B}(\mathcal{D}_{(\cdot)}^*) \times \mathcal{S} \to [0, 1]$ *is a Borel-measurable stochastic kernel (the "transition kernel") on* $\mathcal{D}_{(\cdot)}^*$ *given* $\mathcal{S}$, *which assigns to each* $s = (q, x) \in \mathcal{S}$ *a probability measure on the Borel space* $(\mathcal{D}_q^*, \mathcal{B}(\mathcal{D}_q^*))$: $T(dx|(q, x))$;
- $R : \mathcal{B}(\mathcal{D}_{(\cdot)}^*) \times \mathcal{G} \times \mathcal{Q} \to [0, 1]$ *is a Borel-measurable stochastic kernel (the "reset kernel") on* $\mathcal{D}_{(\cdot)}^*$, *given* $\mathcal{G} \times \mathcal{Q}$, *that assigns to each* $s = (q, x) \in \mathcal{G}$, *and* $q' \in \mathcal{Q}, q' \neq q$, *a probability measure on the Borel space* $(\mathcal{D}_{(q')}^*, \mathcal{B}(\mathcal{D}_{(q')}^*))$: $R(dx|(q, x), q')$. □

The system initialization at the initial time (say $k = 0$) is specified by some probability measure $\pi_0 : \mathcal{B}(\mathcal{S}^*) \to [0, 1]$ on the Borel space $(\mathcal{S}^*, \mathcal{B}(\mathcal{S}^*))$. Here again $\mathcal{B}(\mathcal{S}^*)$ is the σ-field generated by the subsets of $\mathcal{S}^*$ of the form $\cup_q \{q\} \times B_q$, with B_q denoting a Borel set in $\mathcal{D}_q^*$. For details on the measurability and metric properties of $\mathcal{H}$, the reader is invited to refer to [1,5]. Notice that the transition and reset kernels (respectively T and R) have different domains of definition ($\mathcal{S}$ and $\mathcal{G} \times \mathcal{Q}$), but the same support ($\mathcal{D}^*$). Next, we define the notion of execution for the above model (throughout the paper, random processes will be denoted in bold fonts, while random variables in normal typesets).

Definition 2 (Execution). *Consider a dt-SHS* $\mathcal{H} = (\mathcal{Q}, n, \mathcal{G}, T, R)$. *An execution for* $\mathcal{H}$, *associated with an initial distribution* π_0, *is a stochastic process* $\{\mathbf{s}(k), k \in [0, N], N \in \mathbb{N}\}$ *with values in* $\mathcal{S}^*$, *whose sample paths are obtained according to the following algorithm:*

extract from $\mathcal{S}^*$ a value $s_0 = (q_0, x_0)$ for $\mathbf{s}(0)$, according to the distribution π_0;
for $k = 0$ to $N - 1$,

  if there is a $j \neq q_k, j \in \mathcal{Q}$, such that $x_k \in g_{q_k, j}$,

  then extract a value $s_{k+1} \in \mathcal{S}^*$ for $\mathbf{s}(k + 1)$, according to $R(\cdot\,|s_k, j)$;

  else extract a value $s_{k+1} \in \mathcal{S}^*$ for $\mathbf{s}(k + 1)$, according to $T(\cdot\,|s_k)$;

end. □

As mentioned, the introduced (autonomous) dt-SHS is related to the (controlled) SHS in [1], where the additional presence of a stochastic kernel allows for the presence of spontaneous jumps within the invariants. The theory developed in this work can be extended to account for similar terms.

3 Markov Set-Chains

We define here the concept of Markov set-chain, which will be used as an abstraction framework for dt-SHS. We also recall some useful results from [8], which contains a compendium of literature on the subject.

Definition 3 (Transition Set). *Let $P, Q \in \mathbb{R}^{n \times n}$, with $P, Q \geq 0$(that is component-wise nonnegative matrices, not necessarily stochastic), with $P \leq Q$. We define a "transition set" as:*

$$[P, Q] = \{A \in \mathbb{R}^{n \times n} : A \text{ is a stochastic matrix and } P \leq A \leq Q\}. \qquad \square$$

In the proceeding, we assume that the transition set $[P, Q] \neq \varnothing$. When the "bounding matrices" P, Q will be clear from the context, we will use the notation $[\Pi]$ to denote such compact (possibly infinite) set of stochastic matrices. We can define a Markov set-chain as a non-homogeneous, discrete-time Markov chain, where the transition probabilities vary non-deterministically within a compact transition set $[\Pi]$. More formally,

Definition 4 (Markov set-chain). *Let $[\Pi]$ be a transition set, i.e. a compact set of $n \times n$ stochastic matrices. Consider the set of all non-homogeneous Markov chains having all their transition matrices in $[\Pi]$. We call the sequence*

$$[\Pi], [\Pi]^2, \cdots$$

a Markov set-chain, where $[\Pi]^k$ is defined by induction as the compact set of all possible products $A_1, \cdots, A_k$, such that, $\forall i = 1, \cdots, k, A_i \in [\Pi]$.

Similarly, let $[\pi_0]$ be a compact set of $1 \times n$ stochastic vectors, introduced as in Def. 3. We call $[\pi_0]$ the initial distribution set. $\square$

The compact set $[\pi_k] = [\pi_0][\Pi]^k$ is the k-th distribution set and

$$[\pi_0], [\pi_0][\Pi], \cdots$$

is the Markov set-chain with initial distribution set $[\pi_0]$.

It can be shown that each element $[\pi_k]$ is a convex polytope if $[\pi_0]$ is a convex polytope and $[\Pi]$ is a transition set. It should be noticed that the number of vertices of $[\pi_k]$ increases with k, thus the computational burden to obtain $[\pi_k]$ for large values of k should be accounted for. However, it is possible to compute *tight* (see [8]) upper and lower bounding matrices L_k, H_k for $[\pi_k]$ in a very efficient way, in particular the computation of L_k, H_k can be recursively obtained from L_{k-1}, H_{k-1}.

Definition 5 (Coefficient of Ergodicity). *For any stochastic matrix A, its coefficient of ergodicity is defined as follows:*

$$\mathcal{T}(A) = \frac{1}{2} \max_{i,j} ||a_i - a_j||,$$

where a_i is the i–th row of A and $|| \cdot ||$ on a vector is the standard 1–norm. If $\mathcal{T}(A) < 1$, A is said to be scrambling. □

The above definition can be directly extended to Markov set-chains:

Definition 6. *For any transition set $[\Pi]$, its coefficient of ergodicity is defined as follows:*

$$\mathcal{T}([\Pi]) = \max_{A \in [\Pi]} \mathcal{T}(A).$$ □

Notice that since $\mathcal{T}(\cdot)$ is a continuous function and $[\Pi]$ a compact set, the maximum argument of $\mathcal{T}([\Pi])$ exists. Also notice that $\mathcal{T}([\Pi]) \in [0, 1], as \mathcal{T}(A) \in [0, 1]$. This value provides a measure of the "contractive" nature of the Markov set-chain: the smaller $\mathcal{T}([\Pi])$, the more contractive the MSC. This will become clear when studying the asymptotic properties of the MSC, and is related to the regularity properties of the matrices that build up the MSC [8]. The exact value of $\mathcal{T}([\Pi])$ can be hard to compute, but it can be upper bounded as follows:

Theorem 1. *Let $[\Pi]$ be the interval $[P, Q]$ and $A \in [\Pi]$, then:*

$$|\mathcal{T}([\Pi]) - \mathcal{T}(A)| \leq ||Q - P||$$

The above matrix norm is taken from [8] and is a modification of the induced 1-norm. The following notion connects to Definition 5:

Definition 7 (Scrambling Integer). *Suppose $r \geq 1$ is such that $\mathcal{T}(A_1 \cdots A_r) < 1, \forall A_1, \cdots, A_r \in [\Pi]$. Then $[\Pi]$ is said to be product scrambling and r its scrambling integer.* □

We now illustrate some results on the convergence of MSC.

Theorem 2. *Given a product scrambling MSC with transition set $[\Pi]$ and initial distribution set $[\pi_0]$, then there exists a unique limit set $[\pi_\infty]$ such that $[\pi_\infty][\Pi] = [\pi_\infty]$. Moreover, let r be the scrambling integer of $[\Pi]$. Then for any positive integer h, and according to the Hausdorff metric $d(\cdot)$ on compact sets:*

$$d([\pi_h], [\pi_\infty]) \leq K\beta^h \tag{1}$$

where $K = [\mathcal{T}([\Pi]^r)]^{-1} d([\pi_0], [\pi_\infty])$ and $\beta = \mathcal{T}([\Pi]^r)^{\frac{1}{r}} < 1$. Thus

$$\lim_{h \to \infty} [\pi_h] = \lim_{h \to \infty} [\pi_0][\Pi]^h = [\pi_\infty].$$

□

As we argued before, the exact computation of $[\pi_\infty]$ can be expensive. However, it is possible to use the upper and lower bounding matrices L_k, H_k mentioned above to obtain an accurate estimate of $[\pi_\infty]$ with a reasonable computational complexity. In fact, L_k, H_k converge to a value L_∞, H_∞ such that $[\pi_\infty] \subseteq [L_\infty, H_\infty]$. Define the diameter of a compact set (referred to either matrices or vectors) as

$$\Delta([\Pi]) = \max_{A,A' \in [\Pi]} ||A - A'||.$$

The following result provides an efficient procedure to compute an upper bound for the diameter of the limit set $[\pi_\infty]$.

Theorem 3. *Given a product scrambling Markov set-chain with transition set* $[\Pi] = [P, Q]$ *and such that* $\mathcal{T}([\Pi]) < 1$, *then*

$$\Delta([\pi_\infty]) \leq \frac{\Delta([\Pi])}{1 - \mathcal{T}([\Pi])} \leq \frac{||Q - P||}{1 - \mathcal{T}(A) - ||Q - P||},$$

for any $A \in [\Pi]$. *The second inequality holds only if* $\mathcal{T}(A) + ||Q - P|| \leq 1$. □

4 Probabilistic Dynamics

The model described in Definition 1 is quite general and allows for a wealth of possible behaviors. However, even in the case of further knowledge of the structure of the dynamics (beyond the general stochastic kernels T, R that characterize it), is in general not translatable into a closed-form expression for the solution process of $\mathcal{H}$. Thus, in order to study the dynamical properties of $\mathcal{H}$, two directions can be pursued. The first looks at the ensemble of possible realizations that originate from the initial distribution, according to the steps in Definition 2. Monte Carlo simulations are a known example of this approach. The second, instead, characterizes probabilistically the presence of the solution process in certain regions of $\mathcal{S}^*$, as time progresses. More precisely, it is of interest to define the following likelihood: given a point $s_0 \in \mathcal{S}^*$, what is the probability that the solution process $\mathbf{s}(\cdot)$ of $\mathcal{H}$, starting from s_0, is located in the set $A \in \mathcal{B}(\mathcal{S}^*)$ at time $k > 0$? Similarly, given a point $s_0 \in \mathcal{S}^*$, what is the probability that the solution process $\mathbf{s}(\cdot)$ of $\mathcal{H}$ stays within the set $A \in \mathcal{B}(\mathcal{S}^*)$, if $s_0 \in A$, for all the time $k \in [0, N], N < \infty$?

These and similar quantities leverage the ability of defining and computing the concept of *probabilistic reachability* [1]. Interestingly, these stochastic reachability problems are related to the two analogous deterministic approaches taken in [6] for constructing finite abstractions of (deterministic) HS. The two probabilistic kernels T and R depend on, respectively, the invariant and the guard sets. We are thus particularly interested in computing the transition probabilities between these subsets of the hybrid state space. For instance, considering two modes $q, q' \in \mathcal{Q}$, we call $p_{q,q'}(x)$ the probability that a trajectory, starting from a point $(q, x) \in \mathcal{S}$, has to transition in a time step (according to $T(\cdot|(q, x))$) into any other domain $q' \neq q$ by intersecting the corresponding guard, or possibly to continue evolving in $q' = q$:

$$p_{q,q'}(x) \triangleq \int_{g_{q,q'}} T(dy|(q,x)), \text{ if } q' \neq q, \tag{2}$$

$$p_{q,q}(x) \triangleq \int_{\mathcal{D}_q} T(dy|(q,x)) = 1 - \sum_{\substack{q' \in \mathcal{Q} \\ q' \neq q}} \int_{g_{q,q'}} T(dy|(q,x)).$$

The case where $(q,x) \in \mathcal{S}^* \backslash \mathcal{S}$, which is associated to the probability that the trajectory is reset, according to $R(\cdot|(q,x),q')$, into an invariant $q' \neq q$, is similar. Let us denote this probability $p_{(q,q'),q'}(x)$:

$$p_{(q,q'),q'}(x) \triangleq \int_{\mathcal{D}_{q'}} R(dy|(q,x),q'). \tag{3}$$

Notice that, as the support of T and of R coincides, the contribution of both terms is similar, except for the fact that T is associated with a one time-step continuous motion, while R to an instantaneous reset.

Investigating similar quantities for dynamics over a longer time interval involves conditioning the probability backwards in time and referring to the "template quantities" discussed above. For instance, we may be interested in the following transition, for $q,r,s \in \mathcal{Q}, q \neq r, r \neq s$: $x \in g_{q,r} \xrightarrow{R} \mathcal{D}_r \xrightarrow{T} g_{r,s}$; and the associated probability $p_{(q,r),r}(x)p_{r,s}(\cdot)$. This is computed by:

$$\begin{aligned} \mathcal{P}\left(\mathbf{s}(1) \in g_{r,s}|\mathbf{s}(0) = (q,x) \in g_{q,r}\right) &= \int_{\mathcal{D}_r}\int_{g_{r,s}} R(dy|(q,x),r)T(dz|(r,y)) \\ &= \int_{\mathcal{D}_r} R(dy|(q,x),r)p_{r,s}(y) \end{aligned} \tag{4}$$

This quantity shows that the contributions of the one-step probabilities over time have to be necessarily "averaged" over the influence of the stochastic kernels that precede them. This will also hold with reference to a particular initial distribution π_0. As already mentioned, the interplay between transition and reset probabilities is a characteristic feature of SHS.

The terms in (2)-(3), and their multiplications, are then characteristic of the computations we want to perform to study the dynamics of the dt-SHS $\mathcal{H}$. In principle, we may be able to associate a transition probability to each couple of elements taken from the set of invariants and guards. This would allow to abstract the dynamics of $\mathcal{H}$ into those of a discrete m^2-dimensional MC (where $m = \mathtt{card}(\mathcal{Q})$). However, by closely looking at the quantity in (2) [resp. (3)], it becomes clear that it is necessary to compute the transition probabilities over the whole invariant $\mathcal{D}_q$ [over the whole guard $g_{q,q'}$], averaged over the contribution of the incoming reset maps $R(\cdot|(\cdot,\cdot),q)$ [the transition kernel $T(\cdot|(q,\cdot))$]. To fully make sense, these last quantities would have to depend on other probabilities, and so on backwards, until integrating over an initial distribution. This computation is rather unfeasible, and its bottleneck hinges on the dependence of T and R on the continuous component of the hybrid state space.

Rather than aiming, as just proposed, at abstracting the dynamics of the dt-SHS $\mathcal{H}$ into an m^2-dimensional MC, we may instead allow an abstraction into a higher dimensional structure, while improving the precision of the approximation. The technique to achieve this, described in the following section, is based on a continuity assumption on the dynamics, and a state-partitioning procedure.

5 Abstraction Procedure

This section describes the abstraction procedure for the dt-SHS model $\mathcal{H}$ of section 2. The dt-SHS $\mathcal{H}$ will be abstracted into a Markov set-chain $\mathcal{M}$, described by a *one-step* transition set $[\Pi] = [P, Q]$. The computations involved in obtaining the abstraction are reduced to integrations over the continuous part of the hybrid state space. The procedure introduces some necessary approximations in order to perform the computations feasibly. However, explicit bounds on these errors will be obtained, provided some continuity assumptions are raised. The association of these bounds to the computed transition probabilities allows a connection with the theory of MSC, as it provides a direct definition of the transition set $[\Pi]$ of $\mathcal{M}$. The precision of the abstraction will depend on a parameter δ. It is desirable for the abstraction to be endowed, in the limit as $\delta \to 0$, with some convergence properties to the original dt-SHS $\mathcal{H}$.

Approximation of State-Dependent Transitions and Resets

As discussed in section 4, the dependence of transition and reset kernels on, respectively, the invariant and the guard set, and their continuous supports, renders the computation of transition probabilities via nested integrals of product terms as in (4) computationally unattractive. Introducing some "regularity assumptions" on the probabilistic kernels, it is possible to achieve a "state-memoryless" approximation for these transition probabilities, whereby their calculation does not depend on the continuous part of the hybrid state-space $\mathcal{S}$.

Let us suppose that the stochastic kernels T and R, which depend on the continuous component of the hybrid state in Definition 1 of $\mathcal{H}$, admit densities respectively t and r. Similarly, let us assume the initial probability distribution π_0 has a density p_0. It is supposed that p_0, t, and r satisfy the following Lipschitz condition.

Assumption 1 (Lipschitz Continuity of the Stochastic Kernels)

1. $|p_0(s) - p_0(s')| \leq k_0 \|x - x'\|$, *for all* $s = (q, x), s' = (q, x') \in \mathcal{D}_q^*$;
2. $|t(\bar{x}|s) - t(\bar{x}|s')| \leq k_T \|x - x'\|$, *for all* $s = (q, x), s' = (q, x') \in \mathcal{D}_q$, *and* $(q, \bar{x}) \in \mathcal{D}_q^*$;
3. $|r(\bar{x}|s, \bar{q}) - r(\bar{x}|s', \bar{q})| \leq k_R \|x - x'\|$, *for all* $s = (q, x), s' = (q, x') \in \mathcal{D}_q^* \backslash \mathcal{D}_q$, $(\bar{q}, \bar{x}) \in \mathcal{D}_{\bar{q}}^*$, *and* $\bar{q} \in \mathcal{Q}, \bar{q} \neq q$,

where k_0, k_T, *and* k_R *are finite positive constants.* □

Let us also recall the implicit assumption, raised for computations' sake in Definition 1, that for each $q \in \mathcal{Q}$, the continuous domain $\mathcal{D}_q^*$ associated to such mode is a bounded subset of $\mathbb{R}^{n(q)}$.

Let us introduce the following quantities (see Table 1 for a compendium of them), describing the (finite) volume measures of particular subsets of the domains: $\lambda_q^* = \mathcal{L}(\mathcal{D}_q^*), \lambda_q = \mathcal{L}(\mathcal{D}_q), \lambda_{q,r} = \mathcal{L}(g_{q,r}), \lambda = \sum_{q\in\mathcal{Q}} \mathcal{L}(D_q), \lambda^* = \sum_{q\in\mathcal{Q}} \mathcal{L}(D_q^*)$, where $\mathcal{L}$ is the Lebesgue measure of a bounded subset of a Euclidean space. Since $\mathcal{D}_q^* = \mathcal{D}_q \cup \mathcal{G}_q$, it follows that $\forall q \in \mathcal{Q}, \lambda_q = \lambda_q^* - \sum_{\substack{r\in\mathcal{Q}\\ r\neq q}} \lambda_{q,r}$.

Let us now focus on the computation of the transition probabilities. Consider a mode $q \in \mathcal{Q}$, and any two points $(q,x),(q,x') \in \mathcal{D}_q$. Then, with reference to the quantity in (2) and according to Assumption 1, let us compute, $\forall r \in \mathcal{Q}, r \neq q$,

$$\begin{aligned}|p_{q,r}(x) - p_{q,r}(x')| &= \left| \int_{g_{q,r}} T(dz|(q,x)) - \int_{g_{q,r}} T(dz|(q,x')) \right| \\ &\leq \int_{g_{q,r}} |T(dz|(q,x)) - T(dz|(q,x'))| \leq \lambda_{q,r} k_T \|x - x'\|.\end{aligned}$$

A similar bound is obtained for the case $r = q$, which now depends on the quantity λ_q. Furthermore, a similar bound can be found for the quantity in (3): selecting any two points $(q,x),(q,x') \in g_{q,r} \subset \mathcal{D}_q^*, r \neq q$, we have:

$$\begin{aligned}|p_{(q,r),r}(x) - p_{(q,r),r}(x')| &= \left| \int_{\mathcal{D}_r} R(dz|(q,x),r) - \int_{\mathcal{D}_r} R(dz|(q,x'),r) \right| \\ &\leq \int_{\mathcal{D}_r} |R(dz|(q,x),r) - R(dz|(q,x'),r)| \leq \lambda_q k_R \|x - x'\|.\end{aligned}$$

Likewise, it is possible to derive error bounds for more complicated expressions, such as (4).

Hybrid State Space Partition

Let us now introduce a partition of the hybrid state space $\mathcal{S}^*$ (see Table 1). Recall that $\mathcal{S}^*$ can be written as $\mathcal{S}^* = \cup_{q\in\mathcal{Q}} \{q\} \times \mathcal{D}_q^* = \cup_{q\in\mathcal{Q}} \{q\} \times \{\cup_{\substack{r\in\mathcal{Q}\\ r\neq q}} g_{q,r} \cup \mathcal{D}_q\}$.

With regards to a particular mode $q \in \mathcal{Q}$, let us introduce a partition of $\mathcal{D}_q^*$ of cardinality $c_q^\delta = d_q^\delta + \sum_{\substack{r\in\mathcal{Q}\\ r\neq q}} e_{q,r}^\delta$, where the first term d_q^δ refers to the number of sections of the invariant $\mathcal{D}_q$, while the other terms $e_{q,r}^\delta$ refer to the cardinality of the partition of the corresponding guard set $g_{q,r}$. These terms are clearly all greater than or equal to one. Let us introduce their respective measures λ_q^j and $\lambda_{q,r}^k$, which make up the quantities $\lambda_q = \sum_{j=1}^{d_q^\delta} \lambda_q^j$, and $\lambda_{q,r} = \sum_{k=1}^{e_{q,r}^\delta} \lambda_{q,r}^k$ introduced above. This dependence on the parameter δ will be made clear shortly.

We do not impose any structure on the partition, but only require it, within each domain, to respect (that is, not to intersect) the boundaries between invariant and guards, and those between each couple of adjacent guards. It is then possible to express the domain $\mathcal{D}_q^*$, associated to mode $q \in \mathcal{Q}$, as the union of the following disjoint sets:

$$\mathcal{D}_q^* = \{\cup_{\substack{r\in\mathcal{Q}\\ r\neq q}}\{\cup_{j=1}^{e_{q,r}^{\delta}} g_{q,r}^j\}\} \cup \{\cup_{j=1}^{d_q^{\delta}} \mathcal{D}_q^j\}.$$

Let us now associate a discrete state of $\mathcal{M}$ to each of these partitions, by introducing mode q^j for $\mathcal{D}_q^j$, and mode q_r^j for $g_{q,r}^j$. The parameter δ is defined to be

$$\delta = \max_{q\in\mathcal{Q}}\{\max\{\epsilon_q, \gamma_q\}\}, \text{ where}$$
$$\epsilon_q = \max_{\substack{r\in\mathcal{Q}\\ r\neq q}\, j=1,\dots,e_{q,r}^{\delta}} \sup\{\|x - x'\| : x, x' \in g_{q,r}^j\} = \max_{\substack{r\in\mathcal{Q}\\ r\neq q}\, j=1,\dots,e_{q,r}^{\delta}} \epsilon_{q,r}^j,$$
$$\gamma_q = \max_{j=1,\dots,d_q^{\delta}} \sup\{\|x - x'\| : x, x' \in \mathcal{D}_q^j\} = \max_{j=1,\dots,d_q^{\delta}} \gamma_q^j.$$

In other words, δ represents the largest diameter of the partitions defined on $\mathcal{S}^*$.

Let us choose a *representative* point within each single mode introduced through the partition: $\forall q \in \mathcal{Q}, \forall j = 1,\dots,d_q^{\delta}$, let us select a point $\bar{x}_q^j \in \mathcal{D}_q^j$; $\forall q \in \mathcal{Q}, r \neq q, \forall j = 1,\dots,e_{q,r}^{\delta}$, let us select a point $\bar{x}_{q,r}^j \in g_{q,r}^j$.

We will now revisit the computation of the probabilistic quantities in (2)-(3) with the additional knowledge of the derived error bounds, in order to define the elements of the MSC $\mathcal{M}$ that abstracts the original dt-SHS $\mathcal{H}$. Toward this aim, we associate to each discrete state of the above partition a distinct state of the MSC. The values of the error bounds depend on the partition diameter δ, and on the structure of the dynamics of $\mathcal{H}$. To be more precise, we shall approximate the quantities in (2)-(3) with ones that will be based on computations performed on the *representative* points. The new transition probabilities will be intuitively denoted in a similar fashion as the relations in (2)-(3). Let us start from the relation in (2):

$$\forall x \in \mathcal{D}_q^j,\ p_{q^j,r^k}(x) = \int_{g_{q,r}^k} T(dy|(q,x)) \approx p_{q^j,r^k}(\bar{x}_q^j), \tag{5}$$

More precisely, $|p_{q^j,q_r^k}(x) - p_{q^j,q_r^k}(\bar{x}_q^j)| \leq \lambda_{q,r}^k k_T \gamma_q^j \leq \lambda^* k_T \delta$. Notice that, if $x \in \mathcal{D}_q^j \subseteq \mathcal{D}_q, T(dy|(q,x)) = T(dy|(q^j,x))$.

Now, focusing on equation (3), we have:

$$\forall x \in g_{q,r}^j,\ p_{(q,r)^j,r^k}(x) = \int_{\mathcal{D}_r^k} R(dy|(q,x),r) \approx p_{(q,r)^j,r^k}(\bar{x}_{q,r}^j), \tag{6}$$

where $|p_{(q,r)^j,r^k}(x) - p_{(q,r)^j,r^k}(\bar{x}_{q,r}^j)| \leq \lambda_r^k k_R \epsilon_{q,r}^j \leq \lambda^* k_R \delta$. Notice that, if $x \in g_{q,r}^j \subseteq \mathcal{D}_q^*, R(dy|(q,x),r) = T(dy|(g_{q,r}^j,x), D_r^k)$.

Similar transition probabilities and bounds can be referred to the initial distribution π_0. Moreover, it is possible to compute analogous bounds for quantities, such as (4), which involve more than a single step of computation. However, it will become clear in the next section that these bounds can be equivalently derived from direct matrix computations on the MSC $\mathcal{M}$.

Table 1. Relationship between the components of the dt-SHS and the elements of the partition that yields the MSC, with corresponding quantities of interest

component	form	parts	partitions	cardinality	size	diameter
hybrid space of $\mathcal{H}$	$\mathcal{S}^* = \bigcup_{q \in \mathcal{Q}} \{q\} \times \mathcal{D}_q^*$	$\mathcal{D}_q^*$		c^δ	$\lambda^* = \sum_{q \in \mathcal{Q}} \lambda_q^*$	δ
domain	$\mathcal{D}_q^* = \mathcal{D}_q \cup \mathcal{G}_q$	$\mathcal{D}_q, \mathcal{G}_q$		c_q^δ	λ_q^*	$\gamma_q \vee \epsilon_q$
invariant	$\mathcal{D}_q$		$\mathcal{D}_q^j$	d_q^δ	λ_q	γ_q
invariant sections	$\mathcal{D}_q^j$			1	λ_q^j	γ_q^j
guards	$\mathcal{G}_q = \bigcup_{r \in \mathcal{Q}, r \neq q} \{g_{q,r}\}$	$g_{q,r}$	$g_{q,r}^j$	$\sum_{r \in \mathcal{Q}, r \neq q} e_{q,r}^\delta$	$\lambda_q^* - \lambda_q$	ϵ_q
guard sections	$g_{q,r}^j$			1	$\lambda_{q,r}^j$	$\epsilon_{q,r}^j$

6 Steady State Computation Using the MSC Abstraction

In this section we show that it is possible to infer the asymptotic behavior of the dt-SHS $\mathcal{H}$ using the introduced Markov set-chain abstraction $\mathcal{M}$. We start by providing an intuitive justification of why the MSC $\mathcal{M}$ may yield some conclusions about the asymptotic dynamics of the original dt-SHS $\mathcal{H}$.

The values of the MSC, i.e. the explicit bounds for the errors associated to the approximate computations of the transition probabilities of the dt-SHS, allow to introduce a "conservative estimate" of the actual transition probabilities between regions of the state space of the original dt-SHS. By selecting a small enough diameter δ of the partition, the possibly contractive nature of $\mathcal{M}$ may dominate over the approximation errors. The contractivity of $\mathcal{M}$ depends on the dynamics and on the structure of $\mathcal{H}$. By tuning the parameter δ, we may derive conclusions on the asymptotic behavior of $\mathcal{H}$.

We now make the above discussion more quantitative. Given a desired precision $\varepsilon > 0$ on the approximation, we integrate the procedure for the partition of $\mathcal{H}$ into an algorithm to compute the steady state of the MSC abstraction $\mathcal{M}$. The precision ε is related to the partition parameter δ. As discussed above, the steady state vector $[\pi_\infty]$ for $\mathcal{M}$ is an estimate of the invariant measure of $\mathcal{H}$, with a confidence bound given by the diameter $\Delta([\pi_\infty])$. Let us initialize a partition of $\mathcal{H}$ according to a value $\delta = \delta(\varepsilon)$, which guarantees a precision ε for the steady state computation of $[\pi_\infty]$. The transition set $[\Pi] = [P, Q]$, as constructed in the previous section, has the following property:

$$\Delta([\Pi]) \leq ||Q - P|| = \lambda^* \bar{k} \delta(\varepsilon), \tag{7}$$

with $\bar{k} = k_T \vee k_R \vee k_0$. The inequality can be drawn by directly employing the definition of matrix norm, and the bounds derived for equations (5)-(6). Then, by Theorem 3, a sufficient condition to achieve $\Delta([\pi_\infty]) \leq \varepsilon$ is the following:

$$\lambda^* \bar{k} \delta(\varepsilon) \leq \varepsilon \left(1 - \mathcal{T}([\Pi])\right). \tag{8}$$

It is clear that if $\mathcal{T}([\Pi]) < 1$ there always exists a value of $\delta(\varepsilon)$ that satisfies this inequality, since the LHS expression goes to zero as $\delta(\varepsilon)$ goes to zero. Notice however that, without an idea of the transition probabilities that define $[\Pi]$, one cannot estimate $\mathcal{T}([\Pi])$. Since in general $0 \leq \mathcal{T}([\Pi]) \leq 1$, the set of feasible values for $\delta(\varepsilon)$ that satisfy equation (8) ranges from a finite upper bound δ_0 (when $\mathcal{T}([\Pi]) = 0$) to 0 (when $\mathcal{T}([\Pi]) = 1$). This makes sense: until we have no information about the contractive nature of $[\Pi]$, there is no possibility to estimate the limit set behavior. For this reason, it is impossible to establish a priori a value for $\delta(\varepsilon)$ that guarantees a desired precision ε in the steady state computation using the abstraction $\mathcal{M}$.

However, we can choose an "optimistic" initial value δ_0. In the following iterative algorithm, given a partition diameter $\beta(k)$, we define $\Pi(k)$ the transition probabilities computed by the abstraction algorithm described in the previous section from an initial distribution π_0. Moreover, we define $[\Pi(k)] = [P(k), Q(k)]$, the associated MSC. The parameter $\alpha(k)$ represents an upper bound for $\mathcal{T}([\Pi(k)])$.

Algorithm 1 (Compute steady state of $\mathcal{H}$ with precision ε)

input: $(\mathcal{H}, \varepsilon)$;

set integer $k = 0$, real $\alpha(0) = 0$, and real $\beta(0)$ such that $\lambda^* \bar{k} \beta(0) \leq \varepsilon$;

for $k \geq 0$

compute $\Pi(k), [\Pi(k)] = [P(k), Q(k)]$ according to $\beta(k)$;

set $\alpha(k) = \mathcal{T}(\Pi(k)) + ||Q(k) - P(k)||$;

if $\alpha(k) \geq 1$ or $\alpha(k) \geq \alpha(k-1)$ **then** set $\beta(k+1) = a\beta(k), a < 1$;

else if $\frac{||Q(k)-P(k)||}{1-\alpha(k)} > \varepsilon$ **then** set $\beta(k+1)$ s.t. $\lambda^* \bar{k} \beta(k+1) \leq \varepsilon(1 - \alpha(k))$;

else exit;

set $k = k + 1$;

end

compute the steady state π_∞ of $\Pi(k)$;

output: (π_∞). □

Notice that, $\forall k \geq 0, \beta(k+1) < \beta(k)$, thus $\lim_{k \to +\infty} \Delta([\Pi]) = \lim_{k \to +\infty} ||Q(k) - P(k)|| = 0$. Let $\mathcal{T}_\infty = \lim_{k \to +\infty} \mathcal{T}([\Pi(k)]) < 1$: by Theorem 1 it follows that $\lim_{k \to +\infty} \alpha(k) = \mathcal{T}([\Pi(k)]) = \mathcal{T}_\infty$. Namely, if $\mathcal{T}_\infty < 1$ we can arbitrarily increase the accuracy δ of our abstraction until, by equation (8), $\lambda^* \bar{k} \delta \leq \varepsilon (1 - \mathcal{T}_\infty)$. When this happens the algorithm terminates, and we compute the steady state π_∞, or compute $[\pi_\infty]$ using the upper and lower bounding matrices L_∞, H_∞, as described in section 3.

We now discuss the computational burden of our procedure. It is clear that the main bottlenecks are (1) the abstraction procedure for the partitioning of the hybrid state space; and (2) the limit set computation on the abstraction MSC. The first computation directly depends on the parameter δ, which is related to $\mathcal{T}_\infty$ by (8). The second computation depends on two parameters: the cardinality of the MSC and the convergence speed. The state cardinality is $\mathfrak{c}^\delta$, and depends on δ, while the convergence speed can be related to $\mathcal{T}_\infty$ by (1). The main weight in the computational complexity of our abstraction procedure is $\mathcal{T}_\infty$.

For the above arguments, it can be interesting to interpret $\mathcal{T}_\infty$ as the coefficient of ergodicity $\mathcal{T}(\mathcal{H})$ of the dt-SHS $\mathcal{H}$, and possibly compare this value with other convergence bounds directly derived on the structure and the dynamics of $\mathcal{H}$.

7 Numerical Study

We implement the proposed abstraction procedure on a simple one-dimensional dynamical system, whose dynamics is described by the following SDE, defined for $t \geq 0$:

$$d\mathbf{X}_t = f(\mathbf{X}_t)dt + d\mathbf{B}_t, \text{ with } \mathbf{X}_0 \sim \mathcal{U}(A). \tag{9}$$

The drift depends on a function $f : \mathbb{R} \to \mathbb{R}$, assumed to be continuous and bounded. The term $\mathbf{B}_t$ denotes a standard Wiener process. $\mathcal{U}(A)$ is the uniform distribution, over some compact set $A \subset \mathbb{R}$.

The SDE in (9) is discretized in time according to a first-order Euler-Maruyama scheme, with discretization step $\Delta > 0$, which yields the following, for any $n \geq 0$: $\mathbf{X}_{(n+1)\Delta} \sim \mathcal{N}(\mathbf{X}_{n\Delta} + \Delta f(\mathbf{X}_{n\Delta}), \Delta)$, where $\mathcal{N}(m, \sigma^2)$ is a normal random variable with mean m and variance σ^2.

For computational necessity, we shall introduce some approximation outside the compact interval $\mathcal{K} = [-K, K]$. Let us partition this interval $\mathcal{K}$ into $2l$ sections of length 2δ, where $\delta = K/l$, and centered at the *representative* points $\bar{x}_k = -K + (2k-1)\delta, k = 1, 2, \ldots, l$. Call these partitions $\mathcal{D}_k = [-K + 2(k-1)\delta, -K + 2k\delta]$.

Additionally, consider two regions for the open intervals $\mathcal{D}_{lb} = (-\infty, -K], \mathcal{D}_{ub} = [K, +\infty)$, "centered" at the points $\bar{x}_{lb,ub} = \{\pm(K+\delta)\}$. Consider for convenience the extended index set $\mathcal{Q} = \{1, 2, \ldots, l, lb, ub\}$. Conditional on $\mathbf{X}_{n\Delta} = \bar{x}_k$, for any $k \in \mathcal{Q}$, the process at time $(n+1)\Delta$ is distributed according to $T(\cdot|\bar{x}_k) \triangleq \mathcal{N}(\cdot; m_k, \Delta)$, where $m_k = \bar{x}_k + \Delta f(\bar{x}_k)$.

This discretization procedure induces a dt-SHS, where the $l+2$ domains make up the state space as $\mathcal{S} = \bigcup_{k \in \mathcal{Q}} \{k\} \times \mathcal{D}_k$. Let us compute the approximate

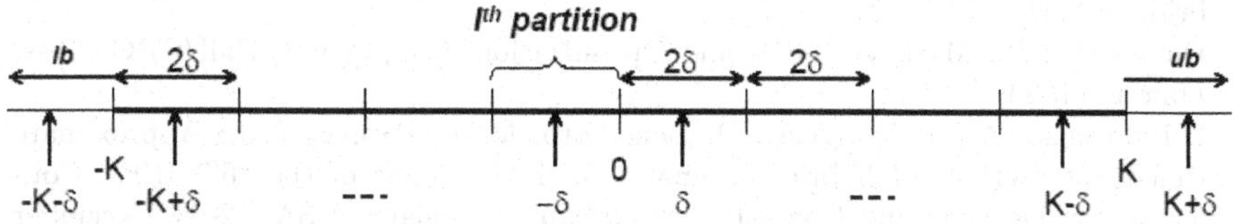

Fig. 1. Abstraction procedure for the one-dimensional system in (9)

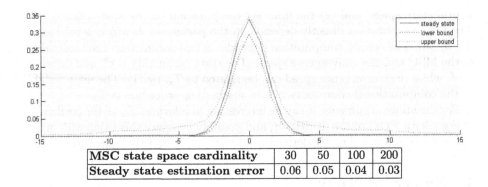

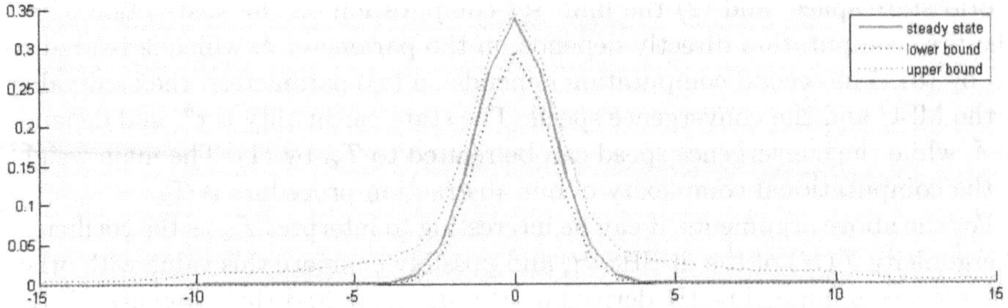

MSC state space cardinality	30	50	100	200
Steady state estimation error	0.06	0.05	0.04	0.03

Fig. 2. Simulation outputs

transition probabilities between the different modes of the introduced dt-SHS based on the representative points, and associate bounds on the errors.

In the following, we implement some computations for the very special linear-drift case, i.e. where $f(x) = -\mu x, \mu > 0$. The knowledge of a closed form distribution for this process [11] enables a comparison of it with the outcome of the simulations. We have chosen the following parameters: $K = 15, \Delta = 1, m = 0, \sigma = 1$. Choosing a $\mu = 0.5$, the solution process of (9) is trivially distributed as $\mathcal{N}(0, 1)$. We have implemented our abstraction procedure and the MSC basic algorithms on Matlab. Figure 2 illustrates that, to obtain a precision (say $\varepsilon = 0.05$) in the steady state computation, we need a MSC abstraction with 50 states. The table below Figure 2 shows that by augmenting the state space of the MSC abstraction, the error bounds for the steady state converge to zero.

References

1. Abate, A., Prandini, M., Lygeros, J., Sastry, S.: Probabilistic reachability and safety for controlled discrete time stochastic hybrid systems. Automatica (accepted, 2007)
2. Alur, R., Henzinger, T., Lafferriere, G., Pappas, G.: Discrete abstractions of hybrid systems. Proceedings of the IEEE 88(2), 971–984 (2000)
3. Aziz, A., Sanwal, K., Singhal, V., Brayton, R.: Model-checking continuous time markov chains. ACM Trans. on Comp. Logic 1(1), 162–170 (2000)
4. Clarke, E.M., Grumberg, O., Peled, D.A.: Model Checking. The MIT Press, Cambridge (2002)
5. Davis, M.H.A.: Markov Models and Optimization. Chapman & Hall/CRC Press, London (1993)
6. D'Innocenzo, A., Julius, A.A., Di Benedetto, M.D., Pappas, G.J.: Approximate timed abstractions of hybrid automata. In: Proceedings of the 46th IEEE Conference on Decision and Control. New Orleans, Louisiana, USA, 12–14 December (2007)
7. Girard, A., Pappas, G.J.: Approximation metrics for discrete and continuous systems. IEEE Transactions on Automatic Control 52(5), 782–798 (2007)

8. Hartfiel, H.J.: Markov Set-Chains. Lecture Notes in Mathematics, vol. 1695. Springer, Heidelberg (1998)
9. Julius, A.A., Pappas, G.J.: Approximate abstraction of stochastic hybrid systems. IEEE Trans. Automatic Control (provisionally accepted)
10. Kushner, H.J.: Approximation and Weak Convergence Methods for Random Processes with Applications to Stochastic Systems Theory. MIT Press, Cambridge (1984)
11. Øksendal, B.: Stochastic Differential Equations: An Introduction with Applications, 6th edn. Springer, Heidelberg (2003)

Co-simulation Tools for Networked Control Systems

Ahmad T. Al-Hammouri[1,2], Michael S. Branicky[1], and Vincenzo Liberatore[1]

[1] Case Western Reserve University
Electrical Engineering and Computer Science Dept.
Cleveland, Ohio 44106 USA
{ata5,mb,vl}@case.edu
[2] Jordan University of Science and Technology,
Computer Engineering Dept.,
Irbid 22110 Jordan
hammouri@just.edu.jo

Abstract. In this paper, we argue that simulation of Networked Control Systems (NCSs) needs to be carried out through *co-simulation*, which requires the joint and simultaneous simulation of both physical and communication networks dynamics. Co-simulation enables construction of synthetic large-scale networks and workloads, replay of collected traces, and obtaining a complete snapshot of both the network behavior and the physical systems states. Therefore, co-simulation provides in-depth understanding of the interaction between communication networks and physical systems dynamics. In this paper, we overview three co-simulation tools that we have developed for NCS co-simulation. The first two tools are extensions to `ns-2` called `Agent/Plant` and `NSCSPlant`; the third tool integrates Modelica and `ns-2`. For each tool, we present demonstrative case studies that highlight its capabilities.

1 Introduction

We are witnessing technological advances in VLSI, in MEMS, and in communication networks that have brought devices with sensing, processing, actuating, and communication capabilities. These devices have contributed to the formation of *Networked Control Systems* (*NCSs*) [1]. The fundamental motivation of NCSs is that they extend the distributed control of the physical world beyond distance barriers [2]; see Fig. 1. Representative applications include industrial automation, distributed instrumentation, unmanned vehicles, home robotics, distributed virtual environments, power distribution, and building structure control [3].

Successful design and implementation of NCSs necessitate the existence of simulation tools that allow verification, validation, and evaluation of different control and network algorithms. In this paper, we argue that simulation of NCSs needs to be carried out through *co-simulation*, which requires the joint and simultaneous simulation of both physical and communication networks dynamics.

The need for co-simulation originates from the fact that the NCS field is an interdisciplinary one that combines the study of control theory and communication

M. Egerstedt and B. Mishra (Eds.): HSCC 2008, LNCS 4981, pp. 16–29, 2008.

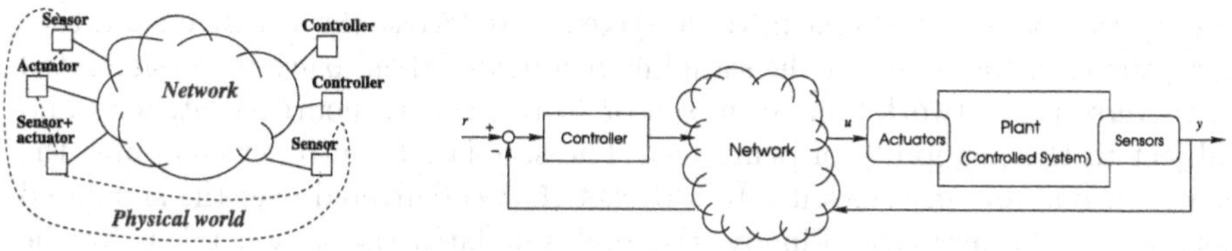

Fig. 1. (left) NCSs integrate sensing, processing, and actuation tasks that enable remote monitoring and control of the physical world. (right) A networked control system with one controlled system (a.k.a. *plant*) and one controller; both the sensor and the actuator are co-located at the plant site. Figures reproduced from [3].

networks. In its simplest form, a NCS consists of a single physical system and a remote controller such as the one in Fig. 1 (right). The sensor samples the values of physical quantities, writes them in a packet, and sends the packet over the network to the controller. The controller examines the received sample to generate a control signal that is then sent over the network to the actuator. Although more complex scenarios are possible, the most fundamental concern is to understand how the communication network and the NCS affect each other as a function of network traffic and topology, and in terms of NCS stability and performance. For example, NCS packets transmitted over the network will incur delays that are often time varying. A central concern is then to understand how these time-varying delays affect the performance or the stability of the NCS. On the other hand, a NCS would sample and transmit sensed data at a rate that is appropriate to achieve some performance levels. However, if this rate is higher than the network bandwidth capacity, the network becomes congested, thus leading to additional packet delays, losses, and jitter [2]. In a nutshell, the study of NCSs necessitates an integrated approach that combines the disciplines of networking and feedback control.

Pursuing a pure analytical approach is likely to be intricate especially when considering multiple NCSs in a wide-area setting, e.g., the Internet. Mathematical formulation and analysis based on fixed delays and on regular sampling intervals may no longer be applicable when packets carrying sensed and control data are subject to long and time-varying delays or the possibility of being lost. Since co-simulation will at least lead to a numerically tractable analysis of the overall system, we believe that co-simulation will be critical to the study of complex systems and of scalable control algorithms in such wide-area settings. In these cases, co-simulation enables us to construct synthetic large-scale networks and workloads, to replay collected traces, and to obtain a complete snapshot of both the network behavior and the physical systems states. For these facts, co-simulation is a key step in NCS co-design, whereby network issues such as bandwidth, quantization, survivability, reliability, scalability, and message delay are considered simultaneously with controlled system issues such as stability, performance, fault tolerance, and adaptability [4].

A common feature for any co-simulation tool is that it needs to capture both the physical and the communication dynamics. For the simple example in Fig. 1

(right), the tool simulates the physical system and derives the system output that is captured by the sensor at the sampling instances. Then, packets are simulated to traverse the network links from sensor to controller, incurring latencies and subject to the possibility of being lost. The simulated controller computes the control signal and inscribes it into a packet that is delivered over the simulated network to the actuator. Finally, the tool simulates the action taken by the actuator. The effectiveness of co-simulation relies on how well a tool describes the dynamics of both the physical systems and communication networks involved. For network dynamics, the tool needs to simulate detailed per-packet events, such as packet forwarding and transmission over communication links, as well as packet enqueueing and dequeueing at different network nodes. As for physical dynamics, the tool should allow the expression of differential algebraic equations (DAEs), be able to solve DAEs, and have the capability of catching events, e.g., zero crossing. In short, it should be capable of simulating general hybrid dynamical systems [5,6].

In this paper, after reviewing the related work (Sect. 2), we present our approach for the NCS co-simulation in Sect. 3. Sections 4 through 6 elaborate on our approach by overviewing three tools we have developed for NCS co-simulation. For each tool, we highlight its capabilities and present demonstrative case studies. Finally, Sect. 7 concludes the paper.

2 Background and Related Work

There have been well-developed simulation tools that target the simulation of either networks or physical systems separately. For example, networks simulators include `ns-2` [7] and OMNet++ [8]. On the other hand, simulations of physical and embedded systems utilize hybrid systems tools, which allow the construction and the simulation of systems involving continuous and discrete dynamics. Examples of hybrid systems simulation tools include Modelica simulation environments [6], Simulink [9], Ptolemy [10], and `adevs` [11].

Simulation of NCSs, which involve the interaction between communication networks and physical systems dynamics, can leverage on the previously mentioned tools. One direction is to utilize and to extend hybrid systems simulation tools to also simulate the events and dynamics of communication networks. An example of a tool that follows this approach is TrueTime [12]. However, TrueTime has support for only local-area networks simulations. Specifically, it allows the simulation of only the physical and the medium-access layers [12]. This limitation inhibits its applicability to more general networks that incorporate higher-layer network protocols, e.g., routing, transport, and application protocols, and geographically distributed networks, such as WANs. Providing support for general network settings in TrueTime can be a formidable task because such higher-protocols in general utilize complex algorithms that are distributed in nature and encompass multi-hop nodes. This same discussion applies to other tools that try to extend hybrid systems simulation tools to support network-side simulations; see for example [13], where Ptolemy was extended to simulate wireless sensor networks. An alternative direction is to extend a network simulator, such as ns-2, to include the capability for physical systems simulations. In Sect. 4 of this paper, we review one such tool, which is an extension of ns-2 called Agent/Plant. With Agent/Plant, physical dynamics of an environment and control algorithms can be modeled by ordinary differential equations (ODEs) and then solved within the simulation script or via a call to an outside utility, e.g., the Ode UNIX utility or Matlab. The same approach was also used in the ns-2 agents NSCSPlant and NSCSController (see Sect. 5 and [2]). A third direction is to marry a full-fledged network simulator and a full-fledged physical dynamics simulator. The integration of the two domain-specific simulators would then furnish a tool that combines the best features of the individual simulators. Such a methodology was sought in [14], where ns-2 was integrated with adevs. Although the tool was developed specifically to simulate power systems and networks, it can be applied to NCSs in general because the discrete-event simulator, adevs, can be used to simulate general hybrid systems. In Sect. 6 of this paper, we present a tool that is similar in spirit to [14], where we combine ns-2 with Modelica. However, in contrast to [14], our tool does not require deriving mathematical modeling equations for system states nor the formulation of input/output and state transition automata. Since Modelica's simulation environments, e.g., Dymola, have the nice features of drag-and-drop and ease-of-use in building physical systems models, our tool can be accessible to a wide spectrum of investigators, especially those with little background in hybrid and physical systems modeling.

Independent of our research, [15] integrates ns-2 with the MoCoNet platform.

3 Our Approach

Our approach is to rely on and to combine well-established simulation tools for networks and for physical systems as much as possible. For example, for the network-side simulations, we employ ns-2 [7], which is a widespread discrete-event simulator developed to facilitate the simulation of network protocols at different layers of the Internet stack, including the MAC, network, transport, and application layers [16]. ns-2 simulates the exact dynamics and events of individual packets while traversing network elements, e.g., communication links and routers. With ns-2, different network topologies can be constructed, and several network technologies can be simulated, such as wireline, wireless, local- or wide-area networks; or a hybrid of these.

Although ns-2 supports some real-time applications, such as multimedia streaming protocols, it still lacks support for applications that involve real-time sensing, actuation, and control. Specifically, ns-2 lacks the ability of simulating continuous-time dynamics, supporting event-catching, and constructing models for physical systems. However, a nice feature of ns-2 is that it is evolvable in the sense that new protocols and algorithms can be added to the already existing ones. In particular, ns-2 exposes well-defined APIs that greatly facilitate developing new traffic sources, traffic destinations, and router queueing algorithms.

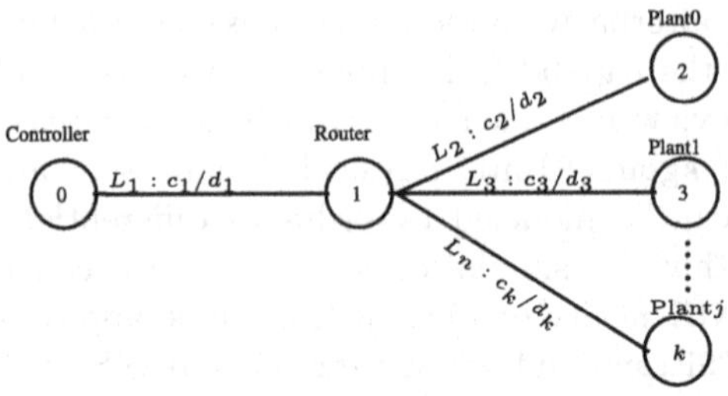

Fig. 2. A network topology consisting of several end-hosts (plants or controllers) connected via a router. Each communication link L_i is characterized by the bandwidth c_i and the propagation delay d_i. The number of plants, j, c_i, and d_i may be varied across experiments.

we discuss how to exploit this to extend ns-2 and combine it with other tools to provide the ability of simulating physical systems dynamics.

For illustration, we next present a short example of setting up a network topology in ns-2. A Tcl simulation script can be written to define the network topology, to define traffic sources and destinations, and to schedule events. For example, the following Tcl snippet defines the network in Fig. 2.

```
# Create nodes and label them
set n0 [$ns node]
$n0 label "Controller"
set n1 [$ns node]
$n1 label "Router"
set n2 [$ns node]
$n2 label "Plant0"

# n3-nk are defined similarly here (code suppressed)

# Connect the nodes with a star topology
$ns duplex-link $n0 $n1 1Mb 1ms DropTail
$ns duplex-link $n1 $n2 1Mb 1ms DropTail

# Links connecting nodes n3-nk to n1 are
# defined similarly here (code suppressed)
```

To simulate network traffic, one can then attach, say, a TCP traffic source at node 0 and a TCP traffic sink at node 2, and then simulate the transfer of a virtual file from node 0 to node 1 using FTP. In the next three sections, we show how to use our contributed packages to simulate the flow of sensory and control packets to accomplish feedback control over a network simulated via ns-2.

4 The Agent/Plant Extension

To support NCS co-simulation in ns-2, we have implemented an extension of ns-2 to simulate physical dynamics and control laws, and the transmission of sensor and control packets between plants and controllers. The extension supports a new type of `ns-2` *agent*, called `Agent/Plant`, that represents the interface between the physical and the network dynamics. An `Agent/Plant` can take the role of a sensor, a controller interface, or an actuator depending on its usage in the simulation script. Pairs of plants are connected to each other, after which they can exchange sampled data and control instructions.

4.1 `Agent/Plant` Usage

`Agent/Plant` is a generic `ns-2` agent, which allows simulation of different configurations of NCSs. For example, it can be used to simulate any combination of time-driven and event-driven plants and controllers. Also, it allows simulation of various plant dynamics (e.g., continuous, discrete, linear, or nonlinear) and various corresponding controllers (e.g., P or PI). To achieve such flexibility, `Agent/Plant` requires two functions to be defined in the Tcl code, which are `sysphy` and `smplschd`; see [17] for fuller details.

`sysphy`: The function `sysphy` is used by plants to simulate the physical dynamics of the controlled system and to apply control signals arriving from controllers (with actuators). Likewise, it is used by controllers upon receiving sensed data packets and when computing the control signals. Physical dynamics and control algorithms can be modeled by ODEs that are solved directly inside `sysphy` or via a call made to external utility, e.g., the `Ode` UNIX utility or Matlab.

`smplschd`: The function `smplschd` schedules a future invocation to sample the system (sensor or controller) output. The function is especially helpful in the case of sensors to implement fixed or variable sampling-rate policies. It is also used at the controller site to trigger the transmission of control messages.

4.2 Example

A pair consisting of a plant (including a time-driven sensor and an event-driven actuator) and a corresponding event-driven controller can be instantiated and attached to nodes 2 and 0 of Fig. 2, respectively, as follows:

```
# The two functions, sysphy and smplschd, are defined
# here to include dynamical equations that simulate
# the plant dynamics and the controller algorithm;
# see [17] for examples how to accomplish this.

# Create a controller agent and attach it to node n0
set c0 [new Agent/Plant]
$ns attach-agent $n0 $c0

# Create a plant and attach it to node n2
set p0 [new Agent/Plant]
$ns attach-agent $n2 $p0
```

```
# Connect the two agents
$ns connect $c0 $p0

# Schedule events
$ns at 0.1 "$p0 sample"
$ns at 16.0 "finish"
```

4.3 Case Studies

To demonstrate the capabilities of `Agent/Plant`, we study the influence of the configuration and the time-dependent dynamics of a network on NCSs. Other experimental results using `Agent/Plant` appeared in [4,18].

The Impact of Buffer Size. We start by considering several *linear scalar* plants that are connected via the network in Fig. 2 (i.e., the plants are attached to nodes 2, 3, ..., k). Each plant is controlled by a proportional controller that is attached to node 0 (see also the sample code in Section 4.2). The plant dynamics and controller law are defined as follows:

$$\dot{x}(t) = ax(t) + u(t)\,, \qquad y(t) = x(t)\,, \qquad u = K(R(t) - y(t))\,, \qquad (1)$$

where $x(t)$ is the plant's state; $y(t)$ is the plant's output; $u(t)$ is the plant's input that is sent by the controller; a is the plant constant; K is the controller proportional gain; $R(t)$ is the reference trajectory the plant is required to follow.

Now, we study the impact of router buffer size on the number of NCSs that can be accommodated by a given network topology. Large buffer sizes lead to long queueing delays but less packet loss; whereas small buffers sizes lead to relatively shorter queueing delays and higher packet loss rates. Because both delays and losses affect the NCSs performance and stability, buffer sizes is expected to be a critical factor on the number of NCSs that can be accommodated in particular network configurations. For the network in Fig. 2, we investigate the impact of the router's buffer size on the number of NCSs for two cases: when the buffer size is four and when it is two. For each buffer size, we vary the number of NCSs from 1 to 39 and for each experiment, we report the packet drop rate at the router. The parameters of each NCS are as follows: $a = 100$; $K = 101$; $R(t) = 1$ (i.e., unit step response); the initial plant state is $x(0) = 0$; and the sampling interval is constant and is drawn from a uniform distribution between 5ms and 15ms. The network parameters are as follows: $c_1 = 1.544$Mbps; $d_1 = 1$ms. For each link L_i, where $i > 1$, $c_i = 100$Mbps and $d_i = 120\mu$s. Finally, all packet sizes are 48B. The results depicted in Figs. 3 and 4 obviously show the striking difference between the performance when using different buffer sizes.

Experimental Sampling Period and Delay Stability Region. `Agent/Plant` provides the flexibility for simulating arbitrarily complicated plant dynamics and networks beyond the previous settings. In particular, `Agent/Plant` can be used to simulate *nonlinear* plant dynamics. In [19,18], we demonstrated the strength of co-simulation by using `Agent/Plant` to characterize an

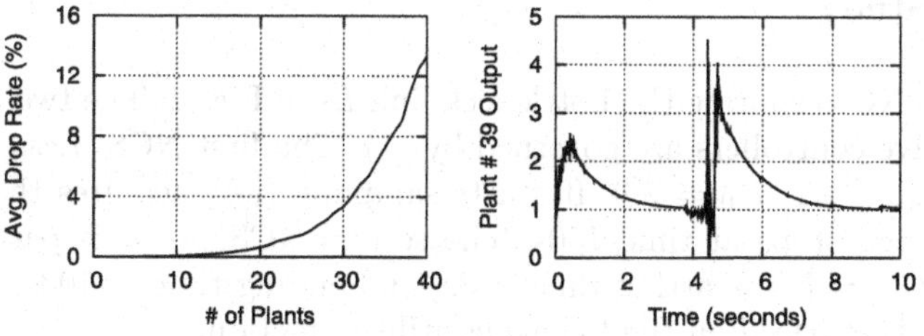

Fig. 3. Buffer of size 4: drop rate for $n = 1, \ldots, 39$; plant response for $n = 39$. Figure is reproduced from [4].

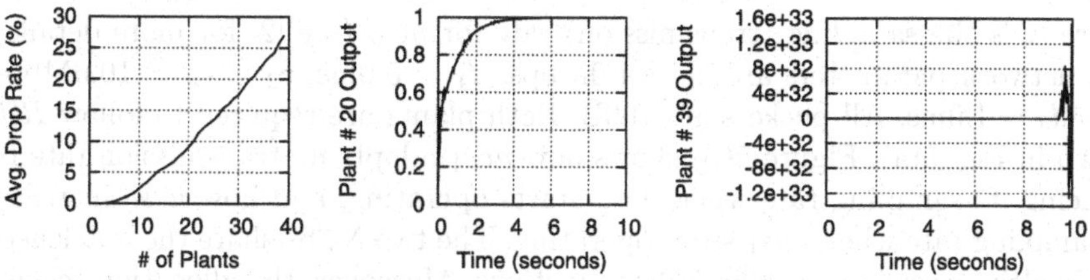

Fig. 4. Buffer of size 2: drop rate for $n = 1, \ldots, 39$; plant response for $n = 20$ and for $n = 39$. Figure is reproduced from [4].

empirical Sampling Period and Delay Stability Region (SPDSR) for a 4-dimensional pendulum-cart system. The empirical SPDSR was compared to the analytical SPDSR, which assumes fixed sampling periods, fixed delays, and no data losses.

5 The `NSCSPlant` and `NSCSController` Extensions

We developed two new `ns-2` agents that are based on the `Agent/Plant` framework. These two agents are referred to by `NSCSPlant` and `NSCSController`, which stand for networked-sensing-and-control-systems plant and controller, respectively. `NSCSPlant` is an abstract agent class, which can be used to instantiate several controlled systems, each of which simulates a physical system; `NSCSController` can be used to instantiate controllers. `NSCSPlant` supports adaptive sampling policies, whereby the sampling rate is adjusted based on a utility (performance) function associated with a particular plant.

The two new agents were used to study the bandwidth allocation problem in NCSs; see [2]. According to the proposed scheme in [2], routers monitor the congestion level on links and convey this information back to plants via a special header in the sensor and controller packets. `NSCSPlant` then regulates its sampling rate based on the associated utility function and using the congestion information fed back from network routers. The proposed scheme of [2] achieves a fair allocation by ensuring that the aggregate utility of all NCSs is maximized.

5.1 Case Study

Consider two NCSs sharing the bottleneck link L_1 of Fig. 2. The two plants and their respective controllers are governed by (1). The first NCS, ncs_0, is parameterized by $a_0 = 0.1$, $K_0 = 2.0$. It starts sampling (i.e., acquires the network) at time 50s, and stops at time 150s. The second NCS, nsc_1, is parameterized by $a_1 = 1.0$, $K_1 = 5.0$, starting time = 0s, and ending time = 100s. Each NCS transmits packets based on the following utility function

$$U_i(r_i) = \frac{a_i - K_i}{a_i} e^{a_i/r_i} , \qquad i \in \{0, 1\} ,$$

where r_i is the sampling (transmission) rate for ncs_i (see [2] for more details). The network parameters are $c_1 = 1.0$Mbps, $d_1 = 5.0$ms, $c_2 = c_3 = 10.0$Mbps, $d_2 = d_3 = 1.0$ms. All packets are 100B. Both plants are required to follow $R(t)$ shown in Fig. 5(a). Figure 5(b) shows how ncs_1 adapts its transmission rate by reducing its sampling rate when ncs_0 starts operating; and how ncs_0 increases its sampling rate when ncs_1 stops operating. The two NCSs share the bottleneck bandwidth according to their utility functions. Moreover, the allocation scheme retains 100% network utilization during all time intervals (this can be inferred by adding transmission rates of ncs_0 and ncs_1 during each interval). Both NCSs stay stable and track the reference signal accurately (Figs. 5(c) and 5(d)). For more experimental results utilizing the two agents `NSCSPlant` and `NSCSController`, see [20,2,21], where we experimented with a larger number of NCSs.

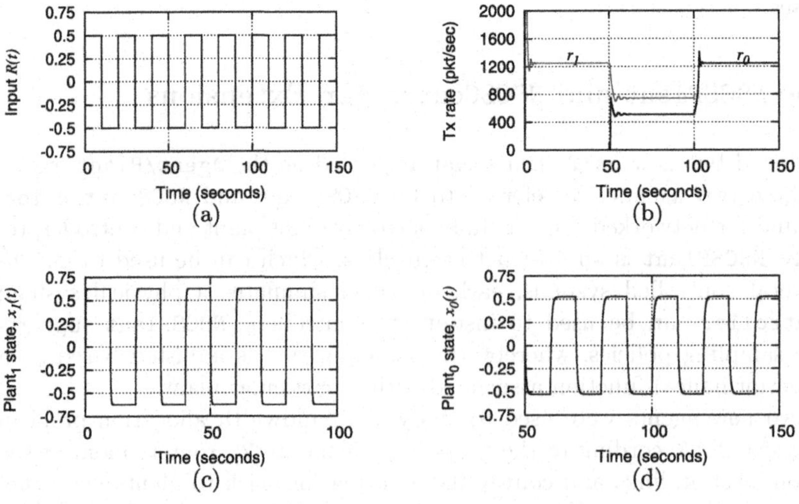

Fig. 5. (a) The input signal, $R(t)$, the two plants are instructed to follow. (b) The transmission/sampling rates r_0 and r_1 for ncs_0 and ncs_1. (c) and (d) The plants states $x_1(t)$ and $x_0(t)$, respectively, while tracking the input signal $R(t)$ in (a).

6 Modelica/ns-2 Integration

Although the `Agent/Plant` has much flexibility, modeling of large physical systems, especially those incorporating systems of subsystems and those including hybrid dynamics, becomes a tedious, and perhaps an error prone, task. Therefore, it would be rational to exploit any of the tools that facilitate the construction and simulation of physical systems models, and combine it with the `Agent/Plant`. One such tool is Modelica. Modelica is a modeling language for large-scale physical systems. It supports model construction and model reusability; supports acausal modeling; has numerous available libraries, e.g., power systems, hydraulics, pneumatics, and power train; and has available commercial and open source simulation environments [6].

Since both Modelica and `ns-2` are not readily interoperable, we integrate them by creating interprocess communication interfaces in `ns-2` and in Modelica. We have created a new `ns-2` *application* that is responsible for communicating to a corresponding Modelica model. For example, the `ns-2` application can receive packets in the `ns-2` simulation and use their payload to set a control signal in a corresponding Modelica actuator. On the Modelica side, we have written inter-simulator communication routines that we can link to generic sensor and actuator models. As a result, simulator communication is achieved by pairs of corresponding modules, one in each of the two simulators [22]. The Modelica/`ns-2` intercommunication mechanics guarantees the synchronization between

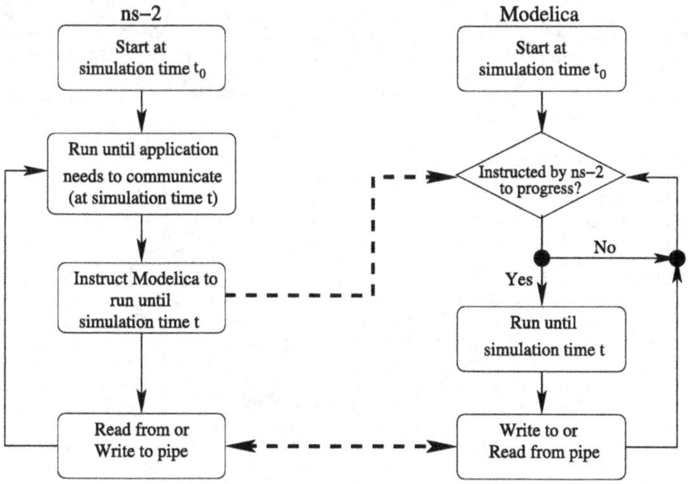

Fig. 6. The Modelica/`ns-2` intercommunication mechanics. `ns-2` runs first and Modelica is paused. When the `ns-2` application is slated by `ns-2`'s event scheduler to receive (deliver) data from (to) a Modelica model at time t, it instructs Modelica to run until time t, and to exchange data at that point. After the data exchange, Modelica simulation time is suspended until the `ns-2` application is scheduled again. Dashed lines represents communication via UNIX named pipes.

the two simulators such that events from one simulator propagate to the other at the appropriate time [22]. The intercommunication relies on UNIX named pipes and is explained in Fig. 6.

In [22], this combined tool was used to simulate a NCS consisting of a power transmission system that is controlled over a wide-area network. In that scenario, the power system involved typical power grid elements, including a permanent-magnet generator, a transmission line, and time-varying loads. The scenario also included a PID controller to regulate the generator's output voltage under varying load, using output measurements sent over the network. Our co-simulation tool enabled us to investigate the influence of network cross-traffic on the NCS's ability to stabilize the voltage.

6.1 Case Study

In this paper, we apply our Modelica/`ns-2` co-simulation tool to a NCS involving a drive train that is controlled by a PI controller (see Fig. 7). The model is constructed using blocks from the Modelica standard library plus our new `Network` block that communicates with `ns-2`.

For the scenario in Fig. 7, the objective is to control the motor inertia (`Inertia1`) to follow the reference speed signal shown in Fig. 8. The reference speed is generated by the two blocks `KinematicPTP` and `Integrator`. The output of the controller is a torque that drives `Inertia1`. The load inertia, `Inertia2`,

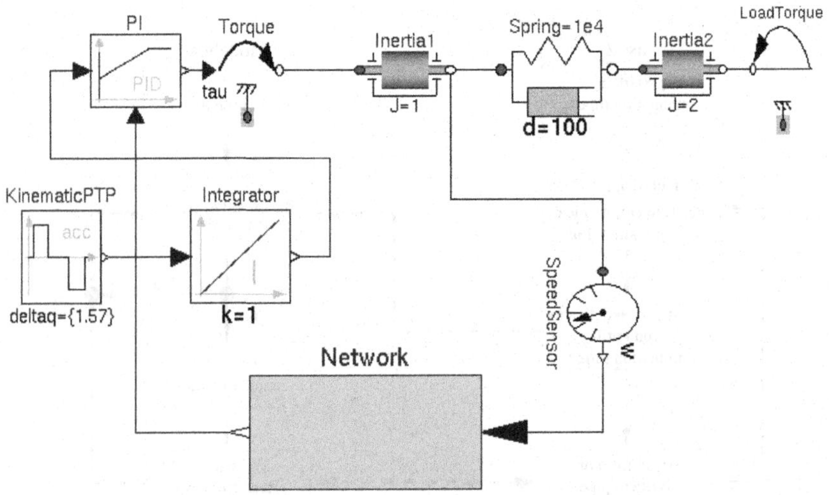

Fig. 7. A drive train NCS created by inserting our `Network` block into an example system that is part of the Modelica standard library [6]. The plant is a cascade of five mechanical elements: `Torque`, `Inertia1`, `Spring`, `Inertia2`, and `LoadTorque`. The Plant is controlled by a PI controller, `PI`, to follow the reference speed generated by the two blocks `KinematicPTP` and `Integrator`. The `SpeedSensor` measures the speed of `Inertia1` at fixed sampling intervals. `Network` is responsible for communicating back and forth with `ns-2` to relay and receive packets.

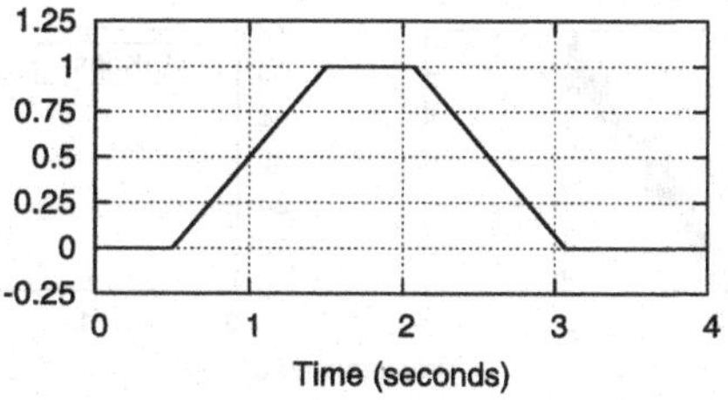

Fig. 8. The reference speed that `Inertia1` is required to follow

is attached to `Inertia1` via a compliant spring-damper component. Also, there is a constant external torque of 10Nm acting on the load inertia. The speed measurements from `Inertia1` are transported to the PI controller over a communication link that is shared with other traffic flows. Finally, `Network` is our newly developed Modelica block that contains the inter-simulator routines to allow Modelica models to communicate with `ns-2`.

Now, assume that the packets carrying the speed measurements flow from node 2 to node 0 of the network in Fig. 2. In this example, the network exists only in the feedback path that connects the plant to the controller but not in the forward path that connects the controller to the plant. Furthermore, we assume that the link L_1 is also traversed by cross-traffic corresponding to a multimedia application whose source and destination are attached to nodes 3 and 0, respectively. The network parameters are the same as those in Sect. 5. The speed is sampled at constant intervals of 2ms, and the samples are inscribed into packets of size 100B. The multimedia source starts injecting packets in the network at time 2sec and lasts for only 1sec. The multimedia packets are 1000B. We consider the effect of cross-traffic on the drive train NCS for two cases: when the multimedia source transmits at a constant rates of 625Kbps and 715Kbps. Figure 9 shows the speed of `Inertia1`, i.e., ω in Fig. 7, for these two cases. Obviously, the multimedia rate of 715Kbps leads to more contention between multimedia and NCS packets than that of 625Kbps. When the aggregate rate of both the NCS and of the multimedia traffic exceeds c_1, packets are enqueued

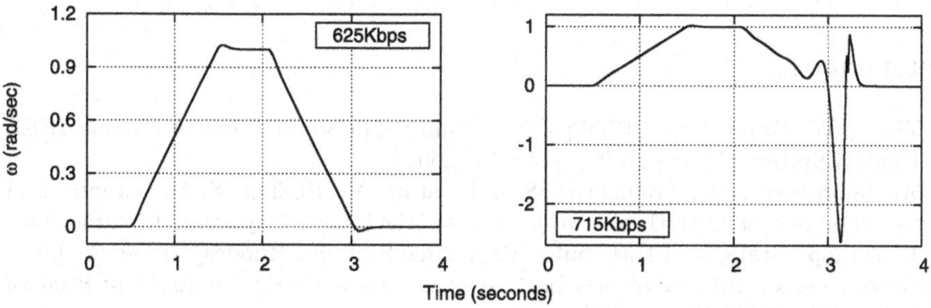

Fig. 9. The speed of `Inertia1`, i.e., ω in Fig. 7, when the multimedia application sends packets at a constant rate of 625Kbps and 715Kbps

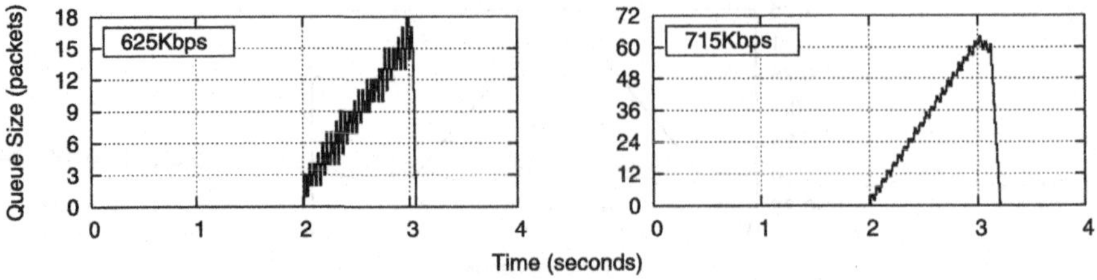

Fig. 10. The queue length at the router of Fig. 2 for the two cases when the multimedia application sends packets at a constant rate of 625Kbps and 715Kbps

in the router buffer (see Fig. 10). As a result, queueing delays deteriorate the control performance and jeopardize the NCS's stability.

7 Conclusions

We overviewed three tools that we have developed for the co-simulation of Networked Control Systems (NCSs). All of our tools use `ns-2` to simulate the communication networks side. The first two tools require modeling of and deriving equations for physical dynamics. Our newly developed tool integrates Modelica with `ns-2` so it reduces physics modeling time, effort, and errors. We argued that co-simulation is indispensable to the study and further progress of NCSs because NCSs, in general, involve hybrid and time-varying dynamics, thus making pure analytical approaches intractable in large scale configurations.

That said, we have not examined the scalability or optimality of our proposed co-simulation paradigm. Specifically, one should examine how the computation time and memory usage of co-simulation scale as the number of plant models and their complexity increase. These matters are the subject of future research.

Acknowledgments

Research supported in part by NSF CCR-0329910, Department of Commerce TOP 39-60-04003, and Department of Energy DE-FC26-06NT42853.

References

1. Zhang, W., Branicky, M., Phillips, S.: Stability of networked control systems. IEEE Control Systems Magazine 21(1), 84–99 (2001)
2. Al-Hammouri, A.T., Branicky, M.S., Liberatore, V., Phillips, S.M.: Decentralized and dynamic bandwidth allocation in networked control systems. In: Proc. Intl. Workshop Parallel and Distributed Real-Time Systems, Rhodes, Greece (2006)
3. Liberatore, V.: Integrated play-back, sensing, and networked control. In: Proc. of IEEE INFOCOM (2006)
4. Branicky, M.S., Liberatore, V., Phillips, S.M.: Networked control system co-simulation for co-design. In: Proc. American Control Conf., Denver (2003)

5. Branicky, M.S., Mattsson, S.E.: Simulation of hybrid systems. In: Antsaklis, P.J., Kohn, W., Nerode, A., Sastry, S.S. (eds.) HS 1996. LNCS, vol. 1273, pp. 31–56. Springer, Heidelberg (1997)
6. Modelica and Modelica Association, `http://www.modelica.org`
7. Network Simulator—**ns-2**, `http://www.isi.edu/nsnam/ns`
8. OMNeT++: Discrete Event Simulation System, `http://www.omnetpp.org`
9. Simulink® version 6.1. The MathWorks Inc. (2004)
10. The Ptolemy Project, `http://ptolemy.eecs.berkeley.edu`
11. ADEVS: A Discrete EVent System simulator, `http://www.ornl.gov/~1qn/adevs/index.html`
12. Cervin, A., Ohlin, M., Henriksson, D.: Simulation of networked control systems using TrueTime. In: Proc. International Workshop on Networked Control Systems: Tolerant to Faults, Nancy, France (2007)
13. Baldwin, P., Kohli, S., Lee, E.A., Liu, X., Zhao, Y.: Modeling of sensor nets in Ptolemy II. In: Proc. Info. Processing in Sensor Networks, Berkeley, CA (2004)
14. Nutaro, J., Kuruganti, P.T., Miller, L., Mullen, S., Shankar, M.: Integrated hybrid-simulation of electric power and communications systems. IEEE Power Engineering Society General Meeting, 1–8 (2007)
15. Nethi, S., Pohjola, M., Eriksson, L., Jantti, R.: Platform for emulating networked control systems in laboratory environments. In: IEEE Intl. Symp. World of Wireless, Mobile and Multimedia Networks, Espoo, Finland (2007)
16. Kurose, J.F., Ross, K.W.: Computer Networking: A Top-Down Approach Featuring the Internet. Addison Wesley Longman, Inc., Amsterdam (2001)
17. Liberatore, V.: `Agent/Plant` extension, `http://vorlon.case.edu/~vxl11/NetBots`
18. Hartman, J.R., Branicky, M.S., Liberatore, V.: Time-dependent dynamics in networked sensing and control. In: Proc. American Control Conf., Portland (2005)
19. Hartman, J.: Networked control system co-simulation for co-design: Theory and experiments. Master's thesis, Case Western Reserve Univ., Cleveland, Ohio (2004)
20. Al-Hammouri, A.T., Liberatore, V.: Optimization congestion control for Networked Control Systems . In: Proc. of IEEE INFOCOM Student Workshop, Miami, FL (abstract) (2005)
21. Al-Hammouri, A.T.: Internet Congestion Control: Complete Stability Region for PI AQM and Bandwidth Allocation in Networked Control. PhD thesis, Case Western Reserve Univ., Cleveland, Ohio (2008)
22. Al-Hammouri, A.T., Liberatore, V., Al-Omari, H., Al-Qudah, Z., Branicky, M.S., Agrawal, D.: A co-simulation platform for actuator networks. In: Proc. ACM Conference on Embedded Networked Sensor Systems, Sydney (demonstration) (2007)

On the Maximum Principle for Impulsive Hybrid Systems

Vadim Azhmyakov[1], Sid Ahmed Attia[2], and Jörg Raisch[2,3]

[1] Departamento de Control Automatico, CINVESTAV, A.P. 14-740, Av. Instituto Politecnico Nacional No. 2508, C.P. 07360, Mexico D.F., Mexico
vazhmyakov@ctrl.cinvestav.mx
[2] Fachgebiet Regelungssysteme, Technische Universität Berlin, Einsteinufer 17, D-10587 Berlin, Germany
attia@ieee.org
[3] Systems and Control Theory Group, MPI for Dynamics of Complex Technical Systems, Sandtorstr. 1, D-39106 Magdeburg, Germany
raisch@control.tu-berlin.de

Abstract. In this contribution, we consider a class of hybrid systems with continuous dynamics and jumps in the continuous state (impulsive hybrid systems). By using a newly elaborated version of the Pontryagin-type Maximum Principle (MP) for optimal control processes governed by hybrid dynamics with autonomous location transitions, we extend the necessary optimality conditions to a class of Impulsive Hybrid Optimal Control Problems (IHOCPs). For these problems, we obtain a concise characterization of the Impulsive Hybrid MP (IHMP), namely, the corresponding boundary-value problem and some additional relations. As in the classical case, the proposed IHMP provides a basis for diverse computational algorithms for the treatment of IHOCPs.

Keywords: impulsive hybrid control systems, optimal control, necessary conditions of optimality, Maximum principle.

1 Introduction

During the last two decades, there has been considerable effort to develop theoretical and computational frameworks for hybrid systems. Of particular importance is the ability to operate such systems in an optimal manner. With the exception of certain special cases, the solution to the optimal problem remains a challenging task. This is due to the fact that the two aspects of system behaviour, i.e., discrete and continuous, are tightly linked, to such an extent that they cannot be decoupled in an effective and simple way. One of the most convenient ways to deal with the problem is to formulate it as a sequential problem, i.e., for a particular execution the time axis is partitioned into intervals, and in each interval, the dynamics are characterized by a set of ODEs, with transitions being triggered internally (autonomous switches) or externally (controlled switches). This is the approach that has been considered since the initial formulation of the corresponding optimal control problem [15,16], [32] and can be

M. Egerstedt and B. Mishra (Eds.): HSCC 2008, LNCS 4981, pp. 30–42, 2008.

seen as a natural way to tackle the problem. For a deeper discussion on the main theoretical questions see e.g., [2,3,6,7,12,13,14,17,18,21,27,28,32,35].

The class of hybrid systems considered in this contribution involves systems driven by continuous control inputs where switching is accompanied by a jump in the state. A similar class has been considered in [33], where the authors focus attention on state delayed systems with controlled switches and where useful gradient formulas have been derived, for an application see [34]. See also [35] and [36] for related problems. In contrast, we consider the case where switches are being triggered by the continuous dynamics but the magnitudes of the corresponding state jumps are part of the optimization variables; see also [3] for a gradient-based approach. This family of systems captures phenomena arising in, e.g., cyclically operated batch processes and certain epidemic propagation models.

A simple transfomation relates the optimal control problem for the aforementioned class of systems to another optimal control problems, for which necessary conditions of optimality have been previously derived by the authors [6]. These results make it possible to use conceptual algorithms and their corresponding convergence results, see e.g., [5]. Note that using transformations is a standard approach in optimal control theory and has been used extensively in the past to formulate different results (see e.g., [11], see also [17], where a transformation is used to derive a version of the Maximum principle for a class of hybrid systems).

The outline of the paper is as follows. In Section 2, we formally describe the IHOCP investigated in this contribution. Section 3 contains an equivalent representation of the impulsive hybrid system under consideration and includes an auxiliary optimal control problem for the given IHOCP. In Section 4, we propose a new variant of the hybrid MP for impulsive hybrid systems, namely the Impulsive Hybrid MP. This principle is derived from the MP for hybrid systems with autonomous location transitions and is closely related to the version of the MP proposed in, e.g., [12,13] and to the gradient-based approach to hybrid optimal control problems proposed in [3,4,5]. In Section 5, we discuss some computational issues of the proposed necessary optimality conditions for IHOCPs. Section 6 summarizes the paper.

2 Modeling Framework and Problem Formulation

Let us formally introduce the class of hybrid systems investigated in this paper:

Definition 1. *An* **impulsive hybrid system** *is a 7-tuple*

$$\mathcal{IHS} = \{\mathcal{Q}, \mathcal{X}, U, \mathcal{U}, F, \Theta, \mathcal{S}\},$$

where

- $\mathcal{Q}$ *is a finite set of locations;*
- $\mathcal{X} = \{\mathcal{X}_q\}_{q \in \mathcal{Q}}$ *is a collection of state sets with* $\mathcal{X}_q \subseteq \mathbb{R}^n$*;*
- $U \subseteq \mathbb{R}^m$ *is a control set;*

– $\mathcal{U}$ *is a set of admissible control functions;*
– $F = \{f_q\}_{q \in \mathcal{Q}}$ *is a family of vector fields* $f_q : [0, t_f] \times \mathcal{X}_q \times U \to \mathbb{R}^n$*;*
– $\Theta = \{\Theta_q\}_{q \in \mathcal{Q}}$ *is a collection of maximal constant amplitudes (state jumps);*
– $\mathcal{S}$ *is a subset of* Ξ*, where*

$$\Xi := \{(q, x, q', x') \ , \ q, q' \in \mathcal{Q}, \ x \in \mathcal{X}_q, \ x' \in \mathcal{X}_{q'}\}.$$

In the following, we consider only impulsive hybrid systems $\mathcal{IHS}$ that satisfy the following assumptions:

A1. The functions $f_q(t, \cdot, \cdot)$, where $q \in \mathcal{Q}$, are continuously differentiable
A2. There exists a constant $K < \infty$ such that $||\partial f_q(t, x, u)/\partial x|| < K$ for all $(t, x, u) \in [0, t_f] \times \mathcal{X}_q \times U$ for all $q \in \mathcal{Q}$
A3. The control set U is compact and convex

Moreover, we assume that smooth functions $m_{q,q'} : \mathbb{R}^n \to \mathbb{R}, \ q, \ q' \in \mathcal{Q}$ with nonzero gradients are given such that the hypersurfaces

$$M_{q,q'} := \{x \in \mathbb{R}^n \ : \ m_{q,q'}(x) = 0\}$$

are pairwise disjoint. Note that in this case a hypersurface $M_{q,q'}$ characterizes the set $\mathcal{S}$ at which a switch from location q to location q' can take place. Evidently, $M_{q,q'}$ is the projection of $\mathcal{S}$ on the product space $\mathcal{X}_q \times \mathcal{X}_{q'}$. The set of admissible control functions from Definition 1 is taken as

$$\mathcal{U} := \{u(\cdot) \in \mathbb{L}^m_\infty(0, t_f) \ : \ u(t) \in U_q, \ \text{a.e. on}[0, t_f]\}.$$

By $\mathbb{L}^m_\infty(0, t_f)$ we denote the standard Lebesque space of measurable and essentially bounded functions. Note that the pair $(q, x(t))$ represents the hybrid state at time t, where q is a location $q \in \mathcal{Q}$ and $x(t) \in \mathbb{R}^n$. Let us introduce some standard spaces, namely, the space $\mathbb{C}^\infty_0(0, t_f)$ of all $\mathbb{C}^\infty$ functions that vanish outside a compact subset of $(0, t_f)$ and the space $\mathcal{D}'(0, t_f)$ of generalized functions (Schwartz distributions). Recall that $\mathcal{D}'(0, t_f)$ can be considered as a space of linear, sequentially continuous functionals with respect to the convergence on the space $\mathbb{C}^\infty_0(0, t_f)$. In the following, we define the notion of a hybrid trajectory of an impulsive hybrid system (see e.g., [4],[5]).

Definition 2. *A* **hybrid trajectory** *of* $\mathcal{IHS}$ *is a triple* $\mathbf{X} = (x(\cdot), \{q_i\}, \tau)$*, where* $x(\cdot) \in \mathcal{D}'(0, t_f)$ *is a discontinuous trajectory,* $\{q_i\}_{i=1,\ldots,r}$ *is a finite sequence of locations and* τ *is the corresponding sequence of switching times*

$$0 = t_0 < \cdots < t_i < \cdots < t_r = t_f$$

such that for each $i = 1, \ldots, r$ *there exists* $u(\cdot) \in \mathcal{U}$ *such that:*

– $x(0) = x_0 \notin \bigcup_{q,q' \in \mathcal{Q}} M_{q,q'}$ *and* $x_i(\cdot) = x(\cdot)|_{(t_{i-1}, t_i)}$ *is an absolutely continuous function on* (t_{i-1}, t_i)*;*
– $x(t_i) \in M_{q_i, q_{i+1}}$ *for* $i = 1, ..., r - 1$*;*

– $\dot{x}_i(t) = f_{q_i}(t, x_i(t), u(t)) + \theta_{q_i}\delta(t - t_i)$ *for almost all* $t \in [t_{i-1}, t_i]$, *where* δ *is the Dirac function and* $||\theta_{q_i}|| \leq \Theta_{q_i}$.

The derivative $\dot{x}_i(\cdot)$ in Definition 2 is considered as a weak derivative of the generalized function $x_i(\cdot)$ defined on the full interval $[t_{i-1}, t_i]$. It is also evident that a function $x(\cdot)$ from Definition 2 consists of absolutely continuous parts defined on the open intervals (t_{i-1}, t_i) and involves jumps of magnitude θ_{q_i} at the switching times t_i, see Figure 1 for an example of the execution. Note that the evolution equation for the trajectory $x(\cdot)$ of a given impulsive hybrid system $\mathcal{IHS}$ can also be represented as follows

$$\begin{aligned} \dot{x}(t) &= \sum_{i=1}^{r} \beta_{[t_{i-1},t_i)}(t) f_{q_i}(t, x(t), u(t)) + \sum_{i=1}^{r} \theta_{q_i}\delta(t - t_i) \text{ a.e. on } [0, t_f] \\ x(0) &= x_0 \end{aligned} \tag{1}$$

where $\beta_{[t_{i-1},t_i)}(\cdot)$ is the characteristic function of the interval $[t_{i-1}, t_i)$

$$\beta_{[t_{i-1},t_i)}(t) = \begin{cases} 1 & \text{if } t \in [t_{i-1}, t_i) \\ 0 & \text{otherwise} \end{cases}$$

for $i = 1, ..., r$. Note that the initial value problem in Equation (1) is also considered in the sense of weak derivatives on the space $\mathcal{D}'(0, t_f)$. Under the assumptions presented above, for each $u(\cdot) \in \mathcal{U}$ and all $||\theta_{q_i}|| \leq \Theta_{q_i}$, $i = 1, ..., r$, the initial value problem (1) has a unique solution in $\mathcal{D}'(0, t_f)$.

Let $f^0 : \mathbb{R} \times \mathbb{R}^n \times \mathbb{R}^m \to \mathbb{R}$ be a continuously differentiable function. Given an impulsive hybrid system $\mathcal{IHS}$ we now formulate a corresponding optimization problem, the following Impulsive Hybrid Optimal Control Problem (IHOCP):

$$\text{minimize} \sum_{i=1}^{r} \int_{t_{i-1}}^{t_i} f^0(t, x(t), u(t))dt \tag{2}$$

over all trajectories $\mathbf{X}$ of $\mathcal{IHS}$.

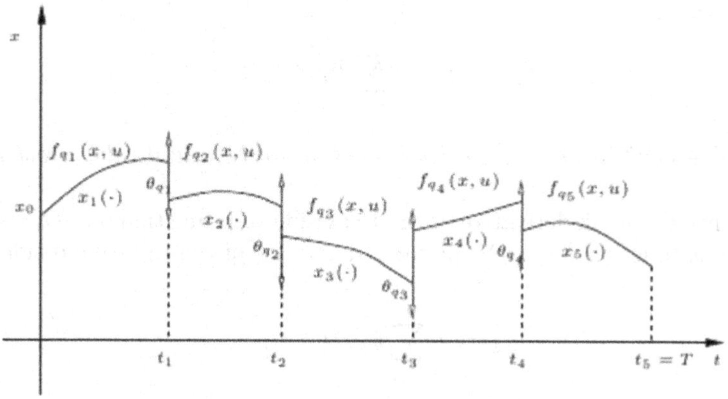

Fig. 1. An example of execution with 4 switches ($r = 5$)

Throughout the paper we assume that the IHOCP (2) has an optimal solution

$$(u^{opt}(\cdot), \theta^{opt}, \mathbf{X}^{opt}(\cdot)) \in \mathcal{C} := \mathcal{U} \times \mathbb{R}^{n\times r} \times \mathcal{D}'(0,t_f) \times \mathcal{Q}^r \times [0,t_f]^r$$

where $\theta^{opt} := (\theta^{opt}_{q_1} ... \theta^{opt}_{q_r})$ is a matrix representing the optimal jumps.

3 Optimization of Impulsive Hybrid Systems

The optimal control problem (2) is an optimization problem formulated on the space $\mathcal{C}$ which involves the space of generalized functions $\mathcal{D}'(0,t_f)$. Our aim is to introduce an auxiliary hybrid optimal control problem governed by a hybrid system with autonomous location transitions without jumps in the continuous state see e.g., [12,13,5,6,7] for further details. For this, consider the following auxiliary initial value problem

$$\begin{aligned} \dot{y}(t) &= \sum_{i=1}^{r} \beta_{[t_{i-1},t_i)}(t) f_{q_i}\big(t, y(t) + \sum_{i=1}^{r} \theta_{q_i}\eta(t-t_i), u(t)\big) \text{ a.e. on } [0,t_f], \\ y(0) &= x_0 \end{aligned} \tag{3}$$

where $i = 1, ..., r$ and $\eta(\cdot)$ is the Heaviside step-function. Note that $\eta(\cdot)$ can also be considered as an element of the space $\mathcal{D}'(0,t_f)$. Under the assumptions stated in the previous section, the initial value problem (3) has a unique absolutely continuous solution for each $u(\cdot) \in \mathcal{U}$ (see, e.g., [9,22]). Next we consider $y(\cdot)$ as an element of the Sobolev space $x(\cdot) \in \mathbb{W}^{1,\infty}_n(0,t_f)$, i.e., the space of absolutely continuous functions with essentially bounded derivatives. We are now able to formulate our first equivalence result.

Theorem 1. *Under the above-mentioned assumptions A1 – A3, the (unique) solution $x(\cdot) \in \mathcal{D}'(0,t_f)$ of the initial value problem (1) can be represented in the following form:*

$$x(t) = y(t) + \sum_{i=1}^{r} \theta_{q_i}\eta(t-t_i), \tag{4}$$

where $y(\cdot) \in \mathbb{W}^{1,\infty}_n(0,t_f)$ is a (unique) solution to the initial value problem (3).

Proof. Since the weak derivative of the Heaviside step-function $\eta(t-t_i)$ is equal to the Dirac function $\delta(t-t_i)$, the weak derivative of the right-hand side of (4) is

$$\dot{y}(t) + \sum_{i=1}^{r} \theta_{q_i}\delta(t-t_i).$$

For an absolutely continuous function $y(\cdot)$ the weak derivative of $y(\cdot)$ coincides with the classical derivative. Using equation (4), the initial value problem (1) can be written in the following form

$$\dot{x}(t) = \dot{y}(t) + \sum_{i=1}^{r} \theta_{q_i} \delta(t - t_i) = \sum_{i=1}^{r} \beta_{[t_{i-1},t_i)}(t) f_{q_i}(t, y(t)$$
$$+ \sum_{i=1}^{r} \theta_{q_i} \eta(t - t_i), u(t)) + \sum_{i=1}^{r} \theta_{q_i} \delta(t - t_i)$$
$$= \sum_{i=1}^{r} \beta_{[t_{i-1},t_i)}(t) f_{q_i}(t, x(t), u(t)) + \sum_{i=1}^{r} \theta_{q_i} \delta(t - t_i)$$

Moreover, for $t = 0$ we obtain $x(0) = y(0)$. The uniqueness arguments for solutions of the initial value problems (1) and (3) complete the proof. □

It is necessary to stress that the proposed representation (4) can also be considered as a transformation of values. This transformation eliminates state jumps at the switching times $t_i \in \tau$ from the original system (1). From the affine structure of (4) we can deduce the following simple characterization of (4) with respect to solutions of the above initial value problems.

Theorem 2. *The transformation* (4) *from* Theorem 1 *is a bijective mapping* $\mathcal{D}'(0, t_f) \to \mathbb{W}_n^{1,\infty}(0, t_f)$ *and the solutions* $x(\cdot) \in \mathcal{D}'(0, t_f)$ *and* $y(\cdot) \in \mathbb{W}_n^{1,\infty}(0, t_f)$ *of the initial value problems* (1) *and* (3) *are related by equation* (4).

Our results, namely, Theorem 1 and Theorem 2, give rise to the study of an auxiliary hybrid system with autonomous location transitions. Recall the corresponding definition.

Definition 3. *A* **hybrid system** *with autonomous location transitions is a 6-tuple*

$$\mathcal{H} = \{\mathcal{Q}, \mathcal{X}, U, \mathcal{U}, F, \mathcal{S}^a\},$$

where

- $\mathcal{Q}$ *is a finite set of locations;*
- $\mathcal{X} = \{\mathcal{X}_q\}_{q \in \mathcal{Q}}$ *is a collection of state sets with* $\mathcal{X}_q \subseteq \mathbb{R}^n$*;*
- $U \subseteq \mathbb{R}^m$ *is a control set;*
- $\mathcal{U}$ *is a set of admissible control functions;*
- $F = \{f_q\}_{q \in \mathcal{Q}}$ *is a family of vector fields* $f_q : [0, t_f] \times \mathcal{X}_q \times U \to \mathbb{R}^n$*;*
- $\mathcal{S}^a$ *is a subset of* Ξ_a*, where*

$$\Xi^a := \{(q, y, q', y') \, , \, q, q' \in \mathcal{Q}, y \in \mathcal{X}_q, y' \in \mathcal{X}_{q'}\}.$$

Moreover, a **hybrid trajectory** *of* $\mathcal{H}$ *is a triple* $\mathbf{Y} = (y(\cdot), \{q_i\}^a, \tau^a)$*, where* $y(\cdot) : [0, T] \to \mathbb{R}^n$ *and for each* $i = 1, \ldots, r$*, there exists* $u(\cdot) \in \mathcal{U}$ *such that:*

- $y(0) = x_0$ *and* $y_i(\cdot) = y(\cdot)|_{(t_{i-1},t_i)}$ *is an absolutely continuous function on* (t_{i-1}, t_i) *continuously prolongable to* $[t_{i-1}, t_i]$*,* $i = 1, ..., r$*;*

- $\dot{y}_i(t) = f_{q_i}(t, y_i(t), u(t))$ *for almost all* $t \in [t_{i-1}, t_i]$, $i = 1, ..., r$;
- *the following switching condition* $(y_i(t_i), y_{i+1}(t_i)) \in S^a_{q_i, q_{i+1}}$ *holds for each value* $i = 1, ..., r-1$, *where*

$$S^a_{q,q'} := \{(y, y') \in \mathcal{X}_q \times \mathcal{X}_{q'} \ : \ (q, y, q'y') \in \mathcal{S}^a\}$$

is a switching set from location $q \in \mathcal{Q}$ *to location* $q' \in \mathcal{Q}$ *with* $y = y'$ *meaning the absence of jumps in the continuous state.*

Under assumptions of Section 2, the switching sets $S^a_{q_i, q_{i+1}}$ can be characterized by the following constructive conditions

$$m_{q_i, q_{i+1}}(y(t) + \sum_{i=1}^{r} \theta_{q_i} \eta(t - t_i)) = 0, \ i = 1, ..., r-1,$$

where functions $m_{q_i, q_{i+1}}$ defines the manifolds $M_{q_i, q_{i+1}}$ from Definition 2.

For the system described by the initial value problem (3), we now formulate the following optimal control problem (see also [5,6,7])

$$\begin{aligned} &\text{minimize} \sum_{i=1}^{r} \int_{t_{i-1}}^{t_i} f^0(t, y(t) + \sum_{i=1}^{r} \theta_{q_i} \eta(t - t_i), u(t)) dt \\ &\text{over all trajectories } \mathbf{Y} \text{ of } \mathcal{H}. \end{aligned} \tag{5}$$

We assume that the optimal control problem (5) has a solution

$$(u^{opt}(\cdot), \theta^{opt}, \mathbf{Y}^{opt}(\cdot)) \in \mathcal{U} \times \mathbb{R}^{n \times r} \times \mathbb{W}^{1,\infty}_n(0, t_f) \times \mathcal{Q}^r \times [0, t_f]^r.$$

The following result establishes the relations between the two optimization problems (2) and (5).

Theorem 3. *Suppose that problems* (2) *and* (5) *have both optimal solutions. Under the assumptions A1 – A3, every optimal solution* $(u^{opt}(\cdot), \theta^{opt}, \mathbf{Y}^{opt})$ *of problem* (5) *defines the corresponding optimal solution* $(u^{opt}(\cdot), \theta^{opt}, \mathbf{X}^{opt}(\cdot))$ *for problem* (2), *where*

$$\begin{aligned} &\{q_i\}^a = \{q_i\}, \ \tau^a = \tau, \\ &x^{opt}(t) = y^{opt}(t) + \sum_{i=1}^{r} \theta^{opt}_{q_i} \eta(t - t^{opt}_i) \end{aligned}$$

Here t^{opt}_i *is an element of the optimal sequence* τ^{opt} *and* $\theta^{opt}_{q_i}$ *are optimal jumps in the original* IHOCP (2).

Note that Theorem 3 is an immediate consequence of Theorem 2.

As evident from the main Definitions 1 and 3, the class of hybrid control systems with autonomous location transitions is a subclass of impulsive hybrid systems. Definition 1 describes hybrid dynamical systems with discontinuous state trajectories. Moreover, the control variable of an impulsive hybrid system $\mathcal{IHS}$ includes external inputs and magnitudes of the jumps in the state. On the other hand, the proposed transformation (4) and the obtained results, namely, Theorems 1-3 make it possible to reduce the general sophisticated IHOCP (2) to the auxiliary optimal control problem of the type (5).

4 The Impulsive Hybrid Maximum Principle

For both hybrid systems (1) and (3) we introduce the extended control vector $v(\cdot) := (u(\cdot), \theta)$, where $\theta := (\theta_{q_1}, ..., \theta_{q_r})$. An admissible extended control vector $v(\cdot)$ satisfies the conditions

$$u(\cdot) \in \mathcal{U}, \ ||\theta_{q_i}|| \leq \Theta_{q_i}, \ i = 1, ..., r.$$

An optimal extended control vector is denoted by $v^{opt}(\cdot)$ and the corresponding elements of this vector are denoted by $u^{opt}(\cdot)$ and θ^{opt}. Now we apply the known MP [6,7].

Theorem 4. *Let the functions f^0, f_{q_i} be continuously differentiable and the optimal control problem* (5) *be regular. Then there exist a function $\psi_i(\cdot)$ from $\mathbb{W}_n^{1,\infty}(0, t_f)$ and a non-zero vector $a = (a_1 \dots a_{r-1})^T \in \mathbb{R}^{r-1}$ such that*

$$\begin{aligned} \dot{\psi}_i(t) &= -\frac{\partial H_{q_i}(y_i^{opt}(t), v^{opt}(t), \psi(t))}{\partial (y + \sum_{j=i}^r \theta_{q_j})} \text{ a.e. on } (t_{i-1}^{opt}, t_i^{opt}), \\ \psi_r(t_f) &= 0, \end{aligned} \tag{6}$$

and

$$\begin{aligned} \psi_i(t_i^{opt}) &= \psi_{i+1}(t_i^{opt}) + \left(a_i \frac{\partial m_{q_i, q_{i+1}}(y^{opt}(t_i^{opt}) + \sum_{j=i}^r \theta_{q_j}^{opt})}{\partial (y + \sum_{j=i}^r \theta_{q_j})} \right), \\ i &= 1, ..., r-1, \end{aligned} \tag{7}$$

Moreover, for every admissible control $v(\cdot)$ the following inequality is satisfied

$$\begin{aligned} &\left(\frac{\partial H_{q_i}(y^{opt}(t), v^{opt}(t), \psi(t))}{\partial v}, (v(t) - v^{opt}(t)) \right) \leq 0 \\ &\text{a.e. on } [t_{i-1}^{opt}, t_i^{opt}], \ i = 1, ..., r \end{aligned} \tag{8}$$

where

$$H_{q_i}(y, v, \psi) := (\psi_i, f_{q_i}(t, y + \sum_{i=1}^r \theta_{q_i} \eta(t - t_i), u)) - f_{q_i}^0(t, y + \sum_{i=1}^r \theta_{q_i} \eta(t - t_i), u)$$

is a "partial" Hamiltonian for the location $q_i \in \mathcal{Q}$, ψ is an adjoint vector and $(\cdot, \cdot)$ denotes the corresponding scalar product.

Using the one-to-one correspondence between the solutions $x^{opt}(\cdot)$ and $y^{opt}(\cdot)$ of the initial value problems (1) and (3) established by Theorem 2 and the transformation from Theorem 1, we are now able to formulate the necessary optimality conditions for the original problem (2), namely the IHMP.

Theorem 5. *Let functions f^0, f_{q_i} be continuously differentiable and the optimal control problem (2) be regular. Then there exist a function $p_i(\cdot)$ from $\mathbb{W}^{1,\infty}_n(0,t_f)$ and a non-zero vector $b = (b_1 \dots b_{r-1})^T \in \mathbb{R}^{r-1}$ such that*

$$\begin{aligned} \dot{p}_i(t) &= -\frac{\partial H_{q_i}(x_i^{opt}(t), v^{opt}(t), p(t))}{\partial x} \text{ a.e. on } (t_{i-1}^{opt}, t_i^{opt}), \\ p_r(t_f) &= 0, \end{aligned} \tag{9}$$

and

$$p_i(t_i^{opt}) = p_{i+1}(t_i^{opt}) + \left(b_i \frac{\partial m_{q_i,q_{i+1}}(x^{opt}(t_i^{opt}))}{\partial x} \right), \quad i = 1, ..., r-1. \tag{10}$$

Moreover, for every admissible control $v(\cdot)$ the following inequalities are satisfied

$$\begin{aligned} &\left(\frac{\partial H_{q_i}(x^{opt}(t), v^{opt}(t), p(t))}{\partial u}, (u(t) - u^{opt}(t)) \right) \leq 0 \\ &\left(\frac{\partial H_{q_i}(x^{opt}(t), v^{opt}(t), p(t))}{\partial \theta}, (\theta - \theta^{opt}) \right) \leq 0 \\ &\text{a.e. on } [t_{i-1}^{opt}, t_i^{opt}], \ i = 1, ..., r \end{aligned} \tag{11}$$

where $H_{q_i}(y, v, p) := \big(p_i, f_{q_i}(t, x, u) + \theta_{q_i}\delta(t - t_i)\big) - f^0_{q_i}(t, x, u)$ is a "partial" Hamiltonian for the location $q_i \in \mathcal{Q}$, p is an adjoint vector and $(\cdot, \cdot)$ denotes the corresponding scalar product.

Note that Theorem 5 is an immediate consequence of Theorem 4 and the above-mentioned ono-to-one correspondence between the solutions of the two initial value problems under consideration. Using the equivalence results from Section 3, we obtain the necessary optimality conditions for the general IHOCP (2) as a consequence of the MP for the auxiliary problem (5). The presented approach allows to avoid the consideration of generalized functions, weak derivatives and some related sophisticated mathematical techniques, which would be necessary for a direct proof of the above IHMP.

When solving constrained optimal control problems based on some necessary conditions for optimality one can obtain singular solutions. There are two possible scenarios for a singularity: the irregularity of the Lagrange multiplier associated with the cost functional [9,22] and the irregularity of the Hamiltonian. In the latter case the Hamiltonian is not an explicit function of the control function during a time interval. Various supplementary conditions (constraint qualifications) have been proposed under which it is possible to assert that the Lagrange Multiplier Rule (and the corresponding Maximum Principle) holds in "normal" form, i.e., that the first Lagrange multiplier is nonequal to zero. In this case the corresponding minimization problem is called regular. We refer to [1,19,23] for theoretical details. Note that some regularity conditions for general constrained optimal control problems can be formulated as controllability conditions for the linearized system [23].

Let us now simplify the Hamiltonian minimization condition (11). Using the given formula for H_{q_i}, we compute

$$\frac{\partial H_{q_i}(x^{opt}(t), v^{opt}(t), p(t))}{\partial \theta} = p_i(t)\delta(t - t_i^{opt}),$$

where $t \in [t_{i-1}^{opt}, t_i^{opt}]$. Then, the second inequality from Theorem 5 can be writen in the following form

$$\left(p_i(t), \theta_{q_i} - \theta_{q_i}^{opt}\right) \delta(t - t_i^{opt}) \leq 0, \; t \in [t_{i-1}^{opt}, t_i^{opt}]. \tag{12}$$

Integrating (12) over $[t_{i-1}^{opt}, t_i^{opt}]$, we obtain

$$\left(p_i(t_i^{opt}), \theta_{q_i} - \theta_{q_i}^{opt}\right) \leq 0. \tag{13}$$

Evidently, in the case $p_i(t_i^{opt}) = 0$ for any index $i = 1, ..., r$, the optimal vector of state jumps θ^{opt} cannot be found directly by globally minimizing H_{q_i}. Note that the partial Hamiltonian H_{q_i} is an affine function of θ_{q_i}. From this it is inferred that in the case of an IHOCP we can have a new kind of singularity, namely, the irregularity of the Hamiltonian with respect to the state jumps. On the other hand, the presented inequality (13) is a condition for a "bang-bang" control with respect to the second part of the extended control vector v.

5 Numerical Aspects

In the previous section we derived a necessary optimality condition (Theorem 4 and Theorem 5) and formulated the Hamiltonian minimization condition in the form of variational inequalities (8) and (11). It is well known that variational inequalities play an important role in optimization theory. We refer to [8] for details. For the numerical treatment of variational inequality see also [24]. It is also well known that the variational inequality (11) is equivalent to the following equation

$$v^{opt}(t) = \Pi_W \left(v^{opt}(t) - \alpha \frac{\partial H_{q_i}(x^{opt}(t), v^{opt}(t), p(t))}{\partial v} v^{opt}(t) \right), \tag{14}$$

where $\alpha > 0$ and Π_W is a projection operator on the set $U \times U_\theta$. Here U_θ is the set of admissible jumps defined by the inequalities $||\theta_{q_i}|| \leq \Theta_{q_i}, \; i = 1, ..., r$. To solve (14) one can use a variety of gradient-type algorithms with a projection procedure. Let N be a sufficiently large positive integer number and

$$G_N := \{t^0 = 0, t^1, \ldots, t^N = T\}$$

be a (possibly nonequidistant) partition of $[0, T]$ with

$$\max_{0 \leq k \leq N-1} |t^{k+1} - t^k| \leq \epsilon$$

for a given accuracy constant ϵ. For every control function $u(\cdot) \in \mathcal{U}$ we introduce the piecewise constant control signals $u^N(\cdot)$ such that

$$u^n(t) := \sum_{k=0}^{N-1} \eta_k(t) u^k, \; u^k = u(t^k), \; k = 0, \ldots, N-1, \; t \in [0, t_f]$$

$$\eta_k(t) = \begin{cases} 1, & \text{if } t \in [t^k, t^{k+1}] \\ 0, & \text{otherwise} \end{cases}$$

Then for an approximate solution of the equation (14) we can consider the following finite-dimensional gradient method

$$\begin{aligned} & u^{N,0} \in U, \; \theta^{N,0} \in U_\theta, \\ & u^{N,(s+1)} = \Pi^1_U \left(u^{N,s} - \alpha_1 \frac{\partial H_{q_i}(x^{N,s}(t), (u^{N,s}(t), \theta^{N,s}), p^{N,s}(t))}{\partial u} u^{N,s} \right), \\ & \theta^{N,s+1} = \Pi^2_{U_\theta} \left(\theta^{N,s} - \alpha_2 \frac{\partial H_{q_i}(x^{N,s}(t), (u^{N,s}(t), \theta^{N,s}), p^{N,s}(t))}{\partial \theta} \theta^{N,s} \right), \end{aligned} \tag{15}$$

where α_1, α_2 are some positive constants, $s = 0, \ldots$, $x^{N,s}(\cdot)$ and $p^{N,s}(\cdot)$ are solutions of the corresponding initial and boundary value problems (1) and (9)-(11) in the actual location $q_i \in \mathcal{Q}$. Here Π^1 and Π^2 are partial projection operators on the set U and U_θ respectively. Moreover, the iteration of the extended control vector is denoted as $(u^{N,s}(\cdot), \theta^{N,s})$. Evidently, U and U_θ are convex sets. Note that in every step of the gradient algorithm (15) we need to solve the corresponding boundary-value problem from Theorem 5. Using inequalities (12) and (13), we can rewrite the second inequality in (15) in the following (integrated) form

$$\theta^{N,s+1} t_f = \Pi^2_{U_\theta} \left(\theta^{N,s} t_f - \alpha_2 p_i^{N,s}(t_i^{opt}) \theta^{N,s} \right). \tag{16}$$

Clearly, the presented inequality (16) must be combined with an effective procedure for estimating the optimal switching time t_i^{opt} for all $i = 1, ..., r$. One can use the iterative algorithm described in [5] for this purpose.

We refer to [29] for convergence properties of the general gradient-type algorithms. Clearly, instead of piecewise constant control signals one can also use possible approximations of higher order (piecewise linear and so on). Finally, note that the gradient technique (15) is analogous to the gradient-based computational approach proposed in [3,4,5,6,7] for optimization of hybrid systems with autonomous transitions.

6 Concluding Remarks

The Hamilton minimization conditions from Theorem 4 and Theorem 5 are presented in the form of variational inequalities. This form is closely related to the

Weierstraß conditions for a strong minimum (see, e.g.,[22]) and to the gradient-based computational approach studied in [3,4,5,6,7]. Finally note that the inequalities conditions (11) from Theorem 5 make it possible to take into consideration some effective methods for numerical treatment of variational inequalities.

Acknowledgements. The authors thank anonymous referees for valuable remarks and suggestions from which the final version of the paper greatly benefited.

References

1. Arutyunov, A.V., Aseev, S.M.: Investigation of the degeneracy phenomenon in the maximum principle for optimal control with state constraints. SIAM Journal on Control and Optimization 35, 930–952 (1997)
2. Attia, S.A., Alamir, M., Canudas de Wit, C.: Suboptimal control of switched nonlinear systems unde location and switching constraints. In: Proceedings of the 16th IFAC World Congress, Prague (2005)
3. Attia, S.A., Azhmyakov, V., Raisch, J.: State jump optimization for a class of hybrid autonomous systems. In: Proceedings of the 2007 IEEE Multi-conference on Systems and Control, Singapore, pp. 1408–1413 (2007)
4. Attia, S.A., Azhmyakov, V., Raisch, J.: On gradient methods for hybrid systems optimization (submitted, 2007)
5. Azhmyakov, V., Raisch, J.: A gradient-based approach to a class of hybrid optimal control problems. In: Proceedings of the 2nd IFAC Conference on Analysis and Design of Hybrid Systems, Alghero, pp. 89–94 (2006)
6. Azhmyakov, V., Attia, S.A., Gromov, D., Raisch, J.: Necessary optimality conditions for a class of hybrid optimal control problems. In: Bemporad, A., Bicchi, A., Buttazzo, G. (eds.) HSCC 2007. LNCS, vol. 4416, pp. 637–640. Springer, Heidelberg (2007)
7. Azhmyakov, V.: Optimal control of hybrid and switched systems. In: Proceedings of the IX Chetaev Conference "Analytical Mechanics, Stability and Control of Motion", Irkutsk, pp. 308–317 (2007)
8. Baiocchi, C., Capello, A.: Variational and Quasivariational Inequalities: Application to Free Boundary Problems. Wiley, New York (1984)
9. Berkovitz, L.D.: Optimal Control Theory. Springer, New York (1974)
10. Branicky, M.S., Borkar, V.S., Mitter, S.K.: A unifed framework for hybrid control: model and optimal control theory. IEEE Transactions on Automatic Control 43, 31–45 (1998)
11. Bryson, A.E., Ho, Y.C.: Applied Optimal Control. Blaisdell Publishing Company, Waltham (1969)
12. Caines, P., Shaikh, M.S.: Optimality zone algorithms for hybrid systems computation and control: From exponential to linear complexity. In: Proceedings of the 13th Mediterranean Conference on Control and Automation, Limassol, pp. 1292–1297 (2005)
13. Caines, P., Shaikh, M.S.: Convergence analysis of Hybrid Maximum Principle (HMP) optimal control algorithms. In: Proceedings of the 17th International Symposium on Mathematical Theory of Networks and Systems, Kyoto, pp. 2083–2088 (2006)
14. Cassandras, C., Pepyne, D.L., Wardi, Y.: Optimal control of a class of hybrid systems. IEEE Transactions on Automatic Control 46, 398–415 (2001)

15. Clarke, F., Vinter, R.: Optimal multiprocesses. SIAM Journal on Control and Optimization 27, 1072–1090 (1989)
16. Clarke, F.H., Vinter, R.B.: Applications of optimal multiprocesses. SIAM Journal on Control and Optimization 27, 1048–1071 (1989)
17. Dmitruk, A.V., Kaganovivh, A.M.: The Hybrid Maximum Principle is a Consequence of Pontryagin Maximum Principle, `http://www.optimization-online.org/`
18. Egerstedt, M., Wardi, Y., Axelsson, H.: Transition-time optimization for switched-mode dynamical systems. IEEE Transactions on Automatic Control 51, 110–115 (2006)
19. Ferreira, M.M.A., Fontes, F.A.C.C., Vinter, R.B.: Nondegenerate necessary conditions for nonconvex optimal control problems with state constraints. Journal of Mathematical Analysis and Applications 233, 116–129 (1999)
20. Filippov, A.F.: Differential Equations with Discontinuous Right-Hand Sides. Kluwer Academic Publishers, Dordrecht (1988)
21. Garavello, M., Piccoli, B.: Hybrid necessary priniple. SIAM Journal on Control and Optimization 43, 1867–1887 (2005)
22. Ioffe, A.D., Tichomirov, V.M.: Theory of Extremal Problems. North Holland, Amsterdam (1979)
23. Jahn, J.: Introduction to the Theory of Nonlinear Optimization. Springer, Berlin (2007)
24. Kaplan, A., Tichatschke, R.: Stable Methods for Ill-Posed Variational Problems. Akademie Verlag, Berlin (1994)
25. Lygeros, J.: Lecture Notes on Hyrid Systems. University of Cambridge, Cambridge (2003)
26. Lygeros, J., Quincampoix, M., Rzezuchowski, T.: Impulse differential inclusions driven by discrete measures. In: Bemporad, A., Bicchi, A., Buttazzo, G. (eds.) HSCC 2007. LNCS, vol. 4416, pp. 385–398. Springer, Heidelberg (2007)
27. Piccoli, B.: Hybrid systems and optimal control. In: Proceedings of the 37th IEEE Conference on Decision and Control, Tampa, pp. 13–18 (1998)
28. Piccoli, B.: Necessary conditions for hybrid optimization. In: Proceedings of the 38th IEEE Conference on Decision and Control, Phoenix, pp. 410–415 (1999)
29. Polak, E.: Optimization. Springer, New York (1997)
30. Rantzer, A.: On relaxed dynamic programming in switching systems. In: IEE Proceedings on Control Theory and Applications, vol. 153, pp. 567–574 (2006)
31. Shaikh, M.S., Caines, P.E.: On the Hybrid Optimal Control Problem: Theory and Algorithms. IEEE Trans. On Aut. Control 52, 1587–1603 (2007)
32. Sussmann, H.J.: A maximum principle for hybrid optimization. In: Proceedings of the 38th IEEE Conference on Decision and Control, Phoenix, pp. 425–430 (1999)
33. Verriest, E., Delmotte, F., Egerstedt, M.: Optimal impulsive control of point delay systems with refractory period. In: Proceedings of the 5th IFAC workshop on Time Delay Systems, Leuven, Belgium (2004)
34. Verriest, E., Delmotte, F., Egerstedt, M.: Control of epidemics by vaccination. In: Proceedings of the American Control Conference, Portland, pp. 985–990 (2005)
35. Xu, X., Antsaklis, P.J.: Optimal Control of Hybrid autonomous Systems with State Jumps. In: Proceedings of the American Control Conference, Denver, pp. 5191–5196 (2003)
36. Xu, X., Antsaklis, P.J.: Results and Perspectives on Computational Methods for Optimal Control of Switched Systems. In: Maler, O., Pnueli, A. (eds.) HSCC 2003. LNCS, vol. 2623, pp. 540–555. Springer, Heidelberg (2003)

Algebraic Identification of MIMO SARX Models

Laurent Bako[1,2] and René Vidal[2]

[1] Ecole des Mines de Douai, Département Informatique et Automatique, 59508, Douai, France
[2] Center for Imaging Science, Johns Hopkins University, Baltimore, MD 21218, USA

Abstract. We consider the problem of identifying the parameters of a multiple-input multiple-output switched ARX model with unknown number of submodels of unknown and possibly different orders. This is a very challenging problem because of the strong coupling between the unknown discrete state and the unknown model parameters. We address this challenge by algebraically eliminating the discrete state from the switched system equations. This algebraic procedure leads to a set of hybrid decoupling polynomials on the input-output data, whose coefficients can be identified using linear techniques. The parameters of each subsystem can then be identified from the derivatives of these polynomials. This exact analytical solution, however, comes with an important price in complexity: The number of coefficients to be identified grows exponentially with the number of outputs and the number of submodels. We address this issue with an alternative scheme in which the input-output data is first projected onto a low-dimensional linear subspace. The projected data is then fit with a single hybrid decoupling polynomial, from which the classification of the data according to the generating submodels can be obtained. The parameters of each submodel are then identified from the input-output data associated with each submodel.

1 Introduction

Hybrid systems are mathematical models of physical processes which exhibit both continuous and discrete behaviors. Such systems can be thought of as a collection of dynamical submodels with interacting behavior resulting from switching among all the submodels. The switches can be exogenous, deterministic, state-driven, event-driven, time-driven or totally random. Given input-output data generated by such a system, the identification problem consists of determining the parameters of each dynamical submodel as well as those of the switching mechanism (if any).

Prior Work. Most of the existing hybrid system identification methods have been developed for the class of piecewise auto-regressive exogenous (PWARX) systems [1,2,3,4,5,6], for which the regressor space is partitioned into polyhedral regions with one ARX submodel associated with each polyhedron. For a comprehensive review of hybrid system identification techniques, we refer the readers to the survey paper [7]. The optimization based method [1] solves the identification problem as a linear or quadratic mixed integer programming problem. The clustering based procedures [2,3,4] use clustering to separate the data into different groups, linear regression to find the boundaries of the polyhedral regions, and linear identification to determine a submodel for each region. Other methods alternate between assigning the data to submodels and estimating simultaneously their parameters by performing a weights learning technique on a

M. Egerstedt and B. Mishra (Eds.): HSCC 2008, LNCS 4981, pp. 43–57, 2008.

fuzzy parameterized model [8], solving a Minimum Partition into Feasible Subsystems (MinPFS) problem [6] or resorting to Bayesian inference [5]. The algebraic approach [9,10] is applicable to the class of Switched ARX (SARX) models, where the switching mechanism can be arbitrary. This approach uses a single decoupling polynomial that vanishes on all the data regardless of their generating submodel. Once this polynomial is computed, the problem reduces to that of recovering the system parameters from the derivatives of the polynomial evaluated at a subset of the regressors.

Unfortunately, most of the aforementioned identification methods can only deal with single-input single-output (SISO) systems. While a few identification methods for multiple-input multiple-output (MIMO) switched linear [11,12,13] and piecewise affine [14,15,16] systems in state-space form do exist, they generally require the restrictive assumption of a minimum dwell time in each discrete state. In addition, they often iterate between data clustering and model estimation, which is quite sensitive to initialization.

Paper Contributions. We present an algebraic solution to the problem of identifying MIMO SARX models. The orders of the submodels are unknown and possibly different and the number of submodels is not available. Our method is based on a technique called Generalized Principal Component Analysis (GPCA) [17], which can cluster data into multiple subspaces by polynomial fitting and differentiation. In contrast to the identification of SISO SARX models [10], where only one vanishing polynomial is used to embed the data lying in a mixture of hyperplanes, the identification of MIMO SARX models involves a potentially unknown number $n_h \geq 1$ of independent homogeneous polynomials that vanish on subspaces of co-dimension higher than one. In order to conveniently construct the regressors to which the embedding is applied, we first estimate the orders of the submodels and the number of discrete states from a rank constraint on the input-output data. Then, given the number of submodels, we compute the number of vanishing polynomials n_h and subsequently identify the ARX parameters from the derivatives of these polynomials. However, the number of coefficients to be estimated grows exponentially with the number of outputs and the number of submodels, thereby making the method computationally expensive. We thus propose an alternative method that first partitions the data according to each submodel using a single vanishing polynomial. Given the classification of the data according to each submodel, the parameters of each submodel are then identified using linear techniques.

2 Problem Statement

We consider a MIMO SARX model of the form

$$y(t) = \sum_{i=1}^{n_{\lambda_t}} A^i_{\lambda_t} y(t-i) + \sum_{i=0}^{n_{\lambda_t}} B^i_{\lambda_t} u(t-i) + e(t), \tag{1}$$

where $y(t) \in \mathbb{R}^{n_y}$ is the output vector, $u(t) \in \mathbb{R}^{n_u}$ is the input vector, $\lambda_t \in \{1, \dots, s\}$ is the discrete state, n_{λ_t} is the order of the j-th submodel for $\lambda_t = j$, s is the number of submodels of the SARX system and $\left\{A^i_j\right\}_{j=1,\cdots,s}^{i=1,\cdots,n_j} \in \mathbb{R}^{n_y \times n_y}$ and $\left\{B^i_j\right\}_{j=1,\cdots,s}^{i=1,\cdots,n_j} \in \mathbb{R}^{n_y \times n_u}$ are the associated parameter matrices. The modeling error or process noise is represented by $e(t) \in \mathbb{R}^{n_y}$. In this representation, there may exist for certain models j an integer $\delta_j < n_j$ such that $B_j^i = 0$ for $i > \delta_j$ but we require that $A_j^{n_j} \neq 0$ for all j.

Given input-output data $\{u(t), y(t)\}_{t=1}^N$ generated by an SARX system of the form (1), and upper bounds on the system orders $\bar{n} \geq \max(n_j)$ and on the number of submodels $\bar{s} \geq s$, the identification problem can be formulated as follows: identify the number of submodels s, their orders $\{n_j\}_{j=1}^s$ and their parameters $\{A_j^i, B_j^i\}_{j=1,\cdots,s}^{i=1,\cdots,n_j}$.

3 Algebraic Identification of MIMO Switched ARX Systems

To begin with the identification procedure, let us define the parameter matrices

$$\begin{aligned} \Gamma_j &= \left[B_j^{n_j}\ A_j^{n_j}\ \cdots\ B_j^1\ A_j^1\ B_j^0\ A_j^0\right] \in \mathbb{R}^{n_y \times (n_j+1)(n_u+n_y)}, \\ P_j &= \left[0_{n_y \times q_j}\ \Gamma_j\right] \in \mathbb{R}^{n_y \times K},\ j = 1, \cdots, s, \end{aligned} \tag{2}$$

and the regressor vector

$$x_n(t) = \left[u(t-n)^\top\ y(t-n)^\top\ \cdots\ u(t-1)^\top\ y(t-1)^\top\ u(t)^\top\ -y(t)^\top\right]^\top \in \mathbb{R}^K, \tag{3}$$

with $n = \max_j(n_j)$, $A_j^0 = I_{n_y}$, $q_j = (n - n_j)(n_u + n_y)$ and $K = (n+1)(n_u + n_y)$.

For now, assume that the data is not corrupted by noise i.e. $e(t) = 0$ in (1). Then, the equations defining an SARX system of the form (1) may be re-written as

$$(P_1 x_n(t) = 0) \vee \cdots \vee (P_s x_n(t) = 0), \tag{4}$$

where $\vee$ refers to the *logical or* operator. To eliminate the discrete state from this set of sn_y equations, similarly to the case of SISO SARX models [9], we take the product of one equation per submodel. The advantage of doing so is that we obtain a set of polynomial constraints $\prod_{j=1}^s \left(\theta_{i_j}^\top x_n(t)\right) = 0$, with $\theta_{i_j}^\top = P_j(i,:)$ for $i = 1, \ldots, n_y$ and $j = 1, \ldots, s$, that are satisfied by all the data regardless of their generating submodel. Consequently, the equations in (4) are equivalent to a set of up to n_y^s (not necessarily independent) homogeneous polynomials $p_{i_1,\cdots,i_s}$ on $x_n(t)$ of the form

$$p_{i_1,\cdots,i_s}(z) = \prod_{j=1}^s \left(\theta_{i_j}^\top z\right) = \sum h_{i_1,\cdots,i_s}^{n_1,\cdots,n_K} z_1^{n_1} \cdots z_K^{n_K} = h_{i_1,\cdots,i_s}^\top \nu_s(z). \tag{5}$$

Here, $\nu_s : \mathbb{R}^K \to \mathbb{R}^{M_s(K)}$, with $M_s(K) = \binom{K+s-1}{s}$, is the Veronese map which associates to $z \in \mathbb{R}^K$ the vector of all monomials of degree s, $z_1^{s_1} \cdots z_K^{s_K}$, $s_1 + \cdots + s_K = s$, organized in a descending lexicographic order. Therefore, each $p_{i_1,\cdots,i_s}$ is a homogeneous polynomial of degree s with coefficient vector $h_{i_1,\cdots,i_s} \in \mathbb{R}^{M_s(K)}$ and all monomials of degree s in K variables stacked as a vector in $\nu_s(z) \in \mathbb{R}^{M_s(K)}$.

3.1 Known Number of Submodels of Known and Equal Orders

In this subsection, we assume that the number of submodels s is known, and that the orders of all the submodels are also known and equal to n. Note that the regressor vectors $x_n(t)$ generated by the hybrid model (1) lie in the union of the s subspaces $\{\text{null}(P_j)\}_{j=1}^s$. A basis for each one of these subspaces can be estimated using the GPCA algorithm [17] as follows. From the entire set $\{u(t), y(t)\}_{t=1}^N$ of input-output data available, construct the matrix of embedded regressor vectors

$$L(n,s) = \left[\nu_s\big(x_n(n+1)\big) \cdots \nu_s\big(x_n(N)\big)\right]^\top \in \mathbb{R}^{(N-n)\times M_s(K)}. \tag{6}$$

Then the coefficient vectors $h_{i_1,\cdots,i_s}$ of the vanishing polynomials must satisfy

$$L(n,s)h_{i_1,\cdots,i_s} = 0. \tag{7}$$

In order to solve for the parameters $h_{i_1,\cdots,i_s}$ from (7), one needs to compute the null space of the embedded data matrix $L(n,s)$. Note that $h_{i_1,\cdots,i_s}$ is the symmetric part of the tensor product of an indexed set of rows $\{\theta_{i_j}\}_{j=1}^s$ taken from $\{P_j\}_{j=1}^s$, i.e. $h_{i_1,\cdots,i_s} = \text{Sym}\,(\theta_{i_1} \otimes \cdots \otimes \theta_{i_s}) \in \mathbb{R}^{M_s(K)}$, where $\otimes$ denotes the Kronecker product. The linear span of all these coefficient vectors gives a subspace of $\mathbb{R}^{M_s(K)}$ that we will refer to as the space of homogeneous polynomials of degree s vanishing on the data. By computing the null space of $L(n,s)$, we obtain a basis for this subspace. In what follows, we will denote such a basis of dimension n_h as $H = \left[h_1 \cdots h_{n_h}\right]$. Notice that the elements of this basis need not have the structure of a symmetric tensor product.

When the data are perfect and rich enough so that the dimension of the null space of $L(n,s)$ is exactly equal to n_h, the matrix of polynomial coefficients H can be computed as a basis for null$(L(n,s))$ using the Singular Value Decomposition (SVD) of $L(n,s)$. A basis for span$(P_{\lambda_t}^\top)$ can then be computed by differentiating the polynomials defined by H at $x_n(t)$. The parameter matrix P_{λ_t} of the submodel generating $x_n(t)$ can then be computed as the basis of span$(P_{\lambda_t}^\top)$ with an identity matrix at the end, as defined in (2). As we do not need to compute the parameter matrices at each time instant, we can alternatively choose s regressors $z_j \in \text{null}(P_j)$ (see §4.1) and obtain the s parameter matrices $\{P_j\}_{j=1}^s$ from the derivatives of the vanishing polynomials at $\{z_j\}_{j=1}^s$. Algorithm 1. gives a basic version of the GPCA algorithm [17] for computing the system parameter matrices $\{P_j\}_{j=1}^s$ from input-output data in a deterministic framework.

In practice the input-output data may be affected by noise. In this case, even with the assumption that the orders and the number of submodels are known, the matrix $L(n,s)$ is likely to be full rank and so, one may not be able to get the right basis H

Algorithm 1. (Identification of MIMO SARX systems using the GPCA algorithm)

Step 1: Compute a basis H for the null space of $L(n,s)$ by SVD and let the corresponding basis of vanishing polynomials of degree s be $\mathcal{Q}(z) = \left[p_1(z) \cdots p_{n_h}(z)\right] = \nu_s(z)^\top H$.

Step 2: Let
$$\nabla\mathcal{Q}(z) = \left[\tfrac{\partial p_1(z)}{\partial z} \cdots \tfrac{\partial p_{n_h}(z)}{\partial z}\right] = \left(\frac{\partial \nu_s(z)}{\partial z}\right)^\top H.$$

Step 3: Obtain by SVD a basis $T_j \in \mathbb{R}^{K\times n_y}$ for span$(P_j^\top)$ as the range space of $\nabla\mathcal{Q}(z_j)$, $j = 1,\cdots,s$, where $z_j \in \text{null}(P_j)$ but is not in null(P_i), for all $i \neq j$.

Step 4: Let $T_j^\top = \left[T_j^1\ T_j^2\right]$ be a partition of $T_j^\top$ such that $T_j^2 \in \mathbb{R}^{n_y\times n_y}$. T_j^2 is necessarily invertible and we can get $P_j = (T_j^2)^{-1}T_j^\top \in \mathbb{R}^{n_y\times K}$, $j = 1,\cdots,s$.

---

of polynomials. Therefore, it is desirable to know in advance the dimension n_h of this basis. In this way, H could be approximated by the right singular vectors of $L(n, s)$ that correspond to its n_h smallest singular values. But since the matrices P_j are not known, it is not easy to compute n_h in a general framework. However, under certain assumptions on the intersection between the null spaces of the matrices P_j, we can derive a closed form formula for n_h as outlined in Proposition 1.

Proposition 1. *Let H be the symmetric tensor product of a set of matrices $B_1, \ldots, B_s$ in $\mathbb{R}^{K\times m}$. That is, H is the matrix whose columns are all vectors in $\mathbb{R}^{M_s(K)}$ of the form* $\mathrm{Sym}\,(b_{i_1} \otimes \cdots \otimes b_{i_s})$, *where $b_{i_1}, \ldots, b_{i_s}$ are, respectively, columns of $B_1, \cdots, B_s$. If $\sum_{i=1}^{s} \mathrm{rank}(B_i) - s < K$ and for all $\{i_1, \cdots, i_q\} \subset \{1, \cdots, s\}$, $q \leq s$,*

$$\mathrm{rank}([B_{i_1}, \cdots, B_{i_q}]) = \min\Big(K, \sum_{j=1}^{q} \mathrm{rank}(B_{i_j})\Big), \tag{8}$$

then $\mathrm{rank}(H) = \prod_{j=1}^{s} \mathrm{rank}(B_j)$.

Assumption (8) of Proposition 1 corresponds to an important property of the subspace arrangement $\cup_{j=1}^{s} \mathrm{null}(B_j^\top)$ that is known as *transversality*. This property states that the dimension of the intersection of any subset of subspaces in the arrangement $\cup_{j=1}^{s} \mathrm{null}(B_j^\top)$ is as small as possible [18]. Under this assumption, the number of independent homogeneous polynomials that vanish on $\cup_{j=1}^{s} \mathrm{null}(B_j^\top)$ is equal to $\mathrm{rank}(H)$. If the same property holds for $\cup_{j=1}^{s} \mathrm{null}(P_j)$ and if $(n+1)\,(n_u + n_y) > (s-1)\,n_y$, then it follows from Proposition 1 that n_h is given by $n_h = \prod_{j=1}^{s} \mathrm{rank}(P_j) = n_y^s$ since $\mathrm{rank}(P_j) = n_y$ for all j. Although our formula is less general than the one derived in [19], it is much easier to compute. In the rest of the section, we will assume that the conditions of Proposition 1 hold, unless stated otherwise.

To summarize, given n and s, the parameter matrices P_j follow directly from Algorithm 1.. If noise is present in the data, the same algorithm still applies but with the difference that the basis H is approximated by the singular vectors of $L(n, s)$ that are associated with its $n_h = n_y^s$ smallest singular values.

3.2 Unknown Number of Submodels of Unknown and Possibly Different Orders

Consider now the more challenging case where neither the orders nor the number of submodels are known and the orders are possibly different. Consequently, n_h is also unknown. This means that we need to derive all the parameters of the SARX model (1) directly from the data. In order to properly estimate these parameters, we shall first identify the orders and the number of submodels. Once this task is accomplished, Algorithm 1. can be applied to a certain submatrix of $L(n, s)$ that will be defined later.

Before proceeding further, we need to introduce some notations. For r and l, positive integers, we use the same definitions for $x_r(t)$ and $L(r, l)$ as before. Without loss of generality, we denote by $n = n_1 \geq n_2 \geq \cdots \geq n_s$ the orders of the different submodels that constitute the SARX system and let $\rho = \begin{bmatrix} n_1 \cdots n_s \end{bmatrix} \in \mathbb{N}^s$ be a vector consisting of all the orders enumerated in a non-increasing order. It follows from (2) and (3) that the equations defining the SARX model (1) may be re-written as

$$(\Gamma_1 x_{n_1}(t) = 0) \vee \cdots \vee (\Gamma_s x_{n_s}(t) = 0), \tag{9}$$

where $x_{n_j}(t) \in \mathbb{R}^{K_j}$, $K_j = (n_j+1)(n_u+n_y)$ and $\Gamma_j \in \mathbb{R}^{n_y \times K_j}$ for $j = 1, \ldots, s$. As before, we may eliminate $\vee$ in (9) by taking the product of one equation per submodel. This leads to a set of polynomial equations on the input-output data of the form

$$(\theta_1^\top x_{n_1}(t)) \cdots (\theta_s^\top x_{n_s}(t)) = h^\top \eta_\rho(x_n(t)), \tag{10}$$

where $\theta_j^\top \in \mathbb{R}^{1 \times K_j}$ is a row of Γ_j, for $j = 1, \ldots, s$, and $\eta_\rho(x_n(t))$ is a vector obtained from $\nu_s(x_n(t))$ after removing some of the monomials. $\eta_\rho(x_n(t))$ does not contain all the monomials, because $n_j \leq n$ for all $j = 1, \ldots, s$, hence $x_{n_j}(t)$ is a sub-vector of $x_n(t)$, and so the product in (10) does not give rise to all the monomials in $\nu_s(x_n(t))$.

In order to define the set of monomials that are to be removed, let $z = x_n(t)$ and consider a monomial $z_1^{\alpha_1} \cdots z_K^{\alpha_K}$, $\alpha_1 + \cdots + \alpha_K = s$. From the definition of $x_n(t)$ in (3), it can be seen that the element $z_j^{\alpha_j}$ is contained in a monomial of $\eta_\rho(x_n(t))$ if the number of regressors $x_{n_i}(t)$ with length $K_i \geq K_1 - j + 1$ (that is the number of regressors where z_j shows up) is greater or equal to α_j. Therefore, in order for the whole monomial $z_1^{\alpha_1} \cdots z_K^{\alpha_K}$ to be included in $\eta_\rho(x_n(t))$, we must have that $k_j \geq \alpha_j$ for all $j = 1, \cdots, K$, where $k_j = \text{card}(\{i : K_i \geq K_1 - j + 1\})$. In view of this analysis, it can shown that the set of monomials to be removed can be indexed by the set $\mathcal{I}_\rho$ of exponents $(\alpha_1, \cdots, \alpha_K)$ satisfying $\alpha_1 + \cdots + \alpha_j > k_j$ for $j \leq K_1 - K_s$.

With this notation, we define a new embedded data matrix in $\mathbb{R}^{(N-n)\times(M_s(K_1)-|\mathcal{I}_\rho|)}$

$$V_\rho := \left[\eta_\rho(x_n(n+1)), \cdots, \eta_\rho(x_n(N))\right]^\top \tag{11}$$

that is simply the matrix $L(n, s)$ with $|\mathcal{I}_\rho|$ missing columns ($n = \rho(1)$). As before, the null space of V_ρ contains the coefficients of the set of vanishing polynomials. However, we may not compute such coefficients directly, because we neither know the system orders ρ nor the number of models s. As it turns out, both ρ and s can be computed from the data under the assumption that the data are rich enough. More specifically:

Definition 1. *We say that the data $\{u(t), y(t)\}_{t=1}^N$ are sufficiently exciting for the SARX system (1) if the null space of V_ρ in in (11) is of dimension exactly equal to n_h, i.e.*

$$\text{rank}(V_\rho) = M_s(K_1) - n_h - |\mathcal{I}_\rho|. \tag{12}$$

Notice that Definition 1 assumes implicitly that all the discrete states have been sufficiently visited. If we denote the matrix of data vectors related to the discrete state j by $\bar{X}_j = \left[x_n(t_1^j) \cdots x_n(t_{N_j}^j)\right]$, where the t_k^j, $k = 1, \ldots, N_j$, are the time instants t such that $\lambda_t = j$, then $\bar{X}_j$ must span completely null(P_j). Otherwise, null(P_j) may not be identifiable from $\cup_{j=1}^s$ null(P_j). We have the following result.

Theorem 1. *Let $\bar{s} \geq s$ be an upper bound on the number of submodels and let r be an integer. Assume that the data are sufficiently exciting in the sense of Definition 1. Assume further that $N_j \gg M_{\bar{s}}(K_1)$ for all $j = 1, \ldots, s$. Then* $\dim\left(\text{null}(L(r, \bar{s}))\right) = 0$ *if and only if* $r < \max(n_j)$.

Proof. Assume $r < n_1$ and let q be the number of submodels whose orders are less than or equal to r. Let $\mathcal{X} = \left[x_r(t_1^o), \cdots, x_r(t_{N_o}^o)\right] \in \mathbb{R}^{f \times N_o}$, with $f = (r+1)(n_u+n_y)$, be a matrix whose columns are regressor vectors formed by data generated by the $(s-q)$ submodels of orders $n_j > r$. Since the data are sufficiently exciting, $\mathcal{X}$ must be full row rank. It follows from Lemma 5 in [20] that $\text{rank}(\nu_{\bar{s}}(\mathcal{X})) = \min(N_o, M_{\bar{s}}(f)) = M_{\bar{s}}(f)$, where $\nu_{\bar{s}}(\mathcal{X}) = \left[\nu_{\bar{s}}(x_r(t_1^o)), \cdots, \nu_{\bar{s}}\left(x_r(t_{N_o}^o)\right)\right]$. Consequently, $L(r, \bar{s})$ is full column rank, because it is equal to a row permutation of $\left[\nu_{\bar{s}}(\mathcal{X}), \nu_{\bar{s}}(\mathcal{X}_{s-q+1}), \cdots, \nu_{\bar{s}}(\mathcal{X}_s)\right]^\top$.

Assume now that $r \geq \max(n_j)$. Then the row nullity of each data matrix X_j is at least one. This means that, for all $j = 1, \ldots, s$, there exists a nonzero $b_j \in \mathbb{R}^f$ satisfying $b_j^\top \mathcal{X}_j = 0$. One can then verify that $\text{Sym}(b_1 \otimes \cdots \otimes b_s \otimes a_{s+1} \otimes \cdots \otimes a_{\bar{s}}) \in \text{null}(L(r, \bar{s}))$ for some $a_i \in \mathbb{R}^f$. Hence, $\dim(\text{null}(L(r, \bar{s}))) \geq 1$. □

Let $\bar{s} \geq s$ and $\bar{n} \geq \max(n_j)$ be upper bounds on the number of submodels and their orders respectively. Thanks to Theorem 1, we can estimate both the number of submodels s and the orders $\{n_j\}$ from the rank of the embedded data matrix $L(r, \bar{s})$. The basic idea is that, whenever r is less than one of the orders, there is no polynomial of degree $\bar{s} \geq s$ vanishing on the entire data set, provided that $N \gg s$ and that the data is sufficiently exciting. Therefore, as shown in Algorithm 2., we can obtain the first order n_1 by setting $\bar{\rho} = \left[r \cdots r\right] \in \mathbb{N}^{\bar{s}}$, so that $V_{\bar{\rho}} = L(r, \bar{s})$, and then start decreasing r from $r = \bar{n}$ to $r = 0$ until $\text{null}(V_{\bar{\rho}}) = \{0\}$ for some r^*. We then have $n_1 = r^* + 1$. Given n_1, we can set $\bar{\rho} = \left[n_1\, r \cdots r\right] \in \mathbb{N}^{\bar{s}}$ and repeat the procedure starting from $r = n_1$ and so on, until all the orders of all the s submodels are identified. Notice that, once all the orders of the s submodels have been correctly estimated, r will go to zero for the $\bar{s} - s$ remaining presumed submodels. Therefore, if one assumes that $n_j > 0$ for all $j = 1, \ldots, s$, then the number of submodels can be estimated as the number of orders n_j strictly greater than zero.

One advantage of Algorithm 2. is that it does not require prior knowledge of the dimension n_h of the space of vanishing polynomials. This is because, if all the orders are correctly identified, then the sufficiency of excitation condition in Definition 1 guarantees that the dimension of the null space of V_ρ is exactly equal to n_h. Given n_h, we can use Algorithm 1. to compute a basis H_ρ of $\text{null}(V_\rho)$. We can then complete that basis with zeros to form a matrix $H \in \mathbb{R}^{M_s(K_1) \times n_h}$ such that the rows indexed by $\mathcal{I}_\rho$ are null. The remaining steps of Algorithm 1. are then performed without additional change.

3.3 Implementation of Algorithm 2 with Noisy Data

The algorithm proposed in the previous subsection will operate correctly in the absence of noise. When dealing with noisy data, however, the multiple rank tests required may cause Algorithm 2. to fail, because the involved matrices may always be full rank. In this subsection, we discuss some possible improvements of the algorithm in order to enhance its ability to deal with noisy data.

Recall first that the purpose of the rank test is to check whether or not the dimension of the null space of $V_{\bar{\rho}}$ is zero for a given vector of orders $\bar{\rho}$. Therefore, we do not need to know the rank of $V_{\bar{\rho}}$ exactly. We just need a measure of how likely it is that there exists a nonzero vector $h_{\bar{\rho}}$ satisfying $V_{\bar{\rho}} h_{\bar{\rho}} = 0$.

One possible way of approaching this problem is to inspect the smallest singular value of $V_{\bar{\rho}}$ for different vectors $\bar{\rho}$. For example, to compute n_1, let $\bar{\rho}_{1,l} = \left[l \cdots l\right] \in$

Algorithm 2. (Identification of the orders and the number of submodels)

Set $j_o \leftarrow 1, n_j \leftarrow \bar{n}$ for $j = 1, \ldots, \bar{s}$,
$K \leftarrow (\bar{n}+1)(n_u + n_y)$, $V \leftarrow L(\bar{n}, \bar{s})$,

1. Determine the maximum order n_1 using Theorem 1
   - **While** $\text{rank}(V) < M_{\bar{s}}(K)$, do
     - $n_j \leftarrow n_1 - 1$ for $j = 1, \ldots, \bar{s}$
     - $K \leftarrow (n_1 + 1)(n_u + n_y)$
     - $V \leftarrow$ last $M_{\bar{s}}(K)$ columns of V
   - **EndWhile**
   - Obtain the maximum order as $n_1 \leftarrow n_1 + 1$ and then set $n_j \leftarrow n_1$ for $j = 1, \ldots, \bar{s}$
   - Set $V \leftarrow L(n_1, \bar{s})$ and $K \leftarrow (n_1 + 1)(n_u + n_y)$
2. Find the remaining orders n_j, $j = 2, \ldots, \bar{s}$ using Theorem 1
   - $j_o \leftarrow j_o + 1$
   - **While** $\text{rank}(V) < M_{\bar{s}}(K) - |\mathscr{I}_{\bar{\rho}}|$
     - $n_j \leftarrow n_{j_o} - 1$ for $j = j_o, \ldots, \bar{s}$
     - $\bar{\rho} \leftarrow \begin{bmatrix} n_1 & \cdots & n_{\bar{s}} \end{bmatrix}$
     - Compute $\mathscr{I}_{\bar{\rho}}$ and remove the corresponding columns of V
   - **EndWhile**
   - Obtain the order n_{j_o}: $n_j \leftarrow n_{j_o} + 1$ for $j = j_o, \ldots, \bar{s}$
   - Set $V \leftarrow L(n_1, \bar{s})$
3. Go to step 2 until $j_o = \bar{s}$ or until one gets $n_{j_o} = 0$
4. Determine the number of submodels $s = \text{card}(\{j : n_j > 0\})$

$\mathbb{N}^{1\times\bar{s}}$, $l = 0, \ldots, \bar{n}$, and define $W_{\bar{\rho}_{1,l}} \doteq \frac{1}{N-\bar{n}} V_{\bar{\rho}_{1,l}} V_{\bar{\rho}_{1,l}}^\top$ as the matrix obtained from $\frac{1}{N-\bar{n}} L(\bar{n}, \bar{s})^\top L(\bar{n}, \bar{s})$ by removing its columns and rows indexed by $\mathscr{I}_{\bar{\rho}_{1,l}}$. Denote by $\sigma_{1,l}$, the smallest eigenvalue of the matrix $W_{\bar{\rho}_{1,l}}$ for $l = 0, \cdots, \bar{n}$. According to Theorem 1, $W_{\bar{\rho}_{1,l}}$ has at least one nonzero vector in its null space for all $l \geq n_1$ and hence, $\sigma_{1,n_1} \approx \cdots \approx \sigma_{1,\bar{n}} \approx \varepsilon_{1,n_1} \doteq \frac{1}{\bar{n}-n_1}(\sigma_{1,n_1+1} + \cdots + \sigma_{1,\bar{n}})$ and are small compared to $\sigma_{1,0}, \cdots, \sigma_{1,n_1-1}$. Therefore, to determine n_1, one needs to look for the smallest integer $l \in \{0, \cdots, \bar{n}\}$ for which $\sigma_{1,l} \approx \varepsilon_{1,l}$ in a certain sense.

Following this procedure, Algorithm 2. can be implemented in a more efficient way for determining the orders. With $\hat{n}_0 = \bar{n}$, and given a user-defined decision threshold ε_0, the following algorithm directly computes the orders starting from $j = 1$ through $j = \bar{s}$, by avoiding the rank tests required in Algorithm 2..

$$
\begin{aligned}
&\bar{\rho}_{j,l} = \begin{bmatrix} \hat{n}_1 & \cdots & \hat{n}_{j-1} & l & \cdots & l \end{bmatrix}, \; l = 0, \cdots, \hat{n}_{j-1}, \\
&\sigma_{j,l} = \min \lambda \left(W_{\bar{\rho}_{j,l}} \right), \; l = 0, \cdots, \hat{n}_{j-1}, \\
&\varepsilon_{j,l} = \frac{1}{\hat{n}_{j-1} - l} \left(\sigma_{j,l+1} + \cdots + \sigma_{j,\hat{n}_{j-1}} \right), \; l = 0, \cdots, \hat{n}_{j-1}, \\
&S_j = \{ l = 0, \cdots, \hat{n}_{j-1} : |\sigma_{j,l} - \varepsilon_{j,l}| < \varepsilon_o \}, \\
&\hat{n}_j = \begin{cases} \min \{ l : l \in S_j \}, & \text{if } \; S_j \neq \emptyset \\ \hat{n}_{j-1} & \text{otherwise,} \end{cases} \\
&j \leftarrow j + 1,
\end{aligned}
$$

where $\lambda(W_{\bar{\rho}_{j,l}})$ is the set of all eigenvalues of the matrix $W_{\bar{\rho}_{j,l}}$. In the notation such as $\bar{\rho}_{j,l}$, the index j indicates which submodel's order is being estimated while l is a possible value of the order sought.

4 Complexity Reduction Using a Projection Approach

The algebraic algorithm proposed in the previous section becomes computationally prohibitive when the dimensions of the SARX system are large. This is because the regressor $x_n(t) \in \mathbb{R}^{K_1}$ constructed from all n_y outputs is large, and so it induces an exponential increase in $M_s(K_1)$, the dimension of the space of homogeneous polynomials space of degree s in K_1 variables. Moreover, the number n_h of polynomials to be estimated is unknown, even when the orders and the number of submodels are given, unless one makes certain assumptions.

In this section, instead of attempting to compute a potentially large and unknown number of polynomials, we propose a computationally simpler method to identify the model parameters. The idea is to transform the MIMO system into a multiple-input single-output (MISO) system, and hence use only one decoupling polynomial to partition the data according to the different ARX submodels. Once all the data are correctly partitioned, the SARX system identification problem reduces to a standard regression problem for each discrete state.

To that end, notice that, without loss of generality, system (1) can transformed into the MISO system[1]

$$y(t) = \sum_{i=1}^{n_{\lambda_t}} a^i_{\lambda_t} y(t-i) + \sum_{i=0}^{n_{\lambda_t}} F^i_{\lambda_t} u(t-i) + e(t), \tag{13}$$

where the $\{a^i_j\}_{i=1,\cdots,n_j}^{j=1,\cdots,s}$ are the coefficients of the polynomial $z^{n_j} - a^1_j z^{n_j-1} - \cdots - a^{n_j}_j$ that encodes the poles of the jth submodel as its roots.

Let $\gamma = \begin{bmatrix}\gamma_1 \cdots \gamma_{n_y}\end{bmatrix}^\top$ be a vector of real nonzero numbers and let $y_o(t) = \gamma^\top y(t) \in \mathbb{R}$ be a weighted combination of all the system outputs. Then, (13) can be transformed into the following single output system

$$y_o(t) = \sum_{i=1}^{n_{\lambda_t}} a^i_{\lambda_t} y_o(t-i) + \sum_{i=0}^{n_{\lambda_t}} \gamma^\top F^i_{\lambda_t} u(t-i) + \gamma^\top e(t). \tag{14}$$

Remark 1. *To the purpose of separating the data according to their generating submodels, one may be tempted to consider a single output $y_j(t)$ from (13) instead of a combination of all the n_y outputs. The problem with proceeding in this way is that, after pole-zero cancellation, the MISO system with output $y_j(t)$ may be common to many different modes and so, we may not be able to differentiate between those modes. By choosing a random linear combination of the outputs, such degenerate situations can be avoided almost surely.*

[1] Note that the orders n_j in (13) may be larger than the ones in (1). By an abuse of notation, we will keep using the same notation for the orders.

By introducing the blended output $y_o(t)$, we obtain only one hybrid decoupling polynomial $g(z)$ that is easier to deal with. However, at the same time the parameters of different submodels are combined. This raises the question of whether this combination of outputs preserves the distinguishability of the different submodels that constitute the SARX system. In fact, depending on the weights vector γ, two submodels which were initially distinct may reduce to the same submodel in (14). To analyze this risk, let

$$F_j = \left[F_j^{n_j} \cdots F_j^1 \; F_j^0\right] \in \mathbb{R}^{n_y \times (n_j+1)n_u} \quad \text{and} \quad a_j = \left[a_j^{n_j} \cdots a_j^1\right]^\top \in \mathbb{R}^{n_j}. \tag{15}$$

It follows from (14) that two different modes i and j become indistinguishable after the previous transformation by γ, if they have the same order ($n_i = n_j$), the same dynamics ($a_i = a_j$) and $\left(F_i^\top - F_j^\top\right)\gamma = 0$, i.e. when γ lies in null$(F_i^\top - F_j^\top)$. If the F_j were known one could readily select a γ which does not satisfy this condition. But these matrices are precisely what we are looking for. The question is, without knowing the F_j, how can we choose γ in such a way that for any $i \neq j$, $\gamma \notin$ null$(F_i^\top - F_j^\top)$. In fact, it is not hard to show that when γ is drawn randomly, this condition is satisfied with probability one. Therefore, two submodels that are distinct in the original system (1) remain so after the transformation. However, the separability of the modes, which is a measure of how close the different submodels are, may be affected.

From (14), let us redefine the parameter vector $\bar{\theta}_j$ and the regressor $\bar{x}_n(t)$ as

$$\bar{\theta}_j = \left[0_{q_j}^\top \; \gamma^\top F_j^{n_j} \; a_j^{n_j} \cdots \gamma^\top F_j^1 \; a_j^1 \; \gamma^\top F_j^0 \; 1\right]^\top \in \mathbb{R}^K, \; j = 1, \cdots, s \tag{16}$$

$$\bar{x}_n(t) = \left[u(t-n)^\top \; y_o(t-n) \cdots u(t)^\top \; -y_o(t)\right]^\top \in \mathbb{R}^K, \tag{17}$$

where $K = (n+1)(n_u+1)$. One can view the smallest singular value $\sigma_0(X(\gamma))$ of $X(\gamma) = \left[\bar{x}_{\bar{n}}(\bar{n}+1) \cdots \bar{x}_{\bar{n}}(N)\right]$, as a certain measure of how likely the data can be fitted to one subspace of $\mathbb{R}^{\bar{K}}$. It is in fact intuitive that the more distinguishable the subspaces are, the larger $\sigma_0(X(\gamma))$ should be. Therefore, to preserve the separability of the modes, we suggest to choose γ for example as $\gamma^* = \arg\max_{\gamma:\|\gamma\|\leq 1} \frac{\sigma_0(X(\gamma))}{\sigma_{max}(X(\gamma))}$, where $\sigma_{max}(X(\gamma))$ is the largest singular value of $X(\gamma)$. Since this could be a hard optimization problem, an alternative is to choose several candidate γs in such a way that $\sigma_0(X(\gamma))$ is in a certain proportion of $\sigma_{max}(X(\gamma))$.

Once γ has been chosen, we can proceed with the identification procedure. As before, we eliminate the dependency of the system equation on the switches by considering the following decoupling polynomial which vanishes on the data independently of their generating submodel:

$$g(\bar{x}_n(t)) = \prod_{j=1}^{s} \left(\bar{\theta}_j^\top \bar{x}_n(t)\right) = h^\top \nu_s(\bar{x}_n(t)) = 0. \tag{18}$$

Solving (18) is a particular and simpler case ($n_y = 1$) of the case studied in section 3. The procedure for the determination of $\bar{\theta}_j$ is roughly the same:

1. Solve for the orders and number of submodels using Algorithm 2..
2. Obtain h_ρ as any nonzero element in null(V_ρ) (which is expected to be one dimensional when the data are sufficiently exciting), and

3. Complete h_ρ with zeros to form a $h \in \mathbb{R}^{M_s(K)}$ so that the entries of h defined by $\mathscr{I}_\rho$ are zero.

Given h, the parameters may be obtained from the derivative of g as shown in [9]:

$$\bar{\theta}_j = \frac{\nabla g(z_j)}{e_K^\top \nabla g(z_j)}, j = 1, \ldots, s, \tag{19}$$

where z_j is a point in $S_j \setminus \cup_{i \neq j}^{s} S_i$, $S_j = \{x \in \mathbb{R}^K : \bar{\theta}_j^\top x = 0\}$, e_K is a vector of length K with 1 in its last entry and 0 everywhere else.

4.1 Classification of the Data

The computation of $\bar{\theta}_j$ for each submodel, involves finding a point lying in S_j but not in any other S_i, $i \neq j = 1, \ldots, s$. We find a point in S_j as $z_j = \bar{x}_n(\tau_j)$, where

$$\tau_j = \arg\min_{t \in \mathcal{D}_j} \left| \frac{\nabla g(\bar{x}_n(t))^\top \bar{x}_n(t)}{e_K^\top \nabla g(\bar{x}_n(t))} \right|, \tag{20}$$

$\mathcal{D}_1 = \{t : \nabla g(\bar{x}_n(t)) \neq 0\}$ and $\mathcal{D}_j = \{t : \nabla g(\bar{x}_n(t)) \neq 0, \bar{\theta}_i^\top \bar{x}_n(t) \neq 0, i = 1, ..., j-1\}$, for $j > 1$. Then one can compute the parameters by (19) using $z_j = \bar{x}_n(\tau_j)$.

Recall that recovering the vectors $\{\bar{\theta}_j\}_{j=1}^{s}$ associated with the blended output $y_o(t)$ is only an intermediate step in achieving the goal of computing the parameters a_j and F_j that define each subsystem of the original system (1). Now, from the parameters $\bar{\theta}_j$ obtained, we can determine the discrete state of (14) which is the same as that of (1) and then, compute finally the system sought. In order to discard possible outliers in the data we set up a performance bound $\varepsilon < 1$ to define the following decision rules:

$$\text{If} \quad \min_j \Delta(\bar{\theta}_j, \bar{x}_n(t)) > \varepsilon \,\|\bar{x}_n(t)\|, \quad \text{then} \quad \lambda_t \quad \text{is undecidable.}$$

$$\text{If} \quad \min_j \Delta(\bar{\theta}_j, \bar{x}_n(t)) \leq \varepsilon \,\|\bar{x}_n(t)\|, \quad \text{then} \quad \lambda_t = \arg\min_j \Delta\left(\bar{\theta}_j, \bar{x}_n(t)\right).$$

Here $\Delta(\bar{\theta}_j, \bar{x}_n(t)) = \dfrac{|\bar{\theta}_j^\top \bar{x}_n(t)|}{\|\bar{\theta}_j\|}$ is the distance from the point $\bar{x}_n(t)$ to the linear hyperplane S_j defined by its normal vector $\bar{\theta}_j$. We define $\mathscr{X}_j = \{t > \bar{n} : \lambda_t = j\} = \left\{t_1^j, \cdots, t_{N_j}^j\right\}$, $j = 1, \ldots, s$ as the set of time instances in which the regressors are generated by the submodel j.

4.2 Estimation of the Submodel Parameters

Based on the results of the previous classification, we know which data correspond to each generating mode. Therefore, we are left with determining the parameters of each mode j from the data indexed by $\mathscr{X}_j$. To begin with, consider a single linear submodel j of order n_j from (1). For any $t \in \mathscr{X}_j$, let us define

$$\Phi_j^y(t) := \left[y(t-1) \cdots y(t-n_j)\right] \in \mathbb{R}^{n_y \times n_j}, \tag{21}$$

$$\phi_j^u(t) := \left[u(t)^\top \cdots u(t-n_j)^\top\right]^\top \in \mathbb{R}^{(n_j+1)n_u}. \tag{22}$$

The parameters of the submodels of system (13) can be computed as the solution to the following linear regression problem

$$y(t) = \left[\Phi_j^y(t)\ \phi_j^u(t)^\top \otimes I_{n_y}\right]\begin{bmatrix} a_j \\ \mathrm{vec}(F_j)\end{bmatrix} + e(t),\ t \in \mathscr{X}_j. \tag{23}$$

This equation is obtained by making use of the identity $\mathrm{vec}(AXB) = (B^\top \otimes A)\mathrm{vec}(X)$, where the symbol $\otimes$ refers to the Kronecker product and $\mathrm{vec}(\cdot)$ is the vectorization operator. Notice that in the whole procedure, the vectors a_j, $j = 1,\ldots,s$, are estimated twice. The first estimate (obtained from $\bar{\theta}_j$) is considered as a raw estimate that is required here just to be able to discriminate among the different modes. The second estimate from (23) is expected to be more accurate.

5 Numerical Results

We test the performance of the proposed approach on an SARX system composed of two submodels of orders 2 and 1, with $n_u = 1$ input and $n_y = 2$ outputs. The system equations are given by

$$y(t) = a_j^1 I_{n_y} y(t-1) + a_j^2 I_{n_y} y(t-2) + b_j^0 u(t) + b_j^1 u(t-1) + b_j^2 u(t-2), \tag{24}$$

where a_j^1 and a_j^2, $j = 1, 2$, are scalar coefficients and b_j^0, b_j^1, b_j^2 are vectors of dimension $n_y = 2$. The coefficients a_j^2 and b_j^2 are zero for the second submodel.

The system is driven by a zero-mean white Gaussian noise input with unit standard deviation and switches periodically from one discrete state to another every 10 samples. The output is corrupted with additive noise with a signal-to-noise ratio (SNR) of 30 dB.

The parameters of the two ARX models are given by the matrices

$$P_1 = \left[\begin{array}{cc|cc|c|c|c} 1.3561, & 0 & 0.6913, & 0, & 0 & 0.3793 & 0.2639 \\ 0, & 1.3561 & 0, & 0.6913, & 1.3001 & 1.8145 & 0.7768 \end{array}\right], \tag{25}$$

$$P_2 = \left[\begin{array}{cc|cc|c|c|c} 0.9485, & 0 & 0, & 0 & 1.7661 & 2.9830 & 0 \\ 0, & 0.9485 & 0, & 0 & 0 & 0.9106 & 0 \end{array}\right], \tag{26}$$

which are defined with respect to the regressor vector

$$\left[y(t-1)^\top \,|\, y(t-2)^\top \,|\, u(t) \,|\, u(t-1) \,|\, u(t-2)\right]^\top.$$

Given input-output data generated by this system on a time window of size 1500, we are interested in extracting the number of constituent submodels, the orders of these submodels and the parameters that describe them. To demonstrate the performance of our algorithm we carried out a Monte-Carlo simulation of size 1000 with the following user-defined set of parameters: $\bar{n} = 3$ and $\bar{s} = 3$. For a threshold of $\varepsilon_0 = 10^{-3}$ in the algorithm of §3.3, the estimation of the orders of both submodels is realized with 100%

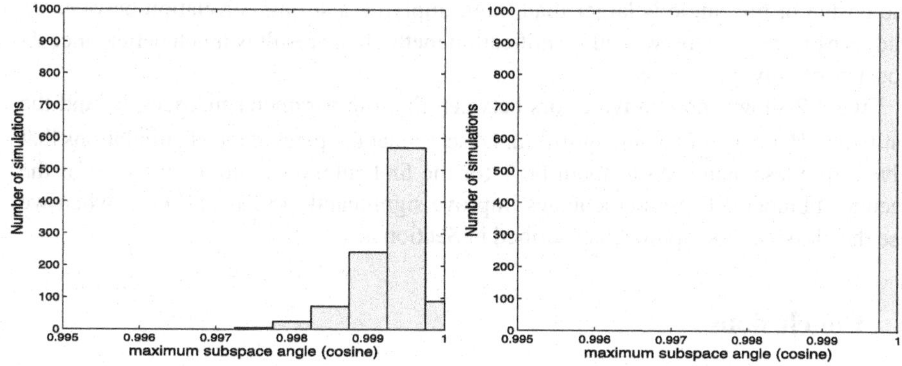

(a) MIMO GPCA method (b) MISO GPCA method

Fig. 1. Histograms of the maximum subspace angle between span(H) and span$(\hat{H})$

of successes. Since we provided $\bar{s} = 3$, the vector of orders is obtained as $\hat{\rho} = \begin{bmatrix} 2 & 1 & 0 \end{bmatrix}$. The means of the estimates $\hat{P}_1$ and $\hat{P}_2$ obtained across all the simulations are given by:

$$\hat{P}_1 = \left[\begin{array}{c|c|c|c|c} 1.3558, \; 0.0043 & 0.6897, \; 0.0036 & 0.0056 & 0.3937, & 0.2639 \\ -0.0012,, \; 1.3558 & -0.0021, \; 0.6907 & 1.3031 & 1.8208 & 0.7753 \end{array}\right], \tag{27}$$

$$\hat{P}_2 = \left[\begin{array}{c|c|c|c|c} 0.9480, \; 0.0045 & -0.0005, \; 0.0050 & 1.7710, & 2.9869, & 0.0050 \\ -0.0003, \; 0.9479 & -0.0001, \; -0.0006 & -0.0012 & 0.9081 & -0.0018 \end{array}\right]. \tag{28}$$

Figure 1 shows a histogram with the maximum angle between the column space of the hybrid parameter matrix H and that of its estimate $\hat{H}$. Notice that for all simulations

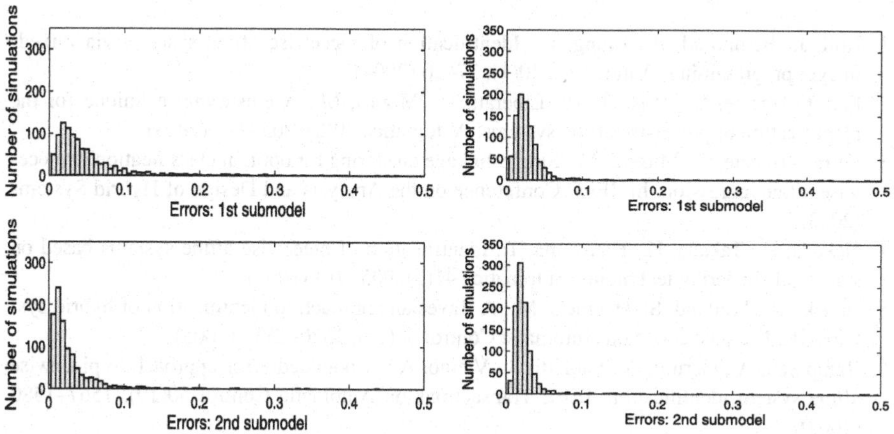

(a) MIMO GPCA method (b) MISO GPCA method

Fig. 2. Histograms of the errors $\|P_1 - \hat{P}_1\|_2 / \|P_1\|_2$ and $\left\|P_2 - \hat{P}_2\right\|_2 / \|P_2\|_2$

the cosine of this angle is larger than 0.99, implying a strong correlation between H and its estimate. For the second identification method, the result is much better since H consists of only one vector.

Figure 2 shows the relative errors between the true parameter matrices P_j and the estimates $\hat{P}_j$ obtained by our algorithm. Observe that the percentage of simulations that give errors less than 0.05 is about 66% for the first submodel and about 85% for the second submodel. These percentages improve significantly (86% and 93%) when we use the classification approach described in Section 4.

6 Conclusions

We have presented an algebraic approach to the identification of MIMO SARX models with unknown number of submodels of unknown and possibly different orders. The number of submodels and their orders are estimated from a rank constraint on the input-output data, and the model parameters using a subspace clustering technique called GPCA. As the complexity of the method is exponential on the number of outputs and submodels, we proposed a simpler approach that applies GPCA to a MISO system built by projecting the original data. Future work includes developing recursive identification algorithms for MIMO SARX systems, such as the one in [20] for SISO systems.

Acknowledgements. The authors thank Mr. Dheeraj Singaraju for his help in proof-reading this paper. This work has been funded by BOURSE-MOBILITE from the Regional Council of Nord-Pas-de-Calais (France), by Johns Hopkins startup funds, and by grants NSF EHS-05-09101, NSF CAREER IIS-04-47739 and ONR N00014-05-1083.

References

1. Roll, J., Bemporad, A., Ljung, L.: Identification of piecewise affine systems via mixed-integer programming. Automatica 40(1), 37–50 (2004)
2. Ferrari-Trecate, G., Muselli, M., Liberati, D., Morari, M.: A clustering technique for the identification of piecewise affine systems. Automatica 39(2), 205–217 (2003)
3. Ferrari-Trecate, G., Muselli, M.: Single-linkage clustering for optimal classification in piecewise affine regression. In: IFAC Conference on the Analysis and Design of Hybrid Systems (2003)
4. Nakada, H., Takaba, K., Katayama, T.: Identification of piecewise affine systems based on statistical clustering technique. Automatica 41(5), 905–913 (2005)
5. Juloski, A., Weiland, S., Heemels, M.: A Bayesian approach to identification of hybrid systems. IEEE Transactions on Automatic Control 50(10), 1520–1533 (2005)
6. Bemporad, A., Garulli, A., Paoletti, S., Vicino, A.: A bounded-error approach to piecewise affine system identification. IEEE Transactions on Automatic Control 50(10), 1567–1580 (2005)
7. Paoletti, S., Juloski, A., Ferrari-Trecate, G., Vidal, R.: Identification of hybrid systems: A tutorial. European Control Journal (2007)
8. Ragot, J., Mourot, G., Maquin, D.: Parameter estimation of switching piecewise linear systems. In: Conference on Decision and Control (2003)

9. Vidal, R., Soatto, S., Ma, Y., Sastry, S.: An algebraic geometric approach to the identification of a class of linear hybrid systems. In: Conference on Decision and Control, pp. 167–172 (2003)
10. Ma, Y., Vidal, R.: Identification of deterministic switched ARX systems via identification of algebraic varieties. In: Morari, M., Thiele, L. (eds.) HSCC 2005. LNCS, vol. 3414, pp. 449–465. Springer, Heidelberg (2005)
11. Bako, L., Mercere, G., Lecoeuche, S.: Online subspace identification of switching systems with possibly varying orders. In: European Control Conference (2007)
12. Huang, K., Wagner, A., Ma, Y.: Identification of hybrid linear time-invariant systems via subspace embedding and segmentation. Conference on Decision and Control 3, 3227–3234 (2004)
13. Verdult, V., Verhaegen, M.: Subspace identification of piecewise linear systems. In: Proceedings of the 43rd IEEE Conference on Decision and Control, pp. 3838–3843 (2004)
14. Münz, E., Krebs, V.: Identification of hybrid systems using a priori knowledge. In: IFAC World Congress (2002)
15. Verdult, V., Verhaegen, M.: Subspace identification of piecewise linear systems. In: IEEE Conference on Decision & Control, pp. 3838–3843 (2004)
16. Münz, E., Krebs, V.: Continuous optimization approaches to the identification of piecewise affine systems. In: IFAC World Congress (2005)
17. Vidal, R., Ma, Y., Sastry, S.: Generalized Principal Component Analysis (GPCA). IEEE Transactions on Pattern Analysis and Machine Intelligence 27(12), 1–15 (2005)
18. Ma, Y., Yang, A., Derksen, H., Fossum, R.: Estimation of subspace arrangements with applications in modeling and segmenting mixed data. In: SIAM Review (to appear, 2008)
19. Derksen, H.: Hilbert series of subspaces arrangements. Journal of Pure and Applied Algebra 209(1), 91–98 (2007)
20. Vidal, R.: Recursive identification of switched ARX systems. Automatica (to appear, 2008)

Contract-Based Design for Computation and Verification of a Closed-Loop Hybrid System

L. Benvenuti[1,2], A. Ferrari[2], E. Mazzi[2,3], and A.L. Sangiovanni Vincentelli[2,4]

[1] Università di Roma "La Sapienza", Roma, Italy
luca.benvenuti@uniroma1.it
[2] PARADES, Via di S.Pantaleo, 66, 00186 Roma, Italy
{aferrari, emazzi}@parades.rm.cnr.it
[3] Centro di Ricerca Interdipartimentale "E. Piaggio", Università di Pisa, Pisa, Italy
[4] Department of Electrical Engineering and Computer Sciences,
University of California at Berkeley, Berkeley, CA 94720, USA
alberto@eecs.berkeley.edu

Abstract. Contract-based design is an approach where the design process is seen as a successive assembly of components where a component is represented in terms of assumptions about its environment and guarantees about its behavior. In the composition, if assumptions of each component are contained in guarantees offered by the others, then the composition is well formed. In this paper, we focus on contract-based design and the use of *Heterogeneous Rich Component* models for embedded controllers where the plant, sensors and actuators are described by hybrid systems. We assume that the components are assembled in a feedback configuration. The problem is to show that this composition satisfies requirements using the assumptions-guarantees of the plant, sensors, actuators and controller. To do so, we give rules on how to compose assumptions and promises for components in cascade and feedback configurations. We then apply these rules to expose the actual calculation involved on a test case, a water-level control problem. We also show how to check that the requirements on the closed-loop configuration are satisfied, i.e, that they are contained in the promises of this configuration using a formal verification tool (Ariadne) for hybrid systems.

1 Introduction

In safety critical applications such as transportation systems, the electronic control system is often a networked system with interacting embedded controllers dedicated to each sub-system. Due to the lack of an overall understanding of the interplay of subsystems and of the difficulties encountered in integrating very complex parts mostly coming by different Tier-1 suppliers, who give scant information about the inner workings of their products, system integration has become a design bottleneck for the leading Original Equipment Manufacturers (OEMs). The source of these problems resides in the complexity of the embedded controllers due to the ever increasing demands on functionality, and in the presence of critical constraints on reliability, cost and time-to-market and on power consumption. As a consequence, a successful design, in which costly and time consuming re-design cycles are avoided, can only be achieved using

M. Egerstedt and B. Mishra (Eds.): HSCC 2008, LNCS 4981, pp. 58–71, 2008.

efficient design methodologies that allow for component reuse and for evaluation of platform requirements at the early stages of the design flow.

The platform-based design methodology proposed in [1] provides concepts and techniques to achieve an efficient design, aimed at maximizing reuse at each design step and early verification with abstracted information from possible implementation platforms. In this context, a platform is a layer of abstraction that hides the unnecessary details of the underlying implementation and yet carries enough information about the layers below to prevent design iterations. The choice of the layers of abstraction and of the corresponding parameters are essential in the quality of the final solution of the design problem. In this framework, the SPEEDS project proposes to describe each subsystem at each abstraction layer by means of common meta-model, called *Heterogeneous Rich Component (HRC)*, with a rigorous formal semantics supporting integration of models [2,3]. The meta-model supports inter-layer relationship (mapping items of one layer to the next layer) and allows splitting and distributing responsibilities between the different actors of the OEM/supplier chain. In particular, a design task called guarantee or *promise* is given to each supplier. This goal involves only entities the supplier is responsible for while those other may be subject to constraints that are given to this supplier as *assumption*. Assumptions are under the responsibility of other actors of the OEM/supplier chain but can be used by this supplier for achieving its own promises. This mechanism of assumption and promises is structured into contracts which define the desired behavior of each component of the system at a given layer of abstraction and supports design across several layers. Integration, reuse and early verification are supported by defining contracts composition, consistency of contract composition, dominance and substitutability relation between contracts [2,4]. The process is general in that no assumption is made on the structure of the composition nor on the type of contracts being considered. This generality is paid in terms of heavy notational complexity and difficulties in implementation. To use contracts efficiently, we need to describe how contracts compose when the corresponding IPs are connected to form a larger system and we also need to identify methods to verify whether the guarantee of the system is valid.

In this paper, we consider the case in which some of the required functionalities for the components call for contracts described by means of hybrid systems. This case is very important when considering embedded controllers where the plant to be controlled is described by Ordinary Differential Equations (ODEs). We assume that the components of the control system are connected in a rather conventional feedback architecture (see figure 5). We give the specific contract composition rules for this architecture. We then examine a case study, a water-level control system, to illustrate how to work with contracts and how to verify that the closed-loop system satisfy the requirements. This is the first step towards an overall contract-based methodology for hybrid systems. We expect to extend the methodology so that the requirements can be decomposed into a set of simpler requirements that if satisfied, guarantees that the overall requirement is satisfied. This step allows to consider then "local" contracts that must be satisfied to guarantee that the overall contract is met. The paper is organized as follows: in Section 2 we describe the HRC formalism and present two different compositions of contracts that are used in the control architecture considered here. In Section 3 we apply the contract-based design approach to the case study of water level control and we demonstrate how to use a formal verification tool to verify that the requirements on the closed-loop configuration are satisfied. Conclusions are offered in Section 4.

2 Heterogeneous Rich Component Formalism

System models expressed in the Heterogeneous Rich Component (HRC) formalism consist of networks of hierarchical components. Each component consists of a set of events and variables and its expected behavior is described by means of some *assumptions A* and *promises G* over these events and variables. Assumptions and promises are identified by the set of admissible runs for some events and/or variables describing the component. The pair (A,G) is referred to as the *contract C* of the component.

The HRC formalism allows to distribute responsibilities regarding the implementation of a complex system among different component providers during the design process. To do that, a methodology to manage contracts composition, its consistency verification (compatibility) and relations among contracts is needed [2,5].

In this paper, we consider the control configuration of figure 5 where components are cascaded and a feedback connection closes the loop. Contract composition formalizes how contracts related to different components have to be combined to represent the composition of the components [2,4]. First, consider two components connected in cascade composition as shown in figure 1. Let $C_1 = (A_1, G_1)$ and $C_2 = (A_2, G_2)$ be the contracts of the two components. The assumptions A_1 can be written as

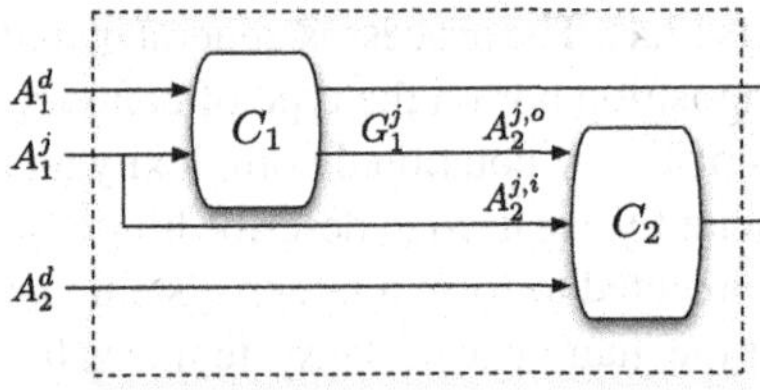

Fig. 1. Cascade composition of two components sharing some events/variables in the interface

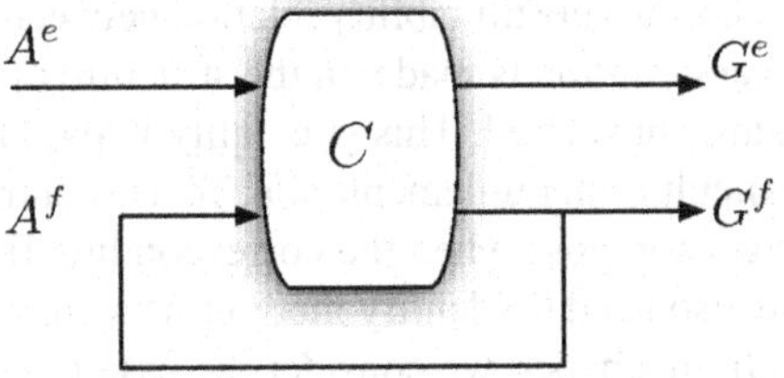

Fig. 2. Feedback composition

$$A_1 = A_1^d \times A_1^j$$

where A_1^d are the assumptions related to the signals (events and variables) acting as inputs only for the first component, and A_1^j are the assumptions on the input signals shared by the two components. Similarly, the assumptions A_2 can be written as

$$A_2 = A_2^d \times A_2^{j,o} \times A_2^{j,i}$$

where A_2^d are the assumptions related to the signals acting as inputs only for the second component, $A_2^{j,o}$ are the assumptions on the output signals of the first component acting as inputs for the second one, and $A_2^{j,i}$ are the assumptions on the input signals shared by the two components.

The promises G_1 can be written as

$$G_1 = G_1^d \times G_1^j$$

where G_1^j are the promises related to the output signals acting as input for the second component and G_1^d those related to the remaining output signals.

The cascade composition is *compatible* if

$$G_1^j \subset A_2^{j,o}$$

that is the promises on the output signals of the first component acting as inputs of the second component define only runs admissible for the second component. In this case, the assumption A_2 can be relaxed neglecting the assumption $A_2^{j,o}$. On the other hand, the assumptions on the disjoint input signals are the conjunction of A_1^d and A_2^d, while as regards those on the shared input signals, one has to consider the tighter ones. In conclusion, the assumption A on the cascade composition are

$$A = A_1^d \times (A_1^j \cap A_2^{j,i}) \times A_2^d.$$

The promise G of a compatible cascade composition is in general not the pure conjunction of promises G_1^d and G_2. In fact, since the cascade composition modifies the assumptions on the input signals of the second component, then the promises G_2 can be refined. Let us denote as G_2' the refinement of promises G_2 under the assumptions

$$A_2^d \times G_1^j \times (A_1^j \cap A_2^{j,i})$$

imposed on the second component by the environment and by the first component. Then, the promise G is given by

$$G = G_1^d \times G_2'$$

Consider now the feedback composition shown in figure 2 where the contract C defining the open loop behavior of the component may obviously be the result of cascade compositions. The assumption A can be written as

$$A = A^e \times A^f$$

where A^e are the assumptions on the events and variables from the environment and A^f are those on the signals feed back from the output. Similarly, the promises G can be written as

$$G = G^e \times G^f$$

where A^e, A^f, G^e and G^f are assumptions and promises of the open loop system.

A sufficient condition for compatibility of the feedback composition is that

$$G^f \subset A^f$$

and in this case, the assumptions of the closed–loop system are only the assumptions from the environment A^e. Also in this case, the promises of the feedback composition are a refinement of the promises G of the open loop component. In particular, the promises of the closed loop system are given by

$$G_e' \times (A^f \cap G^f)$$

where $A^f \cap G^f$ are the promises on the signals used to close the loop and G'_e is the refinement of promises G^e under the assumptions

$$A^e \times (A^f \cap G^f)$$

imposed on the component by the environment and by the feedback signals.

Finally, a contract $C_1 = (A_1, G_1)$ is said to satisfy a contract $C_2 = (A_2, G_2)$ if and only if $A_1 \supset A_2$ and the refinement G'_1 of promises G_1 under the assumptions A_2 are such that $G'_1 \subset G_2$.

3 Contracts Composition and Verification of Contracts Satisfaction

To show how to perform the actual computation for contract composition, we consider a simple hybrid system control problem where we have to control the water level in a cylindric tank (see figure 3), with height $H = 8\ m$ and section $S = 16{,}62\ m^2$, equipped with an inlet pipe at the top and an outlet pipe at the bottom. The outlet flow is assumed to be proportional to the water level, i.e.

$$F_{out}(t) = kx(t) \tag{1}$$

where $x(t)$ denotes the water level in the tank and $k = 1/3\ m^2/s$ is the outlet flow constant. The inlet flow depends on the supply inlet pressure $p(t)$, that is $F_{in}(t) = S_{in}\sqrt{2p(t)/\rho}$ where $S_{in} = 0{,}5\ m^2$ is the inlet pipe cross section and $\rho = 1000\ Kg/m^3$ is the water density.

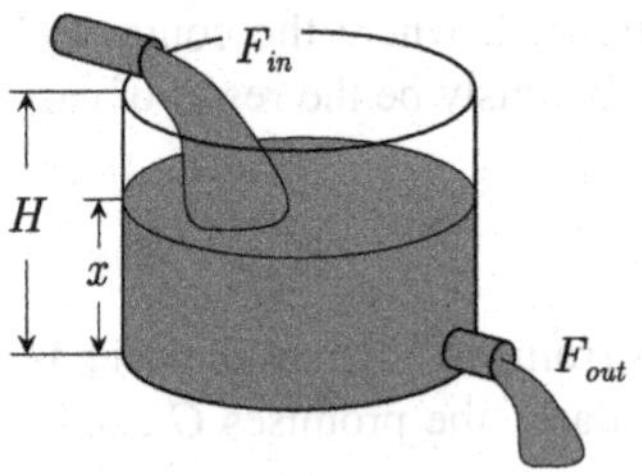

Fig. 3. The tank system

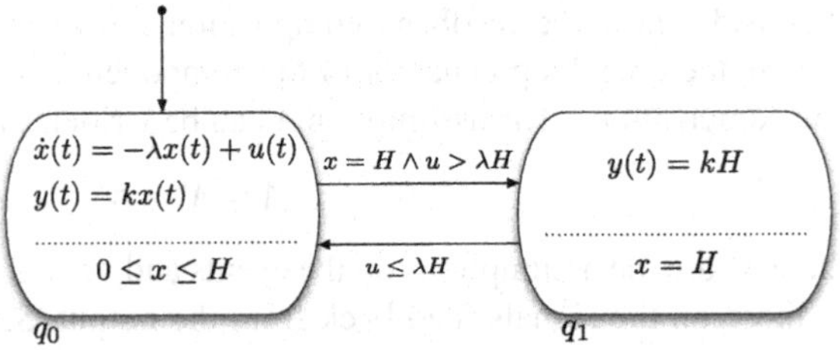

Fig. 4. Tank promise G_{tank}

The behavior of the system can be described by a contract $C_{tank} = (A_{tank}, G_{tank})$ which defines all the possible inlet and outlet flow behaviors. In particular, the evolution of the output flow, that is the promise G_{tank}, can be described by the hybrid system shown in figure 4 where the continuous state variable $x(t)$ represents the water level in the tank, the continuous input variable $u(t)$ is equal to $F_{in}(t)/S$, and the continuous output variable $y(t)$ is the outlet flow $F_{out}(t)$. Location q_0, which is the initial location, represents the situation in which there is no water overflow; in this case, the water level $x(t)$ evolves according to the differential equation associated to the location where

$\lambda = k/S = 0{,}02s^{-1}$. Location $q_1$describes the water overflow situation in which the water level remains constant and equal to H.

The assumptions A_{tank} define the assumption on the system and on the input behavior. In particular, the inlet flow is assumed to be nonnegative and the initial value of the water level an admissible one:

- $u(t) \geq 0$;
- $x(0) \in [0,H]$.

3.1 Contract Specifications

The desired behavior of the system can be described by a contract C_{des} which defines all the admissible inlet and outlet flow behaviors. The aim of the tank, that is the promise G_{des}, is that of providing an outlet flow $F_{out}(t)$ bounded in a given interval

$$y(t) = F_{out}(t) \in [Y^m\ , \ Y^M] = [2/3\ , \ 2] \quad m^3/s$$

at least after a settling time $\bar{t} = 10\ s$ from startup when the inlet pressure $p(t)$ is bounded in the interval

$$p(t) \in [P^m\ , \ P^M] = [5000\ , \ 6000] \quad Pa$$

and the tank is empty at startup. In addition, no water overflow is allowed.

The assumptions A_{des} on the desired behavior can be stated as:

- $u(t) \in [U^m, U^M]$
- $x(0) = 0$.

where the first assumption is due to the assumption on the inlet pressure $p(t) \in [P^m, P^M]$, so that

$$U^m = \frac{S_{in}}{S}\sqrt{\frac{2P^m}{\rho}} = f(P^m), \quad U^M = \frac{S_{in}}{S}\sqrt{\frac{2P^M}{\rho}} = f(P^M)$$

To verify whether the tank satisfies the specifications, one has to check if the contract defining tank behavior satisfies the contract defining system specifications. This relation is true if and only if:

- $A_{tank} \supset A_{des}$;
- $G'_{tank} \subset G_{des}$

where G'_{tank} describes all the possible behaviors of the tank under the assumption A_{des}. As a consequence, as defined by A_{des}, one has to analyze the behavior of the tank in the case in which $u(t) \in [U^m, U^M]$ and the container is empty at startup. To show that the behavior of the tank under the assumption A_{des} does not meet the specification promise G_{des}, it is sufficient to consider the evolution of the outlet flow corresponding to the minimum admissible inlet flow $F_{in}(t)$, that is $u(t) = U^m$ for all t. Since the outlet flow not only goes eventually over the Y^M threshold but even produces water spillage, then one can conclude that to assure contract satisfaction for the C_{tank} with respect to the C_{des} contract, it is necessary to control the outlet flow by regulating the water level $x(t)$. This can be done, for example, using a feedback controller which regulates the water level $x(t)$ acting on the inlet flow by means of a flow rate valve.

3.2 Closed Loop Composition

The controller scheme considered in this section is shown in figure 5. The closed loop includes: (i) the water tank; (ii) an actuator consisting of a flow rate valve; (iii) a water level sensor; (iv) a controller that on the basis of sensor readings and reference signal, actuates the valve. We now introduce the contracts of each element of the configuration and compute the contract of the overall scheme.

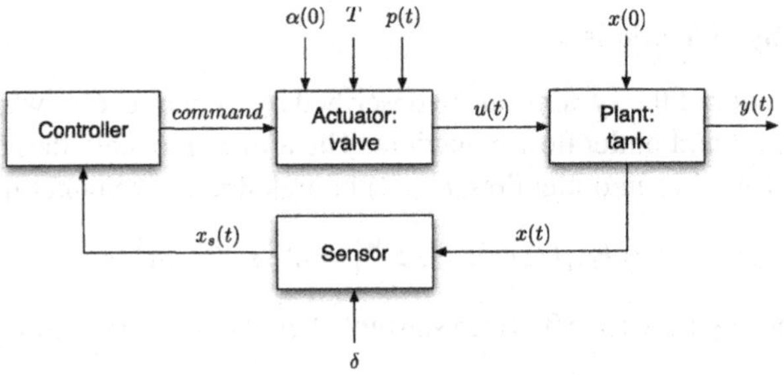

Fig. 5. Feedback composition of the contracts

Valve contract. The inlet flow to the container is controlled by a valve that may get a position command from a controller. It is assumed that, in response to a position command (*open* or *close*), the valve aperture changes linearly in time at rate $1/T$ where $T \in [T^m, T^M] = [2, 4]$ s.

The inlet flow is assumed to be proportional to the valve aperture $\alpha(t)$, where $0 \leq \alpha \leq 1$. As a consequence, the input $u(t)$ to the tank is equal to

$$u(t) = \alpha(t)\frac{S_{in}}{S}\sqrt{\frac{2p(t)}{\rho}} = \alpha(t)f(p(t)) \tag{2}$$

As shown in figure 5 the valve inputs are the *command* signal and the supply inlet pressure $p(t)$ while the output $u(t)$ is given by equation (2).

The assumption of the valve contract is

$$A^d_{valve} = \{p(t) \geq 0\} \times \{T \in [T^m, T^M]\} \times \{\alpha(0) \in [0, 1]\}$$

while the promise G_{valve} is defined on the output $u(t)$ of the valve and can be represented by the hybrid system depicted in figure 6 where the initial location can be either p_1 or p_3. Location p_0 corresponds to the situation in which the valve is closed and the output $u(t)$ toward the container is constantly zero, independently from the value assumed by the inlet pressure $p(t)$. Locations p_1 and p_3 correspond to the situations in which the valve is opening and closing, respectively. In these locations the output $u(t)$ depends on the inlet pressure $p(t)$ and the aperture of the valve $\alpha(t)$. Location p_2 corresponds to the situation in which the valve is open. In this case, the supply outlet flow $u(t)$ depends only on the inlet pressure $p(t)$.

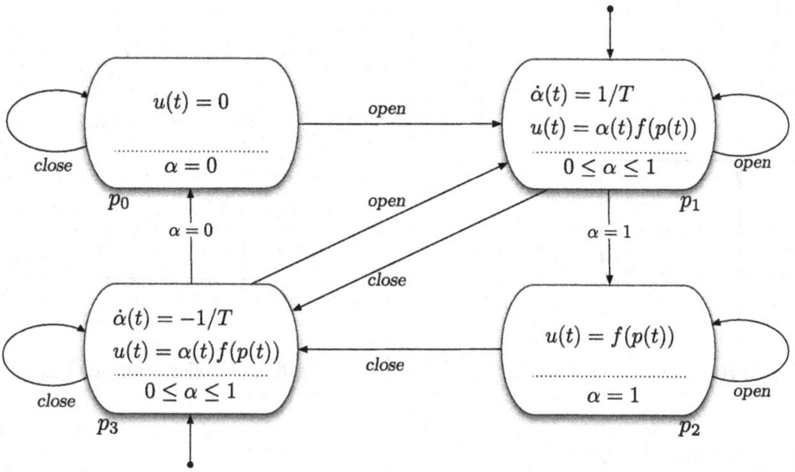

Fig. 6. Valve promise G_{valve}

Sensor contract. As depicted in figure 5 the sensor input is the water level $x(t)$ in the tank, and the output is the measured signal $x_s(t)$ subjected to the sensor error δ. In particular the sensor error δ is assumed to be bounded in a given interval $[-\Delta, \Delta]$ with $\Delta = 0.05\, m$. The assumptions A_{sensor} are the following:

- $A^{d}_{sensor} = \{\delta \in [-\Delta, \Delta]\}$;
- $A^{j,o}_{sensor} = \{x(t) \in [0, H]\}$.

The promise G_{sensor} of the sensor contract is defined as follows:

$$x_s(t) = x(t) + \delta$$

Controller contract. As shown in figure 5 the controller input is the measured water level $x_s(t)$ provided by the sensor, and the output is the command signal *open* or *close* for the regulation of the valve position. The control law is based on the hysteresis loop shown in figure 7. In this case, when the valve is closed and the water level is decreasing, the controller produces the *open* command only for $x_s(t) \leq l = 2.25m$. On the contrary, when the valve is open and the water level is increasing, the controller produces the *close* command only for $x_s(t) \geq h = 5.5m$, with $\Delta < l < h < H - \Delta$. There are no assumptions A_{contr} on the controller behavior, that is any value for $x_s(t)$ is admissible.

The controller promise G_{contr} can be described by the hybrid system shown in figure 8 where c_0 is the initial location.

Contracts composition. We now compose the contracts defining the four blocks of figure 5 to compute the contract of the closed–loop system. First of all consider the cascade composition of the four elements of figure 5 and note that the assumption on the tank behavior can be written as

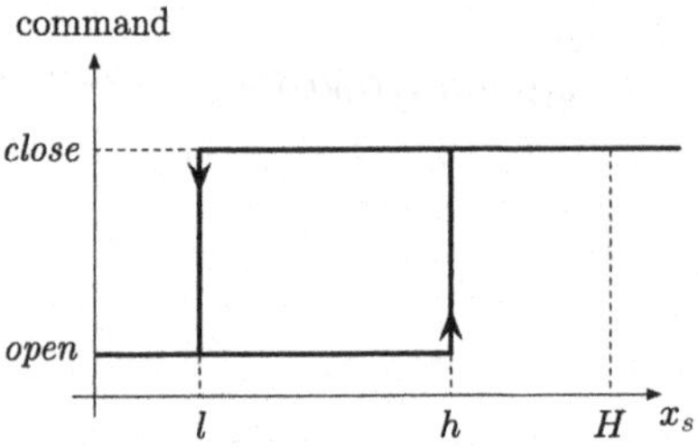

Fig. 7. Hysteresis control law

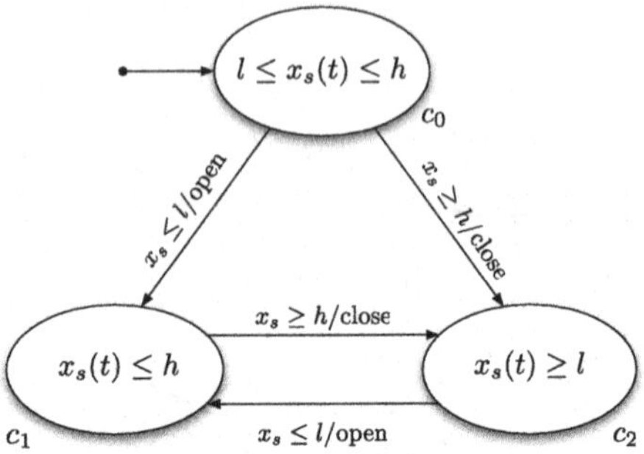

Fig. 8. Controller promise G_{contr}

- $A^d_{tank} = \{x(0) \in [0,H]\}$;
- $A^{j,o}_{tank} = \{u(t) \geq 0\}$.

Compatibility of the cascade composition can be verified considering as a first step the composition of the controller and the valve which is compatible since the valve has no assumptions on the *command* signal. Moreover, in this case, using G_{contr} as assumptions on the valve produces no refinement on G_{valve}.

As a second step, consider the composition of the three components controller–valve–tank by adding the tank component to the previous cascade composition. Since assumption A^d_{valve} ensures $p(t) \geq 0$ and $\alpha(t) \in [0,1]$, then the hybrid system describing G_{valve} is such that $u(t) \geq 0$. As a consequence,

$$G_{valve} = G^j_{valve} \subset A^{j,o}_{tank}$$

so that the composition results to be compatible. In this case, the promise G_{tank} can be refined using G_{valve} as assumption on $u(t)$ thus obtaining a new promise $G'_{tank} \subset G_{tank}$. Consider now the four components cascade composition. Also in this case, it is immediate to check that the hybrid system describing the tank behavior is such that $x(t) \in [0,H]$. As a consequence, the following holds:

$$G'_{tank} \subset G_{tank} \subset A^{j,o}_{sensor}$$

This concludes compatibility verification of the cascade composition.

As a final step, consider the composition obtained by closing the loop. Since there are no assumption A_{contr} on the behavior of $x_s(t)$ as an input to the controller, then

$$G^f = G_{sensor} \subset A_{contr} = A^f$$

and the feedback composition is compatible.

In conclusion, the assumptions on the overall system are the following:

$$A^e = A^d_{valve} \times A^d_{tank} \times A^d_{sensor} = \\ \{p(t) \geq 0\} \times \{T \in [T^m\,,\,T^M]\} \times \{\alpha(0) \in [0\,,\,1]\} \times \{x(0) \in [0,H]\} \times \{\delta \in [-\Delta,\Delta]\} \quad (3)$$

while the promise are given by $G'_e \times G_{sensor}$ where G'_e can be obtained by composing the hybrid systems describing the promises of each component. In fact, the promise of a component can be refined using the promise of the previous[1] component as assumption.

As a first step, consider the composition of the sensor, the controller and the tank. Composing G_{sensor}, G_{contr} and G_{tank} produces a hybrid system with locations belonging to the cartesian product of the location set of the hybrid systems defining G_{contr}, G_{tank}, i.e.

$$\{c_0, c_1, c_2\} \times \{q_0, q_1\}$$

as shown in figure 9. Since there are no continuous dynamics associated to sensor and controller promises, then the continuous dynamics associated to locations (q_i, c_j) are just those associated to q_i. The situation for the invariant conditions is more subtle: the conditions related to $x_s(t)$ in locations c_j can be transformed in conditions on $x(t)$ by using the promise G_{sensor} so that the invariant conditions associated to locations q_i and c_j are related to the same variable $x(t)$. The invariant conditions associated to locations (q_i, c_j) are then the intersection of the conditions associated to locations q_i and c_j. As a consequence, as shown in figure 9, locations (q_1, c_0) and (q_1, c_1) can be neglected since the invariant conditions result to be the an empty set.

As a second step, the hybrid system describing the promise of the tank, sensor and controller cascade composition has to be composed with the hybrid system describing G_{valve} in order to compute the closed–loop promise G'_e. As a consequence, the hybrid system describing G'_e has locations belonging to the cartesian product

$$\{(q_0, c_0), (q_0, c_1), (q_0, c_2), (q_1, c_2)\} \times \{p_0, p_1, p_2, p_3\}$$

and that will be denoted by a triple (p_i, q_j, c_k). Since the continuous dynamics and the invariant conditions associated to locations p_i and (q_j, c_k) are related to different variables, then the continuous dynamics and the invariant conditions associated to location (p_i, q_j, c_k) are just the union of the dynamics and the invariant conditions associated to p_i, and (q_j, c_k) . The hybrid system G'_e is depicted in figure 10. Some locations have been neglected since they cannot be reached from the initial set of locations, i.e. from locations (p_1, q_0, c_0) and (p_3, q_0, c_0).

The resulting hybrid system in figure 10 can be further minimized computing the equivalent minimal realization of the discrete behavior according the methodology illustrated in [6]. First, the hybrid system model is projected into the discrete domain, by abstracting away continuous dynamics and associating to it a finite state machine $\mathscr{F}$. After that, a minimal equivalent realization of $\mathscr{F}$ is computed according to the well-known *Paull-Unger recursive rule* [7,8]. In particular, the pairs of locations $[(p_3, q_0, c_0), (p_3, q_0, c_2)]$, $[(p_0, q_0, c_0), (p_0, q_0, c_2)]$, $[(p_2, q_0, c_0), (p_2, q_0, c_1)]$ and $[(p_1, q_0, c_0), (p_1, q_0, c_1)]$ are equivalent. In figure 10 is represented the minimal equivalent hybrid model describing the contract G'_e.

3.3 Verification of Contracts Satisfaction Relation by Reachability Analysis

In this section, we verify whether the contract defining the behavior of the closed–loop system, (A^e, G^e), satisfies the contract $(A_{des}, G'_e \times G_{sensor})$ defining system

[1] Previous in the cascade composition.

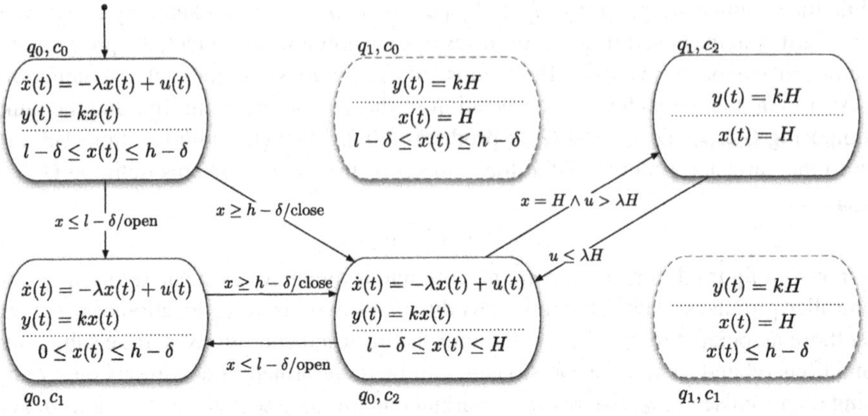

Fig. 9. Tank, sensor and controller cascade composition

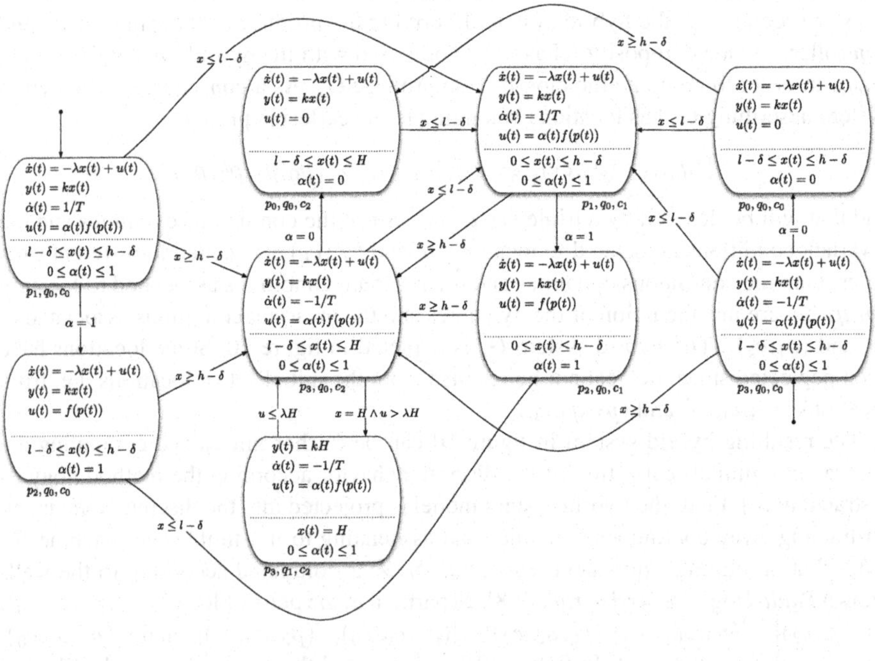

Fig. 10. Closed loop promise G'_e

specifications. To this end, recall that the assumption A^e are given in (3) and the promises G'_e are described by means of the hybrid system shown in figure 10. First, note that $A^e \supset A_{des}$ so that the satisfaction relation is verified if and only if the behavior of the closed–loop system under the assumption A_{des} meets the specification G_{des}. To verify this, an over approximation $\mathscr{R}$ of the infinite–time reachable set of the hybrid

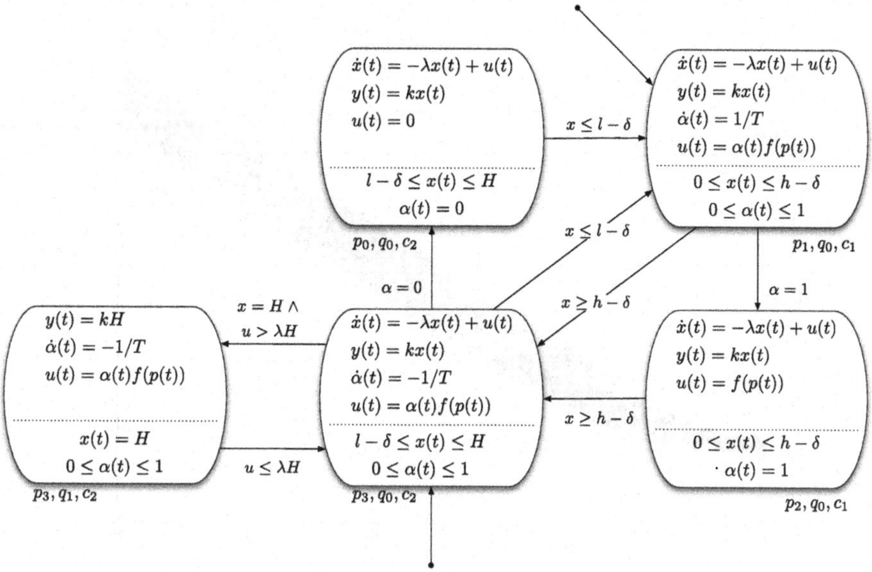

Fig. 11. Closed loop promise G'_e with minimum number of locations

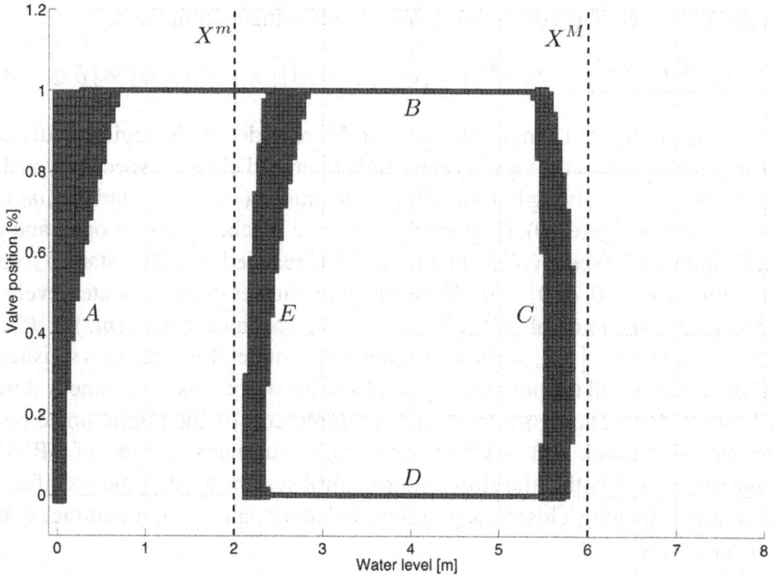

Fig. 12. Over–approximated reachable set

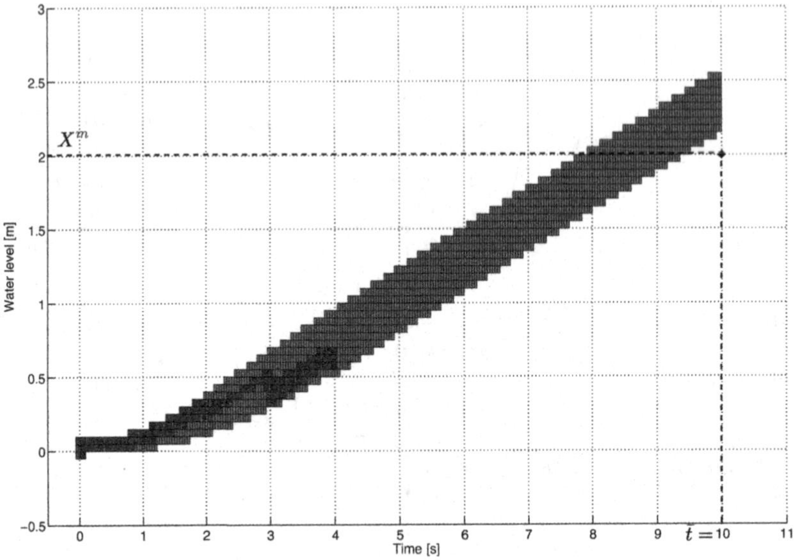

Fig. 13. Over–approximated reachable set against time

system describing G'_e is computed using the formal verification tool ARIADNE [9,10]. More in detail, the set $\mathscr{R}$ is computed under the following assumptions

$$\{p(t) \in [P^m, P^M]\} \times \{T \in [T^m\ ,\ T^M]\} \times \{\alpha(0) \in [0\ ,\ 1]\} \times \{x(0) = 0\} \times \{\delta \in [-\Delta, \Delta]\}$$

and it is depicted in figure 12 in the space $x - \alpha$. More in detail, the regions indicated as B and D are reached when the valve is constantly open and closed respectively and only the water level $x(t)$ is evolving in time (discrete locations (p_2, q_0, c_1) and (p_0, q_0, c_2) of the hybrid model in figure 10). Regions E and C are reached after an open and close controller command, respectively, while region A is reached just after startup from the initial condition $x(0) = 0$, $\alpha(0) \in [0\ ,\ 1]$. As the figure makes clear, the water level $x(t)$ is always bounded in the interval $[X^m, X^M] = [2\ ,\ 6]\ m$. This means that $\forall p(t) \in [P^m, P^M]$, $\forall T \in [T^m, T^M]$ and $\forall \delta \in [-\Delta, \Delta]$ the constraint on the outlet flow (eq. 1) is satisfied. An over approximation of all the possible evolutions of the water tank w.r.t. time is shown in figure 13 for $t \in [0, \bar{t}]$. The figure shows how requirements on the minimum admissible level of water in the tank $x(\bar{t}) > X^m$ are satisfied. In summary, the use of ARIADNE made it possible to verify that the closed-loop control system satisfies the specifications, i.e., the contract defining closed-loop system behavior satisfies the contract defining system specifications.

4 Conclusion

We presented the use of the SPEEDS Heterogeneous Rich Components formalism to design embedded controllers with continuous plants. The rules for composing assumptions-promises that form the basis for HRC for components connected in a generic feedback configuration were described. We then applied these rules to a specific control problem: a water level control problem that, albeit simple, exposes a variety of interesting effects. We showed how to compose hybrid contracts for all the subsystems connected in the closed–loop structure. The verification of closed–loop contracts satisfaction was carried out with ARIADNE, a formal verification tool for hybrid systems.

Acknowledgments

We wish to thank the reviewers for their remarks, which helped in improving the quality of the paper. This research has been supported by the European SPEEDS integrated project number 033471.

References

1. Sangiovanni-Vincentelli, A.: Defining platform-based design. EEdesign (February 2002), http://www.eedesign.com/
2. Bozga, M., Constant, O., Skipper, M., Ma, Q.: SPEEDS meta-model syntax and static semantics. SPEEDS deliverable D2.1b (January 2007)
3. Gössler, G., Graf, S., Cederbaum, M., Martens, M., Sifakis, J.: An approach to modeling and verification of component based systems. In: van Leeuwen, J., Italiano, G.F., van der Hoek, W., Meinel, C., Sack, H., Plášil, F. (eds.) SOFSEM 2007. LNCS, vol. 4362, Springer, Heidelberg (2007)
4. Badouel, E., Benveniste, A., Caillaud, B., Passerone, R.: Heterogeneous rich component definition, mathematical semantics. SPEEDS deliverable D2.1b/sem, annex of deliverable D2.1b (December 2006)
5. Goessler, G., Sifakis, J.: Composition for component-based modeling. Science of Computer Programming, 161–183 (March 2005)
6. Balluchi, A., Mazzi, E., Sangiovanni-Vincentelli, A.: Complexity reduction for the design of interacting controllers. In: Bemporad, A., Bicchi, A., Buttazzo, G. (eds.) HSCC 2007. LNCS, vol. 4416, pp. 46–60. Springer, Heidelberg (2007)
7. Micheli, G.D.: Synthesis and Optimization of Digital Circuits. McGraw-Hill, New York (2001)
8. Katz, R.: Contemporary Logic Design, ch. 1–10. The Benjamin/Cummings Publishing Company (1994)
9. Collins, P.: Continuity and computability of reachable sets. Theoretical Computer Science 341, 162–195 (2005)
10. Balluchi, A., Casagrande, A., Collins, P., Ferrari, A., Villa, T., Sangiovanni-Vincentelli, A.: Ariadne: a framework for reachability analysis of hybrid automata. In: Proceedings of the 17th International Symposium on Mathematical Theory of Networks and Systems (MTNS 2006), Kyoto, Japan (July 2006)

Controller Synthesis with Budget Constraints

Krishnendu Chatterjee[1], Rupak Majumdar[3], and Thomas A. Henzinger[1,2]

[1] EECS, UC Berkeley
[2] CCS, EPFL
[3] CS, UC Los Angeles

Abstract. We study the controller synthesis problem under budget constraints. In this problem, there is a cost associated with making an observation, and a controller can make only a limited number of observations in each round so that the total cost of the observations does not exceed a given fixed budget. The controller must ensure some ω-regular requirement subject to the budget constraint. Budget constraints arise in designing and implementing controllers for resource-constrained embedded systems, where a controller may not have enough power, time, or bandwidth to obtain data from all sensors in each round. They lead to games of imperfect information, where the unknown information is not fixed a priori, but can vary from round to round, based on the choices made by the controller how to allocate its budget.

We show that the budget-constrained synthesis problem for ω-regular objectives is complete for exponential time. In addition to studying synthesis under a fixed budget constraint, we study the budget optimization problem, where given a plant, an objective, and observation costs, we have to find a controller that achieves the objective with minimal average accumulated cost (or minimal peak cost). We show that this problem is reducible to a game of imperfect information where the winning objective is a conjunction of an ω-regular condition and a long-run average condition (or a least max-cost condition), and this again leads to an exponential-time algorithm.

Finally, we extend our results to games over infinite state spaces, and show that the budget-constrained synthesis problem is decidable for infinite state games with stable quotients of finite index. Consequently, the discrete time budget-constrained synthesis problem is decidable for rectangular hybrid automata.

1 Introduction

The *controller synthesis* problem asks, given a model for a plant, to construct a controller that observes the states of the plant and provides inputs to the plant such that the parallel composition of the plant and the controller is guaranteed to satisfy a given specification, provided, e.g., as an ω-regular set [4, 1, 14, 13]. Controller synthesis reduces to solving two-player games on graphs between a controller and the plant [1, 13, 5], where a winning strategy of the controller player for the specification gives a controller.

In constructing the controller, the usual assumption is that the controller can observe the system state completely. This assumption, called *perfect information*,

M. Egerstedt and B. Mishra (Eds.): HSCC 2008, LNCS 4981, pp. 72–86, 2008.

may not hold in many settings of practical interest. For example, an embedded controller may only observe signals up to a finite precision, and a discrete control process may only observe the global state of other processes, not their private variables. Under such observability restrictions, a more relevant model is a game of *imperfect information*, where the controller only observes a part of the state space, and must construct a winning strategy based only on the observed state.

Games with imperfect information have been studied extensively [15, 13, 10, 11, 2]. Usually, the solution to a game of imperfect information proceeds with a subset construction that reduces the imperfect-information game to a game with perfect information (although on an exponentially larger state space). However, so far, most algorithms make the assumption of *fixed* partial information. Roughly, it is assumed that of n state bits, the controller can only observe the first $k < n$ bits, and must come up with a strategy that makes its decisions based on this limited observation. In the context of embedded control systems, especially in low-power settings such as embedded sensor and actuator networks [16], there is often a different kind of partial information. Instead of a fixed set of bits that are visible to the controller in every round of interaction, the partial information can be due to a cost in sensing each bit, and global constraints on the budget available to the controller. For example, in an embedded control system, the controller is free to sense any signal from the system, however, the act of sensing carries a cost (e.g., cost incurred by the energy consumed to sense, or time taken to run the sensing task, or bandwidth required to transmit the sensed value). Thus, in each round, the controller has to make a choice in allocating its resources (energy, time, or bandwidth) to sensing the most crucial data. Moreover, the controller is allowed to select which bits to sense in each round, so the set of bits sensed in one round may be different from the set sensed in the next.

We introduce and study a model of controller synthesis under budget constraints to study imperfect information of this kind. Our model adds a notion of cost associated with controller moves, and the winning conditions constrain possible controls by imposing budgets on the moves either in each round (modeling, e.g., upper bounds on available resources) or in the long run (modeling, e.g., the desire to minimize average cost, or maximize lifetime). In the first model, in each round, the controller may choose to sense a set I of state signals, as long as the total cost of sensing all the signals in I is bounded by B. Practically, the budget represents, e.g., bounds on available energy or bandwidth limitations of the system. Given a two player game with a cost for every state signal, a budget constraint B, and an ω-regular control objective, we construct a B-*restricted* control strategy that satisfies the control objective while always using at most B cost units at any round, if possible. In the second model, we construct a B-*long-run* control strategy that satisfies the control objective while maintaining the long-run average cost of sensing below B. Practically, this represents, e.g., control subject to available battery power. With embedded resource-scarce control problems becoming more and more common, our model presents a realistic generalization of classically studied supervisory control problems.

Dually, we study the *budget optimization problem*, where given the sensing costs for each state signal, we want to find out the minimum budget with which a controller can achieve its goals. Here, we study two different optimization criteria: the first aims to minimize the maximum sensing cost at any single round, the second aims to minimize the long-run average cost of the controller. Optimizations of the first type may be required to find out minimal power or bandwidth requirements for the system: the battery must be able to provide at least this power in order for the controller to effectively satisfy the control objective. Optimizations of the second type are required to maximize the lifetime of the controller.

Technically, there are two steps in our algorithms. For the budget constrained synthesis problem, we construct, from the budget-constrained game, a game of perfect information by a subset construction such that the controller has a winning strategy in the game of perfect information iff it has a winning strategy in the original game. For the budget optimization problem, we perform a similar subset construction, however, the winning objectives on the transformed games are a combination of ω-regular objectives (from the original game) as well as a *quantitative* requirement to reduce either the maximum cost along the path (corresponding to the first optimization criterion) or the long-run average cost along the path (corresponding to the second optimization criterion). From our reduction and solutions of games of perfect information we obtain that both the budget synthesis and the optimization problem are EXPTIME-complete for ω-regular objectives specified as parity conditions (a canonical form to express ω-regular objectives).

We develop the theory both for finite-state, discrete control problems, as well as for discrete time control for rectangular hybrid automata. In the latter, infinite state case, we show that the control problem can be solved by reducing the system to its stable (bisimulation) quotient. Using known results about stable partitions of rectangular automata [6], it follows that the budget constrained synthesis problem is decidable for rectangular automata, and indeed, for any infinite state control problem with a stable quotient of finite index.

2 Definitions

A *game structure* (*of imperfect information*) is a tuple $G = \langle L, l_0, \Sigma, \Delta, \mathcal{O}, \gamma \rangle$, where L is a finite set of states, $l_0 \in L$ is the initial state, Σ is a finite alphabet, $\Delta \subseteq L \times \Sigma \times L$ is a set of labeled transitions, $\mathcal{O}$ is a finite set of observations, and $\gamma : \mathcal{O} \to 2^L \setminus \emptyset$ maps each observation to the set of states that it represents. We require the following two properties on G: (*i*) for all $\ell \in L$ and all $\sigma \in \Sigma$, there exists $\ell' \in L$ such that $(\ell, \sigma, \ell') \in \Delta$; and (*ii*) the set $\{\gamma(o) \mid o \in \mathcal{O}\}$ partitions L. We say that G is a game structure of *perfect information* if $\mathcal{O} = L$ and $\gamma(\ell) = \{\ell\}$ for all $\ell \in L$. We omit $(\mathcal{O}, \gamma)$ in the description of games of perfect information. For $\sigma \in \Sigma$ and $s \subseteq L$, let $\mathsf{Post}^G_\sigma(s) = \{\ell' \in L \mid \exists \ell \in s : (\ell, \sigma, \ell') \in \Delta\}$.

In a game structure, in each turn, Player 1 chooses a letter in Σ, and Player 2 resolves nondeterminism by choosing the successor state. A *play* in G is an infinite sequence $\pi = \ell_0 \sigma_0 \ell_1 \ldots \sigma_{n-1} \ell_n \sigma_n \ldots$ such that (*i*) $\ell_0 = l_0$, and (*ii*) for all $i \geq 0$, we have $(\ell_i, \sigma_i, \ell_{i+1}) \in \Delta$. The *prefix up to* ℓ_n of the play π is denoted by $\pi(n)$; its *length* is $|\pi(n)| = n+1$; and its *last element* is $\mathsf{Last}(\pi(n)) = \ell_n$. The *observation sequence* of π is the unique infinite sequence $\gamma^{-1}(\pi) = o_0\sigma_0 o_1 \ldots \sigma_{n-1} o_n \sigma_n \ldots$ such that for all $i \geq 0$, we have $\ell_i \in \gamma(o_i)$. Similarly, the *observation sequence* of $\pi(n)$ is the prefix up to o_n of $\gamma^{-1}(\pi)$. The set of infinite plays in G is denoted $\mathsf{Plays}(G)$, and the set of corresponding finite prefixes is denoted $\mathsf{Prefs}(G)$. A state $\ell \in L$ is *reachable* in G if there exists a prefix $\rho \in \mathsf{Prefs}(G)$ such that $\mathsf{Last}(\rho) = \ell$. The *knowledge* associated with a finite observation sequence $\tau = o_0\sigma_0 o_1\sigma_1 \ldots \sigma_{n-1} o_n$ is the set $\mathsf{K}(\tau)$ of states in which a play can be after this sequence of observations, that is, $\mathsf{K}(\tau) = \{\mathsf{Last}(\rho) \mid \rho \in \mathsf{Prefs}(G) \text{ and } \gamma^{-1}(\rho) = \tau\}$.

Lemma 1. *Let $G = \langle L, l_0, \Sigma, \Delta, \mathcal{O}, \gamma\rangle$ be a game structure. For $\sigma \in \Sigma$, $\ell \in L$, and $\rho, \rho' \in \mathsf{Prefs}(G)$ with $\rho' = \rho \cdot \sigma \cdot \ell$, let $o_\ell \in \mathcal{O}$ be the unique observation such that $\ell \in \gamma(o_\ell)$. Then $\mathsf{K}(\gamma^{-1}(\rho')) = \mathsf{Post}^G_\sigma(\mathsf{K}(\gamma^{-1}(\rho))) \cap \gamma(o_\ell)$.*

Strategies. A *strategy* in G for Player 1 is a function $\alpha : \mathsf{Prefs}(G) \to \Sigma$. A strategy α for Player 1 is *observation-based* if for all prefixes $\rho, \rho' \in \mathsf{Prefs}(G)$, if $\gamma^{-1}(\rho) = \gamma^{-1}(\rho')$, then $\alpha(\rho) = \alpha(\rho')$. In games of imperfect information we are interested in the existence of observation-based strategies for Player 1. A *strategy* in G for Player 2 is a function $\beta : \mathsf{Prefs}(G) \times \Sigma \to L$ such that for all $\rho \in \mathsf{Prefs}(G)$ and all $\sigma \in \Sigma$, we have $(\mathsf{Last}(\rho), \sigma, \beta(\rho, \sigma)) \in \Delta$. We denote by $\mathcal{A}_G$, $\mathcal{A}^{\mathcal{O}}_G$, and $\mathcal{B}_G$ the set of all Player-1 strategies, the set of all observation-based Player-1 strategies, and the set of all Player-2 strategies in G, respectively.

The *outcome* of two strategies α (for Player 1) and β (for Player 2) in G is the play $\pi = \ell_0\sigma_0\ell_1 \ldots \sigma_{n-1}\ell_n\sigma_n \ldots \in \mathsf{Plays}(G)$ such that for all $i \geq 0$, we have $\sigma_i = \alpha(\pi(i))$ and $\ell_{i+1} = \beta(\pi(i), \sigma_i)$. This play is denoted $\mathsf{outcome}(G, \alpha, \beta)$. The *outcome* of a strategy α for Player 1 in G is the set $\mathsf{Outcome}_1(G, \alpha)$ of plays π such that there exists a strategy β for Player 2 with $\pi = \mathsf{outcome}(G, \alpha, \beta)$. The outcome sets for Player 2 are defined symmetrically.

Qualitative objectives. A *qualitative objective* for G is a set ϕ of infinite sequences of observations and input letters, that is, $\phi \subseteq (\mathcal{O} \times \Sigma)^\omega$. A play $\pi = \ell_0\sigma_0\ell_1 \ldots \sigma_{n-1}\ell_n\sigma_n \ldots \in \mathsf{Plays}(G)$ *satisfies* the objective ϕ, denoted $\pi \models \phi$, if $\gamma^{-1}(\pi) \in \phi$. We assume objectives are Borel measurable, that is, a qualitative objective is a Borel set in the Cantor topology on $(\mathcal{O} \times \Sigma)^\omega$ [9]. Observe that by definition, for all objectives ϕ, if $\pi \models \phi$ and $\gamma^{-1}(\pi) = \gamma^{-1}(\pi')$, then $\pi' \models \phi$.

We specifically consider *parity objectives* [5,17]. Parity objectives are a canonical form to express all ω-regular objectives [17] and lie in the intersection $\Sigma_3 \cap \Pi_3$ of the third levels of the Borel hierarchy. For a play $\pi = \ell_0\sigma_0\ell_1 \ldots$, we write $\mathsf{Inf}(\pi)$ for the set of observations that appear infinitely often in $\gamma^{-1}(\pi)$, that is, $\mathsf{Inf}(\pi) = \{o \in \mathcal{O} \mid \ell_i \in \gamma(o) \text{ for infinitely many } i\text{'s}\}$. For $d \in \mathbb{N}$, let $p : \mathcal{O} \to \{0, 1, \ldots, d\}$ be a *priority function*, which maps each observation to a nonnegative integer priority. The *parity* objective $\mathsf{Parity}(p)$ requires that the minimum priority that appears infinitely often be even. Formally, $\mathsf{Parity}(p) = \{\pi \mid \min\{p(o) \mid o \in \mathsf{Inf}(\pi)\} \text{ is even}\}$.

Quantitative objectives. In addition to parity (ω-regular) objectives, our algorithms will require solving games with quantitative objectives. A *quantitative objective* for G is a Borel measurable function f on infinite sequences of observations and input letters to reals, that is, $f : (\mathcal{O} \times \Sigma)^\omega \to \mathbb{R} \cup \{ \infty, -\infty \}$. We specifically consider mean-payoff, mean-payoff parity and min-parity objectives. Let $r : \Sigma \to \mathbb{R}$ be a reward-function that maps every input letter σ to a real-valued reward $r(\sigma)$, and let $p : \mathcal{O} \to \{ 0, 1, \ldots, d \}$ be a priority function. We define the mean-payoff, mean-payoff parity and min-parity objectives as follows.

1. *Mean-payoff objectives.* For a play $\pi = \ell_0\sigma_0\ell_1 \ldots \sigma_{n-1}\ell_n\sigma_n \ldots$ the mean-payoff objective is the long-run average of the rewards of the input letters [19]. Formally, for a reward function $r : \Sigma \to \mathbb{R}$, the mean-payoff objective is a function $\mathsf{M}(r)$ from plays to reals that maps the play $\pi = \ell_0\sigma_0\ell_1 \ldots \sigma_{n-1}\ell_n\sigma_n \ldots$ to $\mathsf{M}(r)(\pi) = \limsup_{n\to\infty} \frac{1}{n} \sum_{i=0}^{n-1} r(\sigma_i)$.
2. *Mean-payoff parity objectives.* For a play $\pi = \ell_0\sigma_0\ell_1 \ldots \sigma_{n-1}\ell_n\sigma_n \ldots$ the mean-payoff parity objective is the long-run average of the rewards of the input letters if the parity objective is satisfied and $-\infty$ otherwise. Formally, for a reward function $r : \Sigma \to \mathbb{R}$ and a priority function p, the mean-payoff parity objective is a function $\mathsf{MP}(r, p)$ defined on plays as follows: for a play $\pi = \ell_0\sigma_0\ell_1 \ldots \sigma_{n-1}\ell_n\sigma_n \ldots$ we have $\mathsf{MP}(p, r)(\pi) = \mathsf{M}(\pi)$ if $\pi \in \mathsf{Parity}(p)$, and $\mathsf{MP}(p, r)(\pi) = -\infty$ otherwise.
3. *Min-parity objectives.* For a play $\pi = \ell_0\sigma_0\ell_1 \ldots \sigma_{n-1}\ell_n\sigma_n \ldots$ the min-parity objective is the minimum of the rewards of the input letters if the parity objective is satisfied and $-\infty$ otherwise. Formally, for a reward function $r : \Sigma \to \mathbb{R}$ and a priority function p, the min-parity objective is a function $\mathsf{MinP}(r, p)$ defined on plays as follows: for a play $\pi = \ell_0\sigma_0\ell_1 \ldots \sigma_{n-1}\ell_n\sigma_n \ldots$ we have $\mathsf{MinP}(p, r)(\pi) = \min\{r(\sigma_i) \mid i \geq 0\}$ if $\pi \in \mathsf{Parity}(p)$, and $\mathsf{MinP}(p, r)(\pi) = -\infty$ otherwise.

Sure winning and optimal winning. A strategy λ_i for Player i in G is *sure winning* for a qualitative objective ϕ if for all $\pi \in \mathsf{Outcome}_i(G, \lambda_i)$, we have $\pi \models \phi$. A strategy λ_i for Player i in G is *optimal* for a quantitative objective f if for all strategies λ for Player i we have $\inf_{\pi\in\mathsf{Outcome}_i(G,\lambda_i)} f(\pi) \geq \inf_{\pi\in\mathsf{Outcome}_i(G,\lambda)} f(\pi)$. The following theorem from Martin [12] states that perfect-information games with (qualitative or quantitative) Borel objectives are *determined*: from each state, either Player 1 or Player 2 wins (for qualitative objectives), or a value can be defined (for quantitative objectives).

Theorem 1 (Determinacy). [12] *(1) For all perfect-information game structures G and all qualitative Borel objectives ϕ, either there exists a sure-winning strategy for Player* 1 *for the objective ϕ, or there exists a sure-winning strategy for Player* 2 *for the complementary objective* $\mathsf{Plays}(G) \setminus \phi$. *(2) For all perfect-information game structures G and all quantitative Borel objectives f, we have* $\sup_{\alpha\in\mathcal{A}} \inf_{\pi\in\mathsf{Outcome}(G,\alpha)} f(\pi) = \inf_{\beta\in\mathcal{B}} \sup_{\pi\in\mathsf{Outcome}(G,\beta)} f(\pi)$.

3 Imperfect-Information to Perfect-Information Games

First, we use the results of [2] to show that a game structure G of imperfect information can be encoded by a game structure G^{K} of perfect information such that for every qualitative Borel objective ϕ, there is an observation-based sure-winning strategy for Player 1 in G for ϕ if and only if there is a sure-winning strategy for Player 1 in G^{K} for ϕ. We then show that the same construction works for quantitative Borel objectives. We obtain G^{K} using a subset construction. Each state in G^{K} is a set of states of G representing the knowledge of Player 1. In the worst case, the size of G^{K} is exponentially larger than the size of G.

Given a game structure of imperfect information $G = \langle L, l_0, \Sigma, \Delta, \mathcal{O}, \gamma \rangle$, we define the *knowledge-based subset construction* of G as the following game structure of perfect information: $G^{\mathsf{K}} = \langle \mathcal{L}, \{l_0\}, \Sigma, \Delta^{\mathsf{K}} \rangle$, where $\mathcal{L} = 2^L \backslash \{\emptyset\}$, and $(s_1, \sigma, s_2) \in \Delta^{\mathsf{K}}$ iff there exists an observation $o \in \mathcal{O}$ such that $s_2 = \mathsf{Post}^G_\sigma(s_1) \cap \gamma(o)$ and $s_2 \neq \emptyset$. Notice that for all $s \in \mathcal{L}$ and all $\sigma \in \Sigma$, there exists a set $s' \in \mathcal{L}$ such that $(s, \sigma, s') \in \Delta^{\mathsf{K}}$. Given a game structure of imperfect information G we refer to the game structure G^{K} as $\mathsf{Pft}(G)$.

Lemma 2 ([2]). *For all sets $s \in \mathcal{L}$ that are reachable in G^{K}, and all observations $o \in \mathcal{O}$, either $s \subseteq \gamma(o)$ or $s \cap \gamma(o) = \emptyset$.*

By an abuse of notation, we define the *observation sequence* of a play $\pi = s_0\sigma_0 s_1 \ldots \sigma_{n-1} s_n \sigma_n \ldots \in \mathsf{Plays}(G^{\mathsf{K}})$ as the infinite sequence $\gamma^{-1}(\pi) = o_0\sigma_0 o_1 \ldots \sigma_{n-1} o_n \sigma_n \ldots$ of observations such that for all $i \geq 0$, we have $s_i \subseteq \gamma(o_i)$. Since the observations partition the states, and by Lemma 2, this sequence is unique. The play π *satisfies* an objective $\phi \subseteq (\mathcal{O} \times \Sigma)^\omega$ if $\gamma^{-1}(\pi) \in \phi$. As above, we say that a play $\pi = s_0\sigma_0 s_1 \ldots \sigma_{n-1} s_n \sigma_n \cdots \in \mathsf{Plays}(G^{\mathsf{K}})$ *satisfies* an objective ϕ iff the sequence of observations $o_0 o_1 \ldots o_n \ldots$ such that for all $i \geq 0$, $\ell_i \in \gamma(o_i)$ belongs to ϕ. The following lemma follows from the results of [2].

Lemma 3 ([2]). *If Player 1 has a sure-winning strategy in G^{K} for an objective ϕ, then Player 1 has an observation-based sure-winning strategy in G for ϕ. If Player 1 does not have a deterministic sure-winning strategy in G^{K} for a Borel objective ϕ, then Player 1 does not have an observation-based sure-winning strategy in G for ϕ.*

Together with Theorem 1, Lemma 3 implies the first part of the following theorem, also used in [2]. The second part of the theorem generalizes the result to quantitative Borel objectives.

Theorem 2 (Sure-winning reduction). *Let G be a game structure, and $G^{\mathsf{K}} = \mathsf{Pft}(G)$. The following assertions hold. (1) Player 1 has an observation-based sure-winning strategy in G for a qualitative Borel objective ϕ if and only if Player 1 has a sure-winning strategy in G^{K} for ϕ [2]. (2) $\sup_{\alpha \in \mathcal{A}^{\mathcal{O}}_G} \inf_{\pi \in \mathsf{Outcome}(G,\alpha)} f(\pi) = \sup_{\alpha \in \mathcal{A}_{G^{\mathsf{K}}}} \inf_{\pi \in \mathsf{Outcome}(G,\alpha)} f(\pi)$.*

For the second part, let $v = \sup_{\alpha \in \mathcal{A}_{G^{\mathsf{K}}}} \inf_{\pi \in \mathsf{Outcome}(G,\alpha)} f(\pi)$. Given $\epsilon > 0$, consider the qualitative objective $\phi = \{ \pi \mid f(\pi) \geq v - \epsilon \}$. By the first part of the theorem, there is a sure-winning strategy in G^{K} iff there is an observation-based sure-winning strategy in G for the qualitative objective ϕ. Since ϵ is arbitrary, the result follows. It follows from Theorem 2 that to solve a game structure G of imperfect information it suffices to construct the game structure G^{K} of perfect information and solve the corresponding objective on G^{K}.

4 Games with Variables

We now consider game structures whose states are determined by valuations to a set of state variables, and formulate several games of imperfect information by restricting the variables that can be observed.

Games with Variables. A *game with variables* consists of: (1) a finite set $X = \{ x_1, x_2, \ldots, x_n \}$ of n boolean variables; a *valuation* v is a truth value assignment to all the variables, and we write V to denote the set of all valuations; (2) a finite set Γ of input letters; and (3) a non-deterministic transition function $\delta : V \times \Gamma \to 2^V \setminus \emptyset$ given a current valuation and an input letter gives the non-empty possible set of next valuations. We specify the games with variables as a tuple $G = (V, \Gamma, \delta)$. We introduce some notation. Given a natural number n we denote by $[n]$ the set $\{ 1, 2, \ldots, n \}$. For $I \subseteq [n]$ and $v \in V$, we denote by $v \upharpoonright I$ the restriction of the valuation on the set I of variables. Similarly, for $I \subseteq [n]$ we denote by $V \upharpoonright I$ the restriction of the set of valuations on the set I of variables. In games with variables we have two players: the controller and the system. The controller chooses the input letter and the system resolves the non-determinism in the transition function. We will consider several ways to restrict the knowledge of the controller by limiting what variables it can observe.

Games with Fixed-partial-information. To begin with, we consider games with variables where the information of the controller is restricted to a fixed set of size $k \leq n$ of variables. Without loss of generality, we consider the case when the controller can only observe the variables $x_1, x_2, \ldots, x_k$. Such games with variables have *fixed partial-information.*

Reduction. Let $G = (V, \Gamma, \delta)$ be a game with variables. A strategy for the controller in G is $[k]$-restricted if the strategy only observes the variables $\{ x_1, x_2, \ldots, x_k \}$. We present a reduction of games with variables with fixed-partial-information to the class of imperfect information games of Section 2. The reduction to a game with imperfect information $\widehat{G}_{\upharpoonright[k]} = \langle L, l_0, \Sigma, \Delta, \mathcal{O}, \gamma \rangle$ is as follows: (1) the set of states $L = V$, the set of valuations; (2) the input letters $\Sigma = \Gamma$; (3) the set of observations is the set of restrictions of the valuations to $\{ x_1, \ldots, x_k \}$: $\mathcal{O} = V \upharpoonright \{ 1, 2, \ldots, k \}$; (4) $\gamma(o) = \{ l \in L \mid l \upharpoonright \{ 1, 2, \ldots, k \} = o \}$; and (5) $(l, \sigma, l') \in \Delta$ iff $l' \in \delta(l, \sigma)$.

Theorem 3. *Let $G = (V, \Gamma, \delta)$ be a game with variables, and $p : V \to \{0, 1, \ldots, d\}$ be a priority function on V. Let $\widehat{p} : 2^V \setminus \emptyset \to \{ 0, 1, \ldots, d \}$ be a priority function derived from p as follows: for a non-empty set $Y \subseteq V$ we have $\widehat{p}(Y) = \max\{ p(v) \mid v \in Y \}$ if $p(v)$ is even for all $v \in Y$; otherwise $\widehat{p}(Y) = \min\{ p(v) \mid v \in Y, p(v)$ is odd $\}$. There is a $[k]$-restricted strategy for the controller in G to satisfy the objective* $\mathsf{Parity}(p)$ *iff there is a strategy in $\widehat{G}^{\mathsf{K}} = \mathsf{Pft}(\widehat{G}_{\upharpoonright[k]})$ to satisfy* $\mathsf{Parity}(\widehat{p})$.

Example 1. Consider a plant with variables $\{ x_1, x_2, \ldots, x_n \}$ such that the set $\{ x_1, x_2, \ldots, x_k \}$, for $k \leq n$, is the set of *public* variables that can be accessed by the controller and all the other variables are *private*, i.e., cannot be accessed by the controller. Games with fixed-partial-information provide an appropriate framework to model the interaction of the controller and the plant.

Games with Budget Constraints. We now consider games with variables where the set of variables that the controller can observe is not fixed, but there is a hard constraint on the amount of information that the controller can observe at any round. We will again present a reduction to games of imperfect information, but the reduction is more involved than the case of fixed partial-information.

Games with hard constraints. Let $G = (V, \Gamma, \delta)$ be a game with variables, and let c be a cost function that assigns a cost $c(i) > 0$ to variable x_i, i.e., there is a cost $c(i)$ for the controller to know the value of the variable x_i. The controller can choose to know the truth values of a subset of variables and then choose the input letter. For a budget $B > 0$, a strategy of the controller is B-restricted if at each round the controller can ask for the truth values of a subset I of variables such that the sum of the costs of the variables does not exceed B, that is, $\sum_{i \in I} c(i) \leq B$. Observe that the choice of the set of variables is not fixed and can vary in each round. For a set $I \subseteq [n]$ we denote by $c(I) = \sum_{i \in I} c(i)$ the sum of the cost of the variables in I. We present a reduction of games with variables and a budget B to imperfect-information games of Section 2. The reduction to an imperfect-information game $\overline{G}_{\restriction B} = \langle L, l_0, \Sigma, \Delta, \mathcal{O}, \gamma \rangle$ is as follows:

(1) *States.* The set of states is $L = V \times \{ I \subseteq [n] \mid c(I) \leq B \} \cup \overline{V}$, where $\overline{V}$ is a copy of the valuations. That is the set of states consists of a pair of valuation and a subset I such that $c(I)$ does not exceed the budget B, and copy $\overline{V}$ of V.
(2) *Input letters.* The set of input letters is $\Sigma = \Gamma \cup \{ I \subseteq [n] \mid c(I) \leq B \}$. The set of input letters is the set of input letters Γ of the game G and also consists of subsets $I \subseteq [n]$ such that $c(I) \leq B$.
(3) *Observations.* The set of observations is $\mathcal{O} = \{ (o, I) \mid I \subseteq [n], c(I) \leq B, o \in V \restriction I \} \cup \{ \overline{o} \}$. The set of observations consists of pairs (o, I) where $I \subseteq [n]$ and o is a valuation restricted to I, and there is a special observation $\overline{o}$.
(4) *Observation map.* The observation map is as follows: $\gamma(o, I) = \{ (l, I) \in L \mid l \restriction I = o \}$ and $\gamma(\overline{o}) = \overline{V}$. Observe that each state in $\overline{V}$ has the observation $\overline{o}$.
(5) *Transition function.* The transition function is as follows: for $\sigma \in \Gamma$, $((l, I), \sigma, \overline{l'}) \in \Delta$ iff $l' \in \delta(l, \sigma)$ and $(\overline{l}, \sigma, (l, \sigma)) \in \Delta$ for $\sigma = I \subseteq [n]$ such that $c(I) \leq B$. For a state (l, I) if an input letter σ from Γ is chosen, then a next state $\overline{l}'$ is possible iff $l' \in \delta(l, \sigma)$. For a state $\overline{l} \in \overline{V}$ the input letter can be chosen as a subset I such that $c(I) \leq B$, and the next state is (l, I). Observe that we assumed that input letters from Γ can be chosen at states (l, I), and at states from $\overline{V}$ a subset I of $[n]$ can be chosen. However, this can be easily transformed to a game where at every state all input letters are available as follows: we add an auxiliary state that is losing for the controller, and at a state if an input letter is not available, we make it available and add a transition to the losing state. For simplicity, we ignore the details of this reduction.

The set of observation-based strategies of $\overline{G}_{\restriction B}$ represents the set of B-restricted strategies. Let $\overline{G}^{\mathsf{K}}$ be the perfect-information game obtained from the subset construction of $\overline{G}_{\restriction B}$, i.e., $\overline{G}^{\mathsf{K}} = \mathsf{Pft}(\overline{G}_{\restriction B})$.

Theorem 4. *Let $G = (V, \Gamma, \delta)$ be a game with variables with a cost function c on variables and $p : V \to \{0, 1, \ldots, d\}$ be a priority function on V. For $B > 0$, consider the perfect-information game structure $\overline{G}^K = \mathsf{Pft}(\overline{G}_{\restriction B})$. Let $\overline{p}$ be a priority function on $\overline{G}^K$ defined as follows: for $s \subseteq \widetilde{V}$ we have $\overline{p}(s) = d$; and for $s \subseteq L \backslash \widetilde{V}$ we have $\overline{p}(s) = \max\{p(v) \mid (v, I) \in Y\}$ if $p(v)$ is even for all $(v, I) \in s$; otherwise $\overline{p}(s) = \min\{ p(v) \mid (v, I) \in Y, p(v)$ is odd$\}$. There is a B-restricted strategy for the controller in G to satisfy the objective* Parity(p) *iff there is a strategy in $\overline{G}^K$ to satisfy* Parity($\overline{p}$).

Example 2. Consider the interaction of a controller with a plant with variables $\{x_1, x_2, \ldots, x_n\}$ where all the variables are public. Assume the variables are accessed through a network with a bandwidth constraint B. Let c be a cost function that associates with a variable x_i the cost $c(i)$ that specifies the bandwidth requirement to access variable x_i. The games with hard-constraints provide the right framework to model such interactions.

Budget Optimization Problems. We now consider games with soft-constraints. These are games with variables with a cost function on variables. In contrast to games with hard-constraints where the budget B is a hard-constraint, in games with soft-constraints the controller can choose to know the value of a subset I of variables and incur a cost $c(I)$, and the goal is to either minimize the long-run average of the cost, or minimize the maximum cost, along with satisfying a given parity objective. A strategy in such games is called soft-constrained if whenever it asks for the valuation of a set I of variables, then it only observes the valuation of the set I of variables.

Reduction. Let $G = (V, \Gamma, \delta)$ be a game with variables, and let c be a cost function that assigns cost $c(i) > 0$ to variable x_i. We present a reduction of games with variables with soft-constraints to an imperfect-information game $\widetilde{G}_{\mathsf{soft}} = \langle L, l_0, \Sigma, \Delta, \mathcal{O}, \gamma \rangle$ as follows:

(1) *States.* The set of states is $L = V \times \{I \subseteq [n]\} \cup \widetilde{V}$, where $\widetilde{V}$ is a copy of the valuations. That is the set of states consists of a pair of valuation and a subset $I \subseteq [n]$ and copy of the valuations.
(2) *Input letters.* The set of input letters is $\Sigma = \Gamma \cup \{I \subseteq [n]\}$. The set of input letters is the set of input letters Γ of the game G and consists of subsets $I \subseteq [n]$.
(3) *Observations.* The set of observations is $\mathcal{O} = \{(o, I) \mid I \subseteq [n], o \in V \restriction I\} \cup \{\widetilde{o}\}$. The set of observations consists of pairs (o, I) where $I \subseteq [n]$ and o is a valuation restricted to I, and there is a special observation $\widetilde{o}$.
(4) *Observation map.* The observation map is as follows: $\gamma(o, I) = \{(l, I) \in L \mid l \restriction I = o\}$ and $\gamma(\widetilde{o}) = \widetilde{V}$. Observe that each state in $\widetilde{V}$ has the observation $\widetilde{o}$.
(5) *Transition function.* The transition function is as follows: for $\sigma \in \Gamma$, $((l, I), \sigma, \widetilde{l'}) \in \Delta$ iff $l' \in \delta(l, \sigma)$ and $(\widetilde{l}, \sigma, (l, \sigma)) \in \Delta$ for $\sigma = I \subseteq [n]$. For a state (l, I) if an input letter σ from Γ is chosen, then a next state $\widetilde{l'}$ is possible iff $l' \in \delta(l, \sigma)$. For a state $\widetilde{l} \in \widetilde{V}$ the input letter can be chosen as a subset $I \subseteq [n]$. Observe that we assumed that input letters from Γ can be chosen at states (l, I), and at states from $\widetilde{V}$ a subset I of $[n]$ can be chosen.

(6) *Reward function.* The reward function r on input letters is as follows: for input letters $\sigma \in \Gamma$ we have $r(\sigma) = 0$ and for $I \subseteq [n]$ we have $r(I) = -c(I)$, i.e., the reward collected is the negative of the cost.

The set of observation-based strategies of $\widetilde{G}_{\mathsf{soft}}$ represents the set of soft-constrained strategies. Let $\widetilde{G}^{\mathsf{K}}$ be the perfect-information game obtained from the subset construction of $\widetilde{G}_{\mathsf{soft}}$, i.e., $\widetilde{G}^{\mathsf{K}} = \mathsf{Pft}(\widetilde{G}_{\mathsf{soft}})$.

Theorem 5. *Let $G = (V, \Gamma, \delta)$ be a game with variables with a cost function c on variables and $p : V \to \{0, \ldots, d\}$ be a priority function on V. Consider the perfect-information game structure $\widetilde{G}^{\mathsf{K}} = \mathsf{Pft}(\widetilde{G}_{\mathsf{soft}})$. Let $\widetilde{p}$ be a priority function on $\widetilde{G}^{\mathsf{K}}$ defined as: for $s \subseteq \overline{V}$, let $\widetilde{p}(s) = d$; and for $s \subseteq L \setminus \widetilde{V}$, let $\widetilde{p}(s) = \max\{ p(v) \mid (v, I) \in Y \}$ if $p(v)$ is even for all $(v, I) \in s$; otherwise $\widetilde{p}(s) = \min\{ p(v) \mid (v, I) \in Y, p(v) \text{ is odd} \}$. The following assertions hold: (1) there is a soft-constrained strategy for the controller in G to satisfy* $\mathsf{Parity}(p)$ *and ensure the long-run average of the costs is at most λ iff $\sup_{\alpha \in \widetilde{G}^{\mathsf{K}}} \inf_{\pi \in \mathsf{Outcome}(\widetilde{G}^{\mathsf{K}}, \pi)} \mathsf{MP}(\widetilde{p}, r)) \geq -\frac{\lambda}{2}$; and (2) there is a soft-constrained strategy for the controller in G to satisfy* $\mathsf{Parity}(p)$ *and ensure the maximum of the costs is at most λ iff $\sup_{\alpha \in \widetilde{G}^{\mathsf{K}}} \inf_{\pi \in \mathsf{Outcome}(\widetilde{G}^{\mathsf{K}}, \pi)} \mathsf{MinP}(\widetilde{p}, r)) \geq -\lambda$.*

Observe that in item 1 of Theorem 5 the right-hand side is $-\frac{\lambda}{2}$ instead of $-\lambda$. This is because in the modeling of a game with variables with soft-constraints, each step of the original game is simulated in two-steps rather than one, and hence we need a factor of 2 in the result.

Example 3. Consider the interaction of a plant with variables $\{ x_1, x_2, \ldots, x_n \}$ and a controller where all the variables are public. The values of the variables can be obtained through sensors, and the value of variable x_i can be obtained through a sensor by consuming $c(i)$ units of power. Games with soft-constraints provide suitable framework for such games. If the goal is to minimize the average-power consumption, then the long-run average criterion is appropriate, and if the goal is to minimize the peak-power consumption, then the appropriate objective is to minimize the maximum cost.

Solution of perfection-information games. The results of [3] present solutions of perfect-information games with mean-payoff parity objectives. The result of Theorem 5 present a reduction of games with variables with soft-constraints to minimize long run average of the costs along with satisfying a parity objective to perfect-information games with mean-payoff parity objectives. Theorem 5 also presents the reduction of games with variables with soft-constraints to minimize the maximum cost along with satisfying a parity objective to perfect-information games with min-parity objectives. We now briefly describe how to use solutions of perfect-information parity games to obtain solutions of perfect-information min-parity games. The solution of perfect-information games with min-parity objectives can be obtained as follows: (a) sort the rewards on the edges; (b) with a binary search on the range of rewards, keep only edges above a certain reward value and solve the resulting qualitative parity game. The solution of perfect-information games with parity objectives is widely studied in literature, see [8,18,

7] for algorithmic solution of perfect-information parity games. Hence perfect-information min-parity games with n states and m edges can be solved with $\log(m)$ calls to perfect-information parity games. It may be noted that from the above solution we can find the the minimum budget B that is required to satisfy games with variables with hard-constraints to satisfy a given parity objective.

Computational complexity. It follows from the results of [2,15] that games with fixed-partial information are EXPTIME-hard even for reachability objectives. The games with fixed-partial information can be obtained as a special case of games with budget constraints as follows: set the budget as $B = k$, and the cost for bits $1, 2, \ldots, k$ as 1, and $k+1$ for all other bits. Hence it follows that games with budget constraints are EXPTIME-hard; and it also follows that the budget optimization problem is EXPTIME-hard for reachability objectives (and also for the more general parity objectives). From Theorem 4, Theorem 5, and the solution of perfect-information games we obtain an EXPTIME upper bound for the solution of games with budget constraints and the budget optimization problem. Thus we have the following result.

Theorem 6. *Let $G = (V, \Gamma, \delta)$ be a game with variables with a cost function c on variables and $p : V \to \{0, 1, \ldots, d\}$ be a priority function on V. For $B > 0$, it is EXPTIME-complete to decide whether there is a B-restricted strategy for the controller in G to satisfy the objective* $\mathsf{Parity}(p)$; *and the problem is EXPTIME-hard even for reachability objectives.*

5 Discrete Time Control of Rectangular Automata

We now apply the theory of controller synthesis with budget constraints to the discrete time control problem for *rectangular automata* [6]. We obtain our results using a general decidability result about imperfect-information games on infinite state spaces that have a stable partition with a finite quotient.

R-stable games. In this section we drop the assumption of finite state space of games. Let $G = \langle L, l_0, \Sigma, \Delta, \mathcal{O}, \gamma \rangle$ be a game structure of imperfect-information such that L is infinite. Let $R = \{ r_1, r_2, \ldots, r_l \}$ be a finite partition of L. A set $Q \subseteq L$ is *R-definable* if $Q = \bigcup_{r \in Z} r$, for some $Z \subseteq R$. The game G is *R-stable* if the following conditions hold for all $\sigma \in \Sigma$: (a) the set $\{ l \in L \mid \exists l' \in L.(l, \sigma, l') \in \Delta \}$ is R-definable; (b) for all $r \in R$, the set $\mathsf{Post}^G_\sigma(r)$ is R-definable; (c) for all $r, r' \in R$, if for some $x \in r$ we have $\mathsf{Post}^G_\sigma(\{ x \}) \cap r' \neq \emptyset$, then for all $x' \in r$ we have $\mathsf{Post}^G_\sigma(\{ x' \}) \cap r' \neq \emptyset$; and (d) for all $o \in \mathcal{O}$, the set $\gamma(o)$ is R-definable.

Lemma 4. *The following assertions hold. (1) Let G be a game structure of imperfect information, and let R be a finite partition of the state space of G such that the game G is R-stable. Then the perfect-information game* $\mathsf{Pft}(G)$ *is 2^R-stable. (2) Let $\overline{G}$ be a perfect-information game structure with a parity objective with d-priorities. If $\overline{G}$ is $\overline{R}$-stable, for a given finite partition $\overline{R}$, then the sure winning sets in $\overline{G}$ can be computed in time $O(|\overline{R}|^d)$.*

We present the definition of rectangular automata with budget constraints and then reduce the problem to a game of imperfect information. Using a result of [6] we establish the game of imperfect information is R-stable for a finite set R.

Rectangular constraints. Let $Y = \{ y_1, y_2, \ldots, y_k \}$ be a set of real-valued variables. A *rectangular inequality* over Y is of the form $x_i \sim d$, where d is an integer constant, and $\sim \in \{ \leq, <, \geq, > \}$. A *rectangular predicate* over Y is a conjunction of rectangular inequalities. We denote the set of rectangular predicates over Y as $Rect(Y)$. The rectangular predicate ϕ defines the set of vectors $[\phi] = \{ y \in \mathbb{R}^k \mid \phi[Y := y] \text{ is true} \}$. For $1 \leq i \leq k$, let $[\phi]_i$ be the projection on variable y_i of the set $[\phi]$. A set of the form $[\phi]$, where ϕ is a rectangular predicate, is called a rectangle. Given a non-negative integer $m \in \mathbb{N}$, the rectangular predicate ϕ is m-bounded if $|d| \leq m$, for every conjunct $y_i \sim d$ of ϕ. Let us denote by $Rect_m(Y)$ the set of m-bounded rectangular predicates on Y.

Rectangular automata with budget constraints. Let $X = \{x_1, x_2, \ldots, x_n\}$ be a set of boolean variables and V the set of all valuations. A *rectangular automaton with budget constraints* H is a tuple $\langle V, Lab, Edg, Y, Init, Inv, Flow, Jump, c\rangle$ where (a) Lab is a finite set of *labels*; (b) $Edg \subseteq V \times Lab \times V$ is a finite set of *edges*; (c) $Y = \{ y_1, y_2, \ldots, y_k \}$ is a finite set of *variables*; (d) $Init : V \to Rect(Y)$ gives the *initial condition* $Init(v)$ of a valuation v; (e) $Inv : V \to Rect(Y)$ gives the *invariant condition* $Inv(v)$ of valuation v (i.e., the automaton can stay in v as long as the values of variables lie in $[Inv(v)]$); (f) $Flow : V \to Rect(\dot{Y})$ governs the evolution of the variables in each valuation; (g) c is a cost function that assigns cost $c(i)$ to variable x_i, for $1 \leq i \leq n$; and (h) $Jump$ maps each edge e to a predicate $Jump(e)$ of the form $\phi \wedge \phi' \wedge \bigwedge_{i \notin Update(e)} (y_i' = y_i)$, where $\phi \in Rect(Y)$, $\phi' \in Rect(Y')$, and $Update(e) \subseteq \{ 1, 2, \ldots, k \}$. The variables in Y' refer to the updated values of the variables after the edge has been traversed. Each variable y_i with $i \in Update(e)$ is updated nondeterministically to a new value in $[\phi']_i$. A rectangular automaton is m-bounded if all rectangular constraints are m-bounded.

Nondecreasing and bounded variables. Let H be a rectangular automaton, and let $i \in \{ 1, 2, \ldots, k \}$. The variable y_i of H is *nondecreasing* if for all $v \in V$, the invariant interval $[Inv(v)]_i$ and the flow interval $[Flow(v)]_i$ are subsets of the nonnegative reals. The variable y_i of H is *bounded* if for all $v \in V$, the invariant interval $[Inv(v)]_i$ is a bounded set. The automaton H is bounded (resp. nondecreasing) if all the variables are bounded (resp. nondecreasing). In sequel we consider automata that are bounded or nondecreasing.

Game semantics. The rectangular automaton game with a budget constraint B is played as follows: the game starts with a valuation v and values for the continuous variables $y \in [Init(v)]$. At each round the controller can choose to observe a subset I of the boolean variables such that $c(I) \leq B$; and then the controller decides to take one of the enabled edges (if one exists). Then the environment nondeterministically updates the continuous variables according to the flow predicates by letting time pass for 1 time unit. Then the new round of the game starts. We now present a reduction to imperfect-information game, and then show that the game is stable with respect to a finite partition.

Reduction. A rectangular automaton H with a budget constraint B reduces to an imperfect-information game $\overline{H}_{\restriction B} = \langle L, l_0, \Sigma, \Delta, \mathcal{O}, \gamma \rangle$ as follows:

(1) *States.* The set of states is $L = V \times \mathbb{R}^k \times \{ I \subseteq [n] \mid c(I) \leq B \} \cup \overline{V} \times \mathbb{R}^k$, where $\overline{V}$ is a copy of the valuations. That is the set of states consists of a tuple of valuation, values of variables and a subset I such that $c(I)$ does not exceed the budget B, and copy of the valuations and the values of variables.
(2) *Input letters.* The set of input letters is $\Sigma = Lab \cup \{1\} \cup \{I \subseteq [n] \mid c(I) \leq B\}$. The set of input letters is the set of labels Lab of H, unit time 1 and subsets $I \subseteq [n]$ such that $c(I) \leq B$.
(3) *Observations.* The set of observations is $\mathcal{O} = \{ (o, I) \mid I \subseteq [n], c(I) \leq B, o \text{ is a valuation from } V \restriction I \} \cup \{ \overline{o} \}$. The set of observations consists of pairs (o, I) where $I \subseteq [n]$ and o is a valuation restricted to I, and there is a special observation $\overline{o}$.
(4) *Observation map.* The observation map is as follows: $\gamma(o, I) = \{ (l, y, I) \in L \mid l \restriction I = o \}$ and $\gamma(\overline{o}) = \overline{V} \times \mathbb{R}^k$. Observe that each state in $\overline{V} \times \mathbb{R}^k$ has the same observation $\overline{o}$.
(5) *Transition function.* The transition function is as follows: (a) $((\overline{v}, y), \sigma, (v, y, \sigma)) \in \Delta$, for $\sigma = I \subseteq [n]$ such that $c(I) \leq B$; (b) $((v, y, I), \sigma, \overline{v}', y') \in \Delta$, such that there exists $e = (v, \sigma, v') \in Edg$ with $(y, y') \in [Jump(e)]$; and (c) $((v, y, I), 1, (v, y', I)) \in \Delta$ such that there exists a continuously differentiable function $f : [0, 1] \to Inv(v)$ such that $f(0) = y$, $f(1) = y'$ and for all $t \in (0, 1)$ we have $\dot{f}(t) \in [Flow(v)]$.

The set of observation-based strategies of $\overline{H}_{\restriction B}$ represents the set of B-restricted strategies.

Equivalence relation. Let H be a m-bounded rectangular automaton with a budget constraint B, and let $\overline{H}_{\restriction B}$ be the game of imperfect information obtained by the reduction. We define the equivalence relation $\equiv_m$ on the state space as follows: $(v, y, I) \equiv_m (v', y', I)$ (resp. $(\overline{v}, y) \equiv_m (\overline{v}', y')$) iff (a) $v = v'$ (resp. $\overline{v} = \overline{v}'$); and (b) for all $1 \leq i \leq k$, either $\lfloor y_i \rfloor = \lfloor y_i' \rfloor$ and $\lceil y_i \rceil = \lceil y_i' \rceil$, or both y_i and y_i' are greater than m. We denote by $R_{\equiv_m}$ the set of equivalence classes of $\equiv_m$. It is easy to observe that $R_{\equiv_m}$ is finite (in fact exponential in the size of H). An extension of the result of [6] gives us the following result.

Lemma 5. *Let H be a m-bounded rectangular automaton game with a budget constraint B. The imperfect-information game $\overline{H}_{\restriction B}$ is $R_{\equiv_m}$-stable.*

Theorem 7. *Let H be a rectangular automaton with a budget constraint B and let $p : V \to \{ 0, 1, \ldots, d \}$ be a priority function on V. Consider the perfect-information game structure $\overline{H}^{\mathsf{K}} = \mathsf{Pft}(\overline{H}_{\restriction B})$. Let $\overline{p}$ be a priority function on $\overline{H}^{\mathsf{K}}$ defined as follows: for $s \subseteq \overline{V}$ we have $\overline{p}(s) = d$; and for $s \subseteq L \setminus \overline{V}$ we have $\overline{p}(s) = \max\{ p(v) \mid (v, I) \in Y \}$ if $p(v)$ is even for all $(v, I) \in s$; otherwise $\overline{p}(s) = \min\{ p(v) \mid (v, I) \in Y, p(v) \text{ is odd} \}$. There is a B-restricted strategy for the controller in H to satisfy the objective $\mathsf{Parity}(p)$ iff there is a strategy in $\overline{H}^{\mathsf{K}}$ to satisfy $\mathsf{Parity}(\overline{p})$.*

From Lemma 4, Lemma 5, and Theorem 7 we obtain the following corollary.

Corollary 1. *Let H be a rectangular automaton with a budget constraint B and let $p : V \to \{ 0, 1, \ldots, d \}$ be a priority function on V. Whether there is a B-restricted strategy for the controller in H to satisfy the objective* $\mathsf{Parity}(p)$ *can be decided in 2EXPTIME.*

Acknowledgments. This research was supported in part by the NSF grants CCF-0702743, CNS-0720881, CCR-0225610, and CCR-0234690, the Swiss National Science Foundation (NCCR MICS and Indo-Swiss Research Programme), and the ARTIST2 European Network of Excellence.

References

1. Büchi, J.R., Landweber, L.H.: Solving sequential conditions by finite-state strategies. Transactions of the AMS 138, 295–311 (1969)
2. Chatterjee, K., Doyen, L., Henzinger, T.A., Raskin, J.F.: Algorithms for omega-regular games with imperfect information. In: Ésik, Z. (ed.) CSL 2006. LNCS, vol. 4207, pp. 287–302. Springer, Heidelberg (2006)
3. Chatterjee, K., Henzinger, T.A., Jurdziński, M.: Mean-payoff parity games. In: LICS 2005, pp. 178–187. IEEE, Los Alamitos (2005)
4. Church, A.: Logic, arithmetic, and automata. In: Proceedings of the International Congress of Mathematicians, pp. 23–35. Institut Mittag-Leffler (1962)
5. Emerson, E.A., Jutla, C.: Tree automata, mu-calculus and determinacy. In: FOCS 1991, pp. 368–377. IEEE, Los Alamitos (1991)
6. Henzinger, T.A., Kopke, P.W.: Discrete-time control for rectangular hybrid automata. In: Theoretical Computer Science, vol. (221), pp. 369–392. Elsevier, Amsterdam (1999)
7. Jurdziński, M., Paterson, M., Zwick, U.: A deterministic subexponential algorithm for solving parity games. In: SODA 2006, pp. 117–123. ACM-SIAM, New York (2006)
8. Jurdzinski, M.: Small progress measures for solving parity games. In: Reichel, H., Tison, S. (eds.) STACS 2000. LNCS, vol. 1770, pp. 290–301. Springer, Heidelberg (2000)
9. Kechris, A.: Classical Descriptive Set Theory. Springer, Heidelberg (1995)
10. Kumar, R., Shayman, M.: Supervisory control of nondeterministic systems under partial observation and decentralization. SIAM Journal of Control and Optimization (1995)
11. Kupferman, O., Vardi, M.Y.: Synthesis with incomplete informatio. In: Advances in Temporal Logic, pp. 109–127. Kluwer Academic Publishers, Dordrecht (January 2000)
12. Martin, D.A.: Borel determinacy. Annals of Mathematics 102(2), 363–371 (1975)
13. Pnueli, A., Rosner, R.: On the synthesis of a reactive module. In: POPL 1989, pp. 179–190. ACM, New York (1989)
14. Ramadge, P.J.G., Wonham, W.M.: The control of discrete event systems. IEEE Transactions on Control Theory 77, 81–98 (1989)
15. Reif, J.H.: The complexity of two-player games of incomplete information. Journal of Computer and System Sciences 29, 274–301 (1984)

16. Sharp, C., Schenato, L., Schaffert, S., Sinopoli, B., Sastry, S.: Distributed control applications within sensor networks. In: Proceeding of the IEEE, Special Issue on Sensor Networks and Applications (2003)
17. Thomas, W.: Languages, automata, and logic. In: Handbook of Formal Languages. Vol. 3, Beyond Words, ch. 7, pp. 389–455. Springer, Heidelberg (1997)
18. Vöge, J., Jurdziński, M.: A discrete strategy improvement algorithm for solving parity games. In: Emerson, E.A., Sistla, A.P. (eds.) CAV 2000. LNCS, vol. 1855, pp. 202–215. Springer, Heidelberg (2000)
19. Zwick, U., Paterson, M.S.: The complexity of mean payoff games on graphs. Theoretical Computer Science 158, 343–359 (1996)

Trading Infinite Memory for Uniform Randomness in Timed Games*

Krishnendu Chatterjee[1], Thomas A. Henzinger[1,2], and Vinayak S. Prabhu[1]

[1] EECS, UC Berkeley
[2] CCS, EPFL
{c_krish,vinayak}@eecs.berkeley.edu, tah@epfl.ch

Abstract. We consider concurrent two-player timed automaton games with ω-regular objectives specified as parity conditions. These games offer an appropriate model for the synthesis of real-time controllers. Earlier works on timed games focused on pure strategies for each player. We study, for the first time, the use of *randomized* strategies in such games. While pure (i.e., nonrandomized) strategies in timed games require infinite memory for winning even with respect to reachability objectives, we show that randomized strategies can win with finite memory with respect to all parity objectives. Also, the synthesized randomized real-time controllers are much simpler in structure than the corresponding pure controllers, and therefore easier to implement. For safety objectives we prove the existence of pure finite-memory winning strategies. Finally, while randomization helps in simplifying the strategies required for winning timed parity games, we prove that randomization does not help in winning at more states.

1 Introduction

Timed automata [2] are models of real-time systems in which states consist of discrete locations and values for real-time clocks. The transitions between locations are dependent on the clock values. *Timed automaton games* [9,1,7,13,12] are used to distinguish between the actions of several players (typically a "controller" and a "plant"). We shall consider two-player timed automaton games with ω-regular objectives specified as *parity conditions.* The class of ω-regular objectives can express all safety and liveness specifications that arise in the synthesis and verification of reactive systems, and parity conditions are a canonical form to express ω-regular objectives [19]. The construction of a winning strategy for player 1 in such games corresponds to the *controller synthesis problem for real-time systems* [11,16,17,20] with respect to achieving a desired ω-regular objective.

The issue of *time divergence* is crucial in timed games, as a naive control strategy might simply block time, leading to "zeno" runs. Such invalid solutions have often been avoided by putting strong syntactic constraints on the cycles

* This research was supported in part by the NSF grants CCR-0208875, CCR-0225610, CCR-0234690, by the Swiss National Science Foundation, and by the Artist2 European Network of Excellence.

M. Egerstedt and B. Mishra (Eds.): HSCC 2008, LNCS 4981, pp. 87–100, 2008.

of timed automaton games [17,4,13,5], or by semantic conditions that discretize time [14]. Other works [16,11,6,7] have required that time divergence be ensured by the controller —a one-sided, unfair view in settings where the player modeling the plant is allowed to block time. We use the more general, semantic and fully symmetric formalism of [9,15] for dealing with the issue of time divergence. This setting places no syntactic restriction on the game structure, and gives both players equally powerful options for advancing time, but for a player to win, she must not be *responsible* for causing time to converge. It has been shown in [15] that this is equivalent to requiring that the players are restricted to the use of *receptive* strategies [3,18], which, while being required to not prevent time from diverging, are not required to ensure time divergence. More formally, our timed games proceed in an infinite sequence of rounds. In each round, both players simultaneously propose moves, with each move consisting of an action and a time delay after which the player wants the proposed action to take place. Of the two proposed moves, the move with the shorter time delay "wins" the round and determines the next state of the game. Let a set Φ of runs be the desired objective for player 1. Then player 1 has a *winning* strategy for Φ if she has a strategy to ensure that, no matter what player 2 does, one of the following two conditions hold: (1) time diverges and the resulting run belongs to Φ, or (2) time does not diverge but player-1's moves are chosen only finitely often (and thus she is not to be blamed for the convergence of time).

The winning strategies constructed in [9] for such timed automaton games assume the presence of an infinitely precise global clock to measure the progress of time, and the strategies crucially depend on the value of this global clock. Since the value of this clock needs to be kept in memory, the constructed strategies require *infinite memory.* In fact, the following example (Example 2) shows that infinite memory is necessary for winning with respect to reachability objectives. Besides the infinite-memory requirement, the strategies constructed in [9] are structurally complicated, and it would be difficult to implement the synthesized controllers in practice. Before offering a novel solution to this problem, we illustrate the problem with an example of a simple timed game whose solution requires infinite memory.

Example 1 (Signaling hub). Consider a signaling hub that both sends and receives signals at the same port. At any time the port can either receive or send a signal, but it cannot do both. Moreover, the hub must accept all signals sent to it. If both the input and the output signals arrive at the same time, then the output signal of the hub is discarded. The input signals are generated by other processes, and infinitely many signals cannot be generated in a finite amount of time. The time between input signals is not known a priori. The system may be modeled by the timed automaton game shown in Figure 1. The actions b_1 and b_2 correspond to input signals, and a_1 and a_2 to output signals. The actions b_i are controlled by the environment and denote input signals; the actions a_i are controlled by the hub and denote signals sent by the hub. The clock x models the time delay between signals: all signals reset this clock, and signals can arrive or be sent provided the value of x is greater than 0, ensuring that there is a

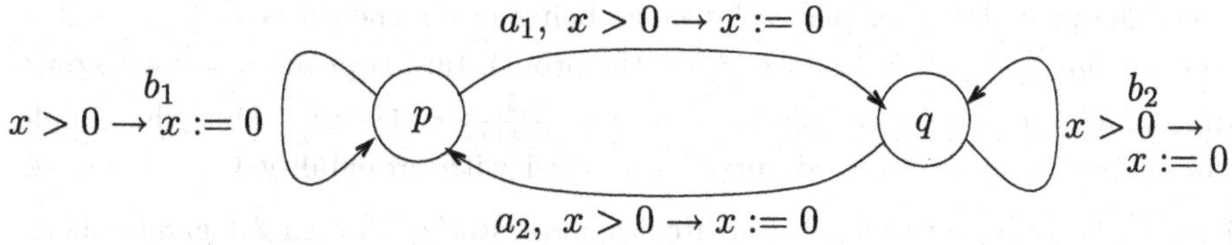

Fig. 1. A timed automaton game

positive delay between signals. The objective of the hub controller is to keep sending its own signals, which can be modeled as the generalized Büchi condition of switching infinitely often between the locations p and q (ie., the LTL objective $\Box(\Diamond p \wedge \Diamond q)$). □

Example 2 (Winning requires infinite memory). Consider the timed game of Figure 1. We let κ denote the valuation of the clock x. We let the special "action" $\perp$ denote a time move (representing time passage without an action). The objective of player 1 is to reach q starting from $s_0 = \langle p, x = 0\rangle$ (and similarly, to reach p from q). We let π_1 denote the strategy of player 1 which prescribes moves based on the history $r[0..k]$ of the game at stage k. Suppose player 1 uses only finite memory. Then player 1 can propose only moves from a finite set when at s_0. Since a zero time move keeps the game at p, we may assume that player 1 does not choose such moves. Let $\Delta > 0$ be the least time delay of these finitely many moves of player 1. Then player 2 can always propose a move $\langle \Delta/2, b\rangle$ when at s_0. This strategy will prevent player 1 from reaching q, and yet time diverges. Hence player 1 cannot win with finite memory; that is, there is no hub controller that uses only finite memory. However, player 1 has a winning strategy with infinite memory. For example, consider the player 1 strategy π_2 such that $\pi_2(r[0..k]) = \langle 1/2^{k+2}, a_1\rangle$ if $r[k] = \langle p, \kappa\rangle$. and $\pi_2(r[0..k]) = \langle 1, \perp\rangle$ otherwise. □

In this paper we observe that the infinite-memory requirement of Example 1 is due to the determinism of the permissible strategies: a strategy is *deterministic* (or *pure*) if in each round of the game, it proposes a unique move (i.e., action and time delay). A more general class of strategies are the randomized strategies: a *randomized* strategy may propose, in each round, a probability distribution of moves. We now show that in the game of Example 2 finite-memory randomized winning strategies do exist. Indeed, the needed randomization has a particularly simple form: player 1 proposes a unique action together with a time interval from which the time delay is chosen uniformly at random. Such a strategy can be implemented as a controller that has the ability to wait for a randomly chosen amount of time.

Example 3 (Randomization instead of infinite memory). Recall the game in Figure 1. Player 1 can play a randomized memoryless strategy π_3 such that $\pi_3(\langle p, \kappa\rangle) = \langle \mathsf{Uniform}((0, 1 - \kappa(x))), a_i\rangle$; that is, the action a_i is proposed to take place at a time chosen uniformly at random in the interval $(0, 1 - \kappa(x))$. Suppose player 2 always proposes the action b_i with varying time delays Δ_j at round j.

Then the probability of player-1's move being never chosen is $\prod_{j=1}^{\infty}(1-\Delta_j)$, which is 0 if $\sum_{j=1}^{\infty}\Delta_j=\infty$ (see [8] for the proof). Interrupting moves with pure time moves does not help player 2, as $1-\frac{\Delta_j}{1-\kappa(x)}<1-\Delta_j$. Thus the simple randomized strategy π_3 is winning for player 1 with probability 1. □

Previously, only deterministic strategies were studied for timed games; here, for the first time, we study randomized strategies. We show that randomized strategies are not more powerful than deterministic strategies in the sense that if player 1 can win with a randomized strategy, then she can also win with a deterministic strategy. However, as the example illustrated, randomization can lead to a reduction in the memory required for winning, and to a significant simplification in the structure of winning strategies. Randomization is therefore not only of theoretical interest, but can improve the implementability of synthesized controllers. It is for this reason that we set out, in this paper, to systematically analyze the trade-off between randomization requirements (no randomization; uniform randomization; general randomization), memory requirements (finite memory and infinite memory) and the presence of extra "controller clocks" for various classes of ω-regular objectives (safety; reachability; parity objectives).

Our results are as follows. First, we show that for safety objectives pure (no randomization) finite-memory winning strategies exist. Next, for reachability objectives, we show that pure (no randomization) strategies require infinite memory for winning, whereas uniform randomized finite-memory winning strategies exist. We then use the results for reachability and safety objectives in an inductive argument to show that uniform randomized finite-memory strategies suffice for all parity objectives, for which pure strategies require infinite memory (because reachability is a special case of parity). In all our uses of randomization, we only use uniform randomization over time, and more general forms of randomization (nonuniform distributions; randomized actions) are not required. This shows that in timed games, infinite memory can be traded against uniform randomness. Finally, we show that while randomization helps in simplifying winning strategies, and thus allows the construction of simpler controllers, randomization does not help a player in winning at more states, and thus does not allow the construction of more powerful controllers. In other words, the case for randomness rests in the simplicity of the synthesized real-time controllers, not in their expressiveness.

We note that in our setting, player 1 (i.e., the controller) can trade infinite memory also against finite memory together with an extra clock. We assume that the values of all clocks of the plant are observable. For an ω-regular objective Φ, we define the following winning sets depending on the power given to player 1: let $[\![\Phi]\!]_1$ be the set of states from which player 1 can win using any strategy (finite or infinite memory; pure or randomized) and any number of infinitely precise clocks; in $[\![\Phi]\!]_2$ player 1 can win using a pure finite-memory strategy and only one extra clock; in $[\![\Phi]\!]_3$ player 1 can win using a pure finite-memory strategy and no extra clock; and in $[\![\Phi]\!]_4$ player 1 can win using a randomized finite-memory strategy and no extra clock. Then, for every timed automaton game, we have $[\![\Phi]\!]_1=[\![\Phi]\!]_2=[\![\Phi]\!]_4$. We also have $[\![\Phi]\!]_3\subseteq[\![\Phi]\!]_1$, with the subset inclusion being in general strict. It can be shown that at least one bit of memory is required for winning of reachability objectives despite player 1 being allowed randomized strategies. We do not know whether memory is required for winning safety objectives (even in the case of pure strategies).

2 Timed Games

In this section we present the definitions of timed game structures, runs, objectives, strategies and the notions of sure and almost-sure winning in timed game structures.

Timed game structures. A *timed game structure* is a tuple $\mathcal{G} = \langle S, A_1, A_2, \Gamma_1, \Gamma_2, \delta \rangle$ with the following components.

- S is a set of states.
- A_1 and A_2 are two disjoint sets of actions for players 1 and 2, respectively. We assume that $\perp \notin A_i$, and write $A_i^\perp$ for $A_i \cup \{\perp\}$. The set of *moves* for player i is $M_i = \mathbb{R}_{\geq 0} \times A_i^\perp$. Intuitively, a move $\langle \Delta, a_i \rangle$ by player i indicates a waiting period of Δ time units followed by a discrete transition labeled with action a_i.
- $\Gamma_i : S \mapsto 2^{M_i} \setminus \emptyset$ are two move assignments. At every state s, the set $\Gamma_i(s)$ contains the moves that are available to player i. We require that $\langle 0, \perp \rangle \in \Gamma_i(s)$ for all states $s \in S$ and $i \in \{1, 2\}$. Intuitively, $\langle 0, \perp \rangle$ is a time-blocking stutter move.
- $\delta : S \times (M_1 \cup M_2) \mapsto S$ is the transition function. We require that for all time delays $\Delta, \Delta' \in \mathbb{R}_{\geq 0}$ with $\Delta' \leq \Delta$, and all actions $a_i \in A_i^\perp$, we have (1) $\langle \Delta, a_i \rangle \in \Gamma_i(s)$ iff both $\langle \Delta', \perp \rangle \in \Gamma_i(s)$ and $\langle \Delta - \Delta', a_i \rangle \in \Gamma_i(\delta(s, \langle \Delta', \perp \rangle))$; and (2) if $\delta(s, \langle \Delta', \perp \rangle) = s'$ and $\delta(s', \langle \Delta - \Delta', a_i \rangle) = s''$, then $\delta(s, \langle \Delta, a_i \rangle) = s''$.

The game proceeds as follows. If the current state of the game is s, then both players simultaneously propose moves $\langle \Delta_1, a_1 \rangle \in \Gamma_1(s)$ and $\langle \Delta_2, a_2 \rangle \in \Gamma_2(s)$. The move with the shorter duration "wins" in determining the next state of the game. If both moves have the same duration, then the move of player 2 determines the next state.[1] We use this setting as our goal is to compute the winning set for player 1 against all possible strategies of player 2. Formally, we define the *joint destination function* $\delta_{\mathsf{jd}} : S \times M_1 \times M_2 \mapsto S$ by

$$\delta_{\mathsf{jd}}(s, \langle \Delta_1, a_1 \rangle, \langle \Delta_2, a_2 \rangle) = \begin{cases} \delta(s, \langle \Delta_1, a_1 \rangle) & \text{if } \Delta_1 < \Delta_2; \\ \delta(s, \langle \Delta_2, a_2 \rangle) & \text{if } \Delta_2 \leq \Delta_1. \end{cases}$$

The time elapsed when the moves $m_1 = \langle \Delta_1, a_1 \rangle$ and $m_2 = \langle \Delta_2, a_2 \rangle$ are proposed is given by $\mathsf{delay}(m_1, m_2) = \min(\Delta_1, \Delta_2)$. The boolean predicate $\mathsf{blame}_i(s, m_1, m_2, s')$ indicates whether player i is "responsible" for the state change from s to s' when the moves m_1 and m_2 are proposed. Denoting the opponent of player i by $\sim i = 3 - i$, for $i \in \{1, 2\}$, we define

[1] Alternatively, we can define the next state to be determined nondeterministically in the case of ties, without changing our results. We give the player-2 move priority only to simplify the presentation.

$$\mathsf{blame}_i(s, \langle \Delta_1, a_1\rangle, \langle \Delta_2, a_2\rangle, s') = \big(\Delta_i \le \Delta_{\sim i} \ \wedge\ \delta(s, \langle \Delta_i, a_i\rangle) = s'\big).$$

Runs. A *run* of the timed game structure $\mathcal{G}$ is an infinite sequence $r = s_0, \langle m_1^0, m_2^0\rangle, s_1, \langle m_1^1, m_2^1\rangle, \ldots$ such that $s_k \in S$ and $m_i^k \in \Gamma_i(s_k)$ and $s_{k+1} = \delta_{\mathsf{jd}}(s_k, m_1^k, m_2^k)$ for all $k \ge 0$ and $i \in \{1,2\}$. For $k \ge 0$, let $\mathsf{time}(r,k)$ denote the "time" at position k of the run, namely, $\mathsf{time}(r,k) = \sum_{j=0}^{k-1} \mathsf{delay}(m_1^j, m_2^j)$ (we let $\mathsf{time}(r,0) = 0$). By $r[k]$ we denote the $(k+1)$-th state s_k of r. The run prefix $r[0..k]$ is the finite prefix of the run r that ends in the state s_k. Let Runs be the set of all runs of $\mathcal{G}$, and let $\mathsf{FinRuns}$ be the set of run prefixes.

Objectives. An *objective* for the timed game structure $\mathcal{G}$ is a set $\Phi \subseteq \mathsf{Runs}$ of runs. We will be interested in the classical reachability, safety and parity objectives. Parity objectives are canonical forms for ω-regular properties that can express all commonly used specifications that arise in verification.

- Given a set of states Y, the *reachability* objective $\mathsf{Reach}(Y)$ is defined as the set of runs that visit Y, formally, $\mathsf{Reach}(Y) = \{r \mid \text{ there exists } i \text{ such that } r[i] \in Y\}$.
- Given a set of states Y, the *safety* objective consists of the set of runs that stay within Y, formally, $\mathsf{Safe}(Y) = \{r \mid \text{ for all } i \text{ we have } r[i] \in Y\}$.
- Let $\Omega : S \mapsto \{0, \ldots, k-1\}$ be a parity index function. The parity objective for Ω requires that the maximal index visited infinitely often is even. Formally, let $\mathsf{InfOften}(\Omega(r))$ denote the set of indices visited infinitely often along a run r. Then the parity objective defines the following set of runs: $\mathsf{Parity}(\Omega) = \{r \mid \max(\mathsf{InfOften}(\Omega(r))) \text{ is even }\}$.

A timed game structure $\mathcal{G}$ together with the index function Ω constitute a *parity timed game* (of index k) in which the objective of player 1 is $\mathsf{Parity}(\Omega)$. We use similar notations for reachability and safety timed games.

Strategies. A *strategy* for a player is a recipe that specifies how to extend a run. Formally, a *probabilistic strategy* π_i for player $i \in \{1,2\}$ is a function π_i that assigns to every run prefix $r[0..k]$ a probability distribution $\mathcal{D}_i(r[k])$ over $\Gamma_i(r[k])$, the set of moves available to player i at the state $r[k]$. *Pure strategies* are strategies for which the state space of the probability distribution of $\mathcal{D}_i(r[k])$ is a singleton set for every run r and all k. We let Π_i^{pure} denote the set of pure strategies for player i, with $i \in \{1,2\}$. For $i \in \{1,2\}$, let Π_i be the set of strategies for player i. Given two strategies $\pi_1 \in \Pi_1$ and $\pi_2 \in \Pi_2$, the set of possible *outcomes* of the game starting from a state $s \in S$ is denoted $\mathsf{Outcomes}(s, \pi_1, \pi_2)$. Given strategies π_1 and π_2, for player 1 and player 2, respectively, and a starting state s we denote by $\Pr_s^{\pi_1,\pi_2}(\cdot)$ the probability space given the strategies and the initial state s.

Receptive strategies. We will be interested in strategies that are meaningful (in the sense that they do not block time). To define them formally we first present the following two sets of runs.

- A run r is *time-divergent* if $\lim_{k\to\infty} \mathsf{time}(r,k) = \infty$. We denote by $\mathsf{Timediv}$ the set of all time-divergent runs.

- The set $\mathsf{Blameless}_i \subseteq \mathsf{Runs}$ consists of the set of runs in which player i is responsible only for finitely many transitions. A run $s_0, \langle m_1^0, m_2^0\rangle, s_1, \langle m_1^1, m_2^1\rangle, \ldots$ belongs to the set $\mathsf{Blameless}_i$, for $i = \{1, 2\}$, if there exists a $k \geq 0$ such that for all $j \geq k$, we have $\neg\, \mathsf{blame}_i(s_j, m_1^j, m_2^j, s_{j+1})$.

A strategy π_i is *receptive* if for all strategies $\pi_{\sim i}$, all states $s \in S$, and all runs $r \in \mathsf{Outcomes}(s, \pi_1, \pi_2)$, either $r \in \mathsf{Timediv}$ or $r \in \mathsf{Blameless}_i$. Thus, no what matter what the opponent does, a receptive strategy of player i cannot be responsible for blocking time. Strategies that are not receptive are not physically meaningful. A timed game structure $\mathcal{G}$ is *well-formed* if both players have receptive strategies. We restrict our attention to well-formed timed game structures. We denote Π_i^R to be the set of receptive strategies for player i. Note that for $\pi_1 \in \Pi_1^R, \pi_2 \in \Pi_2^R$, we have $\mathsf{Outcomes}(s, \pi_1, \pi_2) \subseteq \mathsf{Timediv}$.

Sure and almost-sure winning modes. Let $\mathsf{Sure}_1^{\mathcal{G}}(\Phi)$ (resp. $\mathsf{AlmostSure}_1^{\mathcal{G}}(\Phi)$) be the set of states s in $\mathcal{G}$ such that player 1 has a receptive strategy $\pi_1 \in \Pi_1^R$ such that for all receptive strategies $\pi_2 \in \Pi_2^R$, we have $\mathsf{Outcomes}(s, \pi_1, \pi_2) \subseteq \Phi$ (resp. $\Pr_s^{\pi_1,\pi_2}(\Phi) = 1$). Such a winning strategy is said to be a sure (resp. almost sure) winning receptive strategy. In computing the winning sets, we shall quantify over *all* strategies, but modify the objective to take care of time divergence. Given an objective Φ, let $\mathsf{TimeDivBl}_1(\Phi) = (\mathsf{Timediv} \cap \Phi) \cup (\mathsf{Blameless}_1 \setminus \mathsf{Timediv})$, i.e., $\mathsf{TimeDivBl}_1(\Phi)$ denotes the set of paths such that either time diverges and Φ holds, or else time converges and player 1 is not responsible for time to converge. Let $\underline{\mathsf{Sure}}_1^{\mathcal{G}}(\Phi)$ (resp. $\underline{\mathsf{AlmostSure}}_1^{\mathcal{G}}(\Phi)$) be the set of states in $\mathcal{G}$ such that for all $s \in \underline{\mathsf{Sure}}_1^{\mathcal{G}}(\Phi)$ (resp. $\underline{\mathsf{AlmostSure}}_1^{\mathcal{G}}(\Phi)$), player 1 has a strategy $\pi_1 \in \Pi_1$ such that for all strategies $\pi_2 \in \Pi_2$, we have $\mathsf{Outcomes}(s, \pi_1, \pi_2) \subseteq \Phi$ (resp. $\Pr_s^{\pi_1,\pi_2}(\Phi) = 1$). Such a winning strategy is said to be a sure (resp. almost sure) winning for the non-receptive game. The following result establishes the connection between Sure and $\underline{\mathsf{Sure}}$ sets.

Theorem 1. [15] *For all well-formed timed game structures $\mathcal{G}$, and for all ω-regular objectives Φ, we have* $\underline{\mathsf{Sure}}_1^{\mathcal{G}}(\mathsf{TimeDivBl}_1(\Phi)) = \mathsf{Sure}_1^{\mathcal{G}}(\Phi)$.

We now define a special class of timed game structures, namely, timed automaton games.

Timed automaton games. Timed automata [2] suggest a finite syntax for specifying infinite-state timed game structures. A *timed automaton game* is a tuple $\mathcal{T} = \langle L, C, A_1, A_2, E, \gamma\rangle$ with the following components:

- L is a finite set of locations.
- C is a finite set of clocks.
- A_1 and A_2 are two disjoint sets of actions for players 1 and 2, respectively.
- $E \subseteq L \times (A_1 \cup A_2) \times \mathsf{Constr}(C) \times L \times 2^C$ is the edge relation, where the set $\mathsf{Constr}(C)$ of *clock constraints* is generated by the grammar: $\theta ::= x \leq d \mid d \leq x \mid \neg\theta \mid \theta_1 \wedge \theta_2$, for clock variables $x \in C$ and nonnegative integer constants d. For an edge $e = \langle l, a_i, \theta, l', \lambda\rangle$, the clock constraint θ acts as a guard on the clock values which specifies when the edge e can be taken,

and by taking the edge e, the clocks in the set $\lambda \subseteq C$ are reset to 0. We require that for all edges $\langle l, a_i, \theta', l', \lambda' \rangle, \langle l, a_i, \theta'', l'', \lambda'' \rangle \in E$ with $l' \neq l''$, the conjunction $\theta' \wedge \theta''$ is unsatisfiable. This requirement ensures that a state and a move together uniquely determine a successor state.

- $\gamma : L \mapsto \mathsf{Constr}(C)$ is a function that assigns to every location an invariant for both players. All clocks increase uniformly at the same rate. When at location l, each player i must propose a move out of l before the invariant $\gamma(l)$ expires. Thus, the game can stay at a location only as long as the invariant is satisfied by the clock values.

A *clock valuation* is a function $\kappa : C \mapsto \mathbb{R}_{\geq 0}$ that maps every clock to a nonnegative real. The set of all clock valuations for C is denoted by $K(C)$. A *state* $s = \langle l, \kappa \rangle$ of the timed automaton game $\mathcal{T}$ is a location $l \in L$ together with a clock valuation $\kappa \in K(C)$ such that the invariant at the location is satisfied, that is, $\kappa \models \gamma(l)$. We let S be the set of all states of $\mathcal{T}$. Given a timed automaton game $\mathcal{T}$, the definition of an associated timed game structure $[\![\mathcal{T}]\!]$ is standard [9]. We shall restrict our attention to randomization over time — a random move of a player will consist of a distribution over time over some interval I, denoted $\mathcal{D}^I$, together with a discrete action a_i.

Clock region equivalence. We use the standard *clock-region equivalence* relation from the theory of timed automata [2] (the formal definition is being ommited here as it is fairly standard). We denote two clock-region equivalent clock valuations κ_1, κ_2 by $\kappa_1 \cong \kappa_2$. Two states $\langle l_1, \kappa_1 \rangle, \langle l_2, \kappa_2 \rangle \in S$ are *clock-region equivalent*, denoted $\langle l_1, \kappa_1 \rangle \cong \langle l_2, \kappa_2 \rangle$, iff $l_1 = l_2$ and $\kappa_1 \cong \kappa_2$. A *clock region* is an equivalence class of states with respect to $\cong$. There are finitely many clock regions; more precisely, the number of clock regions is bounded by $|L| \cdot \prod_{x \in C}(c_x + 1) \cdot |C|! \cdot 2^{|C|}$.

For a state $s \in S$, we write $\mathsf{Reg}(s) \subseteq S$ for the clock region containing s. For a run r, we let the *region sequence* $\mathsf{Reg}(r) = \mathsf{Reg}(r[0]), \mathsf{Reg}(r[1]), \cdots$. Two runs r, r' are region equivalent if their region sequences are the same. Given a distribution $\mathcal{D}_{\mathsf{states}}$ over states, we obtain a corresponding distribution $\mathcal{D}_{\mathsf{reg}} = \mathsf{Reg}_d(\mathcal{D}_{\mathsf{states}})$ over regions as follows: for a region R we have $\mathcal{D}_{\mathsf{reg}}(R) = \mathcal{D}_{\mathsf{states}}(\{s \mid s \in R\})$. An ω-regular objective Φ is a region objective if for all region-equivalent runs r, r', we have $r \in \Phi$ iff $r' \in \Phi$. A strategy π_1 is a *region strategy*, if for all prefixes r_1 and r_2 such that $\mathsf{Reg}(r_1) = \mathsf{Reg}(r_2)$, we have $\mathsf{Reg}_d(\pi_1(r_1)) = \mathsf{Reg}_d(\pi_1(r_2))$. The definition for player 2 strategies is analogous. Two region strategies π_1 and π_1' are region-equivalent if for all prefixes r we have $\mathsf{Reg}_d(\pi_1(r)) = \mathsf{Reg}_d(\pi_1'(r))$. A parity index function Ω is a region parity index function if $\Omega(s_1) = \Omega(s_2)$ whenever $s_1 \cong s_2$. Henceforth, we shall restrict our attention to region objectives.

Encoding time divergence by enlarging the game structure. Given a timed automaton game $\mathcal{T}$, consider the enlarged game structure $\widehat{\mathcal{T}}$ with the state space $\widehat{S} \subseteq S \times \mathbb{R}_{[0,1)} \times \{\text{TRUE}, \text{FALSE}\}^2$, and an augmented transition relation $\widehat{\delta} : \widehat{S} \times (M_1 \cup M_2) \mapsto \widehat{S}$. In an augmented state $\langle s, \mathfrak{z}, tick, bl_1 \rangle \in \widehat{S}$, the component $s \in S$ is a state of the original game structure $[\![\mathcal{T}]\!]$, $\mathfrak{z}$ is value of a fictitious clock z which gets reset to 0 every time it hits 1, or if a move of player 1 is chosen, *tick* is true iff z hit 1 at last transition and bl_1 is true if player 1 is to blame for the last transition. Note that any strategy π_i in $[\![\mathcal{T}]\!]$, can be considered a strategy in $\widehat{\mathcal{T}}$. The values of the clock z, *tick* and bl_1 correspond to the values each player keeps in memory in constructing his strategy. Any run r in $\mathcal{T}$ has a corresponding unique run $\widehat{r}$ in $\widehat{\mathcal{T}}$ with $\widehat{r}[0] = \langle r[0], 0, \text{FALSE}, \text{FALSE}\rangle$ such that r is a projection of $\widehat{r}$ onto $\mathcal{T}$. For an objective Φ, we can now encode time-divergence as: $\mathsf{TimeDivBl}(\Phi) = (\Box\Diamond\, tick \rightarrow \Phi) \wedge (\neg\Box\Diamond\, tick \rightarrow \Diamond\Box\neg\, bl_1)$. Let $\widehat{\kappa}$ be a valuation for the clocks in $C \cup \{z\}$. A state of $\widehat{\mathcal{T}}$ can then be considered as $\langle\langle l, \widehat{\kappa}\rangle, tick, bl_1\rangle$. We extend the clock equivalence relation to these expanded states: $\langle\langle l, \widehat{\kappa}\rangle\, tick, bl_1\rangle \cong \langle\langle l', \widehat{\kappa}'\rangle, tick', bl_1'\rangle$ iff $l = l', tick = tick', bl_1 = bl_1'$ and $\widehat{\kappa} \cong \widehat{\kappa}'$. For every ω-regular region objective Φ of $\mathcal{T}$, we have $\mathsf{TimeDivBl}(\Phi)$ to be an ω-regular region objective of $\widehat{\mathcal{T}}$.

We now present a lemma that states for region ω-regular objectives region winning strategies exist, and all strategies region-equivalent to a region winning strategy are also winning.

Lemma 1. *Let $\mathcal{T}$ be a timed automaton game and $\widehat{\mathcal{T}}$ be the corresponding enlarged game structure. Let $\widehat{\Phi}$ be an ω-regular region objective of $\widehat{\mathcal{T}}$. Then the following assertions hold.*

- *There is a pure finite-memory region strategy π_1 that is sure winning for $\widehat{\Phi}$ from the states in $\underline{\mathsf{Sure}}_1^{\widehat{\mathcal{T}}}(\widehat{\Phi})$.*
- *If π_1 is a pure region strategy that is sure winning for $\widehat{\Phi}$ from $\underline{\mathsf{Sure}}_1^{\widehat{\mathcal{T}}}(\widehat{\Phi})$ and π_1' is a pure strategy that is region-equivalent to π_1, then π_1' is a sure winning strategy for $\widehat{\Phi}$ from $\underline{\mathsf{Sure}}_1^{\widehat{\mathcal{T}}}(\widehat{\Phi})$.*

Note that there is an infinitely precise global clock z in the enlarged game structure $\widehat{\mathcal{T}}$. If $\mathcal{T}$ does not have such a global clock, then strategies in $\widehat{\mathcal{T}}$ correspond to strategies in $\mathcal{T}$ where player 1 (and player 2) maintain the value of the infinitely precise global clock in memory (requiring infinite memory).

3 Safety: Pure Finite-Memory Strategies

In this section we show the existence of pure finite-memory sure winning strategies for safety objectives in timed automaton games. Given a timed automaton game $\mathcal{T}$, we define two functions $P_{>0} : C \mapsto \{\text{TRUE}, \text{FALSE}\}$ and $P_{\geq 1} : C \mapsto \{\text{TRUE}, \text{FALSE}\}$. For a clock x, the values of $P_{>0}(x)$ and $P_{\geq 1}(x)$ indicate if the clock x was greater than 0 or greater than or equal to 1 respectively, during the last transition (excluding the originating state). Consider the enlarged game structure $\widetilde{\mathcal{T}}$ with the state space $\widetilde{S} = S \times \{\text{TRUE}, \text{FALSE}\} \times \{\text{TRUE}, \text{FALSE}\}^C \times \{\text{TRUE}, \text{FALSE}\}^C$ and an augmented transition relation $\widetilde{\delta}$. A state of $\widetilde{\mathcal{T}}$ is a tuple $\langle s, bl_1, P_{>0}, P_{\geq 1}\rangle$, where s is a state of $\mathcal{T}$, the component bl_1 is TRUE iff player 1 is to be blamed for the last transition, and $P_{>0}, P_{\geq 1}$ are as defined earlier. The clock equivalence relation can be lifted to states of $\widetilde{\mathcal{T}} : \langle s, bl_1, P_{>0}, P_{\geq 1}\rangle \cong_{\widetilde{A}} \langle s', bl_1', P_{>0}', P_{\geq 1}'\rangle$ iff $s \cong_{\mathcal{T}} s'$, $bl_1 = bl_1'$, $P_{>0} = P_{>0}'$ and $P_{\geq 1} = P_{\geq 1}'$.

Lemma 2. *Let $\mathcal{T}$ be a timed automaton game, and $\widetilde{\mathcal{T}}$ be the corresponding enlarged game. Then player 1 has a receptive strategy from a state s iff $\langle s,\cdot\rangle \in \underline{\mathsf{Sure}}_1^{\widetilde{\mathcal{T}}}(\Phi^*)$, where $\Phi^* = \Box\Diamond(bl_1 = \text{TRUE}) \rightarrow \bigvee_{X\subseteq C} \left(\bigwedge_{x\in X} \Diamond\Box(x > c_x) \wedge \phi_X\right)$, and*

$$\phi_X = \Big(\bigwedge_{x\in C\setminus X} \Box\Diamond(x=0)\Big) \wedge \begin{pmatrix} \left(\bigvee_{x\in C\setminus X} \Box\Diamond((P_{>0}(x)=\text{TRUE})\wedge(bl_1=\text{TRUE}))\right) \\ \vee \\ \left(\bigvee_{x\in C\setminus X} \Box\Diamond((P_{\geq 1}(x)=\text{TRUE})\wedge(bl_1=\text{FALSE}))\right) \end{pmatrix}.$$

The clause $\bigwedge_{x\in X} \Diamond\Box(x > c_x)$ specifies which clocks escape beyond their maximum values (and are never reset). The rest of the clocks hence thus be reset infinitely often in a time diverging run, this is specified by the clause $\bigwedge_{x\in C\setminus X} \Box\Diamond(x = 0)$. Suppose we have $(\bigvee_{x\in C\setminus X} \Box\Diamond((P_{\geq 1}(x) = \text{TRUE})\wedge(bl_1 = \text{FALSE}))$. Then clearly time diverges as some clock x goes from 0 to 1 infinitely often. Suppose we have $(\bigvee_{x\in C\setminus X} \Box\Diamond((P_{>0}(x) = \text{TRUE}) \wedge (bl_1 = \text{TRUE}))$. We note that if a player can take a move from $\widetilde{s}$ to a region $\widetilde{R}$ where the value of some clock x is such that $0 < x \leq c_x$, then there is some clock $y \in C$ (possibly different from x) such that the player can take a move from $\widetilde{s}$ to the region $\widetilde{R}$ such that the value of y will be more than $1/2$ (and less than or equal to c_y). Thus, in this case, some clock goes from 0 to $1/2$ infinitely often and time diverges. It turns out that these conditions are also required. The full proof can be found in [8].

Theorem 2. *Let $\mathcal{T}$ be a timed automaton game and $\widetilde{\mathcal{T}}$ be the corresponding enlarged game. Let Y be a union of regions of $\mathcal{T}$. Then the following assertions hold.*

1. $\mathsf{Sure}_1^{\widetilde{\mathcal{T}}}(\Box Y) = \underline{\mathsf{Sure}}_1^{\widetilde{\mathcal{T}}}((\Box Y) \wedge \Phi^*)$*, where Φ^* is as defined in Lemma 2.*
2. *Player 1 has a pure, finite-memory, receptive, region strategy that is sure winning for the safety objective $\mathsf{Safe}(Y)$ at every state in $\mathsf{Sure}_1^{\widetilde{\mathcal{T}}}(\Box Y)$.*

4 Reachability: Randomized Finite-Memory Strategies

We have seen in Example 2 that pure sure winning strategies require infinite memory in general for reachability objectives. In this section, we shall show that uniform randomized almost-sure winning strategies with finite memory exist. This shows that we can trade-off infinite memory with uniform randomness.

Let S_R be the destination set of states that player 1 wants to reach. We only consider S_R such that S_R is a union of regions of $\mathcal{T}$. For the timed automaton $\mathcal{T}$, consider the enlarged game structure of $\mathcal{T}$. We let $\widehat{S_R} = S_R \times \mathbb{R}_{[0,1]} \times \{\text{TRUE}, \text{FALSE}\}^2$. From the reachability objective (denoted $\mathsf{Reach}(S_R)$) we obtain the reachability parity objective with index function Ω_R as follows: $\Omega_R(\langle s, \mathfrak{z}, tick, bl_1\rangle) = 1$ if $tick \vee bl_1 = \text{TRUE}$ and $s \notin S_R$ (0 otherwise). We assume the states in S_R are absorbing. We let $\widehat{S}_R = S_R \times \mathbb{R}_{[0,1]} \times \{\text{TRUE}, \text{FALSE}\}^2$. We now present a μ-calculus characterization for the sure winning set (using only pure strategies) for player 1 for reachability objectives. We first translate the reachability objective to a parity objective of index 2 (the μ-calculus expression will use the parity index function).

Lemma 3. *For a timed automaton game $\mathcal{T}$, with the reachability objective S_R, consider the enlarged game structure $\widehat{\mathcal{T}}$, and the corresponding reachability parity function Ω_R. Then we have that* $\underline{\mathsf{Sure}}_1(\mathsf{TimeDivBl}(\mathsf{Reach}(S_R)))=\underline{\mathsf{Sure}}_1(\mathsf{Parity}(\Omega_R))$.

The *controllable predecessor* operator for player 1, $\mathsf{CPre}_1 : 2^{\widehat{S}} \mapsto 2^{\widehat{S}}$, defined formally by $\widehat{s} \in \mathsf{CPre}_1(Z)$ iff $\exists m_1 \in \widehat{\Gamma}_1(\widehat{s})\ \forall m_2 \in \widehat{\Gamma}_2(\widehat{s})\,.\,\widehat{\delta}_{\mathsf{jd}}(\widehat{s}, m_1, m_2) \subseteq Z$. Informally, $\mathsf{CPre}_1(Z)$ consists of the set of states from which player 1 can ensure that the next state will be in Z, no matter what player 2 does. From Lemma 3 it follows that the sure winning set can be described as the μ-calculus formula: $\mu Y \nu X \left[(\Omega^{-1}(1) \cap \mathsf{CPre}_1(Y)) \cup (\Omega^{-1}(0) \cap \mathsf{CPre}_1(X))\right]$. The winning set can then be computed as a fixpoint iteration on regions of $\widehat{\mathcal{T}}$. We can also obtain a pure winning strategy π_{pure} of player 1 as in [10]. Note that this strategy π_{pure} corresponds to an infinite-memory strategy of player 1 in the timed automaton game $\mathcal{T}$, as she needs to maintain the value of the clock z in memory.

To compute randomized finite-memory almost-sure winning strategies, we will use the structure of the μ-calculus formula. Let $Y^* = \mu Y \nu X \left[(\Omega^{-1}(1) \cap \mathsf{CPre}_1(Y)) \cup (\Omega^{-1}(0) \cap \mathsf{CPre}_1(X))\right]$. The iterative fixpoint procedure computes $Y_0 = \emptyset \subseteq Y_1 \subseteq \cdots \subseteq Y_n = Y^*$, where $Y_{i+1} = \nu X \left[(\Omega^{-1}(1) \cap \mathsf{CPre}_1(Y_i)) \cup (\Omega^{-1}(0) \cap \mathsf{CPre}_1(X))\right]$. We can consider the states in $Y_i \setminus Y_{i-1}$ as being added in two steps, T_{2i-1} and $T_{2i} (= Y_i)$ as follows:

1. $T_{2i-1} = \Omega^{-1}(1) \cap \mathsf{CPre}_1(Y_{i-1})$. T_{2i-1} is clearly a subset of Y_i.
2. $T_{2i} = \nu X \left[T_{2i-1} \cup (\Omega^{-1}(0) \cap \mathsf{CPre}_1(X))\right]$. Note $(T_{2i} \setminus T_{2i-1}) \cap \Omega^{-1}(1) = \emptyset$.

Thus, in odd stages we add states with index 1, and in even stages we add states with index 0. The *rank* of a state $\widehat{s} \in Y^*$ is j if $\widehat{s} \in T_j \setminus \cup_{k=0}^{j-1} T_k$. The set S_R is a union of regions of $\mathcal{T}$. $T_0 = T_1 = \emptyset$, and T_2 contains the states in $\widehat{S}_R$ together with the states where $tick = bl_1 =$ FALSE, and from where player 1 can ensure that the next state is either in $\widehat{S}_R$, or the next state continues to have $tick = bl_1 =$ FALSE; formally $T_2 = \nu X(\Omega^{-1}(0) \cap \mathsf{CPre}_1(X))$. Henceforth, when we refer to a region R of $\mathcal{T}$, we shall mean the states $R \times \mathbb{R}_{[0,1]} \times \{\text{TRUE}, \text{FALSE}\}^2$ of $\widehat{\mathcal{T}}$.

Lemma 4. *Let $T_2 = \nu X(\Omega^{-1}(0) \cap \mathsf{CPre}_1(X))$. Then player 1 has a (randomized) memoryless strategy π_{rand} such that she can ensure reaching $\widehat{S}_R \subseteq \Omega^{-1}(0)$ with probability 1 against all receptive strategies of player 2 from all states $\widehat{s}$ of a region R such that $R \cap T_2 \neq \emptyset$. Moreover, π_{rand} is independent of the values of the global clock, tick and bl_1.*

We now present the main proof ideas for Lemma 4. For a set T of states, we shall denote by $\mathsf{Reg}(T)$ the set of states that are region equivalent in $\mathcal{T}$ to some state in T. The proof first shows that from every state $\widehat{s}$ in $\mathsf{Reg}(T_2 \setminus \widehat{S}_R)$, either a) player 1 has a move to $\widehat{S}_R$, or b) the invariant of the location of $\widehat{s}$ is closed, such that time can progress from $\widehat{s}$ to the endpoint without the clock z crossing 1, and with player 2 having no moves outside of $\mathsf{Reg}(T_2 \setminus \widehat{S}_R)$. From every state in $\mathsf{Reg}(T_2 \setminus \widehat{S}_R)$, the strategy π_{pure} prescribes a move to either $\widehat{S}_R$, or to the right endpoint of the invariant of the location if it is right closed (effectively relinquishing the move to player 2). If player 1 relinquishes the move in such a manner, then so does π_{rand}. If π_{pure} prescribes a move to $\widehat{S}_R$, there is an earliest destination region $\widehat{R}'$ for player 1 to come to $\widehat{S}_R$, and a corresponding interval I of times which takes her to $\widehat{R}'$. If this interval is left closed, then π_{rand} chooses this leftmost endpoint. If I is not left closed, then π_{rand} proposes a randomized move, with the time being distributed uniformly at random over $(\alpha_l, \alpha_l + 1/2]$ where α_l is the leftmost endpoint of I. We then show that if player 2 plays with a receptive strategy, then if player 1 plays a randomized move infinitely often, then a randomized move with $\alpha_l = 0$ must occur infinitely often. Finally, we demonstrate that for this randomized move (of $\alpha_l = 0$) that player 1 plays infinitely often, the probability of it not being chosen against a receptive strategy of player 2 is 0. The full proof can be found in [8].

The following lemma states that if for some state $s \in \mathcal{T}$, we have $(s, \mathfrak{z}, tick, bl_1) \in T_{2i+1}$, for some i, then for some $\mathfrak{z}', tick', bl_1'$ we have $(s, \mathfrak{z}', tick', bl_1') \in T_{2i}$. Then in Lemma 6 we present the inductive case of Lemma 4. The proof of Lemma 6 is similar to the base case i.e., Lemma 4.

Lemma 5. *Let R be a region of $\mathcal{T}$ such that $R \cap T_{2i+1} \neq \emptyset$. Then $R \cap T_{2i} \neq \emptyset$.*

Lemma 6. *Let R be a region of $\mathcal{T}$ such that $R \cap T_{2i} \neq \emptyset$, and $R \cap T_j = \emptyset$ for all $2 \leq j < 2i$. Then player 1 has a (randomized) memoryless strategy π_{rand} to go from R to some R' such that $R' \cap T_j \neq \emptyset$ for some $j < 2i$ with probability 1 against all receptive strategies of player 2. Moreover, π_{rand} is independent of the values of the global clock, tick and bl_1.*

Once player 1 reaches the target set, she can switch over to the finite-memory receptive strategy of Lemma 2. Thus, using Lemmas 2, 4, 5, and 6 we have the following theorem.

Theorem 3. *Let $\mathcal{T}$ be a timed automaton game, and let S_R be a union of regions of $\mathcal{T}$. Player 1 has a randomized, finite-memory, receptive, region strategy π_1 such that for all states $s \in \mathsf{Sure}_1(\mathsf{Reach}(S_R))$, the following assertions hold: (a) for all receptive strategies π_2 of player 2 we have $\Pr_s^{\pi_1,\pi_2}(\mathsf{Reach}(S_R)) = 1$; and (b) for all strategies π_2 of player 2 we have $\Pr_s^{\pi_1,\pi_2}(\mathsf{TimeDivBl}_1(\mathsf{Reach}(S_R))) = 1$.*

5 Parity: Randomized Finite-Memory Strategies

In this section we show that randomized finite-memory almost-sure strategies exist for parity objectives. Let $\Omega : S \mapsto \{0, \ldots, k\}$ be the parity index function. We consider the case when $k = 2d$ for some d, and the case when $k = 2d-1$, for some d can be proved using similar arguments. Given a timed game structure $\mathcal{T}$, a set $X \subsetneq S$, and a parity function $\Omega : S \mapsto \{0, \ldots, 2d\}$, with $d > 0$, let $\langle \mathcal{T}', \Omega' \rangle = \mathsf{ModifyEven}(\mathcal{T}, \Omega, X)$ be defined as follows: (a) the state space S' of $\mathcal{T}'$ is $\{s^\perp\} \cup S \setminus X$, where $s^\perp \notin S$; (b) $\Omega'(s^\perp) = 2d - 2$, and $\Omega' = \Omega$ otherwise; (c) $\Gamma_i'(s) = \Gamma_i(s)$ for $s \in S \setminus X$, and $\Gamma_i'(s^\perp) = \Gamma_i(s^\perp) = \mathbb{R}_{\geq 0} \times \perp$; and (d) $\delta'(s, m) = \delta(s, m)$ if $\delta(s, m) \notin S \setminus X$, and $\delta'(s, m) = s^\perp$ otherwise. We will use the function ModifyEven to play timed games on a subset of the original structure. The extra state, and the modified transition function are to ensure well-formedness of the reduced structure. We will now obtain receptive strategies for player 1 for the objective $\mathsf{Parity}(\Omega)$ using winning strategies for reachability and safety objectives. We consider the following procedure.

1. $\mathcal{T}_0 = \mathcal{T}$, and $i := 0$;
2. Compute $X_i = \mathsf{Sure}_1^{\mathcal{T}_i}(\Diamond(\Omega^{-1}(2d)))$.
3. Let $\langle \mathcal{T}_i', \Omega' \rangle = \mathsf{ModifyEven}(\mathcal{T}_i, \Omega, X_i)$; and let $Y_i = \mathsf{Sure}_1^{\mathcal{T}_i'}(\mathsf{Parity}(\Omega'))$. Let $L_i = S_i \setminus Y_i$, where S_i is the set of states of $\mathcal{T}_i$.
4. Compute $Z_i = \mathsf{Sure}_1^{\mathcal{T}_i}(\Box(S_i \setminus L_i))$.
5. Let $(\mathcal{T}_{i+1}, \Omega) = \mathsf{ModifyEven}(\mathcal{T}, \Omega, S \setminus Z_i)$ and $i := i + 1$.
6. Go to step 2, unless $Z_{i-1} = S_i$.

It can be shown that (a) when the above procedure terminates, then we have $(S \setminus Z_i) \cap \mathsf{Sure}_1^{\mathcal{T}}(\mathsf{Parity}(\Omega)) = \emptyset$, and (b) there is a randomized, finite-memory, receptive, region almost-sure winning strategy for every state in Z_i, provided that player 1 has access to imprecise clock events such that between any two events, some time more than Δ passes for a fixed real $\Delta > 0$. Player 1 only uses the clock events to observe the passage of some amount of time greater than Δ (it does not have access to the exact amount of time that passes). The details of the winning strategy can be found in [8].

Theorem 4. *Let $\mathcal{T}$ be a timed automaton game, and let Ω be a region parity index function. Suppose that player 1 has access to imprecise clock events such that between any two events, some time more than Δ passes for a fixed real $\Delta >$ 0. Then, player 1 has a randomized, finite-memory, receptive, region strategy π_1 such that for all states $s \in \mathsf{Sure}_1(\mathsf{Parity}(\Omega))$, the following assertions hold: (a) for all receptive strategies π_2 of player 2 we have $\Pr_s^{\pi_1,\pi_2}(\mathsf{Parity}(\Omega)) = 1$; and (b) for all strategies π_2 of player 2 we have $\Pr_s^{\pi_1,\pi_2}(\mathsf{TimeDivBl}_1(\mathsf{Parity}(\Omega))) = 1$.*

Finally, the following theorem shows that though randomization can get rid of infinite memory with respect to almost-sure winning, it does not help to win in more states, and hence that the set of sure and almost-sure winning states coincide for ω-regular objectives.

Theorem 5. *Consider a timed automaton game and an ω-regular objective Φ. For every state $s \notin \mathsf{Sure}_1^{\mathcal{T}}(\Phi)$, every real $\varepsilon > 0$, and every randomized strategy $\pi_1 \in \Pi_1$ for player 1, there is a pure strategy $\pi_2^\varepsilon \in \Pi_2^{\mathsf{pure}}$ for player 2 such that $\Pr_s^{\pi_1,\pi_2^\varepsilon}(\mathsf{TimeDivBl}_1(\Phi)) \leq \varepsilon$.*

References

1. Adler, B., de Alfaro, L., Faella, M.: Average reward timed games. In: Pettersson, P., Yi, W. (eds.) FORMATS 2005. LNCS, vol. 3829, pp. 65–80. Springer, Heidelberg (2005)
2. Alur, R., Dill, D.L.: A theory of timed automata. Theor. Comput. Sci. 126(2), 183–235 (1994)

3. Alur, R., Henzinger, T.A.: Modularity for timed and hybrid systems. In: Mazurkiewicz, A., Winkowski, J. (eds.) CONCUR 1997. LNCS, vol. 1243, pp. 74–88. Springer, Heidelberg (1997)
4. Asarin, E., Maler, O.: As soon as possible: Time optimal control for timed automata. In: Vaandrager, F.W., van Schuppen, J.H. (eds.) HSCC 1999. LNCS, vol. 1569, pp. 19–30. Springer, Heidelberg (1999)
5. Bouyer, P., Cassez, F., Fleury, E., Larsen, K.G.: Optimal strategies in priced timed game automata. In: Lodaya, K., Mahajan, M. (eds.) FSTTCS 2004. LNCS, vol. 3328, pp. 148–160. Springer, Heidelberg (2004)
6. Bouyer, P., D'Souza, D., Madhusudan, P., Petit, A.: Timed control with partial observability. In: Hunt Jr., W.A., Somenzi, F. (eds.) CAV 2003. LNCS, vol. 2725, pp. 180–192. Springer, Heidelberg (2003)
7. Cassez, F., David, A., Fleury, E., Larsen, K.G., Lime, D.: Efficient on-the-fly algorithms for the analysis of timed games. In: Abadi, M., de Alfaro, L. (eds.) CONCUR 2005. LNCS, vol. 3653, pp. 66–80. Springer, Heidelberg (2005)
8. Chatterjee, K., Henzinger, T.A., Prabhu, V.S.: Trading infinite memory for uniform randomness in timed games. Technical Report UCB/EECS-2008-4, EECS Department, University of California, Berkeley (January 2008)
9. de Alfaro, L., Faella, M., Henzinger, T.A., Majumdar, R., Stoelinga, M.: The element of surprise in timed games. In: Amadio, R.M., Lugiez, D. (eds.) CONCUR 2003. LNCS, vol. 2761, pp. 144–158. Springer, Heidelberg (2003)
10. de Alfaro, L., Henzinger, T.A., Majumdar, R.: Symbolic algorithms for infinite-state games. In: Larsen, K.G., Nielsen, M. (eds.) CONCUR 2001. LNCS, vol. 2154, pp. 536–550. Springer, Heidelberg (2001)
11. D'Souza, D., Madhusudan, P.: Timed control synthesis for external specifications. In: Alt, H., Ferreira, A. (eds.) STACS 2002. LNCS, vol. 2285, pp. 571–582. Springer, Heidelberg (2002)
12. Faella, M., La Torre, S., Murano, A.: Automata-theoretic decision of timed games. In: Cortesi, A. (ed.) VMCAI 2002. LNCS, vol. 2294, pp. 94–108. Springer, Heidelberg (2002)
13. Faella, M., La Torre, S., Murano, A.: Dense real-time games. In: LICS 2002, pp. 167–176. IEEE Computer Society, Los Alamitos (2002)
14. Henzinger, T.A., Kopke, P.W.: Discrete-time control for rectangular hybrid automata. Theoretical Computer Science 221, 369–392 (1999)
15. Henzinger, T.A., Prabhu, V.S.: Timed alternating-time temporal logic. In: Asarin, E., Bouyer, P. (eds.) FORMATS 2006. LNCS, vol. 4202, pp. 1–17. Springer, Heidelberg (2006)
16. Maler, O., Pnueli, A., Sifakis, J.: On the synthesis of discrete controllers for timed systems (an extended abstract). In: Mayr, E.W., Puech, C. (eds.) STACS 1995. LNCS, vol. 900, pp. 229–242. Springer, Heidelberg (1995)
17. Pnueli, A., Asarin, E., Maler, O., Sifakis, J.: Controller synthesis for timed automata. In: Proc. System Structure and Control, Elsevier, Amsterdam (1998)
18. Segala, R., Gawlick, R., Søgaard-Andersen, J.F., Lynch, N.A.: Liveness in timed and untimed systems. Inf. Comput. 141(2), 119–171 (1998)
19. Thomas, W.: Languages, automata, and logic. In: Handbook of Formal Languages. Vol. 3, Beyond Words, ch. 7, pp. 389–455. Springer, Heidelberg (1997)
20. Wong-Toi, H., Hoffmann, G.: The control of dense real-time discrete event systems. In: Proc. of 30th Conf. Decision and Control, pp. 1527–1528 (1991)

Solutions to Switched Hamilton-Jacobi Equations and Conservation Laws Using Hybrid Components

Christian G. Claudel[1,*] and Alexandre M. Bayen[2]

[1] Electrical Engineering and Computer Sciences
[2] Systems Engineering, Civil and Environmental Engineering
University of California, Berkeley
Berkeley, CA, 94720-1710
claudel@eecs.berkeley.edu

Abstract. We investigate a class of hybrid systems driven by partial differential equations for which the infinite dimensional state can switch in time and in space at the same time. We consider a particular class of such problems (switched *Hamilton-Jacobi equations*) and define hybrid components as building blocks of hybrid solutions to such problems, using viability theory. We derive sufficient conditions for well-posedness of such problems, and use a generalized *Lax-Hopf formula* to compute these solutions. We illustrate the results with three examples: the computation of the hybrid components of a *Lighthill-Whitham-Richards* equation; a velocity control policy for a highway system; a data assimilation problem using Lagrangian measurements generated from NGSIM traffic data.

1 Introduction

This article investigates a particular class of hybrid systems in which modes are not governed by *ordinary differential equations* (ODEs) as in classical hybrid systems theory [20] but by *partial differential equations* (PDEs). Unlike for ODEs for which modes evolve in finite dimensional spaces, functions solving PDEs evolve in "infinite" dimensional spaces (functional spaces). The framework developed for hybrid systems governed by ODEs [20] can be extended to systems governed by PDEs, though to our best knowledge, no general formalism has been developed to this day to characterize such systems in a unifying way. This is due in part to the fact that for systems driven by PDEs, the switching structure is more complex than in the case of ODEs. Indeed, hybrideness can occur in different ways. We outline three specific structures of interest to us:

- *Switching the PDE in time on the full spatial domain.* This situation is illustrated in Figure 1 (left) and is the PDE counterpart of hybrid systems as defined by [20]. The PDEs – and/or *boundary conditions* (BCs) – are switched sequentially in time. Switching of boundary conditions has been investigated in the context of highway traffic [19,6] and canal systems [2]. Switching PDEs

* Corresponding author.

M. Egerstedt and B. Mishra (Eds.): HSCC 2008, LNCS 4981, pp. 101–115, 2008.

in time sequentially appears in general form in [10] and in the context of highway transportation systems in [6].

- *Switching the PDE on parts of the spatial domain.* This is illustrated in Figure 1 (center). This situation is typical of shape optimization problems, or fluid structure interactions problems [12]. Note that the variable y has been used along the vertical axis instead of t to emphasize that this type of switching is also valid for PDEs not modeling phenomena not depending on time (for example elliptic PDEs depending on space variables only).
- *Switching the PDE on parts of the time-space domain.* This is illustrated in Figure 1 (right). Examples include the *Lighthill-Whitham-Richards* (LWR) PDE with triangular flux function, which can be decomposed into two modes (two one-dimensional wave equations) resulting in a partition of the (x, t) space in regions with forward traveling waves, and regions with backward travelling waves [13,16,1]. This last case is particularly challenging because the switching surfaces are in general not known a priori and must be computed while solving the PDE. If they are known (or if they are derived), additional consistency conditions are needed in order the problem to be well posed, which is the object of the present article.

Not all switched PDE problems fit in one of the three categories above. In particular, the work [18] in the context of biological systems exhibits a source term which is distributed in space and time and can switch modes at every point in the space/time domain. The present article is mostly concerned with the last

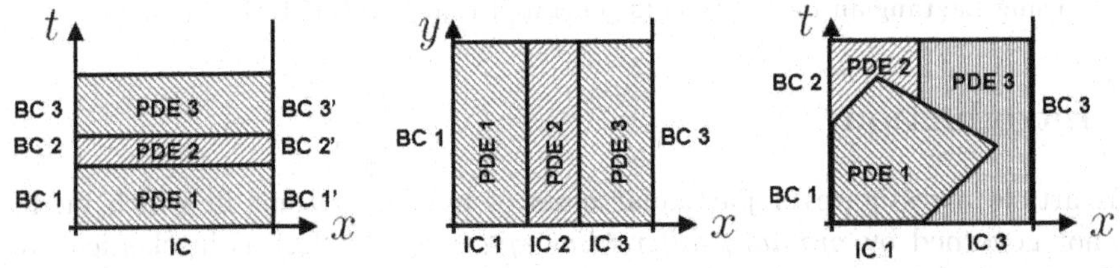

Fig. 1. BC denotes *boundary conditions*; IC denotes *initial conditions.* **Left:** PDEs (and BCs) switched in time. **Middle:** PDEs (and ICs) switched in space; **Right:** PDEs switched in space and time.

case in the list above, in which the switching structure can happen concurrently in space and time. It corresponds to a situation fundamentally different than in the case of hybrid systems driven by ODEs: the infinite dimensional state can be partially switched, based on the (x, t) location in time and space of the point of interest. We develop a method to decompose the (x, t) domain of definition of a solution to a hybrid system problem driven by PDEs into *hybrid components*, which are subsets of the (x, t) space in which a different PDE applies (in Figure 1 right, there would be three hybrid components). The definition of these hybrid components is not trivial, as in general, sufficient conditions for existence and well posedness of such solutions are difficult to find. The contributions of this article is the derivation of sufficient conditions for the use of hybrid components for a class of *Hamilton-Jacobi* (HJ) PDEs. We construct the general solution (denoted $\mathbf{M}(t,x)$) to a class of HJ PDEs (sections 2, 3 and 4), and define hybrid components as parts of the (x,t) solution domain in which we would like another PDE to apply, for which we assume we know a solution $\overline{\mathbf{M}}(t,x)$. We use an inf morphism property to construct the solution $\mathbf{M}(t,x)$ of the HJ PDE, first without hybrid components (section 4), and then with hybrid components (section 5). We compute a sufficient condition for compatibility of the initial and boundary conditions of the HJ PDE problem with the hybrid components added by $\overline{\mathbf{M}}(t,x)$. In section 6, we illustrate the result with three examples. First, we compute the hybrid components of a LWR PDE. Second, we use the method to solve a speed control problem on the highway. Finally, we apply it to data assimilation with NGSIM data.

2 Problem Definition

We consider the class of first order scalar hyperbolic conservation laws with concave flux functions. For illustrative purposes, we will derive the results in the context of highway traffic, which can be modeled by such conservation laws.

Definition 1 *[13,16] **[First order scalar hyperbolic conservation laws].** We consider a density function $\rho(t,x)$ (representing the number of vehicles per unit length located at x, at time t) governed by the following PDE:*

$$\frac{\partial\rho(t,x)}{\partial t}+\frac{\partial\psi(\rho(t,x))}{\partial x}=0 \tag{1}$$

where ψ is a concave flux function ranging in the interval $[0,\omega]$.

In the context of traffic flow, the function ψ is referred to as *fundamental diagram*, and depends on several empirical parameters, such as number of lanes, road geometry and vehicle capabilities. We define $X := [\xi,\chi]$ as the domain in which equation (1) applies (in physical terms, the extent of the highway section of interest). In the case of the highway, if consecutive integer labels are assigned to vehicles entering the highway at location $x=\xi$, one can define a function $\mathbf{M}$ tracking the vehicles on the highway: the *Moskowitz function* $\mathbf{M}(\cdot,\cdot)$. The Moskowitz function is a continuous function satisfying $\lfloor\mathbf{M}(t,x)\rfloor=n$ where n is the label of the vehicle located in x at time t. It was first introduced in [14], appeared later in the famous Newell trilogy [15], and was formally defined by Daganzo in [8,9].

Definition 2 ***[Moskowitz function].*** *The Moskowitz function solves the following HJ PDE [8,9]:*

$$\frac{\partial\mathbf{M}(t,x)}{\partial t}-\psi\left(-\frac{\partial\mathbf{M}(t,x)}{\partial x}\right)=0 \tag{2}$$

Whenever $\mathbf{M}$ is differentiable, the definition of the Moskowitz function implies that $\rho(t,x) = -\frac{\partial \mathbf{M}(t,x)}{\partial x}$, where $\rho(t,x)$ is the density at location x and time t, as defined by [15]. By definition of the Moskowitz function, the iso-level sets of $\mathbf{M}$ represent the vehicles trajectories [9].

Definition 3 ***[Capture basin].*** *[3,4] Given a dynamical system S, two sets $\mathcal{K}$ (called the environment) and $\mathcal{C}$ (called the target) satisfying $\mathcal{C} \subset \mathcal{K}$, the capture basin $\mathrm{Capt}_S(\mathcal{K},\mathcal{C})$ is the subset of states of $\mathcal{K}$ from which there exists at least one evolution solution of S reaching the target $\mathcal{C}$ in finite time while remaining in $\mathcal{K}$.*

The capture basin $\mathrm{Capt}_S(\mathcal{K},\mathcal{C})$ can be numerically computed using the capture basin algorithm [7,17].

Definition 4 ***[Auxiliary dynamical system].*** *The auxiliary system (3) associated to the Moskowitz HJ PDE is defined by:*

$$S := \begin{cases} \tau'(t) &= -1 \\ x'(t) &= u(t) \\ y'(t) &= -\varphi^*(u(t)) \end{cases} \tag{3}$$

where $u(t) \in \mathrm{Dom}(\varphi^*)$, and where the function φ^* is defined by:

$$\varphi^*(u) := \sup_{p \in \mathrm{Dom}(\psi)} [p \cdot u + \psi(p)] \tag{4}$$

Definition 5 ***[Epigraphical target].*** *For any function $\mathbf{f}(t,x)$ defined on a subset $\mathcal{F}$ of $\mathbb{R}_+ \times X$, the associated target function $\mathbf{c}$ is defined as follows:*

$$\mathbf{c}(t,x) := \begin{cases} \mathbf{f}(t,x) & \text{if } (t,x) \in \mathcal{F} \\ +\infty & \text{otherwise} \end{cases}$$

The target $\mathcal{C}$ corresponding to the function $\mathbf{c}(\cdot,\cdot)$ is defined as follows:

$$\mathcal{C} := \mathcal{E}pi(\mathbf{c}) \tag{5}$$

Definition 6 ***[Viability episolution].*** *Let us consider $\mathcal{K} := \mathbb{R}_+ \times [\xi,\chi] \times \mathbb{R}$ and $\mathcal{C}$ defined by (5). The* viability episolution $\mathbf{M}$ *is defined by*

$$\mathbf{M}(t,x) := \inf_{(t,x,y) \in \mathrm{Capt}_S(\mathcal{K},\mathcal{C})} y \tag{6}$$

Proposition 1 ***[Barron-Jensen/Frankowska property].*** *[5] Given an environment $\mathcal{K}$ and a target $\mathcal{C}$ defined by (5), the corresponding viability episolution $\mathbf{M}(t,x)$ is a Barron-Jensen/Frankowska (BJ/F) solution to the Hamilton-Jacobi PDE (2).*

Proof. See [5] for a proof of this property for the CVN function $\mathbf{N}$, and operate the variable change $\mathbf{M}(t,x) = -\mathbf{N}(t,x) + \int_0^t \psi(v(u))du$. ∎

3 Properties of the Viability Episolution

Proposition 2 ***[Generalized Lax Hopf formula].*** *The viability episolution defined by equation (6) can be expressed as:*

$$\mathbf{M}(t,x) = \inf_{(u,T)\in \mathrm{Dom}(\varphi^*)\times\mathbb{R}_+} [\mathbf{c}(t-T, x+Tu) + T\varphi^*(u)] \tag{7}$$

It is well known [3,4,5] that for a given environment $\mathcal{K}$, the capture basin of a finite union of targets is the union of the capture basins of these targets:

$$\mathrm{Capt}_S\left(\mathcal{K}, \bigcup_{i\in I} \mathcal{C}_i\right) = \bigcup_{i\in I} \mathrm{Capt}_S(\mathcal{K}, \mathcal{C}_i) \tag{8}$$

where I is a finite set. This property can be translated in epigraphical form:

Proposition 3 ***[Inf-morphism property].*** *Let $\mathbf{c}_i$ (i belongs to a finite set I) be a family of functions whose epigraphs are the targets $\mathcal{C}_i$. Since the epigraph of the infimum of the functions $\mathbf{c}_i$ is the union of the epigraphs of the functions $\mathbf{c}_i$, the target $\mathcal{C} := \bigcup_{i\in I} \mathcal{C}_i$ is the epigraph of the function $\mathbf{c} := \inf_{i\in I} \mathbf{c}_i$. We thus have the following property:*

$$\forall\, t \geq 0,\ x \in X,\ \ \mathbf{M}_{\mathbf{c}}(t,x) = \inf_{i\in I} \mathbf{M}_{\mathbf{c}_i}(t,x) \tag{9}$$

where $\mathbf{M}_{\mathbf{c}}$ and $\mathbf{M}_{\mathbf{c}_i}$ are the episolutions (6) associated to the targets $\mathcal{C}$ and $\mathcal{C}_i$ respectively.

The inf-morphism property enables us to compute the Moskowitz function using the concept of *hybrid components.*

Definition 7 ***[Components of the Moskowitz function].*** *The component $\mathbf{M}_c$ associated to a target function $\mathbf{c}$ is defined by:*

$$\mathbf{M}_{\mathbf{c}}(t,x) := \inf_{(t,x,y)\in \mathrm{Capt}_S(\mathcal{K}, \mathcal{E}pi(\mathbf{c}))} y \tag{10}$$

Definition 8 ***[Hybrid, initial and boundary components].*** *Let $\mathcal{D}$ be a given set. We consider through the article three functions $\overline{\mathbf{M}}(\cdot,\cdot)$, $\mathbf{M}_0(\cdot,\cdot)$ and $\gamma(\cdot,\cdot)$ satisfying the following properties:*

$$\overline{\mathbf{M}}(t,x) = \begin{cases} \mathbf{M}_{\mathbf{hybrid}}(t,x) \ \ (\textit{given}) & \text{for } (t,x)\in\mathcal{D} \\ +\infty & \text{for } (t,x)\notin\mathcal{D} \end{cases}$$

$$\mathbf{M}_0(t,x) := \begin{cases} \mathbf{M}_{\mathbf{initial}}(x) \ \ (\textit{given}) & \text{for } t=0 \text{ and } x\in[\xi,\chi] \\ +\infty & \forall t\neq 0 \text{ or } \forall x\notin[\xi,\chi] \end{cases}$$

$$\gamma(t,x) := \begin{cases} \mathbf{M}_{\mathbf{boundary}}(t) \ \ (\textit{given}) & \text{for } x=\xi \text{ and } t\geq 0 \\ +\infty & \forall x\neq\xi \text{ or } \forall t<0 \end{cases}$$

The hybrid component $\mathbf{M}_{\overline{\mathbf{M}}}$*, initial condition component* $\mathbf{M}_{\mathbf{M}_0}$ *and boundary condition component* $\mathbf{M}_\gamma$ *respectively associated to* $\overline{\mathbf{M}}$, $\mathbf{M}_0$, *and* γ *are defined by:*

$$\begin{cases} \mathbf{M}_{\overline{\mathbf{M}}}(t,x) := \inf_{(t,x,y)\in \mathrm{Capt}_S(\mathcal{K},\mathcal{E}pi(\overline{\mathbf{M}}))} y \\ \mathbf{M}_{\mathbf{M}_0}(t,x) := \inf_{(t,x,y)\in \mathrm{Capt}_S(\mathcal{K},\mathcal{E}pi(\mathbf{M}_0))} y \\ \mathbf{M}_\gamma(t,x) := \inf_{(t,x,y)\in \mathrm{Capt}_S(\mathcal{K},\mathcal{E}pi(\gamma))} y \end{cases} \tag{11}$$

Proposition 4 ***[Domain of influence].*** *The domain of* $\mathbf{M_c}$*, also called* domain of influence of component $\mathbf{c}$, *is defined by the following formula:*

$$\mathrm{Dom}(\mathbf{M_c}) = \bigcup_{(t,x)\in\mathrm{Dom}(\mathbf{c})} \left(\bigcup_{T\in\mathbb{R}_+} \{t+T\} \times [x - \nu^\sharp T, x + \nu^\flat T] \right) \tag{12}$$

Proof. The generalized Lax Hopf formula (2) implies that

$$\mathrm{Dom}(\mathbf{M_c}) = \{(t,x) \in \mathbb{R}_+ \times X \text{ such that } \exists (T,u) \in \mathbb{R}_+ \times \mathrm{Dom}(\varphi^*) \\ \text{and } (t-T, x+Tu) \in \mathrm{Dom})(\mathbf{c})\}$$

Equation (12) is obtained from the previous formula, observing that u ranges in $\mathrm{Dom}(\varphi^*) := [-\nu^\flat, \nu^\sharp]$. ■

4 The Mixed Initial-Boundary Conditions Problem

Definition 9 ***[Mixed initial boundary condition problem].*** *The mixed initial boundary condition problem is defined as:*

$$\begin{cases} \frac{\partial \mathbf{M}(t,x)}{\partial t} - \psi\left(-\frac{\partial \mathbf{M}(t,x)}{\partial x}\right) = 0 \; \forall (t,x) \in \mathbb{R}_+^* \times]\xi,\chi[\text{ s.t. } \mathbf{M} \text{ is differentiable} \\ \mathbf{M}(0,x) = \mathbf{M}_0(0,x) \quad \forall x \in X \\ \mathbf{M}(t,\xi) = \gamma(t,\xi) \quad \forall t \in \mathbb{R}_+ \end{cases} \tag{13}$$

Remark. The first line of equation (13) has to be understood in the BJ/F sense. □

The initial and boundary condition components of the Moskowitz function can be computed as follows:

$$\begin{aligned} \mathbf{M}_{\mathbf{M}_0}(t,x) &= \inf_{u\in\mathrm{Dom}\,(\varphi^*)} (\mathbf{M}_0(0, x+tu) + t\varphi^*(u)) \\ \mathbf{M}_\gamma(t,x) &= \inf_{u\in\mathrm{Dom}\,(\varphi^*)} \left(\gamma\left(t - \frac{\xi - x}{u}, \xi\right) + \frac{\xi - x}{u}\varphi^*(u)\right) \end{aligned} \tag{14}$$

The initial and boundary condition components satisfy the following properties

$$\begin{cases} \mathbf{M}_{\mathbf{M}_0}(0,x) = \mathbf{M}_0(0,x) \; \forall x \in X \\ \mathbf{M}_\gamma(t,\xi) = \gamma(t,\xi) \qquad \forall t \in \mathbb{R}_+ \end{cases} \tag{15}$$

provided that the growth condition $\forall \tau \in [0, t], \ 0 \leq \gamma(t, \xi) \leq \gamma(t-\tau, \xi) + \tau\varphi^*(0)$ is satisfied. We assume in the rest of the article that this condition and the following consistency condition are satisfied:

$$\inf_{u \in \mathrm{Dom}\,(\varphi^*)} (\mathbf{M}_0(0, \xi + tu) + t\varphi^*(u)) \geq \gamma(t, \xi) \ \forall t \in \mathbb{R}_+ \tag{16}$$

Definition 10 ***[Mixed initial-boundary conditions target].*** *In the specific case of mixed initial-boundary conditions, we define the target function* $\mathbf{c}(t, x)$ *by* $\mathbf{c}(t, x) = \min(\mathbf{M}_0(t, x), \gamma(t, x))$

Theorem 4.1 ***[Solution to the mixed initial-boundary conditions problem].*** *Given this definition, we can express the solution to the mixed initial-boundary conditions problem (13) as:*

$$\mathbf{M}(t, x) \ = \ \min(\mathbf{M}_{\mathbf{M}_0}(t, x), \mathbf{M}_\gamma(t, x)) \tag{17}$$

The solution $\mathbf{M}$ *to the mixed initial-boundary conditions problem is thus expressed in terms of its* initial condition component $\mathbf{M}_{\mathbf{M}_0}$ *and its* boundary condition component $\mathbf{M}_\gamma$.

Proof. The function $\mathbf{M}(\cdot, \cdot)$ defined by equation (17) is a BJ/F solution to the Moskowitz HJ PDE. Equation (15) in conjunction with consistency condition (16) also implies the following properties:

$$\begin{cases} \mathbf{M}(0, x) = \mathbf{M}_0(0, x) \ \forall x \in X \\ \mathbf{M}(t, \xi) = \gamma(t, \xi) \quad \forall t \in \mathbb{R}_+ \end{cases} \tag{18}$$

$\mathbf{M}(t, x)$ is thus solution to problem (13). ∎

5 Hybrid Components in the Moskowitz Function

Definition 11 ***[Hybrid problem].*** *Let a* C^1 *function* $\overline{\mathbf{M}}(\cdot, \cdot)$ *be defined on a given set* $\mathcal{D} \subset \mathbb{R}_+ \times X$. *Our objective is to compute the function* $\mathbf{M}(\cdot, \cdot)$, *solution to the following hybrid problem:*

$$\begin{cases} \frac{\partial \mathbf{M}(t,x)}{\partial t} - \psi\left(\frac{\partial \mathbf{M}(t,x)}{\partial x}\right) \ = \ 0 \ \forall (t, x) \in \mathbb{R}_+^* \times]\xi, \chi[\setminus \mathcal{D} \ s.\ t.\ \mathbf{M} \textit{ is differentiable} \\ \mathbf{M}(0, x) = \mathbf{M}_0(0, x) \qquad \forall x \in X \\ \mathbf{M}(t, \xi) = \gamma(t, \xi) \qquad \forall t \in \mathbb{R}_+ \\ \mathbf{M}(t, x) \ = \ \overline{\mathbf{M}}(t, x) \qquad \forall (t, x) \in \mathcal{D} \end{cases} \tag{19}$$

The function $\mathbf{M}(t, x)$ *is solution to the HJ PDE when* $(t, x) \in \mathbb{R}_+^* \times]\xi, \chi[\setminus \mathcal{D}$, *and satisfies the set of conditions (19).*

The hybrid problem (19) contains an additional hybrid constraint when compared with the mixed initial-boundary conditions problem. Since the mixed initial-boundary is well posed if the consistency condition (16) is satisfied, the hybrid problem is a priori overconstrained. We seek necessary and sufficient conditions on $\overline{\mathbf{M}}$ for the following inequality to hold:

$$\mathbf{M}_{\overline{\mathbf{M}}}(t,x) \geq \overline{\mathbf{M}}(t,x) \quad \forall (t,x) \in \mathcal{D} \tag{20}$$

Note that the converse inequality is always satisfied by definition of the capture basin since $\mathcal{C} \subseteq \mathrm{Capt}_S(\mathcal{K},\mathcal{C})$. When inequality (20) is satisfied, we have $\mathbf{M}_{\overline{\mathbf{M}}}(t,x) = \overline{\mathbf{M}}(t,x)\ \forall (t,x) \in \mathcal{D}$. This condition, similar to conditions (15), is required for the construction of the solution to the hybrid problem. Using the generalized Lax-Hopf formula, we can rewrite condition (20) as:

$$\inf_{(u,T)\in \mathrm{Dom}(\varphi^*)\times \mathbb{R}_+} \left[\overline{\mathbf{M}}(t-T,x+Tu) + T\varphi^*(u)\right] \geq \overline{\mathbf{M}}(t,x) \quad \forall (t,x) \in \mathcal{D} \tag{21}$$

Since equation (21) involves a minimization over two variables, it is difficult in general to assess a priori that a C^1 function $\overline{\mathbf{M}}$ will satisfy this condition.

Proposition 5 ***[Necessary condition for equation (21) to be satisfied].*** *Since $\overline{\mathbf{M}}(\cdot,\cdot)$ is differentiable in a neighborhood of (t,x), condition (21) implies the following necessary condition:*

$$\frac{\partial \overline{\mathbf{M}}(t,x)}{\partial t} \leq \psi\left(-\frac{\partial \overline{\mathbf{M}}(t,x)}{\partial x}\right) \tag{22}$$

Proof. Using the generalized Lax Hopf formula, one can rewrite condition (21) as:

$$\inf_{(u,T)\in \mathrm{Dom}(\varphi^*)\times \mathbb{R}_+} \left[\overline{\mathbf{M}}(t-T,x+Tu) - \overline{\mathbf{M}}(t,x) + T\varphi^*(u)\right] \geq 0 \quad \forall (t,x) \in \mathcal{D} \tag{23}$$

which in turn implies $\forall (t,x) \in \mathcal{D}$ and $\forall (T,u) \in \mathbb{R}_+ \times \mathrm{Dom}(\varphi^*)$

$$\left[\overline{\mathbf{M}}(t-T,x+Tu) - \overline{\mathbf{M}}(t,x) + T\varphi^*(u)\right] \geq 0 \tag{24}$$

Dividing equation (24) by $T > 0$, and taking the limit of the resulting expression when $T \to 0$ enables us to write:

$$\inf_{u\in \mathrm{Dom}(\varphi^*)} \left[-\frac{\partial \overline{\mathbf{M}}(t,x)}{\partial t} + u\frac{\partial \overline{\mathbf{M}}(t,x)}{\partial x} + \varphi^*(u)\right] \geq 0 \quad \forall (t,x) \in \mathcal{D} \tag{25}$$

By definition of the inverse Fenchel transform, we have $\psi(\rho) = \inf_{u\in \mathrm{Dom}(\varphi^*)} (-\rho u + \varphi^*(u))$. Equation (25) thus implies $-\frac{\partial \overline{\mathbf{M}}(t,x)}{\partial t} + \psi(-\frac{\partial \overline{\mathbf{M}}(t,x)}{\partial x}) \geq 0$, which in turn implies formula (22). ■

Remark. In terms of traffic, this necessary condition states that it is not possible to set a traffic state function $\overline{\mathbf{M}}$ which prescribes a flow q higher than the equilibrium flow $\psi(\rho)$ associated to the prescribed density ρ. □

Proposition 6 ***[Sufficient condition for equation (21) to be satisfied].*** *If $\mathcal{D}$ is convex and condition (22) is valid for all $(t,x) \in \mathrm{Dom}(\overline{\mathbf{M}})$ such that $\overline{\mathbf{M}}$ is differentiable, then condition (21) is satisfied.*

Proof. Assume that $\mathcal{D}$ is convex and $\overline{\mathbf{M}}(\cdot,\cdot)$ is C^1, and satisfies equation (22). Condition (21) can be written as:

$$\inf_{(u,T)\in \mathrm{Dom}(\varphi^*)\times\mathbb{R}_+} \left[\overline{\mathbf{M}}(t-T,x+Tu) - \overline{\mathbf{M}}(t,x) + T\varphi^*(u)\right] \geq 0 \ \forall (t,x) \in \mathcal{D} \tag{26}$$

Since $\mathcal{D}$ is convex, the set $\{(t-\tau, x+\tau u), \tau \in [0,T]\}$ is included in $\mathcal{D}$, provided that $(t-T, x+Tu)$ belongs to $\mathcal{D}$. Since $\overline{\mathbf{M}}(\cdot,\cdot)$ is integrable, we can rewrite condition (26) as: $\forall (t,x) \in \mathcal{D}$,

$$\inf_{(u,T)\in \mathrm{Dom}(\varphi^*)\times\mathbb{R}_+} \left[\int_0^T \left(-\frac{\partial \overline{\mathbf{M}}(t-\tau,x+\tau u)}{\partial t} + u\frac{\partial \overline{\mathbf{M}}(t-\tau,x+\tau u)}{\partial x} + \varphi^*(u)\right) d\tau\right] \geq 0 \tag{27}$$

We now prove that condition (22) implies condition (27). Indeed, condition (22) implies that $\forall \tau \in [0,T]$, $\frac{\partial \overline{\mathbf{M}}(t-\tau,x+\tau u)}{\partial t} \leq \psi\left(-\frac{\partial \overline{\mathbf{M}}(t-\tau,x+\tau u)}{\partial x}\right)$. Thus

$$-\int_0^T \psi\left(-\frac{\partial \overline{\mathbf{M}}(t-\tau,x+\tau u)}{\partial x}\right) d\tau \leq \int_0^T -\frac{\partial \overline{\mathbf{M}}(t-\tau,x+\tau u)}{\partial t} d\tau \tag{28}$$

Since $\psi(\cdot)$ is concave and lower semicontinuous, Jensen inequality implies:

$$-\psi\left(\frac{1}{T}\int_0^T -\frac{\partial \overline{\mathbf{M}}(t-\tau,x+\tau u)}{\partial x}\right) d\tau \leq -\frac{1}{T}\int_0^T \psi\left(-\frac{\partial \overline{\mathbf{M}}(t-\tau,x+\tau u)}{\partial x}\right) d\tau \tag{29}$$

We set $f(\cdot,\cdot)$ as $f(T,u) := \frac{1}{T}\int_0^T -\frac{\partial \overline{\mathbf{M}}(t-\tau,x+\tau u)}{\partial x} d\tau$. Equation (22) implicitly implies that $\forall (T,u) \in \mathbb{R}_+ \times \mathrm{Dom}(\varphi^*)$, $-\frac{\partial \overline{\mathbf{M}}(t-\tau,x+\tau u)}{\partial x} \in \mathrm{Dom}(\psi)$ and thus, by integration, that $f(T,u) \in \mathrm{Dom}(\psi)$. We can write the general inequality $\psi(\rho) \leq -\rho u + \varphi^*(u)$ as:

$$\forall (u,T) \in \mathrm{Dom}(\varphi^*) \times \mathbb{R}_+, \quad 0 \leq -\psi(f(T,u)) + uf(T,u) + \varphi^*(u) \tag{30}$$

Equations (28) and (29) imply:

$$-\psi(f(T,u)) + uf(T,u) \leq \int_0^T \left(-\frac{\partial \overline{\mathbf{M}}(t-\tau,x+\tau u)}{\partial t} + u\frac{\partial \overline{\mathbf{M}}(t-\tau,x+\tau u)}{\partial x}\right) d\tau \tag{31}$$

Since u is constant, equation (30) implies:

$$0 \leq \int_0^T \left(-\frac{\partial \overline{\mathbf{M}}(t-\tau,x+\tau u)}{\partial t} + u\frac{\partial \overline{\mathbf{M}}(t-\tau,x+\tau u)}{\partial x} + \varphi^*(u)\right) d\tau \tag{32}$$

Equation (27) is finally obtained from equation (32) by taking the infimum over the parameters $(T,u) \in \mathbb{R}_+ \times \mathrm{Dom}(\varphi^*)$, and by observing that equation (32) is valid for all $(t,x) \in \mathcal{D}$. ■

Definition 12 *[Construction of the hybrid solutions]. In the specific case of mixed initial-boundary-hybrid conditions, we define the target function* $\mathbf{c}(t,x)$ *as follows:*

$$\mathbf{c}(t,x) = \min\left(\mathbf{M}_0(t,x), \gamma(t,x), \overline{\mathbf{M}}(t,x)\right) \tag{33}$$

The function defined by equation

$$\mathbf{M}(t,x) \;=\; \min\left(\mathbf{M}_{\mathbf{M}_0}(t,x), \mathbf{M}_\gamma(t,x), \mathbf{M}_{\overline{M}}(t,x)\right) \tag{34}$$

is associated to the target $\mathcal{C} := \mathcal{E}pi(\mathbf{M}_0) \cup \mathcal{E}pi(\gamma) \cup \mathcal{E}pi(\overline{\mathbf{M}})$. This function is thus a solution to the Moskowitz HJ PDE in the BJ/F sense.

Proposition 7. *We assume that* $\mathcal{D}$ *is a convex subset belonging to the interior of* $\mathbb{R}_+ \times X$*, and that condition (22) is valid for all* $(t,x) \in \mathrm{Dom}(\overline{\mathbf{M}})$*. The function* $\mathbf{M}$ *defined by equation (34) satisfies conditions (19) if and only if the following set of conditions is satisfied:*

$$\begin{cases} \mathbf{M}_{\mathbf{M}_0}(t,x) \geq \overline{\mathbf{M}}(t,x) \text{ and } \mathbf{M}_\gamma(t,x) \geq \overline{\mathbf{M}}(t,x) & \forall (t,x) \in \mathcal{D} \\ \mathbf{M}_{\overline{\mathbf{M}}}(t,\xi) \geq \gamma(t,\xi) \text{ and } \mathbf{M}_{\mathbf{M}_0}(t,\xi) \geq \gamma(t,\xi) & \forall t \in \mathbb{R}_+ \end{cases} \tag{35}$$

Proof. Equation (15) implies that the function $\mathbf{M}$ defined by equation (34) satisfies:

$$\begin{cases} \mathbf{M}(0,x) = \min\left(\mathbf{M}_0(0,x), \mathbf{M}_\gamma(0,x), \mathbf{M}_{\overline{\mathbf{M}}}(0,x)\right) \; \forall x \in X \\ \mathbf{M}(t,\xi) = \min\left(\gamma(t,\xi), \mathbf{M}_{\mathbf{M}_0}(t,\xi), \mathbf{M}_{\overline{\mathbf{M}}}(0,x)\right) \;\; \forall t \in \mathbb{R}_+ \end{cases} \tag{36}$$

Note that we always have $\forall x \in X$, $\mathbf{M}_{\overline{\mathbf{M}}}(0,x) \geq \mathbf{M}_0(0,x)$ and $\mathbf{M}_\gamma(0,x) \geq \mathbf{M}_0(0,x)$, since $\mathbf{M}_\gamma(0,x) = +\infty$ if $x \neq 0$ and $\mathbf{M}_{\overline{\mathbf{M}}}(0,x) = +\infty$ if $\mathcal{D} \subset \mathrm{Int}(\mathbb{R}_+ \times X)$. This consideration and equation (36) imply that $\mathbf{M}$ is solution to equation (19) if and only if equation (35),(2) is satisfied.

The inclusion $\mathcal{C} \subseteq \mathrm{Capt}_S(\mathcal{K}, \mathcal{C})$ (valid for any capture basin) also implies $\forall (t,x) \in \mathcal{D}, \mathbf{M}(t,x) \leq \overline{\mathbf{M}}(t,x)$. Hence, $\mathbf{M}$ satisfies equation (19) if and only if equation (35) is satisfied. ■

6 Applications

We now illustrate the previous results with three numerical applications computed using the generalized Lax Hopf formula, or the viability algorithm [7].

6.1 Switching Solutions of the LWR PDE

In this section, we compute the solution to the LWR PDE (1) with the triangular flux function as the solution to a switched PDE problem. The triangular flux function ψ is defined by:

$$\psi(\rho) \;=\; \begin{cases} \nu^\flat \rho & \text{if } \rho \leq \rho_c \\ \nu^\sharp(\omega - \rho) & \text{if } \rho \geq \rho_c \end{cases} \tag{37}$$

where $\omega = 4$ is the *jam density*, $\nu^\flat = 3$ is the *free flow speed*, $\nu^\sharp = 1$ is the *congestion speed*, and $\rho_c = 1$ is the *critical density*. The two corresponding PDEs are associated to the two modes of propagation of traffic (free flow or congestion):

$$\begin{cases} \frac{\partial \rho}{\partial t} + \nu^\flat \frac{\partial \rho}{\partial x} = 0 & \rho \in [0, \rho_c] \quad \text{(free flow)} \\ \frac{\partial \rho}{\partial t} - \nu^\sharp \frac{\partial \rho}{\partial x} = 0 & \rho \in [\rho_c, \omega] \ \text{(congestion)} \end{cases}$$

where $\nu^\flat$ is the free flow speed and $\nu^\sharp$ the speed of back propagating waves. In Figure 2, we show a numerical example of computation (using the generalized Lax Hopf formula (7)) of the partition of the space time domain on which the free flow and the congested PDE apply, for given initial and boundary conditions. The techniques developed earlier are thus illustrated in this Figure, in which one can see the existence of three modes: highway in free flow (white), highway at maximum capacity (gray) and highway congested (black).

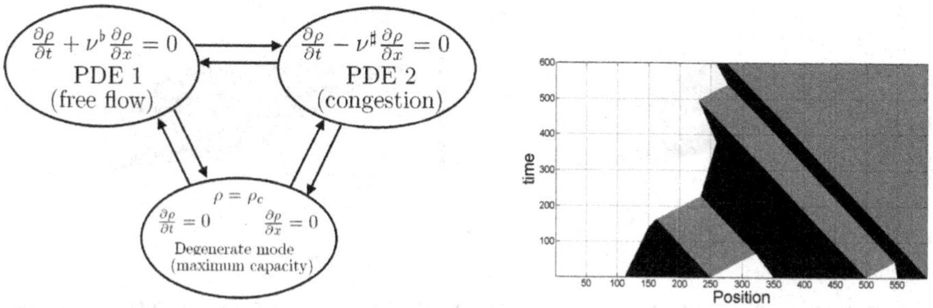

Fig. 2. Illustration of space and time switched PDEs. The solution to the corresponding LWR PDE (1) with triangular flux function (37) leads to three modes: two hybrid components PDE 1 and PDE 2, and a degenerate mode.

6.2 Hybrid Solutions Associated to a Speed Control Policy

We now illustrate the previous results with a variable speed control problem. Variable speed limits are speed limits that are changed by highway operators based on traffic or weather conditions. These speed limits are set for safety or traffic flow management purposes. In this section, we compute the effects of a speed limit set on domain $\mathcal{D} \subset \mathbb{R}_+ \times X$. We consider the following mixed initial-boundary conditions problem:

$$\mathbf{M}_0(0, x) = \begin{cases} -0.7x & \text{if } 0 \le x \le 5 \\ -0.4x - 5.5 & \text{if } 5 \le x \le 14 \\ 41.9 - 3.5x & \text{if } 14 \le x \le 20 \end{cases} \qquad \gamma(t, \xi) = \begin{cases} t & \text{if } 0 \le t \le 4 \\ 2t - 4 & \text{if } 4 \le t \le 8 \\ 1.5t & \text{if } 8 \le t \le 10 \end{cases}$$

We use the triangular flux function defined in the previous section. This set of initial and boundary conditions satisfy condition (16). We now augment this problem using a hybrid component corresponding to a speed control policy. The hybrid solution satisfies the HJ PDE outside of a domain $\mathcal{D}$ defined by

$$\mathcal{D} = \bigcup_{t \in [2,6]} [1 + v(t-2), 7 + v(t-2)] \tag{38}$$

where $v = 1.3$ is the limited speed at which all the vehicles in set $\mathcal{D}$ are running (by effect of the speed control policy). Since the trajectories of the vehicles are the level sets of $\overline{\mathbf{M}}$, we must define $\overline{\mathbf{M}}(t, x)$ as:

$$\forall (t, x) \in \mathcal{D}, \ \ \overline{\mathbf{M}}(t, x) := \mathbf{M_{MIB}}(2, x - v(t-2)) \tag{39}$$

where $\mathbf{M_{MIB}}$ is the solution to the associated mixed initial boundary conditions problem.

We compute the solution to the mixed initial boundary conditions problem, as well as the solution to the hybrid problem. The resulting surface for $\mathbf{M}(t, x)$ is shown in Figure 3.

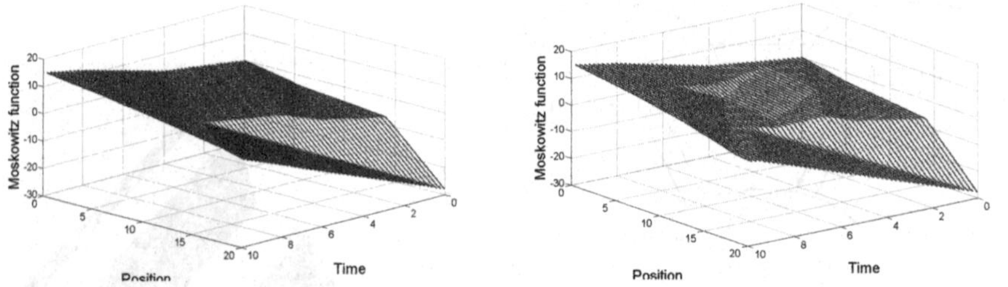

Fig. 3. Solution of the Moskowitz HJ PDE. **Left:** Moskowitz function $\mathbf{M}(t, x)$ corresponding to the mixed initial boundary conditions problem. **Right:** Moskowitz function $\mathbf{M}(t, x)$ solution to the hybrid problem corresponding to a speed control policy for vehicles located in the set $\mathcal{D}$.

The effects of the speed control policy can also be seen in Figure 4, which shows the level sets of the Moskowitz functions associated to the mixed initial boundary condition problem (left) and to the hybrid problem (right). We recall that the integer-level sets of the Moskowitz function correspond by definition to the trajectories of the vehicles.

6.3 Data Assimilation Using Hybrid Components

In this section, we use NGSIM data which contains video extracted trajectories of all vehicles traversing a 0.4 mile section of highway I80 in Emeryville, CA. Since the trajectories of vehicles are the level sets of the Moskowitz function, we can use this data to illustrate the benefits of data assimilation using Lagrangian measurements measurements [11]. We first solve the problem (13) from NGSIM extracted $\mathbf{M}_0(0, x)$ and $\gamma(t, \xi)$. This produces the prediction of shown in Figure 5 (left)[1] and the corresponding error plot of Figure 6 (left). We then add

[1] Note that only a subset of the trajectories is shown on this plot for clarity.

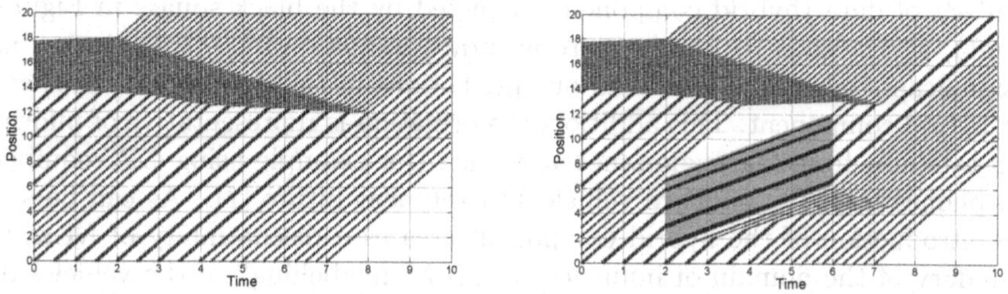

Fig. 4. Vehicle trajectories due to speed control policy. **Left:** trajectories corresponding to the mixed initial boundary conditions problem. **Right:** trajectories corresponding to the hybrid problem. Note the modification of speed of the vehicles in the set $\mathcal{D}$ (shaded), as well as the influence of the speed control policy on $\mathcal{D}$ on the upstream traffic.

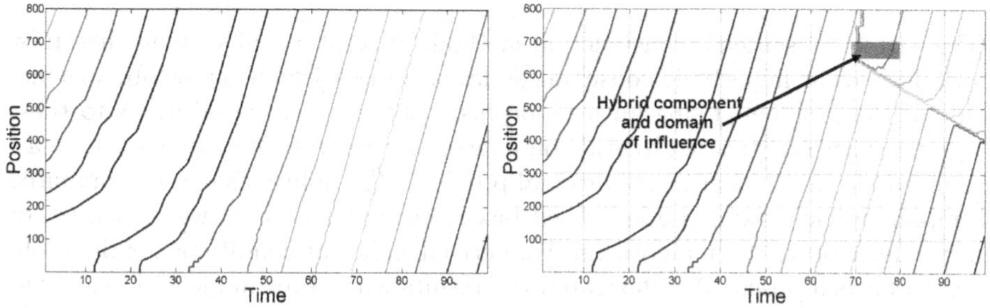

Fig. 5. Trajectories simulated using NGSIM data. **Left:** trajectories simulated using the initial and boundary conditions only and solving (13). **Right:** trajectories obtained by adding the hybrid component $\mathcal{D} = [70, 80] \times [650, 700]$ and solving the hybrid problem (19).

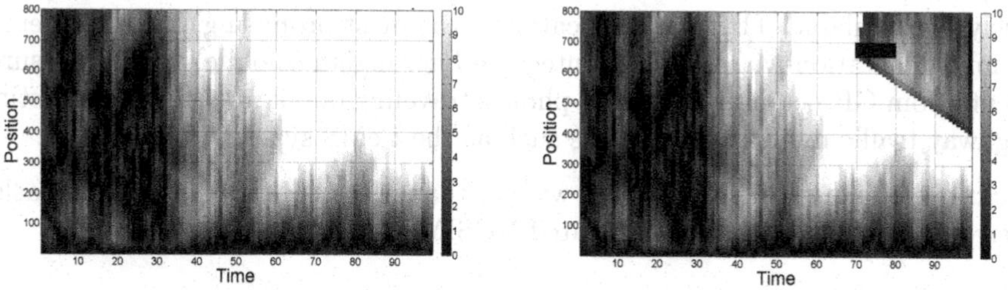

Fig. 6. Simulation using NGSIM data. **Left:** error in the predictions provided by the Moskowitz function simulated using the initial and boundary condition5s only and solving (13). **Right:** error obtained by adding the hybrid component $\mathcal{D} = [70, 80] \times [650, 700]$ and solving the hybrid problem (19). The color scale represents the magnitude of the absolute error. The black color represents a null error, whereas the white color represents an absolute error greater than 10 vehicles.

a subset of data (hybrid component) depicted by the black square in Figure 5 (right), which leads to locally more accurate estimate of the trajectories, and a significant reduction of error in our predictions in the domain of influence of the hybrid component. This additional information is representative of information available from lagrangian measurements (for example using GPS equipped cell phones traveling onboard vehicles) in the near future [11]. As can be seen, the introduction of the hybrid component creates a discontinuity of **M** at the boundary of the domain of influence, which a "relabelling" of the vehicles due to additional information provided by the hybrid component. The corresponding reduction of error can be seen in Figure 6 (right). In Figures 5 and 6, the position is given in units of 2.4 ft (between posts 80 ft and 2000 ft), and the time is given in units of 1.2 s (this corresponds to the two first minutes of the NGSIM experiment).

7 Conclusion

This article presented a construction method for solutions of systems driven by switched scalar hyperbolic conservation laws, using a Hamilton-Jacobi formulation of the problem. Using an inf morphism property of the solutions to these equations, we constructed hybrid components for the problem, which can be assembled into a solution to the original problem. The solutions can be computed semi-analytically using a generalized Lax-Hopf formula which we presented, or using the capture basin algorithm. We derived sufficient conditions for the problem to be well posed. We illustrated the results with three numerical examples. In the first example, we showed how the method can be used to compute hybrid components of the LWR PDE with a triangular flux function. The second example showed how to compute the effects of control on traffic using the Hamilton-Jacobi equation. Finally, the last example used NGSIM data to demonstrate data assimilation capabilities of the method: "internal" boundary conditions which can be added to an original partial differential equation problem in the form of a hybrid component, which "corrects" the model where information was previously not available. This last application is the most promising, and is currently in implementation with Nokia to integrate Lagrangian (mobile) traffic measurements from GPS equipped cellular phones traveling onboard cars inside existing highway traffic monitoring systems such as the PeMS system in California.

Acknowledgments. The authors wish to thank Ryan Herring and Juan Carlos Herrera for computing the aggregated NGSIM data.

References

1. Alvarez-Icaza, L., Munoz, L., Sun, X., Horowitz, R.: Adaptive observer for traffic density estimation. In: American Control Conference, Boston, MA, pp. 2705–2710 (June 2004)
2. Amin, S., Hante, F., Bayen, A.: On stability of switched linear hyperbolic conservation laws with reflecting boundaries. In: Egerstedt, M., Mishra, B. (eds.) HSCC 2008, LNCS, vol. 4981, pp. 602–605. Springer, Heidelberg (2008)

3. Aubin, J.-P.: Viability Theory. In: Systems and Control: Foundations and Applications, Birkhäuser, Boston, MA (1991)
4. Aubin, J.-P.: Viability kernels and capture basins of sets under differential inclusions. SIAM Journal of Control and Optimization 40, 853–881 (2001)
5. Aubin, J.-P., Bayen, A.M., Saint-Pierre, P.: Dirichlet problems for some Hamilton-Jacobi equations with inequality constraints. Technical report, Preprint di Matematica - n. 4, Scuola Normale Superiore, Pisa, Italy (May 2006)
6. Bayen, A.M., Raffard, R.L., Tomlin, C.: Network congestion alleviation using adjoint hybrid control: Application to highways. In: Lynch, N.A., Krogh, B.H. (eds.) HSCC 2000. LNCS, vol. 1790, pp. 95–110. Springer, Heidelberg (2000)
7. Cardaliaguet, P., Quincampoix, M., Saint-Pierre, P.: Set-valued numerical analysis for optimal control and differential games. In: Bardi, M., Raghavan, T.E.S., Parthasarathy, T. (eds.) Stochastic and Differential Games: Theory and Numerical Methods. Annals of the International Society of Dynamic Games, pp. 177–247. Birkhäuser, Basel (1999)
8. Daganzo, C.F.: A variational formulation of kinematic waves: basic theory and complex boundary conditions. Transporation Research B 39B(2), 187–196 (2005)
9. Daganzo, C.F.: On the variational theory of traffic flow: well-posedness, duality and applications. Networks and Heterogeneous Media 1, 601–619 (2006)
10. Hante, F., Leugering, G., Seidman, T.: Modeling and analysis of modal switching in networked transport systems (submitted, 2007)
11. Herrera, J.C., Bayen, A.M.: Traffic flow reconstruction using mobile sensors and loop detector data. In: The 87th Annual Meeting of TRB (to appear, 2007)
12. Koch, H., zuazua, E.: A hybrid system of PDE's arising in multi-structure interaction: coupling of wave equations in n and n-1 space dimensions. Recent Trends in Partial Differential Equations: UIMP-RSME Santaló Summer School, Recent Trends in Partial Differential Equations, Universidad Internacional Menéndez Pelayo, Santander, Spain, 4 (2006)
13. Lighthill, M.J., Whitham, G.B.: On kinematic waves. II. A theory of traffic flow on long crowded roads. Proceedings of the Royal Society of London 229(1178), 317–345 (1956)
14. Moskowitz, K.: Discussion of freeway level of service as influenced by volume and capacity characteristics. In: Drew, D.R., Keese, C.J., Highway Research Record, vol. 99, pp. 43–44 (1965)
15. Newell, G.F.: A simplified theory of kinematic waves in highway traffic. Transporation Research B 27B(4), 281–303 (1993)
16. Richards, P.I.: Shock waves on the highway. Operations Research 4(1), 42–51 (1956)
17. Saint-Pierre, P.: Approximation of the viability kernel. Applied Mathematics and Optimization 29, 187–209 (1994)
18. Seidman, T.I.: A convection/reaction/switching system. Nonlinear Analysis: Theory, Methods & Applications 67(7), 2060–2071 (2007)
19. Strub, I.S., Bayen, A.M.: Weak formulation of boundary conditions for scalar conservation laws 16, 733–748 (2006)
20. Tomlin, C., Lygeros, J., Sastry, S.: A game theoretic approach to controller design for hybrid systems. Proceedings of the IEEE 88(7), 949–970 (2000)

Lost in Translation: Hybrid-Time Flows vs. Real-Time Transitions

P.J.L. Cuijpers and M.A. Reniers

Technische Universiteit Eindhoven (TU/e),
P.O. Box 513, NL-5600 MB Eindhoven, The Netherlands
{P.J.L.Cuijpers, M.A.Reniers}@tue.nl

Abstract. Recently, hybrid-time flow systems have been introduced as an extension to timed transition systems, hybrid automata, continuous time evolutions of differential equations etc. Furthermore, a number of notions of bisimulation have been defined on these flow systems reflecting abstraction from certain timing properties. In this paper, we research the difference in abstraction level between this new semantic model of flow systems, and the more traditional model of real-time transition systems. We explore translations between the old and new semantic models, and we give a necessary and sufficient condition, called *finite-set refutability*, for these translations to be without loss of information. Finally, we show that differential inclusions with an upper-semicontinuous, closed and convex right-hand side, are finite-set refutable, and easily extend this result to impuls differential inclusions and hybrid automata.

1 Introduction

In the literature on hybrid systems, a variety of semantic models is used to describe the combined discrete and continuous behavior of these systems. In Henzinger's early paper on hybrid automata [1], a real-time transition system semantics was used. Later, the timing on the transitions was replaced by flows, resulting in hybrid transition systems. This has enabled the definition of all kinds of compositions of hybrid systems in a more operational way by means of Hybrid I/O automata [2] and a wide range of hybrid process algebras and calculi [3,4,5,6]. Finally, following the behavioral approach of Polderman and Willems [7] and the evolutionary model of Aubin and Dordan [8], *flow systems over hybrid time-lines* have been proposed [9,10,11], which constitute a semantic formalism that is closer to the classical semantics of control theory.

Apart from a difference in ease of use depending on the application area, there is a difference in abstraction level that one should be concerned about when choosing between these semantic models. Perhaps not surprisingly, a hybrid-time flow model contains more detailed information regarding the behavior of a system than a real-time transition model. Furthermore, within the formalism of hybrid-time flow systems, three notions of bisimulation can be distinguished (see [12]) corresponding to different levels of abstraction at which timing can be

M. Egerstedt and B. Mishra (Eds.): HSCC 2008, LNCS 4981, pp. 116–129, 2008.

regarded. The question arises what the exact difference in level of abstraction is when different formalisms and different notions of equivalence are used.

In this paper, we study the difference in abstraction level between hybrid-time flow systems and real-time transition systems. We start, in section 2, with some formal preliminaries on time, transitions and flows. In section 3, we discuss translations from hybrid-time flow systems to real-time transition systems and back. In the translation from transition systems to flow systems, which creates flows by 'pasting' transitions together, no information is lost. The translation in the other direction, which creates transitions based on the presence of a *witnessing flow* (as in hybrid automata theory [1]), turns out to be lossless if and only if the original hybrid-time flows are *finite-set refutable*. I.e. if and only if any flow that is not a valid behavior of the system can be refuted on the basis of observations at only a finite (but well-chosen) set of time-points. The notion of finite-set refutability seems to be connected to the physical intuition that a system can only be observed at a finite number of times, but we are not aware of any previous literature about it. It is likely that finite-set refutability has never been considered in isolation before, since it will usually be replaced by the stronger (topological) notion of compactness (see section 5).

In section 4, we recall three notions of bisimulation equivalence on hybrid-time flow systems [12], and give their corresponding notions on real-time transition systems (one of which is especially introduced in this paper for the purpose). We proceed by proving that the translations preserve these bisimulations. Furthermore, we prove that in case of finite-set refutable flow systems, bisimulation on the real-time transition system resulting from the translation implies bisimulation of the original flow systems. Finally, in section 5, we show that hybrid-time flow systems in which the continuous paths are generated through differential inclusions with an upper-semicontinuous, closed and convex, right-hand side, are finite-set refutable. In section 6, we conclude that the difference in abstraction level between hybrid-time flow systems and real-time transition systems is irrelevant for a very broad class of hybrid systems. We give some suggestions for further research and, amongst others, discuss how hybrid transition systems may come of use if the differential inclusions are not autonomous.

2 Time, Transitions and Flows

Two semantic approaches to the description of dynamical systems are still gaining popularity: (timed) transition system semantics, and flow system semantics. Both make use of a formal notion of time.

A *time-line* is usually defined to be a *linear order* that, depending on the theory to be developed, has certain additional properties. One of those properties, is that it is an *Abelian group*, i.e. it has an addition operator $+$ defined on it. In this paper, it also has a zero element 0, such that $x + 0 = x$, and for notational convenience it has an inverse $-$ such that $x + (-x) = 0$. To denote the passage of time, only the positive numbers are used, which are also referred to as the *future* time-line. The most often used future time-line in control theory is, arguably, that of the non-negative real numbers $\mathbb{R}^{\geq 0}$, with the natural numbers $\mathbb{N} = \mathbb{Z}^{\geq 0}$ at second place. Recently in [9,10], a merge between those two time-lines has arisen known as *hybrid time* $\mathbb{H} = \mathbb{Z} \times \mathbb{R}$, in which the ordering of time-points is lexicographical, i.e. for $(z,r),(z',r') \in \mathbb{H}$ we have $(z,r) < (z',r')$ if and only if $z < z'$ or both $z = z'$ and $r < r'$, and the addition is pointwise, i.e. $(z,r) + (z',r') = (z + z', r + r')$. The future hybrid-time[1] line then consists of the positive quadrant $\mathbb{H}^{\geq 0} = \mathbb{N} \times \mathbb{R}^{\geq 0}$. Paths over this time-line are alternations of continuous changes, i.e. intervals over the 'real' part where the 'discrete' part stays constant, and discrete changes, i.e. changes in the 'discrete' part where the 'real' part stays constant. Thus, hybrid-time provides us with a mechanism to describe hybrid behavior efficiently. For the sake of completeness we mention that the general time-line theory of [10] allows flow systems over even more exotic time-lines, in order to support constructs like *meta hybrid-automata* (automata with hybrid-automata in their states) [13].

The earliest hybrid semantics did not make use of a mechanism like hybrid-time, but rather allowed discontinuous changes in the state of a system that take 0 time. Amongst others, the early hybrid automata frameworks used real-time transition systems [1] as their semantics. Note, that in certain hybrid process algebras and hybrid automata frameworks, the discontinuous changes are not directly associated with a 0-time transition, but rather with an action transition. Such an approach would not fundamentally change the results of this paper, except that the hybrid-time flows would somehow have to accommodate for such actions as well.

Definition 1. *A* real-time transition system *is a tuple* $\mathcal{T} = \langle X, \mathbb{R}^{\geq 0}, \rightarrow \rangle$, *with* X *a* valuation space, $\mathbb{R}^{\geq 0}$ *the future real-time line, and* $\rightarrow \subseteq X \times \mathbb{R}^{\geq 0} \times X$ *the* time transition relation. *A transition* $(x,t,x') \in \rightarrow$ *will be denoted by* $x \xrightarrow{t} x'$.

- $\mathcal{T}$ *is* non-zero prefix-closed *if every transition* $x \xrightarrow{t} x''$, *with* $t > 0$, *can be split into transitions* $x \xrightarrow{t'} x'$ *and* $x' \xrightarrow{t''} x''$ *with* $t = t' + t''$, *and* $t', t'' > 0$;
- $\mathcal{T}$ *is* non-zero concatenation-closed *if for every two transitions* $x \xrightarrow{t} x'$ *and* $x' \xrightarrow{t'} x''$, *with* $t, t' > 0$, *there is also a transition* $x \xrightarrow{t+t'} x''$.

From here on, we will always assume real-time transition systems to be non-zero prefix closed and non-zero concatenation closed.

The latest hybrid semantics use flows over hybrid-time to describe system behaviors [9,10]. This gives a more expressive semantics than obtained by using real-time transition systems, as we will see further on. However, in hybrid time, the usual model of a path being a function from some time-interval to a valuation space no longer applies. An interval $[t_0, t_1] = \{r \mid t_0 \leq r \leq t_1\}$ in future hybrid-time is a 'square' containing all possible ways in which time can proceed from $t_0 = (n_0, r_0)$ to $t_1 = (n_1, r_1)$. An interval does not yet specify in which order the discrete and continuous time-steps are taken. As a result, a path over

[1] For ease of notation, we will write 0 in stead of $(0,0)$ whenever this is convenient.

hybrid-time has a more complicated domain than the interval-domain used in classical control theory. A formal definition is given below.

Definition 2. *A* hybrid-time path[2] *through a valuation space* X *is a partial function* $\phi : \mathbb{H}^{\geq 0} \to X$ *such that* $dom(\phi) = \bigcup_{i \leq N} \{i\} \times [r_i, r_i']$ *with* $r_i' = r_{i+1}$ *for all* $i < N$. *The set of all hybrid-time paths over* X *is denoted* $\mathrm{Path}(\mathbb{H}^{\geq 0}, X)$.

Definition 3. *On a hybrid-time path* $\phi \in \mathrm{Path}(\mathbb{H}^{\geq 0}, X)$ *we define the post-fix operation*

$$\phi^{\geq t}(\tau) \triangleq \phi(\tau + t) \text{ for } \tau + t \in dom(\phi),$$

and the prefix-operation

$$\phi^{\leq t}(\tau) \triangleq \phi(\tau) \text{ for } \tau \leq t \in dom(\phi).$$

On hybrid-time paths ϕ *and* ϕ', *with* $t \in dom(\phi)$ *and* $\phi(t) = \phi'(0)$, *we define the concatenation*

$$(\phi \cdot_t \phi')(\tau) \triangleq \begin{cases} \phi(\tau) & ; \text{ for } \tau \leq t \\ \phi'(\tau - t) ; & \text{ for } \tau \geq t \end{cases}$$

Finally, we define the progress operator which returns the domain of ϕ *up to the first time instance at which a discrete step is taken:*

$$\mathrm{Pro}(\phi) = \{t \in dom(\phi) \mid t > (0,0) \wedge t \leq \min\{(1,r) \mid (1,r) \in dom(\phi)\}\}.$$

Definition 4. *A* hybrid-time flow system *is a tuple* $\mathcal{F} = \langle X, \mathbb{H}^{\geq 0}, \Phi \rangle$, *with* X *a* valuation space, $\mathbb{H}^{\geq 0}$ *the future hybrid-time line, and* $\Phi : X \to 2^{\mathrm{Path}(\mathbb{H}^{\geq 0}, X)}$ *a map from valuations to sets of hybrid-time paths.*

- $\mathcal{F}$ *has* initialization *if the flows associated with a state actually start in that state i.e.* $\phi(0) = x$ *for all* $x \in \mathrm{dom}(\Phi)$ *and* $\phi \in \Phi(x)$;
- $\mathcal{F}$ *is* time-invariant *if the allowed flows do not depend on the current time, i.e.* $\phi^{\geq t} \in \Phi(\phi(t))$ *for all* $x \in \mathrm{dom}(\Phi)$, $\phi \in \Phi(x)$ *and* $t \in dom(\phi)$;
- $\mathcal{F}$ *is* prefix-closed *if breaking off a flow is allowed, i.e.* $\phi^{\leq t} \in \Phi(x)$ *for all* $x \in \mathrm{dom}(\Phi)$, $\phi \in \Phi(x)$ *and* $t \in dom(\phi)$;
- $\mathcal{F}$ *has* property of state *if future flows only depend on the current valuation, and not on the past of the flow, i.e.* $\phi \cdot_t \phi' \in \Phi(x)$ *for all* $x \in \mathrm{dom}(\Phi)$, $\phi \in \Phi(x)$, $t \in dom(\phi)$ *and* $\phi' \in \Phi(\phi(t))$;

From here on, we will always assume hybrid-time flow systems to have initialization, to be time-invariant and prefix-closed, and to have the property of state.

3 Translations

To obtain insight in the difference in abstraction level between real-time transition systems and hybrid-time flow systems, we define straightforward translations between the two. We verify that these translations preserve the desired

[2] The definitions in [10,12] are more general. They start from a more general notion of time-line, of which $\mathbb{H}^{\geq 0}$ is a particular instance.

closure properties, and at the end of the section we study the information that is lost in these translations.

We start out with a translation from hybrid-time flow systems to real-time transition systems, which creates a transition whenever there is a hybrid-time flow witnessing this transition. Note that in the definition below, only witnesses starting in $(0,0)$ are considered. Furthermore, we only consider witnesses for a single discrete change and for a single continuous flow. Due to the assumptions of time-invariance and property of state, any witness can be reduced to a sequence of such 'elementary' witnesses. An alternative translation using 'full' witnesses would not change the theorems obtained in this paper, but would complicate their proofs.

Definition 5. *Given a hybrid-time flow system* $\mathcal{F} = \langle X, \mathbb{H}^{\geq 0}, \Phi\rangle$ *we define the associated real-time transition system* $\mathbf{T}(\mathcal{F}) = \langle X, \mathbb{R}^{\geq 0}, \rightarrow\rangle$ *such that there is a transition* $x \xrightarrow{t} x'$ *of duration* t *from state* $x \in X$ *to state* $x' \in X$ *if and only if:*

- $t = 0$ *and there is a* $\phi \in \Phi(x)$ *such that* $x' = \phi((1,0))$, *or*
- $t > 0$ *and there is a* $\phi \in \Phi(x)$ *such that* $x' = \phi((0,t))$.

Naturally, we must verify that the standard closure properties on real-time transition systems are preserved.

Theorem 1. $\mathbf{T}(\mathcal{F})$ *is non-zero prefix closed and non-zero concatenation closed.*

Proof. Straightforward, but using the general assumptions that $\mathcal{F}$ has initialization, is time-invariant and prefix-closed and has the property of state.

Next, we give a translation from real-time transition systems to hybrid-time flow systems, which creates a hybrid-time flow by pasting real-time transitions in a suitable manner. A hybrid-time flow is only constructed (i.e. extracted from the real-time transition system) if every change of state that appears in the flow is mimicked by some real-time transition.

Definition 6. *Given a real-time transition system* $\mathcal{T} = \langle X, \mathbb{R}^{\geq 0}, \rightarrow\rangle$, *a hybrid-time path* $\phi \in \text{Path}(\mathbb{H}^{\geq 0}, X)$ *is an* extracted path *of* $\mathcal{T}$ *if*

- *for every* $(n,r), (n,r') \in dom(\phi)$ *with* $r < r'$ *there is a transition* $\phi(n,r) \xrightarrow{r'-r} \phi(n,r')$,
- *for every* $(n,r) \in dom(\phi)$ *with also* $(n+1,r) \in dom(\phi)$, *there is a transition* $\phi(n,r) \xrightarrow{0} \phi(n+1,r)$.

Definition 7. *Given a real-time transition system* $\mathcal{T} = \langle X, \mathbb{R}^{\geq 0}, \rightarrow\rangle$ *we define the associated hybrid-time flow system* $\mathbf{F}(\mathcal{T}) = \langle X, \mathbb{H}^{\geq 0}, \Phi\rangle$ *as the set of all extracted paths of* $\mathcal{T}$. *More precisely, for an initial valuation* $x \in X$ *we have* $\phi \in \Phi(x)$ *if and only if* ϕ *is an extracted path of* $\mathcal{T}$ *with* $\phi(0) = x$.

Of course, we verify that the standard closure properties of hybrid-time flow systems are preserved.

Theorem 2. $\mathbf{F}(\mathcal{T})$ *has initialization, is time-invariant and prefix-closed and has the property of state.*

Proof. Straightforward, but using the general assumptions that $\mathcal{T}$ is non-zero prefix closed and non-zero concatenation closed.

In the translation from real-time transition system to hybrid-time flow system no abstraction is applied; the translation is without loss of information. For the translation in the other direction this is not the case. Next, we prove that the abstraction resulting from translating a hybrid-time flow system into a real-time transition system, is that we only observe the behavior of the system at a finite number of points in time. In other words, if a proposed hybrid-time path $\phi \in \mathrm{Path}(\mathbb{H}^{\geq 0}, X)$ cannot be refuted on the basis of a finite set of time-points, then a real-time transition system cannot distinguish it from an actual behavior of the system.

As an example, consider the differential inclusion $\dot{x} \in [-1, 1]$ and the differential inclusion $\dot{x} \in \{-1, 1\}$ which switches between slope -1 and 1 arbitrarily fast. As we prove further on in section 5, the set of solutions of the first inclusion is finite-set refutable, while the set of solutions of the second is not. Furthermore, the behavior defined by the second inclusion is a strict subset of the behavior defined by the first. In particular, the function $x(t) = 0$ is a solution of the first inclusion, but not of the second. Still, given any finite set of time points D, there is a solution $y(t)$ of $\dot{y} \in \{-1, 1\}$ such that $y(d) = x(d) = 0$ for all $d \in D$ (just find an appropriate zig-zag line). In fact, any solution of the first inclusion can be approximated by the second in this way. As a result, the real-time transition systems generated by the two differential inclusions are identical.

Definition 8. *A hybrid-time flow system* $\mathcal{F} = \langle X, \mathbb{H}^{\geq 0}, \Phi\rangle$ *is* finite-set refutable *if for every path* $\psi \in \mathrm{Path}(\mathbb{H}^{\geq 0}, X)$ *such that* $\psi \notin \Phi(\psi(0))$*, there is a finite set* $T_\psi \subseteq dom(\psi)$ *such that for every* $\phi \in \Phi(\psi(0))$ *with* $dom(\phi) = dom(\psi)$ *there is a* $t \in T_\psi$ *with* $\phi(t) \neq \psi(t)$*.*

Theorem 3. *For any real-time transition system* $\mathcal{T}$, $\mathbf{F}(\mathcal{T})$ *is finite-set refutable.*

Proof. Let $\mathcal{T} = \langle X, \mathbb{R}^{\geq 0}, \rightarrow\rangle$. Let $x \in X$, and assume that we have a hybrid-time path $\phi \notin \Phi(x)$, with $\phi(0) = x$. Then, by construction of $\mathbf{F}(\mathcal{T})$, ϕ is not an extracted path of $\mathcal{T}$. Hence, there exist $t_1, t_2 \in dom(\phi)$ with $t_1 = (n_1, r_1)$ and $t_2 = (n_2, r_2)$ such that the transition $\phi(t_1) \overset{r_2 - r_1}{\rightarrow} \phi(t_2)$ is not in $\mathcal{T}$. But then, no extracted path of $\mathcal{T}$ can coincide with ϕ at both t_1 and t_2, and hence the finite set $\{t_1, t_2\}$ is a witness on the basis of which ϕ can be refuted[3].

Theorem 4. *For finite-set refutable hybrid-time flow system* $\mathcal{F}$, $\mathbf{F}(\mathbf{T}(\mathcal{F})) = \mathcal{F}$.

Proof. Let $\mathcal{F} = \langle X, \mathbb{H}^{\geq 0}, \Phi\rangle$. We use $\mathbf{F}(\mathbf{T}(\mathcal{F})) = \langle X, \mathbb{H}^{\geq 0}, \Phi'\rangle$ to denote the result of the translation forwards and backwards. It is trivial to see, for any

[3] Indeed, $\mathbf{F}(\mathcal{T})$ is even 2-point refutable. But, 2-point refutability and finite-set refutability coincide for flow-systems with property of state [14].

$x \in X$, that $\phi \in \Phi(x)$ implies $\phi \in \Phi'(x)$. Hence, we focus on the other direction. Assume that $\phi \in \Phi'(x)$ and that $dom(\phi) = \bigcup_{i \leq N}\{i\} \times [r_i, r_i']$, for some $N \in \mathbb{N}$. Let $t_j = (m_j, s_j) \in dom(\phi)$, with $0 \leq j \leq M \leq 2N$, be any (finite) sequence of times including, at least, all the beginning and end-points of the real-time intervals. I.e. let t_j be a sequence such that for every $i \leq N$ there are $j, k \leq M$ with $t_j = (i, r_i)$ and $t_k = (i, r_i')$. Now, by construction of $\mathbf{F}(\mathbf{T}(\mathcal{F}))$, there are transitions $t_j \overset{s_{j+1}-s_j}{\rightarrow} t_{j+1}$ in $\mathbf{T}(\mathcal{F})$, for each $0 \leq j < M-1$. Hence, by construction of $\mathbf{T}(\mathcal{F})$, there is a path $\psi_j \in \Phi(\phi(t_j))$ with $\psi_j(0, s_{j+1}) = \phi(t_{j+1})$ when $m_j = m_{j+1}$, and with $\psi_j(1, 0) = \phi(t_{j+1})$ when $r_j = r_{j+1}$. The concatenation of these paths ψ_j gives a path $\psi \in \Phi(\phi(0)) = \Phi(x)$ with $dom(\psi) = dom(\phi)$ that furthermore coincides with ϕ at every t_j. In conclusion, for every finite set of times D, we can find a sequence t_j visiting all points in D and all switching points of ϕ. Furthermore, we can construct a path $\psi \in \Phi(x)$ that coincides with ϕ at every t_j, and hence at every $d \in D$. Since $\mathcal{F}$ is assumed to be finite-set refutable, we conclude $\phi \in \Phi(x)$.

Corollary 1. *For any hybrid-time flow system $\mathcal{F}$, $\mathbf{F}(\mathbf{T}(\mathcal{F})) = \mathcal{F}$ if and only if $\mathcal{F}$ is finite-set refutable.*

Proof. Straightforward from the previous two theorems.

Finally, we observe that indeed no information is lost if we start from a real-time transition system.

Theorem 5. *For any real-time transition system $\mathcal{T}$, $\mathbf{T}(\mathbf{F}(\mathcal{T})) = \mathcal{T}$.*

Proof. Straightforward, using the prefix-closure of real-time transition systems to ensure that each transition of $\mathcal{T}$ is represented by some flow in $\mathbf{F}(\mathcal{T})$.

4 Bisimulation Equivalence

In [12], Davoren and Tabuada introduced three notions of bisimulation equivalence on hybrid-time flow systems, in an attempt to preserve properties in the temporal logic GFL* [10]. In this paper, we discuss the relation between these three notions, and three similar notions of bisimulation defined on real-time transition systems (one of which is especially introduced in this paper for the purpose of comparison). The most important topic we adres in this section, is that finite-set refutability as a necessary and sufficient condition for lossless translation, is no guarantee that the notions of bisimulation on real-time transition systems will not abstract from more information than the respective notions of bisimulation on hybrid-time flow systems. Below, we prove that finite-set refutability indeed guarantees that bisimulations on hybrid-time flow systems correspond to their companion bisimulations on real-time transition systems.

The intuition on the definitions give below, is that t-bisimulation preserves the exact timing properties of paths, while p-bisimulation allows paths to be 'compressed', 'stretched', or in some other way cast to a different time-line. The notion of r-bisimulation is not concerned with timing at all, and only preserves the order in which states are reached.

Definition 9. *Given hybrid-time flow systems* $\mathcal{F}_1 = \langle X_1, \mathbb{H}^{\geq 0}, \Phi_1 \rangle$ *and* $\mathcal{F}_2 = \langle X_2, \mathbb{H}^{\geq 0}, \Phi_2 \rangle$*, a relation* $\mathcal{R} \subseteq X_1 \times X_2$ *is called a*

- timed simulation *or* t-simulation[4] *if for every* $x_1 \in X_1$*,* $x_2 \in X_2$ *and* $\phi_1 \in \Phi_1(x_1)$ *with* $x_1 \mathcal{R} x_2$ *there exists* $\phi_2 \in \Phi_2(x_2)$ *with* $dom(\phi_1) = dom(\phi_2)$ *such that for every* $t \in dom(\phi_1)$ *we have* $\phi_1(t) \mathcal{R} \phi_2(t)$*;*
- progress simulation *or* p-simulation *if for every* $x_1 \in X_1$*,* $x_2 \in X_2$*,* $\phi_1 \in \Phi_1(x_1)$ *and* $t_1 \in \text{Pro}(\phi_1)$ *with* $x_1 \mathcal{R} x_2$ *there exists* $\phi_2 \in \Phi_2(x_2)$ *with* $t_2 \in \text{Pro}(\phi_2)$ *such that* $\phi_1(t_1) \mathcal{R} \phi_2(t_2)$ *and for every* $s_2 \in dom(\phi_2)$ *with* $0 < s_2 \leq t_2$ *there is a* $s_1 \in dom(\phi_1)$ *with* $0 < s_1 \leq t_1$ *such that* $\phi_1(s_1) \mathcal{R} \phi_2(s_2)$*;*
- reachable simulation *or* r-simulation *if for every* $x_1 \in X_1$*,* $x_2 \in X_2$*,* $\phi_1 \in \Phi_1(x_1)$ *and* $0 < t_1 \in dom(\phi_1)$ *with* $x_1 \mathcal{R} x_2$ *there exists* $\phi_2 \in \Phi_2(x_2)$ *and* $0 < t_2 \in dom(\phi_2)$ *such that* $\phi_1(t_1) \mathcal{R} \phi_2(t_2)$*.*

In general, a relation $\mathcal{R}$ *is called a* bisimulation *if* $\mathcal{R}$ *and* $\mathcal{R}^{-1}$ *are simulations.*

Next, we give the companion bisimulations defined on (relative-time) real-time transition systems, and show the relation with their hybrid-time flow system originals. As was already pointed out in [12] the notion of t-simulation is, in fact, the usual notion of simulation on real-time transition systems as used, for example, in timed process algebras [15].

Definition 10. *Given real-time transition systems* $\mathcal{T}_1 = \langle X_1, \mathbb{R}^{\geq 0}, \rightarrow_1 \rangle$ *and* $\mathcal{T}_2 = \langle X_2, \mathbb{R}^{\geq 0}, \rightarrow_2 \rangle$*, a relation* $\mathcal{R} \subseteq X_1 \times X_2$ *is called a*

- timed simulation *or* t-simulation *if for every* $x_1, x_1' \in X_1$*,* $x_2 \in X_2$ *and* $t \in \mathbb{R}$ *with* $x_1 \xrightarrow{t}_1 x_1'$ *and* $x_1 \mathcal{R} x_2$ *there exists* $x_2' \in X_2$ *such that* $x_2 \xrightarrow{t}_2 x_2'$ *and* $x_1' \mathcal{R} x_2'$*;*
- progress simulation, *or* p-simulation *if for every* $x_1 \in X_1$*,* $x_2 \in X_2$ *and extracted hybrid-time path* ϕ_1 *from* $\mathcal{T}_1$ *with* $t_1 \in \text{Pro}(dom(\phi_1))$*,* $\phi_1(0) = x_1$ *and* $x_1 \mathcal{R} x_2$*, there exists an extracted hybrid-time path* ϕ_2 *from* $\mathcal{T}_2$ *with* $t_2 \in \text{Pro}(dom(\phi_2))$*,* $\phi_2(0) = x_2$*,* $\phi(t_1) \mathcal{R} \phi(t_2)$ *and for every* $s_2 \in dom(\phi_2)$ *with* $0 < s_2 \leq t_2$ *there is a* $s_1 \in dom(\phi_1)$ *with* $0 < s_1 \leq t_1$ *such that* $\phi(s_1) \mathcal{R} \phi(s_2)$*.*
- reachable simulation *or* r-simulation *if for every* $x_1, x_1' \in X_1$*,* $x_2 \in X_2$ *and* $t \in \mathbb{R}$ *with* $x_1 \xrightarrow{t}_1 x_1'$ *and* $x_1 \mathcal{R} x_2$ *there exists* $x_2' \in X_2$ *and* $t' \in \mathbb{R}$ *such that* $x_2 \xrightarrow{t'}_2 x_2'$ *and* $x_1' \mathcal{R} x_2'$*;*

As before, a relation $\mathcal{R}$ *is called a* bisimulation *if* $\mathcal{R}$ *and* $\mathcal{R}^{-1}$ *are simulations.*

One should note, that in the literature the bisimulation relation $\mathcal{R}$ is also required to preserve other observable aspects of a system, such as the atomic propositions on the state-space in logic [16], and the result of the observation function $y : X \rightarrow Y$ in control theory [17]. The proofs below are robust against adding such observables.

The following theorem shows that the translation from real-time transitions to hybrid-time flows preserves simulations, and consequently preserves bisimulation equivalence.

[4] Despite the more compact formulation we use here, the notions of t- and p- simulation coincide with those of [12].

Theorem 6. *Given real-time transition systems $\mathcal{T}_1 = \langle X_1, \mathbb{R}^{\geq 0}, \rightarrow_1 \rangle$ and $\mathcal{T}_2 = \langle X_2, \mathbb{R}^{\geq 0}, \rightarrow_2 \rangle$, a relation $\mathcal{R} \subseteq X_1 \times X_2$*

- *is a t-simulation of $\mathcal{T}_1$ by $\mathcal{T}_2$ if and only if it is a t-simulation of the translated hybrid-time flow system $\mathbf{F}(\mathcal{T}_1)$ by $\mathbf{F}(\mathcal{T}_2)$,*
- *is a p-simulation of $\mathcal{T}_1$ by $\mathcal{T}_2$ if and only if it is a p-simulation of the translated hybrid-time flow system $\mathbf{F}(\mathcal{T}_1)$ by $\mathbf{F}(\mathcal{T}_2)$,*
- *is a r-simulation of $\mathcal{T}_1$ by $\mathcal{T}_2$ if and only if it is a r-simulation of the translated hybrid-time flow system $\mathbf{F}(\mathcal{T}_1)$ by $\mathbf{F}(\mathcal{T}_2)$.*

Proof. The 'only if' direction in the above theorems is trivial, since having a path ϕ in the translation implies having all transitions $\phi(n_1, r_1) \stackrel{r_2 - r_1}{\rightarrow} \phi(n_2, r_2)$ for $(n_1, r_1), (n_2, r_2) \in dom(\phi)$. The 'if' direction becomes straightforward after observing that with each transition $x \stackrel{t}{\rightarrow} x'$ with $t > 0$ there is also a path $\phi \in \Phi(x)$ such that $\phi(0, t) = x'$, due to the non-zero prefix closedness of $\mathcal{T}$.

For the translation from hybrid-time flows to real-time transition systems we have only the 'only if' direction. The reason for not having the 'if' direction is that simulating a transition in $\mathbf{T}(\mathcal{F}_1)$ by a transition in $\mathbf{T}(\mathcal{F}_2)$ does not guarantee that these transitions were generated by similar paths in $\mathcal{F}_1$ and $\mathcal{F}_2$. For r-simulation, only the actual states that are reached are of importance, not the paths leading to them, which is why we have both directions for r-simulation.

Theorem 7. *For any hybrid-time flow systems $\mathcal{F}_1 = \langle X_1, \mathbb{H}^{\geq 0}, \Phi_1 \rangle$ and $\mathcal{F}_2 = \langle X_2, \mathbb{H}^{\geq 0}, \Phi_2 \rangle$, and a relation $\mathcal{R} \subseteq X_1 \times X_2$*

- *is a t-simulation of $\mathcal{F}_1$ by $\mathcal{F}_2$, only if it is a t-simulation of the real-time transition system $\mathbf{T}(\mathcal{F}_1)$ by $\mathbf{T}(\mathcal{F}_2)$,*
- *is a p-simulation of $\mathcal{F}_1$ by $\mathcal{F}_2$, only if it is a p-simulation of the real-time transition system $\mathbf{T}(\mathcal{F}_1)$ by $\mathbf{T}(\mathcal{F}_2)$,*
- *is a r-simulation of $\mathcal{F}_1$ by $\mathcal{F}_2$, if and only if it is a r-simulation of the real-time transition system $\mathbf{T}(\mathcal{F}_1)$ by $\mathbf{T}(\mathcal{F}_2)$.*

Proof. By construction of the translation.

For the other direction in t-simulation and p-simulation, we need finite-set refutability.

Theorem 8. *For any hybrid-time flow systems $\mathcal{F}_1 = \langle X_1, \mathbb{H}^{\geq 0}, \Phi_1 \rangle$ and $\mathcal{F}_2 = \langle X_2, \mathbb{H}^{\geq 0}, \Phi_2 \rangle$, with $\mathcal{F}_2$ finite-set refutable, and given a relation $\mathcal{R} \subseteq X_1 \times X_2$*

- *$\mathcal{R}$ is a t-simulation of the hybrid time flow system $\mathcal{F}_1$ by $\mathcal{F}_2$, if it is a t-simulation of the real-time transition system $\mathbf{T}(\mathcal{F}_1)$ by $\mathbf{T}(\mathcal{F}_2)$,*
- *$\mathcal{R}$ is a p-simulation of the hybrid time flow system $\mathcal{F}_1$ by $\mathcal{F}_2$, if it is a p-simulation of the real-time transition system $\mathbf{T}(\mathcal{F}_1)$ by $\mathbf{T}(\mathcal{F}_2)$.*

Proof. The proof for the notion of p-simulation is rather straightforward, since by theorem 4 we know for finite-set refutable systems that every extracted path of $\mathbf{T}(\mathcal{F}_2)$ is in fact a path of $\mathcal{F}_2$. In our definition of t-simulation on real-time transition systems we did not make use of the notion of paths, hence we must reconstruct them. This is done in a similar fashion as in theorem 4. Assume that $\mathcal{R}$ is a t-simulation for $\mathbf{T}(\mathcal{F}_1)$ and $\mathbf{T}(\mathcal{F}_2)$. Furthermore, let $x_1 \in X_1$, $x_2 \in X_2$ and $\phi_1 \in \Phi_1(x_1)$ with $x_1 \,\mathcal{R}\, x_2$. Now, like in the proof of theorem 4, we create a sequence $t_j = (m_j, s_j) \subseteq dom(\phi_1)$ of length $M+1$ that at least contains all the discrete steps in ϕ_1. Then, using the simulation relation $\mathcal{R}$ we mimic the transitions $\phi_1(t_j) \overset{s_{j+1}-s_j}{\longrightarrow}_1 \phi_1(t_{j+1})$ by transitions $x_j \overset{s_{j+1}-s_j}{\longrightarrow}_2 x_{j+1}$ such that $\phi_1(t_j) \,\mathcal{R}\, x_j$ for all $j \leq M$. By construction of $\mathbf{T}(\mathcal{F}_2)$ we find paths $\psi_j \in \Phi_2(\phi_1(t_j))$, and concatenating these gives us a path $\phi_D \in \Phi_2(x_2)$ such that for every $t \in dom(\phi_1) \cap D$ we have $\phi_1(t) \,\mathcal{R}\, \phi_D(t)$. The fact that Φ_2 is finite-set refutable then leads to the conclusion that there is also a $\phi_2 \in \Phi_2(x_2)$ such that for every $t \in dom(\phi_1) = dom(\phi_2)$ we have $\phi_1(t) \,\mathcal{R}\, \phi_2(t)$.

5 Impuls Differential Inclusions

Now that we have shown that finite-set refutability captures the loss of information between hybrid-time flow systems and real-time transition systems, we should ask ourselves which systems are finite-set refutable. Our first intuition is that most physical systems should have a finite-set refutable representation, because finite-set refutability is a consequence of the physical principle that we can only distinguish systems on the basis of a well-chosen but finite set of observations. Below, we find mathematical confirmation of this intuition, because the long-standing modeling of physical behavior through continuous differential equations (and more generally, differential inclusions with an upper-semicontinuous, closed and convex, right-hand side) leads to compact, and hence finite-set refutable, real-time flow systems (i.e. hybrid-time flow systems without discrete behavior). The definitions below are taken from [11] and require some formal background in topology and in the theory of (impuls) differential inclusions to understand. See for example also [18].

Definition 11. *An* impulse differential inclusion *is a tuple $H = \langle X, F, R, J \rangle$, consisting of a finite dimensional vector space X, a set valued map $F : X \to 2^X$, regarded as a differential inclusion $\dot{x} \in F(x)$, a set valued map $R : X \to 2^X$, regarded as a reset map, and a set $J \subseteq X$, regarded as a forced transition set.*

Definition 12. *A hybrid-time flow system $\mathcal{F}_H = \langle X, \mathbb{H}^{\geq 0}, \Phi_F \rangle$ is the* solution *of an impulse differential inclusion, $H = \langle X, F, R, J \rangle$ when for all $x \in X$ and all paths $\phi \in \mathrm{Path}(\mathbb{H}^{\geq 0}, X)$ we find $\phi \in \Phi_F(x)$ if and only if*

- *$\phi(0,0) = x$,*
- *for all $(n,r) \in dom(\phi)$ with $(n+1,r) \in dom(\phi)$ we have $\phi(n+1,r) \in R(\phi(n,r))$,*
- *for all $(n,r),(n,r') \in dom(\phi)$ we have that $\phi(\cdot)$ is a solution of the differential inclusion $\dot{x} \in F(x)$ over the interval $[(n,r),(n,r')]$, in the sense of [18][5], and $\phi(t) \notin J$ for $(n,r) \leq t < (n,r')$.*

[5] To explain the complete solution concept on differential inclusions would be out of the scope of this paper.

The solutions of impuls differential inclusions indeed satisfy the properties we require of hybrid-time flow systems in this paper.

Theorem 9. *A hybrid-time flow system $\mathcal{F}_H$ that is the solution of an impuls differential inclusion $H = \langle X, F, R, J \rangle$ has initialization, is time-invariant and prefix-closed and has the property of state.*

Proof. That $\mathcal{F}_H$ has initialization follows from its construction above. Time-invariant, prefix-closedness and the property of state are well-known properties of differential inclusions which, amongst others, follows straightforwardly from the theory explained in [18]. The extension with discontinuous behavior using a reset map R, and the restriction using a forced jump-set J do not influence these properties. The full proof of this claim is omitted for reasons of space.

Next, we show that compactness of the solution to an impuls differential inclusion, is sufficient to guarantee finite-set refutability.

Theorem 10. *Let $\mathcal{F}_H = \langle X, \mathbb{H}^{\geq 0}, \Phi \rangle$ be the solution to an impuls differential inclusion $H = \langle X, F, R, J \rangle$, and furthermore let $\Phi(x)$ be a* compact set *for every $x \in X$. Then $\mathcal{F}_H$ is finite-set refutable.*

Proof. Assume that a path $\psi \in \text{Path}(\mathbb{H}^{\geq 0}, X)$ cannot be refuted on the basis of any finite set of time points, then we must prove $\psi \in \Phi(\psi(0))$. We will first prove that ψ can be approximated by a continuous solution $\phi_\omega \in \Phi(\psi(0))$, and secondly, we prove that ψ is in fact continuous itself (hence equal to ϕ_ω).

We start out by observing that the hybrid-time axis has a countable topology. Therefore, we can construct a sequence $D_i \subseteq dom(\psi)$ of finite sets, which converges to a set D_ω, that is dense in $dom(\psi)$. Also assume that $0 \in D_i$ for each i. Because ψ cannot be refuted on the basis of any of the sets D_i, there exists an associated sequence $\phi_i \in \Phi(\psi(0))$ such that $\phi_i(d) = \psi(d)$ for each i and each $d \in D_i$. Using the assumed compactness of $\Phi(\psi(0))$, we know that this sequence ϕ_i has a subsequence converging in a solution $\phi_\omega \in \Phi(\psi(0))$. This solution coincides with ψ on the dense set D_ω, and furthermore $\phi_\omega \in \Phi(\psi(0))$. Hence we have the promised approximation.

Finally, as the solutions to impuls differential inclusions are continuous (between the countably many jumps due to resets), we know in particular that the approximation ϕ_ω is continuous, regardless of the initial choice of D_ω. This is sufficient to prove by contradiction that ψ is also continuous. Namely, should ψ poses a discontinuity at t_0, then we can start out with $t_0 \in D_\omega$, and we would have found the same discontinuity in ϕ_ω. In conclusion, ϕ_ω and ψ are both found to be continuous, and to coincide on a dense set. Hence, $\psi = \phi_\omega \in \Phi(\psi(0))$.

It is a classical result, that compactness is obtained for differential inclusions (without reset maps) of which the function F is upper-semicontinuous and has a closed and convex right-hand side. (In [11], the strictly stronger condition of F being *Marchaud* is used throughout the whole paper.)

Definition 13. *A function $F : X \to 2^X$ is* upper-semicontinuous *at $x_0 \in X$ if for any open set U containing $F(x_0)$ there exists an open set V containing*

x_0 such that $F(V) \subseteq U$. The function F is upper-semicontinuous if it is upper-semicontinuous at every $x_0 \in X$.

Theorem 11. *Let $\mathcal{F}_H = \langle X, \mathbb{H}^{\geq 0}, \Phi \rangle$ be the solution to an impuls differential inclusion $H = \langle X, F, \emptyset, \emptyset \rangle$, with F upper-semicontinuous, and $F(x)$ closed and convex for every $x \in X$. Under these conditions $\Phi(x)$ is a compact set of paths for every x.*

Proof. Transliterate corollary 4.5 of [18].

Adding a reset map R of forced transition set J to a finite-set refutable differential inclusion will not render it finite-set irrefutable.

Theorem 12. *Let $\mathcal{F}_H = \langle X, \mathbb{H}^{\geq 0}, \Phi_H \rangle$ be the solution to an impuls differential inclusion $H = \langle X, F, R, J \rangle$, with F upper-semicontinuous, and $F(x)$ closed and convex for every $x \in X$. Under these conditions $\mathcal{F}_H$ is finite-set refutable (but not necessarily compact).*

Proof. The proof of this theorem is too long to be presented here completely, but it relies on the observation that $\mathcal{F}_H$ can be constructed by first building the solution $\mathcal{F}_G$ of $G = \langle X, F, \emptyset, \emptyset \rangle$. We build $\mathcal{F}_G$ and translate this solution to a real-time transition system $\mathbf{T}(\mathcal{F}_G)$, which is a lossless translation according to theorems 4, 10 and 11. Then we add transitions $x \xrightarrow{0} x'$ to $\mathbf{T}(\mathcal{F}_G)$ whenever $(x, x') \in R$, and we remove transitions $x \xrightarrow{r} x'$ whenever $r > 0$ and $x \in J$. Thus we obtain a real-time transition system $\mathcal{T}_H$, which we translate back to the hybrid-time flow system $\mathbf{F}(\mathcal{T}_H)$. The omitted part of the proof consists of showing that indeed $\mathbf{F}(\mathcal{T}_H) = \mathcal{F}_H$. Finally, it follows from theorem 3 that this hybrid-time flow system is finite-set refutable.

As a corollary, we now see that the behavior of hybrid automata is indeed finite-set refutable.

Corollary 2. *A hybrid-time flow system $\mathcal{F}$ generated by a hybrid automaton with differential inclusions that satisfy the conditions of the previous theorem, is finite-set refutable.*

6 Conclusions

We have compared the semantic frameworks of hybrid-time flow systems and real-time transition systems in order to obtain insight in the difference in abstraction level between the two. We have captured this difference in the notion of finite-set refutability, which captures a necessary and sufficient condition for lossless translation, even in the context of bisimulations. We have argued that finite-set refutability is a very reasonable condition to impose on models, since it is a result of the physical intuition that we can only distinguish systems on the basis of a finite number of observations. Finally, we have proven that a broad class of differential equations and (impuls) differential inclusions, namely those that are upper-semicontinuous and closed and convex, have a finite-set refutable set of solutions.

These results suggest that the use of real-time transition systems as a model for autonomous physical systems does not introduce additional abstractions compared to hybrid-time flows. But, when the model is still 'open' to inputs and other types of compositions, hybrid-time flow systems may lead to more precise models. In this latter case, however, another alternative is to use hybrid transition systems, with real-time paths as transition-labels. As we show in an earlier technical report [14] on this subject, the definition of finite-set refutability can be adapted to suit the translation to such hybrid transition systems, which means that no unwanted abstractions arise in the hybrid automaton theory of [2] and in the hybrid process algebras of [4,3,5].

A natural question that arises for future research, is whether a given hybrid-time flow system can be made finite-set refutable. In other words, whether there is a convenient operator that closes a system under finite-set refutability. In our counter-example of section 3, we used a non-finite-set refutable differential inclusion $\dot{x} \in \{-1, 1\}$ and its finite-set refutable closure $\dot{x} \in [-1, 1]$. Here, the closure was obtained by taking the convex hull, but in general this approach is likely to add spurious solutions as well. Note, that the given conditions on differential inclusions are only sufficient conditions. Upper-semicontinuity and closedness may not be necessary. As an example, the solutions of the differential inclusion $\dot{x} \in (-1, 1)$, with its right-hand side upper-semicontinuous and convex, but not closed, are not compact, but are still finite-set refutable. It is a consequence of theorem 7, that reachability will not be affected by finite-set refutable closure.

Based on the results in [14], we claimed that the notion of finite-set refutability is still a necessary and sufficient condition for lossless translation when the hybrid-time flow systems are not time-invariant and the real-time transition systems use absolute rather than relative timing. Naturally, the actual translations are different in that case. Note, however, that the conditions for compactness of time-variant differential inclusions are rather complex, as some of the theorems in [18] show.

Acknowledgements. The initial attempts in the direction of this paper were made as part of the Progress/STW project EES5173, and we would like to thank Paul van den Bosch, Jan Friso Groote, Maurice Heemels and Aleksander Juloski, who were a valued source of reflection during this period. We would also like to thank the anonymous reviewers of HSCC, who's comments greatly improved the final version of this paper.

References

1. Henzinger, T.A.: The theory of hybrid automata. In: Proceedings of the 11th Annual IEEE Symposium on Logic in Computer Science (LICS 1996), pp. 278–292. IEEE Computer Society Press, Los Alamitos (1996)
2. Lynch, N., Segala, R., Vaandrager, F.: Hybrid I/O automata. Information and Computation 185(1), 105–157 (2003)

3. Bergstra, J.A., Middelburg, C.A.: Process algebra for hybrid systems. Theoretical Computer Science 335, 215–280 (2005)
4. Cuijpers, P.J.L., Reniers, M.A.: Hybrid process algebra. Journal of Logic and Algebraic Programming 62, 191–245 (2005)
5. van Beek, D.A., Man, K.L., Reniers, M.A., Rooda, J.E., Schiffelers, R.R.H.: Syntax and consistent equation semantics of hybrid chi. Journal of Logic and Algebraic Programming 68, 129–210 (2006)
6. Rounds, W.C., Song, H.: The ϕ-calculus: A language for distributed control of reconfigurable embedded systems. In: Maler, O., Pnueli, A. (eds.) HSCC 2003. LNCS, vol. 2623, pp. 435–449. Springer, Heidelberg (2003)
7. Polderman, J., Willems, J.: Introduction to Mathematical Systems Theory: A Behavioural Approach. In: Texts in Applied Mathematics, vol. 26, Springer, Heidelberg (1998)
8. Aubin, J.P., Dordan, O.: Dynamical qualitative analysis of evolutionary systems. In: Tomlin, C.J., Greenstreet, M.R. (eds.) HSCC 2002. LNCS, vol. 2289, pp. 62–75. Springer, Heidelberg (2002)
9. van der Schaft, A.J., Schumacher, J.M. (eds.): An Introduction to Hybrid Dynamical Systems. Lecture Notes in Control and Information Sciences, vol. 251. Springer-Verlag, London (2000)
10. Davoren, J., Coulthard, V., Markey, N., Moor, T.: Non-deterministic temporal logics for general flow systems. In: Alur, R., Pappas, G.J. (eds.) HSCC 2004. LNCS, vol. 2993, pp. 280–295. Springer, Heidelberg (2004)
11. Aubin, J.P., Lygeros, J., Quincampoix, M., Sastry, S., Seube, N.: Impulse differential inclusions: A viability approach to hybrid systems. IEEE Transactions on Automatic Control 47, 2–20 (2002)
12. Davoren, J.M., Tabuada, P.: On simulations and bisimulation of general flow systems. In: Bemporad, A., Bicchi, A., Buttazzo, G. (eds.) HSCC 2007. LNCS, vol. 4416, pp. 145–158. Springer, Heidelberg (2007)
13. Davoren, J.M.: On hybrid systems and the modal μ-calculus. In: Antsaklis, P.J., Kohn, W., Lemmon, M.D., Nerode, A., Sastry, S.S. (eds.) HS 1997. LNCS, vol. 1567, pp. 38–69. Springer, Heidelberg (1999)
14. Cuijpers, P., Reniers, M., Heemels, W.: Hybrid transition systems. Technical Report CS-Report 02-12, TU/e, Eindhoven, Netherlands (2002)
15. Baeten, J.C.M., Middelburg, C.A.: Process Algebra with Timing. Monographs in Theoretical Computer Science. Springer, Heidelberg (2002)
16. Hennessy, M.C.B., Milner, R.: On observing nondeterminism and concurrency. In: de Bakker, J.W., van Leeuwen, J. (eds.) ICALP 1980. LNCS, vol. 85, pp. 299–309. Springer, Heidelberg (1980)
17. Haghverdi, E., Tabuada, P., Pappas, G.J.: Bisimulation relations for dynamical, control, and hybrid systems. Theoretical Computer Science 342, 229–261 (2005)
18. Smirnov, G.: Introduction to the Theory of Differential Inclusions. Graduate Studies in Mathematics. American Mathematical Society 41 (2002)

A Control Lyapunov Approach to Predictive Control of Hybrid Systems

S. Di Cairano[1], M. Lazar[2], A. Bemporad[1], and W.P.M.H. Heemels[3,*]

[1] Dip. Ingegneria dell'Informazione, Università di Siena,
Via Roma 56, 53100 Siena, Italy
{dicairano, bemporad}@dii.unisi.it
[2] Dept. of Electrical Eng.,
[3] Dept. of Mechanical Eng.,
Eindhoven Univ. of Technology,
P.O. Box 513, 5600 MB Eindhoven, The Netherlands
{m.lazar, m.heemels}@tue.nl

Abstract. In this paper we consider the stabilization of hybrid systems with both continuous and discrete dynamics via predictive control. To deal with the presence of discrete dynamics we adopt a "hybrid" control Lyapunov function approach, which consists of using two different functions. A Lyapunov-like function is designed to ensure finite-time convergence of the discrete state to a target value, while asymptotic stability of the continuous state is guaranteed via a classical local control Lyapunov function. We show that by combining these two functions in a proper manner it is no longer necessary that the control Lyapunov function for the continuous dynamics decreases at each time step. This leads to a significant reduction of conservativeness in contrast with classical Lyapunov based predictive control. Furthermore, the proposed approach also leads to a reduction of the horizon length needed for recursive feasibility with respect to standard predictive control approaches.

1 Introduction

One of the central problems in hybrid systems is the regulation to a desired operating point along with the optimization of a performance criterion. A solution to this problem that can successfully deal with the combination of discrete and continuous dynamics is provided by the model predictive control (MPC) methodology, as illustrated in [1]. One of the major challenges signaled in [1] is constrained stabilization of both continuous and discrete dynamics (in terms of convergence to a desired equilibrium). The solution to this problem presented in [1] consisted in using a terminal equality constraint for both continuous and

* The work by the authors was supported by the European Commission through the HYCON Network of Excellence, contract number FP6-IST-511368. The work by S. Di Cairano and A. Bemporad was also supported by the Italian Ministry for University and Research (MIUR) under project "Advanced control methodologies for hybrid dynamical systems" (PRIN'2005).

M. Egerstedt and B. Mishra (Eds.): HSCC 2008, LNCS 4981, pp. 130–143, 2008.

discrete states. This result was further relaxed in [2, 3] towards using a terminal inequality constraint on the continuous states. However, such relaxations were achieved in the absence of discrete states. In addition, a relatively long prediction horizon was still required for feasibility of the terminal constraints, which resulted in a high computational burden. This is a drawback, as discrete dynamics are indeed one of the fundamental features of hybrid dynamical systems (see e.g. [4, 5, 6]). Discrete dynamics can be used to represent robot tasks and sequences of operations in industrial batch processes, or computer program executions in embedded and software-enabled control systems. Therefore, predictive controllers that stabilize hybrid systems with both continuous and discrete dynamics, preferably in a numerically efficient way, are needed. While we consider stabilization of hybrid systems with discrete dynamics, stability analysis for the autonomous case was considered among the others in [6] (continuous time) and [4] (discrete time).

In this paper we build a framework for predictive control of hybrid systems with discrete dynamics (HSDD, for short), as opposed to piecewise affine systems used in [2, 3], where there are no discrete dynamics, but only a discrete static mapping. Rather than using a terminal constraint setup [7], we employ a hybrid version of the classical control Lyapunov function (CLF) notion [8] to ensure convergence and stability. For the synthesis of CLFs via optimization (including predictive control) we refer to [9, 10, 11]. However, for a general hybrid system it may be too restrictive to enforce a global control Lyapunov function defined over the continuous state only. Instead of using a global CLF defined over the continuous state only, we adopt a "hybrid" CLF defined over the whole hybrid system state and constituted of two functions. A control Lyapunov-like function for the discrete state (*discrete state CLF*) ensures finite-time convergence of the discrete state to the desired value, while asymptotic stability of the continuous state when the discrete state is reached is guaranteed by a standard local CLF (*continuous state CLF*). The main innovations are the combination of the global discrete state CLF and of the local continuous state CLF to address stabilization of hybrid systems, and the construction of the function related to the discrete dynamics, that is defined in terms of the graph distance from the current to the target discrete state over the graph associated with the finite state machine that describes the discrete dynamics. This function is required to decrease over a finite horizon, which is lower bounded by the horizon needed to perform a single transition to a discrete state "closer" to the target, and that is shorter than the horizon needed to reach the target state. Thus, the proposed strategy requires in general a shorter horizon for feasibility with respect to the approach of [1]. In contrast, the CLF associated with the continuous state is allowed *not to* decrease at each time step, until the target discrete state is reached.

The remainder of the paper is organized as follows. Section 2 presents basic definitions and notations, and the system model is defined in Section 3. Section 4 deals with the construction of the hybrid CLF, while Section 5 presents an algorithm that implements the hybrid CLF in a receding horizon control strategy. Conclusions are summarized in Section 6.

2 Preliminaries and Notation

Let $\mathbb{R}$, $\mathbb{R}_+$, $\mathbb{Z}$ and $\mathbb{Z}_+$ denote the field of real numbers, the set of non-negative reals, the set of integers and the set of non-negative integers, respectively. We use the notation $\mathbb{Z}_{\geq c_1}$ and $\mathbb{Z}_{(c_1,c_2]}$ (and similarly with $\mathbb{R}$) to denote the sets $\{k \in \mathbb{Z}_+ \mid k \geq c_1\}$ and $\{k \in \mathbb{Z}_+ \mid c_1 < k \leq c_2\}$, respectively, for some $c_1, c_2 \in \mathbb{Z}$, $c_1 < c_2$. For a set $\mathcal{S} \subseteq \mathbb{R}^n$, we denote by $\text{int}(\mathcal{S})$ its interior. By $\mathbf{0}$ and $\mathbf{1}$ we denote vectors/matrices of appropriate dimensions entirely composed of 0 and 1, respectively. The domains of the discrete state and of the discrete input are the symbolic sets $\mathcal{E} = \{\epsilon_1, \ldots, \epsilon_{n_b}\}$ and $\mathcal{E}_u = \{\epsilon_{u_1}, \ldots, \epsilon_{u_{m_b}}\}$, respectively. The Hölder p-norm of a vector $x \in \mathbb{R}^n$ is defined as $\|x\|_p \triangleq (|[x]_1|^p + \ldots + |[x]_n|^p)^{\frac{1}{p}}$, if $p \in \mathbb{Z}_{[1,\infty)}$ and $\|x\|_\infty \triangleq \max_{i=1,\ldots,n} |[x]_i|$, where $[x]_i$, $i = 1, \ldots, n$, is the i-th component of x and $|\cdot|$ is the absolute value. Let $\|\cdot\|$ denote an arbitrary p-norm.

Given a system $x(k+1) = \phi(x(k), u(k))$, an initial state $x(0)$ and an input sequence $\mathbf{u}_N = \{u(0), \ldots, u(N-1)\}$, $N \in \mathbb{Z}_{\geq 1}$, we use $\mathbf{x} = \{x(0), \ldots, x(N)\}$ to denote the sequence of states obtained by applying from the initial state $x(0)$ the input sequence $\mathbf{u}_N$. Furthermore, let $\phi^i(x(0), \mathbf{u}_i) \triangleq x(i)$, with $\phi^0(x(0), \mathbf{u}_0) \triangleq x(0)$. With some abuse of notation, when useful for clarity, we will separate the discrete and the continuous arguments of a function $f(x, u)$, i.e., given $x = [x_c^T \; x_b^T]^T$, $u = [u_c^T \; u_b^T]^T$, where x_c, u_c are the continuous components of state and input, respectively, and x_b, u_b are the discrete components of state and input, respectively, $f(x_c, x_b, u_c, u_b) \triangleq f(x, u)$.

A function $\varphi : \mathbb{R}_+ \to \mathbb{R}_+$ *belongs to class* $\mathcal{K}$ if it is continuous, strictly increasing and $\varphi(0) = 0$. It *belongs to class* $\mathcal{K}_\infty$ if $\varphi \in \mathcal{K}$ and $\varphi(s) \to \infty$ when $s \to \infty$. A function $\beta : \mathbb{R}_+ \times \mathbb{R}_+ \to \mathbb{R}_+$ *belongs to class* $\mathcal{KL}$ if for each $k \in \mathbb{R}_+$, $\beta(\cdot, k) \in \mathcal{K}$ and for each $s \in \mathbb{R}_+$, $\beta(s, \cdot)$ is non-increasing and $\lim_{k\to\infty} \beta(s, k) = 0$.

2.1 Stability Notions

Consider the discrete-time nonlinear system described by the difference inclusion

$$x(k+1) \in \Phi_c(x(k)), \quad k \in \mathbb{Z}_+, \tag{1}$$

where $x(k) \in \mathbb{R}^n$ is the state at the discrete-time instant k. The mapping $\Phi_c : \mathbb{R}^n \rightrightarrows \mathbb{R}^n$ is an arbitrary nonlinear, possibly discontinuous, set-valued function. We assume that the origin is an equilibrium in (1), i.e. $\Phi_c(0) = \{0\}$.

Definition 1. *We call a set* $\mathcal{P} \subseteq \mathbb{R}^n$ positively invariant (PI) *for system* (1) *if for all* $x \in \mathcal{P}$ *it holds that* $\Phi_c(x) \subseteq \mathcal{P}$.

Next, we state a regional version of the global asymptotic stability property presented in [12, Chapter 4] along with sufficient stabilization conditions.

Definition 2. *Let* $\mathbb{X}$ *with* $0 \in \text{int}(\mathbb{X})$ *be a subset of* $\mathbb{R}^n$. *We call system* (1) asymptotically stable (AS) in $\mathbb{X}$ *if there exists a* $\mathcal{KL}$*-function* $\beta(\cdot, \cdot)$ *such that, for each* $x(0) \in \mathbb{X}$, *it holds that all corresponding state trajectories of* (1) *satisfy* $\|x(k)\| \leq \beta(\|x(0)\|, k)$, $\forall k \in \mathbb{Z}_{\geq 1}$.

Theorem 1. *Let* $\mathbb{X}$ *be a PI set for* (1), *with* $0 \in \text{int}(\mathbb{X})$. *Furthermore, let* $\alpha_1, \alpha_2 \in \mathcal{K}_\infty$, $\rho \in \mathbb{R}_{[0,1)}$ *and let* $V : \mathbb{R}^n \to \mathbb{R}_+$ *be a function such that:*

$$\alpha_1(\|x\|) \leq V(x) \leq \alpha_2(\|x\|) \tag{2a}$$

$$V(x^+) \leq \rho V(x) \tag{2b}$$

for all $x \in \mathbb{X}$ *and all* $x^+ \in \Phi_c(x)$. *Then the system* (1) *is AS in* $\mathbb{X}$.

The proof of Theorem 1 is similar in nature to the proof given in [12, 11] by replacing the difference *equation* with the difference *inclusion* as in (1) and is omitted here for brevity. We call a function $V(\cdot)$ that satisfies the hypothesis of Theorem 1 a *Lyapunov function.*

Consider the system with discrete dynamics

$$x(k+1) = \Phi_b(x(k)), \quad k \in \mathbb{Z}_+, \tag{3}$$

where $\mathcal{E} = \{\epsilon_1, \ldots, \epsilon_{n_b}\}$ is a symbolic set, $x(k) \in \mathcal{E}$ is the state and $\Phi_b : \mathcal{E} \to \mathcal{E}$ is an arbitrary function.

Definition 3. *Let* $x^e \in \mathcal{E}$ *denote a desired target state. We call system* (3) *convergent (with respect to* x^e*) if for all* $x(0) \in \mathcal{E}$ *there exists a* $\bar{k}(x(0)) \in \mathbb{Z}_{\geq 1}$ *such that* $\Phi_b(x(k)) = x^e$ *for all* $k \in \mathbb{Z}_{\geq \bar{k}(x(0))}$.

Consider now the discrete-time system described by the difference equation

$$x(k+1) = \phi_c(x(k), u(k)), \tag{4}$$

where $x(k) \in \mathbb{X} \subseteq \mathbb{R}^n$ is the state, $u(k) \in \mathbb{U} \subseteq \mathbb{R}^m$ is the control input at the discrete-time instant k, and $\phi_c : \mathbb{X} \times \mathbb{U} \to \mathbb{R}^n$ is an arbitrary nonlinear function, possibly discontinuous. We assume $0 \in \text{int}(\mathbb{X})$, $0 \in \text{int}(\mathbb{U})$, and $\phi_c(0,0) = 0$.

Definition 4. *A function* $V : \mathbb{R}^n \to \mathbb{R}_+$ *that satisfies* (2a) *and for which there exists* $\rho \in \mathbb{R}_{[0,1)}$ *such that* $\forall x \in \mathbb{X}$, *there exists a control input* $u \in \mathbb{U}$ *for which*

$$V(\phi_c(x, u)) \leq \rho V(x),$$

is called a Control Lyapunov function (CLF) for system (4).

2.2 Graph Notions

We consider systems with discrete state dynamics defined by a finite state machine, and we employ a directed graph representation for the finite state machine. We introduce here some graph theory notions, that will be used to define the CLF-like function related to the discrete dynamics.

Let $G = (V, E, C)$ be a labelled directed graph, where $V = \{v_1, \ldots, v_s\}$ is the set of *nodes*, and $E \subseteq (V \times V)$ is the set of edges. We indicate by $e_{ij} = (v_i, v_j)$ the edge from node v_i to node v_j, and the label function C associates a positive value to each existing edge, i.e. $C : E \to \mathbb{R}_+$, $C(e_{ij}) = c_{ij}$, and $c_{ii} = 0$, for $i \in \mathbb{Z}_{[1,s]}$. An often employed definition of distance between elements of discrete sets is the *discrete distance* [6], that is $d(v_i, v_j) = 0$ if $i = j$, and $d(v_i, v_j) = 1$, otherwise. Even though this is a proper distance function definition[1], it is not very useful for control problems, since all the discrete states (except the target state itself) appear to be equally far from the target discrete state, and there is no concept of progress with respect to getting "closer" to the target. Thus, we consider a different notion of distance, the *graph distance*.

Definition 5. *Given a directed graph $G = (V, E, C)$, the one-step distance from v_i to v_j, $d_{v_i v_j} \in \mathbb{Z}_+$, is $d_{v_i v_j} = c_{ij}$, if $e_{ij} \in E$, and $d_{v_i v_j} = \infty$, otherwise.*

Definition 6. *Given a directed graph $G = (V, E, C)$, a graph path that starts at v_r and ends at v_s is a sequence of vertices $\tau = \{\nu^{(1)}, \ldots, \nu^{(\ell)}\}$, where $\nu^{(j)} \in V$, for $j \in \mathbb{Z}_{[1,\ell]}$, $(\nu^{(j)}, \nu^{(j+1)}) \in E$, for $j \in \mathbb{Z}_{[1,\ell-1]}$, and $\nu^{(1)} = v_r$, $\nu^{(\ell)} = v_s$. The length of the path is $\mathcal{L}(\tau) \triangleq \sum_{j=1}^{\ell-1} d_{\nu^{(j)}\nu^{(j+1)}}$.*

Definition 7. *Given a directed graph $G = (V, E, C)$, the graph distance between $v_r, v_s \in V$, is the length of the shortest path between them, $d(v_r, v_s) \triangleq \min_{\tau \in \mathcal{T}_{r,s}} \mathcal{L}(\tau)$, where $\mathcal{T}_{r,s}$ is the set of graph paths from v_r to v_s. In the case there is no path between v_r and v_s, $d(v_r, v_s) \triangleq \infty$.*

The graph distance is a proper distance function on undirected graphs, but it lacks the symmetry property on directed graphs, since in general $d(v_i, v_j) \neq d(v_j, v_i)$. Hence, it is a *pseudo-distance.* However, as we will see, this does not affect the problem we consider. In this paper we use $c_{ij} = 1$, $\forall (v_i, v_j) \in E$, that recovers the distance on unlabelled graphs. Once the one-step distances are known, the graph distance $d(v_i, v_j)$, for all $v_i, v_j \in V$ can be computed offline, for instance through a graph search based on Dijkstra's algorithm [13].

3 Reference Model and Problem Formulation

We consider a hybrid dynamical system, with both continuous and discrete states and inputs. The system dynamics are defined by

$$x(k+1) = \begin{bmatrix} x_c(k+1) \\ x_b(k+1) \end{bmatrix} = \begin{bmatrix} \phi_c(x(k), u(k)) \\ \phi_b(x(k), u(k)) \end{bmatrix} = \phi(x(k), u(k)), \tag{5}$$

where $\phi : \mathbb{X} \times \mathbb{U} \to \mathbb{X}$, $\mathbb{X} \subseteq \mathbb{R}^n \times \mathcal{E}$, $\mathbb{U} \subseteq \mathbb{R}^m \times \mathcal{E}_u$ is an arbitrary mapping, $\phi_c(\cdot)$ is the continuous state update function, and $\phi_b(\cdot)$ is the discrete state update function. The sets $\mathbb{X}$ and $\mathbb{U}$ represent physical constraints on state and input vectors, and are assumed to be bounded. Here, the state and input constraints are independent from each other.

Remark 1. $\mathbb{X} = \bigcup_{\epsilon_i \in \mathcal{E}} \mathcal{X}_h(\epsilon_i)$ where $\mathcal{X}_h(\epsilon_i) \triangleq \{x \in \mathbb{X} : x_b = \epsilon_i\}$. The set $\mathcal{X}_c(\epsilon_i) \triangleq \{x_c \in \mathbb{R}^n : \left[\begin{smallmatrix} x_c \\ \epsilon_i \end{smallmatrix}\right] \in \mathbb{X}\}$ is the set of continuous states compatible with discrete state ϵ_i. In [6], $\mathcal{X}_c(\epsilon_i)$ is referred to as the *domain of discrete state* ϵ_i.

[1] Such a definition has nonnegativity, symmetry, and triangle inequality properties.

We assume that the discrete state update function can be represented in the form of a finite state machine, with states $\{\epsilon_1, \ldots, \epsilon_{n_b}\}$ and with transitions $T \subseteq \mathcal{E} \times \mathcal{E}$. Such a finite state machine can be represented as a directed graph where $V \equiv \mathcal{E}$ and $E \equiv T$. The discrete state transitions are affected by the system input and by the continuous state. At time $k \in \mathbb{Z}_+$, if *(i)* $x_b(k) = \epsilon_i$ and *(ii)* $\mathcal{G}_{ij}(x_c, u) = 1$, where the functions $\mathcal{G}_{ij} : \mathcal{X}_c(\epsilon_i) \times \mathbb{U} \to \{0,1\}$, $i, j = 1, \ldots, n_b$, are called *transition guards*, then $x_b(k+1) = \epsilon_j$. In (5), the transition guards are embedded in $\phi_b(\cdot)$. The discrete state affects the continuous dynamics, since x_b modifies the vector field $\phi_c(\cdot)$. We assume that (5) is well posed, i.e., for any $(x, u) \in \mathbb{X} \times \mathbb{U}$, $\phi(x, u)$ is uniquely defined.

An example of a fairly general class of hybrid systems that can be modeled by (5) is the class of discrete hybrid automata [14]. Consider now an autonomous version of system (5), i.e.

$$x(k+1) = \begin{bmatrix} x_c(k+1) \\ x_b(k+1) \end{bmatrix} = \begin{bmatrix} \Phi_c(x(k)) \\ \Phi_b(x(k)) \end{bmatrix} = \Phi(x(k)). \tag{6}$$

Let $x^e = [x_c^{eT} \; x_b^{eT}]^T$ be an equilibrium for (6) (i.e. $\Phi(x^e) = x^e$) and for any $\mathcal{X} \subseteq \mathcal{X}_h(x_b^e)$ define $\bar{\mathcal{X}}_c \triangleq \{x_c \in \mathbb{R}^n : \left[\begin{smallmatrix} x_c \\ x_b^e \end{smallmatrix}\right] \in \mathcal{X}\}$, $\bar{\mathcal{X}}_c \subseteq \mathcal{X}_c(x_b^e)$.

Definition 8. *The hybrid system* (6) *is called* globally asymptotically stable *if there exists a positively invariant set* $\mathcal{X} \subseteq \mathcal{X}_h(x_b^e)$ *for* (6) *with* $x^e \in \mathcal{X}$ *such that for any initial state, the system state converges to* $\mathcal{X}$ *in finite time, and the continuous state dynamics* $x_c(k+1) = \Phi_c(x_c(k), x_b^e)$ *is asymptotically stable in* $\bar{\mathcal{X}}_c$ *(with respect to* $x_c^e \in \mathrm{int}(\bar{\mathcal{X}}_c)$*).*

Definition 8 combines global convergence of the discrete dynamics with local AS in $\bar{\mathcal{X}}_c$ of the continuous dynamics, to obtain a stability-like property for HSDD. This property includes global convergence to x_c^e. The problem considered in this paper can be formulated as follows.

Problem 1. Feedback Control Design Problem: Given a desired equilibrium $x^e \in \mathbb{X}$ for system (5) with steady-state input $u^e \in \mathbb{U}$ (i.e, $\phi(x^e, u^e) = x^e$), synthesize a control law $u(k) = \pi(x(k))$ such that $u(k) \in \mathbb{U}$, $x(k) \in \mathbb{X}$, $\forall k \in \mathbb{Z}_+$ and HSDD in closed-loop with $u(k) = \pi(x(k))$ is globally asymptotically stable in the sense of Definition 8.

In this paper we employ the CLF framework in combination with predictive control to obtain a solution to Problem 1. Let $V(\cdot)$ be a CLF for the continuous dynamics $x_c(k+1) = \phi_c(x_c(k), x_b, u_c(k), u_b(k))$, for all $x_b \in \mathcal{E}$. Then, according to Theorem 1 and Definition 8, it is sufficient to have a feasible control input $u(k)$ at each time $k \in \mathbb{Z}_+$ such that the discrete dynamics $\phi_b(x_c(k), x_b(k), u_c(k), u_b(k))$ converge in finite time to x_b^e and remains there. However, asking the CLF for the continuous dynamics to decrease at each time step $k \in \mathbb{Z}_+$ for all the values of x_b can be overconservative in the hybrid system setting, and it may collide with the objective of steering the discrete state to the target value. This is what may happen for instance in a system with hysteresis such as the one in [5, Example 3.1].

Even for simple hybrid systems it may be impossible to obtain a continuous state CLF on the whole hybrid state space. Rather, to achieve stability, it would be sufficient to keep the continuous state trajectory bounded while the discrete state converges, and have a local continuous state CLF only for the dynamics associated to the target discrete state. To design a control law that yields such a closed-loop behavior, we propose a "hybrid" CLF consisting of two CLF-like functions that depend on each other. More precisely, instead of using a single standard CLF, we exploit the hybrid structure of the problem which consists of two objectives: (*i*) the convergence to the target discrete state; (*ii*) the stabilization of the continuous state while keeping the discrete state at its target value. These objectives are consistent with the existence of two functions, namely $\psi : \mathbb{X} \times \mathbb{U}^N \to \mathbb{Z}_+$ and $V : \mathbb{R}^n \to \mathbb{R}_+$, that satisfy

$$\begin{cases} \psi(x(k), \mathbf{u}_N(k)) < \psi(x(k-1), \mathbf{u}_N(k-1)), \\ V(\phi_c(x(k), u(k))) \leq \rho V(x_c(k)) + M_c \end{cases} \quad \text{if } x_b(k) \neq x_b^e \tag{7a}$$

$$\begin{cases} \psi(x(k), \mathbf{u}_N(k)) \leq \psi(x(k-1), \mathbf{u}_N(k-1)), \\ V(\phi_c(x(k), u(k))) \leq \rho V(x_c(k)), \end{cases} \quad \text{if } x_b(k) = x_b^e \tag{7b}$$

where $\rho \in \mathbb{R}_{[0,1)}$, $M_c \in \mathbb{R}_+$, $V(\cdot)$ is a control Lyapunov function only on the set $\mathcal{P}(x_b^e) = \{x_c \in \mathbb{R}^n : \left[\begin{smallmatrix} x_c \\ x_b^e \end{smallmatrix}\right] \in \mathbb{X}, \ \exists u \in \mathbb{U}, \ \phi_b(x, u) = x_b\}$, and $\psi(\cdot)$ is a CLF-like function that enforces convergence of the discrete state.

4 Synthesis and Properties of the Hybrid CLF

In what follows we show how to synthesize the functions in (7).

4.1 Control Lyapunov Function on the Continuous State

We first design the local CLF on the continuous state according to (7). Let $V : \mathbb{R}^n \to \mathbb{R}_+$ be a CLF for dynamics $x(k+1) = \phi_c(x_c(k), u_c(k), x_b^e, u_b^e)$ in the set $\mathcal{X}_c(x_b^e)$ accordingly to Definition 4. Such a CLF is a relaxed version of a global CLF, since (2b) must hold only in $\mathcal{X}_c(x_b^e)$.

Assumption 1. *For all $x \in \mathcal{X}_h(x^e)$ there exists an input $u \in \mathbb{U}$ such that $V(\phi_c(x, u)) \leq \rho V(x_c)$, and $\phi(x, u) \in \mathcal{X}_h(x^e)$.*

Assumption 1 states that there exists a feasible control law according to the CLF which makes the set $\mathcal{X}_h(x^e)$ positively invariant for the closed-loop dynamics. This only requires that when the discrete state reaches the target, it remains there, which is in general less conservative than requiring the invariance of a generic set $\mathcal{X} \subseteq \mathbb{X} = \bigcup_{\epsilon_i \in \mathcal{E}} \mathcal{X}_h(\epsilon_i)$ containing different dynamics and different discrete states. Assumption 1 can be guaranteed a priori by constraining the continuous state to lie in a pre-defined set of the state space. The tools developed in [11] can be used for this purpose.

4.2 Control Lyapunov-Like Function on the Discrete State

Given the finite state machine representation of function $\phi_b(\cdot)$, we can associate to it a directed graph, where the node v_j is associated to the state ϵ_j. Hence, the distance from ϵ_j to x_b^e can be computed as the distance from v_j to the node corresponding to x_b^e, as defined in Section 2.2. Given a state x, an input sequence $\mathbf{u}_N$, and a target discrete state x_b^e define

$$\psi(x, \mathbf{u}_N) \triangleq \sum_{j=1}^{N} d(\phi_b^j(x, \mathbf{u}_j), x_b^e). \tag{8}$$

Let $h_{x_b^e}(\cdot)$ be the indicator function of the target discrete state, i.e., $h_{x_b^e}(x_b^e) = 1$, and $h_{x_b^e}(x_b) = 0$, for $x_b \neq x_b^e$. For any $k \in \mathbb{Z}_+$ define the *cumulative discrete distance contraction* (CDDC)

$$\psi(x(k), \mathbf{u}_N(k)) - \psi(x(k-1), \mathbf{u}_N(k-1)) \leq -1 + h_{x_b^e}(x_b(k)). \tag{9}$$

Constraint (9) is obtained as a relaxation of the discrete distance contraction constraint $d(\phi_b(x(k), u), x_b^e) < d(x_b(k), x_b^e)$, that requires that at each step the distance to the target discrete state decreases. In general, this constraint will generate infeasibility, because it is not possible that the discrete distance decreases at every step. CDDC (9) relaxes the discrete distance contraction constraint requiring that the sum of the discrete distances along the predicted trajectory at time k is smaller than the one along the predicted trajectory at time $k-1$. The effect of the indicator function $h_{x_b^e}(\cdot)$ is to further relax the constraint when $x_b(k) = x_b^e$. Constraint (9) forces the cumulative discrete distance to decrease until $x_b(k) = x_b^e$ implementing the first inequality of (7a), after which $\psi(x(k), \mathbf{u}_N(k))$ is kept constant. The value $\psi(x(-1), \mathbf{u}_N(-1))$ initializes (9). To achieve feasibility it can be set to a large number, while a more efficient initialization value is proposed later in this section. In what follows we use the shorthand notation $\psi(i) \triangleq \psi(x(i), \mathbf{u}_N(i))$, for $i \in \mathbb{Z}_+$. We show that under suitable assumptions this constraint is feasible and steers the discrete state to the target value in finite time.

Assumption 2. *Given a target state $x^e \in \mathbb{X}$ and given any discrete initial state $x_b = \epsilon_i \neq x_b^e$, there exists a finite value $n_i \in \mathbb{Z}_+$ such that for any initial state $x \in \mathcal{X}_h(\epsilon_i)$, there exists $\epsilon_j \in \mathcal{E}$ and an input sequence $\mathbf{u}_{\ell_i} \in \mathbb{U}^{\ell_i}$, such that $\ell_i \leq n_i$, $\phi^h(x, \mathbf{u}_h) \in \mathbb{X}$, $\phi_b^h(x, \mathbf{u}_h) = \epsilon_i$, $h \in \mathbb{Z}_{[1,\ell_i-1]}$, and $\phi_b^{\ell_i}(x, \mathbf{u}_{\ell_i}) = \epsilon_j$, where $d(\epsilon_j, x_b^e) < d(\epsilon_i, x_b^e)$.*

Definition 9. *Given $x_b = \epsilon_i \neq x_b^e$, the minimum discrete distance progress horizon $\bar{n}_i \in \mathbb{Z}_+$ for discrete state ϵ_i is the minimum value for which Assumption 2 holds for discrete state ϵ_i. For $x_b^e = \epsilon_{\bar{\imath}}$, define $\bar{n}_{\bar{\imath}} \triangleq 1$.*

Assumption 2 requires that given any valid discrete state different from the target, for any continuous state in its domain, there exists a feasible trajectory that brings the discrete state closer to the target discrete state in n_i time steps, which is a sort of finite-time discrete reachability property. The minimum length of input sequences that guarantees such a property is the *minimum discrete progress horizon*, the minimum horizon needed to see the discrete state approaching the target. A (possibly over-approximated) value of $\bar{n}_i$ can be computed by offline reachability analysis.

Note that Assumption 2 requires the existence of a horizon such that the discrete state gets closer to the target discrete state. This is in general less conservative (and requires a shorter horizon) than the condition in [1], which requires the existence of a (finite) horizon such that the target state is reached.

Assumption 3. *For any $x \in \mathcal{X}_h(x_b^e)$, the set $\{u \in \mathcal{U}_f(x) : \phi_b(x,u) = x_b^e\}$ is non-empty, where $\mathcal{U}_f(x) = \{u \in \mathbb{U} : \phi(x,u) \in \mathbb{X}\}$.*

Assumption 2 and 3 are reachability assumptions. Assumption 2 is a finite-time discrete reachability. Assumption 3 requires that for any state value in which the discrete state is at the target, there exists a feasible input that keeps the discrete state constant.

Lemma 1. *Under Assumptions 2 and 3, given $x(k) \in \mathbb{X}$ and a target discrete state x_b^e, for any $M \in \mathbb{Z}_+$, there exists $\mathbf{u}_M \in \mathbb{U}^M$, such that $\phi^i(x(k), \mathbf{u}_i) \in \mathbb{X}$, for $i \in \mathbb{Z}_{[1,M]}$, and $d(\phi_b^{i+1}(x(k), \mathbf{u}_{i+1}), x_b^e) \leq d(\phi_b^i(x(k), \mathbf{u}_i), x_b^e)$, for $i \in \mathbb{Z}_{[0,M-1]}$.*

Proof. Consider the case $x(k) \in \mathcal{X}_h(x_b^e)$. By Assumption 3 there exists $u \in \mathcal{U}_f(x)$ such that $x_b(k+1) = \phi_b(x(k), u(k)) = x_b^e$, hence $d(x_b(k+1), x_b^e) = d(x_b(k), x_b^e)$. Consider the case $x(k) \notin \mathcal{X}_h(x_b^e)$. By Definition 7 and Assumption 2 there exists an input sequence $\mathbf{u}_\ell \in \mathbb{U}^\ell$ such that $\phi_b^i(x(k), \mathbf{u}_i) = x_b(k)$, for $i \in \mathbb{Z}_{[0,\ell-1]}$, and $d(\phi_b^\ell(x(k), \mathbf{u}_\ell), x_b^e) < d(x_b(k), x_b^e)$. In the case $\phi_b^\ell(x(k), \mathbf{u}_\ell) \neq x_b^e$ the procedure can be repeated. In the case $\phi_b^\ell(x(k), \mathbf{u}_\ell) = x_b^e$, we have already proven that there exists $u \in \mathcal{U}_f(x)$ that keeps the discrete state at the target. □

Consider now the system formed by (5) in closed loop with a control law obtained by solving a finite horizon (N) optimization problem (e.g., as done in predictive control) with the constraint (9) added. Suppose that at each time step a sequence of N inputs is computed and only the first element of the sequence is applied to system (5). We show next that constraint (9) is initially feasible and remains feasible at all future time instants under suitable assumptions. The complete control algorithm will be defined later in Section 5, as the following result does not depend on it.

Theorem 2. *Suppose Assumptions 2 and 3 hold. Given a target discrete state x_b^e and any initial state $x(0) \in \mathbb{X}$, let the prediction horizon be $N \geq \max_{\{i:\epsilon_i \in \mathcal{E}\}} \bar{n}_i$, and $\psi(-1) \triangleq Nd(x_b(0), x_b^e)$. Then, (i) constraint (9) is feasible for all $k \in \mathbb{Z}_+$, and (ii) there exists a finite $\bar{k} \in \mathbb{Z}_+$ such that $x_b(k) = x_b^e$, $\forall k \in \mathbb{Z}_{\geq \bar{k}}$.*

Proof. (*i*). Assumption 3 guarantees the constraint feasibility for $x_b(k) = x_b^e$. Due to $N \geq \max_{i:\epsilon_i \in \mathcal{E}} \bar{n}_i$ and by Assumption 2, we have that at $k = 0$ there exists a feasible input sequence $\mathbf{u}_N(0)$ and an index $\bar{\jmath} \in \mathbb{Z}_{[1,N]}$ such that for $j \in \mathbb{Z}_{[0,\bar{\jmath}-1]}$, $\phi_b^j(x(0), \mathbf{u}_j(0)) = x_b(0)$, $d(\phi_b^{\bar{\jmath}}(x(0), \mathbf{u}_j(0)), x_b^e) < d(x_b(0), x_b^e)$ and for $j \in \mathbb{Z}_{[\bar{j}+1,N]}$, $d(\phi_b^j(x(0), \mathbf{u}_j(0)), x_b^e) \leq d(\phi_b^{\bar{j}}(x(0), \mathbf{u}_j(0)), x_b^e)$, by Lemma 1. Hence, constraint (9) is feasible at $k = 0$.

For $k \geq 1$, we have $\psi(k-1) = \sum_{j=1}^{N} d(\phi_b^j(x(k-1), \mathbf{u}_j(k-1)), x_b^e)$ and $x_b(k) = \phi_b^1(x(k-1), \mathbf{u}_1(k-1))$. By Lemma 1, there exists $\mathbf{u}_N(k)$ such that

$$\psi(k) \leq \psi(k-1) - d(x_b(k), x_b^e) + d(\phi_b^N(x(k-1), \mathbf{u}_N(k-1)), x_b^e).$$

If $d(\phi_b(x(k-1), \mathbf{u}_N(k-1)), x_b^e) < d(\phi_b^1(x(k-1), \mathbf{u}_1(k-1)), x_b^e)$, (9) is feasible. If for all $j \in \mathbb{Z}_{[1,N]}$, $\phi_b^j(x(k-1), \mathbf{u}_j(k-1)) = x_b(k-1)$, then by the choice of N, there exists $\mathbf{u}_{\bar{j}}(k) \in \mathbb{U}^{\bar{j}}$, $\bar{j} \leq N$, such that, $d(\phi_b^{\bar{j}}(x(k), \mathbf{u}_{\bar{j}}(k)), x_b^e) < d(\phi_b^1(x(k-1), \mathbf{u}_1(k-1)), x_b^e)$. If needed, the input sequence can be extended to length N enforcing $d(\phi_b^j(x(k), \mathbf{u}_j(k)), x_b^e) \leq d(\phi_b^{\bar{j}}(x(k), \mathbf{u}_{\bar{j}}(k)), x_b^e)$, for $j \in \mathbb{Z}_{[\bar{j}+1,N]}$, as guaranteed by Lemma 1. Such an input sequence is feasible with respect to (9).

(ii). We prove that there exists $\bar{k}$ such that $x_b(\bar{k}) = x_b^e$ by contradiction. Suppose $x_b(k) \neq x_b^e$, for $k \in \mathbb{Z}_+$ and note that by definition $\psi(\cdot) \geq 0$. From *(i)*, for all k such that $x_b(k) \neq x_b^e$, $\Delta\psi(k) \triangleq \psi(k) - \psi(k-1) \leq -1$. Hence,

$$\psi(k) = \psi(0) + \sum_{j=1}^{k} \Delta\psi(j) \leq \psi(0) - k.$$

Thus, $0 \leq \lim_{k\to\infty} \psi(k) \leq \lim_{k\to\infty} \psi(0) - k$. Since $\psi(0)$ is finite, we reached a contradiction. For $k \geq \bar{k}$, (9) guarantees that $x_b(k) = x_b(\bar{k})$. □

5 Stabilizing Predictive Control of HSDD

We propose now a mixed integer linear formulation of the hybrid CLF constraints (7) which can be included in an optimization problem. For computational purposes, we model the discrete state and input of the hybrid system by Boolean vectors. In detail, $u_b \in \{0,1\}^{m_b}$, and we model the discrete state by *one-hot encoding*, i.e., $[x_b]_i \in \{0,1\}$ and $\sum_i [x_b]_i = 1$. In this way, the symbolic variable ϵ_j is represented by the jth unitary vector of $\mathbb{R}^{n_b}$, the vector entirely composed of 0, except for the jth coordinate, which is 1. As a consequence $\mathcal{E}$ is the set of the unitary vectors on $\mathbb{R}^{n_b}$, where n_b is the cardinality of $\mathcal{E}$.

Consider first the function $\psi(\cdot)$. For a given x_b^e, for all $x_b \in \mathcal{E}$, we have

$$d(x_b, x_b^e) = D_{x_b^e}^T x_b, \tag{10}$$

where $D_{x_b^e} \in \mathbb{Z}_+^{n_b}$ is a vector whose i^{th} component is equal to the graph distance from $x_b = \epsilon_i$ to x_b^e. The indicator function $h_{x_b^e}(\cdot)$ can be expressed by

$$h_{x_b^e}(x_b) = \left(1 - \frac{1}{2} H^T \cdot (x_b - x_b^e)\right), \tag{11}$$

where[2] $H = \left(\sum_{j=1, j\neq i}^{n_b} \epsilon_j\right) - \epsilon_i$. Since $H^T \cdot (x_b - x_b^e) = 0$, if $x_b = x_b^e$, and $H^T \cdot (x_b - x_b^e) = 2$, otherwise, (11) implements the desired indicator function.

[2] There are several other definitions of H that obtain the desired behavior. However, we find (11) the most intuitive one.

As a result, via (10) and (11) constraint (9) can be formulated as a set of mixed-integer linear inequalities.

In order to also implement the constraints involving the local CLF on the continuous state via mixed-integer linear inequalities we consider a Lyapunov function defined using the infinity norm, i.e. $V(x_c) = \|Px_c\|_\infty$ for some $P \in \mathbb{R}^{p\times n}$ with full column rank. The constraint on the CLF can be expressed as

$$V(\phi_c^1(x(k)), \mathbf{u}_1) \leq \rho V(x_c(k)) + \frac{M_c}{2} H^T(x_b(k) - x_b^e) \tag{12}$$

where $\rho \in \mathbb{R}_{[0,1)}$, $M_c \in \mathbb{R}_{>0}$ and the rightmost term is responsible for relaxing the constraint when $x_b \neq x_b^e$. Note that, since $\mathbb{X}$ is bounded, we can set $M_c = \max_{x\in\mathbb{X}} V(x_c)$. In this way, constraint (12) can be formulated as a set of mixed-integer linear constraints that ensure that x_c remains bounded when $x_b \neq x_b^e$, while, when $x_b = x_b^e$, ensure that $V(\cdot)$ is a CLF restricted to $\mathcal{X}_c(x_b^e)$.

Given $x(k)$, let $\Gamma(x(k)) = \{\mathbf{u}_N \in \mathbb{U}^N : \phi^i(x(k), \mathbf{u}_i) \in \mathbb{X},\ i \in \mathbb{Z}_{[1,N]},\ (9), (12)\}$ be the set of feasible input sequences, and $\gamma(x(k)) = \{u(0) \in \mathbb{U} : \mathbf{u}_N \in \Gamma(x(k))\}$. The system obtained by (5) in closed-loop with $\gamma(x(k))$ is described, with some abuse of notation, by the difference inclusion

$$x(k+1) \in \phi(x(k), \gamma(x(k))) \triangleq \{\phi(x(k), u) : u \in \gamma(x(k))\}. \tag{13}$$

Theorem 3. *Suppose Assumption 1 and the assumptions of Theorem 2 hold, and set* $M_c = \max_{x\in\mathbb{X}} V(x_c)$. *Then, the closed-loop system described by* (13) *is asymptotically stable in the sense of Definition 8.*

Proof. By Theorem 2 for any sequence $\{u(k)\}_{k=0}^{\infty}$, where $u(k) \in \gamma(x(k))$ for all $k \in \mathbb{Z}_+$, there exists $\bar{k} \in \mathbb{Z}_+$ such that for all $k \geq \bar{k}$, $x_b(k) = x_b^e$. By assumption $\mathbb{X}$ is bounded, hence $M_c = \max_{x\in\mathbb{X}} V(x)$ is finite. Thus, during the time interval $k \in \mathbb{Z}_{[0,\bar{k}-1]}$, since $x_c(k) \in \mathbb{X}$, constraint (12) is satisfied. For $k \geq \bar{k}$ constraint (9) is still feasible by Theorem 2 and it ensures that the discrete state remains at the target. In this case, recursive feasibility of (12) is guaranteed by Assumption 1 and thus, $V(\cdot)$ satisfies inequality (2b) for all $k \geq \bar{k}$. Hence, from Theorem 1 we obtain asymptotic stability of the continuous dynamics in the set $\mathcal{X}_c(x_b^e)$, and the result follows from Definition 8, with $\mathcal{X} = \mathcal{X}_h(x_b^e)$. □

As a consequence of Definition 8, Theorem 3 guarantees convergence to the desired equilibrium for any initial state. Even though the stabilizing properties established in Theorem 3 are guaranteed for any feasible control input, not just for the optimal one, a cost function can be considered to select a $u(k) \in \gamma(x(k))$ that optimizes performance. We introduce now an optimization-based receding horizon control strategy for system (5). Notice that there is no need to keep ρ and M_c fixed in (12). Instead, we will optimize over these two variables which results in improved convergence of the continuous state, when allowed by the condition on the discrete state. Let ρ be the constant that satisfies (12), choose $\bar{\rho} \in \mathbb{R}_{[\rho,1)}$ and let $\eta \in \mathbb{R}_{[0,\bar{\rho}]}$ and $M \in \mathbb{R}_+$ be two additional variables that play the role of ρ and M_c, respectively. Consider the cost function

$$J(x, \mathbf{u}_N, M, \eta) \triangleq w_\eta \eta + w_M M + F(\phi^N(x, \mathbf{u}_N)) + \sum_{i=0}^{N-1} L(\phi^i(x, \mathbf{u}_i), u(i)), \tag{14}$$

where $F(\cdot)$ and $L(\cdot)$ denote suitable terminal and stage costs, respectively, as in standard MPC [7]. The term $w_\eta \eta$, where $w_\eta \in \mathbb{R}_+$, optimizes the reduction of the CLF, while $w_M M$, where $w_M \in \mathbb{R}_{>0}$ penalizes the relaxation of (12) for $x_b(k) \neq x_b^e$. Whenever $M = 0$ the continuous state evolves satisfying (2b).

Algorithm 1. *(Receding Horizon Control of HSDD)*
Initialization. *Set $k = 0$, measure $x(0) \in \mathbb{X}$ and set $\psi(k-1) = N\, D_{x_b^e}^T x_b(0)$.*
Step 1. *Solve the optimization problem*

$$\min_{\mathbf{u}_N, M, \eta} J(x(k), \mathbf{u}_N, M, \eta) \tag{15a}$$

$$\text{s.t.}: \ \mathbf{u}_N \in \mathbb{U}^N,\ \phi^i(x, \mathbf{u}_i) \in \mathbb{X},\ i \in \mathbb{Z}_{[1,N]} \tag{15b}$$

$$M \geq 0,\ \eta \in \mathbb{R}_{[0,\bar{\rho}]} \tag{15c}$$

$$V(\phi_c^1(x(k)), \mathbf{u}_1) \leq \eta V(x_c(k)) + \frac{M}{2} H^T(x_b(k) - x_b^e) \tag{15d}$$

$$\sum_{i=1}^{N} D_{x_b^e}^T \phi^i(x, \mathbf{u}_i) \leq \psi(k-1) - 1 + \left(1 - \frac{1}{2} H^T(x_b - x_b^e)\right). \tag{15e}$$

Step 2. *Let $\bar{\mathbf{u}}_N = \{\bar{u}(0), \ldots, \bar{u}(N)\}$ be a feasible solution of problem* (15) *obtained by minimizing with respect to* (15a) *(possibly, but not necessarily, the optimal one). Set $u(k) = \bar{u}(0)$, and $\psi(k) = \sum_{i=1}^N D_{x_b^e}^T \phi^i(x, \bar{\mathbf{u}}_i)$.*
Step 3. *Set $k \leftarrow k+1$, measure $x(k)$ and go to Step* 1.

Algorithm 1 implements the constraints on the hybrid CLF and minimizes the performance criterion (14). Minimization of the cost (14) ensures finite values of M, and $\eta \leq \bar{\rho} < 1$. Thus, the result of Theorem 3 still applies.

From a computational point of view, constraint (15d) can be formulated as a set of mixed integer linear inequalities as shown in [11]. Furthermore, as (14) is linear in M and η, since $x(k)$ is known (measured) at each step $k \in \mathbb{Z}_+$, if the system dynamics (5) can be described by mixed-integer linear inequalities (e.g., DHA [14]) and $L(\cdot)$, $F(\cdot)$ are linear (quadratic) functions of their arguments, then (15) can be formulated as a mixed integer linear (quadratic) program.

It is worth to point out that, according to Theorem 3, it is not necessary to attain the globally optimal solution in the optimization problem defined in Step 1 of Algorithm 1 to guarantee stability of the resulting closed-loop system. Rather, stability is ensured for any feasible solution.

5.1 Simulation Example

We present a simple example that illustrates the proposed control strategy. Consider a system with: one continuous state, $x_c \in [-5, 35]$, four discrete states $x_b \in \{\epsilon_1, \epsilon_2, \epsilon_3, \epsilon_4\}$, one continuous input $u_c \in [-2.2, 2.2]$ and one discrete input $u_b \in \{0, 1\}$. As a consequence, $\mathbb{U} = [-2.2, 2.2]$, and $\mathbb{X} \subseteq [-5, 35] \times \{\epsilon_1, \epsilon_2, \epsilon_3, \epsilon_4\}$, where in particular $\mathcal{X}_c(\epsilon_4) = [-5, 6]$. The automaton describing the discrete dynamics of the example system is reported in Figure 1. The continuous dynamics are $x(k+1) = A_i x(k) + B_i u(k)$, if $x_b = \epsilon_i$, where $(A_1, B_1) = (1.09, 1)$, $(A_2, B_2) = (0.75, 0.8)$, $(A_3, B_3) = (0.92, 0.75)$, and $(A_4, B_4) = (1.1, 0.7)$.

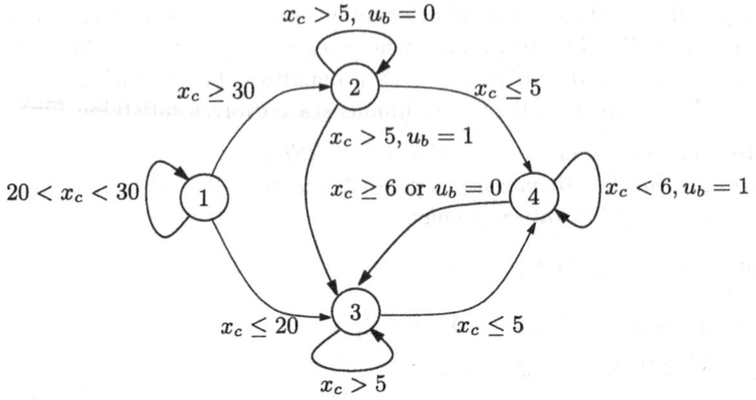

Fig. 1. Automaton describing the discrete dynamics of the example system

The desired equilibrium is $x_c^e = 0$, $x_b^e = \epsilon_4$ for a steady state input $u_c^e = 0$, $u_b^e = 1$. We implemented problem (15) where $L(x, u) = \|Q(x - x^e)\|_\infty + \|R(u - u^e)\|_\infty$, $Q = [\begin{smallmatrix} 1 & 0 \\ 0 & 1 \end{smallmatrix}]$, $R = [\begin{smallmatrix} 0.1 & 0 \\ 0 & 0.1 \end{smallmatrix}]$, $\bar{\rho} = 0.85$, $N = 7$ accordingly to Assumption 2, and $V(x_c) = \|x_c\|_\infty$ as the CLF for the continuous state. The HSDD was implemented as a discrete hybrid automaton using the tools in [14], and problem (15) was formulated as a mixed-integer linear program.

Figure 2 reports the simulation results. The dashed line reports the simulation for the case $x(0) = [22\ \ \epsilon_1]^T$. Note that in this simulation the CLF inequality (2b) holds at every step. The case for $x(0) = [23\ \ \epsilon_1]^T$ is reported as solid lines. Note that there is a discontinuity with respect to the initial conditions, and that in this case the CLF is not monotonically decreasing along the whole trajectory. This is accordingly to (12), since we require the continuous state CLF to decrease only on the set $\mathcal{X}_c(\epsilon_1)$. Moreover, for the same setup the optimization problem formulated as in [1] is infeasible (i.e., it requires a longer horizon).

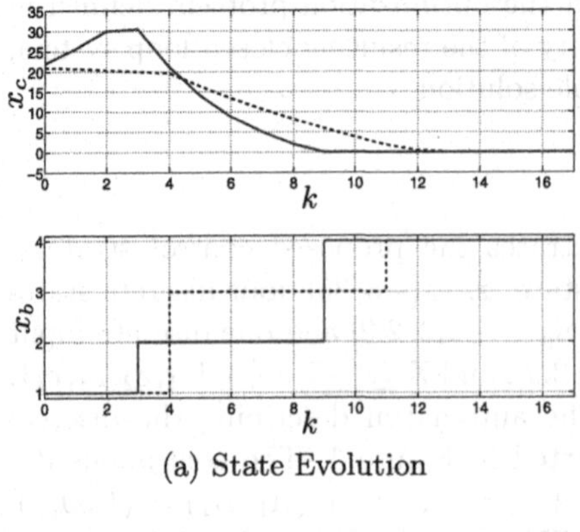

(a) State Evolution

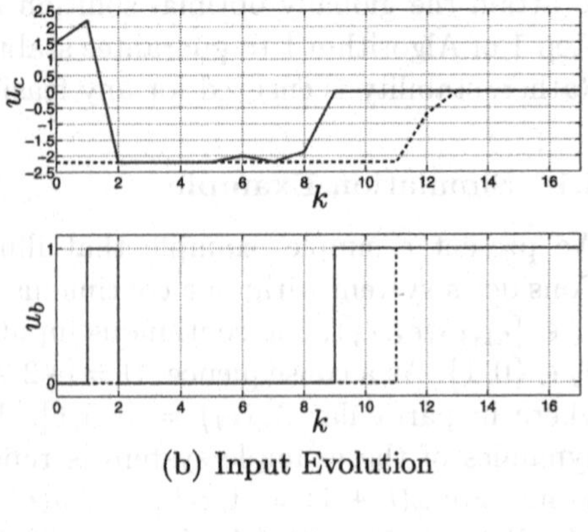

(b) Input Evolution

Fig. 2. Simulation results for $x_c(0) = 23$ (solid lines) and $x_c(0) = 22$ (dashed lines)

6 Conclusions

We have studied the stabilization of hybrid systems with both discrete and continuous dynamics using predictive control based on control Lyapunov functions. We have introduced a hybrid control Lyapunov function constituted of a control Lyapunov-like function that guarantees convergence of the discrete dynamics and of a local control Lyapunov function on the continuous dynamics. The proposed controller is less conservative and less computationally demanding compared to standard predictive control, and it guarantees stability for all the feasible solutions of the optimization problem, not just for the optimal one.

References

1. Bemporad, A., Morari, M.: Control of systems integrating logic, dynamics, and constraints. Automatica 35(3), 407–427 (1999)
2. Kerrigan, E.C., Mayne, D.Q.: Optimal control of constrained, piecewise affine systems with bounded disturbances. In: Proc. 41th IEEE Conf. on Decision and Control, Las Vegas, Nevada, pp. 1552–1557 (2002)
3. Lazar, M., Heemels, W.P.M.H., Weiland, S., Bemporad, A.: Stabilizing model predictive control of hybrid systems. IEEE Trans. Aut. Control 51(11), 1813–1818 (2006)
4. Ferrari-Trecate, G., Cuzzola, F.A., Morari, M.: Lagrange stability and performance analysis of discrete-time piecewise affine systems with logic states. Int. J. Control 76(16), 1585–1598 (2003)
5. Branicky, M.S., Borkar, V.S., Mitter, S.K.: A unified framework for hybrid control: model and optimal control theory. IEEE Trans. Aut. Control 43(1), 31–45 (1998)
6. Lygeros, J., Johansson, K.H., Simic, S.N., Zhang, J., Sastry, S.S.: Dynamical properties of hybrid automata. IEEE Trans. Aut. Control 48, 2–17 (2003)
7. Mayne, D.Q., Rawlings, J.B., Rao, C.V., Scokaert, P.O.M.: Constrained model predictive control: Stability and optimality. Automatica 36(6), 789–814 (2000)
8. Sontag, E.D.: A "universal" construction of Artstein's theorem on nonlinear stabilization. Systems & Control Letters 13, 117–123 (1989)
9. Primbs, J.A., Nevistić, V., Doyle, J.C.: A receding horizon generalization of pointwise min-norm controllers. IEEE Trans. Aut. Control 45(5), 898–909 (2000)
10. Scokaert, P.O.M., Mayne, D.Q., Rawlings, J.B.: Suboptimal model predictive control (feasibility implies stability). IEEE Trans. Aut. Control 44(3), 648–654 (1999)
11. Lazar, M.: Model predictive control of hybrid systems: Stability and robustness. PhD thesis, Eindhoven University of Technology, The Netherlands (2006)
12. Khalil, H.: Nonlinear Systems, 3rd edn. Prentice-Hall, Englewood Cliffs (2002)
13. Dijkstra, E.W.: A note on two problems in connexion with graphs. Numerische Mathematik 1(1), 269–271 (1959)
14. Torrisi, F.D., Bemporad, A.: HYSDEL — A tool for generating computational hybrid models. IEEE Trans. Contr. Systems Technology 12(2), 235–249 (2004)

Discrete and Hybrid Stochastic State Estimation Algorithms for Networked Control Systems

S. Di Cairano[1], K.H. Johansson[2],
A. Bemporad[1], and R.M. Murray[3,*]

[1] Dip. Ingegneria dell'Informazione, Università di Siena, Italy
{dicairano,bemporad}@dii.unisi.it
[2] School of Electrical Engineering, Royal Institute of Technology, Sweden
kallej@ee.kth.se
[3] Division of Engineering and Applied Science, California Institute of Technology
murray@caltech.edu

Abstract. Networked control systems enable for flexible systems operation and reduce cost of installation and maintenance, potentially at the price of increasing the uncertainty due to information exchange over the network. We focus on the problem of information loss in terms of packet drops, which are modelled as stochastic events that depend on the current state of the network. To design reliable control systems the state of the network must be estimated online, together with the state of the controlled process. This paper proposes various approaches to discrete and hybrid stochastic estimation of network and process states, where the network is modelled as a Markov chain and the packet drop probability depends on the states of the Markov chain. The proposed techniques are evaluated on simulations and experimental data.

1 Introduction

Advances in network technology increase the flexibility of modern control systems. Networked control systems[1], in which the controller is remotely located with respect to the plant, are becoming more and more tested and used in industrial applications [2,3]. The advantages of such architectures are in the

* The work by S. Di Cairano and A. Bemporad was supported by the European Commission through the HYCON Network of Excellence (contract FP6-IST-511368), and by the Italian Ministry for University and Research (MIUR) under project "Advanced control methodologies for hybrid dynamical systems" (PRIN'2005). The work by K. H. Johansson was supported by the European Commission through the Network of Excellence HYCON and the Integrated Project SOCRADES, the KTH ACCESS Linnaeus Center, the Swedish Research Council and the Swedish Foundation for Strategic Research. The work by S. Di Cairano and R.M. Murray was partially supported by Boeing through the project Model-Based Design and Qualification of Complex Systems.

M. Egerstedt and B. Mishra (Eds.): HSCC 2008, LNCS 4981, pp. 144–157, 2008.

costs, since a single shared network is less expensive than many point-to-point connections, in the flexibility, since networks are usually capable of automatic reconfiguration, and in the control system maintenance, since the control unit can be deployed far from the plant, that often operates in extreme environmental conditions. Such advantages are further increased when one considers wireless networked control systems, since the absence of wiring further reduces maintenance and deployment costs and increases flexibility. However, when designing a networked control system new issues must be taken into account. The communication network introduces information losses, bandwidth limitations and time-varying delays [4]. These problems are more important in wireless networks [5,6] than in wired networks, as the radio channel performance is affected by many environmental factors and changes rapidly.

When controlling a system over a network, the performance of the network may drastically affect the performance of the system. Several studies have been developed for the particular case in which the network behavior is time invariant, for both, controller and estimator design (see [1,4] for extensive surveys). However, the network characteristics often changes dynamically depending on several factors including network load, number of active users, and environmental conditions [7]. An estimator for a network with piecewise constant statistical properties has been proposed in [8], while a Markov chain model of the network channel has been used for instance in [9,10,11].

When the network is time varying, the overall system state is constituted by the states of the process, of the controller, and of the network. Henceforth, when performing the estimation, it is important to estimate also the current network state. As an example, consider a control system that is composed of a local controller, enforcing stability, and of a remote optimal planner, that communicates via a wireless network, see [12] for a particular example. When the network is reliable, aggressive plans leading to high tracking performances can be safely executed. On the other hand, when the network is unreliable, more cautious plans should be chosen. As another example, consider Alice, the autonomous vehicle of Team Caltech in the 2007 Urban Challenge. Alice's architecture is based on a complex network of sensors, actuators, and computational units. The estimation of the network characteristics can help in revealing whether missing sensor data, such as the localization system data, are not received due to network overload or because the hardware failed, so that the appropriate fault-handling actions can be taken.

This paper analyzes the problem of jointly estimating the network state and the process state under various conditions. Since the physical network models are in general too complicated for control design purposes, we use an abstract model which is simple enough to be analyzable, and still capture the main characteristics of the network phenomena [6]. We focus on networks affected by packet drops, where some of the packets never reach the receiver. The packet drop is an abstract phenomenon representing the loss of information, either physical or logical, in the transmission of a data packet from a sender to a receiver. Many network protocols already provide reliable message delivery through services such as ARQ (automatic repeat request), but these operations introduce delays, and when used in real-time control systems delayed packets can have major influence on closed-loop performance.

We model a discrete-valued network state. Hence, the joint estimation of the continuous-valued process state and of the network state reduces to the estimation of a particular type of hybrid system. We also aim at understanding when the performance of the process state estimation does not affect the network state estimation. In Section 2 we propose the system model and we formulate the estimation problems. In Section 3 we consider the cases in which the network state estimate can be separated from the process estimate. In Section 4 we consider the joint network state and process state estimation. These problems are first analyzed for a networked control system where the network is connecting the controller to the process, and in Section 5 we extend to the different cases involving an additional network between the sensor and the estimator. Simulations of the estimation algorithms are presented in Section 6 together with some experimental results, and the conclusions are summarized in Section 7.

2 Modelling and Problem Formulation

Consider the networked system shown in Figure 1. A discrete-time signal $u(\cdot)$ is transmitted through network $\mathcal{N}_1$ and the received signal $\tilde{u}(\cdot)$ is the input to a dynamical process $\Sigma(x, \tilde{u}, y)$, where x is the process state. The output (or measurement) $y(\cdot)$ is transmitted through network $\mathcal{N}_2$, and the received signal $\tilde{y}(\cdot)$ reaches an estimator $\Theta(u, \tilde{y})$ that knows the signal $u(\cdot)$. The estimator solves a hybrid estimation problem: it provides an estimate $\hat{x}$ of the continuous process state x, and, at the same time, it estimates the discrete states of the networks $\mathcal{N}_1$ and $\mathcal{N}_2$, N_1 and N_2, respectively. Note that the signals u, $\tilde{y}$ available to the estimator may be different from the actual system input $\tilde{u}$ and output y. We call $\mathcal{N}_1$ the *actuation network* and $\mathcal{N}_2$ the *sensing network*, $\tilde{u}(\cdot)$ and $\tilde{y}(\cdot)$ the network filtered input and measurement, and the packets containing u and y are the command packet and the measurement packet, respectively.

Let $\Sigma(x, \tilde{u}, y)$ be a linear discrete-time process subject to disturbances

$$x(k+1) = Ax(k) + B\tilde{u}(k) + w(k), \tag{1a}$$

$$y(k) = Cx(k) + D\tilde{u}(k) + v(k), \quad k \in \mathbb{Z}_{0+} \tag{1b}$$

where $\mathbb{Z}_{0+}$ is the set of nonnegative integers, $x(k) \in \mathbb{R}^n$ is the process state, $y(k) \in \mathbb{R}^p$ is the process output, $\tilde{u}(k) \in \mathbb{R}^m$ is the commanded input, and $w(k)$ and $v(k)$ are the process noise and the measurement noise, respectively. We assume $w(\cdot)$ and $v(\cdot)$ to be white Gaussian random processes with zero mean and covariance matrices Q and R, respectively: for all $k \geq 0$, $w(k) \sim \mathbf{N}(0, Q)$, $v(k) \sim \mathbf{N}(0, R)$. Hence, the state and output dynamics of $\Sigma(x, u, y)$ are Gaussian distributed stochastic processes.

We model the dropping of the packets by a stochastic discrete signal (event) $e(k) \in \{0, 1\}$, where 0 means that the packet at time k has been dropped, while

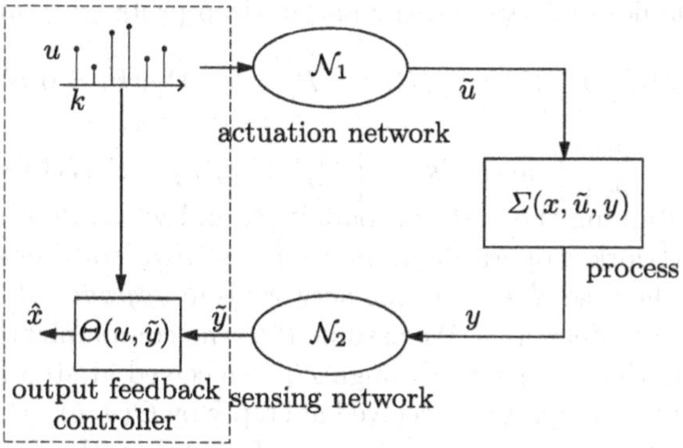

Fig. 1. Process and networked control architecture

1 means that the packet has been received. Consider a discrete-time signal $a(\cdot)$ with domain D_a. In our context $a(\cdot)$ can be either $u(\cdot)$ or $y(\cdot)$. The relation between $a(\cdot)$ and the corresponding network filtered signal $\tilde{a}(\cdot)$ is given by

$$\tilde{a}(k) = \begin{cases} a(k) & \text{if } e(k) = 1 \\ \varepsilon & \text{if } e(k) = 0, \end{cases} \tag{2}$$

where ε is a special symbol indicating the lack of information, and the domain of $\tilde{a}(\cdot)$ is $D_{\tilde{a}} = D_a \cup \varepsilon$. When the loss occurs in $\mathcal{N}_1$ at time step k, we assume the process applies a backup input $\tilde{u}(k) = u_{\text{bu}}(k)$. Common choices for the backup input are $u_{\text{bu}}(k) = 0$, $u_{\text{bu}}(k) = \tilde{u}(k-1)$, and $u_{\text{bu}}(k) = \tilde{u}(k-1) + (\tilde{u}(k-1) - \tilde{u}(k-2))$. The backup input choice depends on the control strategy. In this paper, we consider the strategy as given, and known by the estimator.

We propose a stochastic network model with discrete state $N(k) \in \{0, 1, \ldots, s\}$. The network dynamics are modelled as a Markov chain,

$$\pi(k+1) = M^T \pi(k), \tag{3}$$

where $\pi \in \mathbb{R}^s$ is the vector of state probabilities at time k, i.e. $\pi_i(k) = \mathbf{P}[N(k) = i]$, $i \in \{0, 1, \ldots, S\}$, the superscript ^{T} indicates transposition, and $M \in \mathbb{R}^{s \times s}$ is the transition matrix of the Markov chain. The packet drop probability is state dependent, i.e. $p(k) = p(N(k))$, to represent different operating conditions of the network corresponding to different packet reception rates (PRR).

The proposed network model incorporates common models in the literature. The Poisson process model of packet drops with parameter p, $\mathbf{P}[e(k) = 0] = p$, $\mathbf{P}[e(k) = 1] = 1 - p$, $\forall k \in \mathbb{Z}_{0+}$, that results in a constant drop probability, is a particular case of model (3), where $i \in \{0\}$. Gilbert model [7] is another particular case of model (3), obtained for $i \in \{0, 1\}$, $p(0) = 0$, and $p(1) = 1$.

Two network states can model appropriately behaviors such as network overload and quality of service degradation [7]. We will focus on a two states Markov chain for notational simplicity; the presented approaches can be straightforwardly extended to the case where the Markov chain has a larger number of states. The dynamics of $N(k)$ and the packet drop probability are described by

$$\pi(k+1) = M^T \pi(k),\ \mathbf{P}[e(k)=0|N(k)=R] = p_r,\ \mathbf{P}[e(k)=0|N(k)=U] = p_u, \tag{4}$$

where $M = \begin{bmatrix} p_{R,R} & p_{R,U} \\ p_{U,R} & p_{U,U} \end{bmatrix}$, and $\pi(k) = \begin{bmatrix} \pi_R(k) \\ \pi_U(k) \end{bmatrix}$, $\pi_i(k) = \mathbf{P}[N(k)=i]$, $i \in \{R, U\}$ is the vector containing the state probabilities, and we assume $p_u > p_r$. When $N(k) = R$ the network is operating in *normal (Reliable) state*, ensuring a certain performance. In the case $N(k) = U$ the network is in *degraded (Unreliable) state*, and the performance decreases. We assume that the communications are instantaneous, meaning that $u(k)$ sent through $\mathcal{N}_1$ is received at step k by $\Sigma(x, \tilde{u}, y)$, and that $y(k)$ sent through $\mathcal{N}_2$ is received at step k by $\Theta(u, \tilde{y})$. This is reasonable because in general communications are much faster than the process dynamics.

In general the state of the network is not directly observable since it depends on the interferences among network users sharing the same channel. We can only observe its effects, the packet drops, either by direct knowledge or by inference based on the process measurements. We model this estimation problem as a hidden Markov model (HMM) estimation problem [13]. Let $\mathcal{N}_i = I$ indicate the situation in which the ith communication link is a perfect link, $\tilde{a}(k) = a(k)$, $\forall k \geq 0$. Hence, there is no estimation of $\mathcal{N}_i$. Moreover, let $\mathcal{N}_i = \mathcal{N}_j$, $i \neq j$ indicate that two logical communication links correspond to the same physical network, hence $N_i = N_j$. For the system described in Figure 1 we analyze the problems:

$P1$. Estimate N_1 and x, when $\mathcal{N}_2 = I$.
$P2$. Estimate N_2 and x, when $\mathcal{N}_1 = I$.
$P3$. Estimate N_1, N_2 and x when $\mathcal{N}_1, \mathcal{N}_2 \neq I$, for (a), $\mathcal{N}_1 \neq \mathcal{N}_2$, (b), $\mathcal{N}_1 = \mathcal{N}_2$.

The case where both links are perfect, $\mathcal{N}_2 = I$ and $\mathcal{N}_1 = I$, reduces to the well known problem of estimating the state of a stochastic linear process, easily addressed by Kalman filtering. We first solve Problem $P1$, where we assume to know $e(k)$ (e.g., by an *acknowledge* signal). Then, we extend the approach to the case where $e(k)$ must be inferred from the process output, so that the estimation of the process state and the estimation of the network sate are treated as a single hybrid estimation problem. We show that Problem $P2$ can be solved by the approach proposed for Problem $P1$, where the packet behavior for $\mathcal{N}_2$ is always known. Finally we combine the approaches to solve Problem $P3$.

3 Estimation of Sensing Network State

First, we propose a solution to Problem $P1$, the state estimation of a single network $\mathcal{N}$, assuming to have direct knowledge about the drop events $e(k)$. In this case no process information is used for network state estimation hence process and network state estimation are separated.

Let $\pi_{s|t}(k) = \mathbf{P}[N(k) = s|e(k) = t]$, $s \in \{R, U\}$, $t \in \{0, 1\}$. By Bayes' rule,

$$\pi_{s|t}(k) = \frac{\mathbf{P}[e(k) = t|N(k) = s]\, \pi_s(k)}{\mathbf{P}[e(k) = t]},$$

and then by the total probability theorem

$$\pi_{s|t}(k) = \frac{\mathbf{P}[e(k) = t|N(k) = s]\,\pi_s(k)}{\sum_{j\in\{R,U\}} \mathbf{P}[e(k) = t|N(k) = j]\pi_j(k)}, \tag{5}$$

where $\mathbf{P}[e(k) = t|N(k) = j]$, $j \in \{R, U\}$ is defined by (4). If $e(k)$ is measured, the estimation of the network state is independent from the estimation of the process state. Moreover, if $p_r = 1 - \alpha\varepsilon$, $p_u = \beta\varepsilon$, where $\alpha, \beta > 0$, if $\varepsilon \to 0$, then $\pi_{R|1} = 1$, $\pi_{U|0} = 1$. Hence, estimation (5) applied to the Gilbert model in [7] results in a state with probability 1, and the other with probability 0, because the packet behavior is a perfect indicator of the network state.

In (5) we need to compute $\pi(k)$. We present two estimators that differ on the way such a computation is performed: a static estimator that at each step uses only the current measurement, and a dynamic estimator.

Assumption 1. *Markov chain* (4) *has reached its steady state.*

The stationary probability distribution of the Markov chain states $\lim_{k\to\infty} \mathbf{P}[N(k) = U] = \pi_U^\infty$, $\lim_{k\to\infty} \mathbf{P}[N(k) = R] = \pi_R^\infty$ can be computed from the equilibrium

$$\begin{bmatrix} \pi_R^\infty \\ \pi_U^\infty \end{bmatrix} = M^T \begin{bmatrix} \pi_R^\infty \\ \pi_U^\infty \end{bmatrix}, \tag{6}$$

that has a unique solution for an irreducible Markov chain. The *static estimator* is obtained by plugging the solution of (6) in (5):

$$\pi_{s|t} = \frac{\mathbf{P}[e(k) = t|N(k) = s]\,\pi_s^\infty}{\sum_{j\in\{R,U\}} \mathbf{P}[e(k) = t|N(k) = j]\pi_j^\infty},\quad s \in \{R, U\},\ t \in \{0, 1\}. \tag{7}$$

The maximum likelihood estimate is

$$\hat{N}(k) = \mathrm{argmax}_{j\in\{\mathrm{R,U}\}}\pi_{j|t} \quad \text{if} \quad e(k) = t, \qquad t \in \{0, 1\}. \tag{8}$$

The stationary estimator is simple, since the estimate can be statically computed by evaluating (7) and (8) at every step. In particular, since all the terms in (7) are constant, a lookup table mapping the packet event into the most likely network state can be precomputed and no memory is required. However, such an estimation scheme often leads to poor performance, because only the current measurement is considered, and this information is not used to update the probability of the network state.

We develop a *dynamic estimator* that uses memory to maintain an estimate of the probability of each network state value and uses the measurements on the packet drop to update such an estimate. We can perform estimation by using (3) to compute the predicted state probability to be used in (5), then using the result of (5) as the state probability estimate. This procedure is summarized in Algorithm 3.1, where $\pi_s(k|k) = \mathbf{P}[N(k) = s|e(k)]$, $s \in \{R, U\}$.

The main advantage of Algorithm 3.1 is that the measurements of $e(k)$ are used not only in the decision of the current state, but also to update the state

---

1. set $k = 0$ and let the initial probability vector be $\pi(k|k-1) = \begin{bmatrix} \pi_R(k) \\ \pi_U(k) \end{bmatrix}$;
2. while (TRUE)
   2.1. given $e(k) \in \{0, 1\}$ perform measurement update $\pi(k|k) = \begin{bmatrix} \pi_R(k|k) \\ \pi_U(k|k) \end{bmatrix}$;
   2.2. if $(\pi_R(k|k) \geq \pi_U(k|k))$ then $\hat{N}(k) = R$ else $\hat{N}(k) = U$;
   2.3. perform prediction by flowing the Markov chain $\pi(k+1|k) = M^T \pi(k|k)$;
   2.4. set $k \leftarrow k+1$ and $\pi(k|k-1) \leftarrow \pi(k+1|k)$;

   end

Algorithm 3.1. Dynamic network estimation algorithm

probability, which will affect the future estimation steps. From another point of view, the estimate at time k is directly affected by $e(k)$ and indirectly by $e(j)$, $j = 0, \ldots, k-1$, whose effects are stored in the current state probability. Algorithm 3.1 is the discrete-state version of the Kalman estimator. The algorithm can be initialized by setting $\pi(0|-1)$ to the solution of (6).

Proposition 1. *The network state estimate $\hat{N}$ obtained by Algorithm 3.1 is asymptotically independent of the algorithm initialization value.*

Proposition 1 states that when $k \to \infty$ the value $\hat{N}$ does not depend on the value of $\pi(0|-1)$. This property follows straightforwardly from the *exponential forgetting* property of the HMM filter, that states that for $k \to \infty$, $\pi(k|k)$ is independent of $\pi(0|-1)$. The exponential forgetting property of HMM filters, which include Algorithm 3.1 was proven in [14], where upper bounds on the exponential forgetting rate are also given.

4 Estimation of Sensing Network and Process States

We give now a solution to Problem $P1$, relaxing the hypothesis that $e(k)$ is measured. We modify the estimation algorithm to infer the value of $e(k)$ from the measurement $\tilde{y}(k)$, where $\tilde{y}(k) = y(k)$, since $\mathcal{N}_2 = I$. A simple way to obtain information about $e(k)$ is to add one bit in the measurement packet. The same logic that activates the backup input will also set such a bit to 1 if the command packet has been received, to 0 otherwise. When this strategy is applied, the results of Section 3 hold, and the network state estimation is separated from the process estimation. However, we develop here an estimation approach that is not based on such an additional information, which is useful when the measurement packet cannot be modified, and when $\mathcal{N}_2 \neq I$.

Let $\rho_{t|y}(k) = \mathbf{P}[e(k) = t|y(k)]$, $t \in \{0, 1\}$. Then $\mathbf{P}[N(k) = s|y(k)] = \sum_{t \in \{0,1\}} \mathbf{P}[N(k) = s|y(k), e(k) = t]\rho_{t|y}(k)$, $s \in \{R, U\}$, $t \in \{0, 1\}$. The information given by $y(k)$ about $N(k)$ is entirely contained in the packet event, hence

$\mathbf{P}[N(k) = s|y(k), e(k) = t] = \pi_{s|t}(k)$, and

$$\mathbf{P}[N(k) = s|y(k)] = \sum_{t\in\{0,1\}} \pi_{s|t}(k)\rho_{t|y}(k). \tag{9}$$

In this case the disturbances acting on the process affect also the estimation of the network state. We introduce the joint hybrid-space probability density function $f^{(k)}(e, y)$[1], where $e \in \{0, 1\}$, and y is the process measurement. At a given time $k \in \mathbb{Z}_{0+}$, $f^{(k)}_{y|t}$ is the probability density function of $y(k)$ assuming the event $e(k) = t$. The function $f^{(k)}_{e|y}$ is

$$f^{(k)}_{e|y} = \sum_{t\in\{0,1\}} \frac{f_{y|t}(y(k))}{\sum_{j\in\{0,1\}} f_{y|j}(y(k))}\delta(e(k) - t), \tag{10}$$

where $\delta(\cdot)$ is Dirac's distribution. As a consequence

$$\rho_{t|y}(k) = \frac{f_{y|t}(y(k))}{\sum_{j\in\{0,1\}} f_{y|j}(y(k))}, \tag{11}$$

to be used in (9). Note that the additional uncertainty given by the process noise is contained in the factors $\rho_{t|y}(k)$, $t \in \{0, 1\}$. If the noise vectors in (1) are null and the state is known, there exists $\bar{t} \in \{0, 1\}$ such that $\rho_{\bar{t}|y}(k)$=1, and hence $\rho_{1-\bar{t}|y}(k) = 0$, since the inference on packet behavior is deterministic. Let $\hat{x}(k|k)$ be the estimate of the process state at step k, based on measurements available up to step k, and $f^{(k)}_x$ be the process state distribution function. Algorithm 3.1 is modified into Algorithm 4.1, where $\hat{x}(k|k, t)$ is the estimate of the process state at time k using measurements until time k and assuming $e(k) = t$, $f^{(k)}_{x|i}$, $i \in \{0, 1\}$ is the process state probability density under the assumption the packet has been dropped or received, respectively, and $f^{(k)}_{y|i}$, $i \in \{0, 1\}$ is the corresponding output probability density. In order to compute $f^{(k)}_{y|i}$ which is used in (10), we need to estimate the probability density function of the process state $f^{(k)}_{x|i}$, $i \in \{0, 1\}$, under the assumption the packet has been dropped or received, respectively. Since we consider linear systems subject to Gaussian noise, the obvious choice for the process state estimation is the Kalman filter. The values $\rho_{i|y}(k)$, $i \in \{0, 1\}$ are computed from the output error densities $f^{(k)}_{\varepsilon_y|i}$, $i \in \{0, 1\}$, that are a shifted version of $f^{(k)}_{y|i}$, $i \in \{0, 1\}$. At each step of the process state estimation: (*i*), compute $\hat{y}(k|k, i)$, $i \in \{0, 1\}$, the estimated output under the assumption that the packet has been dropped or received, respectively; (*ii*), compute $\varepsilon_y(k|k, i) = y(k) - \hat{y}(k|k, i)$, $i \in \{0, 1\}$, the output estimation errors in the above cases; (*iii*), compute the probabilities in (11) by the Kalman Filter output error densities estimation $f^{(k)}_{\varepsilon_y|i}$, $i \in \{0, 1\}$. Since only a deterministic

[1] For simplicity, we will drop the superscript $^{(k)}$ when clear from the context.

---

1. set $k = 0$ and let the initial probability vector be $\pi(k|k-1) = \begin{bmatrix} \pi_R(k) \\ \pi_U(k) \end{bmatrix}$;
2. while (TRUE)
   2.1. compute $\hat{x}(k|k,t)$, $f^{(k)}_{x|t}$, $f^{(k)}_{y|t}$, $t \in \{0,1\}$;
   2.2. compute $\rho_{t|y}(k)$, and $\tau = \text{argmax}_{j\in\{0,1\}}\rho_{j|y}(k)$;
   2.3. compute $\pi_{s|t}(k)$ using (5) for $t \in \{0,1\}$, $s \in \{R,U\}$;
   2.4. compute $\pi_s(k|k) = \mathbf{P}[N(k) = s|y(k)]$, $s \in \{R,U\}$, by (9);
   2.5. if $(\pi_R(k|k) \geq \pi_U(k|k))$ then $\hat{N}(k) = R$ else $\hat{N}(k) = U$;
   2.6. perform prediction $\pi(k+1|k) = M^T\pi(k|k)$;
   2.7. update the process state probability density to $f_x(k) = f^{(k)}_{x|\tau}$;
   2.8. set $k \leftarrow k+1$ and $\pi(k|k-1) \leftarrow \pi(k+1|k)$;

   end

Algorithm 4.1. Network estimation algorithm with packet behavior inference

value in the process state is affected by $e(k)$, $f^{(k)}_{y|0}$ and $f^{(k)}_{y|1}$ have the same shape (same covariance), but they are shifted (different average).

By construction, Algorithm 4.1 is the one-step maximum likelihood estimate of the network and process states. The performance of the continuous state estimate affects the discrete estimation by the terms $\rho_{i|y}$, $i \in \{0,1\}$, hence the process and network estimation performances are related.

Remark 1. Algorithm 4.1 assumes that the distribution functions $f^{(k)}_{y|e=1}$ and $f^{(k)}_{y|e=0}$ are different. If this is not the case, $y(k)$ does not give any information about $N(k)$, because the effects of the input on the measurement are delayed. Hence, the estimation must be delayed as well, performing the measurement update to obtain $N(k-\delta|k)$, where $\delta \in \mathbb{Z}_{0+}$ are the steps of delay, followed by δ steps of prediction. Furthermore, when the current input $u(k)$ and the backup input $u_{\text{bu}}(k)$ are the same, it is not possible to distinguish the packet drop and the packet reception from the measurement, similarly to what discussed in [15]. However, this does not degrade the estimation of the process state, since $u(k) = u_{\text{bu}}(k)$.

5 Estimation of Sensing and Actuation Network States

We analyze now Problem $P2$, where packet drops occur in the sensing network, i.e., $\mathcal{N}_2 \neq I$, and all the command packets reach the process, i.e., $\mathcal{N}_1 = I$. The process state can be estimated by applying a Kalman filter modified as in [16], where the authors perform the measurement update only if the measurement packet is received. However, in [16] the network model is static, hence there is no network state estimation. In the case of model (4), the estimation of $N_2(k)$

can be performed by Algorithm 3.1, since the value of $e_2(k)$ is always available to the estimator (it knows whether the measurement packet has been received or not), and the process state estimation does not affect the system state, thus the separation between network state estimation and process state estimation holds. On the other hand, the estimation of the process state is affected by the behavior of the network, since when the measurement packet is dropped, the process state estimate has to be updated in open-loop [16].

Consider now Problem $P3a$, where packet losses occur both in the actuation network and in the sensing network, $\mathcal{N}_i \neq I$, $i = 1, 2$. The uncertainties introduced by $\mathcal{N}_1$ and $\mathcal{N}_2$ are different: a packet loss in $\mathcal{N}_1$ causes the process to evolve in a different way from the commanded one. However, such a drop do not affect the measurements, and the estimation can still be performed by Algorithm 3.1, or by Algorithm 4.1. On the other hand, when packet losses occur in $\mathcal{N}_2$, the measurement is not available, and the only way to update the process state estimate (and the estimate of $\mathcal{N}_1$ if Algorithm 4.1 is used) is by prediction. Thus, losses in $\mathcal{N}_2$ are more critical than losses in $\mathcal{N}_1$ for the estimation problem.

Algorithm 5.1, where e_i is the packet event in $\mathcal{N}_i$, $i = 1, 2$, can be applied for estimation in the case $\mathcal{N}_1, \mathcal{N}_2 \neq I$, $\mathcal{N}_1 \neq \mathcal{N}_2$. We consider the case where $e_1(k)$ is not measured, hence if $e_2(k) = 0$ no measurement is received, and the estimate of $x(k)$ and $N_1(k)$ is updated by prediction. If $e_1(k)$ is measured, the measurement update is always performed also on $\mathcal{N}_1$ (Algorithm 3.1 is used).

---

1. set $k = 0$ and for $\mathcal{N}_i$, $i = 1, 2$, set $\pi^{(i)}(k|k-1) = \begin{bmatrix} \pi_R^{(i)}(k) \\ \pi_U^{(i)}(k) \end{bmatrix}$, respectively;
2. while (TRUE)
   - 2.1. compute $\pi_2(k|k)$ and $\hat{N}_2(k)$ by Algorithm 3.1;
   - 2.2. if $(\pi_R^{(2)}(k|k) \geq \pi_U(k|k))$ then $\hat{N}_2(k) = R$ else $\hat{N}_2(k) = U$;
   - 2.3. if $(e_2(k) = 1)$
     - 2.3.1. compute $\hat{x}(k|k)$;
     - 2.3.2. compute $\pi^{(1)}(k|k)$ and $\hat{N}_1(k)$ by Algorithm 3.1 or by Algorithm 4.1;
   - 2.4. else
     - 2.4.1. set $\hat{x}(k|k) = \hat{x}(k|k-1)$ (open-loop prediction);
     - 2.4.2. set $\pi^{(1)}(k|k) = \pi^{(1)}(k|k-1)$ (open-loop prediction on (4)).
   - 2.5. if $(\pi_R^{(1)}(k|k) \geq \pi_U(k|k))$ then $\hat{N}_2(k) = R$ else $\hat{N}_2(k) = U$;

   end

Algorithm 5.1. Estimation algorithm for the case $\mathcal{N}_1 \neq I$, $\mathcal{N}_2 \neq I$, and $\mathcal{N}_1 \neq \mathcal{N}_2$

We finally consider Problem $P3b$, where the actuation and sensing networks correspond to the same physical network, hence $\mathcal{N}_1 = \mathcal{N}_2$ and $N_1 = N_2 = N$. Since all the packet events refer to the same network, at each step we have up to two measurements that we can use to update the network state estimate.

In (4) the drop probability depends on the state of the network, and not on the behavior of the other packets, hence $\mathbf{P}[e_i(k)|e_j(k), N(k)] = \mathbf{P}[e_i(k)|N(k)]$, $i, j \in \{1, 2\}$, $i \neq j$, and $\mathbf{P}[e_1(k), e_2(k)|N(k)] = \mathbf{P}[e_1(k)|N(k)]\mathbf{P}[e_2(k)|N(k)]$. The measurement update of the network state estimate with two data is

$$\mathbf{P}[N(k)|e_1(k), e_2(k)] = \frac{\mathbf{P}[e_1(k)|N(k)]\mathbf{P}[e_2(k)|N(k)]\mathbf{P}[N(k)]}{\sum_{N(k)=\{U,R\}} \mathbf{P}[e_1(k)|N(k)]\mathbf{P}[e_2(k)|N(k)]}. \tag{12}$$

If the measurement packet is dropped, a single-measurement update (5) is performed, hence packet drops in $\mathcal{N}_2$ results again to be more critical for estimation.

6 Simulations and Experiments

We consider $\mathcal{N}_2 = I$, and $\mathcal{N}_1$ defined by $M_1 = \begin{bmatrix} 0.98 & 0.02 \\ 0.06 & 0.94 \end{bmatrix}$, $p_r^{(1)} = 0.15$, $p_u^{(1)} = 0.80$. The process is a linear system with transfer function $G(s) = \frac{2.44}{s^2+2.4s+2.44}$, sampled at 2 Hz to obtain a discrete-time representation (1), where $A = \begin{bmatrix} 0.96 & -0.60 \\ 0.5 & 0 \end{bmatrix}$, $B = \begin{bmatrix} 0.5 \\ 0 \end{bmatrix}$, $C = \begin{bmatrix} 0.40 & 0.54 \end{bmatrix}$, $D = 0$. We have used as backup strategy $u_{\text{bu}}(k) = 0$, and the noise terms are $v(k) \sim \mathbf{N}(0, 0.6)$, $w(k) \sim \mathbf{N}\left(0, \begin{bmatrix} 2 & 0 \\ 0 & 2 \end{bmatrix}\right)$. All the simulations have been run for 500 steps and the packet drop events $e_1(k)$ and the random signal that generates the transitions of $N_1(k)$ are always the same. An extended discussion on the simulations is available in [17].

Table 1. Results of the simulations of the proposed estimation strategies

$N(k)$ Estimator	$e_1(\cdot)$	$v(k) \neq 0$	$w(k) \neq 0$	$x(k)$ Estimator	$\mathcal{N}_2$	$\mathcal{E}_N$
Static	meas	-	-	-	I	79
Dynamic	meas	-	-	-	I	39
Dynamic	inf	yes	yes	yes	I	48
Dynamic	emb	no	no	no	$\mathcal{N}_2 \neq \mathcal{N}_1 \neq I$	$N_1 : 63$, $N_2 : 31$
Dynamic	emb	no	no	no	$\mathcal{N}_2 = \mathcal{N}_1 \neq I$	27

The simulation results are summarized in Table 1, where $\mathcal{E}_N = \sum_k \varepsilon_N(k)$ is the cumulative network state estimation error, ($\varepsilon_N(k) = |N(k) - \hat{N}(k)|$). Column $e_1(\cdot)$ refers to the knowledge about $e_1(k)$, where *meas* stands for measured, *inf* for inference, and *emb* means that the information on the reception of the command packet is embedded in the measurement packet. First we have simulated the strategies described in Section 3 based on measured $e(k)$. Table 1 shows that the performance of the dynamic estimator is clearly higher than the one of the static estimator. Next, we have simulated Algorithm 4.1 that is based on inference on the process measurements, and we have used a Kalman filter for hypothesis test, as described in Section 4. Table 1 shows that the network state estimate performance is degraded because of the effects of the process noise. The estimation of the process state is shown in Figure 2(a), where the estimated state components $\hat{x}_i(k)$, $i = 1, 2$, are plotted in black, the real state components

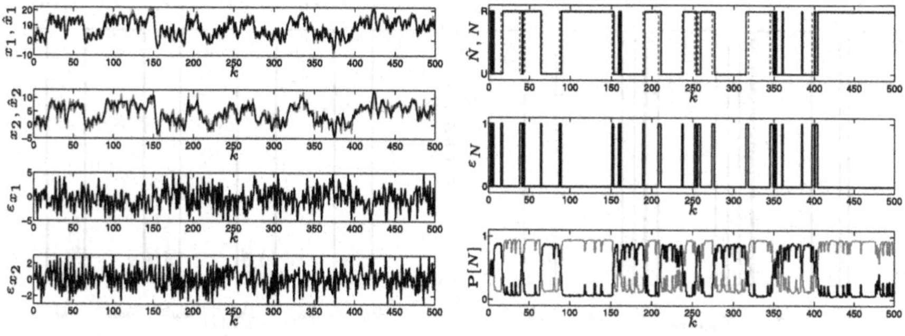

(a) Process state estimation (b) Network state estimation

Fig. 2. Joint actuation network and process states estimation with inference on $e(k)$

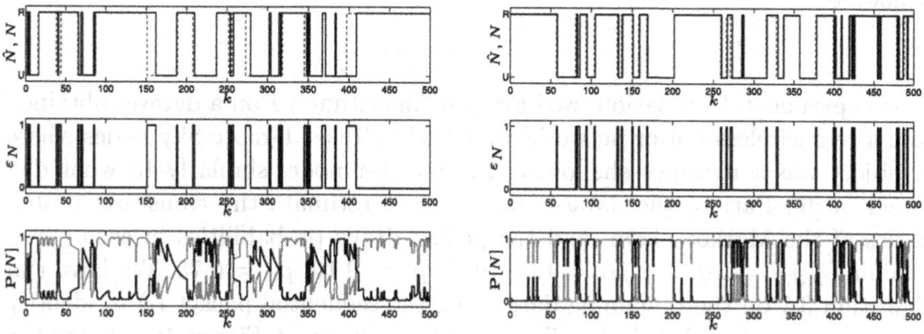

(a) Actuation network ($\mathcal{N}_1$) (b) Sensing network ($\mathcal{N}_2$)

Fig. 3. Actuation and sencing network states estimation $\mathcal{N}_1, \mathcal{N}_2 \neq I$, $\mathcal{N}_1 \neq \mathcal{N}_2$. The measurement packet contains information on command packet reception.

$x_i(k)$, $i = 1, 2$, in gray, and $\varepsilon_{x_i}(k)$ is the estimation error on the ith component of the process state vector at time k. The estimation of the network state is shown in Figure 2(b), where in the upper plot N is the dashed line, and $\hat{N}$ is the solid line, and in the lower plot $\mathbf{P}[N(k) = R]$ is in gray, $\mathbf{P}[N(k) = U]$ is in black.

Finally, we have introduced another network $\mathcal{N}_2 \neq \mathcal{N}_1$ between the process and the estimator. The model of $\mathcal{N}_2$ is described by $M_2 = \left[\begin{smallmatrix} 0.97 & 0.03 \\ 0.09 & 0.91 \end{smallmatrix}\right]$, $p_r^{(2)} = 0.05$, $p_u^{(2)} = 0.87$. We have simulated Algorithm 5.1, in the case where the information about the command packet reception is embedded in the measurement packet. As a consequence, when this is dropped the estimate of N_1 is updated by open-loop prediction. Figure 3 reports the results of the simulation, with the same format as Figure 2(b). Table 1 confirms that the estimation of $\mathcal{N}_2$ is more precise than the estimation of $\mathcal{N}_1$, because it is always known whether the measurement packet has been received or not. The last line of Table 1 refers to a simulation where $\mathcal{N}_2 = \mathcal{N}_1$, which results in the most precise estimation, because at each step at least one data (and at most two) for the network state estimate is available.

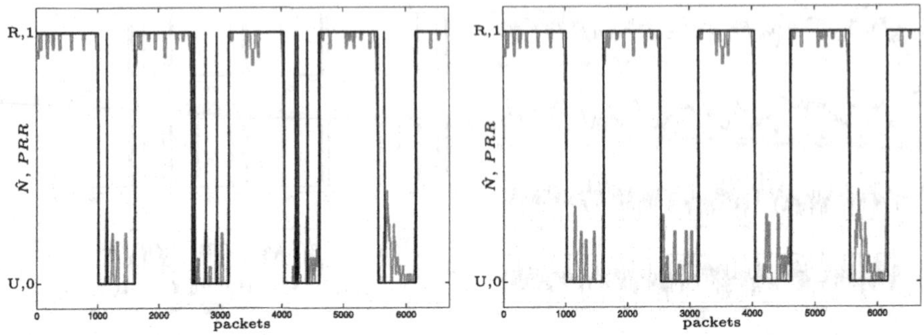

(a) Estimated network state for $p_r = 0.10$, $p_u = 0.75$

(b) Estimated network state for $p_r = 0.20$, $p_u = 0.60$

Fig. 4. Application of the Algorithm 3.1 to a wireless sensor network with intermittent shadowing

As experimental validation, we have run Algorithm 3.1 on a dataset obtained from a real wireless sensor network composed of Telos T-mote Sky nodes where an object was sometimes shadowing the receiver node, similarly to what discussed in [6]. Part of the dataset was used to estimate the transition probabilities of the Markov chain, and the packet drops probabilities in each state, obtaining $p_{R,U} = 10^{-3}$, $p_{U,U} = 1.5 \cdot 10^{-3}$, $p_r = 0.10$, $p_u = 0.75$. We have run Algorithm 3.1 on the remaining data using the sequential packet ID to identify the occurrence of packet drops. The results are shown in Figure 4(a) where the estimated network state is plotted as a black line while the packet reception rate (PRR) obtained by averaging over a symmetric window of 30 packets is plotted as a gray line. The tracking is good, except for some false positives in which nonexistent state switches are detected. These can be removed by tuning the prediction model of the estimator. The behavior obtained by setting $p_r = 0.20$, $p_u = 0.60$ is shown in Figure 4(b), where the false positives are eliminated.

7 Conclusions

This paper has proposed different approaches to estimate the state of a networked control system, composed of the process state and the network state. We have shown the approaches in which the network state estimation can be be separated from the process state estimation and we have shown how the information losses in different places of the networked system affect the estimate. As shown in comparative simulations, the performance of the different approaches varies, and the choice of the one to be applied mainly depends on the overall networked system architecture.

The authors want to thank Pan Gun Park for performing the experiments on the wireless sensor network.

References

1. Zhang, W., Branicky, M.S., Phillips, S.M.: Stability of networked control systems. IEEE Control Systems Magazine 21(1), 84–99 (2001)
2. Årzén, K.E., Bicchi, A., Dini, G., Hailes, S., Johansson, K.H., Lygeros, J., Tzes, A.: A component-based approach to the design of networked control systems. Europ. J. Control 2-3 (2007)
3. Samad, T., McLaughlin, P., Lu, J.: System architecture for process automation: Review and trends. J. Proc. Control 17, 191–201
4. Hespanha, J.P., Naghshtabrizi, P., Xu, Y.: A survey of recent results in networked control systems. Proc. of IEEE, Special Issue on Technology of Networked Control Systems 95(1), 138–162 (2007)
5. Goldsmith, A.: Wireless Communications. Cambridge Univ. Press, Cambridge, U.K (2004)
6. Willig, A., Kubisch, M., Hoene, C., Wolisz, A.: Measurements of a wireless link in an industrial environment using an IEEE 802.11-compliant physical layer. IEEE Trans. Ind. Electr. 49(6), 191–201
7. Yu, X., Modestino, J., Tian, X.: The accuracy of Gilbert models in predicting packet-loss statistics for a single-multiplexer network model. In: INFOCOM. 24th Conf. of IEEE Computer and Communications Societies, pp. 2602–2612 (2005)
8. Jacobsson, K., Hjalmarsson, H., Möller, N., Johansson, K.H.: Some modeling and estimation issues in control of heterogeneous networks. estimation of RTT and bandwidth for congestion control applications in communication networks. In: Proc. 16th Intl. Symposium MTNS (2004)
9. Nilsson, J., Bernhardsson, B.: LQG control over a Markov communication network. In: Proc. 36th IEEE Conf. on Decision and Control., vol. 5, pp. 4586–4591 (1997)
10. Gupta, V., Hassibi, B., Murray, R.M.: On the control of jump linear Markov systems with Markov state estimation. In: American Control Conf., pp. 2893–2898 (2003)
11. Seiler, P., Sengupta, R.: An h_∞ approach to networked control. IEEE Trans. Aut. Control 50(3), 356–364 (2005)
12. Bemporad, A., Di Cairano, S., Henriksson, E., Johansson, K.H.: Hybrid model predictive control based on wireless sensor feedback: An experimental study. In: Proc. 46th IEEE Conf. on Decision and Control., pp. 5062–5067 (2007)
13. Rabiner, L.R., Juang, B.H.: An introduction to hidden Markov models. IEEE Acoustic, Speech, Signal Proc. Mag. 3(1), 4–16 (1986)
14. Shue, L., Anderson, B.D.O., Dey, S.P.: Exponential stability of filters and smoothers for hidden Markov models. IEEE Trans. Signal Proc. 46(8), 2180–2194 (1998)
15. Epstein, M., Shi, L., Murray, R.M.: An estimation algorithm for a class of networked control systems using udp-like communication schemes. In: Proc. 45th IEEE Conf. on Decision and Control., pp. 5597–5603 (2006)
16. Sinopoli, B., Schenato, L., Franceschetti, M., Poolla, K., Jordan, M.I., Sastry, S.S.: Kalman filtering with intermittent observations. IEEE Trans. Aut. Control 49(9), 1453–1464 (2004)
17. Di Cairano, S., Johansson, K.H., Bemporad, A., Murray, R.M.: Dynamic network state estimation in networked control systems. Tech. Report 2007-5 University of Siena (2007), `www.dii.unisi.it/~dicairano/papers/tr07ntwEstim.pdf`

Anytime Control Algorithms for Embedded Real-Time Systems

Daniele Fontanelli[1], Luca Greco[1,2], and Antonio Bicchi[1,*]

[1] Interdepartmental Research Center "E. Piaggio", University of Pisa
{daniele.fontanelli,bicchi}@ing.unipi.it
[2] University of Salerno
greco@dsea.unipi.it

Abstract. In this paper we consider the problem of designing controllers for linear plants to be implemented in embedded platforms under stringent real-time constraints. These include preemptive scheduling schemes, under which the maximum execution time allowed for control software tasks is uncertain. We propose an "anytime control" design approach, consisting in a hierarchy of controllers for the same plant. Higher controllers in the hierarchy provide better closed-loop performance, while typically requiring a larger worst-case execution time. We provide a procedure for the design of controllers which, together with a conditioning process of the stochastic scheduling, provides better performance than prevailing worst case-based design, while guaranteeing almost sure stability of the resulting switching system.

1 Introduction

A general tendency can be observed in embedded systems towards implementation of a great variety of concurrent real-time tasks on the same platform, thus reducing the overall HW cost and development time. Among such tasks, those implementing control algorithms are usually highly time critical, and have traditionally imposed very conservative scheduling approaches, whereby execution time is allotted statically, which makes the overall architecture extremely rigid, hardly reconfigurable for additions or changes of components, and often underperforming.

Modern multitasking Real-Time Operating System (RTOS), running e.g. on embedded ECUs in the automotive domain, schedule their tasks dynamically, adapting to varying load conditions and Quality of Service requirements. Real-time preemptive algorithms, such as e.g. Rate Monotonic (RM) and Earliest Deadline First (EDF) [1,2,3] can suspend the execution of a task in the presence of requests by other, higher priority tasks. Guarantees of schedulability can be provided based on estimates of the Worst-Case Execution Time (WCET) of tasks.

* This work was supported by the EC under contract IST 511368 (NoE) "HYCON - Hybrid Control: Taming Heterogeneity and Complexity of Networked Embedded Systems" and contract IST 045359 "PHRIENDS" - Physical Human-Robot Interaction: Dependability and Safety".

M. Egerstedt and B. Mishra (Eds.): HSCC 2008, LNCS 4981, pp. 158–171, 2008.

However, to make a given set of tasks schedulable and to limit the number of deadline misses, conservative assumptions are typically made which entail underexploitation of the computational platform and, ultimately, cost inefficiencies: for instance, a famous result of [1] shows that RM scheduling can meet all deadlines if the CPU utilization is not larger than 69.3%. On the other hand, when the computational power budget is given and fixed (which is often the case in industrial practice), then control algorithms may have to be drastically simplified to be computable within the allotted time. This clearly reflects in a degradation of the overall performance of the ensuing closed-loop system.

Substantial performance improvement would be gained if less conservative assumptions could be made on the CPU utilization. In particular, it is often the case that, for most of the CPU cycles, a time τ could be made available for a control task which is substantially longer than τ_{min}, although only the latter can be guaranteed in the worst case.

In this paper we propose a strategy to design control algorithms and to schedule their execution, so that the limits of current practice are overcome and better performance could be obtained with the same resources.

2 Anytime Control Algorithms

The key idea is to design controllers which can be implemented so that a useful result is guaranteed whenever the algorithm is run for at least τ_{min}; however, better results can be provided if longer times are allowed.

The idea is borrowed from so-called *anytime algorithms*, that have been proposed in real-time computation [4,5]. The characteristic of anytime algorithms (or of *imprecise computation*, as they are sometimes referred to) is to always return an answer on demand; however, the longer they are allowed to compute, the better (e.g. more precise) an answer they will return. Thus, an anytime algorithm can be interrupted prematurely, still providing a valid result and improving the output accuracy as the available time increases. A periodic task is split in a *mandatory* part and one or more *optional* parts. The criticality of hard RT tasks is preserved ensuring only that the mandatory parts satisfy the time constraints. If all mandatory parts of a set of tasks are schedulable, *feasible mandatory constraint* is satisfied [4].

In digital filter design [6], this philosophy has been pursued by decomposing the full-order filter in a cascade of lower order filters whose execution is prioritized. Execution of code implementing the first block is always guaranteed within τ_{min}; code for blocks in the cascade is then executed sequentially, until a preemption event takes over. The latest computed block output is used as the anytime filter output. The overall performance of the filter was shown in [6] to be superior the the conservative solution of always using only the first filter block.

To adopt the anytime approach in the control domain, a classical monolithic control task should be replaced by a hierarchy of control tasks of increasing complexity, each providing a correspondingly increasing performance of the controlled system. For instance, the simplest control task in the hierarchy, which must be executable within τ_{min}, could be designed to guarantee only stability of the closed loop system, while whenever the scheduler provides "surplus" time, other more sophisticated control algorithms could be executed to obtain better "quality of control".

However, application of the anytime algorithm idea to control is much more challenging than it may superficially appear. The main conceptual roadblock is that, as opposed to most anytime computation and filtering algorithms, anytime controllers interact in feedback with dynamic systems, which fact entails issues such as

Hierarchical Design: The design of a set of controllers as progressive approximations towards a given target design does not typically provide the desired performance hierarchy. Indeed, performances of closed-loop systems are not trivially related to how close approximations are to the target, as it is e.g. in filter design;

Switched System Performance: Unpredictable preemption events introduce stochastic switching among different closed-loop systems, which can subvert naïve expectations — e.g., switching between stabilizing controllers may well result in overall instability. More generally, closed-loop performance is strongly influenced by switching;

Practicality: Implementation of both control and scheduling algorithms must be numerically accurate, yet very simple and non-invasive, not to contradict the very nature of the limited-resource, embedded control problem.

Composability: The computational structure of control algorithms should be inherited through the hierarchy levels, so that the computation of higher controllers in the hierarchy exploits results of computations executed for lower controllers. Although this property is not strictly required, it can greatly enhance effectiveness of anytime control.

3 Prior Work

We will illustrate the relevance of the above issues with reference to prior work in the field. A first attempt to use the anytime control idea is reported in [7,8], where standard system reduction methods (balanced truncation or modal decomposition) are used to decompose a target controller in simpler ones. Unfortunately, these methods do not provide any guarantee on closed-loop performance of the simplified controllers (not even stability, indeed). Even if ad-hoc choices are made that provide stabilizing controllers, stability under switching is not guaranteed by the method in [7,8], unless a substantial dwelling time is assumed between switches, during which the constant use of the same controller is possible.

On the other hand, the substantial literature on *switching system* stability (see e.g. [9,10,11,12] and references therein) provides much inspiration and ideas for the problem at hand, but few results can be used directly. For instance, application of the important results of [13] would provide state-space realizations of different stabilizing controllers such that the overall closed-loop systems would remain stable under *any* switching law. Unfortunately, however, the method is thought for a different application, and assumes all controllers are designed by the internal-model approach, and have the same (rather heavy) computational complexity; most importantly, at each switching instant, a state-space transformation has to be applied, which is of comparable complexity as the controllers themselves. By the same practicality argument, algorithms for switched system stabilization (such as e.g. [14,15,16]) requiring the computation of complex functions of the state to ascertain which subsystem can be activated next time, are not applicable to anytime control.

In [17], the authors proposed a framework for the stability analysis of anytime control algorithms, based on a stochastic model for the scheduler. A set of controllers forming a hierarchy in complexity and performance was assumed to be given. Under these hypotheses, a switching policy capable of conditioning the stochastic properties of the scheduler was designed, such that overall stability (in the probabilistic sense of "almost sure" stability [18,19]) of the resulting Markov Jump Linear System (MJLS) can be guaranteed. This paper complements [17] by providing a constructive design procedure for anytime controllers, and by illustrating the application of the complete methodology to two examples. The modelling framework and the main results of [17] are succinctly reported for the reader's convenience.

4 Scheduling Problem Formulation and Solution

Let $\Sigma \triangleq (A, B, C)$ be the given strictly proper linear, discrete time, invariant plant to be controlled, and let $\Gamma_i \triangleq (F_i, G_i, H_i, L_i)$, $i \in I \triangleq \{1, 2, \dots, n\}$ be a family of feedback controllers for Σ. Assume that all controllers Γ_i stabilize Σ and are ordered by increasing computational time complexity, i.e. $WCET_i > WCET_j$ if $i > j$. Let the closed-loop systems thus obtained be $\Sigma_i \triangleq (\widehat{A}_i, \widehat{B}_i, \widehat{C}_i)$, where

$$\widehat{A}_i = \begin{bmatrix} A + BL_iC & BH_i \\ G_iC & F_i \end{bmatrix}; \widehat{B} = \begin{bmatrix} B_i \\ 0 \end{bmatrix}; \widehat{C}_i = \begin{bmatrix} C_i & 0 \end{bmatrix}.$$

Problems related to jitter and delay are not considered in this work since they can be tackled in the design of the single controllers ([20]). Therefore, we assume that measurements are acquired and control inputs are released at every sampling instant tT_g, $t \in \mathbb{N}$, where T_g is a fixed sampling time. Let $\gamma_t \in [\tau_{min}, \tau_{max}]$, $\tau_{max} < T_g$, denote the time allotted to the control task during the t-th sampling interval. By hypothesis, $WCET_1 \leq \tau_{min}$ and $WCET_n \leq \tau_{max}$.

Define an event set $L_\tau \triangleq \{\tau_1, \dots, \tau_n\}$, and a map

$$\begin{aligned} \mathcal{T} : [\tau_{min}, \tau_{max}] &\to L_\tau \\ \gamma_t &\mapsto \tau(t) \end{aligned}$$

where

$$\tau(t) = \begin{cases} \tau_1, \text{ if } \gamma_t \in [\tau_{min}, WCET_2) \\ \tau_2, \text{ if } \gamma_t \in [WCET_2, WCET_3) \\ \vdots \quad \text{if} \vdots \\ \tau_n, \text{ if } \gamma_t \in [WCET_n, \tau_{max}] \end{cases}$$

Assume a stochastic description of the scheduling process to be given by

$$\Pr\{\tau(t) = \tau_i\} = \bar{\pi}_{\tau_i}, \; 0 < \bar{\pi}_{\tau_i} < 1, \; \sum_{i \in I} \bar{\pi}_{\tau_i} = 1,$$

where $\bar{\pi}_{\tau_i}$ denotes the probability associated to the event that the time slot γ_t is such that all controllers $\Gamma_j, j \leq i$, but no controller $\Gamma_k, k > i$, can be executed. The distribution $\bar{\pi}_\tau = [\bar{\pi}_{\tau_1}, \bar{\pi}_{\tau_2}, \cdots, \bar{\pi}_{\tau_n}]^T$ can be regarded simply as an i.i.d. process, or, in a slightly more complex but general way, as the invariant probability distribution of a finite state discrete-time homogeneous irreducible aperiodic Markov chain given by

$$\pi(t+1) = P^T \pi(t), \; \pi(0) = \pi_0.$$

where $P = (p_{ij})_{n \times n}$ is the transition probability matrix and p_{ij} is the transition probability from state i to state j of the Markov chain (e.g. from controller Γ_i to Γ_j).

Under these hypotheses, the switching process generates a discrete-time Markov Jump Linear System (MJLS)

$$x_{t+1} = \widehat{A}_{\tau_t} x_t \tag{1}$$

Definition 1. *[19] The MJLS (1) is said almost surely stable (AS-stable) if there exists $\mu > 0$ such that, for any $x_0 \in \mathbb{R}^N$ and any initial distribution π_0, the following condition holds*

$$\Pr\left\{\limsup_{t \to \infty} \frac{1}{t} \ln \|x_t\| \leq -\mu\right\} = 1.$$

Let $\|\cdot\|$ be a matrix norm induced by some vector norm. The following sufficient condition for AS-stability was proved in [18]:

Theorem 1 (1–step average contractivity). *[18] If*

$$\xi_1 = \prod_{i \in I} \|\widehat{A}_{\tau_i}\|^{\bar{\pi}_{\tau_i}} < 1 \tag{2}$$

then the MJLS (1) is AS-stable.

4.1 Stochastic Schedule Conditioning

We define a *switching policy* to be a map $s : \mathbb{N} \to I$, $t \mapsto s(t)$, which determines an upper bound to the index i of the controller to be executed at time t, i.e. $i \le s(t)$. In other terms, at time tT_g, the system starts computing the controller algorithm until it can provide the output of $\Gamma_{s(t)}$, unless a preemption event occurs forcing it to provide only $\Gamma_{\tau(t)}$, i.e. the highest controller computed before preemption. Application of a switching policy s to a set of feedback systems Σ_i, $i \in I$ under a scheduler τ generates a switching linear system (Σ_i, τ, s) which, under suitable hypotheses, is also a MJLS. The stochastic characterization of the chain τ is assumed to be a-priori known. Furthermore, in a real application (e.g. automotive domain) different working conditions lead to different stochastic descriptions, thus different Markov chains for the scheduler can be considered.

As an example, the most conservative policy is to set $s(t) \equiv 1$, i.e. forcing always the execution of the simplest controller Γ_1, regardless of the probable availability of more computational time. By assumption, this (non-switching) policy guarantees stability of the resulting closed loop system.

On the opposite, a "greedy" strategy would set $s(t) \equiv n$, which leads to providing $\Gamma_{\tau(t)}$ for all t. Although this policy attempts at maximizing the utilization of the most performing controller, it is well known that switching arbitrarily among asymptotically stable systems Σ_i may easily result in an unstable behavior [21].

A sufficient condition for the greedy switching policy to provide an AS-stable system is provided by Theorem 1. This condition however is rarely satisfied. Indeed, the fact that each matrix $\widehat{A}_{\tau_i}$ is Schur guarantees the existence of a specific norm $\|\cdot\|_{w_i}$ such that $\|\widehat{A}_{\tau_i}\|_{w_i} < 1$, but no single norm $\|\cdot\|_w$ exist in general such that $\|\widehat{A}_{\tau_i}\|_w < 1 \; \forall \tau_i$[1]. The AS stability condition of theorem 1 would require that, for a chosen norm, for all controllers with $\|\widehat{A}_{\tau_i}\|_w > 1$ $\overline{\pi}_{\tau_i}$ is sufficiently small, i.e. they are scheduled by the OS sufficiently rarely.

A switching policy that suitably conditions the scheduler to provide AS-stability was studied in [17], which is illustrated below. Introduce a homogeneous irreducible aperiodic Markov chain σ with the same number n of states as the scheduler chain τ. The states are labelled as σ_i, with the meaning that if the associated process form $\sigma(t)$ is equal to σ_i, then $s(t) = i$, i.e. in the next sampling interval tT_g at most the i–th controller is computed (this will actually happen if no preemption occurs). We will refer to σ as the conditioning Markov chain. The synthesis of such a conditioning Markov chain can be formulated as the following Linear Programming problem:

$$\text{Find a vector } \overline{\pi}_\sigma = \left[\overline{\pi}_{\sigma_1} \cdots \overline{\pi}_{\sigma_n}\right]^T \text{ such that}$$

$$\begin{array}{ll} 1) & \displaystyle\sum_{i=1}^{n} c_i \overline{\pi}_{\sigma_i} < 0 \\ 2) & 0 < \overline{\pi}_{\sigma_i} < 1 \\ 3) & \displaystyle\sum_{i=1}^{n} \overline{\pi}_{\sigma_i} = 1, \end{array} \qquad (3)$$

[1] When this happens, such norm is a common Lyapunov function and the system remains stable for all switching sequences. It is well known that this is rarely the case.

Table 1. Computational complexity (considered as the number of multiplications except by 0 or 1) and numerical reliability of different state-space realizations of a strictly proper transfer function $G(z)$ with N poles. The generic case assumes no particular structure in the systems matrices.

	COMP. COMPL.	NUM. RELIAB.
Generic	$N(N+2)$	–
Companion	$2N$	bad
Jordan	$2N$ to $3N$	good

where

$$c_i = \sum_{h=1}^{n} \overline{\pi}_{\tau_h} \ln\left(\left\|\widehat{A}_{\min(\tau_h,\sigma_i)}\right\|\right).$$

Should this problem not have a feasible solution, multi–step switching policies can be considered, whereby the conditioning Markov chain suggests the sequence of controllers to be executed in the next m steps (see [17] for details). This way, some control patterns, i.e. substrings of symbols in I, are preferentially used with respect to others.

5 Design of a Control Algorithm Hierarchy

In this section we address the problem of designing an ordered set of control algorithms providing increasing closed-loop performance. A top-down design approach to this problem would start with the design of a complex, high-performance controller Γ_n (by e.g. a H_∞ technique); progressively simpler controllers Γ_i, $n-1 \geq i \geq 1$ may then be obtained by e.g. model reduction techniques. As already remarked, however, this approach does not systematically guarantee closed-loop performance under switching. Moreover, most model reduction techniques require state-space realizations with full dynamic matrices F_i, which makes them impractical in real-time embedded applications.

Indeed, practicality requirements imply careful consideration of algorithmic implementations of control laws [22]. Table 1 reports a comparison among three different state space representations for SISO systems.

We propose here a simple, bottom-up design technique which is suitable for addressing the main requirements of anytime control algorithms. The method is based on classical cascade design. Consider the two design stages illustrated in fig. 1, in which controllers are designed to ensure increasing performance by any classical synthesis technique. The scheme in fig. 1 cannot be implemented as a composable anytime control, because after computation of the a) scheme, the input to the $F_1(z)$ block needs to be recomputed completely if the b) scheme is to be applied. However, by simple block manipulations, the scheme in fig. 2 can be obtained, where we set

$$\hat{C}_2(z) = F_1(z)C_2(z).$$

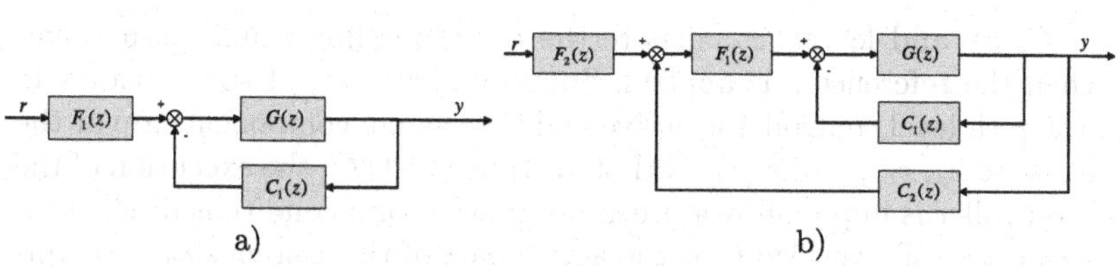

Fig. 1. Two stages of a classical cascade design procedure

The scheme in fig. 2 is suitable for anytime implementation. Indeed the series of $F_1(z)$ and $F_2(z)$ is in open-loop (hence equivalent to an anytime filter), while the parallel connection in the feedback loop is simply obtained by summing the new result by $\hat{C}_2(z)$ to the previous one by $C_1(z)$. Using Jordan form realizations of the blocks provides good numerical accuracy as well as low computational complexity. The cascade design method can be applied iteratively to provide a complete hierarchy of controllers, satisfactorily addressing the issues of hierarchical design, practicality, and composability.

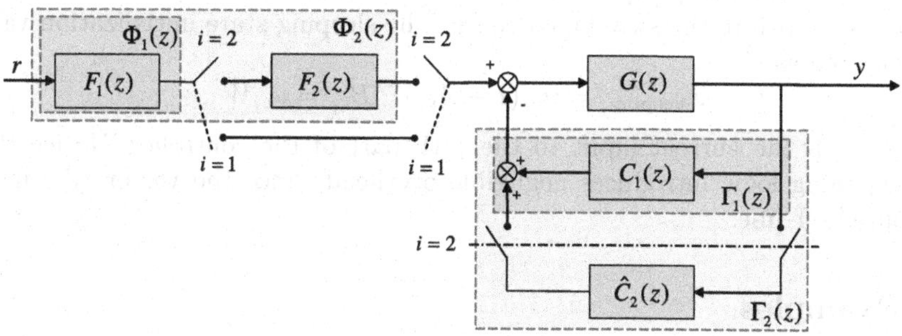

Fig. 2. A switched control scheme suitable for anytime control implementation. The scheme is equivalent to fig. 1-a when the switches are in the $i = 1$ position, and to fig. 1-b for $i = 2$.

6 Tracking Control and Bumpless Transfer

The schedule conditioning technique of section 4.1 is able to address the switched system performance issue satisfactorily when a regulation problem is considered. However, in reference tracking tasks, the performance can be severely impaired by switching between different controllers. This section is devoted to analyze this problem and propose a simple technique to assist in making smooth transitions for the system switching between controllers.

Consider the problem of tracking a constant or slowly-varying set-point r. With reference to the design scheme in fig. 2, the problem can be solved by scaling the reference input r by the steady state gain of each controller Γ_i, $1 \leq i \leq n$. Let x_s denote the state of the controlled plant, and x_{c_i} the state of the i–th controller component $C_i(z)$, and let $\bar{x}_s$, $\bar{x}_{c_i}$ denote the corresponding equilibrium values reached when the reference r is applied. Suppose now that, at some instant in time tT_g, the i–th level controller is active and the system components are at the equilibrium state $\bar{x}_s, \bar{x}_{c_1}, \cdots, \bar{x}_{c_i}$; and that, at time $(t+1)T_g$, the execution of the j–th level controller is imposed by a preemption event or a conditioned schedule. If $j \leq i$, it can be easily verified that the active part of the system state remains at an equilibrium $\bar{x}_s, \bar{x}_{c_1}, \cdots, \bar{x}_{c_j}$. If instead $j > i$ (low-to-high level switching), the state is perturbed from the equilibrium. Indeed, the activation of a higher level controller abruptly introduces the dynamics of the re-activated (sleeping) states.

Sleeping states can be managed such that they are kept constant during their idle period, or they can be zeroed instantaneously or progressively with a simple and computationally inexpensive dynamics. No matter on how they are managed, their re-activation can produce a jump in the state value. Notice that keeping constant their values results in no jumps only if also the reference does not change. These jumps produce an undesirable behavior from a performance point of view. The use of a bumpless-like technique is advisable to cope with this issue. According to this approach, the idle states are re-set to suitable values before re-activation to avoid jumps and to leave the system at its equilibrium, if such was the case before the switching occurs. The sleeping state initialization value is computed as

$$x_{\text{sleeping}_j} = u_{c_j}(I - A_{c_j})^{-1} B_{c_j} = u_{c_j} W$$

where u_{c_j} is the current input to the j–th part of the controller. Notice that the switching logic introduces negligible overhead, since the vector W can be computed off–line.

7 Examples

The control of the two mechanical systems depicted in fig. 3 will be used to illustrate the application of the proposed technique. We report in table 2 the sampled-time linearized dynamics of the two systems (continuous-time models are readily available in the literature, see e.g. [23,24]).

In both examples, the first controller $C_1(z)$ is designed to ensure the stability requirement. The controllers $C_2(z)$ and $C_3(z)$ for the Furuta pendulum example are obtained applying twice in cascade an LQG design technique. For the TORA example, the controllers are instead carefully designed by hand to achieve performance enhancement with minimal complexity increase, i.e more *practical* in the sense of section 2). Prefilters $F_i(z)$ (depicted in fig. 2) are constants used to adapt the steady-state gain and ensure static requirements. The scheduler process is modeled simply by its steady-state probability distribution, which is assumed equal in the two examples and given by $\bar{\pi}_\tau = [1/20, 5/20, 14/20]$.

For the Furuta pendulum example in fig. 3-a, solving the LP problem 3 leads to a steady state conditioning probability distribution $\bar{\pi}_\sigma = [0.017, 0.98, 0.003]$. The resulting conditioned distribution $\bar{\pi}_d = [0.058, 0.94, 0.002]$ thus satisfies the 1-step average contractivity condition (2), hence AS-stability is guaranteed.

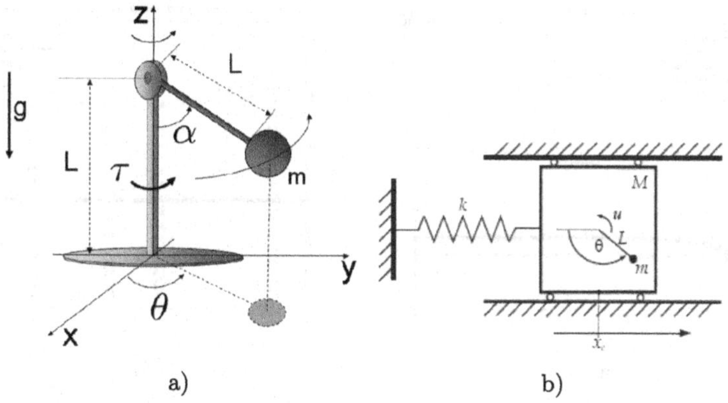

Fig. 3. Mechanical systems adopted for the anytime controller simulations: a Furuta pendulum with zero offset ([23] - a) and a Translational Oscillator/Rotational Actuator (TORA) system ([24] - b)

Table 2. Sampled-time transfer functions for systems in fig. 3 and hierarchical controllers used in simulations

FURUTA PENDULUM SYSTEM $G(z) = \frac{1.2\,10^{-3}(z+3.7)(z+0.3)}{(z-1)(z^2-1.7z+1)}$	
$C_1(z) = \frac{31.6(z^2-1.8z+1.1)}{(z-0.1)(z-0.5)}$	$F_1(z) = 21.28$
$C_2(z) = \frac{117.7(z-1.3)(z-4.7\,10^{-3})(z^2-1.4z+0.7)}{(z-0.5)(z+0.2)(z-0.1)(z^2+0.4z+0.9)}$	$F_2(z) = 0.54$
$C_3(z) = \frac{1370.9(z-0.4)(z-0.6)(z-0.2)(z+0.2)(z-4.7\,10^{-3})(z^2-0.7z+0.2)(z^2-0.4z+0.3)}{(z-0.5)^2(z+0.3)^2(z-0.1)^2(z^2+0.6z+0.8)(z^2+3.4z+4.7)}$	$F_3(z) = 2.73$

TORA SYSTEM $G(z) = \frac{0.27266(z+1)(z^2-1.967z+1)}{(z-1)^2(z^2-1.964z+1)}$	
$C_1(z) = \frac{2.0895(z-0.75)}{(z+0.3761)}$	$F_1(z) = 0.38$
$C_2(z) = \frac{0.8(z-0.4)}{(z+0.6)}$	$F_2(z) = 1.79$
$C_3(z) = \frac{0.73(z^2-0.76z+0.2228)}{(z+0.3)^2}$	$F_3(z) = 1.29$

In fig. 4-a, the *Root Mean Squares* (RMS) of the regulation error for different controllers is shown, corresponding to perturbed initial conditions $x_0 = [0, \pi/10, 0]^T$. Plots labeled Controller 1, 2, and 3, corresponding to results obtained without switching, are reported for reference. Notice the performance increase obtained by more complex controllers. Fig. 4-b shows a sample realization of the stochastic process used to model the OS scheduler. The RMS obtained by the greedy switching policy applied to this schedule shows instability. Notice that the axis labels on the right apply to this plot in fig. 4-a. On the same figure 4-a, the plot labeled "Markov" shows the RMS error obtained by the stochastically conditioned scheduler. Sample realizations of the conditioning and conditioned stochastic schedules used in simulations are reported in fig. 4-b.

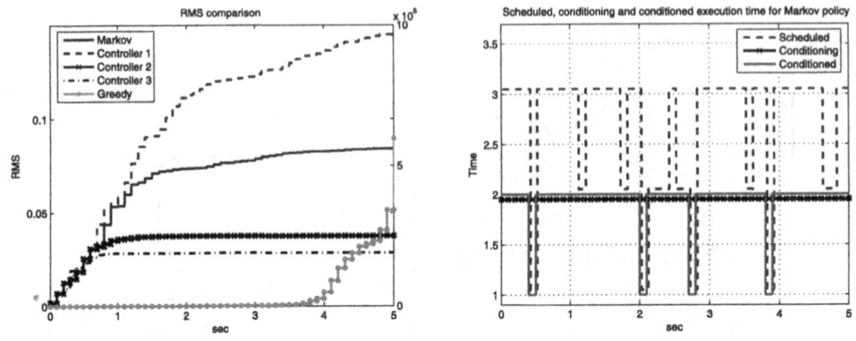

a) b)

Fig. 4. Regulation results for the Furuta pendulum example: a) RMS error of the closed loop system with different control schedulings b) allowable execution times provided by the OS scheduler, and the conditioning and conditioned processes

The example shows how the proposed stochastic switching policy ensures the AS-stability of the closed loop system (which is not guaranteed by the greedy policy), while it obtains a definite performance increase (of the order of 50%) with respect to the conservative scheduler (corresponding to using only Controller 1, see fig. 4-a).

Fig. 5 reports similar plots to illustrate application of the proposed methodology to the TORA example (fig. 3-b), with controllers chosen according to table 2. No solution to the 1-step average contractivity condition could be found in this case. A four-steps lifted version of the problem admits a solution, according to which the conditioning sequence of controllers is a concatenation of the 3^4 possible combinations of length 4 of the three controllers. The steady state conditioning probability distribution $\bar{\pi}_\sigma \in (0,1)^{3^4}$ is not reported here; it is however worth noticing that the particular controller sequence $\Gamma_2 - \Gamma_2 - \Gamma_2 - \Gamma_3$ is by far the most likely, being used in the 89, 204% of cases (except for preemptions). In figure 5-b, the scheduled and the conditioned controllers are depicted: the prevalence of the preferred pattern is apparent.

Results of simulations of the different controllers and scheduling policies are reported in fig. 5-a, for a regulation problem from perturbed initial conditions $X_0 = [0, 0, 0.1, 0]^T$.

The RMS performance plots in fig. 5-a show that the greedy policy (in this particular case) does not lead to divergence. However, it is quite remarkable that our proposed policy performs better than both the greedy and the conservative policies (indeed, slightly better than even using always Controller 2, which is not a feasible choice).

Finally, results of application of the proposed technique for a tracking control problem for the TORA example are reported in fig. 6. The reference to be tracked is a piecewise constant signal of amplitude $\pi/4$, period 10 seconds and pulse width of 30%. The comparison of RMS performance shows that direct

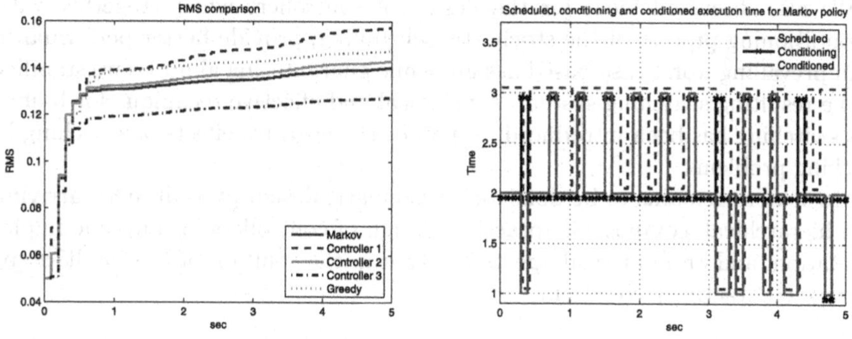

a) b)

Fig. 5. Regulation results for the TORA example: a) RMS error of the closed loop system with different control schedulings b) allowable execution times provided by the OS scheduler, and the conditioning and conditioned processes

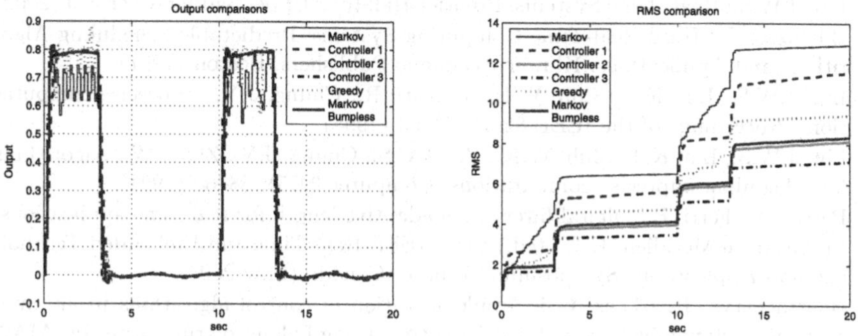

a) b)

Fig. 6. Tracking results for the Tora system: a) output signals; b) RMS errors

application of the conditioned switching policy performs poorly in the tracking case. This is due to the re-activation issues pointed out earlier. Using the simple bumpless switching technique proposed in Section 6, a significant performance improvement is achieved, as shown in both figures 6-a,b. The RMS performance of the bumpless conditioned switching policy is better than both the greedy and the conservative approaches.

8 Conclusions

We have shown that underexploitation of CPU time caused by conservative control scheduling policies can be effectively reduced, and control performance can be significatively enhanced, by adopting a schedule conditioning algorithm that uses a stochastic model of a preemptive RTOS scheduler.

We also discussed ideas for the design of controllers which, together with a conditioning process of the stochastic scheduling, provide better performance than prevailing worst case-based design, while guaranteeing almost sure stability of the resulting switching system. A practical and effective technique for bumpless switching has been introduced, to reduce the negative effects of switching in tracking problems.

Much work remains to be done on a systematic design procedure for arriving at a hierarchical, composable, practical design of controllers for anytime implementation, and on numerical apects involved in the solution of the (multi-step) average contractivity equation.

References

1. Liu, C.L., Layland, J.W.: Scheduling algorithms for multiprogramming in a hard-real-time environment. Journal of the Association for Computing Machinery 20(1) (1973)
2. Liu, J.W.S.: Real–Time Systems. Prentice Hall Inc., Upper Saddle River, NJ (2000)
3. Buttazzo, G.: Hard Real-Time Computing Systems: Predictable Scheduling Algorithms and Applications. Kluwer Academic Publishers, Boston (1997)
4. Liu, J.W.S., Lin, K.J., Shih, W.K., Bettati, R., Chung, J.Y.: Imprecise computation. Proceedings of the IEEE 82(1), 83–93 (1994)
5. Liu, J.W.S., Lin, K.J., Shih, W.K., Yu, A.C.S., Chung, J.Y., Zhao, W.: Algorithms for scheduling imprecise computations. Computer 24(5), 58–68 (1991)
6. Perrin, N., Ferri, B.: Digital filters with adaptive length for real–time applications. In: Le Royal Meridien, K.E., (ed.) Proc. IEEE Real-Time and Embedded Technology and Applications Symposium, Toronto, Canada (May 2004)
7. Bhattacharya, R., Balas, G.J.: Implementation of control algorithms in an environment of dynamically scheduled CPU time using balanced truncation. In: AIAA Guidance, Navigation, and Control Conference and Exhibit, Monterey, CA (August 2002)
8. Bhattacharya, R., Balas, G.J.: Anytime control algorithm: Model reduction approach. Journal of Guidance, Control, and Dynamics 27(5), 767–776 (2004)
9. Branicky, M.S.: Stability of hybrid systems: State of the art. In: Proc. 36th IEEE Conf. On Decision and Control, San Diego, California, USA, pp. 120–125 (December 1997)
10. DeCarlo, R.A., Branicky, M.S., Pettersson, S., Lennartson, B.: Perspectives and results on the stability and stabilizability of hybrid systems. IEEE Proceedings 88(7), 1069–1082 (2000)
11. Liberzon, D., Morse, A.S.: Basic problems in stability and design of switched systems. IEEE Contr. Syst. Mag. 19(5), 59–70 (1999)
12. Ye, H., Michel, A.N., Hou, L.: Stability theory for hybrid dynamical systems. IEEE Trans. Automat. Contr. 43(4), 461–474 (1998)
13. Hespanha, J.P., Morse, A.S.: Switching between stabilizing controllers. Automatica 38(11), 1905–1917 (2002)
14. Wicks, M.A., Peleties, P., DeCarlo, R.: Construction of piecewise Lyapunov functions for stabilizing switched systems. In: Proc. 33rd IEEE Conf. On Decision and Control, Lake Buena Vista, FL, pp. 3492–3497 (December 1994)

15. Wicks, M., DeCarlo, R.: Solution of coupled Lyapunov equations for the stabilization of multimodal linear systems. In: Proc. American Control Conf., Albuquerque, NM, pp. 1709–1713 (June 1997)
16. Pettersson, S., Lennartson, B.: Stabilization of hybrid systems using a min-projection strategy. In: Proc. American Control Conf., Arlington, Virginia, pp. 223–228 (June 2001)
17. Greco, L., Fontanelli, D., Bicchi, A.: Almost sure stability of anytime controllers via stochastic scheduling. In: Proc. IEEE Int. Conf. on Decision and Control, New Orleans, LO (December 2007)
18. Fang, Y., Loparo, K.A., Feng, X.: Almost sure and δ-moment stability of jump linear systems. Int. J. Control 59(5), 1281–1307 (1994)
19. Bolzern, P., Colaneri, P., De Nicolao, G.: On almost sure stability of discrete-time Markov jump linear systems. In: Proc. 43rd IEEE Conf. On Decision and Control, vol. 3, pp. 3204–3208 (2004)
20. Cervin, A., Lincoln, B., Eker, J., Årzén, K.E., Buttazzo, G.: The jitter margin and its application in the design of real-time control systems. In: Proc. 10th Int. Conf. on Real-Time and Embedded Computing Systems and Applications, Gothenburg, Sweden (August 2004)
21. Liberzon, D., Hespanha, J.P., Morse, A.S.: Stability of switched systems: A Lie-algebraic condition. Systems & Control Letters 37(3), 117–122 (1999)
22. Åström, K.J., Wittenmark, B.: Computer Controlled Systems. Prentice-Hall, Englewood Cliffs (1996)
23. Furuta, K., Yamakita, M., Kobayashi, S.: Swing-up control of inverted pendulum using pseudo-state feedback. Proceedings of the Institution of Mechanical Engineers. Pt.I. Journal of Systems and Control Engineering 206(I4), 263–269 (1992)
24. Bupp, R., Bernstein, D., Coppola, V.: A benchmark problem for nonlinear control design: Problem statement, experimental testbed and passive, nonlinear compensation. In: Proc. Amer. Contr. Conf, pp. 4363–4367 (1995)

Stochastic Satisfiability Modulo Theory: A Novel Technique for the Analysis of Probabilistic Hybrid Systems*

Martin Fränzle[1], Holger Hermanns[2], and Tino Teige[1]

[1] Carl von Ossietzky Universität, Oldenburg, Germany
{fraenzle,teige}@informatik.uni-oldenburg.de
[2] Saarland University, Saarbrücken, Germany
hermanns@cs.uni-sb.de

Abstract. The analysis of hybrid systems exhibiting probabilistic behaviour is notoriously difficult. To enable mechanised analysis of such systems, we extend the reasoning power of arithmetic satisfiability-modulo-theory solving (SMT) by a comprehensive treatment of randomized (a.k.a. stochastic) quantification over discrete variables within the mixed Boolean-arithmetic constraint system. This provides the technological basis for a fully symbolic analysis of probabilistic hybrid automata. Generalizing SMT-based bounded model-checking of hybrid automata [2,11], stochastic SMT permits the direct and fully symbolic analysis of probabilistic bounded reachability problems of probabilistic hybrid automata without resorting to approximation by intermediate finite-state abstractions.

1 Introduction

Over the last decade, formal verification of digital systems has evolved from an academic subject to an approach accepted by industry, with dozens of commercial tools now available. Among the most successful verification methods for finite-state systems is *bounded model checking* (BMC), as suggested by Groote et al. in [13] and by Biere et al. in [3]. The idea of BMC is to encode the next-state relation of a system as a propositional formula, to unroll this to some given finite depth k, and to augment it with a corresponding finite unravelling of the tableau of (the negation of) a temporal formula in order to obtain a propositional SAT problem which is satisfiable if and only if an error trace of length k exists. Enabled by the impressive gains in performance of propositional SAT checkers in recent years, BMC can now be applied to very large finite-state designs.

Though originally formulated for discrete transition systems, the concept of BMC also applies to hybrid discrete-continuous systems. The BMC formulae arising from such systems comprise complex Boolean combinations of arithmetic

* This work has been partially supported by the German Research Council (DFG) as part of the Transregional Collaborative Research Center "Automatic Verification and Analysis of Complex Systems" (SFB/TR 14 AVACS, www.avacs.org).

M. Egerstedt and B. Mishra (Eds.): HSCC 2008, LNCS 4981, pp. 172–186, 2008.

constraints over real-valued variables, thus entailing the need for satisfiability-modulo-theory (SMT) solvers over arithmetic theories to solve them. Such SMT procedures are thus currently in the focus of the SAT-solving community (e.g., [10]), as is their application to and tailoring for BMC of hybrid system (e.g., [2]).

The scope of these procedures, however, is confined to purely Boolean queries of the form "can the system ever exhibit an undesirable behavior?", whereas requirements for safety-critical systems frequently take the form of bounds on error probability, requiring the residual probability of engaging into undesirable behavior to be below an acceptable threshold. Automatically answering such queries requires, first, models of hybrid behavior that are able to represent probabilistic effects like component breakdown and, second, algorithms for state space traversal of such hybrid models.

In the context of hybrid systems augmented with probabilities, a wealth of models has been suggested by various authors. These models vary with respect to the degree of continuous dynamics, the support for random phenomena, and the degree to which they support non-determinism and compositionality. The cornerstones are formed by *probabilistic hybrid automata*, where state changes forced by continuous dynamics may involve discrete random experiments [20], *piecewise deterministic Markov processes* [8], where state changes may happen spontaneously in a manner similar to continuous-time Markov processes, and *stochastic differential equations* [1], where, like in Brownian motion, the random perturbation affects the dynamics continuously. In full generality, stochastic hybrid system (SHS) models can cover all such ingredients [16,6]. While such models have a vast potential of application, results related to their analysis and verification are limited, and often based on Monte-Carlo simulation [4,15]. For certain subclasses of piecewise deterministic Markov processes, of probabilistic hybrid automata, and of stochastic hybrid systems, reachability probabilities can be approximated (e.g. [20,7,17]).

In this paper, we present a technology that saves the virtues of SMT-based BMC, namely the fully symbolic treatment of hybrid state spaces, while advancing the reasoning power to probabilistic models and requirements. While the technique is more general, the current paper focuses on depth-bounded reachability of discrete-time probabilistic hybrid automata. With respect to the stochastic dynamics considered this model is very simple and thus constitutes a good attack point to pioneer effective model checking techniques for probabilistic hybrid systems, harvesting recent advances in depth-bounded reachability analysis for ordinary hybrid systems. Albeit being simple, the model of probabilistic hybrid automata has interesting practical applications [20].

In order to achieve this goal, we first define *stochastic satisfiability modulo theory* (SSMT) as the unification of stochastic propositional satisfiability [18] and satisfiability modulo theory. We proceed in Section 3 by defining discrete-time probabilistic hybrid automata. Section 4 formalizes the SSMT encoding of their probabilistic bounded reachability properties. Together with an extension of SMT solving to SSMT solving explained in Section 5, this symbolic encoding provides fully symbolic analysis of probabilistic bounded reachability problems of probabilistic hybrid automata without resorting to approximation by intermediate finite-state abstractions.

2 Stochastic Satisfiability Modulo Theories

The *satisfiability modulo theories* (SMT) problem is a decision problem for logical formulae wrt. combinations of background theories. In this section we extend the SMT problem for arithmetic theories over the real numbers to support *randomized quantification* over discrete variables as known from *stochastic satisfiability* (SSAT) [18] and *stochastic constraint programming* (SCP) [5].

Let φ be an SMT formula in conjunctive normal form (CNF) over some quantifier-free arithmetic theory T. I.e., φ is a logical *conjunction* of clauses, and a *clause* is a logical *disjunction* of (atomic) arithmetic predicates from T, as in $\varphi = (x > 0 \vee 2a + 4b \geq 3) \wedge (y > 0 \vee 2a + 4b < 1)$. An SSMT problem

$$\Phi = Q_1 x_1 \in \mathrm{dom}(x_1) \ldots Q_n x_n \in \mathrm{dom}(x_n) : \varphi$$

is specified by a *prefix* $Q_1 x_1 \in \mathrm{dom}(x_1) \ldots Q_n x_n \in \mathrm{dom}(x_n)$ binding the variables x_i to the quantifier Q_i,[1] and an SMT formula φ, also called *matrix*. We require that the domains $\mathrm{dom}(x)$ of quantified variables x are finite (and thus discrete). A quantifier Q_i, associated with variable x_i, is either *existential*, denoted as $\exists$, or *randomized*, denoted as Я_{d_i} where d_i is a discrete probability distribution over $dom(x_i)$. The value of a variable x_i bound by a randomized quantifier (randomized variable for short) is determined stochastically by the corresponding distribution d_i, while the value of an existentially quantified variable can be set arbitrarily. We usually denote such a probability distribution d_i by a list $\langle (v_1, p_1), \ldots, (v_m, p_m) \rangle$ of value pairs, where p_j is understood as the probability of setting variable x_i to v_j. The list satisfies $v_j \neq v_k$ for $j \neq k$, $\forall j : p_j > 0$, $\sum_{j=1}^{m} p_j = 1$, and $\mathrm{dom}(x_i) = \{v_1, \ldots, v_m\}$. For instance, $\text{Я}_{\{(0,0.2),(1,0.5),(2,0.3)\}} x \in \{0, 1, 2\}$ means that the variable x is assigned the value 0, 1, or 2 with probability 0.2, 0.5, and 0.3, respectively.

The semantics of an SSMT problem is defined by the *maximum probability of satisfaction*. Intuitively, for an SSMT formula $\Phi = \exists x_1 \in \mathrm{dom}(x_1)\ \text{Я}_{d_2} x_2 \in \mathrm{dom}(x_2)\ \exists x_3 \in \mathrm{dom}(x_3)\ \text{Я}_{d_4} x_4 \in \mathrm{dom}(x_4) : \varphi$ determine the maximum probability s.t. there is a value for x_1 s.t. for random values of x_2 there is a value for x_3 s.t. for random values of x_4 the SMT formula φ is satisfiable. (As standard, an SMT formula φ (in CNF) is *satisfiable* iff there exists a valuation σ of the variables in φ s.t. each clause is satisfied under σ, i.e., iff at least one atom in each clause is satisfied under σ. Otherwise, φ is *unsatisfiable.*) More formally, the maximum probability of satisfaction $Pr(\Phi)$ of an SSMT formula Φ is defined recursively by the following rules where φ denotes the matrix.

1. $Pr(\varphi) \;=\; 0$ if φ is unsatisfiable, and 1 otherwise.
2. $Pr(\exists x_i \in \mathrm{dom}(x_i) \ldots Q_n x_n \in \mathrm{dom}(x_n) : \varphi)$
   $= \max_{v \in \mathrm{dom}(x_i)} Pr(Q_{i+1} x_{i+1} \in \mathrm{dom}(x_{i+1}) \ldots Q_n x_n \in \mathrm{dom}(x_n) : \varphi[v/x_i])$.

[1] Not all variables occurring in the formula φ need to be bound by a quantifier.

$$\Phi = \exists x \in \{0,1\} \; \mathrm{H}_{((0,0.6),(1,0.4))} y \in \{0,1\} : (x > 0 \lor 2a + 4b \geq 3) \land (y > 0 \lor 2a + 4b < 1)$$

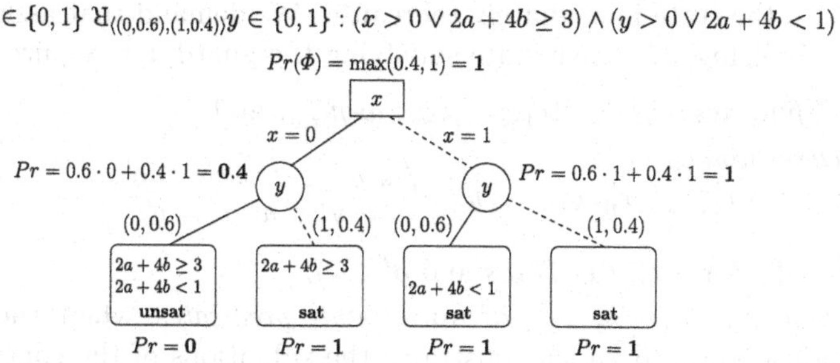

Fig. 1. Semantics of an SSMT formula depicted as a tree

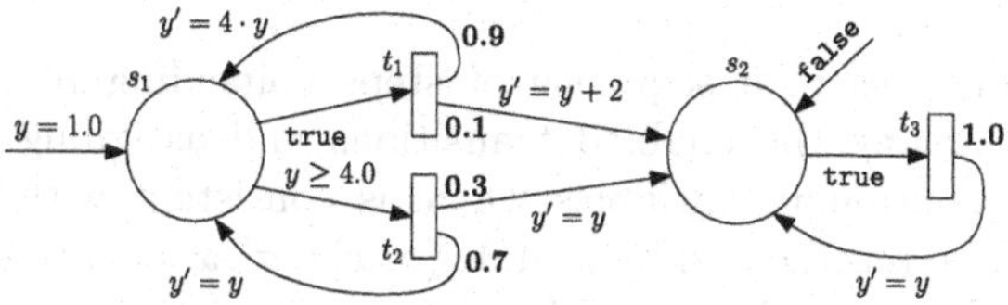

Fig. 2. A probabilistic hybrid automaton A

3. $Pr(\mathrm{H}_{d_i} x_i \in \mathrm{dom}(x_i) \ldots Q_n x_n \in \mathrm{dom}(x_n) : \varphi)$
   $= \sum_{(v,p) \in d_i} p \cdot Pr(Q_{i+1} x_{i+1} \in \mathrm{dom}(x_{i+1}) \ldots Q_n x_n \in \mathrm{dom}(x_n) : \varphi[v/x_i]).$

For an example see Fig. 1.

3   Probabilistic Hybrid Automata

A *discrete-time probabilistic hybrid automaton* $A = (\Sigma, Trans, R, s, p, g, asgn, init)$, as depicted in Fig. 2, consists of

- finite sets Σ of *locations*, *Trans* of *transitions*, and $R = \{x_1, \ldots, x_n\}$ of *continuous state components*, together with mappings $s : Trans \to \Sigma$, assigning to each transition its source location, and $p : Trans \to P(\Sigma)$, assigning to each transition a probability distribution over the target locations,[2]
- a family $g = (g_t)_{t \in Trans}$ assigning to each transition a *transition guard* enabling that transition, where the transition guard is an arithmetic predicate in our arithmetic theory T with free variables in R,
- a family $asgn = (asgn_{t,\sigma'})_{t \in Trans, \sigma' \in \Sigma}$ assigning to each transition and each target location an *assignment* which is defined by means of a T-predicate over variables in R and R', where $R' = \{x_1', \ldots, x_n'\}$ denotes primed variants of the state components in R. Undecorated state components $x \in R$ refer to the state immediately before the transition, while the primed variant $x' \in R'$

---

[2] W.l.o.g., distributions range over the full set Σ as unconnected locations and locations connected with probability 0 are indistinguishable wrt. probabilistic reachability.

refers to the state immediately thereafter. We demand that assignments are uniquely defined for each state satisfying the guard, i.e. require

1. *Definedness:* $g_t \Rightarrow \exists x'_1, \ldots, x'_n : asgn_{t,\sigma'}$ and
2. *Determinacy:*
$$g_t \Rightarrow \forall x'_1, \ldots, x'_n, y'_1, \ldots, y'_n : \left(\begin{array}{l} asgn_{t,\sigma'} \wedge asgn_{t,\sigma'}[y'_1, \ldots, y'_n / x'_1, \ldots, x'_n] \\ \Rightarrow \forall i \leq n : x'_i = y'_i \end{array} \right)$$

to be valid for each $t \in Trans$ and $\sigma' \in \Sigma$.

– a family $init = (init_\sigma)_{\sigma \in \Sigma}$ of *initial state predicates*, where each $init_\sigma$ is a T-predicate over R which constrains the valuations of the continuous state components when control resides *initially* in the discrete location σ.[3] For technical reasons, we demand that for each $\sigma \in \Sigma$, there is at most one $\boldsymbol{x} \in R \to \mathbb{R}$ which satisfies the predicate $init_\sigma$.

The automaton engages in a sequence of steps coinciding to its transitions, thereby selecting among the enabled transitions and assigning a sequence of valuations to the continuous variables which is consistent with the transition effects. A *step* can be represented by a tuple $(\sigma, \boldsymbol{x}, t, \sigma', \boldsymbol{x}')$ consisting of a source location $\sigma \in \Sigma$ and a target location σ', a continuous source state $\boldsymbol{x} \in (R \to \mathbb{R})$ and a continuous target state $\boldsymbol{x}' \in (R \to \mathbb{R})$, plus a transition $t \in Trans$. Such a tuple is a step of automaton A iff there is a transition $t \in Trans$ with $s(t) = \sigma$ such that $\boldsymbol{x}$ satisfies g_t and such that $asgn_{t,\sigma'}$ is satisfied if $\boldsymbol{x}$ is substituted for the variables in R and $\boldsymbol{x}'$ is substituted for the variables in R'. Slightly abusing notation, we will denote the latter fact by $\boldsymbol{x}, \boldsymbol{x}' \models asgn_{t,\sigma'}$ in the sequel. A *run* of A is an alternating sequence $r = (\sigma_0, \boldsymbol{x}_0) \xrightarrow{t_0}, \ldots, \xrightarrow{t_{n-1}} (\sigma_n, \boldsymbol{x}_n)$ of *hybrid states* $(\sigma_i, x_i) \in \Sigma \times (R \to \mathbb{R})$ and transitions $t_i \in Trans$, built from steps of A grounded in a viable initial state. I.e., $\boldsymbol{x}_0$ satisfies $init_{\sigma_0}$ and for all $i < n$, the tuple $(\sigma_i, \boldsymbol{x}_i, t_i, \sigma_{i+1}, \boldsymbol{x}_{i+1})$ is a step of A.

In the sequel, we will be interested in the probability of reaching a given set of undesirable locations within a given number of steps. Owed to the presence of nondeterminism, this probability measure is well-defined only if considering a particular policy (scheduler, adversary) that resolves the nondeterminism. We are interested in the *worst-case*, i.e., *maximum probability of reaching the undesirable states* achieved if ranging over arbitrary policies that may resolve nondeterminism using randomization, the history, etc. Since we are considering step-bounded probabilities, we can avoid the explicit introduction of policies, and instead define the probability of reaching some target state in a set TL of discrete locations within k steps directly as follows.

Definition 1 (Probabilistic bounded reachability). *Given a probabilistic hybrid automaton $A = (\Sigma, Trans, R, s, p, g, asgn, init)$, a set of target locations $TL \subset \Sigma$, a depth $k \in \mathbb{N}$, and a hybrid state $(\sigma, \boldsymbol{x}) \in \Sigma \times (R \to \mathbb{R})$, the* maximum probability of reaching the target TL from $(\sigma, \boldsymbol{x})$ in at most k steps *is denoted $P^k_A(\sigma, \boldsymbol{x}, TL)$. It is defined recursively over the depth k as follows:*

[3] A discrete location σ not to be taken initially takes the predicate $init_\sigma = \texttt{false}$.

$$P_A^k(\sigma, \boldsymbol{x}, TL) = \begin{cases} 1 & \text{if } \sigma \in TL, \\ 0 & \text{if } \sigma \notin TL \wedge k = 0, \\ \max_{t \in Enabled} \sum_{\sigma' \in \Sigma} \left(p(t)(\sigma') \cdot P_{t,\sigma'}^{k-1} \right) & \text{if } \sigma \notin TL \wedge k > 0, \end{cases}$$

where $Enabled = \{t \in Trans, s(t) = \sigma, \boldsymbol{x} \models g(t)\}$ *and* $P_{t,\sigma'}^k = P_A^k(\sigma', \boldsymbol{x}', TL)$ *for the unique* $\boldsymbol{x}'$ *with* $\boldsymbol{x}, \boldsymbol{x}' \models asgn_{t,\sigma'}$.

For an illustration of probabilistic bounded reachability consider the probabilistic hybrid automaton A from Fig. 2 with $TL = \{s_2\}$. Then $P_A^0(s_1, y \mapsto 1.0, TL) = 0.0$, $P_A^1(s_1, y \mapsto 1.0, TL) = 0.1$, $P_A^2(s_1, y \mapsto 1.0, TL) = 0.1 + 0.9 \cdot 0.3 = 0.37$, $P_A^3(s_1, y \mapsto 1.0, TL) = 0.1 + 0.9 \cdot (0.3 + 0.7 \cdot 0.3) = 0.559$.

Based on the worst-case probability of reaching TL, we define the *probabilistic bounded model checking problem (PBMC, for short)* to be the problem of deciding whether the maximum probability of reaching the undesirable states from an initial state within a given number of steps lies below a given threshold:

Definition 2 (Probabilistic bounded model checking). *Given a probabilistic hybrid automaton* $A = (\Sigma, Trans, R, s, p, g, asgn, init)$, *a set of target locations* $TL \subset \Sigma$, *a depth* $k \in \mathbb{N}$, *and a probability threshold* $x \in [0, 1]$, *the* probabilistic bounded model checking problem wrt. target states TL and depth k *is to determine whether* $\max\{P_A^k(\sigma, \boldsymbol{x}, TL) \mid \sigma \in \Sigma, \boldsymbol{x} \models init_\sigma\} \leq x$.

4 Reducing PBMC to SSMT

In order to perform probabilistic bounded model checking (PBMC) we employ a reduction to stochastic satisfiability modulo theory (SSMT) which generalizes the propositional SAT encodings for bounded model checking of finite-state systems [3] and the SMT encodings for BMC of hybrid automata [2,11]. Our construction proceeds in two phases: First, we generate the matrix of the SSMT formula. This matrix is an SMT formula encoding all runs of A of the given length $k \in \mathbb{N}$, akin to [2,11]. Thereafter, we add the quantifier prefix encoding the probabilistic and the non-deterministic choices, whereby a probabilistic choice reduces to a randomized quantifier while a non-deterministic choice yields an existential quantifier.

Phase 1: Constructing the matrix. Let $A = (\Sigma, Trans, R, s, p, g, asgn, init)$ be a discrete-time probabilistic hybrid automaton. In order to encode the runs of A of some given length $k \in \mathbb{N}$ by a matrix formula, we proceed as follows:

1. For encoding the discrete state $\sigma \in \Sigma$, we take $k+1$ variables σ^i, for $0 \leq i \leq k$, each with domain Σ. The value of σ^i coincides with the discrete location which automaton A resides in during step i.
2. For representing transitions $t \in Trans$, we take k variables t^i with domain $Trans$, for $1 \leq i \leq k$. The value of t^i encodes the ith move in the run of A.
3. For each continuous state component $x \in R$ we take $k+1$ real-valued variables x^i. The value of x^{i-1} encodes the value of x before the ith transition in the run (and thus x^i the value thereafter).

4. The interplay between discrete states and transitions requires that t^i implies $\sigma^{i-1} = s(t^i)$. This can be expressed by the $k \cdot |\mathit{Trans}|$ SSMT clauses in

$$\bigwedge_{i=1}^{k} \bigwedge_{t \in \mathit{Trans}} \left(t^i = t \Rightarrow \sigma^{i-1} = s(t)\right) ,$$

where $\varphi \Rightarrow \psi$ abbreviates $\neg\varphi \vee \psi$.

5. Similarly, enabledness of the transition, i.e. validity of the *transition guard* in the pre-state, is enforced through the constraint system

$$\bigwedge_{i=1}^{k} \bigwedge_{t \in \mathit{Trans}} \left(t^i = t \Rightarrow g_t[x_1^{i-1}, \ldots, x_n^{i-1}/x_1, \ldots, x_n]\right) ,$$

where $\{x_1, \ldots, x_n\} = R$. Since g_t need not be a simple T-constraint, the above formula is not necessarily in conjunctive normal form and thus not an SSMT matrix formula. An equisatisfiable CNF can, however, always be obtained by introduction of auxiliary variables as in [12].

6. Likewise, *assignments* are dealt with by

$$\bigwedge_{i=1}^{k} \bigwedge_{t \in \mathit{Trans}} \bigwedge_{\sigma' \in \Sigma} \begin{pmatrix} (t^i = t \wedge \sigma_i = \sigma') \Rightarrow \\ \mathit{asgn}_{t,\sigma'}[x_1^i, \ldots, x_n^i/x_1', \ldots, x_n'][x_1^{i-1}, \ldots, x_n^{i-1}/x_1, \ldots, x_n] \end{pmatrix}$$

Due to the probabilistic choice between variants of the selected transition, the assignment depends on both the transition t^i and the actual target location σ^i.

7. Finally, we complete the matrix by adding constraints describing the allowable initial states through the SSMT constraint system $\bigwedge_{\sigma \in \Sigma} \left(\sigma^0 = \sigma \Rightarrow \mathit{init}_\sigma\right)$.

The conjunction of the above formulae yields the matrix of our SSMT formula encoding the PBMC problem. Satisfying valuations of the matrix thus obtained are in one-to-one correspondence to the runs of A of length k [11]. As in BMC [3], satisfaction of temporal properties on all runs of depth k can thus be checked by adding to the formula the k-fold unrolling of a tableaux of the (negated) property, then checking the resulting formula for unsatisfiability. Using standard techniques from predicative semantics [14], the translation scheme can be extended to both shared variable and synchronous message-passing parallelism, thereby yielding formulae of size linear in the number of parallel components.

Phase 2: Encoding choices. Let φ be the matrix corresponding to the conjunction of the above formulae. As each non-deterministic choice corresponds to selecting a transition while each probabilistic choice amounts to selecting an actual target location, we generate the following SSMT formula:

8. An SSMT formula $\psi = \psi_1$ encoding the probabilitsic and non-deterministic choices along the run is obtained by alternating the quantifiers consistently with the alternation of choices. To permit a homogeneous randomized quantification over all transitions, we first select a finite set $O = \{o_1, \ldots, o_n\}$ of choice options for randomized choices, a probability distribution $p_O : O \to (0, 1]$ over O, and a function $\mathit{pd} : \mathit{Trans} \times \Sigma \to 2^O$ such that these together satisfy

$$\forall t \in \mathit{Trans}, \sigma \in \Sigma : \textstyle\sum_{pc \in pd(t,\sigma)} p_O(pc) = p(t)(\sigma) \text{ and}$$
$$\forall t \in \mathit{Trans}, \sigma_1, \sigma_2 \in \Sigma : \mathit{pd}(t, \sigma_1) \cap \mathit{pd}(t, \sigma_2) = \emptyset .$$

Such a set O and probability distribution p_O do always exist. The worst-case cardinality of O is the number $|\{p(t)(\sigma) \mid t \in \mathit{Trans}, \sigma \in \Sigma\}|$ of different transition probabilities, but can be considerably smaller due to different probability constants being the sums of each other.

Now, we encode the non-deterministic choices by existential quantification over the transitions in *Trans* and the probabilistic choices by randomized quantification over O. The latter quantifiers choose an auxiliary variable pc_i in each step which in turn is mapped to the target location σ_i by means of the mapping pd. Therefore, ψ_i is defined recursively as follows: for $1 \leq i < k$,

$$\psi_i = \exists t^i \in \mathit{Trans} : \text{Я}_{\langle(o_1,p_O(o_1)),\ldots,(o_n,p_O(o_n))\rangle} pc_i \in O : \psi_{i+1} \ , \text{ and}$$

$$\psi_k = \varphi \wedge \bigwedge_{k=1}^{n} \bigwedge_{t \in \mathit{Trans}} \bigwedge_{\sigma \in \Sigma} [(t_i = t \wedge \sigma_i = \sigma) \Rightarrow \bigvee_{o \in pd(t,\sigma)} pc_i = o] \ .$$

9. In order to solve the PBMC problem, it remains to choose the initial state maximizing the probability. This can be accomplished by existential quantification, yielding the formula $\mathit{PBMC}^k_{A,TL} = \exists \sigma^0 \in \Sigma : \psi$. Given the structural similarity between probabilistic bounded reachability and quantification in SSMT, this reduction is correct in the following sense:

Proposition 1 (Correctness of reduction). *$Pr(\mathit{PBMC}^k_{A,TL}) \leq x$ iff A satisfies the PBMC problem wrt. threshold x, depth k, and target states TL.*

5 Algorithm for SSMT

In this section we present our algorithm for calculating the maximum probability of satisfaction of an SSMT formula. More precisely, for a given SSMT formula Φ and a lower and upper threshold $t_l, t_u \in [0,1]$ with $t_l \leq t_u$, the algorithm returns a witness value $p \leq Pr(\Phi)$ s.t. $p > t_u$ iff $Pr(\Phi) > t_u$, a value $p < t_l$ iff $Pr(\Phi) < t_l$, or otherwise (i.e., $t_l \leq Pr(\Phi) \leq t_u$) the value $p = Pr(\Phi)$. It computes the exact value of $Pr(\Phi)$ when taking $t_l = 0$ and $t_u = 1$, but whenever we are interested in a particular target probability x, it saves computational effort by not being forced to be exact about probabilities different from $x = t_l = t_u$. As a proof procedure, we generalize to SSMT the extended Davis-Putnam-Logemann-Loveland (DPLL) algorithm [9] for SSAT described in [18].

Our SSMT algorithm consists of *three layers.* The lowermost layer is a *theory solver TS* for reasoning about a conjunctive system over theory T. As the middle layer, an *SMT solver* for disjunctive systems over T employs the theory solver TS. Finally, the *SSMT solver* is an extension of the SMT layer to deal with existential and randomized quantification.

Theory layer. As in SAT-modulo-theory solving, the theory solver TS decides whether a conjunctive system M of atomic predicates from T is satisfiable over T. Furthermore, we support theory solvers which can deduce new information from the given facts in the form of forward inference, but do not require this functionality to be present or even complete. We denote these capabilities of the theory solver, which following the SMT tradition we assume as given, by three deduction rules:

$$\begin{array}{lll} M \longrightarrow_{TS} \texttt{sat} & \text{iff} & M \text{ is satisfiable.} \\ M \longrightarrow_{TS} \texttt{unsat} & \text{iff} & M \text{ is unsatisfiable.} \\ M \longrightarrow_{TS} M \cdot \langle a \rangle & \text{only if} & M \text{ is satisfiable and } M \models a. \end{array}$$

SMT layer. The SMT layer is described by the following rules. For more details we refer the reader to, e.g., the survey in [19]. In the sequel, let φ be an SMT formula over T in CNF. A *choice* asserts a theory atom occurring in φ or its negation to enforce progress in the backtracking search (rule (1)).

$$\frac{a \in c \in \varphi, b = a \text{ or } b = \neg a, b \notin M}{(\varphi, M) \longrightarrow_{SMT} (\varphi, M \cdot \langle |, b \rangle)} \quad (1)$$

Here, M denotes the list of all asserted atoms and $a \in c \in \varphi$ means that there is a theory atom a occurring in some clause c of φ. In order to facilitate (non-chronological) backtracking, in addition, we intersperse a special marker symbol $|$ into M. When we consider M as a conjunctive system (for the theory solver TS) we neglect the marker symbols $|$ in M.

The rules (2) (*unit propagation*) and (3) (*theory propagation*) are applied if new facts can be deduced. The deduced atoms are added to M.

$$\frac{(a_1 \vee \ldots \vee a_m) \in \varphi, a_i \notin M, \neg a_i \notin M, \forall j \in \mathbb{N}_{\leq m} \text{ with } j \neq i : \neg a_j \in M}{(\varphi, M) \longrightarrow_{SMT} (\varphi, M \cdot \langle a_i \rangle)} \quad (2)$$

$$\frac{M \longrightarrow_{TS} M \cdot \langle a \rangle, a \notin M, \exists c \in \varphi : a \in c \text{ or } \neg a \in c}{(\varphi, M) \longrightarrow_{SMT} (\varphi, M \cdot \langle a \rangle)} \quad (3)$$

If a conflict occurs, i.e. the list of asserted atoms has become infeasible, an (small or even minimal) reason for this conflicting situation can be extracted. To prevent the solver from revisiting the same or a similar conflict, this information can be encoded as an additional, implied clause, a.k.a. *conflict clause*, and added to the formula. This is referred to as *conflict-driven clause learning* (rule (4)).

$$\frac{M = M' \cdot \langle | \rangle \cdot M'', a_1, \ldots, a_{k-1} \in M', a_k \in M'', \langle a_1, \ldots, a_k \rangle \longrightarrow_{TS} \texttt{unsat}}{(\varphi, M) \longrightarrow_{SMT} (\varphi \wedge (\neg a_1 \vee \ldots \vee \neg a_k), M)} \quad (4)$$

Note that there are many different techniques for (efficient) generation of such an infeasible subsystem $a_1, \ldots, a_k$ of M. In rule (4), we use the *unique implication point technique* in order to enforce progress upon non-chronological backtracking in rule (5) (cf., e.g., [19]).

To resolve the conflict, the solver *non-chronologically backtracks* to a previous node in the search tree while often skipping multiple nodes in the tree. The backtrack node can be computed by means of the conflict clause as given by rule (5). Due to the use of unique implication points in conflict clauses, we can enforce a conflict clause to become unit upon backtracking and do directly assert the propagated atom.

$$\frac{M = M' \cdot \langle | \rangle \cdot M'', c \in \varphi, a \in c, \neg a \in M'', \forall a' \in c \text{ with } a' \neq a : \neg a' \in M'}{(\varphi, M) \longrightarrow_{SMT} (\varphi, M' \cdot \langle a \rangle)} \tag{5}$$

If each clause in φ contains at least one asserted atom and the conjunction of all asserted atoms is satisfiable then the SMT formula is satisfiable.

$$\frac{M \longrightarrow_{TS} \mathtt{sat}, \forall c \in \varphi\ \exists a \in c : a \in M}{(\varphi, M) \longrightarrow_{SMT} \mathtt{sat}} \tag{6}$$

If a conflict cannot be resolved, i.e. there is no choice point to be revoked, the formula is unsatisfiable.

$$\frac{| \notin M, M \longrightarrow_{TS} \mathtt{unsat}}{(\varphi, M) \longrightarrow_{SMT} \mathtt{unsat}} \tag{7}$$

SSMT layer. Given the rules of the SMT layer, we construct the SSMT algorithm. Let $\Phi = Pre : \varphi$ be an SSMT formula. W.l.o.g., we assume that all possible value assignments for quantified variables of the SSMT formula Φ are encoded as clauses in the matrix of Φ. More formally, forall $(Qx \in \{v_1, \ldots, v_k\}) \in Pre$ there is a clause $(x = v_1 \vee \ldots \vee x = v_k) \in \varphi$. By this information, the domain emptiness of a quantified variable will be detected by the SMT solver. An SSMT deduction starts from a state $(Pre, \varphi, M, t_l, t_u)$, where $\Phi := Pre : \varphi$ is an SSMT formula, M is a list of asserted atoms, and t_l, t_u are the lower and upper target thresholds. The deduction yields either a new proof state of the same structure or a pair (p, φ') of a satisfaction probability and a new matrix, in which case the deduction terminates. If $(Pre, \varphi, M, t_l, t_u) \longrightarrow^*_{SSMT} (p, \varphi')$ then $p > t_u$ iff $Pr(\Phi) > t_u$ under M, i.e. iff $Pr(Pre : (\varphi \wedge M)) > t_u$, and analogously $p < t_l$ iff $Pr(\Phi) < t_l$ under M, and otherwise $p = Pr(\Phi)$ under M. The new matrix $\varphi' \supseteq \varphi$ potentially contains learned clauses, i.e. $\forall c \in \varphi' - \varphi : (\varphi \models c)$.

The SSMT layer consists of the following rules. To deal with quantified variables, we *branch* the search by assigning values and combine the results according to the semantics of Section 2 (rules (8) and (9)). For the branching SSMT calls we update the target thresholds correspondingly. I.e., in case of an existentially quantified variable we transmit t_l, t_u for the branch $x = v$ and $\max(t_l, p_1), t_u$ for the remaining subtree, since we can neglect probabilities of the remaining subtree less than the already computed value p_1 for branch $x = v$. For randomized variables, we take the probability p_v for the value v and the maximum possible remaining probability $p_r = \sum_{v' \in D - \{v\}, (v', p_{v'}) \in d} p_{v'}$ for all other values $v' \neq v$ into account. I.e., the lower and upper target thresholds for the call where x is assigned to v are $(t_l - p_r)/p_v$ and t_u/p_v, resp., since if $t_l - p_r$ cannot be reached by branch $x = v$ then t_l cannot be reached at all. If t_u is already exceeded by branch $x = v$ then we already exceeded the upper target threshold, which we later will exploit within pruning rules wrt. the threshold parameters. The target thresholds for all remaining branches decrease by the computed probability $p_v \cdot p_1$ for $x = v$.

$$\frac{\begin{array}{c}|D| \geq 2, v \in D, \\ (Pre, \varphi, M \cdot \langle x = v \rangle, t_l, t_u) \longrightarrow^*_{SSMT} (p_1, \varphi_1), consistent(\varphi_1, M), \\ (\exists x \in D \setminus \{v\} \cdot Pre, \varphi_1, M \cdot \langle x \neq v \rangle, \max(t_l, p_1), t_u) \longrightarrow^*_{SSMT} (p_2, \varphi_2)\end{array}}{(\exists x \in D \cdot Pre, \varphi, M, t_l, t_u) \longrightarrow_{SSMT} (\max(p_1, p_2), \varphi_2)} \tag{8}$$

where $consistent(\varphi_1, M) := (\neg\exists c \in \varphi_1 : \forall a \in c : M \cdot \langle a \rangle \longrightarrow_{TS} \textbf{unsat})$ indicates whether the new matrix φ_1 is consistent with the list M of asserted atoms.

$$\frac{\begin{array}{c}|D| \geq 2, v \in D, (v, p_v) \in d, p_r = \sum_{v' \in D - \{v\}, (v', p_{v'}) \in d} p_{v'}, \\ (Pre, \varphi, M \cdot \langle x = v \rangle, (t_l - p_r)/p_v, t_u/p_v) \overset{*}{\longrightarrow}_{SSMT} (p_1, \varphi_1), consistent(\varphi_1, M), \\ (\text{Я}_d x \in D \setminus \{v\} \cdot Pre, \varphi_1, M \cdot \langle x \neq v \rangle, t_l - p_v \cdot p_1, t_u - p_v \cdot p_1) \overset{*}{\longrightarrow}_{SSMT} (p_2, \varphi_2)\end{array}}{(\text{Я}_d x \in D \cdot Pre, \varphi, M, t_l, t_u) \longrightarrow_{SSMT} (p_v \cdot p_1 + p_2, \varphi_2)} \quad (9)$$

If it turns out that the upper target threshold t_u is already reached by the branch under investigation, then we can save visiting any other branch and instead return the positive result immediately via rules (10) and (11). If the remaining branches have insufficient probability mass to reach the lower target threshold t_l then we return the negative result by rule (12) without further exploration. These pruning rules generalize the *thresholding* rules for the propositional case from [18].

$$\frac{\begin{array}{c}v \in D, (Pre, \varphi, M \cdot \langle x = v \rangle, t_l, t_u) \overset{*}{\longrightarrow}_{SSMT} (p, \varphi'), \\ consistent(\varphi', M), p > t_u \text{ or } |D| = 1\end{array}}{(\exists x \in D \cdot Pre, \varphi, M, t_l, t_u) \longrightarrow_{SSMT} (p, \varphi')} \quad (10)$$

$$\frac{\begin{array}{c}v \in D, (v, p_v) \in d, p_r = 0 + \sum_{v' \in D - \{v\}, (v', p_{v'}) \in d} p_{v'}, \\ (Pre, \varphi, M \cdot \langle x = v \rangle, (t_l - p_r)/p_v, t_u/p_v) \overset{*}{\longrightarrow}_{SSMT} (p, \varphi'), \\ consistent(\varphi', M), p_v \cdot p > t_u \text{ or } |D| = 1\end{array}}{(\text{Я}_d x \in D \cdot Pre, \varphi, M, t_l, t_u) \longrightarrow_{SSMT} (p_v \cdot p, \varphi')} \quad (11)$$

$$\frac{\begin{array}{c}|D| \geq 2, v \in D, (v, p_v) \in d, p_r = \sum_{v' \in D - \{v\}, (v', p_{v'}) \in d} p_{v'}, \\ (Pre, \varphi, M \cdot \langle x = v \rangle, (t_l - p_r)/p_v, t_u/p_v) \overset{*}{\longrightarrow}_{SSMT} (p, \varphi'), \\ consistent(\varphi', M), t_l - p_v \cdot p > p_r\end{array}}{(\text{Я}_d x \in D \cdot Pre, \varphi, M, t_l, t_u) \longrightarrow_{SSMT} (p_v \cdot p, \varphi')} \quad (12)$$

It could also happen that after the first SSMT call (for $x = v$), all remaining branches for x lead to probability 0. This is indicated by the returned new matrix φ', in particular by some learned conflict clause in φ', which is inconsistent under the list M of asserted atoms (without assignment $x = v$). In this case, rules (13) and (14) save unnecessary visits of the remaining branches.

$$\frac{v \in D, (Pre, \varphi, M \cdot \langle x = v \rangle, t_l, t_u) \overset{*}{\longrightarrow}_{SSMT} (p, \varphi'), inconsistent(\varphi', M)}{(\exists x \in D \cdot Pre, \varphi, M, t_l, t_u) \longrightarrow_{SSMT} (p, \varphi')} \quad (13)$$

$$\frac{\begin{array}{c}v \in D, (v, p_v) \in d, p_r = 0 + \sum_{v' \in D - \{v\}, (v', p_{v'}) \in d} p_{v'}, \\ (Pre, \varphi, M \cdot \langle x = v \rangle, (t_l - p_r)/p_v, t_u/p_v) \overset{*}{\longrightarrow}_{SSMT} (p, \varphi'), \\ inconsistent(\varphi', M)\end{array}}{(\text{Я}_d x \in D \cdot Pre, \varphi, M, t_l, t_u) \longrightarrow_{SSMT} (p_v \cdot p, \varphi')} \quad (14)$$

where $inconsistent(\varphi', M) := \neg consistent(\varphi', M)$ means that at least one clause in the new matrix φ' is inconsistent with M which forces the solver to backtrack to a previous level (thereby avoiding computation of all other possible branches of x) while keeping the already calculated probability. Note that chained executions of that rule, which occur if the returned matrix φ' is also inconsistent on some previous levels, correspond to *non-chronological backtracking*.

All of the aforementioned SSMT rules are designed to deal with existential and randomized quantification. The following rules embed the SMT layer into the SSMT algorithm. If all quantified variables have a definite value, i.e. the current prefix is empty, we can execute the *choice* rule (15).

$$\frac{(\varphi, M) \longrightarrow_{SMT} (\varphi, M \cdot \langle |, a \rangle)}{(\emptyset, \varphi, M, t_l, t_u) \longrightarrow_{SSMT} (\emptyset, \varphi, M \cdot \langle |, a \rangle, t_l, t_u)} \tag{15}$$

If the SMT solver can propagate new facts from the matrix φ and the list M of asserted atoms, we can do the same in the SSMT layer. I.e., both *unit propagation* and *theory propagation* are lifted to SSMT by rule (16).

$$\frac{(\varphi, M) \longrightarrow_{SMT} (\varphi, M \cdot \langle a \rangle)}{(Pre, \varphi, M, t_l, t_u) \longrightarrow_{SSMT} (update(Pre, a), \varphi, M \cdot \langle a \rangle, t_l, t_u)} \tag{16}$$

where $update(Pre, a)$ prunes the domains $\mathrm{dom}(x)$ in the prefix Pre of the quantified variables x corresponding to the theory atom a. We do not require that *update* is a complete (yet a sound) pruning procedure, i.e., potentially not all but only some non-solutions are removed from $\mathrm{dom}(x)$. E.g., if $a = x > 3$ then the updated domain of x is $\{v_x \in \mathrm{dom}(x) : v_x > 3\}$ or a superset thereof in case of incomplete pruning.

A conflict clause learned by the SMT solver is also valid within the SSMT framework, i.e. *conflict-driven clause learning* is supported by rule (17). Note that implied clauses can be added at any point in the search, in particular even if the current prefix is non-empty.

$$\frac{(\varphi, M) \longrightarrow_{SMT} (\varphi \wedge c, M)}{(Pre, \varphi, M, t_l, t_u) \longrightarrow_{SSMT} (Pre, \varphi \wedge c, M, t_l, t_u)} \tag{17}$$

Rule (18) enables the SSMT solver to *backjump* within the theory part of the search tree.

$$\frac{(\varphi, M \cdot \langle | \rangle \cdot M') \longrightarrow_{SMT} (\varphi, M)}{(\emptyset, \varphi, M \cdot \langle | \rangle \cdot M', t_l, t_u) \longrightarrow_{SSMT} (\emptyset, \varphi, M, t_l, t_u)} \tag{18}$$

Since a marker symbol $|$ is added to the list of asserted atoms only if there is an empty prefix (cf. rule 15), i.e. if all quantified variables are assigned to a value, rule (18) guarantees that value assignments of quantified variables will *not* be removed from the list of asserted atoms (i.e., M' does not contain such assignments).

If a solution of the matrix φ is found by the SMT layer and the prefix Pre does *not* contain randomized quantifiers then the probability 1 is returned by rule (19), since for the remaining existentially quantified variables in Pre there is at least one satisfying branch. However, if some randomized quantifiers are included in Pre, we may not return the probability 1 for the entire subtree, since the initial domain for some randomized variables could be pruned (by rule (16)), and potentially the probability of satisfaction for that subtree could be less 1.

$$\frac{(\varphi, M) \longrightarrow_{SMT} \texttt{sat}, (\text{Ꝁ}_d x \in D) \notin Pre}{(Pre, \varphi, M, t_l, t_u) \longrightarrow_{SSMT} (1, \varphi)} \tag{19}$$

If the SMT solver finds out that the matrix φ is unsatisfiable under M then rule (20) may return the satisfaction probability 0 even if the prefix Pre is non-empty, since no assignment to the quantified variables could counterfeit the unsatisfiability of φ under M.

$$\frac{(\varphi, M) \longrightarrow_{SMT} \texttt{unsat}}{(Pre, \varphi, M, t_l, t_u) \longrightarrow_{SSMT} (0, \varphi)} \tag{20}$$

The above unification of DPLL-based SSAT solving with of SMT is sound and complete in the following sense.

Proposition 2 (Completeness and soundness). *Given an SSMT formula $\Phi = Pre : \varphi$ and the lower and upper probability thresholds t_l, t_u, we have:*

1. *The deduction relation $\longrightarrow_{SSMT}$ is terminating when iteratively applied to $(Pre, \varphi, \emptyset, t_l, t_u)$ as start of the deduction sequence. Each terminal state x has the form $x = (p, \varphi')$ with $p \in [0,1]$ and φ' being an SMT formula.*
2. *If $(Pre, \varphi, \emptyset, t_l, t_u) \longrightarrow^*_{SSMT} (p, \varphi')$ then $p > t_u$ if $Pr(\Phi) > t_u$, and $p < t_l$ if $Pr(\Phi) < t_l$, and $p = Pr(\Phi)$ if $t_l \leq Pr(\Phi) \leq t_u$.*

Example of the SSMT algorithm. Consider target thresholds $t_l = 0.45$ and $t_u = 0.52$ and formula $\Phi = \exists x \in \{0,1\}$ $\text{Ꝁ}_{\langle(0,0.6),(1,0.4)\rangle} y \in \{0,1\} : (x > 0 \vee 2a + 4b \geq 3) \wedge (y > 0 \vee 2a + 4b < 1)$ from Fig. 1. The initial proof state is $(\exists x \in \{0,1\}$ $\text{Ꝁ}_{\langle(0,0.6),(1,0.4)\rangle} y \in \{0,1\}, \varphi, \emptyset, 0.45, 0.52)$, where $\varphi = (x > 0 \vee 2a + 4b \geq 3) \wedge (y > 0 \vee 2a + 4b < 1)$. Only rules (8), (10), or (13) are applicable, each involving a choice over the domain of the leading quantifier. To determine the rule to apply, we choose the value 0 for x and obtain $(\text{Ꝁ}_{\langle(0,0.6),(1,0.4)\rangle} y \in \{0,1\}, \varphi, \langle x = 0\rangle, 0.45, 0.52)$. Then, (16) gives us the theory atom $2a + 4b \geq 3$, i.e. we go to $(\text{Ꝁ}_{\langle(0,0.6),(1,0.4)\rangle} y \in \{0,1\}, \varphi, \langle x = 0, 2a + 4b \geq 3\rangle, 0.45, 0.52)$. Here, we select value 0 with probability 0.6 for the randomized variable y whence the maximum possible remaining probability is 0.4. This gives state $(\emptyset, \varphi, M = \langle x = 0, 2a + 4b \geq 3, y = 0\rangle, t_l', t_u')$ where $t_l' = (0.45 - 0.4)/0.6$ and $t_u' = 0.52/0.6$. This triggers the deduction of $2a + 4b < 1$ again by rule (16). We thus encounter a conflict since the two theory atoms are inconsistent, and learn, e.g., the conflict clause $(x \neq 0 \vee y \neq 0)$. Hence, $(\emptyset, \varphi, M, t_l', t_u') \longrightarrow^*_{SSMT} (0, \varphi')$ where $\varphi' = \varphi \wedge (x \neq 0 \vee y \neq 0)$. By rule (12), this yields $(\text{Ꝁ}_{\langle(0,0.6),(1,0.4)\rangle} y \in \{0,1\}, \varphi, \langle x = 0\rangle, 0.45, 0.52) \longrightarrow_{SSMT} (0, \varphi')$ since t_l can no longer be attained due to $0.45 - (0.6 \cdot 0) > 0.4$. Therefore, neither rule (10) nor rule (13) are applicable wrt. the initial situation. We thus try to establish the preconditions of the remaining rule (8), i.e. we investigate the other branch for x, continuing from proof state $(\exists x \in \{1\}$ $\text{Ꝁ}_{\langle(0,0.6),(1,0.4)\rangle} y \in \{0,1\}, \varphi', \langle x \neq 0\rangle, 0.45, 0.52)$. Selecting value 1 for x by rule (10) and value 0 for y by the choices opening rules (11) and (12) leads to a satisfying branch, i.e. $(\emptyset, \varphi', \langle x \neq 0, x = 1, y =$

$0, 2a+4b < 1\rangle, (0.45-0.4)/0.6, 0.52/0.6) \longrightarrow_{SSMT} (1, \varphi')$. Then, rule (11) matches and we obtain $(\text{Ⅎ}_{\langle(0,0.6),(1,0.4)\rangle} y \in \{0,1\}, \varphi', \langle x \neq 0\rangle, 0.45, 0.52) \longrightarrow_{SSMT} (0.6, \varphi')$ since the computed satisfaction probability 0.6 exceeds $t_u = 0.52$. Finally, application of rule (8) yields $(\exists x \in \{0,1\}\ \text{Ⅎ}_{\langle(0,0.6),(1,0.4)\rangle} y \in \{0,1\}, \varphi, \emptyset, 0.45, 0.52) \longrightarrow_{SSMT} (0.6, \varphi')$. Since the computed probability bound $p = 0.6$ is greater than $t_u = 0.52$, the maximum probability of satisfying Φ must exceed threshold 0.52. The thus computed value p is just a lower bound of $Pr(\Phi)$ (which is 1, cf. Fig. 1), but sufficient as a witness of probabilitistic satisfaction.

6 Conclusion and Future Work

This paper has given a detailed account of a fully symbolic encoding of probabilistic bounded reachability problems of discrete-time probabilistic hybrid automata, together with a generalized SMT procedure permitting the symbolic analysis of that encoding. Together, the two provide the germs of fully symbolic techniques for analyzing probabilistic hybrid systems without resorting to approximation by intermediate finite-state abstractions, thus potentially enhancing accuracy and scalability of the analysis algorithms. Implementation of these algorithms by means of an extension of the iSAT solver [12] with randomized quantifiers and the pertinent deduction rules has recently commenced, with a first prototype being operational, see `http://sisat.gforge.avacs.org/`.

References

1. Arnold, L.: Stochastic Differential Equations: Theory and Applications. Wiley - Interscience (1974)
2. Audemard, G., Bozzano, M., Cimatti, A., Sebastiani, R.: Verifying industrial hybrid systems with MathSAT. BMC, ENTCS 119, 17–32 (2004)
3. Biere, A., Cimatti, A., Zhu, Y.: Symbolic model checking without BDDs. In: Cleaveland, W.R. (ed.) TACAS 1999. LNCS, vol. 1579, pp. 193–207. Springer, Heidelberg (1999)
4. Blom, H.A.P., Krystul, J., Bakker, G.J.: A particle system for safety verification of free flight in air traffic. In: Decision and Control, pp. 1574–1579. IEEE, Los Alamitos (2006)
5. Bordeaux, L., Samulowitz, H.: On the stochastic constraint satisfaction framework. In: SAC, pp. 316–320. ACM Press, New York (2007)
6. Bujorianu, L., Lygeros, J.: Toward a general theory of stochastic hybrid systems. In: Stochastic Hybrid Systems: Theory and Safety Critical Applications, LNCIS, vol. 337, pp. 3–30 (2006)
7. Bujorianu, M.L., Lygeros, J.: Reachability questions in piecewise deterministic Markov processes. In: Maler, O., Pnueli, A. (eds.) HSCC 2003. LNCS, vol. 2623, pp. 126–140. Springer, Heidelberg (2003)
8. Davis, M.: Markov Models and Optimization. Chapman & Hall, London (1993)
9. Davis, M., Logemann, G., Loveland, D.: A machine program for theorem proving. Comm. of the ACM 5, 394–397 (1962)
10. Dutertre, B., de Moura, L.: A Fast Linear-Arithmetic Solver for DPLL(T). In: Ball, T., Jones, R.B. (eds.) CAV 2006. LNCS, vol. 4144, pp. 81–94. Springer, Heidelberg (2006)

11. Fränzle, M., Herde, C.: HySAT: An efficient proof engine for bounded model checking of hybrid systems. Formal Methods in System Design 30, 179–198 (2007)
12. Fränzle, M., Herde, C., Ratschan, S., Schubert, T., Teige, T.: Efficient Solving of Large Non-linear Arithmetic Constraint Systems with Complex Boolean Structure. Journal on Satisfiability, Boolean Modeling and Computation 1, 209–236 (2007)
13. Groote, J.F., Koorn, J.W.C., van Vlijmen, S.F.M.: The Safety Guaranteeing System at Station Hoorn-Kersenboogerd. In: Conference on Computer Assurance, pp. 57–68. National Institute of Standards and Technology (1995)
14. Hehner, E.C.R.: Predicative programming. Comm. of the ACM 27, 134–151 (1984)
15. Hespanha, J.P.: Polynomial stochastic hybrid systems. In: Morari, M., Thiele, L. (eds.) HSCC 2005. LNCS, vol. 3414, pp. 322–338. Springer, Heidelberg (2005)
16. Hu, J., Lygeros, J., Sastry, S.: Towards a theory of stochastic hybrid systems. In: Lynch, N.A., Krogh, B.H. (eds.) HSCC 2000. LNCS, vol. 1790, pp. 160–173. Springer, Heidelberg (2000)
17. Koutsoukos, X.D., Riley, D.: Computational methods for reachability analysis of stochastic hybrid systems. In: Hespanha, J.P., Tiwari, A. (eds.) HSCC 2006. LNCS, vol. 3927, pp. 377–391. Springer, Heidelberg (2006)
18. Littman, M.L., Majercik, S.M., Pitassi, T.: Stochastic Boolean satisfiability. Journal of Automated Reasoning 27(3), 251–296 (2001)
19. Nieuwenhuis, R., Oliveras, A., Tinelli, C.: Solving SAT and SAT Modulo Theories: from an Abstract Davis-Putnam-Logemann-Loveland Procedure to DPLL(T). Journal of the ACM 53(6), 937–977 (2006)
20. Sproston, J.: Model Checking of Probabilistic Timed and Hybrid Systems. PhD thesis, University of Birmingham (2000)

A Counterexample-Guided Approach to Parameter Synthesis for Linear Hybrid Automata

Goran Frehse[1], Sumit Kumar Jha[2], and Bruce H. Krogh[3]

[1] Verimag (UJF-CNRS-INPG), 2, av. de Vignate, 38610 Gières, France
goran.frehse@imag.fr
[2] Computer Science Department, Carnegie Mellon University
[3] ECE Department, Carnegie Mellon University
5000 Forbes Avenue, Pittsburgh, PA 15213, USA
jha@cs.cmu.edu, krogh@ece.cmu.edu

Abstract. Our goal is to find the set of parameters for which a given linear hybrid automaton does not reach a given set of bad states. The problem is known to be semi-solvable (if the algorithm terminates the result is correct) by introducing the parameters as state variables and computing the set of reachable states. This is usually too expensive, however, and in our experiments only possible for very simple systems with few parameters. We propose an adaptation of counterexample-guided abstraction refinement (CEGAR) with which one can obtain an underapproximation of the set of good parameters using linear programming. The adaptation is generic and can be applied on top of any CEGAR method where the counterexamples correspond to paths in the concrete system. For each counterexample, the cost incurred by underapproximating the parameters is polynomial in the number of variables, parameters, and the length of counterexample. We identify a syntactic condition for which the approach is complete in the sense that the underapproximation is empty only if the problem has no solution. Experimental results are provided for two CEGAR methods, a simple discrete version and iterative relaxation abstraction (IRA), both of which show a drastic improvement in performance compared to standard reachability.

1 Introduction

The admissible behaviors of linear hybrid automata (LHA) are determined by sets of linear constraints. The parameters in these constraints represent either physical constants or values chosen by the designer. When the LHA does not satisfy the design specifications, the latter constraints can be adjusted to eliminate the undesirable behaviors. This paper concerns this design problem in the context of reachability specifications: Given a parameterized LHA, determine the set of design parameters, called *good parameters*, for which no bad locations can be reached.

The parameter design problem for LHA was formulated and solved by Henzinger et al. [1], but the proposed solution is tractable for only very simple

M. Egerstedt and B. Mishra (Eds.): HSCC 2008, LNCS 4981, pp. 187–200, 2008.

systems with few parameters. This paper concerns the extension of verification techniques to solve the LHA parameter design problem. Our approach leverages the fact that the feasibility of a given counterexample path corresponds to the satisfiability of a set of linear constraints over instantiations of the initial and final values of the continuous variables in each location along the path, along with variables representing the duration of the continuous state trajectory in each location. Although this observation does not make the parameter design problem tractable, because projection of these constraints into the parameter space is computationally complex and there can be in general an infinite number of counterexample paths, it does lead to a set of heuristics that make it possible to efficiently compute underapproximations of the set of good parameters.

The heuristics we propose are integrated into *counterexample guided abstraction refinement* (CEGAR) [2]. In a standard CEGAR loop, a discrete abstraction of the system is used to find a counterexample, which is a path from the initial states to states considered bad. In a feasibility check, it is then verified whether this path corresponds to a behavior of the concrete hybrid system or whether it was a spurious product of the abstraction. If it is spurious, the abstraction is refined and the loop repeats. If the counterexample corresponds to a concrete behavior, the system is unsafe. Our adaptation consists of replacing the feasibility check with an operator that obtains constraints on the parameters that *make* the counterexample infeasible. If all counterexamples have been eliminated, the resulting constraints describe a set of parameters for which the system is safe. The make-infeasible operator can be implemented approximatively using linear programming, e.g., obtaining rectangular or octagonal underapproximations of the good parameters. Its complexity for each counterexample is polynomial in the number of variables, parameters and the length of the counterexample, compared to exponential complexity of an exact solution. Depending on whether the number of counterexamples or the number of parameters is the dominating cost factor, we apply the underapproximation to each path individually or collectively on sets of paths.

In the general case, the underapproximation may produce an empty set even though good parameters exist. We identify a condition we call *parameter-monotonicity* (intuitively, when parameters function either as lower or upper bounds but not both), under which octagonal approximations are sufficient to prevent this from happening.

The entire approach is generic in the sense that it can be applied to any CEGAR loop in which the counterexamples correspond to paths in the concrete system (as opposed to sets of paths or transitions). It suffices to replace the feasibility check with the make-infeasible operator. We provide experimental results for two different CEGAR implementations: a simple variant of standard discrete CEGAR, and iterative relaxation abstraction (IRA) [3]. Compared to the traditional way of synthesizing parameters using reachability as in [1], we observe a dramatic improvement in speed.

The following section defines the class of LHA with parameters studied in this paper. Section 3 describes the role of counterexamples in defining the set of good parameters. Section 4 discusses the special case when the parameters are *monotonic*, which means each parameter serves as either an upper or lower bound throughout the LHA. Section 5 presents a general counterexample-guided procedure for computing sets of good parameters and Section 6 presents experimental results for two implementations of the procedure. The concluding section discusses directions for further research.

2 Linear Hybrid Automata with Parameters

We consider *linear hybrid automata* (LHA) [4] with explicit parameter variables. An LHA $H = (\mathit{Var}, \mathit{Lab}, \mathit{Loc}, \mathit{Inv}, \mathit{Flow}, \mathit{Trans}, \mathit{ini})$ consists of:

- A finite set of real-valued *variables* $\mathit{Var} = \mathtt{X} \cup \mathtt{P}$, where $\mathtt{X} = \{\mathtt{x_1}, \ldots, \mathtt{x_n}\}$ are the *continuous state variables* and $\mathtt{P} = \{\mathtt{p_1}, \ldots, \mathtt{p_m}\}$ are the *parameters*, which remain constant. We denote the values of variables with $x = (x_1, \ldots, x_n)^\mathsf{T}$ and $p = (p_1, \ldots, p_m)^\mathsf{T}$.
- A finite set of *labels* Lab.
- A finite set of *locations* Loc. A *state* (l, x, p) of the automaton consists of a location $l \in \mathit{Loc}$ and real values $(x, p) \in \mathbb{R}^{n+m}$ for each of the variables.
- For each location l, $\mathit{Inv}(l) \subseteq \mathbb{R}^{n+m}$ is the set of admissible values of the variables in the location.
- $\mathit{Flow}(l) \subseteq \mathbb{R}^n$ is the set of possible time derivatives $(\dot{x}_1, \ldots, \dot{x}_n)^\mathsf{T}$; the derivatives of the parameters are implicitly zero.
- A finite set of *transitions* $\mathit{Trans} \subseteq \mathit{Loc} \times \mathit{Lab} \times 2^{\mathbb{R}^{2n+m}} \times \mathit{Loc}$. A transition indicates that the system state may jump instantaneously from the transition *source state* (l, x, p) to the transition *target state* (l', x', p) if $(x, p, x') \in \mu$, where $\mu \subseteq \mathbb{R}^{2n+m}$ is the transition's *jump relation*. We desire a unique correspondence between sequences of transitions and sequences of labels, so we require that any location l has at most one outgoing transition for each label (the general case can be brought to this form by adding labels and renaming).
- A location $\mathit{ini} \in \mathit{Loc}$ is designated as *initial location* from which all behaviors must start.

The sets $\mathit{Inv}(l)$ and $\mathit{Flow}(l)$ are specified by conjunctions of linear constraints

$$a^\mathsf{T} x + e^\mathsf{T} p \le b, \quad \text{respectively} \quad a^\mathsf{T} \dot{x} \le b, \tag{1}$$

where a, e are vectors of integer coefficients and b is an integer. The jump relation μ of a transition is specified by a conjunction of linear constraints of the form

$$a^\mathsf{T} x + e^\mathsf{T} p + a'^\mathsf{T} x' \le b, \tag{2}$$

where x denotes the values of the variables before the jump, and x' denotes the values after; the values of the parameters do not change. Given a conjunction C of linear constraints over $\mathtt{X}$ and $\mathtt{P}$, we write $[\![C]\!]$ to denote the set of values of (x, p) (a polyhedron) for which all of the constraints are satisfied. We write

$C(p')$ to denote the constraints obtained by substituting p with the values in p', and call $C(p')$ *infeasible* if $[\![C(p')]\!] = \emptyset$.

We define the semantics of a LHA in terms of *feasible paths* for a given parameter value p. This is consistent with the semantics in [4] but reformulated to simplify the use of linear programming. A *path* $\pi = \alpha_0\alpha_1 \ldots \alpha_{z-1}$ is a finite sequence of labels α_i such that the sequence of transitions $(l_i, \alpha_i, \mu_i, l'_i)$ satisfies $l_0 = ini$ and $l'_i = l_{i+1}$ for $i = 0, \ldots, z-1$ (this defines l_z to be the target state of the last transition). The path is *feasible* for a given p if there exist vectors $x_j^{in}, x_j^{out} \in \mathbb{R}^n$ and scalars $\delta_j \in \mathbb{R}$ for $j = 0, \ldots, z$ such that

- $(x_j^{in}, p), (x_j^{out}, p) \in Inv(l_j)$,
- $(x_j^{out} - x_j^{in})/\delta_j \in Flow(l_j)$,
- for $j < z$, $(x_j^{out}, p, x_{j+1}^{in}) \in \mu_j$.

In the above sequence, (l_j, x_j^{in}, p) is the state in which the automaton enters location l_j, and (l_j, x_j^{out}, p) is the state after letting time elapse for δ_j units. If $j < z$, the automaton leaves l_j via the transition identified by α_j, and jumps to the state $(l_{j+1}, x_{j+1}^{in}, p)$. For a given path the above constraints can be written as linear constraints over the $2z(n+1)+m$ variables of x_j^{in}, x_j^{out}, δ_j and p. We call these *path constraints* and denote them by $PathCon(\pi, p)$. Expressed in terms of the path constraints, a counterexample is feasible if $[\![PathCon(\pi, p)]\!] \neq \emptyset$, which can be decided using efficient linear programming techniques [5].

In this paper, we consider reachability problems for LHA. A location l is said to be *reachable* if there is a feasible path $\pi = \alpha_0\alpha_1 \ldots \alpha_{z-1}$ with $l_z = l$. An LHA H is said to be *safe* if none of the locations in a given set of *bad locations* L_B is reachable. We call a path to a bad location a *counterexample*, and write $CE(H, p)$ for the (possibly infinite) set of counterexamples in H for the parameter value p. Let $FCE(H, p)$ denote the set of *feasible counterexamples* in H. The system is safe if and only if $FCE(H, p)$ is empty, i.e., there are no counterexamples or none of the existing counterexamples is feasible. The extension of $CE(H, p)$ and $FCE(H, p)$ to sets of parameter values is straightforward. While we have made some restrictions to our LHA (unique labels) and the reachability problem (unsafe locations), it is straightforward to bring the general problem (unsafe states) to this form by relabeling transitions and introducing an error location reachable by transitions from the unsafe states. We will use the following example throughout the paper:

Example 1. Consider a buffer tank with steady inflow and with a controllable outlet valve resulting in a net level increase $\dot{x} = r$ if the valve is closed, and a net decrease $\dot{x} = -r$ if it is open. A controller is supposed to keep the level between x_{min} and x_{max}. The controller never waits longer than time T to check the level x, and opens (closes) the valve when $x > M$ ($x < m$).

The LHA model H_{tank} of the controlled system is shown in Fig. 1, where for simplicity jump constraints of the form $x' = x$ have been omitted. H_{tank} has the parameters m, M, T, x_{min}, and x_{max}. We assume r to be a given constant (parameters are not allowed in the flows). The forbidden location is *error*.

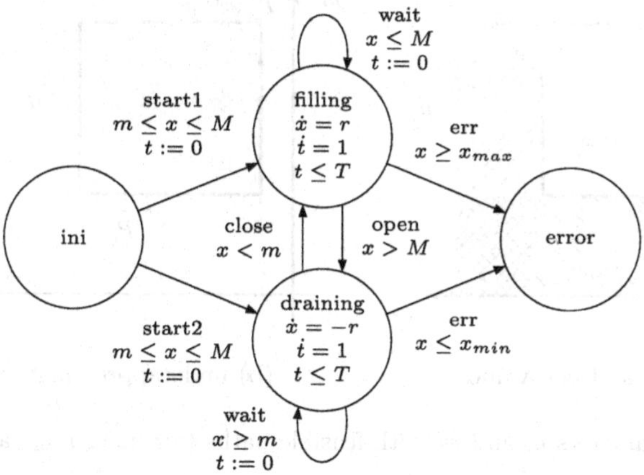

Fig. 1. LHA H_{tank} for the controlled tank example with parameters m, M, T, x_{min}, and x_{max}; r is a given constant since LHA-parameters cannot bound derivatives

H_{tank} has infinitely many counterexamples, a shortest of them being $\pi =$ *start1*, *err*, which covers the locations *ini*, *filling* and *error*, and has the following path constraints (some irrelevant ones are omitted):

$$\begin{array}{llr} m \leq x_0^{out} \leq M, & x_0^{out} = x_1^{in},\ t_1^{in} = 0, & \text{(jump relation)} \\ x_1^{out} - x_1^{in} = r\delta_0, & t_1^{out} - t_1^{in} = \delta_0, & \text{(flow)} \\ t_1^{out} \leq T, & & \text{(invariant)} \\ x_1^{out} \geq x_{max}. & & \text{(jump relation)} \end{array} \quad (3)$$

■

3 Parameter Synthesis Using Counterexamples

We consider the following *good parameters problem*: Given an LHA H and a rectangular parameter domain $P_0 \subseteq \mathbb{R}^m$, what is the largest set of parameter values $P_G \subseteq P_0$ for which the hybrid automaton is safe? Recalling that for a given parameter value p', the set of feasible counterexamples $FCE(H, p')$ is empty exactly if the system is safe, the goal is to compute

$$P_G = \{p' \in P_0 \mid FCE(H, p') = \emptyset\}. \quad (4)$$

We refer to P_G as the *good parameters* and to $P_B := P_0 \setminus P_G$ as the *bad parameters.* A straightforward solution to (4) is via reachability [1]. The set of reachable states $Reach(H)$ is obtained by computing successor states until a fixpoint is reached. Denoting projection onto the parameters (existential quantification over $\mathtt{X}$) with $\downarrow_{\mathtt{P}}$, the set of good parameters is

$$P_G = P_0 \setminus \left(Reach(H) \cap L_B \times \mathbb{R}^{n+m}\right)\downarrow_{\mathtt{P}}. \quad (5)$$

If $Reach(H)$ is obtained as a finite boolean combination of linear constraints for each location, P_G can be computed exactly using Fourier-Motzkin elimination.

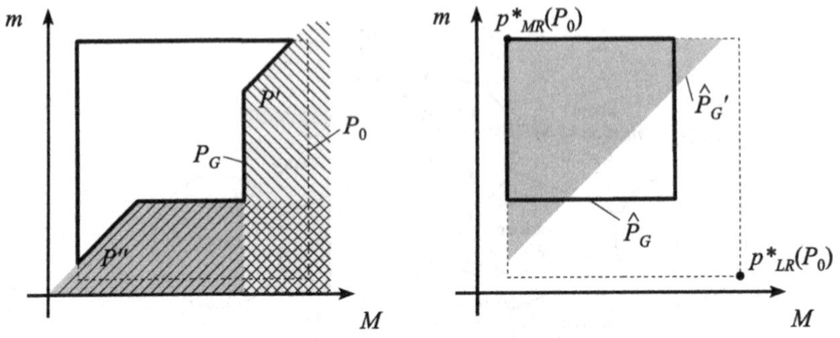

(a) good and bad values (b) underapproximations

Fig. 2. Parameters m and M with feasible paths (for fixed x_{max} and T)

In all but the most simple cases, however, this is prohibitively expensive for three reasons. Firstly, the reachability computation taking into account all parameter values is relatively expensive, since it includes behaviors that will later be excluded in the final solution. Secondly, the projection operation can be very expensive if there are many variables. Thirdly, the difference operation is very expensive if the projection operation produces a disjunction consisting of a large number of convex sets. In this paper, we try to find good parameters by checking individual counterexamples and removing from P_0 those parameters for which the counterexamples are feasible. Using projection (Fourier-Motzkin elimination) onto the parameters, and recalling the definition of FCE, (4) becomes

$$\begin{aligned} P_G &= P_0 \setminus \{p' \mid \exists \pi \in CE(H, P_0) : [\![PathCon(\pi, p')]\!] \neq \emptyset\} \\ &= P_0 \setminus \bigcup_{\pi \in CE(H,P_0)} [\![PathCon(\pi, p)]\!]\!\downarrow_{\mathrm{P}} . \end{aligned} \tag{6}$$

Example 2. Recall the buffer tank from Fig. 1 and the counterexample $\pi = start1, err$ with path constraints (3). We can eliminate x_i^{in}, x_i^{out}, t_i^{in}, t_i^{out} from the path constraints to obtain $m \leq M \wedge M + rT \geq x_{max}$. For values of m, M, T, and x_{max} that satisfy these inequalities, shown as the shaded region P' in Fig. 2(a), the path constraints are feasible and the path is feasible. If we want the system to be safe, we must choose parameter values that violate these inequalities, i.e., make the path constraints infeasible, for the above as well as all other counterexamples (there are infinitely many). For $\pi = start2, err$ the path constraints yield $m \leq M \wedge m - rT \leq x_{min}$, shown as P'' in Fig. 2(a). We finally obtain $P_G = [\![m > M \vee (M + rT < x_{max} \wedge m - rT > x_{min})]\!]$, shown as a solid outline in Fig. 2(a), when taking into account all counterexamples. ■

The method for computing P_G suggested by (6) is conceptually similar to (5), and shares its problems: there may be lots of paths in $CE(H, P_0)$ (possibly infinitely many) and projection is very expensive when there are more than a few variables. Recall that the dimension of the linear program as well as the number of constraints of $PathCon(\pi, p)$ increase linearly with the length of the counterexample. So the projection entails a cost that is exponential in the number of variables and the length of the counterexample. The difference operation also incurs a cost exponential in the number of parameters.

The exact solution being clearly too expensive, we use rectangular or octagonal overapproximations of the bad parameters, and carry out the difference operation on the overapproximation. For a set S of values for the variables of the path constraints, we write $\mathit{OverAppr}_{\mathrm{P}}(S)$ to denote one of the following overapproximations of $S{\downarrow_{\mathrm{P}}}$:

$$\mathit{Box}_{\mathrm{P}}(S) = \bigcap_{i=1,\ldots,m} \{p \mid \min_{(x,p')\in S} p'_i \le p_i \le \max_{(x,p'')\in S} p''_i\}, \tag{7}$$

$$\begin{aligned}\mathit{Oct}_{\mathrm{P}}(S) = & \bigcap_{i,j=1,\ldots,m} \{p \mid \min_{(x,p')\in S} p'_i - p'_j \le p_i - p_j \le \max_{(x,p'')\in S} p''_i - p''_j\} \cap \\ & \bigcap_{i,j=1,\ldots,m} \{p \mid \min_{(x,p')\in S} p'_i + p'_j \le p_i + p_j \le \max_{(x,p'')\in S} p''_i + p''_j\}\end{aligned} \tag{8}$$

These overapproximations are obtained by solving a linear program for each constraint: in total $2m$ programs for rectangular, and $2m^2$ for octagonal overapproximations, where m is the number of parameters. The cost of linear programming is polynomial in the number of variables of the path constraints, which is $2(|\pi|+1)n+m$. In total, the cost for obtaining an overapproximation for a single counterexample is still polynomial.

How these overapproximations should be applied in (6) depends on the dominating cost factor: lots of counterexamples to be checked, or lots of parameters. If we expect few counterexamples, we overapproximate the projection operation, but carry out the difference operation faithfully. We refer to this as *individual overapproximation*:

$$\hat{P}_G = P_0 \setminus \bigcup_{\pi\in CE(H,P_0)} \mathit{OverAppr}_{\mathrm{P}}([\![\mathit{PathCon}(\pi,p)]\!]). \tag{9}$$

For each counterexample, the cost of obtaining the overapproximation is polynomial in the number of parameters, since one linear program needs to be solved for each constraint in the overapproximation. The difference operation incurrs a cost that is exponential in the number of counterexamples, although we did not encounter such a worst case in practice. Consequently, this variant is suitable mainly when a small number of counterexamples is checked.

If the number of counterexamples is excessive, we overapproximate the union operation, which we refer to as *collective overapproximation*:

$$\hat{P}_G = P_0 \setminus \mathit{OverAppr}_{\mathrm{P}}(\bigcup_{\pi\in CE(H,P_0)} [\![\mathit{PathCon}(\pi,p)]\!]). \tag{10}$$

Here $\mathit{OverAppr}_{\mathrm{P}}$ is extended to unions of convex sets as follows. For each counterexample, we compute the bounds of the rectangular or octagonal overapproximation and take the worst case, so there is no explicit union operation. Again, we need to solve a low number of linear programs, but here the complexity of the difference operation depends only on the number of parameters, not the number of counterexamples.

Example 3. Applying rectangular individual overapproximation to our buffer tank example, we obtain $\hat{P}_G$ as shown in Fig. 2(b). For rectangular collective overapproximation we get $\hat{P}_G = \emptyset$, i.e., we fail to find any good parameter at all. With octagonal individual overapproximation we incidentally obtain P_G exactly, for collective overapproximation $\hat{P}'_G$ as shown in Fig. 2(b).

In the general case, neither (9) nor (10) is *complete*, that is, (9) or (10) may return empty sets even though P_G is not empty. This makes the chances of finding a sufficiently good set of parameters look pretty slim. But in practice, many systems do not have an arbitrarily complex set of good parameters, but one with a particularly simple structure, where octagonal overapproximations turn out to be complete. We examine this special case closer in the following section.

4 Monotonic Parameters

It turns out that the set of parameters for which a given counterexample is feasible has a special form if the parameters occur only with one sign (either positive or negative) in the linear constraints defining the automaton. We show that the good parameters have a point that is most restrictive, and that any good point in the parameter space can be relaxed (tightened) toward that point. As a consequence, octagonal constraints are complete when counterexamples are overapproximated individually or collectively.

We call a constraint of the form (1) or (2) *positive in* $\mathtt{p_i}$ if $e_i > 0$, *negative in* $\mathtt{p_i}$ if $e_i < 0$, and *independent of* $\mathtt{p_i}$ if $e_i = 0$, where e_i is the coefficient of p_i from the vector e . We call a parameter $\mathtt{p_i}$ positive (negative) if for all $\pi \in CE(H, P_0)$ with $[\![PathCon(\pi,p)]\!]{\downarrow_{\mathtt{P}}} \neq \emptyset$, all active constraints in $PathCon(\pi,p)$ that are not independent of the parameter are positive (negative) in the parameter.[1] Intuitively, a parameter is negative if it is only relevant as an upper bound, and a positive parameter only as a lower bound. Let *psgn* be a function over the parameters with $psgn(\mathtt{p_i}) = 1$ (-1) if the LHA is positive (negative) in $\mathtt{p_i}$. We call the parameters *monotonic* and the LHA *parameter-monotonic* if all parameters are positive or negative. A syntactic sufficient condition for a parameter $\mathtt{p_i}$ being positive (negative) is that all constraints of invariants and jump relations are positive (negative) in $\mathtt{p_i}$. This is easy to see since the path constraints are made up of simple instantiations of the constraints of invariants, flows and jump relations, with the same coefficients for the parameters. Often, a parameter can be monotonic even though the syntactic condition for monotonicity is not fulfilled because, although the signs of the coefficients differ for some constraints, they are the same for all of the active constraints. In general, we may assume parameter-monotonicity and check for each counterexample whether this assumption is true. If it is not, we are no longer guaranteed to find a good parameter using overapproximations, although we may of course still try.

[1] We call a constraint *active* if removing the constraint leads to a strictly larger set.

Example 4. In our buffer tank example, the parameters x_{max}, T are syntactically positive, x_{min} is syntactically negative, and m and M are neither. In the counterexample $\pi = start1, err$, whose path constraints are given in (3), m is positive and M is negative. It turns out that this is a useful assumption, even though m and M also occur with opposite sign on the transitions switching between *filling* and *draining*. ■

The following results formalize our discussion of parameter-monotonicity. Let $InfeasibleCone_C(p')$ be defined for a set of constraints C as the set of p'' with $p''_i \geq p'_i$ if C is positive in $\mathtt{p_i}$, and $p''_i \leq p'_i$ if C is negative in $\mathtt{p_i}$. Let $FeasibleCone_C(p')$ be the set of p'' with $p''_i \leq p'_i$ if C is positive in $\mathtt{p_i}$, and $p''_i \geq p'_i$ if C is negative in $\mathtt{p_i}$.

Lemma 1. *Given a set of linear constraints C monotonic in all parameters, $[\![C(p')]\!] = \emptyset$ implies $[\![C(p'')]\!] = \emptyset$ for all $p'' \in InfeasibleCone_C(p')$. Symmetrically, $[\![C(p')]\!] \neq \emptyset$ implies $[\![C(p'')]\!] \neq \emptyset$ for all $p'' \in FeasibleCone_C(p')$.*

Proof. We give the proof for $InfeasibleCone_C(p')$; the proof for $FeasibleCone(p')$ is symmetric. Assume $[\![C(p')]\!] = \emptyset$, and the constraints in C are negative in $\mathtt{p_i}$, i.e., of the form $a^\intercal x + e^\intercal p \leq b$ with $e_i \leq 0$. Consider any $p'' \in InfeasibleCone_C(p')$. If $[\![C(p'')]\!] \neq \emptyset$, there exists some x' such that $a^\intercal x' + e^\intercal p'' \leq b$ for all constraints in C. We show that this contradicts the hypothesis. According to the definition of $InfeasibleCone_C(p')$, $e^\intercal p' \leq e^\intercal p''$, since $p''_i \leq p'_i$ and $e_i \leq 0$. Therefore $a^\intercal x' + e^\intercal p' \leq a^\intercal x' + e^\intercal p'' \leq b$, and (x', p') satisfies all constraints in C, which means $[\![C(p')]\!] \neq \emptyset$. □

Under the assumption that the LHA H is parameter-monotonic, a parameter $\mathtt{p_i}$ has the same sign, $psgn(\mathtt{p_i})$, in all path constraints that may occur in (6). Since $InfeasibleCone_C(p')$ is identical for all C with the same parameter sign, we may simply define $InfeasibleCone_H(p')$ over H using $psgn(\mathtt{p_i})$, and similarly with $FeasibleCone_H(p')$. Using the above result, we now show that if the LHA is parameter-monotonic, there is a *most restrictive* and a *least restrictive* combination of parameters out of any rectangular domain P, defined component-wise for parameter $\mathtt{p_i}$ as

$$p^*_{MR,i}(P) = \max_{p' \in P} psgn(\mathtt{p_i}) p'_i, \qquad p^*_{LR,i}(P) = \min_{p' \in P} psgn(\mathtt{p_i}) p'_i. \tag{11}$$

Example 5. Assuming that in the buffer tank example m is a positive and M a negative parameter, we get $p^*_{MR}(P_0)$ and $p^*_{LR}(P_0)$ shown in Fig. 2(b). ■

Proposition 1. *If an LHA H is parameter-monotonic, then for any $p \in P_0$*

$$FCE(H, p^*_{MR}(P_0)) \subseteq FCE(H, p) \subseteq FCE(H, p^*_{LR}(P_0)).$$

Proof. Consider any $\pi \in FCE(H, p^*_{MR}(P_0))$. By definition of FCE, π is a counterexample for which $[\![PathCon(\pi, p^*_{MR}(P_0))]\!] \neq \emptyset$. According to the definition of $p^*_{MR}(P_0)$, any $p \in P_0$ is in $FeasibleCone_H(p^*_{MR}(P_0))$. With Lemma 1 we get $[\![PathCon(\pi, p)]\!] \neq \emptyset$, and consequently $\pi \in FCE(H, p)$. The argument for p^*_{LR} is dual. □

It immediately follows from Prop. 1 that if we substitute the parameters in H with the value $p^*_{LR}(P)$ to obtain H', an LHA without parameters, $FCE(H,P) \subseteq FCE(H')$, i.e., H' is an overapproximation of H. Working with H' may be cheaper since it has less variables than H'.

Proposition 2. *If the parameters are monotonic and $p' \in P_G$, $p'' \in P_B$, then*

$$InfeasibleCone_H(p') \cap P_0 \subseteq P_G \quad \text{and} \quad FeasibleCone_H(p'') \cap P_0 \subseteq P_B.$$

Proof. Since $p' \in P_G$, $[\![PathCon(\pi, p')]\!] = \emptyset$ for all $\pi \in CE(H, P_0)$. According to Lemma 1, the same holds for any $p'' \in InfeasibleCone_H(p')$. Therefore $InfeasibleCone_H(p') \cap P_0 \subseteq P_G$. The argument for *FeasibleCone* is symmetric. □

As a straightforward application of Prop. 2, we can use any feasible counterexamples to obtain an overapproximation of P_G. Similarly, we can use any infeasible counterexamples to obtain an underapproximation of P_G:

Proposition 3. *Given a parameter-monotonic LHA H, a set of z_{feas} parameter valuations $p^1, \ldots, p^{z_{feas}}$ such that there exists a $\pi^i \in FCE(H, p^i)$ for $i = 1, \ldots, z_{feas}$, and a set of z_{infeas} parameter valuations $\bar{p}^1, \ldots, \bar{p}^{z_{infeas}}$ such that $FCE(H, \bar{p}^j) = \emptyset$ for $j = 1, \ldots, z_{infeas}$, then*

$$P_0 \cap \bigcup_j InfeasibleCone_H(\bar{p}^j) \subseteq P_G \subseteq P_0 \setminus \bigcup_i FeasibleCone_H(p^i).$$

We now show that for a parameter-monotonic LHA with rectangular P_0 and a finite number of counterexamples, collective (and therefore also individual) overapproximation with octagonal constraints is complete, i.e., the overapproximation is empty iff $P_G = \emptyset$. This observation follows from the following:

Proposition 4. *If H is parameter-monotonic, $|CE(H)|$ is finite and P_0 is rectangular, $p^*_{MR}(P_0) \in Oct_{\mathrm{P}}(\bigcup_{\pi \in CE(H,P_0)} [\![PathCon(\pi, p) \wedge p \in P_0]\!])$ iff $p^*_{MR}(P_0) \in P_B$.*

Proof. (Sketch) If $p^*_{MR}(P_0) \in P_B$, it follows from Lemma 1, the definition of p^*_{MR} and Prop. 2 that $P_B = P_0$. Since P_0 is rectangular, the octagonal overapproximation of P_B is identical to P_0 and therefore to P_B, and contains $p^*_{MR}(P_0)$. If $p^*_{MR}(P_0) \notin P_B$ and there is a finite number of refining counterexamples, there exists at least one pair of parameters $\mathrm{p_i}, \mathrm{p_j}$ such that for all $\pi \in CE(H, P_0)$

$$max_{p' \in [\![PathCon(\pi,p)]\!]\downarrow_{\mathrm{P}} \cap P_0} psgn(\mathrm{p_i})p'_i + psgn(\mathrm{p_j})p'_j < p^*_{MR,i}(P_0) + p^*_{MR,j}(P_0),$$

since otherwise $p^*_{MR}(P_0)$ would be feasible for some path π. From (8) it follows that $p^*_{MR}(P_0) \notin Oct_{\mathrm{P}}(\bigcup_{\pi \in CE(H,P_0)} [\![PathCon(\pi) \wedge \pi \in CE(H, P_0))]\!]$. □

5 Counterexample-Guided Parameter Synthesis

We adapt the familiar *counterexample guided abstraction refinement* (CEGAR) loop [2] to parameter synthesis based on the results in the previous section. We define a CEGAR loop with the following operators:

- $\Pi' := \mathit{IniAbstr}(H, P)$ constructs a set of paths Π' with $\mathit{FCE}(H, P) \subseteq \Pi'$,
- $\pi := \mathit{SelectCE}(\Pi)$ selects a path in Π, given $\Pi \neq \emptyset$,
- $\Pi' := \mathit{RefineWithSpuriousCE}(\Pi, H, P, \pi)$ refines the set of paths Π using the system H and the spurious counterexample π, i.e., it produces a set of paths Π' such that $\Pi' \subseteq \Pi \setminus \{\pi\}$, and $\mathit{FCE}(H, P) \subseteq \Pi'$ (ensuring that the refinement never removes feasible counterexamples).

A number of CEGAR algorithms, including iterative relaxation abstraction [3], can be brought to this form. Note in general CEGAR constructs and refines a finite abstraction, which may take on various forms. We represent this abstraction as a set of paths Π to simplify and generalize the theoretical discussion, but assume that implementations model this set implicitly, say with an LHA or finite state machine. Algorithm 1 shows our adapted CEGAR loop. Its inputs are the system H and the initial parameter domain $\hat{P}_0$, from which the resulting good parameters are chosen. If it terminates, it outputs an underapproximation of the good parameters $\hat{P}_G$. A conventional CEGAR loop would terminate as soon as the feasibility test in line 6 evaluates to true, reporting π_i as a feasible counterexample. In our adaptation, we instead restrict the parameters such that the counterexample is infeasible and continue to search for other feasible counterexamples. This is accomplished by two additional operators:

- $P' := \mathit{MakeInfeasible}(C, P)$ returns a set $P' \subseteq P$ such that $[\![C]\!]\downarrow_{\mathrm{P}} \cap P' = \emptyset$. Note that the only such set might be $P' = \emptyset$,
- $P' := \mathit{AnalysisParameters}(P)$ returns a set of parameter values P' such that $\mathit{FCE}(H, P) \subseteq \mathit{FCE}(H, P')$.

The exact implementation of $\mathit{MakeInfeasible}(C, P)$ is $P \setminus [\![C]\!]\downarrow_{\mathrm{P}}$, but as discussed in the previous sections, underapproximations similar to (9) and (10) may be advisable. The operator *AnalysisParameters* is used to simplify the set of parameters used in the analysis of H. The condition is that this simplification does not drop any feasible counterexamples. As shown in Sect. 4, one may select a single point in P if the parameters are monotonic, i.e., use $\mathit{AnalysisParameters}(P) := p^*_{LR}(P)$. In that case, the parameters in H can be substituted by constants, thus reducing the number of variables in H. For the general case, a valid implementation is simply $\mathit{AnalysisParameters}(P) := P$.

On the basis of (6) it is straightforward to show that when Alg. 1 terminates, $H(p)$ is safe for any $p \in \hat{P}_G$:

Proposition 5. *If* $\hat{P}_0 \supseteq P_0$ *and Alg. 1 terminates,* $\hat{P}_G \subseteq P_G$.

If the initial abstraction contains all counterexamples and the implementation of $\mathit{MakeInfeasible}(C, P)$ is exact, $\hat{P}_G$ is exact as well:

Proposition 6. *If* $\hat{P}_0 \supseteq P_0$*, Alg. 1 terminates,* $\mathit{IniAbstr}(H, P_0) = \mathit{CE}(H, P_0)$*, and* $\mathit{MakeInfeasible}(C, P) = P \setminus [\![C]\!]\downarrow_{\mathrm{P}}$*,* $\hat{P}_G = P_G$.

We now briefly present a way to check less paths for parameter-monotonic LHA. According to Prop. 1, we may substitute the parameters with the value $p^*_{LR}(P_0)$

Algorithm 1. Counterexample-Guided Parameter Synthesis

Input: LHA H with bad locations L_B, parameter domain $\hat{P}_0$
Output: $\hat{P}_G$ such that $\hat{P}_G \subseteq P_G$

1 $i := 0$;
2 $\tilde{P}_0 := \mathit{AnalysisParameters}(\hat{P}_0)$;
3 $\hat{\Pi}_0 := \mathit{IniAbstr}(H, \tilde{P}_0)$;
4 **while** $\hat{\Pi}_i \neq \emptyset \wedge \hat{P}_i \neq \emptyset$ **do**
5 $\quad \pi_i := \mathit{SelectCE}(\hat{\Pi}_i)$;
6 $\quad$ **if** $[\![\mathit{PathCon}(\pi_i, p) \wedge p \in \hat{P}_i]\!] \neq \emptyset$ **then**
7 $\quad\quad \hat{P}_{i+1} := \mathit{MakeInfeasible}(\mathit{PathCon}(\pi_i, p), \hat{P}_i)$;
8 $\quad\quad \tilde{P}_{i+1} := \mathit{AnalysisParameters}(\hat{P}_{i+1})$;
9 $\quad$ **else**
10 $\quad\quad \hat{P}_{i+1} := \hat{P}_i$; $\tilde{P}_{i+1} := \tilde{P}_i$;
11 $\quad$ **end**
12 $\quad \hat{\Pi}_{i+1} := \mathit{RefineWithSpuriousCE}(\hat{\Pi}_i, H, \tilde{P}_{i+1}, \pi_i)$;
13 $\quad i := i + 1$;
14 **end**
15 $\hat{P}_G := \hat{P}_i$;

to produce an overapproximation of $CE(H, P_0)$. Usually, there is a prohibitively large number of such paths. Instead, we wish to start with a small set of paths, and iteratively add further paths only when necessary. We run Alg. 1 with $\hat{P}_0 = P_0$ and $\mathit{AnalysisParameters}(P) := p^*_{MR}(P)$, to obtain with $\hat{P}_G$ an initial set of parameters checking the least number of paths possible. To check the remaining paths, we run Alg. 1 with $\hat{P}_0 = \hat{P}_G$ and $\mathit{AnalysisParameters}(P) := p^*_{LR}(P)$. Note that we can skip the initialization of $\hat{\Pi}_0$ in line 3 when in running Alg. 1 in step 2 above, and instead continue with $\hat{\Pi}_i$ from step 1.

We use the following two CEGAR implementations, and show experimental results in the next section. *Simple Discrete CEGAR* is a straightforward CEGAR algorithm based on a discrete abstraction of the hybrid system, somewhat similar to [6]. A set of paths is represented by a finite state machine (FSM). $\mathit{IniAbstr}(H, P)$ constructs a FSM $A_0 = (\mathit{Locs}, \Sigma, \rightarrow, \mathit{ini}, \mathit{final})$, where $\Sigma = \mathit{Locs} \times \mathit{Lab}$, and $\rightarrow = \{(l, (l, \alpha), l') \mid \exists \mu : (l, \alpha, \mu, l') \in \mathit{Trans}\}$. $\mathit{SelectCE}(A_i)$ returns a shortest word in the language of A_i. *RefineWithSpurious* works as follows. First, it reduces the counterexample $\pi = \alpha_0, \ldots, \alpha_{z-1}$ by finding the largest k and the smallest j such that the path constraints for $\alpha_k, \ldots, \alpha_j$ are infeasible (starting in the location l_k reached by $\alpha_0, \ldots, \alpha_{k-1}$). For FSM A and language L let $A - L$ denote removing the language L from the language of A. This is a standard automaton operation, implemented by first coding L by an automaton. Let $L_{pre} = \varepsilon$ if $k = 0$ and $L_{pre} = \Sigma^*$ otherwise, and $L_{post} = \varepsilon$ if $j = z - 1$ and $L_{post} = \Sigma^*$ otherwise, Then $A_{i+1} = A_i - L_{pre}(l_k, \alpha_k) \ldots (l_j, \alpha_j) L_{post}$.

Iterative Relaxation Abstraction[3] is similar to Simple Discrete CEGAR, with $A_{i+1} = \mathit{RefineWithSpurious}(A_i, H, P, \pi)$ constructed as follows: First, find an irreducible infeasible subset (IIS) of $\mathit{PathCon}(\pi, p)$, say C. Let V be the variables

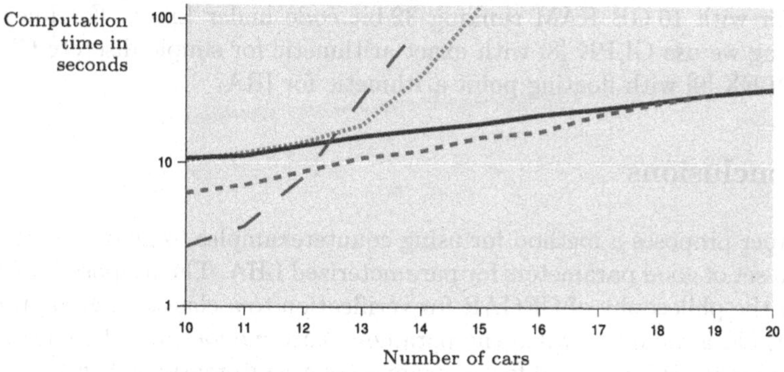

Fig. 3. Parameter synthesis for automated highway controller using standard reachability (wide dashed), simple discrete CEGAR with projection as in (6) (dotted) and with individual octagonal overapproximations as in (9) (solid), and IRA with individual octagonal overapproximations as in (9) (fine dashed)

(including parameters) with nonzero coefficients in C. Let $localize(H, V)$ be the automaton obtained from H by removing all constraints involving variables not in V. Let A' be the language of $localize(H, V)$, which is semi-computable using reachability techniques. Then $A_{i+1} = A_i \cap A' \setminus \pi$.

6 Experimental Results

We consider the model of a central arbiter for an automated highway, roughly similar to the one in [7], and verify that no two vehicles on the automated highway collide with each other. The arbiter provides an allowed range $[a, b]$ for the velocity for each vehicle. When two vehicles come within a distance d_{std} of each other, the arbiter asks the faster car and all behind it to reduce the speed to a' and the slower car and all in front of it to increase the speed to b'. When the distance between the two vehicles involved exceeds d_{normal}, the arbiter goes back to normal. The cars are considered to have crashed if their distance is below c. The LHA model for n cars has n continuous state variables and the parameters d_{std} and d_{normal}. The number of counterexamples is infinite, since the controller can cycle infinitely between normal and recovery mode before a crash occurs.

We consider the constants $a = 40$, $b = 60$, $a' = 41$, $b' = 80$, $c = 0.002$. Using CEGAR and octagonal overapproximations, we synthesize the solution $d_{std} \leq d_{normal} \leq 10 \wedge d_{std} > 0.002$. The plot of the log of the time taken vs. the number of cars in Fig. 3 shows that the cost of standard reachability is double-exponential, while using CEGAR (simple discrete or IRA) it is exponential with a low factor (actually due to the time it takes to compose the system, not the analysis itself). For illustration, we also include the time it takes to obtain the exact solution as in (6) using CEGAR and Fourier-Motzkin elimination – it is also double exponential. These results were obtained on a 1.8 GHz AMD Opteron processor with 16 GB RAM running 32 bit code under Linux. For linear programming we use GLPK [8] with exact arithmetic for simple discrete CEGAR, and CPLEX [9] with floating point arithmetic for IRA.

7 Conclusions

This paper proposes a method for using counterexamples to guide the construction of a set of good parameters for parameterized LHA. The proposed procedure extends the philosophy of CEGAR for verification to a class of design problems. The method is complete when the parameters are monotonic. The effectiveness of the approach is illustrated for an example of an automatic highway controller.

The implications of parameter-monotonicity merit further investigation. If an LHA is not monotonic in the parameters, it can be brought to monotonic form by replacing each parameter $\mathtt{p_i}$ that occurs with both signs with $\mathtt{p_i^+}$ where it occurs with positive sign and $\mathtt{p_i^-}$ where it occurs with negative sign. If P'_G is the set of good parameters for the modified LHA, the set of good parameters for the original system is given by $P_G = P'_G \cap [\![p_i^+ = p_i^-]\!]$. Further research is needed to determine whether or not this leads to any computational advantage for LHA that are not parameter-monotonic.

References

1. Henzinger, T.A., Wong-Toi, H.: Using HyTech to synthesize control parameters for a steam boiler. In: Abrial, J.-R., Börger, E., Langmaack, H. (eds.) Dagstuhl Seminar 1995. LNCS, vol. 1165, pp. 265–282. Springer, Heidelberg (1996)
2. Clarke, E.M., Grumberg, O., Jha, S., Lu, Y., Veith, H.: Counterexample-guided abstraction refinement. In: Emerson, E.A., Sistla, A.P. (eds.) CAV 2000. LNCS, vol. 1855, pp. 154–169. Springer, Heidelberg (2000)
3. Jha, S.K., Krogh, B.H., Weimer, J.E., Clarke, E.M.: Reachability for linear hybrid automata using iterative relaxation abstraction. In: Bemporad, A., Bicchi, A., Buttazzo, G. (eds.) HSCC 2007. LNCS, vol. 4416, Springer, Heidelberg (2007)
4. Henzinger, T.A.: The theory of hybrid automata. In: Proc. 11th Annual IEEE Symposium on Logic in Computer Science, LICS 1996, New Brunswick, New Jersey, July 27-30, 1996, pp. 278–292. IEEE Computer Society Press, Los Alamitos (1996)
5. Li, X., Jha, S.K., Bu, L.: Towards an Efficient Path-Oriented Tool for Bounded Reachability analysis of Linear Hybrid Systems using Linear Programming. In: BMC 2006: Proceedings of the Workshop on Bounded Model Checking (2006)
6. Segelken, M.: Abstraction and counterexample-guided construction of ω-automata for model checking of step-discrete linear hybrid models. In: Damm, W., Hermanns, H. (eds.) CAV 2007. LNCS, vol. 4590, pp. 433–448. Springer, Heidelberg (2007)
7. Horowitz, R., Varaiya, P.: Control design of an automated highway system. Proc. IEEE 88, 913–925 (2000)
8. GNU Linear Programming Kit, v.4.17 (2007), `http://www.gnu.org/software/glpk`
9. ILOG (2007), `http://www.ilog.com/products/cplex/product/simplex.cfm`

Approximately Bisimilar Symbolic Models for Incrementally Stable Switched Systems*

Antoine Girard[1], Giordano Pola[2,3], and Paulo Tabuada[2]

[1] Laboratoire Jean Kuntzmann, Université Joseph Fourier
B.P. 53, 38041 Grenoble, France
Antoine.Girard@imag.fr
[2] Department of Electrical Engineering, University of California at Los Angeles
Los Angeles, CA 90095-1594
{pola,tabuada}@ee.ucla.edu
[3] Department of Electrical and Information Engineering, University of L'Aquila
Poggio di Roio, 67040 L'Aquila, Italy
pola@ing.univaq.it

Abstract. Switched systems constitute an important modeling paradigm faithfully describing many engineering systems in which software interacts with the physical world. Despite considerable progress on stability and stabilization of switched systems, the constant evolution of technology demands that we make similar progress with respect to different, and perhaps more complex, objectives. This paper describes one particular approach to address these different objectives based on the construction of approximately equivalent (bisimilar) symbolic models for a switched system. The main contribution of this paper consists in showing that under standard assumptions ensuring incremental stability of a switched system (i.e. existence of common or multiple Lyapunov functions), it is possible to construct a symbolic model that is approximately bisimilar to the original switched system with a precision that can be chosen a priori. To support the computational merits of the proposed approach we present a realistic example of a boost dc-dc converter and show how to synthesize a switched controller that regulates the output voltage at a desired level.

1 Introduction

Switched systems constitute an important modeling paradigm faithfully describing many engineering systems in which software interacts with the physical world. Although this fact already amply justifies its study, switched systems are also quite intriguing from a theoretical point of view. It is well known that by judiciously switching between stable subsystems one can render the overall system unstable. This motivated several researchers over the years to understand which classes of switching strategies or switching signals preserve stability (see

* This work was partially supported by the ANR SETIN project VAL-AMS and by the NSF CAREER award 0717188.

M. Egerstedt and B. Mishra (Eds.): HSCC 2008, LNCS 4981, pp. 201–214, 2008.

e.g. [1]). Despite considerable progress on stability and stabilization of switched systems, the constant evolution of technology demands that we make similar progress with respect to different, and perhaps more complex, objectives. These comprise the synthesis of control strategies guiding the switched systems through predetermined operating points while avoiding certain regions in the state space, enforcing limit cycles and oscillatory behavior, reconfiguration upon the occurrence of faults, etc.

This paper describes one particular approach to address these different objectives based on the construction of symbolic models in which sets of states in the switched system are represented by abstract states. When the symbolic models are finite, controller synthesis problems can be efficiently solved by resorting to mature techniques developed in the areas of supervisory control of discrete-event systems [2] and algorithmic game theory [3]. The crucial step is therefore the construction of symbolic models that are detailed enough to capture all the behavior of the original system, but not so detailed that their use for synthesis is as difficult as the original model. This is accomplished, at the technical level, by using the notion of approximate bisimulation. Approximate bisimulation has been introduced in [4] as an approximate version of the usual bisimulation relation [5,6]. It generalizes the notion of bisimulation by requiring the outputs of two systems to be close instead of being strictly equal. This relaxed requirement makes it possible to compute symbolic models for larger classes of systems as shown recently for incrementally stable continuous control systems [7].

The main contribution of this paper consists in showing that under standard assumptions ensuring incremental stability of a switched system (i.e. existence of common or multiple Lyapunov functions), it is possible to construct a symbolic model that is approximately bisimilar to the original switched system with a precision that can be chosen a priori. The proof is constructive and it is straightforward to derive a procedure for the computation of these symbolic models. Since in problems of practical interest the state space can be assumed to be bounded, the resulting symbolic model is guaranteed to have finitely many states and can thus be used for algorithmic controller synthesis. The technical contribution extends previous work by the authors that considered only purely continuous systems [7]. To support the computational merits of the proposed approach, we present a realistic example of a boost DC-DC converter and show how to synthesize a switched controller that regulates the output voltage at a desired level.

In the following, the symbols $\mathbb{N}$, $\mathbb{Z}$, $\mathbb{R}$, $\mathbb{R}^+$ and $\mathbb{R}_0^+$ denote the set of natural, integer, real, positive and nonnegative real numbers respectively. Given a vector $x \in \mathbb{R}^n$, we denote by x_i its i-th coordinate and by $\|x\|$ its Euclidean norm.

2 Switched Systems and Incremental Stability

2.1 Switched Systems

We shall consider the class of switched systems formalized in the following definition.

Definition 1. *A switched system is a quadruple $\Sigma = (\mathbb{R}^n, P, \mathcal{P}, F)$, where:*

- *$\mathbb{R}^n$ is the state space;*
- *$P = \{1, \ldots, m\}$ is the finite set of modes;*
- *$\mathcal{P}$ is a subset of $\mathcal{S}(\mathbb{R}_0^+, P)$ which denotes the set of piecewise constant functions from $\mathbb{R}_0^+$ to P, continuous from the right and with a finite number of discontinuities on every bounded interval of $\mathbb{R}_0^+$;*
- *$F = \{f_1, \ldots, f_m\}$ is a collection of vector fields indexed by P. For all $p \in P$, $f_p : \mathbb{R}^n \to \mathbb{R}^n$ is a locally Lipschitz continuous map.*

For all $p \in P$, we denote by Σ_p the continuous *subsystem* of Σ defined by the differential equation:

$$\dot{\mathbf{x}}(t) = f_p(\mathbf{x}(t)). \tag{1}$$

We make the assumption that the vector field f_p is such that the solutions of the differential equation (1) are defined on an interval of the form $]a, +\infty[$ with $a < 0$. Sufficient conditions includes linear growth or compact support of the vector field f_p.

A *switching signal* of Σ is a function $\mathbf{p} \in \mathcal{P}$, the discontinuities of $\mathbf{p}$ are called *switching times*. A piecewise $\mathcal{C}^1$ function $\mathbf{x} : \mathbb{R}_0^+ \to \mathbb{R}^n$ is said to be a *trajectory* of Σ if it is continuous and there exists a switching signal $\mathbf{p} \in \mathcal{P}$ such that, at each $t \in \mathbb{R}_0^+$ where the function $\mathbf{p}$ is continuous, $\mathbf{x}$ is continuously differentiable and satisfies:

$$\dot{\mathbf{x}}(t) = f_{\mathbf{p}(t)}(\mathbf{x}(t)).$$

We will use $\mathbf{x}(t, x, \mathbf{p})$ to denote the point reached at time $t \in \mathbb{R}_0^+$ from the initial condition x under the switching signal $\mathbf{p}$. The assumptions on the vector fields $f_1, \ldots, f_m$ and the fact that the switching signals have only a finite number of discontinuities on every bounded interval, thus ruling out Zeno behaviors, ensure for all initial conditions and switching signals, existence and uniqueness of the trajectory of Σ. Let us remark that a trajectory of Σ_p is a trajectory of Σ associated with the constant switching signal $\mathbf{p}(t) = p$, for all $t \in \mathbb{R}_0^+$. Then, we will use $\mathbf{x}(t, x, p)$ to denote the point reached by Σ_p at time $t \in \mathbb{R}_0^+$ from the initial condition x.

2.2 Incremental Stability

The results presented in this paper rely on some stability notions. A continuous function $\gamma : \mathbb{R}_0^+ \to \mathbb{R}_0^+$ is said to belong to class $\mathcal{K}$ if it is strictly increasing and $\gamma(0) = 0$. Function γ is said to belong to class $\mathcal{K}_\infty$ if it is a $\mathcal{K}$ function and $\gamma(r) \to \infty$ when $r \to \infty$. A continuous function $\beta : \mathbb{R}_0^+ \times \mathbb{R}_0^+ \to \mathbb{R}_0^+$ is said to belong to class $\mathcal{KL}$ if for all fixed s, the map $r \mapsto \beta(r, s)$ belongs to class $\mathcal{K}_\infty$ and for all fixed r, the map $s \mapsto \beta(r, s)$ is strictly decreasing and $\beta(r, s) \to 0$ when $s \to \infty$.

Definition 2. *[8] The subsystem Σ_p is incrementally globally asymptotically stable (δ-GAS) if there exists a $\mathcal{KL}$ function β_p such that for all $t \in \mathbb{R}_0^+$, for all $x, y \in \mathbb{R}^n$, the following condition is satisfied:*

$$\|\mathbf{x}(t, x, p) - \mathbf{x}(t, y, p)\| \le \beta_p(\|x - y\|, t).$$

Intuitively, incremental stability means that all the trajectories of the subsystem Σ_p converge to the same reference trajectory independently of their initial condition. This is an incremental version of the notion of global asymptotic stability (GAS) [9]. Let us remark that when f_p satisfies $f_p(0) = 0$ then δ-GAS implies GAS, as all the trajectories of Σ_p converge to the trajectory $\mathbf{x}(t, 0, p) = 0$. Further, if f_p is linear then δ-GAS and GAS are equivalent. Similarly to GAS, δ-GAS can be characterized by dissipation inequalities.

Definition 3. *A smooth function $V_p : \mathbb{R}^n \times \mathbb{R}^n \to \mathbb{R}_0^+$ is a δ-GAS Lyapunov function*[1] *for Σ_p if there exist $\mathcal{K}_\infty$ functions $\underline{\alpha}_p$, $\overline{\alpha}_p$ and $\kappa_p \in \mathbb{R}^+$ such that:*

$$\forall x, y \in \mathbb{R}^n, \quad \underline{\alpha}_p(\|x - y\|) \leq V_p(x, y) \leq \overline{\alpha}_p(\|x - y\|); \tag{2}$$

$$\forall x, y \in \mathbb{R}^n, \quad \frac{\partial V_p}{\partial x}(x, y) f_p(x) + \frac{\partial V_p}{\partial y}(x, y) f_p(y) \leq -\kappa_p V_p(x, y). \tag{3}$$

The following result completely characterizes δ-GAS in terms of existence of a δ-GAS Lyapunov function.

Theorem 1. *[8] Σ_p is δ-GAS iff it admits a δ-GAS Lyapunov function.*

For the purpose of this paper, we extend the notion of incremental stability to switched systems as follows:

Definition 4. *A switched system $\Sigma = (\mathbb{R}^n, P, \mathcal{P}, F)$ is incrementally globally uniformly asymptotically stable (δ-GUAS) if there exists a $\mathcal{KL}$ function β such that for all $t \in \mathbb{R}_0^+$, for all $x, y \in \mathbb{R}^n$, for all switching signals $\mathbf{p} \in \mathcal{P}$, the following condition is satisfied:*

$$\|\mathbf{x}(t, x, \mathbf{p}) - \mathbf{x}(t, y, \mathbf{p})\| \leq \beta(\|x - y\|, t).$$

Let us remark that the speed of convergence specified by the function β is independent of the switching signal $\mathbf{p}$. Thus, the stability property is uniform over the set of switching signals; hence the notion of incremental global uniform asymptotic stability. Incremental stability of a switched system means that all the trajectories associated with the same switching signal converge to the same reference trajectory independently of their initial condition. This is an incremental version of global uniform asymptotic stability (GUAS) for switched systems [1]. If for all $p \in P$, $f_p(0) = 0$, then δ-GUAS implies GUAS as all the trajectories of Σ converge to the constant trajectory $\mathbf{x}(t, 0, \mathbf{p}) = 0$.

It is well known that a switched system whose subsystems are all GAS may exhibit some unstable behaviors under fast switching signals. The same kind of phenomenon can be observed for switched systems with δ-GAS subsystems. Similarly, the results on common or multiple Lyapunov functions for proving GUAS of switched systems (see e.g. [1]) can be extended to prove δ-GUAS.

---

[1] In [8], (3) is replaced by $\frac{\partial V_p}{\partial x}(x, y) f_p(x) + \frac{\partial V_p}{\partial y}(x, y) f_p(y) \leq -\rho_p(\|x - y\|)$, where ρ_p is a positive definite function. It is known (see e.g. [1]) that there is no loss of generality in considering $\rho_p(\|x - y\|) = \kappa_p V_p(x, y)$, modifying the δ-GAS Lyapunov function V_p if necessary.

Because of the lack of space, we omit the proofs of the following theorems. Let the $\mathcal{K}_\infty$ functions $\underline{\alpha}$, $\overline{\alpha}$ and the real number κ be given by $\underline{\alpha} = \min(\underline{\alpha}_1, \dots, \underline{\alpha}_m)$, $\overline{\alpha} = \max(\overline{\alpha}_1, \dots, \overline{\alpha}_m)$ and $\kappa = \min(\kappa_1, \dots, \kappa_m)$.

Theorem 2. *Consider a switched system $\Sigma = (\mathbb{R}^n, P, \mathcal{P}, F)$. Let us assume that there exists $V : \mathbb{R}^n \times \mathbb{R}^n \to \mathbb{R}_0^+$ which is a common δ-GAS Lyapunov function for subsystems $\Sigma_1, \dots, \Sigma_m$. Then, Σ is δ-GUAS.*

When a common δ-GAS Lyapunov function fails to exist, δ-GUAS of the switched system can be ensured by using multiple δ-GAS Lyapunov functions and a restrained set of switching signals. Let $\mathcal{S}_{\tau_d}(\mathbb{R}_0^+, P)$ denote the set of switching signals with *dwell time* $\tau_d \in \mathbb{R}_0^+$ so that $\mathbf{p} \in \mathcal{S}(\mathbb{R}_0^+, P)$ has dwell time τ_d if the switching times $t_1, t_2, \dots$ satisfy $t_1 \geq \tau_d$ and $t_i - t_{i-1} \geq \tau_d$, for all $i \geq 2$.

Theorem 3. *Let $\tau_d \in \mathbb{R}_0^+$, consider a switched system $\Sigma_{\tau_d} = (\mathbb{R}^n, P, \mathcal{P}, F)$ with $\mathcal{P} \subseteq \mathcal{S}_{\tau_d}(\mathbb{R}_0^+, P)$. Let us assume that for all $p \in P$, there exists a δ-GAS Lyapunov function V_p for subsystem $\Sigma_{\tau_d, p}$ and that in addition there exists $\mu \geq 1$ such that:*

$$\forall x, y \in \mathbb{R}^n,\ \forall p, p' \in P,\ V_p(x, y) \leq \mu V_{p'}(x, y). \tag{4}$$

If $\tau_d > \frac{\log \mu}{\kappa}$, then Σ_{τ_d} is δ-GUAS.

In the following, we show that under the assumptions of Theorems 2 or 3, it is possible to compute approximately equivalent symbolic models of switched systems. We will make the following supplementary assumption on the δ-GAS Lyapunov functions: for all $p \in P$, there exists a $\mathcal{K}_\infty$ function γ_p such that

$$\forall x, y, z \in \mathbb{R}^n,\ |V_p(x, y) - V_p(x, z)| \leq \gamma_p(\|y - z\|). \tag{5}$$

Note that γ_p is not a function of the variable x; let the $\mathcal{K}_\infty$ function γ be given by $\gamma = \max(\gamma_1, \dots, \gamma_m)$. We will discuss this assumption later in the paper and we will show that it is not restrictive provided we are interested in the dynamics of the switched system on a compact subset of the state space $\mathbb{R}^n$.

3 Approximate Bisimulation

In this section, we present a notion of approximate equivalence which will relate a switched system to the symbolic models that we construct. We start by introducing the class of transition systems which allows us to model switched and symbolic systems in a common framework.

Definition 5. *A transition system is a sextuple $T = (Q, L, \longrightarrow, O, H, I)$ consisting of:*

- *a set of states Q;*
- *a set of labels L;*
- *a transition relation $\longrightarrow \subseteq Q \times L \times Q$;*
- *an output set O;*

– *an output function* $H : Q \to O$;
– *a set of initial states* $I \subseteq Q$.

T is said to be metric if the output set O is equipped with a metric d, countable if Q and L are countable sets, finite, if Q and L are finite sets.

The transition $(q, l, q') \in \longrightarrow$ will be denoted $q \xrightarrow{l} q'$. The transition relation captures the dynamics of the transition system: $q \xrightarrow{l} q'$ means that the system can evolve from state q to state q' under the action labelled by l.

Transition systems can serve as abstract models for describing switched systems. Given a switched system $\Sigma = (\mathbb{R}^n, P, \mathcal{P}, F)$ where $\mathcal{P} = \mathcal{S}(\mathbb{R}_0^+, P)$, we define the associated transition system $T(\Sigma) = (Q, L, \longrightarrow, O, H, I)$, where the set of states is $Q = \mathbb{R}^n$; the set of labels is $L = P$; the transition relation is given by $q \xrightarrow{l} q'$ iff there exists a trajectory $\mathbf{x}$ of the subsystem Σ_l such that $\mathbf{x}(\tau, q, l) = q'$ for some $\tau \in \mathbb{R}^+$; the set of outputs is $O = \mathbb{R}^n$; the observation map H is the identity map over $\mathbb{R}^n$; the set of initial states is $I = \mathbb{R}^n$. The transition system $T(\Sigma)$ is metric when the set of outputs $O = \mathbb{R}^n$ is equipped with the metric $d(q, q') = \|q - q'\|$. Note that the state space of $T(\Sigma)$ is infinite.

Usual equivalence relationships between transition systems rely on the equality of the languages. In this paper, we are mostly interested in bisimulation equivalence [5,6]. Intuitively, a bisimulation relation between two transition systems T_1 and T_2 is a relation between their set of states explaining how a trajectory of T_1 can be transformed into a trajectory of T_2 with the same associated sequence of outputs, and vice versa. The requirement of equality of output sequences, as in the classical formulation of bisimulation [5,6] is quite strong for metric transition systems. We shall relax this, by requiring output sequences to be close where closeness is measured with respect to the metric on the output space. This relaxation leads to the notion of approximate bisimulation relation introduced in [4].

Definition 6. *Let $T_1 = (Q_1, L, \underset{1}{\longrightarrow}, O, H_1, I_1)$, $T_2 = (Q_2, L, \underset{2}{\longrightarrow}, O, H_2, I_2)$ be metric transition systems with the same sets of labels L and outputs O equipped with the metric d. Let $\varepsilon \in \mathbb{R}_0^+$ be a given precision, a relation $R \subseteq Q_1 \times Q_2$ is said to be an ε-approximate bisimulation relation between T_1 and T_2 if for all $(q_1, q_2) \in R$:*

– $d(H_1(q_1), H_2(q_2)) \leq \varepsilon$;
– *for all* $q_1 \underset{1}{\xrightarrow{l}} q_1'$, *there exists* $q_2 \underset{2}{\xrightarrow{l}} q_2'$, *such that* $(q_1', q_2') \in R$;
– *for all* $q_2 \underset{2}{\xrightarrow{l}} q_2'$, *there exists* $q_1 \underset{1}{\xrightarrow{l}} q_1'$, *such that* $(q_1', q_2') \in R$.

The transition systems T_1 and T_2 are said to be approximately bisimilar with precision ε (denoted $T_1 \sim_\varepsilon T_2$) if:

– *for all* $q_1 \in I_1$, *there exists* $q_2 \in I_2$, *such that* $(q_1, q_2) \in R$;
– *for all* $q_2 \in I_2$, *there exists* $q_1 \in I_1$, *such that* $(q_1, q_2) \in R$.

4 Approximately Bisimilar Symbolic Models

In the following, we will work with a sub-transition system of $T(\Sigma)$ obtained by selecting the transitions of $T(\Sigma)$ that describe trajectories of duration τ_s for some chosen $\tau_s \in \mathbb{R}^+$. This can be seen as a sampling process. Moreover, we suppose that switching instants can only occur at times of the form $i\tau_s$ with $i \in \mathbb{N}$. This is a natural constraint when the switching in Σ has to be controlled by a microprocessor with clock period τ_s. Given a switched system $\Sigma = (\mathbb{R}^n, P, \mathcal{P}, F)$ where $\mathcal{P} = \mathcal{S}(\mathbb{R}_0^+, P)$, and a time sampling parameter $\tau_s \in \mathbb{R}^+$, we define the associated transition system $T_{\tau_s}(\Sigma) = (Q_1, L_1, \underset{1}{\longrightarrow}, O_1, H_1, I_1)$ where the set of states is $Q_1 = \mathbb{R}^n$; the set of labels is $L_1 = P$; the transition relation is given by $q \overset{l}{\underset{1}{\longrightarrow}} q'$ iff $\mathbf{x}(\tau_s, q, l) = q'$; the set of outputs is $O_1 = \mathbb{R}^n$; the observation map H_1 is the identity map over $\mathbb{R}^n$; the set of initial states is $I_1 = \mathbb{R}^n$. The transition system $T_{\tau_s}(\Sigma)$ is metric when the set of outputs $O_1 = \mathbb{R}^n$ is equipped with the metric $d(q, q') = \|q - q'\|$.

4.1 Common Lyapunov Function

We first examinate the case when there exists a common δ-GAS Lyapunov function V for subsystems $\Sigma_1, \ldots, \Sigma_m$. We start by approximating the set of states $Q_1 = \mathbb{R}^n$ by the lattice:

$$[\mathbb{R}^n]_\eta = \left\{ q \in \mathbb{R}^n \;\middle|\; q_i = k_i \frac{2\eta}{\sqrt{n}},\ k_i \in \mathbb{Z},\ i = 1, ..., n \right\},$$

where $\eta \in \mathbb{R}^+$ is a state space discretization parameter. By simple geometrical considerations, we can see that for all $x \in \mathbb{R}^n$, there exists $q \in [\mathbb{R}^n]_\eta$ such that $\|x - q\| \leq \eta$.

Let us define the transition system $T_{\tau_s,\eta}(\Sigma) = (Q_2, L_2, \underset{2}{\longrightarrow}, O_2, H_2, I_2)$, where the set of states is $Q_2 = [\mathbb{R}^n]_\eta$; the set of labels remains the same $L_2 = L_1 = P$; the transition relation is given by $q \overset{l}{\underset{2}{\longrightarrow}} q'$ iff $\|\mathbf{x}(\tau_s, q, l) - q'\| \leq \eta$; the set of outputs remains the same $O_2 = O_1 = \mathbb{R}^n$; the observation map H_2 is the natural inclusion map from $[\mathbb{R}^n]_\eta$ to $\mathbb{R}^n$, i.e. $H_2(q) = q$; the set of initial states is $I_2 = [\mathbb{R}^n]_\eta$. Note that the transition system $T_{\tau_s,\eta}(\Sigma)$ is countable. Moreover, it is metric when the set of outputs $O_2 = \mathbb{R}^n$ is equipped with the metric $d(q, q') = \|q - q'\|$.

We now give the result that relates the existence of a common δ-GAS Lyapunov function for the subsystems $\Sigma_1, \ldots, \Sigma_m$ to the existence of approximately bisimilar symbolic models for the transition system $T_{\tau_s}(\Sigma)$.

Theorem 4. *Consider a switched system $\Sigma = (\mathbb{R}^n, P, \mathcal{P}, F)$ with $\mathcal{P} = \mathcal{S}(\mathbb{R}_0^+, P)$, time and state space sampling parameters $\tau_s, \eta \in \mathbb{R}^+$ and a desired precision $\varepsilon \in \mathbb{R}^+$. Let us assume that there exists $V : \mathbb{R}^n \times \mathbb{R}^n \to \mathbb{R}_0^+$ which is a common δ-GAS Lyapunov function for subsystems $\Sigma_1, \ldots, \Sigma_m$ and such that equation (5) holds for some $\mathcal{K}_\infty$ function γ. If*

$$\eta \leq \min \left\{ \gamma^{-1}\left((1 - e^{-\kappa\tau_s})\underline{\alpha}(\varepsilon)\right), \overline{\alpha}^{-1}\left(\underline{\alpha}(\varepsilon)\right) \right\} \tag{6}$$

then, the transition systems $T_{\tau_s}(\Sigma)$ and $T_{\tau_s,\eta}(\Sigma)$ are approximately bisimilar with precision ε.

Proof. We start by showing that the relation $R \subseteq Q_1 \times Q_2$ defined by $(q_1, q_2) \in R$ iff $V(q_1, q_2) \leq \underline{\alpha}(\varepsilon)$, is an ε-approximate bisimulation relation. Let $(q_1, q_2) \in R$, then $\|q_1 - q_2\| \leq \underline{\alpha}^{-1}(V(q_1, q_2)) \leq \varepsilon$. Thus, the first condition of Definition 6 holds. Let $q_1 \xrightarrow[1]{l} q_1'$, then $q_1' = \mathbf{x}(\tau_s, q_1, l)$. There exists $q_2' \in [\mathbb{R}^n]_\eta$ such that $\|\mathbf{x}(\tau_s, q_2, l) - q_2'\| \leq \eta$. Then, we have $q_2 \xrightarrow[2]{l} q_2'$. Let us check that $(q_1', q_2') \in R$. From equation (5), $|V(q_1', q_2') - V(q_1', \mathbf{x}(\tau_s, q_2, l))| \leq \gamma(\|q_2' - \mathbf{x}(\tau_s, q_2, l))\|) \leq \gamma(\eta)$. It follows that

$$\begin{aligned} V(q_1', q_2') &\leq V(q_1', \mathbf{x}(\tau_s, q_2, l)) + \gamma(\eta) = V(\mathbf{x}(\tau_s, q_1, l), \mathbf{x}(\tau_s, q_2, l)) + \gamma(\eta) \\ &\leq e^{-\kappa\tau_s} V(q_1, q_2) + \gamma(\eta) \end{aligned} \tag{7}$$

because V is a δ-GAS Lyapunov function for subsystem Σ_l. Then, from equation (6) and since γ is a $\mathcal{K}_\infty$ function, $V(q_1', q_2') \leq e^{-\kappa\tau_s}\underline{\alpha}(\varepsilon) + \gamma(\eta) \leq \underline{\alpha}(\varepsilon)$. Hence, $(q_1', q_2') \in R$. In a similar way, we can prove that, for all $q_2 \xrightarrow[2]{l} q_2'$, there is $q_1 \xrightarrow[1]{l} q_1'$ such that $(q_1', q_2') \in R$. Hence R is an ε-approximate bisimulation relation between $T_\tau(\Sigma)$ and $T_{\tau,\eta}(\Sigma)$.

By definition of $I_2 = [\mathbb{R}^n]_\eta$, for all $q_1 \in I_1 = \mathbb{R}^n$, there exists $q_2 \in I_2$ such that $\|q_1 - q_2\| \leq \eta$. Then, $V(q_1, q_2) \leq \overline{\alpha}(\|q_1 - q_2\|) \leq \overline{\alpha}(\eta) \leq \underline{\alpha}(\varepsilon)$ because of equation (6) and $\overline{\alpha}$ is a $\mathcal{K}_\infty$ function. Hence, $(q_1, q_2) \in R$. Conversely, for all $q_2 \in I_2$, $q_1 = q_2 \in \mathbb{R}^n = I_1$, then $V(q_1, q_2) = 0$ and $(q_1, q_2) \in R$. Therefore, $T_{\tau_s}(\Sigma)$ and $T_{\tau_s,\eta}(\Sigma)$ are approximately bisimilar with precision ε. ■

Let us remark that, for a given time sampling parameter τ_s and a desired precision $\varepsilon \in \mathbb{R}^+$, there always exists $\eta \in \mathbb{R}^+$ sufficiently small such that equation (6) holds. This means that for switched systems admitting a common δ-GAS Lyapunov function there exists approximately bisimilar symbolic models and any precision can be reached for all sampling rates.

4.2 Multiple Lyapunov Functions

If a common δ-GAS Lyapunov function does not exist, it remains possible to compute approximately bisimilar symbolic models provided we restrict the set of switching signals using a dwell time τ_d. In this section, we consider a switched system $\Sigma_{\tau_d} = (\mathbb{R}^n, P, \mathcal{P}, F)$ where $\mathcal{P} = \mathcal{S}_{\tau_d}(\mathbb{R}_0^+, P)$. Let τ_s be a time sampling parameter; for simplicity, we will assume that the dwell time τ_d is an integer multiple of τ_s: there exists $N \in \mathbb{N}$ such that $\tau_d = N\tau_s$. Representing Σ_{τ_d} using a transition system is a bit less trivial than previously as we need to record inside the state of the transition system the time elapsed since the latest switching occured. Thus, the transition system associated with Σ_{τ_d} is $T_{\tau_s}(\Sigma_{\tau_d}) = (Q_1, L_1, \xrightarrow[1]{}, O_1, H_1, I_1)$ where:

- the set of states is $Q_1 = \mathbb{R}^n \times P \times \{0, \dots, N-1\}$, a state $(x, p, i) \in Q_1$ means that the current state of Σ_{τ_d} is x, the current value of the switching signal is p and the time elapsed since the latest switching is exactly $i\tau_s$ if $i < N-1$ or at least $(N-1)\tau_s$ if $i = N-1$.
- the set of labels is $L_1 = P$;
- the transition relation is given by $(x, p, i) \xrightarrow[1]{l} (x', p', i')$ iff $l = p$ and one the following holds:
  - $i < N-1$, $x' = \mathbf{x}(\tau_s, x, p)$, $p' = p$ and $i' = i+1$: switching is not allowed because the time elapsed since the latest switch is strictly smaller than the dwell time;
  - $i = N-1$, $x' = \mathbf{x}(\tau_s, x, p)$, $p' = p$ and $i' = N-1$: switching is allowed but no switch occurs;
  - $i = N-1$, $x' = \mathbf{x}(\tau_s, x, p)$, $p' \neq p$ and $i' = 0$: switching is allowed and a switch occurs.
- the set of outputs is $O_1 = \mathbb{R}^n$;
- the observation map H_1 is given by $H_1((x, p, i)) = x$;
- the set of initial states is $I_1 = \mathbb{R}^n \times P \times \{0\}$.

One can verify that the output trajectories of $T_{\tau_s}(\Sigma_{\tau_d})$ are the output trajectories of $T_{\tau_s}(\Sigma)$ associated with switching signals with dwell time $\tau_d = N\tau_s$. The approximation of the set of states of $T_{\tau_s}(\Sigma_{\tau_d})$ by a symbolic model is done using a lattice, as previously. Let $\eta \in \mathbb{R}^+$ be a state space discretization parameter, we define the transition system $T_{\tau_s,\eta}(\Sigma_{\tau_d}) = (Q_2, L_2, \xrightarrow[2]{}, O_2, H_2, I_2)$ where:

- the set of states is $Q_2 = [\mathbb{R}^n]_\eta \times P \times \{0, \dots, N-1\}$.
- the set of labels remains the same $L_2 = L_1 = P$;
- the transition relation is given by $(x, p, i) \xrightarrow[1]{l} (x', p', i')$ iff $l = p$ and one of the following holds:
  - $i < N-1$, $\|\mathbf{x}(\tau_s, x, p) - x'\| \leq \eta$, $p' = p$ and $i' = i+1$;
  - $i = N-1$, $\|\mathbf{x}(\tau_s, x, p) - x'\| \leq \eta$, $p' = p$ and $i' = N-1$;
  - $i = N-1$, $\|\mathbf{x}(\tau_s, x, p) - x'\| \leq \eta$, $p' \neq p$ and $i' = 0$;
- the set of outputs remains the same $O_2 = O_1 = \mathbb{R}^n$;
- the observation map H_2 is given by $H_2((x, p, i)) = x$;
- the set of initial states is $I_2 = [\mathbb{R}^n]_\eta \times P \times \{0\}$.

Note that the transition system $T_{\tau_s,\eta}(\Sigma_{\tau_d})$ is countable. Moreover, $T_{\tau_s}(\Sigma_{\tau_d})$ and $T_{\tau_s,\eta}(\Sigma_{\tau_d})$ are metric when the set of outputs $O_1 = O_2 = \mathbb{R}^n$ is equipped with the metric $d(x, x') = \|x - x'\|$. The following theorem establishes the approximate equivalence of $T_{\tau_s}(\Sigma_{\tau_d})$ and $T_{\tau_s,\eta}(\Sigma_{\tau_d})$.

Theorem 5. *Consider $\tau_d \in \mathbb{R}_0^+$, a switched system $\Sigma_{\tau_d} = (\mathbb{R}^n, P, \mathcal{P}, F)$ with $\mathcal{P} = \mathcal{S}_{\tau_d}(\mathbb{R}_0^+, P)$, time and state space sampling parameters $\tau_s, \eta \in \mathbb{R}^+$ and a desired precision $\varepsilon \in \mathbb{R}^+$. Let us assume that for all $p \in P$, there exists a δ-GAS Lyapunov function V_p for subsystem $\Sigma_{\tau_d,p}$ and that equations (4) and (5) hold for some $\mu \geq 1$ and $\mathcal{K}_\infty$ functions $\gamma_1, \dots, \gamma_m$. If $\tau_d > \frac{\log \mu}{\kappa}$ and*

$$\eta \leq \min\left\{\gamma^{-1}\left(\frac{\frac{1}{\mu} - e^{-\kappa\tau_d}}{1 - e^{-\kappa\tau_d}}(1 - e^{-\kappa\tau_s})\underline{\alpha}(\varepsilon)\right), \overline{\alpha}^{-1}\left(\underline{\alpha}(\varepsilon)\right)\right\} \tag{8}$$

then, the transition systems $T_{\tau_s}(\Sigma_{\tau_d})$ and $T_{\tau_s,\eta}(\Sigma_{\tau_d})$ are approximately bisimilar with precision ε.

Proof. Let us define the relation $R \subseteq Q_1 \times Q_2$ by

$$R = \{(x_1, p_1, i_1, x_2, p_2, i_2) \in Q_1 \times Q_2 | \, p_1 = p_2 = p, \; i_1 = i_2 = i, V_p(x_1, x_2) \leq \delta_i\}$$

where $\delta_0, \ldots, \delta_N$ are given recursively by $\delta_0 = \underline{\alpha}(\varepsilon), \; \delta_{i+1} = e^{-\kappa\tau_s}\delta_i + \gamma(\eta)$. Let us remark that:

$$\delta_i = e^{-i\kappa\tau_s}\underline{\alpha}(\varepsilon) + \gamma(\eta)\frac{1 - e^{-i\kappa\tau_s}}{1 - e^{-\kappa\tau_s}} = \frac{\gamma(\eta)}{1 - e^{-\kappa\tau_s}} + e^{-i\kappa\tau_s}\left(\underline{\alpha}(\varepsilon) - \frac{\gamma(\eta)}{1 - e^{-\kappa\tau_s}}\right) \quad (9)$$

From equation (4), $\mu \geq 1$; then, from equation (8) and since γ is a $\mathcal{K}_\infty$ function, $\gamma(\eta) \leq (1 - e^{-\kappa\tau_s})\underline{\alpha}(\varepsilon)$. It follows from (9) that $\delta_0 \geq \delta_1 \geq \cdots \geq \delta_{N-1} \geq \delta_N$. From equation (8), and since γ is a $\mathcal{K}_\infty$ function and $\tau_d = N\tau_s$,

$$\delta_N = e^{-\kappa\tau_d}\underline{\alpha}(\varepsilon) + \gamma(\eta)\frac{1 - e^{-\kappa\tau_d}}{1 - e^{-\kappa\tau_s}} \leq e^{-\kappa\tau_d}\underline{\alpha}(\varepsilon) + \left(\frac{1}{\mu} - e^{-\kappa\tau_d}\right)\underline{\alpha}(\varepsilon) = \frac{\underline{\alpha}(\varepsilon)}{\mu}.$$

We can now prove that R is an ε-approximate bisimulation relation between $T_{\tau_s}(\Sigma_{\tau_d})$ and $T_{\tau_s,\eta}(\Sigma_{\tau_d})$. Let $(x_1, p, i, x_2, p, i) \in R$, then

$$\begin{aligned} \|H_1(x_1, p, i) - H_2(x_2, p, i)\| = \|x_1 - x_2\| &\leq \underline{\alpha}^{-1}\left(V_p(x_1, x_2)\right) \\ &\leq \underline{\alpha}^{-1}(\delta_i) \leq \underline{\alpha}^{-1}(\delta_0) = \varepsilon. \end{aligned}$$

Hence, the first condition of Definition 6 holds. Let us prove that the second condition holds as well. Let $(x_1, p, i) \xrightarrow[1]{p} (x_1', p', i')$, then $x_1' = \mathbf{x}(\tau_s, x_1, p)$. There exists a transition $(x_2, p, i) \xrightarrow[2]{p} (x_2', p', i')$ with $\|x_2' - \mathbf{x}(\tau_s, x_2, p)\| \leq \eta$. From equation (5) and since V_p is a δ-GAS Lyapunov function for subsystem Σ_p we can show, similarly to equation (7), that

$$V_p(x_1', x_2') \leq e^{-\kappa\tau_s}V_p(x_1, x_2) + \gamma(\eta) \leq e^{-\kappa\tau_s}\delta_i + \gamma(\eta) = \delta_{i+1}. \quad (10)$$

We now examinate three separate cases:

- $i < N - 1$, then $p' = p$ and $i' = i + 1$; since $V_p(x_1', x_2') \leq \delta_{i+1}$, it follows that $(x_1', p, i + 1, x_2', p, i + 1) \in R$.
- $i = N - 1$ and $p' = p$ then $i' = N - 1$; from (10), $V_p(x_1', x_2') \leq \delta_N \leq \delta_{N-1}$, it follows that $(x_1', p, N - 1, x_2', p, N - 1) \in R$.
- $i = N - 1$ and $p' \neq p$ then $i' = 0$; from (10), $V_p(x_1', x_2') \leq \delta_N \leq \delta_0/\mu$. From equation (5), it follows that $V_{p'}(x_1', x_2') \leq \mu V_p(x_1', x_2') \leq \delta_0$. Therefore, $(x_1', p', 0, x_2', p', 0) \in R$.

Similarly, we can show that for any transition $(x_2, p, i) \xrightarrow[2]{l} (x_2', p', i')$, there exists a transition $(x_1, p, i) \xrightarrow[1]{l} (x_1', p', i')$ such that $(x_1', p', i', x_2', p', i') \in R$. Hence, R is an ε-approximate bisimulation relation.

For all initial states $(x_1, p, 0) \in I_1$, there exists $(x_2, p, 0) \in I_2$ such that $\|x_1 - x_2\| \leq \eta$. Then, $V_p(x_1, x_2) \leq \overline{\alpha}(\eta) \leq \underline{\alpha}(\varepsilon)$ because of equation (8) and $\overline{\alpha}$ is $\mathcal{K}_\infty$ function. Hence, $V_p(x_1, x_2) \leq \delta_0$ and $(x_1, p, 0, x_2, p, 0) \in R$. Conversely, for all $(x_2, p, 0) \in I_2$, $(x_1, p, 0) = (x_2, p, 0) \in I_1$. Then, $V_p(x_1, x_2) = 0 \leq \delta_0$ and $(x_1, p, 0, x_2, p, 0) \in R$. Thus, $T_{\tau_s}(\Sigma_{\tau_d})$ and $T_{\tau_s,\eta}(\Sigma_{\tau_d})$ are approximately bisimilar with precision ε. ■

Provided that $\tau_d > \frac{\log \mu}{\kappa}$, for a given time sampling parameter and a desired precision, there always exists $\eta \in \mathbb{R}^+$ sufficiently small such that equation (8) holds. Thus, if the dwell time is large enough, we can compute symbolic models of arbitrary precision of the switched system. Let us remark that the lower bound we obtain on the dwell time is the same than the one in Theorem 3 ensuring incremental stability of the switched system. Theorem 4 can be seen as a corollary of Theorem 5. Indeed, existence of a common δ-GAS Lyapunov function is equivalent to equation (4) with $\mu = 1$. Then, no constraint is necessary on the dwell time and equation (8) becomes equivalent to (6).

The previous Theorems also give indications on the practical computation of these symbolic models. The sets of states of $T_{\tau_s,\eta}(\Sigma)$ or $T_{\tau_s,\eta}(\Sigma_{\tau_d})$ are countable but infinite. However, if we are interested in the dynamics of the switched system only on a compact subset $C \subseteq \mathbb{R}^n$, then we can restrict the set of states of $T_{\tau_s,\eta}(\Sigma)$ or $T_{\tau_s,\eta}(\Sigma_{\tau_d})$ to the sets $[\mathbb{R}^n]_\mu \cap C$ or $([\mathbb{R}^n]_\mu \cap C) \times P \times \{0, \dots, N-1\}$ which are finite. The computation of the transition relations is then relatively simple since it mainly involves the numerical computation of the points $\mathbf{x}(\tau_s, x, p)$ with $x \in [\mathbb{R}^n]_\mu \cap C$ and $p \in P$. This can be done by simulation of the subsystems $\Sigma_1, \dots, \Sigma_m$. Numerical errors in the computation of these points can be taken into account: it is sufficient to replace η by $\eta + e$, where e is an evaluation of the error, in Theorems 4 and 5.

Finally, we would like to discuss the assumption made in equation (5). This assumption is quite strong because the inequality has to hold for any triple in $\mathbb{R}^n$, and the function γ_p must be independent of x. However, if we are interested in the dynamics of the switched system on the compact subset $C \subseteq \mathbb{R}^n$, we only need this assumption to hold for all $x, y, z \in C$. Then, it is sufficient to assume that V_p is C^1 on C. Indeed, for all $x, y, z \in C$,

$$|V_p(x, y) - V_p(x, z)| \leq \left(\max_{x,y \in C} \left\| \frac{\partial V_p}{\partial y}(x, y) \right\| \right) \|y - z\| = \gamma_p(\|y - z\|).$$

In this case, equation (5) holds. This means that the existence of approximately bisimilar symbolic models on an arbitrary compact subset of $\mathbb{R}^n$ does not need more assumptions than existence of common or multiple Lyapunov functions ensuring incremental stability of the switched system.

5 Symbolic Models for the Boost DC-DC Converter

In this section, we use our methodology to compute symbolic models of a concrete switched system: the boost DC-DC converter (see Figure 1). This is an example

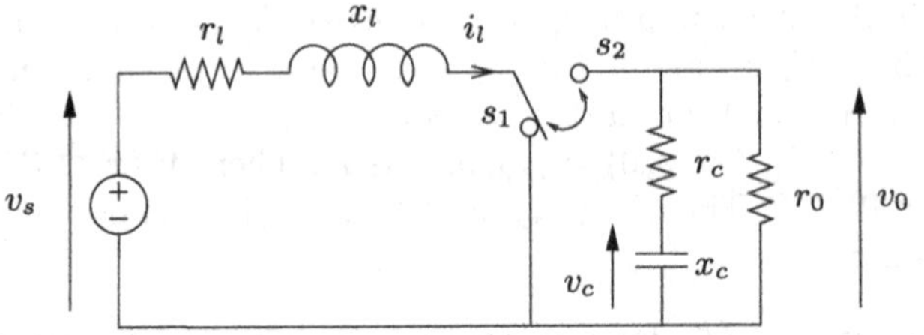

Fig. 1. boost DC-DC converter

of electrical power convertor that has been studied from the point of view of hybrid control in [10,11,12,13].

The boost converter has two operation modes depending on the position of the switch. The state of the system is $x(t) = [i_l(t)\ v_c(t)]^T$ where $i_l(t)$ is the inductor current and $v_c(t)$ the capacitor voltage. The dynamics associated with both modes are affine of the form $\dot{x}(t) = A_p x(t) + b$ $(p = 1, 2)$ with

$$A_1 = \begin{bmatrix} -\frac{r_l}{x_l} & 0 \\ 0 & -\frac{1}{x_c}\frac{1}{r_0+r_c} \end{bmatrix},\ A_2 = \begin{bmatrix} -\frac{1}{x_l}(r_l+\frac{r_0 r_c}{r_0+r_c}) & -\frac{1}{x_l}\frac{r_0}{r_0+r_c} \\ \frac{1}{x_c}\frac{r_0}{r_0+r_c} & -\frac{1}{x_c}\frac{1}{r_0+r_c} \end{bmatrix},\ b = \begin{bmatrix} \frac{v_s}{x_l} \\ 0 \end{bmatrix}.$$

It is clear that the boost DC-DC converter is an example of a switched system. In the following, we use the numerical values from [11], that is, in the per unit system, $x_c = 70$ p.u., $x_l = 3$ p.u., $r_c = 0.005$ p.u., $r_l = 0.05$ p.u., $r_0 = 1$ p.u. and $v_s = 1$ p.u.. The goal of the boost DC-DC converter is to regulate the output voltage across the load r_0. This control problem is usually reformulated as a current reference scheme. Then, the goal is to keep the inductor current $i_l(t)$ around a reference value i_l^{ref}. This can be done, for instance, by synthesizing a controller that keeps the state of the switched system in an invariant set $\mathcal{I}$ centered around the reference value.

It can be shown by solving a set of 2 linear matrix inequalities that the subsystems associated with the two operation modes are both incrementally stable and that they share a common δ-GAS Lyapunov function of the form $V(x,y) = \sqrt{(x-y)^T M (x-y)}$, where M is positive definite symmetric. For a better numerical conditioning, we rescale the second variable of the system (i.e. the state of the system becomes $x(t) = [i_l(t)\ 5v_c(t)]^T$; the matrices A_1, A_2 and vector b are modified accordingly). The δ-GAS Lyapunov function that we obtain has the following characteristics: $\underline{\alpha}(s) = s$, $\overline{\alpha}(s) = \gamma(s) = 1.0127s$, $\kappa = 0.014$, and we set the sampling period to $\tau_s = 0.5$. Then, a symbolic model can be computed for the boost DC-DC converter using the procedure described in Section 4. According to Theorem 4, a desired precision ε can be achieved by choosing a state space discretization parameter η satisfying $\eta \leq \varepsilon/145$. In this example, the ratio between the precision of the symbolic approximation and the state space discretization parameter is quite large. This is explained by the fact that the subsystems are quite weakly stable since the value of κ is small.

We consider two different values of the precision parameter ε. We first choose a precision $\varepsilon = 2.6$ which can be achieved by choosing $\eta = \frac{1}{40\sqrt{2}}$. This precision is

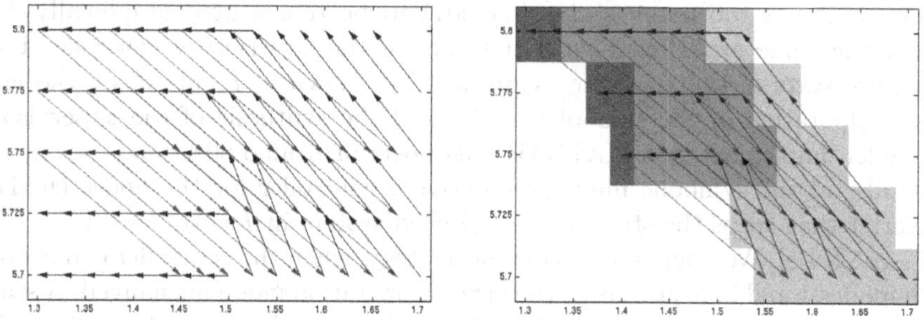

Fig. 2. Symbolic model of the DC-DC converter for $\eta = \frac{1}{40\sqrt{2}}$ (left); Controller for the symbolic model (right) (dark gray: mode 1, light gray: mode 2, medium gray: both modes are acceptable, white: the invariance property cannot be ensured from these states)

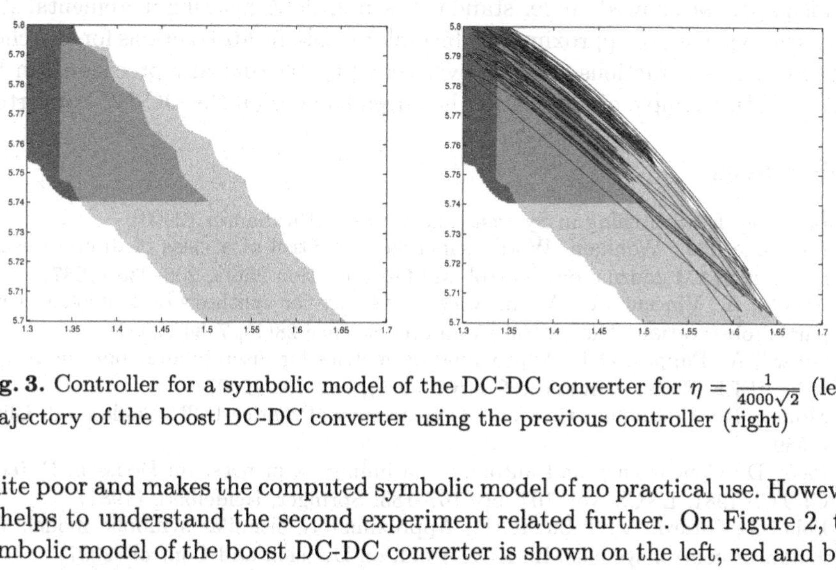

Fig. 3. Controller for a symbolic model of the DC-DC converter for $\eta = \frac{1}{4000\sqrt{2}}$ (left); Trajectory of the boost DC-DC converter using the previous controller (right)

quite poor and makes the computed symbolic model of no practical use. However, it helps to understand the second experiment related further. On Figure 2, the symbolic model of the boost DC-DC converter is shown on the left, red and blue arrows represent the transitions associated with mode 1 and 2, respectively. We only represented the transitions that keep the state of the symbolic model in the set $\mathcal{I}' = [1.3, 1.7] \times [5.7, 5.8]$. Using supervisory control [2], we synthesized a controller that keeps the state of the symbolic model inside $\mathcal{I}'$. It is shown on the right figure: dark and light gray means that for these states of the symbolic model the controller has to use mode 1 and 2, respectively; medium gray means that for these states the controller can use either mode 1 or mode 2; white means that from these states there does not exist any switching sequence that keeps the state of the symbolic model in $\mathcal{I}'$. From this controller, using the approach presented in [14], one could derive a controller for the boost DC-DC converter that keeps the state of the switched system in $\mathcal{I} = [1.3-\varepsilon, 1.7+\varepsilon] \times [5.7-\varepsilon, 5.8+\varepsilon]$ which is not useful in practice.

The second value we consider for the precision parameter is $\varepsilon = 0.026$. This precision can be achieved by choosing $\eta = \frac{1}{4000\sqrt{2}}$. We do not show the symbolic model as it has too many states (642001) to be represented graphically. We repeat the same experiment with this model, the supervisory controller that keeps the state of the symbolic model in $\mathcal{I}'$ is shown in Figure 3, on the left. The computation of the symbolic model and the synthesis of the supervisory controller, implemented in MATLAB, takes overall around 80 seconds. From the controller of the symbolic model, we derive a controller for the boost DC-DC converter that keeps the state of the switched system in $\mathcal{I} = [1.3 - \varepsilon, 1.7 + \varepsilon] \times [5.7 - \varepsilon, 5.8 + \varepsilon]$. We apply a lazy control strategy, when the controller can choose both modes 1 and 2, it just keeps the current operation mode unchanged. A state trajectory of the controlled boost DC-DC converter is shown in Figure 3, on the right. We can see that the trajectory remains in the invariant set.

6 Conclusion

In this paper, we showed, under standard assumptions ensuring incremental stability, the existence of approximately bisimilar symbolic abstractions for switched systems. The abstractions are effectively computable and any precision can be achieved. An example of application has been showed on the DC-DC converter.

References

1. Liberzon, D.: Switching in Systems and Control. Birkhauser (2003)
2. Ramadge, P.J., Wonham, W.M.: Supervisory control of a class of discrete event systems. SIAM Journal on Control and Optimization 25(1), 206–230 (1987)
3. Arnold, A., Vincent, A., Walukiewicz, I.: Games for synthesis of controllers with partial observation. Theoretical Computer Science 28(1), 7–34 (2003)
4. Girard, A., Pappas, G.J.: Approximation metrics for discrete and continuous systems. IEEE Trans. Automatic Control 52(5), 782–798 (2007)
5. Milner, R.: Communication and Concurrency. Prentice-Hall, Englewood Cliffs (1989)
6. Park, D.: Concurrency and automata on infinite sequences. In: Deussen, P. (ed.) GI-TCS 1981. LNCS, vol. 104, pp. 167–183. Springer, Heidelberg (1981)
7. Pola, G., Girard, A., Tabuada, P.: Approximately bisimilar symbolic models for nonlinear control systems. In: IEEE Conf. on Decision and Control (2007)
8. Angeli, D.: A Lyapunov approach to incremental stability properties. IEEE Trans. Automatic Control 47(3), 410–421 (2002)
9. Khalil, H.: Nonlinear Systems. Prentice-Hall, Englewood Cliffs (1996)
10. Senesky, M., Eirea, G., Koo, T.: Hybrid modelling and control of power electronics. In: Maler, O., Pnueli, A. (eds.) HSCC 2003. LNCS, vol. 2623, pp. 450–465. Springer, Heidelberg (2003)
11. Beccuti, A., Papafotiou, G., Morari, M.: Optimal control of the boost dc-dc converter. In: IEEE Conf. on Decision and Control, pp. 4457–4462 (2005)
12. Buisson, J., Richard, P., Cormerais, H.: On the stabilisation of switching electrical power converters. In: Morari, M., Thiele, L. (eds.) HSCC 2005. LNCS, vol. 3414, pp. 184–197. Springer, Heidelberg (2005)
13. Beccuti, A., Papafotiou, G., Morari, M.: Explicit model predictive control of the boost dc-dc converter. In: Analysis and design of hybrid systems, pp. 315–320 (2006)
14. Tabuada, P.: An approximate simulation approach to symbolic control. IEEE Trans. Automatic Control (to appear, 2007)

Zonotope/Hyperplane Intersection for Hybrid Systems Reachability Analysis

Antoine Girard[1] and Colas Le Guernic[2]

[1] Laboratoire Jean Kuntzmann, Université Joseph Fourier
Antoine.Girard@imag.fr
[2] VERIMAG, Université Joseph Fourier
Colas.Le-Guernic@imag.fr

Abstract. In this paper, we are concerned with the problem of computing the reachable sets of hybrid systems with (possibly high dimensional) linear continuous dynamics and guards defined by switching hyperplanes. For the reachability analysis of the continuous dynamics, we use an efficient approximation algorithm based on zonotopes. In order to use this technique for the analysis of hybrid systems, we must also deal with the discrete transitions in a satisfactory (i.e. scalable and accurate) way. For that purpose, we need to approximate the intersection of the continuous reachable sets with the guards enabling the discrete transitions. The main contribution of this paper is a novel algorithm for computing efficiently a tight over-approximation of the intersection of (possibly high-order) zonotopes with a hyperplane. We show the accuracy and the scalability of our approach by considering two examples of reachability analysis of hybrid systems.

1 Introduction

Reachability analysis has been a major research issue in hybrid systems over the past decade [1,2,3,4,5,6,7,8,9]. This research has been motivated by the fact that a successful reachability analysis makes it possible to extend approaches, initially developed in the field of computer science for discrete systems, for analysis and control of hybrid systems [10,11,12,13]. This work resulted in several methods for computing approximations of the reachable sets using, for instance, polytopes [2,3], ellipsoids [4,9] or level sets [5]. The next step was to improve the scalability of these approaches in order to be able to handle larger hybrid systems. Various scalable approaches have been proposed for the reachability analysis of continuous (essentially linear) systems based on classes of polytopes such as hyper-rectangles [6] and zonotopes [7,8], or on ellipsoids [9]. However, in order to use these techniques for the analysis of hybrid systems, we must also deal with the discrete transitions in a satisfactory (i.e. scalable and accurate) way. For that purpose, we need to approximate the intersection of the continuous reachable sets with the guards enabling the discrete transitions.

In this paper, we present a new technique for reachability analysis of hybrid systems with (possibly high dimensional) linear continuous dynamics and guards

M. Egerstedt and B. Mishra (Eds.): HSCC 2008, LNCS 4981, pp. 215–228, 2008.

defined by switching hyperplanes. The reachable set is approximated using zonotopes. The reachability analysis of the continuous dynamics is processed using the algorithm presented in [8]. We handle discrete transitions of the hybrid systems by proposing two new algorithms for computing tight over-approximations of the intersection of a zonotope with a hyperplane. The paper is organized as follows. In section 2, we present briefly the algorithm for reachability analysis of linear systems proposed in [8] and discuss the needs for its extension to hybrid systems reachability. Section 3 is the main contribution of the paper, we first show that the problem of computing a tight over-approximation of the intersection of a zonotope with a hyperplane can be reduced to the problem of computing the intersection of a two dimensional zonotope with a line. Then, we present two efficient algorithms that solve this problem. In section 4, we show the accuracy and the scalability of our approach by considering two examples of reachability analysis of hybrid systems.

2 Reachability of Hybrid Systems

We define informally the class of hybrid systems we consider. The system has several discrete modes; in each mode q, the continuous dynamics of the system is given by a linear differential equation of the form:

$$\dot{x}(t) = A_q x(t) + B_q u(t),\ u(t) \in U_q,$$

where $x(t) \in \mathbb{R}^d$ is the continuous state and $u(t) \in \mathbb{R}^p$ is the continuous input of the system. The system switches from a mode q to mode q' when the continuous state reaches a guard $G_e \subseteq \mathbb{R}^d$ where $e = (q, q')$. We shall assume that the guards are given by switching planes:

$$G_e = \{x \in \mathbb{R}^d : x \cdot n_e = \gamma_e\} \text{ where } n_e \in \mathbb{R}^d \text{ and } \gamma_e \in \mathbb{R}.$$

For simplicity we assume that the reset maps are the identity map, and that there are no Zeno behaviours. In the following, we discuss the over-approximation of the reachable set of the hybrid system by the union of zonotopes.

2.1 Zonotopes

A zonotope is a polytope which can be defined as the Minkowski sum of a finite set of segments. Equivalently it can be seen as the image of a cube by an affine transformation. Formally, a zonotope is a subset of $\mathbb{R}^d$ represented by a center $c \in \mathbb{R}^d$ and a list of generators $g_1, \dots, g_r \in \mathbb{R}^d$:

$$Z = \langle c; g_1, \dots, g_r \rangle = \left\{ c + \sum_{i=1}^{r} \alpha_i g_i : \forall i,\ -1 \le \alpha_i \le 1 \right\}.$$

Each zonotope is a centrally-symmetric convex polytope. Hyper-rectangles and parallelotopes are zonotopes with d generators. The class of zonotopes is closed under arbitrary linear transformations and under the Minkowski sum. The image of a zonotope $Z = \langle c; g_1, \dots, g_r \rangle$ under a linear transformation Φ is the zonotope

$$\Phi Z = \langle \Phi c; \Phi g_1, \dots, \Phi g_r \rangle.$$

The Minkowski sum of two zonotopes $Z = \langle c; g_1, \dots, g_r \rangle$ and $Z' = \langle c'; g'_1, \dots, g'_{r'} \rangle$ is the zonotope

$$Z \oplus Z' = \langle c + c'; g_1, \dots, g_r, g'_1, \dots, g'_{r'} \rangle.$$

Further, it is to be noted that these two operations can be implemented efficiently even in high dimension. This makes the class of zonotopes suitable for reachability analysis.

2.2 Continuous Reachability

We first explain how we handle the continuous dynamics of the hybrid systems. In the following, the results on reachability analysis of linear systems are very briefly described. Details on our approach can be found in [7,8]. Let us consider a linear system of the form:

$$\dot{x}(t) = Ax(t) + Bu(t),\ x(0) \in I,\ u(t) \in U.$$

We want to over-approximate the set of states that are reachable by the linear system within a time interval $[0;T]$ for some initial state in I and admissible input function $u : [0;T] \to U$. We assume that the sets I and U are given by zonotopes. We choose an integration step $\tau = T/(N+1)$ and compute a sequence of zonotopes $\Omega_0, \dots, \Omega_N$ such that Ω_i contains all the states reachable within the time interval $[i\tau, (i+1)\tau]$. We do not detail how the first zonotope of the sequence, Ω_0, is computed (see [7]). Then, the other elements of the sequence can be computed from a recurrence relation of the form:

$$\Omega_{i+1} = \Phi \Omega_i \oplus V,\ i = 0, \dots, N-1 \tag{1}$$

where the matrix $\Phi = e^{\tau A}$ and V is a zonotope that depends on τ, A, B and U (see again [7]). Algorithm 1 is taken from [8] and implements efficiently the computation of the zonotopes $\Omega_1, \dots, \Omega_N$. The time and memory complexities of Algorithm 1 are $\mathcal{O}(Nd^3)$ and $\mathcal{O}(Nd^2)$ respectively.

2.3 Hybrid Reachability

We now discuss the use of Algorithm 1 for reachability analysis of a hybrid system. Again, we keep the discussion informal; our algorithm is similar to the algorithms for reachability analysis of hybrid systems using polytopes [11,2]. Let us assume that the initial discrete mode is q and that the set of initial continuous states is I_q. We start by computing an over-approximation of the reachable set by the continuous dynamics associated with mode q using Algorithm 1; we stop after a zonotope Ω_i has completely crossed a switching plane G_e with $e = (q, q')$

Algorithm 1. Reachability of linear time-invariant systems

Input: The matrix Φ, the sets Ω_0 and U, a positive integer N.
Output: The first N terms of the sequence defined in equation (1).

$X_0 \leftarrow \Omega_0$
$V_0 \leftarrow U$
$S_0 \leftarrow \{0\}$
for i from 0 to $N-1$ **do**
  $X_{i+1} \leftarrow \Phi X_i$ ▷ $X_{i+1} = \Phi^{i+1}\Omega_0$
  $S_{i+1} \leftarrow S_i \oplus V_i$ ▷ $S_{i+1} = \Phi^i U \oplus \cdots \oplus U$
  $V_{i+1} \leftarrow \Phi V_i$ ▷ $V_{i+1} = \Phi^{i+1} U$
  $\Omega_{i+1} \leftarrow X_{i+1} \oplus S_{i+1}$ ▷ $\Omega_{i+1} = \Phi^{i+1}\Omega_0 \oplus \Phi^i U \oplus \cdots \oplus U$
end for
return $\{\Omega_1, \ldots, \Omega_N\}$

or after a specified number of steps is reached. Then, for all transition e of the form $e = (q, q')$ we need to compute a zonotope $I_{q'}$ which over-approximates the intersection of the reachable set with the hyperplane G_e:

$$(\Omega_0 \cup \cdots \cup \Omega_N) \cap G_e \subseteq I_{q'}.$$

Then, we start over with the discrete mode q' and the set of initial continuous states $I_{q'}$. Hence, we can see that the computation of a good over-approximation of the intersection of a zonotope with a hyperplane is required in order to extend Algorithm 1 for reachability analysis of a hybrid system.

3 Intersection of a Zonotope and a Hyperplane

It is known that detecting the intersection between a zonotope and a hyperplane is an easy problem [7]. Given a zonotope $Z = \langle c; g_1, \ldots, g_r \rangle$ and a hyperplane $G = \{x \in \mathbb{R}^d : x \cdot n = \gamma\}$, we have

$$Z \cap G \neq \emptyset \iff c \cdot n - \sum_{i=1}^{r} |g_i \cdot n| \leq \gamma \leq c \cdot n + \sum_{i=1}^{r} |g_i \cdot n|.$$

Furthermore, in the context of reachability analysis, this can be done efficiently while computing the reachable sets [8]. However, computing this intersection (when it is not empty) is actually a much more complicated problem.

This intersection might not be a zonotope, thus a larger class of sets needs to be considered for this computation. Obviously, we can express the zonotope Z as a polytope, and then compute the intersection between the polytope and the hyperplane G. The good news is that computing a H-representation [14] of a zonotope can be done polynomially in the number of its facets [15], the bad news is that a zonotope with r generators in dimension d might have up to $2\binom{r}{d-1}$ facets [16]. Even for relatively small zonotopes, this can be prohibitively large. Further, the zonotope Ω_k computed by Algorithm 1 typically has about

kd generators. Thus, it is clear that this approach is untractable. Another approach is to over-approximate the zonotope before computing the intersection. However, even if the over-approximation of the zonotope is tight (i.e. the over-approximation touches the zonotope in several points), the over-approximation of the intersection is generally not. We propose a third approach which allows to compute a tight over-approximation of the intersection of a zonotope and a hyperplane. Most of the operations are done in two dimensional spaces, thus leading to efficient computations.

3.1 From Dimension d to Dimension 2

Finding a tight polyhedral over-approximation P of a set X can be done by bounding this set using several hyperplanes with normal vectors in a given finite set $\mathcal{D} = \{\ell_1, \dots, \ell_p\}$. The computation involves determining, for each $\ell \in \mathcal{D}$, the infimum m_ℓ and supremum M_ℓ of the sets $\{x \cdot \ell : x \in X\}$. Then, the over-approximation P is given by

$$P = \{x \in \mathbb{R}^d : \forall \ell \in \mathcal{D},\, m_\ell \leq x \cdot \ell \leq M_\ell\}.$$

In our case[1], X is the intersection of the zonotope Z and the hyperplane G. For the reasons we already explained, we can not expect to solve this problem in the full dimensional state-space $\mathbb{R}^d$. The following proposition will allow us to reduce this problem to a two-dimensional problem.

Proposition 1. *Let G be a hyperplane, $G = \{x \in \mathbb{R}^d : x \cdot n = \gamma\}$, Z a set, and ℓ a vector. Let $\Pi_{n,\ell}$ be the following linear transformation:*

$$\begin{aligned} \Pi_{n,\ell} : \mathbb{R}^d &\to \mathbb{R}^2 \\ x &\mapsto (x \cdot n, x \cdot \ell) \end{aligned}$$

Then, we have the following equality

$$\{x \cdot \ell : x \in Z \cap G\} = \{y : (\gamma, y) \in \Pi_{n,\ell}(Z)\}$$

Proof. Let y belongs to $\{x \cdot \ell : x \in Z \cap G\}$, then there exists x in $Z \cap G$ such that $x \cdot \ell = y$. Since $x \in G$, we have $x \cdot n = \gamma$. Therefore $(\gamma, y) = \Pi_{n,\ell}(x) \in \Pi_{n,\ell}(Z)$ because $x \in Z$. Thus, $y \in \{y : (\gamma, y) \in \Pi_{n,\ell}(Z)\}$. Conversely, if $y \in \{y : (\gamma, y) \in \Pi_{n,\ell}(Z)\}$, then $(\gamma, y) \in \Pi_{n,\ell}(Z)$. It follows that there exists $x \in Z$ such that $x \cdot n = \gamma$ and $x \cdot \ell = y$. Since $x \cdot n = \gamma$, it follows that $x \in G$. Thus, $y = x \cdot \ell$ with $x \in Z \cap G$ and it follows that $y \in \{x \cdot \ell : x \in Z \cap G\}$. ■

This proposition states that we can reduce the problem of computing a tight polyhedral over-approximation of the intersection of a set Z and a hyperplane G to the problem of projecting Z on a plane and then computing the intersection of the 2-dimensional set $\Pi_{n,\ell}(Z)$ and the line $L_\gamma = \{(x, y) \in \mathbb{R}^2 : x = \gamma\}$. This must be done for each vector $\ell \in \mathcal{D}$. Algorithm 2 implements this idea.

[1] The results presented in section 3.1 hold for an arbitrary set Z (not only a zonotope).

Algorithm 2. Dimension reduction

Input: A set Z, a hyperplane $G = \{x \in \mathbb{R}^d : x \cdot n = \gamma\}$ and a finite set $\mathcal{D}$ of directions.
Output: A polytope approximating tightly $Z \cap G$ in directions given by $\mathcal{D}$.

```
1: for ℓ in D do
2:     S^π_{n,ℓ} ← Π_{n,ℓ}(Z)
3:     [m_ℓ; M_ℓ] ← BOUND_INTERSECT_2D(S^π_{n,ℓ}, L_γ)
4: end for
5: return {x ∈ R^d : ∀ℓ ∈ D, m_ℓ ≤ x · ℓ ≤ M_ℓ}
```

In our case, the set Z is a zonotope, then the projection $\Pi_{n,\ell}(Z)$ is a two-dimensional zonotope which can be computed efficiently:

$$\Pi_{n,\ell}(\langle c; g_1, \dots, g_r \rangle) = \langle \Pi_{n,\ell}(c); \Pi_{n,\ell}(g_1), \dots, \Pi_{n,\ell}(g_r) \rangle .$$

Remark 1. For each generator g of the zonotope Z, one has to compute $\Pi_{n,\ell}(g)$ for all ℓ in $\mathcal{D}$, but instead of computing these projections independently, which would lead to $2|\mathcal{D}|$ scalar products, one can observe that all the $\Pi_{n,\ell}(g)$ involves computing the scalar product $n \cdot g$, thus only $|\mathcal{D}|+1$ scalar products are necessary for each generator of Z. The projections can thus be done by computing the product of a $(|\mathcal{D}|+1) \times d$ matrix by a $d \times (r+1)$ matrix.

The computation of the intersection of $\Pi_{n,\ell}(Z)$ and the line L_γ is investigated in the next subsection where two algorithms are proposed to solve this problem.

3.2 Intersection of a Zonogon and a Line

Algorithm 2 requires the computation of the intersection of a two dimensional zonotope, with a line. In a two dimensional space, a zonotope is called a zonogon and its number of vertices, as its number of edges, is two times its number of generators. Thus, it is possible to express a zonogon as a polygon (two dimensional polytope) which can easily be intersected with a line. For the simplicity of the notations, we now denote by $Z = \langle c; g_1, \dots, g_r \rangle$ the zonogon that we want to intersect with $L_\gamma = \{(x, y) : x = \gamma\}$. An extremely naive way of determining the list of vertices of a zonogon is to generate the list of points $\{c + \sum_{i=1}^{r} \alpha_i g_i : \forall i, \alpha_i = -1 \text{ or } \alpha_i = 1\}$ and then to take the convex hull of this set. This is clearly not a good approach since we need to compute a list of 2^r points.

Scanning the vertices. It is known that the facets of a zonotope $\langle c; g_1, \dots, g_r \rangle$ are zonotopes whose generators are taken from the list $\{g_1, \dots, g_r\}$. Then, we can deduce that the edges of a zonogon are segments of the form $[P; P + 2g]$ where P is a vertex of the zonogon and g a generator. Therefore, it is sufficient to scan the generators in trigonometric (or anti-trigonometric) order to scan the vertices of the zonogon in a way that is similar to the gift wrapping algorithm [17]. This idea is implemented in Algorithm 3.

Algorithm 3. BOUND_INTERSECT_2D

Input: A zonogon $Z = \langle c; g_1, \ldots, g_r \rangle$ and a line $L_\gamma = \{(x, y) : x = \gamma\}$
Output: A segment $[m; M]$ such that $\{\gamma\} \times [m; M] = Z \cap L_\gamma$.
1: $P \leftarrow c$ ▷ current position
2: $m \leftarrow \infty, M \leftarrow -\infty$
3: **for** i from 1 to r **do**
4:      **if** $y_{g_i} < 0$ or $(y_{g_i} = 0$ and $x_{g_i} < 0)$ **then**   ▷ $g_i = (x_{g_i}, y_{g_i})$
5:          $g_i \leftarrow -g_i$ ▷ Ensure all generators are pointing upward
6:      **end if**
7:      $P \leftarrow P - g_i$ ▷ Drives P toward the lowest vertex of Z
8: **end for**
9: $g_{i_1}, \ldots, g_{i_r} \leftarrow \text{SORT}(g_1, \ldots, g_r)$ ▷ Sort the generators in trigonometric order
10: **for** j from 1 to r **do**
11:     **if** $[P; P + 2g_{i_j}]$ intersects L_γ **then**
12:         $(x, y) \leftarrow [P; P + 2g_{i_j}] \cap L_\gamma$
13:         $m \leftarrow \min(m, y)$
14:         $M \leftarrow \max(M, y)$
15:     **end if**
16:     $P \leftarrow P + 2g_{i_j}$
17: **end for**   ▷ Only half of the vertices of the zonogon have been scanned
18: **for** j from 1 to r **do**
19:     **if** $[P; P - 2g_{i_j}]$ intersects L_γ **then**
20:         $(x, y) \leftarrow [P; P - 2g_{i_j}] \cap L_\gamma$
21:         $m \leftarrow \min(m, y)$
22:         $M \leftarrow \max(M, y)$
23:     **end if**
24:     $P \leftarrow P - 2g_{i_j}$
25: **end for**   ▷ we are back in $P = e$
26: **return** $[m; M]$

All the generators are taken poiting upward for simplicity, this does not change the zonogon since replacing a generator g by it opposite $-g$ does not modify the shape of a zonogon. Then, we compute the lowest vertex of Z, and sort the generators according to the trigonometric order. Scanning the generators in that order allows us to scan the vertices of Z. While scanning these vertices, we check for the intersection with the line L_γ. This leads to an algorithm for the intersection between a line and a zonogon with r generators whose complexity is $\mathcal{O}(r \log r)$. The most time consuming part is to sort the generators.

In practice, the number of generators r can be very large (remember that the zonogon we want to intersect comes from the reachable set Ω_k computed by algorithm 1; Ω_k has about kd generators). Further, each time a discrete transition occurs, this procedure is called several times by algorithm 2 (one call for each direction of approximation). Thus, we need it to be as fast as possible. Hence, instead of scanning all the vertices of Z, we look directly for the two edges that intersect the line L_γ with a dichotomic search.

Dichotomic search of the intersecting edges. We start again from the lowest vertex of Z. At each step of the algorithm, P is a vertex of the zonogon representing the current position and G is a set of generators. We know that the segment $[P; P + \sum_{g \in G} 2g]$ intersects the line L_γ. We choose a pivot vector s and split the generators in G into two sets $G_<$ and $G_>$, the set of generators respectively smaller and bigger (according to the trigonometric order) than s. Then, it is clear that L_γ intersects either $[P; P + \sum_{g \in G_<} 2g]$ or $[P + \sum_{g \in G_<} 2g; P + \sum_{g \in G} 2g]$. We continue either with P and $G_<$ or $P + \sum_{g \in G_<} 2g$ and $G_>$. When the lowest vertex of the intersection is found, we start again from the highest vertex of Z in order to find the highest vertex of the intersection. Algorithm 4 implements this approach. Figure 1 illustrates the execution of the algorithm, both from the lowest and the highest point at the same time.

Algorithm 4. BOUND_INTERSECT_2D

Input: A zonogon $Z = \langle c; g_1, \ldots, g_r \rangle$ and a line $L_\gamma = \{(x, y) : x = \gamma\}$
Output: A segment $[m; M]$ such that $\{\gamma\} \times [m; M] = Z \cap L_\gamma$.
1: $P \leftarrow c$ ▷ current position $P = (x_P, y_P)$
2: $m \leftarrow \infty, M \leftarrow -\infty$
3: **for** i from 1 to r **do**
4:      **if** $y_{g_i} < 0$ or ($y_{g_i} = 0$ and $x_{g_i} < 0$) **then**   ▷ $g_i = (x_{g_i}, y_{g_i})$
5:          $g_i \leftarrow -g_i$ ▷ Ensure all generators are pointing upward
6:      **end if**
7:      $P \leftarrow P - g_i$ ▷ Drives P toward the lowest vertex of Z
8: **end for**
9: **if** $x_p < \gamma$ **then**
10:     $G \leftarrow \{g_1, \ldots, g_r\} \cap (\mathbb{R}^+ \times \mathbb{R})$ ▷ We should look right
11: **else**
12:     $G \leftarrow \{g_1, \ldots, g_r\} \cap (\mathbb{R}^- \times \mathbb{R})$ ▷ or left
13: **end if**
14: $s \leftarrow \sum_{g \in G} 2g$
15: **while** $|G| > 1$ **do**
16:     $(G_1, G_2) \leftarrow$ SPLIT_PIVOT(G, s)
17:     $s_1 \leftarrow \sum_{g \in G_1} 2g$
18:     **if** $[P; P + s_1]$ intersects L_γ **then**
19:         $G \leftarrow G_1$
20:         $s \leftarrow s_1$
21:     **else**
22:         $G \leftarrow G_2$
23:         $s \leftarrow s - s_1$
24:         $P \leftarrow P + s_1$
25:     **end if**
26: **end while**   ▷ Only one generator remains
27: $(x, y) \leftarrow [P; P + s] \cap L_\gamma$
28: $m \leftarrow y$
29: $\ldots$ ▷ Same thing for M, starting from the upper vertex of Z
30: **return** $[m; M]$

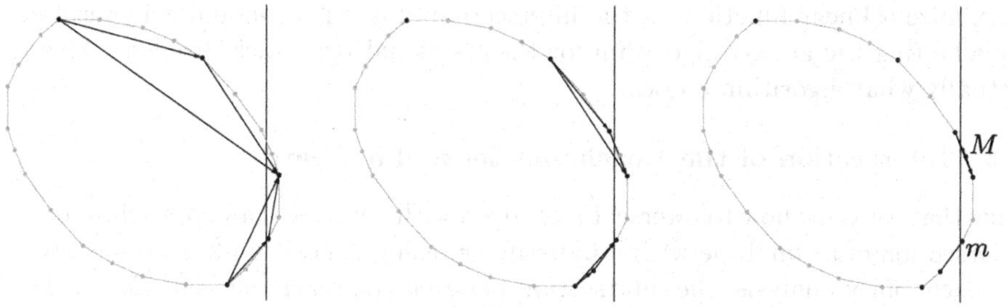

Fig. 1. Dichotomic search of the intersecting edges

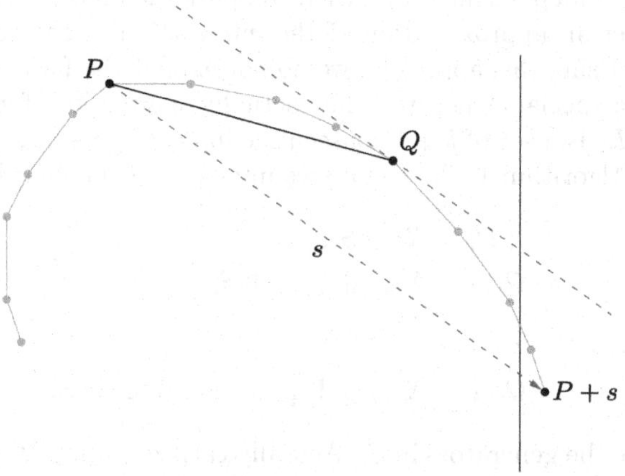

Fig. 2. A good choice for the pivot allows a smart enclosure of the intersection point

With a good pivot selection algorithm [18], the dichotomic search has a linear complexity. For our problem, we choose the sum of the remaining generators as the pivot. Even though this leads to a quadratic theoretical worst case complexity, it improves the practical behavior. Indeed, the sum of the remaining generators is already available and it has a nice geometric interpretation, as illustrated in Figure 2. At each step, P and $P + \sum_{g\in G} 2g$ are both the closest computed vertex to the line $\{(x, y) : x = \gamma\}$, each on a different side of this line, thus defining the best computed under-approximation of the interval $[m; M]$ at this step. A pivot s defines a vertex $Q = P + \sum_{g\in G_<} 2g$ between P and $P + \sum_{g\in G} 2g$. The line of direction s going through Q is "tangent" to Z and its intersection with L_γ defines an over-approximation of the interval $[m; M]$. Choosing $s = \sum_{g\in G} g$ as the pivot ensures that the distance between the over-approximation and the under-approximation of the interval $[m; M]$ is not correlated with γ, the position of the intersecting line.

Remark 2. Algorithm 4 is similar to Bamas and Zemel's algorithm for the fractional Knapsack problem [19]. Eppstein[2] suggested in a talk [20] that one could

[2] The authors wish to thank an anonymous reviewer for pointing out this reference.

maximize a linear function on the intersection of a zonotope and a hyperplane by adapting the greedy algorithm for the fractional Knapsack problem. This is actually what algorithm 3 does.

3.3 Intersection of the Reachable Set and a Guard

Now that we know how to intersect a zonogon with a line, we can approximate the intersection of a zonotope with a hyperplane, using Algorithm 2. In the context of reachability analysis, the intersection between the reachable sets $\Omega_0, \ldots, \Omega_N$ with a guard G generally occurs at several steps. Let $\mathcal{I}_G$ be the set of indices i for which Ω_i intersects the guard G. One can approximate the intersection between each Ω_i and G independently, and then compute the union of these intersections in order to get an approximation of the intersection of the reachable set with the guard G. Using this approach, we do not exploit the fact that the reachable sets Ω_i have a special structure. They actually share a lot of generators. Let us assume that $\mathcal{I}_G$ is a set of $k+1$ consecutive integers i, $i+1$, ..., $i+k$. With the notations of Algorithm 1, the zonotopes intersecting the guards are:

$$\begin{aligned}
\Omega_i &= X_i \oplus S_i, \\
\Omega_{i+1} &= X_{i+1} \oplus V_{i+1} \oplus S_i, \\
&\vdots \\
\Omega_{i+k} &= X_{i+k} \oplus V_{i+k} \oplus \ldots \oplus V_{i+1} \oplus S_i
\end{aligned}$$

They all share the generators in S_i. Actually each zonotope Ω_j shares all its generators but the ones in X_j with the zonotopes of greater index. Consequently, when approximating the intersection at step j in $\mathcal{I}_G$, it is possible to reuse most of the computations already done for smaller indices. Not only the projections of most of the generators of Ω_j have already been computed, but they are also partially sorted. Moreover, at each step of Algorithm 4, one can easily compute an under-approximation and an over-approximation of the intersection, as explained at the end of the previous subsection and on Figure 2. It is then possible to modify Algorithm 4 in order to compute all the intersection concurrently. Since we are interested in $(\cup_{i\in\mathcal{I}_G}\Omega_i)\cap G$ and not in each $\Omega_i\cap G$, we can, at each step, drop the computation of the $\Omega_i\cap G$ whose over-approximation is included in the under-approximation of $(\cup_{i\in\mathcal{I}_G}\Omega_i)\cap G$.

3.4 From Polytopes to Zonotopes

Let us remark that the tight over-approximation of the intersection between the reachable set and the guard G which is computed using Algorithm 2 is a polytope. In order to process the continuous reachability analysis using Algorithm 1 in the next discrete mode, we need this over-approximation to be expressed as a zonotope. To the best of the authors knowledge, there is no known efficient algorithm for the approximation of a general polytope by a zonotope (except in small dimension [21]). In Algorithm 2, we have the choice of the normal vectors to the facets of the approximating polytope. Then, we can choose these vectors such that the resulting polytope can be easily approximated by a zonotope. Even better, we can choose these vectors such that the approximating polytope is a zonotope. Indeed, some polytopes are easily expressed as zonotopes; this is the case for the class of parallelotopes and particularly for hyper-rectangles. Hence, we choose the normal vectors to the facets such that the over-approximation of the intersection of the reachable set with the the guard is a hyper-rectangle.

Initially, we do not have much information on the intersection, so we generate at random (in a way similar to [22]) a set of directions, and only keep the direction ℓ_0 that induces the thinner approximation. Then, we randomly generate a set of directions orthogonal to the directions already chosen, and again we only keep the one for which $M_\ell - m_\ell$ is minimal, until we get a hyper-rectangle, after $d-2$ steps.

4 Examples

The algorithms presented in this paper have been implemented in Ocaml [23]. In this section, we show the effectiveness of our approach on some examples. All computations were performed on a Pentium IV 3.2GHz with 1GB RAM.

4.1 5-Dimensional Benchmark

To evaluate the error introduced by our method, and its usability in a hybrid reachability toolchain, we would like to compare the computed reachable set with the exact one. As explained before, the computation of the exact intersection is untractable. This is why we artificially add a switching hyperplane to a continuous linear system. This guard will allow a transition between two states with the same dynamic (see figure 3).

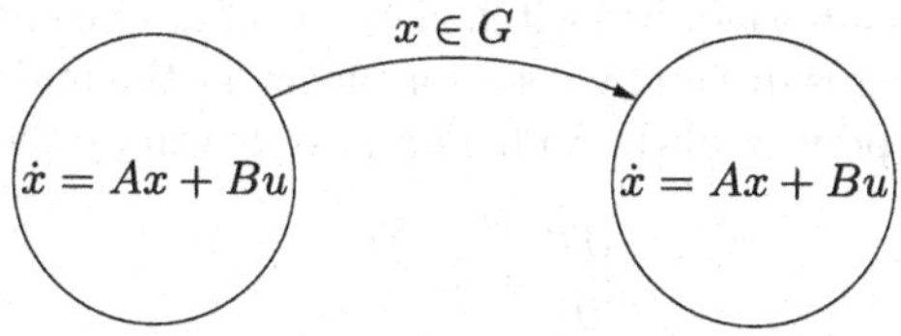

Fig. 3. A *(not so)* hybrid system on which approximate reachable sets can be compared to the exact reachable sets (computed with a non-hybrid view of the system)

The exact (up to initial time discretization errors) reachability analysis of this hybrid system can be done with algorithm 1, by removing the guard. This analysis can then be compared to the one done using our algorithm for approximating the intersection with the guard on the hybrid view of the system. We applied our methods on such a hybrid system contructed on a five dimensional linear system [7,8]. The projection on the first two variables of the computed reachables sets can be seen on figure 4.

The exact reachable set, computed by algorithm 1 on the non-hybrid system, has been plotted in black. After the intersection the error introduced by the

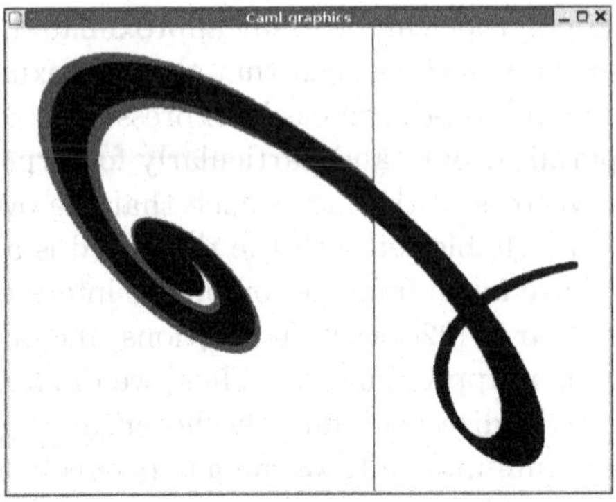

Fig. 4. Error introduced by approximating the intersection (in red)

approximation appears in red. The directions of approximation were chosen as explained in section 3.4, 16 at each step. We only kept 4 out of the 49 computed constraints on the intersection, in order to be able to express it as a zonotope. This first approximation was improved by adding 4 generators, introducing 8 new facets. The whole computation, including intersection and reachability, took 0.2 seconds and 1.4 MB. If we try to compute exactly the intersection, by expressing the intersecting zonotopes as polytopes, we have to deal with more than 10^{11} vertices. Only storing these vertices would require more than 1.8 terabyte, more than one million times what we need for approximate intersection and reachability.

4.2 Thermostat

As a second example, we consider a high dimensional hybrid system with two discrete states. A heat source can be switched on or off at one end of a metal rod of length 1, the switching is driven by a sensor placed at the middle of the rod. The temperature at each point x of the rod, $T(x,t)$ is driven by the Heat equation:

$$\frac{\partial T}{\partial t} = k\frac{\partial^2 T}{\partial x^2}.$$

When the heat source is *ON*, we have $T(0,t) = 1$, and when it is *OFF*, $T(0,t) = 0$. We approximate this partial differential equation by a linear ordinary differential equation using a finite difference scheme on a grid of size $\frac{1}{90}$.

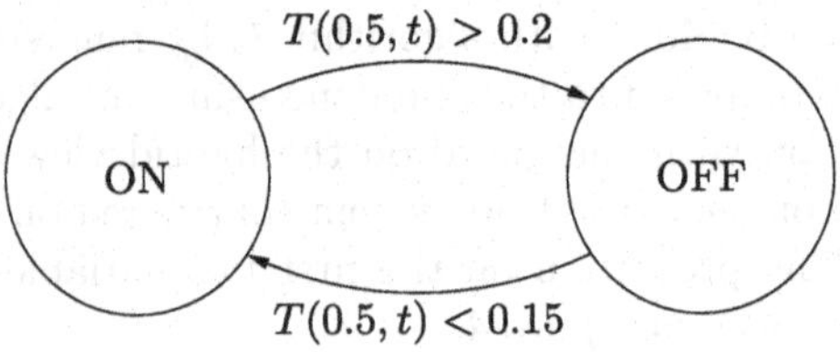

Fig. 5. Hybrid model of a thermostat

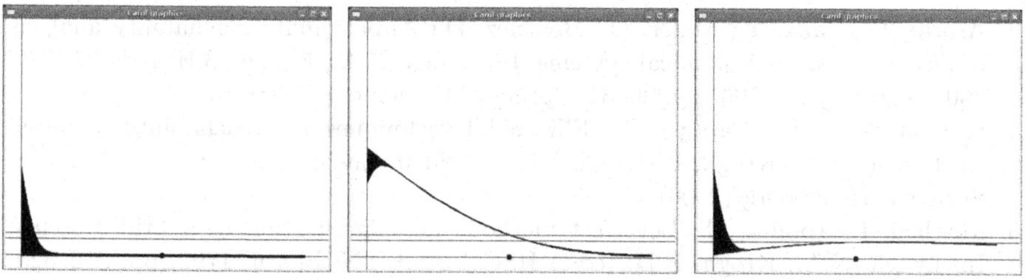

Fig. 6. Reachable set at three different times. The x-axis represents the position in the metal rod, and the y-axis the temperature. The dot on the middle of the x-axis specify the position of the sensor, and the two horizontal line the switching temperatures. The heat source is on the left.

The resulting hybrid system has 89 continuous variables and 2 discrete states (see figure 5). We computed the reachable sets of this system for 1000 times step, during which 10 discrete transitions occured, in 71.6s using 406MB of memory. Figure 6 shows the reachable sets at three different time, each after a discrete transition.

5 Conclusion

In this paper, we presented an efficient algorithm for computing a tight over-approximation of the intersection between a zonotope and a hyperplane. We showed that it can be used in conjunction with a reachability analysis algorithm for continuous linear systems to effectively analyze hybrid systems with high dimensional linear continuous dynamic.

The use of the zonotope representation can be seen as a trick allowing us not to compute the full dimensional Minkowski sum, this trick can in fact be applied to more complex objects and it is possible to adapt our algorithm so that it can handle intersection between a hyperplane and the Minkowski sum of a set of ellipsoids and zonotopes. An other extension should allow us to compute an under-approximation of the intersection. This under-approximation might be useful for the choice of the directions of approximation.

Future work also includes the approximation of a polytope by a zonotope, to avoid loosing most of the computed constraints (in the 5-dimensional example, we only kept 8 out of the 53 computed constraints).

References

1. Varaiya, P.: Reach set computation using optimal control. In: Proc. KIT Workshop on Verification of Hybrid Systems, Verimag, Grenoble (1998)
2. Chutinan, A., Krogh, B.H.: Verification of polyhedral-invariant hybrid automata using polygonal flow pipe approximations. In: Vaandrager, F.W., van Schuppen, J.H. (eds.) HSCC 1999. LNCS, vol. 1569, pp. 76–90. Springer, Heidelberg (1999)

3. Asarin, E., Dang, T., Maler, O., Bournez, O.: Approximate reachability analysis of piecewise-linear dynamical systems. In: Lynch, N.A., Krogh, B.H. (eds.) HSCC 2000. LNCS, vol. 1790, pp. 20–31. Springer, Heidelberg (2000)
4. Kurzhanski, A.B., Varaiya, P.: Ellipsoidal techniques for reachability analysis. In: Lynch, N.A., Krogh, B.H. (eds.) HSCC 2000. LNCS, vol. 1790, pp. 202–214. Springer, Heidelberg (2000)
5. Mitchell, I., Tomlin, C.: Level set methods for computation in hybrid systems. In: Lynch, N.A., Krogh, B.H. (eds.) HSCC 2000. LNCS, vol. 1790, pp. 310–323. Springer, Heidelberg (2000)
6. Stursberg, O., Krogh, B.H.: Efficient representation and computation of reachable sets for hybrid systems. In: Maler, O., Pnueli, A. (eds.) HSCC 2003. LNCS, vol. 2623, pp. 482–497. Springer, Heidelberg (2003)
7. Girard, A.: Reachability of uncertain linear systems using zonotopes. In: Morari, M., Thiele, L. (eds.) HSCC 2005. LNCS, vol. 3414, pp. 291–305. Springer, Heidelberg (2005)
8. Girard, A., Le Guernic, C., Maler, O.: Efficient computation of reachable sets of linear time-invariant systems with inputs. In: Hespanha, J.P., Tiwari, A. (eds.) HSCC 2006. LNCS, vol. 3927, pp. 257–271. Springer, Heidelberg (2006)
9. Kurzhanskiy, A.A., Varaiya, P.: Ellipsoidal techniques for reachability analysis of discrete-time linear systems. IEEE Trans. Automatic Control 52, 26–38 (2007)
10. Asarin, E., Bournez, O., Dang, T., Maler, O., Pnueli, A.: Effective synthesis of switching controllers for linear systems. Proc. of the IEEE 88(7), 1011–1025 (2000)
11. Dang, T.: Vérification et Synthèse des Systèmes Hybrides. PhD thesis, Institut National Polytechnique de Grenoble (2000)
12. Maler, O.: Control from computer science. IFAC Annual Reviews in Control (2003)
13. Tomlin, C., Mitchell, I., Bayen, A., Oishi, M.: Computational techniques for the verification and control of hybrid systems. Proc. of the IEEE 91(7), 986–1001 (2003)
14. Ziegler, G.M.: Lectures on Polytopes. In: Graduate Texts in Mathematics, vol. 152, Springer, Heidelberg (1995)
15. Avis, D., Fukuda, K.: Reverse search for enumeration. Discrete Appl. Math. 65(1-3), 21–46 (1996)
16. Zaslavsky, T.: Facing Up to Arrangements: Face-Count Formulas for Partitions of Space by Hyperplanes. In: Memoirs of the American Mathematical Society. American Mathematical Society, vol. 154 (1975)
17. Jarvis, R.A.: On the identification of the convex hull of a finite set of points in the plane. Inf. Process. Lett. 2(1), 18–21 (1973)
18. Blum, M., Floyd, R.W., Pratt, V.R., Rivest, R.L., Tarjan, R.E.: Time bounds for selection. J. Comput. Syst. Sci. 7(4), 448–461 (1973)
19. Balas, E., Zemel, E.: An algorithm for large zero-one knapsack problems. Operations Research 28(5), 1130–1154 (1980)
20. Bern, M.W., Eppstein, D.: Optimization over zonotopes and training support vector machines (2001) Talk given at WADS
21. Guibas, L.J., Nguyen, A., Zhang, L.: Zonotopes as bounding volumes. In: SODA 2003: Proceedings of the fourteenth annual ACM-SIAM symposium on Discrete algorithms, Society for Industrial and Applied Mathematics, Philadelphia, PA, USA, pp. 803–812 (2003)
22. Muller, M.E.: A note on a method for generating points uniformly on n-dimensional spheres. Commun. ACM 2(4), 19–20 (1959)
23. Leroy, X.: The Objective Caml system. In: INRIA (2007)

Learning and Detecting Emergent Behavior in Networks of Cardiac Myocytes

R. Grosu[1], E. Bartocci[1,2], F. Corradini[2],
E. Entcheva[3], S.A. Smolka[1], and A. Wasilewska[1]

[1] Department of Computer Science, Stony Brook University
Stony Brook, NY 11794-4400, USA
[2] Department of Mathematics and Computer Science, University of Camerino
Camerino (MC), I-62032, Italy
[3] Department of Biomedical Engineering, Stony Brook University
Stony Brook, NY 11794-8181, USA

Abstract. We address the problem of specifying and detecting emergent behavior in networks of cardiac myocytes, spiral electric waves in particular, a precursor to atrial and ventricular fibrillation. To solve this problem we: (1) Apply discrete mode-abstraction to the cycle-linear hybrid automata (CLHA) we have recently developed for modeling the behavior of myocyte networks; (2) Introduce the new concept of *spatial-superposition* of CLHA modes; (3) Develop a new spatial logic, based on spatial-superposition, for specifying emergent behavior; (4) Devise a new method for learning the formulae of this logic from the spatial patterns under investigation; and (5) Apply bounded model checking to detect (within milliseconds) the onset of spiral waves. We have implemented our methodology as the EMERALD tool-suite, a component of our EHA framework for specification, simulation, analysis and control of excitable hybrid automata. We illustrate the effectiveness of our approach by applying EMERALD to the scalar electrical fields produced by our CELLEXCITE simulator.

1 Introduction

One of the most important and intriguing questions in systems biology is how to formally specify *emergent behavior in biological tissue*, and how to efficiently predict and detect its onset. A prominent example of such behavior is electrical *spiral waves* in spatial networks of cardiac myocytes (heart cells). Spiral waves of this kind are a precursor to a variety of cardiac disturbances, including *atrial fibrillation* (AF), an abnormal rhythm originating in the upper chambers of the heart. AF afflicts 2-3 million Americans alone, putting them at risk for clots and strokes. Moreover, the likelihood of developing AF increases with age.

In this paper, we address this question by proposing a simple and efficient method for learning, and automatically detecting the onset of, spiral waves in cardiac tissue. See Figure 1 for an overview of our approach. Underlying our method is a *linear spatial-superposition logic* (LSSL) we have developed for specifying properties of spatial networks. LSSL is discussed in greater detail below. Our

M. Egerstedt and B. Mishra (Eds.): HSCC 2008, LNCS 4981, pp. 229–243, 2008.

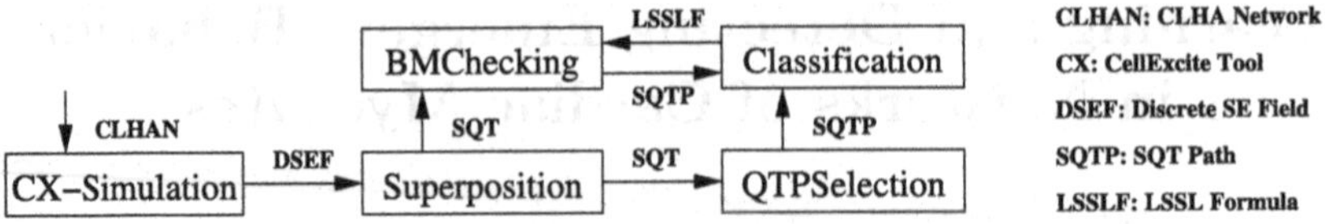

Fig. 1. Overview of our method for learning and detecting spiral waves

method also builds upon hybrid-automata, image-processing, machine-learning, and model-checking techniques to first learn an LSSL formula that characterizes such spirals. The formula is then automatically checked against a *quadtree* representation [15] of the scalar electrical field (SEF), produced by simulating a hybrid automata network modeling the myocytes, at each discrete time step. The quadtree representation is obtained via discrete mode-abstraction and hierarchical superposition of the elementary units within the SEF.

The electrical behavior of cardiac myocytes is hybrid in nature: they exhibit an all-or-nothing electrical response, the so-called *action potential*, to an external excitation. Despite their hybrid nature, networks of myocytes have traditionally been modeled using nonlinear partial differential equations. While highly accurate in describing the molecular processes underlying cell behavior, these models are not particularly amenable to formal analysis and typically do not scale well for the simulation of complex cell networks.

In [11], we showed that it is possible to automatically learn a much simpler *Cycle-Linear Hybrid Automaton* (CLHA) for cardiac myocytes, which describes their action potential up to a specified error margin. Moreover, as we have shown in [2], one can use a variant of this model [19,20] to efficiently (up to an order of magnitude faster) and accurately simulate the behavior of myocyte networks, and, in particular, induce spirals and fibrillation.

A key observation concerning our simulations (see Figure 2) is that mode-abstraction, in which the action-potential value of each CLHA in the network is *discretely abstracted* to its corresponding mode, faithfully preserves the network's waveform and other spatial characteristics. Hence, for the purpose of learning, and detecting the onset of, spirals within CLHA networks, we can exploit mode-abstraction to dramatically reduce the system state space. A similar mode-abstraction is possible for voltage recordings in live cell networks.

The state space of a 400×400 CLHA network is still prohibitively large, even after applying the above-described abstraction: it contains $4^{160,000}$ modes, as each CLHA has four mode values. To combat this state explosion, we use a spatial abstraction inspired by [12]: we regard the mode of each automaton as a probability distribution and define the *superposition* of a set of CLHAs-mode as the probability that an arbitrary CLHA's-mode in this set has a particular value. By successively applying superposition to the network, we obtain a tree structure, the root of which is the mode-superposition of the entire CLHA network, and the leaves of which are the modes of the individual CLHA. The particular superposition tree structure we employ, quadtrees, is inspired by image-processing techniques [15]. We shall refer to quadtrees obtained in this manner as *superposition-quadtrees* (SQT).

Our LSSL logic is an appropriate logic for reasoning about *paths* in SQTs, and the spatial properties of CLHA networks in which we are interested, including spirals, can be cast in LSSL. For example, we have observed that the presence of a spiral can be formulated in LSSL as follows: Given an SQT, is there a path from its root leading to the core of a spiral? Based on this observation, we build a machine-learning classifier, the training-set records for which correspond to the probability distributions associated to the nodes along such paths. Each distribution, for mode value *stimulated*, corresponds to an attribute of a training-set record, with the number of attributes bounded by the depth of the SQT. An additional attribute is used to classify the record as either spiral or non-spiral. For spiral-free SQTs, we simply record the path of maximum distribution.

For training purposes, we use the CellExcite simulator [2] to generate, upon successive time steps, snapshots of a 400×400 CLHA network and their mode-abstraction; see Figures 1,2. Training data for the classifier is then generated by converting the hybrid-abstracted snapshots into SQTs and selecting paths leading to the core of a spiral (if present). The resulting table is input to the decision-tree algorithm of the Weka machine-learning tool suite [8], which produces a classifier in the form of a predicate over the node-distribution attributes.

The syntax of LSSL is similar to that of linear temporal logic, with LSSL's Next operator corresponding to *concretization* (anti-superposition). Moreover, a (finite) sequence of LSSL Next operators corresponds to a path through an SQT. The classifier produced by Weka can therefore be regarded as an LSSL formula. An SQT path can be thought of as a magnifying glass, which starting from the root, produces an increasingly detailed but more focused view of the image. This effect is analogous to *concept hierarchy* in data mining [13] and arguably similar to the way the brain organizes knowledge: a human can recognize a word or a picture without having to look at all of the characters in the word or all of the details in the picture, respectively.

We are now in a position to view spiral detection as a bounded-model-checking problem [3]: Given the SQT Q generated from the discrete SEF of a CLHA network and an LSSL formula φ learned through classification, is there a finite path π in Q satisfying φ? We use this observation to check every second during simulation, whether or not a spiral has been created. More precisely, the LSSL formula we use states that no spiral is present, and we thus obtain as a counterexample one or all the paths leading to the core of a spiral. In the latter case, we can identify the number of spirals in the SEF and their actual position.

The above-described method (including user-guided path selection) has been fully implemented as the Emerald tool suite for automated spiral learning and detection. Emerald is written in Java, and it is a new component of our EHA environment for the specification, simulation, analysis and control of networks of Excitable Hybrid Automata. It is freely available from [10].

The rest of the paper is organized as follows. Section 2 reviews excitable-cell networks and their modeling with CLHA. Section 3 defines superposition and quadtrees, the essential ideas underlying linear spatial-superposition logic, the topic of Section 4. Section 5 describes our learning and bounded-model-checking techniques; their implementation is considered in Section 6, along with our experimental results. Section 7 discusses related work. Section 8 offers our concluding remarks and directions for future research.

2 Biological Background

An excitable cell has the ability to propagate an electrical signal, known at the cellular level as the *Action Potential* (AP), to neighboring cells. An AP corresponds to a change of potential across the cell membrane, and is caused by the flow of ions between the inside and outside of the cell through ion channels. Generally, an AP is an externally triggered event: a cell fires an action potential as an all-or-nothing response to a supra-threshold stimulus, and each AP follows the same sequence of phases and maintains the same magnitude regardless of the applied stimulus. During an AP, generally no re-excitation can occur.

Despite differences in AP duration, morphology and underlying ion currents, the following major AP phases can be identified across different species and different excitable-cell types: *resting*, *stimulated*, *upstroke*, *early repolarization*, *plateau* and *final repolarization*. We shall subsequently use the following abbreviations for these phases: `r` (resting and final repolarization), `s` (stimulated), `u` (upstroke), and `p` (plateau and early repolarization).

Using these AP phases as a guide, we have developed, for several representative excitable-cell types, *Cycle-Linear Hybrid Automata* (CLHA) models that approximates their AP and other bio-electrical properties with reasonable accuracy [19,20,11]. This derivation was first performed manually [19,20]. We subsequently showed in [11] how to fully automate this process by learning various biological aspects of the AP of the different cell types. The CLHA we obtained are fairly compact in nature, employing two or three continuous state variables and four to six modes. The term *Cycle-Linear* is used to highlight the cyclic structure of CLHA, and the fact that while in each cycle they exhibit linear dynamics, the coefficients of the corresponding linear equations and mode-transition guards may vary in interesting ways from cycle to cycle.

The dynamics of excitable-cell networks play an important role in the physiology of many biological processes. For cardiac cells, on each heart beat, an electrical control signal is generated by the sinoatrial node, the heart's internal pacemaking region. Electrical waves then travel along a prescribed path, exciting cells in atria and ventricles and assuring synchronous contractions. Of special interest are cardiac arrhythmias: disruptions of the normal excitation process due to faulty processes at the cellular level, single ion-channel level, or at the level of cell-to-cell communication. The clinical manifestation is a rhythm with altered frequency, tachycardia or bradycardia, or the appearance of multiple frequencies, polymorphic Atrial Tachycardia (AT), with subsequent deterioration to a chaotic signal, Atrial Fibrillation (AF). AF is a serious condition in which there is uncoordinated contraction of the cardiac muscle of the atria in the heart. As a result, the heart fails to adequately pump blood, putting 2-3 million Americans alone at risk for clots and strokes. Moreover, AF likelihood increases with age.

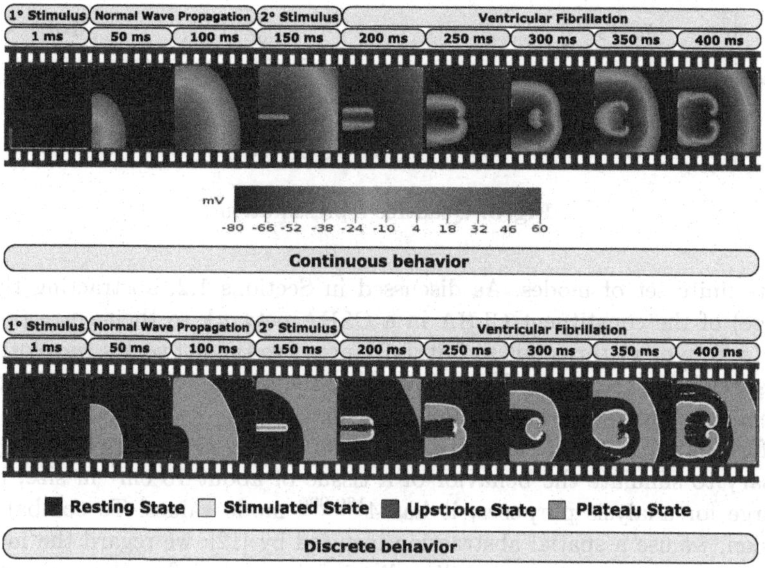

Fig. 2. Simulation of continuous and discrete behavior of CLHA network

In order to simulate the emergent behavior of cardiac tissue, we have developed CELLEXCITE [2], a CLHA-based simulation environment for excitable-cell networks. CELLEXCITE allows the user to sketch a tissue of excitable cells, plan the stimuli to be applied during simulation, and customize the arrangement of cells by selecting the appropriate lattice. Figure 2 presents our simulation results for a 400×400 CLHA network. The network was stimulated twice during simulation, at different regions. The results we obtain demonstrate the feasibility of using CLHA networks to capture and mimic different spatiotemporal behavior of wave propagation in 2D isotropic cardiac tissue, including normal wave propagation (1-150 ms); the creation of spirals, a precursor to fibrillation (200-250 ms); and the break-up of such spirals into more complex spatiotemporal patterns, signaling the transition to ventricular fibrillation (250-400 ms).

As can be clearly seen in Figure 2, a particular form of discrete abstraction, in which the action-potential value of each CLHA in the network is *discretely abstracted* to its corresponding mode, faithfully preserves the network's waveform and other spatial characteristics. Hence, for the purpose of learning and detecting spirals within CLHA networks, we can exploit discrete mode-abstraction to dramatically reduce the system state space.

3 Superposition and Quadtrees

A key benefit of hybrid automata compared to nonlinear ODEs is their explicit support for finite mode abstraction: the infinite range of values of a hybrid automaton's continuous state variables can be abstracted to the automaton's

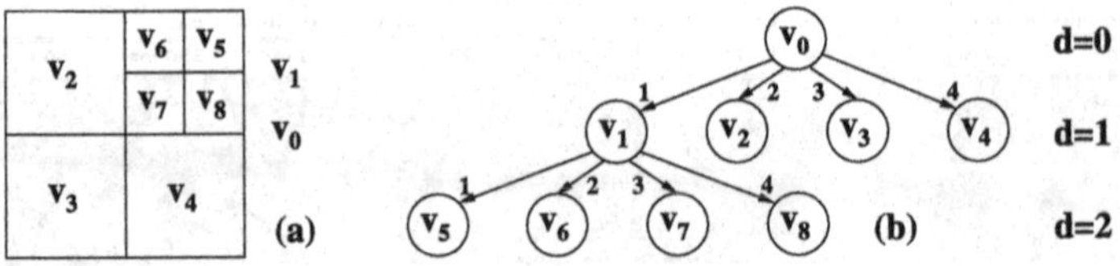

Fig. 3. Quadtree representation

discrete finite set of modes. As discussed in Sections 1,2, abstracting the AP (voltage) of the constituent CLHA in a CLHA network to their corresponding mode (**s**, **u**, **p** or **r**) turns out to faithfully preserve the network's waveform and other spatial characteristics. This allows us to reduce the spiral-onset verification problem to a finite-state verification problem.

Unfortunately, the state space of a 400×400 CLHA network, which would be necessary to simulate the behavior of a tissue of about 16 cm^2 in size, is still too large for analysis purposes: it has $4^{160,000}$ mode values! To combat state explosion, we use a spatial abstraction inspired by [12]: we regard the mode of a CLHA as a degenerate probability distribution and define the *superposition* of a set of (possibly superposed) modes as the mean of their distributions. By successively applying superposition, we obtain a tree whose root is the mode-superposition of the entire CLHA network, and whose leaves are the individual mode of the component CLHA. The particular superposition tree structure we employ, the quadtree, was inspired by image-processing techniques [15].

Let $\mathcal{A}$ be a $2^k * 2^k$ matrix of CLHA modes. A quadtree $Q = (V, R)$ representation of $\mathcal{A}$ is a quaternary tree, such that each vertex $v \in V$ represents a sub-matrix of $\mathcal{A}$. For example, the root v_0 of the quadtree in Figure 3 represents the entire matrix; child v_1 represents the matrix $\{2^{k-1}, \ldots, 2^k\} \times \{0, \ldots, 2^{k-1}\}$; child v_6 represents the matrix $\{2^{k-1}, \ldots, 3 * 2^{k-2}\} \times \{0, \ldots, 2^{k-2}\}$; etc.

Definition 1 (Leaf distribution). *Let $\mathcal{N}$ be a* CLHA *network whose constituent* CLHA *have modes $M = \{s, u, p, r\}$, and let Q be the quadtree representation of $\mathcal{N}$. Then each leaf node $l \in Q$ has an associated degenerate* leaf distribution D_l, *whose probability mass function (*PMF*) satisfies: $\exists m \in M.\ p_l(m) = 1$.*

The intuition is as follows. If the leaf occurs at the maximum depth of the quadtree, then it corresponds to the mode of a CLHA. As CLHA are deterministic, their states assume one of the values in M with probability 1.[1] If the leaf does not occur at the maximum depth of the quadtree, then it corresponds to the superposition of identical degenerate distributions, and no additional information is obtained by decomposing the leaf into its four superposition components. The visual interpretation is that a pixel has one definite color, and that nothing is learned by decomposing an area in which all pixels have the same color.

Definition 2 (Interior-node distribution). *Let $\mathcal{N}$ be a* CLHA *network whose constituent* CLHA *have modes $M = \{s, u, p, r\}$, and let Q be the quadtree*

[1] We will weaken this restriction at the end of the section.

representation of $\mathcal{N}$. Furthermore, let $i \in Q$ be an interior node with children $i1, \ldots, i4$. Then i has an associated superposition distribution D_i *whose* PMF *satisfies:* $\forall m \in M.\ p_i(m) = 1/4 \sum_{j=1}^{4} p_{ij}(m)$.

If all of i's children are leaves, then, for each mode value m, i's superposition is the mean of the occurrences of m. Hence, the probability that the mode of the parent is m is the probability that the mode of an arbitrary child is m. If i's children are interior nodes, it still holds that the probability that i's mode is m is the probability that the mode of an arbitrary leaf below i's children is m.

We call a quadtree whose nodes are labeled with leaf and interior-node distributions a *superposition quadtree* (SQT). The distributions in an SQT are not known in advance. The task of our learning algorithm is to determine these distributions for what we perceive to be spirals. The use of probability distributions is justified by the fact that different spirals might have slightly different shapes; i.e., slightly different values for the leaf nodes of their associated quadtrees.

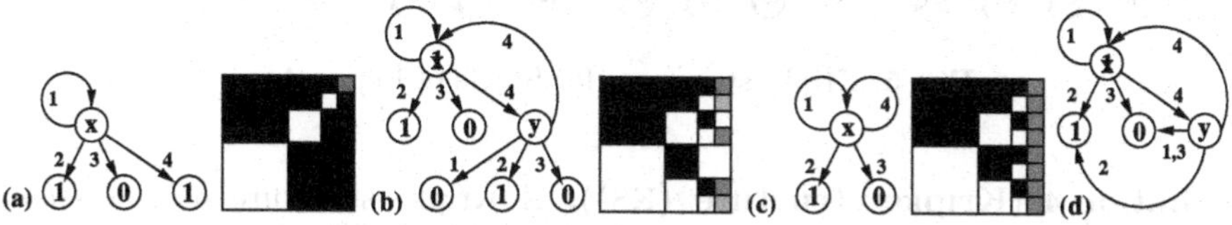

Fig. 4. Fractals as finite SQGs: (a) x = 2/3, (b) x = 5/11, y = 4/11, (c) x = 1/2

The SQTs presented so far were constructed over a finite matrix $\mathcal{A}$ containing $2^k * 2^k$ elements. In general, however, SQTs can be obtained via the finite unfolding of a *superposition quad-graph.* Let $\mathbf{4} = \{1, \ldots, 4\}$.

Definition 3 (Superposition quad-graph (SQG)**).** *A* superposition quad-graph *is a 4-tuple* $G = (V, v_0, R, L)$ *consisting of:*

- *A finite set of* vertices V *with* initial vertex $v_0 \in V$,
- *A* transition relation $R \subseteq V \times \mathbf{4} \times V$ *s.t.* $\forall v \in V, i \in \mathbf{4}\ \exists u \in V.\ (v, i, u) \in R$,
- *A* probability-distribution labeling L *s.t.* $\forall v \in V.\ L(v) = 1/4 \sum_{u \in R(v)} L(u)$.

The condition on R ensures that each vertex in V has precisely four successors in R. The condition on L ensures that the probability distributions are related through superposition. Constructing SQTs as finite unfoldings of SQGs is more powerful as it also supports the definition of infinite SQTs generated by *recursion.* That is, it supports the definition of *fractals.*

Figure 4 gives the specification of three fractals and the unfolding of their SQGs up to depth 3. Recursive nodes are labeled by *distribution variables*, the values for which can be computed by solving a *linear system.* For example, x and y in Figure 4(b) are computed by solving the linear system $x = 1/4\,(x + 1 + y)$ and $y = 1/4\,(1 + x)$. In the pictures on the right, *gray* areas represent recursive nodes. The four self-loops of the leaves are not shown for simplicity. Note that leaves may now be associated with any constant distribution. Also note that graphs (a) and (d) yield equivalent infinite SQTs.

4 Linear Spatial-Superposition Logic

Every finite SQT can be transformed into an SQG by adding to each leaf a self-loop labeled by i, for $i \in \mathbf{4}$. Moreover, an SQG can be transformed into a *Kripke structure* by erasing (forgetting) the transition labeling, collapsing identical transitions, and assuming nondeterminism among transitions emanating from the same node. For example, applying this forgetful transformation to the SQGs of Figure 4 yields the Kripke structures of Figure 5, where the self-loops are made explicit. The Kripke structure of Figure 5(d) can be seen as a minimal-state equivalent of the one of Figure 5(b).

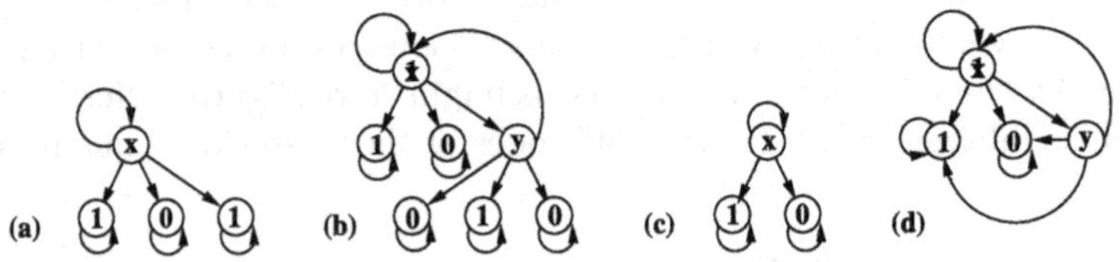

Fig. 5. Kripke structures for SQGs of Figure 4

Definition 4 (Kripke structure (KS)). *A* Kripke structure *over a set of atomic propositions AP is a four-tuple* $M = (S, I, R, L)$ *consisting of:*

- *A countable set of* states S, *with* initial states $I \subseteq S$,
- *A* transition relation $R \in S \times S$ *with* $\forall s \in S\, \exists t \in S.\ (s, t) \in R$,
- *A* labeling (or interpretation) function $L : S \rightarrow 2^{AP}$.

The condition associated with the transition relation R ensures that every state has a successor in R. Consequently, it is always possible to construct an infinite path through the KS, an important property when dealing with reactive systems. In our case, it means that we can reason about recursive SQTs, i.e. fractals.

The labeling function L defines for each state $s \in S$ the set $L(s)$ of atomic propositions that are valid in s. Our atomic propositions are *inequalities over distributions.* Syntactically, they are written as follows: $P(D = m) \sim d$, where D is a distribution function, $m \in M$ for $M \subset R$ is a discrete value (e.g. a mode), $d \in [0..1]$, and $\sim$ is one of $<$, $\leq$, $=$, $\geq$, or $>$.

In order to verify properties of a reactive system modeled as a KS K, it is customary to use either a linear-time or a branching-time temporal logic. A model for a linear-time logic (LTL) formula is an infinite path π in K. A model for a branching-time logic formula is K itself; given a state s of K, this allows one to quantify over the paths originating from s. For our current purposes of specifying, and detecting the onset of, spirals, LTL suffices.

Strictly speaking, our logic is a *linear spatial-superposition logic* (LSSL), as a path π in K represents a sequence of *concretizations* (anti-superpositions). Syntactically, however, our temporal-logic operators are the same as in LTL: the *next* operator X with $X\varphi$ meaning that φ holds in a concretization of the current state; its inverse operator B; the *until* operator U, with $\varphi U \psi$ meaning that φ holds along a path until ψ holds; and the *release* operator R, with $\psi\, R\, \varphi$ meaning that φ holds along a path unless released by ψ.

Definition 5 (LSSL Syntax). *The syntax of* linear space-superposition logic *is defined inductively as follows:*

$$\begin{array}{rcl} \varphi & ::= & \top \mid \bot \mid P[D=m] \sim d \mid \neg\phi \mid \varphi \vee \psi \mid X\varphi \mid B\varphi \mid \varphi\, U \varphi \mid \varphi\, R\, \varphi \\ \sim & ::= & < \mid \leq \mid = \mid \geq \mid > \end{array}$$

Although Kripke structures and the LSSL logic allow us to reason about infinite paths, physical considerations—such as the number of myocytes in a cardiac tissue or the screen resolution—impose a maximum length k on such paths. The length k, however, is maintained as a parameter in LSSL's semantic definition, permitting us to accommodate any number of myocytes or any screen resolution. Defining LSSL's semantics in this manner places us within the framework of *bounded-model-checking* [3].

Definition 6 (LSSL Semantics). *Let K be a* KS *and π a path in K. Then, for $k \geq 0$, π* satisfies an LSSL formula *φ with bound k, written $\pi \models_k \varphi$, if and only if $\pi \models_k^0 \varphi$, where:*

$$\begin{array}{lcl}
\pi \models_k^i \top & \text{and} & \pi \not\models_k^i \bot \\
\pi \models_k^i p & \Leftrightarrow & p \in L(\pi[i]) \\
\pi \models_k^i \neg\varphi & \Leftrightarrow & \pi \not\models_k^i \varphi \\
\pi \models_k^i \varphi \vee \psi & \Leftrightarrow & \pi \models_k^i \varphi \text{ or } \pi \models_k^i \psi \\
\pi \models_k^i X\varphi & \Leftrightarrow & i < k \text{ and } \pi \models_k^{i+1} \varphi \\
\pi \models_k^i B\varphi & \Leftrightarrow & 0 < i \leq k \text{ and } \pi \models_k^{i-1} \varphi \\
\pi \models_k^i \varphi\, U \psi & \Leftrightarrow & \exists j.\ i \leq j \leq k.\ \pi \models_k^j \psi \text{ and } \forall n.\ i \leq n < j.\ \pi \models_k^n \varphi \\
\pi \models_k^i \psi\, R\, \varphi & \Leftrightarrow & \forall j.\ i \leq j \leq k.\ \pi \models_k^j \varphi \text{ or } \exists n.\ i \leq n < j.\ \pi \models_k^n \psi
\end{array}$$

We say that $K \models_k \varphi$ if for all paths π in K, $\pi \models_k \varphi$.

Our release operator R is a bounded version of the LTL's R operator. Similarly, the *globally* operator G, defined as $G\,\varphi \equiv \bot\, R\, \varphi$, is a bounded version of LTL's G operator. The *finally* operator F is defined as usual as $F\varphi \equiv \top\, U\, \varphi$. In general, the unbounded LTL version of G is assumed to not hold. For example, $G\,\varphi$ does not hold as φ could be violated at $k+1$; to decide $G\varphi$ in LTL wrt. a bound k, one needs a more sophisticated analysis of the KS K, as discussed in [3].

As an example, consider an unfolding depth k of the KS in Figure 5(a), and assume the distributions correspond to mode $\mathtt{s}$. This KS has a path π such that $\pi \models_k G(P[D = \mathtt{s}] = 2/3)$ holds: the path that always returns to x. To automatically find π we will model-check the negation of the above formula. This will return π as a counterexample. By using the techniques in [3], one can show that π also satisfies the unbounded LTL version of the formula.

5 Model Checking and Learning

Bounded model checking. Given a Kripke structure K, an LSSL formula φ, and a bound k, a *bounded model checker* (BMC) efficiently verifies if $K \models_k \neg\varphi$. If so, it returns one or more paths π in K that violate φ; otherwise, it returns true. Intuitively, a BMC applies the LSSL semantics inductively defined in Section 4 to each path π in K. We have implemented a simple prototype BMC for Kripke structures K derived from SQTs and LSSL formulae. The BMC first enumerates all paths in K, and then for each path, it applies the LSSL semantics. This BMC is efficient enough to check within milliseconds the onset of spirals. We are currently improving the BMC for safety formulae (formulae without F operator), by traversing the SQT and pruning all subtrees of a vertex as soon as we detect that the current path violates $\neg\varphi$. A more ambitious SAT-based BMC is also under development.

Machine learning. Writing the LTL formulae that a reactive system should satisfy is a nontrivial task. Developers often find it difficult to specify the system properties of interest. The classification of LTL formulae into *safety* (something bad should never happen) and *liveness* properties (something good should eventually happen) provides some guidance, but the task remains difficult.

Writing LSSL formulae describing emerging properties of CLHA networks is even more difficult. For example, what is the LSSL formula for spiral onset? In the following, we describe a surprisingly simple, machine-learning-based approach that we have successfully applied to spiral detection. The main idea is to cast the onset property as follows: *Is there a path in the given* SQT *leading to the core of a spiral?* The implementation is simple as well. For an SEF produced by the CellExcite simulator (see Figure 1), our Emerald tool set allows the user to select a path through the SEF's corresponding SQT simply by clicking on a point in the SEF (e.g. in the core of a spiral). If no spiral is present, the SQT path with maximum PMF (probability mass function) is returned. Note that this method is not restricted to spirals: path selection via clicking on a representative point can be applied to normal wave propagation, wave collision, etc.

The paths so obtained are then used to learn the LSSL formula for the property we are interested in, such as spiral onset. The learning algorithm works as follows: (1) For each path of length k, where k is the height of the SQT, we define k attributes $a_1, \ldots, a_k$ such that each a_i holds the PMF value of vertex v_i, for the mode we are interested in (for spirals, mode $\mathtt{s}$); (2) Each path is classified by Emerald as spiral or non-spiral, depending on whether or not the user clicked on a point (core); the classification is stored as an additional classifier attribute c; (3) All records $(a_i, \ldots, a_k, c)$ are stored in a table, which is provided to the data classification phase; (4) At the end of this phase we obtain a path classifier which we translate into an LSSL formula.

Data classification [17] is generally a two-step process: training and testing. For *training*, we choose a classification algorithm that learns a set of descriptions of our training data set. The form of these descriptions depends on the type of classification algorithm employed. For *testing*, we use a test data set, disjoint from the training set, and containing the class attribute with a known value. The *accuracy* of the classifier on a given test set is the percentage of the test records that are correctly classified. Various techniques can be used to obtain test and training sets from an initial set of records, such as X-Cross Validation [8].

Classification algorithms also come in various flavors. We used a *descriptive* classifier, as this returns a set of if-then rules called *discriminant rules.* Underlying descriptive classifiers are either decision trees, rough sets, classification-by-association analysis, etc. A rule r has the form $(\bigwedge_{i\in I} a_i = v_i) \Rightarrow (c = v)$, where I is a subset of $\mathbf{k}$. Usually, each class c has an associated set of rules $r_1, \ldots, r_n$; i.e. c is characterized by $\bigwedge_{i=1}^{n} r_i$. Using boolean arithmetic, this is equivalent to $(\bigvee_{i=1}^{n} \bigwedge_{j\in I_i} a_{ij} = v_{ij}) \Rightarrow (c = v)$. The antecedent formula $\bigvee_{i=1}^{n} \bigwedge_{j\in I_i} a_{ij} = v_{ij}$ is called the *class description formula* of the class c.

As is customary, we built a classifier for one class only (the class c), called the *target class*, using all other classes as one contrasting class. Hence the classifier consists of only one class-description formula, describing the target class. We say that we *learned* that formula. We have used Weka's decision-tree algorithm, but any other rule-based algorithm could have been used as well. The classifier we have learned for spirals, is as follows:

```
if a7<=0.875 then {if a2<=0.04895 then ~c else c}
else if a3<=0.078359 then {if a0<=0.025021 then ~c else c} else ~c
```

Its translation into linear spatial-superposition generated the following formula:

$$\mathtt{XX}\,(\,\mathtt{P(D=s)} > 0.04895 \wedge \mathtt{XXXXX}\,\mathtt{P(D=s)} \leq 0.875\,) \vee$$
$$\mathtt{P(D=s)} > 0.025021 \wedge \mathtt{XXX}\,(\,\mathtt{P(D=s)} \leq 0.078359 \wedge \mathtt{XXXX}\,\mathtt{P(D=s)} > 0.875\,)$$

This formula is an approximate description of a spiral which we used together with EMERALD's BMC to detect spiral onset within milliseconds. In case the BMC returned a false positive, we add the corresponding record to the classification table as part of a retraining phase; see Figure 1.

6 Implementation and Experimental Results

Our techniques of Sections 2-5 have been implemented as the EMERALD tool suite of the EHA environment. EMERALD is a Java application that can be used to learn an LSSL formula for a particular spatial pattern, and to check the formula against a set of images that reproduce the discrete behavior of a CLHA network. For ease of use, EMERALD provides two graphical panels, one for *Preprocessing* (classification) and the other for *Bounded Model Checking*.

The Preprocessing panel (Figure 6(a)) enables users to browse the various collections of images they have assembled for machine-learning purposes, and to view their SQT representation. It comprises three graphical components: an *image viewer* on the right, a *quadtree viewer* on the top-left, and a *data-table viewer* on the bottom-left, where user-selected paths are displayed. In the image viewer, the user selects a path leading to a spiral core by clicking on an appropriate stimulated point (in yellow) of the image. If the image does not contain a spiral, the user can choose the maximum PMF path or a generic stimulated

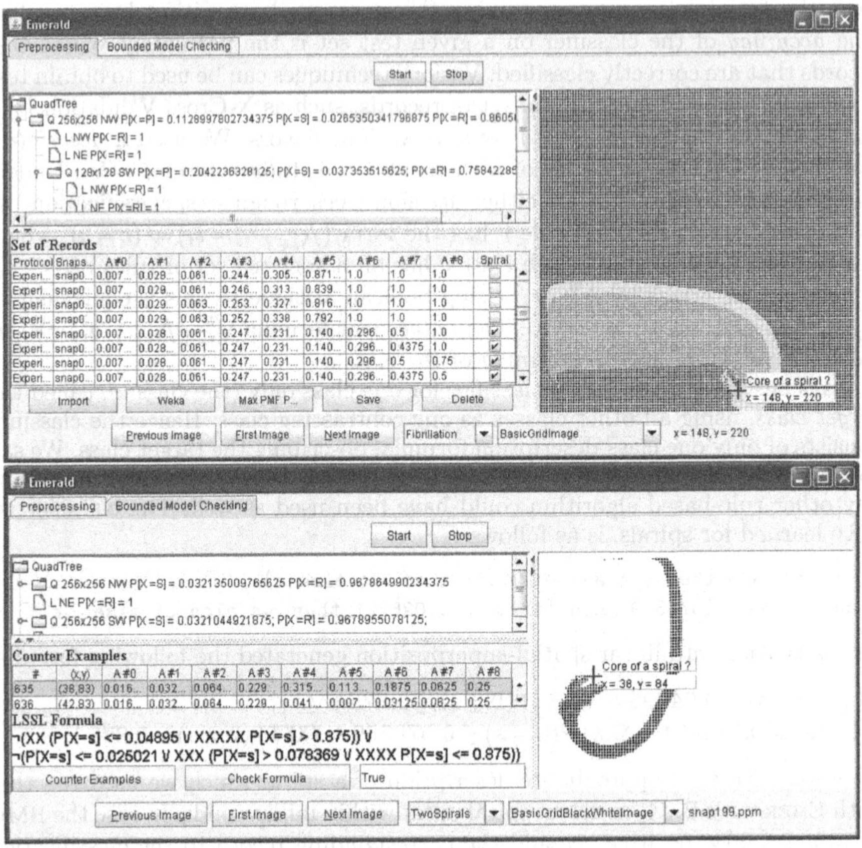

Fig. 6. (a) Top: Preprocessing Panel. (b) Bottom: Bounded Model Checking Panel.

point. Each path selected is stored in a data table in the form of the PMF sequence of stimulated modes in each node of the traversed SQT. All such paths are subsequently exported to Weka in a common format. Presently, we have customized EMERALD for spiral detection, but we plan to extend the tool with the capability to classify any generic spatial pattern.

The BMC panel (Figure 6(b)) enables the user to check an LSSL formula against the SQT representation of a specific image. As discussed in Section 5, the LSSL formula encodes the classifier for the spatial pattern under investigation. If the SQT in question fails to satisfy the formula, the resulting counter-examples (spirals) are reported to the user both as rows in the counter-example table and as red points marking the core of the spiral contained in the image.

Table 1 contains our preliminary experimental results. For training and testing purposes, we used two different sets of images, each containing spirals and normal wave propagation. The first set of images was used to train the classifier; we supervised the training by discriminating between paths leading to a spiral core

Table 1. Experimental Results

Path Classifier	**Test Set 550**	**Test Set 600**	**Test Set 650**
Trained (512 Paths)	87.00%	88.83%	88.23%
Retrained (512 Paths + 67 Counter-Examples)	97.10%	97.33%	93.07%

versus those (of maximum PMF) belonging to images that did not contain a spiral. From this first set we extracted 512 possible paths, and used Weka to build a ruled-based classifier with a very high prediction accuracy (99.25%).

The test set was divided into increasingly larger sets of images: 500, 550, 600 and 650 images. Applying the rule-based classifier on the first 500 images produced 67 wrongly classified paths. We used these paths to obtain a new, retrained classifier. We then used both classifiers on the remaining sets of images, and for each classifier and test set we computed the LSSL *formula accuracy*, as an estimate of how well the formula specifies the spatial pattern. As Table 1 shows, retraining considerably improves accuracy, and can be repeated each time a false classification is returned. Weka's decision-tree algorithm took no more than 9s to construct a rule-based classifier from the training (512 records) and retraining (579 records) tables, respectively. Our model checker took between 1.67s and 7.09s, with an average of 4.72s to model check an SQT for a 400×400 SEF if no spiral was present, and between 1ms and 4.64s, with an average of 230ms if a spiral was present. All results were produced on a PC equipped with a Centrino 2GHz processor with 1.5GB RAM.

7 Related Work

The use of hybrid automata to model and analyze spatial networks is a relatively new subject area, and includes application to Delta-Notch signaling networks [9], coordinated control of autonomous underwater vehicles [14], and aircraft trajectories and landing protocols [7,16]. In contrast, our focus is on emergent behavior (in the form of spiral waves) in networks of cardiac myocytes, and the use of spatial superposition as an abstraction mechanism. Predicting spirals [4] in pure continuous models [18] is a more complicated process than what is implemented in EMERALD, where discrete SQT structures, obtained via mode-abstraction and superposition, are used. Several logics have recently been proposed for describing the behavior and spatial structure of concurrent systems [5,6], and for reasoning about the topological aspects of modal logics and Kripke structures [1]. Unlike LSSL, these logics are not based on an abstraction mechanism like spatial-superposition that can be used to alleviate state explosion during model checking.

8 Conclusions

In this paper, we have presented a framework for specifying and detecting emergent behavior in networks of cardiac myocytes. Our approach, which uses hybrid automata, discrete mode-abstraction, and bounded model checking, is based on a novel notion of spatial-superposition and its related logic LSSL, and a new method for the automated learning of formulae in this logic from the spatial patterns under investigation. Our framework has been fully implemented in the EMERALD tool suite. Our preliminary experimental results are very encouraging, with a prediction accuracy of over 93% on a test set comprising 650 images. As future work, we plan to extend our framework to the learning of branching-time spatial-superposition properties, and the more intricate problem of specifying and detecting spatiotemporal emergent behavior.

References

1. Aiello, M., Benthem, J., Bezhanishvili, G.: Reasoning about space: The modal way. J. Log. Comput. 13(6), 889–920 (2003)
2. Bartocci, E., Corradini, F., Entcheva, E., Grosu, R., Smolka, S.A.: CellExcite: A tool for simulating in-silico excitable cells. BMC Bioinformatics (to appear, 2007)
3. Biere, A., Cimatti, A., Clarke, E., Strichman, O., Zhu, Y.: Bounded model checking. In: Adv. in Comp., Highly Depend. Software, vol. 58, Academic Press, London (2003)
4. Bray, M.A., Lin, S.F., Aliev, R.R., Roth, B.J., Wikswo, J.P.J.: Experimental and theoretical analysis of phase singularity dynamics in cardiac tissue. J Cardiovasc Electrophysiol 12(6), 716–722 (2001)
5. Caires, L., Cardelli, L.: A spatial logic for concurrency (part I). Inf. Comput. 186(2), 194–235 (2003)
6. Caires, L., Cardelli, L.: A spatial logic for concurrency (part II. Theor. Comput. Sci. 322(3), 517–565 (2004)
7. deOliveira, I., Cugnasca, P.: Checking safe trajectories of aircraft using hybrid automata. In: Anderson, S., Bologna, S., Felici, M. (eds.) SAFECOMP 2002. LNCS, vol. 2434, Springer, Heidelberg (2002)
8. Frank, E., Hall, M.A., Holmes, G., Kirkby, R., Pfahringer, B., Witten, I.H., Trigg, L.: WEKA – a machine learning workbench for data mining. In: The Data Mining and Knowledge Discovery Handbook, pp. 1305–1314. Springer, Heidelberg (2005)
9. Ghosh, R., Tiwari, A., Tomlin, C.: Automated symbolic reachability analysis; with application to delta-notch signaling automata. In: Maler, O., Pnueli, A. (eds.) HSCC 2003. LNCS, vol. 2623, pp. 233–248. Springer, Heidelberg (2003)
10. Grosu, R., Bartocci, E., Corradini, F., Entcheva, E., Smolka, S., True, M., Wasilewska, A., Ye, P.: EHA: An environment for the specification, simulation, analysis and control of networks of excitable hybrid automata (2007), `http://www.cs.sunysb.edu/~eha`
11. Grosu, R., Mitra, S., Ye, P., Entcheva, E., Ramakrishnan, I.V., Smolka, S.A.: Learning cycle-linear hybrid automata for excitable cells. In: Bemporad, A., Bicchi, A., Buttazzo, G. (eds.) HSCC 2007. LNCS, vol. 4416, pp. 245–258. Springer, Heidelberg (2007)
12. Kwon, Y., Agha, G.: Scalable modeling and performance evaluation of wireless sensor networks. In: IEEE RT Tech. and App. Symp., pp. 49–58 (2006)
13. Lu, Y.: Concept hierarchy in data mining: Specification, generation and implementation. Master's thesis, Simon Fraser University (December 1997)
14. Pereira, F.L., deSousa, J.B.: Coordinated control of networked vehicles: An autonomous underwater system. Aut. and Remote Ctrl. 65(7), 1037–1045 (2004)

15. Shusterman, E., Feder, M.: Image compression via improved quadtree decomposition algorithms. IEEE Trans. on Image Processing 3(2), 207–215 (1994)
16. Umeno, S., Lynch, N.: Safety verification of an aircraft landing protocol: A refinement approach. In: Bemporad, A., Bicchi, A., Buttazzo, G. (eds.) HSCC 2007. LNCS, vol. 4416, Springer, Heidelberg (2007)
17. Wasilewska, A., Ruiz, E.M.: A classification model: Syntax and semantics for classification. In: Ślęzak, D., Yao, J., Peters, J.F., Ziarko, W., Hu, X. (eds.) RSFDGrC 2005. LNCS (LNAI), vol. 3642, pp. 59–68. Springer, Heidelberg (2005)
18. Wedge, N.A., Branicky, M.S., Cavusoglu, M.C.: Computationally efficient cardiac biolectricity models toward whole-heart simulation. In: Proc.of Intl. Conf. IEEE Engineering in Medicine and Biology Society, pp. 1–4 (2004)
19. Ye, P., Entcheva, E., Grosu, R., Smolka, S.: Efficient modeling of excitable cells using hybrid automata. In: Proc. of CMSB 2005, the 3rd Workshop on Computational Methods in Systems Biology, Edinburgh, Scotland, pp. 216–227 (April 2005)
20. Ye, P., Entcheva, E., Smolka, S., Grosu, R.: A cycle-linear hybrid-automata model for excitable cells. The IET J. of Systems Biology (SYB) (accepted, 2007)

Compositional Modeling and Minimization of Time-Inhomogeneous Markov Chains

Tingting Han[1,2], Joost-Pieter Katoen[1,2], and Alexandru Mereacre[1,3]

[1] RWTH Aachen University, Software Modeling and Verification Group, Germany
{tingting.han,katoen,mereacre}@cs.rwth-aachen.de
[2] University of Twente, Formal Methods and Tools Group, The Netherlands
[3] University of Trento, Dept. of Information and Communication Technology, Italy

Abstract. This paper presents a compositional framework for the modeling of interactive continuous-time Markov chains with time-dependent rates, a subclass of communicating piecewise deterministic Markov processes. A poly-time algorithm is presented for computing the coarsest quotient under strong bisimulation for rate functions that are either piecewise uniform or (piecewise) polynomial. Strong as well as weak bisimulation are shown to be congruence relations for the compositional framework, thus allowing component-wise minimization. In addition, a new characterization of transient probabilities in time-inhomogeneous Markov chains with piecewise uniform rates is provided.

1 Introduction

Modeling large stochastic discrete-event dynamic systems is a difficult task that typically requires human intelligence and ingenuity. To facilitate this process, formalisms are needed that allow for the modeling of such systems in a compositional manner. This allows to construct models of simpler components—usually from first principles—that can be combined by appropriate composition operators to yield complete system models. In concurrency theory, process algebra [20,16] has emerged as an important framework to achieve compositionality: it provides a formal apparatus for compositional reasoning about structure and behavior of systems, and features abstraction mechanisms allowing system components to be treated as black boxes.

Although originally aimed at purely functional behavior, process algebras for stochastic systems have been investigated thoroughly, see e.g., [15,14]. In all these approaches, the dynamics of the stochastic models is assumed to be *time-homogeneous*, i.e., the probabilistic nature of mode transitions as well as the time-driven behavior are independent of the global time. This is, however, a serious drawback to adequately model random phenomena that occur in practice such as failure rates of hardware components (a bath-tub curve), software reliability (which reduces due to memory leaks and increases after a restart), and battery depletion (where the power extraction rate non-linearly depends on the remaining amount of energy [5]), to mention a few. This paper attempts to overcome this deficiency by providing a process algebra for time-*inhomogeneous* continuous-time Markov chains (ICTMCs). This is a very versatile class of models and is a natural stepping-stone towards more full-fledged stochastic hybrid system models such as piecewise deterministic Markov processes (PDPs [6]).

M. Egerstedt and B. Mishra (Eds.): HSCC 2008, LNCS 4981, pp. 244–258, 2008.

We show that ICTMCs can be compositionally modeled by using a time-dependent adaptation of the framework of interactive Markov chains (IMCs) [14]. To facilitate this, ICTMCs are equipped with the potential for interaction, i.e., synchronization. Instrumental to this approach is the memoryless property of ICTMCs.

More importantly though, notions of strong and weak bisimulation are defined and shown to be congruences. Together with efficient quotienting algorithms this allows for the component-wise minimization of hierarchical ICTMC models. Finally, we present an axiomatization for strong and weak bisimulation which allows to simplify models by pure syntactic manipulations as opposed to performing minimization on the model level. As a generalization of results on ordinary lumpability on Markov chains [3], we show that strong bisimulation preserves transient and long-run state probabilities in ICTMCs. This allows to minimize symbolically ICTMCs prior to their analysis.

We present a bisimulation minimization algorithm to obtain the *coarsest* (and thus smallest) *strong bisimulation quotient* of a large class of interactive ICTMCs, viz. those that have piecewise uniform—rate $\mathbf{R}_k(t)$ on piece k is of the form $f_k(t)\cdot\mathbf{R}$ for integrable function $\mathbf{R}$—polynomial, or piecewise polynomial—where each polynomial is of degree three—rate functions. The worst-case time and space complexity is $\mathcal{O}\left(m_a \lg(n) + M m_r \lg(n)\right)$ and $\mathcal{O}\left(m_a + m_r\right)$, respectively, where $M{+}1$ is the number of pieces (or degrees of the polynomial), m_a is the number of action-labeled transitions and m_r the number of rate-labeled transitions in the ICTMC under consideration. This algorithm is based on the partition-refinement bisimulation algorithm for Markov chains by Derisavi *et al.* [7] and Paige-Tarjan's algorithm for labeled transition systems (LTS) [21].

Related work. ICTMCs are related to piecewise deterministic Markov processes (PDPs), a more general class of continuous-time stochastic discrete-event dynamic systems proposed by Davis [6]. The probabilistic nature of mode transitions in PDPs is as for ICTMCs; in fact, ICTMCs are a subclass of PDPs when the global time t has a clock dynamics i.e., $\dot{t} = 1$. The notion of parallel composition of ICTMCs corresponds to that for communicating PDPs (CPDPs) as introduced by Strubbe and van der Schaft [24,23]. Alternative modeling formalisms for PDPs are, e.g., variants of colored Petri nets [9] but they lack a clear notion of compositionality. Compositional modeling formalisms for hybrid systems have been considered by, e.g., [2,1]. Strong bisimulation has been proposed for several classes of (stochastic) hybrid systems, see e.g., [4,12,25]. Our notion of bisimulation is closely related to that for CPDPs [25] but differs in the fact that the maximal progress assumption—a race between one or more rates and a transition that is not subject to interaction with the environment is resolved in favor of the internal transition—is not considered in [25]. Proofs of the major results are contained in [13].

2 Inhomogeneous Continuous Time Markov Chains

Definition 1 (ICTMC). *An inhomogeneous continuous-time Markov chain is a tuple* $\mathcal{C} = (\mathbb{S}, \mathbf{R})$ *where:* $\mathbb{S} = \{1, 2, \ldots, n\}$ *is a finite set of states, and* $\mathbf{R}(t) = [R_{i,j}(t) \geq 0] \in \mathbb{R}^{n \times n}$ *is a time-dependent rate matrix, where* $R_{i,j}(t)$ *is the rate between states* $i, j \in \mathbb{S}$ *at time* $t \in \mathbb{R}_{\geq 0}$.

Let diagonal matrix $\mathbf{E}(t) = \text{diag}\,[E_i(t)] \in \mathbb{R}^{n \times n}$, where $E_i(t) = \sum_{j \in \mathbb{S}} R_{i,j}(t)$ for all $i, j \in \mathbb{S}$, $i \neq j$ i.e., $E_i(t)$ is the total exit rate of state i at time t. Consider a non-homogeneous Poisson process $\{Z(t) | t \geq 0\}$ with rate $R(t)$. The probability of k arrivals in the interval $[t, t + \Delta t]$ is:

$$\Pr\{Z(t+\Delta t) - Z(t) = k\} = \frac{\left[\int_t^{t+\Delta t} R(\ell) d\ell\right]^k}{k!} e^{-\int_t^{t+\Delta t} R(\ell) d\ell}, \quad k = 0, 1, \ldots.$$

The probability that there will be no arrivals in the interval $[t, t + \Delta t]$ is:

$$\Pr\{Z(t+\Delta t) - Z(t) = 0\} = e^{-\int_t^{t+\Delta t} R(\ell) d\ell} = e^{-\int_0^{\Delta t} R(t+\ell) d\ell}. \tag{1}$$

Let the random variable $W_{i,j}(t)$ be the firing time of transition $i \to j$ $(i, j \in \mathbb{S})$ with rate $R_{i,j}(t)$ at time t. From (1) we obtain the cumulative probability distribution of the firing time of transition $i \to j$:

$$\Pr\{W_{i,j}(t) \leq \Delta t\} = 1 - \Pr\{Z(t+\Delta t) - Z(t) = 0\} = 1 - e^{-\int_0^{\Delta t} R_{i,j}(t+\ell) d\ell}. \tag{2}$$

Probability measures. For every ICTMC one can specify measures of interest. These measures are either related to the states or to the transitions of an ICTMC. Consider a random variable $W_i(t)$ which denotes the waiting time in state i.

Property 1

$$\Pr\{W_i(t) \leq \Delta t\} = 1 - e^{-\int_0^{\Delta t} E_i(t+\ell) d\ell}. \tag{3}$$

An intuitive explanation of (3) is that the waiting time $W_i(t)$ in state i is determined by the minimal firing time of all k outgoing transitions from state i, i.e., $W_i(t) = \min\{W_{i,1}(t), \ldots, W_{i,k}(t)\}$. When $R_{i,j}(t) = R_{i,j}$ and $E_i(t) = E_i$ for all $t \in \mathbb{R}_{\geq 0}$, i.e., the ICTMC is a CTMC, $W_i(t)$ has the distribution $1 - e^{-E_i \Delta t}$. An interesting property is that the waiting time in any state i is *memoryless*, i.e.:

$$\Pr\{W_i(t) \leq t' + \Delta t | W_i(t) > t'\} = \Pr\{W_i(t+t') \leq \Delta t\}. \tag{4}$$

This can be shown as follows:

$$\Pr\{W_i(t) \leq t' + \Delta t | W_i(t) > t'\} = \frac{e^{-\int_0^{t'} E_i(t+\ell) d\ell} - e^{-\int_0^{t'+\Delta t} E_i(t+\ell) d\ell}}{e^{-\int_0^{t'} E_i(t+\ell) d\ell}}$$
$$= 1 - e^{-\int_0^{t'+\Delta t} E_i(t+\ell) d\ell + \int_0^{t'} E_i(t+\ell) d\ell} = \Pr\{W_i(t+t') \leq \Delta t\}.$$

Equation (4) will be of importance when we later define a calculus for ICTMCs.

Property 2. The probability $\Pr_{i,j}(t)$ to select transition $i \to j$ $(i \neq j, i, j \in \mathbb{S})$ with rate $R_{i,j}(t)$ at time t is:

$$\Pr_{i,j}(t) = \int_0^\infty R_{i,j}(t+\tau) e^{-\int_0^\tau E_i(t+\ell) d\ell} d\tau. \tag{5}$$

When rates are constant, the measure (5) takes the form $\mathrm{Pr}_{i,j} = \frac{R_{i,j}}{E_i}$ ($\mathrm{Pr}_{i,j}(t) = \mathrm{Pr}_{i,j}$ for all $t \in \mathbb{R}_{\geq 0}$), which corresponds to transition probability in CTMCs.

Property 3. The cumulative probability distribution $\mathrm{Pr}_{i,j}(t, \Delta t)$ to move from state i to state j ($i \neq j$) with rate $R_{i,j}(t)$ in Δt time units starting at time t:

$$\mathrm{Pr}_{i,j}(t, \Delta t) = \int_0^{\Delta t} R_{i,j}(t+\tau) e^{-\int_0^{\tau} E_i(t+\ell)d\ell} d\tau. \tag{6}$$

Notice that (6) is the same as (5) except that the range of the outer-most integral is $[0, \Delta t]$. For CTMCs ($\mathrm{Pr}_{i,j}(t, \Delta t) = \mathrm{Pr}_{i,j}(\Delta t)$ for all $t \in \mathbb{R}_{\geq 0}$), equation (6) results in $\mathrm{Pr}_{i,j}(\Delta t) = \frac{R_{i,j}}{E_i}\left(1 - e^{-E_i \Delta t}\right)$.

Transient probability distribution. One important measure which quantifies the probability to be in a specific state at some time point is the *transient probability distribution.* Consider an ICTMC described by the stochastic process $\{X(t) | t \geq 0\}$. The transient probability distribution $\Pr\{X(t+\Delta t) = j\}$, denoted by $\pi_j(t+\Delta t)$, is the probability to be in state j at time $t + \Delta t$, and is described by the equation:

$$\pi_j(t+\Delta t) = \sum_{i \in \mathbb{S}} \Pr\{X(t) = i\} \cdot \Pr\{X(t+\Delta t) = j | X(t) = i\}. \tag{7}$$

Equation (7) can be expressed in matrix form as: $\boldsymbol{\pi}(t+\Delta t) = \boldsymbol{\pi}(t)\boldsymbol{\Phi}(t+\Delta t, t)$, where $\boldsymbol{\pi}(t) = [\pi_1(t), \ldots, \pi_n(t)]$ and $\boldsymbol{\Phi}(t+\Delta t, t)$ represents the *transition probability matrix.* This equation represents the solution of a system of ODEs:

$$\frac{d\boldsymbol{\pi}(t)}{dt} = \lim_{\Delta t \to 0} \frac{\boldsymbol{\pi}(t+\Delta t) - \boldsymbol{\pi}(t)}{\Delta t} = \lim_{\Delta t \to 0} \boldsymbol{\pi}(t) \frac{[\boldsymbol{\Phi}(t+\Delta t, t) - \mathbf{I}]}{\Delta t}. \tag{8}$$

For the diagonal elements $q_{i,i}(t)$ of the matrix $\lim_{\Delta t \to 0} \frac{[\boldsymbol{\Phi}(t+\Delta t, t) - \mathbf{I}]}{\Delta t}$ from (8), we obtain $q_{i,i}(t) = \lim_{\Delta t \to 0} \frac{\Pr\{X(t+\Delta t) = i | X(t) = i\} - 1}{\Delta t}$. As $\Pr\{X(t+\Delta t) = i | X(t) = i\}$ denotes the probability to stay in state i for at least Δt units of time or the probability to return to state i in two or more steps, it follows:

$$q_{i,i}(t) = \lim_{\Delta t \to 0} \frac{e^{-\int_0^{\Delta t} E_i(t+\ell)d\ell} - 1 + o(\Delta t)}{\Delta t} = -E_i(t),$$

where $o(\Delta t)$ denotes the probability to make two or more transitions in Δt units of time. Notice that $\lim_{\Delta t \to 0} \frac{o(\Delta t)}{\Delta t} = 0$. For the off-diagonal elements $q_{i,j}(t)$ ($i \neq j$) of matrix $\lim_{\Delta t \to 0} \frac{[\boldsymbol{\Phi}(t+\Delta t, t) - \mathbf{I}]}{\Delta t}$, the relation is similar:

$$q_{i,j}(t) = \lim_{\Delta t \to 0} \frac{\Pr\{X(t+\Delta t) = j | X(t) = i\}}{\Delta t} = \lim_{\Delta t \to 0} \frac{\mathrm{Pr}_{i,j}(t, \Delta t) + o(\Delta t)}{\Delta t},$$

which can be reduced using (6) to:

$$q_{i,j}(t) = \lim_{\Delta t \to 0} \frac{\int_0^{\Delta t} R_{i,j}(t+\tau) e^{-\int_0^{\tau} E_i(t+\ell)d\ell} d\tau + o(\Delta t)}{\Delta t} = R_{i,j}(t).$$

The resulting *infinitesimal generator* matrix $\mathbf{Q}(t)$ has the form:

$$\mathbf{Q}(t) = \lim_{\Delta t \to 0} \frac{[\mathbf{\Phi}(t+\Delta t, t) - \mathbf{I}]}{\Delta t} = \mathbf{R}'(t) - \mathbf{E}(t),$$

where $\mathbf{R}'$ equals $\mathbf{R}$ except that $R^{'}_{i,i}(t) = 0$. Plugging $\mathbf{Q}(t)$ into equation (8) yields the system of ODEs which describe the evolution of transient probability distribution over time (Chapman-Kolmogorov equations):

$$\frac{d\boldsymbol{\pi}(t)}{dt} = \boldsymbol{\pi}(t)\mathbf{Q}(t), \qquad \sum_{i=1}^{n} \pi_i(t_0) = 1, \tag{9}$$

where $\boldsymbol{\pi}(t_0)$ is the initial condition. From the literature (see [17, pages 594–631]) it is known that the solution $\boldsymbol{\pi}(t)$ of (9), written as:

$$\boldsymbol{\pi}(t) = \boldsymbol{\pi}(t_0)\mathbf{\Phi}(t, t_0) \tag{10}$$

has the transition probability matrix given by the Peano-Baker series:

$$\mathbf{\Phi}(t, t_0) = \mathbf{I} + \int_{t_0}^{t} \mathbf{Q}(\tau_1)d\tau_1 + \int_{t_0}^{t} \mathbf{Q}(\tau_1) \int_{t_0}^{\tau_1} \mathbf{Q}(\tau_2)d\tau_2 d\tau_1 + \ldots. \tag{11}$$

Note that if $\mathbf{Q}(\tau_1) \int_{t_0}^{\tau_1} \mathbf{Q}(\tau_2)d\tau_2 = \int_{t_0}^{\tau_1} \mathbf{Q}(\tau_2)d\tau_2 \mathbf{Q}(\tau_1)$ then $\mathbf{\Phi}(t, t_0) = e^{\int_{t_0}^{t} \mathbf{Q}(\tau)d\tau}$. If the rate matrix $\mathbf{R}(t)$ is *piecewise constant* i.e., $\mathbf{R}(t) = \mathbf{R}_k$ or $\mathbf{Q}(t) = \mathbf{Q}_k$ for all $t \in [t_k, t_{k+1})$ and $k \leq M \in \mathbb{N}$ ($M+1$ is the total number of constant pieces), equation (10) can also be rewritten as (see [22]):

$$\boldsymbol{\pi}(t) = \begin{cases} \boldsymbol{\pi}(t_0)e^{\mathbf{Q}_0(t-t_0)} & \text{if } t \in [t_0, t_1) \\ \vdots & \vdots \\ \boldsymbol{\pi}(t_M)e^{\mathbf{Q}_M(t-t_M)} & \text{if } t \in [t_M, \infty) \end{cases} \quad \text{and } \boldsymbol{\pi}(t_k) = \boldsymbol{\pi}(t_{k-1})e^{\mathbf{Q}_{k-1}(t_k - t_{k-1})}.$$

The general case is when the rate matrix is *piecewise uniform* i.e., $\mathbf{R}(t) = \mathbf{R}_k(t) = f_k(t)\mathbf{R}_k$ or $\mathbf{Q}(t) = \mathbf{Q}_k(t) = f_k(t)\mathbf{Q}_k$ for any integrable function $f_k(t) : \mathbb{R}_{\geq 0} \to \mathbb{R}_{\geq 0}$ on time interval $[t_k, t_{k+1})$, constant matrices $\mathbf{R}_k$ and $\mathbf{Q}_k$.

Theorem 1. *The transient probability distribution* $\boldsymbol{\pi}(t)$ *of an* ICTMC $\mathcal{C} = (\mathbb{S}, \mathbf{R})$ *with a piecewise uniform rate matrix* $\mathbf{R}(t)$ *and* $M+1$ *pieces is given by:*

$$\boldsymbol{\pi}(t) = \begin{cases} \boldsymbol{\pi}(t_0)e^{\mathbf{Q}_0 \int_{t_0}^{t} f_0(\tau)d\tau} & \textit{if } t \in [t_0, t_1) \\ \vdots & \vdots \\ \boldsymbol{\pi}(t_M)e^{\mathbf{Q}_M \int_{t_M}^{t} f_M(\tau)d\tau} & \textit{if } t \in [t_M, \infty) \end{cases}$$

where $\boldsymbol{\pi}(t_k) = \boldsymbol{\pi}(t_{k-1})e^{\mathbf{Q}_{k-1} \int_{t_{k-1}}^{t_k} f_{k-1}(\tau)d\tau}$.

3 Inhomogeneous Interactive Markov Chains

In order to facilitate the compositional modeling of ICTMCs, we equip these processes with the capability to allow for their mutual interaction. This is established by adding actions to ICTMCs. Let *Act* be the countable universe of actions. The aim of these actions is that certain actions can only be performed together with other processes.

Definition 2 (I^2MC). *An inhomogeneous interactive Markov chain* (I^2MC) *is a tuple* $\mathcal{I} = (\mathbb{S}, Act, \rightarrow, \mathbf{R}, s^0)$ *where* $\mathbb{S}$ *and* $\mathbf{R}$ *are as before,* $\rightarrow \subseteq \mathbb{S} \times Act \times \mathbb{S}$ *is a transition relation and* $s^0 \in \mathbb{S}$ *is the initial state.*

The semantic model of I^2MC represents the time-dependent variant of IMC [14].

Process algebra for I^2MC*.* Originally developed by Hoare and Milner (see [20,16]), process algebras have been developed as a compositional framework for describing the functional behavior of the system. It allows for modeling complex systems in a component-wise manner by offering a set of *operators* to combine component models. Actions are the most elementary notions. The combination of several actions using the operators forms a *process*. We extend this framework by stochastic timing facilities.

Definition 3. *Let X be a process variable, $\lambda(t) \in \mathbb{R}_{\geq 0}$ with $t \in \mathbb{R}_{\geq 0}$, $A \subseteq Act$ and $a \in Act$. The syntax of inhomogeneous interactive Markov language* (I^2ML) *for* I^2MCs *is defined as follows:*

$$P ::= 0 \mid a.P \mid \lambda(t).P \mid P+P \mid P\|_A P \mid P \setminus A \mid X.$$

Process variables are assumed to be defined by recursive equations of the form $X := P$, where P is an I^2ML term. The *null process* 0 is the deadlock process and cannot perform any action. The prefix operators are $a.P$ and $\lambda(t).P$ for actions and rates, respectively. The *choice* operator $P+Q$ chooses between processes P or Q. Process $P\|_A Q$ denotes the *parallel composition* of processes P and Q where synchronization is required only for actions in A; actions not in A are performed autonomously. The process $P \setminus A$ behaves like P except that all actions in A become unobservable to other processes; this is established by relabeling a by the distinguished action $\tau \in Act$. The operational semantics of I^2ML terms is defined by the inference rules in Table 1 where for the sake of conciseness symmetric rules are not shown.

A few remarks concerning time-prefix and choice are in order. The process $\lambda(t).P$ evolves into P within Δt time units with probability:

$$\Pr_{\lambda(t).P,P}(t, \Delta t) = \int_0^{\Delta t} \lambda(t+\tau) e^{-\int_0^{\tau} \lambda(t+\ell)d\ell} d\tau = 1 - e^{-\int_0^{\Delta t} \lambda(t+\ell)d\ell},$$

given that $\lambda(t).P$ is enabled at the global time t. The above relation can be easily proven from (6) by taking $i = \lambda(t).P$, $j = P$, $R_{i,j}(t+\tau) = \lambda(t+\tau)$ and $E_s(t+\ell) = \lambda(t+\ell)$. The process $\lambda(t).P + \mu(t).Q$ can evolve into P if the time delay generated by a stochastic process with rate $\lambda(t)$ is smaller than that generated by a different stochastic process with rate $\mu(t)$. By a symmetric argument it may evolve into Q. Therefore, from (3) it follows that the distribution of time until a choice is made is

Table 1. Inference rules for the operational semantics of I^{2}ML

$\frac{}{a.P \xrightarrow{a} P}$	$\frac{P \xrightarrow{a} P' \text{ and } Q \xrightarrow{a} Q'}{P\parallel_A Q \xrightarrow{a} P'\parallel_A Q'} (a \in A)$	$\frac{}{\lambda(t).P \xrightarrow{\lambda(t)} P}$	$\frac{P \xrightarrow{\lambda(t)} P'}{P\backslash A \xrightarrow{\lambda(t)} P'\backslash A}$
$\frac{P \xrightarrow{a} P'}{P+Q \xrightarrow{a} P'}$	$\frac{P \xrightarrow{a} P'}{P\parallel_A Q \xrightarrow{a} P'\parallel_A Q} (a \notin A)$	$\frac{P \xrightarrow{\lambda(t)} P'}{P+Q \xrightarrow{\lambda(t)} P'}$	$\frac{E[X{:=}E/X] \xrightarrow{\lambda(t)} E'}{X{:=}E \xrightarrow{\lambda(t)} E'}$
$\frac{P \xrightarrow{a} P'}{P\backslash A \xrightarrow{a} P'\backslash A} (a \notin A)$	$\frac{P \xrightarrow{a} P'}{P\backslash A \xrightarrow{\tau} P'\backslash A} (a \in A)$	$\frac{P \xrightarrow{\lambda(t)} P'}{P\parallel_A Q \xrightarrow{\lambda(t)} P'\parallel_A Q}$	$\frac{E[X{:=}E/X] \xrightarrow{a} E'}{X{:=}E \xrightarrow{a} E'}$

$\Pr\{W(t) \leq \Delta t\} = 1 - e^{-\int_0^{\Delta t} \lambda(t+\tau)+\mu(t+\tau)d\tau}$. For a choice between $|J|$ processes (J is a finite index set), the distribution of the waiting time becomes $\Pr\{W(t) \leq \Delta t\} = 1 - e^{-\int_0^{\Delta t} \sum_{i \in J} \lambda_i(t+\tau)d\tau}$. If the rates $\lambda_i(t)$ in the process $\sum_{i \in J} \lambda_i(t).P_i$ are constant ($\lambda_i(t) = \lambda_i$), then the waiting time is exponentially distributed with the sum of the rates λ_i i.e. $\Pr\{W(t) \leq \Delta t\} = 1 - e^{-\sum_{i \in J} \lambda_i \Delta t}$. This corresponds to the interpretation of choice in Markovian process algebras [15]. It is important to note that when $P_i = P$ for all $i \in J$, the process $\sum_{i \in J} \lambda_i(t).P$ will evolve into P with rate $\sum_{i \in J} \lambda_i(t)$.

Parallel composition. When considering just actions the asynchronous parallel composition has the same functionality as that from basic process calculi. On the other hand when considering stochastic delays the composition is more involved. Consider $P := \lambda(t).P'$ and $Q := \mu(t).Q'$. They can evolve into P' and Q' after a time delay governed by a distribution with rate $\lambda(t)$ and $\mu(t)$, respectively. Since the waiting time in any state is memoryless (4), we can show the way by which processes P and Q are composed (see diagram below).

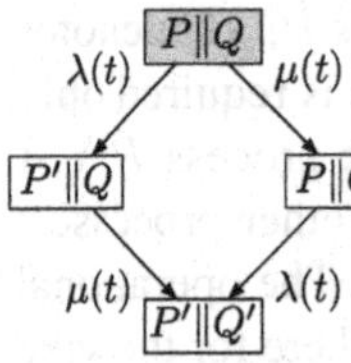

First consider that when both processes start their execution in initial state $P\|Q$ (the shadowed state) they probabilistically select a time delay, say, Δt_λ for P and Δt_μ for Q. If $\Delta t_\lambda < \Delta t_\mu$ then P finishes its execution first and evolves into P'. The same applies to Q when $\Delta t_\mu < \Delta t_\lambda$. By intuition we could think that when it is already in $P'\|Q$, $\Delta t_\lambda = 0$ and the remaining delay for process Q until it finishes its execution is $\Delta t_\mu - \Delta t_\lambda$. What really happens is that on entering state $P'\|Q$ both delays are set to zero i.e., $\Delta t_\lambda = \Delta t_\mu = 0$. As P' has no transitions, Δt_λ remains 0 but for Q its delay is initialized to a new value which might be different from $\Delta t_\mu - \Delta t_\lambda$ due to a probabilistic selection. Due to the memoryless property, however, the remaining delay for Q is fully determined by μ only.

Example 1. Consider two hardware components described by the equations $P := \lambda_1(t).0 + \lambda_2(t).use.P$ and $Q := \mu_1(t).0 + \mu_2(t).use.Q$, respectively. Each of the components may fail with rate $\lambda_1(t)$ and $\mu_1(t)$, respectively. As a result of the failure they evolve into process 0. On the other hand, the components may move to the working state with the rate $\lambda_2(t)$ and $\mu_2(t)$, respectively, where they can *use* some resources. If one of them fails then the entire system fails. Both components can use the resources at the same time if the system is working properly. Figure 1 depicts the I^{2}MC of $P\|_{\{use\}}Q$.

4 Strong and Weak Bisimulation

In order to compare the behavior of ICTMCs (and their interactive variants) we exploit the well-studied and widely accepted notion of bisimulation [3,20,14]. A classical bisimulation relation requires equivalent states to be able to mutually mimic their stepwise behavior. In the probabilistic setting this is interpreted as requiring equivalent states to have equal cumulative rates to move to any equivalence class. Bisimulation is considered as a natural notion of equivalent behavior, is equipped with quotienting algorithms, and has a clear correspondence to equivalence in terms of logical behavioral specifications. In this section, we will define strong bisimulation for I^{2}MC starting from a similar notion on ICTMCs. Some algebraic and probabilistic properties of bisimulation are investigated. The same applies to *weak* bisimulation that allows for the abstraction of internal, i.e., τ actions.

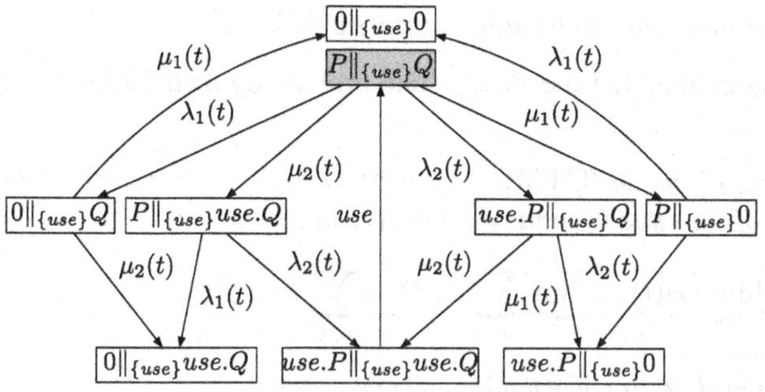

Fig. 1. $P\|_{\{use\}}Q$

Bisimulation for ICTMCs.

Definition 4 (ICTMC strong bisimulation). *An equivalence $\mathcal{R} \subseteq \mathbb{S} \times \mathbb{S}$ is a strong bisimulation whenever for all $(P, Q) \in \mathcal{R}$, $t \in \mathbb{R}_{\geq 0}$ and $C \in \mathbb{S}/\mathcal{R}$:*

$$R(P, C, t) = R(Q, C, t),$$

where $R(P, C, t) = \sum_i \{|\lambda(t)|P \overset{\lambda(t)}{\rightarrow}_i P', P' \in C|\}$. P and Q are strongly bisimilar, denoted $P \sim Q$, if (P, Q) is contained in some strong bisimulation $\mathcal{R}$.

Here, $\{|\ldots|\}$ denotes a multiset. It follows that $\sim$ is the largest strong bisimulation, i.e., it contains any strong bisimulation. To be able to compare ICTMCs by bisimulation, let us equip an ICTMC with an initial state $s^0 \in \mathbb{S}$. Two ICTMCs $\mathcal{C}_P = (\mathbb{S}_P, \mathbf{R}_P, s^0_P)$ and $\mathcal{C}_Q = (\mathbb{S}_Q, \mathbf{R}_Q, s^0_Q)$ are bisimilar, denoted $\mathcal{C}_P \sim \mathcal{C}_Q$, iff their initial states are bisimilar, i.e., $s^0_P \sim s^0_Q$. The quotient of an ICTMC under $\sim$ is defined in the following way.

Definition 5 (Bisimulation quotient). *For the* ICTMC $\mathcal{C} = (\mathbb{S}, \mathbf{R}, s^0)$ *and* $\sim$, *the quotient $\mathcal{C}/\sim$ is defined by $\mathcal{C}/\sim = (\mathbb{S}/\sim, \mathbf{R}_\sim, s^0_\sim)$ where $s^0_\sim = [s^0]_\sim$ and $\mathbf{R}_\sim$ is defined by: $R_\sim([P]_\sim, [P']_\sim, t) = R(P, [P']_\sim, t)$* for all $t \in \mathbb{R}_{\geq 0}$.

Note that $\mathcal{C}$ is strongly bisimilar to $\mathcal{C}/\sim$. An important property of strong bisimulation is that it preserves transient probabilities; in particular, this means that there is a strong relationship between the transient probabilities in an ICTMC and its quotient.

Theorem 2. *Let $\mathcal{C} = (\mathbb{S}, \mathbf{R}, s^0)$ be an* ICTMC. *For every $C \in \mathbb{S}/\!\sim$, the transient probability distribution $\pi_C(t)$ of the state C in the quotient chain $\mathcal{C}/\!\sim$ is:*

$$\pi_C(t) = \sum_{s \in C} \pi_s(t) \quad \text{for all } t \in \mathbb{R}_{\geq 0},$$

where $\pi_s(t)$ is the transient probability distribution of state $s \in \mathbb{S}$ in $\mathcal{C}$.

From Theorem 2 we may conclude that the steady state probability distribution (if it exists) is also preserved.

Corollary 1. *Let $\mathcal{C} = (\mathbb{S}, \mathbf{R}, s^0)$ be an* ICTMC. *For every $C \in \mathbb{S}/\!\sim$, the steady-state probability distribution π_C of the state C in the quotient chain $\mathcal{C}/\!\sim$ is:*

$$\pi_C = \lim_{t \to \infty} \pi_C(t) = \lim_{t \to \infty} \sum_{s \in C} \pi_s(t) = \sum_{s \in C} \pi_s,$$

where π_s is the steady-state probability distribution of state $s \in \mathbb{S}$.

In many cases it is reasonable to assume that two processes P and Q are equal up to time T. For this case we propose the *finite-horizon bisimulation.*

Definition 6. *An equivalence $\mathcal{R} \subseteq \mathbb{S} \times \mathbb{S}$ is a finite-horizon bisimulation whenever for all $(P, Q) \in \mathcal{R}$, $t \in [0, T]$ $(T \in \mathbb{R}_{\geq 0})$ and $C \in \mathbb{S}/\mathcal{R}$: $R(P, C, t) = R(Q, C, t)$. P and Q are finitely-horizon bisimilar, denoted $P \sim^T Q$, if (P, Q) is contained in some finite-horizon bisimulation $\mathcal{R}$.*

Notice that the definition of finite-horizon bisimulation $\sim^T$ is the same except that the time t lies in the interval $[0, T]$. It is easy to see that finite-horizon bisimulation preserves the transient distribution up to time T.

Proposition 1. *For $0 < \cdots < T < \cdots < \infty$ it holds: $\sim^0 \subseteq \cdots \subseteq \sim^T \cdots \subseteq \sim$.*

Thus , $P \sim^{t_i} Q$ implies $P \sim^{t_j} Q$ for every $t_j < t_i$. It follows that for $t_j < t_i$, the quotient under $\sim^{t_j}$ is coarser than under $\sim^{t_i}$.

Bisimulation for I²MCs. So far, we have presented bisimulation for ICTMCs. In order to define bisimulation for I²MCs, unobservable actions (i.e., τ) require special care. Consider four states such that $P_1 \sim P_2 \sim Q_1 \sim Q_2$ (see diagram below).

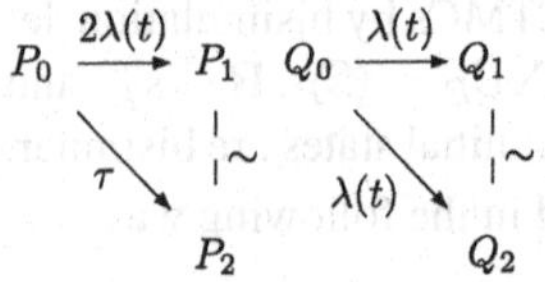

At first sight, it seems natural that $P_0 \sim Q_0$ as $R(P_0, C, t) = R(Q_0, C, t) = 2\lambda(t)$. But, state P_0 can do something more. There is a transition $P_0 \xrightarrow{\tau} P_2$ which consumes no time since a τ-action is an internal one and is not prevented by the environment (maximal progress assumption). The probability that transition $P_0 \xrightarrow{2\lambda(t)} P_1$ will be taken in 0 time units is $\Pr_{P_0,P_1}(t, 0) = \int_0^0 2\lambda(t + \tau) e^{-\int_0^\tau 2\lambda(t+\ell)d\ell} d\tau = 0$. Thus, we may conclude that $P_0 \not\sim Q_0$. When specifying the definition of bisimilarity we have to treat immediate actions (τ) in a special way. Let $\mathbb{S}$ be the state-space of an I²MC.

Definition 7 (I²MC strong bisimulation). *An equivalence $\mathcal{R} \subseteq \mathbb{S} \times \mathbb{S}$ is a strong bisimulation whenever for all $(P, Q) \in \mathcal{R}$, $t \in \mathbb{R}_{\geq 0}$, $a \in Act$ and $C \in \mathbb{S}/\mathcal{R}$:*

Table 2. Sound and complete axioms for $\sim$ on the I^{2}ML sequential fragment

$P + 0 = P$	$a.P + a.P = a.P$	$(P + Q) + R = P + (Q + R)$
$P + Q = Q + P$	$\lambda(t).P + \tau.Q = \tau.Q$	$\lambda(t).P + \mu(t).P = (\lambda(t) + \mu(t)).P$

- $P \xrightarrow{a} P'$ *implies* $Q \xrightarrow{a} Q'$ *for some* Q' *and* $(P', Q') \in \mathcal{R}$.
- $Q \xrightarrow{a} Q'$ *implies* $P \xrightarrow{a} P'$ *for some* P' *and* $(P', Q') \in \mathcal{R}$.
- $P \stackrel{\tau}{\not\rightarrow}$ *(or* $Q \stackrel{\tau}{\not\rightarrow}$*) implies* $R(P, C, t) = R(Q, C, t)$.

P and Q are strongly bisimilar, denoted $P \sim Q$*, if* (P, Q) *is contained in some strong bisimulation* $\mathcal{R}$.

Example 2. Consider the I^{2}MC from Fig. 1 (c) and $\lambda_1(t) = \mu_1(t)$, $\lambda_2(t) = \mu_2(t)$. Its quotient under bisimulation is depicted in Fig. 2. The equivalence classes C_1, C_2 and C_3 contain the following states $C_1 = \{0\|_{\{use\}}Q, P\|_{\{use\}}0\}$, $C_2 = \{P\|_{\{use\}}use.Q, use.P\|_{\{use\}}Q\}$ and $C_3 = \{0\|_{\{use\}}use.Q, use.P\|_{\{use\}}0, 0\|_{\{use\}}0\}$.

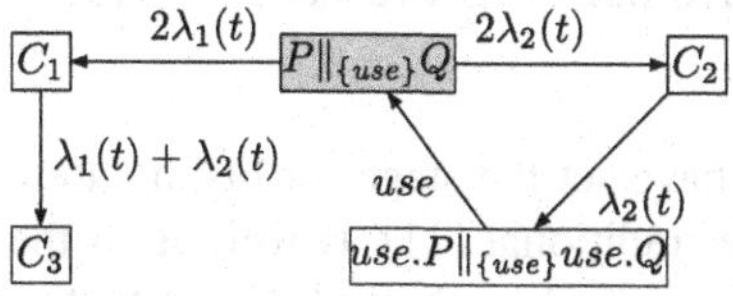

Fig. 2. Bisimulation quotient

In a similar way as for ICTMCs, one can consider the quotient of an I^{2}MC. The compositional nature of I^{2}MC, however, allows in principle for obtaining such quotient in a component-wise manner, e.g., the quotient of $P\|_A Q$ can be obtained by first constructing the quotients of P and Q, then combine them, and quotienting the composition. The necessary requirement that $\sim$ needs to fulfill is that it is a *congruence* relation. The relation $\sim$ is a congruence whenever for processes P and Q it holds: $P \sim Q$ implies $\mathbf{C}[P] \sim \mathbf{C}[Q]$ where $\mathbf{C}[\cdot]$ is any context. (A context is basically a process term containing a hole that may be filled with any process.)

Theorem 3. $\sim$ *is a congruence with respect to all operators in* I^{2}ML.

Finite-horizon bisimulation is a congruence with one additional property.

Proposition 2. *For any processes* P, P', Q, Q' *and intervals* $[0, T_1]$ *and* $[0, T_2]$ *with* $T_1, T_2 \in \mathbb{R}_{\geq 0}$ *we have:*

$$P \sim^{T_1} P' \text{ and } Q \sim^{T_2} Q' \text{ implies } P\|_A Q \sim^{min(T_1,T_2)} P'\|_A Q' \text{ for all } A \subseteq Act.$$

As a next step, we consider the possibility to establish bisimulation symbolically, i.e., on the level of the syntax of the earlier introduced language I^{2}ML. This is facilitated by an axiomatization for $\sim$. The soundness of these axioms ensures that any two terms that are syntactically equal (denoted =) are bisimilar; formally, $P = Q \Rightarrow P \sim Q$. Whenever the axioms are complete, in addition, any strongly bisimilar processes can be represented by the same expressions in I^{2}ML, i.e., $P \sim Q \Rightarrow P = Q$. Summarizing, any bisimulation can be established syntactically, i.e., by just manipulating terms rather than I^{2}MCs, provided the axiom system is sound and complete. Let $\mathcal{A}_\sim$ be the set of axioms listed in Table 2 extended with the expansion law:

$$P\|_A Q = \sum_{i\in J_1} \lambda_i(t).\,(P_i\|_A Q) + \sum_{k\in J_3} \mu_k(t).\,(P\|_A Q_k) + \sum_{a_j=b_l\in A} a_j.\,(P_j\|_A Q_l) +$$
$$+ \sum_{a_j\notin A\wedge a_j\in J_2} a_j.\,(P_j\|_A Q) + \sum_{b_l\notin A\wedge b_l\in J_4} b_l.\,(P\|_A Q_l)$$

where $P := \sum_{i\in J_1} \lambda_i(t).P_i + \sum_{j\in J_2} a_j.P_j$ and $Q := \sum_{k\in J_3} \mu_k(t).Q_k + \sum_{l\in J_4} b_l.Q_l$ with the finite index sets J_1, J_2, J_3 and J_4. Then the following holds:

Theorem 4. *For any $P, Q \in \mathbf{RG}$, $\mathcal{A}_\sim \vdash P = Q$ if and only if $P \sim Q$.*

The term $\mathbf{RG}$ denotes the set of all *regular* (no parallel composition inside recursion) and *guarded* (by actions or rates) expressions. While $\mathcal{A}_\sim \vdash P = Q$ means that $P = Q$ can be deduced from the set of sound and complete axiom system $\mathcal{A}_\sim$. The axiom $\lambda(t).P + \mu(t).P = (\lambda(t) + \mu(t)).P$ is due to the fact that the sum of two Poisson processes with rates $\lambda(t)$ and $\mu(t)$ is a Poisson process with the rate $\lambda(t)+\mu(t)$, whereas the axiom $\lambda(t).P + \tau.Q = \tau.Q$ is due to the maximal progress assumption. Notice that $\mathcal{A}_\sim$ also contains all standard axioms which involve hiding and recursion operators which are standard and omitted here.

Bisimulation minimization. The previous sections have set the stage for bisimulation minimization. Experiments have shown that in the traditional [11] as well as in the stochastic setting [19] exponential state space savings can be achieved. Given that $\sim$ is a congruence, individual processes can be replaced by their bisimilar quotient (under $\sim$) and the peak memory requirements can be reduced significantly. This all, however, requires an efficient bisimulation minimization algorithm. We adopt the *partition-refinement* paradigm to obtain a minimization algorithm for I^{2}MCs. As the problem for arbitrary rate functions is undecidable, we restrict to three classes of rate matrices $\mathbf{R}(t)$: piecewise uniform, polynomial ($\mathbf{R}(t) = t^{M+1}\mathbf{R}_{M+1} + \cdots + t\mathbf{R}_2 + \mathbf{R}_1$, where $\mathbf{R}_i$ with $i \leq M+1 \in \mathbb{N}$ are constant matrices) and piecewise polynomial (each piece is a polynomial of degree three). The same classes have been considered for the transient probability distribution, cf. Theorem 1. Rate comparisons and summations can easily be realized for these classes of functions. For rate matrix $\mathbf{R}$, let $M + 1$ denote the total number of intervals for piecewise uniform $\mathbf{R}(t)$, the polynomial degree when $\mathbf{R}(t)$ is polynomial, and the number of polynomial pieces when $\mathbf{R}(t)$ is piecewise polynomial.

Our bisimulation minimization algorithm for I^{2}MCs is based on a generalization of the algorithm for obtaining the coarsest quotient of a Markov chain under bisimulation by Derisavi *et al.* [7], and Paige-Tarjan's algorithm for LTS. The basic idea is to minimize iteratively over all pieces (or degrees of the polynomials). The bisimulation algorithm exploits an efficient data structure which groups all states with the same outgoing rate. This is in fact a binary tree where each *node* has four parameters: *node.left* and *node.right* - pointers to the left and right child, respectively, *node.sum* - stores the sum of the rates and *node.S* - stores all states with the same *node.sum*. Using such data structures, the time- and space complexity of bisimulation minimization for I^{2}MCs reduces to:

Theorem 5. *The coarsest quotient under $\sim$ of any I^{2}MC can be obtained in a worst-case time complexity $\mathcal{O}(m_a \lg(n) + M m_r \lg(n))$ and space complexity $\mathcal{O}(m_a + m_r)$, where m_a and m_r is the number of action-labeled and rate-labeled transitions, respectively.*

Recall that ICTMCs are I^{2}MCs that contain no action-labeled transitions. As a side result, the above theorem yields that the coarsest bisimulation quotient of a time-inhomogeneous CTMC can be obtained with time and space complexity $\mathcal{O}(M m_r \lg(n))$ and $\mathcal{O}(m_r)$, respectively. (The time complexity for homogeneous Markov chains is $\mathcal{O}(m_r \lg(n))$ [7]). Given the results in this paper that $\sim$ preserves transient and steady state distributions, our algorithm can be used to minimize prior to any such analysis.

Weak bisimulation for I^{2}MCs. Strong bisimulation requires equivalent states to simulate their mutual stepwise behavior. While preserving the branching structure, strong bisimulation also requires mimicking of immediate actions (τ). As immediate actions consume no time it seems reasonable that two states will be equivalent regardless of the number of τ-steps in a sequence that they make. Therefore, the equivalence which will allow for the abstraction of sequences of immediate actions will be denoted as *weak bisimulation*. Let the transition $\stackrel{\tau}{\Longrightarrow}$ be the reflexive and transitive closure of $\stackrel{\tau}{\longrightarrow}^*$ and $\stackrel{a}{\Longrightarrow}$ a shorthand for $\stackrel{\tau}{\Longrightarrow}\stackrel{a}{\longrightarrow}\stackrel{\tau}{\Longrightarrow}$ $(a \neq \tau)$.

Definition 8 (I^{2}MC weak bisimulation). *An equivalence $\mathcal{R} \subseteq \mathbb{S} \times \mathbb{S}$ is a weak bisimulation whenever for all $(P, Q) \in \mathcal{R}$, $t \in \mathbb{R}_{\geq 0}$, $a \in Act$ and $C \in \mathbb{S}/\mathcal{R}$:*

- *$P \stackrel{a}{\longrightarrow} P'$ implies $Q \stackrel{a}{\Longrightarrow} Q'$ for some Q' and $(P', Q') \in \mathcal{R}$.*
- *$P \stackrel{\tau}{\not\rightarrow}$ implies $R(P, C, t) = R(Q'', C, t)$ for some $Q'' \stackrel{\tau}{\not\rightarrow}$ such that $Q \stackrel{\tau}{\Longrightarrow} Q''$ and $(P, Q'') \in \mathcal{R}$.*

For Q symmetric rules apply. P and Q are weakly bisimilar, denoted $P \approx Q$, if (P, Q) is contained in some weak bisimulation $\mathcal{R}$.

It seems intuitive that for the sequence $Q \stackrel{\tau}{\Longrightarrow} Q''$ the rates $R(P, C, t)$ and $R(Q'', C, t)$ have to be compared starting from time $t' = t + \Delta t$ where Δt is the time needed to make all τ in the sequence $Q \stackrel{\tau}{\Longrightarrow} Q''$. As τ transitions take no time the result will be the same even when the rates are compared from time t.

Example 3. Consider the I^{2}MC from Fig. 2 and its abstraction i.e. all actions are transformed into immediate ones (τ). The quotient under $\approx$ is depicted in Fig. 3, with C_1, C_2 and C_3 as in Fig. 2 and $C_0 = \{P\|_{\{use\}}Q,\ use.P\|_{\{use\}}use.Q\}$. It is important to note that after abstraction the transition labeled with use results in an immediate transition which gives the possibility to put the states $P\|_{\{use\}}Q$ and $use.P\|_{\{use\}}use.Q$ in the same equivalence class. Also note that the obtained I^{2}MC has no transitions labeled with actions, i.e., it is an ICTMC. This shows that weak bisimulation may be an effective mechanism to turn an I^{2}MC into an ICTMC, which may be subject to analysis as discussed in Section 2.

Table 3. Sound and complete axioms for $\underline{\approx}$ on the I^{2}ML sequential fragment

$a.\tau.P = a.P$	$P + \tau.P = \tau.P$	$\lambda(t).\tau.P = \lambda(t).P$	$a.(P + \tau.Q) + a.Q = a.(P + \tau.Q)$

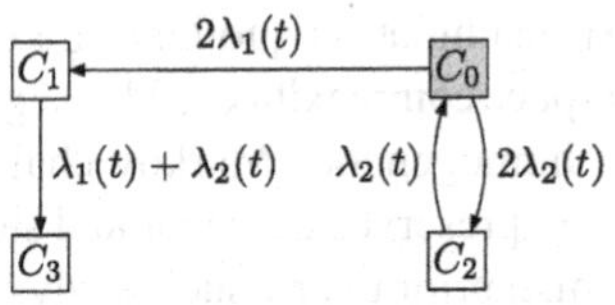

Fig. 3. Weak bisimulation quotient

As in the case of strong bisimulation, weak bisimulation is also a congruence with respect to I^{2}ML operators. But there is an exception. Weak bisimulation is not a congruence with respect to the choice $(P + Q)$ operator [20]. This is due to the fact that weak bisimulation will equate two processes whenever one can do $\stackrel{\tau}{\Longrightarrow}$ and the other one can do nothing. In order to cope with the choice operator one has to differentiate between $\stackrel{a}{\Longrightarrow}$ and $\stackrel{\tau}{\Longrightarrow}\stackrel{a}{\longrightarrow}\stackrel{\tau}{\Longrightarrow}$ when $a = \tau$ as follows:

Definition 9 (Weak congruence). *Pand Q are weakly congruent, denoted by $P \underline{\approx} Q$, whenever for all $a \in Act$, $t \in \mathbb{R}_{\geq 0}$ and $C \in \mathbf{RG}/\approx$:*

- *$P \stackrel{a}{\longrightarrow} P'$ implies $Q \stackrel{\tau}{\Longrightarrow}\stackrel{a}{\longrightarrow}\stackrel{\tau}{\Longrightarrow} Q'$ for some Q' and $P' \approx Q'$.*
- *$Q \stackrel{a}{\longrightarrow} Q'$ implies $P \stackrel{\tau}{\Longrightarrow}\stackrel{a}{\longrightarrow}\stackrel{\tau}{\Longrightarrow} P'$ for some P' and $P' \approx Q'$.*
- *$P \stackrel{\tau}{\not\rightarrow}$ (or $Q \stackrel{\tau}{\not\rightarrow}$) implies $R(P, C, t) = R(Q, C, t)$.*

Theorem 6. *$\underline{\approx}$ is a congruence with respect to all operators in* I^{2}ML.

Consider the set of axioms from Table 2 and 3 together with axioms related to hiding and recursion operators as $\mathcal{A}_{\underline{\approx}}$. As for strong bisimulation the following also holds for weak congruence:

Theorem 7. *For any $P, Q \in \mathbf{RG}$, $\mathcal{A}_{\underline{\approx}} \vdash P = Q$ if and only if $P \underline{\approx} Q$.*

Recall that P and Q are regular and guarded process terms.

5 Concluding Remarks and Future Work

This paper presented a compositional formalism for time-inhomogeneous continuous-time Markov chains (ICTMCs), a subclass of piecewise deterministic Markov processes (PDPs). The main contributions are a full-fledged process algebra for interactive ICTMCs, congruence results for weak and strong bisimulation, and a polynomial-time quotienting algorithm. In addition, a new characterization of transient probabilities is provided for rate functions that are piecewise uniform. In contrast to works on communicating PDPs [24,23,25], this paper considers weak bisimulation, congruence results and axiomatization, and, more importantly a notion of bisimulation which respects maximal progress. Current work consists of investigating improvements to the quotienting algorithm akin to [8], model-checking algorithms [18], and simulation relations for ICTMCs.

Acknowledgment. This research has been performed as part of QUPES project that is financed by the Netherlands Organization for Scientific Research (NWO).

References

1. Alur, R., Grosu, R., Hur, Y., Kumar, V., Lee, I.: Modular specification of hybrid systems in CHARON. In: Lynch, N.A., Krogh, B.H. (eds.) HSCC 2000. LNCS, vol. 1790, pp. 6–19. Springer, Heidelberg (2000)
2. Alur, R., Grosu, R., Sokolsky, O., Lee, I.: Compositional modeling and refinement for hierarchical hybrid systems. J. Log. Algebr. Program. 68(1-2), 105–128 (2006)
3. Buchholz, P.: Exact and ordinary lumpability in finite Markov chains. J. of Applied Probability 31, 59–75 (1994)
4. Bujorianu, M.L., Lygeros, J., Bujorianu, M.C.: Bisimulation for general stochastic hybrid systems. In: Morari, M., Thiele, L. (eds.) HSCC 2005. LNCS, vol. 3414, pp. 198–214. Springer, Heidelberg (2005)
5. Cloth, L., Haverkort, B.R., Jongerden, M.: Computing battery lifetime distributions. In: DSN, pp. 780–789. IEEE Computer Society Press, Los Alamitos (2007)
6. Davis, M.H.A.: Markov Models and Optimization. Chapman and Hall, Boca Raton (1993)
7. Derisavi, S., Hermanns, H., Sanders, W.H.: Optimal state-space lumping in Markov chains. Inf. Processing Letters 87(6), 309–315 (2003)
8. Dovier, A., Piazza, C., Policriti, A.: An efficient algorithm for computing bisimulation equivalence. Theor. Comput. Sci. 311(1-3), 221–256 (2004)
9. Everdij, M., Blom, H.: Piecewise deterministic Markov processes represented by dynamically coloured Petri nets. Stochastics 77(1), 1–29 (2005)
10. Fernandez, J.C.: An implementation of an efficient algorithm for bisimulation equivalence. Science of Computer Programming 13, 219–236 (1989)
11. Fisler, K., Vardi, M.Y.: Bisimulation minimization in an automata-theoretic verification framework. In: Gopalakrishnan, G.C., Windley, P. (eds.) FMCAD 1998. LNCS, vol. 1522, pp. 115–132. Springer, Heidelberg (1998)
12. Haghverdi, E., Tabuada, P., Pappas, G.J.: Bisimulation relations for dynamical, control, and hybrid systems. Theor. Comput. Sci. 342(2-3), 229–261 (2005)
13. Han, T., Katoen, J.-P., Mereacre, A.: Compositional Modeling and Minimization of Time-Inhomogeneous Markov Chains. Technical report AIB200721, RWTH Aachen, Germany (2007)
14. Hermanns, H.: Interactive Markov Chains. LNCS, vol. 2428. Springer, Heidelberg (2002)
15. Hermanns, H., Herzog, U., Katoen, J.-P.: Process algebra for performance evaluation. Theor. Comput. Sci. 274(1-2), 43–87 (2002)
16. Hoare, C.A.R.: Communicating Sequential Processes. Prentice-Hall, Englewood Cliffs (1985)
17. Kailath, T.: Linear Systems. Prentice-Hall, Englewood Cliffs (1980)
18. Katoen, J.-P.: Stochastic model checking. In: Stochastic Hybrid Systems, pp. 79–106. CRC Press, Boca Raton (2006)
19. Katoen, J.-P., Kemna, T., Zapreev, I.S., Jansen, D.N.: Bisimulation minimisation mostly speeds up probabilistic model checking. In: Grumberg, O., Huth, M. (eds.) TACAS 2007. LNCS, vol. 4424, pp. 76–92. Springer, Heidelberg (2007)
20. Milner, R.J.: Communication and Concurrency. Prentice-Hall, Englewood Cliffs (1989)
21. Paige, R., Tarjan, R.: Three partition refinement algorithms. SIAM J. of Computing 16(6), 973–989 (1987)

22. Rindos, A., Woolet, S., Viniotis, I., Trivedi, K.S.: Exact methods for the transient analysis of non-homogeneous continuous-time Markov chains. In: Numerical Solution of Markov Chains (NSMC), pp. 121–134. Kluwer, Dordrecht (1995)
23. Strubbe, S.N., Julius, A.A., van der Schaft, A.J.: Communicating piecewise deterministic Markov processes. In: ADHS, pp. 349–354 (2003)
24. Strubbe, S.N., van der Schaft, A.J.: Compositional modelling of stochastic hybrid systems. In: Stochastic Hybrid Systems, pp. 47–77. CRC Press, Boca Raton (2006)
25. Strubbe, S.N., van der Schaft, A.J.: Bisimulation for communicating piecewise deterministic Markov processes (CPDPs). In: Morari, M., Thiele, L. (eds.) HSCC 2005. LNCS, vol. 3414, pp. 623–639. Springer, Heidelberg (2005)

Observer-Based Control of Linear Complementarity Systems

W.P.M.H. Heemels[1], M.K. Camlibel[2], B. Brogliato[3], and J.M. Schumacher[4]

[1] Eindhoven University of Technology, P.O. Box 513, 5600 MB Eindhoven, The Netherlands
[2] University of Groningen, P.O. Box 800, 9700 AV Groningen, The Netherlands
[3] INRIA, ZIRST Montbonnot, 655 avenue de l'Europe, 38334 Saint Ismier, France
[4] Tilburg University, P.O. Box 90153, 5000 LE Tilburg, The Netherlands

Abstract. In this paper, we will present observer and output-based controller design methods for linear complementarity systems (LCS) employing a passivity approach. Given various inherent properties of LCS, such as the presence of state jumps, mode dynamics described by DAEs, and regions ("invariants") for certain modes being lower dimensional, several proposed observers and controllers for other classes of hybrid dynamical systems do not apply. We will provide sufficient conditions for the observer design for a LCS, which is effective also in the presence of state jumps. Using the certainty equivalence approach we obtain output-based controllers for which we will derive a separation principle.

1 Introduction

Complementarity systems form a class of hybrid dynamical systems that received considerable attention in recent years [1,2,3,4,5,6,7,8,9,10]. The linear complementarity system LCS(A, B, C, D, E, F) is given by

$$\dot{x}(t) = Ax(t) + Bw(t) + Eu(t) \tag{1a}$$
$$z(t) = Cx(t) + Dw(t) + Fu(t) \tag{1b}$$
$$0 \leq z(t) \perp w(t) \geq 0, \tag{1c}$$

where the inequalities are interpreted componentwise and $\perp$ indicates the orthogonality between the vectors $z(t)$ and $w(t)$, i.e, $z^\top(t)w(t) = 0$. The complementarity conditions (1c) constitute a particular set of equalities and inequalities, which are related to the well-known relations between the constraint variables and Lagrange multipliers in the Karush-Kuhn-Tucker conditions for optimality, the voltage-current relationship of ideal diodes, the conditions between unilateral constraints and reaction forces in constrained mechanics, etc. As such, the complementarity framework includes mechanical systems with unilateral constraints, constrained optimal control problems, switched electrical circuits, etc.

Although LCS has its own peculiarities, it has connections to other classes of hybrid systems. Indeed, observe that (1c) implies that $w_i(t) = 0$ or $z_i(t) = 0$ for all $i \in \bar{m} := \{1, \ldots, m\}$. As a consequence, the system (1) has 2^m modes. Each mode can be characterized by the active index set $J \subseteq \bar{m}$, which indicates

M. Egerstedt and B. Mishra (Eds.): HSCC 2008, LNCS 4981, pp. 259–272, 2008.

$z_i = 0$, $i \in J$, and $w_i = 0$, $i \in J^c$, where $J^c := \{i \in \bar{m} \mid i \notin J\}$. For mode J the dynamics is given by the linear differential and algebraic equations (DAEs)

$$\dot{x}(t) = Ax(t) + Bw(t) + Eu(t), \tag{2a}$$

$$z(t) = Cx(t) + Dw(t) + Fu(t), \tag{2b}$$

$$z_i(t) = 0,\ i \in J, \ \text{ and } \ w_i(t) = 0,\ i \in J^c, \tag{2c}$$

The evolution of system (1) will be governed by (2) for mode J as long as the remaining inequalities ("the invariant" in the terminology of hybrid automata [11,12,13]) in (1c)

$$z_i(t) \geq 0,\ i \in J^c \text{ and } w_i(t) \geq 0,\ i \in J \tag{3}$$

are satisfied. Impending violation of (3) will trigger a mode change. As a consequence, during the evolution in time of the system several mode dynamics will be active successively. This indicates that LCS might be recast within the hybrid automaton framework [11,12,13]. However, with exception only of the very simplest cases, the reformulation of LCS dynamics into the hybrid automaton framework leads to voluminous and opaque system descriptions. This effect is already evident in the example worked out in [14], which concerns an electrical circuit with two diodes. Alternatively one can rewrite LCS in the formulation $\dot{x} \in F(x)$ for $x \in C$ and $x^+ \in G(x)$ for $x \in D$, as used for instance in [15]. Again, the transformation is in general cumbersome, and the resulting system data F, G, C and D do generally not satisfy the assumptions adopted in [15] (cf. the example below). Structural properties become harder to study and compactness of descriptions is lost when LCS are translated to such generic frameworks.

To show further links between LCS and other (sub)classes of hybrid dynamical systems, let us consider an LCS with one complementarity pair and $F = 0$:

$$\dot{x} = Ax + bw + eu; \quad z = c^\top x + dw; \quad 0 \leq z \perp w \geq 0 \tag{4}$$

where $A \in \mathbb{R}^{n \times n}$, $b \in \mathbb{R}^{n \times 1}$, $c \in \mathbb{R}^{n \times 1}$, $d \in \mathbb{R}$, and $0 \neq e \in \mathbb{R}^{n \times 1}$. As either $z = 0$ or $w = 0$, this system has two modes. When $d > 0$, one can rewrite (4) as

$$\dot{x} = \begin{cases} Ax + eu & \text{if } c^\top x \geq 0, \\ (A - bd^{-1}c^\top)x + eu & \text{if } c^\top x \leq 0, \end{cases} \tag{5}$$

which is a piecewise linear (PWL) system [16]. When $d = 0$ and $c^\top b > 0$, we have

$$\dot{x} = \begin{cases} Ax + eu & \text{if } (c^\top x > 0) \text{ or } (c^\top x = 0 \text{ and } c^\top Ax + c^\top eu \geq 0), \\ P(Ax + eu) & \text{if } c^\top x = 0 \text{ and } c^\top Ax + c^\top eu < 0. \end{cases} \tag{6}$$

where $P = I - b(c^\top b)^{-1}c^\top$. In this case one has also a bimodal PWL system, but the second subsystem 'lives' on a lower dimensional subspace given by $c^\top x = 0$, which is a situation hardly studied within the realm of PWL systems. Note also that for $c^\top x < 0$, there is no smooth evolution possible and state jumps will occur. In this situation, LCS can also be considered as differential inclusions (DIs) with normal cones as their set values (see e.g. [7]). These DIs do in general not satisfy the boundedness conditions of its values nor the upper semicontinuity properties as often used within the context of DIs. In the case when $d = c^\top b = 0$, $c^\top ab > 0$ and $e = 0$ (no external inputs) the flow set, i.e. the set of states from which the system can continue with a smooth solution temporarily [15], is given by all x_0 such that $(c^\top x_0, c^\top A x_0) \succeq 0$ (see [2, Thm. 6.8]), where $\succeq$ denotes the lexicographic ordering. This indicates that the flow set has no simple closedness properties. This indicates that although LCS have connections to PWL systems and other classes of hybrid systems, they also have their own peculiarities. For instance, the presence of state jumps (think of impacts in constrained mechanical systems) in continuous-time LCS, differentiates them from much of the work done for continuous-time PWL systems. Although for discrete-time LCS strong equivalence links have been established in [17] with piecewise affine systems [16] and other classes of hybrid models such as min-max-plus-scaling systems [18] and mixed logic dynamic systems [19], in the continuous-time framework, which is the natural habitat for most of the LCS applications, such broad equivalence relations are out of the question. There are relations though of LCS to other specific classes of nonsmooth systems such as the mentioned "normal cone DIs" and projected dynamical systems [7,8].

The attention that LCS received recently is not surprising given the broad range of interesting applications. The research [1, 2, 3, 4, 5, 6, 7, 8, 9, 10] focussed on several fundamental system-theoretic issues like well-posedness, discretization (simulation), controllability, observability, stabilizability and stability. In this paper the emphasis will be on observer-based controller design, a topic that is hardly touched upon for LCS. We will adopt a "certainty equivalence control" approach, where one designs output feedback controllers that generate the control input via a state feedback law using an estimate of the state, which is obtained from an observer. For linear systems, the separation principle gives a formal justification of this approach. Due to the absence of a general controller-observer separation principle for nonlinear systems and certainly hybrid systems, the observer-based controller may not result in a stable closed-loop system.

Several interesting papers are available on observer design for hybrid systems, especially in the context of switched and piecewise linear systems, e.g. [20, 21, 22, 23, 24]. Unfortunately, these results do not apply to LCS as LCS typically exhibit lower dimensional regions and state jumps. Observer and observer-based controller design methods for Lur'e type systems as studied in [25, 26, 27, 28] are also related to LCS. Indeed, one can consider LCS as a kind of Lur'e type systems in which the linear system (1a)-(1b) is interconnected with the *non-smooth* and *unbounded* complementarity relations in (1c). Typically, the results in [25,26,27,28] study *locally Lipschitz* slope restricted nonlinearities in the feedback path. As such their conditions do not allow for the non-smoothness and set-valued nonlinearities (and even state jumps) as induced by the complementarity relations. Observer designs for differential inclusions with *bounded* set-values are treated in [29]. Since complementarity conditions are unbounded, [29] does not cover LCS.In summary, although there are various interesting approaches for hybrid observer design, none of them includes (all) the peculiarities of LCS.

Before focussing on controller and observer design for LCS, we will explain the solution concepts for LCS and also extend available well-posedness (existence and uniqueness of solutions) results for LCS to include external inputs. This will result in global existence results thereby excluding the Zeno phenomenon of livelock (an infinite number of discrete actions on one time instant) and providing continuations beyond accumulation points of mode switching times. Next, we will present passivity conditions for state feedback design and observer design for LCS. Interestingly, this means that we will present methods for observer design for systems without knowing the mode and allowing for state resets. Next we will present a separation principle for this class of hybrid dynamical systems.

2 Preliminaries

$\mathbb{R}$ denotes the real numbers, $\mathbb{R}_+ := [0, \infty)$ the nonnegative real numbers, $\mathcal{L}_2(T)$ the square integrable functions on a time-interval $T \subseteq \mathbb{R}$, and $\mathcal{B}$ the Bohl functions (i.e. functions having strictly proper rational Laplace transforms) defined on $\mathbb{R}_+$. Note that sines, cosines, exponentials, polynomials and their sums and products are all Bohl functions. The distribution $\delta_t^{(i)}$ stands for the i-th distributional derivative of the Dirac impulse supported at t. The dual cone of a set $\mathcal{Q} \subseteq \mathbb{R}^n$ is defined by $\mathcal{Q}^* = \{x \in \mathbb{R}^n | x^\top y \geq 0 \text{ for all } y \in \mathcal{Q}\}$. For a positive integer m, the set $\bar{m}$ is defined as $\{1, 2, \ldots, m\}$ and $2^{\bar{m}}$ denotes the collection of all subsets of $\bar{m}$. A vector $u \in \mathbb{R}^k$ is called nonnegative, denoted by $u \geq 0$, if $u_i \geq 0$ for all $i \in \bar{k}$. This means that inequalities for vectors are interpreted componentwise. The orthogonality $u^\top y = 0$ between two vectors $u \in \mathbb{R}^k$ and $y \in \mathbb{R}^k$ is denoted by $u \perp y$. As usual, we say that (A, B, C) (or sometimes (A, B, C, D)) is minimal, when the matrices $[B \; AB \; \ldots \; A^{n-1}B]$ and $[C^\top \; A^\top C^\top \ldots (A^\top)^{n-1}C^\top]$ have full rank. A matrix $M \in \mathbb{R}^{k \times k}$ is called positive definite (not necessarily symmetric), if $x^\top Mx > 0$ for all $x \neq 0$. It is called nonnegative definite, if $x^\top Mx \geq 0$ for all $x \in \mathbb{R}^k$. For a matrix $M \in \mathbb{R}^{k \times l}$ we denote its kernel by $\ker M := \{x \in \mathbb{R}^l \mid Mx = 0\}$ and its image by $\operatorname{im} M := \{Mx \mid x \in \mathbb{R}^l\}$. Finally, for two linear subspaces $\mathcal{V}_1$ and $\mathcal{V}_2$ we write $\mathcal{V}_1 \oplus \mathcal{V}_2 = \mathcal{V}$, if $\mathcal{V} = \mathcal{V}_1 + \mathcal{V}_2 = \{v_1 + v_2 \mid v_1 \in \mathcal{V}_1, \; v_2 \in \mathcal{V}_2\}$ and $\mathcal{V}_1 \cap \mathcal{V}_2 = \{0\}$.

2.1 Linear Complementarity Problem

We define the linear complementarity problem LCP(q, M) (see [30] for a survey) with data $q \in \mathbb{R}^k$ and $M \in \mathbb{R}^{k \times k}$ by the problem of finding $z \in \mathbb{R}^k$ such that $0 \leq z \;\perp\; q + Mz \geq 0$. The solution set of LCP(q, M) will be denoted by SOL(q, M). The notation $K(M)$ will denote the set $\{q \mid \text{LCP}(q, M) \text{ is solvable}\}$.

Let a matrix M of size $k \times k$ and two subsets I and J of $\bar{k}$ of the same cardinality be given. The (I, J)-*submatrix* of M is the submatrix $M_{IJ} := (M_{ij})_{i \in I, j \in J}$. The (I, J)-*minor* is defined as the determinant of M_{IJ}. The (I, I)-submatrices and -minors are also known as the principal submatrices and the principals minors. M is called a *P-matrix* if all its principal minors are positive. P-matrices play an important role in linear complementarity problems, as the following result is well known (cf. [30, thm. 3.3.7]).

Theorem 1. *For a given matrix $M \in \mathbb{R}^{k\times k}$, the problem LCP$(q, M)$ has a unique solution for all vectors $q \in \mathbb{R}^k$ if and only if M is a P-matrix.*

2.2 Passivity of a Linear System

We will recall the notion of passivity as it is defined in [31] for a linear system

$$\Sigma(A,B,C,D): \qquad \dot{x}(t) = Ax(t) + Bu(t); \quad y(t) = Cx(t) + Du(t). \tag{7}$$

Definition 1. *[31] The system $\Sigma(A,B,C,D)$ given by (7) is said to be* passive *if there exists a function $V : \mathbb{R}^n \to \mathbb{R}_+$ (called a* storage function*), such that*

$$V(x(t_0)) + \int_{t_0}^{t_1} u^\top(t)y(t)dt \geq V(x(t_1))$$

holds for all $t_1 \geq t_0$, and for all solutions $(u,x,y) \in \mathcal{L}_2^{m+n+m}(t_0,t_1)$ of (7).

Next, we quote a very well-known characterization of passivity.

Theorem 2. [31] Assume that (A,B,C) is minimal. Then the following statements are equivalent:

1. $\Sigma(A,B,C,D)$ is passive.
2. The following matrix inequalities have a solution

$$P = P^\top > 0 \text{ and } \begin{pmatrix} A^\top P + PA & PB - C^\top \\ B^\top P - C & -(D+D^\top) \end{pmatrix} \leq 0. \tag{8}$$

Moreover, $V(x) = \frac{1}{2}x^\top Px$ defines a quadratic storage function if and only if P satisfies the linear matrix inequalities (8).

Next we will define *strict passivity* of (7).

Definition 2. *$\Sigma(A,B,C,D)$ is called* strictly passive, *if there are P and $\varepsilon > 0$ with*

$$P = P^\top > 0 \textit{ and } \begin{pmatrix} A^\top P + PA + \varepsilon P & PB - C^\top \\ B^\top P - C & -(D+D^\top) \end{pmatrix} \leq 0. \tag{9}$$

The following technical assumption will be used below. Its former part is standard in the literature on dissipative systems, see e.g. [31]. Both conditions are related to removing specific kinds of redundancy in the system description.

Assumption 3. *(A,B,C) is minimal and $\begin{pmatrix} B \\ D+D^\top \end{pmatrix}$ has full column rank.*

3 Linear Complementarity Systems and Initial Solution

We now are going to study the behaviour of the LCS given in (1). Before presenting a global solution concept that incorporates the switching of modes, we will first concentrate on what we call "initial solutions," which are trajectories that satisfy the dynamics of one mode only and that satisfy the inequality conditions possibly only in their beginning. We will employ the theory of distributions in formalizing the solution concept, since the abrupt changes in the trajectories (e.g. impacts in mechanics) can be modeled adequately by Dirac impulses (see also Example 1 below). To do so, we recall the concepts of *Bohl distribution* and *initial solution* [2].

Definition 3. *We call* $\mathtt{w}$ *a* Bohl distribution, *if* $\mathtt{w} = \mathtt{w}_{imp} + \mathtt{w}_{reg}$ *with* $\mathtt{w}_{imp} = \sum_{i=0}^{l} w^{-i}\delta_0^{(i)}$ *for* $w^{-i} \in \mathbb{R}$ *and* $\mathtt{w}_{reg} \in \mathcal{B}$. *We call* $\mathtt{w}_{imp}$ *the impulsive part of* $\mathtt{w}$ *and* $\mathtt{w}_{reg}$ *the regular part of* $\mathtt{w}$. *The space of all Bohl distributions is denoted by* $\mathcal{B}_{imp}$.

Note that Bohl distributions have rational Laplace transforms. It seems natural to call a (smooth) Bohl function $w \in \mathcal{B}$ *initially nonnegative* if there exists an $\varepsilon > 0$ such that $w(t) \geq 0$ for all $t \in [0, \varepsilon)$. Note that a Bohl function w is initially nonnegative if and only if there exists a $\sigma_0 \in \mathbb{R}$ such that its Laplace transform satisfies $\hat{w}(\sigma) \geq 0$ for all $\sigma \geq \sigma_0$. Hence, there is a connection between small time values for time functions and large values for the indeterminate s in the Laplace transform. This fact is closely related to the well-known initial value theorem. The definition of initial nonnegativity for Bohl distributions will be based on this observation (see also [2]).

Definition 4. *We call a Bohl distribution* $\mathtt{w}$ initially nonnegative, *if its Laplace transform* $\hat{\mathtt{w}}(s)$ *satisfies* $\hat{\mathtt{w}}(\sigma) \geq 0$ *for all sufficiently large real* σ.

To relate the definition to the time domain, note that a scalar-valued Bohl distribution $\mathtt{w}$ without derivatives of the Dirac impulse (i.e. $\mathtt{w}_{imp} = w^0\delta$ for some $w^0 \in \mathbb{R}$) is initially nonnegative if and only if either $w^0 > 0$, or $w^0 = 0$ and there exists an $\varepsilon > 0$ such that $\mathtt{w}_{reg}(t) \geq 0$ for all $t \in [0, \varepsilon)$. With these notions we can recall the concept of an initial solution [2]. Loosely speaking, an initial solution to (1) with initial state x_0 and Bohl input $u \in \mathcal{B}^k$ is a triple $(\mathtt{w}, \mathtt{x}, \mathtt{z}) \in \mathcal{B}_{imp}^{m+n+m}$ satisfying (2) for some mode I and satisfying (3) either on a time interval of positive length or on a time instant at which Dirac distributions are active.

At this point we only allow Bohl functions (combinations of sines, cosines, exponentials and polynomials) as inputs. In the global solution concept we will allow the inputs to be concatenations of Bohl functions (i.e., piecewise Bohl), which may be discontinuous.

Definition 5. *The distribution* $(\mathtt{w}, \mathtt{x}, \mathtt{z}) \in \mathcal{B}_{imp}^{m+n+m}$ *is said to be an* initial solution *to (1) with initial state* x_0 *and input* $u \in \mathcal{B}^k$ *if*

1. $\dot{\mathtt{x}} = A\mathtt{x} + B\mathtt{w} + Eu + x_0\delta_0$ *and* $\mathtt{z} = C\mathtt{x} + D\mathtt{w} + Fu$ *as equalities of distributions.*

2. *there exists an* $J \subseteq \overline{m}$ *such that* $\mathtt{w}_i = 0$, $i \in I^c$ *and* $\mathtt{z}_i = 0$, $i \in J$ *as equalities of distributions.*
3. $\mathtt{w}$ *and* $\mathtt{z}$ *are initially nonnegative.*

The statements 1 and 2 in the definition above express that an initial solution satisfies the dynamics (2) for mode J on the time-interval $\mathbb{R}_+$ and the initial condition $x(0) = x_0$.

Example 1. Consider the system $\dot{x}(t) = w(t)$, $z(t) = x(t)$ together with (1c). This represents an electrical network consisting of a capacitor connected to a diode. The current is equal to w and the voltage across the capacitor is equal to $z = x$. For initial state $x(0) = 1$, $(\mathtt{w}, \mathtt{x}, \mathtt{z})$ with $\mathtt{w} = 0$ and $\mathtt{z}(t) = \mathtt{x}(t) = 1$ for all $t \in \mathbb{R}$ is an initial solution. This corresponds to the case that the diode is blocking and there is no (nonzero) current in the network. To show that the distributional framework is convenient, consider the initial state $x(0) = -1$, for which $(\mathtt{w}, \mathtt{x}, \mathtt{z})$ with $\mathtt{w} = \delta$, $\mathtt{x}(t) = \mathtt{z}(t) = 0$, $t > 0$ is the unique initial solution. This corresponds to an instantaneous discharge of the capacitor at time instant 0 resulting in a state jump from $x(0) = -1$ to 0 at time 0 induced by the impulse.

This circuit example indicates that there is a clear physical interpretation of the impulses in initial solutions to model the abrupt changes in trajectories of electrical circuits (see also [3, 14]). Also for mechanical systems, these initial solutions induce state jumps with a clear physical meaning (related to inelastic restitution laws) as shown in [2].

4 Initial and Local Well-Posedness

In this section, we are interested in existence and uniqueness of initial solutions, and we will provide an extension to a local well-posedness result.

Definition 6. *A rational matrix* $H(s) \in \mathbb{R}^{l \times l}(s)$ *is said to be of index* r, *if it is invertible as a rational matrix and* $s^{-r}H^{-1}(s)$ *is proper. It is said to be totally of index* r, *if all its principal submatrices* $H_{JJ}(s)$ *for* $J \subset \bar{l}$ *are of index* r.

The theorem below is an extension of a result proven in [5] that used $F = 0$.

Theorem 4. *Consider an LCS with external inputs given by* (1) *such that* $G(s) = C(sI - A)^{-1}B + D$ *is totally of index* 1 *and* $G(\sigma)$ *is a P-matrix for sufficiently large* σ. *Define* $\mathcal{Q}_D := SOL(0, D) = \{v \in \mathbb{R}^m \mid 0 \leq v \perp Dv \geq 0\}$ *and let* $K(D)$ *be the set* $\{q \in \mathbb{R}^m \mid LCP(q, D) \text{ solvable}\}$.

1. *For arbitrary initial state* $x_0 \in \mathbb{R}^n$ *and any input* $u \in \mathcal{B}^k$, *there exists exactly one initial solution, which will be denoted by* $(\mathtt{w}^{x_0,u}, \mathtt{x}^{x_0,u}, \mathtt{z}^{x_0,u})$.
2. *No initial solution contains derivatives of the Dirac distribution. Moreover,*

$$\mathtt{w}_{imp}^{x_0,u} = w^0\delta_0;\ \mathtt{x}_{imp}^{x_0,u} = 0;\ \mathtt{z}_{imp}^{x_0,u} = Dw^0\delta_0 \text{ for some } w^0 \in \mathcal{Q}_D.$$

3. *For all* $x_0 \in \mathbb{R}^n$ *and* $u \in \mathcal{B}^k$ *it holds that* $Cx_0 + Fu(0) + CBw^0 \in \mathcal{K}(D)$.

4. *The initial solution* $(\mathtt{w}^{x_0,u}, \mathtt{x}^{x_0,u}, \mathtt{z}^{x_0,u})$ *is smooth (i.e., has a zero impulsive part) if and only if* $Cx_0 + Fu(0) \in K(D)$.

The impulsive part $\mathtt{w}_{imp}^{x_0,u} = w^0\delta_0$ of the initial solution induces a state jump from x_0 to $x_0 + Bw^0$, which in circuits might correspond to infinitely large currents related to instantaneous discharges of capacitors (see Example 1) and in mechanical systems to infinite reaction forces that cause resets in the velocities of impacting bodies.

Theorem 5. *Consider an LCS with* (A, B, C, D) *is passive and Assumption 3 holds. Then* $G(s) = C(sI - A)^{-1}B + D$ *is totally of index* 1 *and both* $G(\sigma)$ *and* $D + s^{-1}CB$ *are P-matrices for sufficiently large* σ. *In this case the results of Theorem 4 hold for* (1) *with* $K(D) = \mathcal{Q}_D^*$.

For brevity we skip the proof (see e.g. [3] for the case $F = 0$.) Theorem 4 gives explicit conditions for existence and uniqueness of solutions.The second statement indicates that derivatives of Dirac distributions are absent in the behaviour of LCS of index 1. The fourth statement gives necessary and sufficient condition for an initial solution to be smooth. In particular, a LCS satisfying the conditions of Theorem 5 is "*impulse-free*" (no state jumps), if $\mathcal{Q}_D = \text{SOL}(0, D) = \{0\}$ (or, in terms of [30], if D is an R_0-matrix). Note that in this case $\mathcal{Q}_D^* = \mathbb{R}^m$. In case the matrix $[C\ F]$ has full row rank, this condition is also necessary. Other sufficient conditions, that are more easy to verify, are D being a positive definite matrix, or $\text{Ker}(D + D^\top) \cap \mathbb{R}_+^m = \{0\}$. For the general case of (not necessarily passive) systems with transfer functions totally of index 1, Theorem 4 implies that $K(D) = \mathbb{R}^m$ (in terms of [30] this means that the matrix D should be a so-called Q-matrix) is sufficient for the system being impulse-free. One condition that guarantees this is that $w^T Dw > 0$ for all $w \in \mathbb{R}_+^m$ and $w \neq 0$.

Note that the first statement in Theorem 4 by itself does not immediately guarantee the existence of a solution on a time interval with positive length. The reason is that an initial solution with a non-zero impulsive part may only be valid at the time instant on which the Dirac distribution is active. If the impulsive part of the (unique) initial solution is equal to $w^0\delta_0$, the state after re-initialization is equal to x_0+Bw^0. From this "next" initial state again an initial solution has to be determined, which might in principle also have a non-zero impulsive part, which results in another state jump. As a consequence, the occurrence of infinitely many jumps at $t = 0$ without any smooth continuation on a positive length time interval is not immediately excluded (sometimes called "livelock" in hybrid systems theory). However, Theorem 4 excludes this kind of Zeno phenomenon: if smooth continuation is not directly possible from x_0, it is possible after one re-initialization. Indeed, since $C(x_0 + Bw^0) + Fu(0) = Cx_0 + Fu(0) + CBw^0 \in K(D)$, it follows from the fourth claim that the initial solution corresponding to $x_0 + Bw^0$ and input u is smooth. This initial solution satisfies the (in)equalities in (1) on an interval of the form $(0, \varepsilon)$ with $\varepsilon > 0$ by definition and hence, we proved a local existence and uniqueness result. However, we still have to show global existence of solutions as other kinds of Zeno behaviour (accumulation of mode switching times) might prevent this.

5 Global Well-Posedness

Before we can formulate a global well-posedness theorem, we need to define a class of allowable input functions and the global solution concept.

Definition 7. *A function $u : \mathbb{R}_+ \to \mathbb{R}$ is called* a piecewise Bohl *function, if*

- *u is right-continuous, i.e. $\lim_{t\downarrow\tau} u(t) = u(\tau)$ for all $\tau \in \mathbb{R}_+$*
- *for all $\tau \in \mathbb{R}_+$ there are $\varepsilon > 0$ and $v \in \mathcal{B}$ such that $u(t) = v(t)$ for all $t \in (\tau, \tau+\varepsilon)$*
- *u is locally bounded in the sense that for any interval $[0,T]$ there is a constant M such that $|u(t)| \leq M$ for all $t \in [0,T]$.*

We denote this function space as $\mathcal{PB}$. A distribution $\mathtt{u} : \mathbb{R}_+ \to \mathbb{R}$ is called piecewise Bohl with first order impulses, *if $\mathtt{u}$ is the sum of a piecewise Bohl* function *$\mathtt{u}_{reg}$ and the distribution $\mathtt{u}_{imp} = \sum_{\theta\in\Gamma} w^\theta \delta_\theta$, where $\Gamma = \{\tau_i\}_i$ is a finite or countable subset of $\mathbb{R}_+$, which is isolated* [1]. *We denote this distribution space by $\mathcal{PB}_0$.*

Definition 8. *Let $(\mathtt{w}, \mathtt{x}, \mathtt{z}) \in \mathcal{PB}_0^{m+n+m}$ be given with*

$$\mathtt{w}_{imp} = \sum_{\theta\in\Gamma} w^\theta \delta_\theta,\ \mathtt{x}_{imp} = \sum_{\theta\in\Gamma} x^\theta \delta_\theta,\ \mathtt{z}_{imp} = \sum_{\theta\in\Gamma} z^\theta \delta_\theta$$

for $w^\theta \in \mathbb{R}^m$, $x^\theta \in \mathbb{R}^n$ and $w^\theta \in \mathbb{R}^m$ for $\theta \in \Gamma$ and some Γ. Then we call $(\mathtt{w}, \mathtt{x}, \mathtt{z})$ a (global) solution *to LCS (1) with input function $u \in \mathcal{PB}$ and initial state x_0, if the following properties hold.*

1. *For any interval (a,b) such that $(a,b) \cap \Gamma = \emptyset$ the restriction $\mathtt{x}_{reg}\,|_{(a,b)}$ is (absolutely) continuous and satisfies (1) for almost all $t \in (a,b)$*
2. *For each $\theta \in \Gamma$ the corresponding impulse $(w^\theta\delta_\theta, x^\theta\delta_\theta, z^\theta\delta_\theta)$ is equal to the impulsive part of the unique initial solution*[2] *to (1) with initial state $\mathtt{x}_{reg}(\theta-) := \lim_{t\uparrow\theta} \mathtt{x}_{reg}(t)$ (taken equal to x_0 for $\theta = 0$) and input $t \mapsto u(t-\theta)$.*
3. *For times $\theta \in \Gamma$ it holds that $\mathtt{x}_{reg}(\theta+) = \mathtt{x}_{reg}(\theta-) + Bw^\theta$ with w^θ the multiplier of Dirac pulse supported at θ.*

Theorem 6. *Consider an LCS with external inputs given by (1) such that $G(s) = C(sI-A)^{-1}B + D$ is totally of index 1 and $G(\sigma)$ is a P-matrix for sufficiently large σ. The LCS (1) has a unique (global) solution $(\mathtt{w}, \mathtt{x}, \mathtt{z}) \in \mathcal{PB}_0^{k+n+k}$ for any initial state x_0 and input $u \in \mathcal{PB}^k$. Moreover, $\mathtt{x}_{imp} = 0$ and impulses in $(\mathtt{w}, \mathtt{z})$ can only show up at the initial time and times for which Fu is discontinuous (i.e. Γ in Definition 8 can be taken as a subset of $\{0\} \cup \Gamma^d_{Fu}$).*

[1] The set $\Gamma \subseteq \mathbb{R}$ is called isolated, if for all $\tau \in \Gamma$ there is an $\varepsilon > 0$ such that $\Gamma \cap (\tau-\varepsilon, \tau+\varepsilon) = \{\tau\}$.

[2] Note that we shift time over θ to be able to use the definition of an initial solution, which is given for an initial condition at $t = 0$.

Proof. The proof follows along similar lines as the proof of the case $F = 0$ as given in the thesis [5] by carefully incorporating the presence of impulses (see also [3] for the passive case). □

This theorem implies that if Fu is continuous, jumps of the state can only occur at the initial time instant 0.

6 Stability and State Feedback Design for LCS

Let us first define formally what we mean by stability of LCS.

Definition 9. *The LCS* (1) *without inputs (i.e. $E = F = 0$) is called globally asymptotically stable (GAS), if*

Global existence: *for each x_0 there exists a global solution to* (1) *and moreover, for each $T \geq 0$ all solutions $(\mathtt{w}, \mathtt{x}, \mathtt{z}) \in \mathcal{P}\mathcal{B}_0^{m+n+m}$ to* (1) *for initial state x_0 defined on $[0, T)$ can be continued to a global solution on $[0, \infty)$;*

Lyapunov stability: *for each $\varepsilon > 0$ there exists a $\delta > 0$ such that $\|\mathtt{x}_{reg}(t)\| < \varepsilon$, for all $t \geq 0$ when $\|x_0\| < \delta$, where $(\mathtt{w}, \mathtt{x}, \mathtt{z}) \in \mathcal{P}\mathcal{B}_0^{m+n+m}$ is a global solution in the sense of Definition 8 to* (1) *for initial state x_0;*

Attractiveness: $\lim_{t\to\infty} \mathtt{x}_{reg}(t) = 0$ *for any global solution $(\mathtt{w}, \mathtt{x}, \mathtt{z}) \in \mathcal{P}\mathcal{B}_0$.*

In this section we aim at designing a state feedback controller

$$u(t) = Kx(t) \tag{10}$$

that renders the system (1) GAS.

Assumption 7. *$(A + EK, B, C + FK, D)$ is strictly passive and minimal.*

For necessary and sufficient conditions of "passifiability" for the case $D = 0$ (i.e. finding K such that $(A + EK, B, C + FK, 0)$ is strictly passive), see [25].

Theorem 8. *Consider the LCS* (1) *and the state feedback* (10) *and suppose that Assumptions 3 and 7 hold. Then the closed-loop system* (1)-(10) *is GAS.*

In [3] it was shown that a sufficient condition for GAS is the strict passivity of the underlying system. The above theorem on state feedback design is a consequence of that result. After these preparatory steps, we continue with the main results of this paper related to observer design and output-based controller design.

7 Observer Design

Consider the LCS (1) and assume that only

$$y(t) = Gx(t) \in \mathbb{R}^p \tag{11}$$

is measured instead of the complete state being available for feedback. Based on this output measurement, we aim at estimating the continuous state $x(t)$ of (1) using an observer. For the observer design to be meaningful, we have to assume some conditions of the existence of solutions to the observed system (1).

Assumption 9. *For any initial state* x_0 *and for any input function* $u \in \mathcal{PB}^k$ *there exists a global solution* $(\mathtt{w}, \mathtt{x}, \mathtt{z}) \in \mathcal{PB}_0^{m+n+m}$ *to system* (1) *in the sense of Definition 8.*

The well-posedness theory derived before can be used to guarantee this property. For instance, Theorem 6 shows that under the assumption that $G(s) = C(sI - A)^{-1}B + D$ is totally of index 1 and $G(\sigma)$ is a P-matrix for sufficiently large σ, Assumption 9 is indeed satisfied.

We propose the following observer for LCS (1) with measured output (11):

$$\dot{\hat{x}}(t) = A\hat{x}(t) + B\hat{w}(t) + Eu(t) + L(y(t) - \hat{y}(t)) \tag{12a}$$
$$\hat{z}(t) = C\hat{x}(t) + D\hat{w}(t) + Fu(t) + M(y(t) - \hat{y}(t)) \tag{12b}$$
$$0 \leq \hat{z}(t) \perp \hat{w}(t) \geq 0. \tag{12c}$$
$$\hat{y}(t) = G\hat{x}(t), \tag{12d}$$

where we have two observer gains (L and M).

Assumption 10. $(A - LG, B, C - MG, D)$ *is strictly passive and minimal.*

First of all, one has to show that the observer structure (12) produces estimates $\hat{x}$ of the state x, i.e. that existence of global solutions to (12) is guaranteed given an initial estimate $\hat{x}_0$ and external inputs $u \in \mathcal{PB}^k$ and $y \in \mathcal{PB}^p$. Using Theorem 5 the following result can be proven.

Theorem 11. *Consider the observer* (12) *with external inputs* $u \in \mathcal{PB}^k$ *and* $y \in \mathcal{PB}^p$, *where* y *is obtained from the LCS given by* (1) *and* (11) *for some initial state* x_0 *and input* u. *If Assumption 3 and Assumption 10 are satisfied, then for any initial state* $\hat{x}_0$ *there exists a unique global solution* $(\hat{\mathtt{w}}, \hat{\mathtt{x}}, \hat{\mathtt{z}})$ *to* (12).

Since we proved global existence of $\hat{x}$, we can consider the observation error $e := x - \hat{x}$, which evolves according to the following dynamics

$$\dot{e}(t) = (A - LG)e(t) + Bw(t) - B\hat{w}(t) \tag{13a}$$
$$z(t) = Cx(t) + Dw(t) + Fu(t) \tag{13b}$$
$$\hat{z}(t) = C\hat{x}(t) + D\hat{w}(t) + Fu(t) + M(y(t) - \hat{y}(t)) \tag{13c}$$
$$0 \leq z(t) \perp w(t) \geq 0, \quad \text{and} \quad 0 \leq \hat{z}(t) \perp \hat{w}(t) \geq 0 \tag{13d}$$

Theorem 12. *Consider the error dynamics* (13) *such that Assumption 3, Assumption 9 and Assumption 10 hold. Then the error dynamics is GAS*[3].

Proof. See the report [32]. □

The theorem shows (under the given hypothesis) that the observer (12) recovers asymptotically the state of the LCS (1) based on the output (11), even when the state of the system or observer exhibits state jumps. Since the jumps in

[3] Note that the definition of GAS has to be slightly generalized to allow for exogenous signals.

both the observer and the observed plant are triggered by discontinuities in the external signal (due to the low index of the underlying linear system), the time instants of the jumps coincide for the observer and controller, which is exploited in the proof. For higher index systems (e.g. mechanical systems with unilateral constraints) this property is lost, which complicates observer design significantly.

8 Separation Principle: Observer-Based Controller

To design an output-based controller for (1) with (11), we will employ a "certainty equivalence" approach by using the estimate $\hat{x}$ obtained from the designed observer in the state feedback controller, i.e. $u(t) = K\hat{x}(t) = Kx(t) - Ke(t)$. The closed-loop system consisting of the system (1), the observer (12) and the controller $u(t) = K\hat{x}(t)$ becomes

$$\begin{pmatrix} \dot{x} \\ \dot{e} \end{pmatrix} = \underbrace{\begin{pmatrix} (A+EK) & -EK \\ 0 & A-LG \end{pmatrix}}_{=:A_{cl}} \begin{pmatrix} x \\ e \end{pmatrix} + \underbrace{\begin{pmatrix} B & 0 \\ B & -B \end{pmatrix}}_{=:B_{cl}} \begin{pmatrix} w \\ \hat{w} \end{pmatrix} \tag{14a}$$

$$\begin{pmatrix} z \\ \hat{z} \end{pmatrix} = \underbrace{\begin{pmatrix} C+FK & -FK \\ C+FK & -(C+FK-MG) \end{pmatrix}}_{=:C_{cl}} \begin{pmatrix} x \\ e \end{pmatrix} + \underbrace{\begin{pmatrix} D & 0 \\ 0 & D \end{pmatrix}}_{=:D_{cl}} \begin{pmatrix} w \\ \hat{w} \end{pmatrix} \tag{14b}$$

$$0 \leq \begin{pmatrix} z \\ \hat{z} \end{pmatrix} \perp \begin{pmatrix} w \\ \hat{w} \end{pmatrix} \geq 0 \tag{14c}$$

We focus on the so-called *basic observer*, which is the observer (12) with $M = 0$ implying that there is only an innovation (output injection) term in the differential equation (12a) and not in the complementarity relation (12b). We will return to the *extended observer* with $M \neq 0$ in Remark 1. We will start by proving closed-loop well-posedness.

Theorem 13. *Consider the system* (14) *such that Assumptions 3, 7 and 10 with $M = 0$ are satisfied. The system* (14) *has for each initial condition x_0 and e_0 a unique global solution in the sense of Definition 8. Moreover, only on time 0, there can be a discontinuity in the state trajectory x.*

Proof. See the report [32]. □

Now we can state a separation principle for LCS.

Theorem 14. [Separation principle] *Consider the closed-loop LCS* (14). *If Assumptions 3, 7 and 10 with $M = 0$ are satisfied, then the LCS* (14) *is GAS.*

Proof. See the report [32].

Once the observer (12) is included in an observer-based control configuration for the LCS (1), jumps in the state variable of (14) can only take place at the initial time (under the given hypothesis of the theorem above). The reason is that for the 'open' LCS (1) the state jumps are triggered by the external signal u, while the closed-loop system (14) is a 'closed' system without external inputs. Note, however, that when the observer is applied to an 'open' LCS (1), the state of (1) is still recovered asymptotically (under the hypothesis of Theorem 12) even when state jumps (triggered by discontinuities in u) remain to be persistently present. The fact that jumps only occur at the initial time is related to the low index of the underlying linear system of the LCS (14). In general for systems of higher index (like constrained mechanical systems) discontinuities are not only externally triggered by exogenous signals, but also by internal events (impacts).

Remark 1. The extended observer case (i.e. $M \neq 0$) can be covered in a similar manner as above under the assumption that $F = 0$.

9 Conclusion

We presented observer and output-based controller design methods for linear complementarity systems (LCS) employing a passivity approach. We provided sufficient conditions for the observer design for a LCS, which is effective also in the presence of state jumps. Using the certainty equivalence approach we obtained output-based controllers for which we provided a separation principle in case the basic observer ("$M = 0$") is used or there is no direct feedthrough of the input in the complementarity conditions ("$F = 0$"). Future work will involve the study of the full separation principe for both F and M nonzero. Another important line of future research is the observer and observer-based control design of LCS for which the underlying linear system is of higher index (such as constrained mechanical systems.)

References

1. van der Schaft, A.J., Schumacher, J.M.: Complementarity modeling of hybrid systems. IEEE Transactions on Automatic Control 43, 483 (1998)
2. Heemels, W., Schumacher, J., Weiland, S.: Linear complementarity systems. SIAM Journal on Applied Mathematics, 1234–1269 (2000)
3. Camlibel, M., Heemels, W., Schumacher, J.: On linear passive complementarity systems. European Journal of Control 8, 220–237 (2002)
4. Shen, J., Pang, J.: Semicopositive lineaer complementarity systems. Intern. J. Robust and Nonlinear Control 17(15), 1367–1386 (2007)
5. Camlibel, M.: Complementarity methods in the analysis of piecewise linear dynamical systems. PhD thesis Tilburg University (2001)
6. Brogliato, B.: Some perspectives on the analysis and control of complementarity systems. IEEE Trans Automatic Control 48, 918–935 (2003)
7. Brogliato, B., Daniilidis, A., Lemaréchal, C., Acary, V.: On the equivalence between complementarity systems, projected systems and differential inclusions. System and Control Letters 55, 45–51 (2006)
8. Heemels, W., Schumacher, J., Weiland, S.: Projected dynamical systems in a complementarity formalism. Operations Research Letters 27(2), 83–91 (2000)
9. Camlibel, M., Heemels, W., van der Schaft, A., Schumacher, J.: Switched networks and complementarity. IEEE Trans. Circuits Systems-I 50, 1036–1046 (2003)

10. Camlibel, M., Heemels, W., Schumacher, J.: Consistency of a time-stepping method for a class of piecewise-linear networks. IEEE Trans. Circuits Systems-I 49(3), 349–357 (2002)
11. Lynch, N., Segala, R., Vaandrager, F., Weinberg, H.: Hybrid I/O automata. In: Proc. Workshop Verification and Control of Hybrid Systems, pp. 496–510 (1996)
12. Branicky, M., Borkar, V., Mitter, S.: A unified framework for hybrid control: model and optimal control theory. IEEE Trans. Automatic Control 43(1), 31–45 (1998)
13. Lygeros, J., Johansson, K., Simic, S., Zhang, J., Sastry, S.: Dynamical properties of hybrid automata. IEEE Trans. Aut. Control 48(1) (2003)
14. Heemels, W., Camlibel, M., van der Schaft, A., Schumacher, J.: Modelling, well-posedness, and stability of switched electrical networks. In: Maler, O., Pnueli, A. (eds.) HSCC 2003. LNCS, vol. 2623, pp. 249–266. Springer, Heidelberg (2003)
15. Cai, C., Teel, A., Goebel, R.: Smooth Lyapunov functions for hybrid systems. Part I: Existence is equivalent to robustness. IEEE Trans. Automatic Control 52(7), 1264–1277 (2007)
16. Sontag, E.: Nonlinear regulation: The piecewise linear approach. IEEE Trans. Automatic Control 26(2), 346–358 (1981)
17. Heemels, W., De Schutter, B., Bemporad, A.: Equivalence of hybrid dynamical models. Automatica 37(7) (2001)
18. De Schutter, B., van den Boom, T.: On model predictive control for max-min-plus-scaling discrete event systems. Automatica 37(7), 1049–1056 (2001)
19. Bemporad, A., Morari, M.: Control of systems integrating logic, dynamics, and constraints. Automatica 35, 407–427 (1999)
20. Alessandri, A., Coletta, P.: Design of Luenberger observers for a class of hybrid linear systems. In: Di Benedetto, M.D., Sangiovanni-Vincentelli, A.L. (eds.) HSCC 2001. LNCS, vol. 2034, pp. 7–18. Springer, Heidelberg (2001)
21. Iulia Bara, G., Daafouz, J., Kratz, F., Iung, C.: State estimation for a class of hybrid systems. In: Int. Conf. Automation of Mixed Processes, pp. 313–316 (2000)
22. Petterson, S.: Switched state jump observers for switched systems. In: Proceedings of the IFAC World Congress, Prague, Czech Republic (2005)
23. Juloski, A., Heemels, W., Weiland, S.: Observer design for a class of piecewise linear systems. Intern. J. Robust and Nonlinear Control 17(15), 1387–1404 (2007)
24. Pavlov, A., van de Wouw, N., Nijmeijer, H.: Convergent piecewise affine systems: analysis and design. In: Proc. CDC/ECC, Sevilla, Spain (2005)
25. Arcak, M., Kokotović, P.: Observer based control of systems with slope-restricted nonlinearities. IEEE Trans. Automatic Control 46(7), 1146–1150 (2001)
26. Arcak, M.: Certainty-equivalence output-feedback design with circle-criterion observers. IEEE Trans. Automatic Control 50, 905–909 (2005)
27. Fan, X., Arcak, M.: Observer design for systems with multivariable monotone nonlinearities. Systems and Control Letters 50, 319–330 (2003)
28. Rajamani, R.: Observers for Lipschitz nonlinear systems. IEEE Trans. Aut. Control 43, 397–401 (1998)
29. Osorio, M., Moreno, J.: Dissipative design of observers for multivalued nonlinear systems. In: Proc. CDC, pp. 5400–5405 (2006)
30. Cottle, R., Pang, J.S., Stone, R.: The Linear Complementarity Problem. Academic Press, Boston (1992)
31. Willems, J.: Dissipative dynamical systems. Archive for Rational Mechanics and Analysis 45, 321–393 (1972)
32. Heemels, W., Camlibel, M., Brogliato, B., Schumacher, J.: Observer-based control of linear complementarity systems. Technical report, Eindhoven University of Technology, Department of Mechanical Engineering, DCT report DCT 2008.002 (2008)

Complementarity Systems in Constrained Steady-State Optimal Control

A. Jokic, M. Lazar, and P.P.J. van den Bosch

Dept. of Electrical Eng., Eindhoven Univ. of Technology,
P.O. Box 513, 5600 MB Eindhoven, The Netherlands
{a.jokic, m.lazar, p.p.j.v.d.bosch}@tue.nl

Abstract. This paper presents a solution to the problem of regulating a general nonlinear dynamical system to a time-varying economically optimal operating point. The system is characterized by a set of exogenous inputs as an abstraction of time-varying loads and disturbances. The economically optimal operating point is implicitly defined as a solution to a given constrained convex optimization problem, which is related to steady-state operation. The system outputs and the exogenous inputs represent respectively the decision variables and the parameters in the optimization problem. Complementarity systems are employed as building blocks to construct a dynamic controller that solves the considered regulation problem. The complementarity solution arises naturally via a dynamic extension of the Karush-Kuhn-Tucker optimality conditions for the steady-state related optimization problem.

1 Introduction

Although there has been earlier substantial work in specific research areas where combinations of differential equations are coupled with complementarity conditions, it is since their formal introduction in 1996 by Van der Scahft and Schumacher [1], see also [2], that complementarity systems (CS) have become an extensive topic of research in the hybrid systems community. This particular class of systems has certain structural properties that have already been successfully exploited in answering some of the fundamental theoretical questions like well-posedness [2, 3], certain control synthesis problems [4], and recently also Lyapunov stability analysis [5]. Complementarity systems naturally arise in many application areas, such as constrained mechanical systems, electrical circuit theory, dynamic optimization problems, oligopolistic markets and Leontiev economy. For a more detailed presentation see the excellent overview given in [6]. In this paper we present a new application, namely constrained steady-state optimal control, where complementarity systems provide an attractive solution. In contrast to the vast majority of previously considered applications where CS come in as a natural *modeling* framework, here CS arise as a suitable *control synthesis* framework. More precisely, we propose a specific dynamic extension of the Karush-Kuhn-Tucker (KKT) optimality conditions to obtain a novel feedback control structure as a solution to the problem of regulating a general nonlinear

M. Egerstedt and B. Mishra (Eds.): HSCC 2008, LNCS 4981, pp. 273–286, 2008.

dynamical system to a time-varying economically optimal operating point. The considered dynamical system is characterized with a set of exogenous inputs as an abstraction of time-varying loads and disturbances acting on the system. Economic optimality is defined through a convex constrained optimization problem with system outputs as decision variables, and with the values of exogenous inputs as parameters in the optimization problem. In the following paragraph we give a flavor of possible regulation problems that motivate the results presented in this paper.

In many production facilities, the optimization problem reflecting economical benefits of production is associated with a *steady-state operation* of the system. The control action is required to maintain the production in an optimal regime in spite of various disturbances, and to efficiently and rapidly respond to changes in demand. Furthermore, it is desirable that the system settles in a steady-state that is optimal for novel operating conditions. The vast majority of control literature is focused on regulation and tracking with respect to known setpoints or trajectories, while coping with different types of uncertainties and disturbances in both the plant and its environment. Typically, setpoints are determined off-line by solving an appropriate optimization problem and they are updated in an open-loop manner. The optimization problem typically reflects variable costs of production and economical benefits under the current market conditions, e.g. fuel or electricity prices, and accounts for physical and security limits of the plant. If a production system is required to follow a time-varying demand in real-time, e.g., if produced commodities cannot be efficiently stored in large amounts, it becomes crucial to perform economic optimization on-line. A typical example of such a system are electrical power systems. Increase of the frequency with which the economically optimal setpoints are updated can result in a significant increase of economic benefits accumulated in time. If the time-scale on which economic optimization is performed approaches the time-scale of the underlying physical system, i.e. of the plant dynamics, dynamic interaction in between the two has to be considered. Economic optimization then becomes a challenging control problem, especially since it has to cope with inequality constraints that reflect the physical and security limits of the plant.

1.1 Nomenclature

For a matrix $A \in \mathbb{R}^{m\times n}$, $[A]_{ij}$ denotes the element in the i-th row and j-th column of A. For a vector $x \in \mathbb{R}^n$, $[x]_i$ denotes the i-th element of x. A vector $x \in \mathbb{R}^n$ is said to be nonnegative (nonpositive) if $[x]_i \geq 0$ ($[x]_i \leq 0$) for all $i \in \{1, \dots n\}$, and in that case we write $x \geq 0$ ($x \leq 0$). The nonnegative orthant of $\mathbb{R}^n$ is defined by $\mathbb{R}^n_+ := \{x \in \mathbb{R}^n \mid x \geq 0\}$. The operator $\mathrm{col}(\cdot, \dots, \cdot)$ stacks its operands into a column vector. For $u, v \in \mathbb{R}^k$ we write $u \perp v$ if $u^\top v = 0$. We use the compact notational form $0 \leq u \perp v \geq 0$ to denote the complementarity conditions $u \geq 0$, $v \geq 0$, $u \perp v$. The matrix inequalities $A \succ B$ and $A \succeq B$ mean A and B are Hermitian and $A - B$ is positive definite and positive semi-definite, respectively. For a scalar-valued differentiable function $f : \mathbb{R}^n \to \mathbb{R}$, $\nabla f(x)$ denotes its gradient at $x = \mathrm{col}(x_1, \dots, x_n)$ and is defined as a *column vector*, i.e. $\nabla f(x) \in \mathbb{R}^n$, $[\nabla f(x)]_i = \frac{\partial f}{\partial x_i}$. For a vector-valued differentiable function $f : \mathbb{R}^n \to \mathbb{R}^m$, $f(x) = \mathrm{col}(f_1(x), \dots, f_m(x))$, the Jacobian at $x = \mathrm{col}(x_1, \dots, x_n)$ is the matrix $Df(x) \in \mathbb{R}^{m \times n}$ and is defined by $[Df(x)]_{ij} = \frac{\partial f_i(x)}{\partial x_j}$. For a vector valued function $f : \mathbb{R}^n \to \mathbb{R}^m$, we will use $\nabla f(x)$ to denote the transpose of the Jacobian, i.e. $\nabla f(x) \in \mathbb{R}^{n \times m}$, $\nabla f(x) \triangleq Df(x)^\top$, which is consistent with the gradient notation ∇f when f is a scalar-valued function. *With a slight abuse of notation we will often use the same symbol to denote a signal, i.e. a function of time, as well as possible values that the signal may take at any time instant.*

2 Problem Formulation

In this section we formally present the constrained steady-state optimal control problem considered in this paper. Furthermore, we list several standing assumptions, which will be instrumental in the subsequent sections.

Consider a dynamical system

$$\dot{x} = f(x, w, u), \tag{1a}$$
$$y = g(x, w), \tag{1b}$$

where $x(t) \in \mathbb{R}^n$ is the state, $u(t) \in \mathbb{R}^m$ is the control input, $w(t) \in \mathbb{R}^{n_w}$ is an exogenous input, $y(t) \in \mathbb{R}^m$ is the measured output, $f : \mathbb{R}^n \times \mathbb{R}^{n_w} \times \mathbb{R}^m \to \mathbb{R}^n$ and $g : \mathbb{R}^n \times \mathbb{R}^{n_w} \to \mathbb{R}^m$ are arbitrary nonlinear functions.

For a constant $w \in W$, with $W \subset \mathbb{R}^{n_w}$ denoting a known bounded set, consider the following convex optimization problem associated with the output y of the dynamical system (1):

$$\min_y \quad J(y) \tag{2a}$$

subject to

$$Ly = h(w), \tag{2b}$$
$$q_i(y) \leq r_i(w), \quad i = 1, \dots, k, \tag{2c}$$

where $J : \mathbb{R}^m \to \mathbb{R}$ is a strictly convex and continuously differentiable function, $L \in \mathbb{R}^{l \times m}$ is a constant matrix, $h : \mathbb{R}^{n_w} \to \mathbb{R}^l$ and $r_i : \mathbb{R}^{n_w} \to \mathbb{R}$, $i = 1, \dots, k$ are continuous functions, while $q_i : \mathbb{R}^m \to \mathbb{R}$, $i = 1, \dots, k$ are convex, continuously differentiable functions. For the matrix L we require $\operatorname{rank} L = l < m$.

For a constant exogenous signal $w(t) = w \in W$, the optimization problem (2) implicitly defines the optimal operating point in terms of the steady-state value of the output vector y in (1). The constraints in (2) represent the security-type "soft" constraints for which some degree of transient violation may be accepted, but whose feasibility is required in steady-state. Note that in general not all of the elements of y that appear in the constraints (2b), (2c) need to appear in the objective function $J(\cdot)$, and *vice versa.* The objective of the control input u is to drive the output y to the optimal steady-state operating point given by (2).

We continue by listing several assumptions concerning the dynamics (1) and the optimization problem (2). Let $\mathcal{I}_l$ denote the set of indices i for which the function q_i in (2c) is a linear function, and let $\mathcal{I}_n$ denote the set of indices corresponding to nonlinear q_i.

Assumption 1. For each $w \in W$ the set

$$\{y \mid Ly = h(w),\ \ q_i(y) < r_i(w) \text{ for } i \in \mathcal{I}_n,\ q_i(y) \leq r_i(w) \text{ for } i \in \mathcal{I}_l\}$$

is nonempty. □

Assumption 1 states that the convex optimization problem (2) satisfies Slater's constraint qualification [7] for each $w \in W$, implying that strong duality holds for the considered problem. Note also that due to strict convexity of the objective function in (2), the optimization problem has an unique minimizer $\tilde{y}(w)$ for each $w \in W$.

Assumption 2. For each $w \in W$, in the optimization problem (2) the minimum is attained. □

Assumption 3. For each $w \in W$, there is a unique pair $(\tilde{x}(w), \tilde{u}(w))$ such that

$$0 = f(\tilde{x}(w), w, \tilde{u}(w)), \tag{3a}$$

$$\tilde{y}(w) = g(\tilde{x}(w), w), \tag{3b}$$

where $\tilde{y}(w)$ denotes the corresponding minimizer in (2). □

Assumption 3 guarantees that for all constant $w(t) = w \in W$, the output vector y can be driven to the corresponding optimal steady-state point, which is then characterized by a unique, constant value of the input signal u. In other words, Assumption 3 implies that the steady-state relations from (1) do not pose any additional constraints to the optimization problem (2), i.e. any constraint on the steady-state imposed by (1) is already included in (2).

Assumption 4. The values of all components of w that appear in (2) are available at all time instants. □

Assumption 4 implies that violations of the constraints (2b) and (2c) can be measured. Hence, they can be used for control purposes.

With the definitions and assumptions made so far, we are now ready to formally state the control problem considered in this paper.

Problem 1. Constrained steady-state optimal control.
For a dynamical system given by (1), design a feedback controller that has y as input signal and u as output signal, such that the following objective is met for any constant-valued exogenous signal $w(t) = w \in W$: the closed-loop system globally converges to an equilibrium point with $y = \tilde{y}(w)$, where $\tilde{y}(w)$ denotes the corresponding minimizer of the optimization problem (2). □

Note that Problem 1 includes the standard regulation problem, see e.g. Chapter 12 in [8], as a special case. More precisely, if (2) is modified to include only equality constraints and $J(y) = 0$, then Problem 1 reduces to the problem of regulating the output $\hat{y} := Ly$ to the constant reference signal $\hat{r} := h(w)$. Furthermore, note that for a dynamical system (1) we have assumed the same dimension of the output signal y and the control input signal u. However, this assumption can be relaxed. A typical example of such a relaxation is presented in the illustrative example in Section 5.

3 Dynamic KKT Controllers

In this section we present a controller that guarantees the existence of an equilibrium point with $y = \tilde{y}(w)$ as described in Problem 1. This is done using an appropriate dynamic extension of the Karush-Kuhn-Tucker optimality conditions for the optimization problem (2).

Assumption 1 implies that for each $w \in W$, the first order Karush-Kuhn-Tucker (KKT) conditions are *necessary and sufficient* conditions for optimality. For the optimization problem (2) these conditions are given by the following set of equalities and inequalities:

$$\nabla J(y) + L^\top \lambda + \nabla q(y)\mu = 0, \tag{4a}$$
$$Ly - h(w) = 0, \tag{4b}$$
$$0 \le -q(y) + r(w) \;\perp\; \mu \ge 0, \tag{4c}$$

where $q(y) := \operatorname{col}(q_1(y), \ldots, q_k(y))$, $r(w) := \operatorname{col}(r_1(w), \ldots, r_k(w))$ and $\lambda \in \mathbb{R}^l$, $\mu \in \mathbb{R}^k$ are Lagrange multipliers. Since the above conditions are necessary and sufficient conditions for optimality, it is apparent that the existence of an equilibrium point with $y = \tilde{y}(w)$ is implied if for each $w \in W$ the controller guarantees the existence of the vectors λ and μ, such that that the conditions (4) are fulfilled in a steady-state of the closed-loop system.

In what follows, we present two controllers that achieve this goal. Later in this section it will be shown that there are certain insightful differences as well as similarities between these two control structures.

Max-based KKT controller. Let $K_\lambda \in \mathbb{R}^{l\times l}$, $K_\mu \in \mathbb{R}^{k\times k}$, $K_c \in \mathbb{R}^{m\times m}$ and $K_o \in \mathbb{R}^{k\times k}$ be diagonal matrices with non-zero elements on the main diagonal and $K_\mu \succ 0$, $K_o \succ 0$. Consider a dynamic controller with the following structure:

$$\dot{x}_\lambda = K_\lambda(Ly - h(w)), \tag{5a}$$
$$\dot{x}_\mu = K_\mu(q(y) - r(w)) + v, \tag{5b}$$
$$\dot{x}_c = K_c(L^\top x_\lambda + \nabla q(y)x_\mu + \nabla J(y)), \tag{5c}$$
$$0 \le v \;\perp\; K_o x_\mu + K_\mu(q(y) - r(w)) + v \ge 0, \tag{5d}$$
$$u = x_c, \tag{5e}$$

where x_λ, x_μ and x_c denote the controller states and the matrices K_λ, K_μ, K_c and K_o represent the controller gains. Note that the input vector $v(t) \in \mathbb{R}^k$ in (5b) is at any time instant required to be a solution to a finite-dimensional linear complementarity problem (5d). □

Saturation-based KKT controller. Let $K_\lambda \in \mathbb{R}^{l\times l}$, $K_\mu \in \mathbb{R}^{k\times k}$ and $K_c \in \mathbb{R}^{m\times m}$ be diagonal matrices with non-zero elements on the main diagonal and $K_\mu \succ 0$. Consider a dynamic controller with the following structure:

$$\dot{x}_\lambda = K_\lambda(Ly - h(w)), \tag{6a}$$
$$\dot{x}_\mu = K_\mu(q(y) - r(w)) + v, \tag{6b}$$
$$\dot{x}_c = K_c(L^\top x_\lambda + \nabla q(y)x_\mu + \nabla J(y)), \tag{6c}$$
$$0 \leq v \perp x_\mu \geq 0, \tag{6d}$$
$$u = x_c, \tag{6e}$$
$$x_\mu(0) \geq 0, \tag{6f}$$

where x_λ, x_μ and x_c denote the controller states and the matrices K_λ, K_μ and K_c represent the controller gains. Note that the input vector $v(t) \in \mathbb{R}^k$ in (6b) is at any time instant required to be a solution to a finite-dimensional linear complementarity problem (6d). The initialization constraint (6f) is required as a necessary condition for well-posedness, conform with the inequality in the complementarity condition (6d). □

The choice of names *max-based KKT controller* and *saturation-based KKT controller* will become clear later in this section. Notice that both controllers belong to the class of complementarity systems [1,2].

Theorem 1. *Let $w(t) = w \in W$ be a constant-valued signal, and suppose that Assumption 1 and Assumption 3 hold. Then the closed-loop system, i.e. the system obtained from the system* (1) *connected with controller* (5) *or* (6) *in a feedback loop, has an equilibrium point with $y = \tilde{y}(w)$, where $\tilde{y}(w)$ denotes the corresponding minimizer of the optimization problem* (2).

Proof. We first consider the closed-loop system with the max-based KKT controller, i.e. controller (5). By setting the time derivatives of the closed-loop system states to zero and by exploiting the non-singularity of the matrices K_λ, and K_c, we obtain the following complementarity problem:

$$0 = f(x, w, x_c), \tag{7a}$$
$$y = g(x, w), \tag{7b}$$
$$0 = Ly - h(w), \tag{7c}$$
$$0 = K_\mu(q(y) - r(w)) + v, \tag{7d}$$
$$0 = L^\top x_\lambda + \nabla q(y)x_\mu + \nabla J(y), \tag{7e}$$
$$0 \leq v \perp K_o x_\mu + K_\mu(q(y) - r(w)) + v \geq 0, \tag{7f}$$

with the closed-loop system state vector $x_{cl} := \mathrm{col}(x, x_\lambda, x_\mu, x_c)$ and the vector v as variables. Any solution x_{cl} to (7) is an equilibrium point of the closed-loop system. By substituting $v = -K_\mu(q(y) - r(w))$ from (7d) and utilizing $K_\mu \succ 0$ and $K_o \succ 0$, the complementarity condition (7f) reads as $0 \leq -q(y) + r(w) \perp x_\mu \geq 0$. With $\lambda := x_\lambda$ and $\mu := x_\mu$, the conditions (7c),(7d),(7e),(7f) therefore correspond to the KKT conditions (4) and, under Assumption 1, they necessarily have a solution. Furthermore, for any solution (y, x_λ, x_μ, v) to (7c),(7d),(7e),(7f), it necessarily holds that $y = \tilde{y}(w)$. It remains to show that (7a), (7b) admit a solution in (x, x_c) for $y = \tilde{y}(w)$. This is, however, the hypothesis of Assumption 3. Moreover, Assumption 3 implies uniqueness of x and x_c in an equilibrium.

Now, consider the closed-loop system with the saturation-based KKT controller, i.e. controller (6). The difference in this case comes only through (6b) and (6d). It is therefore sufficient to show that (6b) and (6d) imply $0 \leq -q(y) + r(w) \perp x_\mu \geq 0$. This implication is obvious since $K_\mu \succ 0$. □

In the following subsection we concentrate on those parts of the KKT controllers that are directly affected by the algebraic complementarity conditions (5d) and (6d). We present a systematic procedure for implementing these conditions, which involves the definition of complementary integrators as the basic building blocks for imposing steady-state complementarity conditions. In turn, complementarity integrators form the basic building blocks of the developed dynamic KKT controllers.

3.1 Complementarity Integrators

The main distinguishing feature between the max-based KKT controller (5) and the saturation-based KKT controller (6) is in the way the steady-state complementarity slackness condition (4c) is enforced. Although characterized by the same steady-state relations, the two controllers, and therefore the corresponding closed-loop systems, have some significantly different *dynamical* features which will be discussed further in this section. In the following two paragraphs our attention is on the equations (5b),(5d) and (6b),(6d), and the goal is to show the following:

- The *max-based KKT controller*, i.e. controller (5), can be represented as a dynamical system in which certain variables are coupled by means of static, continuous, piecewise linear characteristics;
- The *saturation-based KKT controller*, i.e. controller (6), can be represented as a dynamical system with state saturations.

Max-based complementarity integrator. Let $\eta = [q(y) - r(w)]_i$, $\xi = [x_\mu]_i$, $\nu = [v]_i$, $k_o = [K_o]_{ii}$ and $k_\mu = [K_\mu]_{ii}$, for some $i \in \{1, \ldots, k\}$. Then the i-th row in (5b) and (5d) is respectively given by

$$\dot{\xi} = k_\mu \eta + \nu, \tag{8a}$$

$$0 \leq \nu \perp k_o \xi + k_\mu \eta + \nu \geq 0, \tag{8b}$$

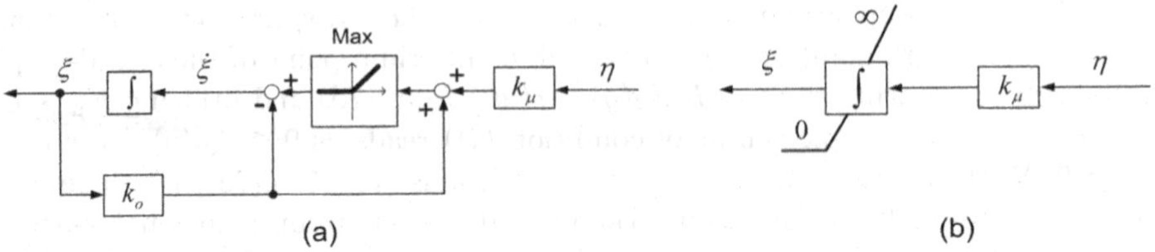

Fig. 1. Complementarity integrators. (a) Max-based complementarity integrator. (b) Saturation-based complementarity integrator.

where $k_o > 0$ and $k_\mu > 0$. Let a, b and c be real scalars related through the complementarity condition $0 \leq c \perp a + b + c \geq 0$. It is easily verified, e.g. by checking all possible combinations, that this complementarity condition is equivalent to $b + c = \max(a + b, 0) - a$. Now, by taking $c = \nu$, $a = k_o\xi$ and $b = k_\mu\eta$, it follows that (8) can be equivalently described by

$$\dot{\xi} = \max(k_o\,\xi + k_\mu\eta, 0) - k_o\,\xi. \tag{9}$$

Figure 1a presents a block diagram representation of (9). The block labeled "Max" in the figure, represents the scalar max relation as a static piecewise linear characteristic.

With $k_o > 0$ and $k_\mu > 0$, it is easy to verify that, if the system in Figure 1a is in steady-state, then the value of its input signal η and the value of its output signal ξ necessarily satisfy the complementarity condition $0 \leq \xi \perp -\eta \geq 0$. □

Saturation-based complementarity integrator. Let $\eta = [q(y) - r(w)]_i$, $\xi = [x_\mu]_i$, $\nu = [v]_i$ and $k_\mu = [K_\mu]_{ii}$, for some $i \in \{1, \ldots, k\}$. Then the i-th row in (6b),(6d) and (6f) is respectively given by

$$\dot{\xi} = k_\mu\eta + \nu, \tag{10a}$$

$$0 \leq \nu \perp \xi \geq 0, \tag{10b}$$

$$\xi(0) \geq 0, \tag{10c}$$

where $k_\mu > 0$. The dynamical system (10) can equivalently be described by

$$\dot{\xi} = \phi_{SCI}(\xi, \eta) := \begin{cases} 0 & \text{if } \xi = 0 \text{ and } k_\mu\eta < 0, \\ k_\mu\eta & \text{if } \xi = 0 \text{ and } k_\mu\eta \geq 0, \\ k_\mu\eta & \text{if } \xi > 0. \end{cases} \tag{11}$$

Figure 1b presents a block diagram representation of (11), which is a saturated integrator with the lower saturation point equal to zero. The equivalence of the dynamics (10) and the saturated integrator defined by (11) directly follows from the equivalence of *gradient-type complementarity systems* (GTCS) ((10) belongs to the GTCS class) and *projected dynamical systems* (PDS) ((11) belongs to the PDS class). For the precise definitions of GTCS and PDS system classes and for the equivalence results see [9] and [10].

With $k_\mu > 0$, it is easy to verify that if the system in Figure 1b is in steady-state, the value of the input signal η and the value of its output signal ξ necessarily satisfy the complementarity condition $0 \leq \xi \perp -\eta \geq 0$. □

The above presented complementarity integrators provide the basic building blocks for imposing steady-state complementarity conditions. We will use the term *max-based complementarity integrator* (MCI) to refer to the system (8), i.e. the system with the structure as depicted in Figure 1a, and we will use the term *saturation-based complementarity integrator* (SCI) for the system (10), i.e. the system in Figure 1b. Together with a pure integrator, complementarity integrators form the basic building block of a KKT controller.

Remark 1. For the MCI given by (8) the following holds:

(*i*) If $\xi(0) < 0$ then $\xi(t) \to 0$ as $t \to \infty$. Indeed for $\xi(t) < 0$, from (8) it follows that $\dot{\xi}(t) > 0$, irrespective of the value of the input signal $\eta(t)$.
(*ii*) If $\xi(0) \geq 0$, then $\xi(t) \geq 0$ for all $t \in \mathbb{R}_+$. Indeed for $\xi(t) = 0$, from (8) it follows that $\dot{\xi}(t) \geq 0$, irrespective of the value of the input signal $\eta(t)$. Therefore, similarly to the behavior of the saturation-based KKT controller, if $x_\mu(0) \geq 0$ in the max-based KKT controller (5), then $x_\mu(t) \geq 0$ for all $t \in \mathbb{R}_+$.

In what follows, we point out an interesting relation between the dynamical behavior of the two types of complementarity integrators. Consider the MCI (8) and let $\xi(0) \geq 0$. Note that according to Remark 1 it follows that $\xi(t) \geq 0$ for all $t \in \mathbb{R}_+$. For $\xi(t) \geq 0$, the dynamics (8) can be equivalently represented in a piecewise-linear form as follows:

$$\dot{\xi} = \phi_{MCI}(\xi, \eta) := \begin{cases} k_\mu \eta & \text{if } \ \xi \geq -\frac{k_\mu}{k_o}\eta, \\ -k_o \xi & \text{if } \ \xi < -\frac{k_\mu}{k_o}\eta. \end{cases} \tag{12}$$

Now, suppose that the gain k_μ has the same value in (11) and (12). For a given $\eta(t) < \infty$, we define the set $\mathcal{D} := \{\xi \mid \xi \geq 0, \ \phi_{SCI}(\xi, \eta) \neq \phi_{MCI}(\xi, \eta)\}$. By inspection it can easily be observed that for any $\eta(t) < \infty$, the Lebesgue measure of the set $\mathcal{D}$ tends to zero as k_o tends to ∞. This implies that the SCI can be considered as a special case of the MCI when the gain k_o is set to infinity. In the same sense, the saturation-based KKT controller can be considered as a special case of the max-based KKT controller.

4 Well-Posedness and Stability of the Closed-Loop System

In this subsection we shortly present some results concerning the well-posedness and stability analysis problems of the closed-loop system, i.e. of the system (1) interconnected with a dynamic KKT controller in a feedback loop. We refer to [11] for a more detailed treatment of these topics.

4.1 Well-Posedness

Since the function $max(\cdot, 0)$ is globally Lipschitz continuous, for checking well-posedness of the closed-loop system with max-based KKT controller one can resort on standard Lipschitz continuity conditions.

Notice that the system (1) in closed loop with a saturation-based KKT controller belongs to a specific class of gradient-type complementarity systems for which sufficient conditions for well-posedness have been presented in [9] and [10]. More precisely, it was shown that the *hypermonotonicity* property plays a crucial role in establishing well-posedness, see [9] and [10] for details.

It can be easily verified, see [11] for details, that Lipschitz continuity implies hypermonotonicity, and therefore we can state the following unified condition for well-posedness of the system (1) in closed loop with a dynamic KKT controller (irrespective of the KKT controller type):

Proposition 1. *Suppose that the functions q, ∇J and all entries in ∇q are globally Lipschitz. Then the system* (1) *in closed loop with a dynamic KKT controller of the form* (5) *or* (6) *is globally well-posed.*

4.2 Stability Analysis

Stability analysis for a fixed $w \in W$. Theorem 1 states that for any constant-valued exogenous signal $w(t) \in W$, the closed-loop system necessarily has an equilibrium. Furthermore, from the proof of this theorem it follows that for *all* corresponding equilibrium points the values of the state vectors (x, x_c) are *unique*. For a given $w(t) = w \in W$, the necessary and sufficient condition for uniqueness of the remaining closed-loop system state vectors (x_λ, x_μ), and therefore a necessary and sufficient condition for uniqueness of the closed-loop system equilibrium, corresponds to the condition for uniqueness of the Lagrange multipliers in (4). This condition is known as the *strict Mangasarian-Fromovitz constraint qualification* (SMFCQ) and is presented in [12].

Since both types of complementarity integrators can be presented in a piecewise affine framework [13], for a given $w(t) = w \in W$ characterized by a *unique equilibrium*, one can perform a global asymptotic stability analysis based on: *i)* the analysis procedures from [14, 15] in case when (2) is a quadratic program and (1) is a linear system; *ii)* the analysis procedure from [16] in case when (2) is given by a (higher order) polynomial objective function and (higher order) polynomial inequality constraints, while (1) is a general polynomial system.

In the case when $w(t) = w \in W$ is such that the SMFCQ does not hold, the closed-loop system is characterized by a *set of equilibria* (not a singleton), which is then an invariant set for the closed-loop system. Each equilibrium in this set is characterized by different values of the state vectors (x_λ, x_μ), but unique values of the remaining states. Under additional generalized Slater constraint qualification, see [17] for details, the set of equilibria is guaranteed to be bounded. For stability analysis with respect to this set, one could invoke a suitable extension of LaSalle's invariance theorem [18].

Stability analysis for all $w \in W$. A possibility to perform stability analysis for *all possible* constant values of the exogenous signal $w(t)$, i.e. for all $w(t) = w$ where w is *any* constant in W, is to formulate a corresponding robust stability analysis problem. For instance, consider the max-based KKT control structure, which is particulary suitable for this approach. Let $\mathcal{M}$ denote the set of autonomous systems that contains all the closed-loop systems that correspond to one fixed $w \in W$. Furthermore, suppose that each system in $\mathcal{M}$ has the origin as equilibrium, after an appropriate state transformation. Then, it can be shown that for any closed-loop system in $\mathcal{M}$ the static nonlinearity of the MCI, see Figure 1a, fulfills certain sector bound conditions. Therefore, stability of all the closed-loop systems in the set $\mathcal{M}$ can be established using the integral quadratic constraint approach [19]. See [11] for a complete description that also deals with non-unique equilibria.

5 Illustrative Example

To illustrate the theory, in this section we present the following example that includes nonlinear constraints on the steady-state operating point. Consider a third-order system of the form (1) given by

$$\begin{pmatrix} \dot{x}_1 \\ \dot{x}_2 \\ \dot{x}_3 \end{pmatrix} = \begin{pmatrix} -2.5 & 0 & -5 \\ 0 & -5 & -15 \\ 0.1 & 0.1 & -0.2 \end{pmatrix} \begin{pmatrix} x_1 \\ x_2 \\ x_3 \end{pmatrix} + \begin{pmatrix} 0 \\ 0 \\ -0.1 \end{pmatrix} w + \begin{pmatrix} 2.5 & 0 \\ 0 & 5 \\ 0 & 0 \end{pmatrix} \begin{pmatrix} u_1 \\ u_2 \end{pmatrix}, \tag{13a}$$

$$y = \mathrm{col}(x_1, x_2, x_3), \tag{13b}$$

and let $u := \mathrm{col}(u_1, u_2)$ collect the control inputs.

With $x_p := \mathrm{col}(x_1, x_2)$, the associated steady-state related optimization problem is defined as follows:

$$\min_{x_p} \quad \frac{1}{2} x_p^\top H x_p + a^\top x_p \tag{14a}$$

subject to

$$x_1 + x_2 = w, \tag{14b}$$

$$(x_1 - 4.7)^2 + (x_2 - 4)^2 \leq 3.5^2, \tag{14c}$$

where $H = \mathrm{diag}(6, 2)$, $a = \mathrm{col}(-4, -4)$, and the value of the exogenous signal w is limited in the interval $W = [4, 11.5]$. It can be verified that for this W and the constraints (14b) and (14c), Assumption 1 holds. Furthermore, it can easily be verified that Assumption 3 holds. From the dynamics of the state x_3, it follows that in steady-state the equality $x_1 + x_2 - 2x_3 = w$ holds. Therefore, in steady-state, $x_3 = 0$ implies fulfilment of the constraint (14b). This implies that for control purposes we can directly use the value of the state x_3 as a measure of violation of this constraint. Hence, explicit knowledge of w is not required.

Simulations of the closed-loop system response to stepwise changes in the exogenous input $w(t)$, which is presented in Figure 2a, have been performed.

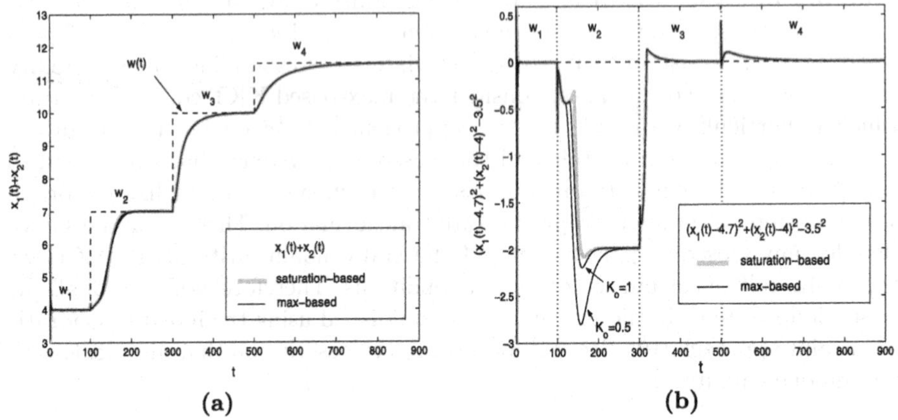

Fig. 2. (a) The values of w and $x_1 + x_2$, i.e. the right hand and the left hand side of the equality constraint (14b), as a function of time. (b) Violation of the inequality constraint (14c) as a function of time. When the curves are above zero (horizontal dashed line), the constraint is violated.

Figure 2 and Figure 3 present the results of the simulation when the system is controlled with both a saturation-based and a max-based KKT controller with different values of the gain K_o. Both controllers were implemented with the gains $K_\lambda = 0.15$, $K_\mu = 0.1$, $K_c = -0.7I_2$, and the gain K_o in the max-based controller was set to 0.5 and 1. In each figure, a legend is included to indicate which trajectory belongs to each controller.

Figure 2a and Figure 2b clearly illustrate that the controllers continuously drive the closed-loop system towards the steady-state where the constraints (14b), (14c) are satisfied. Figures 2b and 3a show fulfilment of the complementarity slackness condition (4c) in steady-state.

Finally, Figure 3b illustrates that the controllers drive the system towards the correspondent optimal operating point as defined by (14). In this figure the straight dashed lines labeled w_i, $i = 1, \ldots, 4$, represent the equality constraint $x_1 + x_2 = w_i$ where the values of $w_i, i = 1, \ldots, 4$ are the ones given in Figure 2a. The dashed circle represents the inequality constraint (14c), i.e. the steady-state feasible region for x_p is within this circle. Thin dotted lines represent the contour lines of the objective function (14a), while the dash-dot line represents the locus of the optimal point $\tilde{x}_p(w)$ for the whole range of values w in the case when the inequality constraint (14c) would be left out from the optimization problem.

From the simulations we can observe that by increasing the gain K_o in the max-based controller, the trajectory of the closed-loop system with the max-based KKT controller approaches the trajectory of the closed-loop system with saturation-based KKT controller.

Remark 2. The presented KKT control methodology has a great potential for application in real-time, price-based power balance and network congestion

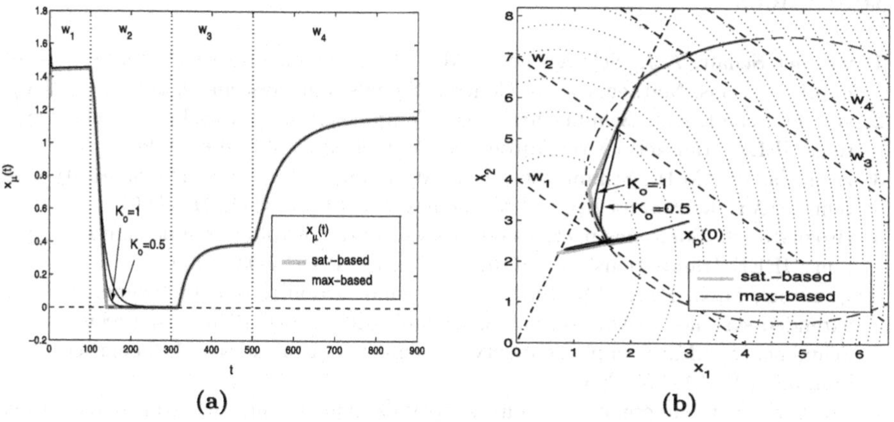

Fig. 3. (a) Simulated trajectory of the controller state x_μ. (b) Simulated trajectory of the state vector x_p for the close-loop system.

control of electrical energy transmission systems. This is considered to be one of the toughest problems in operation and control of market-based power systems [20]. This topic has recently gained a significant attention in power systems community, following the large restructuring processes occurring in this sector. Specifically, the KKT control structure is suitable for this particular application since it explicitly manipulates with the Lagrange multipliers, which, in power systems, have the interpretation of nodal prices for electricity. The interested reader is refereed to [11] for more details on this topic.

6 Conclusions

In this paper we have considered the problem of regulating a general nonlinear dynamical system to a time-varying economically optimal operating point. The economically optimal operating point was implicitly defined as a solution to a given constrained convex optimization problem, which is related to steady-state operation. We have shown that complementarity systems arise naturally as a solution to this problem. More precisely, the solution that we proposed in this paper is based on the specific dynamic extension of the Karush-Kuhn-Tucker optimality conditions for the steady-state related optimization problem. An advantageous feature of the proposed solution is that it offers an explicit control law, i.e. the implementation of the controller does not require solving on-line the corresponding optimization problem. Some results and tools that can be used for well-posedness and stability analysis of the resulting closed-loop system have also been discussed.

Acknowledgments. The authors would like to thank Dr. Maurice Heemels for valuable discussions.

References

1. van der Schaft, A.J., Schumacher, J.M.: The complementarity-slackness class of hybrid systems. Mathematics of Control, Signals, and Systems 9, 266–301 (1996)
2. van der Schaft, A.J., Schumacher, J.M.: Complementarity modeling of hybrid systems. IEEE Transactions on Automatic Control 43(3), 483–490 (1998)
3. Heemels, W.P.M.H., Schumacher, J.M., Weiland, S.: Linear complementarity systems. SIAM Journal on Applied Mathematics 60(4), 1234–1269 (2000)
4. Brogliato, B.: Some perspectives on analysis and control of complementarity systems. IEEE Transactions on Automatic Control 48, 918–935 (2003)
5. Çamlibel, M.K., Pang, J.S., Shen, J.: Lyapunov stability of complementarity and extended systems. SIAM Journal on Optimization 17(4), 1056–1101 (2006)
6. Schumacher, J.M.: Complementarity systems in optimization. Mathematical programming B 101, 263–296 (2004)
7. Boyd, S., Vandenberghe, L.: Convex optimization. Cambridge University Press, Cambridge (2004)
8. Khalil, H.K.: Nonlinear Systems, 3rd edn. Prentice-Hall, Englewood Cliffs (2002)
9. Heemels, W.P.M.H., Schumacher, J.M., Weiland, S.: Projected dynamical systems in a complementarity formalism. Operations Research Letters 27(2), 83–91 (2000)
10. Brogliato, B., Daniilidis, A., Lemaréchal, C., Acary, V.: On the equivalence between complementarity systems, projected systems and differential inclusions. Systems and Control Letters 55, 45–51 (2006)
11. Jokic, A.: Price-based optimal control of electrical power systems. PhD thesis, Eindhoven University of Technology, The Netherlands (2007)
12. Kyparisis, J.: On uniqueness of Kuhn-Tucker multipliers in nonlinear programming. Mathematical Programming 32, 242–246 (1985)
13. Sontag, E.D.: Nonlinear regulation: the piecewise linear approach. IEEE Transactions on Automatic Control 26(2), 346–357 (1981)
14. Johansson, M., Rantzer, A.: Computation of piecewise quadratic Lyapunov functions for hybrid systems. IEEE Transactions on Automatic Control 43(4), 555–559 (1998)
15. Gonçalves, J.M., Megretski, A., Dahleh, M.A.: Global analysis of piecewise linear systems using impact maps and surface Lyapunov functions. IEEE Transactions on Automatic Control 48(12), 2089–2106 (2003)
16. Prajna, S., Papachristodoulou, A.: Analysis of swiched and hybrid systems - beyond piecewise quadratic methods. In: American Control Conference, USA (2003)
17. Pomerol, J.C.: The boundedness of the Lagrange multipliers set and duality in mathematical programming. Zeitschrift für Operations Research 25, 191–204 (1981)
18. LaSalle, J.P.: The stability of dynamical systems. In: SIAM, (ed.) Regional Conference Series in Applied Mathematics. Philadelphia, vol. 25 (1976)
19. Megretski, A., Rantzer, A.: System analysis via integral quadratic constraints. IEEE Transactions on Automatic Control 42(6), 819–830 (1997)
20. Stoft, S.: Power System Economics: Designing Markets for Electricity. Kluwer Academic Publishers, Dordrecht (2002)

Dealing with Nondeterminism in Symbolic Control*

Marius Kloetzer and Calin Belta

Center for Information and Systems Engineering
Boston University
15 Saint Mary's Street, Boston, MA 02446
{kmarius,cbelta}@bu.edu

Abstract. Abstractions (also called symbolic models) are simple descriptions of continuous and hybrid systems that can be used in analysis and control. They are usually constructed in the form of transition systems with finitely many states. Such abstractions offer a very attractive approach to deal with complexity, while at the same time allowing for rich specification languages. Recent results show that, through the abstraction process, the resulting transition systems can be nondeterministic (*i.e.,* if an input is applied in a state, several next states are possible). However, the problem of controlling a nondeterministic transition system from a rich specification such as a temporal logic formula is not well understood. In this paper, we develop a control strategy for a nondeterministic transition system from a specification given as a Linear Temporal Logic formula with a deterministic Büchi generator. Our solution is inspired by LTL games on graphs, is complete, and scales polynomially with the size of the Büchi automaton. An example of controlling a linear system from a specification given as a temporal logic formula over the regions of its triangulated state space is included for illustration.

1 Introduction

In control problems, trajectories of "complex" mathematical models, such as systems of differential equations, are usually checked against "simple" specifications, such as stability of equilibria and set invariance. In formal verification, "rich" specifications, such as formulas of temporal logics, are checked against "simple" models of software programs and digital circuits, such as (finite) transition graphs. There has been a lot of interest lately in developing theoretical frameworks and computational tools for bridging in this gap, and therefore allowing for specifying the properties of continuous and hybrid systems in a rich language, with automatic verification and controller synthesis. Most of the existing approaches are centered at the concept of abstraction, *i.e.,* the process through which a system with infinitely many states (such as a control system in continuous space and time) is mapped to a system with finitely many states, called symbolic, or abstract model. Roughly, the abstract model can be seen as a transition graph, whose states label "equivalent" sets of states of the initial system.

* This work is partially supported by NSF CAREER 0447721 and NSF 0410514 at Boston University.

M. Egerstedt and B. Mishra (Eds.): HSCC 2008, LNCS 4981, pp. 287–300, 2008.

The abstract model can be either equivalent with the initial system with respect to the satisfaction of the specification, or it can provide an approximation, with the guarantee that the satisfaction of the specification for the abstract model is sufficient for the satisfaction of the specification by the initial system. Equivalent abstractions are based on the notion of bisimulation [1], while sufficient abstractions can be derived using simulation relations. The class of systems for which equivalent finite models exist include systems with very simple continuous dynamics, such as timed automata [2], multirate automata [3], rectangular automata [4], or systems with more complex continuous dynamics but simpler discrete dynamics, such as o-minimal hybrid systems [5]. More recent results provide conditions for the existence of equivalent abstractions for discrete-time continuous-space linear systems [6] and for more general systems through a relaxed notion of approximate bisimulation [7,8]. Recent works on constructing sufficient abstractions focus on systems with linear dynamics and polyhedral partitions [9] and systems with polynomial dynamics and partitions given by semi-algebraic sets [10]. In these works, the construction of sufficient or equivalent abstractions (if they exist) is expensive, and involves either the integration of vector fields [9] or quantifier elimination for real closed fields and theorem proving [10].

There are two classes of systems for which checking the existence of equivalent abstractions and the construction of sufficient abstractions can be reduced to polyhedral operations only [11]: affine systems with simplicial partitions (*e.g.*, triangulations in the 2D case) and multi-affine systems with rectangular partitions. Roughly, such constructions are possible because necessary and sufficient conditions for the existence of controllers driving all initial states of an affine (multi-affine) system in a simplex (rectangle) through a facet in finite time and for making a simplex (rectangle) an invariant can be reduced to checking the non-emptiness of polyhedral sets [12,13]. If in a simplicial (rectangular) partition of the state space of an affine (multi-affine) system, feedback controllers can be designed such that all states either stay inside or leave through a facet (to a neighbor region), then the corresponding quotient transition system is an equivalent abstraction (bisimulation quotient). Moreover, this finite transition system is deterministic, since an applied control uniquely determines the next state. If the control specification for the initial system is given as a Linear Temporal Logic (LTL) formula over the regions of the partitioned state space, then the problem reduces to controlling a deterministic transition system from an LTL formula over its states. This problem is relatively easy, since it can be solved by adapting standard tools from LTL model checking [14]. We proposed a solution in [15], and used it to develop a fully automated procedure for control of linear systems from specifications given as arbitrary LTL formulas over arbitrary linear predicates in the state variables.

This paper is motivated by recent results [16,17] extending the work from [12,13]. Specifically, in [16], the authors showed that, for an affine system in a simplex, even though a controller driving all states through a facet (*i.e.*, to a neighbor) might fail to exist, controllers driving the system through a set of facets (*i.e.*, to a set of neighbors) might be found. Similar results were proved for multi-affine systems and rectangles in [17]. While reducing the conservativeness introduced through the abstraction process, these results raise a new problem: since a controller does not guarantee a transition to exactly one neighbor, the abstract transition system is non-deterministic. On the other hand, the problem of controlling a non-deterministic transition system from a rich specification such as an LTL formula over its states is currently not solved.

In this paper, we focus on specifications given as formulas of a fragment of LTL [14] for which the corresponding languages are generated by deterministic Büchi automata. We propose a solution inspired from (infinite) LTL games [18,19,20], which are played by two players on a graph. Roughly said, we generalize this problem to transition systems with inputs, and treat non-determinism as an adversary. The solution is presented in the form of a feedback automaton, which at each step reads the current state of the transition system and generates the applied control. We approached this problem in our previous work [21], where we mapped it to a classical LTL game played on a modified transition system by assigning its states to the two players. As opposed to [21], the solution that we propose here is *complete*, in the sense that we find a solution if one exists. The algorithms proposed in this paper were implemented as a user-friendly software tool under Matlab, which is freely downloadable from `http://iasi.bu.edu/~software/nondet.htm`.

2 Case Study

To motivate the problem and illustrate our approach, we consider an example of controlling an affine system from a specification given as a temporal logic statement about the reachability of simplices in a triangulation of its state space. Consider the following affine system:

$$\dot{x} = \begin{bmatrix} -0.4 & 0.2 \\ 0.5 & -0.8 \end{bmatrix} x + \begin{bmatrix} 1 & 0 \\ 0 & 1 \end{bmatrix} u + \begin{bmatrix} 0.7 \\ 0.5 \end{bmatrix}, \tag{1}$$

where the state and controls are restricted to rectangular sets $x \in [2, 10] \times [1, 7]$ and $u \in [-1, 1] \times [-1, 1]$, respectively. Assume the (planar) state space of the system is triangulated as shown in Fig. 1 (a).

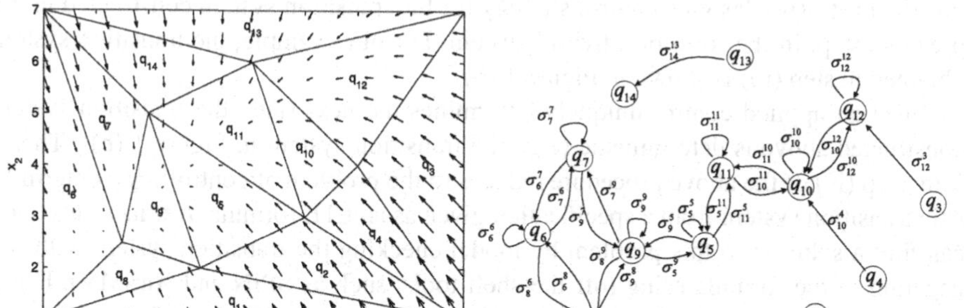

(a) (b)

Fig. 1. (a) Triangular partition of the planar state space of system (1) and the vector field corresponding to the uncontrolled system. (b) The deterministic transition system modelling controllers driving all states in a simplex through a facet or making a simplex an invariant (σ_j^i with $i \neq j$ is a feedback controller for q_i guaranteeing exit to q_j in finite time; σ_i^i is a feedback controller making q_i an invariant.

Assume we want to find initial states and control strategies for system (1) such that all the trajectories of the closed loop system satisfy the following specification:

$$\text{“}\textit{eventually visit } q_6 \textit{ and } q_{12}, \textit{ in any order}\text{”} \tag{2}$$

In other words, it is desired that the trajectories of the closed loop system evolve in the triangulated environment such that, at some point in the future, the regions labelled by q_6 and q_{12} (not necessarily in this order), are reached. Note that this specification contains temporal (“eventually”) and logical (“and”) information. Temporal logics [14] offer formal frameworks for such temporal and logical statements. Specifically, in our case, the specification translates to the following Linear Temporal Logic (LTL) formula over the set of symbols $\{q_1, \ldots, q_{14}\}$:

$$\phi = \Diamond q_6 \wedge \Diamond q_{12}, \tag{3}$$

where “$\Diamond$” means “eventually” and “$\wedge$” is the well known notation for “and”. Therefore, the problem translates to controlling the affine system (1) from a specification given as the temporal logic formula (3) over triangles in its partitioned state space.

This problem can be seen as a particular case of the framework we developed in [15], where an arbitrary linear system was controlled from LTL formulas over arbitrary linear predicates in its state variables. In short, the computational tool developed in [15] consists of the following steps: (i) construct a polyhedral partition of the state space using the linear predicates in the specification, (ii) for each of the polytopes in the partition, find feedback controllers making the polytope an invariant, and, for each of its facets, find feedback controllers driving all the initial states in the polytope through the facet (to a neighbor polytope) in finite time, (iii) arrange the results of the previous two steps in the form of a transition system (or transition graph), where the states (nodes) label the polytopes, and the transitions (included in the adjacency relations between polytopes) are labelled by the corresponding controllers designed in the previous step (a self transition corresponds to a controller making the corresponding polytope an invariant set), (iv) design a control strategy for the transition system constructed in the previous step, in the form of a hybrid system. For our example, the transition system obtained in step (iii) is shown in Figure 1 (b).

Since an applied control uniquely determines the next state, the transition system constructed above is deterministic (*e.g.*, the transition system in Figure 1 (b)). Therefore, step (iv) of the above procedure reduces to the problem of controlling a deterministic transition system from a specification given as an LTL formula over its states. One can find a solution to this problem by model checking the transition system with the negation of the formula using (off-the-shelf tools, such as SPIN and NuSMV). However, there is no control over the produced counterexample, which might be too long, or simply not implementable by the initial continuous system. To overcome this, in [15], we proposed another solution for the problem, which will be also briefly reviewed in Remark 3. The solution consists of the following steps: (a) construction of a Büchi automaton accepting the language satisfying the formula, (b) synchronization of the transition system with the Büchi automaton by taking their product, (c) finding a run in the product automaton that is implementable by the initial continuous system and is optimal with respect to a cost imposed by the particular application, and (d) finding the control strategy in the form of the sequence of controls producing the run from the previous step. Step (d) is possible because, in a deterministic transition system, a run is uniquely determined by a sequence of applied controls.

By applying the procedure from [15] to our example, we find that the set of initial states for which control strategies can be designed such that all trajectories of the closed loop system satisfy the formula is given by the union of all triangles except for q_1, q_2, q_{13}, q_{14}. The solution is of course conservative, in the sense that, even though we label some triangles as not containing initial states for trajectories satisfying the formula, there might exist states in these triangles such that trajectories originating there satisfy the formula. There are two sources of conservativeness in this approach: (1) the initial states are treated as whole sets given by the initial triangles (no subpartition is performed), and (2) only controllers either driving all initial states to a facet or making a triangle an invariant are allowed. Related to the latter source of conservativeness, one can imagine that, even though controllers driving all initial states to a facet might fail to exist, controllers guaranteeing exiting through a set of facets might be found. For example, by using the techniques from [12], no feedback controllers can be found to drive the states in triangle q_1 through the separating facet with q_8, or through the separating facet with q_2. However, by using the more general conditions from [16], a feedback controller can be found which guarantees that all initial states in q_1 will eventually reach either q_8 or q_2. However, if such controllers are allowed, the quotient transition system becomes nondeterministic. For our example, the resulting transition system is shown in Figure 2 (b). By applying the general method for controlling nondeterministic transition systems proposed in this paper, coupled with feedback controllers as in [16], we show in Section 6 that control strategies producing trajectories satisfying the formula can be found for all initial states in $q_1, q_2, \ldots, q_{14}$. In other words, the conservatism from our previous method is considerably reduced.

3 Preliminaries

Throughout the paper, for a finite set A, we will use the notations $|A|$, A^ω, and 2^A to denote its cardinality, the set of all infinite words over A, and its power set (the set of all its subsets), respectively.

Definition 1 (Transition system). *A finite (nondeterministic) transition system is a tuple $T = (Q, \Sigma, \delta)$, where:*

- *Q is a finite set of states,*
- *Σ is a finite input alphabet,*
- *$\delta : Q \times \Sigma \to 2^Q$ is a (nondeterministic) transition function.*

For a given state $q \in Q$, the set of available (feasible) inputs is denoted by Σ_q (*i.e.*, Σ_q is the set of $\sigma_i \in \Sigma$ for which $|\delta(q, \sigma_i)| \geq 1$). An *input word* $\sigma \in \Sigma^\omega$ is denoted by $\sigma = \sigma_1\sigma_2\sigma_3 \ldots$ A *trajectory* or *run* of T produced by an input word σ starting from q is an infinite sequence $w \in Q^\omega$, $w = w_1w_2w_3 \ldots$ with the property that $w_1 = q$ and $\forall i \geq 1$, $w_{i+1} \in \delta(w_i, \sigma_i)$.

A formal definition of the syntax and semantics of Linear Temporal Logic (LTL) formulas is beyond the scope of this paper. Intuitively, an LTL formula over the set Q

is any "sensible" combination of elements from Q, logical operators $\neg$ (negation), $\wedge$ (conjunction), $\vee$ (disjunction), $\Rightarrow$ (implication), $\Leftrightarrow$ (equivalence), and temporal operators $\bigcirc$ (next), $\mathcal{U}$ (until), $\diamondsuit$ (eventually), $\square$ (always). The semantics of LTL formulas are given over runs of transition system T. For example, if the states Q of T are labels for regions in a partitioned state space of a control system, then the control specification "visit region q_1, then region q_2, and then go to final target q_3, while avoiding q_1" translates to formula

$$\diamondsuit(q_1 \wedge \diamondsuit(q_2 \wedge (\neg q_1)\mathcal{U}q_3)) \tag{4}$$

which is true for any run in which q_1 appears at some position, then q_2 appears, and then eventually q_3 appears, while q_1 does not appear before this happens.

For every LTL formula over Q, there exists a Büchi automaton (also called a generator of the LTL formula) accepting all and only the words satisfying it [22].

Definition 2 (Büchi automaton). *A Büchi automaton is a tuple $B = (S, S_0, Q, \delta_B, F)$, where:*

- *S is a finite set of states,*
- *$S_0 \subseteq S$ is the set of initial states,*
- *Q is the input alphabet,*
- *$\delta_B : S \times Q \to 2^S$ is a nondeterministic transition function,*
- *$F \subseteq S$ is the set of accepting (final) states.*

The semantics of a Büchi automaton is defined over infinite input words. Let $w = w_1w_2w_3...$, $w \in Q^\omega$, be an infinite input word of automaton B. We denote by $\mathcal{R}_B(w)$ the set of all initialized runs of B that can be produced by w:

$$\mathcal{R}_B(w) = \{r = s_1s_2s_3...|\ s_1 \in S_0,\ s_{i+1} \in \delta_B(s_i, w_i),\ \forall i \geq 1\} \tag{5}$$

Definition 3 (Büchi acceptance). *A word $w \in Q^\omega$ is accepted by the Büchi automaton B if and only if $\exists r \in \mathcal{R}_B(w)$ so that $inf(r) \cap F \neq \emptyset$, where $inf(r)$ denotes the set of states appearing infinitely often in the run r.*

In words, an input word w is accepted by B if and only if there exists at least a run induced by w that visits F infinitely often.

Remark 1. Motivated by the particular control application, we use simplified definitions of transition system, Büchi automaton, and Büchi acceptance. We refer to [14] for more general definitions.

4 Problem Formulation and Approach

Problem 1. Given a transition system $T = (Q, \Sigma, \delta)$ and a Büchi automaton $B = (S, S_0, Q, \delta_B, F)$, find a set of initial states $Q_0 \subseteq Q$ and a control strategy for T such that all runs of T are accepted by B.

The Büchi automaton B from the above problem should be seen as a generator for an LTL formula ϕ over Q, which is the high-level control specification. Due to some complexity issues that go beyond the scope of this paper, in this work we assume that the Büchi automaton B from Problem 1 is *deterministic* (*i.e.*, $S_0 = \{s_0\}$ is a singleton, and $\delta_B : S \times Q \to S$ is a partial function). Intuitively, the current state of a deterministic Büchi automaton shows the progress towards the satisfaction of the LTL formula, and this information is used in developing the strategy from that point on. If a deterministic Büchi automaton does not exist for a given formula, the nondeterministic Büchi generator has to be translated into a more complicated type of deterministic automaton, like Muller or Rabin.

Remark 2. It is important to note at this point that, although for any LTL formula a generator Büchi automaton can be constructed, this automaton is in general nondeterministic, and cannot be always determinized [23]. However, the assumption that the Büchi generator is deterministic does not seem restrictive from an expressivity point of view [24], since most LTL formulas capturing control tasks (including the formulas in Eqn. (3), (4), as well as specifications like safety and liveness) belong to some isolated fragments of LTL, for which (partially-ordered) deterministic generators can be constructed [25].

Remark 3. If the transition system T were deterministic (*i.e.* $\delta : Q \times \Sigma \to Q$), then a solution to Problem 1 could be found by using an idea similar to model checking [14,15]: the product automaton $T \times B$ is computed and in this product automaton an accepting run with a specific structure is found and projected to a run of T. Since T is deterministic, a control strategy implementing the desired run can be constructed. This approach also works in the case of nondeterministic Büchi automata.

Problem 1 is related to the problem of controlling a discrete event system modelled as a transition system with inputs [26]. However, in this latter case, the specification is given as an ω-regular expression over inputs (rather than an LTL formula over states). In this paper, we propose a method inspired by the theory of LTL games. An LTL game is defined on a graph $G = (V, E)$ and it is played by two players: a protagonist and an adversary. The set of nodes (states) V is partitioned into a set of protagonist's states V_p, from which the protagonist can choose the next state, and a set of adversary's states V_a, from which the adversary chooses the next state [18]. A play consists of an infinite sequence of states resulted from an infinite sequence of transitions (edges) chosen by the two players. The specification for an LTL game is an LTL formula over the set of states V. A play is won by the protagonist if the produced run satisfies the LTL formula.

The protagonist has a winning strategy if, whenever the current state is in V_p, she manages to choose transitions such that she wins the current game, no matter what transitions the adversary chooses when the current state is in V_a. The goal of an LTL game is to find the set of initial states from where the protagonist has winning strategies and a winning strategy for plays starting in those initial states. The existing algorithms for solving LTL games are complete, in the following sense: when starting from the found set of initial states, the winning strategy guarantees that the protagonist wins the game, no matter how smart the adversary is, and when starting from any other state, the adversary has a strategy prohibiting the protagonist's winning [19].

Intuitively, we can think of control Problem 1 as an LTL game in which the adversary uses the non-determinism in the problem in the smartest way possible to prevent us from producing runs of T satisfying the formula. More precisely, while we have full control in choosing the current input of the transition system T in every state from Q, the adversary can choose the next state in the case when the chosen input produces nondeterministic transitions.

Maybe the simplest way of transforming our problem into a standard LTL game would be to partition the set of states Q in two sets: a protagonist's set Q_p, with each state having only deterministic outgoing transitions, and an adversary's set Q_a, with each state having at least one input producing non-deterministic transitions. Then, a graph with vertices Q can be easily constructed, where the adversary has full control in choosing any existing transition from states in Q_a. An algorithm for solving LTL games can be applied to this graph, and the resulting winning strategy (if any) can be adapted for the initial T as follows: in states from Q_p, the winning strategy (giving the next state to be reached) is easily mapped to the input producing the deterministic transition to the desired next state, and in states from Q_a any feasible input can be applied (since we gave full control to the adversary). Obviously, this strategy is conservative because we don't use our power of choosing inputs in every state, but instead we give all the transitions (inputs) from some states to the adversary. An attempt to reduce this conservatism can be as follows: first, place all states from Q in Q_p. Then, for each non-deterministic input in a node, replace the non-deterministic transitions with a deterministic one to a newly added state in Q_a, and assign the removed non-deterministic transitions to this new state. The solution is correct only for some LTL fragments, it is more complex, and it still cannot be proved to be complete.

In [21], Problem 1 was mapped to an LTL game for an augmented transition system obtained by splitting the states of T and by assigning them to the protagonist and the adversary. However, this procedure led to a conservative, incomplete solution. In the next section, we present a different approach, which is based on an adaptation of the LTL game algorithms, and which leads to a complete solution to Problem 1.

5 Solution to Problem 1

In this section, we show how the main steps involved in solving an LTL game [19] can be adapted to our problem. We first construct a product automaton P between the transition system T and the Büchi automaton B (Sect. 5.1). We then solve a Büchi game on P and find a set of initial states, together with a memoryless (positional) winning strategy (Sect. 5.2). Finally, the set of initial states and the winning strategy for T are obtained by projecting the initial states of P into Q and by adapting the winning strategy of P for T, respectively (Sect. 5.3). Unlike the winning strategy for P, the one corresponding to T will have memory.

5.1 Constructing the Product Automaton

Definition 4 (Product automaton). *The product automaton* $P = T \times B$ *between the nondeterministic transition system* $T = (Q, \Sigma, \delta)$ *and the deterministic Büchi automaton* $B = (S, S_0, Q, \delta_B, F)$ *is defined as the tuple* $P = (S_P, S_{P0}, \Sigma, \delta_P, F_P)$, *where:*

- $S_P = Q \times S$ *is the finite set of states,*
- $S_{P0} = Q \times S_0$ *is the set of initial states,*
- Σ *is the input alphabet,*
- $\delta_P : S_P \times \Sigma \to 2^{S_P}$ *is the transition function, defined as* $\delta_P((q,s),\sigma) = \{(q',s') \in S_P \mid q' \in \delta(q,\sigma) \text{ and } s' = \delta_B(s,q)\}$*, where* $(q,s) \in S_P$ *and* $\sigma \in \Sigma$*,*
- $F_P = Q \times F$ *is the set of accepting (final) states.*

The product automaton P is in fact a nondeterministic Büchi automaton with input alphabet Σ. Its acceptance condition is formulated as in Definition 3, but with respect to input words from Σ^ω. The product automaton in Definition 4 can be regarded as a match between the states and transitions of T and B. The transition function of P captures both the nondeterministic behavior of T and the way of deterministically tracking the progress towards the satisfaction on the LTL formula corresponding to B (infinitely visiting set F of B).

Let $w_P \in \Sigma^\omega$ be an accepted input of automaton P and let $r_P = (q_{i1}, s_{j1})\,(q_{i2}, s_{j2})\,(q_{i3}, s_{j3})...$ be a resulted run such that $inf(r_P) \cap F_P \neq \emptyset$. Then, a result from the model checking theory states that the projection of r_P to states in Q is a run $r_T = q_{i1}, q_{i2}, q_{i3}...$ of T accepted by B. Furthermore, a run of T accepted by B exists if and only if P has an accepted run. However, since T is nondeterministic, we cannot make sure that a certain run will be followed, as we could for the deterministic case mentioned in Remark 3. Therefore, our goal becomes to design a controller that applies to T inputs guaranteeing that any possible run will be accepted by B. Looking at P, this goal translates to designing a strategy of applying inputs to P such that any possible run r_P satisfies $inf(r_P) \cap F_P \neq \emptyset$.

This problem resembles a Büchi game, which is an intermediate step in solving a classical LTL game. The results from the next section can be seen as an extension of the solution to the Büchi game from partitioned graphs [18] to transition systems with inputs, where the protagonist can choose inputs and the adversary can choose the next state in nondeterministic transitions.

5.2 Solving a Büchi Game

As stated in the previous subsection, we want to apply inputs to P such that the subset of states F_P will be visited infinitely often. Whenever a nondeterministic transition is encountered, even though we are able to choose the input, the adversary will decide the next state, and we have to make sure that we will be able to accomplish the goal, no matter what state the adversary chooses. Eventually, by using a fixed-point strategy, we will be able to isolate a set of states $W_P \subseteq S_P$ (the winning region), from where we can guarantee infinitely many visits to F_P. An immediate adaptation of a result from the theory of LTL games [18] states that if a nonempty set W_P together with winning strategy of applying inputs exist, then there also exists a memoryless (positional) strategy, which applies a certain input in each state from W_P. In other words, a memoryless strategy will be a map $\pi_P : W_P \to \Sigma$.

In the following three definitions, which are adapted from [19], A is an arbitrary subset of the set of states S_P.

Definition 5 (Recurrent set). *The recurrent set of A, denoted by $\mathcal{R}(A)$, is defined as the set of all $s \in A$ from which there can be enforced infinitely many revisits to set A.*

The recurrent set will be recursively computed by starting with $\mathcal{R}_0(A) = A$ and by finding, at each step $i \geq 1$, the set $\mathcal{R}_i(A)$, which is the set of all $s \in A$ from which there can be enforced at least i revisits to set A. Then, because A is finite, the decreasing sequence $A \supseteq \mathcal{R}_1(A) \supseteq \mathcal{R}_2(A) \ldots$ will reach a stationary value (which can be the empty set) for some $i \leq |A|$, and that value is $\mathcal{R}(A)$. The actual details of computing $\mathcal{R}_i(A)$ will be given after Definition 7.

Definition 6 (Attractor set). *The attractor set of A, denoted by $\mathcal{A}(A)$, is the set of all $s \in S_P$ from which there can be enforced a visit to set A in zero or more steps.*

Enforcing a visit in zero steps is equivalent to starting from A and applying no input. The attractor set will be the stationary value of an increasing sequence: $\mathcal{A}_0(A) \subseteq \mathcal{A}_1(A) \subseteq \mathcal{A}_2(A) \ldots$, where $\mathcal{A}_i(A)$ is the set of all $s \in S_P$ from which there can be enforced a visit to set A in at most i steps. It is easy to see that the recursion starts with $\mathcal{A}_0(A) = A$ and, at each step, $\mathcal{A}_{i+1}(A)$ is computed as the union of $\mathcal{A}_i(A)$ with the set of all $s \in S_P \setminus \mathcal{A}_i(A)$ from which there can be enforced a visit to set $\mathcal{A}_i(A)$ in one step, for $i \geq 0$. The stationary set ($\mathcal{A}_{i+1}(A) = \mathcal{A}_i(A)$) will again be reached in a finite number of steps $i \leq |S_P|$.

The winning region W_P is given by $W_P = \mathcal{A}(\mathcal{R}(F_P))$: once $\mathcal{R}(F_P)$ is reached, we are certain that we can revisit states from F_P infinitely often. However, in order to effectively compute the recurrent set of a given subset of states, we need one more definition.

Definition 7 (Proper attractor). *The proper attractor of A, denoted by $\mathcal{A}^+(A)$, is defined as the set of all $s \in S_P$ from which there can be enforced a visit to set A in one or more steps.*

The proper attractor is computed similarly to the attractor set, but the following differences appear: we start with $\mathcal{A}_0^+(A) = \emptyset$ and, at each iteration, we compute $\mathcal{A}_{i+1}^+(A)$ as the union of $\mathcal{A}_i^+(A)$ with the set of all $s \in S_P \setminus \mathcal{A}_i^+(A)$ from which there can be enforced a visit to set $\mathcal{A}_i(A) \cup A$ in one step. This comes from the fact that the proper attractor set requires at least one step to be taken (one input to be applied) in order to visit set A, while the regular attractor from Definition 6 consider as a visit the situation of starting from set A and taking no transition. Because of this difference, the proper attractor is suitable for computing the recurrent set, by using the recurrence $\mathcal{R}_{i+1}(A) = \mathcal{R}_i(A) \cap \mathcal{A}^+(\mathcal{R}_i(A))$: at each step, keep only states from $\mathcal{R}_i(A)$ from where a revisit to $\mathcal{R}_i(A)$ can be enforced in a strictly positive number of steps.

We now have all the tools for solving the Büchi game on the product automaton P. Due to space constraints, we do not include the corresponding algorithm here, and we refer to the technical report from `http://iasi.bu.edu/~software/nondet.htm`. The idea of solving the Büchi game on P is to first compute $\mathcal{R}(F_P)$ (using the recurrence given after Definition 7), and then, if the resulting set is nonempty, the set $W_P = \mathcal{A}(\mathcal{R}(F_P))$ is computed (as described after Definition 6). The winning strategy π_P is constructed during the computation of these sets, by searching inputs from Σ

guaranteeing the satisfaction of definitions for recurrent and attractor sets, respectively. The obtained solution is the set W_P and the memoryless strategy $\pi_P : W_P \to \Sigma$. If the set $W_{P0} = S_{P0} \cap W_P$ is nonempty, then there exist initial states of P from where F_P will be visited infinitely often. Otherwise, our Büchi game with inputs has no solution, and correspondingly Problem 1 is infeasible. The solution from this section is complete, and its correctness is guaranteed by construction.

5.3 Constructing the Control Strategy for T

If there is a solution for winning the Büchi game on the product automaton P (set W_{P0} is nonempty), we have to adapt this solution to our initial transition system T. First, the set of initial states of T from where the LTL formula can be satisfied is $Q_0 = \alpha(W_{P0})$, where map $\alpha : S_P \to Q$ is just the projection of states from P to Q. Second, the control strategy for T will be an automaton C obtained from the memoryless strategy π_P in the winning region W_P. The input applied to C will be the current state of T, and the output of C will give the next input to be applied to T.

The control automaton C is the tuple $C = (S, Q, s_0, \tau, \pi, \Sigma)$, where:

- S is the set of states of B,
- Q is the input set, equal with the set of states of T,
- s_0 is the initial state of the deterministic Büchi automaton B,
- $\tau : S \times Q \to S$ is the memory update function, $\tau(s, q) = \delta_B(s, q)$ if $(q, s) \in W_P$, and $\tau(s, q)$ undefined otherwise,
- $\pi : S \times Q \to \Sigma$ is the output function, $\pi(s, q) = \pi_P((q, s))$ if $(q, s) \in W_P$, and $\pi(s, q)$ undefined otherwise.

The correctness of the control automaton C can be verified as follows: if we equip C with the set of final states F, then the product automaton $T \times C$ will have the same states as P, its transitions will be the subset of transitions of P that can appear during the winning of a Büchi game, and the strategy for applying inputs is exactly π_P.

To summarize, the solution to Problem 1 is given by the set of initial states $Q_0 = \alpha(W_{P0})$ and the feedback control automaton C. Whenever T starts from an initial state in set Q_0, the satisfaction of the LTL formula corresponding to the Büchi automaton B is guaranteed by the controller C, which, at each step, reads the current state of T, uses map π to determine the next input to be applied to T, and updates its own internal state by using the map τ.

Since the solution from section 5.2 is complete, the overall procedure proposed in this paper for solving Problem 1 is complete. On complexity, the running time of the overall three-step procedure is $O(|Q|^2 \cdot |S|^2 \cdot |\Sigma|)$ (proofs are omitted due to space constraints). If the specification is given as an LTL formula, to this we need to add the running time for the conversion of the formula to a Büchi generator, which is at most double exponential in the length of the formula [25]. If smaller fragments of LTL are considered, then the construction of the Büchi generator can be more efficient. For example, for the LTL fragment which includes the example in Eqn. (4), exponential complexity can be achieved [25]. Moreover, note that this upper bounds for complexity are very rarely attained in practice.

The three-step procedure proposed in this paper has been implemented in Matlab. The user-friendly interface takes as input the transition system T and the Büchi automaton B, and returns the control automaton C. The software package is freely downloadable from `http://iasi.bu.edu/~software/nondet.htm`.

6 Case Study Revisited

Let us now revisit the case study from Section 2, which requires to find initial states and feedback controllers for system (1) such that all trajectories of the corresponding closed loop system satisfy specification (2), *i.e.,* LTL formula (3). The deterministic Büchi automaton corresponding to the formula (not shown due to space constraints) has 4 states, one final state, and 56 transitions, out of which 52 are self transitions.

We start by constructing a transition system T with states $Q = \{q_1, \ldots, q_{14}\}$ corresponding to the partition elements and with transitions capturing the ability of designing affine feedback controllers such that a triangle either becomes an invariant for the closed loop system, or it is left in finite time to one or several neighbors. To compute such controllers, we used the method developed in [16], which consists of polyhedral operations only. We first check transitions to one neighbor. Then, if some neighbor(s) cannot be reached, we check transitions to the possible pairs of neighbors that include the non-reachable one(s). We stop either when every neighbor can be reached (through deterministic or non-deterministic transitions), or when all combinations of exit facets were checked (including the set of all three facets). The resulting transition system (shown in Figure 2 (b)) has 38 transitions, out of which 27 are deterministic.

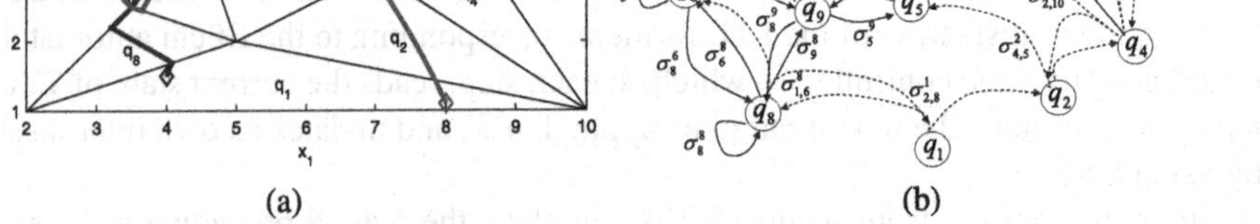

(a) (b)

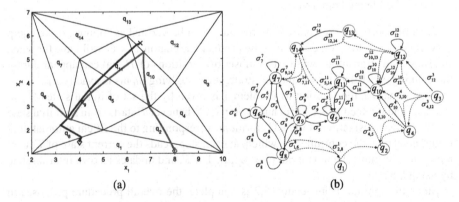

Fig. 2. (a) Two continuous trajectories of the controlled system, starting from the points marked with "◇" ($x = (4, 1.5)$ and $x = (8, 1.1)$, respectively) and asymptotically converging to the points marked with "X". (b) The nondeterministic transition system modelling feedback controllers making a triangle an invariant and driving all states to one or several neighbors. Deterministic transitions are shown in solid line, while non-deterministic transitions are shown in dashed line. $\sigma^i_{j,k}$ labels a controller driving all initial states in q_i to q_j or q_k.

By using the three-step approach from Sect. 5, we conclude that formula ϕ can be satisfied by trajectories starting from any triangle q_i, $i = 1, \ldots, 14$. The product automaton has 56 states, which appear all in the winning region W_P. The control automaton C has 4 states. The computation for all three steps took less than one second. We skip the exact details on how this discrete control strategy is applied to the continuous system (1). Roughly, a discrete transition in T takes place when the current triangle is left. Each input to be applied to T is mapped to an affine feedback controller, and applied as long as the continuous trajectory evolves in the current triangle.

In Fig. 2 (a), we show two continuous trajectories starting in region q_1 and corresponding to the strategy imposed by the control automaton C. Even though the continuous trajectories reach different sequences of triangles, they both satisfy the formula. Each trajectory converges to a point marked by "X", inside q_6 and q_{12}, respectively. Note that the solution presented here is less conservative than the one shown in Section 2, which was based on control-to-facet problems and deterministic transition systems. We also solved the (discrete part of the) problem by using two other (conservative) approaches: (1) direct translation to an LTL game on a graph (see Sect. 4), and (2) LTL game played on an augmented transition system (see [21]). Notably, as in Section 2, these two methods returned that the formula can be satisfied by starting from any triangle except q_1, q_2, q_{13}, q_{14}.

7 Conclusion

We developed a method for control of a nondeterministic transition system from a specification given as a temporal logic formula generated by a deterministic Büchi automaton. The method is complete and scales polynomially with the size of the Büchi generator. We illustrated the application of the method to the control of a continuous planar affine system from a specification given as an LTL formula over regions in a triangulated environment.

The method proposed here is quite general, and can be used whenever a finite transition system representation of a control problem can be constructed (*e.g.*, multi-affine dynamics and rectangular partitions). Therefore, it provides the first steps towards the construction of expressive specification languages for symbolic control. An immediate application is automatic planning and control of robot motion, where triangulation and rectangular grids are the most used partitioning schemes, and task specifications are naturally given as temporal and logic statements about the reachability of regions of interest in the robot environment.

References

1. Milner, R.: Communication and concurrency. Prentice-Hall, Englewood CliDs, NJ (1989)
2. Alur, R., Dill, D.L.: A theory of timed automata. Theoretical Computer Science 126(2), 183–235 (1994)
3. Alur, R., Courcoubetis, C., Henzinger, T.A., Ho, P.H.: Hybrid automata: An algorithmic approach to the specification and verification of hybrid systems. In: Grossman, R.L., Ravn, A.P., Rischel, H., Nerode, A. (eds.) HS 1991 and HS 1992. LNCS, vol. 736, pp. 209–229. Springer, Heidelberg (1993)
4. Henzinger, T.A., Kopke, P.W., Puri, A., Varaiya, P.: What is decidable about hybrid automata? J. Comput. Syst. Sci. 57, 94–124 (1998)

5. Lafferriere, G., Pappas, G.J., Sastry, S.: O-minimal hybrid systems. Math. Control, Signals, Syst 13(1), 1–21 (2000)
6. Tabuada, P., Pappas, G.J.: Linear time logic control of discrete-time linear systems. IEEE Transactions on Automatic Control 51(12), 1862–1877 (2006)
7. Tabuada, P.: Symbolic control of linear systems based on symbolic subsystems. IEEE Transactions on Automatic Control 51(6), 1003–1013 (2006)
8. Girard, A.: Approximately bisimilar finite abstractions of stable linear systems. In: Bemporad, A., Bicchi, A., Buttazzo, G. (eds.) HSCC 2007. LNCS, vol. 4416, pp. 231–244. Springer, Heidelberg (2007)
9. Alur, R., Dang, T., Ivancic, F.: Reachability analysis of hybrid systems via predicate abstraction. In: Tomlin, C.J., Greenstreet, M.R. (eds.) HSCC 2002. LNCS, vol. 2289, Springer, Heidelberg (2002)
10. Tiwari, A., Khanna, G.: Series of abstractions for hybrid automata. In: Tomlin, C.J., Greenstreet, M.R. (eds.) HSCC 2002. LNCS, vol. 2289, Springer, Heidelberg (2002)
11. Belta, C., Habets, L.: Constructing decidable hybrid systems with velocity bounds. In: 43rd IEEE Conference on Decision and Control, Paradise Island, Bahamas (2004)
12. Habets, L., van Schuppen, J.: A control problem for affine dynamical systems on a full-dimensional polytope. Automatica 40, 21–35 (2004)
13. Belta, C., Habets, L.: Control of a class of nonlinear systems on rectangles. IEEE Transactions on Automatic Control 51(11), 1749–1759 (2006)
14. Clarke, E.M., Grumberg, O., Peled, D.A.: Model Checking. MIT Press, Cambridge (1999)
15. Kloetzer, M., Belta, C.: A fully automated framework for control of linear systems from LTL specifications. In: Hespanha, J.P., Tiwari, A. (eds.) HSCC 2006. LNCS, vol. 3927, pp. 333–347. Springer, Heidelberg (2006)
16. Habets, L., Collins, P., van Schuppen, J.: Reachability and control synthesis for piecewise-affine hybrid systems on simplices. IEEE Trans. Aut. Control 51, 938–948 (2006)
17. Kloetzer, M., Habets, L., Belta, C.: Control of rectangular multi-affine hybrid systems. In: 45th IEEE Conference on Decision and Control, San Diego, CA (2006)
18. Thomas, W.: Infinite games and verification. In: Brinksma, E., Larsen, K.G. (eds.) CAV 2002. LNCS, vol. 2404, pp. 58–64. Springer, Heidelberg (2002)
19. Wallmeier, N., Hütten, P., Thomas, W.: Symbolic synthesis of finite-state controllers for request-response specifications. In: H. Ibarra, O., Dang, Z. (eds.) CIAA 2003. LNCS, vol. 2759, pp. 113–127. Springer, Heidelberg (2003)
20. Piterman, N., Pnueli, A., Sa'ar, Y.: Synthesis of reactive(1) designs. In: Emerson, E.A., Namjoshi, K.S. (eds.) VMCAI 2006. LNCS, vol. 3855, pp. 364–380. Springer, Heidelberg (2005)
21. Kloetzer, M., Belta, C.: Managing non-determinism in symbolic robot motion planning and control. In: IEEE International Conference on Robotics and Automation, Rome, Italy (2007)
22. Wolper, P., Vardi, M., Sistla, A.: Reasoning about infinite computation paths. In: Nagel, E., et al. (eds.) Proceedings of the 24th IEEE Symposium on Foundations of Computer Science, Tucson, AZ, pp. 185–194 (1983)
23. Safra, S.: Complexity of automata on infinite objects. PhD thesis, The Weizman Institute of Science, Rehovot, Israel (1989)
24. Fainekos, G.E., Loizou, S.G., Pappas, G.J.: Translating temporal logic to controller specifications. In: 45th IEEE Conference on Decision and Control, San Diego, CA (2006)
25. Alur, R., Torre, S.L.: Deterministic generators and games for LTL fragments. In: 16th IEEE Symposium on Logic in Computer Science, LICS 2001, pp. 291–300 (2001)
26. Kumar, R., Garg, V.K.: Modeling and Control of Logical Discrete Event Systems. Kluwer, Boston, MA (1995)

Safety and Liveness in Intelligent Intersections*

Hemant Kowshik[1], Derek Caveney[2], and P.R. Kumar[1]

[1] CSL and ECE, University of Illinois, Urbana-Champaign
1308, West Main Street, Urbana, IL-61801, USA
[2] The Toyota Technical Center,
2350 Green Road, Ann Arbor, MI-48105, USA
kowshik2@uiuc.edu, derek.caveney@tema.toyota.com, prkumar@uiuc.edu

Abstract. Automation of driving tasks is becoming of increasing interest for highway traffic management. Technologies for on-board sensing, combined with global positioning and inter-vehicular wireless communications, can potentially provide remarkable improvements in safety and efficiency. We address the problem of designing intelligent intersections where traffic lights and stop signs are removed, and cars negotiate the intersection through a combination of centralized and distributed decision making. Such intelligent intersections are representative of complex distributed hybrid systems which need architectures and algorithms with provable safety and liveness.

We propose a hybrid architecture which involves an appropriate interplay between centralized coordination and distributed freedom for the cars. Our approach is based on each car having an open-loop infinite horizon contingency plan, which is updated at each sampling time in a distributed fashion. We also define a partial order relation between cars which specifies to each car a set of cars whose worst case behaviors it should guard against. We prove the safety and liveness of the overall scheme. Concerning performance, we conduct a simulation study that shows the benefits over stop signs and traffic lights.

1 Introduction

In the near future, cars will have access to a wide range of information from GPS and onboard sensors such as radar, lidar, camera, gyroscopes, etc. Further, vehicle to vehicle wireless communication enabled by Dedicated Short Range Communication (DSRC) radios will enable the exchange of this information with other cars. This has opened up a plethora of opportunities in the area of Intelligent Transportation systems [5]. In this paper, we will focus on safety applications. Accidents currently account for 42,000 fatalities every year and an estimated 18 percent of the healthcare expenditure in the U.S. [3]. Developing

* This material is based upon work partially supported by the Toyota Technical Center, Ann Arbor, MI, under Contract Number 2006-06246, NSF under Contract Nos. NSF ECCS-0701604, CNS-07-21992, NSF CNS 05-19535, and CCR-0325716, and USARO under Contract No. W-911-NF-0710287.

M. Egerstedt and B. Mishra (Eds.): HSCC 2008, LNCS 4981, pp. 301–315, 2008.

technologies to enhance vehicular and passenger safety is of great interest, and an important application vis-a-vis safety is collision avoidance. Collision avoidance technologies today are *passive*, and depend on the human driver to respond accurately. Automation of driving tasks is becoming increasingly prominent, with the introduction of Adaptive Cruise Control (ACC), Lane Keeping Assist (LKA) and Advanced Parking Guidance (APG). Such automated systems which improve safety, comfort and efficiency are the motivation for this paper.

Our focus in this paper is on *intelligent intersections.* An intelligent intersection is one in which conventional traffic control devices are removed. Vehicles coordinate their movement across the intersection through a combination of centralized and distributed real-time decision making, that leverages global positioning, wireless communications and in-vehicle sensing and computation. Smooth coordination of vehicles through intersections will provide overall improvements in fuel efficiency, vehicle wear and travel time. Most importantly, intelligent intersections can provide *guaranteed* safety.

Intelligent intersections are representative of complex distributed hybrid systems which require architectures and algorithms that guarantee safety and liveness, as a prerequisite for their acceptance. For safety, we pose the problem of collision avoidance in a worst case setting. One needs to safeguard not only against the worst-case behaviors of the other agents, but also against uncertainties in sensing and communication. *Systemwide* safety requires coordination between vehicles. This raises the issue of what is the appropriate division of functionalities between distributed agents and centralized coordination.

We consider the design of a time-slot based architecture for intersection collision avoidance. Our approach to distributed safety is built on each car possessing, at each time step, an *infinite horizon contingency plan* called the "failsafe maneuver." At any time, if the car chooses to ignore all future information updates and simply executes the failsafe maneuver, this maneuver still ensures safety with respect to some subset of cars in the system. Alternatively, given updated state information, each car can modify its infinite horizon contingency plan while still preserving the safety property. This is reminiscent of receding horizon control [14] except that we are computing *infinite* horizon plans at each time step. Systemwide safety is guaranteed by inducing an ordering on the set of cars, which clearly defines the subset of cars to which a given car must defer. We provide a precise description of the *hybrid architecture* and algorithms for distributed agents, culminating in a proof of systemwide safety and liveness. For the last challenge of performance evaluation, we test our overall solution by simulation and compare it with stop signs and traffic lights. A precise mathematical evaluation of performance may be impracticable.

2 Related Work

We first provide a brief flavor of the vast literature in this area. In the collision warning approach, various warning and overriding algorithms decide thresholds to raise an alarm, or apply the brakes. These algorithms are mostly ad hoc and are designed to take into account brake system delay and driver reaction time; see [15] and [2]. In the driver assistance domain, cooperative collision warning systems [9] and cooperative ACC [4] have been studied. These technologies already represent a move towards automatic control of vehicles. However, they do not provide any safety guarantees and are only expected to aid the human.

Reference [13] helps to put the larger problem in perspective, decoupling the various technical, technological and policy issues. In [6], a cooperative collision warning system was designed based on future trajectory prediction and conflict detection. This approach closely resembles the approach taken in aircraft collision avoidance [7], where the state of the system is estimated and propagated through a model which could be deterministic, probabilistic or worst case, and conflicts are detected. In the automotive domain, however, prediction based approaches could lead to unacceptable false alarm rates.

In the area of safety verification of multi agent systems, [11] proposes a method to design controllers for safety specifications in hybrid systems. In [12], a game-theoretic approach is used to design provably safe conflict resolution maneuvers in air traffic management. In this approach, we need to compute solutions to Hamilton-Jacobi-Isaacs partial differential equations, which could be computationally complex. In [10], the problem of systemwide safety is addressed using a cooperative avoidance control approach. Strategies which minimize worst case performance are studied in [1] where the authors use a dynamic programming like recursion can be used to arrive at the min-max strategy.

3 Perpetual Collision Avoidance

Consider two agents A and B, with state spaces X_A and X_B respectively. Their states $x_A \in X_A$ and $x_B \in X_B$ could be vectors containing various elements of interest like position, velocity, etc. We adopt a discrete time perspective and describe their dynamics through *One-step reachability set mappings.*

Definition 1 (One-step reachability set mapping). *The one-step reachability set for A is specified by $\mathcal{R}_A : X_A \to 2^{X_A}$, which specifies the set of points $\mathcal{R}_A(x_A) \subseteq X_A$ reachable from a state x_A in one discrete time step. Similarly, the reachability set for B is specified by $\mathcal{R}_B : X_B \to 2^{X_B}$.*

We can extend this to the set of states reachable from a *set of initial states* in one time step. Thus, $\mathcal{R}_A(\Gamma_A)$ is the set of states which can be reached from some point in Γ_A. $\mathcal{R}_A(\Gamma_A) := \bigcup_{x_A \in \Gamma_A} \mathcal{R}_A(x_A)$, $\quad \mathcal{R}_B(\Gamma_B) := \bigcup_{x_B \in \Gamma_B} \mathcal{R}_B(x_B)$.

We define a "collision relation" between points in the sets X_A and X_B, corresponding to some notion such as "being within K meters of each other."

Definition 2 (Collision relation). *Let $\mathcal{C}_{AB}$ be a subset of $X_A \times X_B$. We say that agents A and B have* collided *if their states x_A and x_B are such that $(x_A, x_B) \in \mathcal{C}_{AB}$. Alternatively, we can simply define a "collision set" $\mathcal{C}_A(x_A) := \{x_B : (x_A, x_B) \in \mathcal{C}_{AB}\}$.*

3.1 Perpetually Maintainable Relations

In the sequel, we address a scenario where A is free to move around, while B has to make worst case assumptions about A's behaviour and is responsible for perpetual collision avoidance. We suppose that we are given a "desirable relation," i.e., a set valued mapping $\mathcal{P}_A : X_A \to 2^{X_B}$ between states x_A and x_B in the sense that we want $x_B \in \mathcal{P}_A(x_A)$ maintained at *all* times. We extend this mapping to sets by taking an intersection: $\mathcal{P}_A(\Gamma_A) := \bigcap_{x_A \in \Gamma_A} \mathcal{P}_A(x_A)$ for any $\Gamma_A \subseteq X_A$. This is the set of points in X_B that forms a desirable relationship with *every* point in Γ_A.

Given a desirable relationship $\mathcal{P}_A$, the question that arises is whether it can be indefinitely maintained by Agent B if one were to start with initial states that satisfied the relationship. This is to be guaranteed under worst case assumptions on Agent A, provided only that $x_A(t+1) \in \mathcal{R}_A(x_A(t))$, and that Agent B gets to observe $(x_A(t), x_B(t))$ at each time t before picking $x_B(t+1)$, which is constrained to lie in $\mathcal{R}_B(x_B(t))$. If this is so, then we will say that the relation $\mathcal{P}_A$ is *perpetually maintainable* by Agent B.

Theorem 1. *A relation $\mathcal{P}_A$ is* perpetually maintainable *by Agent B if and only if $\mathcal{R}_B(x_B) \cap \mathcal{P}_A(\mathcal{R}_A(x_A)) \neq \phi$ for all $x_A \in X_A$ and $x_B \in \mathcal{P}_A(x_A)$.*[1]

3.2 Perpetually Avoiding Collisions

We would like to ensure that there are never any collisions, i.e., $x_B(t) \notin \mathcal{C}_A(x_A(t))$ for all t. Hence we would like to *determine* a perpetually maintainable relation $\mathcal{P}_A$ with the additional property that $\mathcal{P}_A(x_A) \cap \mathcal{C}_A(x_A) = \phi$ for all $x_A \in X_A$. Given, $x_A \in X_A$, we can try to compute such a $\mathcal{P}_A(x_A)$ as follows:

(i) We create a first iterate for $\mathcal{P}_A(x_A)$: $\mathcal{P}_A^{(0)}(x_A) := \{x_B \in X_B : x_A \mathcal{C} x_B\}^c$.
(ii) Given $\mathcal{P}_A^{(k)}(x_A)$, calculate $\mathcal{P}_A^{(k+1)}(x_A) := \mathcal{R}_B^{-1}(\mathcal{P}_A^{(k)}(\mathcal{R}_A(x_A))) \bigcap \mathcal{P}_A^{(k)}(x_A)$.
(iii) $\mathcal{P}_A(x_A) := \lim_{k\to\infty} \mathcal{P}_A^{(k)}(x_A)$.

Theorem 2. *(i) $\mathcal{P}_A^{(k+1)}(x_A) \subseteq \mathcal{P}_A^{(k)}(x_A)$ for all $x_A \in X_A$.*
(ii) Hence $\lim_{k\to\infty} \mathcal{P}_A^{(k)} =: \mathcal{P}_A(x_A)$ exists for each $x_A \in X_A$.
(iii) If $\overline{\mathcal{P}}_A : X_A \to 2^{X_B}$ is also perpetually maintainable and it satisfies $\overline{\mathcal{P}}_A(x_A) \cap \mathcal{C}_A(x_A) = \phi$ for all $x_A \in X_A$, then $\mathcal{P}_A(x_A) \supseteq \overline{\mathcal{P}}_A(x_A)$ for all $x_A \in X_A$.

Definition 3 (Safety relation). *We shall call a relation $\mathcal{P}_A$ satisfying:*
(i) $\mathcal{P}_A$ is perpetually maintainable,
(ii) $\mathcal{P}_A(x_A) \cap \mathcal{C}_A(x_A) = \phi$ for all $x_A \in X_A$,
a safety relation, *and such a set $\mathcal{P}_A(x_A)$ a* safety set *for $x_A \in X_A$.*

4 Cars on a Lane

Consider two point cars A and B on a single lane, where the rear car B, makes worst case assumptions about the front car A, and is responsible for perpetual

[1] For details of all proofs, we refer the reader to [8].

safety. Each car is restricted to non-negative velocity, i.e., it cannot travel backwards. Each car also has both an upper bound as well as a lower bound on its acceleration, where the latter is a negative quantity. Let $x_A \equiv \binom{s_A}{v_A}$ be the state vector for the front car with position s_A and velocity v_A; similarly for $x_B \equiv \binom{s_B}{v_B}$. Note that $s_B < s_A$, $v_A \geq 0$ and $v_B \geq 0$. Let $\underline{a}_A$, $\underline{a}_B$ be the minimum acceleration that A and B are capable of applying, respectively.

We declare a collision if the two cars are separated by less than K meters.

Theorem 3 (Perpetual safety for two cars on a lane). *The necessary and sufficient condition for perpetual collision avoidance (perpetual safety) of two cars A and B, with $s_A > s_B$, is*

$$K + s_B + \int_0^t (v_B + \underline{a}_B\tau)^+ d\tau \quad \leq \quad s_A + \int_0^t (v_A + \underline{a}_A\tau)^+ d\tau \qquad \forall t \geq 0.$$

Less conservatively, it is easy to see that we can choose any open-loop input $\{a_B(t) : t \geq 0\}$ resulting in velocity trajectory $\{v_B(t) : t \geq 0\}$ which satisfies:

$$K + s_B + \int_0^t v_B(\tau)d\tau \leq s_A + \int_0^t (v_A + \underline{a}_A\tau)^+ d\tau \quad \forall t \geq 0. \qquad (1)$$

Note that the above theorem only guarantees *safety*. However, there is also the issue of whether traffic will actually flow on a street where cars follow such safe behaviour. This is the issue of *liveness*. Liveness will be guaranteed by an aggressive choice of the rear car strategy $a_B(\cdot)$, as described in Section 4.2.

4.1 Sampling with Intermediate Safety

Suppose the acceleration of A is constrained to lie in the interval $[\underline{a}_A, \overline{a}_A]$ and that of B in $[\underline{a}_B, \overline{a}_B]$, and that the rear car B receives updates on the state of the front car every T seconds, the *sampling interval.* Based on the information about the lead car A at time nT, B chooses an acceleration input $\{a_B(t) : t \in [nT, (n+1)T)\}$. For simplicity, let us restrict ourselves to *T-horizon strategies*, where if the current time is 0, $a_B(\cdot)$ is chosen identically equal to $\underline{a}_B$, except on the interval $[0, T]$.

4.2 Maximally Aggressive but Safe Strategies

Definition 4 (Maximally aggressive strategy). *A* maximally aggressive strategy *$a_B^*(\cdot)$ is one which maximizes the distance travelled in each interval $[nT, (n+1)T)$, while still satisfying the safety condition (1) at each time nT.*

Let a_B^* denote the constant accleration in [0,T] for the *maximally aggressive constant control input strategy.* The condition (1) yields that a_B^* is the maximal acceleration in $[\underline{a}_B, \overline{a}_B]$ which satisfies the following two conditions:

$$K + s_B + \textstyle\int_0^t (v_B + a_B^*\tau)^+ d\tau \leq s_A + \int_0^t (v_A + \underline{a}_A\tau)^+ d\tau \quad 0 \leq t \leq T,$$

$$\begin{aligned} K + s_B + \textstyle\int_0^T (v_B + a_B^*\tau)^+ d\tau + \int_0^t ((v_B + a_B^* T)^+ + \underline{a}_B\tau)^+ d\tau \\ \leq \quad s_A + \textstyle\int_0^{T+t} (v_A + \underline{a}_A\tau)^+ d\tau \qquad \text{for } 0 \leq t \leq \frac{v_B + a_B^* \cdot T}{-\underline{a}_B}. \end{aligned}$$

Note that all accelerations in the interval $[\underline{a}_B, a^*_B]$ yield perpetual safety. When car B receives fresh information at time T, it can simply repeat the same procedure, as in receding horizon control [14]. We thus arrive at a *piecewise constant input*, $a^*_B(t) = a_{B,n}$ for $nT \leq t < (n+1)T$, with $a_{B,n} \in [\underline{a}_B, a^*_{B,n}] \subseteq [\underline{a}_B, \overline{a}_B]$.

Remark 1. The above approach can be easily extended to multiple cars on a lane by simply following the rule that *each car makes worst case assumptions about the car immediately in front of it*; see [8].

Remark 2. We can handle noisy information, random delays and packet loss, with minor modifications to the scheme described above; see [8].

5 Collision Avoidance at Intersections

Now we turn to the more general problem where there are two or more streams of cars crossing at an intersection. We need to devise a scheme which achieves two objectives. First, all cars cross the intersection without collisions and second, once cars are on their destination lanes, the perpetual safety condition continues to be satisfied for any pair of adjacent cars. Another issue of interest is liveness, in terms of avoiding deadlock. To solve these problems, we introduce a "hybrid" architecture. It is based on an interaction between cars and the intersection infrastructure based on time slot assignment by the intersection infrastructure, with the cars responsible for distributed safety with respect to collisions.

5.1 Description of System

We consider a four road intersection, with four incoming and four outgoing roads as shown in Figure 1(a). The incoming and outgoing roads are indexed by the directions N, W, E and S, as shown. Consider a system of m cars indexed $\{1, 2, 3 \ldots m\}$. Car i's acceleration is constrained to lie in an interval $[\underline{a}_i, \overline{a}_i]$ where

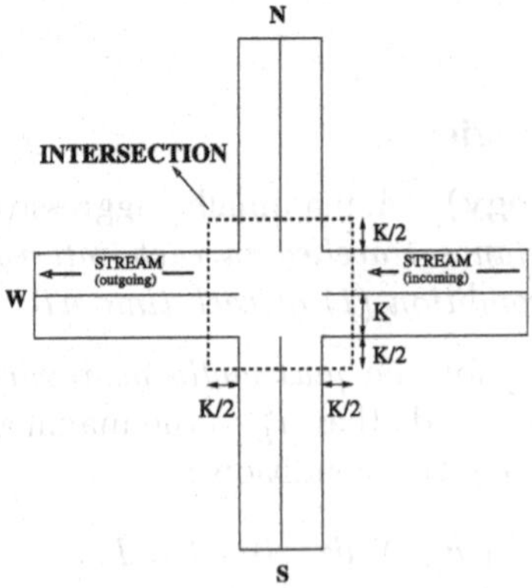

(a) Intersection

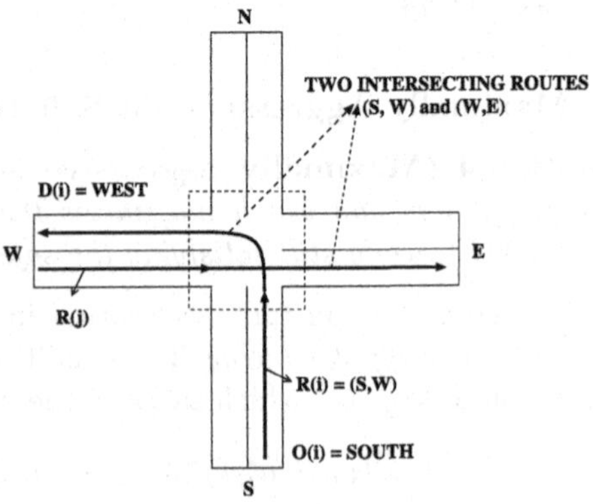

(b) Intersecting routes

Fig. 1. Description of system

$\underline{a}_i < 0$ and $\overline{a}_i > 0$. We assume that each car employs a *piecewise constant input.* We also assume that all cars have a *maximum speed limit* v_M. The following vocabulary will be useful.

By *intersection* we refer to the square consisting of the intersection proper as well as $K/2$ meters along each incoming and outgoing lane; see Figure 1(a). The *route* taken by a car i is described by an ordered pair $R(i) = (O(i), D(i))$, consisting of origin and destination respectively. Two routes are said to be *intersecting* if they cross each other; see Figure 1(b). For clarity, we add that two routes $R(i)$ and $R(j)$ are considered to be non-intersecting if $O(i) = O(j)$ or $D(i) = D(j)$. Thus, we have an "intersection relation" $\mathcal{I}$ defined on the set of routes. If two routes $R(i)$ and $R(j)$ are intersecting, we say $R(i)\ \mathcal{I}\ R(j)$.

We associate with each route a one-dimensional coordinate system, assuming that the position coordinate increases in the direction of traffic flow along the route. Hence each car i has its own coordinate system associated with its route $R(i)$. Let $s_i(t)$ and $v_i(t)$ denote the position and velocity of car i at time t in i's coordinate system. Further, along $R(i)$, let s_i^α and s_i^β denote the position coordinates of the beginning and end of the intersection, respectively.

5.2 Hybrid Architecture

We propose a *hybrid architecture* for collision avoidance at intersections. The intersection infrastructure functions as a *scheduler* which assigns a *time slot* to a car when it comes within communication range of the intersection, with the instruction that the car should be *strictly outside* the area covered by the intersection during all times *other* than its time-slot. This is done by the *Time Slot Allocation Algorithm* implemented at the intersection. Note that this does *not* mean that the car is required to be *in* the intersection during its time slot. Given a time slot, the car has to determine if it can safely get through the intersection and onto its destination lane in the allotted time slot, and compute acceleration inputs appropriately. If the car cannot get through the intersection in its time slot, or cannot safely get onto the destination lane, then it prepares to come to a halt before the intersection and receives a new slot. All this is done by the *Intersection Crossing Algorithm* implemented by each car in the system.

Time slot assignment policy. The *time slot assignment* is a mapping σ which maps each car i in $\{1, 2, \ldots m\}$ to an interval of time $\sigma(i) = [t_{start}(i), t_{end}(i))$, called the *time slot* allocated to i. We will also allow for a *new* (or "revised") slot to be assigned to a car that has missed its earlier assigned time slot. This corresponds to modifying the time slot assignment. Hence we are interested in a sequence of time slot assignments $\{\sigma^{(0)}(\cdot), \sigma^{(1)}(\cdot), \ldots\}$, with the understanding that $\sigma^{(n)}(\cdot) : i \to [t_{start}^{(n)}(i), t_{end}^{(n)}(i))$ is the time slot assignment applicable during the time interval $[nT, (n+1)T)$. We will say that a car i *conforms* to the slot $\sigma(i)$ if it never occupies the intersection at any time outside $\sigma(i)$.

Suppose that we have a *strict partial ordering relation* "$\prec$" on the set of slots, established by comparing slot start times, that is, we say, $\sigma(i) \prec \sigma(j)$ if and only if $t_{start}(i) < t_{start}(j)$.

Definition 5 (Admissible Time Slot Assignment sequence). *We say that a time slot assignment sequence* $\{\sigma^{(0)}(\cdot), \sigma^{(1)}(\cdot), \ldots\}$ *is* admissible *if it satisfies the following properties.*

(a) *For any two cars* i *and* j, *if* $R(i) \mathcal{I} R(j)$, *then* $\sigma^{(n)}(j) \cap \sigma^{(n)}(i) = \phi$ *for all* n. *This ensures that two cars with intersecting routes have non-intersecting slots.*
(b) *For any car* i, *define* $I(i) := \{j : D(j) = D(i), O(j) \neq O(i)\}$. *Then we must have* $\sigma^{(n)}(i) \prec \sigma^{(n)}(\bar{i})$ *or* $\sigma^{(n)}(\bar{i}) \prec \sigma^{(n)}(i)$, *for all* n, *for all* i *and for all* $\bar{i} \in I(i)$.

In the sequel, for each car i *at time* nT, *we will have an available* open loop sequence *of inputs called the* failsafe maneuver, *denoted by* $\{a_i^{F,n}(k)\}_{k \geq n}$. *This determines an open-loop future trajectory for car* i, *which it can thereafter follow and stay perpetually safe.*

Reallocation Policy: *Suppose car* i *gets a "revised" slot at time* nT, *i.e.,* $\sigma^{(n-1)}(i) \neq \sigma^{(n)}(i)$. *Then the following conditions must be satisfied:*

(i) *The reallocated slot must be in the future, i.e.,* $t^{(n)}_{start}(i) \geq nT$.
(ii) *Under the available failsafe maneuver at time* nT, *if it is implemented at time* nT, *then car* i *will come to a stop before the intersection.*
(iii) *Reallocation cannot be done too early; reallocation is permitted at time* nT *only if* $nT \geq t^{(n-1)}_{end}(i) - \tau_{max} + T$, *where* τ_{max} *is the length of time enough for any car starting from rest to get through the intersection.*
(iv) *Consider the set of cars* $\{j : R(j) = R(i), t^{(n-1)}_{end}(j) > nT\}$; *let* ζ *be the car in this set which is highest in the ordering* $\prec$ *(this need not be unique). Then we must have,* $\sigma^{(n-1)}(k) \prec \sigma^{(n)}(i)$ *for all* $\{k \in I(i) : \sigma^{(n-1)}(k) \prec \sigma^{(n-1)}(\zeta)\}$. *If such a* ζ *does not exist, we must have* $\sigma^{(n-1)}(k) \prec \sigma^{(n)}(i)$ *for all* $k \in I(i)$.

Three Maneuvers. We now define three maneuvers, a "braking" maneuver, a "parking" maneuver and a "tailing" maneuver. These maneuvers will be used in what follows to compose more complex behavior that ensures safety.

We adopt a discrete-time viewpoint and suppose that information about other cars in the system refreshes periodically every T seconds. We denote by $\{s_i(n)\}$, $\{v_i(n)\}$ the sampled position and velocity in car i's coordinate system, and by $\{a_i(n)\}$ the piecewise constant input, all of car i, in the time interval $[nT, (n+1)T)$. We say that a *car* j *is on* i*'s route at time* nT, if either

(i) $O(j) = O(i)$ and car j is located $< K$ meters from a point on $R(i)$, or
(ii) $D(j) = D(i)$ and car j is located at a point on $R(i)$ and $t^{(n)}_{end}(j) \leq nT$.

Given a car i, consider any other car j with $O(j) = O(i)$ or $D(j) = D(i)$. We can project the position and velocity of car j onto i's coordinate system as follows. If car j is not on i's route at time nT, we set $s_{ji}(n) := s_i^{\alpha} + K$ and $v_{ji}(n) := 0$. If car j is on i's route at time t, we have two cases. If $O(j) = O(i)$, we set $s_{ji}(n) := s_i^{\alpha} + s_j(n) - s_j^{\alpha}$ and $v_{ji}(n) := v_j(n)$; if $D(j) = D(i)$, we set $s_{ji}(n) := s_i^{\beta} + s_j(n) - s_j^{\beta}$ and $v_{ji}(n) := v_j(n)$.

For a car i at time nT, we define its *lead car* $l(i, nT)$ as the car immediately in front of car i on i's route at time t. If there is no such lead car in front of car i on

i's route, a *virtual lead car* is assumed to be situated at $+\infty$ along i's route. We declare a *collision* between two cars i and j if they are less than K meters apart. Consider two cars i and j with $O(j) = O(i)$ or $D(j) = D(i)$. If $s_{ji}(n) > s_i(n)$, the minimum value of $s_{ji}(n) - s_i(n)$ required to ensure a "physical" separation of K meters between car i and car j at time nT, is denoted by K_{ji}. If $O(j) = O(i)$ and $D(j) \neq D(i)$, K_{ji} is the distance along $R(j)$ beyond s_j^{α}, after which j is no longer on i's route, or $K_{ji} = K$ otherwise.

Maximum braking maneuver. A car i is said to execute the *maximum braking* (MB) maneuver at time nT, if $a_i(k) = \underline{a}_i \quad \forall k \geq n$.

Parking maneuver. For car i at time nT, a *parking maneuver* stopping at s_{park} consists of a choice of $\{a_i(k)\}_{k \geq n}$ and an $n^* \geq n$, such that $s_i(k) = s_{park}$ for all $k \geq n^*$. Applying this sequence of inputs will result in car i parking (i.e., coming to a standstill) at s_{park} and staying there for all further time. We note that such a maneuver may be infeasible for certain values of s_{park}. The *minimum-time parking maneuver* is the parking maneuver with the smallest value of n^*.

Tailing maneuver. Consider two cars i and j with $R(i) = R(j)$. A *tailing maneuver* for car i behind car j at time nT is a sequence of acceleration inputs $\{a_i(k)\}_{k \geq n}$ which guarantees $s_j(t) - s_i(t) \geq K$ for all $t \geq nT$ under worst case assumptions (viz., maximum braking) on car j, and results in car i parking at $s_j(n) + \frac{v_j(n)^2}{-2\underline{a}_j} - K$. A specific extremal tailing maneuver of interest is the *minimum-time tailing maneuver* which stops in minimum time.

Downstream cars: Real and Virtual. It is necessary for cars to take responsibility to avoid collisions with the other cars that are "ahead" of them.

Potential Downstream Cars. The set of potential downstream cars $\mathcal{D}(i, nT)$ for car i at time nT, is defined as the set of cars that consists of:

(i) All cars $j \neq i$ on i's route at time nT, with $s_{ji}(n) \geq s_i(n)$.
(ii) All cars j not on i's route at time nT, with $D(j) = D(i)$, $nT < t_{end}^{(n)}(j)$ and $\sigma^{(n)}(j) \prec \sigma^{(n)}(i)$.
(iii) A virtual car 0 with $\{s_0(\cdot)\} \equiv \infty$, $\{v_0(\cdot)\} \equiv \infty$ and $\underline{a}_0 = 0$.

The above is a *set* of cars. We now define one car, the *immediate downstream car*, that car i will need to take responsibility for avoiding.

Immediate Downstream Car. The immediate downstream car $d(i)$ for a car i is a *virtual car* with location and velocity given as follows:

$$s_{d(i)}(n) = \min_{j \in \mathcal{D}(i,nT)} s_{ji}(n), \qquad a_{d(i)}(n) = \underline{a}_i,$$
$$s_{d(i)}(n) + \frac{v_{d(i)}^2(n)}{-2\underline{a}_i} - K = \min_{j \in \mathcal{D}(i,nT)} \left\{ s_{ji}(n) + \frac{v_{ji}^2(n)}{-2\underline{a}} - K_{ji} \right\},$$

where $\underline{a} = \min_{1 \leq j \leq m} \underline{a}_j$. Now we show that it is enough to make worst case assumptions on the virtual car $d(i)$ instead of all cars in $\mathcal{D}(i, nT)$.

Lemma 1. *Given a car i at time nT, the continuous time evolution of the state $(s_j(t), v_j(t))$ of any car $j \in \mathcal{D}(i, nT)$ satisfies*

$$\left(s_{d(i)}(nT) + \int_0^{\tau} (v_{d(i)}(nT) + \underline{a}_i s)^+ ds - K\right) \leq s_{ji}(nT + \tau) - K_{ji} \; \forall \tau \geq 0.$$

Outline of Algorithm for Perpetual Safety. Let us suppose that the following two properties hold for each car i. In the sequel we will show how to maintain them.

Property P1: Each car i conforms to its slot sequence $\{\sigma^{(0)}(i), \sigma^{(1)}(i), \ldots\}$.

Property P2: Each car i does not collide with any car in $\mathcal{D}(i, nT)$ in the interval $[nT, (n+1)T)$ for all n.

Lemma 2. *Given an admissible time slot assignment sequence, if the two properties P1 and P2 are satisfied by each car i, then there is perpetual collision avoidance for all cars in the system.*

Failsafe maneuver update algorithm. Our scheme for perpetual collision avoidance is predicated upon each car having a so called *failsafe maneuver* at every time, which it can apply from that time forward in an open-loop fashion, and guarantee safety. The algorithm to ensure perpetual collision avoidance for all cars in the system is based on the iterative update of the available failsafe maneuver at each time nT. Given a failsafe maneuver $\{a_i^{F,n}(k)\}_{k \geq n}$, for car i at time nT, and information about other cars at time nT, we prescribe the current input $a_i(n)$ and the failsafe maneuver $\{a_i^{F,n+1}(k)\}_{k \geq n+1}$ at time $(n+1)T$.

Step 1. *(Determine if car i will stop before the intersection if it executes the one-step Modified Maximum Braking maneuver $\equiv \{\overline{a}_i, \underline{a}_i, \underline{a}_i, \ldots\}$ at time nT).*

Suppose car i executes the one step Modified Maximum Braking (MMB) maneuver at time nT. This will result in car i stopping at $s_i^{MMB}(\infty)$.

If $s_i^{MMB}(\infty) < s_i^{\alpha}$, then
Car i chooses any $a_i(n)$ which ensures that car i stays in the safety set of the lead car $l(i, nT)$ (as described in Section 4), and sets $a_i^{F,n+1}(k) = \underline{a}_i \quad \forall k \geq n+1$.

Else, go to Step 2.

Step 2. *(Ensure that car i does not enter the intersection before the start of the assigned slot. In particular, if, even under maximum braking, car i is inside the intersection at the start of its slot, it must execute the failsafe maneuver).*

Let $\{s_i^{MB}(k)\}_{k \geq n}$, $\{v_i^{MB}(k)\}_{k \geq n}$ and $\{a_i^{MB}(k)\}_{k \geq n}$ denote the resulting position, velocity and acceleration profiles of car i if car i were to execute the Maximum Braking (MB) maneuver at time nT.

If $s_i^{MB}(\frac{t^{(n)}_{start}(i)}{T}) > s_i^{\alpha}$, then
Car i does go ahead and execute the current failsafe maneuver, i.e., car i chooses $a_i(n) = a_i^{F,n}(n)$ and sets $a_i^{F,n+1}(k) = a_i^{F,n}(k) \quad \forall k \geq n+1$.

Else, go to Step 3.

Step 3. *(Ensure that car i exits the intersection before $t^{(n)}_{end}(i)$, and is in the safety set of its lead car upon exit. This is done by checking if car i can safely tail the immediate downstream car).*

Construct the Minimum-Time Tailing (MTT) maneuver behind the immediate downstream car $d(i)$, for car i at time nT. For convenience, let $\{s_i^{MTT}(k)\}_{k\geq n}$, $\{v_i^{MTT}(k)\}_{k\geq n}$ and $\{a_i^{MTT}(k)\}_{k\geq n}$ denote the resulting position, velocity and acceleration profiles of car i, if car i were to execute the MTT maneuver.

If the tailing maneuver behind $d(i)$ is infeasible, or if $s_i^{MTT}\left(\frac{t^{(n)}_{end}(i)}{T}\right) \leq s_i^{\beta}$, then Car i goes ahead and does execute the current failsafe maneuver, i.e., car i chooses $a_i(n) = a_i^{F,n}(n)$ and sets $a_i^{F,n+1}(k) = a_i^{F,n}(k) \quad \forall k \geq n+1$.

Else, go to Step 4.

Step 4. *(Given that the MTT maneuver behind $d(i)$ is feasible, check if, under this maneuver, car i conforms to its time slot).*

If $s_i^{MTT}(\frac{t^{(n)}_{start}(i)}{T}) \leq s_i^{\alpha}$, then
Car i goes ahead and executes the MTT maneuver, i.e., car i chooses $a_i(n) = a_i^{MTT}(n)$ and sets $a_i^{F,n+1}(k) = a_i^{MTT}(k) \quad \forall k \geq n+1$.

Else, go to Step 5.

Step 5. *(Synthesize a failsafe maneuver using the MB maneuver and the MTT maneuver behind $d(i)$. Check that, under this synthesized maneuver, car i conforms to its time slot).*

Define a sequence of acceleration inputs $\{a_i^*(k)\}_{k\geq n}$ as follows. First, define $a_i^*(k) := \lambda.a_i^{MTT}(k) + (1-\lambda).\underline{a}_i$ for all $k \in \{n, \ldots, \frac{t^{(n)}_{start}(i)}{T} - 1\}$ where $\lambda = \frac{s_i^{\alpha} - s_i^{MB}(\frac{t^{(n)}_{start}(i)}{T})}{s_i^{MTT}(\frac{t^{(n)}_{start}(i)}{T}) - s_i^{MB}(\frac{t^{(n)}_{start}(i)}{T})}$. For $k \geq \frac{t^{(n)}_{start}(i)}{T}$, $a_i^*(k)$ is the sequence of acceleration inputs corresponding to the Minimum-Time Parking maneuver behind $s_{d(i)}(n) + \frac{v^2_{d(i)}(n)}{-2\underline{a}_{d(i)}}$ for car i, with initial time set to $\frac{t^{(n)}_{start}(i)}{T}$, initial position $s_i^*(\frac{t^{(n)}_{start}(i)}{T})$ and initial velocity $v_i^*(\frac{t^{(n)}_{start}(i)}{T})$.

If $s_i^*(\frac{t_{end}(i)}{T}) \leq s_i^{\beta}$, then
Car i goes ahead and executes the current failsafe maneuver, i.e., car i chooses $a_i(n) = a_i^{F,n}(n)$ and sets $a_i^{F,n+1}(k) = a_i^{F,n}(k) \quad \forall k \geq n+1$.

Else, go to Step 6.

Step 6
Car i simply chooses $a_i(n) = a_i^*(n)$ and sets $a_i^{F,n+1}(k) = a_i^*(k) \quad \forall k \geq n+1$.

The Intersection Crossing Algorithm. Now we are ready to specify the algorithm that cars use in the hybrid architecture.

At time zero, each car i sets the failsafe maneuver $\{a_i^{F,0}(k)\}_{k\geq 0}$ to be the maximum braking maneuver. At every time step nT, car i has two choices. It can

(i) Choose the current input $a_i(n)$ and update the failsafe maneuver by running the update algorithm using information from other cars at time nT,
(ii) Or, it can simply execute the failsafe maneuver at time nT, i.e., $a_i(n) = a_i^{F,n}(n)$

and set $\{a_i^{F,n+1}(k)\}_{k\geq n+1} = \{a_i^{F,n}(k)\}_{k\geq n+1}$. This corresponds to following the "contingency plan" at time nT, possibly due to lost packets.

Once car i exits the intersection, it sets $s_i^\alpha, s_i^\beta = +\infty$, and continues the failsafe maneuver update. This will simply amount to repeatedly executing Step 1 of the update algorithm.[2]

Safety of the Intersection Crossing Algorithm. In order to establish safety, we need to analyze the evolution of positions of the cars, their failsafe maneuvers, and the time slots allocated to them. Let $x(n) \in \mathcal{X}$ represent the "physical state" of the system at time nT, which includes position, velocity, etc., of all cars in the system. Let $\pi^{n|x(n-1)} \in \Pi$ be the "planning state" at time nT, which is the set of failsafe maneuvers at time nT; $\pi^{n|x(n-1)} = \{p_1^{n|x(n-1)}, p_2^{n|x(n-1)}, \ldots, p_m^{n|x(n-1)}\}$. Finally, let $\sigma^{(n)} \in \Sigma$ be the time slot assignment during $[nT, (n+1)T)$.

The *superstate* of the system at time nT is given by $(\underline{x(n)}, \pi^{n|x(n-1)}, \sigma^{(n)}) \in \mathcal{X} \times \Pi \times \Sigma$, where the underlining of $x(n)$ is to indicate that this information is *private*. The superstate evolves in four steps as follows:

$$(\underline{x(n)}, \pi^{n|x(n-1)}, \sigma^{(n)}) \stackrel{StepA}{\longrightarrow} (x(n), U(n) \times \pi^{n+1|x(n)}, \sigma^{(n)})$$
$$\stackrel{StepB}{\longrightarrow} (x(n), u(n) \in U(n), \pi^{n+1|x(n)}, \sigma^{(n)}) \stackrel{StepC}{\longrightarrow} (\underline{x(n+1)}, \pi^{n+1|x(n)}, \sigma^{(n)})$$
$$\stackrel{StepD}{\longrightarrow} (\underline{x(n+1)}, \pi^{n+1|x(n)}, \sigma^{(n+1)}).$$

Step A: When the cars exchange physical state information at time nT, each car i can run the Intersection Crossing Algorithm, which prescribes a set of feasible current inputs $U_i(n)$ and the updated failsafe maneuver $p_i^{n+1|x(n)}$ for car i. This results in a set of feasible inputs $U(n) = U_1(n) \times U_2(n) \ldots U_m(n)$ for the system and an updated planning state $\pi^{n+1|x(n)}$.
Step B: Each car i can then choose a particular input $a_i(n) \in U_i(n)$, which results in the system choosing $u(n) \in U(n)$.
Step C: The physical state of the system evolves from $x(n)$ to $x(n+1)$.
Step D: Finally, the time slot assignment is updated from $\sigma^{(n)}$ to $\sigma^{(n+1)}$.

We prove the safety property of the intersection crossing algorithm by showing that there is an *invariant set* $\mathcal{A} \subset \mathcal{X} \times \Pi \times \Sigma$ for the superstate. $\mathcal{A}$ will comprise of all those superstates $(x(n), \pi^{n|x(n-1)}, \sigma^{(n)})$ for which, under the maneuver $p_i^{n|x(n-1)}$ for each car i at time nT, it results that

$(C1^{(n)})$: Car i conforms at all future times to the slot $\sigma^{(n)}(i)$, i.e., if the time slot $\sigma^{(n)}(i)$ is never changed in the future and is kept "frozen."
$(C2^{(n)})$: Car i does not collide with any car in $\mathcal{D}(i, nT)$ under worst case assumptions on cars in $\mathcal{D}(i, nT)$.

Theorem 4. *Suppose we have an admissible Time Slot Assignment Sequence and that all cars are following the intersection crossing algorithm described above. Let us suppose that* $(\underline{x(n)}, \pi^{n|x(n-1)}, \sigma^{(n)}) \in \mathcal{A}$ *at time* nT*. Then,*

[2] In a road network, set the values of s_i^α and s_i^β to correspond to the next intersection.

(a) The set of superstates $(x(n), U(n) \times \pi^{n+1|x(n)}, \sigma^{(n)}) \subseteq \mathcal{A}$.
(b) If each car i chooses the current input $a_i(n)$ *as described, then there are no collisions in* $[nT, (n+1)T)$. *Further* $(\underline{x(n+1)}, \pi^{n+1|x(n)}, \sigma^{(n)}) \in \mathcal{A}$.
(c) Under the slot reallocation policy, we have $(\underline{x(n+1)}, \pi^{n+1|x(n)}, \sigma^{(n+1)}) \in \mathcal{A}$.

Perpetual Systemwide safety. It remains to prove *perpetual systemwide safety* of the hybrid architecture. We make the following assumptions:

(A1) We have an admissible time slot assignment sequence.
(A2) At time zero, all cars are at least a braking distance away from the intersection. Further, each car i is in the safety set of its lead car at time zero.

Theorem 5. ***Systemwide Safety of the Intersection Crossing Algorithm*** *Under conditions (A1) and (A2), if each car follows the Intersection Crossing Algorithm, there is perpetual collision avoidance for the whole system of cars.*

Liveness of the Intersection Crossing algorithm. As noted earlier, in addition to safety, it is also important to ensure that any finite system of cars does not fall into deadlock, i.e., every car must cross the intersection in finite time. We can ensure liveness under the following additional conditions:

(A3) Suppose that all cars in the system are *α-aggressive*, i.e., in Step 1 of the failsafe maneuver update algorithm, if the maximum permissible acceleration ($a_i^{max}(n)$) for a car i at time nT is positive, then the chosen input must be at least $\alpha \cdot a_i^{max}(n)$ where $0 < \alpha \leq 1$.
(A4) The partial ordering relation "$\prec$" satisfies the condition:
$\sigma(i) \prec \sigma(j) \Rightarrow l(\sigma(j) \cap \sigma^c(i)) \geq \tau_{max}$, where $l(A)$ is the maximum length of an interval contained in A, and τ_{max} is a length of time enough for any car starting from rest to traverse through the intersection.
(A5) A new slot is reallocated within Δ seconds of missing an earlier slot.

Theorem 6. ***Liveness of the Intersection Crossing Algorithm.*** *Under conditions (A1) through (A5), if each car follows the Intersection Crossing Algorithm, then there is guaranteed liveness for the whole system of cars.*

6 Performance Evaluation

The algorithm and architecture described above ensure systemwide safety and liveness, while still providing freedom in the design space. We would like to find time slot assignments which satisfy conditions (A1)-(A2), and locally maximize an appropriate performance metric. In order to find such efficient slot assignments, we use a local improvement heuristic, specifically a gradient approach based on forward simulation. We run the simulation with an arbitrary initial slot assignment and record the average travel time and the final slot assignment. We systematically tweak this to obtain modified time slot assignments, which we again evaluate by forward simulation. When we obtain an assignment which entails lower average travel time, we switch to it, and continue this procedure

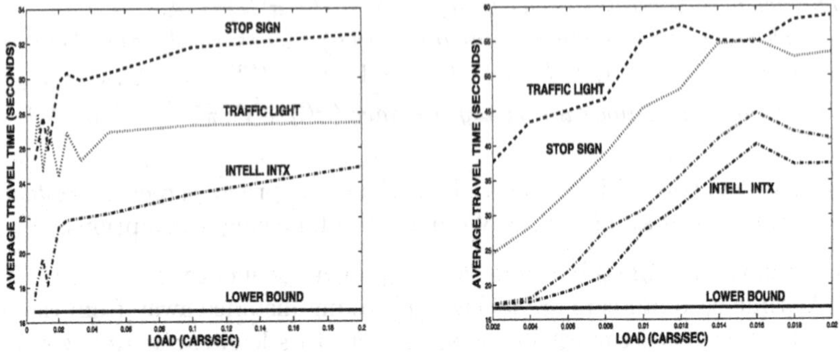

(a) Clearing 10 cars (b) Clearing 30 cars

Fig. 2. Average travel time comparison

recursively. The algorithm terminates when we obtain a slot assignment, all of whose modifications result in higher average travel time.

We have built a simulator of the entire system. We consider a system of m cars which desire to get through the intersection. The performance metric under consideration is the average time taken to travel from 200m away from the start of the intersection to 200m beyond the end of the intersection. The routes of all cars are independent and identically distributed according to a probability mass function which assigns a mass of 1/6 to each of the four straight line routes, and a mass of 1/24 to each of the eight turning routes. All cars start from at least 200m away from the start of the intersection, with each subsequent car being positioned at a distance of $(K+ exp(\lambda)RV)$ behind its lead car with $K = 5m$. The parameter λ of the exponential distribution is a measure of the *load on the intersection.* All cars start at maximum velocity equal to $25m/s$, and are assumed to have braking power equal to $-3.5m/s^2$.

Using this simulation framework, we can compare the performance of our scheduler against traffic regualation mechanisms such as stop signs and traffic lights; see Figure 2. We see that our intelligent intersection outperforms both traffic lights and stop signs at low and moderate loads by fairly good margins. It even appears to perform comparably or better at high loads. However, we should note that these conclusions deserve a much more thorough simulation study.

7 Concluding Remarks

This paper has examined an important safety application, intelligent intersections, that can provide provable safety with improved efficiency. We have proposed a design based on distributed updates of infinite horizon contingency plans by distributed agents, with centralized coordination. We have also demonstrated by a simulation study the performance benefit of our approach over stop signs and traffic lights. It is hoped that this approach may be useful in the design of other tractable complex, distributed, hybrid systems.

References

1. Başar, T., Kumar, P.R.: On worst case design strategies. Computers and Mathematics with Applications 13(1-3), 239–245 (1987)
2. Doi, A., Butsuen, T., Niibe, T., Yakagi, T., Yamamoto, Y., Seni, H.: Development of a rear-end collision avoidance system with automatic braking control. JSAE Review 15, 335–340 (1994)
3. National Center for Statistics and Analysis. In: 2006 Traffic Safety Annual Assessment - A Preview, DOT HS 810 791 (July 2007)
4. Girard, A.R., de Sousa, J.B., Misener, J.A., Hedrick, J.K.: A control architecture for integrated cooperative cruise control and collision warning systems. In: Proceedings of the 40th Conference on Decision and Control, vol. 2, pp. 1491–1496.
5. Intelligent transportation systems, California Center for Innovative Transportation (August 2007), [Online], http://www.calccit.org/itsdecision
6. Huang, J., Tan, H.S.: Design and implementation of a cooperative collision warning system. In: Proceedings of the IEEE Intelligent Transportation Systems Conference, Toronto, Canada, pp. 1017–1022 (2006)
7. Kuchar, J.K., Yang, L.C.: A review of conflict detection and resolution modeling methods. IEEE Transactions on Intelligent Transportation Systems 1, 179–189 (2000)
8. Kowshik, H., Caveney, D., Kumar, P.R.: Provable Systemwide Safety in Intelligent Intersections. IEEE Transactions Automatic Control (submitted, 2007)
9. Misener, J.A., Sengupta, R., Krishnan, H.: Cooperative collision warning: Enabling crash avoidance with wireless technology. In: 12th World Congress on Intelligent Transportation Systems, San Francisco, p. 1960 (2005)
10. Stipanovic, D.M., Hokayem, P.F., Spong, M.W., Siljak, D.D.: Avoidance control for multi-agent systems. ASME Journal of Dynamic Systems, Measurement and Control 129(5), 699–707 (2007)
11. Tomlin, C., Lygeros, J., Sastry, S.: A game theoretic approach to controller design for hybrid systems. Proceedings of the IEEE 88(7), 949–970 (2000)
12. Tomlin, C., Pappas, G., Sastry, S.: Conflict resolution of air traffic management: A study in multiagent hybrid systems. IEEE Transactions on Automatic Control 43(4), 509–521 (1998)
13. Varaiya, P.: Smart cars on smart roads: Problems of control. IEEE Transactions on Automatic Control 38, 195–207 (1993)
14. Ydstie, B.E., Liu, L.K.: Single- and multi-variable control with extended prediction horizons. In: American Control Conference, vol. 21, pp. 1303–1308.
15. Zhang, Y., Antonsson, E.K., Grote, K.: A new threat assessment measure for collision avoidance systems. In: Proceedings of the IEEE Intelligent Transportation Systems Conference, Toronto, Canada, pp. 968–975 (2006)

LTLC: Linear Temporal Logic for Control

YoungMin Kwon and Gul Agha*

[1] Microsoft Corporation
ykwon4@cs.uiuc.edu
[2] Department of Computer Science
University of Illinois at Urbana Champaign
agha@cs.uiuc.edu

Abstract. Linear systems are one of the most commonly used models to represent physical systems. Yet, only few automated tools have been developed to check their behaviors over time. In this paper, we propose a linear temporal logic for specifying complex properties of discrete time linear systems. The proposed logic can also be used in a control system to generate control input in the process of model checking. Although, developing a full feedback control system is beyond the scope of this paper, authors believe that a feedback loop can be easily introduced by adopting the receding horizon scheme of predictive controllers. In this paper we explain the syntax, the semantics, a model checking algorithm, and an example application of our proposed logic.

1 Introduction

Linear systems have been widely used as mathematical models for physical systems because they can accurately represent the actual systems despite their simple structure. Thus, not surprisingly, many control systems are developed based on this simple mathematical model. In designing a control system, one of the fundamental questions about the system is the *controllability* of the system: whether we can drive the system from any state to any state [1]. Nowadays, with the popular use of versatile digital controllers, control systems can perform ever complex tasks and so become the requirements. In this challenging environment, one may want to know more than the traditional notion of controllability. For example, in a vehicle control system, we want to know, whether the vehicle can maintain certain speed even though we cannot keep accelerate it for longer than a duration to prevent overheating. The traditional controllability does not address this type of problem. Also, this seemingly simple problem has too many cases to be checked by hand: feasible set of state at each step depends on its past computational path – whether we accelerate or not at the current step affects the feasible set of state after the duration.

One obvious problem here is that we need a way to describe the complex requirements. Combinations of linear constraints can be a building block for the description: conjunctions of linear constraints define a convex region in the state space of the system

* The authors thank Eunhee Kim for revising the paper. This research has been supported in part by the DARPA IXO NEST program under contract F33615-01-C-1907, by NSF under grant CNS 05-09321 and by ONR under DoD MURI award N0014-02-1-0715.

M. Egerstedt and B. Mishra (Eds.): HSCC 2008, LNCS 4981, pp. 316–329, 2008.

and any arbitrary regions can be described by union or complements of them. However, these combinations of constraints can be too complex to generate or to modify by hand for nontrivial requirements. In this paper, we propose a logic, called *Linear Temporal Logic for Control* (LTLC) on linear systems to describe the requirements in a highly abstract manner. LTLC uses logical and temporal operators to combine the constraints so that the complex path-dependent behaviors can be easily expressed. The usefulness of LTLC is not limited to checking the refined notion of controllability: it can also be used to compute a sequence of control input that can obtain control objectives.

Temporal logics like LTL, CTL, and CTL* are initially developed to specify behaviors of concurrent systems and later they are introduced to model checking [2,3,4]. Because their reasoning process is automated, model checking has been widely used in verifying complex hardware and software systems. However, the models of these logics are finite state machines whereas the model of LTLC is a linear system which has uncountably many states. Thus, in order to introduce these logics to linear systems we need different ways of expressing the states and different model checking algorithms. There has been approaches to address the problems of specifying and model checking in infinite state spaces. For example, Alur and Dill developed *timed automaton*, which is a finite state automaton with finite number of real valued clocks associated with the states, to model hybrid systems [5]. A decidability result for LTL model checking on controllable linear systems has been reported where a control system defined on a space of grid blocks bisimilar to the original linear system is built to divide the uncountable state space into finite partitions [6]. This result is extended to build a framework for designing controllers [7]. In iLTL, properties of Discrete Time Markov Chains (DTMC) are specified in the form of inequalities about expected rewards [8]. In iLTL the set of atomic propositions partitions the uncountable *probability mass function* (pmf) space into a finite number of equivalent classes. Although these approaches address the uncountable state space problem, none of these approaches address the question: "Given a system and a requirement, is there an initial state and a sequence of input that can drive the system to satisfy the specification?"

From the perspective of automatic control, *Model Predictive Control* (MPC) has similarity with our approach. MPC is an optimal control method minimizing a cost function of the error between the predicted output and the reference and of the energy to change the system state [9,10]. One of the merits of MPC is that because it computes the predicted output it can follow non-constant references while satisfying other physical constraints. The key idea in the success of MPC is the use of finite input/output horizons where the input and output to and from the system become constant. These finite horizons enable us to express the output of the system in terms of a finite sequence of input. This conversion removes the dependency between input and output defined by the system dynamics equation during the optimization process. In LTLC model checking we adopt the key idea of MPC: adopt the input/output horizons and remove the input/output dependencies from the model checking process. However, unlike MPC where *always* enforced constraints are hard coded in the controller in the form of quadratic programming, LTLC provides a high level abstraction logic to generate complex sets of constraints. Note that this hard coded control objectives are difficult generate or modify because of the lack of the abstractions. Note that LTLC model checking can also be used to compute a sequence of control input to satisfy a complex control objective described in LTLC: a counter example of the negated control objective is a sequence of input that will satisfy the original goal.

2 Discrete Linear Time Invariant System Model

Our system model is a Discrete Linear Time Invariant System which can be represented by a seven-tuple $\mathcal{M} = (\mathcal{U}, \mathcal{Y}, \mathcal{X}, \mathrm{A}, \mathrm{B}, \mathrm{C}, \mathrm{D})$, where $\mathcal{U} = \{u_1, \ldots, u_{nu}\}$ is a set of inputs, $\mathcal{Y} = \{y_1, \ldots, y_{ny}\}$ is a set of outputs, $\mathcal{X} = \{x_1, \ldots, x_{nx}\}$ is a set of states, and $\mathrm{A} \in \mathbb{R}^{nx \times nx}$, $\mathrm{B} \in \mathbb{R}^{nx \times nu}$, $\mathrm{C} \in \mathbb{R}^{ny \times nx}$, and $\mathrm{D} \in \mathbb{R}^{ny \times nu}$ are system matrices that describe the difference equations for the dynamics of the system. Our model describes a Multiple Input and Multiple Output (MIMO) system which has nu inputs and ny outputs.

In this paper, we overload the definitions of u_i, y_i, and x_i with the functions $u_i : \mathbb{N} \to \mathbb{R}$, $y_i : \mathbb{N} \to \mathbb{R}$, and $x_i : \mathbb{N} \to \mathbb{R}$ that map discrete time t to the value of input, output, and state at that time. We also define the following vector functions:

$$\begin{aligned}
\mathbf{u} : \mathbb{N} \to \mathbb{R}^{nu \times 1} &\text{ such that } \mathbf{u}(t)_i = u_i(t), \text{ for } i = 1, \ldots, nu,\\
\mathbf{y} : \mathbb{N} \to \mathbb{R}^{ny \times 1} &\text{ such that } \mathbf{y}(t)_i = y_i(t), \text{ for } i = 1, \ldots, ny,\\
\mathbf{x} : \mathbb{N} \to \mathbb{R}^{nx \times 1} &\text{ such that } \mathbf{x}(t)_i = x_i(t), \text{ for } i = 1, \ldots, nx,
\end{aligned}$$

where the subscript i of a vector is the ith element of the vector.

The relations among input, output, and state functions are given by the following difference equations.

$$\begin{aligned}
\mathbf{x}(t+1) &= \mathrm{A} \cdot \mathbf{x}(t) + \mathrm{B} \cdot \mathbf{u}(t), \\
\mathbf{y}(t) &= \mathrm{C} \cdot \mathbf{x}(t) + \mathrm{D} \cdot \mathbf{u}(t).
\end{aligned} \tag{1}$$

Note that in the first difference equation, the next state $\mathbf{x}(t+1)$ is solely determined by the current state $\mathbf{x}(t)$ and the current input $\mathbf{u}(t)$. Thus, while inputs do not change, if two consecutive states remains the same, then the system is in a steady state from then on. That is, if $\mathbf{x}(t+1) = \mathbf{x}(t)$ and $\mathbf{u}(t+i) = \mathbf{u}(t)$ for $i \geq 0$ then $\mathbf{x}(t+j) = \mathbf{x}(t)$ for $j \geq 0$.

Given an input $\mathbf{u}$ and an initial state $\mathbf{x}(0)$, we can compute the state and the output of the system at time t as follows by recursively applying the equation (1).

$$\begin{aligned}
\mathbf{x}(t) &= \mathrm{A}^t \cdot \mathbf{x}(0) + \sum_{i=0}^{t-1} \mathrm{A}^{t-i-1} \cdot \mathrm{B} \cdot \mathbf{u}(i), \\
\mathbf{y}(t) &= \mathrm{C} \cdot \mathbf{x}(t) + \mathrm{D} \cdot \mathbf{u}(t).
\end{aligned} \tag{2}$$

3 Linear Temporal Logic for Control (LTLC)

In this section, we describe the syntax and the semantics of LTLC. LTLC has the same temporal and logical operators as *Linear Temporal Logic* (LTL). However, LTLC has different ways of describing atomic propositions than conventional LTL. A commonly used model for LTL is a Kripke structure [11] which is a finite state automaton with a set of atomic propositions associated with each state. In LTLC, with its uncountable state model, atomic propositions are given as a predicate function of states: equalities or inequalities about linear combinations of input, output, and state variables. With this form of atomic propositions, we can easily describe many useful properties of physical systems.

3.1 Syntax

The syntax of an LTLC formula ψ is as follows:

$$\begin{aligned} \psi ::= &\; \mathtt{T} \mid \mathtt{F} \mid ap \\ &\neg\psi \mid \psi \vee \phi \mid \psi \wedge \phi \mid \psi \rightarrow \phi \mid \psi \leftrightarrow \phi \\ &\mathtt{X}\,\psi \mid \psi\,\mathtt{U}\,\phi \mid \psi\,\mathtt{R}\,\phi \mid \Box\,\psi \mid \Diamond\,\psi, \\ ap(t) ::= &\; c_1 \cdot v_1(texp_1) + \cdots + c_n \cdot v_n(texp_n) \bowtie d, \end{aligned}$$

where ap is an atomic proposition, $texp_i$ is a polynomial of variable t, $c_1, \ldots, c_n$, and d are real numbers, $v \in \mathcal{U} \cup \mathcal{Y} \cup \mathcal{X}$ is one of input, output, or state variables, and $\bowtie$ is one of $\{<, \leq, >, \geq, =\}$.

As MPC enforces input and output *horizon constraints*, LTLC also enforces them. Note that they are not just constraints but an important control objective as well: drive the system to a steady state in finite time horizon. These constraints may restrict the scope of LTLC model checking but they play crucial roles in deriving the decidability result of Theorem 2. Also those computational paths pruned by these constraints are less interesting from an automatic control perspective: we are interested in those sequences of input that will drive the system to a steady state rather than arbitrary sequences of input. Let Hy be an output horizon when the system arrives a steady state and Hu be an input horizon ($Hu \leq Hy$) from which the inputs to the system do not change. This horizon constraint can be expressed as follows:

$$\bigwedge_{i=1}^{nx} x_i(Hy+1) = x_i(Hy) \wedge \bigwedge_{i=1}^{nu} u_i(Hu+j) = u_i(Hu) \text{ for } j > 0. \tag{3}$$

The *texp* of LTLC is a polynomial of time variable t. The use of *texp* enriches the expressiveness of LTLC such that some formula cannot be expressed otherwise. For example, in Pharmacokinetics, an instruction like take medicine at every three hours can be easily expressed in LTLC as: `always` ($dose(3 \cdot t + 0) > 0$ and $dose(3 \cdot t + 1) = 0$) and $dose(3 \cdot t + 2) = 0$). However, improper use of *texp* can hamper the steady state constraints (3). Thus, we assume that all non-constant *texp* for state and output variables, $texp(t) \geq Hy$ for $t \geq Hy$ and that all non-constant *texp* for input variables, $texp(t) \geq Hu$ for $t \geq Hu$, where $texp(t)$ is the value of *texp* at time t.

3.2 Semantics

An LTLC formula has atomic propositions, logical connectives, $\neg$, $\vee$, $\wedge$, $\rightarrow$, and $\leftrightarrow$, and temporal connectives $\mathtt{X}$, $\mathtt{U}$, $\mathtt{R}$, $\Box$, and $\Diamond$. An atomic proposition of LTLC is a linear constraint on time-indexed variables (input, output, and state variables) with a

$\mathcal{M},\mathbf{u},\mathbf{x}(0),t \models \mathrm{T}$		
$\mathcal{M},\mathbf{u},\mathbf{x}(0),t \not\models \mathrm{F}$		
$\mathcal{M},\mathbf{u},\mathbf{x}(0),t \models \sum_i c_i \cdot v_i(texp_i) \bowtie d$	$\Leftrightarrow$	$\sum_i c_i \cdot v_i(texp_i(t)) \bowtie d$
$\mathcal{M},\mathbf{u},\mathbf{x}(0),t \models \neg\psi$	$\Leftrightarrow$	$\mathcal{M},\mathbf{u},\mathbf{x}(0),t \not\models \psi$
$\mathcal{M},\mathbf{u},\mathbf{x}(0),t \models \psi \wedge \phi$	$\Leftrightarrow$	$\mathcal{M},\mathbf{u},\mathbf{x}(0),t \models \psi$ and $\mathcal{M},\mathbf{u},\mathbf{x}(0),t \models \phi$
$\mathcal{M},\mathbf{u},\mathbf{x}(0),t \models \psi \vee \phi$	$\Leftrightarrow$	$\mathcal{M},\mathbf{u},\mathbf{x}(0),t \models \psi$ or $\mathcal{M},\mathbf{u},\mathbf{x}(0),t \models \phi$
$\mathcal{M},\mathbf{u},\mathbf{x}(0),t \models \mathbf{X}\,\psi$	$\Leftrightarrow$	$\mathcal{M},\mathbf{u},\mathbf{x}(0),t+1 \models \psi$
$\mathcal{M},\mathbf{u},\mathbf{x}(0),t \models \psi\,\mathbf{U}\,\phi$	$\Leftrightarrow$	there is $j \geq 0$ such that $\mathcal{M},\mathbf{u},\mathbf{x}(0),t+j \models \phi$ and $\mathcal{M},\mathbf{u},\mathbf{x}(0),t+i \models \psi$ for $i = 0,\ldots,j-1$
$\mathcal{M},\mathbf{u},\mathbf{x}(0),t \models \psi\,\mathbf{R}\,\phi$	$\Leftrightarrow$	for all $i \geq 0$ if $\mathcal{M},\mathbf{u},\mathbf{x}(0),t+j \not\models \psi$ for $0 \leq j < i$ then $\mathcal{M},\mathbf{u},\mathbf{x}(0),t+i \models \phi$.

Fig. 1. Quintuple satisfaction relation $\models$

comparator $\bowtie$. The meaning of an atomic proposition at any given time t is whether the linear constraint at time $texp(t)$ satisfies the usual meaning of $\bowtie$. Note that the value of state variables and the output variables can be rewritten in terms of an initial state and a sequence of inputs as can be seen in equation (2).

The meaning of logical operators $\neg$, $\vee$, and $\wedge$ are: $\neg\psi$ is true if and only if ψ is false, $\psi \vee \phi$ is true if and only if ψ or ϕ is true, and $\psi \wedge \phi$ is true if and only if ψ and ϕ are both true. The meaning of implies ($\rightarrow$) is $\psi \rightarrow \phi \Leftrightarrow \neg\psi \vee \phi$ and that of equivalent ($\leftrightarrow$) is $\psi \leftrightarrow \phi \Leftrightarrow \psi \rightarrow \phi \wedge \phi \rightarrow \psi$.

The meaning of temporal operators $\mathbf{X}$, $\mathbf{U}$, and $\mathbf{R}$ are: $\mathbf{X}\,\psi$ is true if and only if ψ is true at the next step, $\psi\,\mathbf{U}\,\phi$ is true if and only if ϕ eventually becomes true and before ϕ becomes true ψ is true, and $\psi\,\mathbf{R}\,\phi$ is true if and only if ϕ is true while ψ is false and if ψ becomes true then ϕ is true until that moment. The meaning of $\Box\,\psi$ is always ψ is true which is equivalent to $\mathrm{F}\ \mathbf{R}\,\psi$ and the meaning of $\Diamond\,\psi$ is eventually ψ becomes true which is equivalent to $\mathrm{T}\ \mathbf{U}\,\psi$.

Formally, the semantics of LTLC formula is defined by a binary satisfaction relation $\models\subset \mathcal{M}\times\psi$. In order to help explain the binary satisfaction relation $\models$, we overload the symbol and define a quintuple satisfaction relation $\models\subset \mathcal{M}\times(\mathbb{N}\rightarrow\mathbb{R}^{nu})\times\mathbb{R}^{nx}\times\mathbb{N}\times\psi$ which is described in Figure 1. For simplicity we write $\mathcal{M} \models \psi$ for $(\mathcal{M},\psi) \in \models$ and $\mathcal{M},\mathbf{u},\mathbf{x}(0),t \models \psi$ for $(\mathcal{M},\mathbf{u},\mathbf{x}(0),t,\psi) \in \models$.

The quintuple satisfaction relation is about a single path: whether a sequence of transitions from an initial state by a sequence of input satisfies the given LTLC formula. Using the definition of the quintuple satisfaction relation, the binary satisfaction relation $\models$ is defined as:

$$\mathcal{M} \models \psi \Leftrightarrow \mathcal{M},\mathbf{u},\mathbf{x}(0),0 \models \psi \text{ for all } \mathbf{u},\mathbf{x}(0).$$

The binary satisfaction relation is about all paths: whether the transitions from all initial states by all sequences of input satisfy the quintuple satisfaction relation.

In order to bring more insight into the syntax, the semantics, and usages of LTLC we explain the following example about drug administration. In Pharmacokinetics, drug concentrations in our body is often modeled as linear systems.

Example 1. Suppose that there is a patient who has disease in his lung. In order to cure the disease certain level of drug concentration (say, 5 mg/l) should be maintained in the lung for certain period of time (say, 3 hour). However, because this drug is toxic to liver, its concentration at the liver should not exceed certain level (say, 3 mg/l). Also, in order to increase absorption of the drug, it should be taken after dining, or say, every 4 hours. As a final condition, the drug should be cleared from the body eventually.

Let *dose* be the dose of medicine, *liver* is the concentration of the drug at the liver, and *lung* is the concentration of the drug at the lung.

The constraint that the drug should be taken at every 4 hours can be written as $\square\,(dose(4\cdot t+1) = 0 \wedge dose(4\cdot t+2) = 0 \wedge dose(4\cdot t+3) = 0)$. In this formula the *always* operator $\square$ provides t from 0 to infinity. A similar but different formula is: $\square\,(dose(t) > 0 \rightarrow (dose(t+1) = 0 \wedge dose(t+2) = 0 \wedge dose(t+3) = 0))$. This formula can be read as, once he took the medicine he shouldn't take it again within 4 hours. Similarly, the drug concentration constraint in the liver can be written as $\square(liver(t) < 3)$.

The goal, the condition about the drug concentration in the lung can be written as $\diamond\,(lung(t) > 5 \wedge \mathbf{X}\,lung(t) > 5 \wedge \mathbf{X}\,\mathbf{X}\,lung(t) > 5)$. Note that the *eventually* operator $\diamond$ ensures that the condition should happen.

The last clearance condition can be written as: $\diamond\,\square\,(lung(t) = 0 \wedge liver(t) = 0)$. Note that the combined operators $\diamond\,\square$ specify properties at a steady state.

Finally, we can express the whole problem in LTLC as follows:

$$\begin{aligned}
&\square\,(dose(4\cdot t+1) = 0 \wedge dose(4\cdot t+2) = 0 \wedge dose(4\cdot t+3) = 0)\\
\wedge\ &\square\,(liver(t) < 3)\\
\wedge\ &\diamond\,(lung(t) > 5 \wedge \mathbf{X}\,lung(t) > 5 \wedge \mathbf{X}\,\mathbf{X}\,lung(t) > 5)\\
\wedge\ &\diamond\,\square\,(lung(t) = 0 \wedge liver(t) = 0).
\end{aligned}$$

■

4 Model Checking

In this section, we describe an LTLC model checking algorithm. We first transform variables at different times into normal form, which is a fixed length coefficient vector. We then remove all temporal operators from the specification using the horizon constraints. Finally, we prove the decidability of LTLC model checking.

4.1 Converting Timed Variables to a Normal Form

The atomic propositions of LTLC are equality or inequality constraints about linear combinations of input, output, or state variables. These variables are related to others by the system dynamics equation (1). In this section we convert these timed variables into a normal form so that the dependencies among variables are eliminated during the model checking process. This is a standard technique in MPC to compute an optimal solution [9,10]. In Section 3.1 we described the steady state constraint of LTLC. This constraint not only is a useful control objective but also makes LTLC model checking decidable. The constraint also plays a key role in defining the *normal form* explained below.

For a constant c: $\mathbf{c}(c,t)_j = \begin{cases} c \text{ if } j = 1 \\ 0 \text{ otherwise} \end{cases}$	For an input variable $u_i(t)$: $\mathbf{c}(u,t)_j = \begin{cases} 1 \text{ if } j = 1 + nx + nu \cdot t_u + i \\ 0 \text{ otherwise} \end{cases}$
For a state variable $x_i(t)$: $\mathbf{c}(x,t)_1 = 0$ $\mathbf{c}(x,t)_{1+j} = (A^{t_y})_{ij}$ for $1 \leq j \leq nx$ $\mathbf{c}(x,t)_{1+nx+j \cdot nu+k} = \begin{cases} 0 & \text{if } j > t_y - 1 \\ \left(A^{t_y-j-1} \cdot B\right)_{ik} & \text{else if } j < Hu \\ \left(\Sigma_{j'=j}^{t_y-1} A^{j'} \cdot B\right)_{ik} & \text{else if } j = Hu \end{cases}$ for $0 \leq j \leq Hu, 1 \leq k \leq nu$	For an output variable $y_i(t)$: $\mathbf{c}(y,t)_1 = 0$ $\mathbf{c}(y,t)_{1+j} = (C \cdot A^{t_y})_{ij}$ for $1 \leq j \leq nx$ $\mathbf{c}(y,t)_{1+nx+j \cdot nu+k} = \begin{cases} \mathbf{c}'(y,t)_{j \cdot nu+k} + D_{ik} & \text{if } j = \min(Hu, t_y) \\ \mathbf{c}'(y,t)_{j \cdot nu+k} & \text{otherwise} \end{cases}$ for $0 \leq j \leq Hu, 1 \leq k \leq nu$, where $\mathbf{c}'(y,t)_{j \cdot nu+k} = \begin{cases} 0 & \text{if } j > t_y - 1 \\ \left(C \cdot A^{t_y-j-1} \cdot B\right)_{ik} & \text{else if } j < Hu \\ \left(\Sigma_{j'=j}^{t_y-1} C \cdot A^{j'} \cdot B\right)_{ik} & \text{else if } j = Hu \end{cases}$

Fig. 2. The conversion function **c**

Let t_y be $\min(t, Hy)$ and let t_u and i_u be $\min(t, Hu)$ and $\min(i, Hu)$ respectively. If the steady state constraint (3) is satisfied then the system dynamics equation (2) can be rewritten as:

$$\mathbf{x}(t) = \mathrm{A}^{t_y} \cdot \mathbf{x}(0) + \sum_{i=0}^{t_y-1} \mathrm{A}^{t_y-i-1} \cdot \mathrm{B} \cdot \mathbf{u}(i_u), \tag{4}$$
$$\mathbf{y}(t) = \mathrm{C} \cdot \mathbf{x}(t) + \mathrm{D} \cdot \mathbf{u}(t_u).$$

Note that in equation (4), $\mathbf{x}(t)$ or $\mathbf{y}(t)$ at any time t can be expressed in terms of $\mathbf{x}(0)$ and $\mathbf{u}(i)$ for $i = 0, \ldots, Hu$. Let $\mathbf{v}$ be a vector of these variables defined as:

$$\mathbf{v} = [1, x_1(0), \ldots, x_{nx}(0), u_1(0), \ldots, u_{nu}(0), \ldots, u_1(H_u), \ldots, u_{nu}(H_u)]^T.$$

Then, the normal form for a variable $z(t)$ is a coefficient vector, say $\mathbf{z}$, such that $z(t) = \mathbf{z} \cdot \mathbf{v}$, where z is one of input, output, or state variables. The conversion function $\mathbf{c}$: $(\mathcal{U} \cup \mathcal{Y} \cup \mathcal{X} \cup \mathbb{R}) \times \mathbb{N} \rightarrow \mathbb{R}^{1+nx+nu \cdot (Hu+1)}$ is defined in Figure 2. For simplicity, we overload the function $\mathbf{c} : (\mathcal{U} \cup \mathcal{Y} \cup \mathcal{X} \cup \mathbb{R}) \times \mathbb{N} \rightarrow \mathbb{R}^{1+nx+nu \cdot (Hu+1)}$ with $\mathbf{c} : AP \times \mathbb{N} \rightarrow AP$ as follows.

$$\mathbf{c}(c_1 \cdot v_1(texp_1) + \cdots + c_n \cdot v_n(texp_n) \bowtie d, t) =$$
$$(c_1 \cdot \mathbf{c}(v_1, texp_1(t)) + \cdots + c_n \cdot \mathbf{c}(v_n, texp_n(t)) - \mathbf{c}(d, 0)) \cdot \mathbf{v} \bowtie 0.$$

With the normal form

$$c_1 \cdot v_1(texp_1(t)) + \cdots + c_n \cdot v_n(texp_n(t)) \bowtie d \Leftrightarrow$$
$$\mathbf{c}(c_1 \cdot v_1(texp_1) + \cdots + c_n \cdot v_n(texp_n) \bowtie d, t).$$

The horizon constraint (3) can be written in LTLC formula as follows:

$$H : \bigwedge_{i=1}^{nx} (x_i(Hy+1) = x_i(Hy)) \wedge \bigwedge_{i=1}^{nu} \Box\ (u_i(Hu+t) = u_i(Hu))$$

Thus, given an LTLC formula ψ we implicitly mean $H \rightarrow \psi$.

4.2 Model Checking as a Feasibility Checking

Before we explain the details of model checking algorithm, we first show an example that illustrates how to convert an LTLC model checking problem into a feasibility checking problem.

Example 2. Let a linear system $\mathcal{M}$ be $\left(\{u\}, \{y\}, \{x_1, x_2\}, \begin{bmatrix} 1 & 1 \\ 2 & 1 \end{bmatrix}, \begin{bmatrix} 2 \\ 1 \end{bmatrix}, [1\ 1], \mathbf{0}\right)$, an atomic proposition $a(t)$ be $y(t) < 3$, horizon constraints be $Hu = 2$ and $Hy = 2$, and suppose that we want to find an initial state and a sequence of input such that $H \wedge \mathbf{X}\, a \wedge \mathbf{X}\,\mathbf{X}\, a$.

For this problem, we do LTLC model checking for the system $\mathcal{M}$ against a specification $\psi : H \rightarrow \neg(\mathbf{X}\, a \wedge \mathbf{X}\,\mathbf{X}\, a)$. Note that any counter example of $\mathcal{M} \models \psi$ satisfies the original goal. In practice, we search for $\mathbf{u}(t)$ and $\mathbf{x}(0)$ such that $\mathcal{M}, \mathbf{u}, \mathbf{x}(0), 0 \models \neg\psi$. That is,

$$\begin{aligned}
&\mathcal{M}, u, \mathbf{x}(0), 0 \models H \wedge \mathbf{X}\, a \wedge \mathbf{X}\,\mathbf{X}\, a \\
&\Leftrightarrow \begin{cases} u(t+2) = u(2) \text{ for } t \geq 0 \wedge & \text{(input horizon constraint)} \\ x_1(2) = x_1(3) \wedge x_2(2) = x_2(3) \wedge & \text{(output horizon constraint)} \\ y(1) < 3 \wedge y(2) < 3 & (\mathbf{X}\, a \wedge \mathbf{X}\,\mathbf{X}\, a) \end{cases} \\
&\Leftrightarrow \begin{matrix} [0,4,3,4,3,2] \cdot \mathbf{v} = 0 \wedge \ [0,6,2,6,3,1] \cdot \mathbf{v} = 0 \wedge \\ [-3,3,2,3,0,0] \cdot \mathbf{v} < 0 \wedge [-3,7,5,7,3,0] \cdot \mathbf{v} < 0 \end{matrix}\ ,
\end{aligned}$$

where $\mathbf{v}$ is $[1, x_1(0), x_2(0), u(0), u(1), u(2)]$. Thus,

$$\mathcal{M} \not\models \psi \Leftrightarrow \left\{ \mathbf{v} : \begin{matrix} [0,4,3,4,3,2] \cdot \mathbf{v} = 0 \wedge \ [0,6,2,6,3,1] \cdot \mathbf{v} = 0 \wedge \\ [-3,3,2,3,0,0] \cdot \mathbf{v} < 0 \wedge [-3,7,5,7,3,0] \cdot \mathbf{v} < 0 \end{matrix} \right\} \neq \emptyset.$$

Note that the emptiness of $\mathbf{v}$ can be checked by linear programming and any feasible $\mathbf{v}$ is the counter example that we are seeking. ■

We now show how to transform an LTLC model checking problem into a feasibility checking problem and use it to prove the decidability of LTLC model checking. If the horizon constraint H is satisfied then the system arrives at a steady state from Hy step onward and the atomic propositions of the specification become constants. Otherwise, the system simply is not a model of the specification. If H is satisfied, then for $t \geq Hy$,

$$\begin{aligned}
\mathcal{M}, \mathbf{u}, \mathbf{x}(0), t \models \mathbf{X}\,\psi &\Leftrightarrow \mathcal{M}, \mathbf{u}, \mathbf{x}(0), t \models \psi, \\
\mathcal{M}, \mathbf{u}, \mathbf{x}(0), t \models \psi\, \mathbf{U}\, \phi &\Leftrightarrow \mathcal{M}, \mathbf{u}, \mathbf{x}(0), t \models \phi, \\
\mathcal{M}, \mathbf{u}, \mathbf{x}(0), t \models \psi\, \mathbf{R}\, \phi &\Leftrightarrow \mathcal{M}, \mathbf{u}, \mathbf{x}(0), t \models \phi.
\end{aligned} \tag{5}$$

```
f(ψ,t) {
  if(ψ is T)      return T
  if(ψ is F)      return F
  if(ψ is an AP) return c(ψ,t)
  if(ψ is ¬φ)     return ¬f(φ,t)
  if(ψ is φ∨η)   return f(φ,t) ∨ f(η,t)
  if(ψ is φ∧η)   return f(φ,t) ∧ f(η,t)
  if(ψ is Xφ)
    if(t ≥ Hy)  return f(φ,t)
    else        return f(φ,t+1)
  if(ψ is φUη)
    if(t ≥ Hy)  return f(η,t)
    else        return f(η,t) ∨ ( f(φ,t) ∧ f(ψ,t+1) )
  if(ψ is φRη)
    if(t ≥ Hy)  return f(η,t)
    else        return ( f(φ,t) ∧ f(η,t) ) ∨ ( f(η,t) ∧ f(ψ,t+1) )
}
```

Fig. 3. Function f removes all temporal operators from an LTLC formula ψ

The use of normal form for timed variables and the fact that the system arrives at a steady state enable us to remove all the temporal operators from LTLC specifications. Figure 3 shows an algorithm to remove all temporal operators of an LTLC formula that is equivalent to the original formula if H is satisfied.

Theorem 1. $\mathcal{M} \models H \rightarrow \psi \Leftrightarrow \mathcal{M} \models H \rightarrow \mathtt{f}(\psi, 0)$.

Outline of proof: We prove the equivalence by induction on the structural tree of LTLC formula ψ. The induction base are T , F , and the atomic propositions which can easily proved. Induction steps on the logical connectives can be proved by the definitions of f and the quintuple satisfaction relation $\models$. Induction steps on the temporal connectives can be proved using the equivalence relations

$$\psi \,\mathbf{U}\, \phi \equiv \phi \vee (\psi \wedge \mathbf{X}\,(\psi \,\mathbf{U}\, \phi)), \qquad (6)$$
$$\psi \,\mathbf{R}\, \phi \equiv (\psi \wedge \phi) \vee (\phi \wedge \mathbf{X}\,(\psi \,\mathbf{R}\, \phi)),$$

the steady state relation of equation (5), and the definition of f about the X formula. We divide the induction step on temporal operators in two cases: before time t reaches the steady state horizon, where we use the equivalence relation (6), and after the steady state, where we use the equation (5). ■

Theorem 2. *Model checking LTLC formulas $H \rightarrow \psi$ is decidable* .

Proof. Given an LTLC formula ψ with an implicit output horizon Hy, we can get a formula $\phi = \mathtt{f}(\psi, 0)$, which is equivalent to ψ, for the runs where H is true. Because ϕ does not have any temporal operators, we can transform it to Disjunctive Normal Form (DNF) whose satisfiability can be checked by checking the satisfiability of each

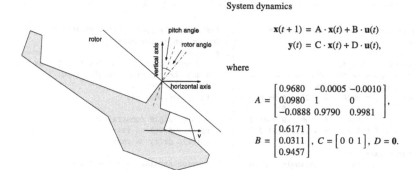

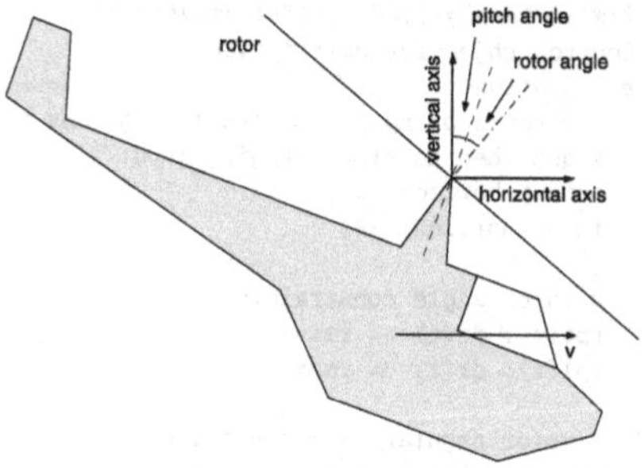

System dynamics

$$\mathbf{x}(t+1) = \mathrm{A} \cdot \mathbf{x}(t) + \mathrm{B} \cdot \mathbf{u}(t)$$
$$\mathbf{y}(t) = \mathrm{C} \cdot \mathbf{x}(t) + \mathrm{D} \cdot \mathbf{u}(t),$$

where

$$A = \begin{bmatrix} 0.9680 & -0.0005 & -0.0010 \\ 0.0980 & 1 & 0 \\ -0.0888 & 0.9790 & 0.9981 \end{bmatrix},$$

$$B = \begin{bmatrix} 0.6171 \\ 0.0311 \\ 0.9457 \end{bmatrix}, \; C = \begin{bmatrix} 0 & 0 & 1 \end{bmatrix}, \; D = \mathbf{0}.$$

Fig. 4. A helicopter diagram and its discrete time dynamics

conjunctive subformula. The subformula is a conjunction of linear equalities and inequalities in the normal form. Thus, the satisfiability of each subformula is equivalent to the feasibility of linear constraints which can be checked by linear programming. Because ϕ has only finite number of conjunctive subformulas and linear programming can be done in finite number of steps, LTLC model checking is decidable. ■

Note that in LTLC model checking we do not make transitions of states explicitly. Instead, we transform the atomic propositions at different times into normal form. In model checking hybrid systems, one of the difficulties is the uncountably large state space. LTLC model checking addresses the difficulty in this framework. Thus, at any moment we can partition the state space into at most $|2^{AP}|$ equivalent classes which are not further distinguishable by AP.

Although the method described in this section is intuitive, when converted to a DNF, the number of conjunctive subformulas of an LTLC formula can grow exponentially in terms of the output horizon Hy. For example, the conjunctive subformulas of $\Box\,(a \vee b)$ have $\bigwedge_{t=0}^{Hy} (a(t) \mid b(t))$, where $\mid$ is a choice operator. Thus, the number of conjunctive terms is 2^{Hy+1} and with large Hy model checking becomes practically impossible. Fortunately, however, there are many common terms in the conjunctive subformulas. If infeasibility is found in the common terms then we can skip checking all of the terms with the common infeasible terms. To leverage this computational benefit, we build a Büchi automaton [12] which can be thought as a generator of the conjunctive subterms. Each path of length Hy of the Büchi automaton is a conjunctive subformula. We can check the feasibility of common prefixes together and skip large number of redundant checks.

5 Experiment

In this section we illustrate how LTLC model checking can be used in controlling linear systems. The example system is a helicopter at near hover speed. Figure 4 shows a diagram of the example helicopter and its dynamics equations. The helicopter is composed of a body (fuselage) and a main rotor whose angle to the body is our control variable.

```
########################################
# System description
system:
    const pi = 3.141592;
    const rmin  = -pi*20/180, rmax = -rmin,
          rrmax =  pi*10/180;
    const A = [ 0.9608, -0.0005, -0.0010;
                0.0980,  1,       0;
               -0.0888,  0.9790,  0.9981 ],
          B = [ 0.6171;  0.0311;  0.9457 ];

    # System variables
    #   x:  pitch rate, pitch angle, speed
    #   dr: rotor angle
    #   v:  speed
    var x[3]: state,
        dr:   input,
        v:    output;

    # System dynamics equation
    x = A * x + B * dr;
    v = [0, 0, 1] * x;
```

```
########################################
# Control objective description
specification:
    # when to bring the system to a steady state
    # and when to stop changing input
    output horizon: 25;
    input horizon: 24;

    # rotor angle constraints
    rp0(t): dr(t) >= rmin;
    rp1(t): dr(t) <= rmax;

    # rotor angular rate constraints
    rr0(t): dr(t+1) - dr(t) <= rrmax;
    rr1(t): dr(t+1) - dr(t) >= -rrmax;

    # initial state
    #   pitch rate and angle are both 0
    x0(t): x[0](t) = 0;
    x1(t): x[1](t) = 0;

    # initial and finial vehicle speed
    vi(t): v(t) = 2;      #initial speed
    vs(t): v(t+16) = 0; #stop at 1.6 sec
    vr(t): v(t) >= 5;    #finial speed

    # negated control objective
    ! (   [] ( rp0 /\ rp1 /\ rr0 /\ rr1 )
                    # physical constraints
       /\  x0 /\ x1  # initial state
       /\  vi        # initial speed
       /\  ([] vs \/ <> [] vr )
                    # either stop or speedup
    );
```

Fig. 5. LTLC specification for the experiment

The angle between the body and the horizontal plane is called *pitch* angle (nose down is positive). The speed of the helicopter (v in Figure 4) is defined at the center of mass. In this example we consider only the horizontal component of the velocity vector. The angle between the rotor plane and the direction of body is called *rotor angle*. The attitude (pitch angle pa, and pitch rate $pr = \dot{pa}$) and the speed (v) of a helicopter can be controlled by changing the rotor angle (dr).

Our system model for the helicopter is $\mathcal{M} = (\mathcal{U}, \mathcal{Y}, \mathcal{X}, \mathrm{A}, \mathrm{B}, \mathrm{C}, \mathrm{D})$, where $\mathcal{U} = \{dr\}$, $\mathcal{Y} = \{v\}$, $\mathcal{X} = \{pr, pa, v\}$, and the system dynamics equation is given in Figure 4. We obtain the discrete time dynamics by sampling a continuous time dynamics equations in [1] at a sampling rate of 10 samples per sec. We also consider physical constraints to the control variable (the rotor angle) to make the system more realistic: its maximum and minimum angles are +20 ° and -20 ° respectively, and its maximum and minimum angular rates are +100 °/sec and -100 °/sec respectively.

Figure 5 shows a model and specification description written in our LTLC checker [13]. It has two main components: a system description block that begins with `system:` tag and a specification block that begins with `specification:` tag. One can define scalar or matrix constants and type annotated variables in this block. Using the constants and the variables system dynamics equations are finally defined in this block. Note that the LHS of the dynamics equations are a state variable or an output variable.

The specification block begins with the implicit horizon constraints. The output horizon *Hy* and the input horizon *Hu* are first defined in this block as can be seen in Figure 5. Optional definitions of atomic propositions follow the horizon constraints. A definition of an atomic proposition has its name with a time variable and a linear constraint. A constraint is a comparison between linear combinations of input, output, and state variables. Also, each variable is associated with a time expression. In Figure 5, *rp0* and *rp1* describe the physical limits of the rotor angle, and *rr0* and *rr1* describe the limits of the rotor angular rate. The next two constraints *x0* and *x1* are about the state variable `x` (pitch rate and pitch angle). We use these equalities to specify an initial condition. The last part of LTLC checker description is an LTLC formula using the previously defined atomic propositions. Usually, the topmost operator of the LTLC specification is the negation operator because we want to model check the negation of our control objective.

Now, suppose that the helicopter is flying at the speed of 2 m/sec and there is another vehicle approaching to it. In order to avoid collision we need to stop the helicopter within 1.6 sec or accelerate it to a speed faster than 5 m/sec within 2.5 sec. We want to know whether this control objective is achievable and if it is possible we want to know the input sequence also.

The subformula $x0 \wedge x1$ is about the initial state condition: the helicopter's initial pitch rate and pitch angle are both zero. Note that an LTLC formula without any temporal operator is about the initial step (at time 0). The subformula $\Box(rp0 \wedge rp1 \wedge rr0 \wedge rr1)$ means that the physical constraints on the rotor control are always imposed. The always operator $\Box$ ensures the binding of the time variable of inequalities and actual time during the process of model checking. Note the time expression *t+16* in *vs(t)*. Because the first time index of *vs(t)* is 16, the formula $\Box vs$ means that the helicopter stops from 1.6 sec onward. The formula $vi \wedge (\Box vs \vee \Diamond\Box vr)$ specifies that a vehicle initially flying at 2 m/sec speed stops within 1.6 sec or speeds up to a speed faster than 5 m/sec within 2.5 sec. Note how easily and intuitively the goal is expressed in LTLC. Even this simple disjunctive form of goal would be very difficult to write by hand.

The model checking result is:

```
result: F
state=   [ -0.000  0.000  2.000 ]^T
input[0]=[ -0.349 -0.349 -0.237 -0.063  0.112  0.286  0.349  0.349  0.175  0.287
            0.113  0.000  0.000 -0.157 -0.332 -0.157  0 0 0 0 0 0 0 0 0          ]
```

In the model checking result '`result: F`' means that the helicopter is not the model of the negated specification. In other words, there is an initial state and a sequence of input that drive the system to meet the original control objective. As a counter example the model checker prints out the initial state and the sequence of input. Thus, by applying the input sequence in that order, the system will arrive at a steady state with all the control objectives satisfied.

Figure 6 shows the result of applying the computed input to the system from the computed initial state. In the second graph of Figure 6, the solid line is the control input, the dashed line is the resulting pitch rate, and the dot-dashed line is the resulting

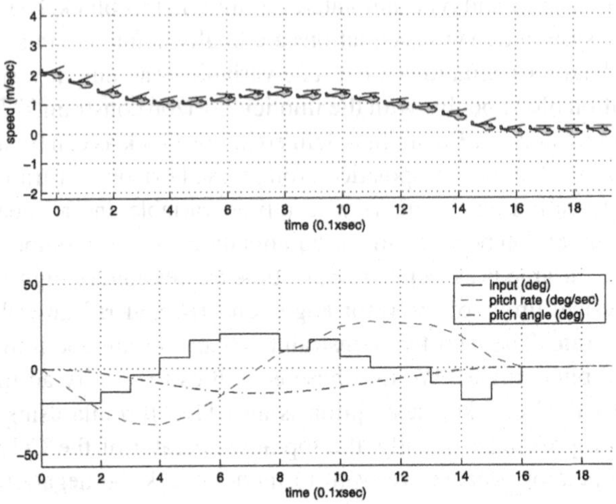

Fig. 6. Transitions of the model system driven by the computed input

pitch angle of the helicopter. Notice the difference that the input sequence in the counter example is in radian whereas the graph is plotted in degree. From this graph we can see that the physical constraints on the rotor angle and its angular rate are always satisfied. The first graph of Figure 6 shows the helicopter's speed. This graph also shows the vehicle's pitch attitude and the rotor angle at the same time in order to give more insight into the dynamics of the system. Note that the vertical axis is the speed of the vehicle not the elevation. This graph shows how the vehicle comes to stop within 1.6 sec and the input also becomes constant from that moment.

6 Discussions

We developed a temporal logic called LTLC for specifying properties of linear systems and its model checking algorithm. LTLC model checking is decidable if we control the system to arrive at a steady state within a specified horizon. Although the implicit steady state constraints prevent LTLC model checking from using arbitrary input, many practical interest for the system require these constraints. LTLC can also be used to explicitly describe complex control objectives. A sequence of control input that can achieve the control objective can be computed in the process of model checking.

The use of *texp* in atomic propositions makes writing specification easy and intuitive. Also, *texp* extends the expressiveness of LTLC such that some properties cannot be expressed without it. Thus, *texp* can be regarded as a special temporal operator. However, on the other hand, its use can obscure the definition of state and requires a refinement in semantics. An interpretation of *texp* can be done in two layers: the first layer is a path determined by the choice of initial state and input; the second layer consists of the parallel compositions of reordered sequences of the path for each *texp* sampled at *texp(t)*.

The implicit horizon constraints could be removed if we adopt the semantics of bounded model checking [14]. In this case, we can still enforce the constraints by explicitly specifying them. As far as assuring system stability goes, the bounds for input horizon *Hu* and output horizon *Hy* are well known in predictive control literature [9]. A general guideline from [9] is, set *Hu* less than the number of states and set *Hy* larger than twice the number of states. Also, the LTLC model checking for control described in this paper is for an ideal open loop control. The closed loop feedback control can be achieved by adopting the Receding Horizon Scheme [9].

We believe, LTLC can be used as a high level abstraction tool that can hide the complexities of the underlying physical systems. We also believe that composing the abstractions to define higher level abstractions will be an important technique for handling the scalability problem in large systems.

References

1. Franklin, G.F., Powell, J.D., Emami-Naeini, A.: Feedback Control of Dynamic Systems, 3rd edn. Addison Wesley, Reading (1994)
2. Lichtenstein, O., Pnueli, A.: Checking that finite state concurrent programs satisfy their linear specification. In: Proc of 12th ACM Symposium on Principles of Programming Languages, pp. 97–107 (1985)
3. Clarke, E., Emerson, E.: Design and synthesis of synchronization skeletons using branching time temporal logic. In: Kozen, D. (ed.) Logic of Programs 1981. LNCS, vol. 131, Springer, Heidelberg (1982)
4. Clarke, E.M., Emerson, E.A., Sistla, A.P.: Automatic verification of finite-state concurrent systems using temporal logics specification: A practical approach. In: Proc. 10th Int. ACM Symposium on Principles of Programming Languages, pp. 117–126 (1983)
5. Alur, R., Dill, D.: A theory of timed automata. Theoretical Computer Science 126, 183–235 (1994)
6. Tabuada, P., Papas, G.J.: Model checking LTL over controllable linear systems is decidable. In: Maler, O., Pnueli, A. (eds.) HSCC 2003. LNCS, vol. 2623, pp. 498–513. Springer, Heidelberg (2003)
7. Tabuada, P., Papas, G.J.: Linear time logic control of discrete-time linear systems. IEEE Transictions on Automatic Control 51, 1862–1877 (2006)
8. Kwon, Y., Agha, G.: Linear inequality LTL (iLTL): A model checker for discrete time markov chains. In: Davies, J., Schulte, W., Barnett, M. (eds.) ICFEM 2004. LNCS, vol. 3308, pp. 194–208. Springer, Heidelberg (2004)
9. Clarke, D., Mohtai, C.: Properties of generalized predictive control. Automatica 25, 859–875 (1989)
10. Clarke, D., Scattolini, R.: Constrained receding-horizon predictive control. IEE Proc. Part D 138, 347–354 (1991)
11. Hughes, G., Creswell, M.: Introduction to Modal Logic. Methuen (1997)
12. Büchi, J.: On a decision method in restricted second order arthmetic. In: Proc. of the Int. Conf. on Logic, Methodology and Philosophy of Science, pp. 1–11. Stanford University Press (1960)
13. LTLC Checker: (2007), `http://osl.cs.uiuc.edu/~ykwon4/cgi/LTLC.html`
14. Biere, A., Cimatti, A., Clarke, E., Zhu, Y.: Symbolic model checking without bdds. In: Cleaveland, W.R. (ed.) TACAS 1999. LNCS, vol. 1579, pp. 193–207. Springer, Heidelberg (1999)

Switched and PieceWise Nonlinear Hybrid System Identification

Fabien Lauer and Gérard Bloch

Centre de Recherche en Automatique de Nancy (CRAN UMR 7039),
Nancy–University, CNRS, France
fabien.lauer@esstin.uhp-nancy.fr, gerard.bloch@esstin.uhp-nancy.fr

Abstract. Hybrid system identification aims at both estimating the discrete state or mode for each data point, and the submodel governing the dynamics of the continuous state for each mode. The paper proposes a new method based on kernel regression and Support Vector Machines (SVM) to tackle this problem. The resulting algorithm is able to compute both the discrete state and the submodels in a single step, independently of the discrete state sequence that generated the data. In addition to previous works, nonlinear submodels are also considered, thus extending the class of systems on which the method can be applied from PieceWise Affine (PWA) and switched linear to PieceWise Smooth (PWS) and switched nonlinear systems with unknown nonlinearities. Piecewise systems with nonlinear boundaries between the modes are also considered with some preliminary results on this issue.

1 Introduction

Context. Hybrid systems are usually described by both a continuous state and a discrete state, where the vector field defining the evolution of the continuous state depends on the discrete state. In this framework, a system can be seen as switching between n different subsystems, which are usually modeled by AutoRegressive with eXogenuous inputs (ARX) models in the discrete-time case. Two types of identification problems may arise in this setting depending on whether the discrete state sequence that generated the data is known or not. If it is, then the problem can be simply recast as n common identification problems, each one using only the data for a given discrete state. However, in most cases this sequence is unknown and the problem becomes nontrivial.

Models of hybrid systems. The predicted output y_t of a hybrid model in ARX form is given as a function of the continuous state $\boldsymbol{x}_t = [u_{t-n_c} \cdots u_{t-1}, y_{t-n_a} \cdots y_{t-1}]^T$, containing the lagged inputs u_{t-j} and outputs y_{t-j}, and the discrete state λ_t. Considering n submodels f_j, the hybrid model is written as

$$y_t = f_{\lambda_t}(\boldsymbol{x}_t) + e_t, \tag{1}$$

where e_t is a noise term. Hybrid models can be classified with respect to the nature of the submodels f_j and of the evolution of the discrete state $\lambda_t \in \{1, \dots, n\}$.

M. Egerstedt and B. Mishra (Eds.): HSCC 2008, LNCS 4981, pp. 330–343, 2008.

Table 1. Nomenclature of the hybrid models in ARX form

ARX model	abbr.	models f_j	discrete state λ_t	domains S_j
PieceWise	PWARX	affine	function of $\boldsymbol{x}$	polyhedral
PieceWise Nonlinear	PWNARX	nonlinear	function of $\boldsymbol{x}$	polyhedral
Nonlinearly PieceWise	NPWARX	affine	function of $\boldsymbol{x}$	arbitrary
Nonlinearly PieceWise Nonlinear	NPWNARX	nonlinear	function of $\boldsymbol{x}$	arbitrary
Switched	SARX	affine	arbitrary	
Switched Nonlinear	SNARX	nonlinear	arbitrary	

Table 1 defines the nomenclature that will be used in the paper. SARX and SNARX models assume that the system is arbitrarily switched. On the other hand, PWARX models consider a dependency between the discrete state and the continuous state. They can thus be defined by PieceWise Affine (PWA) maps of the type $f(\boldsymbol{x}) = f_j(\boldsymbol{x})$, if $\boldsymbol{x} \in S_j = \{\boldsymbol{x} \,:\, \boldsymbol{H}_j[\boldsymbol{x}^T \; 1]^T \leq 0\}$, $j = 1, \dots, n$, where the matrices $\boldsymbol{H}_j$ represent a set of hyperplanes that define the polyhedral domains S_j partitioning the continuous state space. Similarly, PWNARX models can be defined by PieceWise Smooth (PWS) maps, where f_j are smooth nonlinear functions instead of affine functions. Extensions of the PWARX and PWNARX models to "nonlinearly piecewise" models, where the domains S_j are no more constrained to be polyhedral, will be denoted NPWARX and NPWNARX.

Related work. Five main approaches have been devised for hybrid system identification: the clustering-based approach [1], the mixed integer programming based approach [2], the Bayesian approach [3], the bounded error approach [4] and the algebraic approach [5,6]. The first four focus on the problem of PieceWise Affine (PWA) system identification, where the discrete state depends on the continuous state. However, both the bounded error and Bayesian approaches can also be used to identify a broader class of systems, known as switched linear systems, where the discrete state evolves independently of the continuous state. The algebraic approach [5] focuses on this latter problem, but without taking the noise into account in its development. This leads to an algorithm very sensitive to noise, compared to the clustering-based or bounded error methods, as shown by [7]. Besides, the bounded error method [4] provides a convenient way of dealing with noisy data by looking for a model with a predefined accuracy. However, the hyperparameters of the method, such as the model accuracy that determines the number of modes, may be difficult to tune to get a prescribed structure, e.g. if prior knowledge on the number of modes is available [7].

Tools and proposed method. The paper proposes a new method for hybrid system identification based on kernel regression and Support Vector Machines (SVMs). Stemming from statistical learning theory, Support Vector Machines (SVMs) [8] quickly became a state-of-the-art tool for classification and are already commonly used, either in their original form or through closely related methods [9], in hybrid system identification to estimate the switching boundary between modes [1,4]. Based on the same theoretical concepts, Support Vector Regression (SVR) retains properties of SVMs, such as a good generalization ability from few samples, and offers an interesting alternative both for regression and system identification [10,11,12]. SVR uses an ε-insensitive loss function which does not take into account errors that are less than ε [13]. This loss function ignoring errors below a predefined threshold is close in spirit to the bounded error approach. However, the origin is different. In learning theory, this effect is justified in order to minimize the generalization error of the model, whereas the bounded error approach was developed to allow the automatic determination of the number of linear submodels required to approximate a non-linear function with a given accuracy.

In the past decade, kernel methods have attracted much attention in a large variety of fields and applications: classification and pattern recognition, regression, density estimation, etc. Indeed, using kernel functions, many linear methods can be extended to the nonlinear case in an almost straightforward manner, while avoiding the curse of dimensionality by transposing the focus from the data dimension to the number of data.

The proposed method uses the SVR framework to estimate hybrid models with submodels in kernel expansion form. The resulting algorithm is able to compute both the discrete state and the submodels in a single step, independently of the discrete state sequence that generated the data. Nonlinear submodels with unknown types of nonlinearities can be easily treated, thus extending the class of systems on which the method can be applied from switched linear to switched nonlinear systems and from piecewise affine to piecewise smooth systems by considering models in SARX, SNARX, PWARX or PWNARX form. Nonlinearly PWA and PWS maps with nonlinear mode boundaries are also considered in the paper with some preliminary results using nonlinear SVM classifiers. The idea is that since the method estimates the discrete state without any assumption on the switching sequence, labeling data points generated from nonlinearly separable modes is possible.

Contribution. The paper proposes solutions for two problems that have not yet been extensively studied and solved in the literature: identification of hybrid systems switching between unknown nonlinear dynamics and identification of nonlinearly piecewise systems with nonlinear boundaries between the modes in the continuous state space.

Paper organization. The paper starts by some preliminaries on kernel functions and Support Vector Regression (Sect. 2.1) before using these to develop a hybrid system identification algorithm in Sect. 2.2. The problem of estimating nonlinear boundaries between modes is then discussed in Sect. 2.3 and Section 3 provides an interpretation of the method based on previous approaches from the literature. Finally, Section 4 gives some numerical examples of application.

Notations. All vectors are column vectors written in boldface and lowercase letters whereas matrices are boldface and uppercase. The vectors $\mathbf{0}$ and $\mathbf{1}$ are vectors of appropriate dimensions with all their components respectively equal to 0 and 1. For $\boldsymbol{A} \in \mathbb{R}^{d \times m}$ and $\boldsymbol{B} \in \mathbb{R}^{d \times n}$ containing d-dimensional sample vectors and the kernel function $k : \mathbb{R}^d \times \mathbb{R}^d \to \mathbb{R}$, the "kernel" $\boldsymbol{K}(\boldsymbol{A}, \boldsymbol{B})$ maps $\mathbb{R}^{d \times m} \times \mathbb{R}^{d \times n}$ in $\mathbb{R}^{m \times n}$ with $\boldsymbol{K}(\boldsymbol{A}, \boldsymbol{B})_{i,j} = k(\boldsymbol{A}_i, \boldsymbol{B}_j)$, where $\boldsymbol{A}_i$ and $\boldsymbol{B}_j$ are the ith and jth columns of $\boldsymbol{A}$ and $\boldsymbol{B}$. In particular, if $\boldsymbol{x} \in \mathbb{R}^d$ is a column vector then $\boldsymbol{K}(\boldsymbol{x}, \boldsymbol{B})$ is a row vector in $\mathbb{R}^{1 \times n}$. The matrix $\boldsymbol{X} \in \mathbb{R}^{N \times d}$ contains all the training samples $\boldsymbol{x}_i$, $i = 1, \dots, N$, as rows. The vector $\boldsymbol{y} \in \mathbb{R}^N$ gathers all the target values y_i for these samples. The kernel matrix $\boldsymbol{K}(\boldsymbol{X}^T, \boldsymbol{X}^T)$ will be written $\boldsymbol{K}$ for short.

2 Nonlinear Hybrid System Identification

This section presents a new method based on kernel regression and support vector machines (SVMs) for hybrid system identification. The basics of nonlinear function approximation by kernel methods are first recalled, before describing the proposed method itself. The section ends with a discussion on piecewise systems with nonlinear boundaries between modes.

2.1 Kernels and Support Vector Regression

A simple method to approximate a nonlinear function is to first map the data to a higher dimensional feature space and then perform linear regression in that space. This approach usually suffers from the so-called *curse of dimensionality*, which can however be avoided thanks to the "kernel trick" depicted below.

First, consider the nonlinear mapping $\boldsymbol{\Phi}$ that maps the data $\boldsymbol{x}$ from the input space $\mathcal{X} \subset \mathbb{R}^p$ to a vector $\boldsymbol{\Phi}(\boldsymbol{x})$ in a feature space $\mathcal{F}$. Assume now that the function f is given by an expansion based on the N training samples $\boldsymbol{x}_i \in \mathbb{R}^p$ in that feature space, i.e. $f(\boldsymbol{x}) = \sum_{i=1}^N \alpha_i \boldsymbol{\Phi}(\boldsymbol{x})^T \boldsymbol{\Phi}(\boldsymbol{x}_i) + b$. Clearly, though being a nonlinear function in the input space, f is a linear function in $\mathcal{F}$. Note that in order to compute $f(\boldsymbol{x})$, it is not necessary to explicitly compute the images $\boldsymbol{\Phi}(\boldsymbol{x}_i)$ of the points but only the result of their inner product. This is the "kernel trick" which replaces the inner products between images of points by a *kernel function* $k(\boldsymbol{x}, \boldsymbol{x}_i) = \boldsymbol{\Phi}(\boldsymbol{x})^T \boldsymbol{\Phi}(\boldsymbol{x}_i)$. In kernel regression, the training data $(\boldsymbol{x}_i, y_i)$, $i = 1, \dots, N$, stacked in the matrix $\boldsymbol{X}$ and the vector $\boldsymbol{y}$, are thus approximated by a kernel expansion

$$f(\boldsymbol{x}) = \sum_{i=1}^{N} \alpha_i k(\boldsymbol{x}, \boldsymbol{x}_i) + b = \boldsymbol{K}(\boldsymbol{x}, \boldsymbol{X}^T)\boldsymbol{\alpha} + b \,, \tag{2}$$

where $\boldsymbol{\alpha} = [\alpha_1 \ \dots \ \alpha_i \ \dots \ \alpha_N]^T$ and b are the parameters of the model and $k(.,.)$ is the kernel function. Typical kernel functions are the linear ($k(\boldsymbol{x}, \boldsymbol{x}_i) = \boldsymbol{x}^T \boldsymbol{x}_i$), Gaussian RBF ($k(\boldsymbol{x}, \boldsymbol{x}_i) = \exp(-\|\boldsymbol{x} - \boldsymbol{x}_i\|_2^2 / 2\sigma^2)$ and polynomial ($k(\boldsymbol{x}, \boldsymbol{x}_i) = (\boldsymbol{x}^T \boldsymbol{x}_i + 1)^d$) kernels. The kernel function defines the feature space $\mathcal{F}$ in which the data are implicitly mapped. The higher the dimension of $\mathcal{F}$ is, the higher the approximation capacity of the function f is, up to the universal approximation capacity obtained for an infinite feature space, as with Gaussian RBF kernels. It is also possible to build kernel functions from prior knowledge on the task at hand, see for instance [14] for the properties of kernel functions and the construction of new kernels or [15] for examples of application in pattern recognition. In the hybrid system identification framework, this can be useful for instance when the type of nonlinearity of a particular mode is known beforehand.

In kernel regression via linear programming (LP), the ℓ_1-norm of the parameters $\boldsymbol{\alpha}$ of the kernel expansion is minimized together with the ℓ_1-norm of the errors $y_i - f(\boldsymbol{x}_i)$ by

$$\min_{(\boldsymbol{\alpha},b)} \|\boldsymbol{\alpha}\|_1 + C\sum_{i=1}^{N} |f(\boldsymbol{x}_i) - y_i| , \tag{3}$$

where a hyperparameter C is introduced to tune the trade-off between the minimization of the model complexity (measured by $\|\boldsymbol{\alpha}\|_1$) and the error on the data (measured by $\sum_{i=1}^{N} |f(\boldsymbol{x}_i) - y_i|$). Minimizing the complexity of the model allows to control its generalization capacity. In practice, this amounts to penalize non-smooth functions and implements the general smoothness assumption that two samples close in input space tend to give the same output.

Instead of the ℓ_1-norm of the errors, the ε-insensitive loss function, defined by [8] as

$$l(e) = |e|_\varepsilon = \begin{cases} 0 & \text{if } |e| \leq \varepsilon , \\ |e| - \varepsilon & \text{otherwise} , \end{cases} \tag{4}$$

can also be used to yield Linear Programming Support Vector Regression (LP-SVR). This loss function builds a tube of insensitivity in which the errors are meaningless. Errors larger than the tube width[1] ε are penalized linearly.

A possible formulation of the LP-SVR problem involves $4N + 1$ design variables [16]. In the remaining of the paper, we will follow the approach of [17] that involves only $3N + 1$ variables. Introducing two sets of optimization variables, in two positive slack vectors $\boldsymbol{a}$ and $\boldsymbol{\xi}$, this problem can be implemented as a linear program solvable by standard optimization softwares such as the MATLAB *linprog* function. In this scheme, the LP-SVR problem may be written as

$$\begin{aligned} &\min_{(\boldsymbol{\alpha},b,\boldsymbol{\xi}\geq\mathbf{0},\boldsymbol{a}\geq\mathbf{0})} && \mathbf{1}^T\boldsymbol{a} + C\mathbf{1}^T\boldsymbol{\xi} \\ &\text{s.t.} && -\boldsymbol{\xi} - \varepsilon\mathbf{1} \leq \boldsymbol{K}\boldsymbol{\alpha} + b\mathbf{1} - \boldsymbol{y} \leq \varepsilon\mathbf{1} + \boldsymbol{\xi} \\ & && -\boldsymbol{a} \leq \boldsymbol{\alpha} \leq \boldsymbol{a} . \end{aligned} \tag{5}$$

The last set of constraints ensures that $\mathbf{1}^T\boldsymbol{a}$, which is minimized, bounds $\|\boldsymbol{\alpha}\|_1$. In practice, sparsity is obtained as a certain number of parameters α_i will tend to zero. The input vectors $\boldsymbol{x}_i$ for which the corresponding α_i are non-zero are called *support vectors*.

[1] Actually, ε does not stand for the tube width but for half of the tube section with respect to y.

2.2 Hybrid System Identification with Kernels

The bounded error approach, developed by [4] for the identification PWARX models, aims at finding a model with a predefined accuracy, i.e. that allows the error on all the training points $(\boldsymbol{x}_i, y_i)$ to be bounded by

$$|y_i - f_{\lambda_i}(\boldsymbol{x}_i)| = |e_i| \leq \delta, \; i = 1, \dots, N \; . \tag{6}$$

The following presents a new method based on kernel regression to achieve this goal. As a direct benefit, nonlinear submodels f_j are easily handled by the choice of the kernel functions, thus providing a method for the estimation of both piecewise and switched nonlinear ARX models.

Following the SVR approach, submodels in kernel expansion form

$$f_j(\boldsymbol{x}) = \sum_{i=1}^{N} \alpha_{ij} k_j(\boldsymbol{x}, \boldsymbol{x}_i) + b_j = \boldsymbol{K}_j(\boldsymbol{x}, \boldsymbol{X}^T)\boldsymbol{\alpha}_j - b_j, \tag{7}$$

are trained by minimizing the ℓ_1-norm of the parameters $\boldsymbol{\alpha}_j$. As indicated by the subscript j, various kernel functions k_j can be associated to the different models f_j. This leads to vectors $\boldsymbol{K}_j(\boldsymbol{x}, \boldsymbol{X}^T)$ and kernel matrices $\boldsymbol{K}_j = \boldsymbol{K}_j(\boldsymbol{X}^T, \boldsymbol{X}^T)$, as defined in the notations at end of the introduction. It is thus possible to take prior information into account such as the number of modes governed by linear dynamics or knowledge on the type of a particular nonlinearity. In this setting, the problem of training n models under the bounded error constraint may be written as

$$\begin{aligned} &\min_{\boldsymbol{\alpha}_j, b_j, \boldsymbol{a}_j \geq \boldsymbol{0}} \sum_{j=1}^{n} \boldsymbol{1}^T \boldsymbol{a}_j \\ &-\delta\boldsymbol{1} \leq \boldsymbol{y} - \boldsymbol{K}_j\boldsymbol{\alpha}_j - b_j\boldsymbol{1} \leq \delta\boldsymbol{1}, \; \forall \boldsymbol{x}_i \in S_j, \; j = 1, \dots, n, \\ &-\boldsymbol{a}_j \leq \boldsymbol{\alpha}_j \leq \boldsymbol{a}_j, \; j = 1, \dots, n \; . \end{aligned} \tag{8}$$

where $\boldsymbol{y} = [y_1 \; y_2 \; \dots \; y_N]^T$ and the absolute error $|e_{ij}| = |f_j(\boldsymbol{x}_i) - y_i|$ is constrained to be less than δ only for the model j corresponding to the discrete state λ_i of the point $\boldsymbol{x}_i$. However, without further information on the classification of the data into modes, S_j are unknown and the problem is intractable. To circumvent this issue, consider the equivalent problem using the ε-insensitive loss function (4) for $\varepsilon = \delta$ implemented with slack variables ξ_{ij}, $i = 1, \dots, N$, $j = 1, \dots, n$, stacked in the n vectors $\boldsymbol{\xi}_j \in \mathbb{R}^N$ as in (5):

$$\begin{aligned} &\min_{\boldsymbol{\alpha}_j, b_j, \boldsymbol{a}_j \geq \boldsymbol{0}, \boldsymbol{\xi}_j \geq \boldsymbol{0}} \sum_{j=1}^{n} \boldsymbol{1}^T \boldsymbol{a}_j \\ &-\boldsymbol{\xi}_j - \delta\boldsymbol{1} \leq \boldsymbol{y} - \boldsymbol{K}_j\boldsymbol{\alpha}_j - b_j\boldsymbol{1} \leq \delta\boldsymbol{1} + \boldsymbol{\xi}_j, \; j = 1, \dots, n, \\ &-\boldsymbol{a}_j \leq \boldsymbol{\alpha}_j \leq \boldsymbol{a}_j, \; j = 1, \dots, n, \\ &\prod_{j=1}^{n} \xi_{ij} = 0, \; i = 1, \dots, N \; . \end{aligned} \tag{9}$$

The last equalities stand for the fact that all points must be estimated with accuracy δ by at least one submodel f_j. In other words, for a given sample $(\boldsymbol{x}_i, y_i)$, there is at least one j for which $\xi_{ij} = 0$. As nonlinear equalities are not easy to deal with from an optimization point of view, these are approximated by

$$\min_{\boldsymbol{\alpha}_j, b_j, \boldsymbol{a}_j \geq \boldsymbol{0}, \boldsymbol{\xi}_j \geq \boldsymbol{0}} \sum_{j=1}^{n} \boldsymbol{1}^T \boldsymbol{a}_j + C \sum_{i=1}^{N} \prod_{j=1}^{n} \xi_{ij} \tag{10}$$
$$-\boldsymbol{\xi}_j - \delta \boldsymbol{1} \leq \boldsymbol{y} - \boldsymbol{K}_j \boldsymbol{\alpha}_j - b_j \boldsymbol{1} \leq \delta \boldsymbol{1} + \boldsymbol{\xi}_j, \; j = 1, \dots, n,$$
$$-\boldsymbol{a}_j \leq \boldsymbol{\alpha}_j \leq \boldsymbol{a}_j, \; j = 1, \dots, n \; .$$

Solving this problem with a sufficiently large constant C leads to functions f_j solutions of the former problem (8). Moreover, the discrete state λ_i, in which the system was for each data point $\boldsymbol{x}_i$ is readily available from the variables ξ_{ij} vanishing to zero as $\hat{\lambda}_i = j$, for $\xi_{ij} = 0$. The cases where the bounded error constraint is not satisfied, i.e. no ξ_{ij} is zero, can be further discriminated by letting $\hat{\lambda}_i = \arg\min_j(\xi_{ij})$. On the other hand, for cases where more than one ξ_{ij} is zero, the absolute error is considered and $\hat{\lambda}_i = \arg\min_j |e_{ij}|$, with $e_{ij} = y_i - f_j(\boldsymbol{x}_i)$.

In the case of PWARX or PWNARX models where the modes are linearly separable in the continuous state space, undetermined points can be reclassified after the training of separating hyperplanes (the boundaries between the sets S_j) based on the determined cases only. The linear classification issue is not discussed here due to size constraints and the reader is referred to [8] and [9] for an introduction to state-of-the-art methods, whereas multi-class pattern recognition is considered for instance by [18]. In the next Section, extensions of the PWARX and PWNARX models to nonlinearly piecewise models, where the domains S_j are no more constrained to be polyhedral, will be discussed.

An advantage of the proposed approach is the possibility to deal easily with a noise level that also switches with the model. In order to do so, multiple loss functions with different parameters δ_j for each mode can be used and implemented in the following final problem

$$\min_{\boldsymbol{\alpha}_j, b_j, \boldsymbol{a}_j \geq \boldsymbol{0}, \boldsymbol{\xi}_j \geq \boldsymbol{0}} \sum_{j=1}^{n} \boldsymbol{1}^T \boldsymbol{a}_j + C \sum_{i=1}^{N} \prod_{j=1}^{n} \xi_{ij} \tag{11}$$
$$-\boldsymbol{\xi}_j - \delta_j \boldsymbol{1} \leq \boldsymbol{y} - \boldsymbol{K}_j \boldsymbol{\alpha}_j - b_j \boldsymbol{1} \leq \delta_j \boldsymbol{1} + \boldsymbol{\xi}_j, \; j = 1, \dots, n,$$
$$-\boldsymbol{a}_j \leq \boldsymbol{\alpha}_j \leq \boldsymbol{a}_j, \; j = 1, \dots, n \; .$$

Another possible formulation with $n \times N$ less variables and constraints involves the minimization of the squares of the parameters α_{ij} as

$$\min_{\boldsymbol{\alpha}_j, b_j, \boldsymbol{\xi}_j \geq \boldsymbol{0}} \sum_{j=1}^{n} \boldsymbol{\alpha}_j^T \boldsymbol{\alpha}_j + C \sum_{i=1}^{N} \prod_{j=1}^{n} \xi_{ij} \tag{12}$$
$$-\boldsymbol{\xi}_j - \delta_j \boldsymbol{1} \leq \boldsymbol{y} - \boldsymbol{K}_j \boldsymbol{\alpha}_j - b_j \boldsymbol{1} \leq \delta_j \boldsymbol{1} + \boldsymbol{\xi}_j, \; j = 1, \dots, n \; .$$

The solution of this problem is not sparse as the one of (11) but can usually be computed in less time.

Remark 1. In the case of a linear kernel $k_j(\boldsymbol{x}, \boldsymbol{x}_i) = \boldsymbol{x}^T \boldsymbol{x}_i$, the parameters of the linear model $f_j(\boldsymbol{x}) = \boldsymbol{w}_j^T \boldsymbol{x} + b_j$ can be explicitly recovered by $\boldsymbol{w}_j = \boldsymbol{X}^T \boldsymbol{\alpha}_j$.

Remark 2. The hyperparameters of the method are the kernel types, the number n of modes, the bounds δ_j, the regularization parameter C and the number of lagged inputs and outputs (dynamic order). They can be tuned on a subset of the data put aside for validation. When too few data are available, cross-validation techniques can be used. Moreover, the algorithms (11) and (12) can be extended to automatically tune the bounds δ_j to the noise level by using a trick similar to the one introduced in ν-SVR [16,17]. This is studied in [19] for linear submodels and directly applicable to the problems above. Besides, the proposed method is well adapted when some basic prior knowledge on the system is available such as the number n of modes. However, due to the universal approximation capability of kernel models, the tuning of n is less crucial than when using linear or affine submodels. For piecewise maps, a good fit can be obtained with an underestimated n.

Remark 3. Problems (11) and (12) are linearly constrained nonlinear programs. They involve the minimization of a criterion composed of a linear (11) or quadratic (12) term and a product of nonnegative variables subject to linear constraints. These problems are not convex and have multiple minima. This can be seen from their symmetric structure, leading to multiple solutions for simple permutations of models. All these solutions are acceptable and yield the same objective function value corresponding to a global optimum. However, care must be taken when using different kernels for different models, in which case permuting models is no more without effect and may lead to local minima.

A possible initialization of the optimization can be obtained by solving the feasibility problems corresponding to the constraints of (11) and (12), which are simple linear programs.

2.3 Nonlinear Boundaries between Modes

A direct extension of the PWARX and PWNARX models, in which the discrete state is determined by a set of separating hyperplanes in the continuous state space, is obtained by introducing nonlinear boundaries or arbitrary regions (also pointed out in the conclusion of [4]). In these "nonlinearly piecewise" models (denoted by NPWARX and NPWNARX, see Table 1 in the introduction), the discrete state is still a function of the continuous state, but the separating surfaces are no more restricted to hyperplanes. This can lead to a decrease of the number of submodels if the true system corresponds to this description. Indeed, in this case, the linear separability assumption may require to build multiple identical submodels for different regions of the continuous state space that are however governed by the same dynamics. Moreover, regrouping the data available in several regions of the continuous state space into one submodel may help to get better estimates for regions with few samples.

Nonlinear classification methods have to be used in this case and are readily available in number (KPCA, KFD, SVM...) [14] thanks to the kernel trick used above. In particular, SVMs are similarly very easily extended to nonlinear classification by an appropriate choice of kernel function. Moreover, the final classifier is given as a sparse kernel expansion allowing for relatively fast estimation of the mode for a new sample. For the binary case (only 2 modes), the nonlinear separating surface $\mathcal{S}$ is given by

$$h(\boldsymbol{x}) = \sum_{i=1}^{N} \beta_i k_c(\boldsymbol{x}, \boldsymbol{x}_i) + b_c = 0 \ , \tag{13}$$

where $k_c(.,.)$ is a kernel function and the β_i, b_c are the trainable parameters of the classifier. Simply taking the sign of the function h yields the class of a pattern $\boldsymbol{x}$, i.e. $+1$ if $h(\boldsymbol{x}) \geq 0$ and -1 otherwise.

The method proposed in Sect. 2 can deal with nonlinearly piecewise maps (themselves either affine or nonlinear) without any modification and provide the labeling of the data, required to train a classifier, through $\hat{\lambda}_i$. Indeed, any method (including the bounded-error, Bayesian or algebraic approaches) that estimates the discrete state without dependency on the continuous state, and thus without any assumption regarding the linear separability of the data in the continuous state space, can deal with nonlinearly piecewise maps. In practice, the procedure is as follows.

1. Train a hybrid model on the input-output data $(\boldsymbol{x}_i, y_i)$, $i = 1, \dots, N$, by solving (11) or (12),
2. Estimate the discrete states, e.g. by $\hat{\lambda}_i = \arg\min_j |e_{ij}|$, $i = 1, \dots, N$,
3. Train a classifier on the labeled data $(\boldsymbol{x}_i, \hat{\lambda}_i)$, $i = 1, \dots, N$.

Additionally, in a refinement step, the training points could be re-assigned to the different modes by the classifier and the submodels f_j retrained one by one on the relevant data only.

An illustrative example of this procedure is given in Sect. 4.2, where the method is applied to estimate a Nonlinearly PieceWise Affine (NPWA) map.

3 Interpretation and Links with other Approaches

The proposed method can be interpreted as a bridge between the bounded error approach [4], that can deal easily with noise, and the algebraic procedure [5], that can deal with arbitrarily switched systems, while providing nonlinear extensions to these. More precisely, it amounts to a bounded error relaxation of the hybrid decoupling constraint used in the algebraic procedure as follows.

The hybrid decoupling constraint of the algebraic procedure can be expressed as a function of the submodel errors, $e_{ij} = y_i - f_j(\boldsymbol{x}_i)$, by

$$\prod_{j=1}^{n} e_{ij} = 0, \ i = 1, \dots, N. \tag{14}$$

These constraints account for the fact that there must be at least one of the submodels f_j that can estimate the ith point with zero error. In the case of noisy data, these constraints cannot be satisfied for all the N points. Considering the bounded error approach, "decoupling" can be however enforced. The bounded error constraints (6) act similarly to (14), though being less restrictive on the estimation error (with a threshold δ). Combining these two approaches results in constraints of the form

$$\prod_{j=1}^{n}[|e_{ij}| \geq \delta] = 0, \ i = 1, \dots, N \ , \tag{15}$$

where $[\cdot] = 1$, if the bracketed expression is true, and 0 otherwise. Using these constraints, the absolute value of the error $|e_i| = \min_j |e_{ij}|$ (assuming that $\hat{\lambda}_i = \arg\min_j |e_{ij}|$) of the hybrid model is bounded by the threshold δ. Approximating $[|e_{ij}| \geq \delta]$ for all j by an ε-insensitive loss function and minimizing their product leads to the algorithm (11).

4 Numerical Examples

The following presents three examples of application. The first one shows the simultaneous estimation of two functions, one linear and one nonlinear, from datasets overlapping in the input space, while the second one is concerned with the estimation of a nonlinearly piecewise affine (NPWA) map. The last example shows the identification of a SNARX model of a hybrid system arbitrarily switching between linear and nonlinear dynamics. For examples 1 and 3, the discrete state is arbitrarily switched and the type of nonlinearity is unknown. In all the examples, the problems are formulated as the optimization program (11) and solved by the MATLAB function *fmincon*.

4.1 Switching Function with Unknown Nonlinearity

In this one-dimensional example, the data are generated by two models: a linear submodel $y_1(x) = ax + b + e = 2x - 1 + e$ and a polynomial submodel $y_2(x) = 0.5x^2 + e$, where e is a zero-mean Gaussian noise of standard deviation 0.5. The discrete state λ, determining which submodel is active, is independent of the variable x. Two data points, $(x, y_1(x))$ and $(x, y_2(x))$, are generated for 30 values of x in the interval $]-5, 1[$. Beside these 60 data, the only prior knowledge is that one submodel is linear and the other is nonlinear. The aim of this example is to show that the proposed method can discriminate between the two submodels and correctly approximate each one without further knowledge on the type of nonlinearity. Figure 1 shows the results obtained for $\delta_1 = \delta_2 = 0.5$, $C = 100$, a linear kernel k_1 and a Gaussian RBF kernel k_2 with $\sigma = 2$. The estimated parameters for the linear submodel are $\hat{a} = 1.999$ and $\hat{b} = -0.863$. The overall Mean Square Error (MSE) is $\text{MSE} = \frac{1}{N}\sum_{i=1}^{N}(y_i - f_{\hat{\lambda}_i}(x_i))^2 = 0.205$, which is rather good compared to the noise variance $\sigma_b^2 = 0.25$.

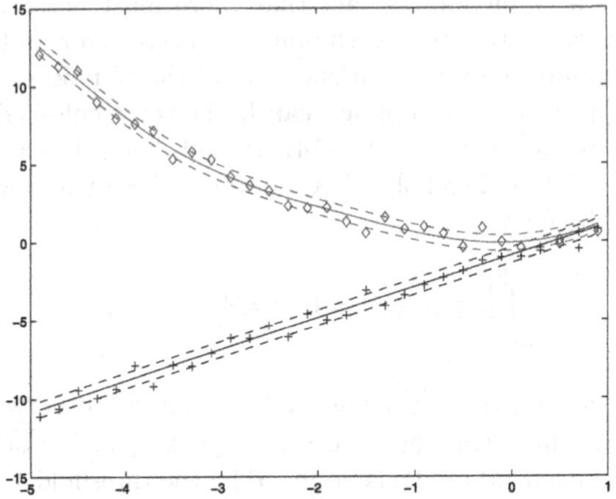

Fig. 1. One-dimensional example of the simultaneous estimation of two functions on noisy data. Points associated to the linear and RBF models are respectively represented by crosses (+) and diamonds ($\diamond$).

4.2 Nonlinearly Piecewise Affine Map Estimation

In this illustrative example, the problem is to estimate a Nonlinearly PieceWise Affine (NPWA) map defined as $y = x + 0.5 + e$, for $x \in]-\infty, -1] \bigcup [1, \infty[$, and $y = -0.5x - 1 + e$, for $x \in]-1, 1[$, where e is a zero-mean Gaussian noise of standard deviation 0.1. This problem could be solved by considering a PWA map with 3 modes linearly separable in the x variable, or, as proposed in this example, by considering only 2 modes with a nonlinear boundary between mode 1 and mode 2. Thus, two models with linear kernels are trained on $N = 60$ data points for $\delta_1 = \delta_2 = 0.1$ and $C = 100$. The resulting models, shown on Fig. 2, are $y = 1.01x + 0.53$ and $y = -0.48x - 1.02$. All the points are associated to the correct model except for one point, $(x_i, y_i) = (-0.9, -0.31)$, close to the mode boundary. The training of a SVM classifier, with a polynomial kernel $k_c = (xx_i + 1)^3$, on the data labeled by $\hat{\lambda}_i$, $i = 1, \dots, N$, yields a nonlinear boundary $\mathcal{S}$ between the modes given by 2 support vectors $x_1 = -3$ and $x_{60} = 2.9$. As the data x_i are in $\mathbb{R}$, this nonlinear separating surface is a set of points defined as $\mathcal{S} = \{x \ : \ h(x) = -0.24(-3x + 1)^3 - 0.22(2.9x + 1)^3 + 10.3 = 0\}$, as shown on the right hand side of Fig. 2. This classifier yields no classification error with respect to the target labels $\hat{\lambda}_i$.

4.3 Simulated Hybrid System Identification

Consider the hybrid system switching between mode 1: $y_t = -0.905y_{t-1} + 0.9u_{t-1} + e_t$, and mode 2: $y_t = -0.4y_{t-1}^2 + 0.5u_{t-1} + e_t$, where e_t is a zero-mean Gaussian noise of standard deviation $\sigma_b = 0.1$. An output trajectory of $N = 100$ points of this system is generated with a random initial condition y_0, a random input sequence u_t uniformly distributed in the interval $[0, 1]$ and

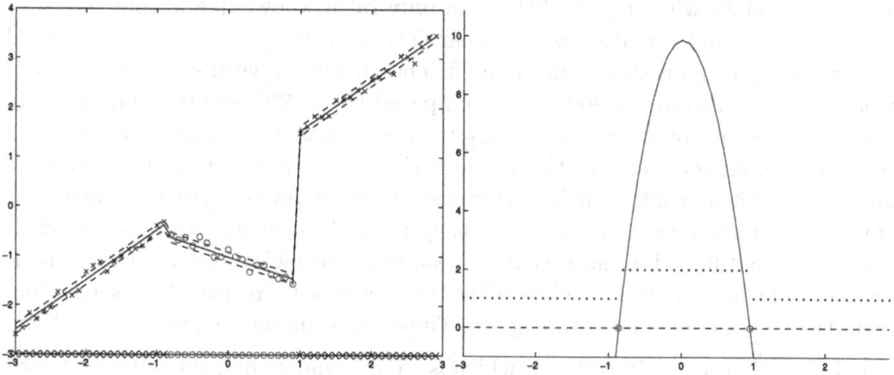

Fig. 2. Nonlinear boundary between 2 modes. *Left*: Hybrid model (—) with its insensitivity tube (- -) approximating the data points represented by '×' for $\hat{\lambda}_i = 1$ and "∘' for $\hat{\lambda}_i = 2$. The estimated mode $\hat{\lambda}_i$ also appears on the x-axis as '×' for mode 1 and '∘' for mode 2 to highlight the partition of the input space $\mathcal{X}$. *Right*: Class labels $\hat{\lambda}_i$ (.) for each data point x_i used to learn the nonlinear boundary $\mathcal{S}$ (∘), defined as the zeros of $h(x)$ (—).

a mode switch from mode 1 to mode 2 at time $t = 41$. The signal-to-noise ratio of this trajectory is 12 dB corresponding to a variance of the noise free trajectory of 0.20 and a noise variance of 0.012. These data are then used to train a SNARX model with $C = 1000$, $\delta_1 = \delta_2 = 0.1$, a linear kernel k_1 and

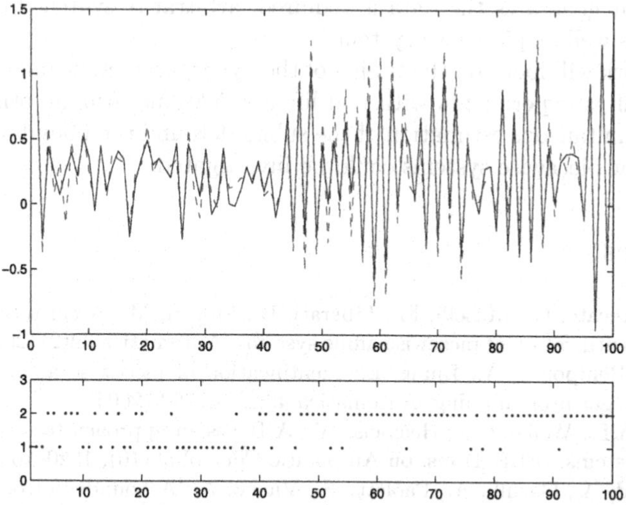

Fig. 3. Simulated hybrid system identification. *Top*: Trajectory of the system (blue plain line) and of the model (red dash line) in simulation mode (only the initial condition and the input is given to the model). *Bottom*: Estimated discrete state $\hat{\lambda}_t$.

a RBF kernel k_2 with $\sigma = 1$. Thus, the only prior knowledge is that one submodel is linear and the other is nonlinear. The trajectory of the resulting model $\hat{y}_t = f_{\hat{\lambda}_t}(\hat{y}_{t-1}, u_{t-1})$ is shown on Figure 3. The estimated parameters of the linear mode 1 are -0.929 and 0.960, to be compared to -0.905 and 0.9. The discrete state is estimated by $\hat{\lambda}_t = \arg\min_j(\xi_{tj})$. As shown at the bottom of Fig. 3, 22 classification errors occur on the whole trajectory. The effect of these errors is limited and their origin can be explained. Most of them occur on ambiguous points for which $f_1(y_{t-1}, u_{t-1}) = f_2(y_{t-1}, u_{t-1}) \pm (\delta_1 + \delta_2)$. Here, a switched system is identified, but note that in case of a piecewise system, these ambiguities could be removed by classifying the points with respect to a separating boundary in the continuous state space. The overall simulation error is RMSEsim $= \sqrt{1/N \sum_{t=1}^{N}(y_t - \hat{y}_t)^2} = 0.154$, which is slightly more than the noise standard deviation $\sigma_b = 0.1$. Only 8 support vectors with nonzero α_{ij} are selected from the 100 training samples to build the kernel expansion f_2.

5 Conclusion

In this paper, a new system identification method has been proposed to deal with nonlinear hybrid systems. In particular, this method is applicable to systems switching between unknown nonlinear dynamics and nonlinearly piecewise systems with arbitrary nonlinear boundaries between the modes. It also bridges the gap between the bounded error approach and the algebraic procedure by making use of the ε-insensitive loss function proposed in the machine learning community for Support Vector Regression. Since no assumption on the discrete sequence that generates the data is required, arbitrarily switched systems can be treated as well as piecewise systems.

Future work will focus on the tuning of the hyperparameters and optimization issues as well as experiments with real life applications. Among other perspectives, the simultaneous estimation of the submodels and the boundaries between the modes for piecewise systems could be investigated.

References

1. Ferrari-Trecate, G., Muselli, M., Liberati, D., Morari, M.: A clustering technique for the identification of piecewise affine systems. Automatica 39(2), 205–217 (2003)
2. Roll, J., Bemporad, A., Ljung, L.: Identification of piecewise affine systems via mixed-integer programming. Automatica 40(1), 37–50 (2004)
3. Juloski, A.L., Weiland, S., Heemels, W.: A Bayesian approach to identification of hybrid systems. IEEE Trans. on Automatic Control 50(10), 1520–1533 (2005)
4. Bemporad, A., Garulli, A., Paoletti, S., Vicino, A.: A bounded-error approach to piecewise affine system identification. IEEE Trans. on Automatic Control 50(10), 1567–1580 (2005)
5. Vidal, R., Soatto, S., Ma, Y., Sastry, S.: An algebraic geometric approach to the identification of a class of linear hybrid systems. In: Proc. of the 42nd IEEE Conf. on Decision and Control, Maui, Hawaï, USA, pp. 167–172 (2003)

6. Ma, Y., Vidal, R.: Identification of deterministic switched ARX systems via identification of algebraic varieties. In: Morari, M., Thiele, L. (eds.) HSCC 2005. LNCS, vol. 3414, pp. 449–465. Springer, Heidelberg (2005)
7. Juloski, A., Heemels, W., Ferrari-Trecate, G., Vidal, R., Paoletti, S., Niessen, J.H.G.: Comparison of four procedures for the identification of hybrid systems. In: Morari, M., Thiele, L. (eds.) HSCC 2005. LNCS, vol. 3414, pp. 354–369. Springer, Heidelberg (2005)
8. Vapnik, V.N.: The nature of statistical learning theory. Springer, New York (1995)
9. Mangasarian, O.: Generalized support vector machines. In: Smola, A., Bartlett, P., Schölkopf, B., Schuurmans, D. (eds.) Advances in Large Margin Classifiers, pp. 135–146. MIT Press, Cambridge (2000)
10. Drezet, P., Harrison, R.: Support vector machines for system identification. In: Proc. of the UKACC Int. Conf. on Control, Swansea, UK, vol. 1, pp. 688–692 (1998)
11. Mattera, D., Haykin, S.: Support vector machines for dynamic reconstruction of a chaotic system. In: Schölkopf, B., Burges, C.J., Smola, A.J. (eds.) Advances in kernel methods: support vector learning, pp. 211–241. MIT Press, Cambridge (1999)
12. Zhang, L., Xi, Y.: Nonlinear system identification based on an improved support vector regression estimator. In: Yin, F.-L., Wang, J., Guo, C. (eds.) ISNN 2004. LNCS, vol. 3173, pp. 586–591. Springer, Heidelberg (2004)
13. Smola, A.J., Schölkopf, B.: A tutorial on support vector regression. Statistics and Computing 14(3), 199–222 (2004)
14. Shawe-Taylor, J., Cristianini, N.: Kernel Methods for Pattern Analysis. Cambridge University Press, Cambridge (2004)
15. Lauer, F., Bloch, G.: Incorporating prior knowledge in support vector machines for classification: a review. Neurocomputing (2007)
16. Smola, A.J., Schölkopf, B., Rätsch, G.: Linear programs for automatic accuracy control in regression. In: Proc. of the 9th Int. Conf. on Artificial Neural Networks, Edinburgh, UK, vol. 2, pp. 575–580 (1999)
17. Mangasarian, O.L., Musicant, D.R.: Large scale kernel regression via linear programming. Machine Learning 46(1-3), 255–269 (2002)
18. Crammer, K., Singer, Y.: On the algorithmic implementation of multiclass kernel-based vector machines. Journal of Machine Learning Research 2, 265–292 (2001)
19. Lauer, F., Bloch, G.: A new hybrid system identification algorithm with automatic tuning. In: Proc. of the 17th IFAC World Congress, Seoul, Korea (2008)

Verification of Supervisory Control Software Using State Proximity and Merging*

Flavio Lerda[1,**], James Kapinski[2], Edmund M. Clarke[1], and Bruce H. Krogh[2]

[1] School of Computer Science
flerda@cs.cmu.edu, emc@cs.cmu.edu
[2] Department of Electrical and Computer Engineering
jpk3@ece.cmu.edu, krogh@ece.cmu.edu
Carnegie Mellon University
Pittsburgh, PA 15213

Abstract. This paper describes an approach for bounded-time verification of safety properties of supervisory control software interacting with a continuous-time plant. A combination of software Model Checking and numerical simulation is used to compute a conservative approximation of the reachable states. The technique verifies system properties in the presence of nondeterministic behavior in the software due to, for instance, interleaving of tasks. A notion of *program equivalence* is used to characterize the behaviors of the controller, and the bisimulation functions of Girard and Pappas are employed to characterize the behaviors of the plant. The approach can conservatively merge traces that reach states that are in proximity to each other. The technique has been implemented for the case of affine plant dynamics, which allows efficient operations on ellipsoidal sets based on convex optimization involving linear matrix inequalities (LMIs). We present an illustrative example for a model of the position controller of an unmanned aerial vehicle (UAV).

1 Introduction

Model-based design of embedded control systems is becoming standard practice. Applying formal methods to embedded control design is important for reducing time to market and for meeting safety and performance requirements, but formal methods are difficult to apply to systems that interact with a continuous dynamic environment. We present a formal verification technique based on the combination of software Model Checking and numerical simulation of a continuous dynamic plant. We use level sets of bisimulation functions [1] to represent sets of plant trajectories and a notion of *program equivalence* for the controller

* This research was sponsored by the Air Force Research Office (AFRO) under contract no. FA9550-06-1-0312, and by the National Science Foundation (NSF) under grant no. CCR-0411152. The views and conclusions contained in this document are those of the author and should not be interpreted as representing the official policies, either expressed or implied, of AFRO, NSF, or the U.S. government.
** The first author was supported by General Motors under grant no. GM9100096UMA.

M. Egerstedt and B. Mishra (Eds.): HSCC 2008, LNCS 4981, pp. 344–357, 2008.

to guarantee safety bounds and provide an efficient and exhaustive search of the system behaviors. The approach narrows the gap between simulation and Model Checking of control systems.

A nonconservative approach that combines Model Checking [2,3] and simulation was first proposed in [4]. That approach provides a means of efficiently searching for counterexamples, but since it is not conservative, it cannot guarantee safety. The approach presented here formalizes and extends that technique by employing conservative approximations of the set of reachable states. Reachable set estimation is a central problem in performing verification of safety properties. Other techniques compute the reachable set of states forward in time and merge the reachable trajectories that are in proximity to each other in the state space [5,6]. In the approach proposed here, the safety requirements are used to construct sets of states that are guaranteed to be safe and these sets are propagated backwards in time.

The work by Julius et al. provides a means for determining maximum safety bounds for simulation traces [7], but the technique does not handle nondeterminism in the discrete transitions and it does not consider the semantics of the control software. The work presented here deals efficiently with the proliferation of reachable paths that occurs due to nondeterministic behaviors in the controller.

2 System Model

We consider *supervisory controllers*, by which we mean feedback controllers that select operating modes for continuous dynamic systems. The supervisor may select plant operating modes directly or manage lower-level feedback control loops. Lower-level control loops are modeled as part of the plant. This is appropriate if the lower-level controller has a significantly higher sampling rate than the supervisor. A sampled-data supervisor observes the state of the plant only at fixed times, called sample instants. We assume that the sample instants are multiples of a fixed sampling period, $t_s > 0$. We model systems where the supervisor is implemented by a set of tasks, and the plant is described by a set of differential equations. We assume that the code of the supervisor executes instantaneously, which is a reasonable assumption if the sampling period of the supervisor is large compared to the actual execution time of the code. Also, we assume that all tasks share the same clock. This assumption is appropriate for analyzing control software implemented as a set of concurrent tasks on one processor or on multiple processors if the clock skew and jitter are small relative to the sampling period of the tasks.

Consider a set of m supervisor variables taking values from a finite set V, and a set of n real-valued plant variables. Let $\mathbf{v} \in V^m$ be the value of the supervisor variables, and $\mathbf{x} \in \mathbb{R}^n$ be the value of the plant variables, called the plant state.

Definition 1 (Supervisor Task). *Given a set of m supervisor variables with domain V^m and a set of plant states $\mathbb{R}^n$, a supervisor task is a tuple $\mathcal{T}_i = \langle Loc_i, l_{i,initial}, l_{i,final}, \delta_i \rangle$ where:*

- *Loc_i is a finite set of control locations;*
- *$l_{i,initial}, l_{i,final} \in Loc_i$ are two specially designated locations, called the initial and final control locations of $\mathcal{T}_i$; and*
- *$\delta_i : \mathbb{R}^n \to 2^{Loc_i \times V^m \times Loc_i \times V^m}$ is the transition relation of $\mathcal{T}_i$. We assume that there are no transitions from the final control location $l_{i,final}$.*

At each sample instant, the task starts executing at the initial control location $l_{i,initial}$ and executes until it reaches the final control location $l_{i,final}$. We assume that every sequence of task transitions is finite and eventually reaches the control location $l_{i,final}$, i.e., the code has no deadlock or livelock. A Model Checker can be used to detect deadlocks and livelocks, but these aspects have been omitted from the presentation for the sake of clarity. An approach that takes into account these aspects is described in [4]. Notice that the transition relation δ_i depends on the current plant state $\mathbf{x}$. Given $l_i, \hat{l}_i \in Loc_i$, $\mathbf{v}, \hat{\mathbf{v}} \in V^m$, and $\mathbf{x} \in \mathbb{R}^n$, there exists a transition from $(l_i, \mathbf{v})$ to $(\hat{l}_i, \hat{\mathbf{v}})$ when the plant state is equal to $\mathbf{x}$ if and only if $(l_i, \mathbf{v}, \hat{l}_i, \hat{\mathbf{v}}) \in \delta_i(\mathbf{x})$.

Definition 2 (Sampled-Data Control System). *A sampled-data control system is a tuple $SDCS = \langle\{\mathcal{T}_1, \ldots, \mathcal{T}_p\}, V, f_{\mathbf{v}}, t_s, Init\rangle$ where:*

- *$\{\mathcal{T}_1, \ldots, \mathcal{T}_p\}$ is a finite set of supervisor tasks;*
- *V is a finite domain for the supervisor variables;*
- *For each $\mathbf{v} \in V^m$, $f_{\mathbf{v}} : \mathbb{R}^n \to \mathbb{R}^n$ is a Lipschitz continuous function that describes the flow of the plant and depends on the value of the supervisor variables;*
- *t_s is the sampling period; and*
- *$Init \subseteq Loc_1 \times \ldots \times Loc_p \times V^m \times \mathbb{R}^n$ is a set of initial states.*

Let Loc denote the set $Loc_1 \times \ldots \times Loc_p$ of the control locations for all of the tasks. A state of an $SDCS$ is a tuple $(q, \mathbf{x})$ where: $q = (L, \mathbf{v})$ is the supervisor state, $L \in Loc$ specifies the control locations of each task, $\mathbf{v} \in V^m$ is the value of the supervisor variables, and $\mathbf{x} \in \mathbb{R}^n$ is the plant state. Given a value $\mathbf{v}$ for the supervisor variables and a plant state $\mathbf{y}$, let $\xi_{\mathbf{v}}^{\mathbf{y}} : \mathbb{R} \to \mathbb{R}^n$ denote a solution to the initial value problem $\dot{\mathbf{x}}(t) = f_{\mathbf{v}}(\mathbf{x}(t)), \mathbf{x}(0) = \mathbf{y}$. Since we assumed that $f_{\mathbf{v}}(\cdot)$ is Lipschitz continuous, there exists a unique $\xi_{\mathbf{v}}^{\mathbf{y}}(\cdot)$ for every $\mathbf{y} \in \mathbb{R}^n$.

Definition 3 (Transitions). *Given two states $s = (q, \mathbf{x})$ and $\hat{s} = (\hat{q}, \hat{\mathbf{x}})$ of an SDCS, there exists a transition from s to $\hat{s}$, denoted by $s \longrightarrow \hat{s}$, if either:*

- *$q = ((l_1, \ldots, l_p), \mathbf{v})$, $\hat{q} = ((\hat{l}_1, \ldots, \hat{l}_p), \hat{\mathbf{v}})$, and there exists a task $\mathcal{T}_j$ such that $\mathbf{x} = \hat{\mathbf{x}}$, $(l_j, \mathbf{v}, \hat{l}_j, \hat{\mathbf{v}}) \in \delta_j(\mathbf{x})$ and, for every task $\mathcal{T}_i$ not equal to $\mathcal{T}_j$, $l_i = \hat{l}_i$. This is called a supervisor transition.*
- *$q = (L_{final}, \mathbf{v})$, $\hat{q} = (L_{initial}, \mathbf{v})$, and $\hat{\mathbf{x}} = \xi_{\mathbf{v}}^{\mathbf{x}}(t_s)$. This is called a plant transition.*

A trace of an $SDCS$ is a finite sequence of states $\sigma = s_0 \ldots s_K$, for some K, such that $s_k \longrightarrow s_{k+1}$ for all $0 \le k < K$. Figure 1 provides an illustration of traces of an SDCS. In the figure, the plant states have two dimensions, corresponding

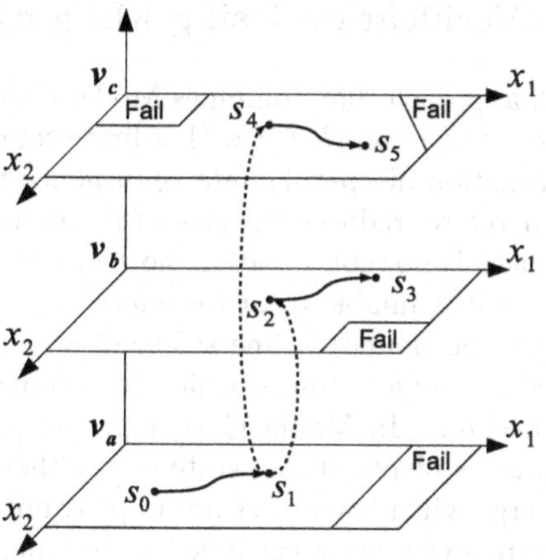

Fig. 1. An illustration of traces of an SDCS. Solid arrows connecting points represent plant transitions. Dotted lines connecting points represent supervisor transitions.

to the axes labeled x_1 and x_2. The vertical axis represents the value of the supervisor variables: each plane corresponds to a different value of the supervisor variables, namely $\mathbf{v}_a$, $\mathbf{v}_b$, and $\mathbf{v}_c$. The initial state is $s_0 = (L_{final}, \mathbf{v}_a, \mathbf{x}_{init})$, and the first transition is a plant transition, $s_0 \longrightarrow s_1$, where $s_1 = (L_{initial}, \mathbf{v}_a, \hat{\mathbf{x}})$ for some $\hat{\mathbf{x}}$. From s_1, nondeterminism in the supervisor leads to two separate states, $s_2 = (L_{final}, \mathbf{v}_b, \hat{\mathbf{x}})$ and $s_4 = (L_{final}, \mathbf{v}_c, \hat{\mathbf{x}})$. From each of these states a plant transition is taken, $s_2 \longrightarrow s_3$, where $s_3 = (L_{initial}, \mathbf{v}_b, \mathbf{y})$ for some $\mathbf{y}$, and $s_4 \longrightarrow s_5$, where $s_5 = (L_{initial}, \mathbf{v}_c, \mathbf{z})$ for some $\mathbf{z}$.

Definition 4 (Duration). *The duration of a trace σ is the amount of time elapsed between its first state and its last state, and it is defined inductively as follows:*

- *If $\sigma = s_0$, $duration(\sigma) = 0$.*
- *If $\sigma = s_0 \dots s_K$ and $s_{K-1} \longrightarrow s_K$ is a supervisor transition then $duration(\sigma) = duration(s_0, \dots s_{K-1})$, since we assume that supervisor transitions execute instantaneously.*
- *If $\sigma = s_0 \dots s_K$ and $s_{K-1} \longrightarrow s_K$ is a plant transition then $duration(\sigma) = duration(s_0, \dots s_{K-1}) + t_s$.*

A state s of an *SDCS* is reachable within a time bound T if and only if there exists a trace $\sigma = s_0 \dots s_K$, for some K, such that $s_0 \in Init$, $s_K = s$ and $duration(\sigma) \leq T$. Given a time bound T and a set of states $Fail \subset Loc \times V^m \times \mathbb{R}^n$, a state s is safe for time bound T if and only if for every trace $\sigma = s_0 \dots s_K$, of arbitrary length K, such that $s_0 = s$ and $duration(\sigma) \leq T$, we have that $s_K \notin Fail$. For example, state s_0 in Figure 1 is safe for time bound $2t_s$.

Definition 5 (Bounded-Time Safety). *Given an SDCS, a set $Fail \subset Loc \times V^m \times \mathbb{R}^n$ of fail states, and a time bound T, the SDCS is safe for time bound T if and only if all initial states are safe for time bound T.*

3 Conservative Verification Using Merging

In [4], we presented an approach that combines Model Checking and simulation to check bounded-time safety of an *SDCS* with a finite set of initial states. That work also introduces a notion of *approximate equivalence* that is used to prune the state space and, therefore, reduces the size of the state space that needs to be explored. The approach is not conservative, however; it can be used to search for counterexamples, but it is unable to prove safety.

Our approach for proving bounded-time safety of an *SDCS* is able to prune parts of the state space by *merging traces*, which corresponds to merging a state with a previously visited one. In Model Checking, merging can be done only when a state on one trace is identical to a state on another trace. Our approach is able to perform a merge when two states are in proximity to each other if the pruned parts of the state space are guaranteed to be safe. In the following, we show how to determine safe sets of plant states around the points in a trace. These sets correspond to a set of traces that are in proximity of the visited trace and are guaranteed to be safe. When a state that is within a safe set is reached, the trace can be merged conservatively and the successors of such a state do not need to be explored further.

In general, given a dynamical system and two initial states that are in proximity to each other, the trajectories starting at those initial states may diverge. This paper uses bisimulation functions to bound the distance between future evolutions. Bisimulation functions were introduced by Girard and Pappas as a way to determine the relation between states of a dynamical system [1]. In this work, we use bisimulation functions to approximate conservatively the plant transitions.

Definition 6 (Bisimulation Function). [1] *Given an autonomous dynamical system Σ described by $\dot{\mathbf{x}}(t) = f_{\mathbf{v}}(\mathbf{x}(t))$ where $\mathbf{x} : \mathbb{R} \to \mathbb{R}^n$ and $f : \mathbb{R}^n \to \mathbb{R}^n$, a differentiable function $\varphi_{\mathbf{v}} : \mathbb{R}^n \times \mathbb{R}^n \to \mathbb{R}$ is a bisimulation function of Σ if and only if*

- $\varphi_{\mathbf{v}}(\mathbf{y}, \mathbf{z}) \geq 0$, *for all* $\mathbf{y}, \mathbf{z} \in \mathbb{R}^n$*; and*
- $\nabla_{\mathbf{y}}\varphi_{\mathbf{v}}(\mathbf{y}, \mathbf{z}) \cdot f_{\mathbf{v}}(\mathbf{y}) + \nabla_{\mathbf{z}}\varphi_{\mathbf{v}}(\mathbf{y}, \mathbf{z}) \cdot f_{\mathbf{v}}(\mathbf{z}) \leq 0$, *for all* $\mathbf{y}, \mathbf{z} \in \mathbb{R}^n$.

Definition 7 (Sublevel Sets). *Given $\mathbf{x} \in \mathbb{R}^n$, a bisimulation function φ of $\dot{\mathbf{x}}(t) = f(\mathbf{x}(t))$, and a real value $r \geq 0$, the sublevel set of the bisimulation function φ centered at $\mathbf{x}$ and of size r, denoted by $\mathcal{N}_\varphi(\mathbf{x}, r)$, is defined as*

$$\mathcal{N}_\varphi(\mathbf{x}, r) = \{\mathbf{z} \in \mathbb{R}^n \mid \varphi(\mathbf{x}, \mathbf{z}) \leq r\}.$$

In the following, we assume that the bisimulation functions are symmetric, i.e., $\varphi(\mathbf{y}, \mathbf{z}) = \varphi(\mathbf{z}, \mathbf{y})$ for every $\mathbf{y}, \mathbf{z} \in \mathbb{R}^n$. If a bisimulation function $\varphi(\cdot, \cdot)$ is a metric on $\mathbb{R}^n$, then it is called a *contraction metric* [8]. We assume that for every value of the supervisor variables $\mathbf{v}$, a bisimulation function $\varphi_{\mathbf{v}}$ of the autonomous dynamical system $\dot{\mathbf{x}}(t) = f_{\mathbf{v}}(\mathbf{x}(t))$ is given. We can now state the following theorem about bisimulation functions and plant transitions, based on a theorem from Julius et al. [7].

Theorem 1 (Plant Approximation). *Given two states $s = ((L_{final}, \mathbf{v}), \mathbf{y})$ and $\hat{s} = ((L_{initial}, \mathbf{v}), \hat{\mathbf{y}})$ such that $s \longrightarrow \hat{s}$ is a plant transition, and a bisimulation function $\varphi_{\mathbf{v}}$ for the differential equation $\dot{\mathbf{x}}(t) = f_{\mathbf{v}}(\mathbf{x}(t))$, for every $r \geq 0$ and for every $\mathbf{z} \in \mathcal{N}_{\varphi_{\mathbf{v}}}(\mathbf{y}, r)$, if $((L_{final}, \mathbf{v}), \mathbf{z}) \longrightarrow ((L_{initial}, \mathbf{v}), \hat{\mathbf{z}})$ is a plant transition, then $\hat{\mathbf{z}} \in \mathcal{N}_{\varphi_{\mathbf{v}}}(\hat{\mathbf{y}}, r)$.*

Proof. The theorem is a direct consequence of Corollary 1 of [7].

Given a program state q and a time bound T, a set $X \subseteq \mathbb{R}^n$ of plant states is safe for T at q if and only if, for every $\mathbf{x} \in X$, $s = (q, \mathbf{x})$ is safe for time bound T. Given a program state q, the set of fail plant states at q is defined as $Fail_q = \{\mathbf{x} \in \mathbb{R}^n \mid (q, \mathbf{x}) \in Fail\}$.

Theorem 2 (Plant Transition Approximation). *Given two states $(q, \mathbf{y})$ and $(\hat{q}, \hat{\mathbf{y}})$ such that $q = (L_{final}, \mathbf{v})$, $\hat{q} = (L_{initial}, \mathbf{v})$, and $(q, \mathbf{y}) \longrightarrow (\hat{q}, \hat{\mathbf{y}})$ is a plant transition, if $\hat{\mathcal{X}} \subseteq \mathbb{R}^n$ is safe for T at $\hat{q}$, then for all $r \geq 0$, if $\mathcal{N}_{\varphi_{\mathbf{v}}}(\hat{\mathbf{y}}, r) \subseteq \hat{\mathcal{X}}$ and $\mathcal{N}_{\varphi_{\mathbf{v}}}(\mathbf{y}, r) \subseteq \overline{Fail_q}$ then $\mathcal{N}_{\varphi_{\mathbf{v}}}(\mathbf{y}, r)$ is safe for $(T + t_s)$ at q.*

Proof. We prove this theorem by contradiction. Assume that $\mathcal{N}_{\varphi_{\mathbf{v}}}(\mathbf{y}, r)$ is not safe for $(T + t_s)$ at q. This means that there exists a plant state $\mathbf{z} \in \mathcal{N}_{\varphi_{\mathbf{v}}}(\mathbf{y}, r)$ and a trace $\sigma = s_0 s_1 \ldots s_K$, for some K, such that $s_0 = (q, \mathbf{z})$, $s_K \in Fail$, and $duration(\sigma) \leq T + t_s$. Since $\mathbf{z} \in \mathcal{N}_{\varphi_{\mathbf{v}}}(\mathbf{y}, r) \subseteq \overline{Fail_q}$, we have that $s_0 \notin Fail$ and therefore the trace must contain at least two states ($K \geq 1$). Let $\hat{\sigma}$ denote $s_1 \ldots s_K$. By Definition 4 we have that $duration(\hat{\sigma}) = duration(\sigma) - t_s \leq T$. By Definition 3, $s_1 = (\hat{q}, \hat{\mathbf{z}})$ for some $\hat{\mathbf{z}} \in \mathbb{R}^n$. By Theorem 1 we can deduce that $\hat{\mathbf{z}} \in \mathcal{N}_{\varphi_{\mathbf{v}}}(\hat{\mathbf{y}}, r)$. But, by hypothesis, $\mathcal{N}_{\varphi_{\mathbf{v}}}(\hat{\mathbf{y}}, r) \subseteq \hat{\mathcal{X}}$ and therefore $\hat{\mathbf{z}} \in \hat{\mathcal{X}}$. Since $\hat{\mathcal{X}}$ is safe for T at $\hat{q}$, there does not exists any trace starting at $(\hat{q}, \hat{\mathbf{z}})$ that reaches a state in *Fail* and whose duration is less than or equal to T. However, $\hat{\sigma}$ is such a trace, which is a contradiction. Therefore $\mathcal{N}_{\varphi_{\mathbf{v}}}(\mathbf{y}, r)$ must be safe for $(T + t_s)$ at q. □

Figure 2-(a) illustrates the notion of safe plant states and plant transition approximations. On each plane, the areas marked by *Fail* correspond to the parts of the plant state space that are unsafe for the corresponding value of the supervisor variables. Plant transitions correspond to continuous lines within a given plane; supervisor transitions correspond to dotted lines from one plane to another. The two sets N_3 and N_5 are safe for time bound zero as they do not intersect the *Fail* plant states in the corresponding planes. By Theorem 2, the sets N_2 and N_4 are safe for time bound t_s, the sampling period, as they are guaranteed to avoid the *Fail* region if the system evolves for one sampling period.

Theorem 2 allows us to determine a set of plant states that are safe for $(T + t_s)$ at a given supervisor state q given a set of plant states that are safe for T at the supervisor state $\hat{q}$ obtained by performing a plant transition. Below we show how to compute a set of plant states that is safe for T at a supervisor state q for the case of discrete transitions. While continuous transitions are always deterministic, supervisor transitions may lead from one state to a number of successor states. In order to deal with this, we define a notion of equivalence between continuous states with respect to a supervisor state.

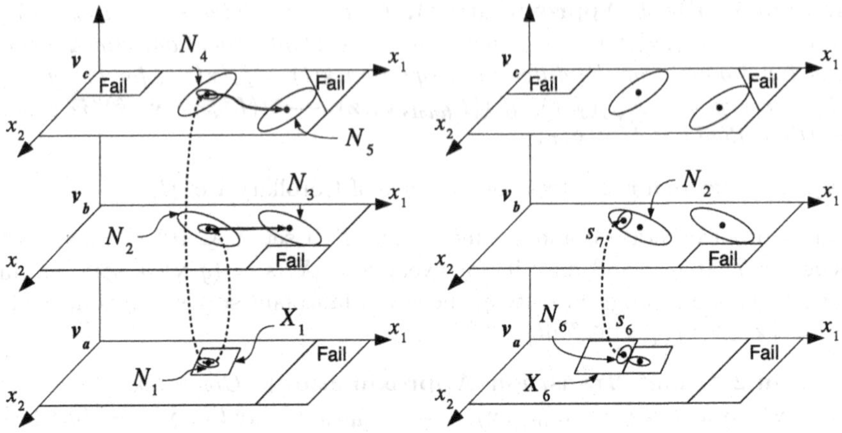

(a) (b)

Fig. 2. (a) An illustration of sets safe for a time bound T. N_3 and N_5 are safe for time bound zero. N_1, N_2, and N_4 are safe for t_s; (b) An illustration of merging. N_6 is safe for t_s since all of its states make transitions into the set N_2, which is safe for t_s.

Definition 8 (Program Equivalence). *Given a supervisor state q and a pair of plant states $\mathbf{y}, \mathbf{z} \in \mathbb{R}^n$, we say that $\mathbf{y}$ is program equivalent to $\mathbf{z}$ at q, denoted by $\mathbf{y} \approx_q \mathbf{z}$, if the set of successors of q at plant state $\mathbf{y}$ is the same as the set of successors of q at plant state $\mathbf{z}$, i.e., $\hat{Q}_q(\mathbf{y}) = \hat{Q}_q(\mathbf{z})$ where, given a supervisor state q and a plant state $\mathbf{x}$, $\hat{Q}_q(\mathbf{x}) = \{\hat{q} \,|\, (q, \mathbf{x}) \longrightarrow (\hat{q}, \mathbf{x})\}$.*

The relation $\approx_q$ defined above is an equivalence relation. Therefore, for every supervisor state q, $\approx_q$ defines a set of equivalence classes. Given a supervisor state q and a plant state $\mathbf{y}$, let $[\mathbf{y}]_{\approx_q}$ denote the equivalence class of $\mathbf{y}$ defined by $\approx_q$, that is $[\mathbf{y}]_{\approx_q} = \{\mathbf{z} \in \mathbb{R}^n \,|\, \mathbf{y} \approx_q \mathbf{z}\}$.

Theorem 3 (Supervisor Transition Approximation). *Given a state $(q, \mathbf{y})$ with $q = (L, \mathbf{v})$ and $L \neq L_{final}$, for each $\hat{q} \in \hat{Q}_q(\mathbf{y})$, let $\hat{\mathcal{X}}_{\hat{q}} \subseteq \mathbb{R}^n$ be a set of plant states safe for some time bound $T_{\hat{q}}$ at $\hat{q}$. Let $T = \min_{\hat{q} \in \hat{Q}_q(\mathbf{y})} T_{\hat{q}}$ denote the minimum of the time bounds for each $\hat{q}$. The set*

$$\mathcal{X} = [\mathbf{y}]_{\approx_q} \cap \overline{Fail_q} \cap \bigcap_{\hat{q} \in \hat{Q}_q(\mathbf{y})} \hat{\mathcal{X}}_{\hat{q}}$$

is safe for time bound T at q.

Proof. We prove this theorem by contradiction. Assume $\mathcal{X}$ is not safe for T at q. This means that there exists a plant state $\mathbf{z} \in \mathcal{X}$ and a trace $\sigma = s_0 s_1 \ldots s_K$, for some K, such that $s_0 = (q, \mathbf{z})$, $s_K \in Fail$, and $duration(\sigma) \leq T$. Since $\mathbf{z} \in \mathcal{X} \subseteq \overline{Fail_q}$, we know that $s_0 \notin Fail$ and therefore the trace must contain at least two states ($K \geq 1$). The first transition of σ must be a discrete transition because $L \neq L_{final}$ by hypothesis. Let $s_1 = (\hat{q}, \mathbf{z})$ and $\hat{\sigma} = s_1 \ldots s_K$. Since

$\mathbf{z} \in \mathcal{X} \subseteq [\mathbf{y}]_{\approx_q}$, by hypothesis, we know that there exists a discrete transition $(q, \mathbf{y}) \longrightarrow (\hat{q}, \mathbf{y})$. Therefore, by hypothesis, $\hat{q} \in \hat{Q}_q(\mathbf{y})$. Since we assumed that $\mathbf{z} \in \mathcal{X}$ and, by hypothesis, $\mathcal{X} \subseteq \hat{\mathcal{X}}_{\hat{q}}$, we have that $\mathbf{z} \in \hat{\mathcal{X}}_{\hat{q}}$. But, by hypothesis, $\hat{\mathcal{X}}_{\hat{q}}$ is safe for time bound $T_{\hat{q}}$ at $\hat{q}$. This means that there does not exist any trace starting at $(\hat{q}, \mathbf{z})$ that reaches a state in *Fail* and whose duration is less than or equal to $T_{\hat{q}}$. But $\hat{\sigma}$ is such a trace because $\mathit{duration}(\hat{\sigma}) \leq T_{\hat{q}}$. This is true since $\mathit{duration}(\hat{\sigma}) = \mathit{duration}(\sigma) \leq T_{\hat{q}}$, by assumption, and $T \leq T_{\hat{q}}$. This is a contradiction and therefore $\mathcal{X}$ must be safe for T at q. □

Figure 2-(a) shows an application of the theorem above. In this case, the state $s_1 = (q, \mathbf{y})$ has two successors, states s_2 and s_4. We assume that the sets N_2 and N_4 are safe for time bound t_s. The set X_1 in the figure denotes the equivalence class $[\mathbf{y}]_{\approx_q}$ corresponding to s_1. Then N_1 is safe for t_s, because N_1 does not intersect the fail states of q, every state of N_1 is program equivalent to $\mathbf{y}$, and N_1 is contained within both N_2 and N_4.

The conservative merging occurs when a trace reaches a state within a safe set of plant states. State s_7 in Figure 2-(b) is within N_2, which we assume to be safe for time bound t_s. The state s_6 has a single successor, namely s_7. The set X_6 in the figure denotes the equivalence class corresponding to state s_6. The set N_6 does not intersect the fail region, N_6 is a subset of N_2, and N_6 is a subset of the equivalence class X_6. Therefore, by Theorem 3, we can deduce that N_6 is safe for t_s: any trace starting from a plant state within N_6 leads to a state within N_2.

3.1 Bounded-Time Safety Verification Algorithm

This section gives an algorithm to check bounded-time safety of an *SDCS*. This algorithm is based on the explicit-state Model Checking algorithm [3], but uses level sets of a bisimulation function and the notion of program equivalence to determine sets of plant states that are safe. The standard explicit-state Model Checking algorithm is a depth first search of the set of reachable states for each of the initial states. By using bisimulation functions and the notion of program equivalence, the algorithm presented here is able to determine, without looking at every trace, if a certain state encountered during the analysis is guaranteed not to lead to a fail state.

The procedures `main` and `explore` in Figure 3 implement the depth first search. For each initial state $(q, \mathbf{x})$, the procedure `explore` is invoked to perform a depth first search up to the time bound T (lines 5-10). If the initial state is safe, a set of states that are safe for T at q is returned: this set is added to the set of initial states that are guaranteed to be safe ($\text{Safe}_{\mathit{Init}}$ on line 8). Otherwise, if an error was detected, it is returned immediately (line 10). After analyzing each initial state, the set of safe initial states is returned on line 11. The procedure `explore` takes as arguments a state $(q, \mathbf{x})$, a time bound τ, and a trace σ which leads to $(q, \mathbf{x})$. The time bound τ represents the amount of time remaining from the given state; that is, $\tau = T - \mathit{duration}(\sigma)$. It performs the actual depth first

1: **global** SDCS, *Fail*, T;
2: **global** safe_sets ← ∅; *Sets of safe plant states, initially empty.*

3: **main:** *Check bounded-time safety of SDCS*
4:     Safe*Init* ← ∅ *Set of safe initial states.*
5:     **foreach** ((q, **x**) ∈ Init) *Depth-first search for each initial state.*
6:         result ← explore(q, **x**, T, [(q, **x**)]);
7:         **if**(result = (*SAFE*, 𝒳))
8:             Safe*Init* ← Safe*Init* ∪ {(q, **x**) | **x** ∈ 𝒳} *Add to safe initial states.*
9:         **else**
10:            **return** result; *An error was detected.*
11:    **return** (*SAFE*, Safe*Init*); *Return the set of safe initial states.*

12: **function** explore(q, **x**, τ, σ) *Depth-first search from (q, **x**) up to time τ.*
13:     **if** ((q, **x**) ∈ *Fail*) **return** (*UNSAFE*, σ); *Check for fail states.*
14:     **if** (∃ (q̂, 𝒳̂, τ̂) ∈ safe_sets: q = q̂ ∧ **x** ∈ 𝒳̂ ∧ τ ≤ τ̂)
15:         **return** (*SAFE*, 𝒳̂); *Merge traces if within a safe set.*
16:     **if** (q.L = L*final*)
17:         result = plant_transition(q, **x**, τ, σ); *Plant transition*
18:     **else**
19:         result = supervisor_transitions(q, **x**, τ, σ); *Supervisor transitions*
20:     **if** (result = (*SAFE*, 𝒳))
21:         safe_sets ← safe_sets ∪ {(q, 𝒳, τ)}; *Plant states safe for τ at q.*
22:     **return** result;

23: **function** plant_transition(q, **x**, τ, σ)
24:     **if** (τ < t_s) *Stop if time bound is less than sampling time*
25:         **return** (*SAFE*, {**x** | (q, **x**) ∉ *Fail*});
26:     **x̂** ← sim(**x**, f_{q.v}); *Numerical simulation*
27:     q̂ ← (L_{initial}, q.**v**);
28:     result = explore(q̂, **x̂**, τ - t_s, σ · (q̂, **x̂**));
29:     **if** (result = (*SAFE*, 𝒳̂))
30:         r_{max} ← max {r | 𝒩_{φ_{q.v}}(**x̂**, r) ⊆ 𝒳̂}; *Safe set of plant states*
31:         **return** (*SAFE*, 𝒩_{φ_{q.v}}(**x**, r_{max}));
32:     **else**
33:         **return** result;

34: **function** supervisor_transitions(q, **x**, τ, σ)
35:     Q̂ ← {q̂ | ∃i: (q, q̂) ∈ δ_i(**x**)}; *Explore each successor*
36:     𝒳 ← [**x**]_{≈_q} ∩ $\overline{Fail}$;
37:     **foreach** (q̂ ∈ Q̂)
38:         result ← explore(q̂, **x**, τ, σ · (q̂, **x**));
39:         **if** (result = (*SAFE*, 𝒳̂))
40:             𝒳 = 𝒳 ∩ 𝒳̂;
41:         **else**
42:             **return** result;
43:     **return** (*SAFE*, 𝒳);

Fig. 3. The conservative merging verification algorithm

search starting from the given state up to the time bound. The trace σ is used to generate a counterexample if a fail state is reached (line 13). The current state is compared with the sets of safe states that have been determined so far (lines 14-15). If there exists a set of plant states $\hat{\mathcal{X}}$ that is safe for the current supervisor state q and a longer time bound $\hat{\tau} \geq \tau$, the search of this branch can terminate and the set of plant states $\hat{\mathcal{X}}$ is returned to the caller as safe.

Two ways of computing the successor states are possible. If the current control state is equal to L_{final}, then a plant transition is performed by calling the function `plant_transition` (line 17). Otherwise, the transitions of the supervisor are explored by calling the function `supervisor_transitions` (line 19). In either case, if the result is that the current state is safe, the set $\mathcal{X}$ of plant states that are computed to be safe for state q and time bound τ is added to the list of safe sets (line 21).

The result of a plant transition is computed by the function `plant_transition` in Figure 3. Line 25 is executed if the time bound has been reached, i.e., there is not enough time left to complete an additional plant transition. The set of plant states that are safe for time bound τ at q is simply the set of plant states that are not fail states at supervisor state q, since $\tau < t_s$ (line 24). Otherwise, the successor state $(\hat{q}, \hat{\mathbf{x}})$ of the current state $(q, \mathbf{x})$ is computed using numerical simulation (line 26) and by setting the current control location to $L_{initial}$ (line 27). The search continues from the new state by calling `explore`. The recursive call uses a smaller time bound and adds one state to the trace being constructed (line 28). If the result at line 28 is that state $(\hat{q}, \hat{\mathbf{x}})$ is safe, the set of states $\hat{\mathcal{X}}$ that are safe for time bound $\tau - t_s$ at $\hat{q}$ is used to determine the maximum size of a sublevel set of the bisimulation function centered around $\mathbf{x}$ that is safe for time bound τ at q by solving the optimization problem:

$$r_{max} = \max\left\{r \in \mathbb{R} \,|\, \mathcal{N}_{\varphi_{\mathbf{v}}}(\hat{\mathbf{x}}, r) \subseteq \hat{\mathcal{X}}\right\},$$

where $\mathbf{v}$ is the current value of the supervisor variables and $\varphi_{\mathbf{v}}$ is the bisimulation function for $\dot{\mathbf{x}} = f_{\mathbf{v}}(\mathbf{x})$ (line 30). The set $\mathcal{N}_{\varphi_{\mathbf{v}}}(\mathbf{x}, r_{max})$ is returned to the caller since it is safe for time bound τ at q.

The function `supervisor_transitions` in Figure 3 computes and explores the successors of a state $(q, \mathbf{x})$ that originate from transitions of the supervisor. The set of successors $\hat{Q}$ is generated by using the transition relations $\delta_1, \ldots, \delta_p$ of the tasks that make up the supervisor (line 35). Each successor $\hat{q}$ is visited by calling the function `explore` over $(\hat{q}, \mathbf{x})$ with the same time bound τ (since supervisor transitions are instantaneous) and with a trace that adds the new state $(\hat{q}, \mathbf{x})$ to σ (line 38). If the state $(\hat{q}, \mathbf{x})$ is safe, a set of safe plant states $\hat{\mathcal{X}}$ is returned by the recursive call. The set of safe plant states that is returned to the caller by this call (line 43), computed by lines 36 and 40, is

$$X = [\mathbf{x}]_{\approx_q} \cap \overline{Fail_q} \cap \bigcap_{\hat{q} \in \hat{Q}} \hat{\mathcal{X}}_{\hat{q}}.$$

This concludes the description of the algorithm. The following theorems establish correctness and termination of the procedure. The proofs are omitted for the sake of brevity.

Theorem 4 (Correctness). *Consider an SDCS, a set of fail states Fail, and a time bound T. If the algorithm of Figure 3 returns (SAFE,* Safe_{Init}*) then the SDCS is safe for time bound T, Init* $\subseteq \text{Safe}_{Init}$*, and all states in* Safe_{Init} *are safe for time bound T. If the algorithm returns (UNSAFE, σ) then SDCS is not safe for time bound T and σ is a trace of duration less than T that ends at a state in Fail.*

Theorem 5 (Termination). *Given an SDCS* $= \langle\{\mathcal{T}_1,\ldots,\mathcal{T}_p\}, V, f_{\mathbf{v}}, t_s, Init\rangle$ *such that Init is finite, the algorithm of Figure 3 always terminates.*

3.2 Ellipsoidal Sets for Affine Dynamics

In this subsection, we discuss properties related to our technique for the case of stable affine plant dynamics and sets of fail states defined by linear inequalities

Bisimulation Functions. For the special case of stable, affine plant dynamics, $f_{\mathbf{v}}(\mathbf{x}) = \mathbf{A_v x} + \mathbf{B_v}$, a bisimulation function is given by

$$\varphi_{\mathbf{v}}(\mathbf{y},\mathbf{z}) = (\mathbf{z}-\mathbf{y})^T\mathbf{P_v}(\mathbf{z}-\mathbf{y}),$$

where $\mathbf{P_v}$ satisfies the Lyapunov inequality $\mathbf{A_v}^T\mathbf{P_v}+\mathbf{P_v}\mathbf{A_v} \leq \mathbf{0}$. The level sets are given by $\mathcal{N}_{\varphi_{\mathbf{v}}}(\mathbf{x},r) = \{\mathbf{z}\in\mathbb{R}^n \mid (\mathbf{z}-\mathbf{x})^T\mathbf{P_v}(\mathbf{z}-\mathbf{x}) \leq r\}$, which are ellipsoidal.

Maximum Ellipsoid Within an Ellipsoid. In the case of affine dynamics, one operation required in line 30 of the procedure given in Figure 3 is the computation of the maximum sized ellipsoid contained in a second ellipsoid. Given a set $\mathcal{N}_{\varphi_{\mathbf{v}}}(\mathbf{z},r_{\mathbf{z}})$ and a point $\mathbf{y}\in\mathbb{R}^n$, we want to find the maximum $r_{\mathbf{y}}$ such that $\mathcal{N}_{\varphi_{\mathbf{v}}}(\mathbf{y},r_{\mathbf{y}}) \subseteq \mathcal{N}_{\varphi_{\mathbf{v}}}(\mathbf{z},r_{\mathbf{z}})$. It is shown in [9] that this is equivalent to the following:

$$\max_{\lambda,c}\ c$$
$$\text{s.t.}\ \begin{bmatrix} -r_{\mathbf{z}}\mathbf{Q_v} & (\mathbf{z}-\mathbf{y}) & c\sqrt{\mathbf{Q_v}} \\ (\mathbf{z}-\mathbf{y})^T & \lambda-1 & 0 \\ c\sqrt{\mathbf{Q_v}} & 0 & -\lambda\mathbf{I} \end{bmatrix} \leq \mathbf{0}, \lambda\geq 0, c\geq 0,$$

where $c=\sqrt{r_{\mathbf{y}}}$, $\mathbf{Q_v}=\mathbf{P_v}^{-1}$, $\mathbf{I}$ is the identity matrix, and $\sqrt{\mathbf{Q_v}}$ is the matrix that satisfies $\mathbf{Q_v}=\sqrt{\mathbf{Q_v}}\sqrt{\mathbf{Q_v}}$, which exists since $\mathbf{Q_v}$ is positive semidefinite. This is a convex problem with LMI constraints. Numerical tools exists for solving such problems in polynomial time.

Maximum Ellipsoid Within a Set of Linear Constraints. Another operation required in line 30 of the procedure given in Figure 3 for the case of affine dynamics is the computation of an ellipsoid of maximum size that satisfies a conjunction of linear constraints. We want to maximize r subject to constraints of the form $\bigwedge_{i=1}^{i_{max}} \mathbf{c}_i^T \mathbf{y} \le b_i$ for all $\mathbf{y} \in \mathcal{N}_{\varphi_{\mathbf{v}}}(\mathbf{x}, r) = \{\mathbf{z} \in \mathbb{R}^n \mid (\mathbf{z}-\mathbf{x})^T \mathbf{P_v} (\mathbf{z}-\mathbf{x}) \le r\}$, where $b_i \in \mathbb{R}$, $\mathbf{c}_i \in \mathbb{R}^n$ for each i. Let $\mathbf{Q_v} = \mathbf{P_v}^{-1}$. The maximum r that satisfies the linear constraints is then given by [10]

$$r^* = \min_{i \in \{1,\ldots,i_{max}\}} \frac{(b_i - \mathbf{c}_i^T \mathbf{x})^2}{\mathbf{c}_i^T \mathbf{Q_v} \mathbf{c}_i}.$$

4 Experimental Results

The technique presented in the previous section was implemented using an existing explicit-state source-code Model Checker. The tool we chose is Java PathFinder [11]. The main purpose of the tool is to verify Java programs, but it also handles the subset of C that is common to the two languages. This prototype implementation handles systems where the plant dynamics are affine. We use the LMI tool CVX with the semidefinite program solver SDPT3 [12,13] to solve the optimization problems that arise during the verification.

Java PathFinder was extended as follows. The state of a system was enhanced to include the plant state $\mathbf{x}$, represented by a set of floating-point variables. Our extension stores sets of plant states that are safe with respect to a given supervisor state and time bound. Safe sets are represented as ellipsoidal sets, and program equivalence classes and system requirements are represented as sets of linear constraints. Ellipsoidal sets are represented by their size parameter r and their center, while the shape and orientation are determined by the bisimulation function given for each set of plant dynamics. The set of constraints used to express the set of fail states as well as the program equivalence classes are given as annotations. Moreover, since the plant dynamics are affine, it is possible to convert the continuous-time dynamics into discrete-time difference equations over the fixed sampling period t_s.

We applied our technique to an example based on the Stanford Testbed of Autonomous Rotorcraft for Multi-Agent Control (STARMAC), a quadrotor unmanned aerial vehicle (UAV) under development at Stanford University [14]. The vehicle is a square frame with four rotors mounted on its corners and a computer controller and power supply at its center. The controller sends thrust commands to the four rotors. The supervisor makes its decisions based on measurements of the state of the vehicle. We consider a model of the STARMAC system with six plant state variables: the horizontal position and velocity (x and $\dot{x}$), the vertical position and velocity (z and $\dot{z}$), and the rotation about the y-axis and the corresponding rotational velocity (θ and $\dot{\theta}$). The y position and rotation around the x-axis and z-axis are not included in this model. Motors 1 and 3 provide lift and torque around the y-axis, while motors 2 and 4 only provide lift. The forces applied by motors 2 and 4 lie on the y-axis. Equivalent force is applied by motors 2 and 4 at all times.

The equations of motion are nonlinear. We linearized the equations and designed a linear quadratic regulator (LQR) to drive the system to a given set point.

	Model-Checking-Guided Simulation without Merging	Model Checking with Safe Sets and Merging
Visited states	43,134	25,493
Running time	17 sec	107 sec
Memory usage	90.2MB	77.0MB

Fig. 4. Visited states, running time, and memory usage for the time bound $T = 90\,\text{sec}$ with and without merging of safe states. The number of state merges was 282.

The LQR controller is modeled as part of the plant. The system we obtained is of the form $\dot{\mathbf{x}} = \mathbf{A}\mathbf{x} + \mathbf{B}\mathbf{x}^*$, where $\mathbf{x}^*$ is the set point we want to reach and

$$\mathbf{A} = -\mathbf{B} = \begin{bmatrix} -0.6 & 0.0 & 0.0 & 0.0 & 0.0 & 9.8 \\ 1.0 & 0.0 & 0.0 & 0.0 & 0.0 & 0.0 \\ 0.0 & 0.0 & -1.1 & -0.4 & 0.0 & 0.0 \\ 0.0 & 0.0 & 1.0 & 0.0 & 0.0 & 0.0 \\ -35.4 & -22.1 & 0.0 & 0.0 & -70.2 & -2221.7 \\ 0.0 & 0.0 & 0.0 & 0.0 & 1.0 & 0.0 \end{bmatrix}.$$

The supervisory controller for this system is implemented by two concurrent tasks: one task determines the target position based on a given list of waypoints; the other sends position commands to the plant. Due to the interleaving of the two tasks, the plant might receive the updated target position with a sampling period delay, and the system will follow slightly different traces every time a new waypoint is generated.

We performed the analysis both with and without state merging. The results, presented in Figure 4 show a significant reduction in number of visited states and memory usage. The space overhead due to the ellipsoidal sets that need to be associated with each visited state was limited and it was offset by the reduction in memory consumption due to the drastic reduction in number of visited states. Such a reduction was obtained with just a handful of conservative state merges: even a single merge can lead to a large reduction because every state reachable from the merged state no longer needs to be visited. The approach as implemented showed a significant overhead in terms of running time, however, which could be reduced by further optimizing the operations involving storing and lookup of ellipsoids.

5 Conclusions

This paper presents a formal verification technique for embedded control systems based on the combination of software Model Checking and numerical simulation of a continuous dynamic plant. The technique can provide a guarantee that a continuous dynamic plant controlled by a supervisor implemented in software satisfies safety requirements over a given time bound.

The algorithm presented in this work can be applied to system with nonlinear plant dynamics; however, the process of identifying bisimulation functions for nonlinear systems is difficult, in general. The work by Parrilo et al. on identifying Lyapunov functions for a class of nonlinear systems is related to the work presented here [15]. Due to the similarity between Lyapunov functions and bisimulation functions, similar techniques can be used to compute bisimulation functions for nonlinear systems.

References

1. Girard, A., Pappas, G.J.: Approximation Metrics for Discrete and Continuous Systems. Technical Report MS-CIS-05-10, University of Pennsylvania (2005)
2. Clarke, E.M., Emerson, E.A.: Synthesis of Synchronization Skeletons for Branching Time Temporal Logic. In: Proc. of Workshop on Logic of Programs (1981)
3. Clarke, E.M., Grumberg, O., Peled, D.: Model Checking. MIT Press, Cambridge (2000)
4. Lerda, F., Kapinski, J., Maka, H., Clarke, E.M., Krogh, B.H.: Model Checking In-The-Loop. In: The 27th American Control Conference (submitted, 2007)
5. Kapinski, J., Krogh, B.H., Maler, O., Stursberg, O.: On Systematic Simulation of Open Continuous Systems. In: Maler, O., Pnueli, A. (eds.) HSCC 2003. LNCS, vol. 2623, pp. 283–297. Springer, Heidelberg (2003)
6. Donzé, A., Maler, O.: Systematic Simulation using Sensitivity Analysis. In: Bemporad, A., Bicchi, A., Buttazzo, G. (eds.) HSCC 2007. LNCS, vol. 4416, pp. 174–189. Springer, Heidelberg (2007)
7. Julius, A.A., Fainekos, G.E., Anand, M., Lee, I., Pappas, G.J.: Robust Test Generation and Coverage for Hybrid Systems. In: Bemporad, A., Bicchi, A., Buttazzo, G. (eds.) HSCC 2007. LNCS, vol. 4416, pp. 329–342. Springer, Heidelberg (2007)
8. Aylward, E., Parrilo, P.A., Slotine, J.J.E.: Algorithmic Search for Contraction Metrics via SOS Programming. In: Proc. of the 2006 American Control Conference (2006)
9. Boyd, S., Ghaoui, L.E., Feron, E., Balakrishnan, V.: Linear Matrix Inequalities in System and Control Theory. In: SIAM Studies in Applied Mathematics, vol. 15. SIAM, Philadelphia (1994)
10. Kurzhanski, A.B., Vályi, I.: Ellipsoidal Calculus for Estimation and Control. Birkhäuser, Boston (1997)
11. Visser, W., Havelund, K., Brat, G., Park, S., Lerda, F.: Model Checking Programs. Automated Software Engineering 10(2), 203–232 (2003)
12. Grant, M., Boyd, S., Ye, Y.: CVX User's Guide (2007)
13. Toh, K.C., Todd, M.J., Tütüncü, R.H.: SDPT3 4.0. MIT Press, Cambridge (2006)
14. Hoffmann, G.M., Huang, H., Waslander, S.L., Tomlin, C.J.: Quadrotor Helicopter Flight Dynamics and Control: Theory and Experiment. In: Proc. of the AIAA Guidance, Navigation, and Control Conference (2007)
15. Parrilo, P.A.: Structured Semidefinite Programs and Semialgebraic Geometry Methods in Robustness and Optimization. PhD thesis, California Institute of Technology (2000)

Optimotaxis: A Stochastic Multi-agent Optimization Procedure with Point Measurements*

Alexandre R. Mesquita, João P. Hespanha, and Karl Åström

Center for Control, Dynamical Systems and Computation
University of California, Santa Barbara, CA 93106

Abstract. We consider the problem of seeking the maximum of a scalar signal using a swarm of autonomous vehicles equipped with sensors that can take point measurements of the signal. Vehicles are not able to measure their current position or to communicate with each other. Our approach induces the vehicles to perform a biased random walk inspired by bacterial chemotaxis and controlled by a stochastic hybrid automaton. With such a controller, it is shown that the positions of the vehicles evolve towards a probability density that is a specified function of the spatial profile of the measured signal, granting higher vehicle densities near the signal maxima.

1 Introduction

This paper addresses the problem of controlling a team of autonomous vehicles so as to find the maximum of a scalar function defined over a region of interest, without position and gradient measurements. In the stochastic framework adopted, our goal is to enforce a probability density for the vehicles' positions whose maximum coincides with the maximum of the scalar function. This is achieved by inducing the vehicles into a random motion that mimicks the chemotactic behavior observed in the bacterium *Escherichia coli.* Being unable to directly sense chemical gradients because of its reduced dimensions, this organism is still able to follow the gradient of a chemical attractant, despite the rotational diffusion that constantly changes the bacterium orientation. This is accomplished by switching between two alternate behaviors known as *run* and *tumble* [1,2].

The problem of finding the maximum of a spatially defined function by moving agents (that we also call vehicles) is often called *source-seeking.* This terminology refers to a specific application of this problem, which consists of finding the source of a chemical substance that is being produced at one particular location, but spreads over a region through a diffusion process. Potential applications for source-seeking include chemical plant safety, hydrothermal vent prospecting and pollution and environmental monitoring.

* This material is based upon work supported by the Inst. for Collaborative Biotechnologies through grant DAAD19-03-D-0004 from the U.S. Army Research Office. The first author was partially funded by CAPES (Brazil) grant BEX 2316/05-6.

M. Egerstedt and B. Mishra (Eds.): HSCC 2008, LNCS 4981, pp. 358–371, 2008.

We are interested in source-seeking under very limited sensing by the vehicles. Gradient information is often not directly available, either because of noisy and turbulent environments or because the vehicle size is too small to provide accurate gradient measurements, challenges also faced by *E. coli*. In addition, dispensing position measurements is necessary in applications for which inertial navigation systems are expensive, GPS is not available or not sufficiently accurate (as in underwater navigation or cave exploration), or the vehicles are too small or weight-constrained to carry this type of equipment.

Classical techniques from numerical optimization have been adapted for single- and multi-vehicle search strategies when gradients are not explicitly available [3,4,5]. In [3], the local gradient is estimated by means of a circular movement. The simplex method is implemented with a network of autonomous vehicles in [4]. However, this approach requires the ability to measure the vehicles relative position. Mayhew et al. [5] proposed a hybrid control algorithm to perform a conjugate directions method without position measurements. Control algorithms for networks of vehicles inspired by collective behavior such as fish schooling and chemotaxis are designed in [6,7]. An extremum seeking strategy is adopted in [8]. Statistical approaches have also been proposed for the case of turbulent environments, but assuming the availability of vehicle's position measurements [9,10]. In general, when convergence is proven in the above mentioned references, this is done exclusively under the assumption that the signal spatial profile is quadratic-like. Bio-inspired techniques have a strong appeal in optimization. Examples are the well-known genetic algorithms and the solutions for the traveling salesman problem inspired by ant colonies [11]. Mimicking chemotaxis is not a new approach to the source-seeking problem, see e.g. [6,10,12,13].

In the *E. coli*, chemotaxis consists of an alternation of two modes of motion called the *run* and *tumble* phases. In the run phase the bacterium swims with constant velocity by rotating its flagella in the counter-clockwise direction. In the tumble phase, by rotating its flagella in the clockwise direction, the bacterium spins around without change in its position and in such a way that it enters the next run phase with arbitrary orientation. Berg and Brown [1] observed that the only parameter that is affected by the concentration of a chemical attractant is the duration of runs. Roughly speaking, the less improvement the bacterium senses in the concentration of the attractant during the run phase, the more probable a direction change (tumble) becomes. Such a motion leads to a distribution whose peak usually coincides with the optimum of the sensed quantity. Whereas the previous works on chemotaxis-based source-seeking rely on a heuristic approach, we present a technique that allows one to control the probability density of the vehicle's position to permit the estimation of not only the peak of the sensed signal, but also the whole spatial profile of that signal. In fact, with the algorithm proposed, the probability density of the vehicle's position converges to a pre-specified function of the signal spatial profile. We adopt the suggestive name of *optimotaxis* to designate this search procedure. An important feature of optimotaxis is that it can be used with a broad class of signal profiles, including the ones with multiple maxima, a feature that is shared with a few other stochastic optimization algorithms which are not constrained by vehicle kinematics [14,15].

Optimotaxis is motivated by scenarios in which source-seeking is to be solved by a team of autonomous agents. Since the probability density of the agents' position is guaranteed to converge to a pre-specified function of the sensed signal, a supervisor that can sense the positions of the individual agents will be able to monitor the profile of the sensed signal and discern the location of its optimum. Our convergence results (cf. Theorems 1–2) show that by averaging the observations of the position of a single agent over time one recovers the signal profile. In fact, optimotaxis can be performed effectively by a single vehicle. However, given that optimotaxis was specially designed for use with small and cheap vehicles, one should take advantage of the more accurate estimates obtained with multiple vehicles, as we explain in Section 4.

2 Problem Description and Controllers

We consider vehicles with position $\mathbf{x} \in \Omega := \mathbb{R}^d$ and velocity $\mathbf{v} \in V := \rho\mathbb{S}^{d-1}$, where $\rho > 0$, $d \in \{2,3\}$, and $\mathbb{S}$ is the unit sphere equipped with the Lebesgue measure $d\mu$. We denote by $F(x)$ the scalar function describing the intensity of the sensed signal at position $x \in \Omega$. We define $p(x,v,t)$ as the probability density of finding a vehicle at position x with velocity v at time t. For each fixed time t, $p(x,v,t) \in L^1(\Omega \times V)$, where $\Omega \times V$ is equipped with the product measure $dx \otimes d\mu$.

The objective of optimotaxis is to design a control law to select the velocity $\mathbf{v}(t)$ as a function of the measurements $\{F(\mathbf{x}(\tau)); 0 \leq \tau \leq t\}$ collected up to time t such that the marginal $\int_V p(x,v,t)d\mu(v)$ converges to some density $Q(F(x))$. The function $Q(\cdot)$ is a design parameter called the shaping function which is used to guarantee that $Q(F)$ is a valid probability density function and perhaps to accentuate the maxima of the sensed signal. For example, if $F(x) = 1 - \|x\|^2$, a valid nonnegative shape would be attained with

$$Q(F) = \begin{cases} cF & , \text{if } F > \delta \\ c\delta e^{F-\delta} & , \text{if } F \leq \delta \end{cases} , \tag{1}$$

where $\delta > 0$ and c is a normalizing constant. Alternatively, if one is mainly interested in the position of the maxima of $F(x)$, a possible choice would be $Q(F)$ equal to some power of F, which would make maxima more distinct.

Two different controllers inspired by bacterial chemotaxis are presented below.

2.1 Run and Tumble Controller

The jump-diffusion framework that we adopt for optimotaxis was introduced for bacterial chemotaxis in [16,17]. We consider here a vehicle moving with constant velocity between tumbles. The conditional probability that a tumble does not

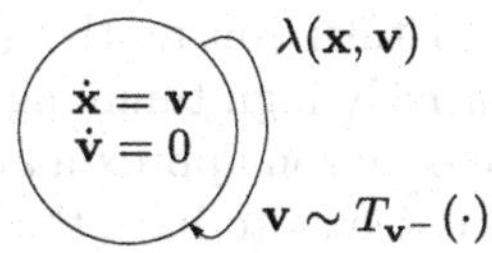

Fig. 1. Hybrid automaton for optimotaxis

occur between the time instants t and s, given that the vehicle was at position x with velocity v at time s is given by

$$\exp\left(-\int_s^t \lambda(x+\tau v, v)d\tau\right) , \tag{2}$$

where the positive function $\lambda(\cdot,\cdot) \in L^\infty(\Omega \times V)$ is the tumbling rate. At each tumble, the velocity jumps to a random value $\mathbf{v} \in V$ with probability density $T_{\mathbf{v}^-}$ that may depend on the velocity $\mathbf{v}^-$ just before the tumble. In the bacterial case, the quantities λ and T_v were characterized by Alt [2]. In our work, these should be viewed as control parameters which we will select and that may depend on x and v through the measurements $\{F(\mathbf{x}(\tau)); 0 \le \tau \le t\}$.

This controller for optimotaxis is captured by several stochastic hybrid system models that appeared in the literature, including Piecewise-Deterministic Markov Processes (PDPs) [18], our stochastic hybrid models discussed in [19], or the hybrid models initially proposed in [20] by Hu, Lygeros, and co-workers and further expanded in a series of subsequent papers. Fig. 1 depicts a schematic representation of our hybrid model for optimotaxis.

The probability density $p(x, v, t)$ was shown to satisfy the following integro-differential equation [16,17]:

$$\frac{\partial p}{\partial t}(x, v, t) + v \cdot \nabla_x p(x, v, t) = -\lambda p(x, v, t) + \int_V T_{v'}(v)\lambda(x, v')p(x, v', t)d\mu(v') . \tag{3}$$

We note that (3) has been indifferently used in the literature for p as a probability density or simply the density of individuals. When p is regarded as the density of individuals, (3) has a simple intuitive interpretation. On the left-hand side we find a drift term $v \cdot \nabla_x p$ corresponding to the vehicles straight runs, on the right-hand side we find an absorption term $-\lambda(x, v)p(x, v)$, that corresponds to vehicles leaving the state (x, v), and an integral term corresponding to the vehicles jumping to the state (x, v). Equation (3) is also known in linear transport theory, where it models the particular case of pure scattering [21,22]. In that framework, the absorption and the integral terms account for elastic collisions between particles.

2.2 Diffusion Controller

In the limit as the tumbling rate and the velocity approach infinity the jump-diffusion process may approach a pure diffusion process [17]. Inspired by this observation, we present in this section an alternative controller for optimotaxis that requires the vehicle to turn constantly. This could be applied when the vehicles are capable of relatively high tumbling rates. We do not claim that the model in this section is the diffusion approximation for the model in the run and tumble controller, though it seems to have the same desirable properties of the diffusion approximation. For simplicity we adopt $d = 2$. Let $\mathbf{x} = [\mathbf{x}_1\ \mathbf{x}_2]' \in \Omega$ be the position vector in the plane and θ be such that $\mathbf{v} = [\rho\cos\theta\ \rho\sin\theta]' \in V$. We propose a controller given by the following stochastic differential equation:

$$\begin{aligned} d\mathbf{x}_1 &= \rho\cos\theta dt \\ d\mathbf{x}_2 &= \rho\sin\theta dt \\ d\theta &= \sigma(\mathbf{x},\theta)d\mathbf{w}\ , \end{aligned} \tag{4}$$

where $\mathbf{w}(t)$ is a continuous Wiener process with $\mathrm{E}d\mathbf{w}^2 = 1$ and $\sigma(x,\theta)$ is the turning intensity, which we select to attain the desired behavior. The rationale for this controller involves the same original idea of having a turning intensity proportional to the improvement in the measurements. This model with continuous turning allows us to write the Fokker-Planck equation for the probability density of agents $p(x,v,t)$ [23]:

$$\frac{\partial p}{\partial t}(x,v,t) + v\cdot\nabla_x p(x,v,t) = \frac{1}{2}\frac{\partial^2}{\partial\theta^2}\left(\sigma^2 p(x,v,t)\right)\ . \tag{5}$$

3 Control Law

To obtain the control law we substitute the desired stationary density in equations (3) or (5) for the evolution of the density and then solve for λ and T_v or σ. We will subsequently verify convergence to the desired density. For simplicity, we set the desired stationary density to be independent of v such that $p(x,v,t) = Q(F(x))$. In the following we write $Q(F(x))$ simply as $Q(x)$.

3.1 Run and Tumble Controller

As we substitute $p(x,v,t) = Q(x)$ in the steady state version of (3), we obtain

$$v\cdot\nabla_x Q(x) = -\lambda(x,v)Q(x) + Q(x)\int_V T_{v'}(v)\lambda(x,v')d\mu(v')\ . \tag{6}$$

At this point we need to make the assumption that $Q(x) > 0$ for all $x \in \Omega$. This important assumption will be made throughout this paper. Dividing (6) by $Q(x)$ and rearranging the terms we conclude that we must have

$$\lambda(x,v) = \int_V T_{v'}(v)\lambda(x,v')d\mu(v') - v\cdot\nabla_x \ln Q(x)\ . \tag{7}$$

In the case of a uniformly distributed velocity jump, namely,

$$T_{v'}(v) = \frac{1}{\mu(V)}\ , \tag{8}$$

it is straightforward to solve for $\lambda(x, v)$:

$$\lambda(x, v) = \eta(x) - v \cdot \nabla_x \ln Q(x) \ , \tag{9}$$

where $\eta(x) = \int_V T_{v'}(v)\lambda(x, v')d\mu(v')$ is some function chosen by the designer to depend on x only through $F(x)$.

This control law is implementable using the past measurements $\{F(\mathbf{x}(\tau)); 0 \leq \tau \leq t\}$ since the tumbling rate depends only on the projection of the gradient in the direction of motion. In fact,

$$\mathbf{v}(t) \cdot \nabla_x Q(\mathbf{x}(t)) = \frac{dQ(\mathbf{x}(t))}{dt} \ . \tag{10}$$

Notice that $\eta(x)$ is the average tumbling rate at the position x and it must be chosen larger than or equal to $\rho \sup \|\nabla_x \ln Q(x)\|$ to make sure that the tumbling rate λ is positive. In this paper we only consider finite tumbling rates. Thus, here comes a second important restriction on $Q(x)$: $\|\nabla_x \ln Q(x)\|$ must be uniformly bounded. When this happens, we can take η to be independent of x and, according to (2), the probability of an agent maintaining a run with the same direction during the interval $[0, t]$ is given by

$$\begin{aligned} \exp\left(-\int_0^t \lambda(\mathbf{x}(\tau), \mathbf{v}(\tau))d\tau\right) &= \exp\left(-\int_0^t \eta - \frac{d}{d\tau}(\ln Q(\mathbf{x}(\tau)))d\tau\right) \\ &= e^{-\eta t}\frac{Q(\mathbf{x}(t))}{Q(\mathbf{x}(0))} \ . \end{aligned} \tag{11}$$

This provides a simple and useful expression for the practical implementation of the search procedure: Suppose that an agent tumbled at time t_k, at that time pick a random variable P uniformly distributed in the interval $[0, 1]$ and tumble when the following condition holds

$$Q(\mathbf{x}(t)) \leq P e^{\eta(t-t_k)} Q(\mathbf{x}(t_k)), \ \ t \geq t_k \ . \tag{12}$$

As opposed to what (10) seems to imply, one does not need to take derivatives to implement (9). Also, the control law is not changed if a constant scaling factor is applied to $Q(x)$. It is important to remark that η may be adjusted online. An agent may begin a search with $\eta = \epsilon > 0$ and if at some time t it observes that $\eta < \bar{\eta} = t^{-1} \ln Q(\mathbf{x}(t))/Q(\mathbf{x}(0))$, then it updates η to $\bar{\eta} + \epsilon$. The use of a small residue ϵ grants a positive λ. In this case, one can prove that the probability to have the vehicle visiting any neighborhood in space is positive. Hence, η will eventually converge to $\rho \sup \|\nabla_x \ln Q(x)\| + \epsilon$. A more elaborate adaptation can be obtained by having $\eta(x)$ as a function of the measurements $F(x)$, which would reduce the number of unnecessary tumbles.

We note that most physical quantities propagate with spatial decay not faster than exponential, which allows for the uniform boundedness of $\|\nabla_x \ln Q(x)\|$. If, however, $F(x)$ has a faster decay rate, it may still be possible to achieve boundedness of $\|\nabla_x \ln Q(x)\|$ via reshaping (i.e. selecting an appropriate Q) as long as $F(x) > 0$ for all $x \in \Omega$ and one knows its maximum decay rate.

3.2 Diffusion Controller

Substituting $p(x, v, t) = Q(x)$ in (5) and integrating twice in θ one obtains:

$$v \cdot \nabla_x Q(x) + \frac{1}{2}\sigma^2(x, \theta)Q(x) = \theta c_1(x) + c_2(x) \ . \tag{13}$$

Solving for $\sigma^2(x, \theta)$ we have

$$\sigma^2(x, \theta) = \theta d_1(x) + d_2(x) - 2v \cdot \nabla_x \ln Q(x) \ . \tag{14}$$

We set $d_1(x) = 0$ since there is no advantage in having $\sigma^2(x, \theta)$ growing linearly with θ. Thus, we can rewrite (14) as

$$\sigma^2(x, v) = \eta(x) - 2v \cdot \nabla_x \ln Q(x) \ . \tag{15}$$

Again, the only information needed to implement $\sigma^2(x, v)$ is the measurements $F(\mathbf{x}(t))$ collected along the vehicle's trajectory. As before, boundedness of $\|\nabla_x \ln Q(x)\|$ is an important condition and $\eta(x)$ may be adjusted online. A simple implementation of (4) with $\sigma(x, v)$ given by (15) can be done using Euler's approximation.

The addition of exogenous white Gaussian noise to $\dot{\theta}$ in (4) leads to the addition of a positive constant to $\sigma^2(x, v)$ in (5), which is equivalent to an increased η. Thus, this kind of disturbance does not change the stationary density. The same conclusion is true if we consider white Gaussian noise added to $\dot{\rho}$ in (5). Therefore, an important property of this controller is that the stationary density is robust to additive white Gaussian noise applied in the vehicle's bodyframe.

4 Convergence to the Steady-State

In this section we analyze the convergence of solutions to the desired stationary density $Q(x)$. We consider mild solutions [24] to the initial value problem defined by (3) and an initial density $p(x, v, 0) \in \mathcal{D} := \{f \in L^1(\Omega \times V); f \geq 0, \|f\| = 1\}$. The main result is stated in Theorem 1, which implies that $Q(x)$ can be estimated through the time average of the observed vehicles' position. In particular, with a proper choice of $Q(x)$, the maximum of $F(x)$ will be located in the neighborhood that is most often visited by the vehicle.

Theorem 1. *Assume that $Q(x) > 0$ and $\|\nabla_x \ln Q(x)\| \in L^\infty(\Omega)$. If T_v and λ are chosen according to (8) and (9), respectively, such that λ is uniformly bounded and strictly positive, then*

1. *A mild solution $p(x, v, t)$ to (3) exists and is unique for all $t \geq 0$ and all initial densities $p(x, v, 0) \in \mathcal{D}$.*
2. *$Q(x)$ is the unique stationary density for (3).*
3. *For any initial density $p(x, v, 0) \in \mathcal{D}$,*

$$\lim_{N\to\infty} \left\| \frac{1}{N} \sum_{k=0}^{N-1} p(x, v, k\tau) - Q(x) \right\| = 0 \tag{16}$$

for all $\tau > 0$.

We note that the continuous time average

$$\frac{1}{t}\int_0^t p(x,v,t)dt \tag{17}$$

also converges in norm to $Q(x)$ as $t \to \infty$, see e.g. [25, Cor. VIII.7.4].

Theorem 1 provides the basis for a procedure to estimate $Q(x)$ by observing the position of N agents: We start by partitioning the region of interest into a family of sets $\{A_i \subset \Omega\}$ and then we sample the vehicles' positions at times $k\tau \in \{0, \tau, 2\tau, \ldots, (K-1)\tau\}$, for some $\tau > 0$, and count the number of times that a vehicle is observed in each set A_i. It turns out that the fraction of samples corresponding to vehicles observed over the set A_i provides an asymptotically correct estimate of the average value of $Q(x)$ on the set A_i. To see why this is the case, we define

$$f_{N,K} = \frac{1}{NK}\sum_{n=0}^{N-1}\sum_{k=0}^{K-1} f(\mathbf{x}_n(k\tau)) , \tag{18}$$

for some $f \in L^\infty(\Omega)$. Assuming that the agents have mutually independent motion, by the law of large numbers we have that $f_{N,K}$ converges almost surely as $N \to \infty$. Moreover, by the specific version of the law of large numbers in [26], we also have that $f_{N,K}$ converges almost surely as $K \to \infty$. In particular, if f is the characteristic function of a measurable set A_i, then

$$f_{N,K} \to \int_{A_i} Q(x)dx \text{ a.s.} \tag{19}$$

as $K \to \infty$. This shows that $Q(x)$ can be estimated by averaging the observations of the agents position as in (18). The use of multiple agents ($N > 1$) improves the estimates according to the relation

$$\mathrm{var}(f_{N,K}) = \frac{\mathrm{var}(f_{1,K})}{N} . \tag{20}$$

Proof of Theorem 1 (outline). A complete proof is given in [27]. The existence and uniqueness results rely on previous results on linear transport theory [21] using semigroups of linear operators. To prove the uniqueness of the stationary density we take $q(x,v,t)$ and $r(x,v,t)$ to be two convex combinations of a stationary density $p(x,v,t)$ and $Q(x)$. We consider the Kullback-Leibler divergence between $q(x,v,t)$ and $r(x,v,t)$

$$H(t) = \int_\Omega\int_V q(x,v,t)\ln\frac{q(x,v,t)}{r(x,v,t)}\, dxd\mu(v) , \tag{21}$$

and show that $\dot{H}(t) = 0$ for all $t > 0$ implies $p = Q$. The convergence of the Cesàro averages in part 3 of the theorem is a direct consequence of the mean ergodic theorem provided that $Q(x) > 0$ is the unique invariant density. See e.g. Theorem 5.2.2 of [28] or [29, Chap. 2]. □

It is worthwhile to remark that $p(x,v,t)$ actually converges to $Q(x)$ in norm if λ is bounded away from zero. The proof of this result is based on a result from [30] that states that, if $V(t)$ is a Harris operator for every $t>0$ and $Q(x)>0$ is its unique invariant density, then $V(t)f$ converges to $Q(x)$ in norm for all $f \in \mathcal{D}$. It turns out that one can prove that the semigroup generated by (3) consists of Harris operators [27]. In addition, we conjecture that convergence is exponential. The proof of this result would be possible with a generalization of some results in the spectral theory of linear transport operators in unbounded domains presented in [31]. However, such a generalization is not yet available.

Next, we state the corresponding result for the diffusion controller.

Theorem 2. *Assume that $Q(x)>0$ and $\|\nabla_x \ln Q(x)\| \in L^\infty(\Omega)$. If σ^2 is chosen according to (15) such that σ^2 is uniformly bounded and strictly positive, then*

1. *A mild solution $p(x,v,t)$ to (5) exists and is unique for all $t \geq 0$ and all initial densities $p(x,v,0) \in \mathcal{D}$.*
2. *$Q(x)$ is the unique stationary density for (5).*
3. *For any initial density $p(x,v,0) \in \mathcal{D}$,*

$$\lim_{N\to\infty} \left\| \frac{1}{N} \sum_{k=0}^{N-1} p(x,v,k\tau) - Q(x) \right\| = 0 \tag{22}$$

for all $\tau > 0$.

The proof of this result is also presented in [27].

5 Numerical Results and Discussion

In this section we present numerical experiments to illustrate the proposed optimization procedure. We adopt preferentially the run and tumble controller with a constant function $\eta(x)$. The results for the diffusion case are similar but with slightly faster convergence. The desired stationary density is taken to be $Q(F(x)) = cF^n(x)$, where c is a normalizing constant and n is an integer.

The main capability of optimotaxis, the localization of the global maximum, is stressed in Fig. 2. We observe a swarm of agents that starts from the upper left corner (1), initially clusters around a local maximum (2) and then progressively migrates to the global maximum (3,4). When the equilibrium is reached, most agents concentrate in a neighborhood of the global maximum. Yet, a portion of the agents clearly indicates the existence of the local maximum. We notice that the center of mass of the swarm goes straight through the local maximum to the global one. This feature is not shared with most deterministic optimization procedures and even with some stochastic ones. As a bonus, the information on secondary sources (local maxima) is not lost.

We use the Kullback-Leibler divergence $H(t)$ (defined in Section 4) between $p(x,v,t)$ and the convex combination $10Q(x)/11 + p(x,v,t)/11$ to analyze the speed of convergence to the desired stationary density. One useful property of this

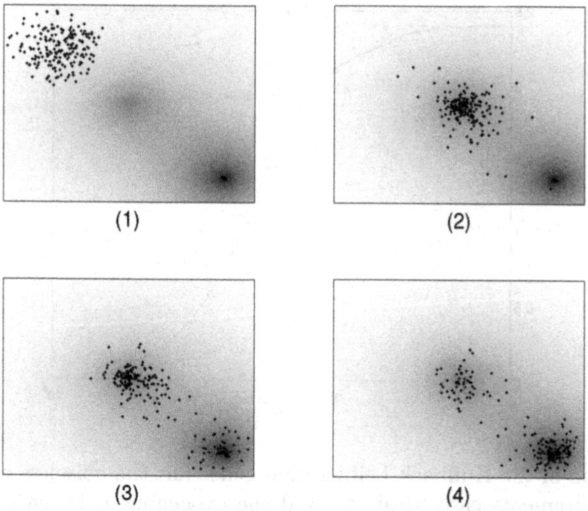

Fig. 2. Different stages of optimotaxis in the presence of two maxima. Black dots represent agents position whereas the background intensity represents the signal intensity. $F(x) = 0.4e^{-\|x\|} + 0.6e^{-\|x-[1.5\ -1.5]'\|}$, $Q(x) = F^n(x)$ with $n = 10$, and $\rho = 1$.

Kullback-Leibler divergence is that $H = 0$ iff $p = Q$. Moreover, $\alpha(\|p - Q\|) \leq H(t) \leq \beta(\|p - Q\|)$, where α, β are class $\mathcal{K}$ functions [32]. Using a space grid with resolution 0.068, we calculate $H(t)$, which is shown to converge to zero in Fig. 3.

Also included in Fig. 3 is the evolution of $H(t)$ when the measurements are quantized and when exogenous noise is added. In the quantization case, we used the quantized version of the desired density $Q(x)$ to calculate $H(t)$. Interestingly, the addition of noise does not seem to affect considerably the transient response. Nevertheless, the residual error is greater due to the fact that the stationary density is not the one expected. On the other hand, quantization has a much more negative impact on optimotaxis performance. Yet, we believe that convergence to a quantized $Q(x)$ does happen but at a low speed.

The sensitivity of the procedure with respect to the parameter n of the shaping function is studied with Fig. 4. The mean-square error of the vehicles position with respect to the maximum is used as a performance index. One notices that the performance degrades for n too low or too high. In particular, the sensitivity to noise and quantization increases with n. This suggests that an interesting strategy to reduce the effect of uncertainties and quantization is to assign agents with different values of n. In this case, the observed density would converge to an arithmetic average of the powers $F^n(x)$. Thus, the mean-square error would be smaller than the error corresponding to the maximum or minimum value of the chosen n.

5.1 Chemotaxis and Optimotaxis

It is remarkable that the expression for λ in (9) has the same structure of some biochemical models for the tumbling rate of the *E. coli*; see, for instance, Alt

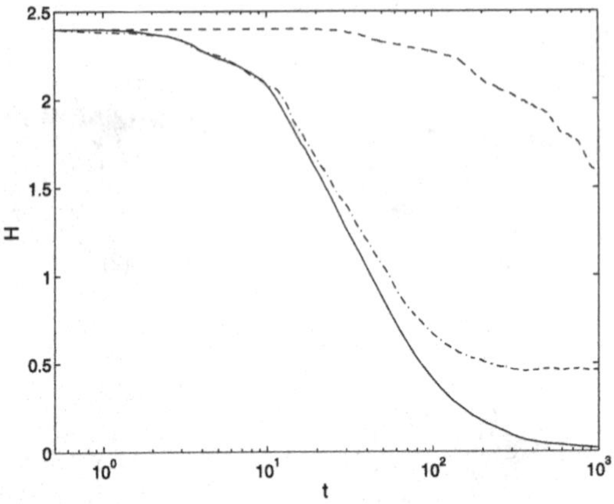

Fig. 3. Evolution of the Kullback-Leibler divergence for: the noiseless case (solid), the quantized measurements case (dashed), and the exogenous noise case (dash-dotted). The number of quantization levels is 128. The noise added to $\dot{v}$ is white Gaussian with standard deviation 10^{-2} along each axis. 100 agents were uniformly deployed in the rectangle $[-2.5, 2.5] \times [-2.5, 2.5] \times V$. Refer to Fig. 2 for more details.

[2, Equation 4.8]. This author essentially proposed the existence of a chemical activator for the locomotion mechanism such that a tumble would occur each time the concentration of this activator would become less than a certain value. The concentration of this activator would jump to a high value at tumbles and decrease at a rate corresponding to η in (9). A receptor-sensor-mechanism would then regulate the additional generation of the activator (this corresponds to $v \cdot \nabla_x Q(x)$ in (9)), which would modulate the run length. We find surprising that our reverse engineering design resulted in an expression for λ similar to the one in bacterial chemotaxis. In fact, though the use of tumble and run in optimotaxis is inspired by chemotaxis, one would not necessarily expect that our choice of the tumbling rate would lead to control laws similar to the biochemical models in bacteria. This fact suggests that the bacteria evolutionary process might have selected a taxis mechanism with the same desirable properties of our model.

To understand what these desired properties might be, let us suppose that bacteria are performing optimotaxis as it is described in this paper. Let $p(x, v, t)$ be the spatial density of bacteria and let $Q(x)$ be some function related to the concentration of nutrients. From Section 4, we know that $p(x, v, t)$ converges in norm, which implies that

$$H(t) = -\int_{\Omega}\int_{V} p(x,v,t) \ln\left(\frac{1}{2} + \frac{1}{2}\frac{Q(x)}{p(x,v,t)}\right) \, dx d\mu(v) \to 0 \ . \tag{23}$$

Thus, $H(t)$ can be regarded as a cost functional that is being minimized by optimotaxis/chemotaxis. More specifically, we notice that what is being maximized is the expected value of a concave function of Q/p, which is the ratio of the

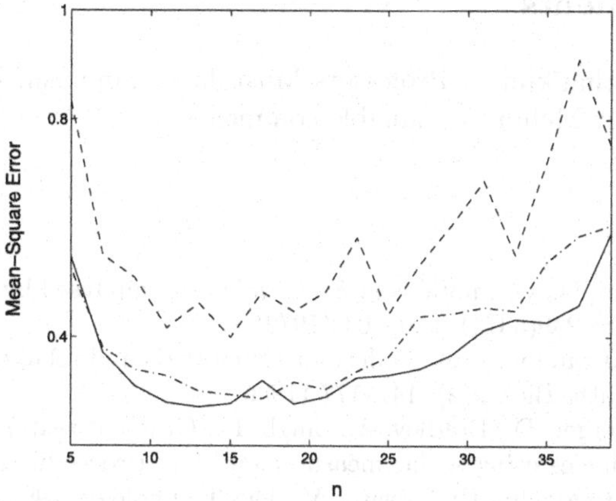

Fig. 4. Mean-square error with respect to the maximum of $F(x) = e^{-\|x\|}$ as a function of n. Noiseless case (solid), quantized $F(x)$ (dashed), and exogenous noise (dash-dotted). The number of quantization levels is 128. The noise added to $\dot{v}$ is white Gaussian with standard deviation 10^{-3} in each axis. $\rho = 1$.

concentration of nutrients per the density of organisms. This is a meaningful cost for the population of bacteria as a whole.

It is important to remark that the jump velocity probability density function T_v is not uniform in bacteria. This supports our belief that better results for optimotaxis might be obtained with more sophisticated choices for T_v.

6 Conclusion

A random optimization algorithm based on bacterial chemotaxis was presented. This algorithm is mainly intended for application in a swarm of agents whose mission is to find the maximum of a measured quantity. The most attractive features of the procedure are its simplicity and low cost of implementation as well as the identification of both global and local maxima. The only measurement needed by the agents is the signal of interest and the only information that must be known a priori is a bound on the spatial decay of the measured quantity. The convergence of the agents probability density to a specified function was demonstrated. Some robustness to exogenous disturbance was also demonstrated. In addition, insight was gained on what bacterial chemotaxis might try to optimize.

We note that the proposed choice of control parameters may not be optimal. Hence, alternative choices for the tumbling rate and for the probability density of velocity jumps are important themes for further investigation. Future research directions also include the study of optimotaxis in compact spatial domains and signal spatial profiles with discontinuities. Alternatively, it may be worth to explore the application of these ideas to solve problems in numerical optimization by arrays of independent processors.

Acknowledgments

The authors are thankful to Professors Mustafa Khammash, Upamanyu Madhow, and Prashant Mehta for valuable comments.

References

1. Berg, H., Brown, D.: Chemotaxis in *Escherichia coli* analysed by three-dimensional tracking. Nature 239(5374), 500–504 (1972)
2. Alt, W.: Biased random walk models for chemotaxis and related diffusion approximations. J. Math. Biol. 9(2), 147–177 (1980)
3. Burian, E., Yoerger, D., Bradley, A., Singh, H.: Gradient search with autonomous underwater vehicles using scalar measurements. In: Proceedings of the 1996 Symposium on Autonomous Underwater Vehicle Technology, 1996. AUV 1996, June 1996, pp. 86–98 (1996)
4. Sousa, J., Johansson, K., Silva, J., Speranzon, A.: A verified hierarchical control architecture for co-ordinated multi-vehicle operations. International Journal of Adaptive Control and Signal Processing 21(2-3), 159–188 (2007)
5. Mayhew, C., Sanfelice, R., Teel, A.: Robust source-seeking hybrid controllers for autonomous vehicles. In: Proceedings of the 2007 American Control Conference. ACC 2007, July 2007, pp. 1185–1190 (2007)
6. Hoskins, D.A.: Least action approach to collective behavior. In: Parker, L.E. (ed.) Proc. SPIE, vol. 2593, pp. 108–120; Microrobotics and Micromechanical Systems. In: Parker, L.E. (ed.) The Society of Photo-Optical Instrumentation Engineers (SPIE) Conference. vol. 2593, pp. 108–120 (December 1995)
7. Bachmayer, R., Leonard, N.: Vehicle networks for gradient descent in a sampled environment. In: Proceedings of the 41st IEEE Conference on Decision and Control, pp. 112–117 (December 2002)
8. Zhang, C., Arnold, D., Ghods, N., Siranosian, A., Krstic, M.: Source seeking with non-holonomic unicycle without position measurement and with tuning of forward velocity. Systems & Control Letters 56(3), 245–252 (2007)
9. Pang, S., Farrell, J.: Chemical plume source localization. IEEE Transactions on Systems, Man and Cybernetics, Part B 36(5), 1068–1080 (2006)
10. Vergassola, M., Villermaux, E., Shraiman, B.: 'infotaxis' as a strategy for searching without gradients. Nature 445(7126), 406–409 (2007)
11. Dorigo, M., Gambardella, L.M.: Ant colony system: A cooperative learning approach to the traveling salesman problem. IEEE Transactions on Evolutionary Computation 1(1), 53–66 (1997)
12. Ferrée, T., Lockery, S.: Computational rules for chemotaxis in the nematode C. Elegans. Journal of Computational Neuroscience 6, 263–277 (1999)
13. Dhariwal, A., Sukhatme, G.S., Requicha, A.A.: Bacterium-inspired robots for environmental monitoring. In: IEEE International Conference on Robotics and Automation, New Orleans, Louisiana, April 2004, pp. 1436–1443. IEEE, Los Alamitos (2004)
14. Aluffipentini, F., Parisi, V., Zirilli, F.: Global optimization and stochastic differential-equations. Journal of Optimization Theory and Applications 47(1), 1–16 (1985)
15. Dekkers, A., Aarts, E.: Global optimization and simulated annealing. Math. Program. 50(3), 367–393 (1991)

16. Stroock, D.: Some stochastic processes which arise from a model of the motion of a bacterium. Probability Theory and Related Fields 28(4), 305–315 (1974)
17. Papanicolaou, G.: Asymptotic analysis of transport processes. Bulletin of the American Mathematical Society 81(2), 330–392 (1975)
18. Davis, M.H.A.: Markov models and optimization. In: Monographs on statistics and applied probability, Chapman & Hall, London, UK (1993)
19. Hespanha, J.P.: Modeling and analysis of stochastic hybrid systems. IEE Proc — Control Theory & Applications, Special Issue on Hybrid Systems 153(5), 520–535 (2007)
20. Hu, J., Lygeros, J., Sastry, S.: Towards a theory of stochastic hybrid systems. In: Lynch, N.A., Krogh, B.H. (eds.) HSCC 2000. LNCS, vol. 1790, pp. 160–173. Springer, Heidelberg (2000)
21. Kaper, H.G., Lekkerkerker, C.G., Hejtmanek, J.: Spectral Methods in Linear Transport Theory. Birkhäuser Verlag, Basel (1982)
22. Mokhtar-Kharroubi, M.: Mathematical Topics in Neutron Transport Theory. World Scientific, Singapore (1997)
23. Risken, H.: The Fokker-Planck Equation - Methods of Solution and Applications. Springer Series in Synergetics. Springer, Berlin (1984)
24. Pazy, A.: Semigroup of Linear Operators and Applications to Partial Differential Equations. Springer, New York (1983)
25. Dunford, N., Schwartz, J.: Linear Operators. In: Pure and Applied Mathematics, vol. VII, Interscience Publishers, New York (1957)
26. Derriennic, Y., Lin, M.: Uniform ergodic convergence and averaging along markov chain trajectories. Journal of Theoretical Probability 7(3), 483–497 (1994)
27. Mesquita, A., Hespanha, J., Åstrom, K.: Optimotaxis: A stochastic multi-agent optimization procedure with point measurements: Extended version. Technical report, University of California, Santa Barbara (October 2007), http://www.ece.ucsb.edu/~hespanha/techreps.html
28. Lasota, A., Mackey, M.: Chaos, Fractals, and Noise. Stochastic Aspects of Dynamics. In: Applied Mathematical Sciences, vol. 97, Springer, New York (1994)
29. Krengel, U.: Ergodic Theorems. de Gruyer Studies in Mathematics. vol. 6, Walter de Gruyter, Berlin, New York (1985)
30. Pichór, K., Rudnicki, R.: Continuous markov semigroups and stability of transport equations. Journal of Mathematical Analysis and Applications 249, 668–685 (2000)
31. Mokhtar-Kharroubi, M., Sbihi, M.: Spectral mapping theorems for neutron transport, l^1-theory. Semigroup Forum 72, 249–282 (2006)
32. Lin, J.: Divergence measures based on shannon entropy. IEEE Transactions on Information Theory 37(1), 145–151 (1991)

Noncausal Optimal Tracking of Linear Switched Systems

Gou Nakura

Osaka University, Department of Engineering
2-1, Yamadaoka, Suita, Osaka, 565-0871, Japan
nakura@watt.mech.eng.osaka-u.ac.jp

Abstract. In this paper we consider the noncausal optimal tracking problem on the finite time interval for linear switched systems. We consider the problem to obtain the solution of both optimal switching sequences and optimal control inputs such that the tracking error is minimized. In this paper we assume that information of reference signals is known *a priori* for the whole time interval and utilize its information so that the tracking performace becomes better. We study a computation method of the optimal performance including some information of tracking errors and present an iterative algorithm to determine the optimal timing and optimal tracking performance numerically.

Keywords: Switched systems; Optimal control; GSLQ problems; Noncausal tracking theory; Riccati equations.

1 Introduction

On optimal control problems for switched systems, the problem to obtain the solution of both the optimal switching sequences and the optimal inputs is very important, and so much works have been done by many researchers recently ([1,2,6,19,20,22]).

In particular, X. Xu and P. J. Antsaklis have studied the optimal timing and control problem by the parametrization approach([19,22]). They have decomposed the problem into two stages. In the first stage, they have considered a cost optimization problem over fixed switching sequences. In the second stage, they have considered a nonlinear optimization problem to find local switching sequences. In order to solve these two problems, they have presented an algorithm based on the gradient projection method and its variations([3]). For linear qudratic (LQ) problem, they have constructed the optimization algorithm by using the general Riccati equation parametrized by switching instants. The embedded control system theory is a more general control theory than the theory by their time parametrization approach for the switched systems. The switched systems can be "embedded" into a larger class of systems. Recently the relationship between the switched and embedded systems has been researched([2]).

M. Egerstedt and B. Mishra (Eds.): HSCC 2008, LNCS 4981, pp. 372–385, 2008.

It is well known that, for design of tracking control systems, preview information of reference signals is very useful for improving the performance of the closed-loop systems, and much work has been done for preview control systems([4,5,7,8,9,10,11,12,13,14,15,16,17,18]). U. Shaked and C. E. de Souza have presented the H_∞ tracking theory with preview by a game theoretic approach ([17]). Their theory can be restricted to optimal tracking theory and also extended to robust H_∞ tracking control theory([18]) or stochastic H_∞ tracking control theory([7,8,9]). Their theory has been applied to various types of systems, for example, continuous-time systems([8,17,18]), discrete-time systems([4,7]), impulsive systems ([13,14,15,16]) and so on. In this paper we describe that their tracking theory can be applied to the switched systems.

There exist two structures on preview information. One is the fixed preview type that information of reference signals is known until fixed preview time length ahead. The other is the perfectly noncausal type that information of reference signals is known *a priori* for the whole time interval. In this paper we assume that the structure of the preview information is the perfectly noncausal type.

In this paper we study the noncausal optimal timing and tracking control problem for linear switched systems based on the time parametrization approach by X. Xu and P. J. Antsaklis([19,22]). In order to design noncausal feedforward compensators, we consider a vector and its dynamics introducing future information of reference signals([17]). As the cases of the previous various preview or noncausal tracking control theory([4,5,7,8,9,10,11,12,13,14,15,16,17,18]), we can expect improvement of tracking performance by introducing future information. We present a practical optimization algorithm, which is an extension of the time parametrization method by X. Xu and P.J. Antsaklis([19,22]). Their algorithm is feasible for numerical computation in the sense of not demanding more than solving a set of ODEs (ordinary differential equations) with boundary conditions. Compared with it, our algorithm on the tracking problem needs some numerical integration to add to the task of solving the set of ODEs.

The organization of this paper is as follows. In section 2 we describe our systems and problem formulation. In section 3 we present the equivalent noncausal GSLQ(General Switched Linear Quadratic) tracking problem and, under the assumption of the fixed switching instants, give the necessary and sufficient conditions of the solvability and a control strategy for this problem. In section 4 we construct the optimization algorithm of both switching instants and tracking performance, based on the theory described in the section 3. In the appendix we describe the proof of Proposition 1, which gives the necessary and sufficient conditions of the solvability and a control strategy for the equivalent noncausal GSLQ tracking problem under the assumption of the fixed switching instants.

Notations: Throughout this paper the subscript "$'$" stands for the matrix transposition, $\|\cdot\|$ denotes the Euclidian vector norm and $\|v\|_R^2$ also denotes the weighted norm $v'Rv$.

2 Problem Formulation

Consider the following switched systems with effects of reference signal.

$$\begin{aligned} \dot{x}(t) &= A_1x(t) + B_{2,1}u(t) + B_{3,1}r_c(t),\ t_0 \le t < t_1, x(t_0) = x_0, \\ \dot{x}(t) &= A_2x(t) + B_{2,2}u(t) + B_{3,2}r_c(t),\ t_1 \le t \le T \\ z_c(t) &= C_1x(t) + D_{12}u(t) + D_{13}r_c(t) \end{aligned} \tag{1}$$

where $x \in \mathbf{R}^{\mathbf{n}}$ is the state, $u \in \mathbf{R}^{\mathbf{m}}$ is the control input, $z_c \in \mathbf{R}^{\mathbf{k_c}}$ is the controlled output, $r_c(t) \in \mathbf{R}^{\mathbf{r_c}}$ is an known or mesurable reference signal. x_0 is a given initial state. t_0 and T is given initial and terminal times, and t_1 is a switching time to be sought such that the tracking performance becomes optimal. We assume that all system matrices are constant and of compatible dimensions.

Remark 1. The generalized system with K switching instants of the system (1) can be represented as follows:

$$\begin{aligned} \dot{x}(t) &= A_1x(t) + B_{2,1}u(t) + B_{3,1}r_c(t),\ t_0 \le t < t_1,\ x(t_0) = x_0, \\ \dot{x}(t) &= A_2x(t) + B_{2,2}u(t) + B_{3,2}r_c(t),\ t_1 \le t < t_2 \\ &\cdots \\ \dot{x}(t) &= A_{K+1}x(t) + B_{2,K+1}u(t) + B_{3,K+1}r_c(t),\ t_K \le t \le T \end{aligned} \tag{2}$$

Throughout this paper, for simplification, we mainly consider the system (1), which has only one switching instant.

For the system (1), we assume the following condition.

$$\mathbf{A1}:\ D_{12}'D_{12} > O$$

We define the following performance index for the system (1)

$$J := \int_{t_0}^{T} \|z_c(t)\|^2 dt + x'(T)Q_f x(T) \tag{3}$$

where $Q_f \ge O$. Partially, in this paper, in order to clarify the switching intants, we denote J as $J(t_1)$ and etc.

Remark 2. On defining the performance index, U. Shaked and C.E. de Souza ([17]) have introduced the expectation $\mathbf{E}_{\bar{R}_s}$ considering the average of the performance index over the statistics of the unknown part $\bar{R}_{s+h} := \{r_c(l); s + h < l \le T\}$ of the reference signal r_c where h is a fixed preview length. Note that, compared with it, we do not introduce any expectation operators. As U. Shaked and C.E. de Souza have described in [17], the expectation operator is superfluous in the case of perfectly noncausal settings because we don't have to consider both of causal and noncausal parts on the whole time interval, i.e., we don't have to consider any unknown parts of reference signals *at the current time* on the whole time interval $[t_0, T]$.

For the system (1) and the performance index (3), we consider the following noncausal optimization problem.

Noncausal Optimal Timing and Tracking Problem
Consider the system (1) and the performance index (3), and assume the condition **A1**. Assume also that the reference signal $\{r_c(t)\}$ is known *a priori* for the whole time interval $t \in [t_0, T]$. Then, find $\{u^*\}$ and a switching instant t_1 minimizing the performance index (3).

In order to solve this problem, we consider the following optimization algorithm as [19,22]. However, note that our performance index can include any noncausal information of tracking signals.

– *Algorithm 1*
1) Set the iteration index $j = 0$. Choose an initial t_1^j.
2) By solving an optimal noncausal tracking problem, find $J(t_1^j)$.
3) Compute $(\partial J/\partial t_1)(t_1^j)$ (and $(\partial^2 J/\partial t_1^2)$ if second-order method is to be used).
4) Use some feasile direction method to update to be $t_1^{j+1} = t_1^j + \alpha^j\ (\partial J/\partial t_1)(t_1^j)$ (the stepsize α^j can be chosen using some stepsize rule, e.g., Armijo's rule ([3])). Set the iteration index $j = j + 1$.
5) Repeat Steps 2), 3), 4) and 5), until, for a given small number $\epsilon > 0$, $|\partial J/\partial t_1| < \epsilon$.

How can we compute this gradient of the performance index? X. Xu and P.J. Antsaklis([19,22]) have presented how to compute the gradient for the GSLQ problem using the generalized Riccati equation denpendent on the parameter, but not considering any exogeneous tracking signals nor noncausal information. We present an algorithm including how to compute the gradient with the tracking error, considering the effects of the exogeneous and noncausal tracking error over the whole time interval $[0, T]$. In order to construct the algorithm, we utilize the dynamics which gives the noncausal information of the tracking signal with the parametrized general Riccati equation by X. Xu and P.J. Antsaklis together.

3 Approach Based on the Parametrization of the Switching Instants

In order to realize the algorithm for the **Noncausal Optimal Timing and Tracking Problem** in the previous section, we take the following steps.

Step 1: We parameterized and reduce our problem to the equivalent GSLQ Tracking Problem.

Step 2: We seek the solution of the equivalent GSLQ Tracking Problem for the fixed x_{n+1}.

Step 3: Minimize J with respect to varying x_{n+1}.

First we introduce a state variable x_{n+1} corresponding to the switching instant t_1. Let x_{n+1} satisfy

$$\frac{dx_{n+1}}{dt} = 0,\ x_{n+1}(0) = t_1.$$

Moreover, we introduce a new independent time variable τ and define a piecewise linear relationship between t and τ as follows:

$$t = \begin{cases} t_0 + (x_{n+1} - t_0)\tau, & 0 \le \tau \le 1 \\ x_{n+1} + (T - x_{n+1})(\tau - 1), & 1 \le \tau \le 2. \end{cases} \quad (4)$$

By this parametrization of the switching time, our **Noncausal Optimal Timing and Tracking Problem** is transcribed into the following equivalent problem.

Equivalent Noncausal GSLQ (General Switched Linear Quadratic) Tracking Problem

Consider the system

$$\frac{dx(\tau)}{d\tau} = (x_{n+1} - t_0)(A_1 x(\tau) + B_{2,1}u(\tau) + B_{3,1}r_c(\tau)), \quad \frac{dx_{n+1}(\tau)}{d\tau} = 0 \quad (5)$$

for $\tau \in [0, 1)$ and

$$\frac{dx(\tau)}{d\tau} = (T - x_{n+1})(A_2 x(\tau) + B_{2,2}u(\tau) + B_{3,2}r_c(\tau)), \quad \frac{dx_{n+1}(\tau)}{d\tau} = 0 \quad (6)$$

for $\tau \in [1, 2]$. t_0, T and $x(0)$ are given. Assume that the reference signal $\{r_c(t)\}$ is known *a priori* for the whole time interval $\tau \in [0, 2]$. Find an x_{n+1} and a $u(\tau)$ such that the parametrized performance index

$$J = x'(2)Q_f x(2) + \int_0^1 (x_{n+1} - t_0)\|z_c(\tau)\|^2 d\tau + \int_1^2 (T - x_{n+1})\|z_c(\tau)\|^2 d\tau \quad (7)$$

is minimized.

Note that this problem no longer includes any varying switching instants. However, it is difficult to solve this problem because of the nonlinearity of the whole system including the variable x_{n+1}. In order to solve this problem, first we assume that x_{n+1} is fixed. Now we consider the following general Riccati equation and terminal condition parametrized by x_{n+1}.

$$-\frac{\partial X}{\partial \tau} = (x_{n+1} - t_0)(A_1'X + XA_1 + C_1'C_1 - \tilde{S}_1'\tilde{R}^{-1}\tilde{S}_1) \text{ for } \tau \in [0, 1), \quad (8)$$

$$-\frac{\partial X}{\partial \tau} = (T - x_{n+1})(A_2'X + XA_2 + C_1'C_1 - \tilde{S}_2'\tilde{R}^{-1}\tilde{S}_2) \text{ for } \tau \in [1, 2] \quad (9)$$

and $X(2, x_{n+1}) = Q_f$ where

$$\tilde{R} = D_{12}'D_{12}, \; \tilde{S}_1(\tau) = B_{2,1}'X(\tau) + D_{12}'C_1, \; \tilde{S}_2(\tau) = B_{2,2}'X(\tau) + D_{12}'C_1.$$

Remark 3. This type of Riccati equation is the same as the one for the standard GSLQ problem by [19,22] not considering the effects of any reference signals nor noncausal information.

Then we have the following proposition, which gives the solvability and an optimal control strategy for our equivalent GSLQ tracking problem under the assumption of the fixed x_{n+1}. This proposition is an extension of the noncausal tracking control theory by U. Shaked and C. E. de Souza([17]).

Proposition 1. *Consider the system (5)-(6) and the performance index (7), and suppose* **A1**. *Assume that x_{n+1} is fixed. Then the equivalent GSLQ tracking problem is solvable by state feedback if and only if there exists a matrix $X(\tau, x_{n+1})$ satisfying the conditions $X(\tau, x_{n+1}) = X'(\tau, x_{n+1})$ and $X(2, x_{n+1}) = Q_f$ such that the equation (8)-(9) holds over $\tau \in [0, 2]$. Then an optimal control strategy for our noncausal tracking problem (5)-(6) and (7) is given by*

$$u^*_{c,1}(\tau, x_{n+1}) = -\tilde{R}^{-1}\tilde{S}_1 x(\tau, x_{n+1}) \\ -\mathbf{C}_u r_c(\tau, x_{n+1}) - \mathbf{C}_{\theta u,1}\theta(\tau, x_{n+1}) \text{ for } 0 \le \tau < 1, \quad (10)$$

$$u^*_{c,2}(\tau, x_{n+1}) = -\tilde{R}^{-1}\tilde{S}_2 x(\tau, x_{n+1}) \\ -\mathbf{C}_u r_c(\tau, x_{n+1}) - \mathbf{C}_{\theta u,2}\theta(\tau, x_{n+1}) \text{ for } 1 \le \tau \le 2 \quad (11)$$

where

$$\mathbf{C}_{\theta u,1} = \tilde{R}^{-1}B'_{2,1}, \ \mathbf{C}_{\theta u,2} = \tilde{R}^{-1}B'_{2,2}, \ \mathbf{C}_u = \tilde{R}^{-1}D'_{12}D_{13}.$$

$\theta(t)$, $t \in [0, T]$, satisfies the dynamics

$$\frac{\partial}{\partial\tau}\theta(\tau, x_{n+1}) = (x_{n+1} - t_0)\{-\bar{A}'_{c,1}(\tau, x_{n+1})\theta(\tau, x_{n+1}) \\ +\bar{B}_{c,1}(\tau, x_{n+1})r_c(\tau, x_{n+1})\}, \ 0 \le \tau < 1, (12)$$

$$\frac{\partial}{\partial\tau}\theta(\tau, x_{n+1}) = (T - x_{n+1})\{-\bar{A}'_{c,2}(\tau, x_{n+1})\theta(\tau, x_{n+1}) \\ +\bar{B}_{c,2}(\tau, x_{n+1})r_c(\tau, x_{n+1})\}, \ 1 \le \tau \le 2 \ (13)$$

and the terminal condition $\theta(2, x_{n+1}) = 0$ where

$$\bar{A}_{c,i}(\tau, x_{n+1}) = A_i - B_{2,i}\tilde{R}^{-1}\tilde{S}_i(\tau, x_{n+1}), \\ \bar{B}_{c,i}(\tau, x_{n+1}) = -(X(\tau, x_{n+1})B_{3,i} + C'_1 D_{13}) + \tilde{S}'_i(\tau, x_{n+1})\mathbf{C}_u \text{ for } i = 1, 2.$$

Moreover, the parametrized value at $\tau = 0$ of performance index by the optimal input $u^*_{c,i}$ for $i = 1, 2$ is

$$J(t_1) = J(x_{n+1}) = V(x_0, 0, x_{n+1}) \\ = x'_0 X(0, x_{n+1})x_0 + 2\theta'(0, x_{n+1})x_0 + (x_{n+1} - t_0)\int_0^1 \delta\bar{J}_{c,1}(r_c, \tau, x_{n+1})d\tau \\ +(T - x_{n+1})\int_1^2 \delta\bar{J}_{c,2}(r_c, \tau, x_{n+1})d\tau \quad (14)$$

where

$$\delta\bar{J}_{c,i}(r_c, \tau, x_{n+1}) = \delta J_c(r_c, \tau, x_{n+1}) \\ +2\theta'(\tau, x_{n+1})B_{3,i}r_c(\tau, x_{n+1}) \\ -2\theta'(\tau, x_{n+1})\mathbf{C}'_{\theta u,i}\tilde{R}'\mathbf{C}_u r_c(\tau, x_{n+1}) - \|\tilde{R}^{1/2}\mathbf{C}_{\theta u,i}\theta(\tau, x_{n+1})\|^2, \ i = 1, 2$$

and

$$\delta J_c(r_c, \tau, x_{n+1}) = \|D_{13} r_c(\tau, x_{n+1})\|^2 - \|\tilde{R}^{1/2} \mathbf{C}_u r_c(\tau, x_{n+1})\|^2.$$

Proof: See appendix.

Remark 4. In the case of the **causal** tracking problem, in which we do not consider any future information of tracking signals, the control strategy is

$$u^*_{c,1}(\tau, x_{n+1}) = -\tilde{R}^{-1}\tilde{S}_1 x(\tau, x_{n+1}) - \mathbf{C}_u r_c(\tau, x_{n+1}) \text{ for } 0 \leq \tau < 1, \quad (15)$$

$$u^*_{c,2}(\tau, x_{n+1}) = -\tilde{R}^{-1}\tilde{S}_2 x(\tau, x_{n+1}) - \mathbf{C}_u r_c(\tau, x_{n+1}) \text{ for } 1 \leq \tau \leq 2, \quad (16)$$

using the solution of the Riccati equation (8)-(9), and the parametrized value at $\tau = 0$ of performance index by the optimal input $u^*_{c,i}$ for $i = 1, 2$ is

$$\begin{aligned} J(t_1) &= J(x_{n+1}) = V(x_0, 0, x_{n+1}) \\ &= x_0' X(0, x_{n+1}) x_0 + (x_{n+1} - t_0) \int_0^1 \delta J_c(r_c, \tau, x_{n+1}) d\tau \\ &\qquad + (T - x_{n+1}) \int_1^2 \delta J_c(r_c, \tau, x_{n+1}) d\tau. \end{aligned} \quad (17)$$

By comparing the value of performance index in the case of the **noncausal** tracking with the one in the case of the **causal** numerically, we can quantitatively verify whether or not the tracking performance becomes better by the noncausal information of the tracking signal.

We can obtain the value of $J(x_{n+1})$ at $\tau = 0$ by solving (8)-(9) and (12)-(13) (for a fixed x_{n+1}) backward in τ along with the terminal conditions $X(T, x_{n+1}) = Q_f$ and $\theta(T, x_{n+1}) = 0$. Moreover how can we numerically calculate the gradient $dJ(x_{n+1})/dx_{n+1}$? We will describe the method of calculus of the gradient $dJ(x_{n+1})/dx_{n+1}$ in the next section.

4 Construction of an Algorithm for Numerical Computation

Our issue is to find the optimal point x_{n+1} at which the performance index including the tracking error is minimized. For this purpose, we need calculate the gradient $dJ(x_{n+1})/dx_{n+1}$.

Hence, throughout in this section, we assume the following condition for the reference signal $r_c(t)$.

A2 : r_c is at least C^2 class function.

We need calculate the gradient $dJ(x_{n+1})/dx_{n+1}$ according to the optimization algorithm. From (14), we obtain

$$\frac{dJ(x_{n+1})}{dx_{n+1}} = x_0' \frac{\partial X(0, x_{n+1})}{\partial x_{n+1}} x_0 + 2 \left(\frac{\partial \theta'(0, x_{n+1})}{\partial x_{n+1}} \right) x_0$$

$$+\int_0^1 \delta\bar{J}_{c,1}(r_c,\tau,x_{n+1})d\tau - \int_1^2 \delta\bar{J}_{c,2}(r_c,\tau,x_{n+1})d\tau$$
$$+(x_{n+1}-t_0)\int_0^1 \frac{\partial\delta\bar{J}_{c,1}}{\partial x_{n+1}}(r_c,\tau,x_{n+1})d\tau$$
$$+(T-x_{n+1})\int_1^2 \frac{\partial\delta\bar{J}_{c,2}}{\partial x_{n+1}}(r_c,\tau,x_{n+1})d\tau. \quad (18)$$

In order to obtain the value at x_{n+1} of this right hand side, we make calculus as follows.

By differentiatting (8) and (9), we have the following equation.

$$-\frac{\partial}{\partial\tau}\left(\frac{\partial X}{\partial x_{n+1}}\right) = A_1'X + XA_1 + C_1'C_1 - \tilde{S}_1'\tilde{R}^{-1}\tilde{S}_1$$
$$+(x_{n+1}-t_0)\left(\frac{\partial X}{\partial x_{n+1}}A_1 + A_1'\frac{\partial X}{\partial x_{n+1}}\right.$$
$$-(B_{2,1}'\frac{\partial X}{\partial x_{n+1}} + D_{12}'C_1)'\tilde{R}^{-1}(B_{2,1}'X + D_{12}'C_1)$$
$$\left.-(B_{2,1}'X + D_{12}'C_1)'\tilde{R}^{-1}(B_{2,1}'\frac{\partial X}{\partial x_{n+1}} + D_{12}'C_1)\right) \quad (19)$$

over the time interval $\tau \in [0,1)$ and

$$-\frac{\partial}{\partial\tau}\left(\frac{\partial X}{\partial x_{n+1}}\right) = -(A_2'X + XA_2 + C_1'C_1 - \tilde{S}_2'\tilde{R}^{-1}\tilde{S}_2)$$
$$+(T-x_{n+1})\left(\frac{\partial X}{\partial x_{n+1}}A_2 + A_2'\frac{\partial X}{\partial x_{n+1}}\right.$$
$$-(B_{2,2}'\frac{\partial X}{\partial x_{n+1}} + D_{12}'C_1)'\tilde{R}^{-1}(B_{2,2}'X + D_{12}'C_1)$$
$$\left.-(B_{2,2}'X + D_{12}'C_1)'\tilde{R}^{-1}(B_{2,2}'\frac{\partial X}{\partial x_{n+1}} + D_{12}'C_1)\right) \quad (20)$$

over the time interval $\tau \in [1,2]$. Note that $(\partial/\partial x_{n+1})(\partial/\partial\tau) = (\partial/\partial\tau)(\partial/\partial x_{n+1})$ and we have used the general Riccati equation (8)-(9) on these calculus.

Moreover, with respect to the terms including the tracking errors, we have

$$\frac{\partial\delta\bar{J}_{c,i}}{\partial x_{n+1}} = \frac{\partial\delta J_c}{\partial x_{n+1}}$$
$$+2\left(\frac{\partial\theta}{\partial x_{n+1}}\right)' B_{3,i}r_c(\tau,x_{n+1}) + 2\theta'(\tau,x_{n+1})B_{3,i}\frac{\partial r_c}{\partial x_{n+1}}$$
$$-\left\{2\left(\frac{\partial\theta}{\partial x_{n+1}}\right)' \mathbf{C}_{\theta u,i}'\tilde{R}'\mathbf{C}_u r_c(\tau,x_{n+1}) + 2\theta'(\tau,x_{n+1})\mathbf{C}_{\theta u,i}'\tilde{R}'\mathbf{C}_u\frac{\partial r_c}{\partial x_{n+1}}\right\}$$
$$-2\theta'(\tau,x_{n+1})\mathbf{C}_{\theta u,i}'\tilde{R}\mathbf{C}_{\theta u,i}\frac{\partial\theta}{\partial x_{n+1}},\ i=1,2$$

and

$$\frac{\partial \delta J_c}{\partial x_{n+1}} = 2r_c'(\tau, x_{n+1})D_{13}'D_{13}\frac{\partial r_c}{\partial x_{n+1}} - 2r_c'(\tau, x_{n+1})\mathbf{C}_u'\tilde{R}\mathbf{C}_u\frac{\partial r_c}{\partial x_{n+1}}.$$

Now we need the value of $\partial\theta/\partial x_{n+1}$ at $\tau \in [0, 2]$. By differentiatting $\partial\theta/\partial x_{n+1}$ with respect to $\tau \in [0, 2]$ and using the dynamics (12)-(13) of θ, we obtain the following equality.

$$\begin{aligned}
&\frac{\partial}{\partial \tau}\left(\frac{\partial \theta}{\partial x_{n+1}}\right) = \frac{\partial}{\partial x_{n+1}}\left(\frac{\partial \theta}{\partial \tau}\right) \\
&= -\bar{A}_{c,1}'\theta(\tau, x_{n+1}) - (x_{n+1} - t_0)\left\{\bar{A}_{c,1}'\frac{\partial \theta}{\partial x_{n+1}} + \frac{\partial \bar{A}_{c,1}'}{\partial x_{n+1}}\theta(\tau, x_{n+1})\right\} \\
&\quad +\bar{B}_{c,1}r_c(\tau, x_{n+1}) + (x_{n+1} - t_0)\left\{\frac{\partial \bar{B}_{c,1}}{\partial x_{n+1}}r_c(\tau, x_{n+1}) + \bar{B}_{c,1}\frac{\partial r_c}{\partial x_{n+1}}\right\}, \quad (21)
\end{aligned}$$

for $\tau \in [0, 1)$, where

$$\begin{aligned}
\frac{\partial \bar{A}_{c,1}}{\partial x_{n+1}} &= -B_{2,1}\tilde{R}^{-1}\frac{\partial \tilde{S}_1}{\partial x_{n+1}} = -B_{2,1}\tilde{R}^{-1}B_{2,1}'\frac{\partial X}{\partial x_{n+1}}, \\
\frac{\partial \bar{B}_{c,1}}{\partial x_{n+1}} &= -\frac{\partial X}{\partial x_{n+1}}B_{3,1} + \frac{\partial X}{\partial x_{n+1}}B_{2,1}\mathbf{C}_u.
\end{aligned}$$

Similarly, for $\tau \in [1, 2]$,

$$\begin{aligned}
&\frac{\partial}{\partial \tau}\left(\frac{\partial \theta}{\partial x_{n+1}}\right) = \frac{\partial}{\partial x_{n+1}}\left(\frac{\partial \theta}{\partial \tau}\right) \\
&= \bar{A}_{c,2}'\theta(\tau, x_{n+1}) - (T - x_{n+1})\left\{\bar{A}_{c,2}'\frac{\partial \theta}{\partial x_{n+1}} + \frac{\partial \bar{A}_{c,2}'}{\partial x_{n+1}}\theta(\tau, x_{n+1})\right\} \\
&\quad -\bar{B}_{c,2}r_c(\tau, x_{n+1}) + (T - x_{n+1})\left\{\frac{\partial \bar{B}_{c,2}}{\partial x_{n+1}}r_c(\tau, x_{n+1}) + \bar{B}_{c,2}\frac{\partial r_c}{\partial x_{n+1}}\right\} \quad (22)
\end{aligned}$$

where

$$\begin{aligned}
\frac{\partial \bar{A}_{c,2}}{\partial x_{n+1}} &= -B_{2,2}\tilde{R}^{-1}\frac{\partial \tilde{S}_2}{\partial x_{n+1}} = -B_{2,2}\tilde{R}^{-1}B_{2,2}'\frac{\partial X}{\partial x_{n+1}}, \\
\frac{\partial \bar{B}_{c,2}}{\partial x_{n+1}} &= -\frac{\partial X}{\partial x_{n+1}}B_{3,2} + \frac{\partial X}{\partial x_{n+1}}B_{2,2}\mathbf{C}_u.
\end{aligned}$$

Note that these equalities (8)-(9), (12)-(13), (19)-(20) and (21)-(22) are a set of ODEs for $X(\tau, x_{n+1})$, $\theta(\tau, x_{n+1})$, $\partial X/\partial x_{n+1}$ and $\partial\theta/\partial x_{n+1}$ with the boundary conditions

$$X(2, x_{n+1}) = Q_f, \quad \frac{\partial X}{\partial x_{n+1}}(2, x_{n+1}) = O, \quad \theta(2, x_{n+1}) = 0, \quad \frac{\partial \theta}{\partial x_{n+1}}(2, x_{n+1}) = 0$$

at $\tau = 2$.

Now we obtain the following modified algorithm to obtain the values of the gradients of the performance index and the optimal timing numerically.

– *Algorithm 2* (Modified Algorithm)

1) Set the iteration index $j = 0$. Choose an initial $x_{n+1}^j (= t_1^j)$. (Then $\tau = 1$.)
2) By solving an optimal noncausal tracking problem, find $J(x_{n+1}^j)$.
   In order to compute $J(x_{n+1}^j)$ numerically,
   2a) For the given x_{n+1}^j, solve (8)-(9) with $X(2, x_{n+1}) = O$.
   2b) For the given x_{n+1}^j, solve (12)-(13) with $\theta(2, x_{n+1}) = 0$ based on the information of r_c over the whole time interval $\tau \in [0, 2]$.
   2c) Collectting the values over $\tau \in [0, 2]$ obtained in 2a) and 2b), we do a numerical integration to obtain the value of $J(x_{n+1}^j)$ (cf.(14) in the non-causal case and (17) in the causal case)
3) Compute $(\partial J/\partial x_{n+1})(x_{n+1}^j)$ (and $(\partial^2 J/\partial^2 x_{n+1})(x_{n+1}^j)$ if second-order method is to be used).
   In order to compute $(\partial J/\partial x_{n+1})(x_{n+1}^j)$ numerically,
   3a) For the given x_{n+1}^j, solve (19)-(20) with $\partial X/\partial x_{n+1}(2, x_{n+1}) = O$ utilizing the result of 2a).
   3b) For the given x_{n+1}^j, solve (21)-(22) with $\partial \theta/\partial x_{n+1}(2, x_{n+1}) = 0$ utilizing the result of 2a), 2b) and 3a)
   3c) Collectting the values over $\tau \in [0, 2]$ obtained in 2a), 2b), 3a) and 3b), we do a numerical integration to obtain the value of $(\partial J/\partial x_{n+1})(x_{n+1}^j)$ (cf.(18)) Or, instead of 2) and 3),

2-3) For the given x_{n+1}^j, solve a set of ODEs (8)-(9), (12)-(13), (19)-(20) and (21)-(22) with $X(2, x_{n+1}) = O$, $\theta(2, x_{n+1}) = 0$, $\partial X/\partial x_{n+1}(2, x_{n+1}) = O$ and $\partial \theta/\partial x_{n+1}(2, x_{n+1}) = 0$ to obtain the value of $J(x_{n+1}^j)$ and $(\partial J/\partial x_{n+1})$ (x_{n+1}^j) numerically. (cf.(14)(17)(18))

4) Use some feasile direction method to update to be $x_{n+1}^{j+1} = x_{n+1}^j + \alpha^j$ $(\partial J/\partial x_{n+1})(x_{n+1}^j)$ (in the case of second-order method, $x_{n+1}^{j+1} = x_{n+1}^j - \alpha^j$ $(\partial^2 J/\partial x_{n+1}^2)^{-1}(\partial J/\partial x_{n+1})(x_{n+1}^j)$, e.g., refer to [21])
   (the stepsize α^j can be chosen using some stepsize rule, e.g.,Armijo's rule[3]).
   Set the iteration index $j = j + 1$.
5) Repeat Steps 2), 3), 4) and 5), until, for a given small number ϵ, $|\partial J/\partial x_{n+1}| < \epsilon$.

Remark 5. In order to obtain not only the initial value but also the value of the tracking error term numerically, we need not only the initial value but also the intermediate value of the solutions for the set of ODEs (8)-(9), (12)-(13), (19)-(20) and (21)-(22). For example, we set a sufficiently small sampling time and approximately calculate the value of the integral to obtain the values of the gradients dJ/dx_{n+1} at the switching instants.

Remark 6. Note that, as we have described in *Remark 4*, in the case of the **causal** tracking problem, we do not need any information with respect to the values of θ and $\partial\theta/\partial x_{n+1}$, which is different from the case of the **noncausal** tracking problem.

Remark 7. The Cases of More Than One Switching Times: It can be seen that there is no difficulty in applying the previous method to GSLQ tracking problems in the cases with more than one switchings as GSLQ problems not considering any tracking signals. In detail, we can construction the algorithm for the optimization as follows: Assuming that there exist K switchings, we can transcribe the original optimal tracking problem into an equivalent problem by introducing K new state variables x_{n+i}, $i = 1, \cdots, K$ which correspond to the switching instants t_i and satisfy

$$\frac{dx_{n+1}}{dt} = 0, \; x_{n+i}(0) = t_i.$$

The new independent time variable τ has the following piecewise linear relationship between t and τ.

$$t = \begin{cases} t_0 + (x_{n+1} - t_0)\tau, & 0 \leq \tau \leq 1 \\ x_{n+1} + (x_{n+2} - x_{n+1})(\tau - 1), & 1 \leq \tau \leq 2 \\ \cdots & \cdots \\ x_{n+K} + (T - x_{n+K})(\tau - K), & K \leq \tau \leq K+1. \end{cases}$$

Note that $\tau = 0$ corresponds to $t = t_0$, $\tau = 1$ corresponds $t = t_1$,..., and $\tau = K+1$ corresponds to $t = T$. Then, differentiating the Riccati equations and the dynamics of θ parametrized by $x_{n+1}, \cdots, x_{n+K}$, we can obtain additional equations for $\partial X/\partial x_{n+i}$ and $\partial \theta/\partial x_{n+i}$. Along with the boundary conditions $X(K+1, x_{n+1}, \cdots, x_{n+K}) = Q_f$, $\theta(K+1, x_{n+1}, \cdots, x_{n+K}) = 0$, $\partial\theta/\partial x_{n+i}(K+1, x_{n+1}, \cdots, x_{n+K}) = 0$ and $\partial X/\partial x_{n+i}(K+1, x_{n+1}, \cdots, x_{n+K}) = O$ for $1 \leq i \leq K$, we can resultant ODEs backwards in τ to find the values of X, θ and their derivatives with respect to x_{n+i} over $\tau \in [0, K+1]$.

Remark 8. With Regard to Second-Order Derivatives: If we need the second order derivatives of $J(x_{n+1})$ (e.g., refer to [21]) on the above nonlinear optimization algorithm, we can obtain the values by the following similar methods to the first order derivatives. In order to obtain the values of the second order derivatives of $J(x_{n+1})$, we need the values of $\partial^2 X/\partial x_{n+1}^2(\tau, x_{n+1})$ and $\partial^2\theta/\partial x_{n+1}^2(\tau, x_{n+1})$ over the whole time interval $\tau \in [0, 2]$. By taking the first and second-order differentiations of (8)-(9) and (12)-(13) with respect to x_{n+1}, we can form a set of ODEs. Along with the terminal and boundary conditions $X(2, x_{n+1}) = Q_f$, $\theta(2, x_{n+1}) = 0$, $\partial X/\partial x_{n+1}(2, x_{n+1}) = O$, $\partial\theta/\partial x_{n+1}(2, x_{n+1}) = O$, $\partial^2 X/\partial x_{n+1}^2(2, x_{n+1}) = O$, and $\partial^2\theta/\partial x_{n+1}^2(2, x_{n+1}) = O$, we can easily solve the set of ODEs for X, θ, $\partial X/\partial x_{n+1}$, $\partial\theta/\partial x_{n+1}$, $\partial^2 X/\partial x_{n+1}^2$, and $\partial^2\theta/\partial x_{n+1}^2$ and obtain the value of $d^2 J(\tau, x_{n+1})/dx_{n+1}^2$ at each x_{n+1}.

5 Conclusion

In this paper, we have studied the noncausal optimal timing and tracking problem for the switched systems. We have presented an optimization algorithm based on the time parametrization approach by X. Xu and P.J. Antsaklis ([19,22]). In order to obtain the values of the gradients of the performance index, we need to do numerical integration and have assumed the appropriate smoothness on the reference signals. In spite of these task of numerical integration and assumption on the reference signals, we can expect better tracking performance and more appropriate switching timings by the noncausal information of the reference signals. Our noncausal tracking theory can be also applied to more general embedded systems. To clarify relationship between switched and more general embedded systems from the point of view of noncausal tracking control is a very important issue to research.

References

1. Azuma, S.-i., Egerstedt, Wardi, Y.: Output-Based Optimal Timing Control of Switched Systems. In: Hespanha, J.P., Tiwari, A. (eds.) HSCC 2006. LNCS, vol. 3927, pp. 64–78. Springer, Heidelberg (2006)
2. Bengea, S.C., DeCarlo, R.A.: Optimal Control of Switching Systems. Automatica 41(1), 11–27 (2005)
3. Bertsekas, D.P.: Nonlinear Programming, 2nd edn., Athena Scientific (1999)
4. Cohen, A., Shaked, U.: Linear Discrete-Time H_∞-Optimal Tracking with Preview. IEEE Trans. Automat. Contr. 42, 270–276 (1997)
5. Devasia, S., Chen, D., Paden, B.: Nonlinear Inversion-Based Output Tracking. IEEE Trans. Automat. Contr. 41, 930–942 (1996)
6. Egerstedt, M., Azuma, S.-i., Wardi, Y.: Optimal Timing Control of Switched Linear Systems Based on Partial Information. Nonlinear Analysis 65, 1736–1750 (2006)
7. Gershon, E., Limebeer, D.J.N., Shaked, U., Yaesh, I.: Stochastic H_∞ Tracking with Preview for State-Multiplicative Systems. IEEE Trans. Automat. Contr. 49, 2061–2068 (2004)
8. Gershon, E., Shaked, U., Yaesh, I.: H_∞ Tracking of Linear Continuous-Time Systems with Stochastic Uncertainties and Preview. Int. J. Robust and Nonlinear Control 14, 607–626 (2004)
9. Gershon, E., Shaked, U., Yaesh, I.: H_∞ Control and Estimation of State-Multiplicative Linear Systems. LNCIS, vol. 318 (2005)
10. Kojima, A., Ishijima, S.: H_∞ performance of preview control systems. Automatica 39, 693–701 (2003)
11. Kojima, A., Ishijima, S.: H_∞ preview tracking in output feedback setting. Int. J. Robust and Nonlinear Control 14, 627–641 (2004)
12. Kojima, A., Ishijima, S.: Formulas on Preview and Delayed H^∞ Control. IEEE Trans. Automat. Contr. 51(12), 1920–1937 (2006)
13. Nakura, G.: H_∞ Tracking with Preview by State Feedback for Linear Jump Systems. Trans. of the Society of Instrument and Control Engneers (SICE) (in Japanese) 42(6), 628–635 (2006)
14. Nakura, G.: Stochastic H_∞ Tracking with Preview by State Feedback for a Linear Jump System. In: 35th Symposium on Control Theory in Japan, pp. 237–242 (2006)
15. Nakura, G.: H_∞ Tracking with Preview for Linear Systems with Impulsive Effects -State Feedback and Full Information Cases. In: The 17th IFAC World Congress, Seoul (accepted, to appear, 2008)
16. Nakura, G.: H_∞ Tracking with Preview by Output Feedbak for Linear Systems with Impulsive Effects. In: The 17th IFAC World Congress, Seoul (accepted, to appear, 2008)

17. Shaked, U., de Souza, C.E.: Continuous-Time Tracking Problems in an H_∞ Setting: A Game Theory Approach. IEEE Trans. Automat. Contr. 40(5), 841–852 (1995)
18. de Souza, C.E., Shaked, U., Fu, M.: Robust H_∞-Tracking: A Game Theory Approach. Int. J. Robust and Nonlinear Control 5, 223–238 (1995)
19. Xu, X., Antsaklis, P.J.: An Approach for Solving General Switched Linear Quadratic Optimal Control Problems. In: Proc. 40th IEEE Conf. Decision Control, pp. 2478–2483 (2001)
20. Xu, X., Antsaklis, P.J.: Optimal Control of Switched systems via Nonlinear Optimization Based on Direct Differentiations of Value Functions. Int. J. Contr. 75, 1406–1426 (2002)
21. Xu, X., Antsaklis, P.J.: Optimal Timing Control of a Class of Hybrid Autonomous Systems. International Journal of Hybrid Systems 3(1), 33–60 (2003)
22. Xu, X., Antsaklis, P.J.: Optimal Control of Switched Systems Based on Parameterization of the Switching Instants. IEEE Trans. Automat. Contr. 49(1), 2–16 (2004)

Appendix: Proof of Proposition 1

In this appendix, we give the proof of Proposition 1. This is the modification of the preview tracking control theory by U. Shaked and C.E. de Souza([17]) for the noncausal GSLQ tracking problem.

Proof of Proposition 1
Sufficiency: For $\tau \in [0, 1)$, not considering any preview or noncausal information, we can easily show

$$\begin{aligned}
&\frac{d}{d\tau}\{x'(\tau, x_{n+1})P(\tau, x_{n+1})x(\tau, x_{n+1})\} \\
&= (x_{n+1} - t_0)\{-\|z_c(\tau, x_{n+1})\|^2 \\
&\qquad +\|u(\tau, x_{n+1}) + \tilde{R}^{-1}\tilde{S}_1 x(\tau, x_{n+1}) + \mathbf{C}_u r_c(\tau, x_{n+1})\|^2_{\tilde{R}} \\
&\qquad -2x'(\tau, x_{n+1})\bar{B}_{c,1}(\tau, x_{n+1})r_c(\tau, x_{n+1}) + \delta J_c(r_c, \tau, x_{n+1})\}
\end{aligned}$$

where we have used the general Riccati equation (8)-(9). Now introducing the vector θ, which can include some preview information of the tracking signals,

$$\begin{aligned}
&\frac{d}{d\tau}\{\theta'(\tau, x_{n+1})x(\tau, x_{n+1})\} \\
&= \frac{\partial}{\partial\tau}\theta'(\tau, x_{n+1})x(\tau, x_{n+1}) \\
&\quad +(x_{n+1} - t_0)\theta'(\tau, x_{n+1})(\bar{A}_{c,1}x(\tau, x_{n+1}) + B_{2,1}\hat{u}_{c,1}(\tau, x_{n+1}) + B_{3,1}r_c(\tau, x_{n+1}))
\end{aligned}$$

where $\hat{u}_{c,1}(\tau, x_{n+1}) = u(\tau, x_{n+1}) + \tilde{R}^{-1}\tilde{S}_1 x(\tau, x_{n+1})$. As a result,

$$\begin{aligned}
&\frac{d}{d\tau}\{x'(\tau, x_{n+1})X(\tau, x_{n+1})x(\tau, x_{n+1})\} + 2\frac{d}{d\tau}\{\theta'(\tau, x_{n+1})x(\tau, x_{n+1})\} \\
&= (x_{n+1} - t_0)\{-\|C_1 x(\tau, x_{n+1}) + D_{12}u(\tau, x_{n+1}) + D_{13}r_c(\tau, x_{n+1})\|^2 \\
&\qquad +\|\hat{u}_{c,1}(\tau, x_{n+1}) + \mathbf{C}_u r_c(\tau, x_{n+1}) + \mathbf{C}_{\theta u,1}\theta(\tau, x_{n+1})\|^2_{\tilde{R}} \\
&\qquad +\delta\bar{J}_{c,1}(r_c, \tau, x_{n+1})\} \qquad (23)
\end{aligned}$$

where we have used the dynamics (12). Similarly, for $\tau \in [1,2]$, using the dynamics (13), we obtain

$$\begin{aligned}
&\frac{d}{d\tau}\{x'(\tau,x_{n+1})X(\tau,x_{n+1})x(\tau,x_{n+1})\} + 2\frac{d}{d\tau}\{\theta'(\tau,x_{n+1})x(\tau,x_{n+1})\} \\
&= (T - x_{n+1})\{-\|C_1 x(\tau,x_{n+1}) + D_{12}u(\tau,x_{n+1}) + D_{13}r_c(\tau,x_{n+1})\|^2 \\
&\qquad +\|\hat{u}_{c,2}(\tau,x_{n+1}) + \mathbf{C}_u r_c(\tau,x_{n+1}) + \mathbf{C}_{\theta u,2}\theta(\tau,x_{n+1})\|^2_{\tilde{R}} \\
&\qquad +\delta \bar{J}_{c,2}(r_c,\tau,x_{n+1})\} \qquad (24)
\end{aligned}$$

where $\hat{u}_{c,2}(\tau,x_{n+1}) = u(\tau,x_{n+1}) + \tilde{R}^{-1}\tilde{S}_2 x(\tau,x_{n+1})$. Integrating (23) and (24) from $\tau = 0$ to $\tau = 2$ piecewise, we obtain

$$\begin{aligned}
&x'(2,x_{n+1})P(2,x_{n+1})x(2,x_{n+1}) - x'(0,x_{n+1})P(0,x_{n+1})x(0,x_{n+1}) \\
&\qquad +2\theta'(2,x_{n+1})x(2,x_{n+1}) - 2\theta'(0,x_{n+1})x(0,x_{n+1}) \\
&= (x_{n+1} - t_0)\int_0^1 \{-\|z_c(\tau,x_{n+1})\|^2 + \delta \bar{J}_{c,1}(r_c,\tau,x_{n+1}) \\
&\qquad +\|\hat{u}_{c,1}(\tau,x_{n+1}) + \mathbf{C}_u r_c(\tau,x_{n+1}) + \mathbf{C}_{\theta u,1}\theta(\tau,x_{n+1})\|^2_{\tilde{R}}\}d\tau \\
&\qquad +(T - x_{n+1})\int_1^2 \{-\|z_c(\tau,x_{n+1})\|^2 + \delta \bar{J}_{c,2}(r_c,\tau,x_{n+1}) \\
&\qquad +\|\hat{u}_{c,2}(\tau,x_{n+1}) + \mathbf{C}_u r_c(\tau,x_{n+1}) + \mathbf{C}_{\theta u,2}\theta(\tau,x_{n+1})\|^2_{\tilde{R}}\}d\tau.
\end{aligned}$$

Including the noncausal part $\theta(\tau,x_{n+1})$ at time τ, we adopt

$$\begin{aligned}
\hat{u}^*_{c,1}(\tau,x_{n+1}) &= -\mathbf{C}_u r_c(\tau,x_{n+1}) - \mathbf{C}_{\theta u,1}\theta(\tau,x_{n+1}) \text{ for } \tau \in [0,1), \\
\hat{u}^*_{c,2}(\tau,x_{n+1}) &= -\mathbf{C}_u r_c(\tau,x_{n+1}) - \mathbf{C}_{\theta u,2}\theta(\tau,x_{n+1}) \text{ for } \tau \in [1,2]
\end{aligned}$$

as the optimal control strategy. By the terminal conditions $P(2,x_{n+1}) = Q_T$ and $\theta(2,x_{n+1}) = 0$, we get the result.

Necessity: Because of arbitrality of the reference signal $r_c(\cdot)$, by considering the case of $r_c(\cdot) \equiv 0$, one can easily deduce the necessity for the solvability of our GSLQ tracking problem. For the purpose, one can get the parametrized general Hamiltion-Jacobi equation by applying the standard dynamic programming method based on the principle of optimality. We can obtain the parametrized general Riccati equation (8)-(9) by restricting the form of the value function to be quadratic as follows:

$$V(x,\tau,x_{n+1}) = x'X(\tau,x_{n+1})x$$

(QED.)

Realization Theory for Discrete-Time Semi-algebraic Hybrid Systems

Mihály Petreczky[1,2] and René Vidal[2]

[1] Eindhoven University of Technology, P.O. Box 513, 5600 MB Eindhoven, The Netherlands
[2] Center for Imaging Science, Johns Hopkins University, Baltimore MD 21218, USA

Abstract. We present realization theory for a class of autonomous discrete-time hybrid systems called *semi-algebraic hybrid systems*. These are systems in which the state and output equations associated with each discrete state are defined by polynomial equalities and inequalities. We first show that these systems generate the same output as semi-algebraic systems and implicit polynomial systems. We then derive necessary and almost sufficient conditions for existence of an implicit polynomial system realizing a given time-series data. We also provide a characterization of the dimension of a minimal realization as well as an algorithm for computing a realization from a given time-series data.

1 Introduction

Realization theory is one of the central topics of control and systems theory. Its goals are to study the conditions under which the observed behavior of a system can be represented by a state-space representation of a certain type and to develop algorithms for finding a (preferably minimal) state-space representation of the observed behavior. Realization theory forms the theoretical foundation of model reduction and systems identification. It also plays an important role in filtering and control design.

The goal of this paper is to develop realization theory and algorithms for the class of *autonomous discrete-time semi-algebraic hybrid systems*. Semi-algebraic hybrid systems (SAHSs) are characterized by the following two properties. First, the state and output trajectories are obtained by switching between various continuous subsystems. Second, the state-transition and output maps of each continuous subsystem are semi-algebraic functions, that is functions defined by polynomial equalities and inequalities. Particular examples of semi-algebraic functions are polynomial maps, piecewise-polynomial maps and piecewise-affine maps. The class of SAHSs includes important classes of discrete-time dynamical systems, such as *linear systems*, *polynomial systems*, and *piecewise-affine* hybrid systems. Furthermore, notice that semi-algebraic continuous state-transition maps can be used to encode discrete-state transition maps, semi-algebraic resets maps and guards. Hence, the class of SAHSs does implicitly allow for guards and resets. In this paper, we will deal only with *autonomous* SAHSs.

Papers contributions. We present a necessary condition for existence of an SAHS realization. The condition is formulated in terms of the finiteness of the (Krull) dimension of the algebra generated by the system outputs. We call this condition the *algebraic Hankel-rank* condition, as it is a natural generalization of the well-known Hankel-rank condition for linear systems. We show that the dimension of a minimal realization is

M. Egerstedt and B. Mishra (Eds.): HSCC 2008, LNCS 4981, pp. 386–400, 2008.

bounded from below by the algebraic Hankel-rank. We also present an algorithm for computing an almost minimal SAHS realization from a given time-series data.

The results of the paper are based on the following behavioral relationships.

1. **Semi-algebraic hybrid systems = semi-algebraic systems.** We will show that the output of an SAHS can be generated by a discrete-time system with semi-algebraic state-transition and output maps. The converse is trivially true.
2. **Semi-algebraic systems $\subseteq$ implicit polynomial systems.** We will show that the output of a dynamical system with semi-algebraic equations can be expressed as the output of a dynamical system defined by means of implicit polynomial equations.
3. **Implicit polynomial systems $\subseteq$ semi-algebraic hybrid systems.** We will show that the output of a dynamical system given by implicit polynomial equations can be generated by an SAHS. In fact, the switching signal of the hybrid system indicates which solution of the implicit polynomial equations should be chosen at each time.

By exploring the above relationships, we will be able to solve the realization problem for SAHSs by solving the realization problem for implicit polynomial systems. The solution of the latter problem is closely related to, and is inspired by, the work of Sontag [2] on discrete-time polynomial systems. The main difference with respect to [2] is that the algebras we work with are no longer integral domains.

The approach proposed in this paper bears a close resemblance to the algebraic-geometric approach to identification of switched autoregressive exogenous (SARX) systems of Vidal et al. [19,20,21]. In fact, the reduction of the realization problem for hybrid systems to finding implicit polynomial equations is analogous to the idea of the *hybrid decoupling polynomial* of [19,20,21]. The main differences lie in the classes of systems that are investigated and in the goals. The work of [19,20,21] investigates SARX systems and aims to obtain an SARX representation. Here we study systems which are autonomous, but otherwise more general than SARX systems, and aim to obtain a *more general* semi-algebraic hybrid system representation from the output data.

Prior work. The realization problem is well studied for deterministic and stochastic linear systems thanks to the works of Kalman and others (see e.g., [29,30]). For bilinear and smooth/analytic nonlinear systems, the realization problem is also well understood thanks to the works of Sussmann, Jakubczyk, Sontag, Fliess, Isidori and others (see e.g., [1,5,6,7,2,3,4]). However, the algorithmic aspects of the theory are not fully developed for general nonlinear systems. There are important results on realization theory of polynomial and rational systems developed by Bartoszewicz, Sontag, Wang, etc., [8,2,9]. However, the study of minimality and realization algorithms is not well understood. The work of Grossmann and Larson [10] is one of the first attempts to tackle realization of hybrid systems. However, a formal realization theory is not presented. More recently, several papers have dealt with realization theory of switched linear/bilinear systems [11,12,13], linear/bilinear hybrid systems without guards and with partially observed discrete states [14,13], nonlinear hybrid systems without guards [13,15], piecewise-linear hybrid systems [16,13], and stochastic jump-Markov linear systems [17,18].

Paper outline. The paper is organized as follows. §2 presents the necessary algebraic preliminaries. §3 formulates the realization problem and states the main result of the paper formally. §4 contains the sketch of the proofs of the main results along with the realization algorithm. §5 presents the conclusions and directions for future work.

2 Algebraic Preliminaries

In this section we review some basic results from commutative algebra and semi-algebraic geometry. The reader is referred to [22,23,24,25] for more details. In particular, the reader is encouraged to consult [23,22] for the definition and basic properties of Gröbner bases and Noether normalization. In what follows the term *algebra* denotes a commutative algebra over the field of real numbers $\mathbb{R}$, equipped with a unit element.

Polynomials in finitely many commuting variables. Let A be an algebra. Recall from [22,23] that $A[X_1, X_2, \ldots, X_n]$ is the algebra of polynomials in the commuting variables $X_1, \ldots, X_n$ over the algebra A. The elements of $A[X_1, X_2, \ldots, X_n]$ are finite formal sums

$$P = \sum_{\alpha_1,\ldots,\alpha_n \in I} a_{\alpha_1,\ldots,\alpha_n} X_1^{\alpha_1} X_2^{\alpha_2} \cdots X_n^{\alpha_n},$$

where $a_{\alpha_1,\ldots,\alpha_n} \in A$ and I is a finite set of natural numbers (possibly including zero). We will identify X_i^0 with the unit element 1 of A for all $i = 1, \ldots, n$. If we want to emphasize the dependence of P on the variables $X_1, X_2, \ldots, X_n$, we will write $P(X_1, X_2, \ldots, X_n)$ instead of P.

Semi-algebraic sets and maps. Recall from [24,25] that a subset $S \subseteq \mathbb{R}^n$ is called *semi-algebraic* if it is of the form

$$S = \{(x_1, \ldots, x_n) \in \mathbb{R}^n \mid \bigvee_{i=1}^{d} \bigwedge_{j=1}^{m_i} (P_{i,j}(x_1, \ldots, x_n) \;\; \epsilon_{i,j} \;\; 0)\},$$

where for each $i = 1, \ldots, d$ and $j = 1, \ldots, m_i$ the symbol $\epsilon_{i,j}$ belongs to the set of symbols $\{<, >, \leq, \geq, =\}$ and $P_{i,j}$ is a polynomial in $\mathbb{R}[X_1, \ldots, X_n]$. Here $\bigvee$ stands for the *logical or* operator and $\bigwedge$ stands for the *logical and* operator. Consider a subset V of $\mathbb{R}^n$ and a map $f : V \to \mathbb{R}^m$. Recall from [24,25] that the map f is said to be a *semi-algebraic map*, if the graph of f is a semi-algebraic set.

Finitely generated algebra. Let A be an algebra and let $x_1, \ldots, x_n \in A$. Denote by $\mathbb{R}[x_1, \ldots, x_n]$ the smallest sub-algebra of A which contains $x_1, \ldots, x_n$. We will call $\mathbb{R}[x_1, \ldots, x_n]$ the *algebra generated* by $x_1, \ldots, x_n$. The algebra A is called *finitely generated* if there exist finitely many elements $x_1, \ldots, x_n$ of A such that $A = \mathbb{R}[x_1, \ldots, x_n]$.

Krull-dimension of a finitely generated algebra. Consider a finitely generated algebra $A = \mathbb{R}[x_1, \ldots, x_n]$. Consider elements $z_1, \ldots, z_d$ of A. We will say that $z_1, \ldots, z_d$ are *algebraically independent*, if the only polynomial $Q \in \mathbb{R}[Z_1, \ldots, Z_d]$ such that $Q(z_1, \ldots, z_d) = 0$ is the zero polynomial. Here, $Q(z_1, \ldots, z_n)$ is the element of A obtained from Q by substituting for each variable Z_i the element z_i and evaluating the resulting expression using the addition and multiplication operations in A. The Krull-dimension of A is the *maximal number of algebraically independent elements of* A. We refer to the *Krull-dimension* of A simply as the *dimension* of A and denote it by $\dim A$.

Algebra of time-series. The algebra of time-series plays a crucial role in this paper. Consider the set $\mathbb{R}^\infty$ of all infinite sequences of real numbers. A typical element of $\mathbb{R}^\infty$ is of the form $(b(n))_{n\in\mathbb{N}}$, where $b(n) \in \mathbb{R}$ for all n. We will also refer to the elements of $\mathbb{R}^\infty$ as time-series, by interpreting a sequence as a sequence of measured system outputs. We define the addition and multiplication of time-series point-wise. That is, given two time-series $(a(n))_{n\in\mathbb{N}}$ and $(b(n))_{n\in\mathbb{N}}$, their sum is defined as the time-series $(a(n))_{n\in\mathbb{N}} + (b(n))_{n\in\mathbb{N}} = (a(n) + b(n))_{n\in\mathbb{N}}$, and their product is defined as the time-series $(a(n))_{n\in\mathbb{N}} \cdot (b(n))_{n\in\mathbb{N}} = (a(n)b(n))_{n\in\mathbb{N}}$. It is easy to see that, with the operations above, $\mathbb{R}^\infty$ forms an algebra. Its null element is the time-series in which every element is zero. Its identity element is the time-series where each element is 1. Moreover, each real number x can be identified with the time-series where each element is equal to x.

3 Problem Formulation and Statement of the Main Results

The goals of this section are to define formally the notions of semi-algebraic systems (§3.1), semi-algebraic hybrid systems (§3.2) and implicit polynomial systems (§3.3), and to state the main results on realization theory and minimality for these classes of systems (§3.4). The proofs of these results together with a realization algorithm will be presented in the next section.

Before proceeding further, let us fix some notation and terminology. Throughout the paper we will look at discrete-time systems, i.e. our time axis will be the set of natural numbers including zero. We will denote the time axis by $\mathbb{N}$ and hence $0 \in \mathbb{N}$. Also, we will use $(\tilde{\mathbf{y}}(k))_{k\in\mathbb{N}} \in \mathbb{R}^p$ to denote $\mathbb{R}^p$ valued time-series, i.e. $\tilde{\mathbf{y}}(k) \in \mathbb{R}^p$, $k \in \mathbb{N}$. For each $i = 1, 2, \ldots, p$, we will denote by $\tilde{\mathbf{y}}_i(k)$ the ith coordinate of the vector $\tilde{\mathbf{y}}(k)$.

3.1 Semi-algebraic Systems

A *semi-algebraic system* (SAS) is a discrete-time system of the form

$$\mathcal{S}_p : \begin{cases} \mathbf{x}(k+1) = f(\mathbf{x}(k)), & \mathbf{x}(0) = \mathbf{x}_0, \\ \mathbf{y}(k) = h(\mathbf{x}(k)), & \end{cases} \tag{1}$$

where for each $k \in \mathbb{N}$, the *state* $\mathbf{x}(k)$ at time k belongs to $\mathbb{R}^n$ and the *output* $\mathbf{y}(k)$ at time k belongs to $\mathbb{R}^p$. The *state-transition* map $f : \mathbb{R}^n \to \mathbb{R}^n$ and the *readout map* $h : \mathbb{R}^n \to \mathbb{R}^p$ are semi-algebraic maps. The state $\mathbf{x}_0$ is the *initial state* of the system. It is clear that the external behavior of (1) can be characterized by the time-series $(\mathbf{y}(k))_{k\in\mathbb{N}}$.

Definition 1 (Realization by SASs). *We will say that a system $\mathcal{S}_p$ of the form* (1) *is a realization of $\mathcal{Y} = (\tilde{\mathbf{y}}(k))_{k\in\mathbb{N}} \in \mathbb{R}^p$ if for all time instants $k \in \mathbb{N}$, $\tilde{\mathbf{y}}(k) = \mathbf{y}(k)$.*

We define the *dimension* of $\mathcal{S}_p$, denoted by $\dim \mathcal{S}_p$, as the number of state variables, i.e. $\dim \mathcal{S}_p = n$. Assume that $\mathcal{S}_p$ is a realization of a time-series $\mathcal{Y}$. We will say that $\mathcal{S}_p$ is a *minimal realization* of $\mathcal{Y}$ if $\mathcal{S}_p$ is a realization of $\mathcal{Y}$ that has the smallest possible dimension among all possible SASs that realize $\mathcal{Y}$.

3.2 Semi-algebraic Hybrid Systems

A *semi-algebraic hybrid system* (SAHS) is a discrete-time hybrid (switched) system of the form

$$\mathcal{H}_p : \begin{cases} \mathbf{x}(k+1) = f_{q(k)}(\mathbf{x}(k)), & \mathbf{x}(0) = \mathbf{x}_0, \\ \mathbf{y}(k) = h_{q(k)}(\mathbf{x}(k)), \end{cases} \tag{2}$$

where $\mathbf{x}(k) \in \mathbb{R}^n$ denotes the *continuous state* at time $k \in \mathbb{N}$, $\mathbf{x}_0$ denotes the *initial state* of the system, $\mathbf{y}(k) \in \mathbb{R}^p$ denotes the *continuous output* at time $k \in \mathbb{N}$, and $q(k) \in Q$ denotes the *discrete mode* at time $k \in \mathbb{N}$. Here we assume that the set Q is *finite*. The switching signal $(q(k))_{k\in\mathbb{N}}$ is assumed to be arbitrary. Also, for each discrete mode $q \in Q$, the maps $f_q : \mathbb{R}^n \to \mathbb{R}^n$ and $h_q : \mathbb{R}^n \to \mathbb{R}^p$ are assumed to be semi-algebraic, hence the name semi-algebraic hybrid systems. The definition of a realization for an SAHS is analogous to Definition 1.

Definition 2 (Realization by SAHSs). *An SAHS $\mathcal{H}_p$ of the form* (2) *is a realization of $\mathcal{Y} = (\tilde{\mathbf{y}}(k))_{k\in\mathbb{N}} \in \mathbb{R}^p$ if for all $k \in \mathbb{N}$, $\tilde{\mathbf{y}}(k) = \mathbf{y}(k)$.*

We will call the number continuous state variables n the *dimension* of $\mathcal{H}_p$, and we will denote it by $\dim \mathcal{H}_p$, i.e. $\dim \mathcal{H}_p = n$. We will call an SAHS $\mathcal{H}_p$ a *minimal* realization of $\mathcal{Y}$ if $\mathcal{H}_p$ is a realization of $\mathcal{Y}$ with the smallest dimension among all possible SAHS realizations of $\mathcal{Y}$. One may wonder whether this definition of minimality is justified, as it does not take into the account the number of discrete modes. We think this is an interesting direction to explore. However, we are not aware of any work in this direction.

3.3 Implicit Polynomial Systems

An *implicit polynomial system* (IPS) is a discrete-time dynamical system of the form

$$\mathcal{P}_p : \begin{cases} Q_i(\mathbf{x}_i(k+1), \mathbf{x}_1(k), \dots, \mathbf{x}_n(k)) = 0 \text{ for all } i = 1, \dots, n \\ P_j(\mathbf{y}_j(k), \mathbf{x}_1(k), \dots, \mathbf{x}_n(k)) = 0 \text{ for all } j = 1, \dots, p. \end{cases} \tag{3}$$

In the above equation, $\mathbf{x}(k) = (\mathbf{x}_1(k), \dots, \mathbf{x}_n(k))^\top \in \mathbb{R}^n$ is the *continuous state* at time $k \in \mathbb{N}$, $\mathbf{y}(k) = (\mathbf{y}_1(k), \mathbf{y}_2(k), \dots, \mathbf{y}_p(k))^\top \in \mathbb{R}^p$ is the *continuous output* at time $k \in \mathbb{N}$, $\mathbf{x}(0) = \mathbf{x}_0$ is the *initial state* of the system, and for each $i = 1, \dots, n$ and $j = 1, \dots, p$, $Q_i(Z_0, Z_1, \dots, Z_n)$ and $P_j(Z_0, Z_1, \dots, Z_n)$ are polynomials in the variables $Z_0, \dots, Z_n$ with real coefficients. In addition, we will assume the following.

Assumption 1. *For all $k \in \mathbb{N}$, $i = 1, \dots, n$, and $j = 1, \dots, p$, $P_j(Z_0, \mathbf{x}_1(k), \dots, \mathbf{x}_n(k))$ and $Q_i(Z_0, \mathbf{x}_1(k), \dots, \mathbf{x}_n(k))$ are non-zero polynomials in Z_0.*

If the assumption above fails for some k, then one of the components of $\mathbf{y}(k)$ or $\mathbf{x}(k+1)$ can be chosen indepently of the state $\mathbf{x}(k)$.

Notice that the state and output of (3) at time k are not determined solely by the initial state $\mathbf{x}(0) = \mathbf{x}_0$. The reason for this is that the current state determines the next state and the current output *implicitly*, and hence several valid choices for the output and next state may exist. In the sequel, whenever we speak of an IPS of the form (3), we will always assume that a specific state trajectory $(\mathbf{x}(k))_{k\in\mathbb{N}}$ and output trajectory $(\mathbf{y}(k))_{k\in\mathbb{N}}$ is fixed, such that $(\mathbf{x}(k))_{k\in\mathbb{N}}$ and $(\mathbf{y}(k))_{k\in\mathbb{N}}$ satisfy (3).

Definition 3 (Realization by IPSs). *An IPS $\mathcal{P}_p$ of the form (3) with state trajectory $(\mathbf{x}(k))_{k\in\mathbb{N}} \in \mathbb{R}^n$ and output trajectory $(\mathbf{y}(k))_{k\in\mathbb{N}} \in \mathbb{R}^p$ is said to be a realization of the time-series $\mathcal{Y} = (\tilde{\mathbf{y}}(k))_{k\in\mathbb{N}} \in \mathbb{R}^p$ if for all $k \in \mathbb{N}$, $\tilde{\mathbf{y}}(k) = \mathbf{y}(k)$.*

As before, we define the *dimension* of an IPS $\mathcal{P}_p$ of the form (3), denoted by $\dim \mathcal{P}_p$, to be the number of state variables, i.e. $\dim \mathcal{P}_p = n$. An IPS $\mathcal{P}_p$ is said to be a *minimal realization* of $\mathcal{Y}$ if $\mathcal{P}_p$ is a realization of $\mathcal{Y}$ that has the smallest dimension among all possible IPSs that realize $\mathcal{Y}$.

3.4 Main Results

In what follows, we state the main results of the paper on realization of SASs, SAHSs, and IPSs. We begin with Theorem 1, which states the main result on output equivalence of these systems. Then in Theorems 2–4 we state the main results on existence and minimality of realizations. The proof of Theorem 1 (see §4.1) yields a number of procedures for converting systems from one of these classes to the others. Before stating the theorem formally, we need to introduce some notation for each one of these transformations.

Notation 1. *The proof of Theorem 1 yields the following transformations.*

Procedure for transforming SAHSs to SASs. *Given an SAHS $\mathcal{H}_p$, we will denote by $SA(\mathcal{H}_p)$ the SAS which is the outcome of this procedure if applied to $\mathcal{H}_p$.*

Procedure for transforming SASs to IPSs. *Given an SAS $\mathcal{S}_p$, we will denote by $IP(\mathcal{S}_p)$ the IPS which is the outcome of this procedure if applied to $\mathcal{S}_p$.*

Procedure for transforming IPSs to SAHSs. *Given an IPS $\mathcal{P}_p$, we will denote by $SAH(\mathcal{P}_p)$ the SAH which is the outcome of this procedure if applied to $\mathcal{P}_p$.*

With this notation, we are ready to state the main result on equivalence of the output behaviors generated by these systems.

Theorem 1 (Equivalence of SASs, SAHSs and IPSs). *Let $\mathcal{S}_p$ be an SAS, $\mathcal{H}_p$ be an SAHS, and $\mathcal{P}_p$ be an IPS satisfying Assumption 1. Let $\mathcal{Y} = (\tilde{\mathbf{y}}(k))_{k\in\mathbb{N}} \in \mathbb{R}^p$ be a time-series. Then the following holds.*

- *$\mathcal{H}_p$ is a realization of $\mathcal{Y}$ if and only if $SA(\mathcal{H}_p)$ is a realization of $\mathcal{Y}$. In addition, $\dim SA(\mathcal{H}_p) = \dim \mathcal{H}_p + 1$.*
- *$\mathcal{S}_p$ is a realization of $\mathcal{Y}$ if and only if $IP(\mathcal{S}_p)$ is a realization of $\mathcal{Y}$. In addition, $\dim IP(\mathcal{S}_p) = \dim \mathcal{S}_p + 1$ and $IP(\mathcal{S}_p)$ satisfies Assumption 1.*
- *If $\mathcal{P}_p$ is a realization of $\mathcal{Y}$, then $SAH(\mathcal{P}_p)$ is a realization of $\mathcal{Y}$. In addition, $\dim SAH(\mathcal{P}_p) = \dim \mathcal{P}_p$.*

We now state the main result on existence of a realization by an IPS, and hence by an SAHS or SAS. To that end, recall from linear systems theory the definition of the Hankel-matrix $H_{\mathcal{Y}}$ associated with the time-series $\mathcal{Y} = (\tilde{\mathbf{y}}(k))_{k\in\mathbb{N}} \in \mathbb{R}^p$. The matrix $H_{\mathcal{Y}} \in \mathbb{R}^{\infty\times\infty}$ has an infinite number of rows and columns indexed by natural numbers, and the entry of $H_{\mathcal{Y}}$ indexed by $((l-1)p+i, j)$ with $j, l = 1, 2, 3, \ldots$, and $i = 1, \ldots, p$ equals $\tilde{\mathbf{y}}_i(l + j - 2)$. Let $H_{\mathcal{Y},N} \in \mathbb{R}^{pN\times\infty}$ be the matrix formed by all rows of $H_{\mathcal{Y}}$

indexed by indices of the form $k = lp + i$ with $l = 0, \ldots, N$ and $i = 1, \ldots, p$. That is, $H_{\mathcal{Y},N}$ is of the form

$$H_{\mathcal{Y},N} = \begin{bmatrix} \widetilde{\mathbf{y}}_1(0) & \widetilde{\mathbf{y}}_1(1) & \cdots & \widetilde{\mathbf{y}}_1(j) & \cdots \\ \vdots & \vdots & \vdots & \vdots & \vdots \\ \widetilde{\mathbf{y}}_i(l) & \widetilde{\mathbf{y}}_i(l+1) & \cdots & \widetilde{\mathbf{y}}_i(l+j) & \cdots \\ \vdots & \vdots & \vdots & \vdots & \vdots \\ \widetilde{\mathbf{y}}_p(N) & \widetilde{\mathbf{y}}_p(N+1) & \cdots & \widetilde{\mathbf{y}}_p(N+j) & \cdots \end{bmatrix}. \tag{4}$$

A classical result from linear systems theory is that the time-series $\mathcal{Y}$ admits an autonomous linear system realization if and only if the rank of the Hankel-matrix $H_{\mathcal{Y}}$ is finite, or equivalently, there is an upper bound on the ranks of the set of matrices $\{H_{\mathcal{Y},N}, N \in \mathbb{N}\}$. Below we will extend this well-known finite Hankel-rank condition to IPSs, by introducing the notion of *algebraic rank* of $H_{\mathcal{Y}}$.

Definition 4 (Hankel-algebra). *Define the sub-algebra $\mathcal{A}_{\mathcal{Y},N}$ of $\mathbb{R}^{\infty}$ as the sub-algebra generated by the rows of the matrix $H_{\mathcal{Y},N}$ viewed as scalar time-series. We will call the sub-algebra $\mathcal{A}_{\mathcal{Y},N}$ the* N-Hankel-algebra of $\widetilde{\mathbf{y}}$.

Definition 5 (Algebraic rank of the Hankel-matrix). *Define the algebraic rank of the Hankel-matrix $H_{\mathcal{Y}}$, denoted by alg-rank $H_{\mathcal{Y}}$, as the supremum of the Krull-dimensions of the N-Hankel-algebras. That is,*

$$\textit{alg-rank } H_{\mathcal{Y}} = \sup_{N \in \mathbb{N}} \dim \mathcal{A}_{\mathcal{Y},N}. \tag{5}$$

Remark 1 (Finite rank of the Hankel-matrix implies finite algebraic rank). *Notice that if the rank of the Hankel-matrix is finite, then its algebraic rank is also finite.*

Theorem 2 (Existence and minimality of an IPS realization). *A time-series $\mathcal{Y} = (\widetilde{\mathbf{y}}(k))_{k \in \mathbb{N}} \in \mathbb{R}^p$ has a realization by an IPS satisfying Assumption 1 only if the algebraic rank of the Hankel-matrix $H_{\mathcal{Y}}$ is finite. In addition, the dimension of any IPS realization $\mathcal{P}_p$ of $\mathcal{Y}$ satisfying Assumption 1 is at least alg-rank $H_{\mathcal{Y}}$. Moreover, if alg-rank $H_{\mathcal{Y}} = n < +\infty$, then we can construct an IPS realization of $\mathcal{Y}$ whose dimension is n, but which does not necessarily satisfy Assumption 1.*

We will say that an SAHS $\mathcal{H}_p$ is an *almost minimal* realization of $\mathcal{Y} = (\widetilde{\mathbf{y}}(k))_{k \in \mathbb{N}}$ if $\dim \mathcal{H}_p =$ alg-rank $H_{\mathcal{Y}}$ and $\mathcal{H}_p$ is a realization of $\mathcal{Y}$. We will say that an SAS $\mathcal{S}_p$ is an *almost minimal* realization of $\mathcal{Y}$ if $\mathcal{S}_p$ is a realization of $\mathcal{Y}$ and $\dim \mathcal{S}_p =$ alg-rank $H_{\mathcal{Y}}+1$. Combining Theorem 2 with Theorem 1 we get the following realization theorems.

Theorem 3 (Existence and minimality of an SAHS realization). *A time-series $\mathcal{Y} = (\widetilde{\mathbf{y}}(k))_{k \in \mathbb{N}} \in \mathbb{R}^p$ has a realization by an SAHS only if alg-rank $H_{\mathcal{Y}} < +\infty$. In addition, the dimension of a minimal SAHS realization of $\mathcal{Y}$ is at least alg-rank $H_{\mathcal{Y}}-2$. Moreover, if $\mathcal{Y}$ admits an IPS realization $\mathcal{P}_p$ such that $\dim \mathcal{P}_p =$ alg-rank $H_{\mathcal{Y}}$ and $\mathcal{P}_p$ satisfies Assumption 1, then $SAH(\mathcal{P}_p)$ is an almost minimal SAHS realization of $\mathcal{Y}$.*

Theorem 4 (Existence and minimality of an SAS realization). *A time-series $\mathcal{Y} = (\tilde{y}(k))_{k\in\mathbb{N}} \in \mathbb{R}^p$ has a realization by an SAS only if alg-rank $H_{\mathcal{Y}} < +\infty$. In addition, the dimension of a minimal SAS realization of $\mathcal{Y}$ is at least alg-rank $H_{\mathcal{Y}} - 1$. Moreover, if $\mathcal{Y}$ has an IPS realization $\mathcal{P}_p$ such that $\dim \mathcal{P}_p$ = alg-rank $H_{\mathcal{Y}}$ and $\mathcal{P}_p$ satisfies Assumption 1, then $SA(SAH(\mathcal{P}_p))$ is an almost minimal SAS realization of $\mathcal{Y}$.*

Theorems 2-4 establish conditions for existence and minimality of IPS, SAHS, and SAS realizations of $\mathcal{Y} = (\tilde{y}(k))_{k\in\mathbb{N}} \in \mathbb{R}^p$. In §4.3, we will show that under suitable assumptions one can actually construct a minimal IPS realization $\mathcal{P}_p$ from the rows of $H_{\mathcal{Y}}$. Furthermore, we will show that one can use $\mathcal{P}_p$ to construct an almost minimal SAHS realization of $\mathcal{Y}$ and an almost minimal SAS realization of $\mathcal{Y}$. Before delving into the details of these constructions, together with the corresponding realization algorithms, we shall provide in §4.1-§4.2 the proofs for Theorems 1-4.

4 Realization Construction

In this section, we sketch the constructions that lie at the heart of the proofs of Theorems 1–4. In §4.1 we present the proof of Theorem 1. In §4.2 we present the proof of Theorems 2–4. Finally, in §4.3 we discuss the algorithmic aspects of realization theory.

4.1 Proof of Theorem 1

The proof of Theorem 1 will be divided into the following three parts.

Definition of $SA(\mathcal{H}_p)$ and its properties. Consider an SAHS $\mathcal{H}_p$ of the form (2) and let $w = (q(k))_{k\in\mathbb{N}} \in Q$ be its switching signal. Since the set of discrete modes Q is finite, we can assume without loss of generality that Q is of the form $Q = \{1, 2, \ldots, d\}$. As shown in [16,27], this allows one to encode the switching signal w as a real number in the interval $[0, 1]$ by using the following procedure. Define the *encoding* $\psi(w)$ of w as $\psi(w) = \sum_{k=0}^{\infty} \frac{(q(k)-1)}{(2d)^{k+1}}$. It is easy to see that this series is absolutely convergent and that $0 \le \psi(w) < 1$. Recall also from [16,27] that there exist piecewise-affine operations $H : [0, 1] \to \mathbb{R}$ and $M : [0, 1] \to [0, 1]$ such that $H(\psi(w)) = q(0)$ and $M(\psi(w)) = \psi((q(k + 1))_{k\in\mathbb{N}})$. That is, $H(\psi(w))$ returns the first element of the sequence w, and $M(\psi(w))$ returns the encoding of the *shift* of w. For each $z \in [0, 1]$, these operations can be written explicitly as:

$$
\begin{aligned}
H(z) &= \begin{cases} i+1 & \text{if } i \le 2dz < i+1 \text{ for some } i = 0, \ldots, d-1 \\ d & \text{otherwise} \end{cases} \\
M(z) &= \begin{cases} 2dz - i & \text{if } i \le 2dz < i+1 \text{ for some } i = 0, \ldots, d-1 \\ z & \text{otherwise} \end{cases} .
\end{aligned} \tag{6}
$$

Furthermore, it is easy to see that H and M can be extended to piecewise-affine maps defined on the whole $\mathbb{R}$. We can then obtain $SA(\mathcal{H}_p)$ from $\mathcal{H}_p$ by adding a new state variable $\mathbf{z}(k)$ that equals the encoding $\psi((q(l+k))_{l\in\mathbb{N}})$ of the future switching sequence. That is

$$SA(\mathcal{H}_p):\begin{cases}\begin{bmatrix}\mathbf{x}(k+1)\\ \mathbf{z}(k+1)\end{bmatrix}=\begin{bmatrix}\widetilde{f}(\mathbf{x}(k),\mathbf{z}(k))\\ M(\mathbf{z}(k))\end{bmatrix}\\ \mathbf{y}(k)=\widetilde{h}(\mathbf{x}(k),\mathbf{z}(k))\end{cases}\tag{7}$$

where $\mathbf{x}(0)=\mathbf{x}_0$ coincides with the initial state of $\mathcal{H}_p$ and $\mathbf{z}(0)=\mathbf{z}_0=\psi(w)$, and the maps $\widetilde{f}$ and $\widetilde{h}$ are defined as

$$\begin{aligned}\widetilde{f}(x,z)&=\begin{cases}f_q(x) & \text{if } H(z)=q \text{ for some } q\in Q\\ f_d(x) & \text{otherwise}\end{cases}\\ \widetilde{h}(x,z)&=\begin{cases}h_q(x) & \text{if } H(z)=q \text{ for some } q\in Q\\ h_d(x) & \text{otherwise}\end{cases}\end{aligned}\tag{8}$$

It is easy to see that $\widetilde{f}$ and $\widetilde{h}$ are semi-algebraic maps. It is also easy to see that $\mathbf{y}(k)$ and $\mathbf{x}(k)$ in (7) are the same as $\mathbf{y}(k)$ and $\mathbf{x}(k)$ in (2) for all time instances $k\in\mathbb{N}$. Hence, the system in (7) is a well-defined SAS. Furthermore, it is a realization of $(\widetilde{\mathbf{y}}(k))_{k\in\mathbb{N}}$ if and only if $\mathcal{H}_p$ is a realization of $(\widetilde{\mathbf{y}}(k))_{k\in\mathbb{N}}$, and $\dim SA(\mathcal{H}_p)=\dim\mathcal{H}_p+1$.

Definition of $IP(\mathcal{S}_p)$ and its properties. Consider an SAS $\mathcal{S}_p$ of the form (1) with state transition map $f:\mathbb{R}^n\to\mathbb{R}^n$ and readout map $h:\mathbb{R}^n\to\mathbb{R}^p$. For all $i=1,\dots,n$ and $j=1,\dots,p$, denote by $f_i:\mathbb{R}^n\ni x\mapsto f_i(x)\in\mathbb{R}$ and $h_j:\mathbb{R}^n\ni x\mapsto h_j(x)\in\mathbb{R}$ the semi-algebraic maps obtained from the ith and jth coordinates of f and h, respectively. It follows from the proof of Proposition 8.13.7 in [24] that there exist polynomials in $\mathbb{R}[Z_0,\dots,Z_{n+1}]$, $\{Q_i(Z_0,\dots,Z_n,Z_{n+1})\}_{i=1}^n$ and $\{P_j(Z_0,\dots,Z_n,Z_{n+1})\}_{j=1}^p$, such that the following holds: There exists a *finite* subset of $\mathbb{R}$, $\mathcal{D}=\{d_1,\dots,d_M\}\subseteq\mathbb{R}$, such that for all $x_1,\dots,x_n\in\mathbb{R}$ there exists $\gamma=\gamma(x_1,\dots,x_n)\in\mathcal{D}$ such that $P_j(Z_0,x_1,\dots,x_n,\gamma)$ and $Q_i(Z_0,x_1,\dots,x_n,\gamma)$ are nonzero polynomials in Z_0, and

$$Q_i(f_i(x),x_1,\dots,x_n,\gamma)=0 \text{ and } P_j(h_j(x),x_1,\dots,x_n,\gamma)=0$$

for all $i=1,\dots,n$ and $j=1,\dots,p$. We can then define $IP(\mathcal{S}_p)$ as

$$\begin{aligned}Q_i(\mathbf{x}_i(k+1),\mathbf{x}_1(k),\dots,\mathbf{x}_{n+1}(k))&=0 \text{ for all } i=1,\dots,n+1\\ P_j(\mathbf{y}_j(k),\mathbf{x}_1(k),\dots,\mathbf{x}_{n+1}(k))&=0 \text{ for all } j=1,\dots,p\end{aligned}\tag{9}$$

where the polynomials Q_i,P_j for $i=1,\dots,n$, $j=1,\dots,p$ are as defined above and $Q_{n+1}(Z_0,\dots,Z_{n+1})=\Pi_{l=1}^M(Z_0-d_l)$. The first n state components $\mathbf{x}_1(k),\dots,\mathbf{x}_n(k)$ of $IP(\mathcal{S}_p)$ coincide with those of $\mathcal{S}_p$. The $n+1$st state is defined as $\mathbf{x}_{n+1}(k)=\gamma(\mathbf{x}_1(k),\dots,\mathbf{x}_n(k))\in\mathcal{D}$. The output trajectory of $IP(\mathcal{S}_p)$ is the same as that of $\mathcal{S}_p$. It follows that $IP(\mathcal{S}_p)$ is a well defined IPS satisfying Assumption 1. Moreover, $\mathcal{S}_p$ is a realization of $\mathcal{Y}$ if and only if $IP(\mathcal{S}_p)$ is a realization of $\mathcal{Y}$, and $\dim IP(\mathcal{S}_p)=\dim\mathcal{S}_p+1$.

Definition of $SAH(\mathcal{P}_p)$ and its properties. Let $\mathcal{P}_p$ be an IPS of the form (3) satisfying Assumption 1. Recall that by specifying $\mathcal{P}_p$ we fix a state-trajectory $(\mathbf{x}(k))_{k\in\mathbb{N}}$ and an output-trajectory $(\mathbf{y}(k))_{k\in\mathbb{N}}$ satisfying the equations in (3). Let d_i and r_j be, respectively, the degrees of the polynomials $Q_i(Z_0,Z_1,\dots,Z_n)$ and $P_j(Z_0,Z_1,\dots,Z_n)$ with respect to Z_0, for $i = 1, \ldots, n$, $j = 1, \ldots, p$. It follows from Proposition A.5 in [24] that there are semi-algebraic functions from $\mathbb{R}^n$ to $\mathbb{R}$, $\psi_{j,1}, \ldots, \psi_{j,r_j}$ and $\chi_{i,1}, \ldots, \chi_{i,d_i}$, $i = 1, \ldots, n$, $j = 1, \ldots, p$, such that for all $x_1, \ldots, x_n \in \mathbb{R}$, $Q_i(Z_0, x_1, \ldots, x_n)$ and $P_j(Z_0, x_1, \ldots, x_n)$ are non-zero polynomials over Z_0; if $Q_i(z, x_1, \ldots, x_n) = 0$, then $z = \chi_{i,l}(x_1, \ldots, x_n)$ for a unique $l = 1, \ldots, d_i$, and if $P_j(z, x_1, \ldots, x_n) = 0$, then $z = \psi_{j,k}(x_1, \ldots, x_n)$ for a unique $k = 1, \ldots, r_j$. We can then define $SAH(\mathcal{P}_p)$ as in (2), with the system parameters defined as follows. Let the set of discrete modes of $SAH(\mathcal{P}_p)$ be the set Q of all $n + p$ tuples $(\alpha_1, \ldots, \alpha_p, \beta_1, \ldots, \beta_n)$, where $\alpha_j = 1, \ldots, r_j$, and $\beta_i = 1, \ldots, d_i$, for all $j = 1, \ldots, p, i = 1, \ldots, n$. For each discrete mode $q \in Q$ of the form $q = (\alpha_1, \ldots, \alpha_p, \beta_1, \ldots, \beta_n)$ define

$$\begin{aligned} f_q(x_1, \ldots, x_n) &= \left[\chi_{1,\beta_1}(x_1, \ldots, x_n)\ \chi_{2,\beta_2}(x_1, \ldots, x_n) \cdots \chi_{n,\beta_n}(x_1, \ldots, x_n)\right]^T \\ h_q(x_1, \ldots, x_n) &= \left[\psi_{1,\alpha_1}(x_1, \ldots, x_n)\ \psi_{2,\alpha_2}(x_1, \ldots, x_n) \cdots \psi_{p,\alpha_p}(x_1, \ldots, x_n)\right]^T \end{aligned} \tag{10}$$

It is easy to see that f_q and h_q are semi-algebraic functions for all discrete modes $q \in Q$. It is left to define the initial state and the switching signal of $SAH(\mathcal{P}_p)$. Recall that $(\mathbf{x}(k))_{k\in\mathbb{N}}$ and $(\mathbf{y}(k))_{k\in\mathbb{N}}$ are, respectively, the state and output trajectory of $\mathcal{P}_p$. It follows from the discussion above and Assumption 1 that for each time instant $k \in \mathbb{N}$ there exist indices $\beta_i(k) \in \{1, \ldots, d_i\}$, $i = 1, \ldots, n$ and $\alpha_j(k) \in \{1, \ldots, r_j\}$, $j = 1, \ldots, p$, such that $\mathbf{x}_i(k + 1)$ equals $\chi_{i,\beta_i(k)}(\mathbf{x}_1(k), \ldots, \mathbf{x}_n(k))$ and $\mathbf{y}_j(k)$ equals $\psi_{j,\alpha_j(k)}(\mathbf{x}_1(k), \ldots, \mathbf{x}_n(k))$. Choose the switching signal $w = (q(k))_{k\in\mathbb{N}}$ as $q(k) = (\alpha_1(k), \ldots, \alpha_p(k), \beta_1(k), \ldots, \beta_n(k)) \in Q$ and the initial state as $\mathbf{x}(0) = \mathbf{x}_0$. We get that $(\mathbf{x}(k))_{k\in\mathbb{N}}$ and $(\mathbf{y}(k))_{k\in\mathbb{N}}$ are the state and output trajectories of $SAH(\mathcal{P}_p)$. In particular, this implies that $SAH(\mathcal{P}_p)$ is a realization of $(\widetilde{\mathbf{y}}(k))_{k\in\mathbb{N}}$. It is easy to see from the construction of $SAH(\mathcal{P}_p)$ that $\dim SAH(\mathcal{P}_p) = \dim \mathcal{P}_p$.

4.2 Proof of Theorems 2-4

Theorems 3 and 4 follow easily from Theorems 1 and 2. Therefore, it is enough to prove Theorem 2. We divide the proof of Theorem 2 into the following three parts.

Necessity. Assume that $\mathcal{Y} = (\widetilde{\mathbf{y}}(k))_{k\in\mathbb{N}}$ has an IPS realization $\mathcal{P}_p$ of the form (3) satisfying Assumption 1. Notice that the time-series $(\mathbf{x}_i(k))_{k\in\mathbb{N}} \in \mathbb{R}$, $i = 1, \ldots, n$, formed by the components of the state trajectory belong to $\mathbb{R}^\infty$. In addition, for each $j = 1, \ldots, p$ the time-series $(\widetilde{\mathbf{y}}_j(k))_{k\in\mathbb{N}} \in \mathbb{R}$, coincides with the time-series $(\mathbf{y}_j(k))_{k\in\mathbb{N}}$ formed by the jth coordinates of the output trajectory of $\mathcal{P}_p$. For each N denote by $\mathcal{B}_{\mathcal{P}_p,N}$ the sub-algebra of $\mathbb{R}^\infty$ generated by the rows of $H_{\mathcal{Y},N}$ and by the time-series $(\mathbf{x}_i(k + l))_{k\in\mathbb{N}}$, $i = 1, \ldots, n$ and $l = 0, \ldots, N$. It is easy to see that the N-Hankel-algebra $\mathcal{A}_{\mathcal{Y},N}$ is a sub-algebra of $\mathcal{B}_{\mathcal{P}_p,N}$. Moreover, using Corollary 3.7 of [22] we see that for each N, $\dim \mathcal{A}_{\mathcal{Y},N} \leq \dim \mathcal{B}_{\mathcal{P}_p,N}$. If we can show that $\dim \mathcal{B}_{\mathcal{P}_p,N} \leq n$, then it follows that alg-rank $H_{\mathcal{Y}} \leq n < +\infty$. To that end, consider any minimal prime ideal P of $\mathcal{B}_{\mathcal{P}_p,N}$ (see [22] for the definition of a minimal prime ideal of an algebra) and the sub-algebra $\mathcal{A}_x = \mathbb{R}[(\mathbf{x}_1(k))_{k\in\mathbb{N}}, \ldots, (\mathbf{x}_n(k))_{k\in\mathbb{N}}]$ of $\mathcal{B}_{\mathcal{P}_p,N}$. Using Assumption 1 it can be shown that $\mathcal{B}_{\mathcal{P}_p,N}/P$ is algebraic over $\mathcal{A}_x/(\mathcal{A}_x \cap P)$, and hence $\dim \mathcal{B}_{\mathcal{P}_p,N}/P \leq n$ for any minimal prime P. Since $\dim \mathcal{B}_{\mathcal{P}_p,N} = \max\{\dim \mathcal{B}_{\mathcal{P}_p,N}/P \mid P \text{ is a minimal prime}\}$ we get that $\dim \mathcal{B}_{\mathcal{P}_p,N} \leq n$.

Sufficiency. Assume that alg-rank $H_{\mathcal{Y}} = n < +\infty$. It follows that there exists N^* such that for all $k > 0$, $n = \dim \mathcal{A}_{\mathcal{Y},N^*} = \dim \mathcal{A}_{\mathcal{Y},N^*+k}$. Choose a Noether Normalization (see [22]) $(\mathbf{z}_i(k))_{k\in\mathbb{N}} \in \mathbb{R}$, $i = 1,\ldots,n$, of $\mathcal{A}_{\mathcal{Y},N^*}$. Then the time-series $(\mathbf{z}_1(k))_{k\in\mathbb{N}},\ldots,(\mathbf{z}_n(k))_{k\in\mathbb{N}}$ are algebraically independent and $\mathcal{A}_{\mathcal{Y},N^*+1}$ is algebraic over the algebra $\mathbb{R}[(\mathbf{z}_1(k))_{k\in\mathbb{N}},\ldots,(\mathbf{z}_n(k))_{k\in\mathbb{N}}]$. Therefore, there exist polynomials $Q_i(T_0,Z_1,\ldots,Z_n)$ and $P_j(T_0,Z_1,\ldots,Z_n)$, $i = 1,\ldots,n$, $j = 1,\ldots,p$ such that

$$\begin{aligned} Q_i(\mathbf{z}_i(k+1),\mathbf{z}_1(k),\ldots,\mathbf{z}_n(k)) &= 0 \text{ for all } i = 1,\ldots,n, k \in \mathbb{N} \\ P_j(\widetilde{\mathbf{y}}_j(k),\mathbf{z}_1(k),\ldots,\mathbf{z}_n(k)) &= 0 \text{ for all } j = 1,\ldots,p, k \in \mathbb{N}. \end{aligned} \tag{11}$$

It is then easy to see that (11) defines an IPS realization of $\mathcal{Y}$ with the state trajectory $(\mathbf{z}(k))_{k\in\mathbb{N}}$, $\mathbf{z}(k) = (\mathbf{z}_1(k),\ldots,\mathbf{z}_n(k)) \in \mathbb{R}^n$, $k \in \mathbb{N}$, and output trajectory $(\widetilde{\mathbf{y}}(k))_{k\in\mathbb{N}} \in \mathbb{R}^p$. We will call this IPS the *free realization* of $\mathcal{Y}$ and we will denote it by $\mathcal{P}_{\widetilde{\mathbf{y}}}$. Notice that $\mathcal{P}_{\widetilde{\mathbf{y}}}$ need not satisfy Assumption 1.

Minimality. The proof of the statement of Theorem 2 is now rather simple. First, from the proof of necessity of the finite algebraic rank of the Hankel-matrix, it follows that if $\mathcal{P}_p$ is an IPS realization of $(\widetilde{\mathbf{y}}(k))_{k\in\mathbb{N}}$ and $\mathcal{P}_p$ satisfies Assumption 1, then alg-rank $H_{\mathcal{Y}} \leq \dim \mathcal{P}_p$. From the proof of sufficiency it follows that the free realization $\mathcal{P}_{\widetilde{\mathbf{y}}}$ is an IPS realization of $(\widetilde{\mathbf{y}}(k))_{k\in\mathbb{N}}$ and $\dim \mathcal{P}_{\widetilde{\mathbf{y}}} =$ alg-rank $H_{\mathcal{Y}}$.

4.3 Realization Algorithms

In this section, we present realization algorithms for constructing an almost minimal IPS, SAS and SAHS realization of a time series. We first present a realization algorithm that returns the polynomials of an IPS realization $\mathcal{P}_p$ of the measured data along with a finite portion of the state trajectory. We then discuss how to use this algorithm for computing a minimal SAHS and SAS realization of the same series.

Throughout the section we will assume that the first $2M$ elements of the time series $\mathcal{Y} = (\widetilde{\mathbf{y}}(k))_{k\in\mathbb{N}}$ are measured for some $M \in \mathbb{N}$.

Realization algorithm for IPSs. The main idea behind the realization algorithm we are about to present is that each Hankel-algebra $\mathcal{A}_{\mathcal{Y},N}$, $N \in \mathbb{N}$, can be represented as a quotient of a polynomial ring with a suitable ideal I_N. Then, given a Gröbner basis for I_N, the computation of the polynomials defining $\mathcal{P}_p$ can be done using Gröbner-basis techniques. The following paragraphs describe the algorithm in more detail.

For each N, let $\mathbb{R}[T_N]$ be the ring of polynomials $\mathbb{R}[T_1,\ldots,T_{(N+1)p}]$ in the variables $T_1,\ldots,T_{(N+1)p}$. Also let I_N be the ideal of $\mathbb{R}[T_N]$ generated by all the polynomials that vanish on the set

$$V_N = \{(\widetilde{\mathbf{y}}(k)^\top,\ldots,\widetilde{\mathbf{y}}(k+N)^\top)^\top \in \mathbb{R}^{p(N+1)} \mid k \in \mathbb{N}\}. \tag{12}$$

Then, it is easy to see that $\mathcal{A}_{\mathcal{Y},N}$ is isomorphic to the quotient $\mathcal{A}_{\mathcal{Y},N} \cong \mathbb{R}[T_N]/I_N$. Denote by G_N the Gröbner-basis of I_N. Choose a number $D > 0$ representing our guess on the maximal degree of polynomials generating the ideals I_N. We are now ready to formulate the partial realization algorithm IPPartReal(M, D) for IPSs.

IPPartReal(M, D)

1: Set $N := 0$.
2: Compute the Gröbner basis of I_N and I_{N+1}
   $G_N :=$ ApproxIdeal(M, D, N), $G_{N+1} :=$ ApproxIdeal$(M, D, N+1)$.
3: Compute the Noether Normalization of G_N and G_{N+1}
   $(\{Y_1^l, \dots, Y_{d_l}^l\}, d_l) =$ NoetherNorm(l, G_l) for $l = N, N+1$.
4: If $(d_{N+1} > d_N)$ and $(N + 2 \leq M)$, then go back to Step 2 with $N := N+1$.
5: Compute the polynomials of the free IPS realization $\mathcal{P}_{\tilde{\mathbf{y}}}$ as follows.
   Let $d := d_N = d_{N+1}$.
   For each $i = 1, \dots, d$, let $Z_i(T_1, \dots, T_{(N+2)p}) := Y_i^N(T_{p+1}, T_{p+2}, \dots, T_{(N+2)p})$.
   For each $i = 1, \dots, d$, let $Q_i :=$ DepPoly$(N+1, Y_1^N, \dots, Y_d^N, Z_i, G_{N+1})$.
   For each $j = 1, \dots, p$, let $P_j :=$ DepPoly$(N+1, Y_1^N, \dots, Y_d^N, T_j, G_{N+1})$.
   For each $i = 1, \dots, d$, define $\mathbf{z}_i(k) := Y_i^N((\tilde{\mathbf{y}}(k)^\top, \dots, \tilde{\mathbf{y}}(k+N)^\top)^\top)$.
6: Return the IPS $\mathcal{P}_{\tilde{\mathbf{y}}}$ defined as

$$\mathcal{P}_{\tilde{\mathbf{y}}} \begin{cases} Q_i(\mathbf{z}_i(k+1), \mathbf{z}_1(k), \dots, \mathbf{z}_d(k)) = 0 \text{ for all } i = 1, \dots, d \\ P_j(\tilde{\mathbf{y}}_j(k), \mathbf{z}_1(k), \dots, \mathbf{z}_d(k)) = 0 \text{ for all } j = 1, \dots, p \end{cases} \tag{13}$$

Notice that the algorithm IPPartReal depends on several other algorithms, such as ApproxIdeal, NoetherNorm and ComputeDepPoly. Each one of these algorithms can be implemented using techniques from commutative algebra, as we describe next.

The algorithm ApproxIdeal(D, M, N) computes an approximation of the Gröbner-basis of I_N and proceeds as follows.

ApproxIdeal(D, M, N)

1: For each $l = 0, \dots, M$, let $I_{l,N}$ be the ideal generated by the polynomials $T_{kp+j} - \tilde{\mathbf{y}}_j(k+l)$ for each $k = 0, \dots, N$, and $j = 1, \dots, p$.
2: Compute the Gröbner-basis $G_{N,M}$ of the ideal $I_{N,M} = \bigcap_{l=0,\dots,M} I_{l,N}$ using the grlex ordering (see [23]). Return a Gröbner-basis of the ideal generated by those elements of $G_{N,M}$ that are of degree less than D.

The algorithm NoetherNorm(N, G_N) returns $d = \dim A_{\mathcal{Y},N}$ and a set of polynomials $Y_1, \dots, Y_d$ in $\mathbb{R}[\mathcal{T}_N]$ such that the substitutions

$$\mathbf{z}_i = Y_i((\tilde{\mathbf{y}}_1(k))_{k\in\mathbb{N}}, \dots, (\tilde{\mathbf{y}}_p(N+k))_{k\in\mathbb{N}}) \in \mathbb{R}^\infty \text{ for each } i = 1, \dots, d$$

yield a *Noether Normalization* $\mathbf{z}_1, \dots, \mathbf{z}_d$ of $\mathcal{A}_{\mathcal{Y},N}$. This algorithm is known to be computable from any finite basis G_N of the ideal I_N, as can be seen from the proof of the Noether Normalization Theorem (see [22]).

The algorithm DepPoly$(N, Y_1, \dots, Y_d, Z, G_N)$ returns a nontrivial polynomial Q in $d+1$ variables such that $Q(Z, Y_1, \dots, Y_d) \in I_N$ for polynomials $Z, Y_1, \dots, Y_d \in \mathbb{R}[\mathcal{T}_N]$, provided that such a polynomial Q exists. The algorithm proceeds as follows.

ComputeDepPoly($N, Y_1, \ldots, Y_d, Z, G_N$)

1: Introduce new variables $S_0, S_1, \ldots, S_d$ and define the ideal J of the polynomial ring $\mathbb{R}[S_0, \ldots, S_d, T_1 \ldots T_{(N+1)p}]$ as the ideal generated by the elements of the Gröbner-basis of G_N and the polynomials $S_0 - Z$ and $S_i - Y_i, i = 1, \ldots, d$.
2: Compute the Gröbner-basis $\hat{G}$ of the intersection $J \cap \mathbb{R}[S_0, S_1, \ldots, S_d]$, see [23] for an algorithm. Return an element Q of $\hat{G}$.

From the Algebraic Sampling Theorem stated in [28] it follows that if M and D are large enough, then ApproxIdeal(D, M, N) returns a Gröbner-basis of I_N. Hence, we get the following.

Lemma 1 (Partial realization). *Assume alg-rank $H_{\mathcal{Y}} < +\infty$. Then, if M and D are large enough, then the IPS $\mathcal{P}_{\tilde{\mathbf{y}}}$ returned by* IPPartReal(M, D) *is a realization of $\mathcal{Y} = (\tilde{\mathbf{y}}(k))_{k \in \mathbb{N}}$, and the dimension of $\mathcal{P}_{\tilde{\mathbf{y}}}$ is at most alg-rank $H_{\mathcal{Y}}$. If $\mathcal{P}_{\tilde{\mathbf{y}}}$ satisfies Assumption 1, then* $\dim \mathcal{P}_{\tilde{\mathbf{y}}} =$ *alg-rank $H_{\mathcal{Y}}$.*

The question that arises is how to check if the output of IPPartReal satisfies Assumption 1. To this end, we can assume without loss of generality that the polynomials from (13) are of the form $P_j = \sum_{r=0}^{K} Z_0^r P_{j,r}$ and $Q_i = \sum_{l=0}^{K} Z_0^l Q_{i,l}$ for some $K > 0$, where $P_{j,r}$ and $Q_{i,l}$ are polynomials in $Z_1, \ldots, Z_n$ for all $i = 1, \ldots, n$, and $j = 1, \ldots, p$. Assume that the Groebner-basis G_N of I_N is known. Denote by $\hat{Q}_{i,l}$ and $\hat{P}_{j,r}$ the polynomials in $\mathbb{R}[\mathcal{T}_N]$ obtained from $Q_{i,l}$ and $P_{j,r}$ by substituting Y_m for Z_m, $m = 1, \ldots, n$. It is easy to see that the IPS $\mathcal{P}_p$ returned by IPPartReal satisfies Assumption 1 if the zero set in $\mathbb{R}^{(N+1)p}$ of the ideal S_a generated by the set of polynomials $G_N \cup \{\hat{Q}_{i,l}, \hat{P}_{j,r} \mid i = 1, \ldots, n, j = 1, \ldots, p, l, r = 0, \ldots, K\}$ is empty. Checking emptiness of S_a can be done using techniques from algebraic geometry, for example, by using procedures for deciding emptiness of semi-algebraic sets, see [26].

Realization algorithm for SAHSs. Assume that $\mathcal{P}_p$ is the IPS returned by the algorithm IPPartReal. Assume that $\mathcal{P}_p$ satisfies Assumption 1 and it is a realization of $\mathcal{Y}$. Then, it follows that $SAH(\mathcal{P}_p)$ is an almost minimal SAH system realization of $\mathcal{Y}$ and $\dim SAH(\mathcal{P}_p) =$ alg-rank $H_{\mathcal{Y}}$. If the equations of the IPS $\mathcal{P}_p$ are known, then the equations of $SAH(\mathcal{P}_p)$ can be computed. However, in order to compute the initial state and the switching sequence of $SAH(\mathcal{P}_p)$ the knowledge of the states of $\mathcal{P}_p$ is required. Notice that IPPartReal also computes the state variables for time instances $k = 0, \ldots, M$.

Realization algorithm for SASs. We can proceed as follows. Use IPPartReal an IPS realization $\mathcal{P}_p$ of $\mathcal{Y}$. If $\mathcal{P}_p$ satisfies Assumption 1, we can use the procedure above to compute the equations and possibly the state of $\mathcal{H}_p = SAH(\mathcal{P}_p)$. It is easy to see that the knowledge of the equations of $\mathcal{H}_p$ allows us to compute the equations of $SA(\mathcal{H}_p)$. Unfortunately, the computation of the initial state of $SA(\mathcal{H}_p)$ is problematic, as it requires the knowledge of the whole infinite switching sequence. It follows that $SA(\mathcal{H}_p)$ is a realization of $\mathcal{Y}$ and $\dim SA(\mathcal{H}_p) =$ alg-rank $H_{\mathcal{Y}} + 1$.

5 Discussion and Future Work

We have presented necessary and an almost sufficient conditions for existence of a realization for implicit polynomial systems, semi-algebraic systems, and semi-algebraic hybrid systems, along with a characterization of minimality and a realization algorithm.

There are several potential directions for future research. To begin with, it would be desirable to find a sufficient condition for existence of a semi-algebraic realization. In addition, the relationship between minimality and such important properties as observability and reachability are not well-understood for semi-algebraic hybrid systems. Another potential research direction is to extend the results of the paper to systems with inputs, possibly stochastic. A third research direction could be to explore further the relationship between the approach presented in this paper and the works on identification using GPCA, see [19,20,21]. Extending the results of the paper to the continuous-time case represents a potential research direction as well. Investigating the computation complexity of the presented realization algorithm, remains a topic of future research.

Acknowledgements. This work was supported by grants NSF EHS-05-09101, NSF CAREER IIS-04-47739, and ONR N00014-05-1083.

References

1. Isidori, A.: Nonlinear Control Systems. Springer, Heidelberg (1989)
2. Sontag, E.D.: Polynomial Response Maps. Lecture Notes in Control and Information Sciences, vol. 13. Springer, Heidelberg (1979)
3. Sontag, E.D.: Realization theory of discrete-time nonlinear systems: Part I – the bounded case. IEEE Transaction on Circuits and Systems CAS-26(4) (1979)
4. Fliess, M.: Matrices de Hankel. J. Math. Pures Appl. (23), 197–224 (1973)
5. Sussmann, H.: Existence and uniqueness of minimal realizations of nonlinear systems. Mathematical Systems Theory 10, 263–284 (1977)
6. Jakubczyk, B.: Realization theory for nonlinear systems, three approaches. In: Fliess, M., Hazewinkel, M., (eds.) Algebraic and Geometric Methods in Nonlinear Control Theory, pp. 3–32. D. Reidel Publishing Company (1986)
7. Wang, Y., Sontag, E.: Generating series and nonlinear systems: analytic aspects, local realizability and I/O representations. Forum Mathematicum (4), 299–322 (1992)
8. Bartosiewicz, Z.: Realizations of polynomial systems. In: Algebraic and geometric methods in nonlinear control theory., Math. Appl., vol. 29, pp. 45–54. Dordrecht, Reidel (1986)
9. Wang, Y., Sontag, E.: Algebraic differential equations and rational control systems. SIAM Journal on Control and Optimization (30), 1126–1149 (1992)
10. Grossman, R., Larson, R.: An algebraic approach to hybrid systems. Theoretical Computer Science 138, 101–112 (1995)
11. Petreczky, M.: Realization theory for linear switched systems: Formal power series approach. Systems and Control Letters 56(9-10), 588–595 (2007)
12. Petreczky, M.: Realization theory for bilinear switched systems: A formal power series approach. In: Proc. of 44th IEEE Conference on Decision and Control, pp. 690–695 (2005)
13. Petreczky, M.: Realization Theory of Hybrid Systems. PhD thesis, Vrije Universiteit, Amsterdam (2006), `http://www.cwi.nl/~mpetrec`
14. Petreczky, M.: Hybrid formal power series and their application to realization theory of hybrid systems. In: Proc. 17th International Symposium on Mathematical Theory of Networks and Systems (2006)

15. Petreczky, M., Pomet, J.B.: Realization theory of nonlinear hybrid systems. In: Proceedings of CTS-HYCON Workshop on Hybrid and Nonlinear Control Systems (2006)
16. Petreczky, M.: Realization theory for discrete-time piecewise-affine hybrid systems. In: Proc 17th Internation Symposium on Mathematical Theory of Networks and Systems (2006)
17. Petreczky, M., Vidal, R.: Metrics and topology for nonlinear and hybrid systems. In: Bemporad, A., Bicchi, A., Buttazzo, G. (eds.) HSCC 2007. LNCS, vol. 4416, pp. 459–472. Springer, Heidelberg (2007)
18. Petreczky, M., Vidal, R.: Realization theory of stochastic jump-Markov linear systems. In: Proceedings 46th IEEE Conference on Decision and Control (2007)
19. Ma, Y., Vidal, R.: Identification of deterministic switched ARX systems via identification of algebraic varieties. In: Morari, M., Thiele, L. (eds.) HSCC 2005. LNCS, vol. 3414, pp. 449–465. Springer, Heidelberg (2005)
20. Vidal, R.S.S., Sastry, S.: An algebraic geometric approach to the identification of linear hybrid systems. In: IEEE Conference on Decision and Control, pp. 167–172 (2003)
21. Vidal, R.: Identification of PWARX hybrid models with unknown and possibly different orders. In: Proceedings of the IEEE American Conference on Control, pp. 547–552 (2004)
22. Kunz, E.: Introduction to commutative algebra and algebraic geometry. Birkhaeuser, Stuttgard (1985)
23. Cox, D., Little, J., O'Shea, D.: Ideal, varieties, and algorithms. Springer, New York (1997)
24. Brumfiel, G.W.: Partialy Ordered Rings and Semi-Algebraic Geometry. Cambridge University Press, Cambridge (1979)
25. Bochnak, J., Coste, M., Roy, M.F.: Real Algebraic Geometry. Springer, Heidelberg (1998)
26. Basu, S., Pollack, R., Roy, M.F.: Algorithms in Real Algebraic Geometry. Springer, Heidelberg (2003)
27. Collins, P., van Schuppen, J.H.: Observability of hybrid systems and Turing machines. In: Proceedings of the 43rd IEEE Conference on Decision and Control, pp. 7–12 (2004)
28. Ma, Y., Yang, A., Derksen, H., Fossum, R.: Estimation of subspace arrangements with applications in modeling and segmenting mixed data. SIAM Review (to appear, 2007)
29. Ho, B.L., Kalman, R.E.: Effective construction of linear state-variable models from input/output data. In: Proc. 3rd Allerton Conf. on Circuit and System Theory, pp. 449–459 (1965)
30. Caines, P.: Linear Stochastic Systems. John Wiley and Sons, New-York (1988)

A Decidable Class of Planar Linear Hybrid Systems

Pavithra Prabhakar, Vladimeros Vladimerou, Mahesh Viswanathan, and Geir E. Dullerud

University of Illinois at Urbana-Champaign

Abstract. The paper shows the decidability of the reachability problem for planar, monotonic, linear hybrid automata without resets. These automata are a special class of linear hybrid automata with only two variables, whose flows in all states is monotonic along some direction in the plane, and in which the continuous variables are not reset on a discrete transition.

1 Introduction

The use of embedded devices in safety critical systems, has prompted extensive research in the formal modeling and analysis of hybrid systems. *Hybrid automata* [1] are a widely used formalism for modeling such systems. These are machines with finitely many control states and finitely many real-valued variables that evolve continuously with time. The transitions depend on the values of the continuous variables and they change both the discrete control state as well as the values of the variables. The safety of systems modelled by such automata can often be reduced to the question of whether a certain state or *region* of the state space can be reached during an execution. This is called the *reachability problem*.

Due to its importance, the reachability problem for hybrid automata has been carefully investigated in the past couple of decades. The problem has been shown to be decidable for special kinds of hybrid automata including *timed automata* [2], certain special classes of *rectangular hybrid automata* [6], and *o-minimal hybrid automata* [8]. These decidability results often rely on demonstrating the existence of a finite, computable partition of the state space that is *bisimilar* to the original system.

However, such decidability results are the exception rather than the norm. The reachability problem remains stubbornly undecidable even for very simple and special classes of hybrid automata, not just in the general case. One such special class is that of *linear hybrid automata*. In these automata each variable is constrained to evolve along a constant slope (with time), and despite such simple dynamics, have been unamenable to algorithmic analysis even in low dimension (i.e., with very few continuous variables). Timed automata, where each variable evolves synchronously with a global clock, but where the machine is allowed to compare clock values at the time of discrete transitions[1], is undecidable even for systems with 6 clocks [2]. The case of general linear hybrid automata in which variables are constrained to be compared only to constants,

[1] The decidability result for timed automata holds when clocks are only compared with constants.

M. Egerstedt and B. Mishra (Eds.): HSCC 2008, LNCS 4981, pp. 401–414, 2008.

remains undecidable even for just 3 variables [1]. Undecidability results for dynamical systems with piecewise constant derivative in 3 dimensions, and piecewise affine maps in 2 dimensions [5] provide further evidence.

In this paper, we prove the decidability for a special class of linear hybrid automata that are *planar, monotonic* and *don't have resets*. Planar refers to the fact that the automata has only two variables. Monotonic refers to the fact that we require the existence of a vector ρ such that the derivatives of the variables (viewed as a vector in the plane) in all states have a positive projection along ρ; note, this does not mean that both variables have positive derivatives in each state. Finally, the automaton does not reset/change the values of the variables when taking a discrete transition.

The automaton model that we consider here is more general in some aspects, and at the same time more restrictive in some aspects, when compared with other hybrid automata models for which decidability results are known. First variables are not restricted to clocks, like timed automata. Second, variables are not required to have the same slope in all states, or for them to be reset when the flow is changed, as in some rectangular hybrid automata. Next, transitions don't have strong resets that decouple the continuous dynamics from the discrete, as in o-minimal systems. Finally, the guards and invariants are not required to be disjoint, as in dynamical systems with piecewise constant derivatives [3] or polygonal hybrid systems [4]. On the other hand, our automata only have 2 variables, no resets, and monotonic flows.

Despite the restrictive dynamics and planarity, the decidability proof is very challenging. Like many decidability proofs in this area, we first partition the plane into *regions*, which in our case are convex polygons formed by considering lines associated with the constraints appearing in the automaton description, and lines perpendicular to the direction along which the flow is monotonic. Such regions have a very special geometric structure in that they are bounded by 2 to 4 line segments, at least one of which is a line segment perpendicular to the monotonic direction. The first key idea in the proof is to observe the existence of a line ℓ, perpendicular to the monotonic direction, such that the behavior of the automaton beyond ℓ is bisimilar to a finite state system. Then reachability computation is broken up into two phases: the first phase computes all points before ℓ that are reachable, and the second phase constructs the finite bisimulation for the points beyond ℓ and does the search in the bisimilar transition system.

The computation of the reachable regions before ℓ itself relies on observing that any execution of the automaton can be seen as a concatenation of a series of *almost-inside executions*. An almost-inside execution is an execution that starts at the boundary of a region R, enters R, and then leaves to another boundary of R, all the while staying inside R, while taking both discrete and time steps. The first lemma we prove is that the effect of such almost-inside executions is computable for all regions. However, in order for the decidability proof to go through we need a stronger result for certain special regions that we call *right pinched triangles*; we need to show that the effect of concatenating finitely many almost-inside executions can be computed. We do this through a tree construction reminiscent of the Karp-Miller tree [7] for vector addition systems. Finally, we solve the reachability result for regions before ℓ by another tree construction. A carefully counting argument coupled with the monotonicity of flows ensures that this tree will be finite and hence effectively constructable. Space constraints prevent us from giving detailed proofs of the decidablity result here; complete proofs can be found in [9].

2 An Example

We will first illustrate our algorithm for deciding reachability on an example. Consider the hybrid system $\mathbb{H}$ given in Figure 1. It has five locations $s_1, \cdots, s_5$, with flows $f_1, \cdots, f_5$, respectively, associated with them. The locations are labelled by their invariants. For example, the invariant associated with location s_1 is $y < 1$, and this says that the control of the system can be in s_1 only if the value of the variable y is less than 1. When in a certain location the values of the variables change according to their flow. If the system starts with $x = 0$ and $y = 0$ at location s_1, and spends a unit time, then the values of the variables would be $x = 1$ and $y = 2$. However in this case the system is forced by the invariant to leave the location before half time unit. We note that $\mathbb{H}$ is a *monotone linear* hybrid system, where by linear we mean that the flows associated with the locations are constants, and by monotone that the flows have a positive projection along some direction, in this case the x-axis as shown in Figure 2.

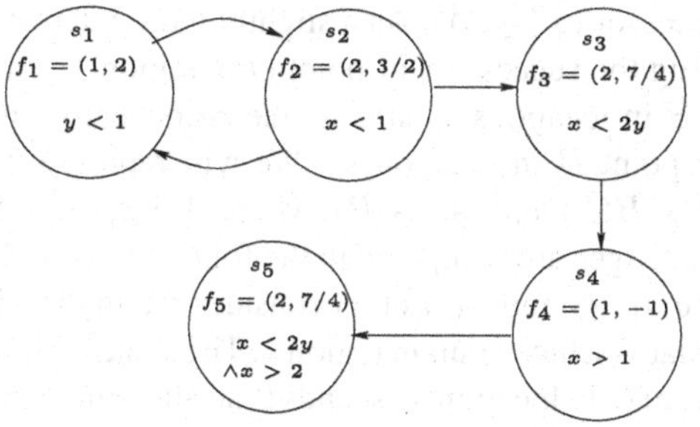

Fig. 1. Linear hybrid system $\mathbb{H}$

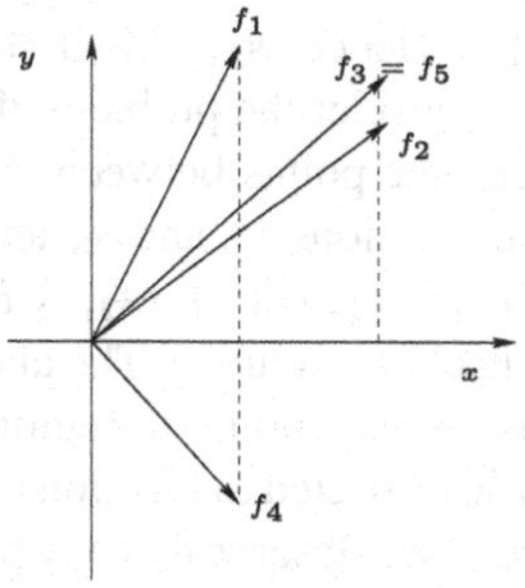

Fig. 2. Flows of the hybrid system $\mathbb{H}$

We will consider the following reachability problem: Is the location s_5 reachable starting from s_1 with $x = 0$ and $y = 0$? As shown in Figure 3, this translates to checking if starting in s_1 at point O, we can reach the shaded region in location s_5.

We first divide the plane into regions depending on the constraints in $\mathbb{H}$. Corresponding to each constraint of $\mathbb{H}$, there is a straight line, as shown by the solid lines in Figure 3. We also add lines parallel to the y-axis passing through the points of intersections of these lines, if one does not already exist. As is easily seen, the interior of a region is invariant with respect to the locations in that either it is contained in the invariant of a location or is disjoint from it. Hence with each element of a region which is its interior, its edge without the end-points or its vertex, we can associate a set of locations whose invariants contain the element. For example, the set of locations corresponding to the interior of region 1 is $\{s_1, s_2, s_3\}$.

The idea of the algorithm is to compute successors for the regions. Given a part of an edge, called a subedge, and a location, the successor with respect to a region is the set

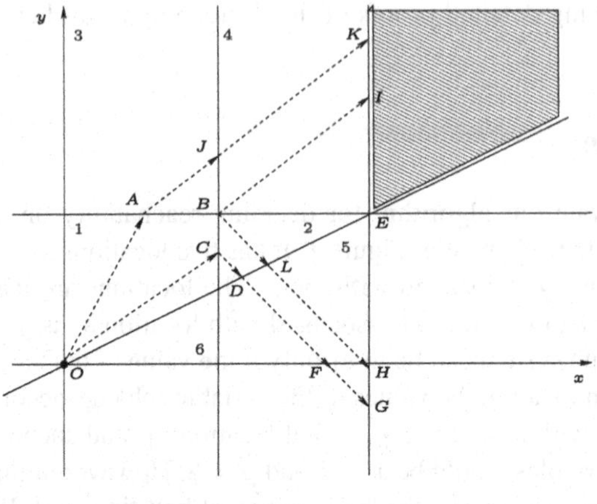

Fig. 3. Regions of the hybrid system $\mathbb{H}$

of all points on the boundary of the region reachable by moving only in its interior, and leaving and entering the boundary at most once. For example, starting from point A in location s_3, we can reach J by following flow f_3 of s_3 and moving only in the interior of region 3. Hence (s_3, J) is in the successor of (s_3, A). As a slightly more interesting example, consider the problem of finding the successors of point O in region 1. These are exactly the points between A and B in locations s_2 and s_3, the points between B and C in locations s_1 and s_3 and the point B in location s_3. We will represent this succinctly as $(s_1, B'C')$, $(s_2, A'B')$, (s_3, BC') and $(s_3, A'B)$, where A' indicates that point A itself is excluded. The above subedges are computed in the following way. The locations corresponding to region 1 are s_1, s_2 and s_3. Let us consider the underlying graph of $\mathbb{H}$ restricted to locations and guards which contain region 1. The same is shown in Figure 4. We observe that any path from O in location s_1 spends time alternately in s_1

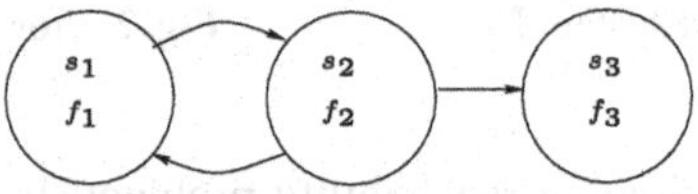

Fig. 4. Underlying graph of $\mathbb{H}$ restricted to region 1

and s_2, and then possibly makes a transition to s_3 where it spends additional time before reaching the boundary. We will show that the set of all points reachable by alternating between s_1 and s_2 is exactly the set of point in the cone generated by f_1 and f_2 which are also in the interior of region 1, namely, the points inside the parallelogram $OABC$ in the figure. This is true only because s_1 and s_2 belong to the same strongly connected component of the underlying graph corresponding to region 1. We then show how to compute the set of points reachable starting from these points with respect to the next maximal strongly connected component, in this case s_3. In this example it turns out that the points reachable by moving along f_3 from points in the parallelogram $OABC$ is $OABC$ itself.

Now coming back to our original problem of finding if there is an execution of $\mathbb{H}$ starting at point O in location s_1 to some point in the shaded region in location s_5, we will build a rooted tree, called the *reachability tree*. Its nodes are labelled with pairs of locations and subedges and the root is labelled $(s_1, 0)$. The children of any node are labelled with the elements of the successors of the label of the current node with respect to every region it is adjacent to. The above computation is carried out with respect to every region to the left of the line $x = 2$. This gives us the set of all pairs of locations and points reachable on this line. Figure 5 shows some part of this tree.

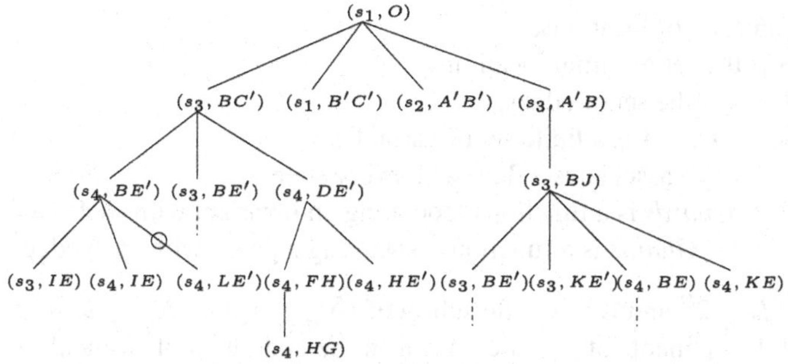

Fig. 5. Reachability tree

Our next goal is to show that this tree is finite. As a first step to achieve this, we prune some branches of the tree. The node (s_4, LE') is removed from the tree as its parent (s_4, BE') contains all the required information. The finiteness of the tree follows from two observations, namely, the number of children of any node is finite and every path in the tree is bounded. We can then apply Konig's Lemma to conclude that the tree is finite. To show that a path is finite, we have from the monotonicity of the flows that the leftmost point of any child of a node is to the right of the leftmost point of the node. For example, the x-coordinate of the left-most point of O which is O itself is less than that of A which is the leftmost point of $A'B$, which is in its successor. However, there is a priori no *minimum* distance by which this shift to the right occurs. Such a bound exists if the successor is with respect to a region which is a trapezium, like region 1. It is not clear for a "left-pinched triangle" like region 6. However for this case we argue that though a global minimum does not exist, given any path of the tree such a minimum exists. In case of a "right-pinched triangle" like region 2, even such a local minimum does not exist. Hence, instead, in this case we compute the "transitive closure" of the successor with respect to the region, which is the set of all points reachable on the boundary by moving within R and touching the boundary any number of times. We show that this is computable when the constraints corresponding to the boundary are strict. We then use the assumption that there are no adjacent right-pinched triangles, to argue that the paths of the tree are finite.

We cannot continue with the construction of the tree beyond the line $x = 2$, because all regions to the right of this line are unbounded. This might potentially lead to infinite paths in the tree. So we stop building the tree at the line l which passes through the leftmost vertex, and show that there is a finite bisimulation of the states corresponding to the regions to the right of this line. This bisimulation can be computed. Hence we can decide the reachability.

3 Preliminaries

3.1 Linear Hybrid Systems

A *linear hybrid system* (*LHS*) $\mathbb{H}$ is a tuple $(S, S_0, E, X, \mathit{flow}, \mathit{inv}, \mathit{guard})$ where

- S is a finite set of locations,
- $S_0 \subseteq S$ is the set of initial locations,
- $E \subseteq S \times S$ is the set of edges,
- $X = \{y_1, \cdots, y_n\}$ is a finite set of variables,
- $\mathit{flow} : S \to \mathbb{Q}^n$ associates a flow with every state,
- $\mathit{inv} : S \to \mathit{Guards}$ is a function associating an invariant with each state, and
- $\mathit{guard} : E \to \mathit{Guards}$ is a function associating a guard with each edge,

where $\mathit{Guards} = 2^{\mathbb{C}}$ and $\mathbb{C}$ is a finite subset of $\{\sum_{i=1}^{n} a_i y_i \sim b_i \mid a_i, b_i \in \mathbb{Q}, \sim \in \{<, >\}\}$. We call the elements of $\mathbb{C}$ which occur in the codomain of *inv* and *guard*, the set of *constraints* associated with $\mathbb{H}$. The size of X is called the *dimension* of $\mathbb{H}$.

We note that the definition of the hybrid system above deviates from the standard definition in that we do *not* allow *resets* and the constraints are restricted to be *strict*.

We define the semantics of an *LHS* in terms of a *transition system*. The transition system of $\mathbb{H}$ is a triple $(X, X_0, \to)$, where $X = S \times \mathbb{R}^n$ is the set of states of $\mathbb{H}$, $X_0 \subseteq X$ called the set of initial states consists of state (s, v) such that $s \in S_0$ and $v \in \mathit{inv}(s)$, and the *transition relation* $\to$ is a binary relation on the set of *states* X. The transition relation $\to$ is defined as the union of *discrete* transitions $\to_d$ and *continuous* transitions $\to_c$, which are defined as:

- $(s, v) \to_d (s', v')$ if $v = v'$ and there exists $e = (s, s') \in E$ such that $v \in \mathit{inv}(s) \cap \mathit{inv}(s') \cap \mathit{guard}(e)$.
- $(s, v) \to_c (s', v')$ if $s = s'$ and there exists $t \in \mathbb{R}$ such that $t \geq 0$ and $v' = v + \mathit{flow}(s)t$, and for all $t' \in [0, t]$, $v + \mathit{flow}(s)t' \in \mathit{inv}(s)$.

An *execution* of $\mathbb{H}$ from a state (s_1, v_1) is a sequence of states $(s_1, v_1) \cdots (s_n, v_n)$ such that for all $1 \leq i < n$, $(s_i, v_i) \to (s_{i+1}, v_{i+1})$. We then say that (s_n, v_n) is *reachable* from (s_1, v_1), and denote it by $(s_1, v_1) \to^* (s_n, v_n)$. We can represent an execution $(s_1, v_1)(s_2, v_2) \cdots (s_n, v_n)$ as a function $\sigma : [0, t] \to S^+ \times \mathbb{R}^n$. We define σ as a pair of functions (σ^1, σ^2), where $\sigma^1 : [0, t] \to S^+$ gives the sequence of locations at any time point and $\sigma^2 : [0, t] \to \mathbb{R}^n$ gives the values of the variables. With each $(s_i, v_i) \to (s_{i+1}, v_{i+1})$ we associate a *delay* d_i, where $d_i = 0$ if $v_i = v_{i+1}$, and $d_i = (v_{i+1} - v_i)/\mathit{flow}(s_i)$ otherwise. Let $t_i = \sum_{j=1}^{i} d_j$. We set $t = t_{n-1}$. We define $\sigma^1(t') = s_i$ if $t' \in (t_{i-1}, t_i)$, otherwise $\sigma^1(t') = s_i \cdots s_j$, where $t' = t_i$ and $t_{i-1} \neq t_i = t_{i+1} = \cdots = t_j \neq t_{j+1}$. We define $\sigma^2(t')$ for $t' \in [t_{i-1}, t_i]$ inductively. We set $\sigma^2(0) = v_1$ and $\sigma^2(t') = \sigma^2(t_{i-1}) + \mathit{flow}(s_i)(t' - t_{i-1})$ for $t' \in [t_{i-1}, t_i]$. A *run* of $\mathbb{H}$ is an execution starting from an initial state.

3.2 Elements of the Two Dimensional Plane

We define some elements of the two dimensional plane formed by straight lines. A *convex closed polygonal set* P is the intersection of finitely many closed half-planes. We simply call P a convex polygon. The *interior* of P, denoted *interior*(P), is the intersection of finitely many open half-planes corresponding to the closed half-planes of P. The *boundary* of P, denoted *boundary*(P), is P – *interior*(P). An *edge* of P is a maximal convex subset of *boundary*(P). We denote the set of all edges of P by *edges*(P). A *vertex* of P is a point of intersection of two distinct edges of P. The set of all vertices of P will be denoted by $vertices(P)$.

We call a convex subset of an edge, a *subedge*. The end-points of a subedge e are points a and b such that e consists of all points on the line segment joining a and b, except possibly a and b themselves. We denote this by *end-points*$(e) = \{a\} \cup \{b\}$. The subset of e without the end-points will be denoted *open*(e), which is e – *end-points*(e). The elements of the subedge e are then its end-points which are contained in e and the *open*(e). This is denoted by *elements*$(e) = \{open(e)\} \cup \{a \mid a \in \textit{end-points}(e), a \in e\}$. From now on, by a convex set, we mean a polygon, interior of a polygon, or a subedge of a polygon.

3.3 Restricted Hybrid Systems

We call an *LHS* $\mathbb{H}$ *monotone* if there exists an $f \in \mathbb{R}^n$ such that for all locations s of $\mathbb{H}$, $flow(s).f > 0$, where . is the standard dot product. We call such an f a *direction* of $\mathbb{H}$.

We will call a linear hybrid system *planar*, if its dimension is two. A planar linear hybrid system is said to be *simple* if no three distinct lines corresponding to its constraints intersect at a common point, where the line corresponding to a constraint $\sum_{i=1}^{n} a_i y_i \sim b_i$ is the set of points satisfying $\sum_{i=1}^{n} a_i y_i = b_i$.

3.4 Notations for Planar Hybrid Systems

Let us fix a simple monotone planar linear hybrid system $\mathbb{H} = (S, S_0, E, X, flow, inv, guard)$ for the rest of the paper. Let $X = \{x, y\}$ and $f_{\mathbb{H}}$ be a direction of $\mathbb{H}$. Let us fix our coordinate system such that the x-axis is parallel to $f_{\mathbb{H}}$ and the y-axis is perpendicular to it. Given a subedge e we define *left*(e) to be the infimum of the x-coordinates of the points in e and *right*(e) to be the supremum of the x-coordinates of the points in e.

Let V be the set consisting of the points of intersections of the lines corresponding to the constraints in $\mathbb{H}$. Let us associate with $\mathbb{H}$ a *set of lines* which are parallel to the y-axis and contain some point in V. We denote this by *lines*$(\mathbb{H})$. We can order the lines of $\mathbb{H}$ as $l_1, l_2, \cdots, l_k$ such that for any $1 \leq i < j \leq k$, if v_i and v_j are the points in V which are contained in l_i and l_j respectively, then *left*$(v_i) <$ *left*(v_j).

Let L be a set of lines which contains *lines*$(\mathbb{H})$ and the lines corresponding to the constraints in $\mathbb{H}$. We associate a set of *regions* with $\mathbb{H}$ which consists of polygons whose interiors are non-empty and which are formed by choosing exactly one closed half-plane corresponding to each line in L. We denote this by *regions*$(\mathbb{H})$. We use *regions*$(\mathbb{H}, i, j)$

to denote the regions of $\mathbb{H}$ which are contained in the set of points between lines l_i and l_j of *lines*($\mathbb{H}$). Also *regions*($\mathbb{H}, 0, j$) and *regions*($\mathbb{H}, i, k+1$) denote the set of regions contained in the set of points which occur to the left of l_j and the set of points which occur to the right of l_i, respectively. Note that two distinct regions in *regions*($\mathbb{H}$) have non-intersecting interiors, and the union of all the regions gives us the whole plane $\mathbb{R}^2$.

Following are a few observations about the regions of $\mathbb{H}$:

1. The regions in *regions*($\mathbb{H}, 0, 1$) are unbounded and have two or three edges.
2. The regions in *regions*($\mathbb{H}, 1, k$) are either triangles, or trapeziums, or unbounded regions with three edges. For the triangles, one of the edges is contained in some l_i and its vertex not on that edge is contained in either l_{i+1} or l_{i-1}. If the vertex is contained in l_{i+1}, then we call the triangle a *right-pinched triangle* otherwise we call it a *left-pinched triangle*. For the trapeziums in this region, we will call its edge a *parallel* edge if it lies on one of the l_i's.
3. The regions in *regions*($\mathbb{H}, k, k+1$) are unbounded with two or three edges.

From now on by a subedge we mean a subedge of the edge of some region in *regions*($\mathbb{H}$). We abuse notation and call a pair (s, e) where $s \in S$ is a location and e a subedge, also a subedge. However it will be clear from the context which one we mean. The subedge (s, e) is said to contain the state (s, v) where $v \in e$. Two subedges (s, e) and (s', e') are said to be disjoint if the do not contain any common state. By a state (s, v) or a subedge (s, e) being on a subedge e' or a line l we mean v or e is contained in e' or l. Similarly we use regions also for pairs of states and regions.

We will focus on the following problems in the rest of the paper: the point-to-point reachability and the region-to-region reachability. The *point-to-point reachability problem* is to decide given two states (s_1, v_1) and (s_2, v_2), if $(s_1, v_1) \rightarrow^* (s_2, v_2)$. The *region-to-region* reachability problem is to decide given two location-region pairs (s_1, R_1) and (s_2, R_2), if there exist points $v_1 \in R_1$ and $v_2 \in R_2$ such that $(s_1, v_1) \rightarrow^* (s_2, v_2)$.

4 Decidability of the Reachability Problem

In this section we show that the point-to-point and region-to-region reachability problems for simple monotone planar linear hybrid systems is decidable. We will continue to use the notations introduced in the previous section. We first present a sketch of the proof of decidability.

1. We first show that the *edge-to-edge reachability* problem is decidable: given a subedge (s, e) of a region $R \in$ *regions*($\mathbb{H}, 0, k$), we can compute the set of all states on l_k which are reachable from the states on the subedge.
2. We then show that there exists a computable finite bisimulation of the transition system of $\mathbb{H}$ restricted to the states on and after l_k which respects the partition created by the elements of the regions in *regions*($\mathbb{H}, k, k+1$).
3. We then use the above results to decide the point-to-point and region-to-region reachability.

4.1 Edge-to-Edge Reachability

In this section we solve the problem of finding the set of all states on the line l_k reachable from a subedge (s, e) of some region $R \in$ *regions*$(\mathbb{H}, 0, k)$. Any execution from a state in (s, e) to a state on l_k can be broken up into a sequence of executions each of which is such that they move within a single region and leave or enter its boundary at most once. Our approach is to build a tree whose nodes represent subedges, and the states corresponding to the nodes of the children of a node give the set of all points reachable from the states in the parent node by executions which move within a region. Then any path in the tree would correspond to executions starting from states in the root. We call this the *reachability* tree. We show that the tree is computable and finite. Then the set of all states in the tree which correspond to the states on l_k will give us the required.

We first compute the set of all states reachable from a subedge by moving only within a region. We define an *almost-inside execution* with respect to a region to be an execution which leaves the boundary of the region at most once and enters the boundary of the region at most once, and at all times during the execution is in the region. An almost-inside execution (*AI*-execution) from a state (s, v) to a state (s', v') with respect to a region R is an execution $\sigma : [0, t]$ such that $\sigma^1(0)$ contains s and $\sigma^2(0) = v$, $\sigma^1(t)$ contains s' and $\sigma^2(t) = v'$, and there exist $t_1, t_2 \in [0, t]$ such that for all $t' \in (0, t_1] \cup [t_2, t), \sigma^2(t') \in$ *boundary*(R), and for all $t' \in (t_1, t_2), \sigma^2(t') \in$ *interior*(R). We say that a subedge (s', e') is reachable from a subedge (s, e) by almost-inside executions with respect to a region R, if for every $v' \in e'$, there exists a $v \in e$ and an *AI*-execution from (s, v) to (s', v'). The successor of a subedge (s, e) with respect to a region R is a subedge of R reachable from (s, e) by *AI*-executions with respect to R. We denote by *succ*$((s, e), R)$ the maximal successors of (s, e) with respect to R, where a successor (s', e') is maximal if for every successor $(s', e''), e'' \subseteq e'$.

In the next lemma, we show that *succ*$((s, e), R)$ is computable. A notion that we use is that of the underlying graph of the hybrid system restricted to those locations and edges whose invariants and guards respectively are satisfied by the elements of a region. Given a set of points V, we define the underlying graph of $\mathbb{H}$ with respect to V to be *graph*$(\mathbb{H}, V) = (V_{\mathbb{H}}, E_{\mathbb{H}},)$ such that $V_{\mathbb{H}} = \{s \in S \,|\, V \subseteq inv(s)\}$ and $E_{\mathbb{H}} = \{e \in E \,|\, V \subseteq guard(e)\}$.

Lemma 1. *Given a region $R \in$ regions$(\mathbb{H})$ and a subedge (s, e) of R, succ$((s, e), R)$ is computable.*

Proof. We consider the maximal strongly connected components of the underlying graph *graph*$(\mathbb{H}$, *interior*$(R))$, and first compute the set of all states on the boundary reachable by moving in a single component. Then we show how this can be used to compute all the states reachable.

Given a graph G, let us call the graph with these strongly connected components as vertices, the component graph of G, and denote it as *SCC*(G). There is an edge between two vertices in *SCC*(G) if there is one between two states of the components in the original graph. Note that maximality of the components gives us that *SCC*(G) is a directed acyclic graph.

We observe that any *AI*-execution from a state in (s, e) to a state on the boundary of R would correspond to a path in $SCC(G)$. For each such path $\pi = C_1 C_2 \cdots C_n$ where C_i's are the strongly connected components, we compute the states on the boundary of R reachable by *AI*-executions which follow this path. We do the computation iteratively. We first find the states reachable by moving only in the component C_1.

To compute the above, we need a notion of *post* of a convex subset of a region with respect to a set of flows, which is the set of all points in the region reachable by following the flows and always remaining in the interior of the region except possibly at the end-points. We can show that $post(P, F, R)$ is computable, where P is a convex subset of region R and F is a set of at most two flows, and that it can be expressed as a finite union of convex subsets. A crucial observation is that corresponding to a trajectory following F from a point in P to any point in R, there is one which moves only within R. The only exceptions are the vertices of R, but it can be tested separately if they can be reached. It turns out that the set of all points in R reachable from a point in P are those in the cone generated by the flows in F. This can also be extended to any convex subset by taking the convex hull of the sets corresponding to the vertices of P. The details of the computation of $post(P, F, R)$ are given in [9].

Now the set of all points reachable on the boundary by following flows in the component C_1 is given by $post(e, F, R)$, where F contains those flows associated with the locations in C_1 which make a maximum or a minimum angle with $f_{\mathbb{H}}$. Further the points in $post(e, F, R)$ which are in the interior of R can be reached in any location of C_1. A points p in $post(e, F, R)$ which is on the boundary and is reached from some point in e by moving in R for some non-zero time, can only be reached if there is a location which is in both C_1 and $graph(\mathbb{H}, e)$, that is, there is an execution which can move into the interior, and there is a location which is in both C_1 and $graph(\mathbb{H}, p)$, that is, there is an execution which moves from the interior to the boundary. We then compute the set of all states on an edge reached by moving along the boundary from points on the boundary given by $post(e, F, R)$. Suppose that we have found the set of all states on the interior and boundary reachable by the prefix of the path π till C_i. We can then compute the post of the interior points with respect to the flows of C_{i+1}, and compute the states reached when in C_{i+1} similar to above. Again the details can be found in [9].

Once we have found the set of states reachable along π, we can take the union of all the states over all the π's to get the set of all states on the boundary reachable. Since at each point in the procedure above we get a representation of the set of states on the boundary reachable as a finite union of subedges, and the number of paths π is finite, we can compute $succ((s, e), R)$. □

Now that we have shown that $succ((s, e), R)$ is computable, we can construct the reachability tree. However we also want to show that the tree is finite, and we will show this by ensuring that the paths in the tree are finite. We will do this by showing that along any path the successors move to the right by at least some minimum distance. In the case of a right-pinched triangle such a minimum does not exist. Hence we will compute the transitive closure of *succ*, called *succ** where we consider points reachable by a sequence of *AI*-executions such that the last state of an execution is same as the first state of the next execution. The intuition behind this is that if we compute *succ** instead of *succ* for a subedge with respect to a region then we will not need to consider the *succ* of the elements in *succ** with respect to the region, as those states are already included in *succ**. We will see that the simplicity of the system can then be used to argue that the paths in the reachability tree are finite. Next lemma says that *succ** is computable.

Lemma 2. *Given a right-pinched triangle R in regions$(\mathbb{H}, 1, k)$ and a subedge (s, e) of R, succ$^*((s, e), R)$ is computable.*

Proof. Let the right-pinched triangle R be abc with the edge ab on some l_i and c on l_{i+1} as shown in Figure 6. Let (s, e) be a subedge of ac. We first compute the set of all states

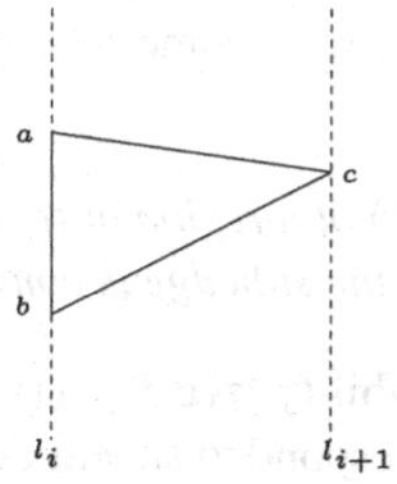

Fig. 6. Right-pinched triangle abc

on ac reachable by a sequence of one or more AI-executions. For this, we build a tree $T^*(s, e)$ rooted at node (s, e). We will need the following new notion of successor. Let us denote by $succ_1((s_1, e_1), R)$ the set of states reachable on ac by executions which touch bc at most once in the following sense: $succ_1((s_1, e_1), R) = \{(s_2, e_2) \mid (s_2, e_2) \in succ((s_1, e_1), R), e_2 \subseteq ac\} \cup \{(s_3, e_3) \mid (s_3, e_3) \in succ(s_2, e_2), e_3 \subseteq ac, (s_2, e_2) \in succ((s_1, e_1), R), e_2 \subseteq bc\}$.

We now define how the tree is constructed. We will simultaneously mark nodes in the partial tree constructed. The children of a node (s_1, e_1) are the elements (s_2, e_2) in $succ_1((s_1, e_1), R)$ such that there is no node $(s_2, -)$ along the path from the root to the node (s_1, e_1). For every element (s_2, e_2) in $succ_1((s_1, e_1), R)$ such that there is a node (s_2, e'_2) along the path from the root to the node (s_1, e_1), we mark the node (s_2, e'_2). Note that a node could get marked twice. The construction of tree will terminate since it is finite, which is due to the fact that the number of children of any node is finite and the height of the tree is bounded by the number of locations.

We now describe how to compute $succ^*((s, e))$ from the tree constructed above. We form a set A which contains all the nodes of $T^*(s, e)$, and for each node (s_1, e_1) which belongs to a subtree of some marked node, it contains $(s_1, full(e_1))$, where $full(e_1)$ is the subedge e_2 of ac such that $left(e_2) = left(e_1)$ and $right(e_2) = right(c)$ and e_2 contains the points $left(e_1)$ and c if and only if e_1 contains them. A contains all points on ac' reachable from (s, e) by moving only within the triangle and touching the boundary any number of times. This is because if from a state (s, v_1) we can reach a state (s, v_2) by an execution σ, where v_2 is strictly to the right of v_1, then we can reach any point to the right of v_1 by taking a sequence of one or more executions whose transition sequence is same as that of σ but with possibly less time spent in each location. Similarly if (s_1, e_1) can reach (s_2, e_2), then $(s_1, full(e_1))$ can reach $(s_2, full(e_2))$. For details, see [9]. Hence it makes to sense to take the *full* of all nodes in the subtree of a marked node.

To compute the set of states on bc' reachable, we observe that such a state is reachable only from an AI-execution starting from some state on ac'. Hence the reachable states on bc' B can be computed by taking the *succ* of the maximal subedges of A. Finally, if c is reachable then it is reachable by an AI-execution starting from a state on ac' or bc', hence will be included in the *succ* of the subedges in A or that of B. Hence all points in $succ^*((s,e),R)$ can be computed. □

We show below that the set of all states reachable on the line l_k is computable. As already said before, we construct a tree using the *succ* and *succ** to compute the children of the nodes. The nodes of the tree will correspond exactly to the states on edges of regions in $regions(\mathbb{H},0,k)$ reachable from some subedge of some region in it for which the tree is built.

Lemma 3. *Given a subedge (s^*,e^*) of a region in $regions(\mathbb{H},0,k)$, the set of all states on l_k reachable from some state on the subedge is computable.*

Proof. Construction of the reachability tree $T_{reach}((s^*,e^*))$. We construct the reachability tree, in which the nodes correspond to subedges, and the children of a node capture the set of all states reachable from the states of the current node by *AI*-executions. A particular child of a node corresponds to *AI*-executions with respect to a single region.

We first define *tsucc* of a subedge with respect to a region which consists of states reachable by *AI*-executions in this region. We break up the subedges into its elements, because when computing *tsucc*, we require that all points of a subedge belong to the same set of regions. Note that otherwise, the end-point of a subedge which is a vertex could belong to a different set of regions than the subedge without the end-points.

For a subedge (s,e) of a region R, $tsucc((s,e,R))$ is given by:

- If R is not a right-pinched triangle, $tsucc((s,e,R)) = \{(s',el,R') \mid (s',e') \in succ((s,e),R), el \in elements(e'), el \subseteq R', R' \in regions(\mathbb{H},0,k)\}$.
- If R is a right-pinched triangle, $tsucc((s,e,R)) = \{(s',el,R') \mid (s',e') \in succ^*((s,e),R), el \in elements(e'), el \subseteq R', R' \in regions(\mathbb{H},0,k), R \neq R'\}$.

The root of $T_{reach}((s^*,e^*))$ is $*$. The children of $*$ are the element of the set $\{(s^*,e^*,R) \mid e^* \in R, R \in regions(\mathbb{H},0,k)\}$. The children of any node (s,e,R) are the elements of $tsucc((s,e,R))$ which contain at least one state which has not occurred in the current node or any of its ancestors, that is, an element (s_1,e_1,R_1) is present in the *tsucc* of the current node (s,e,R) if for all nodes (s_1,e_2,R_1) which is the current node or its ancestor, there exists a v such that $v \in e_1 - e_2$.

We sketch below a proof of finiteness of the tree $T_{reach}((s^*,e^*))$. Details are given in [9]. First we make a few observations which are crucial in arguing the finiteness.

1. Let (s,e) and (s',e') be elements of subedges of a region R. Then if $(s',e') \in tsucc((s,e),R)$, then $left(e) \leq left(e')$ and $right(e) \leq right(e')$. This follows from the monotonicity of the flows in $\mathbb{H}$.
2. Given any region $R \in regions(\mathbb{H},1,k)$, and (s,e) and (s',e') elements of subedges of R which are not on the l_i's such that $(s',e') \in tsucc((s,e),R)$, we have:
   (a) If R is a trapezium or an unbounded region, then either $right(e')$ is on some l_i or there exists a $d_R > 0$ such that $right(e') \geq right(e) + d_R$.

(b) If R is a left-pinched triangle, then either *right*(e') is on some l_i or there exists a d which increases monotonically with *right*(e) such that *right*$(e') \geq$ *right*$(e)+d$.

Now turning to the proof, by construction the above tree is finitely branching. To see that every path in the tree is also finite, we can deduce from the above observations that (a) there is a bound on the number of consecutive children whose right-end points do not move closer to l_k (the bound is the number of locations), (b) when the successors are computed with respect to a trapezium and the right-end moves strictly to the right, there is a minimum distance by which the shift occurs namely the minimum of all the d_R's, (c) when the successors are computed with respect to a left-pinched triangle the minimum distance is non-zero and depends on the right-end point of the first occurrence on the path of one of its elements not contained in any l_i. This along with the simplicity of the system which guarantees that two right-pinched triangles are never adjacent to each other, we obtain a bound on the length of any path. Finally, from Konig's Lemma, we have that the tree is finite. □

4.2 Finite Bisimulation

We show that the states of $\mathbb{H}$ corresponding to the regions in *regions*$(\mathbb{H}, k, k+1)$ have a finite bisimulation. A binary relation $\sim$ over a set of states is a *bisimulation* if it is symmetric and for every pair of states (s_1, v_1) and (s_2, v_2), if $(s_1, v_1) \sim (s_2, v_2)$ and $(s_1, v_1) \rightarrow ({s'}_1, {v'}_1)$, then there exists a state $({s'}_2, {v'}_2)$ such that $(s_2, v_2) \rightarrow ({s'}_2, {v'}_2)$ and $({s'}_1, {v'}_1) \sim ({s'}_2, {v'}_2)$. We will show that there exists a computable equivalence relation $\sim$ of finite index on the set of states in *regions*$(\mathbb{H}, k, k+1)$ which is a bisimulation and which respects the partition created by the elements of the regions in *regions*$(\mathbb{H}, k, k+1)$. By partition created by l_k we mean the two parts, one consisting of the states on l_k and the other consisting of the rest of the states in *regions*$(\mathbb{H}, k, k+1)$.

We define $\sim$ as follows. $(s_1, v_1) \sim (s_2, v_2)$ if $s_1 = s_2$ and v_1, v_2 belong to the same element of a region. To see that this is a bisimulation consider (s, v_1) and (s, v_2) where v_1 and v_2 belong to the same element of some region. If (s, v_1) takes a discrete transition to (s', v_1), then so can (s, v_2) to (s', v_2) as the guards and invariants respect the elements of the regions. Suppose (s, v_1) takes a continuous transition to $(s, {v'}_1)$, then there is a straight line from the v_1 to ${v'}_1$ which passes through a finite sequence of infinite edges and interiors of the regions. There exists a straight line from v_2 parallel to the above which moves through the same sequence of edges and regions. Hence we can find a point ${v'}_2$ in the required region.

Since the number of regions in *regions*$(\mathbb{H}, k, k+1)$ is finite, the number of elements of these regions is also finite. Hence we have a finite bisimulation.

4.3 Point-to-Point and Region-to-Region Reachability

Theorem 1. *Point-to-point and region-to-region reachability problems are decidable for simple monotone linear hybrid systems.*

Proof. To check if state (s', v') is reachable from (s, v), add two more lines to *lines*$(\mathbb{H})$ which pass through v and v', and are parallel to y-axis. Then check if (s', v') corresponds to any node in $T_{reach}((s, v))$.

To decide if (s', R') is reachable from (s, R), where $R, R' \in$ *regions*$(\mathbb{H})$, first compute the set of subedges *init*(R) of R reachable from points in R. For each subedge $(s^*, e^*) \in$ *init*(R), compute the set of subedges in l_k reachable, and then take their union. If $R' \in$ *regions*$(\mathbb{H}, k, k+1)$, then construct the finite bisimulation to decide if R' is reachable. Otherwise check if any state in (s', R') is reachable from the set of subedges on its boundary reachable from states in *init*(R). □

5 Conclusions

In this paper we identified a new class of planar linear hybrid automata that have a decidable reachability problem. The key aspect in defining the class was requiring flows to be monotonic. One can prove that the reachability problem is undecidable in 4 dimensions; see [9] for details. The 3 dimensional case is an interesting open problem.

References

1. Alur, R., Courcoubetis, C., Halbwachs, N., Henzinger, T.A., Ho, P.-H., Nicollin, X., Olivero, A., Sifakis, J., Yovine, S.: The algorithmic analysis of hybrid systems. Theoretical Computer Science 138(1), 3–34 (1995)
2. Alur, R., Dill, D.L.: A theory of timed automata. Theoretical Computer Science 126(2), 183–235 (1994)
3. Asarin, E., Maler, O., Pnueli, A.: Reachability analysis of dynamical systems having piecewise-constant derivatives. Theoretical Computer Science 138(1), 35–65 (1995)
4. Asarin, E., Schneider, G., Yovine, S.: Algorithmic analysis of polygonal hybrid systems, part I: Reachability. Theor. Comput. Sci. 379(1-2), 231–265 (2007)
5. Blondel, V.D., Bournez, O., Koiran, P., Papadimitriou, C.H., Tsitsiklis, J.N.: Deciding stability and mortality of piecewise affine dynamical systems. Theoretical Computer Science 255(1–2), 687–696 (2001)
6. Henzinger, T.A., Kopke, P.W., Puri, A., Varaiya, P.: What's decidable about hybrid automata? In: Proc. 27th Annual ACM Symp. on Theory of Computing (STOC), pp. 373–382 (1995)
7. Karp, R.M., Miller, R.E.: Parallel program schemata. Journal of Computer and System Sciences 3(2), 147–195 (1969)
8. Lafferriere, G., Pappas, G., Sastry, S.: O-minimal hybrid systems (1998)
9. Prabhakar, P., Vladimerou, V., Viswanathan, M., Dullerud, G.E.: A Decidable Class of Planar Linear Hybrid Systems. Technical Report UIUCDCS-R-2008-2927, UIUC (January 2008)

Reachability of Uncertain Nonlinear Systems Using a Nonlinear Hybridization

Nacim Ramdani[1], Nacim Meslem[2], and Yves Candau[2]

[1] INRIA Sophia-Antipolis Méditerranée and LIRMM UMR 5506 CNRS UM2, 161 rue Ada, 34392 Montpellier Cedex 5, France
[2] CERTES, Univ. Paris 12-Val de Marne, 61 av. Gl. de Gaulle, 94000 Créteil, France

Abstract. In this paper, we investigate nonlinear reachability computation in presence of model uncertainty, via guaranteed set integration. We show how this can be done by using the classical Müller's existence theorem. The core idea developed is to no longer deal with whole sets but to derive instead two nonlinear dynamical systems which involve no model uncertainty and which bracket in a guaranteed way the space reachable by the original uncertain system. We give a rule for building the bracketing systems. In the general case, the bracketing systems obtained are only piecewise C^k-continuously differential nonlinear systems and hence can naturally be modeled with hybrid automata. We show how to derive the hybrid model and how to address mode switching. An example is given with a biological process.

1 Introduction

Computing reachable sets for hybrid systems is an important step when one addresses verification or synthesis taks. A key issue then lays in the calculation of the reachable space for continuous dynamics with nonlinear models. In this paper, we will also emphasize the presence of parameter uncertainty in the nonlinear dynamical models used for characterizing the continuous dynamics.

Consider an *uncertain* dynamical system described by non-autonomous differential equations with the following form:

$$\left\{ \dot{\boldsymbol{x}}(t) = f(\boldsymbol{x}, \boldsymbol{p}, t), \quad \boldsymbol{x}(t_0) \in \mathcal{X}_0 \subseteq \mathcal{D}, \quad \boldsymbol{p} \in \mathcal{P} \right\} \tag{1}$$

where function $f : \mathcal{D} \times \mathcal{P} \times \mathbb{R}^+ \mapsto \mathbb{R}^n$ is possibly nonlinear, $\mathcal{D} \subseteq \mathbb{R}^n$, $\mathcal{X}_0$ is the initial domain for state vector $\boldsymbol{x}$ at time $t_0 \geq 0$ and $\mathcal{P}$ is an uncertainty domain for parameter vector $\boldsymbol{p}$. The reachable space of system (1) is then defined as follows

$$\mathcal{R}([t_0, t]\,; \mathcal{X}_0) = \left\{ \begin{array}{c} \boldsymbol{x}(\tau),\ t_0 \leq \tau \leq t\ | \\ (\dot{\boldsymbol{x}}(\tau) = f(\boldsymbol{x}, \boldsymbol{p}, \tau)) \wedge (\boldsymbol{x}(t_0) \in \mathcal{X}_0) \wedge (\boldsymbol{p} \in \mathcal{P}) \end{array} \right\} \tag{2}$$

Several methods have been developed recently for the explicit computation of the reachable space, however, most of them do not address the presence of model parameter uncertainty. When the continuous dynamics are linear, these

M. Egerstedt and B. Mishra (Eds.): HSCC 2008, LNCS 4981, pp. 415–428, 2008.

methods compute over-approximations of the reachable sets by combining time discretization, numerical integration and computational geometry. They use various representations for the reachable sets such as polytopes [1,3,6], zonotopes [8] or ellipsoids [5,13]. Some other methods proceed with hybrid abstractions [9,7,14]. When the continuous dynamics are modelled with a nonlinear differential equation, the computation of the reachable set becomes much harder which forms one of the main obstacle in safety verification of hybrid systems [14]. Most computationnal methods rely on an hybridization of the continuous-time models, i.e. the use of piecewise simpler, possibly affine approximations of the analysed system on cells defined on the state space [2]. Unfortunately, these reachability computations are tractable only for systems where the dimension of the continuous state component is small.

Few authors investigated the computation of reachable set by using guaranteed set integration. In [10], interval Tayor models [16] were used for the verification of hybrid systems, but no parameter uncertainty were considered. They were also used for the simulation of uncertain hybrid systems where the dimension of vectors were small [17]. Nevertheless, it is well-known that in general the size of the reachable space derived with interval Taylor models diverges after few computation steps when the size of initial state domain or parameter uncertainty domain are large. This shortcoming is mainly caused by the *wrapping* effect, i.e. the overestimation of the solution due to the bracketing of any set by an axis-aligned box.

Hence, the contribution of this paper is to show how one can address nonlinear continuous reachability computation in presence of model uncertainty, in a more efficient way by using the classical Müller's theorem [15,18,12] allied with interval Taylor models. We will recall the classical Müller's existence theorem and we will indicate how it can be used for guaranteed set integration and hence reachability computation.

The core idea developped in the sequel is to no longer perform set integration with whole domains but to only compute guaranteed bounds for the reachable spaces. To do so, we will first show how the Müller's theorem makes it possible to derive two dynamical systems which enclose the original uncertain dynamical system and thus bound the flow pipe between a minimal solution, i.e. a flow that is always lower than the solution flow pipe, and a maximal solution, i.e. a flow that is always larger. Since the two bounding systems involve no more uncertainty, interval Taylor models can be used for the guaranteed computation of the minimal and maximal solutions. We will show how to build the bracketing systems by analyzing function f partial derivatives signs. Since the latter may change over integration time period, the bounding systems are in general defined by continuous but only piecewise C^k-differentiable functions. We will show how to use hybrid automata to model them and how to address mode switching. In summary, the computation of the reachable set for an uncertain continuous dynamical system boils down to running two hybrid dynamical systems involving no uncertainty in neither model parameters nor initial state.

2 Guaranteed Set Integration with Interval Taylor Models

In this section, we will recall how to perform guaranteed set integration with interval Taylor models.

2.1 Interval Analysis

Interval analysis was initially developed to account for the quantification errors introduced by the floating point representation of real numbers with computers and was extended to validated numerics ([11] and the references therein). A real interval $[a] = [\underline{a},\ \overline{a}]$ is a connected and closed subset of $\mathbb{R}$. We have $\text{Inf}[a] = \underline{a}$ and $\text{Sup}[a] = \overline{a}$. The set of all real intervals of $\mathbb{R}$ is denoted by $\mathcal{IR}$. Real arithmetic operations are extended to intervals. Consider an operator $\circ \in \{+, -, *, \div\}$ and $[a]$ and $[b]$ two intervals. Then:

$$[a] \circ [b] = [\inf_{u\in[a],v\in[b]} u \circ v, \quad \sup_{u\in[a],v\in[b]} u \circ v] \tag{3}$$

An interval vector $[\boldsymbol{a}]$ is a subset of $\mathbb{R}^n$ that can be defined as the Cartesian product of n intervals. One can write $[\boldsymbol{a}] = [a_1] \times [a_2] \times \ldots \times [a_n]$ where $[a_i] = [\underline{a}_i, \overline{a}_i]$. Consider $g : \mathbb{R}^n \longmapsto \mathbb{R}^m$; the range of this function over an interval vector $[\boldsymbol{a}]$ is given by:

$$g([\boldsymbol{a}]) = \{g(\boldsymbol{u}) \mid \boldsymbol{u} \in [\boldsymbol{a}]\} \tag{4}$$

where the inclusion $\boldsymbol{u} \in [\boldsymbol{a}]$ means that $u_i \in [a_i]$ for all $i = 1, \ldots, n$. The interval function $[g] : \mathcal{IR}^n \longmapsto \mathcal{IR}^m$ is an inclusion function for g if

$$\forall [\boldsymbol{a}] \in \mathcal{IR}^n,\ g([\boldsymbol{a}]) \subseteq [g]([\boldsymbol{a}]) \tag{5}$$

An inclusion function for g can be obtained by replacing each occurrence of a real variable by the corresponding interval and each standard function by its interval counterpart. The resulting function is called the natural inclusion function. The performances of this inclusion function depend on the formal expression for g.

Given a bounded set $\mathcal{E}$ of complex shape, one usually defines an axis-aligned box or a paving, i.e. a union of non-overlaping boxes, $\overline{\mathcal{E}}$ which contains the set $\mathcal{E}$: this is known as an *outer* approximation of it. Likewise, one also defines an *inner* approximation $\underline{\mathcal{E}}$ which is contained in the set $\mathcal{E}$. Hence, we have the following properties

$$\underline{\mathcal{E}} \subseteq \mathcal{E} \subseteq \overline{\mathcal{E}} \tag{6}$$

$$vol(\underline{\mathcal{E}}) \leq vol(\mathcal{E}) \leq vol(\overline{\mathcal{E}}) \tag{7}$$

where $vol(.)$ is the volume of a set.

2.2 Interval Taylor Models

Consider now the differential equation (1) and define a time grid $t_0 < t_1 < t_2 < \ldots < t_{n_T}$ which is not necessarily equally spaced. The objective is to compute interval vectors $[\boldsymbol{x}_j], j = 1, \ldots, n_T$, that are *guaranteed* to contain the solution of (1) at time t_j.

Effective methods for solving such a problem are based on Taylor expansions. These methods are usually one-step methods which proceed with two phases:

1. they first verify existence and uniqueness of the solution using the fixed point theorem and the Picard-Lindelöf operator, compute an *a priori* enclosure $[\tilde{\boldsymbol{x}}_j]$ such that
$$\forall t \in [t_j, t_{j+1}] \quad \boldsymbol{x}(t) \in [\tilde{\boldsymbol{x}}_j] \tag{8}$$
and adapt integration time step size $h_j = t_{j+1} - t_j$ if necessary in order to keep the width of $[\tilde{\boldsymbol{x}}_j]$ and hence the global truncation error smaller than a given threshold;
2. then they compute a tighter enclosure $[\boldsymbol{x}_{j+1}]$ of the solution of (1) at t_{j+1}, i.e.
$$[\boldsymbol{x}_{j+1}] = [\boldsymbol{x}_j] + \sum_{i=1}^{k-1} h_j^i \boldsymbol{f}^{[i]}([\boldsymbol{x}_j], [\boldsymbol{p}], t_j) + h_j^k \boldsymbol{f}^{[k]}([\tilde{\boldsymbol{x}}_j], [\boldsymbol{p}], [t_j, t_{j+1}]) \tag{9}$$
which corresponds to a Taylor expansion of order k where $[\tilde{\boldsymbol{x}}_j]$ is used to compute the remainder term. The coefficients $\boldsymbol{f}^{[i]}$ are the Taylor coefficients of the solution $\boldsymbol{x}(t)$ which can be computed either numerically by automatic differentiation or analytically via formal methods.

The enclosures thus obtained are said *validated* which is in contrast with conventional numerical integration techniques which derive approximations with unknown global error and where the accumulation of both truncation and round-off errors may cause the computed solution to deviate widely from the real one. Unfortunately, the *wrapping* effect makes the explicit scheme (9) width-increasing and thus not suitable for numerical implementation. To solve such a drawback, one can use mean value forms, matrices preconditioning and linear transforms [16].

Remark 1. *When the size of the initial domain or the parameter vector box is too large, guaranteed numerical integration is often doomed to diverge. In such cases, pessimism might be controled by bisection, i.e. perfoming a partition of the initial state vector or parameter vector domains. Nevertheless, such a procedure increases computation times very significantly. Hence, the method introduced in this paper investigates the possibility to achieve numerical integration without employing bisection.*

3 Guaranteed Set Integration Using Müller's Existence Theorem

In this section, we address set integration by using the classical Müller's existence theorem [15,18] as reported in [12].

Theorem 1 ([18,12]). *Consider the dynamical system (1), where function f is continuous over a domain $\mathcal{T}$ defined by*

$$\mathcal{T} : \begin{cases} \omega(t) \leq \boldsymbol{x}(t) \leq \Omega(t) \\ \underline{\boldsymbol{p}} \leq \boldsymbol{p} \leq \overline{\boldsymbol{p}} \\ t_0 \leq t \leq t_{n_T} \end{cases} \tag{10}$$

where $\boldsymbol{a} \leq \boldsymbol{b}$ means $a_i \leq b_i$ for all i. Assume that functions $\omega_i(t)$ and $\Omega_i(t)$ are continuous over $[t_0, t_{n_T}]$ for all i and satisfy the following properties

1. *$\omega(t_0) = \underline{\boldsymbol{x}}_0$ and $\Omega(t_0) = \overline{\boldsymbol{x}}_0$*
2. *the lower Dini derivatives $D^-\omega_i(t)$ and $D^-\Omega_i(t)$ and the upper Dini derivatives $D^+\omega_i(t)$ and $D^+\Omega_i(t)$ of $\omega_i(t)$ and $\Omega_i(t)$ are such that*

$$\forall i,\ D^{\pm}\omega_i(t) \leq \min_{\underline{\mathcal{T}}_i(t)} f_i(\boldsymbol{x}, \boldsymbol{p}, t) \tag{11}$$

$$\forall i,\ D^{\pm}\Omega_i(t) \geq \max_{\overline{\mathcal{T}}_i(t)} f_i(\boldsymbol{x}, \boldsymbol{p}, t) \tag{12}$$

where $\underline{\mathcal{T}}_i(t)$ is the subset of $\mathcal{T}(t)$ defined by

$$\underline{\mathcal{T}}_i : \left\{ x_i = \omega_i(t),\quad \omega_j(t) \leq x_j \leq \Omega_j(t),\ j \neq i,\quad \underline{\boldsymbol{p}} \leq \boldsymbol{p} \leq \overline{\boldsymbol{p}} \right\} \tag{13}$$

and where $\overline{\mathcal{T}}_i(t)$ is the subset of $\mathcal{T}(t)$ defined by

$$\overline{\mathcal{T}}_i : \left\{ x_i = \Omega_i(t),\quad \omega_j(t) \leq x_j \leq \Omega_j(t),\ j \neq i,\quad \underline{\boldsymbol{p}} \leq \boldsymbol{p} \leq \overline{\boldsymbol{p}} \right\} \tag{14}$$

Then for all $\boldsymbol{x}_0 \in [\underline{\boldsymbol{x}}_0, \overline{\boldsymbol{x}}_0]$, $\boldsymbol{p} \in [\underline{\boldsymbol{p}}, \overline{\boldsymbol{p}}]$, system (1) admits a solution $\boldsymbol{x}(t)$ that stays in the domain

$$\mathcal{X} : \begin{cases} t_0 \leq t \leq t_{n_T} \\ \omega(t) \leq \boldsymbol{x}(t) \leq \Omega(t) \end{cases} \tag{15}$$

and takes the value $\boldsymbol{x}_0$ at t_0. If, in addition, for all $\boldsymbol{p} \in [\underline{\boldsymbol{p}}, \overline{\boldsymbol{p}}]$, function $f(\boldsymbol{x}, \boldsymbol{p}, t)$ is Lipschitzian with respect to $\boldsymbol{x}$ over $\mathcal{D}$ then this solution is unique for any given $\boldsymbol{p}$.

Finally, an enclosure for the solution of (1) is given by

$$\forall t \in [t_0,\, t_{n_T}],\quad [\boldsymbol{x}](t) = [\omega(t),\, \Omega(t)] \tag{16}$$

Denote $[\tilde{\omega}_j]$ and $[\tilde{\Omega}_j]$ *a priori* solutions for bracketing systems (11-12). It is easy to prove that the enclosures

$$[\tilde{\boldsymbol{x}}_j] = \left[\mathrm{Inf}([\tilde{\omega}_j]),\, \mathrm{Sup}([\tilde{\Omega}_j]) \right],\quad j = 1, \ldots, n_T - 1 \tag{17}$$

satisfy (8) and hence are *a priori* solutions for (1).

The main difficulty now, is to obtain suitable bracketing functions $\omega(t)$ and $\Omega(t)$ in the general case. However, when the components of f are monotonic with respect to each parameter and each state vector component, it is quite easy to define these systems [12].

Rule 1. *[Use of monotonicity property – Analysis of the partial derivatives signs] Here we adapt the idea introduced in [12]. Let's assume that the sign of the partial derivatives* $\frac{\partial f_i}{\partial p_k}$ *and* $\frac{\partial f_i}{\partial x_j}$ *is constant over the time period considered. Define* $\overline{\delta}^i(p_k)$ *as follows*

$$\overline{\delta}^i(p_k) = \begin{cases} \overline{p}_k & \text{if } \frac{\partial f_i}{\partial p_k} \geq 0 \\ \underline{p}_k & \text{if } \frac{\partial f_i}{\partial p_k} < 0 \end{cases} \tag{18}$$

and $\overline{\delta}^i(\mathbf{p}) = [\overline{\delta}^i(p_1), ..., \overline{\delta}^i(p_k), ...]^T$. *In a similar way, define* $\underline{\delta}^i(p_k)$ *as follows*

$$\underline{\delta}^i(p_k) = \begin{cases} \underline{p}_k & \text{if } \frac{\partial f_i}{\partial p_k} \geq 0 \\ \overline{p}_k & \text{if } \frac{\partial f_i}{\partial p_k} < 0 \end{cases} \tag{19}$$

and $\underline{\delta}^i(\mathbf{p}) = [\underline{\delta}^i(p_1), ..., \underline{\delta}^i(p_k), ...]^T$. *Now define* $\overline{\gamma}^i(x_j)$ *as follows*

$$\overline{\gamma}^i(x_j) = \begin{cases} \Omega_i & \text{if } i = j \\ \Omega_j & \text{if } (i \neq j) \wedge \frac{\partial f_i}{\partial x_j} \geq 0 \\ \omega_j & \text{if } (i \neq j) \wedge \frac{\partial f_i}{\partial x_j} < 0 \end{cases} \tag{20}$$

and $\overline{\gamma}^i(\boldsymbol{x}) = [\overline{\gamma}^i(x_1), ..., \overline{\gamma}^i(x_j), ...]^T$. *In a similar way, define* $\underline{\gamma}^i(x_j)$ *as follows*

$$\underline{\gamma}^i(x_j) = \begin{cases} \omega_i & \text{if } i = j \\ \omega_j & \text{if } (i \neq j) \wedge \frac{\partial f_i}{\partial x_j} \geq 0 \\ \Omega_j & \text{if } (i \neq j) \wedge \frac{\partial f_i}{\partial x_j} < 0 \end{cases} \tag{21}$$

and $\underline{\gamma}^i(\boldsymbol{x}) = [\underline{\gamma}^i(x_1), ..., \underline{\gamma}^i(x_k), ...]^T$. *Now the components of the differential equations which make it possible to compute the upper and lower solutions are obtained as follows*

$$i = 1, \ldots, n, \quad \begin{cases} \dot{\omega}_i(t) = f_i(\underline{\gamma}^i(\boldsymbol{x}), \underline{\delta}^i(\mathbf{p}), t) \\ \dot{\Omega}_i(t) = f_i(\overline{\gamma}^i(\boldsymbol{x}), \overline{\delta}^i(\mathbf{p}), t) \end{cases} \tag{22}$$

Denote

$$\underline{f}_i(\omega, \Omega, \underline{\mathbf{p}}, \overline{\mathbf{p}}, t) = f_i(\underline{\gamma}^i(\boldsymbol{x}), \underline{\delta}^i(\mathbf{p}), t) \tag{23}$$

$$\overline{f}_i(\omega, \Omega, \underline{\mathbf{p}}, \overline{\mathbf{p}}, t) = f_i(\overline{\gamma}^i(\boldsymbol{x}), \overline{\delta}^i(\mathbf{p}), t) \tag{24}$$

then obviously $\omega(t)$ *and* $\Omega(t)$ *are in general, solutions of a system of coupled differential equations, i.e.*

$$\begin{cases} \dot{\omega}(t) = \underline{f}(\omega, \Omega, \underline{\mathbf{p}}, \overline{\mathbf{p}}, t), & \omega(t_0) = \underline{\boldsymbol{x}}_0 \\ \dot{\Omega}(t) = \overline{f}(\omega, \Omega, \underline{\mathbf{p}}, \overline{\mathbf{p}}, t), & \Omega(t_0) = \overline{\boldsymbol{x}}_0 \end{cases} \tag{25}$$

which involve no uncertain quantity. Therefore interval Taylor models such as the one introduced in the previous section can be used for efficiently solving (25). Indeed when these methods are used for solving differential equations with no uncertainty, they are usually able to curb the pessimism induced by the wrapping effect, even over long integration time.

Remark 2. *Althoug interval Taylor models can be used for solving in an efficient way the system (25), there is no guaranty that the size of the enclosure* $[\omega(t), \Omega(t)]$ *will not diverge.*

In practice, when rule 1 is used with functions the monotonicity of which changes along the time interval $[t_0, t_{n_T}]$, the obtained bracketing functions $\{\underline{f}, \overline{f}\}$ are not continuously differentiable. Therefore interval Taylor models cannot be used directly for numerical integration. In the sequel, we will show how we can overcome this difficulty by using hybrid automata as bracketting systems. But first, let us recall how to compute the reachable sets with set integration.

4 Computing Reachable Sets with Set Integration

For $j = 0, \ldots, n_T - 1$ and $t \in [t_j, t_{j+1}]$ define

$$[\boldsymbol{x}](t) = [\boldsymbol{x}_j] + \sum_{i=1}^{k-1} (t - t_j)^i \boldsymbol{f}^{[i]}([\boldsymbol{x}_j], [\boldsymbol{p}], t_j) + (t - t_j)^k \boldsymbol{f}^{[k]}([\boldsymbol{\psi}_j], [\boldsymbol{p}], [t_j, t_{j+1}]) \quad (26)$$

Proposition 1

$$\text{If } [\boldsymbol{\psi}_j] \supseteq [\tilde{\boldsymbol{x}}_j] \quad \text{then } \forall t \in [t_j, t_{j+1}],\ \boldsymbol{x}(t) \in [\boldsymbol{x}](t), \quad j = 0, \ldots, n_T - 1 \quad (27)$$

Proof 1. *It suffices to write a Taylor series expansion at time* t_j *and use* $[\tilde{\boldsymbol{x}}_j]$ *for evaluating the remainder term (see [16]).*

Define $\overline{\mathcal{R}}$ as an over-approximation of a reachable space $\mathcal{R}$, as follows

$$\forall t, t' \in [t_0, t_{N_T}],\ \overline{\mathcal{R}}([t, t']; [\boldsymbol{x}](t)) \supseteq \mathcal{R}([t, t']; [\boldsymbol{x}](t)) \quad (28)$$

Proposition 2. *A conservative over-approximation of (28) is given by*

$$\forall t \in [t_j, t_{j+1}],\ \overline{\mathcal{R}}([t_j, t]; [\boldsymbol{x}_j]) = \cup_{\tau \in [t_j, t]} [\boldsymbol{x}](\tau), \quad j = 0, \ldots, n_T - 1 \quad (29)$$

and satisfies

$$\forall t \in [t_j, t_{j+1}],\ \overline{\mathcal{R}}([t_j, t]; [\boldsymbol{x}_j]) \subseteq [\tilde{\boldsymbol{x}}_j], \quad j = 0, \ldots, n_T - 1 \quad (30)$$

Proof 2. *Obvious from (27) and (8).*

Define $\overline{\mathcal{R}}([t_0, t_0]; [\boldsymbol{x}_0]) = [\boldsymbol{x}_0]$.

Proposition 3. *An over-approximation of the reachable space 2 is given by*

$$\forall t \in [t_j, t_{j+1}],\ \overline{\mathcal{R}}([t_0, t]; [\boldsymbol{x}_0]) = \overline{\mathcal{R}}([t_0, t_j]; [\boldsymbol{x}_0]) \cup \overline{\mathcal{R}}([t_j, t]; [\boldsymbol{x}_j]), \quad j = 1, \ldots, n_T - 1 \quad (31)$$

and satisfies

$$\forall t \in [t_j, t_{j+1}], \quad \overline{\mathcal{R}}([t_0, t]; [\boldsymbol{x}_0]) \subseteq \cup_{i \in \{0, j\}} [\tilde{\boldsymbol{x}}_i], \quad j = 1, \ldots, n_T - 1 \quad (32)$$

Proof 3. *Obvious from (27) and proposition (2).*

As a conclusion, it is clear that thanks to (26) and (31), one can derive explicit formulas which characterize the boundaries of the reachable space. In practice however, one can use instead of (31) the over-approximation (32) obtained by using the *a priori* solutions $[\tilde{\boldsymbol{x}}_j]$ only.

5 Computing a Reachable Set by Using Hybrid Automata as Bounding Systems

In this section, we introduce a new approach for enclosing the reachable space of uncertain dynamical systems, for which the signs of the partial derivatives $\partial f_i/\partial x_j$ and $\partial f_i/\partial p_k$ change along the integration time interval $[t_0, t_{n_T}]$. In such a case, the Müller's theorem and rule 1 make it possible to build system (25) over each time interval where functions f_i are monotonic with respect to both variables x_j and p_k. When system (1) is analysed over the whole time interval $[t_0, t_{n_T}]$, the bounding systems given by rule 1 are only piecewise C^k-times continuously differentiable. System (25) can then be regarded as a hybrid dynamical system, and thus be modelled by the following hybrid automaton

$$\mathcal{H} = (\mathcal{Q}, \mathcal{E}, \mathcal{D}, \mathcal{P}, \mathcal{F}, \mathcal{T}, \mathcal{J}) \tag{33}$$

where:

1. $\mathcal{Q}$ is a finite set of modes. For each mode corresponds a continuous-time system which provides the maximal and minimal solution of (1). These systems are built using rule 1.
2. $\mathcal{E} \subseteq \mathcal{Q} \times \mathcal{Q}$ is the set of the transitions. It contains all the possible commutations between the continuous systems which bracket (1).
3. $\mathcal{D}$ is the state space of (1).
4. $\mathcal{P} = [\boldsymbol{p}] = [\underline{\boldsymbol{p}}, \overline{\boldsymbol{p}}]$ represents a feasible domain for model parameters for (1).
5. $\mathcal{F} = \{(\underline{f}_q, \overline{f}_q), q \in \mathcal{Q}\}$ is the collection of bracketing systems obtained with rule 1
$$\forall q \in \mathcal{Q}, \quad \begin{cases} \underline{f}_q : \mathcal{D}^2 \times \mathcal{P}^2 \longrightarrow \mathcal{D} \\ \overline{f}_q : \mathcal{D}^2 \times \mathcal{P}^2 \longrightarrow \mathcal{D} \end{cases} \tag{34}$$
6. $\mathcal{T} = \{t_e, e \in \mathcal{E}\}$ is the collection of switching time instants. Define $g_{i,r}(.) = \frac{\partial f_i}{\partial p_r}(.)$ and $h_{i,l}(.) = \frac{\partial f_i}{\partial x_l}(.)$ with $i \in \{1, ..., n, \}, r \in \{1, ..., n_p, \}$ and $l \in \{1, ..., n\}$. The set $\mathcal{T}$ is defined as
$$\mathcal{T} = \left\{ \begin{array}{c} t_e \in [t_0\, t_{n_T}] \,|\, \exists i, \exists l, \exists r, \exists \boldsymbol{p} \in [\boldsymbol{p}], \exists \boldsymbol{x} \in [\boldsymbol{x}](t_e) \\ ((g_{i,r}(\boldsymbol{x}, \boldsymbol{p}, t_e) = 0) \vee (h_{i,l}(\boldsymbol{x}, \boldsymbol{p}, t_e) = 0)) \end{array} \right\} \tag{35}$$
That is to say that if the monotonicity of f with respect to a parameter or state vector component changes at t_e, a transition $e = (q, q') \in \mathcal{E}$ occurs and the bracketing systems changes too.
7. $\mathcal{J} = \{\mathcal{J}_e, e \in \mathcal{E}\}$ is the collection of reset functions. They initialize the field vectors $\overline{f}_{q'}$ (resp.$\underline{f}_{q'}$) after the activation of a transition $e = (q, q')$: $\{\underline{\boldsymbol{x}}_{q'}(t_e), \overline{\boldsymbol{x}}_{q'}(t_e)\} = \mathcal{J}_e(\underline{\boldsymbol{x}}_q(t_e), \overline{\boldsymbol{x}}_q(t_e))$.

Now, in order to use rule 1, we will split the experiment time period $[t_0, t_{n_T}]$ into a succession of integration time intervals $[t_j, t_{j+1}]$ where $t_{j+1} = t_j + h_j$ and where integration time steps h_j are either chosen a priori or adapted on-line as in the preceding sections.

Denote $\mathcal{I}_M$, the set of time intervals $[t_j, t_{j+1}]$ over which no switching occurs, i.e., all the components of the field vectors of f of (1) are monotonic with respect to each parameter and state vector

$$\mathcal{I}_M = \{[t_j, t_{j+1}] \subseteq [t_0, t_{n_T}] | \forall e \in \mathcal{E}, t_e \notin [t_j, t_{j+1}]\} \tag{36}$$

Next proposition shows how to compute an inner approximation $\underline{\mathcal{I}_M}$ for $\mathcal{I}_M$, i.e. a set which satisfies the property

$$[t, t'] \in \underline{\mathcal{I}_M} \Rightarrow [t, t'] \in \mathcal{I}_M \tag{37}$$

Proposition 4 (Inner approximation of $\mathcal{I}_M$) *An inner approximation $\underline{\mathcal{I}_M} \subseteq \mathcal{I}_M$ is given by*

$$\underline{\mathcal{I}_M} \equiv \left\{ \begin{array}{c} [t_j,\, t_{j+1}] \subseteq [t_0, t_{n_T}] \,|\, \forall i,\, \forall l,\, \forall k, \\ ((0 \notin [g]_{i,k}([\tilde{\boldsymbol{x}}_j], [\boldsymbol{p}]), [t_j,\, t_{j+1}]) \wedge (0 \notin [h]_{i,l}([\tilde{\boldsymbol{x}}_j], [\boldsymbol{p}]), [t_j,\, t_{j+1}])) \end{array} \right\} \tag{38}$$

Proof 4. *Since the a priori solution $[\tilde{\boldsymbol{x}}_j]$ of (1) as given by (8) or (17) encloses the whole state trajectory over $[t_j, t_{j+1}]$, we can write*

$$\begin{array}{c} \forall i,\, \forall j,\, \forall \boldsymbol{x}(t_j) \in [\boldsymbol{x}_j],\, \forall \boldsymbol{p} \in [\boldsymbol{p}],\, \forall t \in [t_j, t_{j+1}] \\ g_{i,j}(\boldsymbol{x}, \boldsymbol{p}, t) \in [g]_{i,j}([\tilde{\boldsymbol{x}}], [\boldsymbol{p}], [t_j, t_{j+1}]) \end{array} \tag{39}$$

Consequently

$$0 \notin [g]_{i,j}([\tilde{\boldsymbol{x}}], [\boldsymbol{p}], [t_j, t_{j+1}]) \Rightarrow \forall t \in [t_j, t_{j+1}],\, g_{i,j}(\boldsymbol{x}, \boldsymbol{p}, t) \neq 0 \tag{40}$$

We have similar results for function $h_{i,l}$. This ends the proof.

Similarly, define the set $\mathcal{I}_S$ of intervals where a switching occurs, i.e.,

$$\mathcal{I}_S = \{[t_j, t_{j+1}] \subset [t_0, t_{n_T}] \,|\, \exists e \in \mathcal{E}, t_e \in [t_j, t_{j+1}]\} \tag{41}$$

Since we have

$$[t_0, t_{n_T}] = \mathcal{I}_M \cup \mathcal{I}_S \tag{42}$$

then an outer approximation $\overline{\mathcal{I}_S}$ of $\mathcal{I}_S$, i.e. a set which satisfies the property

$$[t, t'] \in \mathcal{I}_S \Rightarrow [t, t'] \in \overline{\mathcal{I}_S} \tag{43}$$

can be obtained as follows

$$\overline{\mathcal{I}_S} = [t_0, t_{n_T}] \setminus \underline{\mathcal{I}_M} \tag{44}$$

Now, we can use rule (1) over each time intervals $[I_m] \in \underline{\mathcal{I}_M}$ in order to derive $\underline{f}_m$ and $\overline{f}_m$ to bracket all the possible solutions of the uncertain system (1)

$$\begin{array}{c} \forall [I_m] \in \underline{\mathcal{I}_M},\, \forall m \in \mathcal{Q},\, \forall \boldsymbol{p} \in [\boldsymbol{p}],\, \forall \boldsymbol{x} \in \mathcal{D}, \\ \forall t \in [I_m],\, \underline{f}_m(\omega, \Omega, \underline{\boldsymbol{p}}, \overline{\boldsymbol{p}}, t) \leq \boldsymbol{f}(\boldsymbol{x}, \boldsymbol{p}, t) \leq \overline{f}_m(\omega, \Omega, \underline{\boldsymbol{p}}, \overline{\boldsymbol{p}}, t) \end{array} \tag{45}$$

where $(\underline{f}_m, \overline{f}_m) \in \mathcal{F}$.

One difficulty remains as the actual time instant, i.e., t_e in (35) when the hybrid system reaches one of its switching time instant is unknown a priori. By using a validated interval Taylor model integration method we will be able to solve this problem *on-the-fly* in an efficient and guaranteed way. By doing so, we keep the guarantee property for the enclosures without having to derive the actual time instant where the commutation occurs. Let us use *mode* 0 to denote the original *uncertain* dynamical system and *modes* $q \neq 0$ to denote coupled bounding systems. The following propositions will make it possible to detect on-the-fly the switching between modes, i.e. $q \neq 0 \mapsto q' = 0$ and $q = 0 \mapsto q' \neq 0$ and to instantiate the new mode.

Proposition 5 (Switching $q \neq 0 \mapsto q' = 0$)

$$\begin{aligned}&\textit{If}(\ (q \neq 0) \wedge \\ &\quad (\exists i,\ \exists l,\ \exists k,\ (0 \in [g]_{i,k}([\tilde{\boldsymbol{x}}_j], [\boldsymbol{p}], [t_j,\ t_{j+1}])) \vee (0 \in [h]_{i,l}([\tilde{\boldsymbol{x}}_j], [\boldsymbol{p}], [t_j,\ t_{j+1}])))) \\ &\Rightarrow ((e = (q, q') \wedge (q' = 0)) \wedge ([\tilde{\boldsymbol{x}}_j] \ \textit{must be re-computed via (8)})\end{aligned} \tag{46}$$

Proof 5. *When mode $q \neq 0$ and one of the partial derivatives $g(.)$ or $h(.)$ changes sign at $t_e \in [t_j, t_{j+1}]$ then a transition occurs and the new mode is necessarily $q' = 0$. Indeed in this case, the sign of the partial derivative cannot be ascertained for all t in $[t_j, t_{j+1}]$. Now, recall that $[\tilde{\boldsymbol{x}}_j]$ is computed via (17). But, since solutions $\omega(t)$ and $\Omega(t)$ computed with the bounding systems derived for mode q are valid only over $[t_j,\ t_e]$, $[\tilde{\boldsymbol{x}}_j]$ does not contain $[\boldsymbol{x}](t)$ for $t \in]t_e,\ t_{j+1}]$. $[\tilde{\boldsymbol{x}}_j]$ must be re-computed with the original* uncertain *system.*

Proposition 6 (Switching $q = 0 \mapsto q' \neq 0$)

$$\begin{aligned}&\textit{If}(\ (q = 0) \wedge \\ &\quad (\forall i,\ \forall l,\ \forall k,\ (0 \notin [g]_{i,k}([\tilde{\boldsymbol{x}}_j], [\boldsymbol{p}], [t_j,\ t_{j+1}])) \wedge (0 \notin [h]_{i,l}([\tilde{\boldsymbol{x}}_j], [\boldsymbol{p}], [t_j,\ t_{j+1}])))) \\ &\Rightarrow (e = (q, q') \wedge (q' \neq 0))\end{aligned} \tag{47}$$

Proof 6. *When mode $q = 0$ and it becomes possible to ascertain the sign of all the partial derivatives $g(.)$ and $h(.)$ for all t in $[t_j, t_{j+1}]$ which is done by using the inclusion functions, then a transition occurs and the new mode is necessarily $q' \neq 0$. $[\tilde{\boldsymbol{x}}_j]$ is computed with interval Taylor models and is always valid. Numerical integration can then be taken forward from t_{j+1}.*

Finally, the algorithm for computing the reachable space of (1) is as follows

Algorithm **Hybrid-Bounding**
(in:$t_0, t_{n_T}, \boldsymbol{f}, \boldsymbol{F}, [\boldsymbol{x}_0], [\boldsymbol{p}]$; out:$[\tilde{\boldsymbol{x}}_0], [\tilde{\boldsymbol{x}}_1], \ldots, [\tilde{\boldsymbol{x}}_{n_T}], [\boldsymbol{x}_1], \ldots, [\boldsymbol{x}_{n_T}]$)

$j := 0$;
$q :=$ ***Initialize***$(f, [\boldsymbol{x}_0], [\boldsymbol{p}])$;
while ($j < n_T$) do
  $\{h_j, [\boldsymbol{x}_{j+1}], [\tilde{\boldsymbol{x}}_j]\} :=$ **Integrate-one-step-ahead**$(q, \{f\}, \mathcal{F}, t_j, [\boldsymbol{x}_j], [\boldsymbol{p}])$;
  $\{\_jump\_, q'\} :=$ **Check-Switching**$(q, \{f\}, [\tilde{\boldsymbol{x}}_j])$;

6. if (_*jump*_) then
7.   if ($q = 0$) then
8. $q := q'$; $j := j + 1$;
9.   else
10. $q := 0$;
11.   endif
12. else
13. $j := j + 1$;
14. endif
15. end

where algorithm **Integrate-one-step-ahead** computes the one-step ahead solution for an uncertain differential equation. It is summarized in the following algorithm

Algorithm **Integrate-one-step-ahead**
(in : $q, \{f\}, \mathcal{F}, t_j, [\boldsymbol{x}_j], [\boldsymbol{p}]$; out : $h_j, [\boldsymbol{x}_{j+1}], [\tilde{\boldsymbol{x}}_j]$)
1. if $q := 0$ then
2. $\{h_j, [\boldsymbol{x}_{j+1}], [\tilde{\boldsymbol{x}}_j]\}$:= **Interval-Integrate**($f, [\boldsymbol{x}_j], [\boldsymbol{p}], t_j$);
3. else
4. $(\underline{f}_q, \overline{f}_q)$:= **Select-Boundings**($q, \mathcal{F}$);
5. $[\omega_j] := [\underline{\boldsymbol{x}}_j]$;
6. $[\Omega_j] := [\overline{\boldsymbol{x}}_j]$;
7. $\{h_j, [\omega_{j+1}], [\Omega_{j+1}], [\tilde{\omega}_j], [\tilde{\Omega}_j])\} :=$
            Interval-Integrate($\underline{f}_q, \overline{f}_q, [\omega_j], [\Omega_j], [\underline{\boldsymbol{p}}], [\overline{\boldsymbol{p}}], t_j$);
8. $[\tilde{\boldsymbol{x}}_j] := [Inf([\tilde{\omega}_j]), Sup([\tilde{\Omega}_j])]$;
9. $[\boldsymbol{x}_{j+1}] := [Inf([\omega_{j+1}]), Sup([\Omega_{j+1}])]$;
10. end

In algorithm **Hybrid-Bounding**, line 2 initializes the initial mode, i.e. at time t_0. While integration time is smaller that t_{n_T}, algorithm integrates one step ahead from t to $t+h$ (line 4), then checks if a mode switching occurs during the time interval $[t, t+h]$ (line 5). This is done by cheking if the signs of the partial derivatives $g_{i,r}$ and $h_{i,l}$ have changed. If this is the case, variable _*jump*_ is set to *true*, otherwise it is set to $false$. If there is a switching, then action will depend on the current mode. If the current mode is $q = 0$ then it suffices to switch to the new mode $q' \neq 0$ and carry on integration (lines 8-9) according to proposition 6. To the contrary, if current mode is not 0, then algorithm has to re-do computation for current time step with the *uncertain* model in order to cross the switching condition in a guaranteed way (lines 11) according to proposition 5.

In algorithm **Integrate-one-step-ahead**, numerical integration is done via interval Taylor models with the original uncertain system when $q = 0$ (line 2). When $q \neq 0$, the bounding systems are selected at line 4 and bounding solutions $\omega(t_j)$ and $\Omega(t_j)$ are set at line 5 and 6. The numerical integration is performed at line 7. In order to have guaranteed results, we have choosen to use the same interval Taylor model method as in line 2 for solving the coupled system (25), but with intervals of zero width.

6 Example

We consider the Haldane model to simulate the biotechnological process in a stirred reactor. The model is taken from [4] but addresses the existence of one specy on a chemostat with a single substrate. Consider the following equations:

$$\begin{cases} \dot{x} = f_x(x,s) = (\mu_0 \frac{s}{s+k_s+s^2/k_i} - \alpha d)x \\ \dot{s} = f_s(x,s) = -k\mu_0 \frac{s}{s+k_s+s^2/k_i} x + (s_{in} - s)d \end{cases} \tag{48}$$

where x designates the biomass density, s the substrate concentration, d the dilution rate of the chemostat, s_{in} the concentration of input substrate. The coefficients k, k_s, k_i and α are positive constans which are defined as follows $k = 42.14$, $k_s = 9.28mmol/l$, $k_i = 256mmol/l$ and $\alpha = 0.5$. $s_{in}(t) = s_{in}^0 + 15\cos(1/5t)$ and $d = 2$. The coefficients μ_0 and s_{in}^0 are assumed uncertain : $\mu_0 = 0.75$ with relative uncertainty $\pm 1\%$ and $s_{in}^0 = 65$ with relative uncertainty $\pm 1.5\%$. Initial state is taken uncertain and is defined as follows $x(t_0) \times s(t_0) = [9.5, 10.5] \times [36, 44]$.

It easy to check that the signs of the partial derivatives needed to apply rule 1 are as follows

$$\text{sign}(\partial f_x/\partial s) = \text{sign}(k_s k_i - s^2) \tag{49}$$

$$\forall t > t_0,\ (\partial f_x/\partial \mu_0 > 0) \wedge (\partial f_s/\partial x < 0) \wedge (\partial f_s/\partial \mu_0 < 0) \wedge (\partial f_s/\partial s_{in}^0 > 0) \tag{50}$$

Hence, the automaton (33) which must be used with algorithm **Hybrid-Bounding** contains only 3 modes:

- mode $q = 0$ corresponds to the original system (48) ;
- mode $q = 1$ is active when $s > \sqrt{k_s k_2}$, i.e. $\partial f_x/\partial s < 0$ and system (25) writes

$$\begin{cases} \dot{\underline{x}} = \underline{\mu}_0 \frac{\overline{s}}{\overline{s}+k_s+\overline{s}^2/k_i} \underline{x} - \alpha u \underline{x} \\ \dot{\underline{s}} = -k\overline{\mu}_0 \frac{\underline{s}}{\underline{s}+k_s+\underline{s}^2/k_i} \overline{x} + u(\underline{s}_{in} - \underline{s}) \\ \dot{\overline{x}} = \overline{\mu}_0 \frac{\underline{s}}{\underline{s}+k_s+\underline{s}^2/k_i} \overline{x} - \alpha u \overline{x} \\ \dot{\overline{s}} = -k\underline{\mu}_0 \frac{\overline{s}}{\overline{s}+k_s+\overline{s}^2/k_i} \underline{x} + u(\overline{s}_{in} - \overline{s}) \end{cases} \tag{51}$$

- mode $q = 2$ is active when $s < \sqrt{k_s k_2}$ and system (25) writes

$$\begin{cases} \dot{\underline{x}} = \underline{\mu}_0 \frac{\underline{s}}{\underline{s}+k_s+\underline{s}^2/k_i} \underline{x} - \alpha u \underline{x} \\ \dot{\underline{s}} = -k\overline{\mu}_0 \frac{\underline{s}}{\underline{s}+k_s+\underline{s}^2/k_i} \overline{x} + u(\underline{s}_{in} - \underline{s}) \\ \dot{\overline{x}} = \overline{\mu}_0 \frac{\overline{s}}{\overline{s}+k_s+\overline{s}^2/k_i} \overline{x} - \alpha u \overline{x} \\ \dot{\overline{s}} = -k\underline{\mu}_0 \frac{\overline{s}}{\overline{s}+k_s+\overline{s}^2/k_i} \underline{x} + u(\overline{s}_{in} - \overline{s}) \end{cases} \tag{52}$$

Algorithm **Interval-Integrate** is implemented with the extended mean value algorithm [16] with a constant integration time step $h = 0.03$s. Profil/BIAS C++ class library is used for interval computations and FADBAD++ package is used for computing the Taylor coefficients. The reachable space as obtained, in 16.75s CPU time, by algorithm **Hybrid-Bouding** for the integration time interval $[t_0 = 0\text{s}, t_{n_T} = 20\text{s}]$ is ploted in figure 1. Note also the switching hyperplane defined by $s = \sqrt{k_s k_2}$. To the contrary, the reachable space as obtained by a state-of-the-art interval Taylor model based method diverges after few steps only.

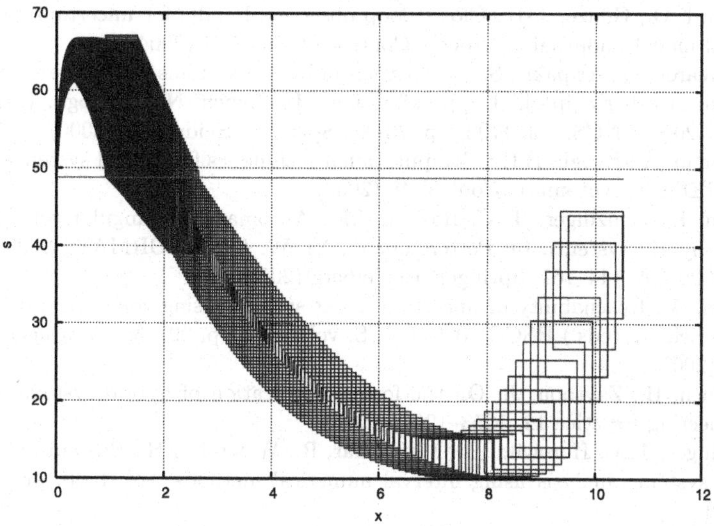

Fig. 1. Reachable space of (48) for $[t_0 = 0\text{s}, t_{n_T} = 20\text{s}]$. CPU time = 16.75s PIV 2GHz.

7 Conclusion

In this paper we have addressed the issue of computing the reachable space for non-autonomous uncertain nonlinear continuous dynamical systems by guaranteed set integration by employing the Müller's existence theorem and hybrid automata as bounding systems. We have shown that this *hybrid bounding* method is capable of computing the reachable space for non-linear systems with fairly large uncertainty in both parameter and state vectors. Used with state-of-the-art hybrid system verification tools, it should make it easier to solve hybrid reachability issues when the continuous dynamical systems are described via nonlinear differential equations. Further work will address error and convergence issues, i.e. how to ensure that the reachable space for a stable nonlinear system is tractable with the introduced method. Also we will study how to optimize the performance of the algorithms introduced when using a bisection strategy for crossing switching hyperplanes. Constraint propagation shall then be of great help.

References

1. Alur, R., Courcoubetis, C., Halbwachs, N., Henzinger, T.A., Ho, P.-H., Nicollin, X., Olivero, A., Sifakis, J., Yovine, S.: The algorithmic analysis of hybrid systems. Theoretical Computer Science 138, 3–34 (1995)
2. Asarin, E., Dang, T., Girard, A.: Hybridization methods for the analysis of nonlinear systems. Acta Informatica 43, 451–476 (2007)
3. Asarin, E., Maler, O., Pnueli, A.: Reachability analysis of dynamical systems having piecewise-constant derivatives. Theoretical Computer Science 138, 35–65 (1995)

4. Bernard, O., Gouzé, J.-L.: Closed loop observers bundle for uncertain biotechnological models. Journal of Process Control 14, 765–774 (2004)
5. Botchkarev, O., Tripakis, S.: Verification of hybrid systems with linear differential inclusions using ellipsoidal approximations. In: Lynch, N.A., Krogh, B.H. (eds.) HSCC 2000. LNCS, vol. 1790, pp. 73–88. Springer, Heidelberg (2000)
6. Chutinan, A., Krogh, B.H.: Computational techniques for hybrid systems verification. IEEE T. Automatic Control 48 (2003)
7. Doyen, L., Henzinger, T.A., Raskin, J.F.: Automatic rectangular refinement of affine hybrid systems. In: Pettersson, P., Yi, W. (eds.) FORMATS 2005. LNCS, vol. 3829, pp. 144–161. Springer, Heidelberg (2005)
8. Girard, A.: Reachability of uncertain linear systems using zonotopes. In: Morari, M., Thiele, L. (eds.) HSCC 2005. LNCS, vol. 3414, pp. 291–305. Springer, Heidelberg (2005)
9. Guéguen, H., Zaytoon, J.: On the formal verification of hybrid systems. Control Engineering Practice 12, 1253–1267 (2004)
10. Henzinger, T.A., Horowitz, B., Majumdar, R., Wong-Toi, H.: Beyond hytech: Hybrids systems analysis using interval numerical methods, vol. 1790, pp. 130–144 (2000)
11. Jaulin, L., Kieffer, M., Didrit, O., Walter, E.: Applied Interval Analysis: with examples in parameter and state estimation, robust control and robotics. Springer, London (2001)
12. Kieffer, M., Walter, E., Simeonov, I.: Guaranteed nonlinear parameter estimation for continuous-time dynamical models. In: Proceedings 14th IFAC Symposium on System Identification, Newcastle, Aus., pp. 843–848 (2006)
13. Kurzhanski, A.B., Varaiya, P.: Ellipsoidal techniques for hybrid dynamics: The reachability problem. In: Dayawansa, W.P., Lindquist, A., Zhou, Y. (eds.) New Directions and Applications in Control Theory. Lecture Notes in Control and Information Sciences, vol. 321, pp. 193–205. Springer, Heidelberg (2005)
14. Lefebvre, M.-A., Guéguen, H.: Hybrid abstractions of affine systems. Nonlinear Analysis 65(6), 1150–1167 (2006)
15. Müller, M.: Uber das fundamentaltheorem in der theorie der gewöhnlichen differentialgleichungen. Mathematische Zeitschrift 26, 619–645 (1927)
16. Nedialkov, N.S., Jackson, K.R., Corliss, G.F.: validated solutions of initial value problems for ordinary differential equations. Applied Mathematics and Computation 105, 21–68 (1999)
17. Rauh, A., Kletting, M., Aschemann, H., Hofer, E.P.: Interval methods for simulation of dynamical systems with state-dependent switching characteristics. In: Proceedings of the 2006 IEEE International Conference on Control Applications, Munich, pp. 355–360 (2006)
18. Walter, W.: Differential inequalities and maximum principles: Theory, new methods and applications. Nonlinear Analysis, Theory, Methods & Applications 30(8), 4695–4711 (1997)

Modeling and Simulation of Biochemical Processes Using Stochastic Hybrid Systems: The Sugar Cataract Development Process

Derek Riley[1], Xenofon Koutsoukos[1], and Kasandra Riley[2]

ISIS/EECS
[1] Vanderbilt University
Nashville, TN 37235, USA
Derek.Riley, Xenofon.Koutsoukos@vanderbilt.edu
Howard Hughes Medical Institute
[2] Yale University
New Haven, CT, USA
Kasandra.Riley@yale.edu

Abstract. As biomedical research advances there is an increasing need to model and simulate more complicated systems to better understand them. Since biochemical processes are inherently stochastic and often contain both continuous and discrete behavior, stochastic hybrid systems are an ideal modeling paradigm for capturing their dynamics. In this paper we present a framework for modeling biochemical systems and demonstrate the approach for the sugar cataract development process including two methods of modeling drug treatment. Further, we present a simulation method that uses second-order Taylor approximations for the continuous dynamics and an improved method for detecting boundary hits. We use the sugar cataract development process to demonstrate the results of the method.

1 Introduction

As biomedical research advances into more complicated systems, there is an increasing need to model and simulate these systems to better understand them. Since biochemical processes are inherently stochastic and often contain both continuous and discrete behavior, Stochastic Hybrid Systems (SHS) are an ideal modeling paradigm for capturing their complex dynamics. Such systems are often too large and complex for exhaustive verification techniques, so accurate, efficient simulation techniques are very important.

Recently, a renewed interest in the field of biochemical system modeling has increased the quality and diversity of the models created. Biological protein regulatory networks have been modeled with hybrid systems using linear differential equations to describe the changes in protein concentrations and discrete switches to activate or deactivate the continuous dynamics based on protein thresholds [1]. Biomolecular network modeling using hybrid systems is accomplished by using differential equations to model feedback mechanisms and discrete switches to

M. Egerstedt and B. Mishra (Eds.): HSCC 2008, LNCS 4981, pp. 429–442, 2008.

model changes in the underlying dynamics [2]. A modeling technique that uses polynomial SHS to construct models for chemical reactions is presented in [3]. A SHS model of a genetic regulatory network is compared to a deterministic model in [4]. Switching thresholds for piecewise-affine models of genetic regulatory networks are studied in [5]. SHS models of biochemical systems using reaction rate analysis have been developed and simulated in [6]. A biochemical system drug model based on physical interactions at the molecular level has been developed in [7].

Sugar Cataract Development (SCD) has been studied previously because it is a biomedically significant process, and the dynamics of the system are complex and difficult to test experimentally [8]. After a brief description of the SCD model presented in [6] and establishment of realistic parameters for its simulation, we present two new models of medication-controlled SCD. The first model incorporates the medication and models the effect that the medication has on the system. The second new model adds probabilistic delays to capture both the absorption of the drug into the system and drug metabolism.

Simulation of SHS is challenging because it must combine numerical integration methods for Stochastic Differential Equations (SDEs) and methods for detection of boundary crossings. Numerical integration of SDEs is accurate if the trajectory is sufficiently far from any boundaries; however, when the trajectory is close to a boundary, large errors can be incurred. A technique for accurately detecting absorbing boundaries has been developed for one-dimensional systems [9], and extensions have been proposed that scale to higher dimensional systems [10]. The boundary crossing detection algorithm presented in [11] uses analysis of moments to improve the accuracy of the approximation.

To improve upon previous SHS simulation techniques we present the Hybrid Milstein Method (HMM) which utilizes a second order Taylor-based approximation for the stochastic continuous dynamics in conjunction with a technique for accurately approximating the boundary hitting times. We validate the SCD models by comparing simulation trajectories of the SHS and the stochastic simulation algorithm (SSA), which is considered to be an accurate but computationally inefficient approximation.

The organization for the rest of the paper is as follows: Section 2 describes the biochemical modeling framework as well as three SCD models, Section 3 describes the SHS simulation technique, Section 4 presents our simulation results, and Section 5 concludes the work.

2 Modeling Biochemical Reactions Using SHS

2.1 Dynamics of Biochemical Reactions

Discrete models are a natural modeling paradigm for biochemical systems because they can capture the changes of the concentrations of the involved reactants and products based on the stoichiometry defined by the biochemical reaction. In a discrete model, when the reaction fires, the concentrations of the reactants and products are reset to the appropriate updated values.

To accurately model the reactions, the rate at which the individual reactions fire must be calculated. The rate at which chemical reactions occur is calculated using the stoichiometry defined by the type of reaction assuming temperature and pressure are constant. For example, the reaction $V + X \rightarrow Y + Z$, has a reaction rate $a = kvx$ where chemical species V, X, Y, and Z have concentrations v, x, y, and z, and k is the reaction's kinetic coefficient. The rates of other types of reactions can be calculated similarly [3].

Chemical reactions are inherently probabilistic because of the unpredictability of molecular motion [12]. Discrete stochastic models of reactions describe a reaction as firing at a rate which is calculated using the chemical concentrations and the kinetic coefficient. Slow reactions occur when reaction rates and concentrations are small enough and they can be modeled and simulated efficiently using discrete stochastic techniques. However, discrete simulations become inefficient when there are large concentrations of molecules and/or fast reaction rates. When discrete models become inefficient, reactions can be accurately modeled as continuous stochastic models [6].

The rate of change of each chemical species in a fast reaction is calculated using the chemical dynamics from the biochemical reactions. Suppose that we have a system of M chemical reactions and N chemical species. We define x_i as the concentration of the ith chemical species in micro-Molarity (μM), M_{fast} as the number of fast reactions, a_j as the reaction rate of the jth reaction, w as an M_{fast}-dimensional Wiener process, and the stoichiometric matrix v as a $(M_{fast} \times N)$ matrix whose values represent the concentration of chemical species lost or gained in each reaction. The dynamics for each of the i chemical species are described by

$$dx_i = \sum_{j=1}^{M_{fast}} v_{ji} a_j(x(t))dt + \sum_{j=1}^{M_{fast}} v_{ji} \sqrt{a_j(x(t))} dw_j. \tag{1}$$

Biochemical systems can contain a mixture of both fast and slow reactions. When fast and slow dynamics must both be considered it is most efficient to use a combined, hybrid modeling approach to take advantage of the efficiency of continuous modeling for the fast reactions while still keeping the accuracy of discrete modeling for the slow reactions. Determining which reactions are fast or slow is based on analysis of the rates using the kinetic coefficients and chemical concentrations. To determine the slowest rate, the smallest possible concentrations for each chemical species are used. Similarly, the fastest rate can be determined by using the highest possible concentrations. Since the reaction rates depend on the concentrations, reactions may be classified as either fast or slow dynamically based on the system state.

2.2 Medication Modeling

Understanding how a biochemical system will operate under normal conditions is important; however, in many systems, it is advantageous to understand how the system will act when it is perturbed by outside influences such as a medication. The interaction of a drug with a biochemical system is important to model and analyze because often the anticipated affect of the drug is altered by unforeseen influences, and theoretical modeling and testing can help to demonstrate the safety of a medication before it is tested on real subjects.

Drugs are administered to patients to improve their health by altering the equilibrium of the reactions responsible for their symptoms. There are several defining characteristics of drugs that are considered when modeling their behavior. Drugs can generally be classified as either stimulants or inhibitors, which respectively increase or decrease reaction rates. The efficacy of a drug is the potential therapeutic response that it could produce. Drugs are metabolized by the body at varying rates further complicating the system, so the decay of the drug must be understood to accurately model its behavior.

The most direct drug modeling approach is to add the drug's chemical species and reactions to the original model. While this may appear to be a logical approach, it adds significant complexity to the system. A simpler technique is to model the behavior of a drug as an inhibitor or stimulant and avoid increasing the number of chemical reactions or chemical species considered.

Because stimulants and inhibitors alter the reaction rates of certain reactions, modeling the effect of a drug on a given chemical reaction can be accomplished by altering the kinetic coefficients. The amount of change of the kinetic coefficients is determined by the efficacy and metabolism rate of the drug. For the SCD model, discrete modes describe the system under different drug influences, and discrete transitions model the application and metabolism of the drug.

2.3 Stochastic Hybrid Systems

We adopt the model presented in [13]. To establish the notation, we let Q be a set of discrete states. For each $q \in Q$, we consider the Euclidean space $\mathbb{R}^{d(q)}$ with dimension $d(q)$ and we define an invariant as an open set $X^q \subseteq \mathbb{R}^{d(q)}$. The hybrid state space is denoted as $S = \bigcup_{q \in Q} \{q\} \times X^q$. Let $\bar{S} = S \cup \partial S$ and $\partial S = \bigcup_{q \in Q} \{q\} \times \partial X^q$ denote the completion and the boundary of S respectively. The Borel σ-field in S is denoted as $\mathcal{B}(S)$.

To define the execution of the system, we denote $(\Omega, \mathcal{F}, P)$ the underlying probability space, and consider an $\mathbb{R}^p$-valued Wiener process $w(t)$ and a sequence of stopping times $\{t_0 = 0, t_1, t_2, \ldots\}$. Let the state at time t_i be $s(t_i) = (q(t_i), x(t_i))$ with $x(t_i) \in X^{q(t_i)}$. While the continuous state stays in $X^{q(t_i)}$, $x(t)$ evolves according to the SDE

$$dx = b(q, x)dt + \sigma(q, x)dw \tag{2}$$

where the discrete state $q(t) = q(t_i)$ remains constant. A sample path of the stochastic process is denoted by $x_t(\omega), t > t_i, \omega \in \Omega$.

The next stopping time t_{i+1} represents the time when the system transitions to a new discrete state. The discrete transition occurs either because the continuous state x exits the invariant $X^{q(t_i)}$ of the discrete state $q(t_i)$ (guarded transition) or based on an exponential distribution with nonnegative transition rate function $\lambda : \bar{S} \rightarrow \mathbb{R}_+$ (probabilistic transition). At time t_{i+1} the system will transition to a new discrete state and the continuous state may jump according to the transition measure $R : \bar{S} \times \mathcal{B}(\bar{S}) \rightarrow [0, 1]$. The evolution of the system is then governed by the SDE (2) with $q(t) = q(t_{i+1})$ until the next stopping time. If $t_{i+1} = \infty$, the system continues to evolve according to (2) with $q(t) = q(t_i)$.

The following assumptions are imposed on the model. The functions $b(q, x)$ and $\sigma(q, x)$ are bounded and Lipschitz continuous in x for every q, and thus the SDE (2) has a unique solution for every q. The transition rate function λ is a bounded and measurable function which is assumed to be integrable for every $x_t(\omega)$. For the transition measure, it is assumed that $R(\cdot, A)$ is measurable for all $A \in \mathcal{B}(S)$ and $R(s, \cdot)$ is a probability measure for all $s \in \bar{S}$, and $R((q, x), dz)$ is a stochastic continuous kernel. Let $N_t = \sum_i I_{t \geq t_i}$ denote the number of jumps in the interval $[0, t]$. It is assumed that the expected number of jumps is finite for every initial state $s \in S$, that is $E_s[N_t] < \infty$. A sufficient condition for ensuring finitely many jumps can be formulated by restricting $R(s, A)$ [14,15].

2.4 Sugar Cataract Modeling

This section describes three SHS models of the biochemical process of SCD. The first model describes the biochemical process of SCD. The two subsequent models extend the first model to include the effect of medication on the system. The first medicated model assumes that the effect of the drug on the system is instantaneous, while the final model is designed to incorporate probabilistic delay to model absorption and metabolization.

Sugar Cataract Development Model (SCD1). A sugar cataract distorts the light passing through the lens of an eye by attracting water to the lens when an excess of sorbitol is present. Often these cataracts are formed in the eyes of diabetic patients who have highly fluctuating blood sugar levels. Several factors affect the accumulation of sorbitol including the amount of the enzyme SDH. SDH catalyzes the reversible oxidation of sorbitol and other polyalcohols to the corresponding keto-sugars [8]. There are 8 chemical species involved in the reaction: $NADH(x_1)$, $E - NADH(x_2)$, $NAD^+(x_3)$, $E - NAD^+(x_4)$, SDH (x_5), Fructose(x_6), Sorbitol(x_7), and the inactive form of SDH (Z).

A SHS model for SCD (SCD1) has been previously presented in [6,16]. The ranges are bounded and are estimated using realistic concentration values derived from experimental data and Michaelis-Menten constants (Km) defined as the rate of the reaction at half-maximal velocity [8]. Table 1 describes the seven reactions and rates involved in SCD. The rates are calculated based on the concentrations and the kinetic coefficients presented in Table 1.

Each of the six fast reactions are modeled using the SDE (1). The inactive form of SDH (Z) is not a reactant in any of the chemical equations, so its concentration is not modeled. The equations describe the rates of change of the individual chemical species and are

Table 1. Sugar cataract reactions and kinetic coefficients

Reaction	Kinetic coefficient	Rate
$SDH + NADH \rightarrow E - NADH$	$k_1 = 6.2$	31.1
$E - NADH \rightarrow SDH + NADH$	$k_2 = 33$	151
$E - NADH + F \rightarrow E - NAD^+ + S$	$k_3 = 0.0022$	6
$E - NAD^+ + S \rightarrow E - NADH + F$	$k_4 = 0.0079$	19.5
$E - NAD^+ \rightarrow SDH + NAD^+$	$k_5 = 227$	998
$SDH + NAD^+ \rightarrow E - NAD^+$	$k_6 = .61$	3.2
$SDH \rightarrow Z$	$k_7 = 0.0019$	0.002

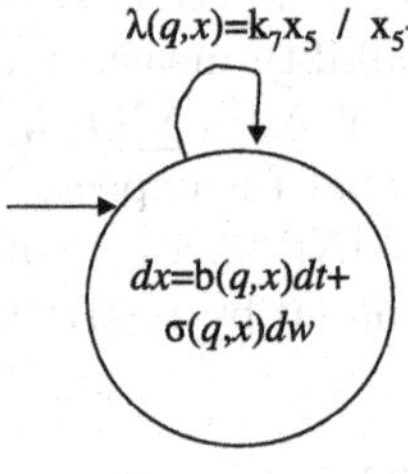

Fig. 1. SHS model of SCD1

$$
\begin{aligned}
dx_1 &= (-k_1x_1x_5 + k_2x_2)dt - \sqrt{k_1x_1x_5}dw_1 + \sqrt{k_2x_2}dw_2 \\
dx_2 &= (k_1x_1x_5 - k_2x_2 - k_3x_2x_6 + k_4x_4x_7)dt + \sqrt{k_1x_1x_5}dw_1 \\
&\quad -\sqrt{k_2x_2}dw_2 - \sqrt{k_3x_2x_6}dw_3 + \sqrt{k_4x_4x_7}dw_4 \\
dx_3 &= (k_5x_4 - k_6x_3x_5)dt + \sqrt{k_5x_4}dw_5 - \sqrt{k_6x_3x_5}dw_6 \\
dx_4 &= (k_3x_2x_6 - k_4x_4x_7 - k_5x_4 + k_6x_3x_5)dt + \sqrt{k_3x_2x_6}dw_3 \\
&\quad -\sqrt{k_4x_4x_7}dw_4 - \sqrt{k_5x_4}dw_5 + \sqrt{k_6x_3x_5}dw_6 \\
dx_5 &= (-k_1x_1x_5 + k_2x_2 + k_5x_4 - k_6x_3x_5)dt - \sqrt{k_1x_1x_5}dw_1 \\
&\quad +\sqrt{k_2x_2}dw_2 + \sqrt{k_5x_4}dw_5 - \sqrt{k_6x_3x_5}dw_6 \\
dx_6 &= (-k_3x_2x_6 + k_4x_4x_7)dt - \sqrt{k_3x_2x_6}dw_3 + \sqrt{k_4x_4x_7}dw_4 \\
dx_7 &= (k_3x_2x_6 - k_4x_4x_7)dt + \sqrt{k_3x_2x_6}dw_3 - \sqrt{k_4x_4x_7}dw_4
\end{aligned}
$$

The single slow reaction $SDH \rightarrow Z$ describes the conversion of the enzyme (SDH) into its inactive form at a rate of k_7x_5. When the reaction occurs, the number of molecules of x_5 is decreased by one and the concentration is decreased by $d_1 = 10^{-21}$ μM. The SHS model can be seen in Figure 1. The reset on the transition ($x_5- = d_1$) describes the effect of the single slow reaction on the concentration of x_5. For the SCD system, the classifications of the reactions do not change dynamically because the kinetic coefficients are significantly different and the chemical concentrations do not fluctuate widely.

SCD Model with Medication Control (SCD2). Drugs can help patients who are at high risk of developing sugar cataracts. These drugs work by inhibiting the enzyme SDH thereby reducing the rate at which SDH reacts with other molecules in the system. This initially results in less sorbitol production; however, since the reversible reactions are tightly coupled, the results can have side effects such as increasing the fructose levels.

We have created a new SHS model (SCD2), shown in Figure 2, of drug-modulated SCD to include the effect that drug has on the system. The application of the drug is represented as a new discrete mode that represents drug-influenced dynamics where the reaction rates k_1,k_6, and k_7 are reduced by 50% to model the inhibition of the enzyme. Since the drug is metabolized slowly and the amount that the rates are reduced is directly proportional to the concentration of the drug, modeling a constant concentration is a reasonable approximation.

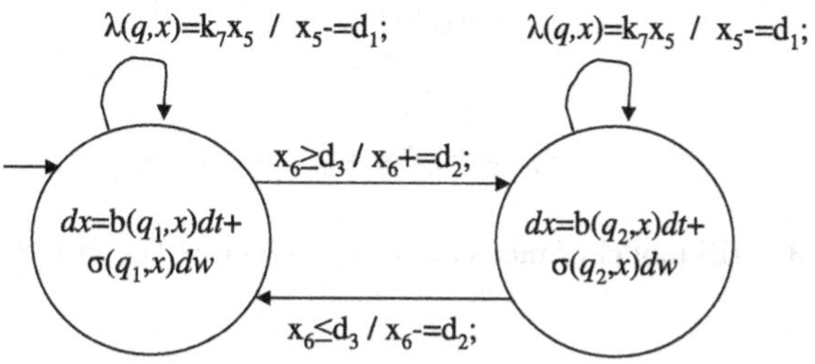

Fig. 2. SHS model of medication-controlled SCD2

We have modeled the drug administration based on an elevated level of fructose. It is assumed that patients self-monitor and self-administer the medication. When the amount of fructose in the blood rises above a threshold $d_3 = 250\ \mu$M, we use a guarded transition to drive the system to a new state which introduces the effect of the drug. When the fructose level drops back below d_3, we use another guarded transition to transition to the original state effectively removing the effect of the drug. We also include resets on the mode transitions to avoid infinitely fast switching that arises due to the stochastic nature of the Wiener process. The reset increases or decreases the fructose concentration by $d_2 = 1\ \mu$M.

SCD Model with Probabilistically-Delayed Medication Effect (SCD3). The SCD2 model is effective for demonstrating the effect of medication on the reactions; however, realistically the effect of the drug will not be immediate because of variable drug metabolism rates. Drugs are generally administered in a form called a prodrug which allows the transport of the actual drug to the appropriate cells. This prodrug is metabolized into an active form of the drug at different rates for different people. Furthermore, once a patient discontinues taking a drug, the body can metabolize the residual drug at variable rates depending on many factors.

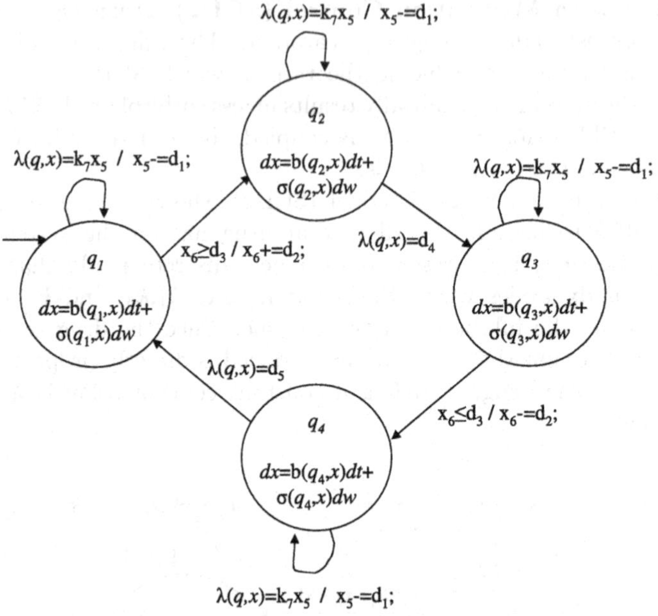

Fig. 3. SHS model of medication-controlled SCD3 with delays

We have developed a model (SCD3), seen in Figure 3, which incorporates two new states to model the delay of the conversion from prodrug to drug (q_2) and metabolism after dosage is discontinued (q_4). We use guarded transitions to model exiting the medicated and non-medicated states and entering the respective delay states. We then use probabilistic transitions to model the exit from the delay states to model the stochastic nature of the conversion and metabolism rates. The value $d_4 = 0.05$ is the rate of an exponential distribution that models the delay incurred by the conversion of prodrug to drug, and $d_5 = 0.05$ is the value which models the exponential distribution corresponding to the drug metabolism delay. These values were chosen so the average delay is on the order of one hour which is reasonable for the SCD system, but the values could be easily changed to model other types of medications. SHS can also incorporate the continuous state into the transition rate if such a model is necessary.

The continuous dynamics of the medicated (q_3) and non-medicated (q_1) states are consistent with SCD2. The dynamics of the delay state q_2 are the same as those in state q_1 to reflect the lack of change while the prodrug is being converted into the drug. The dynamics in the delay state q_4 model the metabolism of the drug after the administration is removed, so the kinetic coefficients are adjusted to reflect their half-life values. The coefficients can be adjusted to model various drugs.

3 SHS Simulation

3.1 Background

Simulating SHS is an important task because it can be used to understand and validate models. However, it is challenging because the interplay between the stochastic continuous and discrete dynamics can cause large errors if handled incorrectly. Errors can be decreased by reducing the step size of the approximation, but this comes at the cost of efficiency. Therefore, care must be taken to ensure that the simulation techniques used are accurate and efficient.

For numerical integration of SDEs, the order of convergence is used to quantify the quality of the approximation. An approximation $X^{\Delta t}(T)$ at time T with step size Δt converges with order γ strongly to the actual trajectory $x(T)$ if there exists $c > 0$ such that $E\left(\left|x(T) - X^{\Delta t}(T)\right|\right) \leq c\Delta t^{\gamma}$. $X^{\Delta t}(T)$ converges with order γ weakly to $x(T)$ if there exists $c > 0$ such that $E\left(\left|f(x(T)) - f(X^{\Delta t}(T))\right|\right) \leq c\Delta t^{\gamma}$ for a given class of measurable functions f [17]. Strong convergence implies that the trajectory is a possible trajectory of the system, and weak convergence implies that the computed trajectory only preserves the moments of the actual trajectory.

Simulation of SDEs can be performed using Taylor-based approximation techniques which have strong order of convergence of $\gamma = 0.5$ to $\gamma = 3.0$ and weak order of convergence of $\gamma = 1.0$ to $\gamma = 6.0$ depending on the number of approximating terms [17]. The computation of higher order terms requires many more operations and can be prohibitively expensive; therefore, a tradeoff must be reached to achieve the appropriate accuracy and efficiency.

Numerical integration methods for SDEs assume that the solution is far away from any boundaries; however, this assumption does not hold for SHS where the effect of the switching boundaries must be taken into account. Large errors can be incurred if the boundary conditions are not handled properly. Let us assume a system has an invariant X^q with a boundary ∂X_q, and the state at time t is $X(t)$. As shown in Figure 4, if Δt is large, it is possible that $X(t), X(t+\Delta t) \in X^q$, but $\exists \tau \in [t, t+\Delta t]$ where $x(\tau) \notin X^q$. In this case, a discrete transition will occur in the actual execution of the SHS but not in the approximating solution, and this discrepancy may cause a significant error.

3.2 Simulation of SDEs

Simulation of SDEs can be performed using the Euler Maruyama (EM) method which is a first-order Taylor scheme [17]. Assuming a d-dimensional drift coefficient b and a $d \times m$ diffusion coefficient σ, the kth component of the EM scheme is given by

$$X_{n+1}^{k} = X_{n}^{k} + b^{k}\Delta t + \sum_{j=1}^{m} \sigma^{k,j} \Delta W^{j}$$

for $k = 1, 2, ..., d$ where ΔW^{j} is the normally-distributed increment of the jth component of the m-dimensional Wiener process W. The EM method is simple

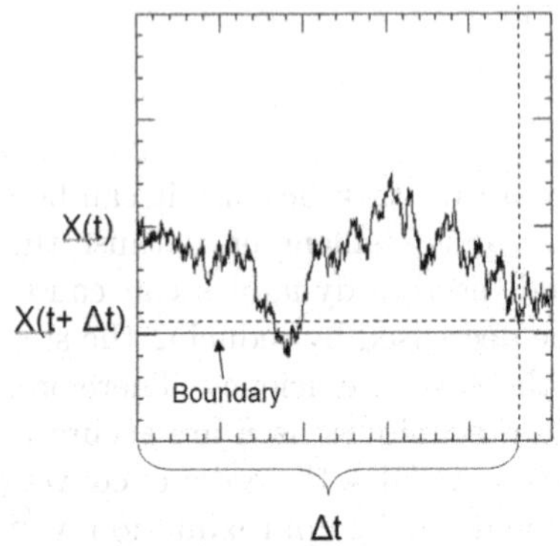

Fig. 4. A SHS trajectory close to a boundary

to implement, but achieves a strong convergence of $\gamma = 0.5$ and weak convergence $\gamma = 1.0$, so small time steps must be used to generate accurate approximations.

The Milstein Method (MM) is a second-order Taylor scheme and has a strong order of convergence $\gamma = 1.0$ while maintaining an acceptable efficiency. The kth component of the MM scheme is described by

$$X_{n+1}^k = X_n^k + b^k \Delta t + \sum_{j=1}^{m} \sigma^{k,j} \Delta W^j + \sum_{j_1,j_2=1}^{m} L^{j_1} \sigma^{k,j_2} I_{(j_1,j_2)}$$

where

$$L^j = \sum_{k=1}^{d} \sigma^{k,j} \frac{d}{dx^k} \text{ and } I_{(j_1,j_2)} = \int_{\tau_n}^{\tau_{n+1}} \int_{\tau_n}^{s_1} dw_{s_2}^{j_1} dw_s^{j_2}.$$

A method for approximating the multiple stochastic integrals is given in [17].

3.3 Switching Boundaries

Once the execution of the SHS hits a switching boundary, the current process is stopped (absorbed) and re-started in a new state; therefore, switching boundaries can be treated as absorbing boundaries. It is important to accurately estimate the time and location that the process is absorbed to minimize the error introduced into the approximation.

The naive technique to detect that a boundary was hit is to analyze the trajectory at each time step to determine if it has crossed the boundary or not. This method has a strong order of convergence of $\gamma = 0.5$ [11]. The technique developed in [18] determines whether or not the trajectory has hit an absorbing boundary with weak order $\gamma = 1.0$ assuming that the boundary is sufficiently smooth. We assume that the switching boundaries are hyperplanes $\partial X^q = \left\{x \in \mathbb{R}^{d(q)} : n.(x - X_b) = 0\right\}$ where n is the unit vector normal to the boundary ∂X^q, X_b is the position of the boundary, and denote X_t, $X_{t+\Delta t}$ the computed continuous state at time t and $t + \Delta t$ respectively. If $X_{t+\Delta t}$ hasn't crossed the boundary, but is close, the probability that the state trajectory has hit the boundary between t and $t + \Delta t$ is

$$P(hit) = exp\left(\frac{-2(n.(X_t - X_b))(n.(X_{t+\Delta t} - X_b))}{n.(\sigma\sigma^*(X_t)n)\Delta t}\right).$$

For this approximation to be accurate, $\sigma\sigma^T(X_t)$ must be non-degenerate in the direction normal to the boundary [18]. In between steps of the MM, the probability $P(hit)$ is tested against a uniform random value U in $[0, 1]$, and when $P(hit) < U$, we assume that the absorbing boundary has been hit.

Firing of the probabilistic transitions (according to the transition rate λ) occurs according the technique described in [15]. We draw a sample from a uniform distribution and test the exponential decay at various times to determine the jump time for each probabilistic transition. When the exponential decay is greater than or equal to the random value, the transition is fired.

We combine the absorbing boundary version of the MM and probabilistic firing technique to create the Hybrid Milstein Method (HMM) simulation technique for SHS. The resulting algorithm has a weak convergence of $\gamma = 1.0$. The following algorithm describes a version of one step of the simulation method.

Algorithm 3.1: HIGHORDERSHSSIMSTEP(X_t^k, $SimLength$)

$X_{t+\Delta t}^k = X_t^k + b^k\Delta t + \sum_{j=1}^m \sigma^{k,j}\Delta W^j + \sum_{j_1,j_2=1}^m L^{j_1}\sigma^{k,j_2} I_{(j_1,j_2)}$
$t{+}{+}$
if $U1 = rand(0,1) < exp(\frac{-2(n.(X_t^k - X_b))(n.(X_{t+\Delta t}^k - X_b))}{n.(\sigma\sigma^*(X_t)n)\Delta t})$
  then $FireGuardedTransition$
if $U2 = rand(0,1) < exp(-\lambda(t - TimeOfLastFire))$
  then $FireProbabilisticTransition$

4 Simulation Results

To better understand and validate our models, we present simulation results using variants of the SSA, EM, and MM methods. The SSA simulates chemical reactions consuming reactants and creating products one reaction at a time. Individual reactions in a system are assigned probabilities of occurrence, and probability distributions are used to choose which reaction fires at each iteration. Once a reaction fires, the quantities of reactants and products are updated [19]. The SSA is very accurate, but it can be inefficient for large systems or fast reactions because many iterations must be completed before results can be observed. To efficiently handle practical systems, computational improvements such as R-leaping have been devised for the SSA [20]. R-leaping increases the number of reactants consumed and products produced in each step by a factor of R. This increases the efficiency of the approximation, but will decrease the accuracy. Since updates are made based on concentrations, the overall time step can vary throughout the simulation.

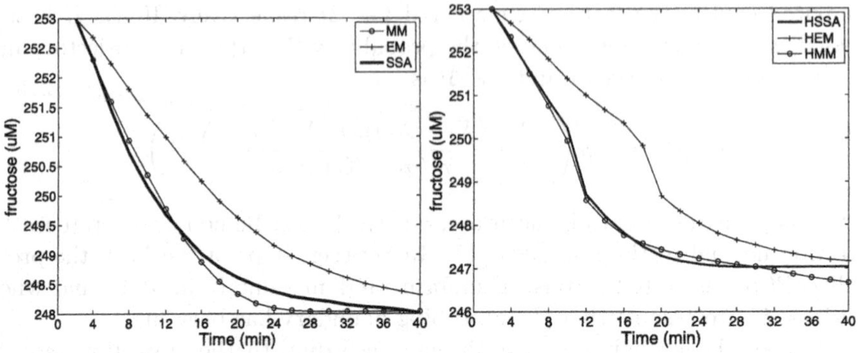

Fig. 5. Simulation results for SCD1 and SCD2

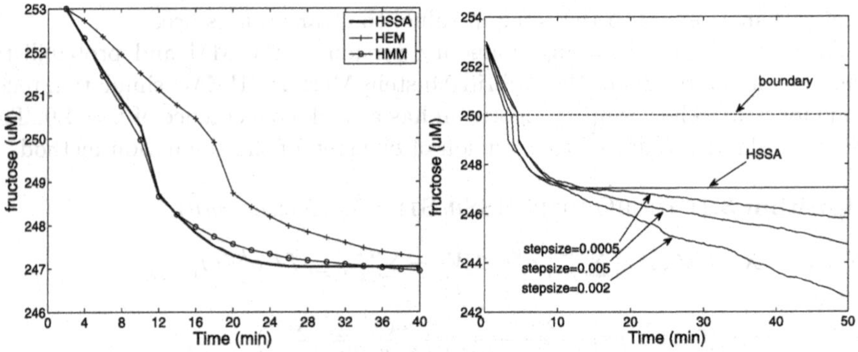

Fig. 6. Simulation results for SCD3 and stepsize comparison

For simulation of SCD2 and SCD3, we have created a new algorithm, the Hybrid Stochastic Simulation Algorithm (*HSSA*), which implements the SSA using R-leaping and discrete transitions between modes. After each iteration of the SSA, the guards for all valid transitions are tested, and a transition which validates its guard conditions is fired if possible. Once the transition resets have been executed, the SSA algorithm resumes in the new state.

The stochastic continuous dynamics of the SCD models can be simulated using EM approximations [17]. To accurately model the discrete transitions of the SCD models, we have developed a variant of the EM approximations called the Hybrid EM (*HEM*). In *HEM*, discrete transitions are incorporated into the EM approximations by analyzing transition guards between steps of the continuous dynamics simulation and executing the resets when a boundary crossing is detected. Once the state is updated, the EM algorithm continues in the new discrete state. We use the *HMM* as described in the previous section to provide a more accurate simulation result.

Since the SSA algorithm is considered to be an accurate approximation of a well-stirred chemical system [20], we compare the results of our *HSSA*, *HEM*, and *HMM* algorithms to demonstrate accuracy of the three SHS models and the accuracy of the approximations in Figures 5 and 6. We also present a comparison of the accuracy of the *HMM* for SCD3 at various resolutions in Figure 6. We chose to display the concentration of fructose because it is directly correlated with the development of cataracts, and it affects the administration of the medication. The initial conditions of the system are: $x_1 = 5.0$, $x_2 = 0.0$, $x_3 = 5.0$, $x_4 = 0.0$, $x_5 = 1.0$, $x_6 = 253.0$, and $x_7 = 0$. The figures display the average concentration at each time step for fructose for 100 runs of the three models. These results show that the high order simulation technique results in a more accurate simulation with a larger step size resulting in a faster simulation. The 100 *HSSA* simulations completed in 98 hours, the 100 *HEM* simulations took approximately 6 hours (with step size $\Delta t = 0.00001$), and the *HMM* simulations took approximately 3 hours (with step size $\Delta t = 0.0005$, and $p = 10$[1]) on a 3GHz desktop computer.

5 Conclusions and Future Work

Accurate and efficient simulation of SHS is an important task because it is an important tool which can expose the intricacies of the complicated dynamics of highly-coupled systems. The interplay between the continuous and discrete dynamics in SHS can introduce large errors into the simulations, so they must be handled carefully. Our technique using high-order methods for simulating SDEs combined with probabilistic boundary detection improves the accuracy and efficiency of the simulator when compared with the naive approaches. This work only addresses absorbing boundaries, so in the future we will also incorporate boundary conditions for reflecting boundaries that are required for practical systems such as biochemical processes.

Acknowledgements. This research is partially supported by the National Science Foundation (NSF) CAREER grant CNS-0347440.

References

1. Ghosh, R., Tomlin, C.: Symbolic reachable set computation of piecewise affine hybrid automata and its application to biological modeling: Delta-notch protein signalling. Sys. Bio. 1, 170–183 (2004)
2. Alur, R., Belta, C., Ivanicic, F., Kumar, V., Mintz, M., Pappas, G., Rubin, H., Schug, J.: Hybrid modeling and simulation of biomolecular networks. In: Di Benedetto, M.D., Sangiovanni-Vincentelli, A.L. (eds.) HSCC 2001. LNCS, vol. 2034, pp. 19–33. Springer, Heidelberg (2001)
3. Hespanha, J., Singh, A.: Stochastic models for chemically reacting systems using polynomial stochastic hybrid systems. Int. J. on Robust Cont., Special Issue on Control at Small Scales 15, 669–689 (2005)

[1] p is a parameter used to approximate the Stratonovich integrals as described in [17].

4. Hu, J., Wu, W., Sastry, S.: Modeling subtilin production in bacillus subtilis using stochastic hybrid systems. In: Alur, R., Pappas, G.J. (eds.) HSCC 2004. LNCS, vol. 2993, pp. 417–431. Springer, Heidelberg (2004)
5. Drulhe, S., Ferrari-Trecate, G., de Jong, H., Viari, A.: Reconstruction of switching thresholds in piecewise-affine models of genetic regulatory networks. In: Hespanha, J.P., Tiwari, A. (eds.) HSCC 2006. LNCS, vol. 3927, pp. 184–199. Springer, Heidelberg (2006)
6. Salis, H., Kaznessis, Y.: Accurate hybrid stochastic simulation of a system of coupled chemical or biochemical reactions. J. Chem. Phys. 122, 54–103 (2005)
7. Ramos, M., Melo, A., Henriques, E., Gomes, J., Reuter, N., Maigret, B., Floriano, W., Nascimento, M.: Modeling enzyme-inhibitor interactions in serine proteases. Int. J. Quant. Chem. 74(3), 299–314 (1999)
8. Marini, I., Bucchioni, L., Borella, P., Corso, A.D., Mura, U.: Sorbitol dehydrogenase from bovine lens: Purification and properties. Arch. Biochem. and Biophy. 340, 383–391 (1997)
9. Mannella, R.: Absorbing boundaries and optimal stopping in a stochastic differential equation. Phys. Lett. A 254, 257–262 (1999)
10. Lamm, G.: Extended brownian dynamics. iii. three dimensional diffusion. J. Chem. Phys. 80(6), 2845–2855 (1983)
11. Peters, E., Barenbrug, T.: Efficient brownian dynamics simulation of particles near walls. i. reflecting and absorbing walls. Physical Review 66, 1–7 (2002)
12. Elowitz, M., Levine, A., Siggia, E., Swain, P.: Stochastic gene expression in a single cell. Science 1183(297) (2002)
13. Bujorianu, M., Lygeros, J.: Theoretical foundations of general stochastic hybrid systems: Modeling and optimal control. In: IEEE Conf. on Dec. and Cont. (2004)
14. Koutsoukos, X., Riley, D.: Computational methods for reachability analysis of stochastic hybrid systems. In: Hespanha, J.P., Tiwari, A. (eds.) HSCC 2006. LNCS, vol. 3927, pp. 377–391. Springer, Heidelberg (2006)
15. Bernadskiy, M., Sharykin, R., Alur, R.: Structured modeling of concurrent stochastic hybrid systems. In: Lakhnech, Y., Yovine, S. (eds.) FORMATS 2004 and FTRTFT 2004. LNCS, vol. 3253, pp. 309–324. Springer, Heidelberg (2004)
16. Riley, D., Koutsoukos, X., Riley, K.: Safety analysis of sugar cataract development using stochastic hybrid systems. In: Bemporad, A., Bicchi, A., Buttazzo, G. (eds.) HSCC 2007. LNCS, vol. 4416, pp. 758–761. Springer, Heidelberg (2007)
17. Kloeden, P., Platen, E.: Numerical Solution of Stochastic Differential Equations. Springer, Heidelberg (1999)
18. Gobet, E.: Euler schemes and half-space approximation for the simulation of diffusion in a domain. ESAIM: Probability and Statistics 5, 261–297 (2001)
19. Gillespie, D.: A general method for numerically simulating the stochastic time evolution of coupled chemical reactions. J. Comp. Phys. 22, 403–434 (1976)
20. Auger, A., Chatelain, P., Koumoutsakos, P.: R-leaping: Accelerating the stochastic simulation algorithm by reaction leaps. J. Chem. Phys. 125, 84–103 (2006)

Distributed Lyapunov Functions in Analysis of Graph Models of Software*

Mardavij Roozbehani[1], Alexandre Megretski[1], Emilio Frazzoli[1], and Eric Feron[2]

[1] Laboratory for Information and Decision Systems
Massachusetts Institute of Technology (MIT), Cambridge, MA
mardavij@mit.edu, ameg@mit.edu, frazzoli@mit.edu
[2] Department of Aerospace Engineering
Georgia Institute of Technology, Atlanta, GA
feron@gatech.edu

Abstract. In previous works, the authors introduced a framework for software analysis, which is based on optimization of Lyapunov invariants. These invariants prove critical software properties such as absence of overflow and termination in finite time. In this paper, graph models of software are introduced and the software analysis framework is further developed and extended on graph models. A distributed Lyapunov function is assigned to the software by assigning a Lyapunov function to every node on its graph model. The global decremental condition is then enforced by requiring that the Lyapunov functions on each node decrease as transitions take place along the arcs. The concept of graph reduction and optimality of graphs for Lyapunov analysis is briefly discussed.

1 Introduction

Verification of safety-critical software systems presents itself with many challenges, including verification of the functional requirements, line-by-line verification of the code at the implementation level, and the need to prove absence of run-time errors. Due to its great potential to address these issues, static analysis has attracted computer scientists for decades. The book [13] provides an extensive collection of available results and techniques developed by computer scientists. Formal methods, including *Abstract Interpretation* [7], and *Model Checking* [5,6] were developed in this endeavor to advance software verification.

While software verification has attracted little attention in the control community, recently, there have been renewed efforts at establishing properties of software systems by the combined use of abstractions and control theoretic principles. Much of the relevant literature in that regard may be found in the recent field of *hybrid systems* [10]. See for instance [8]. In general, it was found that

* This work was supported by the National Science Foundation (NSF-0715025). Any opinions, findings, conclusions or recommendations expressed in this paper are those of the authors and do not necessarily reflect the views of the supporting organization.

M. Egerstedt and B. Mishra (Eds.): HSCC 2008, LNCS 4981, pp. 443–456, 2008.

many methods developed in system and control theory for systems driven by differential equations were in principle applicable to hybrid systems, possibly at the price of having to re-develop some elements of theory, e.g. optimal control theory on hybrid systems [12,4,2], computation of Lyapunov functions for hybrid systems [9], or control of hybrid systems using bisimulations [11].

The premise of using control theoretic tools for software verification is that such tools appear to adapt very well for analysis of software in aerospace, automotive, and many other safety-critical systems. For instance, in flight control systems, the software provides the control law to actuators that control the position of surfaces based on the pilot input and the current states. Our proposition is that since the embedded software implements a control law that is designed via system theoretic tools, such tools are best suited for verification at the implementation level. The analysis relies on a discrete event dynamical systems modeling of computer programs, and the verification method relies on numerical optimization in searching for system invariants. This paper complements existing results on software verification by further extending a previously established framework for transferring control theoretic tools to software analysis. This paper focuses on graph models in analysis of software systems via distributed Lyapunov functions.

1.1 Automated Software Analysis: Preliminaries

In this section we briefly review the principals of software analysis via dynamical system models. Interested readers are referred to [17],[15],[16] for more details.

Computer programs as dynamical systems

Exact and abstract representations of computer programs. We will consider models defined in general by a *state space* set X with selected subsets $X_0 \subseteq X$ of *initial states* and $X_\infty \subset X$ of *terminal states*, and by a set-valued function $f : X \to 2^X$, such that $f(x) \subseteq X_\infty$, $\forall x \in X_\infty$. Thus, a computer program $\mathcal{P}$, represented by the dynamical system $\mathcal{S}(X, f, X_0, X_\infty)$ with parameters X, f, X_0, X_∞ is understood as the set of all sequences $\mathcal{X} := (x(0), x(1), \ldots, x(t), \ldots)$ of elements from X, satisfying

$$x(0) \in X_0, \qquad x(t+1) \in f(x(t)) \quad \forall t \in \mathbb{Z}_+ \tag{1}$$

Definition 1. *Consider a computer program $\mathcal{P}$ and its dynamical system representation $\mathcal{S}(X, f, X_0, X_\infty)$. Program $\mathcal{P}$ is said to terminate in finite time if every solution $\mathcal{X} \equiv x(.)$ of (1) satisfies $x(t) \in X_\infty$ for some $t \in \mathbb{Z}_+$.*

Definition 2. *Consider a computer program $\mathcal{P}$ and its dynamical system representation $\mathcal{S}(X, f, X_0, X_\infty)$. Program $\mathcal{P}$ is said to run without an overflow runtime error if for every solution $\mathcal{X} \equiv x(.)$ of (1) and for every $t \in \mathbb{Z}_+$, $x(t)$ does not belong to a certain (unsafe) subset X_- of X.*

In addition to *exact* dynamical systems models of computer programs, we also define *abstracted* models. We say that the model $\mathcal{S}(\hat{X}, \hat{f}, \hat{X}_0, \hat{X}_\infty)$ is an *abstraction* of $\mathcal{S}(X, f, X_0, X_\infty)$ (or simply an *abstraction* of $\mathcal{P}$), if $X \subseteq \hat{X}$, $X_0 \subseteq \hat{X}_0$, $\hat{X}_\infty \subseteq X_\infty$, and $f(x) \subseteq \hat{f}(x)$ for all $x \in X$.

Proposition 1. *[17] Consider a computer program $\mathcal{P}$ and its dynamical system representation $\mathcal{S}(X, f, X_0, X_\infty)$. Let $\mathcal{S}(\hat{X}, \hat{f}, \hat{X}_0, \hat{X}_\infty)$ be an abstraction of $\mathcal{P}$. Let X_- and $\hat{X}_-$, representing the overflow regions of $\mathcal{P}$ and its abstraction respectively, be such that $X_- \subseteq \hat{X}_-$. Assume that absence of overflow has been certified for the abstracted model of $\mathcal{P}$. Then, an overflow RTE will not occur during any execution of $\mathcal{P}$. In addition, if finite-time termination has been certified for the abstracted model, then program $\mathcal{P}$ will terminate in finite time.*

1.2 Lyapunov Invariants as Behavior Certificates

We introduce Lyapunov-like invariants as *certificates* for the behavior of computer programs. We then describe the conditions under which, finding these Lyapunov-like invariants can be formulated as a convex optimization problem.

Definition 3. *A rate-θ Lyapunov invariant for system $\mathcal{S}(X, f, X_0, X_\infty)$ is defined to be a function $V : X \to \mathbb{R}$ such that*

$$V(x_+) - \theta V(x) < 0 \quad \forall x \in X,\ x_+ \in f(x) : x \notin X_\infty. \tag{2}$$

where $\theta > 0$ is a constant. Thus, a rate-θ Lyapunov invariant satisfies an invariant property ($V(x_+) - \theta V(x) < 0$) along the trajectories of (1) until they reach a terminal state.

Lemma 1. *[15] Consider a computer program $\mathcal{P}$, and its dynamical system model $\mathcal{S}(X, f, X_0, X_\infty)$ and assume that $\theta > 1$. If there exists a rate-θ Lyapunov invariant $V : X \to \mathbb{R}$, uniformly bounded on X, satisfying*

$$V(x) < 0 \quad \forall x \in X_0 \tag{3}$$

then $\mathcal{P}$ terminates in finite time.

Theorem 1. *[15] Consider a program $\mathcal{P}$, and let $\mathcal{S}(X, f, X_0, X_\infty)$ be its dynamical system model. Let θ be constant and let $\mathcal{V}$ denote the set of all rate-θ Lyapunov invariants for program $\mathcal{P}$. An overflow run-time error will not occur during any execution of $\mathcal{P}$, if there exists $V \in \mathcal{V}$ satisfying*

$$\inf_{x \in X_-} V(x) \geq \sup_{x \in X_0} V(x) \tag{4}$$

and at least one of the following three conditions holds:

$$(i)\ \ \theta = 1 \tag{5}$$

$$(ii)\ \ 0 < \theta < 1\ ,\ \text{and} \inf_{x \in X_-} V(x) \geq 0 \tag{6}$$

$$(iii)\ \ 0 < \theta\ ,\ \text{and}\ 0 \geq \sup_{x \in X_0} V(x) \tag{7}$$

2 Graph Models in Analysis of Computer Programs

In this section we further extend and develop our software analysis framework on graph models. Practical considerations such as expressivity, convenience for automated parsing, existence of efficient relaxation techniques and compatibility with available numerical optimization engines render graph models an efficient and applicable model for analysis of real-time embedded software. In addition, graph models provide a convenient platform for mapping the proofs of correctness and certificates of performance from the model to the actual line of code at the implementation level. We will also see that graph models allow for trading off computational efforts at the parsing/modeling phase for computational efforts at the convex optimization phase and vice versa.

A graph model is essentially a generalized version of the model previously introduced for *Linear Programs with Conditional Switching* (LPwCS) [16], [17]. A graph model is defined on a directed graph $G(\mathcal{N},\mathcal{E})$ with a set of nodes (*"effective"* lines of code) $\mathcal{N} := \{0,1,\ldots,m\} \cup \{\bowtie\}$, and a set of arcs $\mathcal{E} := \{(i,j,k) \mid i \in \mathcal{N},\ j \in \mathcal{O}(i)\}$, where $\mathcal{O}(i)$ is the set of all nodes to which transition from node i is possible in one time step. Multiple arcs between nodes are allowed and the third element in the triplet (i,j,k) is the index of the k-th arc between nodes i and j. This model, has state space $X := \mathcal{N} \times \mathbb{R}^n$, with initial and terminal subsets defined as

$$X_0 := \{0\} \times v_0,\ v_0 \subseteq \mathbb{R}^n,\ X_\infty := \{\bowtie\} \times \mathbb{R}^n$$

where v_0 is a selected subset of $\mathbb{R}^n$, constrained by linear, quadratic or polynomial equalities and inequalities. On this graph, node 0 represents a (perhaps fictitious) line containing all the available information about the initial conditions of the continuous states. Node $\bowtie$ represents the terminal location and the definition of X_∞ as $\{\bowtie\} \times \mathbb{R}^n$ implies that our characterization of the terminal states depends only on the discrete component of the state space, i.e., a specific line of code, and is not (explicitly) dependent on the analog components of the state space. The set-valued map $f : X \to 2^X$, is defined by the transitions associated with the arcs on this graph, subject to certain rules associated with each arc.

The only possible transition involving node 0 is a transition from node 0 to node 1. The only possible transition from/to node $\bowtie$ is the identity transition to node $\bowtie$. Multiple arcs between nodes are allowed. The set $\mathcal{A}(i,j) := \{1,..,\overline{\kappa}_{ij}\}$ denotes the set of all indices of the arcs from node i to node j, where $\overline{\kappa}_{ij}$ denotes the total number of arcs from node i to j. We denote the k-th arc from node i to node j by (i,j,k). We attribute two labels to every arc (i,j,k) on this graph: (i) A *transition* label T_{ji}^k, to be understood as an operator defined on $\mathbb{R}^n$, which represents a set-valued function mapping the state (i,v) to all possible states $(j,\overline{v})$, where $\overline{v} \in T_{ji}^k v$. ($ii$) A *passport* label I_{ji}^k, to be understood as the indicator function of a semi-algebraic set, defined by a set of linear, quadratic, or polynomial equalities and inequalities.

$$P_{ji}^k := \left\{v \mid H_{ji}^k(v) = 0,\ Q_{ji}^k(v) \leq 0\right\},\ I_{ji}^k[v] := \begin{cases} 1 \text{ if } v \in P_{ji}^k \\ 0 \text{ if } v \notin P_{ji}^k \end{cases}$$

According to this definition, transition along arc (i, j, k) is possible if and only if $I_{ji}^k[v] = 1$. A passport label $I1_{ji}^k \wedge I2_{ji}^k$ is understood as $I1_{ji}^k \cdot I2_{ji}^k$. Finally, the state transition map $f : X \to 2^X$ is given by

$$f(i, v) = \left\{ \left(j, T_{ji}^k v\right) \mid j \in \mathcal{O}(i),\ I_{ji}^k[v] = 1 \right\}.$$

We have defined all the elements of the model. In reference to the graph model of a computer program, we will use the concise notation $G(\mathcal{N}, \mathcal{E})$, with the convention that the nodes and arcs of G are appropriately labeled to define a valid model $\mathcal{S}(X, f, X_0, X_\infty)$ according to our previous discussion.

Remark 1. Multiple arcs between nodes enable modeling "or" or "xor" type conditional transitions. The passport labels associated with multiple arcs between nodes are not necessarily exclusive. Thus, multiple transitions along different arcs may be possible. This allows for nondeterministic modeling.

2.1 Lyapunov Analysis of Graph Models

Consider a computer program $\mathcal{P}$, and its graph model $G(\mathcal{N}, \mathcal{E})$. We are interested in finding Lyapunov functions that prove certain properties of $\mathcal{P}$. As we described before, the state in this model is defined by $x = (i, v)$ where i is the discrete component and v is the continuous component of the state vector. We define Lyapunov functions for this model in the following way:

$$V(x) \equiv V(i, v) := \sigma_i(v) \tag{8}$$

where for every $i \in \mathcal{N}$ the function $\sigma_k : \mathbb{R}^n \to \mathbb{R}$ is a quadratic, polynomial or an affine functional. This means that we assign a quadratic/linear/polynomial Lyapunov function to every node $i \in \mathcal{N}$ on graph $G(\mathcal{N}, \mathcal{E})$. We will refer to Lyapunov functions defined according to (8) as node-wise Lyapunov functions.

Proposition 2. *Let $V(x)$ be defined according to (8). The Lyapunov invariance condition*

$$V(x_+) < \theta V(x) \qquad \forall x \in X \setminus X_\infty,\ x_+ \in f(x)$$

holds true if and only if

$$\sigma_j(T_{ji}^k v) - \theta\sigma_i(v) < 0,\ \forall i \in \mathcal{N} \setminus \{\bowtie\},\ j \in \mathcal{O}(i),\ k \in \mathcal{A}(i, j),\ I_{ji}^k[v] = 1. \tag{9}$$

Let $N_a := \sum_{(i,j)\in\mathcal{E}} |\mathcal{A}(i, j)|$ denote the total number of arcs on $G(\mathcal{N}, \mathcal{E})$, excluding the identity transformation arc $(\bowtie, \bowtie)$. Then, according to proposition 2 the Lyapunov invariance condition is enforced via N_a constraints. Assume for the moment that each σ_i is a quadratic functional, and also that

$$P_{ji}^k[v] := \left\{ v \mid E_i^k(v) = 0,\ I_i^k(v) \leq 0 \right\}$$

where E_i^k and I_i^k are quadratic functionals. Each of the constraints in (9) expresses that a quadratic form must be negative whenever certain quadratic constraints are satisfied. Various forms of convex relaxations such as the $\mathcal{S}$-Procedure in positivity of quadratic forms can be employed to formulate (9) as a convex optimization problem. In this case, the resulting optimization problem will be a semidefinite program [1]. In the presence of polynomial constraints, or if we allow $\sigma_i(v)$ to be polynomial functionals of v, the resulting optimization problem can be formulated as a sum of squares program [14]. Similarly, linear invariants subject to linear constraints lead to linear programming [3].

Finite-time termination. In node-wise Lyapunov analysis of graph models, we often do not impose the same invariance rate θ along all the arcs, as this may lead to either infeasibility or to weak invariants. While computing the optimal value of θ per arc is neither possible nor necessary, depending on the state transitions along the arcs, certain choices of θ may be more reasonable than others. The following theorem provides a finite-time termination criterion via node-wise Lyapunov invariants defined on graph models.

Definition 4. *A cycle $\mathcal{C}_m$ on a graph $G(\mathcal{N},\mathcal{E})$ is an ordered list of m triplets (n_1,n_2,k_1), (n_2,n_3,k_2), ..., (n_m,n_{m+1},k_m), where $n_1=n_{m+1}$ and for all $j\in\{1,...,m\}$ we have $(n_j,n_{j+1},k_j)\in\mathcal{E}$. A simple cycle is a cycle that does not visit any node more than once. Thus, a simple cycle has the following property:*

$$\text{If } (n_i,n_{i+1},k_i)\in\mathcal{C}_m \text{ and } (n_j,n_{j+1},k_j)\in\mathcal{C}_m \text{ then}$$
$$n_{j+1}=n_i \Longrightarrow i=1 \text{ and } j=m$$

Theorem 2. *Consider a computer program $\mathcal{P}$ and its graph model $G(\mathcal{N},\mathcal{E})$. Let $V(i,v):=\sigma_i(v)$ be a variable-rate invariant defined on G, in the sense that*

$$\sigma_0(v)<0,\ \forall v\in v_0 \tag{10a}$$

$$\sigma_j(T_{ji}^k v)<\theta_{ji}^k\sigma_i(v),\ \forall i\in\mathcal{N}\backslash\{\bowtie\},\ j\in\mathcal{O}(i),\ k\in\mathcal{A}(i,j),\ v\in P_{ji}^k[.] \tag{10b}$$

In addition, assume that V is bounded from below. Then, (10) proves that $\mathcal{P}$ terminates in finite time if and only if for every simple cycle $\mathcal{C}\in G$, we have

$$\prod_{(i,j,k)\in\mathcal{C}}\theta_{ij}^k>1,\ \mathcal{C}\in G \tag{11}$$

Proof. Proof of sufficiency proceeds by contradiction. Assume that (10) and (11) hold, but $\mathcal{P}$ does not terminate in finite time. Then, there exists a sequence $\mathcal{X}\equiv(x(0),x(1),\ldots,x(t),\ldots)$ of elements from X satisfying (1) that does not reach a terminal state in finite time. Let $L:X\to\mathcal{N}$ be an operator mapping every element x from X, to the discrete component of x. The sequence $L\mathcal{X}\equiv(0,1,\ldots)$ is then a sequence of infinite length that takes only finitely many different values. Therefore, there exists at least one element which repeats infinitely often in $\mathcal{X}$. Let $\omega\in\mathcal{N}\backslash\{0,\bowtie\}$ be an element that repeats infinitely often in $L\mathcal{X}$ and let $\mathcal{C}[\omega]$ denote the set of all cycles on $G(\mathcal{N},\mathcal{E})$ that begin and end at ω. Define

$$\theta=\min_{\mathcal{C}\in\mathcal{C}[\omega]}\prod_{(i,j,k)\in\mathcal{C}}\theta_{ij}^k.$$

Note that (11) implies that $\theta > 1$. Let $\mathcal{W}$ be a subsequence of $\mathcal{X}$ consisting of all the elements from $\mathcal{X}$ that satisfy $Lx = \omega$, and rename the analog component of x at the k-th appearance of ω in $L\mathcal{X}$ by v_k to obtain the sequence $\mathcal{W} := ((\omega, v_1), (\omega, v_2), ..., (\omega, v_t), ...)$. Then we have $V_\omega(v_1) < 0$, and $V_\omega(v_{i+1}) < \theta V_\omega(v_i)$, and $\theta > 1$. The result follows immediately from Lemma 1. It is easy to construct counter examples to prove necessity. We do not give a counter-example here due to space limitation.

Absence of overflow. The following result is a corollary of Theorems 1 and 2.

Corollary 1. *Consider a program $\mathcal{P}$ and its graph model $G(\mathcal{N}, \mathcal{E})$. Suppose that the overflow limit is defined by a positive real number M. That is, $X_- := \{x \in X \mid |x_i| \geq M\}$. Let $V(i, v) := \sigma_i(v)$ be a variable-rate invariant defined on G, as in (10a) and (10b). Assume that $V(i, v)$ additionally satisfies*

$$\sigma_i(v) > \left\| \frac{v}{M} \right\|^2 - 1 \qquad \forall v \in F_i,\ i \in \mathcal{N} \backslash \{0, \bowtie\}.$$

Then, an overflow runtime error will not occur during any execution of $\mathcal{P}$. In addition, if (11) holds, then $\mathcal{P}$ terminates in at most T steps, where

$$T = \sum_{\mathcal{C} \in G} \frac{\log M - \log \sup_{v \in v_0} |\sigma_0(v)|}{\log \theta(\mathcal{C})}, \quad \theta(\mathcal{C}) := \prod_{(i,j,k) \in \mathcal{C}} \theta_{ij}^k.$$

2.2 Towards Optimal Graph Models

Consider now the following two programs, $\mathcal{P}_1$ and $\mathcal{P}_2$.

```
program P1

loc 0 :  % pre: x1, x2 ∈ [−100, 100];
loc 1 :  while True,
loc 2 :  if x1^2 − x2^2 ≤ 0
loc 3 :      x1 = 0.99x1 + 0.01x2;
             x2 = −0.05x1 + 0.99x2;
         else
loc 5 :      x1 = 0.99x1 + 0.05x2;
             x2 = −0.01x1 + 0.99x2;
         end
loc ⋈:   end
```

```
program P2

loc 0 :  % pre: x1, x2 ∈ [−100, 100];
loc 1 :  while True,
loc 2 :  while x1^2 − x2^2 ≤ 0
loc 3 :      x1 = 0.99x1 + 0.01x2;
             x2 = −0.05x1 + 0.99x2;
         end
loc 4 :  while x1^2 − x2^2 > 0
loc 5 :      x1 = 0.99x1 + 0.05x2;
             x2 = −0.01x1 + 0.99x2;
         end
loc ⋈:   end
```

The two programs $\mathcal{P}_1$ and $\mathcal{P}_2$ define exactly the same evolution path for the state variables x_1 and x_2. In other words the set of all sequences $\mathcal{X}(\mathcal{P}_1) := (x(0), x(1), \ldots, x(t), \ldots)$ of the dynamical system model $\mathcal{S}_1(X, f, X_0, X_\infty)$ of program $\mathcal{P}_1$, and the set of all sequences $\mathcal{X}(\mathcal{P}_2) := (x(0), x(1), \ldots, x(t), \ldots)$ of the dynamical system model $\mathcal{S}_2(X, f, X_0, X_\infty)$ of program $\mathcal{P}_2$ are identical. Thus, program $\mathcal{P}_1$ is correct if and only if program $\mathcal{P}_2$ is correct (indeed, both programs are correct in the sense of absence of overflow and their trajectories converge to the origin). Below, we construct the graph models of both programs and discuss analysis of the models via Lyapunov invariants. Let T_1 and T_2 be the transformations that take place upon leaving nodes 3 and 5 respectively, that is,

$$T_1 \begin{bmatrix} x_1 \\ x_2 \end{bmatrix} = \begin{bmatrix} 0.99x_1 + 0.01x_2 \\ -0.05x_1 + 0.99x_2 \end{bmatrix}, \text{ and } T_2 \begin{bmatrix} x_1 \\ x_2 \end{bmatrix} = \begin{bmatrix} 0.99x_1 + 0.05x_2x_2 \\ -0.01x_1 + 0.99x_2 \end{bmatrix}.$$

Also, define $P := \{x \mid x_1^2 - x_2^2 \leq 0\}$, $Q := \{x \mid x_1^2 - x_2^2 > 0\}$, $C_{1\bowtie} := \varnothing$.

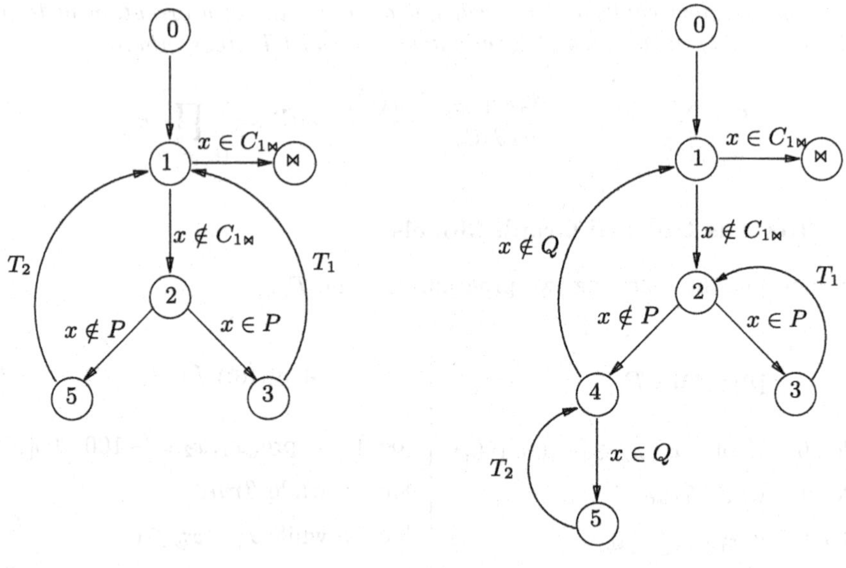

Fig. 1. Graph Models of Programs $\mathcal{P}1$ (left) and $\mathcal{P}2$ (right)

The graph models of programs $\mathcal{P}_1$ and $\mathcal{P}_2$ are shown in Figure 1. The graph model of $\mathcal{P}_1$ is of degree 4, and the graph model of $\mathcal{P}_2$ is of degree 5 (nodes 0 and $\bowtie$ are not counted). The transition labels associated with identity transitions along the arcs are dropped from the diagrams. As discussed before, we assign a quadratic Lyapunov function $\sigma_i(x) := x^T S_i x$ to every node on the graph and write the Lyapunov invariance condition according to Proposition (2). For these programs we get

For program $\mathcal{P}_1$

$$\sigma_0(x) < 0, \text{ s.t. } x^2 \in [0, 10^4]$$
$$\sigma_1(x) < \sigma_0(x)$$
$$\sigma_2(x) < \sigma_1(x) \text{ s.t. } x \notin C_{1\bowtie}$$
$$\sigma_3(x) < \sigma_2(x) \text{ s.t. } x_1^2 - x_2^2 \leq 0$$
$$\sigma_5(x) < \sigma_2(x) \text{ s.t. } x_1^2 - x_2^2 > 0$$
$$\sigma_1(T_1 x) < \sigma_3(x)$$
$$\sigma_1(T_2 x) < \sigma_5(x)$$
$$\sigma_{\bowtie}(x) < \sigma_1(x) \text{ s.t. } x \in C_{1\bowtie}$$

For program $\mathcal{P}_2$

$$\sigma_0(x) < 0, \text{ s.t. } x^2 \in [0, 10^4]$$
$$\sigma_1(x) < \sigma_0(x)$$
$$\sigma_2(x) < \sigma_1(x) \text{ s.t. } x \notin C_{1\bowtie}$$
$$\sigma_3(x) < \sigma_2(x) \text{ s.t. } x_1^2 - x_2^2 \leq 0$$
$$\sigma_4(x) < \sigma_2(x) \text{ s.t. } x_1^2 - x_2^2 > 0$$
$$\sigma_2(T_1 x) < \sigma_3(x)$$
$$\sigma_5(x) < \sigma_4(x) \text{ s.t. } x_1^2 - x_2^2 > 0$$
$$\sigma_4(T_2 x) < \sigma_5(x)$$
$$\sigma_1(x) < \sigma_4(x) \text{ s.t. } x_1^2 - x_2^2 \leq 0$$
$$\sigma_{\bowtie}(x) < \sigma_1(x) \text{ s.t. } x \in C_{1\bowtie}$$

We can then use the $\mathcal{S}$-Procedure to convert the above constraints on $\sigma_i := x^T S_i x$ to semidefinite constraints and solve for the parameters of S_i. The result of this experiment is somewhat surprising. Although the two programs define the exact same trajectories for the state variables x_1 and x_2, the optimization problem arising from node-wise quadratic Lyapunov invariant analysis on graph model of $\mathcal{P}_2$ is feasible, while the optimization problem turns out infeasible for $\mathcal{P}_1$. Interestingly, this has nothing to do with the fact that there are more nodes in the graph model of $\mathcal{P}_2$, and that the Lyapunov function defined on the graph model of $\mathcal{P}_2$ has more parameters. To understand this situation better, we introduce the notions of reduction and minimality of graph models.

Definition 5. *A node $i \in \mathcal{N} \backslash \{0, \bowtie\}$ is called a focal node, if there exists a non-identity transition arc from node i to itself, that is,*

$$\exists k, \text{ s.t. } (i, i, k) \in \mathcal{E} \text{ and } T_{ii}^k \neq I$$

A node $i \in \mathcal{N} \backslash \{0, \bowtie\}$ is called an auxiliary node if it is not a focal node, that is,

$$\forall k : (i, i, k) \in \mathcal{E} \implies T_{ii}^k = I$$

Informally speaking, focal nodes are nodes with nontrivial self arcs and auxiliary nodes are nodes without nontrival self arcs. A graph model of a computer program $\mathcal{P}$ is called irreducible, if every node $i \in \mathcal{N} \backslash \{0, \bowtie\}$ is a focal node.

Consider a graph $G(\mathcal{N}, \mathcal{E})$ and let $\alpha \in \mathcal{N} \backslash \{0, \infty\}$ be an auxiliary node. A *reduced* graph $G_r(\mathcal{N}_r, \mathcal{E}_r)$ can be obtained from G in the following way: 1. Remove the auxiliary node α, and all the pertinent incoming and outgoing arcs 2. For every pair of arcs $\{(i, \alpha, r), (\alpha, j, s)\}$ where $i \in \mathcal{I}(\alpha)$ and $j \in \mathcal{O}(\alpha)$, add a new arc (i, j, k) with the transition label $T_{ji}^k := T_{j\alpha}^s T_{\alpha i}^r$ and passport label $P_{ji}^k := P_{j\alpha}^s T_{\alpha i}^r \wedge P_{\alpha i}^r$. If $G_r(\mathcal{N}_r, \mathcal{E}_r)$ is a reduced graph model obtained from $G(\mathcal{N}, \mathcal{E})$, we write $G_r \sqsubseteq G$. An irreducible model of G can be obtained by repeating the above process until every auxiliary node is eliminated. Note that the irreducible graph of G is not unique, neither is its degree. Among all the irreducible offspring graphs of G, we call the one(s) with minimal degree, a minimal realization of G. The degree of a minimal realization of G, is called the effective or minimal degree of G. Similarly, among all the irreducible offsprings of G, we call the one(s) with maximal degree, a maximal realization of G. The degree of a maximal realization of G, is called the maximal degree of G, and is equal to the degree of G if and only if G is irreducible. If G is reducible, the minimal or maximal realizations of G are may not be unique either. Note that if $G_r \sqsubseteq G$, then $\mathcal{N}_r \subset \mathcal{N}$, while $\mathcal{E}_r \nsubseteq \mathcal{E}$. Also note that the set of all reduced graphs of G do not form an ordered set, in the sense that if $G_{r_1} \sqsubseteq G$ and $G_{r_2} \sqsubseteq G$, neither $G_{r_1} \sqsubseteq G_{r_2}$ nor $G_{r_2} \sqsubseteq G_{r_1}$ has to hold.

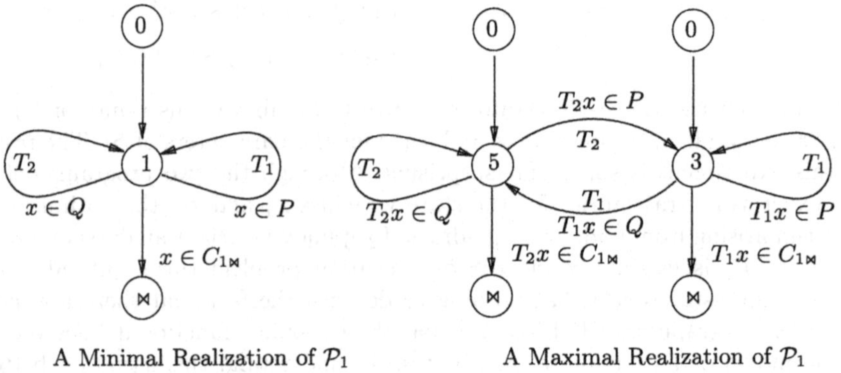

Fig. 2. Minimal and Maximal realizations of program $\mathcal{P}_1$

The graph model of Program $\mathcal{P}_1$ is of minimal degree 1, and maximal degree 2. A particular minimal and a particular maximal realization are show in Figure 2. It can be verified that the graph model of $\mathcal{P}_2$ is of minimal degree 2, and maximal degree 3. The minimal realization of $\mathcal{P}_2$ can be obtained via a reduction process that eliminates nodes 3, 5, and 1, exactly in that order. The maximal realization of $\mathcal{P}_2$ can be obtained via a reduction process that eliminates nodes 2, and 4, exactly in that order.

The following theorem states that assigning node-wise Lyapunov functions to graph models results in sufficient conditions for existence of Lyapunov invariants within a specific class of functions, e.g. quadratic functions, that are weaker than (i.e. always imply) the sufficient conditions imposed by assigning node-wise Lyapunov invariants to reduced models of the same graph. In other words, existence of node-wise Lyapunov invariants within a specific class of functions for the reduced model is a necessary but not sufficient condition for existence of node-wise Lyapunov invariants within the same class for the original graph model of a computer program.

Theorem 3. *Consider a computer program $\mathcal{P}$, and its graph model $G(\mathcal{N},\mathcal{E})$. Let $G_r(\mathcal{N}_r,\mathcal{E}_r) \sqsubseteq G(\mathcal{N},\mathcal{E})$ be any reduced model of G. If*

$$V(i,v) := \sigma_i(v), \ i \in \mathcal{N}$$

is a nodewise quadratic Lyapunov invariant on graph $G(\mathcal{N},\mathcal{E})$, then there exists a nodewise quadratic Lyapunov invariant $V_r(i,v)$ that is valid on $G_r(\mathcal{N}_r,\mathcal{E}_r)$. However, if

$$V_r(i,v) := \sigma_i(v), \ i \in \mathcal{N}_r$$

is a node-wise quadratic Lyapunov invariant on graph $G_r(\mathcal{N}_r,\mathcal{E}_r)$, a node-wise quadratic Lyapunov invariant that is valid on $G(\mathcal{N},\mathcal{E})$ may not even exist.

Proof. If $G_r \sqsubseteq G$, then there exists a sequence of reduced graph models G_i, $i = 1...q$, where $G_1 = G$, $G_{i+1} \sqsubseteq G_i$, and $G_q = G_r$ with the property that $|\mathcal{N}_{i+1}| = |\mathcal{N}_i| - 1$, that is, G_{i+1} is obtained by removing one auxiliary node from G_i. Further, assume that G_{i+1} is derived from G_i by eliminating node n, and that V is a Lyapunov invariant for G. Then,

$$V_n(T_{nm}^r v) - \theta V_m(v) < 0, \ m \in \mathcal{I}(n), \ r \in \mathcal{A}(m,n), \ I_{nm}^r[v] = 1,$$

$$V_l(T_{ln}^s v) - \theta V_n(v) < 0, \ l \in \mathcal{O}(n), \ s \in \mathcal{A}(n,l), \ I_{ln}^s[v] = 1.$$

Necessary conditions for the latter conditions to hold are that:

$$V_l(T_{ln}^s T_{nm}^r v) - \theta V_n(T_{nm}^r v) < 0, \ I_{ln}^s[T_{nm}^r v] = 1,$$
$$m \in \mathcal{I}(n), \ l \in \mathcal{O}(n), \ s \in \mathcal{A}(n,l), \ r \in \mathcal{A}(m,n).$$

This, and the first set of conditions imply that:

$$V_l(T_{ln}^s T_{nm}^r v) - \theta^2 V_m(v) < 0, \ I_{nm}^r[v] = 1, \ I_{ln}^s[T_{nm}^r v] = 1,$$
$$r \in \mathcal{A}(m,n), \ s \in \mathcal{A}(n,l).$$

By definition, this implies that V_l and V_m satisfy the Lyapunov conditions along all the arcs that were added in the reduction process. Since V_l and V_m satisfy all Lyapunov conditions along all the existing arcs (before reduction), we conclude that V is also a Lyapunov invariant for the reduced model. The result holds by induction. The proof also shows that

$$V_r(i,v) := \sigma_i(v), \ i \in \mathcal{N}_r$$

is a valid Lyapunov invariant on G_r.

In analysis of programs via Lyapunov invariants, an important issue is to determine whether a computer program admits certain type of Lyapunov invariants, e.g. quadratic, piece-wise quadratic, etc. For instance, consider program $\mathcal{P}_1$, which is known not to admit a quadratic Lyapunov invariant, while a piecewise quadratic Lyapunov invariant is known to exist. Recall that the graph model of this program is of degree 4 (not counting nodes 0, and $\bowtie$), of minimal degree 1, and maximal degree 2. Theorem 3 states that a Lyapunov invariant cannot be found by assigning four different quadratic Lyapunov functions to the four nodes on the graph. However, a Lyapunov function may be found by assigning two Lyapunov functions to each of the two nodes on the maximal realization of $\mathcal{P}_1$. As far as existence of Lyapunov functions is concerned, assigning different Lyapunov functions to an immediate graph model of a program is only as good as assigning fewer many Lyapunov functions to its minimal realization. In other words, more Lyapunov functions assigned to auxiliary nodes do not add more flexibility/power in Lyapunov analysis. The latter statement of the theorem is even more interesting since it states that performing analysis on reduced models may even be beneficial. This is indeed the case for the program $\mathcal{P}_1$. Since $\mathcal{P}_1$ does not admit a quadratic Lyapunov invariant, the optimization problem arising from the original graph of $\mathcal{P}_1$ is infeasible. So is the optimization problem arising from analysis of the minimal graph of $\mathcal{P}_1$. However, the optimization problem arising from analysis of the maximal graph of $\mathcal{P}_1$ (which is of degree 2) is feasible and a Lyapunov invariant was indeed found. On the other hand, since the minimal graph of $\mathcal{P}_2$ is of degree 2, the optimization problem arising from the original graph of $\mathcal{P}_2$ is readily feasible and a Lyapunov invariant is found. Same is true for analysis of minimal and maximal realization of $\mathcal{P}_2$.

So far, we have established that, at least from a theoretical point of view, it is beneficial to search for Lyapunov invariants on the reduced graph models rather than the original graph models of computer programs. From an optimization point of view, Theorem 3 compares two generally nonconvex optimization problems. It states that if the nonconvex optimization problem associated with the original graph model is feasible, then so is the nonconvex optimization problem associated with the reduced graph model. A natural question that arises here is about the computational procedure that will be used to compute the Lyapunov invariants on the two graph models. More specifically, the effects of convex relaxations on the computation of such invariants on the original and the reduced models must be investigated. It is interesting that the statement of Theorem 3 remains valid even after convex relaxations are applied to these nonconvex optimization problems. More specifically, the Lyapunov invariant $V_r(i,v)$ can be computed using the same convex relaxations that render the computation of $V(i,v)$ a feasible convex optimization problem. To make this concept clearer, let us consider a specific case. Consider a graph G, and assume that G_r is obtained by eliminating node 2, where, $\mathcal{I}(2) := \{1\}$, $\mathcal{O}\{2\} := \{3,5\}$ (this is like the graph of program $\mathcal{P}_1$). Assume that each transition label T_{ji} is a finite-dimensional linear operator defined by the matrix of T_{ji}, and each passport label is defined by a single quadratic constraint: $P_{ji}[u] = \{u \mid u^T Q_{ji} u \leq 0\}$. The Lyapunov conditions as imposed on G, are:

$$\sigma_2(T_{21}v) - \theta\sigma_1(v) < 0, \text{ s.t. } v^T Q_{21} v \leq 0, \quad (12a)$$

$$\sigma_3(T_{32}v) - \theta\sigma_2(v) < 0, \text{ s.t. } v^T Q_{32} v \leq 0, \quad (12b)$$

$$\sigma_5(T_{52}v) - \theta\sigma_2(v) < 0, \text{ s.t. } v^T Q_{52} v \leq 0. \quad (12c)$$

The Lyapunov conditions as imposed on the reduced model G_r, are:

$$\sigma_3\left(T_{32}T_{21}v\right) - \theta\sigma_1\left(v\right) < 0, \text{ s.t. } v^TQ_{21}v \le 0, \; v^TT_{21}^TQ_{32}T_{21}v \le 0, \tag{13a}$$

$$\sigma_4\left(T_{42}T_{21}v\right) - \theta\sigma_1\left(v\right) < 0, \text{ s.t. } v^TQ_{21}v \le 0, \; v^TT_{21}^TQ_{52}T_{21}v \le 0. \tag{13b}$$

Now, let each σ_i be a quadratic functional, $\sigma_i\left(v\right) := v^TP_iv$. Note that each of the conditions in (12) express negativity of a quadratic form subject to a single quadratic constraint, while each of the conditions in (13), express negativity of a quadratic form subject to two quadratic constraints. It may be misleading to think that using the $\mathcal{S}$-Procedure as the convex relaxation method for (13) would be more conservative than for (12). However, as we have already suggested, this is not the case. Using the $\mathcal{S}$-Procedure, conditions (12) are converted to LMIs in the following way:

$$T_{21}^TP_2T_{21} - \theta P_1 - \tau_{21}Q_{21} < 0, \; \tau_{21} > 0, \tag{14a}$$

$$T_{32}^TP_3T_{32} - \theta P_2 - \tau_{32}Q_{32} < 0, \; \tau_{32} > 0, \tag{14b}$$

$$T_{52}^TP_5T_{52} - \theta P_2 - \tau_{52}Q_{52} < 0, \; \tau_{52} > 0, \tag{14c}$$

while (13) becomes:

$$T_{21}^TT_{32}^TP_3T_{32}T_{21} - \theta P_1 - \tau_{21}Q_{21} - \tau_{32}T_{21}^TQ_{32}T_{21} < 0, \; \tau_{21} > 0, \; \tau_{32} > 0, \tag{15a}$$

$$T_{21}^TT_{52}^TP_5T_{52}T_{21} - \theta P_1 - \tau_{21}Q_{21} - \tau_{52}T_{21}^TQ_{52}T_{21} < 0, \; \tau_{21} > 0, \; \tau_{52} > 0. \tag{15b}$$

It is not difficult to see that if P_1, P_2, P_3, P_5, τ_{21}, τ_{32}, τ_{52} are a feasible solution to the set of LMIs in (14), then P_1, θP_3, θP_5, τ_{21}, $\theta\tau_{32}$, $\theta\tau_{52}$ are a feasible solution to the set of LMIs is (15): To obtain (15a) from (14), multiply (14b) on both sides by $T_{21}^T/\sqrt{\theta}$ and $T_{21}\sqrt{\theta}$, and add it to (14a). Inequality (15b) can be obtained similarly. We have shown for a special case, that computation of the Lyapunov invariants on the reduced graph is not more difficult than the original graph. The result is true in general, and the same type of relaxations that make convex optimization of the Lyapunov invariants feasible on the original graph, are applicable to the reduced graph. In light of Theorem (3), the conclusion of the above discussion is that analysis of the reduced models are always beneficial, regardless of the convex relaxations that are used at the optimization phase.

3 Conclusions and Future Work

Concepts and tools from control and optimization can be exploited to build a framework for software verification. This framework is particularly appealing for analysis of safety-critical software in embedded systems. Our framework consists of the following four procedures: 1. Model the software as a dynamical system. 2. Given the functional and the safety specifications, formulate Lyapunov invariants whose existence prove the desired properties of the model and hence, the program itself. 3. Apply convex relaxations such that finding the proposed invariants can be formulated as a convex optimization problem. 4. Use the relevant numerical optimization tools, e.g. semidefinite programming, to compute these invariants. In this paper, we focused on graph models of software and further developed the framework on such models. Some future works include in-depth study of optimality of graph models in the reduction process and improving scalability. Computing the minimal and maximal degrees, and the corresponding realizations of a computer program are interesting problems that arise in this context.

References

1. Boyd, S., Ghaoui, L.E., Feron, E., Balakrishnan, V.: Linear Matrix Inequalities in Systems and Control Theory. Society for Industrial and Applied Math. (1994)
2. Bemporad, A., Mignone, D., Morari, M.: Moving horizon estimation for hybrid systems and fault detection. In: Proc. American Control Conf., pp. 2471–2475 (1999)
3. Bertsimas, D., Tsitsikilis, J.: Introduction to Linear Optimization. Athena Scientific (1997)
4. Branicky, M.S., Borkar, V.S., Mitter, S.K.: A unified framework for hybrid control: Model and optimal control theory. IEEE Trans. Automatic Control 43(1), 31–45 (1998)
5. Clarke, E.M., Emerson, E.A., Sistla, A.P.: Automatic verification of finite-state concurrent systems using temporal logic specifications. ACM Trans. on Programming Languages and Systems 8(2), 244–263 (1986)
6. Clarke, E.M., Grumberg, O., Peled, D.A.: Model Checking. MIT Press, Cambridge (1999)
7. Cousot, P., Cousot, R.: Abstract interpretation: A unified lattice model for static analysis of programs by construction or approximation of fixpoints. In: Proc. 4th Symposium on Principles of Programming Languages, pp. 238–252 (1977)
8. Prajna, S., Jadbabaie, A., Pappas, G.: A Framework for Worst-Case and Stochastic Safety Verification Using Barrier Certificates. IEEE Trans. on Automatic Control 52(8), 1415–1428 (2007)
9. Johansson, M., Rantzer, A.: Computation of piecewise quadratic Lyapunov functions for hybrid systems. IEEE Trans. on Automatic Control 43(4), 555–559 (1998)
10. Alur, R., Pappas, G.J. (eds.): HSCC 2004. LNCS, vol. 2993. Springer, Heidelberg (2004)
11. Lafferriere, G., Pappas, G.J., Sastry, S.: Hybrid systems with finite bisimulations. In: Antsaklis, P.J., Kohn, W., Lemmon, M.D., Nerode, A., Sastry, S.S. (eds.) HS 1997. LNCS, vol. 1567, Springer, Heidelberg (1999)
12. Lygeros, J., Tomlin, C., Sastry, S.: Controllers for reachability specifications for hybrid systems. Automatica 35(3), 349–370 (1999)
13. Peled, D.A.: Software Reliability Methods. Springer, New York (2001)
14. Parrilo, P.A.: Minimizing Polynomial Functions. In: Algorithmic and Quantitative Real Algebraic Geometry. DIMACS Series in Discrete Mathematics and Theoretical Computer Science, vol. 60, pp. 83–99. AMS
15. Roozbehani, M., Feron, É., Megrestki, A.: Modeling, Optimization and Computation for Software Verification. In: Morari, M., Thiele, L. (eds.) HSCC 2005. LNCS, vol. 3414, pp. 606–622. Springer, Heidelberg (2005)
16. Roozbehani, M., Megretski, A., Feron, E.: Convex optimization proves software correctness. In: Proc. American Control Conf., pp. 1395–1400 (2005)
17. Roozbehani, M., Megretski, A., Feron, E.: Optimization of Lyapunov Invariants for Certification of Software Systems. IEEE Trans. Automatic Control (submitted, 2007)

On the Optimality of Dubins Paths across Heterogeneous Terrain

Ricardo G. Sanfelice and Emilio Frazzoli

Laboratory for Information and Decision Systems
Massachusetts Institute of Technology
Cambridge, MA 02139-4307
{sricardo,frazzoli}@mit.edu

Abstract. We derive optimality conditions for the paths of a Dubins vehicle when the state space is partitioned into two patches with different vehicle's forward velocity. We recast this problem as a hybrid optimal control problem and solve it using optimality principles for hybrid systems. Among the optimality conditions, we derive a "refraction" law at the boundary of the patches which generalizes the so-called Snell's law of refraction in optics to the case of paths with bounded maximum curvature.

1 Introduction

Control algorithms that are capable of steering autonomous vehicles to satisfy a given set of specifications, like initial and final constraints, and at the same time, guarantee certain optimality conditions are very appealing to applications in robotics and aerospace. This has led researchers to strive for control design tools that adequately incorporate both trajectory constraints and measures of optimality. As a consequence, many results from the theory of optimal control, in particular, those that guarantee time optimality, have found wide applicability in autonomous vehicle control problems.

Perhaps, the earliest result on time-optimal control laws for autonomous vehicles modeled as a particle moving with constant, positive forward velocity and with constrained minimum turning radius is the work by Dubins [1]. While Dubins used only geometric arguments to establish his results, a few years later, the appearance of Pontryagin's Maximum Principle in [2] enabled the authors in [3] to systematically recover Dubins results. Moreover, building from the work of Reeds and Shepp [4], the application of Pontryagin's optimality principle permitted the authors in [5,3] to derive similar results for a vehicle model without forward velocity constraints.

In this paper, we consider autonomous vehicles with dynamics governed by

$$|u| \leq 1 \, , \qquad \begin{cases} \dot{x} &= v \sin\theta \\ \dot{y} &= v\cos\theta \\ \dot{\theta} &= u \end{cases} , \tag{1}$$

where (x, y) is the vehicle's position, θ is the angle between the vehicle and the vertical axis determining the vehicle's orientation, u is the angular acceleration

M. Egerstedt and B. Mishra (Eds.): HSCC 2008, LNCS 4981, pp. 457–470, 2008.

input for the vehicle, and v is the vehicle's forward velocity. This vehicle model is usually referred to as Dubins vehicle. We consider the case of heterogeneous velocity along the terrain where the vehicle is deployed. Two different velocities, v_1 and v_2, define the constant, forward velocity of Dubins vehicle on two patches of the plane, patch $\mathcal{P}_1$ and patch $\mathcal{P}_2$, depicted in Figure 1. We are interested in the following problem:

Find the minimum-time path for Dubins vehicle from an initial point and angle in patch $\mathcal{P}_1$ to a final point and angle in patch $\mathcal{P}_2$.

Figure 1 shows possible initial and final vehicle configurations, which are denoted by (x^0, y^0, θ^0) and (x^1, y^1, θ^1), respectively, for which a minimum-time path is to be found. To the best of our knowledge, the problem described above has not been addressed in the past, perhaps due to the fact that the classical Pontryagin's Maximum Principle is not applicable because of the discontinuous behavior at the common boundary between the patches.

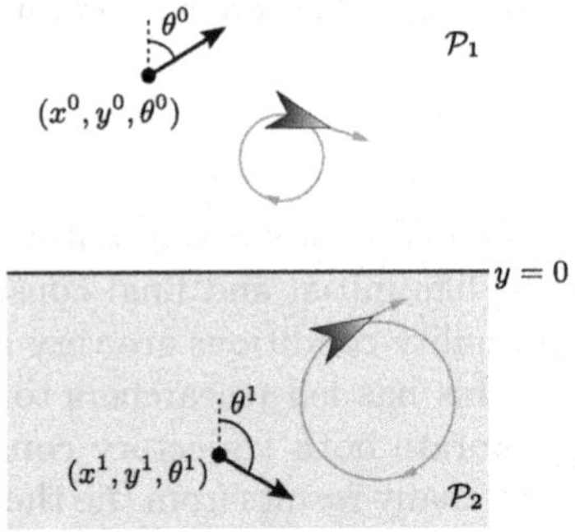

Fig. 1. Dubins vehicle on an heterogeneous terrain. The initial configuration is given by (x^0, y^0, θ^0) and the final configuration by (x^1, y^1, θ^1). The forward velocity in patch $\mathcal{P}_1$ is smaller than the forward velocity in patch $\mathcal{P}_2$.

By recasting this problem into an optimal hybrid control problem and applying principles of optimality for hybrid systems, we establish the following conditions that illuminate important characteristics of optimal paths:

- *The portions of the paths that remain in either patch are Dubins optimal.*
- *Optimal paths are such that, at the boundary between the patches, their type does not change; that is, the type of path right before and after crossing the boundary are the same.*
- *Optimal paths that cross the boundary describing a straight line are orthogonal to the boundary.*
- *The angles of the path pieces before and after crossing the boundary satisfy a "refraction" law, which consists of a generalization of Snell's law of refraction in optics.*

Applications of these results include optimal motion planning of autonomous vehicles in environments with obstacles, different terrains properties, and other topological constraints. Strategies that steer autonomous vehicles across heterogeneous terrain using Snell's law of refraction have already been recognized in the literature and applied to point-mass vehicles; see, e.g., [6,7]. Our results extend those to the case of autonomous vehicles with Dubins dynamics.

The remainder of the paper is organized as follows. Section 2 discusses related background to the optimal control problem outlined above and introduces general notation. In Section 3, we present a hybrid model which, as shown in that same section, enable us to formulate the problem of study in an optimal hybrid control framework. In Section 4, we establish necessary conditions for optimality of paths including a refraction law at the boundary of the patches. Due to space constraints, the technical proofs are omitted and will be published elsewhere.

2 Background

Pontryagin's Maximum Principle [2] is a very powerful tool to derive necessary conditions for optimality of solutions to a dynamical system. In words, this principle establishes the existence of an adjoint function with the property that, along optimal system solutions, the Hamiltonian obtained by combining the system dynamics and the cost function associated to the optimal control problem is minimized. In its original form, this principle is applicable to optimal control problems with dynamics governed by differential equations with continuously differentiable right-hand sides.

The shortest path problem between two points with specific tangent direction and bounded maximum curvature has received wide attention in the literature. In his pioneer work in [1], by means of geometric arguments, Dubins showed that optimal paths to this problem consist of a smooth concatenation of no more than three pieces, each of them describing either a straight line, denoted by $\mathcal{L}$, or a circle, denoted by $\mathcal{C}$ (when the circle is traveled clockwise, we write $\mathcal{C}^+$, while when the circle is traveled counter-clockwise, we write $\mathcal{C}^-$), and are either of type $\mathcal{CCC}$ or $\mathcal{CLC}$, that is, they are among the following six types of paths

$$\mathcal{C}^-\mathcal{C}^+\mathcal{C}^-,\ \mathcal{C}^+\mathcal{C}^-\mathcal{C}^+,\ \mathcal{C}^-\mathcal{L}\mathcal{C}^-,\ \mathcal{C}^+\mathcal{L}\mathcal{C}^+,\ \mathcal{C}^+\mathcal{L}\mathcal{C}^-,\ \mathcal{C}^-\mathcal{L}\mathcal{C}^+, \tag{2}$$

in addition to any of the subpaths obtained when some of the pieces (but not all) have zero length. More recently, the authors in [3] recovered Dubins' result by using Pontryagin's Maximum Principle; see also [5]. Further investigations of the properties of optimal paths to this problem and other related applications of Pontryagin's Maximum Principle include [8,9,10], to just list a few.

Optimal control problems exhibiting discontinuous/impulsive behavior, like the heterogeneous version of Dubins' problem outlined in Section 1, cannot be solved using the classical Pontryagin's Maximum Principle. Extensions of this principle to systems with discontinuous right-hand side appeared in [11] while extensions to hybrid systems include [12], [13], and [14]. These principles establish the existence of an adjoint function which, in addition to conditions that parallel the necessary optimality conditions in the principle by Pontryagin, satisfies certain conditions at times of discontinuous/jumping behavior. The applicability of these principles to relevant problems have been highlighted in [12,15,16]. These will be the key tool in deriving the results in this paper.

2.1 Notation

We use the following notation throughout the paper. $\mathbb{R}^n$ denotes n-dimensional Euclidean space. $\mathbb{R}$ denotes the real numbers. $\mathbb{R}_{\geq 0}$ denotes the nonnegative real numbers, i.e., $\mathbb{R}_{\geq 0} = [0, \infty)$. $\mathbb{N}$ denotes the natural numbers including 0, i.e., $\mathbb{N} = \{0, 1, \ldots\}$. Given $k \in \mathbb{N}$, $\mathbb{N}_{\leq k}$ denotes $\{0, 1, \ldots, k\}$. Given a set S, $\overline{S}$ denotes its closure and S° denotes its interior. Given a vector $x \in \mathbb{R}^n$, $|x|$ denotes the Euclidean vector norm. Given $U := [-1, 1]$, $\mathcal{U}$ denotes the set of all piecewise-continuous functions u from subsets of $\mathbb{R}_{\geq 0}$ to U.

3 Problem Statement

In this section, we formulate the problem of steering Dubins vehicle across heterogeneous terrain as a hybrid optimal control problem. We present a hybrid model and introduce the optimal control problem. An alternative approach is to treat this problem as a differential equation with discontinuous right-hand side and use the results in [11]. However, a hybrid control systems approach is not only more convenient from a modeling point of view as it enables the use of a sound concept of solution but also facilitates the application of more explicit optimality principles for hybrid systems, like the ones in [12].

3.1 Hybrid Model

We denote by $\mathcal{H}_v$ the hybrid system that captures the dynamics of Dubins vehicle along the patches. Let $v_1, v_2 \in \mathbb{R}_{>0}$, $v_1 \neq v_2$, be the forward velocity of the vehicle on patch $\mathcal{P}_1$ and patch $\mathcal{P}_2$, respectively, where

$$\mathcal{P}_1 := \left\{ [x\ y\ \theta]^\top \in \mathbb{R}^3 \mid y \geq 0 \right\}, \qquad \mathcal{P}_2 := \left\{ [x\ y\ \theta]^\top \in \mathbb{R}^3 \mid y \leq 0 \right\},$$

which share a common boundary $\mathcal{P}_1 \cap \mathcal{P}_2 = \left\{ [x\ y\ \theta]^\top \in \mathbb{R}^3 \mid y = 0 \right\}$; see Figure 1. Let q be a discrete state taking value in $Q := \{1, 2\}$ that indicates the current patch to which the vehicle belongs to. Following the vehicle's dynamics in (1),

$$\begin{bmatrix} \dot{\xi} \\ \dot{q} \end{bmatrix} = \begin{bmatrix} f_q(\xi, u) \\ 0 \end{bmatrix} \qquad \xi \in \mathcal{P}_q \tag{3}$$

with

$$\xi := \begin{bmatrix} x \\ y \\ \theta \end{bmatrix} \in \mathbb{R}^3 \qquad \text{and} \qquad f_q(\xi, u) := \begin{bmatrix} v_q \sin\theta \\ v_q \cos\theta \\ u \end{bmatrix}$$

define the continuous dynamics (or *flows*) of $\mathcal{H}_v$, where ξ is the continuous state and $u \in \mathcal{U}$ is the control input. Then, during flows, ξ captures the vehicle dynamics on the q-th patch while q remains constant. We model the change of patch so that it occurs when y is zero and the vehicle is moving away from the current patch. Then, defining a function $s : Q \to \{-1, 1\}$ where $s(1) = -1$ and $s(2) = 1$, the discrete dynamics (or *jumps*) of $\mathcal{H}_v$ are given by

$$\begin{bmatrix} \xi^+ \\ q^+ \end{bmatrix} = \begin{bmatrix} \xi \\ 3 - q \end{bmatrix} \qquad \xi \in \mathcal{P}_1 \cap \mathcal{P}_2 \ \text{ and } \ s(q) v_q \cos\theta > 0 \,, \tag{4}$$

which implies that at jumps ξ does not change while q is toggled between 1 and 2. Finally, we denote by $\zeta := [\xi^\top \; q]^\top$ the full state of $\mathcal{H}_v$.

Following the hybrid systems framework outlined in [17] and further established in [18,19], we can rewrite $\mathcal{H}_v$ as

$$\mathcal{H}_v : \begin{cases} \dot{\zeta} = f(\zeta, u) & \zeta \in C \\ \zeta^+ = g(\zeta) & \zeta \in D \end{cases}$$

by defining

$$f(\zeta, u) := \begin{bmatrix} f_q(\xi, u) \\ 0 \end{bmatrix}, C := \bigcup_{q \in Q} (C_q \times \{q\}), g(\zeta) := \begin{bmatrix} \xi \\ 3 - q \end{bmatrix}, D := \bigcup_{q \in Q} (D_q \times \{q\}),$$

where $C_q := \mathcal{P}_q$ and $D_q := \left\{ \xi \in \mathbb{R}^3 \mid y = 0, s(q) v_q \cos\theta > 0 \right\}$ for each $q \in Q$. Then, $\mathcal{H}_v$ is determined by the data (f, C, g, D), where f is the *flow map*, C is the *flow set*, g is the *jump map*, and D is the *jump set*. As in [17], solutions to $\mathcal{H}_v$ are given by *hybrid arcs* on *hybrid time domains*. Hybrid time domains use a variable t to indicate flow time and an index j to keep track of the number of jumps, and hence, parametrize solutions by (t, j). A subset E of $\mathbb{R}_{\geq 0} \times \mathbb{N}$ is a *hybrid time domain* if it is the union of infinitely many intervals of the form $[t_j, t_{j+1}] \times \{j\}$, where $0 = t_0 \leq t_1 \leq t_2 \leq \ldots$, or of finitely many such intervals, with the last one possibly of the form $[t_j, t_{j+1}] \times \{j\}$, $[t_j, t_{j+1}) \times \{j\}$, or $[t_j, \infty) \times \{j\}$. (Note that the t component of elements $(t, j) \in E$ does not uniquely define the index j since, in this framework, multiple jumps at the same t are possible.) Then, given a control input $u \in \mathcal{U}$, solutions to $\mathcal{H}_v$ are given by functions, called *hybrid arcs*, $\zeta : \operatorname{dom} \zeta \to \mathbb{R}^4$, where $\operatorname{dom} \zeta$ is a hybrid time domain, $t \mapsto \xi(t, j)$ is a locally absolutely continuous function for each fixed j, $t \mapsto q(t, j)$ is a piecewise constant function for each fixed j, and ζ satisfies the flow and jump conditions mentioned above. More precisely, given an input $u \in \mathcal{U}$, a hybrid arc ζ is a *solution to the hybrid system* $\mathcal{H}_v$ if $\zeta(0,0) \in C \cup D$, $\operatorname{dom} \zeta = \operatorname{dom} u$, and:

(S1) For all $j \in \mathbb{N}$ and almost all t such that $(t, j) \in \operatorname{dom} \zeta$ [1],

$$\zeta(t, j) \in C, \quad \dot{\zeta}(t, j) = f(\zeta(t, j), u(t, j)) \,.$$

[1] $\dot{\zeta}(t, j)$ denotes the derivative of $t \mapsto \zeta(t, j)$ with respect to t for a fixed j, which exists for almost every t such that $(t, j) \in \operatorname{dom} \zeta \cap ([t_j, t_{j+1}] \times \{j\})$.

(S2) For all $(t, j) \in \operatorname{dom} \zeta$ such that $(t, j+1) \in \operatorname{dom} \zeta$,

$$\zeta(t, j) \in D, \quad \zeta(t, j+1) = g(\zeta(t, j)) .$$

Inputs u given as signals $t \mapsto u(t)$ for each $t \in \mathbb{R}_{\geq 0}$ can be rewritten on a hybrid time domain E by defining, with some abuse of notation, $u(t, j) := u(t)$ for each $(t, j) \in E$. Note that solutions to $\mathcal{H}_v$ exist from every point in $C \cup D = \mathbb{R}^3 \times Q$. In particular, solutions are allowed to flow in the boundary $\mathcal{P}_1 \cap \mathcal{P}_2$ with either $q = 1$ or $q = 2$; such a feature cannot be captured with a differential equation with discontinuous right-hand side or with a (regular) differential inclusion without adding extra solutions. Also note that since the sets D_q are not closed subsets of $\mathbb{R}^3$, the regularity property for D required in [18,19] does not hold (the flow map, jump map, and jump set of $\mathcal{H}_v$ satisfy the properties therein). While such a regularity is not required for the results in this paper to be true, it turns out that, as shown in [19], it highlights the presence of undesirable solutions if the sets D_q were to be closed or small noise entered through the state.

3.2 Hybrid Optimal Control Problem

We consider the following hybrid optimal control problem. Given $(x^0, y^0, \theta^0) \in C_1^\circ$ and $(x^1, y^1, \theta^1) \in C_2^\circ$:

($\star$) Minimize the transfer time $T \in \mathbb{R}_{\geq 0}$ subject to:
- (C1) Dynamical constraint: dynamics of $\mathcal{H}_v$ given in (3)-(4).
- (C2) Input constraint: $u \in \mathcal{U}$.
- (C3) Initial and terminal constraints: every optimal solution (ξ, q) to $\mathcal{H}_v$ satisfies the initial constraint $(x(0,0), y(0,0), \theta(0,0)) = (x^0, y^0, \theta^0)$ and the terminal constraint $(x(T,J), y(T,J), \theta(T,J)) = (x^1, y^1, \theta^1)$ for some $(T, J) \in \operatorname{dom}(\xi, q)$.

The number of jumps required to solve ($\star$) is finite, given by $J - 1$, and no smaller than one; hence, optimal solutions to ($\star$) are not Zeno. The initial and final constraints are such that solutions can flow from some time before their first jump and after their final jump (that is, the first jump is at some $(t_1, 0)$ with $t_1 > 0$ and the last jump is at some $(t_J, J-1)$ with $t_J < T$). This is a technical requirement for the application of the hybrid maximum principle in [12] in the next section.

4 Necessary Conditions for Optimality

Necessary optimality conditions for solutions to $\mathcal{H}_v$ solving ($\star$) can be obtained using the principle of optimality for hybrid systems in [12] (see also [20] and [15]). Under further technical assumptions, Theorem 1 in [12] establishes that there exists an *adjoint pair* $(\lambda, \lambda_\circ)$, where λ is a function and $\lambda_\circ$ is a constant, which, along optimal solutions to ($\star$), satisfies certain *Hamiltonian maximization, nontriviality, transversality,* and *Hamiltonian value conditions.* In particular, [12, Theorem 1] can be applied to the optimal control problem ($\star$) to deduce the following optimality conditions for the paths.

Proposition 1 (properties of ($\star$)). *For each optimal solution (ξ, q) to ($\star$) with optimal control u, minimum transfer time T, and $J-1$ number of jumps, there exists a function $\lambda : \operatorname{dom}\lambda \to \mathbb{R}^3$, $\lambda := [\alpha\ \beta\ \gamma]^\top$, $\operatorname{dom}\lambda = \operatorname{dom}(\xi, q)$, where $t \mapsto \lambda(t,j)$ is absolutely continuous for each j, $(t,j) \in \operatorname{dom}\lambda$, and a constant $\lambda_\circ \in \mathbb{R}$ defining the adjoint pair $(\lambda, \lambda_\circ)$ satisfying:*

a) $\lambda_\circ \geq 0$ *and* $\dot{\lambda}(t,j) = -\dfrac{\partial H_{q(t,j)}}{\partial \xi}(\xi(t,j), \lambda(t,j), \lambda_\circ, u(t,j))$ *for almost every* $t \in [t_j, t_{j+1}]$, $(t,j) \in \operatorname{dom}\lambda$, *where, for each* $q \in \{1,2\}$, $H_q : \mathbb{R}^3 \times \mathbb{R}^3 \times \mathbb{R} \times$ $\times U \to \mathbb{R}$ *is the Hamiltonian associated with the continuous dynamics of* $\mathcal{H}_v$, *which is given by*

$$H_q(\xi, \lambda, \lambda_\circ, u) = \alpha v_q \sin\theta + \beta v_q \cos\theta + \gamma u - \lambda_\circ$$

for each $q \in Q$.

b) There exist $\overline{\alpha}, \overline{\beta} \in \mathbb{R}$ *and, for each* $j \in \mathbb{N}_{\leq J}$, *there exists* $p_j \in \mathbb{R}$ *such that* $\alpha(t,j) := \overline{\alpha}$ *for all* $(t,j) \in \operatorname{dom}(\xi,q)$, $\beta(t,j) := \overline{\beta} + p_j$ *for almost all* $t \in [0,T]$, $(t,j) \in \operatorname{dom}(\xi,q)$, *and* $\gamma(t,j) = \gamma(t,j+1)$ *for each* (t,j) *such that* $(t,j), (t,j+1) \in \operatorname{dom}\lambda$.

c) For every $(t,j) \in \operatorname{dom}(\xi,q)$ *such that* $\gamma(t,j) \neq 0$, $u(t,j) = sgn(\gamma(t,j))$; *and for every* $(t,j) \in \operatorname{dom}(\xi,q)$ *such that* $\gamma(t,j) = 0$, $u(t,j) = 0$.

d) For every $(t,j) \in \operatorname{dom}(\xi,q)$ *such that* $\gamma(t,j) = 0$, $\beta(t,j)\tan\theta(t,j) = \alpha(t,j)$.

Remark 1. The proof of Proposition 1 uses the fact that $\mathcal{H}_v$ can be associated with a hybrid system $\mathcal{H}_v^*$ given in the framework in [12] and that every solution to $\mathcal{H}_v$ solving ($\star$) is also a solution to $\mathcal{H}_v^*$ (agreeing with the concept of solution in [12][2]). This property follows by construction of $\mathcal{H}_v^*$. Hybrid systems in [12] and [15] have a continuous state ξ with flows governed by $\dot{\xi} = f_q(\xi, u)$ when ξ belongs to a smooth manifold $\mathcal{M}_q$, where $q \in Q$ is a discrete state (which remains constant during flows). Jumps from mode q to mode q' satisfy: 1) the switching condition $(\xi, \xi') \in \mathcal{S}_{q,q'}$, where ξ is the continuous state before the jump, ξ' is the continuous state after the jump, and $\mathcal{S}_{q,q'}$ is the switching set; and 2) a temporal constraint enforcing that the jump time for the current mode is in the set $J_q \subset \mathbb{R}$. To obtain $\mathcal{H}_v^*$, the sets C_q in $\mathcal{H}_v$ are replaced by smooth

[2] In [12], solutions to hybrid systems are given on compact time intervals by absolutely continuous functions ξ_j on $[t_j, t_{j+1}]$ such that, for each $j \in \{1, 2, \dots, \nu\}$ (with finite $\nu \in \mathbb{N}$) and for finite sequences of logic states $\{q_j\}$ and control inputs $\{u_j\}$, satisfy the flow condition $\dot{\xi}_j = f_{q_j}(\xi_j(t), u_j(t))$ for almost all $t \in [t_j, t_{j+1}]$ and the jump condition $(\xi_j(t_j), \xi_{j+1}(t_j)) \in \mathcal{S}_{q_j, q_{j+1}}$ for each t_j, where t_j denotes the jump time (which is assumed to belong to the interior of the compact time interval where solutions are defined) and $\mathcal{S}_{q_j, q_{j+1}}$ is the switching set at the j-th jump (see [12, Definition 3] for more details). Hence, passing from a solution ζ on a bounded hybrid time domain $\operatorname{dom}\zeta$ with jumps at different (t_j, j)'s, first jump at $(t_1, 0)$ with $t_1 > t_0$, and last jump at $(t_J, J-1)$ with $t_J < T$, where $T := \sup\{t \in \mathbb{R}_{\geq 0} \mid \exists j \in \mathbb{N} \text{ such that} (t,j) \in \operatorname{dom}\zeta\}$ and $J := \sup\{j \in \mathbb{N} \mid \exists t \in \mathbb{R}_{\geq 0} \text{ such that} (t,j) \in \operatorname{dom}\zeta\}$), to a solution as in [12, Definition 3] is straightforward.

manifolds $\mathcal{M}_q$, $C_q \subset \mathcal{M}_q$, while the jump set and the jump map are replaced by the switching condition given by

$$\mathcal{S}_{1,2} = \mathcal{S}_{2,1} = \hat{\mathcal{S}} := \left\{(\xi, \xi) \;\middle|\; y = 0, \xi \in \mathbb{R}^3\right\} ,$$

and $J_1 = J_2 = \mathbb{R}$. Then, the properties of the adjoint pair guaranteed by [12, Theorem 1] automatically imply item a) in Proposition 1 (see [12, Definition 9]). The condition for optimality at switches for the adjoint state λ implies that only the second component of λ, i.e. β, has a jump while the other two components are continuous (see Remark 2). This implies item b) in Proposition 1. The Hamiltonian maximization condition guaranteed to hold by [12, Theorem 1] implies that

$$H_{q(t,j)}(\xi(t,j), \lambda(t,j), \lambda_\circ, u(t,j)) = \max_{w \in U} H_{q(t,j)}(\xi(t,j), \lambda(t,j), \lambda_\circ, w)$$

for almost every $t \in [t_j, t_{j+1}]$, $(t,j) \in \operatorname{dom} \lambda$ (see [12, Definition 10]). It follows that the control law in item c) in Proposition 1 maximizes H_q. By integrating the adjoint state λ when $u = 0$, Proposition 1.d follows automatically. ∎

Remark 2. [12, Theorem 1] implies that at jumps, the optimal solution, optimal control, and adjoint pair satisfy the switching condition $(-\lambda(t,j), \lambda(t,j+1)) \in K_j^{\perp}$ for each j for which there exists $t \in [0,T]$ such that $(t,j), (t,j+1) \in \operatorname{dom} \lambda$, where $K_j^{\perp}$ is the polar of the Boltyanskii approximating cone to $\mathcal{S}_{q(t,j),q(t,j+1)} (= \hat{\mathcal{S}})$. The set $\hat{\mathcal{S}}$ is such that $K_j^{\perp}$ is given by $\left\{w \in \mathbb{R}^3 \times \mathbb{R}^3 \;\middle|\; \langle w, v\rangle \le 0 \;\forall v \in \hat{\mathcal{S}}\right\}$ since the Boltyanskii approximating cone to $\hat{\mathcal{S}}$ is the set itself. Then, since by definition of $\hat{\mathcal{S}}$ the second and fourth components of v in $K_j^{\perp}$ are zero, $(-\lambda(t,j), \lambda(t,j+1)) \in K_j^{\perp}$ if and only if $\alpha(t,j) = \alpha(t,j+1)$, $\gamma(t,j) = \gamma(t,j+1)$, which implies that only β can have a jump. This property can also be obtained using the optimality principles in [14]. ∎

4.1 Optimality of Paths

The properties of the adjoint pair $(\lambda, \lambda_\circ)$ and the control input u in Proposition 1 can be related to properties of the continuous component ξ of the solutions to $(\star)$. These characterize the optimal paths from given initial and terminal constraints, as the following theorem states.

Theorem 1 (optimality conditions of solutions to $(\star)$). *Each optimal solution (ξ, q) to $(\star)$ with optimal control u, minimum transfer time T, and $J-1$ number of jumps is such that:*

a) The continuous component ξ is a smooth concatenation of finitely many pieces from the set $\{\mathcal{C}^+, \mathcal{C}^-, \mathcal{L}\}$.
b) The input component u is piecewise constant with finitely many pieces taking value in $\{-1, 0, 1\}$.

c) Each piece of the continuous component ξ contained in C_q, $q \in Q$, is Dubins optimal between the first and last point of such piece, i.e., it is given as in (2).

d) For each $(t,j) \in \mathrm{dom}(\xi, q)$ for which $(x(t,j), y(t,j), \theta(t,j)) \in D_{q(t,j)}$, the solution has a jump and:

d.1) If the path before the jump is $\mathcal{C}$ then the path after the jump is $\mathcal{C}$.

d.2) If the path before the jump is $\mathcal{L}$ then the path after the jump is $\mathcal{L}$ and $\theta(t,j)$ is zero or any multiple of π.

Remark 3. The proof of Theorem 1 uses Proposition 1 and the fact that, since the jump condition in $\mathcal{H}_v$ is time independent (that is, $J_1 = J_2 = \mathbb{R}$), the Hamiltonian value condition guaranteed to hold by [12, Theorem 1] implies that there exists $h^* \in \mathbb{R}$ such that

$$h^* = H_{q(t,j)}(\xi(t,j), \lambda(t,j), \lambda_\circ, u(t,j))$$

for almost every $t \in [t_j, t_{j+1}]$, $(t,j) \in \mathrm{dom}\,\lambda$ (see [12, Definition 13]). ∎

Figure 2 depicts optimal paths around the boundary of the patches. Item d.1) in Theorem 1 implies that optimal paths that cross the boundary are of the same type at each side of it. More precisely, if before crossing the boundary, the optimal path is of type $\mathcal{C}$ ($\mathcal{C}^+$ or $\mathcal{C}^-$), then the optimal path after crossing the boundary is also of type $\mathcal{C}$ ($\mathcal{C}^+$ or $\mathcal{C}^-$, respectively). Figure 2(a) depicts an optimal path of type $\mathcal{C}^+$. Statement d.2) in Theorem 1 implies that $\mathcal{L}$-type paths at the boundary are optimal only if they are orthogonal to the boundary. Figure 2(b) depicts this situation.

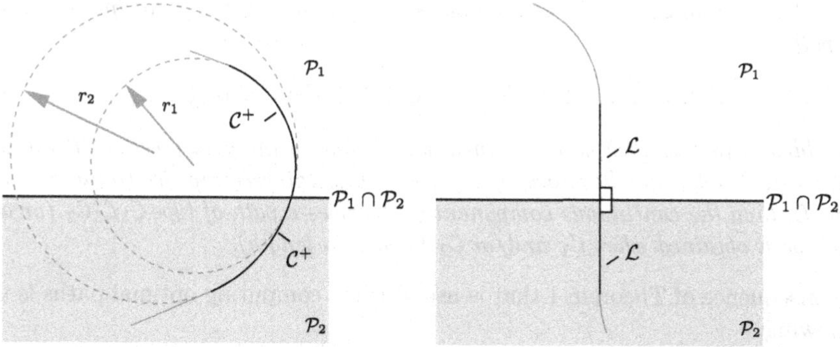

(a) $\mathcal{C}^+$-type of path at the boundary. Path pieces $\mathcal{C}^+$ in patch $\mathcal{P}_1$ with radius $r_1 = v_1$ and in patch $\mathcal{P}_2$ with radius $r_2 = v_2$, $v_2 > v_1$.

(b) $\mathcal{L}$-type of path at the boundary. The angle between the path and the boundary in each patch is $\pi/2$.

Fig. 2. Optimal paths nearby the boundary: paths of types $\mathcal{C}^+$ and $\mathcal{L}$ satisfying the necessary conditions in Theorem 1

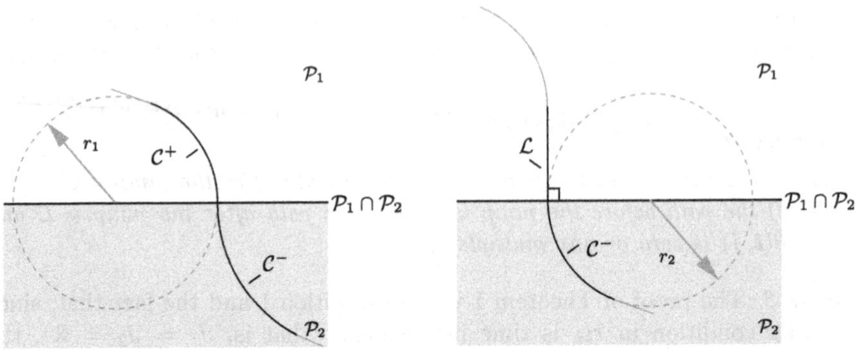

(a) Nonoptimal $\mathcal{C}^+/\mathcal{C}^-$-type path at the boundary. Path piece $\mathcal{C}^+$ in patch $\mathcal{P}_1$ with radius $r_1 = v_1$ and path piece $\mathcal{C}^-$ in patch $\mathcal{P}_2$ with radius $r_2 = v_2$, $v_2 > v_1$.

(b) Nonoptimal $\mathcal{L}/\mathcal{C}^-$-type path at the boundary. Path piece $\mathcal{C}^-$ in patch $\mathcal{P}_2$ with radius $r_2 = v_2$.

Fig. 3. Nonoptimal paths at the boundary: paths of type $\mathcal{C}^+/\mathcal{C}^-$ and $\mathcal{L}/\mathcal{C}^-$ changing at the boundary and hence, not satisfying the necessary conditions for optimality in Theorem 1

Using Theorem 1, it is possible to determine optimal families of paths for a class of solutions to $(\star)$. The following statements follow directly from Dubins' result and Theorem 1.

Corollary 1 (optimal paths w/one jump). *Every optimal solution* (ξ, q) *to* $(\star)$ *with only one jump is such that the continuous component* ξ *is a smooth concatenation of* $\mathcal{C}, \mathcal{L}$ *paths pieces and is given by one of the following four types of paths*

$$\mathcal{C}_1\mathcal{L}_1\mathcal{C}_2\mathcal{L}_2\mathcal{C}_3,\ \mathcal{C}_1\mathcal{C}_2\mathcal{C}_3\mathcal{L}_1\mathcal{C}_4,\ \mathcal{C}_1\mathcal{C}_2\mathcal{C}_3\mathcal{C}_4\mathcal{C}_5,\ \mathcal{C}_1\mathcal{L}_1\mathcal{C}_2\mathcal{C}_3\mathcal{C}_4\ , \tag{5}$$

in addition to any such path obtained when some of the path pieces (but not all) have zero length. Furthermore, if the path piece intersecting the boundary is of type $\mathcal{L}$*, then the continuous component* ξ *describes a path of type* $\mathcal{C}_1\mathcal{L}_1\mathcal{C}_2$ *(or any such path obtained when* $\mathcal{C}_1$ *and/or* $\mathcal{C}_2$ *have zero length).*

A consequence of Theorem 1 that is useful when computing optimal paths is the following.

Corollary 2 (nonoptimal paths). *For the optimal control problem* $(\star)$*, solutions to* $\mathcal{H}_v$ *satisfying (C1)-(C3) with the continuous component* ξ *describing paths that change at the boundary are nonoptimal, that is, paths that before and after the boundary are given by* $\mathcal{C}^+$ *and* $\mathcal{L}$*,* $\mathcal{C}^-$ *and* $\mathcal{L}$*,* $\mathcal{L}$ *and* $\mathcal{C}^+$*,* $\mathcal{L}$ *and* $\mathcal{C}^-$*,* $\mathcal{C}^+$ *and* $\mathcal{C}^-$*, or* $\mathcal{C}^-$ *and* $\mathcal{C}^+$*, respectively, are nonoptimal.*

Figure 3 depicts two of the path types that Corollary 2 determines to be nonoptimal.

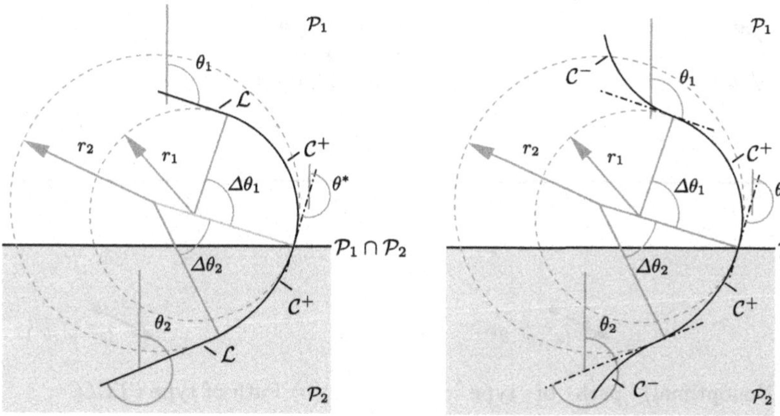

(a) Refraction for $\mathcal{LCL}$-type of path nearby the boundary. The $\mathcal{L}$ path pieces define the angles θ_1, θ_2 and their variations $\Delta\theta_1, \Delta\theta_2$.

(b) Refraction for $\mathcal{CCC}$-type of path nearby the boundary. The tangents (plotted with .– lines) at the point of path change define the angles θ_1, θ_2 and their variations $\Delta\theta_1, \Delta\theta_2$.

Fig. 4. Refraction law for paths at the boundary. The initial and final angles of optimal paths intersecting the boundary given by θ_1 and θ_2, respectively, and their variations $(\Delta\theta_1, \Delta\theta_2)$ satisfy equation (6), which is a generalization of Snell's law of refraction.

4.2 Refraction Law at Boundary

The optimal control law given in Proposition 1.c and the properties of the component γ of the adjoint state λ given in Proposition 1.b imply that the control law is constant at jumps of $\mathcal{H}_v$ (note that u is piecewise continuous for each fixed j with discontinuities at (t, j)'s where the path type changes). While θ remains constant at the boundary, the initial and final angles (and their variations) of the paths intersecting the boundary satisfy the following algebraic condition involving the patch velocities v_1 and v_2.

Theorem 2 (refraction law for ($\star$)). *Let (ξ, q) be an optimal solution to ($\star$). Let θ_1 and θ_2 denote the initial and final angle, respectively, of a path piece intersecting the boundary $\mathcal{P}_1 \cap \mathcal{P}_2$, as show in Figure 4. Let $\Delta\theta_1, \Delta\theta_2 \in \mathbb{R}$ be given by $\Delta\theta_1 := \theta^* - \theta_1$, $\Delta\theta_2 := \theta_2 - \theta^*$, where θ^* is the angle between the path and the boundary $\mathcal{P}_1 \cap \mathcal{P}_2$ at their intersection (with respect to the vertical axis). If the path piece intersecting $\mathcal{P}_1 \cap \mathcal{P}_2$ is of type $\mathcal{C}$, then $v_1, v_2, \theta_1, \theta_2, \Delta\theta_1$ and $\Delta\theta_2$ satisfy*

$$\frac{v_1}{v_2} = \frac{1 + \cot\theta_2 \cot\left(\frac{\Delta\theta_1 - \Delta\theta_2}{2} + \frac{\theta_1 + \theta_2}{2}\right)}{1 + \cot\theta_1 \cot\left(\frac{\Delta\theta_1 - \Delta\theta_2}{2} + \frac{\theta_1 + \theta_2}{2}\right)}, \tag{6}$$

and if the path piece intersecting $\mathcal{P}_1 \cap \mathcal{P}_2$ is of type $\mathcal{L}$, then θ_1 and θ_2 are equal to π.

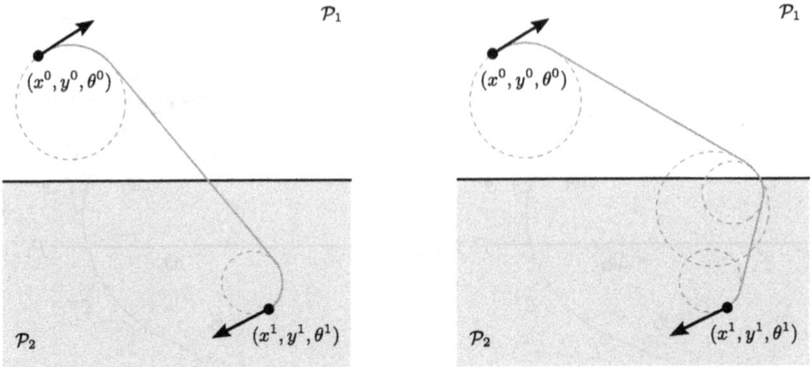

(a) (Nonoptimal) path of type $\mathcal{CLC}$

(b) Path of type $\mathcal{CLCLC}$

Fig. 5. Optimal control of Dubins vehicle on patches with velocities $v_1 = 2v_2$. The path depicted in (a) is nonoptimal since its $\mathcal{L}$-type piece is not orthogonal to the boundary $\mathcal{P}_1 \cap \mathcal{P}_2$ (it is also nonoptimal since it does not exploit the fact that the maximum velocity in patch $\mathcal{P}_1$ is twice faster than in patch $\mathcal{P}_2$). The path depicted in (b) is a candidate for optimality as it satisfies the conditions in Theorem 1 and Corollary 1.

Remark 4. Equation (6) in Theorem 2 implies that for a path of type $\mathcal{C}$ intersecting $\mathcal{P}_1 \cap \mathcal{P}_2$ to be optimal, $\theta_1, \theta_2, \Delta\theta_1$ and $\Delta\theta_2$ shown in Figure 4 must satisfy (6). When the path intersecting $\mathcal{P}_1 \cap \mathcal{P}_2$ is of type $\mathcal{L}$, by Corollary 1, the path $\mathcal{L}$ is orthogonal to $\mathcal{P}_1 \cap \mathcal{P}_2$ and consequently, there is no "refraction" at the boundary. This is depicted in Figure 2(b). The proof of Theorem 2 follows from the properties of the optimal solution and adjoint state at jumps stated in Theorem 1 and Proposition 1.d. ■

Equation (6) can be interpreted as a refraction law at the boundary of the two patches for the angles (and their variations) θ_1, θ_2 (and $\Delta\theta_1, \Delta\theta_2$). This parallels Snell's law of refraction in optics, which states a relationship between the angles of rays of light when passing through the boundary of two isotropic media with different refraction coefficients. More precisely, given two media with different refraction indexes v_1 and v_2, Snell's law of refraction states that

$$\frac{v_1}{v_2} = \frac{\sin\theta_1}{\sin\theta_2}, \tag{7}$$

where θ_1 is the angle of incidence and θ_2 is the angle of refraction. This law can be derived by solving a minimum-time problem between two points, one in each medium. Moreover, the dynamics of the rays of light can be associated to the differential equations $\dot{x} = v_i$, where v_i is the velocity in the i-th medium, $i = 1, 2$. Theorem 2 generalizes Snell's law to the case when the dynamics of the rays of light are given by (1). In fact, (6) reduces to (7) when $\Delta\theta_1 = \theta_1$ and $\Delta\theta_2 = \theta_2$. In the context of autonomous vehicles, (6) consists of a generalization of the refraction law for optimal steering of a point-mass vehicle, as in [6,7], to the Dubins vehicle case.

To further illustrate our results, consider $v_1 = 2v_2 > 0$, (x^0, y^0, θ^0), and (x^1, y^1, θ^1) as depicted in Figure 5. A path corresponding to a solution to $\mathcal{H}_v$ matching the initial and terminal constraints is shown in Figure 5(a). Since the $\mathcal{L}$-type path piece smoothly connecting the $\mathcal{C}$-type paths at (x^0, y^0, θ^0) and (x^1, y^1, θ^1) does not intersect the boundary $\mathcal{P}_1 \cap \mathcal{P}_2$ orthogonally, Theorem 1.d implies that it is nonoptimal (see also Corollary 1). Note that this path is not taking advantage of the fact that in patch $\mathcal{P}_1$, the vehicle can travel twice faster than in patch $\mathcal{P}_2$. Paths candidate for being optimal are like the one depicted in Figure 5(b) as it satisfies the conditions in Theorem 1 and Corollary 1.

5 Conclusions

We have derived necessary conditions for the optimality of paths with bounded maximum curvature. To establish our results, we formulated the problem as a hybrid optimal control problem and used optimality principles from the literature. Our results provide verifiable conditions for optimality of paths. These include conditions both in the interior of the patches and at their common boundary, as well as a refraction law for the angles which generalizes Snell's law of refraction in optics to the current setting. Applications of our results include optimal motion planning tasks for autonomous vehicles with Dubins vehicle dynamics.

Acknowledgments

This research has been partially supported by ARO through grant W911NF-07-1-0499, and by NSF through grant 0715025. Any opinions, findings, and conclusions or recommendations expressed in this publication are those of the authors and do not necessarily reflect the views of the supporting organizations.

References

1. Dubins, L.E.: On curves of minimal length with a constraint on average curvature, and with prescribed initial and terminal positions and tangents. American Journal of Mathematics 79, 497–516 (1957)
2. Pontryagin, L.S., Boltyanskij, V.G., Gamkrelidze, R.V., Mishchenko, E.F.: The mathematical theory of optimal processes. Wiley, Chichester (1962)
3. Boissonnat, J.D., Cérézo, A., Leblond, J.: Shortest paths of bounded curvature in the plane. Journal of Intelligent and Robotic Systems 11, 5–20 (1994)
4. Reeds, J.A., Shepp, L.A.: Optimal paths for a car that goes both forwards and backwards. Pacific Journal of Mathematics 145, 367–393 (1990)
5. Sussmann, H.J., Tang, G.: Shortest paths for the Reeds-Shepp car a worked out example of the use of geometric techniques in nonlinear optimal control. Technical report, Rutgers Center for Systems and Control Technical Report (1991)

6. Alexander, R.S., Rowe, N.C.: Path planning by optimal-path-map construction for homogeneous-cost two-dimensional regions. In: Proc. IEEE International Conference on Robotics and Automation, pp. 1924–1929 (1990)
7. Rowe, N.C., Alexander, R.S.: Finding optimal-path maps for path planning across weighted regions. The International Journal of Robotics Research 19, 83–95 (2000)
8. Shkel, A.M., Lumelsky, V.: Classification of the Dubins' set. Robotics and Autonomous Systems 34, 179–202 (2001)
9. Balkcom, D.J., Mason, M.T.: Time optimal trajectories for bounded velocity differential drive vehicles. The International J. Robotics Research 21, 199–217 (2002)
10. Chitsaz, H., LaValle, S.M., Balkcom, D.J., Mason, M.T.: Minimum wheel-rotation paths for differential-drive mobile robots. In: Proceedings IEEE International Conference on Robotics and Automation (2006)
11. Sussmann, H.J.: Some recent results on the maximum principle of optimal control theory. In: Systems and Control in the Twenty-First Century, 351–372 (1997)
12. Sussmann, H.J.: A maximum principle for hybrid optimal control problems. In: Proc. 38th IEEE Conference on Decision and Control, pp. 425–430 (1999)
13. Garavello, M., Piccoli, B.: Hybrid necessary principle. SIAM J. Control Optim. 43(5), 1867–1887 (2005)
14. Shaikh, M.S., Caines, P.E.: On the hybrid optimal control problem: Theory and algorithms. IEEE Transactions on Automatic Control 52, 1587–1603 (2007)
15. Piccoli, B.: Necessary conditions for hybrid optimization. In: Proceedings of the 38th IEEE Conference on Decision and Control, pp. 410–415 (1999)
16. D'Apice, C., Garavello, M., Manzo, R., Piccoli, B.: Hybrid optimal control: Case study of a car with gears. International Journal of Control 76, 1272–1284 (2003)
17. Goebel, R., Hespanha, J., Teel, A., Cai, C., Sanfelice, R.: Hybrid systems: Generalized solutions and robust stability. In: Proc. 6th IFAC Symposium in Nonlinear Control Systems, pp. 1–12 (2004)
18. Goebel, R., Teel, A.: Solutions to hybrid inclusions via set and graphical convergence with stability theory applications. Automatica 42(4), 573–587 (2006)
19. Sanfelice, R., Goebel, R., Teel, A.: Generalized solutions to hybrid dynamical systems. In: ESAIM: Control, Optimisation and Calculus of Variations (to appear, 2008)
20. Sussmann, H.J.: A nonsmooth hybrid maximum principle. In: Stability and Stabilization of Nonlinear Systems. Lecture Notes in Control and Information Sciences, pp. 325–354. Springer, Heidelberg (1999)

Switching Surface Design for Periodically Operated Discretely Controlled Continuous Systems

Axel Schild and Jan Lunze

Institute of Automation and Computer Control, Ruhr-Universitaet Bochum, Universitaetsstrasse 150, 44780 Bochum, Germany
{Schild, Lunze}@atp.rub.de

Abstract. Discretely controlled continuous systems (DCCS) represent an important class of hybrid systems, in which a continuous process is regulated by a discrete controller. The paper introduces a novel model-based design procedure for periodically operated DCCS with the objective to produce a periodic stationary operation. The method exploits an equivalence to periodic control systems to obtain an event-driven switching strategy that locally stabilizes a predetermined limit cycle and enforces a desired transient behavior. In contrast to earlier results, the controller responds to deviations without a dead time.

1 Introduction

Discretely controlled continuous systems (DCCS) have recently received much attention throughout the hybrid systems community [1,2,3,4,5,6,7]. Such systems form a control loop composed of a continuous plant and a discrete-event controller (Fig. 1(a)). This structure is found in many application domains, such as power electronics, manufacturing systems, process engineering, mechanics and robotics. The control task of DCCS is to switch the plant's mode of operation at opportune moments to meet specifications defined in terms of the continuous variables at stationary operation. As a central characteristic, the working principle of these systems demands a never ending switching action, which prevents the continuous state trajectory to converge towards an equilibrium state. Instead, a periodic or even a chaotic stationary motion is observed.

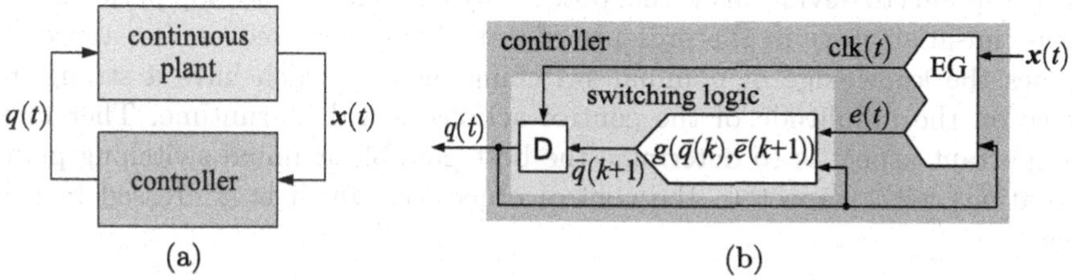

Fig. 1. Structure of a DCCS: (a) control loop, (b) discrete controller

M. Egerstedt and B. Mishra (Eds.): HSCC 2008, LNCS 4981, pp. 471–485, 2008.

This paper presents a novel model-based design procedure for the event generator included in the discrete controller. The presented approach produces *static switching planes* and allows to influence the local loop properties systematically. Compared to previously published approaches, the discrete controller is of lower complexity and its control actions are instantaneously applied without any delay. The method does not impose any restrictions on the number of continuous states or the number of operation modes. Furthermore, it allows for a partial design, if a subset of system-inherent switching surface must not be altered.

The paper is organized as follows: Section 2 recalls the model of a DCCS. Following the problem formulation (Sect. 3), all design steps are presented in Sect. 4. The key idea is to recast the original problem into a periodic linear control problem (Sect. 4.1). With the equivalence stated in Theorem 1, novel results for checking the local stabilizability of a DCCS along a closed orbit are derived (Sect. 4.2) and summarized in Theorem 3. Section 4.3 classifies modes as effective or ineffective, which is crucial for obtaining feasible design results. Section 4.4 summarizes the design algorithm, which is successfully applied to a laboratory plant in Sect. 5. The experimental data demonstrate the excellent loop performance, which is attained by this discrete controller.

Literature. In the past, research work on DCCS primarily focused on analysis methods, whereas model-based design approaches have only been scarcely developed. Recently, the optimal start-up of DCCS under known initial conditions was addressed in [8, 9] and extended to unknown initial states in [10, 11]. Lyapunov-based switching with application to switching power converters was discussed in [12, 13]. The primary objective considered in these publications is to drive the continuous trajectory into a neighborhood of a desired terminal state.

The problem of *stabilizing limit cycles* of smooth nonlinear systems, on the other hand, has been investigated over the past two decades starting with [14]. It was extended to non-smooth dynamical systems in [15], where the authors advocate the use of switching and state-resetting to affect the stability of recurrent motions. The question of how to systematically design the "control law" in case of multiple control interactions over one period remained unanswered, until a model-based solution was presented in [16]. The approach proposed therein relies on the *dynamic adjustment* of nominal switching surfaces by means of a *switching surface controller* (SSC). Because the resulting controller responds to deviations with a potentially large delay, the loop performance may be unsatisfactory in the presence of disturbances. Moreover, the approach assumes the knowledge of nominal switching planes, which have a strong influence on the amplitude of the control actions issued at runtime. Therefore, an important aspect is to determine the best possible nominal switching plane orientations with respect to the control objective, which is addressed in this paper.

2 Modeling of Periodically Operated Discretely Controlled Continuous Systems

2.1 Hybrid Model

The main contribution of this paper is a novel model-based design method for the event generator of periodically operated discretely controlled continuous systems (DCCS), i.e. systems that recurrently execute a predetermined sequence

$$Q_{\mathrm{LC}} = \left(\bar{q}_0^\star \bar{q}_1^\star \cdots \bar{q}_{p-1}^\star\right) \tag{1}$$

of p distinct operation modes $\bar{q}_i^\star \neq \bar{q}_j^\star$. This section summarizes a model, which reflects all relevant aspects of the closed-loop behavior and represents a tailored version of the general hybrid model introduced in [16, 17].

The model consists of three components: a continuous plant, an event generator and a discrete switching logic (Fig. 1(b)). The continuous dynamics are governed by the state equation

$$\dot{\boldsymbol{x}}(t) = \boldsymbol{f}(\boldsymbol{x}(t)\,, q(t))\,, \quad \boldsymbol{x}(0) = \boldsymbol{x}_0 \ , \tag{2}$$

where $\boldsymbol{x} \in \mathbb{R}^n$ is the continuous state. The plant's sole accessible input $q(t)$ is restricted to the finite set $\mathcal{Q} = \left\{\bar{q}_0^\star, \ldots, \bar{q}_{p-1}^\star\right\}$ of *operation modes*. For each mode $\bar{q}_k^\star$, the continuous dynamics (2) possess a different equilibrium state.

The event generator implements a piecewise affine *event function*

$$\Phi(\boldsymbol{x}, q) = \boldsymbol{c}^{\mathrm{T}}(q)\; \boldsymbol{x}(t) - d(q) \ , \tag{3}$$

which implicitly defines a switching hyperplane

$$\mathcal{S}\,(q) = \{\boldsymbol{x} \,:\, \Phi(\boldsymbol{x}, q) = 0\} \tag{4}$$

for each mode q. The vector $\boldsymbol{c}^{\mathrm{T}}(q)$ and the scalar $d(q)$ determine a plane's orientation and its location in the state space. The event generator outputs a trigger signal

$$\mathrm{clk}(t) = \begin{cases} 0\,, & \text{if } |\Phi(\boldsymbol{x}(t)\,, q(t))| > 0 \\ 1\,, & \text{if } \Phi(\boldsymbol{x}(t)\,, q(t)) = 0 \ , \end{cases}$$

which initiates an update of the memory (D) according to

$$\bar{q}(k{+}1) = q\big(\bar{t}(k{+}1)^+\big) = \bar{q}^\star_{((k+1) \bmod p)}\,, \ \bar{q}(0) = \bar{q}_0^\star \tag{5}$$

at the *switching time*

$$\bar{t}(k{+}1) = \min_{t>\bar{t}(k)} \ t \,:\, \mathrm{clk}(t) = 1 \ .$$

Here $\bar{t}(k)^+$ denotes the limit from above. As the DCCS is assumed to execute the predetermined mode sequence Q_{LC}, the second output $e(t)$ of the event generator (Fig. 1) can be omitted. In the following, signals

$$\bar{\boldsymbol{x}}(k) = \boldsymbol{x}(\bar{t}(k))\,, \ \bar{q}(k) = q\big(\bar{t}(k)^+\big)$$

sampled at switching instants are indicated by a bar and enumerated by a counter k. The time span

$$\bar{\tau}(k) = \bar{t}(k+1) - \bar{t}(k) > 0$$

is called the *activation duration* of mode $\bar{q}(k)$ and τ denotes the elapsed time since the last switching. A DCCS *execution* over N switchings is denoted by

$$\chi(\boldsymbol{x}_0^h, t_0, N) = (\boldsymbol{x}(t)\,,\, q(t)\,,\, \mathcal{T}(N)) \quad , \quad \boldsymbol{x}_0^h = \begin{pmatrix}\boldsymbol{x}_0 & \bar{q}_0^\star\end{pmatrix}^{\mathrm{T}},\ t \in [t_0,\, \bar{t}(N)] \qquad (6)$$

with $\mathcal{T}(N) = (([t_0, \bar{t}(0)]\,,\, (\bar{t}(0), \bar{t}(1)]\,,\, ...)$ being a finite sequence of N activation intervals. The continuous state evolution starting in $\begin{pmatrix}\boldsymbol{x}_0 & \bar{q}_0^\star\end{pmatrix}^{\mathrm{T}}$ is referred to as $\boldsymbol{x}(\tau, \boldsymbol{x}_0, \bar{q}_0^\star)$. Executions $\chi^\star(\boldsymbol{x}_0^{h,\star}, 0, N)$ that satisfy

$$\begin{gathered}\bar{q}^\star(k+p) = \bar{q}^\star(k)\\ \boldsymbol{x}^\star(\tau, \bar{\boldsymbol{x}}^\star(k+p), \bar{q}^\star(k+p)) = \boldsymbol{x}^\star(\tau, \bar{\boldsymbol{x}}^\star(k), \bar{q}^\star(k))\,,\ \ \forall \tau \in (0,\, \bar{\tau}^\star(k)]\end{gathered}$$

for all $k \leq N-p$ are called *periodic* of *order* p and are indicated by a star. The corresponding closed orbit $\mathcal{L}_{\mathrm{LC}}$ traced out by $\chi^\star(\boldsymbol{x}_0^{h,\star}, 0, p)$ is called the *limit cycle.* For notational convenience, let $\bar{\boldsymbol{x}}^\star(\bar{q}_k^\star)$ denote the switch point $\bar{\boldsymbol{x}}^\star(k) \in \mathcal{L}_{\mathrm{LC}}$, at which the mode $\bar{q}^\star(k) = \bar{q}_k^\star$ is activated for the next $\bar{\tau}^\star(\bar{q}_k^\star)$ time units.

Remark 1. Any periodic execution $\chi^\star(\boldsymbol{x}_0^h, 0, p)$ satisfies

$$\min_{\tau \in [0,\, \bar{\tau}^\star(\bar{q}_k^\star))} \left|\boldsymbol{c}^{\mathrm{T}}(\bar{q}_k^\star)\ \left(\boldsymbol{x}^\star(\tau, \bar{\boldsymbol{x}}^\star(\bar{q}_k^\star)\,, \bar{q}_k^\star) - \bar{\boldsymbol{x}}^\star\left(\bar{q}_{k+1}^\star\right)\right)\right| > 0 \qquad (7)$$

for all $k = 0 \ldots (p-1)$, since the first intersection of $\boldsymbol{x}^\star(\tau, \bar{\boldsymbol{x}}^\star(\bar{q}_k^\star)\,, \bar{q}_k^\star)$ and the planes $\mathcal{S}\left(\bar{q}_k^\star\right)$ must occur at $\bar{\boldsymbol{x}}^\star\left(\bar{q}_{k+1}^\star\right)$. Accordingly, (7) constitute critical constraints, if the event function (3) is not given but must be synthesized to enforce a particular periodic execution.

2.2 Sampled Data Model

Sampling an execution (6) at switching instants yields the sampled execution

$$\bar{\chi}(\boldsymbol{x}_0^h, t_0, N) = \left(\left(\bar{\boldsymbol{x}}(0)\ \bar{q}(0)\ \bar{t}(0)\right)^{\mathrm{T}}, \ldots,\ \left(\bar{\boldsymbol{x}}(N)\ \bar{q}(N)\ \bar{t}(N)\right)^{\mathrm{T}}\right) \ , \qquad (8)$$

which is obtained by N iterated applications of the system's embedded map [18]. To synthesize switching planes (4) by means of a model, an analytic expression of this map's continuous component

$$\bar{\boldsymbol{x}}(k+1) = \boldsymbol{H}_x(\bar{\boldsymbol{x}}(k)\,,\, \bar{q}(k)\,,\, \bar{\tau}(k)) \qquad (9)$$

is needed. Unfortunately, a closed form representation of $\boldsymbol{H}_x$ is only possible for very simple DCCS. Concerning the vicinity of a stationary periodic execution $\chi^\star(\boldsymbol{x}_0^{h,\star}, 0, p)$ that transversally intersects with all switching planes, i.e.

$$\left|\boldsymbol{c}^{\mathrm{T}}(\bar{q}_k^\star)\, \boldsymbol{f}\left(\bar{\boldsymbol{x}}^\star\left(\bar{q}_{k+1}^\star\right), \bar{q}_k^\star\right)\right| > 0,\ \forall \bar{q}_k^\star \in \mathcal{Q}\ , \qquad (10)$$

at least a linear approximation of (9) for $\bar{q}(k) = \bar{q}_k^\star$ can be obtained as [19]

$$\begin{aligned}\delta\bar{\boldsymbol{x}}(k+1) &= \frac{\mathrm{d}\boldsymbol{H}_x}{\mathrm{d}\boldsymbol{x}}(\bar{\boldsymbol{x}}^\star(\bar{q}_k^\star)\,,\,\bar{q}_k^\star,\,\bar{\tau}^\star(\bar{q}_k^\star))\,\delta\bar{\boldsymbol{x}}(k)\\ &= \left(\boldsymbol{I} - \frac{\boldsymbol{f}\left(\bar{\boldsymbol{x}}^\star\left(\bar{q}_{k+1}^\star\right),\bar{q}_k^\star\right)\boldsymbol{c}^{\mathrm{T}}(\bar{q}_k^\star)}{\boldsymbol{c}^{\mathrm{T}}(\bar{q}_k^\star)\,\boldsymbol{f}\left(\bar{\boldsymbol{x}}^\star\left(\bar{q}_{k+1}^\star\right),\bar{q}_k^\star\right)}\right)\frac{\partial\bar{\boldsymbol{x}}^\star\left(\bar{q}_{k+1}^\star\right)}{\partial\bar{\boldsymbol{x}}^\star(\bar{q}_k^\star)}\delta\bar{\boldsymbol{x}}(k)\;. \end{aligned} \tag{11}$$

Here, $\partial\bar{\boldsymbol{x}}^\star\left(\bar{q}_{k+1}^\star\right)/\partial\bar{\boldsymbol{x}}^\star(\bar{q}_k^\star)$ is the fundamental matrix of (2) for $q = \bar{q}_k^\star$ and $\boldsymbol{x}(0) = \bar{\boldsymbol{x}}^\star(\bar{q}_k^\star)$ at $t = \bar{\tau}^\star(\bar{q}_k^\star)$. The difference $\delta\bar{\boldsymbol{x}}(k) = \bar{\boldsymbol{x}}(k) - \bar{\boldsymbol{x}}^\star(\bar{q}_k^\star)$ denotes the sampled deviation of $\boldsymbol{x}(t)$ from the stationary periodic execution. Clearly, the approximation (11) is only well defined, if the transversality condition (10) holds.

A composition of (9) over a complete cycle Q_{LC} yields a first return map

$$\bar{\boldsymbol{x}}(c+1) = \boldsymbol{P}_x(\bar{\boldsymbol{x}}(c)\,,\,\bar{q}(c)\,,\,\bar{\tau}(c)) = \boldsymbol{H}_x\circ\ldots\circ\boldsymbol{H}_x(\bar{\boldsymbol{x}}(c)\,,\,\bar{q}(c)\,,\,\bar{\tau}(c))\;, \tag{12}$$

which describes the evolution $\bar{\boldsymbol{x}}(c)$ of the switch points in the switching plane $\mathcal{S}\left(\bar{q}(c)\right)$ associated to mode $\bar{q}(c+1) = \bar{q}(c)$. The counter c is used to enumerate the executed cycles. Similar to (12), the linearized return map

$$\begin{aligned}\delta\bar{\boldsymbol{x}}(c+1) &= \frac{\mathrm{d}\boldsymbol{P}_x}{\mathrm{d}\boldsymbol{x}}(\bar{\boldsymbol{x}}^\star(\bar{q}_0^\star)\,,\,\bar{q}_0^\star,\,\bar{\tau}^\star(\bar{q}_0^\star))\,\delta\bar{\boldsymbol{x}}(c)\\ &= \left(\prod_{k=0}^{p-1}\frac{\mathrm{d}\boldsymbol{H}_x}{\mathrm{d}\boldsymbol{x}}(\bar{\boldsymbol{x}}^\star(\bar{q}_k^\star)\,,\,\bar{q}_k^\star,\,\bar{\tau}^\star(\bar{q}_k^\star))\right)\delta\bar{\boldsymbol{x}}(c)\end{aligned} \tag{13}$$

is obtained by composing (11) over a complete cycle Q_{LC}, in this case starting at $\bar{q}_0^\star$. Note that (13) represents a linear autonomous discrete-time periodic system, which carries information about the local orbital stability of $\boldsymbol{x}^\star(t)$ [17].

Remark 2. In case of a piecewise constant vector field $\boldsymbol{f}(\boldsymbol{x}, q) = \boldsymbol{b}(q)$, the expressions (11) and (13) describe $\boldsymbol{H}_x$ and $\boldsymbol{P}_x$ exactly [5].

Remark 3. Assuming a transversal intersection of $\chi^\star(\boldsymbol{x}_0^{h,\star}, 0, p)$ with all switching planes $\mathcal{S}\left(\bar{q}_k^\star\right)$, the map $\boldsymbol{H}_x$ is a local C^1-diffeomorphism in a neighborhood of all $\bar{\boldsymbol{x}}^\star(\bar{q}_k^\star)$ [19]. As $\boldsymbol{P}_x$ results from the composition of $\boldsymbol{H}_x$ over a switching cycle, it is a local C^1-diffeomorphism in a neighborhood of $\bar{\boldsymbol{x}}^\star(\bar{q}_0^\star)$ as well.

3 Problem Formulation

Problem 1. Consider a continuous plant (2), a switching logic (5) that cyclically generates the mode sequence Q_{LC} (1) and a predetermined stationary periodic execution $\chi^\star(\boldsymbol{x}_0^{h,\star}, 0, p)$ starting in $\boldsymbol{x}_0^{h,\star} = \left(\bar{\boldsymbol{x}}^\star(\bar{q}_0^\star)\;\bar{q}_0^\star\right)^{\mathrm{T}}$. The task considered in this paper is to find an event function (3) that renders the limit cycle $\mathcal{L}_{\mathrm{LC}}$ associated to $\chi^\star(\boldsymbol{x}_0^{h,\star}, 0, p)$ locally orbitally stable [16].

According to Prob. 1, the task is to find switching planes (4) that implicitly parameterize the activation duration $\bar{\tau}(\bar{q}(k)\,,\,\delta\boldsymbol{x}(\tau)) = \bar{\tau}^\star(\bar{q}(k)) + \delta\bar{\tau}(\bar{q}(k)\,,\,\delta\boldsymbol{x}(\tau))$

in terms of the mode and the deviation $\delta\boldsymbol{x}(\tau)=\mathrm{dist}(\boldsymbol{x}(\tau,\bar{\boldsymbol{x}}(k)\,,\bar{q}(k))\,,\mathcal{L}_{\mathrm{LC}})$ and thereby assure local orbital stability of $\mathcal{L}_{\mathrm{LC}}$. The latter implies that all multipliers

$$m_i = \lambda_i \left(\prod_{k=0}^{p-1} \frac{\mathrm{d}\boldsymbol{H}_x}{\mathrm{d}\boldsymbol{x}} (\bar{\boldsymbol{x}}^\star(\bar{q}_k^\star)\,,\, \bar{q}_k^\star,\, \bar{\tau}^\star(\bar{q}_k^\star)) \right) \tag{14}$$

of the return map's Jacobian (13) must lie inside the unit circle.

4 Switching Surface Design

4.1 Equivalent Discrete-Time Periodic Linear System

According to (11), the event generator design concentrates on finding vectors $\boldsymbol{c}^{\mathrm{T}}(\bar{q}_k^\star)$ that ensure orbital stability of $\mathcal{L}_{\mathrm{LC}}$. The sequel shows that by solving a classical linear periodic control problem, a set of feasible vectors $\boldsymbol{c}^{\mathrm{T}}(\bar{q}_k^\star)$ for $k = 1\dots(p-1)$ is obtained, which result in multipliers (14) satisfying $|m_i| < 1$.

In the first step, the denominator of (11) is removed, by which the normals $\boldsymbol{c}^{\mathrm{T}}(\bar{q}_k^\star)$ enter the linearized return map (13) nonlinearly. This nonlinear dependence vanishes, iff the design procedure generates vectors $\boldsymbol{c}^{\mathrm{T}}(\bar{q}_k^\star)$ that satisfy

$$\boldsymbol{c}^{\mathrm{T}}(\bar{q}_k^\star)\, \boldsymbol{f}(\bar{\boldsymbol{x}}^\star(\bar{q}_{k+1}^\star)\,,\bar{q}_k^\star) = 1,\ \ \forall \bar{q}_k^\star \in \mathcal{Q}\ . \tag{15}$$

The following Lemma translates the constraints (15) into equivalent conditions that can be explicitly accounted for in the design.

Lemma 1. *A vector $\boldsymbol{c}^{\mathrm{T}}(\bar{q}_k^\star)$ satisfies the constraint* (15), *iff*

$$\det\left(\boldsymbol{I} - \boldsymbol{f}(\bar{\boldsymbol{x}}^\star(\bar{q}_{k+1}^\star)\,,\, \bar{q}_k^\star)\, \boldsymbol{c}^{\mathrm{T}}(\bar{q}_k^\star)\right) = 0\ . \tag{16}$$

Proof. The equivalence of (15) and (16) readily follows from the matrix determinant lemma [20], which says that $\det(\boldsymbol{I} - \boldsymbol{a}\boldsymbol{b}^{\mathrm{T}}) = 1 - \boldsymbol{a}^{\mathrm{T}}\boldsymbol{b}$. □

With Lemma 1, a key result of the paper follows. Recall that two periodic linear system $\Sigma_i = \{\boldsymbol{A}_i(k)\,,\, \boldsymbol{b}_i(k)\}\,,\ i = 1,2$ are equivalent, if their monodromy matrices $\boldsymbol{\Psi}_i(p,0) = \prod_{k=0}^{p-1} \boldsymbol{A}_i(k)$ are similar.

Theorem 1. *The p-periodic linear system $\Sigma = \{\boldsymbol{A}_d(k)\,,\, \boldsymbol{b}_d(k)\}$ given by*

$$\boldsymbol{\zeta}(k{+}1) = \boldsymbol{A}_d(k)\,\boldsymbol{\zeta}(k) + \boldsymbol{b}_d(k)\,\boldsymbol{u}(k)\ \ \textit{with} \tag{17}$$

$$\boldsymbol{A}_d(k{+}p) = \boldsymbol{A}_d(k) = \partial\bar{\boldsymbol{x}}^\star(\bar{q}_{k+2}^\star)\,/\partial\bar{\boldsymbol{x}}^\star(\bar{q}_{k+1}^\star) \tag{18}$$

$$\boldsymbol{b}_d(k{+}p) = \boldsymbol{b}_d(k) = \boldsymbol{A}_d(k)\, \boldsymbol{f}(\bar{\boldsymbol{x}}^\star(\bar{q}_{k+1}^\star)\,,\, \bar{q}_k^\star) \tag{19}$$

under a p-periodic state feedback

$$\boldsymbol{u}(k) = -\boldsymbol{k}^{\mathrm{T}}(k)\ \boldsymbol{\zeta}(k)\ \ \textit{with}\ \boldsymbol{k}^{\mathrm{T}}(k{+}p) = \boldsymbol{k}^{\mathrm{T}}(k) \tag{20}$$

is equivalent to the periodic system (13), *iff for all k the following is true:*

1. $\alpha(k) = \boldsymbol{c}^{\mathrm{T}}(\bar{q}_k^\star)\, \boldsymbol{f}(\bar{\boldsymbol{x}}^\star(\bar{q}_{k+1}^\star)\,,\bar{q}_k^\star) \neq 0$ (21)
2. $\boldsymbol{k}^{\mathrm{T}}(k) = \boldsymbol{c}^{\mathrm{T}}(\bar{q}_k^\star)\,/\alpha(k)$ (22)
3. $\det\left(\boldsymbol{A}_d(k) - \boldsymbol{b}_d(k)\, \boldsymbol{k}^{\mathrm{T}}(k)\right) = 0$. (23)

Proof. First, define the scaled normal vectors

$$\tilde{\boldsymbol{c}}^{\mathrm{T}}(\bar{q}_k^\star) = \boldsymbol{c}^{\mathrm{T}}(\bar{q}_k^\star)/\alpha(k) \;, \tag{24}$$

which is only feasible, if (21) holds. Then applying the periodic equivalence transformation

$$\delta\bar{\boldsymbol{x}}(k) = \boldsymbol{T}(k)\,\boldsymbol{\zeta}(k)\,, \quad \boldsymbol{T}(k) = \left(\partial\bar{\boldsymbol{x}}^\star(\bar{q}_{k+1}^\star)/\partial\bar{\boldsymbol{x}}^\star(\bar{q}_k^\star)\right)^{-1}$$

to the linearized return map (13) and considering (11) and (24) yields

$$\boldsymbol{\zeta}(c+1) = \prod_{k=0}^{p-1}\left(\frac{\partial\bar{\boldsymbol{x}}^\star(\bar{q}_{k+2}^\star)}{\partial\bar{\boldsymbol{x}}^\star(\bar{q}_{k+1}^\star)} - \frac{\partial\bar{\boldsymbol{x}}^\star(\bar{q}_{k+2}^\star)}{\partial\bar{\boldsymbol{x}}^\star(\bar{q}_{k+1}^\star)}\boldsymbol{f}\left(\bar{\boldsymbol{x}}^\star(\bar{q}_{k+1}^\star), \bar{q}_k^\star\right)\tilde{\boldsymbol{c}}^{\mathrm{T}}(\bar{q}_k^\star)\right)\boldsymbol{\zeta}(c) \;. \tag{25}$$

To assure the identity of the loop (17), (20) and (25), $\boldsymbol{A}_d(k)$, $\boldsymbol{b}_d(k)$ and $\boldsymbol{k}^{\mathrm{T}}(k)$ must be equal to the expressions (18), (19) and (22). Moreover, the state transition matrix $\partial\bar{\boldsymbol{x}}^\star(\bar{q}_{k+2}^\star)/\partial\bar{\boldsymbol{x}}^\star(\bar{q}_{k+1}^\star)$ is regular and $\tilde{\boldsymbol{c}}^{\mathrm{T}}(\bar{q}_k^\star)\,\boldsymbol{f}\left(\bar{\boldsymbol{x}}^\star(\bar{q}_{k+1}^\star), \bar{q}_k^\star\right) = 1$ holds. Hence, by Lemma 1 the last constraint (23) must be satisfied as well. □

From (22) it follows that $\boldsymbol{k}^{\mathrm{T}}(k)$ and $\boldsymbol{c}^{\mathrm{T}}(\bar{q}_k^\star)$ are colinear vectors, which can be directly exploited for solving Problem 1.

Theorem 2. *By defining the event function* (3) *as*

$$\Phi(\boldsymbol{x}(t), \bar{q}_k^\star) = \boldsymbol{k}^{\mathrm{T}}(k)\left(\boldsymbol{x}(t) - \bar{\boldsymbol{x}}^\star(\bar{q}_{k+1}^\star)\right) \;, \tag{26}$$

where the periodic state feedback gain $\boldsymbol{k}^{\mathrm{T}}(k)$ *stabilizes the equivalent periodic system* Σ *and* (26) *satisfies the condition* (7), *local orbital stability of the limit cycle* $\mathcal{L}_{\mathrm{LC}}$ *is guaranteed.*

Proof. Theorem 1 states that the eigenvalues

$$\lambda_{p,i}\left(\boldsymbol{\Psi}_{\mathrm{cl}}(p,0)\right) = \lambda_{p,i}\left(\prod_{k=0}^{p-1}\left(\boldsymbol{A}_d(k) - \boldsymbol{b}_d(k)\,\boldsymbol{k}^{\mathrm{T}}(k)\right)\right)$$

of the closed-loop monodromy matrix $\boldsymbol{\Psi}_{\mathrm{cl}}(p,0)$ of system (17)–(20) are identical to the characteristic multipliers m_i of (14). Hence, if these eigenvalues satisfy the condition $|\lambda_{p,i}| < 1$, then all m_i are stable as well. Moreover, the event function (26) vanishes at all switch points $\bar{\boldsymbol{x}}^\star(\bar{q}_{k+1}^\star)$ of the limit cycle, which under the assumption (7) guarantees that any trajectory $\boldsymbol{x}(t)$ starting in a local neighborhood of $\mathcal{L}_{\mathrm{LC}}$ actually converges to $\mathcal{L}_{\mathrm{LC}}$. The constraints (10) are trivially satisfied because (15) holds for all $\bar{q}_k^\star$. □

By Theorems 1 and 2, the event generator design amounts to solving a constrained pole placement problem for the periodic discrete-time linear system (17)-(19). For the unconstrained problem, a well developed theory exists. How to integrate the constraint sets (7) and (23) in the design procedure is explained in Sect. 4.4. Besides ensuring stability, the equivalence stated in Theorem 1 allows a goal-oriented shaping of the local loop behavior, if the target eigenvalues $\lambda_{p,i}^d$ are specified appropriately.

4.2 Local Stabilizability along a Limit Cycle

A solution to the control problem only exists if the DCCS is locally stabilizable along the orbit $\mathcal{L}_{\mathrm{LC}}$. A definition of this property on the basis of the concept of local controllability along a trajectory [21] is given here.

Definition 1. *Let* $\mathcal{B}_\delta(\mathcal{L}_{\mathrm{LC}}) = \{\boldsymbol{x} \;:\; \mathrm{dist}(\boldsymbol{x}, \mathcal{L}_{\mathrm{LC}}) < \delta\}$, $\delta > 0$ *define a local neighborhood of the limit cycle* $\mathcal{L}_{\mathrm{LC}}$. *A state* $\boldsymbol{x}_0 \in \mathcal{B}_\delta(\mathcal{L}_{\mathrm{LC}})$ *is* locally stabilizable along the orbit $\mathcal{L}_{\mathrm{LC}}$, *if there exists an* $\epsilon > 0$, *a mode sequence* $q(t)$ *and a trigger signal* clk(t), *such that the following holds:*

$$1.\ \boldsymbol{x}(t, \boldsymbol{x}_0, q(0)) \in \mathcal{B}_\epsilon(\mathcal{L}_{\mathrm{LC}}), \quad \forall t > 0$$
$$2.\ \lim_{t\to\infty} \mathrm{dist}(\boldsymbol{x}(t, \boldsymbol{x}_0, q(0)), \mathcal{L}_{\mathrm{LC}}) = 0 \ .$$

Definition 2. *A periodically operated DCCS is called locally stabilizable along the orbit* $\mathcal{L}_{\mathrm{LC}}$, *if all states* $\boldsymbol{x}_0$ *in an open neighborhood* $\mathcal{B}_\delta(\mathcal{L}_{\mathrm{LC}})$, $\delta > 0$ *of* $\mathcal{L}_{\mathrm{LC}}$ *are locally stabilizable.*

From the results of Theorems 1 and 2 a sufficient condition immediately follows, which ensures local stabilizability along a limit cycle for a DCCS.

Theorem 3. *A periodically operated DCCS* (2), (5) *is locally stabilizable along the orbit* $\mathcal{L}_{\mathrm{LC}}$, *if the equivalent system* $\Sigma = \{\boldsymbol{A}_d(k), \boldsymbol{b}_d(k)\}$ *is stabilizable.*

Proof. To prove Theorem 3, pick any mode $\bar{q}_k^\star \in \mathcal{Q}$ and assume that the equivalent periodic system Σ is stabilizable. Then by Theorems 1 and 2, stabilizing gains $\boldsymbol{k}^{\mathrm{T}}(k)$ exists, which translate into stabilizing normal directions $\boldsymbol{c}^{\mathrm{T}}(\bar{q}_k^\star)$. As the return map $\boldsymbol{P}_x$ is a local C^1 diffeomorphism, there exists a non-empty invariant open region $\mathcal{B}_\gamma(\bar{\boldsymbol{x}}^\star(\bar{q}_k^\star)) = \{\boldsymbol{x} \mid (\boldsymbol{x} - \bar{\boldsymbol{x}}^\star(\bar{q}_k^\star))^{\mathrm{T}} \boldsymbol{V} (\boldsymbol{x} - \bar{\boldsymbol{x}}^\star(\bar{q}_k^\star)) < \gamma\}$ with $\boldsymbol{V}, \gamma > 0$ in the plane $\mathcal{S}(\bar{q}_k^\star)$, for which all trajectories that emanate from $\mathcal{B}_\gamma(\bar{\boldsymbol{x}}^\star(\bar{q}_k^\star))$ asymptotically converge to the limit cycle. The backward reachable set of $\mathcal{B}_\gamma(\bar{\boldsymbol{x}}^\star(\bar{q}_k^\star))$ then defines a non-empty neighborhood of stabilizable states along $\mathcal{L}_{\mathrm{LC}}$, from which the values $\epsilon > 0$ and $\delta > 0$ can be extracted (Fig. 2). Now, for all $\boldsymbol{x}_0 \in \mathcal{B}_\delta(\mathcal{L}_{\mathrm{LC}})$ the event generator equipped with the event function (26) generates a trigger signal clk(t), such that $\boldsymbol{x}(t, \boldsymbol{x}_0, q(0))$ converges towards $\mathcal{L}_{\mathrm{LC}}$. Therefore, stabilizability of Σ is sufficient for the local stabilizability of the underlying DCCS along $\mathcal{L}_{\mathrm{LC}}$. □

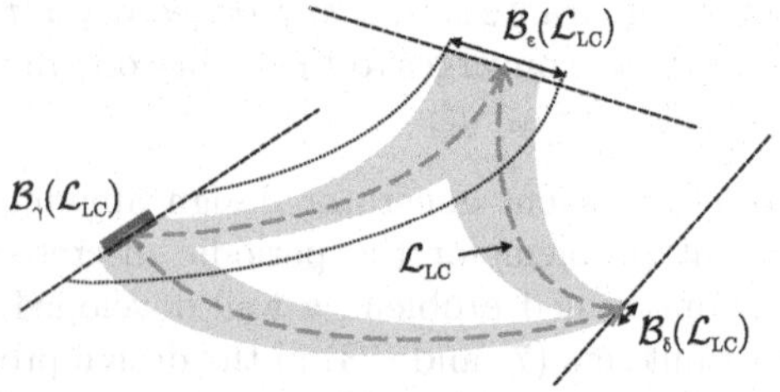

Fig. 2. Limit cycle $\mathcal{L}_{\mathrm{LC}}$, backward reachable set of $\mathcal{B}_\gamma(\mathcal{L}_{\mathrm{LC}})$ and neighborhoods $\mathcal{B}_\delta(\mathcal{L}_{\mathrm{LC}})$, $\mathcal{B}_\epsilon(\mathcal{L}_{\mathrm{LC}})$ defining the region of locally stabilizable states

Stabilizability of periodic systems is defined in [22] and can be checked numerically as described in [23].

4.3 Local Effectivity of Operation Modes

Regarding the design task, it is crucial to identify all *effective* mode transitions, which can be employed for altering the continuous evolution.

Definition 3. *A mode $\bar{q}_k^\star \in \mathcal{Q}$ of a periodically operated DCCS is called* locally effective *with respect to the limit cycle $\mathcal{L}_{\mathrm{LC}}$, if it is deactivated upon a controlled switching and a perturbation of $\bar{\tau}^\star(\bar{q}_k^\star)$ affects the future run of $\boldsymbol{x}(t)$.*

All modes $\bar{q}_k^\star$, which do not meet these two properties, are called *ineffective.* Modes that are deactivated by an autonomous switching are ineffective, since the corresponding switching conditions must not be altered in the design process. As a result of the above, the periodic sequence $Q_{\mathrm{LC}} = Q_{\mathrm{LC}}^{\mathrm{eff},1} Q_{\mathrm{LC}}^{\mathrm{ineff},1} \dots Q_{\mathrm{LC}}^{\mathrm{eff},j}$ can be decomposed into effective and ineffective subsequences.

Proposition 1. *A mode $\bar{q}_k^\star$ is locally effective, if it is deactivated by a controlled switching and the mode transition causes a discontinuity in the vector field:*

$$\boldsymbol{f}\left(\bar{\boldsymbol{x}}^\star\left(\bar{q}_{k+1}^\star\right), \bar{q}_k^\star\right) \neq \boldsymbol{f}\left(\bar{\boldsymbol{x}}^\star\left(\bar{q}_{k+1}^\star\right), \bar{q}_{k+1}^\star\right) \ . \tag{27}$$

Proof. While the first part of the proposition is clear, the last part can be proved by contradiction. Assume that (27) is violated. Then, concatenating the linearized embedded map (11) over two consecutively activated modes $\bar{q}_k^\star$ and $\bar{q}_{k+1}^\star$ yields the expression

$$\delta\bar{\boldsymbol{x}}(k+2) \;=\; \left(\boldsymbol{I} - \frac{\boldsymbol{f}\left(\bar{\boldsymbol{x}}^\star\left(\bar{q}_{k+2}^\star\right), \bar{q}_{k+1}^\star\right) \boldsymbol{c}^{\mathrm{T}}\left(\bar{q}_{k+1}^\star\right)}{\boldsymbol{c}^{\mathrm{T}}\left(\bar{q}_{k+1}^\star\right) \boldsymbol{f}\left(\bar{\boldsymbol{x}}^\star\left(\bar{q}_{k+2}^\star\right), \bar{q}_{k+1}^\star\right)}\right) \frac{\partial \bar{\boldsymbol{x}}^\star\left(\bar{q}_{k+2}^\star\right)}{\partial \bar{\boldsymbol{x}}^\star\left(\bar{q}_{k+1}^\star\right)} \frac{\partial \bar{\boldsymbol{x}}^\star\left(\bar{q}_{k+1}^\star\right)}{\partial \bar{\boldsymbol{x}}^\star\left(\bar{q}_{k}^\star\right)} \delta\bar{\boldsymbol{x}}(k)$$

and reveals that $\delta\bar{\boldsymbol{x}}(k+2)$ is independent of $\boldsymbol{c}^{\mathrm{T}}(\bar{q}_k^\star)$. Therefore, the mode $\bar{q}_k^\star$ is ineffective with respect to the control task. □

Identifying all ineffective modes prior to performing the design is crucial, as ineffective modes lead to infeasible design results, which include switching planes that violate assumption (10). To reduce computational effort, locally ineffective subsequences $Q_{\mathrm{LC}}^{\mathrm{ineff},j}$ may be condensed into single modes.

4.4 Design Algorithm

Design procedure for $Q_{\mathrm{LC}} = Q_{\mathrm{LC}}^{\mathrm{eff},1}$. With the results of Theorems 1 and 2, an event function that guarantees the loop properties specified in Sect. 3 can be obtained as follows:

Algorithm 1. *Determination of a stabilizing event function.*

Given: *a DCCS (2), (5) and an admissible sampled periodic execution $\chi^\star(\boldsymbol{x}_0^h, 0, p)$ evolving on the limit cycle $\mathcal{L}_{\mathrm{LC}}$ to be stabilized.*

1. *Compute the periodic matrices* $\boldsymbol{A}_d(k)$, $\boldsymbol{b}_d(k)$ *according to* (18), (19).
2. *Verify stabilizability of the equivalent periodic system* $\Sigma = \{\boldsymbol{A}_d(k), \boldsymbol{b}_d(k)\}$.
3. *Apply periodic pole placement [24] to obtain a periodic feedback gain* $\boldsymbol{k}^{\mathrm{T}}(k)$ *that simultaneously satisfies the conditions* (23) *and places the eigenvalues at desired locations* m_i^d *in the complex plane.*
4. *According to* (26), *set the event function coefficients to* $\boldsymbol{c}^{\mathrm{T}}(\bar{q}_k^\star) = \boldsymbol{k}^{\mathrm{T}}(k) / \|\boldsymbol{k}^{\mathrm{T}}(k)\|$ *and compute* $d(\bar{q}_k^\star) = \boldsymbol{c}^{\mathrm{T}}(q)\, \bar{\boldsymbol{x}}^\star(\bar{q}_{k+1}^\star)$.
5. *Verify the constraints* (7), *otherwise introduce additional "counter modes".*

Result: *Event generator* (3), *that guarantees local orbital stability of the limit cycle* $\mathcal{L}_{\mathrm{LC}}$ *and enforces a desired local transient behavior.*

The scaling of the normal vectors in Step 4 is admissible, because the Jacobian $\mathrm{d}\boldsymbol{P}_x/\mathrm{d}t$ is independent of the length of $\boldsymbol{c}^{\mathrm{T}}(\bar{q}_k^\star)$. If stabilizability of (17) is given, the existences of a periodic state feedback $\boldsymbol{k}^{\mathrm{T}}(k)$ that stabilizes the equivalent periodic system is assured for the *unconstrained control problem.* How to cope with the constraints introduced earlier is explained next.

Handling Constraints (23)**.** To explicitly account for the constraints (23) in the design procedure is easy. These conditions only reduce the space of admissible multipliers m_i^d by one or more dimensions, but a stabilizing solution always exists. The number of multipliers, which must be placed at the origin, depends on the structure of the system (17). It is in general enough to place just one m_i at zero, while the remaining ones can be freely assigned in order to shape the transient loop behavior as desired.

Handling Constraints (7)**.** Constraints of type (7) are accounted for after the pole assignment. Assume, that Step 5 of Algorithm 1 identifies a mode $\bar{q}_k^\star$, for which (7) is violated. Then, there exist one or more additional intersections of $\boldsymbol{x}^\star(\tau, \bar{\boldsymbol{x}}^\star(\bar{q}_k^\star), \bar{q}_k^\star)$ with $\mathcal{S}(\bar{q}_k^\star)$ in the time interval $[0, \bar{\tau}^\star(\bar{q}_k^\star))$. Since the periodic execution $\chi^\star(\boldsymbol{x}_0^h, 0, p)$ requires all mode transitions $\bar{q}_k^\star \rightarrow \bar{q}_{k+1}^\star$ to exactly occur at $\bar{\tau}^\star(\bar{q}_k^\star)$, the cyclic mode sequence $\mathcal{Q}_{\mathrm{LC}}$ must be extended by auxiliary *counter modes* $\bar{q}_{k,j}^\star$ (Fig. 3). These counter modes are inserted in between $\bar{q}_k^\star$ and $\bar{q}_{k+1}^\star$ and keep track of the number of previous intersections of $\boldsymbol{x}(t)$ and $\mathcal{S}(\bar{q}_k^\star)$. They

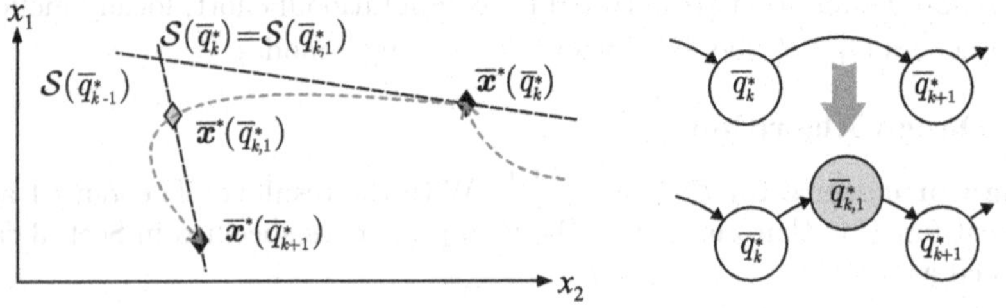

Fig. 3. Introduction of a counter mode into the cyclic mode sequence, due to violation of the constraint (7)

are associated to the same continuous dynamics $\boldsymbol{f}(\boldsymbol{x}, \bar{q}^{\star}_{k,j}) = \boldsymbol{f}(\boldsymbol{x}, \bar{q}^{\star}_{k})$ as $\bar{q}^{\star}_{k}$ and require to augment the event function (3) by

$$\Phi\left(\boldsymbol{x}, \bar{q}^{\star}_{k,j}\right) = \boldsymbol{c}^{\mathrm{T}}(\bar{q}^{\star}_{k})\, \boldsymbol{x} - d(\bar{q}^{\star}_{k}) + \epsilon(-1)^{j}, \quad \epsilon \ll d(\bar{q}^{\star}_{k}) \ .$$

Design in the Presence of Ineffective Modes. If a subset of modes is locally ineffective, Algorithm 1 is still applicable. In this case, the system matrices (18) and (19) of all ineffective modes become

$$\begin{aligned} \boldsymbol{A}_d(k+p) &= \boldsymbol{A}_d(k) = \partial \bar{\boldsymbol{x}}^{\star}(\bar{q}^{\star}_{k+2}) \,/ \partial \bar{\boldsymbol{x}}^{\star}(\bar{q}^{\star}_{k+1}) \left(\boldsymbol{I} - \boldsymbol{f}(\bar{q}^{\star}_{k}, \bar{\boldsymbol{x}}^{\star}(\bar{q}^{\star}_{k+1}))\, \boldsymbol{c}^{\mathrm{T}}_{0}(\bar{q}^{\star}_{k})\right) \\ \boldsymbol{b}_d(k+p) &= \boldsymbol{b}_d(k) = \boldsymbol{0} \ . \end{aligned}$$

In this expression, $\boldsymbol{c}^{\mathrm{T}}_{0}(\bar{q}^{\star}_{k})$ represents a nominal normal that satisfies the condition $\boldsymbol{c}^{\mathrm{T}}_{0}(\bar{q}^{\star}_{k})\, \boldsymbol{f}(\bar{q}^{\star}_{k}, \bar{\boldsymbol{x}}^{\star}(\bar{q}^{\star}_{k+1})) = 1$. Its orientation is either determined from the associated autonomous switching condition or it must be properly chosen, in case $\bar{q}^{\star}_{k}$ is ineffective, because it violates (27).

5 Experimental Validation

To compare the performance of the novel design approach with earlier results from [16], the new method was successfully applied to the same 2-Tank system consisting of two coupled tanks and a controllable number of inlets and outlets (Fig. 4(a)). For the design, the linear 2-Tank model, its parameters and the desired stationary limit cycle listed in [16] are adopted here again. At stationary operation, the plant recurrently executed the mode sequence $Q_{\mathrm{LC}} = (1234)$. For this sequence, the matrices (18), (19) of the equivalent periodic system Σ are

$$\boldsymbol{A}_{\mathrm{d}}(1) = \begin{pmatrix} 0.5572 & 0 \\ 0.3544 & 0.6575 \end{pmatrix}, \qquad \boldsymbol{A}_{\mathrm{d}}(2) = \begin{pmatrix} 0.6421 & 0 \\ 0.2693 & 0.5747 \end{pmatrix},$$

$$\boldsymbol{A}_{\mathrm{d}}(3) = \begin{pmatrix} 0.6534 & 0 \\ 0.2637 & 0.5874 \end{pmatrix}, \qquad \boldsymbol{A}_{\mathrm{d}}(4) = \begin{pmatrix} 0.8004 & 0 \\ 0.1839 & 0.8525 \end{pmatrix},$$

$$\boldsymbol{b}_{\mathrm{d}}(1) = \left(-0.001007 \; -9.117e-005\right)^{\mathrm{T}}, \qquad \boldsymbol{b}_{\mathrm{d}}(2) = \left(0.0009182 \; 0.001224\right)^{\mathrm{T}},$$

$$\boldsymbol{b}_{\mathrm{d}}(3) = \left(0.0006 \; -0.0001484\right)^{\mathrm{T}}, \qquad \boldsymbol{b}_{\mathrm{d}}(4) = \left(-0.001808 \; -0.001525\right)^{\mathrm{T}} .$$

Since Σ turns out to be stabilizable, the underlying DCCS is locally stabilizable along $\mathcal{L}_{\mathrm{LC}}$. It shows that all multipliers m_i can be arbitrarily assigned by only using one of the four available feedback gains $\boldsymbol{k}^{\mathrm{T}}(k)$. The large surplus of design parameters is exploited here to maximize the local convergence rate and obtain a dead-beat behavior. Therefore, all desired eigenvalues λ^{d}_{i} are set to zero.

The event function coefficients resulting from the application of Algorithm 1 are listed in Tab. 1. They define the switching planes depicted in Figure 4(b) (dashed black lines). The diamonds indicate the switch points $\bar{\boldsymbol{x}}(k)$ of the depicted execution. Note that all switching planes touch the simulated limit cycle $\mathcal{L}_{\mathrm{LC}}$ tangentially (thick grey dashed line), which is a characteristic feature of a dead-beat switching law. For reasons of comparison, the additional thin grey

Table 1. Event function parameters derived from the model-based design procedure. These parameters maximize the convergence rate towards $\mathcal{L}_{\mathrm{LC}}$.

q	1	2	3	4
$c^{\mathrm{T}}(q)$	$(-0.3096\ \ 0.9509)^{\mathrm{T}}$	$(0.7875\ \ 0.6163)^{\mathrm{T}}$	$(0.1889\ \ -0.9820)^{\mathrm{T}}$	$(-0.5449\ \ -0.8385)^{\mathrm{T}}$
$d(q)$	0.005	0.0286	0.0266	0.0058

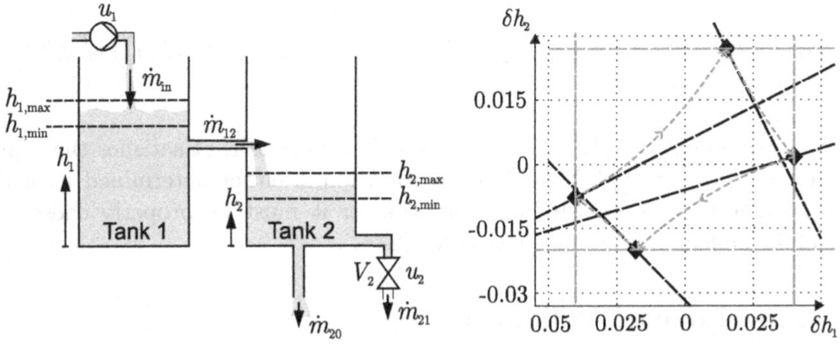

(a) (b)

Fig. 4. 2-Tank system: (a) experimental setup, (b) switching surfaces resulting in local dead-beat behavior

dashed lines illustrate the paraxial switching planes of the heuristic switching policy explained in [16].

Figure 5 presents a series of state space plots showing experimental data obtained at the laboratory system. They disclose the strong influence of disturbances and model uncertainties, which cause orbital instability when applying the heuristic switching policy. Under the model-based strategy, however, stability is preserved. The experiment was conducted as follows: At runtime, the event function coefficients $c^{\mathrm{T}}(\bar{q}_k^{\star})$, $d(\bar{q}_k^{\star})$ were toggled every 1000 seconds between the values listed in Tab. 1 and the values implementing the paraxial planes of the heuristic switching policy. Afterwards, the observed behavior was plotted in a separate figure for each switching policy. For example, the data acquired in the first interval [0s, 1000s] until the substitution of the switching strategy, is plotted in the top-left subplot. Likewise, the behavior observed in the second interval [1000s, 2000s] associated to the heuristic policy is plotted in the top-middle subplot and so on.

As can be concluded from every other subplot, the heuristic switching policy does not succeed in stabilizing $\mathcal{L}_{\mathrm{LC}}$, while the model-based switching policy generates the expected, fast decaying transient loop behavior. The latter is best verified from the subplot "bottom-middle", where the transition onto the limit cycle is finished two switchings after toggling the switching policy. Indeed, the desired periodic operation is preserved even under the influence of considerable disturbances, which is crucial in practical applications.

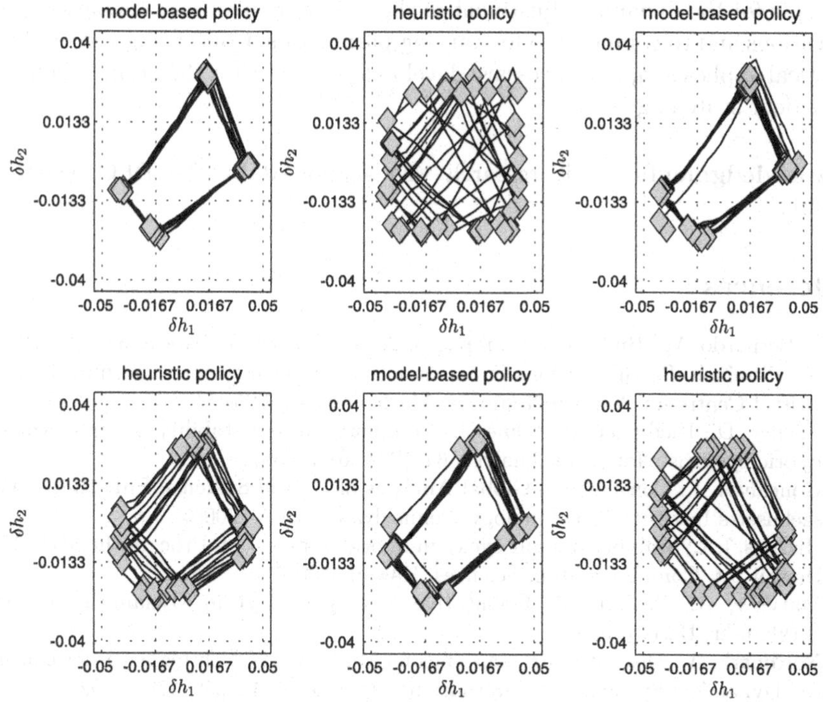

Fig. 5. State space snapshots showing experimental data obtained at the laboratory 2-Tank system. For comparison, the event-generator was toggled between a heuristic and a model-based event-driven policy.

6 Conclusion

The main contribution of this paper is a novel model-based design methodology for the event generator of a periodically operated discretely controlled continuous system. The approach applies to systems of arbitrary state dimension and imposes no restrictions on the number of operation modes. It allows for a goal-oriented shaping of the system's local behavior, in particular to achieve local orbital stability and a fast transient response. Compared to earlier control concepts, the resulting controller issues its actions instantaneously instead of postponing them to the next switching. Thus, the implemented switching strategy guarantees the best possible local loop behavior in the presence of disturbances. As a core feature, the proposed design procedure exploits an equivalence between the original design problem and a classical periodic linear control problem. Based on this idea, the local stabilizability of the DCCS can be investigated. Furthermore, the design is simplified through the application of well known pole placement algorithms for periodic systems.

Future research directions focus on ways for exploiting excessive degrees of freedom to maximize the region of attraction of the stabilized cycle and on concepts for the dynamic adjustment of the switching planes to enable set-point transitions and to compensate for varying parameters. Concerning the method's practical application, it is necessary develop approaches for the design of output-dependent switching laws.

Acknowledgments. This research was supported by the DFG grant LU 462 |21.

References

1. di Bernardo, M., Budd, C., Champneys, A., Kowalczyk, P., Nordmark, A., Olivar, G., Piiroinen, P.: Bifurcations in nonsmooth dynamical systems. Technical report, Bristol Centre for Applied Nonlinear Mathematics (2005)
2. Flieller, D., Riedinger, P., Louis, J.: Computation and stability of limit cycles in hybrid systems. Nonlinear Analysis 64, 352–367 (2006)
3. Goncalves, J.: Constructive Global Analysis of Hybrid Systems. PhD thesis, Massachusetts Institute of Technology, Pennsylvania, USA (2000)
4. Hiskens, I.A.: Stability of limit cycles in hybrid systems. In: Proc. of the 34th IEEE Hawaii Int. Conf. on System Sciences, Hawaii (2001)
5. Matveev, A., Savkin, A.: Qualitative Theory of Hybrid Dynamical Systems. Birkhauser, Basel (2000)
6. Nordmark, A.: Discontinuity mappings for vector fields with higher order continuity. Dynamical Systems: An International Journal 17(4), 359–376 (2002)
7. Rubensson, M., Lennartson, B., Pettersson, S.: Convergence to limit cycles in hybrid systems: An example. In: Proc. IFAC-LSS 1998, Rio Patras, pp. 704–709 (1999)
8. Boccadoro, M., Wardi, Y., Egerstedt, M., Verriest, E.: Optimal control of switching surfaces in hybrid systems. Discrete Event Dynamic Systems 15(4), 433–448 (2005)
9. Egerstedt, M., Wardi, Y., Axelsson, H.: Transition-time optimization for switched-mode dynamical systems. IEEE Trans. Autom. Control 51, 110–115 (2006)
10. Axelsson, H., Boccadoro, M., Wardi, Y., Egerstedt, M.: Optimal mode-switching for hybrid systems with unknown initial state. In: Proceedings of the 2nd IFAC Conf. on Analysis and Design of Hybrid Systems, Alghero, Alghero, pp. 95–100 (2006)
11. Boccadoro, M., Valigi, P., Wardi, Y.: A method for the design of optimal switching surfaces for autonomous hybrid systems. In: Bemporad, A., Bicchi, A., Buttazzo, G. (eds.) HSCC 2007. LNCS, vol. 4416, pp. 650–655. Springer, Heidelberg (2007)
12. Buisson, J., Richard, P.Y., Comerais, H.: On the stabilisation of switching electrical power converters. In: Morari, M., Thiele, L. (eds.) HSCC 2005. LNCS, vol. 3414, pp. 185–197. Springer, Heidelberg (2005)
13. Sanders, R., Verghese, G.: Lyapunov-based control for switched power converters. IEEE Transactions on Power Electronics 7, 17–23 (1992)
14. Ott, E., Grebogi, C., Yorke, J.: Controlling chaos. Physical Review Letters 64(11), 1196–1199 (1990)
15. Dankowicz, H., Piiroinen, P.: Exploiting discontinuities for stabilization of recurrent motions. Dynamical Systems 17(4), 317–342 (2002)
16. Schild, A., Lunze, J.: Stabilization of limit cycles of discretely controlled continuous systems by controlling switching surfaces. In: Bemporad, A., Bicchi, A., Buttazzo, G. (eds.) HSCC 2007. LNCS, vol. 4416, pp. 515–528. Springer, Heidelberg (2007)

17. Krupar, J., Schild, A., Schwarz, W., Lunze, J.: Modeling and analysis of a class of hybrid systems by return maps. In: Proc. of NOLTA, Bologna, pp. 59–62 (2006)
18. Krupar, J., Lunze, J., Schwarz, W., Schild, A.: Modelling and analysis of discretely controlled continuous systems by means of embedded maps. IEICE Trans. on Fundamentals of Electronics, Communication and Computer Science 89, 2697–2705 (2006)
19. Chua, L.O., Parker, T.S.: Practical Numerical Algorithms for Chaotic Systems. Springer, Heidelberg (1989)
20. Bernstein, D.: Matrix Mathematics. Princeton University Press, Princeton (2007)
21. Sontag, E.D.: Mathematical Control Theory. Springer, Heidelberg (1991)
22. Bittanti, S., Bolzern, P.: Stabilizability and detectability of linear periodic systems. Syst. Control Lett. 6(2), 141–146 (1985)
23. Sreedhar, J., Dooren, P.V.: An orthogonal method for the controllable subspace of a periodic system. In: Proc. Conf. on Inf. Sciences & Systems, Baltimore (1993)
24. Sreedhar, J., Dooren, P.V.: Pole placement via the periodic schur decomposition. In: Proc. American Control Conference, San Fransisco (1993)

Discrete Dynamics of Two-Dimensional Nonlinear Hybrid Automata

Lorenzo Sella and Pieter Collins

Centrum voor Wiskunde en Informatica,
Kruislaan 413, 1098 SJ Amsterdam, The Netherlands
{Lorenzo.Sella,Pieter.Collins}@cwi.nl

Abstract. In this paper, we develop an algorithm to compute under- and over-approximations to the discrete dynamics of a hybrid automaton. We represent the approximations to the dynamics as *sofic shifts*, which can be generated by a discrete automaton. We restrict to two-dimensional systems, since these give rise to one-dimensional return maps, which are significantly easier to study. Given generic non-degeneracy conditions, the under- and over-approximations computed by our algorithm converge to the discrete dynamics of the hybrid automaton. We apply the algorithms to two simple nonlinear hybrid systems, an affine switching system with hysteresis, and the singularly forced van der Pol oscillator.

Keywords: hybrid automata, symbolic dynamics, interval computation, van der Pol equation.

1 Introduction

Hybrid automata are dynamic systems which combine both discrete and continuous behaviour. Hybrid automata are frequently used to modelling systems in which dynamics occurs on different time scales, such as a slow-moving physical object controlled using a fast-switching digital controller. In many cases, the exact details of the continuous dynamics is relatively unimportant, and only the qualitative behaviour given by the discrete dynamics is of interest. It is therefore of interest to have numerical methods for computing approximations to the discrete dynamics of a hybrid automaton.

Existing work on finding discrete abstractions to hybrid automata has mostly focused on bisimulation by discrete automata [1]. However, since the class of systems admitting nontrivial finite bisimulations is highly restricted (generalisations of timed automata), this approach can only be used for simple classes of system. More complex classes of systems can only be studied by computing discrete abstractions which either simulate, or are simulated by, the exact discrete dynamics of the hybrid automaton. Sequences of discrete abstractions simulating the hybrid automaton were constructed in [2] for polynomial hybrid automata using first-order logic over the reals. Discrete abstractions simulating the hybrid automaton based on quantising the state space were given by [3] and

M. Egerstedt and B. Mishra (Eds.): HSCC 2008, LNCS 4981, pp. 486–499, 2008.

used for reachability analysis, and by [4] and used for supervisory control. Two-dimensional hybrid systems have been studied in [5], and the singular limit of the van der Pol oscillator was studied in [6,7].

In this paper, we present a method for computing both over- and under approximations to the discrete dynamics. In the language of symbolic dynamics, we construct sofic shifts over- and under approximating the exact shift of the hybrid automaton. In the language of transition systems, we construct discrete automata simulating of the hybrid automaton, and discrete automata simulated by the hybrid automaton. Our method is generically optimal in the sense that under certain nondegeneracy conditions the shift maps obtained converge to the exact discrete dynamics as the accuracy in increased. In the current work, we concentrate on two-dimensional hybrid systems, since these can be reduced to one-dimensional return maps which are easier to analyse.

The results of this paper extend the validity of existing methods by constructing under-approximations as well as over-approximations to the discrete dynamics, by applying to general nonlinear systems, and by being convergent for generic systems.

The paper is organised as follows. In Section 2, we give technical preliminaries on hybrid systems, shift spaces symbolic dynamics and interval methods which we need later. In Section 3, we present algorithms for computing over- and under-approximations to the symbolic dynamics and prove their convergence. In Section 4 we demonstrate the effectiveness of the method by computing the discrete dynamics of an affine switching hybrid automaton and the singular limit of the Van Der Pol oscillator. Finally, in Section 5 we give some conclusions and suggestions for further research.

The main mathematical techniques used in this article include interval analysis and validated solution of differential equations, one-dimensional dynamical systems and symbolic dynamics. Good references to these topics are include the books [8,9,10,11,12,13].

2 Theoretical Preliminaries

We now introduce the basic definitions, terminology and results on hybrid automata, symbolic dynamics and interval analysis which we will need. Throughout, we write $f :\subset X \to Y$ to denote a function from a subset of X to Y, and $f : X \rightrightarrows Y$ to denote a multivalued function from X to Y.

2.1 Hybrid Automata

A hybrid automaton is a dynamic system in which continuous-time evolution is interspersed with discrete jumps.

Definition 1 (Hybrid Automaton). *A* hybrid automaton *is a tuple* $\mathscr{H} = (Q, E, X, G, \phi, r)$ *where* Q *is a finite set of* modes, E *is a finite set of* events, $X = \bigsqcup\{X_q \mid q \in Q\}$ *is the* state space, $G = \bigcup\{G_e \subset X \mid e \in E\}$ *is the* guard set, $\phi :\subset X \times \mathbb{R} \to X$ *is the* continuous dynamic, *and* $r :\subset G \times E \to X$ *is the* reset map. *We write* $r_e : G_e \to X$ *for the reset map corresponding to event* e. *Typically,* ϕ_q *is defined by a differential equation* $\dot{x} = \chi_q(x)$ *for* $x \in X_q$.

An *execution* of a hybrid automaton is an alternating sequence of continuous and discrete transitions:

$$\xi : x_0 \xrightarrow{\phi_{t_0}} y_0 \xrightarrow{r_{e_0}} x_1 \xrightarrow{\phi_{t_1}} y_1 \xrightarrow{r_{e_1}} x_2 \cdots \tag{1}$$

Often the quantitative behaviour of a hybrid automaton is unimportant, and only the qualitative behaviour given by the sequence of discrete locations visited and the sequence of discrete events which occur.

Definition 2 (Discrete Dynamics). *The* discrete dynamics *of a hybrid automaton* $\mathscr{H}$ *is the set of all transition sequences*

$$q_0 \xrightarrow{e_0} q_1 \xrightarrow{e_1} q_2 \cdots \tag{2}$$

such that there exists an execution ξ *given by* (1) *with* $y_i \in X_{q_i}$ *for all* i.

In order to compute the discrete dynamics we need only look at the state just before each transition, giving rise to the *return map*.

Definition 3 (Return Map). *The* return map f *of a hybrid automaton* $\mathscr{H}$ *is the transition system* $f :\subset G \times E \rightrightarrows G$ *with* $f_e :\subset G_e \rightrightarrows G$ *given by*

$$f_e(x) := \{y \in G \mid \exists t \in \mathbb{R}^+ \ s.t. \ y = \phi_t(r_e(x))\}. \tag{3}$$

In other words, f_e is defined by the transitions $\phi_t \circ r_e$, where the continuous evolution ϕ_t proceeds until the state enters a guard set.

If we ignore the discrete-event labels, the return map is a dynamical system $f :\subset G \rightrightarrows G$ defined by

$$f(x) := \{y \in G \mid \exists e \in E, \ t \in \mathbb{R}^+ \text{ s.t. } y = \phi_t(r_e(x))\}. \tag{4}$$

Note that the return map need not be everywhere defined since a point need not have any further discrete transitions. As shown in Figure 1, the return map may also be discontinuous and multivalued if the initial state starts on the boundary of two guard sets (a) or the continuous evolution grazes the guard set and returns to the interior of the state set X before later hitting the guard set (b).

Typically, the return map is piecewise-continuous on the guard set. We therefore need to develop an algorithm for computing discrete dynamics for piecewise-continuous maps.

2.2 Shift Spaces and Finite Automata

If A is a finite alphabet of symbols, recall that the sequence space A^ω is compact under the *product topology* defined by the metric $d(\vec{s}, \vec{t}) = 2^{-m}$ where $m = \min\{n \in \mathbb{N} \mid s_n \neq t_n\}$. In other words, two sequences are "close" if they agree on a long initial subword.

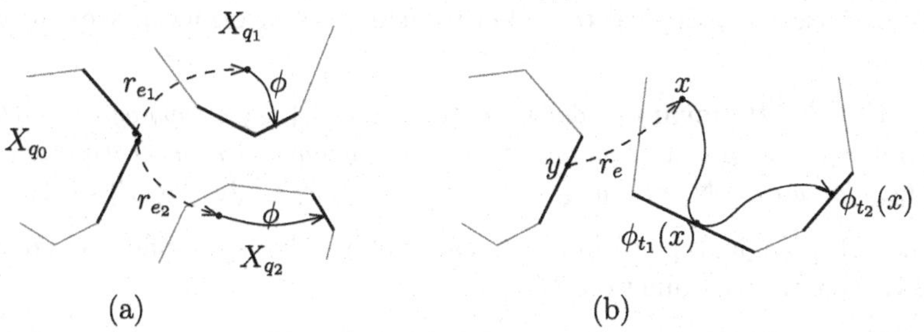

Fig. 1. Discontinuities of the return map. (a) Discontinuity at the boundary of a guard set. (b) Discontinuity caused by tangential contact with a guard set.

Definition 4 (Shifts). *Let A be a finite alphabet. The* shift map σ *on sequences A^ω is defined by $(\sigma\vec{s})_i = s_{i+1}$ for $i \in \mathbb{N}$. A* shift space *on A is a compact subset Σ of A^ω which is invariant under σ. A* shift *is the restriction of the shift map σ to a shift space Σ.*

A shift $\sigma|_\Sigma$ is a *subshift* of $\sigma|_{\widehat{\Sigma}}$ if $\Sigma \subset \widehat{\Sigma}$. Since shift spaces are compact subsets of a metric space, we can measure the difference between two shift spaces using the Hausdorff distance. If $\Sigma \subset \widehat{\Sigma}$, an alternative measure of the difference between Σ and $\widehat{\Sigma}$ is the difference in the topological entropies of $\sigma|_\Sigma$ and $\sigma|_{\widehat{\Sigma}}$.

A shift is *sofic* if it is generated by a finite automaton (as the sequence. Since the set of sofic shifts is dense in the space of all shifts on an alphabet A, sofic shifts are a convenient way of approximating arbitrary shifts.

2.3 Symbolic Dynamics of Piecewise-Continuous Maps

Symbolic dynamics is a powerful tool to analyse discrete-time dynamical systems. The basic idea is to compute the *itineraries* of orbits in terms of the regions of state space. The main complicating factor is that there is no nontrivial partition of a connected space M into compact pieces, so we instead use open sets whose closures cover the space.

Definition 5 (Topological Partition). *A* topological partition *of a space M is a finite collection $\mathcal{P} = \{P_1, P_2, ..., P_n\}$ of mutually disjoint open sets such that $M = \bigcup_{i=1}^{n} \overline{P}_i$. The* boundary points *of $\mathcal{P}$ are elements of $\partial\mathcal{P} := \bigcup_{P\in\mathcal{P}} \partial P$.*

Given topological partitions $\mathcal{P}$ and $\mathcal{Q}$, we say that $\mathcal{P}$ is a refinement *of $\mathcal{Q}$ if for all $P \in \mathcal{P}$, there exists $Q \in \mathcal{Q}$ such that $P \subset Q$. The* join *of $\mathcal{P}$ and $\mathcal{Q}$ is defined by $\mathcal{P} \vee \mathcal{Q} = \{P \cap Q \mid P \in \mathcal{P},\ Q \in \mathcal{Q}$ and $P \cap Q \neq \emptyset\}$.*

We shall consider piecewise-continuous functions defined as follows:

Definition 6 (Piecewise-Continuous Map). *Let $\mathcal{P}$ be a topological partition of M. A function $f : M \to M$ is* $\mathcal{P}$-continuous *if for all $P \in \mathcal{P}$, $f|_P$ is continuous and extends to a continuous function over $\overline{P}$. system*

We define $f^\circ_P = f|_P$, $\bar{f}_P$ to be the continuous extension of $f|_P$ to $\overline{P}$, $f^\circ :\subset X \to X$ by $f^\circ(x) = \bigcup_{P\in\mathcal{P}} f^\circ_p(x)$ and $\bar{f} = \bigcup_{P\in\mathcal{P}} \bar{f}_p(x)$.

We can use a topological partition to define an encoding of sequences in the space M.

Definition 7 (Itinerary). *Let $\mathcal{Q} = \{Q_s \mid s \in S\}$ be a topological partition of M, and $\vec{x} = (x_i)_{i \in \mathbb{N}}$ a sequence in M. A sequence $\vec{s}$ is a $\mathcal{Q}$-*itinerary *of $\vec{x}$ if $x_i \in Q_{s_i}$ for all $i \in \mathbb{N}$, and a $\overline{\mathcal{Q}}$-*itinerary *of $\vec{x}$ if $x_i \in \overline{Q}_{s_i}$ for all $i \in \mathbb{N}$.*

Given a topological partition, we can define the symbolic dynamics of a piecewise-continuous function f.

Definition 8 (Symbolic Dynamics). *Let $\mathcal{Q} = \{Q_s \mid s \in S\}$ be a topological partition, $\mathcal{P}$ a refinement of $\mathcal{Q}$, and $f : M \to M$ a $\mathcal{P}$-continuous function.*

- *The* lower symbolic dynamics $\underline{\Sigma}(f)$ *of f is the closure of the set of all $\mathcal{Q}$-itineraries of orbits of f°.*
- *The* upper symbolic dynamics $\overline{\Sigma}(f)$ *of f is the closure of the set of all $\overline{\mathcal{Q}}$-itineraries of orbits of $\bar{f}$.*

The lower symbolic dynamics is a subshift of the upper symbolic dynamics. Intuitively, the lower symbolic dynamics consists of itineraries which are "robustly" present, and the upper symbolic dynamics excludes those itineraries which are "robustly" absent.

In order to prove that an itinerary $\vec{s}$ is not part of the upper shift, we use the following trivial result, which is valid in any dimension.

Proposition 1. *If there is an orbit $\vec{x}$ of $\bar{f}$ such that $x_i \in P_{s_i}$ for all i, then $\bar{f}(P_{s_i}) \cap P_{s_i+1} \neq \emptyset$ for all i.*

Symbolic dynamics for one-dimensional maps is substantially easier than in higher dimensions. The partition elements P are intervals, so can easily be represented by their boundary points. The symbolic dynamics can be computed using the kneading theory of [14] or by the following result.

Theorem 1. *Suppose $(R_0, R_1, \ldots)$ is a sequence of compact intervals such that f is continuous on each R_i and $f(R_i) \supset R_{i+1}$ for all i. Then there is an orbit $(x_0, x_1, \ldots)$ of f such that $x_i \in R_i$ for all i.*

For general piecewise-continuous functions, the lower symbolic dynamics may differ considerably from the upper symbolic dynamics. Under certain conditions, the lower symbolic dynamics $\underline{\Sigma}(f)$ and the upper symbolic dynamics $\overline{\Sigma}(f)$ coincide.

Theorem 2. *let $\mathcal{Q}$ be a partition of M, let $\mathcal{P}$ be a refinement of $\mathcal{Q}$, and let f be a $\mathcal{P}$-continuous map satisfying assumptions (A1-2) below. Then the lower symbolic dynamics $\underline{\Sigma}(f)$ equals the upper symbolic dynamics $\overline{\Sigma}(f)$.*

A1. *The image under f° of every open subset of M contains an open set.*
A2. *The forward orbits of all boundary points of $\mathcal{Q}$, all discontinuity points of f, and all critical points of f are disjoint from the boundary points of $\mathcal{Q}$.*

Assumption A1 is valid for any non-constant analytic map, and assumption A2 is valid for generic continuous functions.

2.4 Interval Arithmetic

Since we typically cannot compute the return map of a hybrid system exactly, we resort to numerical approximation. In order to ensure that we can obtain rigorous conclusions from approximate numerics, we compute error bounds for all quantities. Hence a numerical approximation to a real number x is represented by an interval $\lfloor x \rceil = [\underline{x}, \overline{x}]$ such that $\underline{x} < x < \overline{x}$.

If f is a continuous function, then an *interval extension* $[f]$ of f is a function from intervals to intervals such that:

1. if $x \in \lfloor x \rceil$, then $f(x) \in [f](\lfloor x \rceil)$,
2. if $\lfloor x_2 \rceil \subset \lfloor x_1 \rceil$, then $[f](\lfloor x_2 \rceil) \subset \lfloor x_1 \rceil$, and
3. if $\lfloor y \rceil$ is any interval containing $y = f(x)$ in its interior, then there exists an interval $\lfloor x \rceil$ containing x such that $[f](\lfloor x \rceil) \subset \lfloor y \rceil$.

When computing an interval extension of f in practice, we set an a-priori numerical precision ϵ, and perform all computations to that precision. If the results are not sufficiently accurate, then we increase the precision and repeat the computations.

If f is n-times differentiable, we also assume that an interval extension is available for derivatives $f^{(i)}(x)$ for $i = 1, \ldots, n$. If f is piecewise-continuous, then an interval extension to f consists of:
1. interval approximations $\lfloor d_i \rceil$ to the discontinuity points d, and
2. an interval extension of f_P over all continuous branches P.

If $[\underline{x}, \overline{x}]$ is an interval containing x, and $\lfloor y \rceil$ and $\lfloor z \rceil$ are intervals such that $[f](\lfloor y \rceil) < \underline{x}$ and $[f](\lfloor z \rceil) > \overline{x}$, then there is a point w in $\lfloor w \rceil = [\overline{y}, \underline{z}]$ such that $f(w) = x$. By using a modified version of the bisection algorithm, we can therefore compute preimages of points under f. We have the following result.

Lemma 1. *If f is strictly monotone on an interval P, then it is possible to compute an interval extension of $(f|_P)^{-1}$ from an interval extension of f.*

3 Algorithms for Computing the Discrete Dynamics

In this section we present a numerical algorithm for computing the discrete dynamics of a two-dimensional hybrid automaton with one-dimensional guard sets, under assumptions which ensure that the return map is piecewise-continuous. We first briefly outline how to rigorously compute the return map and its derivatives arbitrarily accurately. We describe the algorithms to compute the symbolic dynamics of the return map, and finally state some convergence results.

3.1 Numerical Computation of the Return Map

We now outline the numerical procedure to compute approximations to the return map. We consider hybrid automata such that:

B1. The state space X is a two-dimensional manifold with piecewise-differentiable boundary, and the guard set G is a subset of ∂X.

B2. The reset maps r_e are differentiable on their domains G_e.
B3. The continuous dynamics ϕ is given by a Lipschitz differential equation $\dot{x} = \chi(x)$.

We will also need a mild regularity assumption on the crossings of the continuous dynamics with the guard set. The following condition is sufficient:

B4. Whenever the continuous evolution $\xi(t)$ hits the guard set G, it either crosses G transversely, or touches G at a corner point or a quadratic tangency and continuous within X.

Under the assumptions $(B1 - 4)$, the return map is piecewise-differentiable, though may not be everywhere defined on G. Locally, we can represent the guard set G as $\{x \in X \mid g(x) = 0\}$ for some differentiable function g. The return map is then given by $y = f(x) = \phi_t(r(x))$ under the constraint $g(y) = 0$. Using a rigorous high order integration scheme, such as Lohner's method or Taylor methods [15,16,17],it is possible to compute $f(x)$ and $f'(x)$ to arbitrary accuracy away from corners of the guard set and grazing points of the flow.

We obtain a numerical discretisation of the return map f in terms of interval arithmetic. More specifically:

Theorem 3. *Let $\mathcal{H}$ be a hybrid system satisfying hypotheses (B1-4). Let f be the return map of $\mathcal{H}$. Then it is possible to compute an interval extension of f and its derivative f'.*

In the subsequent analysis, we shall only use information about the numerically-computable interval extension $[f]$, and not assume that we have an analytic description of the map itself.

3.2 Computing the Discrete Dynamics

In this section we show how to compute the symbolic dynamics of a map f which is piecewise continuous on branches $\mathcal{C}$ relative to a partition $\mathcal{Q}$. The basic strategy is outlined in the following procedure:

Algorithm 4. *Let $\mathcal{Q}$ be a partition of X, $\mathcal{E}$ be a topological partition of X and f be a piecewise-continuous function with nondegenerate critical points.*

1. *Fix a numerical precision ϵ and a maximum number of steps n.*
2. *Compute an approximate topological partition $\mathcal{C}$ refining $\mathcal{Q}$ and $\mathcal{E}$ such that f is continuous on each piece of $\mathcal{C}$*
3. *Refine the partition $\mathcal{C}$ to obtain an approximate topological partition $\mathcal{M}$ such that f is monotone on each partition element.*
4. *Refine the partition $\mathcal{M}$ by repeating the one of the following partitioning strategies at most n times to obtain a partition $\mathcal{R}$.*
   - *Forward refinement: Refine a partition $\mathcal{P}$ by introducing new partition boundary points at $f(p)$ for boundary points $p \in \partial\mathcal{P}$.*
   - *Backward refinement: Refine a a partition $\mathcal{P}$ by introducing new partition boundary points at $f^{-1}(p)$ for $p \in \partial\mathcal{P}$*

In either strategy, do not introduce any new points $\lfloor y \rceil$ *which overlap existing boundary points* $\lfloor p \rceil$.

5. *For each pair* $R, R' \in \mathcal{R}$, *compute whether* $\bar{f}(\overline{R}) \cap \overline{R}' \neq \emptyset$, $f(R) \supset R'$ *or* $f(R) \subset R'$.
6. *Define the under-approximation* $\Lambda = \Lambda_{\epsilon,n}$ *and the over-approximation* $\Upsilon = \Upsilon_{\epsilon,n}$ *to the symbolic dynamics to consist of all sequences* $(Q_0, Q_1, \ldots)$ *for which there exists* $(R_0, R_1, \ldots) \in \mathcal{R}^\omega$ *with* $R_i \subset Q_i$ *and*
   Λ: $\exists\, k \in \mathbb{N} \cup \{\infty\}$ *s.t.* $f(R_i) \supset R_{i+1}\ \forall i < k$, *and* $f(R_i) \subset R_{i+1}\ \forall i \geq k$.
   Υ: $\bar{f}(\overline{R}) \cap \overline{R}' \neq \emptyset\ \forall i \in \mathbb{N}$.

The data type representing a boundary point p of a partition $\mathcal{P}$ has two fields, a `value` field which is an interval approximation $\lfloor p \rceil$ to p, and a `image` field which is a reference or pointer to the object representing $f(p)$. If p is a discontinuity point, then we store two image points, namely the image of p under both branches of $\bar{f}$ at p.

To compute the critical points, we need information on the derivative f. A point c is a critical point if $f'(c) = 0$, and the zeros of f' can easily be computed to arbitrary accuracy by a bisection strategy.

In certain degenerate cases, we may not be able to distinguish two discontinuity points of f, or a discontinuity point and a critical point. Although it is possible to handle these cases in a consistent way, in this paper we assume for simplicity that these cases do not arise.

The forward refinement of a partition $\mathcal{P}$ can be easily computed, since we need simply compute the images of all boundary points of $\mathcal{P}$. The boundary points of the backward refinement of $\mathcal{P}$ can be computed using Lemma 1. The main advantage of the forward refinement strategy are that better results can usually be obtained with fewer partition points, but convergence to the symbolic dynamics using forward refinement need not be monotone.

If $\mathcal{P}$ is a partition with monotone branches, then the n-step backward refinement of $\mathcal{P}$ consists of sets $P_{i_0,i_1,\ldots,i_{n-1}}$ defined recursively by $P_{i_0} \in \mathcal{P}$ and $P_{i_0,i_1,\ldots,i_{n-1}} = P_{i_0} \cap f^{-1}(P_{i_1,\ldots,i_{n-1}})$. For any $x \in P_{i_0,i_1,\ldots,i_{n-1}}$, we have $f^k(x) \in P_{i_k}$, so each partition element of an n-step backward refinement of $\mathcal{P}$ determines the first n elements of a $\mathcal{P}$-itinerary.

In order to determine whether $f(R) \supset R'$ or $\bar{f}(\overline{R})$ is disjoint from $\overline{R}'$, we need to know the relative ordering of the boundary points i.e. whether $r_i < r_j$, $r_i = r_j$ or $r_i > r_j$, and the image point r_k of r_i under f. As long as the interval approximations to the boundary points do not overlap, we can determine the relative ordering. Further, since when refining we compute each $\lfloor r_{i+1} \rceil$ as an image or preimage of some $p_i \in \lfloor r_i \rceil$, we have exact information about the images by construction.

3.3 Convergence to the Discrete Dynamics

We now describe how the sofic shifts computed by Algorithm 4 approximate the symbolic dynamics of f, and give sufficient conditions under which the approximations converge.

Theorem 5. *Let Λ and Υ be the shifts obtained by Algorithm 4. Then Λ is a subshift of $\underline{\Sigma}(f)$ and $\overline{\Sigma}(f)$ is a subshift of Υ.*

The following result shows that if the upper symbolic dynamics and the lower symbolic dynamics are equal, then the algorithm converges.

Theorem 6. *Suppose f is a piecewise-continuous map satisfying assumptions (A1-2). Then the under- and over-approximations $\Lambda_{\epsilon,n}$ and $\Upsilon_{\epsilon,n}$ to the discrete dynamics computed by Algorithm 4 using backwards refinement converge to the symbolic dynamics of f as the accuracy $1/\epsilon$ and maximum number of steps n increase.*

The proof is technical and will be published elsewhere. The main observation is that under condition A2, there is essentially no difference between an algorithm using interval arithmetic, and an algorithm using exact values. Under weaker assumptions, it is possible to prove that lower approximations $\Lambda_{\epsilon,n}$ and upper approximations $\Upsilon_{\epsilon,n}$ converge to the lower shift $\underline{\Sigma}$ and the upper shift $\overline{\Sigma}$.

3.4 Representing the Symbolic Dynamics by Discrete Automata

We can represent the discrete dynamics of the hybrid automaton by a discrete automaton whose states are the elements of $\mathcal{R}$, with two types of arrows. We draw a solid arrow $R \rightarrow R'$ if $f(R) \supset R$, and a dashed arrow $R\dashrightarrow R'$ if merely $\bar{f}(\overline{R}) \cap \overline{R}' \neq \emptyset$. Further, if there is a sequence $(R_{s_0}, R_{s_0}, \ldots)$ such that $f(R_{s_i}) \subset R_{s_{i+1}}$ for all i, then we replace all dashed arrows $R_{s_i}\dashrightarrow R_{s_{i+1}}$ with solid arrows $R_{s_i} \rightarrow R_{s_{i+1}}$. The shift Γ is generated by the solid arrows, and Υ is generated by both dashed and solid arrows.

We can label an arrow starting in R with the event e if $R \subset G_e$. If $\vec{s}$ is a sequence of symbols and there is a *solid* path:

$$R_{s_0} \xrightarrow{e_0} R_{s_1} \xrightarrow{e_1} R_{s_2} \cdots \tag{5}$$

then there must be an orbit $\vec{x} = (x_0, x_1, \ldots)$ of the return map f such that $x_i \in R_i$ for all i and $f_{e_i}(x_i) = x_{i+1}$. Hence there is an exectution of the hybrid automaton with itinerary:

$$q_0 \xrightarrow{e_0} q_1 \xrightarrow{e_1} q_2 \cdots \tag{6}$$

where $R_{s_i} \subset X_{q_i}$ for all i. From the construction of Υ and Proposition 1, we see that if there is an orbit of the return map with $x_i \in \overline{R}_i$ for all i, then there must be a *broken* path (which may consist of both dashed and solid arrows):

$$R_{s_0} \overset{e_0}{\dashrightarrow} R_{s_1} \xrightarrow{e_1} R_{s_2} \overset{e_k}{\dashrightarrow} R_{s_3} \cdots . \tag{7}$$

4 Case Studies

In this section, we present two case studies: a simple hysteresis system and the singular limit of the van der Pol equation.

4.1 A Hysteresis Switching System

We now consider a piecewise-affine model of a system governed by hysteresis switching [18]. We let $H(x)$ be the hysteresis map $H(x) = 0$ for $x \leq 1$, the first mode, and $H(x) = 1$ for $x \geq 0$, the second mode, and consider the system:

$$\begin{aligned} \dot{x} &= y + a_1 H(x/b) \\ \dot{y} &= -x - 2\sigma y + a_2 H(x/b). \end{aligned} \tag{8}$$

The return map is defined on the set $P = \{(x, y) \in \mathbb{R}^2 \mid x = 0,\ y > 0\}$ and maps a point $p \in P$ to a point $q \in P$ such that q belongs to the same orbit of p, and q is the next intersection after p in forward time of this orbit with P in the first mode. We have computed symbolic dynamics for the return map with parameter values $a_1 = -1$, $a_2 = -1$, $b = 0.3$ and $\sigma = -0.2$. The graph of the return map is shown in Fig. 2. We take an initial partition $\mathcal{Q}$ which are the domains of the monotone branches. The partition elements are $Q_0 = [p_0, p_1]$, $Q_1 = [p_1, p_3]$, $Q_2 = [p_3, p_5]$, $Q_3 = [p_5, p_7]$ and $Q_4 = [p_7, p_8]$ where the boundary points are

$$p_0 = 0.0,\ p_1 \approx 0.20894,\ p_3 \approx 0.39278,\ p_5 \approx 0.73329,\ p_7 \approx 0.92580,\ p_8 = 1.0.$$

The associated symbolic dynamics is in Fig. 3(a). The two points of discontinuity are p_1 and p_5 and they can be proved to have the same left and right images. The partition after one iteration of forward refinements has the following additional endpoints:

$$\begin{aligned} p_2 = f(p_7) \approx 0.33792,\ p_4 = f(p_1^+) = f(p_5^+) \approx 0.59890, \\ p_6 = f(p_1^-) = f(p_5^-) \approx 0.75340. \end{aligned}$$

The symbolic dynamics generated by this partition is approximated by the graph in Fig. 3(b).

We notice that the lower approximation of the dynamics of the refined partition misses some sequences of the lower approximation of dynamics of the

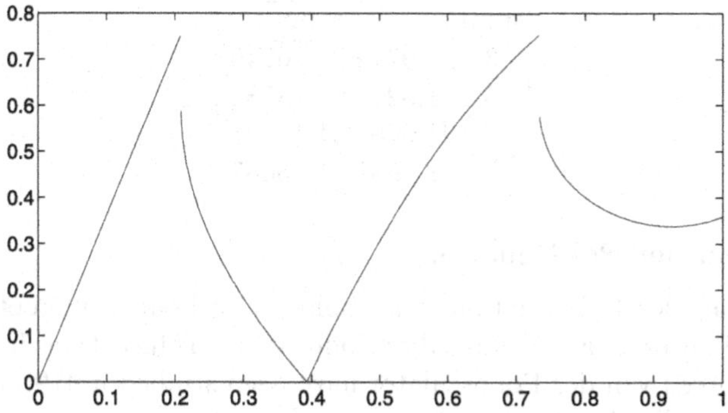

Fig. 2. The return map for the hysteresis system (9)

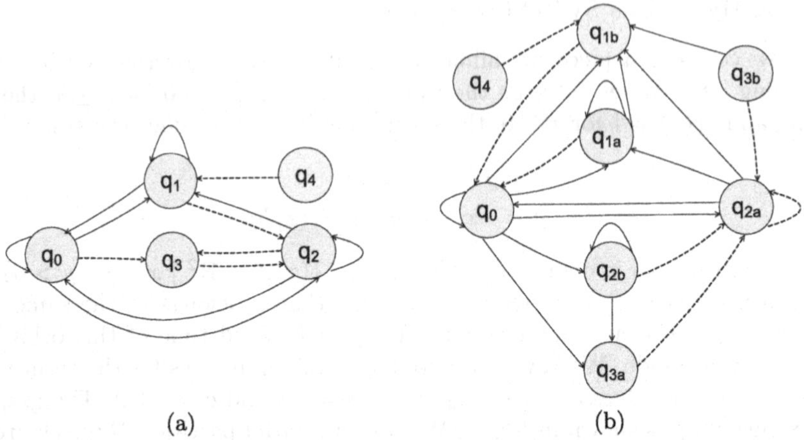

Fig. 3. Lower and upper approximation of symbolic dynamics for the hysteresis system (9) for (a) the initial partition and (b) the forward refinement of the initial partition

initial partition. This is due to the fact that although region $Q_1 = [p_1, p_3]$ covers $Q_0 = [p_0, p_1]$ under one iterate of the return map, neither of the subdivided regions $P_{1;0} = [p_1, p_2]$ and $P_{1;1} = [p_2, p_3]$ cover Q_0. Hence the convergence of the lower approximations to the symbolic dynamics computed using forward refinement is not monotone. With backward refinement the convergence can be shown to be monotone, but backward refinements have the disadvantage of being slower to compute than forward refinements.

The lower shift for the initial partition can be written as the regular expression

$$(q_0^* q_2)^*(q_0^\omega + q_1^\omega) + (q_0^* q_2 q_0)^*(q_1^\omega + q_2^\omega) + (q_0^* q_2)^\omega.$$

We can see for instance that the periodic sequence $(q_0 q_3 q_2 q_1)^\omega$ belongs to the upper shift but not to the lower shift. From the two shifts we can show that the topological entropy lies in the interval [0.80958, 1.27020]. The topological entropies obtained for further refinement are shown in the table :

steps	entropy
3	[0.97494,1.26249]
5	[1.02407,1.18582]
7	[1.04636,1.16493]
12	[1.06873,1.15087]

4.2 The van der Pol Equation

The forced van der Pol equation is a nonlinear ordinary differential equation modeling oscillation in a vacuum tube triode circuit. Bifurcations in the singular limit of the forced van der Pol oscillator have been studied in [19]. In this paper we analyse the following version of the equation:

$$\ddot{x} + \mu(x^2 - 1)\dot{x} + x = a(x^2 - 1)\sin(2\pi\nu\tau) \tag{9}$$

in the singular limit as $\mu \to \infty$. To obtain a form more convenient for analysis, we rescale time $t = \tau/\mu$, introduce new parameters $\varepsilon = \frac{1}{\mu^2}$, $\omega = \nu\mu$ and $\theta = \omega t$, and define the new variable $y = \dot{x}/\mu^2 + x^3/3 - x$. We obtain the following autonomous system:

$$\varepsilon\dot{x} = y + x - x^3/3; \tag{10}$$
$$\dot{y} = -x + a(x^2 - 1)\sin(2\pi\theta); \tag{11}$$
$$\dot{\theta} = \omega.$$

The *fast subsystem* is defined by (10), since the dynamics of the fast variable x occurs on a time scale which is fast relative to the evolution of the *slow variables* y and θ.

We see that on the *critical manifold* $y + x - x^3/3 = 0$ the system evolves on a time scale of order t. However, the critical manifold is unstable for the fast system if $|x| \leq 1$, and that when this occurs, the value of x jumps instantaneously to one of the stable fixed points of (10).

We can therefore view the singular limit as a hybrid system in which the continuous dynamics is given by the slow flow on the stable sheet of the critical manifold, and the reset map is given by the fast flow. By eliminating y, we obtain the following dynamics for the slow subsystem:

$$\dot{x} = -x + a(x^2 - 1)\sin(2\pi\theta) \tag{12}$$
$$\dot{\theta} = \omega(x^2 - 1)$$

The fast dynamics is described by the guard set and reset map

$$G = \{(x, \theta) \mid |x| = 1\}; \qquad r(x, \theta) = (-2\,\mathrm{sgn}(x), \theta). \tag{13}$$

In other words, when the guard condition $|x| = 1$ becomes satisfied the state jumps to $x = \mp 2$.

Since the dynamics is symmetric under the transformation $T(x, \theta) = (-x, \theta + 1/2)$, we can post-compose the return map from the guard set $x = 1$ to the guard set $x = -1$ with T to obtain the *half return map* f taking $\{(r, \theta) \mid r = 1\}$ into itself. The graph of the half return map for parameter values $a = 5$ and $\omega = 3$ is shown in Fig. 4. We have computed the lower and upper symbolic dynamics with respect to the partition given by the continuous branches using forward refinement.

In the return map there are 5 discontinuity points:

$$p_2 \approx 0.05816,\; p_3 \approx 0.25226,\; p_5 \approx 0.69356,\; p_6 \approx 0.81553,\; p_7 \approx 0,98495.$$

and 2 critical points, a local maximum $p_1 \approx 0.02183$ and a local minimum $p_4 \approx 0.47872$. These points with the extremes of the interval $p_0 = 0$ and $p_8 = 1$ generate an initial partition of 9 pieces. After one forward iteration we obtain 11 pieces.

$$q_0 = f(p_0) \approx 0.15520,\; q_1 = f(p_1) \approx 0.17825,\; q_2 = f(p_4) \approx 0.29017,$$

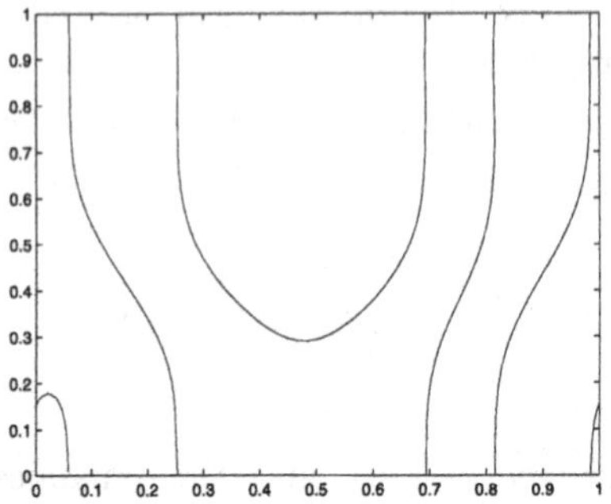

Fig. 4. The half return map for the singular limit of the forced van der Pol oscillator (12)

The lower and upper discrete automata are not included for reasons of space. After one step of refinement, the discrete automaton representing the symbolic dynamics separate into two strongly connected components. Both the lower and upper shifts include the component with the highest entropy, while the lower shift does not include the smallest.

Therefore the topological entropy of the lower and upper shifts are equal and can be computed exactly yielding a numerical value of approximately 1.55705. From Fig. 4 we could already infer the entropy is at least $\log(3) \approx 1.09861$ because there are 3 continuous pieces of the partition which map the whole interval. From numerical computation we can deduce the existence of an attracting periodic orbit close to the local minimum. This let us infer the existence of a chaotic invariant Cantor set, every point non belonging to this set converges to the attracting periodic orbit.

5 Conclusion

In this paper, we have presented a method for computing the discrete dynamics of a hybrid automaton with a two-dimensional state space. We obtain sequences of sofic shifts which approximate the actual discrete dynamics from above and below. We have given nondegeneracy conditions under which the method is optimal, in the sense that the resulting shift spaces converge to the actual shift space. In future work, we plan to remove the nondegeneracy conditions on the method, and extend the method to hybrid automata in higher dimensions.

References

1. Alur, R., Henzinger, T.A., Lafferriere, G., Pappas, G.J.: Discrete abstractions of hybrid systems. Proc. IEEE 88, 971–984 (2000)
2. Tiwari, A., Khanna, G.: Series of abstractions for hybrid automata. In: Tomlin, C.J., Greenstreet, M.R. (eds.) HSCC 2002. LNCS, vol. 2289, pp. 465–478. Springer, Heidelberg (2002)

3. Lunze, J., Nixdorf, B.: Discrete reachability of hybrid systems. Internat. J. Control 76(14), 1453–1468 (2003)
4. Moor, T., Raisch, J., O'Young, S.: Discrete supervisory control of hybrid systems based on l-complete approximations. Discrete Event Dyn. Syst. 12(1), 83–107 (2002); WODES 1998, Cagliari
5. Guckenheimer, J., Johnson, S.: Planar hybrid systems. In: Antsaklis, P.J., Kohn, W., Nerode, A., Sastry, S.S. (eds.) HS 1994. LNCS, vol. 999, pp. 202–225. Springer, Heidelberg (1995)
6. Grasman, J., Nijmeijer, H., Veling, E.J.M.: Singular perturbations and a mapping on an interval for the forced van der Pol relaxation oscillator. Phys. D 13(1–2), 195–210 (1984)
7. Bold, K., Edwards, C., Guckenheimer, J., Guharay, S., Hoffman, K., Hubbard, J., Oliva, R., Weckesser, W.: The forced van der Pol equation. II. Canards in the reduced system. SIAM J. Appl. Dyn. Syst. 2(4), 570–608 (2003) (electronic)
8. Moore, R.E.: Interval analysis. Prentice-Hall Inc., Englewood Cliffs (1966)
9. Jaulin, L., Kieffer, M., Didrit, O., Walter, É.: Applied interval analysis. Springer, London (2001)
10. Aberth, O.: Introduction to Precise Numerical Methods. Academic Press, London (2007)
11. Lind, D., Marcus, B.: An introduction to symbolic dynamics and coding. Cambridge University Press, Cambridge (1995)
12. Kitchens, B.P.: Symbolic dynamics. In: Universitext. Springer, Berlin (1998) (one-sided, two-sided and countable state Markov shifts)
13. Katok, A., Hasselblatt, B.: Introduction to the modern theory of dynamical systems. In: Encyclopedia of Mathematics and its Applications, vol. 54. Cambridge University Press, Cambridge (1995)
14. Milnor, J., Thurston, W.: On iterated maps of the interval. In: Dynamical systems (College Park, MD, 1986–1987). Lecture Notes in Math., vol. 1342, pp. 465–563. Springer, Berlin (1988)
15. Berz, M., Makino, K.: Verified integration of ODEs and flows using differential algebraic methods on high-order Taylor models. Reliab. Comput. 4(4), 361–369 (1998)
16. Nedialkov, N.S., Jackson, K.R., Corliss, G.F.: Validated solutions of initial value problems for ordinary differential equations. Appl. Math. Comput. 105(1), 21–68 (1999)
17. Wilczak, D., Zgliczynski, P.: C^r Lohner algorithm. oai:arXiv.org:0704.0720 (2007)
18. Newcomb, R.W., El-Leithy, N.: Chaos generation using binary hysteresis. Circuits Systems Signal Process 5(3), 321–341 (1986)
19. Guckenheimer, J., Hoffman, K., Weckesser, W.: The forced van der Pol equation. I. The slow flow and its bifurcations. SIAM J. Appl. Dyn. Syst. 2(1), 1–35 (2003) (electronic)

Input-to-State Stabilization with Quantized Output Feedback*

Yoav Sharon and Daniel Liberzon

Coordinated Science Laboratory, Department of Electrical Engineering,
University of Illinois at Urbana Champaign, Urbana, IL, U.S.A
{ysharon,liberzon}@control.csl.uiuc.edu

Abstract. We study control systems where the output subspace is covered by a finite set of quantization regions, and the only information available to a controller is which of the quantization regions currently contains the system's output. We assume the dimension of the output subspace is strictly less than the dimension of the state space. The number of quantization regions can be as small as 3 per dimension of the output subspace. We show how to design a controller that stabilizes such a system, and makes the system robust to an external unknown disturbance in the sense that the closed-loop system has the Input-to-State Stability property. No information about the disturbance is required to design the controller. Achieving the ISS property for continuous-time systems with quantized measurements requires a hybrid approach, and indeed our controller consists of a dynamic, discrete-time observer, a continuous-time state-feedback stabilizer, and a switching logic that switches between several modes of operation. Except for some properties that the observer and the stabilizer must possess, our approach is general and not restricted to a specific observer or stabilizer. Examples of specific observers that possess these properties are included.

1 Introduction

Many tools developed in control theory assume a system where the measurement that enters the controller is either the state of the system (state-feedback) or some linear transformation of the state (output-feedback). In many practical applications, however, the measurement available to the controller is only a quantized version of the aforementioned signals. More specifically, the measurement available to the controller is confined to a finite set of values. While the size of this finite set of values is assumed to be fixed, we do assume that the mapping from the output-subspace into this set depends on a few parameters that can be changed by the controller. This is referred to as dynamic quantization. Quantization can result from the physical properties of the sensors in the system. For example a coarse temperature sensor which can only measure "normal", "too hot", or "too low", but its threshold can be adjusted. Another example is a low

* This work was supported by NSF ECS-0134115 CAR and NSF ECCS-0701676 awards.

M. Egerstedt and B. Mishra (Eds.): HSCC 2008, LNCS 4981, pp. 500–513, 2008.

resolution camera whose orientation and optical zoom can be adjusted. Quantization can also result from a link with a limited data rate between the sensors and the controller. The approach in this paper is especially designed for systems where each sensor is connected, through some limited data rate link, directly to the controller. In particular this means there is no need for a processing unit on the "sensor side" to collect the information from all the sensors, and generate a state estimate from the partial output measurements, before transmitting it to the controller. Basic references on quantized control include [1], [2] and [3].

Several different notions of stability exist in the literature. We chose the notion of Input-to-State Stability (ISS), first presented in [4] for continuous-time systems. Roughly speaking, a system is ISS if every state trajectory corresponding to a bounded disturbance remains bounded, and the trajectory eventually becomes small if the disturbance is small (no matter what the initial state is). The notion of ISS was extended to discrete-time systems in [5]. Our choice of ISS as the desired property is natural because we want to have a bounded response to arbitrary bounded disturbances. This implies, in particular, that no information about the disturbance bound is given to the controller.

Recent papers on how to achieve stabilization under quantization include: [6], [7], [8] and [9] which assume only disturbance-free systems; [10] and [11] which deal only with disturbances whose bound is known to the controller; [12] which only requires the controller to know some statistical information about the disturbance but not its bound; and [13] and [14] in which the controller does not have any information about the disturbance. Even though in [12] and [13] the controller does not know the disturbance bound, neither shows ISS — [12] shows mean square stability in the stochastic setting and [13] shows stability in probability. The paper [14] does show ISS; however, the approach in [14] is considerably different from our approach and in particular it does not guarantee a minimum number of quantization regions or a minimum data rate. Of the papers that deal with disturbances, only [12] and [13] also deal with the output-feedback case. However, in contrast to our paper, in these papers it is assumed that the quantization is applied after a state estimate is constructed by some observer that has direct access to the measurements. This approach is arguably less relevant in applications since it does not address the case where the quantization is due to physical or practical limitations of the sensors (and not only due to a limited data rate).

The work presented in this paper is built on our recent work [15], which was the first to show how to achieve ISS under state-quantization and minimum data rate. In the work presented here, we show how to extend that scheme to output-feedback systems where only the projection of the state into a lower dimensional subspace is measured (and then quantized). Achieving the ISS property for continuous-time systems with quantized measurements requires a hybrid approach, and indeed our controller consists of a dynamic, discrete-time observer, a continuous-time state-feedback stabilizer, and a switching logic that switches between several modes of operation.

The paper is organized as follows. In §2 we define the system and the quantizer. In §3 we give an overview of and the motivation for the three modes of operation of our controller. In §4 we define a general form of an observer, and then present the controller that achieves the objectives listed above. Our main result is presented in that section, and it is followed by a simulation. In §5 we give examples of specific observers that can be used with our control system. We conclude in §6. Due to paper length limitations we are unable to include here the proof of our result. It will appear in the journal version of this work, while in the meantime it can be viewed in the appendix of the review version of this paper, which is available at `http://decision.csl.uiuc.edu/~ysharon/hscc08_full.pdf`

2 System Definition

The continuous-time dynamical system we are to stabilize is as follows ($t \in \mathbb{R}_{\geq 0}$, $k \in \mathbb{N} \cup \{0\}$):

$$\begin{aligned} \dot{\boldsymbol{x}}(t) &= A\boldsymbol{x}(t) + B\boldsymbol{u}(t) + D\boldsymbol{w}(t) \\ \boldsymbol{y}(k) &= C\boldsymbol{x}\left(kT_s\right) \qquad \boldsymbol{z}(k) = Q\left(\boldsymbol{y}(k); \boldsymbol{c}(k), \mu(k)\right) \end{aligned} \tag{1}$$

where $\boldsymbol{x} \in \mathbb{R}^{n_x}$ is the state of the system, $\boldsymbol{u} \in \mathbb{R}^{n_u}$ is the control input that the control system will need to generate, $\boldsymbol{w} \in \mathbb{R}^{n_w}$ is an unknown disturbance which is injected to the system and $\boldsymbol{y} \in \mathbb{R}^{n_y}$ is the projection of the state space into the output subspace which is measured by the sensors. Finally, $\boldsymbol{z} \in \mathbb{R}^{n_y}$ is the information available to the controller. We use T_s for the time interval between subsequent measurement. We will refer to each instance in time when a measurement is taken as a time sample. A, B, D, C are real matrices of appropriate dimensions. We assume that A and B are a controllable pair and that A and C are an observable pair.

We use N for the number of quantization regions per observed dimension. It can be determined by the physical properties of the sensor or from the data rate. Given N, the data rate required, in bits per time sample, is $R = \log_2\left(N^{n_y}\right)$. Our quantizer, denoted by Q, is parameterized by $\boldsymbol{c} \in \mathbb{R}^{n_y}$ and $\mu \in \mathbb{R}$ as follows (see Figure 1 for an illustration):

$$Q_i\left(\boldsymbol{x}; \boldsymbol{c}, \mu\right) \doteq c_i + \begin{cases} (-N+1)\mu & x_i - c_i \leq (-N+2)\mu \\ (-N+3)\mu & (-N+2)\mu < x_i - c_i \leq (-N+4)\mu \\ \vdots & \vdots \\ 0 & -\mu < x_i - c_i \leq \mu \\ \vdots & \vdots \\ (N-3)\mu & (N-4)\mu < x_i - c_i \leq (N-2)\mu \\ (N-1)\mu & (N-2)\mu < x_i - c_i . \end{cases} \tag{2}$$

We will refer to $\boldsymbol{c}$ as the center of the quantizer, and to μ as zoom factor. Note that what will actually be transferred from the quantizer to the observer will be an index to one of the quantization regions. The observer, which knows the

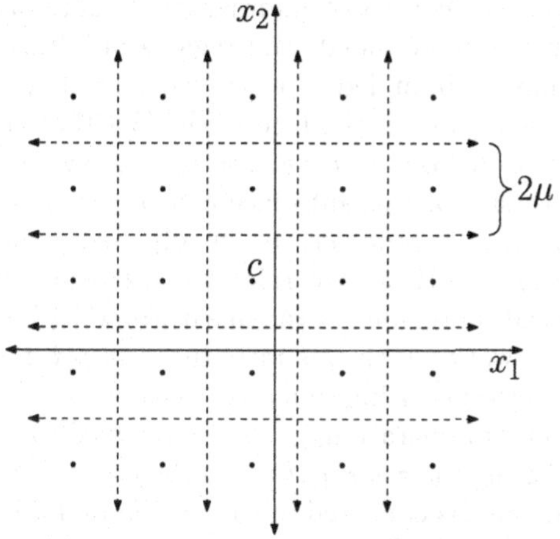

Fig. 1. Illustration of the quantizer for the two-dimensional output subspace, $N = 5$. The dashed lines define the boundaries of the quantization regions. The black dots define where the quantizer estimates the projection of the state to be, given the index of the quantization region that currently contains the projection.

values of $\boldsymbol{c}$ and μ, will use this information to convert the received index to the value of Q as given in (2). The controller sets $\boldsymbol{u}$, $\boldsymbol{c}$ and μ, and the only signal directly observed by the controller is $\boldsymbol{z}$. The system model, represented by the matrices A, B, D, C, is known to the controller.

Adopting the standard ISS notion to the class of hybrid systems that we design here, we will say that the closed-loop system is ISS if its solution satisfies

$$|\boldsymbol{x}(t)| \leq \beta_{cl}\left(|\boldsymbol{x}(0)|, t\right) + \gamma_{cl}\left(\|\boldsymbol{w}\|\right), \qquad \forall t \geq 0 \tag{3}$$

for some $\mathcal{K}_\infty$-function[1] γ_{cl} and some $\mathcal{KL}$-function[2] β_{cl}. See also [16] for a study of ISS in the framework of impulsive systems.

In this paper we will use the ∞-norm unless otherwise specified: for vectors, $|\boldsymbol{x}| \doteq |\boldsymbol{x}|_\infty \doteq \max_i |x_i|$; for matrices, $\|M\| \doteq \max_{\boldsymbol{x}} \frac{|M\boldsymbol{x}|}{|\boldsymbol{x}|} \equiv \max_i \left(\sum_j |M_{ij}|\right)$; for continuous-time signals, $\|\boldsymbol{w}\|_{[t_1,t_2]} \doteq \max_{t\in[t_1,t_2]} |\boldsymbol{w}(t)|_\infty$, $\|\boldsymbol{w}\| \doteq \|\boldsymbol{w}\|_{[0,\infty)}$; and for discrete-time signals, $\|\boldsymbol{y}\|_{\{k_1\ldots k_2\}} \doteq \max_{k\in\{k_1\ldots k_2\}} |\boldsymbol{y}(k)|_\infty$, $\|\boldsymbol{y}\| \doteq \|\boldsymbol{y}\|_{\{0\ldots\infty\}}$.

3 Overview of the Controller Design

Our controller operates in three different modes of operation. The motivation for each of these modes is given in this section.

---

[1] A function $\alpha : [0, \infty) \to [0, \infty)$ is said to be of class $\mathcal{K}$ if it is continuous, strictly increasing, and $\alpha(0) = 0$. A function $\alpha : [0, \infty) \to [0, \infty)$ is said to be of class $\mathcal{K}_\infty$ if it is of class $\mathcal{K}$ and also unbounded.

[2] A function $\beta : [0, \infty) \times [0, \infty) \to [0, \infty)$ is said to be of class $\mathcal{KL}$ if $\beta(\cdot, t)$ is of class $\mathcal{K}$ for each fixed $t \geq 0$ and $\beta(s, t)$ decreases to 0 as $t \to \infty$ for each fixed $s \geq 0$.

A general quantizer may consist of quantization regions of finite size, for which the estimation error can be bounded, and regions of infinite size, where the estimation error can not be bounded. We will refer to these regions as bounded and unbounded regions, respectively. Due to the fact that there are only a finite number of quantization regions to cover the infinite-size $\mathbb{R}^{n_y}$ output subspace, only a region of finite size of this subspace can be covered by the bounded regions. The size of this region, however, can be adjusted dynamically by changing the parameters of the quantizer. We refer to this region which is covered by only bounded quantization regions as the unsaturated region. Our controller follows the general framework which was introduced in several previous papers to achieve disturbance rejection using dynamic quantization. This framework consists of two main modes of operation, generally referred to as a "*zoom-in*" and a "*zoom-out*" mode. During the *zoom-out* mode the unsaturated region is enlarged until the measured output is captured in this region and a bound on the estimation error can be established. This is followed by a switch to the *zoom-in* mode. During the *zoom-in* mode the size of the quantization regions is reduced in order to have the state estimate converge to the true state. The reduction of the size of the quantization regions inevitably reduces the size of the unsaturated region. As the size of this region is reduced, eventually the unknown disturbance will drive the measured output outside the unsaturated region. To regain a bounded estimation error, the controller will switch back to the *zoom-out* mode. By switching repeatedly between these two modes, ISS relation can be established. In this paper we use the name "*capture*" mode for the *zoom-out* mode.

In our quantizer there are $2n_y$ unbounded quantization regions. If each sensor measures only one dimension of the output subspace, then this setting allows for an independent reading by each sensor. This setting also allows the use of as little as 3 quantization regions per dimension. To achieve the minimum data-rate, however, we are required to use the unbounded regions not only to detect saturation (as is done in previous papers), but also to reduce the estimation error. Consider for example the case of only 3 quantization regions for each dimension. In this case there is only one bounded region which can not be used by itself to reduce the estimation error. This dual use is done by dividing the *zoom-in* mode into two modes: a "*measurement-update*" mode and an "*escape-detection*" mode. After receiving r successive measurements in bounded quantization regions, where r is the observability index, and assuming there are no disturbances, we are able to define a containment region in the state space which must contain the state. We enlarge this region by a constant to accommodate some disturbance. In the *measurement-update* mode we cover this containment region using both the bounded and the unbounded regions of the quantizer. This way we are able to use the smallest quantization regions, which leads to the fastest reduction in the estimation error. The "problem" with this mode is that if a strong disturbance comes in, we will not be able to detect it. Therefore, in the *escape-detection* mode we use larger quantization regions, but cover the containment region using only the bounded regions. Thus, if a strong disturbance does come in, we will be able to detect it as it will drive the measured output to one of the unbounded regions.

The precise details on how to design to controller are given in the next section.

4 Controller Design

We define the sampled-time versions of A, $\boldsymbol{u}$ and $\boldsymbol{w}$ as:

$$A_d \doteq \exp\left(T_s A\right), \qquad \boldsymbol{u}_d\left(k\right) \doteq \int_0^{T_s} \exp\left(A\left(T_s - t\right)\right) B\boldsymbol{u}\left(kT_s + t\right) dt,$$

$$\boldsymbol{w}_d\left(k\right) \doteq \int_0^{T_s} \exp\left(A\left(T_s - t\right)\right) D\boldsymbol{w}\left(kT_s + t\right) dt,$$

so we can write $\boldsymbol{x}\left(\left(k+1\right)T_s\right) = A_d\boldsymbol{x}\left(kT_s\right) + \boldsymbol{u}_d(k) + \boldsymbol{w}_d(k)$. We assumed that A and B are a controllable pair, so there exists a control gain K such that $A+BK$ is Hurwitz. By construction A_d is full rank, and in general (unless T_s belongs to some set of measure zero) the observability of A and C implies that A_d and C are an observable pair. Thus there exists r such that:

$$\widetilde{C} \doteq \begin{pmatrix} CA_d^{-r+1} \\ \vdots \\ CA_d^{-1} \\ C \end{pmatrix} = \begin{pmatrix} C \\ CA_d \\ \vdots \\ CA_d^{r-1} \end{pmatrix} A_d^{-r+1} \tag{4}$$

has full column rank.

Our controller consists of three elements: an observer which generates a state estimate; a switching logic which sets the parameters for the quantizer and for the observer; and a stabilizing control law which computes the control input based on a state estimate. For simplicity of presentation, we assume the stabilizing control law is a simple static gain given by K. However, any control law that will render the closed-loop system ISS with respect to the disturbance and the estimation error, will work with our controller. Note that it is sufficient for K to be such that $A+BK$ is Hurwitz in order to satisfy this ISS requirement. In the next subsection we present a general structure for an observer, and specify the properties it is required to satisfy. In subsection 4.2 we present the algorithm for the switching logic and state our main theorem.

4.1 Desired Observer Properties

The first element in our control system is the observer. The observer is required to generate an estimate of the state based on current and previous quantized measurements. We assume that the observer is linear, and that there exists a sequence of linear gains, G_0, G_1, …, G_{d-1}, $d > r$, where $G_k \in \mathbb{R}^{n_x \times (k+r)n_y}$, such that the state estimate can be written for $k \in \{0 \ldots d-1\}$ as:

$$\hat{\boldsymbol{x}}_u(k_0+k) = G_k \begin{bmatrix} \boldsymbol{z}(k_0-r+1) + C\sum_{i=1}^{k+r-1} A_d^{-i}\boldsymbol{u}_d(k_0-r+i) \\ \vdots \\ \boldsymbol{z}(k_0+k-1) + CA_d^{-1}\boldsymbol{u}_d(k_0+k-1) \\ \boldsymbol{z}(k_0+k) \end{bmatrix}.$$

Note that we must have at least r successive measurements to generate a state estimate. Therefore, (5) is defined only for $k_0 \geq r-1$. We use the subscript u to indicate that $\hat{\boldsymbol{x}}_u(k)$ is our estimate of $\boldsymbol{x}(k)$ based on measurements up to $\boldsymbol{z}(k)$. We will later also use the subscript p to indicate that $\hat{\boldsymbol{x}}_p(k)$ is our estimate of $\boldsymbol{x}(k)$ based on measurements up to $\boldsymbol{z}(k-1)$. The subscripts u and p stand for *update* and *predict*, respectively, which are common notations in the Kalman filter. We denote the quantization error by $\boldsymbol{e}_q(k) \doteq \boldsymbol{z}(k) - \boldsymbol{y}(k)$ and the state estimation error by $\boldsymbol{e}_x(k) \doteq \hat{\boldsymbol{x}}_u(k) - \boldsymbol{x}(kT_s)$.

The first requirement for our approach to succeed is that the linear gains $G_0, G_1, \ldots, G_d$ are such that if no disturbance is injected into the system, and $\boldsymbol{e}_q \equiv 0$, then the state estimate is exact: $\boldsymbol{e}_x \equiv 0$. In the presence of estimation errors, $\boldsymbol{e}_q \neq 0$, and bounded disturbances, the state estimate cannot be exact, but we will need it to converge to the true state. This is achieved by having $\mu(k+d) < \mu(k)$. We cannot, however, decrease μ arbitrarily, since we need the quantization regions to cover the projection of the containment region into the output subspace. The containment region is the region where we expect the state to be based on previous measurements, and given that the disturbances are small enough. If at time sample $k-1$ the gain G_p was used then at time sample k the radius (in ∞-norm) of the projection of this containment region is given by $F(\mu, k, p) + \alpha \|\mu\|_{\{k-p-r\ldots k-p-1\}}$. F (see (6) below for a precise definiton) is the radius if there are no disturbances, and α is used as a "slack" for the disturbance. Note that the only variable on which this radius depends is μ, and the dependence is linear. Thus we can arbitrarily choose the initial values of μ in order to verify if we get convergence. The requirement is thus formulated as follows: there exist $\alpha \in \mathbb{R}_{>0}$ and $\sigma < 1$ ($\sigma \in \mathbb{R}_{>0}$) such that if we set

$$\begin{aligned} \mu'(k) &= 1, && k \in \{0\ldots r-1\} \\ \mu'(k) &= \frac{F(\mu'; k; k-r) + \alpha}{N}, && k \in \{r \ldots d-1\} \\ \mu'(k) &= \frac{F(\mu'; k; k-r) + \alpha}{N-2}, && k \in \{d \ldots d+r-1\}, \end{aligned} \tag{5}$$

where

$$F(\mu; k; p) \doteq \max_{i\in\{1\ldots n_x\}} \sum_{l=-r}^{p-1} \sum_{m=1}^{n_y} \left|(CA_dG_p)_{i,(l+r)n_y+m}\right| \mu(k-p+l). \tag{6}$$

then

$$\|\mu'\|_{k\in\{d\ldots d+r-1\}} \leq \sigma. \tag{7}$$

The first line in (5) corresponds to our arbitrary choice of initial values for μ. The second and third lines correspond to the minimal possible value for μ in the *measurement-update* mode and in the *escape-detection* mode, respectively. If the observer satisfies this second requirement for some α, we say that it has the *convergence property* for this α. Note that if it has this property for some α_0 then it will have it for all $\alpha < \alpha_0$. Note also that it is possible to satisfy this requirement just by increasing N sufficiently.

4.2 Switching Logic

The controller will operate in one of three modes which will be determined by the switching logic: *capture*, *measurement update* or *escape detection*. The initial mode will be *capture*. The current mode will be stored in the variable $mode(k) \in \{capture, update, detect\}$. The controller will also use[3] $\hat{\boldsymbol{x}}_p(k) \in \mathbb{R}^{n_x}$, $\hat{\boldsymbol{x}}_u(k) \in \mathbb{R}^{n_x}$, $\hat{\boldsymbol{x}}(t) \in \mathbb{R}^{n_x}$, $p(k) \in \mathbb{Z}$ and $saturated \in \{true, false\}$ as auxiliary variables. We initialize $\hat{\boldsymbol{x}}_p(0) = \mathbf{0}$. The initial value of $\mu(0)$, the zoom factor for the quantizer, can be any positive value and it will be regarded as a design parameter. The controller will also have three other design parameters: $\alpha \in \mathbb{R}_{>0}$, $s \in \mathbb{R}_{>0}$, and $\Omega_{\text{out}} \in \mathbb{R}$, $\Omega_{\text{out}} > \|A\|$. With a slight abuse of notation we define:

$$G(\boldsymbol{z}; \boldsymbol{u}_d; k; p) \doteq G_p \begin{bmatrix} \boldsymbol{z}(k-r-p+1) + C\sum_{i=1}^{p+r-1} A_d^{-i}\boldsymbol{u}_d(k-r-p+i) \\ \vdots \\ \boldsymbol{z}(k-1) + CA_d^{-1}\boldsymbol{u}_d(k-1) \\ \boldsymbol{z}(k) \end{bmatrix}.$$

At each time sample, k, the following switching logic will be executed:

---

1. Preliminaries

if $mode(k) = capture$ **then**
  set $\mu_k = \Omega_{out}\mu_{k-1}$
else if $mode(k) = update$ **then**
  set

$$\mu_k = \frac{F(\mu; k; p(k-1)) + \alpha\|\mu\|_{\{k-r-p(k-1)\ldots k-1-p(k-1)\}}}{N} \tag{8}$$

else if $mode(k) = detect$ **then**
  set

$$\mu_k = \frac{F(\mu; k; p(k-1)) + \alpha\|\mu\|_{\{k-r-p(k-1)\ldots k-1-p(k-1)\}}}{N-2} \tag{9}$$

end if
have the observer record $\boldsymbol{z}(k) = Q(\boldsymbol{y}(k); C\hat{\boldsymbol{x}}_p(k), \mu_k)$
if $\exists i$ such that $\boldsymbol{z}_i(k) = (C\hat{\boldsymbol{x}}_p(k))_i \pm (N-1)\mu_k$ **then**
  set $saturated(k) =$ **true**
else
  set $saturated(k) =$ **false**
end if
by default the mode will not change – set $mode(k+1) = mode(k)$

---

[3] The distinction between $\hat{\boldsymbol{x}}_u$, $\hat{\boldsymbol{x}}_p$ and $\hat{\boldsymbol{x}}$ is only to make the proofs easier to read. The controller can be implemented using just one variable.

2. *capture* mode

if $mode(k) = capture$ **then**
  if $saturated(k)$ **then**
    set $p(k) = 0$ and use the observer to update $\hat{\boldsymbol{x}}_u(k) = \hat{\boldsymbol{x}}_p(k)$
  else
    set $p(k) = p(k-1) + 1$
    if $p(k) = r$ **then**
      set $p(k) = 0$ and use the observer to compute $\hat{\boldsymbol{x}}_u(k) = G(\boldsymbol{z}; \boldsymbol{u}_d; k; 0)$
      switch to the *measurement update* mode: set $mode(k+1) = update$
    else
      use the observer to update $\hat{\boldsymbol{x}}_u(k) = \hat{\boldsymbol{x}}_p(k)$
    end if
  end if
end if

3. *measurement update* mode

if $mode(k) = update$ **then**
  set $p(k) = p(k-1)+1$ and use the observer to compute $\hat{\boldsymbol{x}}_u(k) = G(\boldsymbol{z}; \boldsymbol{u}_d; k; p(k))$
  if $p(k) = d - r$ **then**
    switch to the *escape detection* mode: set $mode(k+1) = detect$
  end if
end if

4. *escape detection* mode

if $mode(k) = detect$ **then**
  if not $saturated(k)$ **then**
    set $p(k) = p(k-1) + 1$
    if $p(k) < d$ **then**
      use the observer to compute $\hat{\boldsymbol{x}}_u(k) = G(\boldsymbol{z}; \boldsymbol{u}_d; k; p(k))$
    else
      set $p(k) = 0$ and use the observer to compute $\hat{\boldsymbol{x}}_u(k) = G(\boldsymbol{z}; \boldsymbol{u}_d; k; 0)$
      switch to the *measurement update* mode: set $mode(k+1) = update$
    end if
  else
    set $p(k) = 0$, $\mu(k) = s$ and use the observer to update $\hat{\boldsymbol{x}}_u(k) = \hat{\boldsymbol{x}}_p(k)$
    switch to *capture* mode: set $mode(k+1) = capture$
  end if
end if

Between the time samples the following will be executed:

5. Control input generation

use the observer to update $\hat{\boldsymbol{x}}(kT_s) = \hat{\boldsymbol{x}}_u(k)$; $\boldsymbol{u}_d(k) = 0$
for $t \in [0, T_s)$ **do**
use the stabilizing control law to set the control action $\boldsymbol{u}(kT_s + t) = K\hat{\boldsymbol{x}}(kT_s + t)$
use the observer to update:

$$\begin{aligned}\dot{\hat{\boldsymbol{x}}}(kT_s + t) &= A\hat{\boldsymbol{x}}(kT_s + t) + B\boldsymbol{u}\left(kT_s + t\right)\\ \dot{\boldsymbol{u}}_d(k) &= \exp\left(A\left(T_s - t\right)\right) B\boldsymbol{u}\left(kT_s + t\right)\end{aligned}$$

end for
use the observer to update $\hat{\boldsymbol{x}}_p\left(k+1\right) = \lim_{t \nearrow T_s} \hat{\boldsymbol{x}}\left(kT_s + t\right)$

We are now ready to state our main result (see the last paragraph in §1 for a reference to the proof):

Theorem 1. *Consider the system* (1). *If we implement the controller with the algorithm above, and the observer has the convergence property for the α chosen for the implementation, then the closed-loop system will be input-to-state stable with respect to the disturbances.*

An illustrative simulation of this controller is given in figure 2.

5 Observer Examples

In §4.1 we gave a somewhat cumbersome definition for an observer. The reason was to allow for our approach to be implemented with a wide range of observers. In this section we give two examples of observers for which our definition is valid.

5.1 Pseudo-Inverse Observer

Perhaps the most obvious observer is the pseudo-inverse observer[4]:

$$G_0 = \left(\widetilde{C}^T\widetilde{C}\right)^{-1}\widetilde{C}^T, \qquad G_i = \left[0_{n_x \times n_y} \mid G_{i-1}\right], \quad \forall i \in \{1 \ldots d-1\} \qquad (10)$$

where $\widetilde{C}$ is defined in (4). Since our assumption is that $\widetilde{C}$ has full column rank, then $G_0\widetilde{C} = I$, the identity matrix. Thus if no disturbance is injected into the system, and there is no quantization error, then indeed the state estimate will be exact. This satisfies the first requirement from §4.1. A sufficient condition for this observer to satisfy the second requirement from §4.1 is

$$\sigma_{pi} \doteq \frac{1}{N}\left\|CA_dG_0\right\| < 1. \qquad (11)$$

To see that indeed this condition is sufficient note first that from (6):

[4] $0_{n_x \times n_y}$ is the zero matrix of dimension $n_x \times n_y$.

$$F(\mu;k;k-r)=\max_{i\in\{1\dots n_x\}}\sum_{l=k-2r}^{k-r-1}\sum_{m=1}^{n_y}\left|(CA_dG_0)_{i,(l+2r-k)n_y+m}\right|\mu(r+l)$$
$$\le\left(\max_{i\in\{1\dots n_x\}}\sum_{m=1}^{n_yr}\left|(CA_dG_0)_{i,m}\right|\right)\|\mu\|_{k-r\dots k-1}=\|CA_dG_0\|\,\|\mu\|_{k-r\dots k-1},$$

so that

$$\frac{F(\mu';k;k-r)+\alpha}{N}\le\sigma_{pi}\|\mu'\|_{k-r\dots k-1}+\frac{\alpha}{N}. \tag{12}$$

Assume d is a multiple of r and α satisfies $\sigma_{pi}+\frac{a}{N}\le 1$ so that $\forall l\in\mathbb{N}$: $\sigma_{pi}^{l+1}+\sum_{m=0}^{l}\sigma_{pi}^{m}\frac{\alpha}{N}\le\sigma_{pi}^{l}+\sum_{m=0}^{l-1}\sigma_{pi}^{m}\frac{\alpha}{N}$. With these assumptions, and from (12) we have by induction that for all $l\in\{1\dots d/r-1\}$:

$$\|\mu'\|_{lr\dots(l+1)r-1}\le\sigma_{pi}^{l}+\sum_{m=0}^{l-1}\sigma_{pi}^{m}\frac{\alpha}{N}\doteq V(l)\qquad\text{and}$$
$$\|\mu'\|_{d-r\dots d-1}\le\max\left\{\frac{N}{N-2}\sigma_{pi}V(d/r-1)+\frac{\alpha}{N-2},\right.$$
$$\left.\left(\frac{N}{N-2}\sigma_{pi}\right)^{r}V(d/r-1)+\sum_{m=0}^{r-1}\left(\frac{N}{N-2}\sigma_{pi}\right)^{m}\frac{\alpha}{N-2}\right\}$$

It can now be easily seen that by taking d to be large enough, and α to be small enough, we can make $\|\mu'\|_{d-r\dots d-1}<1$ which satisfies the convergence property.

5.2 Luenberger-Type Observer

Another commonly used observer for unquantized, output feedback systems is the Luenberger observer:

$$\hat{\boldsymbol{x}}(k+1)=A_d\hat{\boldsymbol{x}}(k)+\boldsymbol{u}_d(k)+L(\boldsymbol{y}(k)-C\hat{\boldsymbol{x}}(k)), \tag{13}$$

where $L\in\mathbb{R}^{n_x\times n_y}$ is chosen so that A_d-LC is Schur[5]. Given that A_d and C are an observable pair, such an L is guaranteed to exist. Since the Luenberger observer requires some initialization, we can use G_0 as in the pseudo-inverse observer (10). We can then replace in the algorithm all the computations of the state estimate, $\hat{\boldsymbol{x}}_u(k)=G(\boldsymbol{z};\boldsymbol{u}_d;k;p)$, when $p>0$, with

$$\hat{\boldsymbol{x}}_u(k)=\hat{\boldsymbol{x}}_p(k)+L(\boldsymbol{z}(k-1)-C\hat{\boldsymbol{x}}_u(k-1)).$$

Using this alternative is equivalent to using

$$G_i=\left[*\,|\,(A_d-LC)^{i-2}L\,|\dots|\,L\,|\,0_{n_x\times n_y}\right],\qquad i\in\{1\dots d-1\} \tag{14}$$

where

$$*\doteq(A_d-LC)^{i}G_0+\left[0_{n_x\times(r-1)n_y}\,|\,(A_d-LC)^{i-1}L\right].$$

[5] All the eigenvalues of a Schur matrix are inside the unit ball on the complex plane. This is the discrete counterpart to a Hurwitz matrix.

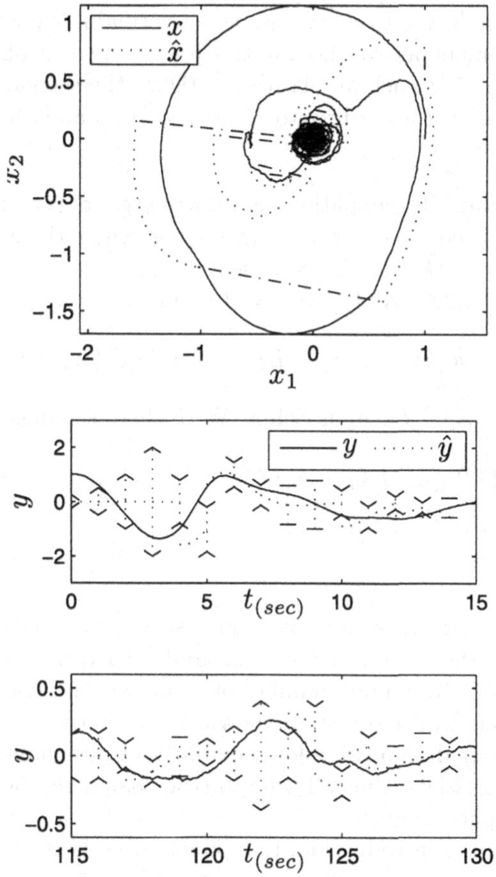

Fig. 2. Simulation of the proposed controller. Simulated here is a two dimensional dynamical system: $\dot{\boldsymbol{x}}(t) = [0.1, -1; 1, 0.1]\, \boldsymbol{x}(t) + [0; 1]\, \boldsymbol{u}(t) + [1, 0; 0, 1]\, \boldsymbol{w}(t)$, where only the first dimension is observed, $\boldsymbol{y}(k) = [0, 1]\, \boldsymbol{x}(kT_s)$, through a quantizer with $N = 3$. The solid line in the left plot is the trajectory of the system (starting at $\boldsymbol{x}(0) = [1; 0]$). The dotted line in that plot is the state estimate. The dashed-dot lines represent the jumps in the state estimate after a new measurement is received. The top right plot shows the first 15 seconds of the measured output ($T_s = 1s$). The vertical dotted lines depict the only one bounded quantization region. The controller is in the *capture* mode where these vertical lines are bounded by arrows facing outward; in the *update* mode where the arrows are facing inward; and in the *detect* mode where the vertical lines are bounded by small horizontal lines. The bottom right plot shows 15 seconds of the steady-state behavior of the simulation, where an escape of the trajectory due to disturbances is detected at $t = 119s$, and then the trajectory is recaptured at $t = 122s$. The pseudo-inverse observer (see §5.1) was used in this simulation. The other design parameters were: $d = 6$, $\mu(0) = 0.25$, $\Omega_{out} = 2$, $\alpha = 0.02$, $s = 0.05$, $K = [0.6, -1.5]$. The disturbances followed the zero-mean normal distribution with standard deviation of 0.2.

Remark 1. This observer will satisfy the first requirement from §4.1. However, we have not been able yet to derive an easily verifiable sufficient condition for the second requirement as we did for the pseudo-inverse observer with (11). Therefore, to verify that such an observer satisfies the second requirement, one has to generate the μ''s according to (5) using (14), and then verify that (7) holds.

Remark 2. The standard formulation for a Luenberger observer is (13). However, note that when we need to construct $\hat{\boldsymbol{x}}_u(k+1)$, on which the control inputs from $t = (k+1)T_s$ to $t = (k+2)T_s$ are based, we already have the measurement $\boldsymbol{z}(k+1)$. Therefore, instead of (13) it will be better to use

$$\hat{\boldsymbol{x}}(k+1) = A_d\hat{\boldsymbol{x}}(k) + \boldsymbol{u}_d(k) + L\left(\boldsymbol{y}(k+1) - C\left(A_d\hat{\boldsymbol{x}}(k) + \boldsymbol{u}_d(k)\right)\right),$$

which requires that $A_d - LCA_d$ is Schur. With these settings (14) becomes:

$$G_i = \left[(A_d - A_dLC)^i G_0 \mid (A_d - A_dLC)^{i-1} L \mid \ldots \mid L\right], \qquad i \in \{1 \ldots d-1\}.$$

6 Conclusion

In this paper we showed how to implement a stabilizing controller when only a partial subspace of the state space is measured, and furthermore the measurements are quantized with a finite number of quantization regions. The controller is also robust, in the ISS sense, to unknown disturbance which can be injected to the system. In our design, we allow flexibility in designing the observer and the stabilizing control law, thus allowing further balancing between ease of implementation and performance.

As mentioned in the introduction, this paper extends the results in [15] from the state-feedback scenario to the output-feedback scenario. Future developments will be to extend the results further to systems with delays and nonlinear systems.

Acknowledgments

We are grateful to the anonymous reviewers for their constructive comments.

References

1. Miller, R.K., Mousa, M.S., Michel, A.N.: Quantization and overflow effects in digital implementaitions of linear dynamic controllers. IEEE Trans. Automat. Control 33, 698–704 (1988)
2. Delchamps, D.F.: Stabilizing a linear system with quantized state feedback. IEEE Trans. Automat. Control 35(8), 916–924 (1990)
3. Brockett, R.W., Liberzon, D.: Quantized feedback stabilization of linear systems. IEEE Trans. Automat. Control 45(7), 1279–1280 (2000)

4. Sontag, E.D.: Smooth stabilization implies coprime factorization. IEEE Trans. Automat. Control 34, 435–443 (1989)
5. Jiang, Z.P., Wang, Y.: Input-to-state stability for discrete-time nonlinear systems. Automatica 37, 857–869 (2001)
6. Petersen, I.R., Savkin, A.V.: Multi-rate stabilization of multivariable discrete-time linear systems via a limited capacity communication channel. In: Proc. 40th IEEE Conf. on Decision and Control, pp. 304–309 (2001)
7. Liberzon, D.: On stabilization of linear systems with limited information. IEEE Trans. Automat. Control 48(2), 304–307 (2003)
8. Nair, G.N., Evans, R.J., Mareels, I.M.Y., Moran, W.: Topological feedback entropy and nonlinear stabilization. IEEE Trans. Automat. Control 49(9), 1585–1597 (2004)
9. Liberzon, D., Hespanha, J.P.: Stabilization of nonlinear systems with limited information feedback. IEEE Trans. Automat. Control 50(6), 910–915 (2005)
10. Hespanha, J.P., Ortega, A., Vasudevan, L.: Towards the control of linear systems with minimum bit-rate. In: Proc. 15th Int. Symp. on Mathematical Theory of Networks and Systems (MTNS) (2002)
11. Tatikonda, S., Mitter, S.: Control under communication constraints. IEEE Trans. Automat. Control 49(7), 1056–1068 (2004)
12. Nair, G.N., Evans, R.J.: Stabilizability of stochastic linear systems with finite feedback data rates. SIAM J. Control Optim. 43(2), 413–436 (2004)
13. Matveev, A.S., Savkin, A.V.: Stabilization of stochastic linear plants via limited capacity stochasitc communication channel. In: Proc. 45th IEEE Conf. on Decision and Control, pp. 484–489 (2006)
14. Liberzon, D., Nesic, D.: Input-to-state stabilization of linear systems with quantized state measurements. IEEE Trans. Automat. Control 52(5), 767–781 (2007)
15. Sharon, Y., Liberzon, D.: Input-to-state stabilization with minimum number of quantization regions. In: Proc. 46th IEEE Conf. on Decision and Control (2007)
16. Hespanha, J.P., Liberzon, D., Teel, A.R.: Lyapunov characterizations of input-to-state stability for impulsive systems. Automatica (to appear)

Bisimilar Finite Abstractions of Interconnected Systems

Yuichi Tazaki and Jun-ichi Imura

Tokyo Institute of Technology,
Ōokayama 2-12-1, Meguro, Tokyo, Japan
{tazaki, imura}@cyb.mei.titech.ac.jp
http://www.cyb.mei.titech.ac.jp

Abstract. This paper addresses the design of approximately bisimilar finite abstractions of systems that are composed of the interconnection of smaller subsystems. First, it is shown that the ordinary notion of approximate bisimulation does not preserve the interconnection structure of the concrete model. Next, a new definition of approximate bisimulation that is compatible with interconnection is proposed. Based on this definition of approximate bisimulation, the design of interconnection-compatible finite abstractions of linear subsystems is discussed.

1 Introduction

Discrete abstractions simplify concrete continuous systems by cutting off the details, while preserving the essential characteristics. Moreover, it reduces the computational cost of numerical methods such as reachability analysis and controller synthesis. During this decade, there have been a variety of researches on this topic. Lafferriere et al [1] investigated a class of autonomous planar hybrid systems with finite bisimulations. Alur et al [2] presented algorithms for reachability analysis of hybrid systems by combining the notion of predicate abstraction with polytopic approximation of reachable sets. Lunze [3] considered continuous-time, continuous-state systems that can only be observed through discrete events triggered when the state hits one of the boundaries placed on the state space, and modeled the occurrence of discrete-event sequences as stochastic automata. Tsumura [4] considered systems whose state is stored in a digital memory and analyzed the relation between necessary bit-length to achieve a certain bound on input-to-output approximation error, and systems properties such as stability.

Recently, there has been several researches on finite-state abstractions using the notion of approximate bisimulation [6], which is an extension of the classical bisimulation. Girard [7] derived a procedure for constructing approximately bisimilar finite abstractions of stable discrete-time linear systems. Tabuada [8] addressed a design of approximately similar finite abstractions of continuous-time nonlinear dynamical systems under a certain stabilizability assumption. Tazaki [12] discussed the application of approximate bisimilar abstractions to optimal control problems.

M. Egerstedt and B. Mishra (Eds.): HSCC 2008, LNCS 4981, pp. 514–527, 2008.

To date, these approaches on discrete abstractions have been successful only to systems of a relatively small size. This is mainly due to the fact that the number of the state of discrete abstractions often grows exponentially with respect to the state dimension of the concrete system. If one knows the internal interconnection structure of a complex system, it is natural to take advantage of such knowledge to reduce the complexity of the computation of the abstraction process and that of the resultant abstraction itself. Tabuada et al [9] discussed the relation between bisimulations and compositional operators in a general setting. They showed that for a concrete system given by a composition of subsystems, there exists a bisimilar abstraction that is expressed as a composition of bisimilar abstractions of subsystems. Julius et al [11] addressed approximate syncronization and showed that approximate (bi)simulation is preserved under approximate syncronization. However, in the case of input-output interconnection, which is a special class of composition, the interconnection structure of the concrete system is not in general preserved in its abstraction. This means that, under the conventional bisimulation, one cannot simply interconnect the abstractions of subsystems to construct an abstraction of the original interconnected system.

In this research, motivated by the above background, we propose a new variant of approximate bisimulation that is compatible with interconnected systems. Furthermore, based on the proposed interconnection-compatible bisimulation, the design of finite abstractions of linear subsystems is developed.

The rest of this paper is organized as follows. In Section 2, we define the basic form of discrete-time dynamical systems treated in this paper, and the notion of approximate simulation and approximate bisimulation on this class of systems. In Section 3, after introducing the framework of input-output interconnected systems, we show with a simple example that the ordinary approximate bisimulation does not preserve the interconnection structure. To overcome this problem, we propose a new notion of approximate bisimulation that is compatible with interconnection. In Section 4 we discuss the finite abstraction problem of linear subsystems, according to the definition of approximate bisimulation introduced in Section 3. Section 5 concludes this paper with some remarks for future works.

Notation: The symbol $[\boldsymbol{v}_1; \boldsymbol{v}_2; ...; \boldsymbol{v}_N]$ denotes the vertical concatenation of vectors or that of matrices, which is equivalent to $[\boldsymbol{v}_1^{\mathrm{T}}\ \boldsymbol{v}_2^{\mathrm{T}}\ \ldots\ \boldsymbol{v}_N^{\mathrm{T}}]^{\mathrm{T}}$. Throughout the paper, the symbol $\|\cdot\|$ denotes the 2-norm unless otherwise stated. Moreover, the symbol $\|\boldsymbol{v}\|_M$ is defined as $\sqrt{\boldsymbol{v}^{\mathrm{T}} M \boldsymbol{v}}$. For matrices, $\|A\|$ denotes the largest singular value of A.

2 Approximate Simulations and Bisimulations of Discrete-Time Dynamical Systems

In this section, we introduce the definition of approximate (bi)simulation on a class of discrete-time dynamical systems. Let us first define the basic form of discrete-time dynamical systems.

Definition 1. *Discrete-time dynamical system*
A discrete-time dynamical system (or simply a system) is a 5-tuple $\langle X, U, Y, f, h \rangle$*, where* $X \subset \mathbb{R}^n$ *is the set of states,* $U \subset \mathbb{R}^m$ *is the set of inputs,* $Y \subset \mathbb{R}^l$ *is the set of outputs,* $f : X \times U \mapsto X$ *is the state transition function, and* $h : X \times U \mapsto Y$ *is the measurement function. The state, input, and output of the system at time* $t \in \mathcal{T} = \{0\} \cup \mathbb{N}$ *are expressed as* $\boldsymbol{x}_t \in X$*,* $\boldsymbol{u}_t \in U$*, and* $\boldsymbol{y}_t \in Y$*, respectively. The state transition and the measurement at time* t *are expressed as*

$$\boldsymbol{x}(t+1) = f(\boldsymbol{x}(t), \boldsymbol{u}(t)), \tag{1}$$

$$\boldsymbol{y}(t) = h(\boldsymbol{x}(t), \boldsymbol{u}(t)), \tag{2}$$

respectively.

Throughout this paper, we use the symbol $\Sigma\langle X, U, Y, f, h \rangle$ or simply Σ to express a system. Let us introduce the notion of approximate simulation and approximate bisimulation on the class of systems just defined.

Definition 2. *Approximate simulation of dynamical systems*
Consider two systems $\Sigma\langle X, U, Y, f, h \rangle$*,* $\hat{\Sigma}\langle \hat{X}, \hat{U}, Y, \hat{f}, \hat{h} \rangle$ *and positive constant* ϵ*. A binary relation* $R \subset X \times \hat{X}$ *is called an* ϵ*-approximate simulation relation from* Σ *to* $\hat{\Sigma}$ *if and only if for every* $(\boldsymbol{x}, \hat{\boldsymbol{x}}) \in R$*, the following holds:*
for all $\boldsymbol{u} \in U$*, there exists a* $\hat{\boldsymbol{u}} \in \hat{U}$ *such that*

$$\|h(\boldsymbol{x}, \boldsymbol{u}) - \hat{h}(\hat{\boldsymbol{x}}, \hat{\boldsymbol{u}})\| \leq \epsilon, \tag{3}$$

$$(f(\boldsymbol{x}, \boldsymbol{u}), \hat{f}(\hat{\boldsymbol{x}}, \hat{\boldsymbol{u}})) \in R. \tag{4}$$

Moreover, if such an R *exists,* $\hat{\Sigma}$ *is said to be approximately similar to* Σ *with respect to* R *and the precision* ϵ*.*

Definition 3. *Approximate bisimulation of dynamical systems*
Consider two systems $\Sigma\langle X, U, Y, f, h \rangle$*,* $\hat{\Sigma}\langle \hat{X}, \hat{U}, Y, \hat{f}, \hat{h} \rangle$ *and positive constant* ϵ*. A binary relation* $R \subset X \times \hat{X}$ *is called an* ϵ*-approximate bisimulation relation between* Σ *and* $\hat{\Sigma}$ *if and only if* R *is an* ϵ*-approximate simulation relation from* Σ *to* $\hat{\Sigma}$ *and its inverse relation* $R^{-1} = \{(\hat{\boldsymbol{x}}, \boldsymbol{x}) \mid (\boldsymbol{x}, \hat{\boldsymbol{x}}) \in R\}$ *is an* ϵ*-approximate simulation relation from* $\hat{\Sigma}$ *to* Σ*. Moreover, if such an* R *exists,* Σ *and* $\hat{\Sigma}$ *are said to be approximately bisimilar with respect to* R *and the precision* ϵ*, and this relation is denoted by* $\Sigma \sim_\epsilon \hat{\Sigma}$*.*

The major difference between the above definitions and those introduced in the literature (see [6], for example) is that the measurement variable of dynamical systems depend not only on states but also on control inputs, and therefore the definitions of approximate (bi)simulation are extended accordingly.

3 Approximate Bisimulation of Interconnected Systems

3.1 Expression of Interconnected Systems

This subsection introduces the general expression of interconnected systems treated in this paper. Consider a complex system composed of N subsystems

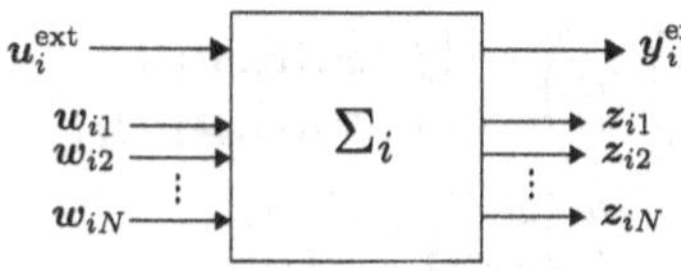

(a) i-th subsystem of interconnected system.

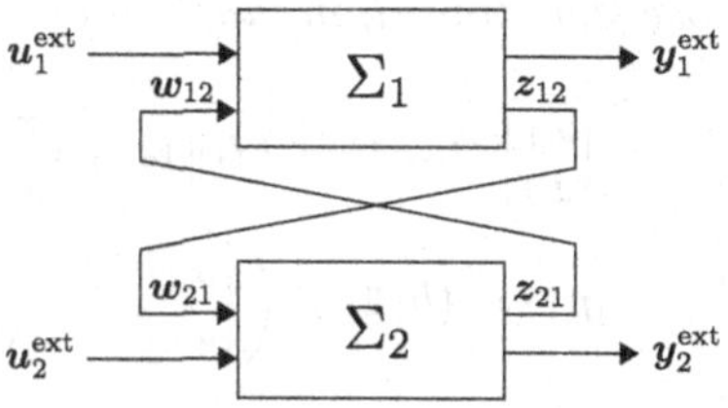

(b) Interconnection of two sub-systems.

Fig. 1. Schematics of interconnected system

interconnected with each other. The i-th subsystem is described as

$$\Sigma_i\langle X_i, U_i, Y_i, f_i, h_i\rangle.$$

Here, the input variable $\boldsymbol{u}_i \in U_i$ and the output variable $\boldsymbol{y}_i \in Y_i$ are decomposed into subvectors as shown below.

$$\boldsymbol{u}_i = \left[\boldsymbol{u}_i^{\text{ext}}; \boldsymbol{w}_i\right], \quad \boldsymbol{w}_i = \begin{cases} \left[\boldsymbol{w}_{i2}; \ldots; \boldsymbol{w}_{iN}\right] & (i=1) \\ \left[\boldsymbol{w}_{i1}; \ldots; \boldsymbol{w}_{i,N-1}\right] & (i=N) \\ \left[\boldsymbol{w}_{i1}; \ldots; \boldsymbol{w}_{i,i-1}; \boldsymbol{w}_{i,i+1}; \ldots; \boldsymbol{w}_{iN}\right] & \text{otherwise.} \end{cases} \tag{5}$$

$$\boldsymbol{y}_i = \left[\boldsymbol{y}_i^{\text{ext}}; \boldsymbol{z}_i\right], \quad \boldsymbol{z}_i = \begin{cases} \left[\boldsymbol{z}_{i2}; \ldots; \boldsymbol{z}_{iN}\right] & (i=1) \\ \left[\boldsymbol{z}_{i1}; \ldots; \boldsymbol{z}_{i,N-1}\right] & (i=N) \\ \left[\boldsymbol{z}_{i1}; \ldots; \boldsymbol{z}_{i,i-1}; \boldsymbol{z}_{i,i+1}; \ldots; \boldsymbol{z}_{iN}\right] & \text{otherwise.} \end{cases} \tag{6}$$

Each subsystem has two groups of input signals ($\boldsymbol{u}_i^{\text{ext}}$ and $\boldsymbol{w}_i$) and two groups of output signals ($\boldsymbol{y}_i^{\text{ext}}$ and $\boldsymbol{z}_i$). The signals $\boldsymbol{w}_i$ and $\boldsymbol{z}_i$ are *internal signals*, used to construct interconnections between other subsystems. On the other hand, $\boldsymbol{u}_i^{\text{ext}}$ and $\boldsymbol{y}_i^{\text{ext}}$ are *external signals*, which compose, together with those of other subsystems, the input/output interface of the whole interconnected system.

Here, for simplicity of discussion, we introduce the following assumption to ensure that the interconnected system is well-posed.

Assumption 1. *The internal output variables at time t, $\boldsymbol{z}_i(t)$, are independent of the internal input variables at time t, $\boldsymbol{w}_i(t)$.*

The measurement function is then decomposed as

$$\boldsymbol{y}_i = \begin{bmatrix} \boldsymbol{y}_i^{\text{ext}} \\ \boldsymbol{z}_i \end{bmatrix} = \begin{bmatrix} h_i^y(\boldsymbol{x}_i, \boldsymbol{u}_i^{\text{ext}}, \boldsymbol{w}_i) \\ h_i^z(\boldsymbol{x}_i, \boldsymbol{u}_i^{\text{ext}}) \end{bmatrix}. \tag{7}$$

We first define the parallel composition of two subsystems.

Definition 4. *Parallel composition*
Suppose two systems $\Sigma_i\langle X_i, U_i, Y_i, f_i, h_i\rangle$ $(i = 1, 2)$ are given. The parallel composition of Σ_1 and Σ_2 is the system $\langle X_1 \times X_2, U_1 \times U_2, Y_1 \times Y_2, f_1 \| f_2, h_1 \| h_2\rangle$

whose state transition function and measurement function are defined as follows.

$$\begin{aligned} \begin{bmatrix} \boldsymbol{x}_1 \\ \boldsymbol{x}_2 \end{bmatrix}(t+1) &= (f_1 \| f_2)\left(\begin{bmatrix} \boldsymbol{x}_1 \\ \boldsymbol{x}_2 \end{bmatrix}(t), \begin{bmatrix} \boldsymbol{u}_1 \\ \boldsymbol{u}_2 \end{bmatrix}(t) \right) = \begin{bmatrix} f_1(\boldsymbol{x}_1(t), \boldsymbol{u}_1(t)) \\ f_2(\boldsymbol{x}_2(t), \boldsymbol{u}_2(t)) \end{bmatrix}, \\ \boldsymbol{y}(t) &= (h_1 \| h_2)\left(\begin{bmatrix} \boldsymbol{x}_1 \\ \boldsymbol{x}_2 \end{bmatrix}(t), \begin{bmatrix} \boldsymbol{u}_1 \\ \boldsymbol{u}_2 \end{bmatrix}(t) \right) = \begin{bmatrix} h_1(\boldsymbol{x}_1(t), \boldsymbol{u}_1(t)) \\ h_2(\boldsymbol{x}_2(t), \boldsymbol{u}_2(t)) \end{bmatrix}. \end{aligned} \tag{8}$$

We denote by $\Sigma_1 \| \Sigma_2$ the parallel composition of Σ_1 and Σ_2. The parallel composition of more than two systems are defined recursively as follows.

$$\Sigma_1 \| \Sigma_2 \| \dots \| \Sigma_N := \Sigma_1 \| (\Sigma_2 \| \dots \| \Sigma_N). \tag{9}$$

The interconnection of subsystems are obtained by imposing restrictions representing the interconnections of the internal signals on their parallel composition.

Definition 5. *Interconnection of subsystems*
Suppose N subsystems $\Sigma_i \langle X_i, U_i, Y_i, f_i, h_i \rangle$ $(i = 1, 2, \dots, N)$, whose input vectors and output vectors are decomposed as in (5) and (6), respectively, are given. Moreover, suppose the size of subvectors $\boldsymbol{w}_{ij}$ and $\boldsymbol{z}_{ji}$ matches for all $i \in \{1, 2, \dots, N\}, j \in \{1, 2, \dots, N\} \backslash \{i\}$. The interconnection of $\Sigma_1, \Sigma_2, \dots,$ and Σ_N, denoted by $\mathcal{I}(\Sigma_1, \Sigma_2, \dots, \Sigma_N)$, is defined as the parallel composition $\Sigma_1 \| \Sigma_2 \| \dots \| \Sigma_N$ subject to the constraints

$$\boldsymbol{w}_{ij} = \boldsymbol{z}_{ji} \ (i \in \{1, 2, \dots, N\}, j \in \{1, 2, \dots, N\} \backslash \{i\}) \tag{10}$$

and whose input and output variables are defined as

$$\bar{\boldsymbol{u}} = \left[\boldsymbol{u}_1^{\mathrm{ext}}; \boldsymbol{u}_2^{\mathrm{ext}}; \dots; \boldsymbol{u}_N^{\mathrm{ext}}\right], \ \bar{\boldsymbol{y}} = \left[\boldsymbol{y}_1^{\mathrm{ext}}; \boldsymbol{y}_2^{\mathrm{ext}}; \dots; \boldsymbol{y}_N^{\mathrm{ext}}\right]. \tag{11}$$

Fig. 1(a) illustrates the block diagram of the i-th subsystem, and Fig. 1(b) shows the interconnected system with two subsystems.

3.2 Composition-Compatible Bisimulation

There are some important aspects that the abstractions of interconnected systems should be equipped with. First, it should preserve the interconnection structure of the original system. In addition, it is preferable if we could design the abstraction separately for each subsystem. However, using the ordinary definition of bisimulation, the interconnection of the bisimilar abstractions of subsystems is *not* in general bisimilar with the original interconnected system. This can be shown in the following simple example.

Let us consider two systems Σ_1 and Σ_2 connected in a cascade (Fig. 2(a)). We denote by $\hat{\Sigma}_i$ an abstraction of Σ_i, which is ϵ_i-approximately bisimilar to Σ_i with the binary relation R_i. Our question is whether the cascade of the abstractions (shown in Fig 2(b)) is approximately bisimilar to the cascade of the original systems, under the notion of the conventional bisimulation.

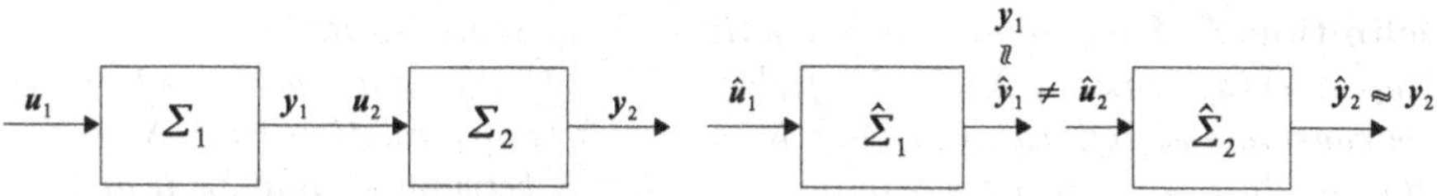

(a) Cascade of subsystems. (b) Cascade of abstractions.

Fig. 2. Cascade of two subsystems

In the cascade of Σ_1 and Σ_2, the equality

$$\boldsymbol{y}_1 = \boldsymbol{u}_2 \tag{12}$$

holds. In the cascade of $\hat{\Sigma}_1$ and $\hat{\Sigma}_2$, on the other hand, assuming that the interconnection is temporarily cut off, approximate bisimilarity implies that

$$\|\boldsymbol{y}_i - \hat{\boldsymbol{y}}_i\| \leq \epsilon_i \ \ (i = 1, 2)$$

hold for some $\hat{\boldsymbol{y}}_1, \hat{\boldsymbol{y}}_2, \hat{\boldsymbol{u}}_1$ and $\hat{\boldsymbol{u}}_2$. The equality constraint $\hat{\boldsymbol{y}}_1 = \hat{\boldsymbol{u}}_2$ is in general not met, unless $\epsilon_1 = 0$ (meaning that $\hat{\Sigma}_1$ is strictly similar to Σ_1) and $\hat{\Sigma}_2 = \Sigma_2$. Thus, the conventional bisimulation is not compatible even with this simple interconnection.

In the following, we propose a new variation of approximate bisimulation that is compatible to interconnection operation.

Definition 6. *Interconnection-compatible approximate simulation*
Suppose subsystems $\Sigma_i\langle X_i, U_i, Y_i, f_i, h_i\rangle$, $\hat{\Sigma}_i\langle \hat{X}_i, \hat{U}_i, \hat{Y}_i, \hat{f}_i, \hat{h}_i\rangle$, and a set of positive constants

$$\boldsymbol{\epsilon}_i = \{\epsilon_i^y,\ \{\epsilon_{ij}^w\}_{j\in\{1,\ldots,N\}\backslash\{i\}},\ \{\epsilon_{ij}^z\}_{j\in\{1,\ldots,N\}\backslash\{i\}}\} \tag{13}$$

are given. A binary relation $R_i \in X_i \times \hat{X}_i$ is an interconnection-compatible (IC in short) $\boldsymbol{\epsilon}_i$-approximate simulation relation from Σ_i to $\hat{\Sigma}_i$ if and only if for every $(\boldsymbol{x}_i, \hat{\boldsymbol{x}}_i) \in R_i$, the following holds:
for all $\boldsymbol{u}_i = [\boldsymbol{u}_i^{\text{ext}}; \boldsymbol{w}_i]$ $(\boldsymbol{w}_i = [\boldsymbol{w}_{i1}; \ldots; \boldsymbol{w}_{iN}])$, there exists a $\hat{\boldsymbol{u}}_i^{\text{ext}}$ that satisfies the following two conditions.
1. For $[\boldsymbol{z}_{i1}; \ldots; \boldsymbol{z}_{iN}] = h_i^z(\boldsymbol{x}_i, \boldsymbol{u}_i^{\text{ext}})$ and $[\hat{\boldsymbol{z}}_{i1}; \ldots; \hat{\boldsymbol{z}}_{iN}] = \hat{h}_i^z(\hat{\boldsymbol{x}}_i, \hat{\boldsymbol{u}}_i^{\text{ext}})$,

$$\|\boldsymbol{z}_{ij} - \hat{\boldsymbol{z}}_{ij}\| \leq \epsilon_{ij}^z \ \ (j \in \{1, \ldots, N\}\backslash\{i\}). \tag{14}$$

2. For all $\hat{\boldsymbol{w}}_i = [\hat{\boldsymbol{w}}_{i1}; \ldots; \hat{\boldsymbol{w}}_{iN}]$ within the range $\|\boldsymbol{w}_{ij} - \hat{\boldsymbol{w}}_{ij}\| \leq \epsilon_{ij}^w$,

$$\|h_i^y(\boldsymbol{x}_i, \boldsymbol{u}_i^{\text{ext}}, \boldsymbol{w}_i) - \hat{h}_i^y(\hat{\boldsymbol{x}}_i, \hat{\boldsymbol{u}}_i^{\text{ext}}, \hat{\boldsymbol{w}}_i)\| \leq \epsilon_i^y \ \ (j \in \{1, \ldots, N\}\backslash\{i\}) \tag{15}$$

and

$$(f_i(\boldsymbol{x}_i, \boldsymbol{u}_i^{\text{ext}}, \boldsymbol{w}_i),\ \hat{f}_i(\hat{\boldsymbol{x}}_i, \hat{\boldsymbol{u}}_i^{\text{ext}}, \hat{\boldsymbol{w}}_i)) \in R_i \tag{16}$$

hold.

Definition 7. *Interconnection-compatible approximate bisimulation*
Suppose subsystems $\Sigma_i\langle X_i, U_i, Y_i, f_i, h_i\rangle$, $\hat{\Sigma}_i\langle \hat{X}_i, \hat{U}_i, \hat{Y}_i, \hat{f}_i, \hat{h}_i\rangle$ and a set of positive constants $\boldsymbol{\epsilon}_i$ defined as in (13) are given. A binary relation $R_i \subset X_i \times \hat{X}_i$ is called an IC $\boldsymbol{\epsilon}_i$-approximate bisimulation relation between Σ_i and $\hat{\Sigma}_i$ if and only if R_i is an IC $\boldsymbol{\epsilon}_i$-approximate simulation relation from Σ_i to $\hat{\Sigma}_i$ and its inverse relation R_i^{-1} is an IC $\boldsymbol{\epsilon}_i$-approximate simulation relation from $\hat{\Sigma}_i$ to Σ_i. Moreover, if such an R_i exists, Σ_i and $\hat{\Sigma}_i$ are said to be IC-approximately bisimilar with respect to R_i and the precision $\boldsymbol{\epsilon}_i$, and this relation is denoted by $\Sigma_i \sim^{\mathcal{I}}_{\boldsymbol{\epsilon}_i} \hat{\Sigma}_i$.

The major difference between the above definition and the ordinary approximate bisimulation is that, the internal input signals $\hat{\boldsymbol{w}}_{ij}$ are regarded as disturbances rather than control inputs.

Remark 1. For systems without internal input signals, Definition 7 reduces to the definition of ordinary approximate bisimulation with the output error bound separately specified to $\boldsymbol{y}_i^{\text{ext}}$ and $\boldsymbol{z}_{ij}$s. For systems without external input signals, Definition 7 becomes a bounded output error condition under bounded disturbances.

The following theorem states that IC-approximately bisimilar abstractions are actually compatible with interconnection.

Theorem 1. *Suppose N subsystems Σ_i $(i = 1, \ldots, N)$ are given, and for each of them, $\hat{\Sigma}_i$ is an IC-approximately bisimilar abstraction with respect to the binary relation R_i and the precision set $\boldsymbol{\epsilon}_i$. If the condition*

$$\epsilon^w_{ij} \geq \epsilon^z_{ji} \; (i \in \{1, 2, \ldots, N\}, j \in \{1, 2, \ldots, N\} \backslash \{i\}) \tag{17}$$

is satisfied, the two interconnected systems $\mathcal{I}(\Sigma_1, \ldots, \Sigma_N)$ and $\mathcal{I}(\hat{\Sigma}_1, \ldots, \hat{\Sigma}_N)$ are approximately bisimilar (in the sense of Definition 3) with respect to the relation

$$R = \{((\boldsymbol{x}_1; \boldsymbol{x}_2; \ldots; \boldsymbol{x}_N), (\hat{\boldsymbol{x}}_1; \hat{\boldsymbol{x}}_2; \ldots; \hat{\boldsymbol{x}}_N)) \,|\, (\boldsymbol{x}_i, \hat{\boldsymbol{x}}_i) \in R_i \;\; (i = 1, 2, \ldots, N)\} \tag{18}$$

and the precision

$$\epsilon = \sum_i \epsilon^y_i. \tag{19}$$

The proof is given in Appendix A.

Now let us return to the previous cascade system example and make sure that the cascade of abstractions based on Definition 7 is actually approximately bisimilar to the original system. Suppose $\Sigma_1 \sim^{\mathcal{I}}_{\boldsymbol{\epsilon}_1} \hat{\Sigma}_1$ with respect to the relation R_1 and $\Sigma_2 \sim^{\mathcal{I}}_{\boldsymbol{\epsilon}_2} \hat{\Sigma}_2$ with respect to the relation R_2, where $\boldsymbol{\epsilon}_1 = \{\epsilon^z_{12}\}$, $\boldsymbol{\epsilon}_2 = \{\epsilon^y_2, \epsilon^w_{21}\}$. For any $\boldsymbol{u}_1^{\text{ext}}$, there exists $\hat{\boldsymbol{u}}_1^{\text{ext}}$ that satisfies $\|\boldsymbol{z}_{12} - \hat{\boldsymbol{z}}_{12}\| \leq \epsilon^z_{12}$ (and vice versa). Moreover, the condition $\|\boldsymbol{y}_2^{\text{ext}} - \hat{\boldsymbol{y}}_2^{\text{ext}}\| \leq \epsilon^y_2$ holds as long as the condition $\|\boldsymbol{w}_{21} - \hat{\boldsymbol{w}}_{21}\| \leq \epsilon^w_{21}$ is satisfied. Therefore, if the condition $\epsilon^w_{21} \geq \epsilon^z_{12}$

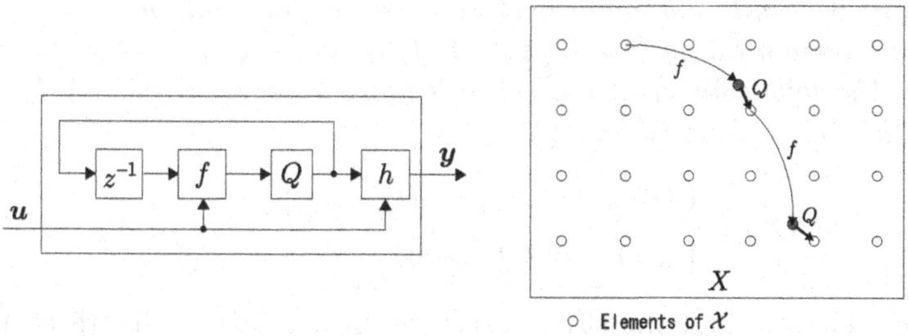

(a) Block diagram of $Q(\Sigma)$ (b) State transition of $Q(\Sigma)$

Fig. 3. System with state quantizer

holds, the cascade of $\hat{\Sigma}_1$ and $\hat{\Sigma}_2$ is approximately bisimilar to the cascade of Σ_1 and Σ_2 with the precision $\epsilon = \epsilon_2^y$.

In order to design the abstractions of subsystems that preserve approximate bismilarity under interconnection, one should first divide the input-output signals into groups of those used for external interface and those used for interconnection, and then design the abstractions satisfying the conditions stated in Theorem 1. Moreover, the precision parameter of each abstraction should be chosen according to the condition (17). The proposed method enables us to design the abstraction of each subsystem in a separate way by regarding errors on internal signals as disturbances. One should keep in mind, however, that this could produce a conservative result compared to designing the abstraction by viewing the original interconnected system as a whole, if such a method is available.

4 Finite Abstractions of Linear Subsystems

In the previous section, we have introduced the notion of interconnection-compatible approximate bisimulation. As the next step, in this section we address the design of approximately bisimilar finite abstractions of subsystems of interconnected systems. The term *finite abstraction* refers to a finite state system that approximates a continuous-state system.

4.1 Expression of Finite Abstractions Via State Quantization

One of the most important issues of the finite abstraction problem is about the expression of finite automata. In the following, we propose a way of expressing finite automata via *state-quantization* of continuous-state systems.

First of all, a quantization function is defined as follows.

$$Q : X \mapsto \mathcal{X}. \tag{20}$$

Here, the set $\mathcal{X} = \{\boldsymbol{x}_1, \ldots, \boldsymbol{x}_N\}$ is a finite subset of X.

The following definition introduces the notion of finite automata induced by the state-quantization of continuous-state systems.

Definition 8. *Finite automata induced by state quantization*
Consider a dynamical system $\Sigma\langle X, U, Y, f, h\rangle$ and a quantization function $Q : X \mapsto \mathcal{X}$. The following system is called a finite automaton induced by the state quantization of Σ, denoted by $Q(\Sigma)$.

$$Q(\Sigma) : \begin{cases} \boldsymbol{x}(t+1) = Q(f(\boldsymbol{x}(t), \boldsymbol{u}(t))) \\ \boldsymbol{y}(t) = h(\boldsymbol{x}(t), \boldsymbol{u}(t)) \end{cases} \quad (\boldsymbol{x}(0) \in \mathcal{X}). \tag{21}$$

The block diagram and the state transition of a $Q(\Sigma)$ is illustrated in Fig. 3. Notice that, in this state equation, the state transition is closed in $\mathcal{X}$ as long as the initial state is chosen from $\mathcal{X}$. To clarify this property, we define the subset of the input set as

$$\mathcal{U}_{ij} = \{\boldsymbol{u} \in U \mid Q(f(\boldsymbol{x}_i, \boldsymbol{u})) = \boldsymbol{x}_j\}, \tag{22}$$

which refers to the set of control inputs that drives the state $\boldsymbol{x}_i$ to $\boldsymbol{x}_j$. Note that from the property of the quantization function Q, $\{\mathcal{U}_{ij}\}_j$ forms a partition of U for each i. Using this notation, the state transition of $Q(\Sigma)$ is rewritten as

$$\boldsymbol{x}(t) = \boldsymbol{x}_i \ \wedge\ \boldsymbol{u}(t) \in \mathcal{U}_{ij} \ \Rightarrow\ \boldsymbol{x}(t+1) = \boldsymbol{x}_j. \tag{23}$$

In this way, the input set is also discretized as a class induced from the state transition over finite states. Therefore, the partition of the input set is dependent on the current state. This implicit fashion of the input discretization differs from the other researches (like [7],[8]), where explicit input quantization or originally discrete input systems are considered. Moreover, in the case that the measurement function is a function of states only (written as $h(\boldsymbol{x})$), the state quantization results in indirect quantization of the output set; i.e., $Y \mapsto \mathcal{Y} = \{h(\boldsymbol{x}) \mid \boldsymbol{x} \in \mathcal{X}\}$.

4.2 Approximate Bisimulation Condition of Finite Abstraction

In this subsection, we address the design of finite abstractions of linear subsystems. Linear subsystems are expressed as follows.

$$\Sigma_i : \begin{cases} \boldsymbol{x}_i(t+1) = A_i \boldsymbol{x}_i(t) + B_i^u \boldsymbol{u}_i^{\text{ext}}(t) + \displaystyle\sum_{j \in \{1,2,\ldots,N\} \backslash \{i\}} B_{ij}^w \boldsymbol{w}_{ij}, \\ \boldsymbol{y}_i^{\text{ext}}(t) = C_i^y \boldsymbol{x}_i(t) + D_i^{yu} \boldsymbol{u}_i^{\text{ext}}(t) + \displaystyle\sum_{j \in \{1,2,\ldots,N\} \backslash \{i\}} D_{ij}^{yw} \boldsymbol{w}_{ij}, \\ \boldsymbol{z}_{ij}(t) = C_{ij}^z \boldsymbol{x}_i(t) \qquad (j \in \{1,2,\ldots,N\} \backslash \{i\}). \end{cases} \tag{24}$$

We assume that the state set X_i of Σ_i is bounded. For systems of this form, we express their abstractions as state-quantized systems $Q_i(\Sigma_i)$, defined in the previous subsection. Then the problem of concern reduces to deriving a quantization function Q_i whose resultant $Q_i(\Sigma_i)$ is IC-approximately bisimilar to Σ_i with respect a binary relation R_i satisfying the condition.

$$\text{For any } \boldsymbol{x} \in X_i, \text{ there exists a } \hat{\boldsymbol{x}} \in \mathcal{X}_i \text{ such that } (\boldsymbol{x}, \hat{\boldsymbol{x}}) \in R_i, \tag{25}$$

where $\mathcal{X}_i$ denotes the state set of $Q_i(\Sigma_i)$.

Remark 2. The condition (25) is necessary for applying bisimilar abstractions to actual analysis and control problems, assuming that the initial state is arbitrarily chosen from X_i. In [11], this condition is imposed in the definition of approximate (bi)simulation.

Theorem 2. *Interconnection-compatible approximately bisimilar finite abstractions of linear subsystems*
Let Σ_i be an (A_i, B_i^u)-stabilizable discrete-time linear system defined by (24) and let $\boldsymbol{\epsilon}_i$ be a set of positive constants defined by (13). There exist a matrix F_i, a positive definite matrix M_i and a constant $\lambda_i \in (0,1)$ satisfying the conditions

$$(A_i + B_i^u F_i)^{\mathrm{T}} M_i (A_i + B_i^u F_i) \leq \lambda_i^2 M_i, \tag{26}$$

$$\begin{aligned} M_i &\geq \frac{1}{(1-\lambda_i)^2 \alpha_i^2}(C_i^y + D_i^{yu} F_i)^{\mathrm{T}}(C_i^y + D_i^{yu} F_i), \\ M_i &\geq \frac{1}{(1-\lambda_i)^2 {\epsilon_{ij}^z}^2}(C_{ij}^z + D_{ij}^{zu} F_i)^{\mathrm{T}}(C_{ij}^z + D_{ij}^{zu} F_i) \quad (j \in \{1,2,\ldots,N\}\backslash\{i\}) \end{aligned} \tag{27}$$

where the constant α_i is given by

$$\alpha_i := \epsilon_i^y - \sum_{j \in \{1,2,\ldots,N\}\backslash\{i\}} ||D_{ij}^{yw}|| \epsilon_{ij}^w. \tag{28}$$

Furthermore, if α_i and the constant defined as

$$\beta_i := 1 - \sum_{j \in \{1,2,\ldots,N\}\backslash\{i\}} ||{B_{ij}^w}^{\mathrm{T}} M_i B_{ij}^w|| \epsilon_{ij}^w \tag{29}$$

are both positive, then for a quantization function Q_i satisfying the condition

$$||\boldsymbol{x}_i - Q_i(\boldsymbol{x}_i)||_{M_i} \leq \beta_i \ \ \forall \boldsymbol{x}_i \in X_i, \tag{30}$$

the systems Σ_i and $Q_i(\Sigma_i)$ are IC-approximately bisimilar with respect to the precision $\boldsymbol{\epsilon}_i$ and the relation

$$R_i = \{(\boldsymbol{x}, \hat{\boldsymbol{x}}) \,|\, ||\boldsymbol{x} - \hat{\boldsymbol{x}}||_{M_i} \leq 1/(1-\lambda_i)\}, \tag{31}$$

which satisfies (25).

A rough explanation of Theorem 2 is as follows: Bisimulation can be captured as a tracking problem of two systems. If one system can track the other system's output trajectory with a constant error bound (say ϵ), then this system is similar to the other with the precision ϵ. Moreover, if both systems can track their opponent's trajectory, then they are bisimilar to each other. Therefore, in those cases when both systems are linear, the problem can be viewed as the stabilization problem of the error system, and in such cases, the bisimulation relation is related to the invariant set of the error system. A detailed proof is given in Appendix B.

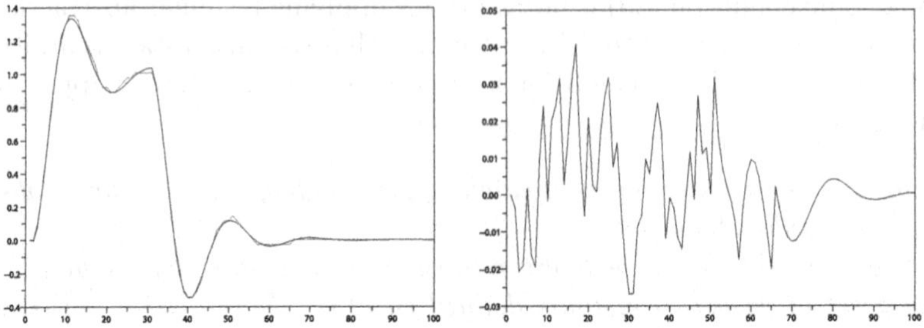

(a) Output response.

(b) Difference of the output trajectories of $\mathcal{I}(\hat{\Sigma}_1, \Sigma_2)$ and $\mathcal{I}(\Sigma_1, \Sigma_2)$.

Fig. 4. Output response of $\mathcal{I}(\hat{\Sigma}_1, \Sigma_2)$ and $\mathcal{I}(\Sigma_1, \Sigma_2)$

Finally, an explicit expression of the quantizer Q_i satisfying the condition (30) is given as follows.

$$Q_i(\boldsymbol{x}) = \left(\frac{\sqrt{n}}{2}U_i\right)^{-1}\left[\left(\frac{\sqrt{n}}{2}U_i\right)\boldsymbol{x}\right] \tag{32}$$

Here, the matrix U_i is given by $U_i^{\mathrm{T}}U_i = M_i/\beta_i^2$, n is the size of $\boldsymbol{x}$ and $[\boldsymbol{x}]$ is the rounding function, which maps each element of $\boldsymbol{x}$ to its nearest integer.

4.3 Example

This section shows a simple example. Consider an interconnected system composed of two subsystems. The parameters of the subsystems are given as follows.

$$\Sigma_1 : \begin{cases} \boldsymbol{x}_1(t+1) = \begin{bmatrix} 1.0 & 0.1 \\ -1.0 & 0.7 \end{bmatrix} \boldsymbol{x}_1(t) + \begin{bmatrix} 0.0 & 0.0 \\ 1.0 & 0.1 \end{bmatrix} \begin{bmatrix} u_1^{\mathrm{ext}}(t) \\ w_{12} \end{bmatrix} \\ \begin{bmatrix} y_1^{\mathrm{ext}} \\ z_{12} \end{bmatrix}(t) = \begin{bmatrix} 1.0 & 0.0 \\ 0.0 & 0.1 \end{bmatrix} \boldsymbol{x}_1(t) \end{cases}$$

$$\Sigma_2 : \begin{cases} \boldsymbol{x}_2(t+1) = \begin{bmatrix} 0.7 & 0.1 \\ -1.0 & 0.5 \end{bmatrix} \boldsymbol{x}_2(t) + \begin{bmatrix} 0.0 \\ 0.2 \end{bmatrix} w_{21}(t) \\ z_{21}(t) = \begin{bmatrix} 0.0 & 0.2 \end{bmatrix} \boldsymbol{x}_2(t) \end{cases}$$

Let us derive an abstraction of this system by first designing a finite abstraction of Σ_1 only, and next making its interconnection with Σ_2.

The following parameters are chosen to meet the conditions in Theorem 2.

$$\epsilon_1^y = 0.1,\ \epsilon_{12}^z = \epsilon_{21}^w = 0.1,\ \epsilon_{21}^z = \epsilon_{12}^w = 0.05$$

$$M_1 = \begin{bmatrix} 2.3\text{e}3 & 2.2\text{e}2 \\ 2.2\text{e}2 & 4.3\text{e}1 \end{bmatrix},\ F_1 = \begin{bmatrix} -4.1 & -1.2 \end{bmatrix},\ \lambda_1 = 0.7$$

$$M_2 = \begin{bmatrix} 1.6\text{e}3 & 1.6\text{e}2 \\ 1.6\text{e}2 & 1.9\text{e}2 \end{bmatrix},\ \lambda_2 = 0.7$$

Substituting the above values of M_1 and $\beta_1 = 0.97$ to (32) we obtain the quantizer Q_1 and hence $\hat{\Sigma}_1 = Q_1(\Sigma_1)$.

Fig. 4 shows the output response of the two systems $\mathcal{I}(\hat{\Sigma}_1, \Sigma_2)$ and $\mathcal{I}(\Sigma_1, \Sigma_2)$. The input signal

$$u_1^{\mathrm{ext}}(t) = \begin{cases} 1.0 & (t < 30) \\ 0.0 & (t \geq 30) \end{cases}$$

is applied to $\mathcal{I}(\Sigma_1, \Sigma_2)$, and the input signal for $\mathcal{I}(\hat{\Sigma}_1, \Sigma_2)$ is given by $\hat{u}_1^{\mathrm{ext}} = u_1^{\mathrm{ext}}(t) + F_1(\hat{\boldsymbol{x}}_1(t) - \boldsymbol{x}_1(t))$. It is observed from the figure that the specified output error bound is achieved.

5 Conclusion

In this paper we discussed the design of finite abstractions of interconnected systems. In a general setting of interconnected systems, we introduced an extended notion of approximate bisimulation, which is compatible with interconnection. This means that the abstractions of subsystems that are based on the presented approximate bisimulation can be connected with each other to form an abstractions of the whole system. We have also presented a design procedure for the finite abstraction of linear subsystems under this new notion of approximate bisimulation. In future works, we should extend the class of subsystems whose finite abstractions are computable.

References

1. Lafferriere, G., Pappas, G.J., Sastry, S.: Hybrid Systems with Finite Bisimulations. In: Antsaklis, P.J., Kohn, W., Lemmon, M.D., Nerode, A., Sastry, S.S. (eds.) HS 1997. LNCS, vol. 1567, pp. 186–203. Springer, Heidelberg (1999)
2. Alur, R., Verimag, T.D., Ivančić, F.: Predicate Abstractions for Reachability Analysis of Hybrid Systems. ACM Trans. on Embedded Computing Systems 5(1), 152–199 (2006)
3. Lunze, J.: A timed discrete-event abstraction of continuous-variable systems. International Journal of Control 72(13), 1147–1164 (1999)
4. Tsumura, K.: Stabilization of Linear Systems by Bit-Memory Controllers under Constraints of Bit-Length. In: 45th IEEE Conference on Decision and Control, San Diego, CA, USA, pp. 5507–5512 (December 2006)
5. Milner, R.: Communication and Concurrency. Prentice-Hall, Englewood Cliffs (1989)
6. Girard, A., Pappas, G.J.: Approximation Metrics for Discrete and Continuous Systems. IEEE Transactions on Automatic Control 52(5), 782–798 (2007)
7. Girard, A.: Approximately Bisimilar Finite Abstractions of Stable Linear Systems. In: Bemporad, A., Bicchi, A., Buttazzo, G. (eds.) HSCC 2007. LNCS, vol. 4416, pp. 231–244. Springer, Heidelberg (2007)
8. Tabuada, P.: Approximate Simulation Relations and Finite Abstractions of Quantized Control Systems. In: Bemporad, A., Bicchi, A., Buttazzo, G. (eds.) HSCC 2007. LNCS, vol. 4416, pp. 529–542. Springer, Heidelberg (2007)

9. Tabuada, P., Pappas, G.J., Lima, P.: Composing Abstractions of Hybrid Systems. In: Tomlin, C.J., Greenstreet, M.R. (eds.) HSCC 2002. LNCS, vol. 2289, pp. 436–450. Springer, Heidelberg (2002)
10. Tabuada, P., Pappas, G.J., Lima, P.: Compositional Abstractions of Hybrid Control Systems. Discrete Event Dynamic Systems: Theory and Applications 14, 203–238 (2004)
11. Julius, A.A., Pappas, G.J.: Approximate Equivalence and Approximate Synchronization of Metric Transition Systems. In: The Proc. 45th IEEE Conf. Decision and Control, San Diego, USA (2006)
12. Tazaki, Y., Imura, J.: Finite Abstractions of Discrete-time Linear Systems and Its Application to Optimal Control. In: 17th IFAC World Congress, Seoul, Korea (to appear, 2008)

A Proof of Theorem 1

We only prove the approximate similarity from $\mathcal{I}(\Sigma_1,\dots,\Sigma_N)$ to $\mathcal{I}(\hat{\Sigma}_1,\dots,\hat{\Sigma}_N)$. The opposite case is treated in the same manner. Suppose, for each i, the state $\boldsymbol{x}_i$ of the subsystem Σ_i and the state $\hat{\boldsymbol{x}}_i$ of its abstraction $\hat{\Sigma}_i$ are in the relation R_i. Moreover, suppose that the input $\bar{\boldsymbol{u}} = [\boldsymbol{u}_1^{\text{ext}};\dots;\boldsymbol{u}_N^{\text{ext}}]$ of $\mathcal{I}(\Sigma_1,\dots,\Sigma_N)$ is arbitrarily chosen. Then, for each i, the internal output, internal input, external output and state transition are subsequently determined as $\boldsymbol{z}_i = h_i^z(\boldsymbol{x}_i,\boldsymbol{u}_i^{\text{ext}})$, $\boldsymbol{w}_{ij} = \boldsymbol{z}_{ji}$, $\boldsymbol{y}_i^{\text{ext}} = h_i^y(\boldsymbol{x}_i,\boldsymbol{u}_i^{\text{ext}},\boldsymbol{w}_i)$, and $\boldsymbol{x}_i' = f_i(\boldsymbol{x}_i,\boldsymbol{u}_i^{\text{ext}},\boldsymbol{w}_i)$. From the approximate bisimilarity of Σ_i and $\hat{\Sigma}_i$, there exists $\hat{\bar{\boldsymbol{u}}} = [\hat{\boldsymbol{u}}_1^{\text{ext}};\dots;\hat{\boldsymbol{u}}_N^{\text{ext}}]$ satisfying (14) and also, under the assumption

$$\|\boldsymbol{w}_{ij} - \hat{\boldsymbol{w}}_{ij}\| \le \epsilon_{ij}^w, \tag{33}$$

satisfying (15) and (16). From the condition (17), the assumption (33) is actually fulfilled. Finally, it is straightforward from (15) that $\|\bar{\boldsymbol{y}} - \hat{\bar{\boldsymbol{y}}}\| \le \epsilon$ holds with ϵ defined by (19).

□

B Proof of Theorem 2

From the stabilizability assumption, there exists a matrix F_i making the eigenvalues of $(A_i + B_i^u F_i)$ strictly inside the unit circle and hence one can show that M_i and λ_i satisfying (26),(27) exist by following the line of Proposition 3 in [6]. Let us denote the state, the input and the output of $Q_i(\Sigma_i)$ by $\hat{\boldsymbol{x}}_i$, $\hat{\boldsymbol{u}}_i$ and $\hat{\boldsymbol{y}}_i$, respectively. We first derive the condition for $Q_i(\Sigma_i)$ to be approximately similar to Σ_i. Taking the difference of the state equations of $Q_i(\Sigma_i)$ and Σ_i, we obtain the error system

$$\boldsymbol{e}_i(t+1) = A_i\boldsymbol{e}_i(t) + B_i^u\delta\boldsymbol{u}_i^{\text{ext}}(t) + \sum_{j\in\{1,2,\dots,N\}\setminus\{i\}} B_{ij}^w\delta\boldsymbol{w}_{ij} + \boldsymbol{d}_i(t) \tag{34}$$

where $\boldsymbol{e}_i = \hat{\boldsymbol{x}}_i - \boldsymbol{x}_i$, $\delta \boldsymbol{u}_i^{\text{ext}} = \hat{\boldsymbol{u}}_i^{\text{ext}} - \boldsymbol{u}_i^{\text{ext}}$, $\delta \boldsymbol{w}_{ij} = \hat{\boldsymbol{w}}_{ij} - \boldsymbol{w}_{ij}$ and $\boldsymbol{d}_i$ is the quantization error defined by $\boldsymbol{d}_i(t) = Q_i(A_i\hat{\boldsymbol{x}}_i(t)+B_i\hat{\boldsymbol{u}}_i(t))-(A_i\hat{\boldsymbol{x}}_i(t)+B_i\hat{\boldsymbol{u}}_i(t))$. Here, we specify the control input $\hat{\boldsymbol{u}}_i^{\text{ext}}(t)$ as a function of $\boldsymbol{x}_i(t), \hat{\boldsymbol{x}}_i(t)$ and $\boldsymbol{u}_i^{\text{ext}}(t)$ defined by $\hat{\boldsymbol{u}}_i^{\text{ext}}(t) = \boldsymbol{u}_i^{\text{ext}}(t) + F_i(\hat{\boldsymbol{x}}_i(t) - \boldsymbol{x}_i(t))$ where F_i is a matrix making the matrix $(A_i + B_i^u F_i)$ asymptotically stable. Then the error dynamics is written as

$$\boldsymbol{e}_i(t+1) = (A_i + B_i^u F_i)\boldsymbol{e}_i(t) + \sum_{j\in\{1,2,\ldots,N\}\setminus\{i\}} B_{ij}^w \delta\boldsymbol{w}_{ij}(t) + \boldsymbol{d}_i(t) \tag{35}$$

and moreover, the following inequality holds.

$$\|\boldsymbol{e}_i(t+1)\|_{M_i} \le \lambda_i \|\boldsymbol{e}_i(t)\|_{M_i} + 1 - \beta_i + \|\boldsymbol{d}_i(t)\|_{M_i}.$$

Here, M_i is the positive definite matrix satisfying (26),(27) and the constant β_i is defined by (29). From the condition $\|\boldsymbol{d}_i(t)\|_{M_i} \le \beta_i$, the set E_i defined as

$$E_i = \{\boldsymbol{e} \mid \|\boldsymbol{e}\|_{M_i} \le 1/(1-\lambda_i)\} \tag{36}$$

is an invariant set of the error system. Moreover, from (27) and (28), every element $\boldsymbol{e} \in E_i$ satisfies the conditions

$$\|\hat{\boldsymbol{y}}_i^{\text{ext}} - \boldsymbol{y}_i^{\text{ext}}\| \le \|(C_i^y + D_i^{yu}F_i)\boldsymbol{e}\| + \sum_{j\in\{1,2,\ldots,N\}\setminus\{i\}} \|D_{ij}^{yw}\| \epsilon_{ij}^w \le \epsilon_i^y,$$
$$\|\hat{\boldsymbol{z}}_{ij} - \boldsymbol{z}_{ij}\| = \|(C_{ij}^z + D_{ij}^z F_i)\boldsymbol{e}\| \le \epsilon_{ij}^z \qquad (j = 1, \ldots, N,\ j \ne i).$$

Therefore it follows that the binary relation R_i defined as $R_i = \{(\boldsymbol{x}, \hat{\boldsymbol{x}}) \mid (\hat{\boldsymbol{x}} - \boldsymbol{x}) \in E_i\}$, which is written equivalently as (31), is an IC-approximate simulation relation from Σ_i to $Q_i(\Sigma_i)$ with the precision $\boldsymbol{\epsilon}_i$.

In the opposite case, choosing the control input $\boldsymbol{u}_i^{\text{ext}}(t)$ as $\boldsymbol{u}_i^{\text{ext}}(t) = \hat{\boldsymbol{u}}_i^{\text{ext}}(t) + F_i(\boldsymbol{x}_i(t) - \hat{\boldsymbol{x}}_i(t))$ yields the same error system as (35). Therefore, the relation (31) is an IC-approximate bisimulation relation between Σ_i and $Q_i(\Sigma_i)$.

□

On Controllability of Timed Continuous Petri Nets

C. Renato Vázquez[1], Antonio Ramírez[2], Laura Recalde[1], and Manuel Silva[1,*]

[1] Dep. de Informática e Ingeniería de Sistemas, Centro Politécnico Superior, Universidad de Zaragoza, María de Luna 1, E-50018 Zaragoza, Spain
{cvazquez,lrecalde,silva}@unizar.es
[2] CINVESTAV-IPN Unidad Guadalajara, 45090 Guadalajara, Mexico
art@gdl.cinvestav.mx

Abstract. Continuous Petri Nets is a subclass of hybrid models representing relaxed views of discrete events systems, in which timing may adopt different semantics. Even if no semantics is strictly superior, we proved in [1] that for an important subclass of models infinite server semantics provides always a better approximation of the underlying discrete model than finite server. This paper then concentrates on controllability under this semantics. First we propose a notion of controllability over subsets of the reachable polytope, and provide a necessary and sufficient condition for markings with no null elements (interior points); later the transformation of an arbitrary initial marking into an interior one is done. The technically more involved part of the paper is the extension of those results to the case in which some transitions are non controllable. An interesting point is that all characterizations depend only on the structure and firing speeds of the timed continuous net.

1 Introduction

Petri Nets constitute a well-known paradigm useful to model discrete event systems. In many practical cases, an enumeration approach has to be used to verify some properties of net models. Unfortunately, for highly marked systems, even for bounded, the reachability graph can be so large that many properties cannot be analyzed. This problem is known as the state explosion problem. Systems that frequently appear in practice, for instance in manufacturing, telecommunications, traffic or logistic, lead to Petri net models with many states. So, to analyze such systems fluidification has been proposed.

Fluidification constitutes a relaxation technique to study discrete systems through a "similar" but continuous model. Using fluid models, more analytical techniques can be used for the analysis of some interesting properties. In Petri Nets, fluidification has been introduced from different perspectives ([2,3]). Here we consider the approach adopted in [4]. In this work, timed continuous Petri net (TCPN) models under infinite server semantics are considered. The continuous model thus obtained is piecewise linear with bounded and nonnegative inputs.

* This work was partially supported by project CICYT and FEDER DPI2006-15390.

M. Egerstedt and B. Mishra (Eds.): HSCC 2008, LNCS 4981, pp. 528–541, 2008.

In recent years, a lot of research has been done on controllability of switched linear systems. For instance, [5] and [6] give sufficient and necessary conditions for controllability of 3-dimensional systems and single switching sequence systems, respectively, but always under the assumption of unconstrained inputs. Classic works ([7] and [8]) deal with controllability on linear systems (non piecewise) with bounded and nonnegative inputs, respectively. Camlibel [9] has extended the results of Brammer to a particular class of piecewise linear systems known as linear complementary systems. In [10] optimal control of switched piecewise affine autonomous systems is studied, assuming that the decision variables are the switching instants and the sequence of operating modes.

However, in timed continuous Petri net (TCPN) systems switching is not controllable. Moreover, in [11] it is shown that these systems are not controllable in the classical sense. In [12] it is proven that for Join Free Timed Continuous Petri Nets there exists an invariant set, named Controllability Space (CS), in which the system exhibits the controllability property, i.e. any state of CS is reachable from any other state of CS. In that work, the set CS is characterized.

Here the study of controllability and reachability properties for general timed continuous Petri nets under infinite server semantics is addressed. A controllability notion is presented for TCPN systems. It deals with the possibility that the state evolves from any state, of a given set, to another; so it is an appropriate adaptation of the classical controllability concept of linear continuous systems (see [13]). Based on this controllability definition, a structural characterization of controllable TCPN systems is obtained. It is worth to remark that this property does not depend on the initial marking, but on the structure and timing of the net as it is proved in the sequel.

This work is organized as follows: in Section 2 an overview of continuous and timed continuous Petri nets is presented, while in Section 3, a concept of controllability is formally introduced. In Section 4, necessary and sufficient conditions for controllability are given, under the hypothesis that all transitions are controllable, while the controllability of systems with uncontrollable transitions is studied in Section 5. Finally, some conclusions are presented in Section 6.

2 Basic Concepts

The structure $\mathcal{N} = \langle P, T, \mathbf{Pre}, \mathbf{Post} \rangle$ of *continuous Petri nets* is the same as the structure of discrete PN. That is, P is a finite set of places, T is a finite set of transitions with $P \cap T = \emptyset$, **Pre** and **Post** are $|P| \times |T|$ sized, natural valued, *pre- and post- incidence matrices.* The main difference is in the evolution rule, since in continuous PN firing is not restricted to be done in integer amounts, and so the marking is not forced to be integer. More precisely, a transition t is *enabled* at $\mathbf{m}$ iff for every $p \in {}^\bullet t$, $\mathbf{m}[p] > 0$, and its *enabling degree* is $enab(t, \mathbf{m}) = \min_{p \in {}^\bullet t}\{\mathbf{m}[p]/\mathbf{Pre}[p,t]\}$. The firing of t in a certain amount $\alpha \leq enab(t, \mathbf{m})$ leads to a new marking $\mathbf{m}' = \mathbf{m} + \alpha \cdot \mathbf{C}[P, t]$, where $\mathbf{C} = \mathbf{Post} - \mathbf{Pre}$ is the token-flow matrix. Right and left rational annullers of $\mathbf{C}$ are called

T- and *P-flows*, respectively. If there exists $\mathbf{y} > \mathbf{0}$ ($\mathbf{x} > \mathbf{0}$) such that $\mathbf{y} \cdot \mathbf{C} = \mathbf{0}$ ($\mathbf{C} \cdot \mathbf{x} = \mathbf{0}$), the net is said to be *conservative* (*consistent*). A set of places Σ is a *siphon* iff ${}^\bullet\Sigma \subseteq \Sigma^\bullet$ (the set of input transitions is contained in the set of output transitions). For reachability, as in [14], the limit concept is used, and a marking reached in the limit of an infinitely long sequence is considered reachable.

For the timing interpretation we will use a first order (or deterministic) approximation of the discrete case ([4]). Hence, a *Timed Continuous Petri Net (TCPN)* is a continuous PN together with a vector $\boldsymbol{\lambda} \in \mathbb{R}^{|T|}_{>0}$. Here infinite server semantics is considered, thus the flow through a timed transition t is the product of the speed, $\boldsymbol{\lambda}[t]$, and $enab(t, \mathbf{m})$, the instantaneous enabling representing the number of active serves, i.e., $\mathbf{f}(\mathbf{m})[t] = \boldsymbol{\lambda}[t] \cdot enab(t, \mathbf{m}) = \boldsymbol{\lambda}[t] \cdot \min_{p \in {}^\bullet t}\{\mathbf{m}[p]/\mathbf{Pre}[p, t]\}$ (see [1,4] for a more detailed study of the semantics used in continuous PNs). For the flow to be well defined we will assume that $\forall t \in T, |{}^\bullet t| \geq 1$. The "*min*" in the definition leads to the concept of *configurations*: a configuration assigns to a transition one place that for some markings will control its firing rate (i.e. it is constraining that transition). The number of configurations is upper bounded by $\prod_{t \in T} |{}^\bullet t|$.

The flow through the transitions can be written in a vectorial form as $\mathbf{f}(\mathbf{m}) = \boldsymbol{\Lambda}\boldsymbol{\Pi}(\mathbf{m})\mathbf{m}$ (see [11]), where $\boldsymbol{\Lambda}$ is a diagonal matrix whose elements are those of $\boldsymbol{\lambda}$, and $\boldsymbol{\Pi}(\mathbf{m})$ is the configuration operator matrix, defined by elements as

$$\boldsymbol{\Pi}(\mathbf{m})[i, j] = \begin{cases} \frac{1}{\mathbf{Pre}[p_j, t_i]} & \text{if } p_j \text{ is constrainting } t_i \\ 0 & \text{otherwise} \end{cases}$$

If more than one place is constrainting the flow of a transition at a given marking, any of them can be used, but only one is taken.

Control action may only be a reduction of the flow through the transitions. That is, transitions (machines for example) cannot work faster than their nominal speed. Transitions in which a control action can be applied are called controllable. The effective flow through a controllable transition can be represented as: $\mathbf{f}_i(\tau) = \boldsymbol{\lambda}(t_i) \cdot enab(\tau)\,[t_i] - u(\tau)[t_i]$, where $0 \leq u(\tau)[t_i] \leq \lambda(t_i) \cdot enab(\tau)[t_i]$.

The control vector $\mathbf{u} \in \mathbb{R}^{|T|}$ is defined s.t. $\mathbf{u}_i$ represents the control action on t_i. If t_i is not controllable then $\mathbf{u}_i = 0$. The set of all controllable transitions is denoted by T_c, and the set of uncontrollable transitions is $T_{nc} = T - T_c$.

The behavior of a TCPN forced system is described by the state equation:

$$\begin{array}{c} \dot{\mathbf{m}} = \mathbf{C}\boldsymbol{\Lambda}\boldsymbol{\Pi}(\mathbf{m})\mathbf{m} - \mathbf{C}\mathbf{u} \\ \mathbf{0} \leq \mathbf{u} \leq \boldsymbol{\Lambda}\boldsymbol{\Pi}(\mathbf{m})\mathbf{m} \end{array} \tag{1}$$

Given a marking trajectory, an input $\mathbf{u}(\mathbf{m})$ (as a function of $\mathbf{m}$) such that $\mathbf{0} \leq \mathbf{u}(\mathbf{m}) \leq \boldsymbol{\Lambda}\boldsymbol{\Pi}(\mathbf{m})\mathbf{m}$, and $\forall t_i \in T_{nc}\ \mathbf{u}_i = 0$ along the marking trajectory, is called *suitably bounded.* Notice that if an input is not suitably bounded for a marking trajectory, then it cannot be applied in this. A marking $\mathbf{m}$ for which $\exists \mathbf{u}$ suitably bounded such that $\mathbf{C}[\boldsymbol{\Lambda}\boldsymbol{\Pi}(\mathbf{m})\mathbf{m} - \mathbf{u}] = \mathbf{0}$ is called *equilibrium marking.*

Marking $\mathbf{m}_2$ is said to be reachable from $\mathbf{m}_1$ if there exists an input $\mathbf{u}$ that transfers the marking from $\mathbf{m}_1$ to $\mathbf{m}_2$ in either finite or infinite time (lim-reachable) and it is suitably bounded. A marking reachable from the initial one is simply called reachable. The set of reachable markings can be defined for autonomous continuous PN and TCPN systems [14]. In the sequel, the term reachability *always* refer to timed systems.

3 Controllability Definition

If $\mathbf{y}$ is a *P-flow*, then for any reachable marking $\mathbf{m}$, $\mathbf{y}^T\mathbf{m} = \mathbf{y}^T\mathbf{m_0}$. So, whenever a TCPN system has *P-flows*, linear dependencies between marking variables appear, introducing state invariants. So, systems with P-flows are not controllable in the classical sense [11]. However, we are interested in the study of controllability "over" this invariant. In the sequel, we refer to this state invariant as $Class(\mathbf{m_0})$, since it is the equivalence class of $\mathbf{m_0}$ under the relation β defined as: $\mathbf{m}_1\beta\mathbf{m}_2$ iff $\mathbf{B_y}^T\mathbf{m}_1 = \mathbf{B_y}^T\mathbf{m}_2$, where $\mathbf{B_y}$ is a basis of P-flows.

Notice that, for a general TCPN system, every reachable marking belongs to $Class(\mathbf{m_0})$. The set $Class(\mathbf{m_0})$ can be divided into subsets of markings associated to the same configuration, which are named *regions* and are denoted by $\Re_i = \{\mathbf{m} \in Class(\mathbf{m_0}) | \mathbf{\Pi}(\mathbf{m}) = \mathbf{\Pi}_i\}$. Notice that such regions are convex sets, and inside each one, the state equation (1) is linear ($\mathbf{\Pi}(\mathbf{m})$ is constant). In the sequel, let us denote by $int(Class(\mathbf{m_0}))$ and $int(\Re_i)$ the sets of interior markings of $Class(\mathbf{m_0})$ and $\Re_i$, respectively, considering the space generated by the columns of $\mathbf{C}$. Next, linear systems controllability definition is recalled [13].

Definition 1. *A state equation is fully controllable if there exists an input such that for any two states* $\mathbf{x}_1$ *and* $\mathbf{x}_2$ *of the state space, it is possible to transfer the state from* $\mathbf{x}_1$ *to* $\mathbf{x}_2$ *in finite time.*

Notice that this definition cannot be applied to TCPN systems because the set of reachable markings never compose a vector space, as it is inside $Class(\mathbf{m_0})$. Moreover, in TCPN systems the input must be suitably bounded (i.e. $\mathbf{0} \leq \mathbf{u} \leq \mathbf{\Lambda\Pi}(\mathbf{m})\mathbf{m}$, $\mathbf{u}_i = 0, \forall t_i \in T_{nc}$). Therefore, the following adaptation of the classical controllability definition is proposed.

Definition 2. *The* TCPN *system* $\langle \mathcal{N}, \boldsymbol{\lambda}, \mathbf{m_0}\rangle$ *is controllable with bounded input (*BIC*) over* $S \subseteq Class(\mathbf{m_0})$ *if for any two markings* $\mathbf{m}_1, \mathbf{m}_2 \in S$ *there exists an input* $\mathbf{u}_{12}$ *that transfers the system from* $\mathbf{m}_1$ *to* $\mathbf{m}_2$ *in finite or infinite time, and it is suitably bounded (i.e.* $\mathbf{0} \leq \mathbf{u}_{12} \leq \mathbf{\Lambda\Pi}(\mathbf{m})\mathbf{m}$, *and* $\forall t_i \in T_{nc}$ $u_i = 0$ *along the marking trajectory). Furthermore, if* $S = Class(\mathbf{m_0})$ *then the system is said to be fully controllable with bounded input (*BIFC*).*

It is important to remark that controllability is a *structural* property. Even when, under this definition, it is said that a system is controllable over some subset of $Class(\mathbf{m_0})$, is the dynamical behavior of the system, which is determined by the structure and timing, that makes the system be controllable or not.

4 The Case Where All Transitions Are Controllable

In [14] reachability is studied for untimed continuous Petri net systems. An important result introduced in that paper is that a marking $\mathbf{m}$ is reachable iff

$\exists \boldsymbol{\sigma} \geq \mathbf{0}$ such that $\mathbf{m} = \mathbf{m_0} + \mathbf{C}\boldsymbol{\sigma} \geq \mathbf{0}$ and the transitions in the support of $\boldsymbol{\sigma}$ are fireable. This result can be extended for TCPN in the following way [11]:

Proposition 1. *Let $\langle \mathcal{N}, \boldsymbol{\lambda}, \mathbf{m_0} \rangle$ be a* TCPN *system in which $T_c = T$. A marking $\mathbf{m_1} \in Class(\mathbf{m_0})$ is reachable from $\mathbf{m_0} \in int(Class(\mathbf{m_0}))$ iff $\exists \boldsymbol{\sigma} \geq \mathbf{0}$ such that $\mathbf{C}\boldsymbol{\sigma} = (\mathbf{m_1} - \mathbf{m_0})$.*

The following proposition gives a necessary and sufficient condition for controllability over the interior of $Class(\mathbf{m_0})$.

Proposition 2. *Let $\langle \mathcal{N}, \boldsymbol{\lambda}, \mathbf{m_0} \rangle$ be a* TCPN *system, and let S be defined as $S = \{\mathbf{m} \in Class(\mathbf{m_0}) | \mathbf{m} > \mathbf{0}\}$. The system $\langle \mathcal{N}, \boldsymbol{\lambda}, \mathbf{m_0} \rangle$ is* BIC *over S iff the net is consistent.*

Proof. Proposition 2 in [11] states that if the net is consistent then the system is BIC over S. Now, for the other implication, consider any vector $\mathbf{d} \in span(\mathbf{C})$ and a marking $\mathbf{m_1} \in S$. Then, there exists a scalar $\beta > 0$ such that $\mathbf{m_1} + \beta\mathbf{d} \geq \mathbf{0}$. Let $\mathbf{m_2} = \mathbf{m_1} + \beta\mathbf{d}$, then $\mathbf{m_2} \in Class(\mathbf{m_0})$. Since the system is *BIC* over the interior of $Class(\mathbf{m_0})$, $\mathbf{m_2}$ is a particular solution of the fundamental equation, so $(\mathbf{m_2} - \mathbf{m_1}) = \beta\mathbf{d} = \mathbf{C}\boldsymbol{\sigma}$, where $\boldsymbol{\sigma} \geq \mathbf{0}$. Therefore, $\forall \mathbf{d} \in span(\mathbf{C}), \exists \boldsymbol{\sigma}$ such that $\mathbf{C}\boldsymbol{\sigma} = \mathbf{d}$. Finally, it can be proved that this property implies that $\exists \mathbf{x} > \mathbf{0}$ such that $\mathbf{C}\mathbf{x} = \mathbf{0}$, i.e. the net is consistent. □

Notice that the condition for controllability (consistency) is purely structural. Actually, the TCPN is BIC over the interior of $Class(\mathbf{m_0})$ iff the TCPN is BIC over the interior of $Class(\mathbf{m_1})$, for every $\mathbf{m_1} \geq \mathbf{0}$. Next proposition gives a condition to transfer the marking from the border of $Class(\mathbf{m_0})$ to its interior.

Proposition 3. *Let $\langle \mathcal{N}, \boldsymbol{\lambda}, \mathbf{m_0} \rangle$ be a* TCPN *system. An input* $\mathbf{u}$*, such that every enabled transition is always fired, transfers the marking from $\mathbf{m_0}$ to some $\mathbf{m}_f$, where $\mathbf{m}_f$ has not null elements, iff there are not empty siphons at $\mathbf{m_0}$.*

Proof. If there exists an empty siphon then $\nexists \mathbf{u}$ that transfers the marking to some $\mathbf{m} > \mathbf{0}$. Now, suppose that an input $\mathbf{u}$ such that for any enabled transition t_j, $\mathbf{u}_j < [\boldsymbol{\Lambda}\boldsymbol{\Pi}(\mathbf{m})\mathbf{m}]_j$ is being applied. If there exists a place p_i that remains unmarked for all time, then for each input transition t_j to this place, it must exists an input place p_k to t_j, which remains unmarked for all time. Repeating this reasoning, it can be seen that p_i belongs to an unmarked siphon. □

The following theorem introduces necessary and sufficient conditions for controllability over $Class(\mathbf{m_0})$. The proof is immediate from previous propositions.

Theorem 1. *The* TCPN *system $\langle \mathcal{N}, \boldsymbol{\lambda}, \mathbf{m_0} \rangle$ is* BIFC *iff $\mathcal{N}$ is consistent and there do not exist empty siphons at any marking in $Class(\mathbf{m_0})$.*

Example 1. Consider the TCPN systems of Figure 1, where $\mathbf{m_0} = [1, 2, 3, 1]^T$, $\mathbf{m_1} = [2, 1, 3, 1]^T$ and $\mathbf{m_2} = [1, 2, 1, 3]^T$. Since both systems have 2 P-semiflows, only the marking of two places are needed to represent the whole state.

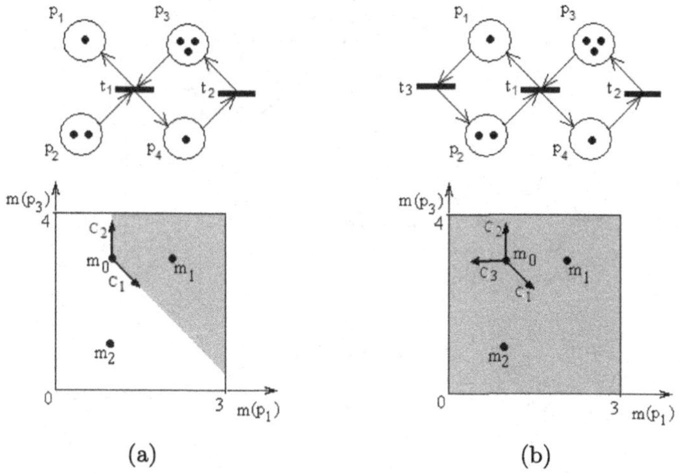

Fig. 1. (a) TCPN that is not BIFC. (b) A BIFC TCPN system.

For the system in Figure 1(a), $\exists \boldsymbol{\sigma} \geq \mathbf{0}$ such that $\mathbf{C}\boldsymbol{\sigma} = (\mathbf{m}_1 - \mathbf{m}_0)$, but $\nexists \boldsymbol{\sigma} \geq \mathbf{0}$ such that $\mathbf{C}\sigma = (\mathbf{m}_2 - \mathbf{m}_0)$, so, according to Proposition 1, $\mathbf{m}_1$ is reachable but $\mathbf{m}_2$ is not. Therefore it is not BIFC. The same conclusion (i.e. the system is not BIFC) can be obtained using Theorem 1. The shadowed area in Figure 1(a) corresponds to the set of reachable markings, notice that it is the convex defined by vectors $\mathbf{C}_1$ and $\mathbf{C}_2$, which represent the columns of $\mathbf{C}$ restricted to p_1 and p_3. Now, consider the system of Figure 1(b). This system is consistent, so, according to Proposition 2, it is BIC over the interior of $Class(\mathbf{m}_0)$. Therefore $\mathbf{m}_1$ and $\mathbf{m}_2$ are reachable from $\mathbf{m}_0$. Moreover, since at the border markings of $Class(\mathbf{m}_0)$ there are not unmarked siphons, according to Theorem 1, the system is BIFC.

5 Controllability with Uncontrollable Transitions

The study of controllability with uncontrollable transitions is more complicated than previous case. In this, consistency is no longer sufficient to guarantee controllability over the interior of $Class(\mathbf{m}_0)$. So, it is first necessary to define a suitable set of markings, and then, study the controllability over it. In this work only sets of equilibrium markings are considered, because they represent the "stationary operating points" of the modeled system. The set of all equilibrium markings is defined as:

$$E_qS = \{m \in Class(\mathbf{m}_0) | \exists \mathbf{u} \text{ suitably bounded such that } \mathbf{C}(\mathbf{\Lambda\Pi}(\mathbf{m})\mathbf{m} - \mathbf{u}) = 0\}$$

Notice that if all transitions are controllable then $E_qS = Class(\mathbf{m}_0)$. The set of all equilibrium markings in the i-th region is defined as $E_i = \{\mathbf{m} | \mathbf{m} \in E_qS \cap \Re_i\}$.

In the sequel, the following notation is adopted. Let $\mathbf{m}^q \in E_qS$. An equilibrium input for $\mathbf{m}^q$ is a vector $\mathbf{u}^q$ such that $\mathbf{C}(\mathbf{\Lambda\Pi}(\mathbf{m}^q)\mathbf{m}^q - \mathbf{u}^q) = \mathbf{0}$ and it is suitably

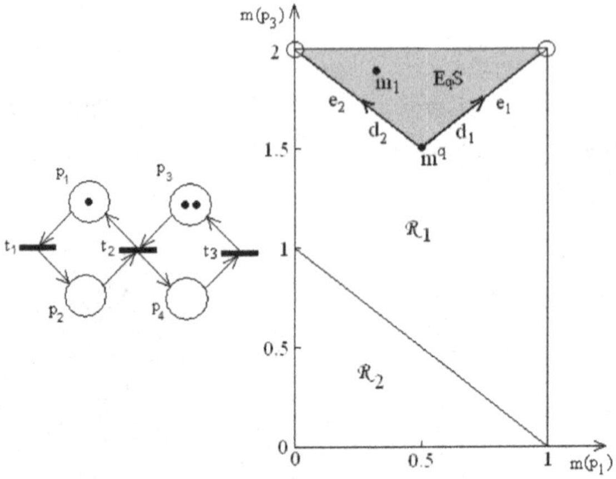

Fig. 2. The set E_qS, and subsets E_i, E_i^+ and E_i^*

bounded. The equilibrium flow through the transitions for $\mathbf{m}^q$ and $\mathbf{u}^q$ is denoted as $\mathbf{w}^q$, i.e. $\mathbf{w}^q = \mathbf{\Lambda\Pi}(\mathbf{m}^q)\mathbf{m}^q - \mathbf{u}^q$.

Example 2. Consider the system of figure 2 where $\mathbf{\Lambda} = \mathbf{I}$ and $T_c = \{t_1, t_2\}$. There exist two possible configurations: that in which t_2 is constrained by p_2, denoted by $\mathcal{C}_1$, and the other in which t_2 is constrained by p_3, denoted by $\mathcal{C}_2$. $\Re_1$ and $\Re_2$ are the regions related to $\mathcal{C}_1$ and $\mathcal{C}_2$, respectively. The whole triangle with all its edges and vertices corresponds to E_1. Actually, in this example $E_1 = E_qS$ and $E_2 = \varnothing$.

Since the system is linear inside each region, we will first investigate the controllability over each E_i. For that, it is necessary to represent a given E_i in a matrix form. The following definition introduces this representation.

Definition 3. *Let $\langle \mathcal{N}, \boldsymbol{\lambda}, \mathbf{m_0} \rangle$ be a* TCPN *system. A* Generator *of $E_i \neq \varnothing$ is a full column rank matrix $\mathbf{G}_i$ with $|P|$ rows, such that:*

a) *$\forall \mathbf{m}_1, \mathbf{m}_2 \in E_i$, the vector $(\mathbf{m}_1 - \mathbf{m}_2)$ is in the range of $\mathbf{G}_i$ (i.e. it is a linear combination of the columns of $\mathbf{G}_i$).*

b) *$\mathbf{G}_i$ is minimal (if one of its columns is removed then **a** is false).*

Notice that $\mathbf{G}_i$ is a kind of basis for E_i, but, formally speaking, E_i is not a vector space, then, it does not have a basis.

Coming back to the system of figure 2, a generator of E_1 is given by

$$\mathbf{G}_1 = \begin{bmatrix} 0.5, -0.5, 0.5, & 0.5 \\ -0.5, & 0.5, 0.5, -0.5 \end{bmatrix}^T$$

The restriction of the columns of $\mathbf{G}_1$ to the places p_1 and p_3 are represented in figure 2 by vectors $\mathbf{d}_1$ and $\mathbf{d}_2$.

In order to deal with the variable boundedness of the input, controllability is studied through the reachability over neighborhoods of equilibrium markings, because the bounds of the input are almost constant in these. Let us detail this idea. Consider again the system of figure 2. Let $\mathbf{m}_1$ be a marking in the interior E_1. The evolution of the system, taking $\mathbf{m}_1$ as the origin, is described by:

$$(\mathbf{m} \overset{\bullet}{-} \mathbf{m}_1) = \mathbf{C}\boldsymbol{\Lambda}\boldsymbol{\Pi}(\mathbf{m} - \mathbf{m}_1) - \mathbf{C}(\mathbf{u} - \mathbf{u}_1)$$

where $(\mathbf{u} - \mathbf{u}_1)$ is the new input. Since $\mathbf{u}_1$ is such that $[\boldsymbol{\Lambda}\boldsymbol{\Pi}\mathbf{m}_1]_j > \mathbf{u}_{1j} > 0$ for every $t_j \in T_c$ ($\mathbf{m}_1$ is in the interior of E_1), then the entries of $(\mathbf{u}-\mathbf{u}_1)$, related to the controllable transitions, can be settled as either negative or positive values, at least at the markings in a small enough neighborhood of $\mathbf{m}_1$. So, the reachability in such neighborhood can be studied through the classical Kalman's reachability condition (see [13]). However, the Kalman condition cannot be directly applied for all equilibrium markings. Consider the marking $\mathbf{m}^q$, depicted in figure 2, instead $\mathbf{m}_1$. The equilibrium input for this marking is $\mathbf{u}^q = \mathbf{0}$, so, the entries of the input $(\mathbf{u}-\mathbf{u}^q)$ can only be settled as nonnegative values (to apply the Kalman condition it is necessary that the input could take either positive or negative values). Therefore, it is important to know at which markings and at which entries the input can take negative values. For that, the following definitions are introduced.

Definition 4. *Let T_c be the set of controllable transitions. A transition $t_j \in T_c$ is said to be fully controllable at E_i if there exists an equilibrium marking $\mathbf{m}^q \in E_i$ with an equilibrium input $\mathbf{u}^q$ such that $[\boldsymbol{\Lambda}\boldsymbol{\Pi}_i\mathbf{m}^q]_j > \mathbf{u}^q_j > 0$. In other case, t_j is said to be partially controllable. The set of fully (partially) controllable transitions at E_i is denoted as T^i_{cf} (T^i_{cp}).*

Definition 5. *The subset of E_i, in which the equilibrium flow can be positive, is defined as*

$$E^+_i = \{\mathbf{m}^q \in E_i | \exists \mathbf{u}^q \text{ such that } \mathbf{w}^q > \mathbf{0}\}$$

The subset of E_i, in which the equilibrium flow can be positive and the entries of the input related to transitions T^i_{cf} are positive, is defined as

$$E^*_i = \{\mathbf{m}^q \in E^+_i | \exists \mathbf{u}^q \text{ such that } \mathbf{u}^q_j > 0,\ \forall t_j \in T^i_{cf}\}$$

Notice that $\forall \mathbf{m}^q \in E^+_i\ \exists \mathbf{u}^q$ such that $\mathbf{u}^q_j < [\boldsymbol{\Lambda}\boldsymbol{\Pi}_i\mathbf{m}^q]_j$, $\forall t_j \in T_c$. For all marking $\mathbf{m}^q \in E^*_i$ the input $\mathbf{u}$, at a neighbor marking $\mathbf{m}$, can be increased or decreased with respect to $\mathbf{u}^q$, at those entries related to the transitions in T^i_{cf} (i.e. fully controllable transitions). On the other hand, the entries of $\mathbf{u}$ related to the transitions in T^i_{cp} can only be increased with respect to $\mathbf{u}^q$ (i.e. partially controllable). For instance, the interior of the triangle in figure 2 corresponds to E^*_1, while the union of E^*_1 and the edges e_1 and e_2 (without the circled points) corresponds to E^+_1. Furthermore, $T^1_{cf} = T_c$ and $T^1_{cp} = \emptyset$. Therefore, for any marking in the interior of the triangle (i.e. for any $\mathbf{m}_1 \in E^*_1$) the value of $(\mathbf{u}-\mathbf{u}_1)$ can be settled as either positive or negative at those entries related to the transitions $\{t_1, t_2\}$ (i.e. T^1_{cf}).

Remark 1. E_i^*, E_i^+, E_i are convex sets, and $E_i^* \subseteq E_i^+ \subseteq E_i$. The markings of $\{E_i^+ - E_i^*\}$ are limit points, not interiors, of E_i^* (in the space generated by $\mathbf{G}_i$).

In the sequel, let us denote as $\mathbf{C}_c$, $\mathbf{C}_{cf}^i$ and $\mathbf{C}_{cp}^i$ the matrices built with the columns of $\mathbf{C}$ related to the transitions that belong to T_c, T_{cf}^i and T_{cp}^i, respectively. In the same way, denote with $\mathbf{u}_c$, $\mathbf{u}_{cf}^i$ and $\mathbf{u}_{cp}^i$ the vectors built with the entries of $\mathbf{u}$ related to the transitions that belong to T_c, T_{cf}^i and T_{cp}^i, respectively. In this way: $\mathbf{Cu} = \mathbf{C}_c\mathbf{u}_c = \mathbf{C}_{cf}^i\mathbf{u}_{cf}^i + \mathbf{C}_{cp}^i\mathbf{u}_{cp}^i$.

Now, we are ready to introduce the following theorem, which gives a sufficient and necessary condition for controllability over a set E_i^+.

Theorem 2. *Let $\langle \mathcal{N}, \boldsymbol{\lambda}, \mathbf{m_0} \rangle$ be a* TCPN *system. Consider E_i^+ such that $E_i^+ \cap int(\Re_i) \neq \varnothing$ and let $\mathbf{G}_i$ be a generator of it.*

The system is BIC *over E_i^+, considering all marking trajectories in $\Re_i$, iff there exist an index k and a matrix $\mathbf{b} \geq \mathbf{0}$ such that*

$$Cont^k\left(\mathbf{C}\boldsymbol{\Lambda}\boldsymbol{\Pi}_i, \left[-\mathbf{C}_{cf}^i, \mathbf{C}_{cf}^i, -\mathbf{C}_{cp}^i\right]\right) \cdot \mathbf{b} = \left[\mathbf{G}_i, -\mathbf{G}_i\right]$$

where the matrix function $Cont^k(\mathbf{A}, \mathbf{B}) = \left[\mathbf{B},\ \mathbf{AB},\ \ldots\ \mathbf{A}^k\mathbf{B}\right]$.

The proof is large and to improve readability it is shown in the appendix. This theorem also includes the result introduced in previous section, in which consistency is sufficient to guarantee controllability over $int(Class(\mathbf{m_0}))$, where $T_c = T$. This is easy to see noting that matrix $\left[-\mathbf{C}_{cf}^i, \mathbf{C}_{cf}^i, -\mathbf{C}_{cp}^i\right]$ includes all columns of the incidence matrix, and since the net is consistent, there always exists $\mathbf{b} \geq 0$ that fulfills the condition (consider $k = 0$).

The condition of previous theorem could be difficult to check, since there is no bound for the index k. Next corollary separates this condition into a necessary and a sufficient conditions that can be checked in polynomial time.

Corollary 1. *Let $\langle \mathcal{N}, \boldsymbol{\lambda}, \mathbf{m_0} \rangle$ be a* TCPN *system. Consider some E_i^+ such that $E_i^+ \cap int(\Re_i) \neq \varnothing$, as previously defined, and let $\mathbf{G}_i$ be a generator of it. Then:*

1. *If $\exists \mathbf{b}$ such that $Cont^{|P|-1}(\mathbf{C}\boldsymbol{\Lambda}\boldsymbol{\Pi}_i, -\mathbf{C}_{cf}^i) \cdot \mathbf{b} = \mathbf{G}_i$, then the system is controllable over E_i^+. Furthermore, if $T_{cf}^i = T_c$ then it is also a necessary condition for controllability over E_i^+, considering all the marking trajectories in $\Re_i$.*
2. *If $\nexists \mathbf{b}$ such that $Cont^{|P|-1}(\mathbf{C}\boldsymbol{\Lambda}\boldsymbol{\Pi}_i, -\mathbf{C}_c) \cdot \mathbf{b} = \mathbf{G}_i$, then the system is not controllable over E_i^+, considering all marking trajectories in $\Re_i$.*

Proof. Statement 1). Suppose that $\exists \mathbf{b}$ such that $Cont^{|P|-1}(\mathbf{C}\boldsymbol{\Lambda}\boldsymbol{\Pi}_i, -\mathbf{C}_{cf}^i) \cdot \mathbf{b} = \mathbf{G}_i$. Then, $\exists \mathbf{b}' \geq \mathbf{0}$ such that $Cont^{|P|-1}(\mathbf{C}\boldsymbol{\Lambda}\boldsymbol{\Pi}_i, [-\mathbf{C}_{cf}^i, \mathbf{C}_{cf}^i]) \cdot \mathbf{b}' = [\mathbf{G}_i, -\mathbf{G}_i]$. So, according to Theorem 2, the system is BIC over E_i^+. On the other hand, suppose that $T_c = T_{cf}^i$, so $\mathbf{C}_{cf} = \mathbf{C}_c$. If $\mathbf{G}_i$ is not in the range of $Cont^{|P|-1}(\mathbf{C}\boldsymbol{\Lambda}\boldsymbol{\Pi}_i, -\mathbf{C}_{cf}^i)$ then it is not in the range of $Cont^{|P|-1}(\mathbf{C}\boldsymbol{\Lambda}\boldsymbol{\Pi}_i, -\mathbf{C}_c^i)$. This condition is equal to that of statement 2).

Statement 2). Suppose that $\nexists \mathbf{b}$ such that $Cont^{|P|-1}(\mathbf{C}\boldsymbol{\Lambda}\boldsymbol{\Pi}_i, -\mathbf{C}_c) \cdot \mathbf{b} = \mathbf{G}_i$, then $\mathbf{G}_i$ is not in the range of $Cont^k(\mathbf{C}\boldsymbol{\Lambda}\boldsymbol{\Pi}_i, [-\mathbf{C}_{cf}^i, \mathbf{C}_{cf}^i, -\mathbf{C}_{cp}^i])$, for $k = |P|-1$, and according to the Cayley-Hamilton theorem, $\mathbf{G}_i$ is not in the range for any index k, so, the system is not BIC over E_i^+ (Theorem 2). □

Notice that previous corollary does not consider all possible cases, for that, next proposition introduces an equivalent condition to that of Theorem 2.

Proposition 4. *Suppose that all the coefficients of the characteristic polynomial of a matrix* $\mathbf{A}$ *are nonnegative.*

There exist k *and* $\mathbf{X}_k \leq \mathbf{0}$ *such that* $Cont^k(\mathbf{A},\mathbf{B}) \cdot \mathbf{X}_k = \mathbf{Y}$ iff $\exists \mathbf{X}_{2n-1} \leq \mathbf{0}$ *such that* $Cont^{2n-1}(\mathbf{A},\mathbf{B}) \cdot \mathbf{X}_{2n-1} = \mathbf{Y}$, *where* n *is the order of* $\mathbf{A}$.

Proof. Let m be the number of columns of $\mathbf{B}$. The sufficiency is obvious (just consider k as $2n-1$). Now, according to the Cayley-Hamilton theorem, $\mathbf{I}\alpha_0 + \mathbf{A}\alpha_1 + ... + \mathbf{A}^n\alpha_n = \mathbf{0}$, where $\{\alpha_0, \alpha_1, ..., \alpha_n\}$ are the coefficients of the characteristic polynomial of $\mathbf{A}$. Without lost of generality, suppose that $\alpha_n = 1$. Then, defining $\hat{\mathbf{a}} = \left[\mathbf{I}\alpha_0, \mathbf{I}\alpha_1, ..., \mathbf{I}\alpha_{n-1}\right]^T$, it can be seen that $Cont^{n-1}(\mathbf{A},\mathbf{B}) \cdot \hat{\mathbf{a}} = -\mathbf{A}^n\mathbf{B}$. Actually, for every $k \geq 0$, $-\mathbf{A}^{n+k}\mathbf{B} = Cont^{n+k-1}(\mathbf{A},\mathbf{B}) \cdot \left[\mathbf{0}_{m\times km},\ \hat{\mathbf{a}}^T\right]^T$, where $\mathbf{0}_{m\times km}$ is a null matrix of order $m \times km$. With this property, it is easy to prove that every solution $\mathbf{X}_k$ for

$$Cont^k(\mathbf{A},\mathbf{B}) \cdot \mathbf{X}_k = \mathbf{Y} \tag{2}$$

has the form

$$\mathbf{X}_k = \begin{bmatrix} \\ \mathbf{X}_{n-1} \\ \\ \mathbf{0} \\ \vdots \\ \mathbf{0} \\ \mathbf{0} \end{bmatrix} + \begin{bmatrix} \mathbf{I}\alpha_0 & \mathbf{0} & \cdots & \mathbf{0} \\ \mathbf{I}\alpha_1 & \mathbf{I}\alpha_0 & \cdots & \mathbf{0} \\ \vdots & \vdots & & \vdots \\ \mathbf{I}\alpha_{n-1} & \mathbf{I}\alpha_{n-2} & & \mathbf{0} \\ -\mathbf{I} & \mathbf{I}\alpha_{n-1} & \cdots & \mathbf{0} \\ \mathbf{0} & -\mathbf{I} & \cdots & \mathbf{I}\alpha_0 \\ \vdots & \vdots & & \vdots \\ \mathbf{0} & \mathbf{0} & \cdots & -\mathbf{I} \end{bmatrix} \begin{bmatrix} \gamma_n \\ \vdots \\ \gamma_k \end{bmatrix} \tag{3}$$

where $\mathbf{X}_{n-1}$ is any solution of equation (2) for $k = n-1$, and $\left[\gamma'_n \cdots \gamma'_k\right]^T$ is any column vector.

Now, suppose that for some $k > 2n-1$ there exists $\mathbf{X}'_k \leq \mathbf{0}$ that fulfills equation (2). Then, there exist $\mathbf{X}'_{n-1}$ and $\left[\gamma'_n \cdots \gamma'_k\right]^T$ that fulfill equation (3) (with $\mathbf{X}_k = \mathbf{X}'_k$). Since $\hat{\mathbf{a}} \geq \mathbf{0}$ and $\mathbf{X}'_k \leq \mathbf{0}$, it is easy to see, following a backward substitution reasoning in equation (3), that $\left[\gamma'_n \cdots \gamma'_k\right]^T \geq \mathbf{0}$. Then, considering the equation (3) with $k = 2n-1$, the values of $\mathbf{X}'_{n-1}$ and $\left[\gamma'_n \cdots \gamma'_{2n-1}\right]^T \geq \mathbf{0}$ lead to a solution $\mathbf{X}'_{2n-1} \leq \mathbf{0}$ for equation (2). □

Example 3. Consider the system of figure 3 with $T_c = \{t_4\}$, $\lambda_1 = \lambda_2 = \lambda_3 = 1$ and $\lambda_4 = 2$. Four configurations are realizable in the net, those are characterized by: $\mathcal{C}_1 = \{(t_2, p_2), (t_3, p_4)\}$, $\mathcal{C}_2 = \{(t_2, p_3), (t_3, p_4)\}$, $\mathcal{C}_3 = \{(t_2, p_2), (t_3, p_5)\}$ and $\mathcal{C}_4 = \{(t_2, p_3), (t_3, p_5)\}$, (the arcs (t_1, p_1) and (t_4, p_6) are also present in all the configurations). Moreover, given the initial marking of this system, $\mathcal{C}_2$ cannot occur. The lines inside the polytope correspond to set E_qS. The markings in

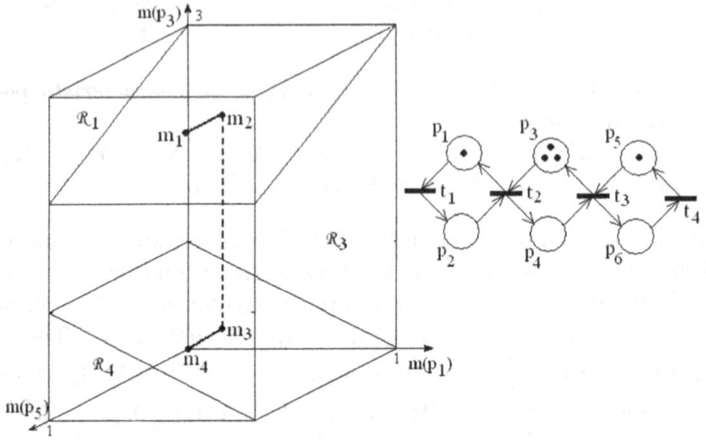

Fig. 3. TCPN system with its E_qS. Transition t_4 is the only controllable one.

the segments $[\mathbf{m}_1, \mathbf{m}_2]$, $[\mathbf{m}_2, \mathbf{m}_3]$ and $[\mathbf{m}_3, \mathbf{m}_4]$ correspond to E_1, E_3 and E_4, respectively. For this system we have that $T^1_{cf} = T^3_{cf} = T^4_{cf} = \{t_4\}$, and

$$\begin{array}{l} \mathbf{G}_1 = [\ 0,\quad 0,\quad 0,\quad 0,\ -1/2, 1/2\ ]^T \\ \mathbf{G}_3 = [\ 0,\quad 0,\ -1,\quad 1,\quad 0,\quad 0\ ]^T \\ \mathbf{G}_4 = [\ -1/3, 1/3, -1/3, 1/3, -1/3, 1/3\ ]^T \end{array}$$

Since $T^i_{cf} = T_c$ for the three configurations, we can check for the condition of Corollary 1 to investigate the controllability over each E_i^+. In this case the system fulfills that condition for the three E_i^+, so, it is BIC over each one.

Now, consider the same system but with $\mathbf{\Lambda} = \mathbf{I}$. In this case, the sets E_3 and E_4 remain unchanged, and so $\mathbf{G}_3$ and $\mathbf{G}_4$, but $E_1 = \{\mathbf{m}_2\}$. Also $T^3_{cf} = \varnothing$, then we cannot apply corollary 1 in order to investigate the controllability over E_3, however, the coefficients of the characteristic polynomial of $\mathbf{C\Lambda\Pi}_3$ are nonnegative, so we can use the Proposition 4, therefore the system is BIC over E_3^+ iff $\exists \mathbf{b} \geq \mathbf{0}$ such that $Cont^{2|P|-1}(\mathbf{C\Lambda\Pi}_3, -\mathbf{C}^3_{cp}) \cdot \mathbf{b} = [\mathbf{G}_3, -\mathbf{G}_3]$. Since it does not exists such vector, then the system is not BIC over E_3^+.

Finally, next proposition introduces sufficient conditions for controllability over the union of sets of equilibrium markings of different regions.

Proposition 5. *Let* $\langle \mathcal{N}, \boldsymbol{\lambda}, \mathbf{m_0} \rangle$ *be a* TCPN *system. Consider some equilibrium sets* E_1^+, E_2^+,..., E_j^+ *as defined above. If the system is* BIC *over each one and their union (i.e.* $\bigcup_{i=1}^{j} E_i^+$*) is connected, then the system is* BIC *over the union.*

Proof. Consider two of those sets E_1^+, E_2^+ such that $E_1^+ \cap E_2^+ \neq \varnothing$. Let $\mathbf{m}^q$ be a marking such that $\mathbf{m}^q \in E_1^+ \cap E_2^+$. Since the system is controllable over E_1^+ and E_2^+, there exists a marking $\mathbf{m}_2 \in E_2^+ - E_1^+$ that is reachable, in finite time, from another marking in $\mathbf{m}_1 \in E_1^+ - E_2^+$, due to the fact that both are reachable from

$\mathbf{m}^q$, in finite time, and to the continuity of the flow function. Then, any marking of E_2^+ is reachable from any marking of E_1^+, via $\mathbf{m}_1$ and $\mathbf{m}_2$. Following a similar reasoning, it can be concluded that the system is controllable over $\bigcup_{i=1}^{j} E_i^+$. □

Example 4. Consider the system of figure 3, where $T_c = \{t_4\}$, $\lambda_1 = \lambda_2 = \lambda_3 = 1$ and $\lambda_4 = 2$. In the previous example it was shown that the system is controllable over each E_i^+. Now, since the union of E_1^+, E_3^+ and E_4^+ is connected, then, according to Proposition 5, the system is BIC over $E_1^+ \cup E_3^+ \cup E_4^+$. Notice that, the union of those sets is equal to $E_qS - \{\mathbf{m}_4\}$.

6 Conclusions

This work addresses the controllability of timed continuous Petri Nets ($TCPN$) from a structural point of view. The main contributions of this work are focused in defining the controllability property and its characterization. For the case where all transitions are controllable, a polynomial characterization of controllable TCPN systems is presented. For systems with uncontrollable transitions, sufficient and necessary conditions for controllability, over subsets of equilibrium markings, are introduced, and sufficient conditions for controllability, over the union of those subsets, are given.

References

1. Mahulea, C., Recalde, L., Silva, M.: On performance monotonicity and basic servers semantics of continuous Petri nets. In: 8th Int. Workshop on Discrete Event Systems WODES 2006, Ann Arbor, USA, pp. 345–351. IEEE Computer Society Press, Los Alamitos (2006)
2. Alla, H., David, R.: Continuous and hybrid Petri nets. Journal of Circuits, Systems, and Computers 8(1), 159–188 (1998)
3. Recalde, L., Teruel, E., Silva, M.: Autonomous continuous P/T systems. In: Donatelli, S., Kleijn, J. (eds.) ICATPN 1999. LNCS, vol. 1639, pp. 107–126. Springer, Heidelberg (1999)
4. Silva, M., Recalde, L.: Petri nets and integrality relaxations: A view of continuous Petri nets. IEEE Trans. on Systems, Man, and Cybernetics 32(4), 314–327 (2002)
5. Sun, Z., Zheng, D.: On stabilization of switched linear control systems. IEEE Trans. on Automatic Control 46(2), 291–295 (2001)
6. Xie, G., Wang, L.: Controllability and stabilization of switched linear systems. Systems and Control Letters 48(2), 135–155 (2002)
7. Sontag, E.: An algebraic approach to bounded controllability of linear systems. Int. Journal of Control 39, 181–188 (1984)
8. Brammer, R.: Controllability in linear autonomous systems with positive controllers. SIAM J. Control 10(2), 329–353 (1972)
9. Camlibel, M.: Popov-belevitch-hautus type controllability for linear complementary systems. IEEE Trans. on Software Engineering 56(5), 381–387 (2007)
10. Seatzu, C., Corona, D., Giua, A., Bemporad, A.: Optimal control of continuous-time switched affine systems. IEEE Trans. on Automatic Control 51(5), 726–741 (2006)

11. Mahulea, C., Ramirez-Trevino, A., Recalde, L., Silva, M.: Steady state control reference and token conservation laws in continuous Petri net systems. IEEE Trans. on Automation Science and Engineering (to appear, 2007)
12. Jiménez, E., Júlvez, J., Recalde, L., Silva, M.: On controllability of timed continuous Petri net systems: the join free case. In: Proc. of the 44th IEEE Conf. on Decision and Control (Joint CDC-ECC), Seville, Spain, pp. 7645–7650 (2005)
13. Chen, C.: Linear system theory and design. Oxford University Press, USA (1984)
14. Júlvez, J., Recalde, L., Silva, M.: On reachability in autonomous continuous Petri net systems. In: van der Aalst, W.M.P., Best, E. (eds.) ICATPN 2003. LNCS, vol. 2679, pp. 221–240. Springer, Heidelberg (2003)

Appendix: Proof of Theorem 2

Proof. If $E_i^* = \varnothing$ then consider the set E_i^+ instead of E_i^*. Consider an equilibrium marking $(\mathbf{m}^q, \mathbf{u}^q)$, where $\mathbf{m}^q \in E_i^* \cap int(\Re_i)$. The state equation for any marking in $\Re_i$ can be expressed as: $\dot{\mathbf{m}} = (\mathbf{m} \overset{\bullet}{-} \mathbf{m}^q) = \mathbf{C\Lambda\Pi}_i(\mathbf{m} - \mathbf{m}^q) - \mathbf{C}(\mathbf{u} - \mathbf{u}^q)$. The solution of this state equation is given by:

$$\mathbf{m}(\tau) - \mathbf{m}^q = e^{\mathbf{C\Lambda\Pi}_i\tau}(\mathbf{m_0} - \mathbf{m}^q) - \int_0^\tau e^{\mathbf{C\Lambda\Pi}_i\zeta}\mathbf{C}\left(\mathbf{u}(\tau-\zeta) - \mathbf{u}^q\right)d\zeta \quad (4)$$

Now, let us analyze the boundedness of the input. By definition of T_{cf}^i, T_{cp}^i and $\mathbf{m}^q$, the input $\mathbf{u}^q$ is such that $[\mathbf{\Lambda\Pi}_i\mathbf{m}^q]_j > \mathbf{u}_j^q > \mathbf{0}$ $\forall t_j \in T_{cf}^i$, $\mathbf{u}_j^q = 0$ $\forall t_j \in T_{cp}^i$, and $\mathbf{u}_j = 0$ $\forall t_j \in T_{nc}$. Then, at any marking of a small enough neighborhood of $\mathbf{m}^q$ the value of $(\mathbf{u}(\tau-\zeta) - \mathbf{u}^q)_j$ can be settled as either positive or negative $\forall t_j \in T_{cf}^i$, as nonnegative $\forall t_j \in T_{cp}^i$, and zero $\forall t_j \in T_{nc}$. Furthermore, since $\mathbf{m}^q \in E_i^* \cap int(\Re_i)$, it can be demonstrated that $\mathbf{m}^q$ is an interior point of this neighborhood, considering the space generated by the columns of $Cont^k(\mathbf{C\Lambda\Pi}_i, \mathbf{C}_c)$. Therefore, considering the notation previously introduced, we can define column vectors $\mathbf{u}^+$ and $\mathbf{u}^-$ such that $\mathbf{C}_{cf}^i(\mathbf{u}_{cf}^i - \mathbf{u}_{cf}^{qi}) = [\mathbf{C}_{cf}^i, -\mathbf{C}_{cf}^i]\cdot[\mathbf{u}^+, \mathbf{u}^-]^T$ where $\mathbf{u}^+, \mathbf{u}^- \geq \mathbf{0}$. Then $\mathbf{Cu} = [\mathbf{C}_{cf}^i, -\mathbf{C}_{cf}^i, \mathbf{C}_{cp}^i]\mathbf{u}^*$ where $\mathbf{u}^* = [\mathbf{u}^+, \mathbf{u}^-, (\mathbf{u}_{cp}^i - \mathbf{u}_{cp}^{qi})]^T \geq 0$ at any marking in a neighborhood of $\mathbf{m}^q$.

Considering $\mathbf{m_0} = \mathbf{m}^q$ and substituting previous equation into (4), we obtain:

$$\mathbf{m}(\tau) - \mathbf{m}^q = -\int_0^\tau e^{\mathbf{C\Lambda\Pi}_i\zeta}\left[\mathbf{C}_{cf}^i, -\mathbf{C}_{cf}^i, \mathbf{C}_{cp}^i\right]\mathbf{u}^*(\tau-\zeta)d\zeta$$

Expanding the exponential matrix and reordering the terms:

$$\mathbf{m}(\tau) - \mathbf{m}^q = \left[\mathbf{I}, (\mathbf{C\Lambda\Pi}_i), (\mathbf{C\Lambda\Pi}_i)^2 \ldots\right]\cdot$$
$$\left[-\mathbf{C}_{cf}^i, \mathbf{C}_{cf}^i, -\mathbf{C}_{cp}^i\right]\begin{bmatrix}\int_0^\tau \mathbf{u}^*(\tau-\zeta)d\zeta \\ \int_0^\tau \zeta\mathbf{u}^*(\tau-\zeta)d\zeta \\ \int_0^\tau \frac{\zeta^2}{2}\mathbf{u}^*(\tau-\zeta)d\zeta \\ \vdots\end{bmatrix} \quad (5)$$

Notice that the entries of the right side vector are linearly independent and non-negative functions, for a small enough neighborhood of $\mathbf{m}^q$. Moreover, previous equation constitutes a necessary and sufficient condition for reachability.

If the condition of this theorem is fulfilled then, by definition of $\mathbf{G}_i$, for any equilibrium marking $\mathbf{m}^r$ in $\Re_i$ there exists $\mathbf{b}^r \geq \mathbf{0}$ such that

$$\mathbf{m}^r - \mathbf{m}^q = \left[\mathbf{I}, (\mathbf{C\Lambda\Pi}_i), (\mathbf{C\Lambda\Pi}_i)^2 \ldots\right] \cdot \left[-\mathbf{C}^i_{cf}, \mathbf{C}^i_{cf}, -\mathbf{C}^i_{cp}\right] \mathbf{b}^r$$

The entries of $\mathbf{b}^r \geq \mathbf{0}$ could be as small as desired (just considering $\mathbf{m}^r$ close enough to $\mathbf{m}^q$), so, comparing this equation with (5), it can be concluded that $\mathbf{m}^r$ is reachable from $\mathbf{m}^q$. Then, there exists a neighborhood of $\mathbf{m}^q$ in which all equilibrium markings are reachable from $\mathbf{m}^q$. Finally, since $E^*_i \cap int(\Re_i)$ is a convex set and $\forall \mathbf{m}^q \in E^*_i \cap int(\Re_i)$ there exists such reachable neighborhood, in which $\mathbf{m}^q$ is an interior point, then the set $E^*_i \cap int(\Re_i)$ is covered by these reachable neighborhoods and the system is BIC over $E^*_i \cap int(\Re_i)$.

On the other hand, notice that at any marking in $\Re_i$ the input is such that $\mathbf{u}^* \geq \mathbf{0}$. So, if the condition asked for the theorem is not fulfilled, then $\exists \mathbf{m}^r$ for which $\nexists \mathbf{b}^r \geq \mathbf{0}$ that fulfills previous equation, and according to equation (5), there does not exist a marking trajectory from $\mathbf{m}^q$ to $\mathbf{m}^r$ in $\Re_i$ in which $\mathbf{u}^* \geq \mathbf{0}$, therefore, $\mathbf{m}^r$ is not reachable from $\mathbf{m}^q$, considering all the marking trajectories in $\Re_i$ and so, the system is not BIC over E^*_i.

Now, let us demonstrate that controllability over $E^*_i \cap int(\Re_i)$ implies controllability over E^+_i. For this, suppose that the system is controllable over $E^*_i \cap int(\Re_i)$. Consider any marking $\mathbf{m}^r \in E^+_i - (E^*_i \cap int(\Re_i))$ and the markings $\mathbf{m}^q, \mathbf{m}^{r\prime}, \mathbf{m}^{q\prime} \in E^*_i \cap int(\Re_i)$, such that $(\mathbf{m}^r - \mathbf{m}^q) = \alpha(\mathbf{m}^{r\prime} - \mathbf{m}^{q\prime})$ with $\alpha \in \mathbb{R}_{>0}$.

Since the system is BIC over $E^*_i \cap int(\Re_i)$, then $\exists \mathbf{u}'$ that transfers the state from $\mathbf{m}^{r\prime}$ to $\mathbf{m}^{q\prime}$. So, by linearly, an input $\mathbf{u}$ such that $(\mathbf{u} - \mathbf{u}^q) = \alpha(\mathbf{u}' - \mathbf{u}^{q\prime})$ transfers the state from $\mathbf{m}^r$ to $\mathbf{m}^q$ (this is easy to prove by using equation (4)). Actually, $(\mathbf{m}(\tau) - \mathbf{m}^q) = \alpha(\mathbf{m}'(\tau) - \mathbf{m}^{q\prime})$, where $\mathbf{m}(\tau)$ $(\mathbf{m}'(\tau))$ is the marking at time τ if $\mathbf{m_0} = \mathbf{m}^q$ $(\mathbf{m_0} = \mathbf{m}^{q\prime})$ and $\mathbf{u}$ $(\mathbf{u}')$ is applied. So, choosing a suitable trajectory for $\mathbf{m}'(\tau)$ in $E^*_i \cap int(\Re_i)$, we can make $\mathbf{m}(\tau)$ stay always inside $\Re_i$. Since $\mathbf{0} \leq \mathbf{u}' \leq \mathbf{\Lambda\Pi}_i\mathbf{m}'$ then $-\alpha\mathbf{u}^{q\prime} \leq \alpha(\mathbf{u}' - \mathbf{u}^{q\prime}) \leq \alpha(\mathbf{\Lambda\Pi}_i\mathbf{m}' - \mathbf{u}^{q\prime})$. Now, substituting $\mathbf{u}'$ and $\mathbf{m}'$ and arranging the terms, we obtain: $(\mathbf{u}^q - \alpha\mathbf{u}^{q\prime}) \leq \mathbf{u} \leq \mathbf{\Lambda\Pi}_i\mathbf{m} - (\mathbf{w}^q - \alpha\mathbf{w}^{q\prime})$. Since $\mathbf{w}^q > \mathbf{0}$ and $(\mathbf{u}^{q\prime}_j > 0 \Rightarrow \mathbf{u}^q_j > 0)$, then $\exists\alpha > 0$ small enough such that $\mathbf{u}^q \geq \alpha\mathbf{u}^{q\prime}$ and $\mathbf{w}^q \geq \alpha\mathbf{w}^{q\prime}$, so, $\mathbf{0} \leq \mathbf{u} \leq \mathbf{\Lambda\Pi}_i\mathbf{m}$, i.e. $\mathbf{u}$ is s.b..

Therefore, for any $\mathbf{m}^r \in E^+_i - (E^*_i \cap int(\Re_i))$ there exists $\mathbf{m}^q \in E^*_i \cap int(\Re_i)$ reachable from $\mathbf{m}^r$. Furthermore, since the points of $E^+_i - (E^*_i \cap int(\Re_i))$ are limit points of $E^+_i \cap int(\Re_i)$, then every marking in $E^+_i - (E^*_i \cap int(\Re_i))$ can be reached (at least in infinite time) from any marking in $E^*_i \cap int(\Re_i)$, following a trajectory in $E^*_i \cap int(\Re_i)$. So, the system is controllable over E^+_i if it is controllable over $E^*_i \cap int(\Re_i)$. Finally, by definition, if the system is not controllable over $E^*_i \cap int(\Re_i)$, considering all marking trajectories in $\Re_i$, then it is not BIC over E^+_i.

Parameter Synthesis for Piecewise Affine Systems from Temporal Logic Specifications

Boyan Yordanov and Calin Belta*

Boston University, Boston MA
yordanov@bu.edu, cbelta@bu.edu

Abstract. In this paper, we consider discrete-time continuous-space Piecewise Affine (PWA) systems with parameter uncertainties, and study temporal logic properties of their trajectories. Specifically, given a PWA system with polytopal parameter uncertainties, and a Linear Temporal Logic (LTL) formula over linear predicates in the states of the system, we attempt to find subsets of parameters guaranteeing the satisfaction of the formula by all trajectories of the system. We illustrate our method by applying it to a PWA model of a two-gene network.

Keywords: Piecewise Affine Systems, Formal Verification.

1 Introduction

Temporal logics and model checking [1] are customarily used for specifying and verifying the correctness of digital circuits and computer programs. However, due to their resemblance to natural language, expressivity, and existence of off-the-shelf algorithms for model checking, temporal logics have the potential to impact several other areas. Examples include analysis of systems with continuous dynamics [2], control of linear systems from temporal logic specifications [3,4], task specification and controller synthesis in mobile robotics [5,6] and specification and analysis of qualitative behavior of genetic circuits [7,8,9].

In this paper we focus on piecewise affine systems (PWA) that evolve along different affine dynamics (in discrete time) in different polytopal regions of the (continuous) state space. PWA systems are widely used as models in many areas, including systems and synthetic biology, where they are particularly fitting for describing gene circuits [8]. PWA systems are also attractive because of the existence of tools for model identification [10]. Additionally, PWA systems are quite general, since they can approximate nonlinear dynamics with arbitrary accuracy [11], and are proven to be equivalent with several other classes of hybrid systems [12]. Even so, a PWA system with fixed parameters might not provide a good model of a real system. This is especially true for gene networks, where processes depend on various, hard to control external factors such as temperature and concentrations of chemicals not part of the system. To develop a model that

* This work is partially supported by NSF CAREER 0447721 and NSF 0410514 at Boston University.

M. Egerstedt and B. Mishra (Eds.): HSCC 2008, LNCS 4981, pp. 542–555, 2008.

can capture the rich behavior of systems under a range of conditions, a PWA model with uncertain parameters can be used. For such models, the dynamics in each region of the state space can take on parameters from a polytopal range.

A rich spectrum of properties of dynamical systems are naturally expressed in Linear Temporal Logic (LTL) [1] formulas over linear predicates in the state variables. Examples include remaining within certain regions (invariance), getting to certain target regions (reachability), or avoiding dangerous regions (safety). In this paper, we consider a parameter synthesis problem: given a PWA system with polytopal parameter uncertainties, and a Linear Temporal Logic (LTL) formula over linear predicates in the states of the system, we attempt to find subsets of parameters guaranteeing the satisfaction of the formula by all trajectories of the system. Our approach is based on the construction of finite simulation quotients, model checking, and use of counterexamples for determining ranges of allowed parameters.

From a theoretical and computational point of view, this work can be seen in the context of literature focused on the construction of finite quotients of infinite systems (see [13] for a review), and is closely related to [14,3,4] and our previous work on formal analysis of PWA systems with fixed parameters [15]. Unlike counterexample guided refinement [16], where violating trajectories of the quotient are checked against the concrete model and, if spurious, removed by refinement, we use counterexamples to remove a set of (possibly spurious) violating transitions from the quotient. From an application point of view, this paper relates to [8,17,18,19,9], where temporal logics are used to specify properties of biomolecular networks. These works analyze whether the trajectories of a system satisfy a temporal logic formula. In contrast, we search parameter sets guaranteeing the satisfaction of a formula. We implemented our method as a software tool for parameter synthesis in PWA systems, which is freely downloadable from `http://iasi.bu.edu/~cbelta/software.htm`.

2 Preliminaries

2.1 Transition Systems, Simulations, and Bisimulations

Definition 1. *A transition system is a tuple $T = (Q, Q_0, \to, \Pi, \vDash)$, where Q is a set of states, $Q_0 \subseteq Q$ is the set of initial states, $\to \subseteq Q \times Q$ is a transition relation, Π is a finite set of atomic propositions, and $\vDash \subseteq Q \times \Pi$ is a satisfaction relation.*

A transition $(q, q') \in \to$ is also denoted by $q \to q'$. The transition system T is called *finite* if its set of states Q is finite, and infinite otherwise. The transition system T is called *non-blocking* if, for every state $q \in Q$, there exists $q' \in Q$ such that $(q, q') \in \to$ (*i.e.*, the relation $\to$ is total). The transition system T is called *deterministic* if, for all $q \in Q$, there exists at most one $q' \in Q$ such that $(q, q') \in \to$ (the case $q = q'$ is included in the definitions above).

For an arbitrary state $q \in Q$, we define $\Pi_q = \{\pi \in \Pi \mid q \vDash \pi\}$, $\Pi_q \in 2^{\Pi}$ as the set of all atomic propositions satisfied at q. A *trajectory* or *run* of T

starting from $q \in Q_0$ is an infinite sequence $r = r(1)r(2)r(3)\ldots$ with the property that $r(1) = q$, $r(i) \in Q$, and $(r(i), r(i+1)) \in \rightarrow$, for all $i \geq 1$. A trajectory $r = r(1)r(2)r(3)\ldots$ defines a *word* $w = w(1)w(2)w(3)\ldots$, where $w(i) = \Pi_{r(i)}$. The set of all words generated by the set of all trajectories starting at $q \in Q_0$ is called the *language* of T originating at q and is denoted by $L_T(q)$. The language of the transition system T is defined as $L_T(Q_0)$ or L_T for simplicity.

A subset X of the state set Q ($X \subseteq Q$) is called a *region* of T. For an arbitrary region X, we define the set of states $Post(X)$ that can be reached from X in one step as

$$Post(X) = \{q' \in Q \mid \exists q \in X,\ q \rightarrow q'\} \tag{1}$$

and the set of states that can reach X in one step as

$$Pre(X) = \{q' \in Q \mid \exists q \in X,\ q' \rightarrow q\} \tag{2}$$

An equivalence relation $\sim \subseteq Q \times Q$ over the state space of T is *proposition preserving* if for all $q_1, q_2 \in Q$ and all $\pi \in \Pi$, if $q_1 \sim q_2$ and $q_1 \vDash \pi$, then $q_2 \vDash \pi$. Among the several proposition preservation equivalence relations that can be defined, *propositional equivalence* defined as $q_1 \sim q_2$ if and only if $\Pi_{q_1} = \Pi_{q_2}$ is of special interest. A proposition preserving equivalence relation naturally induces a *quotient transition system* $T/_\sim = (Q/_\sim, Q_0/_\sim, \rightarrow_\sim, \Pi, \vDash_\sim)$. $Q/_\sim$ is the quotient space (the set of all equivalence classes) and $Q_0/_\sim = \{X \in Q/_\sim \mid \exists q \in X$ such that $q \in Q_0\}$ is the set of all initial equivalence classes. The transition relation $\rightarrow_\sim$ is defined as follows: for $X_1, X_2 \in Q/_\sim$, $X_1 \rightarrow_\sim X_2$ if and only if there exist $q_1 \in X_1$ and $q_2 \in X_2$ such that $q_1 \rightarrow q_2$. The satisfaction relation is defined as follows: for $X \in Q/_\sim$, we have $X \vDash_\sim \pi$ if and only if there exist $q \in X$ such that $q \vDash \pi$. It is easy to see that $L_T(X) \subseteq L_{T/_\sim}(X)$, for any $X \in Q_0/_\sim$ (with a slight abuse of notation, we use the same symbol X to denote both a state of $T/_\sim$ and the corresponding region of equivalent states of T). The quotient transition system $T/_\sim$ is said to *simulate* the original system T, which is written as $T/_\sim \geq T$.

Definition 2. *A proposition preserving equivalence relation $\sim$ is a bisimulation of a transition system $T = (Q, Q_0, \rightarrow, \Pi, \vDash)$ if, for all states $p, q \in Q$, if $p \sim q$ and $p \rightarrow p'$, then there exist $q' \in Q$ such that $q \rightarrow q'$ and $p' \sim q'$.*

If $\sim$ is a bisimulation, then the quotient transition system $T/_\sim$ is called a *bisimulation quotient* of T, and the transition systems T and $T/_\sim$ are called *bisimilar*, denoted by $T/_\sim \cong T$. An immediate consequence of bisimulation is language equivalence, *i.e.*, $L_T(X) = L_{T/_\sim}(X)$, for all $X \in Q_0/_\sim$.

2.2 Linear Temporal Logic and Model Checking

To specify temporal logic properties for trajectories of PWA systems, in this paper we use Linear Temporal Logic [1]. Informally, the LTL formulas are recursively defined over a set of atomic propositions Π, by using the standard Boolean operators (*e.g.*, $\neg$ (negation), $\vee$ (disjunction), $\wedge$ (conjunction)) and temporal operators, which include $\mathcal{U}$ ("until"), $\Box$ ("always"), $\Diamond$ ("eventually"). LTL formulas are interpreted over infinite words in 2^{Π}, as are those generated by the transition system T from Definition 1. If ϕ_1 and ϕ_2 are two LTL formulas over Π, formula $\phi_1 \mathcal{U} \phi_2$ intuitively means that (over some word) ϕ_2 will eventually become true and ϕ_1 is true until this happens. For an LTL formula ϕ, formula $\Diamond\phi$ means that ϕ becomes eventually true, whereas $\Box\phi$ indicates that ϕ is true at all positions of a word. More expressiveness can be achieved by combining the mentioned operators. For example, $\Diamond\Box\phi$ means that ϕ will eventually become true and then remain true forever, while $\Box\Diamond\phi$ means that ϕ is true infinitely often.

Given a finite transition system $T = (Q, Q_0 \rightarrow, \Pi, \models)$ and a formula ϕ over Π, checking whether the words of T starting from a region X satisfy ϕ (written as $T(X) \models \phi$) is called *model checking* [1]. If we denote by L_ϕ the set of all words (language) satisfying ϕ, then model checking means deciding the language inclusion $L_T(X) \subseteq L_\phi$. We also say that a transition system satisfies a formula ($T \models \phi$) if and only if $T(Q_0) \models \phi$.

If $T/_\sim$ is a quotient of T, then for any equivalence class $X \in Q_0/_\sim$ and formula ϕ, we have:

$$T/_\sim(X) \models \phi \Rightarrow T(X) \models \phi. \tag{3}$$

In addition, if $\sim$ is a bisimulation, then

$$T/_\sim(X) \models \phi \Leftrightarrow T(X) \models \phi \tag{4}$$

Properties (3) and (4) allow one to model check finite quotients and extend the results to the (possibly infinite) original transition system.

3 Problem Formulation

Let $\mathcal{X}, \mathcal{X}_l$, $l \in L$ be a set of open polytopes in $\mathbb{R}^N$ and $\mathcal{P}_l$ be a set of open polytopes in $\mathbb{R}^{(N^2+N)}$, where L is a finite index set, such that $\mathcal{X}_{l_1} \bigcap \mathcal{X}_{l_2} = \emptyset$ for all $l_1, l_2 \in L$, $l_1 \neq l_2$ and $\bigcup_{l \in L} cl(\mathcal{X}_l) = cl(\mathcal{X})$, where $cl(\mathcal{X})$ is the closure of $\mathcal{X}$.

A discrete-time continuous-space piecewise affine (PWA) system Σ with polytopal parameter uncertainty is defined as:

$$\Sigma\ :\ x_{k+1} = A(p)x_k + b(p),\ x_0 \in \mathcal{X}_{in},\ x_k \in \mathcal{X}_l,\ p \in \mathcal{P}_l,\ l \in L,\ k = 0, 1, , \dots \tag{5}$$

where $\mathcal{X}_{in} \subseteq \mathcal{X}$ is a set of initial conditions and $\mathcal{P}_l$ is the allowed set of parameters in region $l \in L$. The linear functions $A : \mathbb{R}^{(N^2+N)} \rightarrow \mathbb{R}^{N \times N}$ and $b : \mathbb{R}^{(N^2+N)} \rightarrow \mathbb{R}^{N \times 1}$ simply take the first N^2 and the last N components of $p \in \mathbb{R}^{(N^2+N)}$ and form a $N \times N$ matrix and $N \times 1$ vector, respectively.

$\mathcal{X}$ is assumed to be an invariant for the trajectories of Σ under all values of the parameters. We are interested in studying properties of trajectories of system (5) specified in terms of a set of linear predicates of the form

$$\Pi = \{\pi_i \,|\, \pi_i\ :\ a_i^T x + b_i < 0,\ i = 1, \dots, K\}, \tag{6}$$

where $x, a_i \in \mathbb{R}^N$ and $b_i \in \mathbb{R}, i = 1, \ldots, K$. Without loss of generality, we assume that the set of initial states $\mathcal{X}_{in}$ from the definition of the PWA system (5) is a union of polytopes from the set of polytopes determined by the regions $\mathcal{X}_l$ and the linear predicates from Π (if this is not the case, more linear predicates can be added to Π in Equation (6)).

Informally, the semantics of system (5) can be understood in the following sense: a trajectory $x_0 x_1 x_2 \ldots$ of the system can be obtained by selecting an initial condition $x_0 \in \mathcal{X}_{in}$, finding an $l \in L$, such that $x_0 \in \mathcal{X}_l$, selecting a parameter $p \in \mathcal{P}_l$, applying the affine map of Equation (5) and repeating this procedure for each subsequent step. A trajectory produces a word $w_0 w_1 w_2 \ldots$, where each $w_i \in 2^{\Pi}$ lists the propositions from Π which are satisfied by x_i. Then, such words can be checked against satisfaction of LTL formula ϕ over Π. A formal definition is given in Section 4 through an embedding transition system. We consider the following problem:

Problem 1. Given a PWA system (Equation (5)) and an LTL formula ϕ over a set of linear predicates Π (Equation (6)), find sets of parameters such that all the trajectories of the system satisfy the formula, under all identified parameters.

In other words, we are interested in excluding parameters from the allowed sets for each region, for which the formula is not satisfied. As it will become clear later, for each region $l \in L$, the solution will be in the form of a union of disjoint open subpolytopes of the allowed polytope $\mathcal{P}_l$.

To provide a solution to Problem 1, we first embed the PWA system (5) into an infinite transition system T_e. By using the equivalence classes induced by the predicates from (6), we then construct a finite overapproximation quotient transition system $\overline{T_e/_\sim}$ whose language includes the language of T_e (see Section 4). We then use model checking to cut transitions from $\overline{T_e/_\sim}$ (see Section 5.1) and, correspondingly, sets of parameters from (5) (see Section 5.2), until all its trajectories satisfy the formula. Alternatively, in Section 6, we propose a method for the direct construction of a bisimulation quotient. In both approaches, our method is conservative, as it will become clear later.

Remark 1. There are several simplifying assumptions that we make in the formulation of Problem 1. First, we assume that the polytope $\mathcal{X}$ is an invariant for all trajectories of (5). However, this assumption is not restrictive, since $\mathcal{X}$ can be assumed large enough to contain all possible state values in a particular process. Second, we assume that the predicates in Equation (6) are given over strict inequalities, and only the reachability of open full dimensional polytopes is captured in the semantics of the embedding and of the quotients[1]. However, this seems to be enough for practical purposes, since only sets of measure zero are disregarded, and it is unreasonable to assume that equality constraints can be detected in a real world application.

[1] Throughout the rest of the paper, unless clearly specified, we refer to an "open polytope" simply as "polytope."

4 Construction of Finite Quotients

To formally define the satisfaction of a formula ϕ over Π by the PWA system (5), we embed it into a transition system:

Definition 3. *An embedding transition system for (5) and the set of predicates Π can be defined as $T_e = (Q_e, Q_{0e}, \rightarrow_e, \Pi_e, \models_e)$, where*

- $Q_e = \bigcup_{l \in L} \mathcal{X}_l$,
- $Q_{0e} = \mathcal{X}_{in}$,
- $(x, x') \in \rightarrow_e$ *if and only if there exist $l \in L$, $x \in \mathcal{X}_l$ and $p \in \mathcal{P}_l$ such that $x' = A(p)x + b(p)$,*
- $\Pi_e = L \bigcup \Pi$,
- $\models_e$ *is defined as follows: if $\pi = l \in L$, then $x \models_e \pi$ if and only if $x \in \mathcal{X}_l$; if $\pi = \pi_i \in \Pi$, then $x \models_e \pi$ if and only if $a_i^T x + b_i < 0$,*

Definition 4. *Given a subset $X \subseteq Q_{0e}$, we say that all trajectories of system (5) originating in X satisfy formula ϕ if and only if $T_e(X)$ satisfies ϕ (as defined in Section 2.1).*

The embedding transition system T_e has infinitely many states and cannot be model checked directly. Given a polytopal, proposition preserving equivalence relation $\sim$ on Q_e, one can try to construct (and model check) the quotient transition system $T_e/_\sim = \{Q_e/_\sim, Q_{0e}/_\sim, \rightarrow_{e\sim}, \Pi_e, \models_e\}$ (see Section 2.1). The construction of the states $Q_e/_\sim$ and initial states $Q_{0e}/_\sim$ amounts to checking the non-emptiness of polyhedral sets and intersections of polyhedral sets, respectively. Satisfaction of each state is induced directly from the equivalence relation. If the *Post*() (or *Pre*()) operator can be computed, transitions in the quotient can be assigned as follows: $(X_i, X_j) \in \rightarrow_{e\sim}$ if and only if $Post(X_i) \cap X_j \neq \emptyset$ (or $Pre(X_j) \cap X_i \neq \emptyset$).

In our previous work [15], we focused on PWA systems with fixed parameters (*i.e.*, $\mathcal{P}_l$ in Equation (5) were singletons), and showed that for the propositional equivalence relation $\sim$, the quotient $T_e/_\sim$ can be efficiently constructed, based on the computation of the *Pre*() operator, which was a polyhedral set. Moreover, we showed that all the steps in the "bisimulation algorithm" for the iterative construction of simulation quotients leading to the coarsest bisimulation quotient [20,21] (if one exists) are implementable.

Under parameter uncertainty, $T_e/_\sim$ cannot always be constructed, since in general, there are no algorithms capable of exact computations of *Pre*() or *Post*() operators. In fact, it can be proven that when parameters are allowed to vary in polyhedral sets, both operators might return a non-convex set even when applied to a polyhedral set [22].

If we denote by $Post_e()$ the "*Post*()" operator of the embedding transition system T_e, then from Equation (1) and Definition 3, for an arbitrary polytope $X \subseteq \mathcal{X}_l, l \in L$ we have

$$Post_e(X) = \{x' \in \mathbb{R}^N \mid \exists p \in \mathcal{P}_l,\ \exists x \in X \text{ such that } x' = A(p)x + b(p)\} \quad (7)$$

Proposition 1. *A polyhedral overapproximation of $Post_e(X)$ is given by*

$$\overline{Post_e(X)} = Conv\{A(w)v + b(w), w \in \mathcal{V}(\mathcal{P}_l), v \in \mathcal{V}(X)\} \tag{8}$$

where $\mathcal{V}(X)$ and $\mathcal{V}(\mathcal{P}_l)$ denote the sets of vertices of $\mathcal{X}$ and $\mathcal{P}_l$, respectively.

Proof. See `http://iasi.bu.edu/~yordanov/papers/HSCC2008full.pdf`.

Similarly to [23], we use the smallest convex set containing $Post_e()$ as an overapproximation. Although a precise distance between the real set and its overapproximation has not been determined, it has been established through extensive simulation that in general, the volume of $Post_e()$ is not significantly increased by the approximation.

By using $\overline{Post_e(X)}$ instead of the regular $Post_e()$ operator, transitions in an overapproximation quotient can be efficiently obtained as described for the general case.

Formally, if $\sim$ is the propositional equivalence relation, the overapproximation quotient can be given as $\overline{T_e/_\sim} = \{Q_e/_\sim, Q_{0e}/_\sim, \overline{\to_{e\sim}}, \Pi_e, \models_e\}$, where $\to_{e\sim} \subseteq \overline{\to_{e\sim}}$. This implies that

$$L_{T_e} \subseteq L_{T_e/_\sim} \subseteq L_{\overline{T_e/_\sim}} \tag{9}$$

and therefore the overapproximation quotient simulates the exact quotient and the embedding system. As a result, model checking can be performed on the overapproximation quotient and satisfaction of a formula can be extended to the embedding.

5 Counterexample Guided Parameter Synthesis

In Section 4 we showed that an overapproximation quotient $\overline{T_e/_\sim}$ can be constructed, and all operations involved are computable. In this section, we propose to use LTL model checking to "cut" transitions from $\overline{T_e/_\sim}$ until we obtain a transition system $\overline{T_e/_\sim}^{\phi}$ satisfying the formula. Then we go back to the initial system (5) and remove parameter values such that the language of the new embedding transition system is included in the language of $\overline{T_e/_\sim}^{\phi}$, which guarantees the satisfaction of the formula by the PWA system (5).

5.1 Construction of Satisfying Quotients

Using our LTL model checker described in [4], we start by searching for a shortest run[2] of $\overline{T_e/_\sim}$ satisfying the negation of the formula $\neg\phi$. If such a run exists, then we eliminate it by removing one of its transitions. Then we reiterate the process until we obtain the transition system $\overline{T_e/_\sim}^{\phi}$ satisfying ϕ.

[2] A standard representation of an infinite run includes finite prefix and suffix, where the suffix is repeated an infinite number of times. The length of a run is defined as the sum of the lengths of the prefix and suffix.

Since, in general, several different transitions are taken during the generation of a counterexample, removing any one of them will remove the counterexample from the language of the quotient. It is impossible to determine which transition's removal will lead to a solution (or to the best solution when more than one exists). Therefore, in this paper, we exhaustively generate all solutions. This process can be seen as generating a tree, having the initial finite quotient as its root. Each child node in the tree represents a quotient that has the same set of states as the parent, but only a subset of its transitions. The children for each node are generated by removing one different transition, appearing in the shortest counterexample, from the parent.

When transitions are removed, a state of the quotient might become blocking, resulting in the appearance of finite words in its language. Since the semantics of LTL are defined only over infinite ω-words, we make all blocking states unreachable by removing all their incoming transitions. It is also possible that one or more of the initial states become blocking, in which case we ignore the corresponding quotient (further removal of transitions will not lead to a solution).

A leaf node in the tree represents a quotient for which computation stopped, since no additional counterexamples can be generated. The quotients represented by such nodes satisfy the LTL formula, since their languages are nonempty (all initial states are non-blocking), do not contain finite words (no blocking states are reachable), and have an empty set of counterexamples.

5.2 Parameter Synthesis

The finite quotient $T_e/_\sim$ is constructed so that it captures all possible transitions of the embedding T_e. By Definition 3, transitions are included in the embedding if and only if appropriate parameters for such a transition are allowed. Therefore, we can relate the transitions present in the finite quotient to sets of allowed parameters for the PWA system.

Definition 5. *Given two polytopes X and Y in $\mathbb{R}^N$, the set of parameters $P^{X \not\to Y}$, for which the image of X does not have an intersection with Y, is defined as:*

$$P^{X \not\to Y} = \{p \in \mathbb{R}^{(N^2+N)} \mid A(p)x + b(p) \notin Y \text{ for all } x \in X\} \tag{10}$$

Proposition 2. *Let X and Y be polytopes in $\mathbb{R}^N$ given in V-representation as $X = Conv\{v_1, \dots v_m\}$ and H-representation as $Y = \{x \in \mathbb{R}^N \mid c_i^T x + d_i < 0,\ i = 1, \dots, n\}$, respectively. Then,*

$$\underline{P^{X \not\to Y}} = \bigcup_{i=1}^{n} \{p \in \mathbb{R}^{(N^2+N)} \mid c_i^T (A(p)v_j + b(p)) + d_i > 0, \text{ for all } j = 1, \dots, m\}$$

is an underapproximation of $P^{X \not\to Y}$ (i.e., $\underline{P^{X \not\to Y}} \subseteq P^{X \not\to Y}$)

Proof. See `http://iasi.bu.edu/~yordanov/papers/HSCC2008full.pdf`.

In other words, a conservative underapproximation $\underline{P^{X \not\to Y}}$ of $P^{X \not\to Y}$ can be obtained as the union of polyhedral sets from the V-representation of X and the H-representation of Y.

We use the underapproximation from Proposition 2 to find sets of parameters for each region $l \in L$, such that, for each node of the tree described in Section 5.1, the corresponding PWA system is simulated by the quotient transition system at that node. Specifically, for two polytopes $X \subseteq \mathcal{X}_l$ and Y, if the parameters in region $l \in L$ are restricted to the set $\mathcal{P}_l \cap \underline{P^{X \not\to Y}}$, then, by Proposition 2, the transition $x \rightarrow_e y$ will not appear in the embedding T_e, for any $x \in X$ and $y \in Y$. This means that, in the corresponding quotient, the transition $X \rightarrow_{e\sim} Y$ will not exist. As already stated, we cannot compute $T_e/_\sim$. However, by restricting the parameters as described above, we can ensure that, at every node of the tree constructed in Section 5.1, the PWA system with restricted parameters is simulated by the quotient transition system at that node. As previously stated, the leaf nodes of the computation tree contain quotients satisfying the formula and their corresponding PWA systems provide a solution to Problem 1.

Because of the overapproximation used in the construction of the quotient, a spurious transition might appear in place of a deleted one ($(X,Y) \in \overline{\rightarrow}_{e\sim}$ but $(X,Y) \not\in \rightarrow_{e\sim}$). We prevent this by enforcing that a deleted transition never reappears in the quotient. Additionally, the structure of PWA systems allows different polytopes (determined by the set of linear predicates) to share the same sets of parameters, and therefore, it is possible that other transitions are removed from the quotient besides the target one. To account for this, we reconstruct the quotient every time parameters are cut. If, during the removal of parameters, a set $\mathcal{P}_l$ becomes empty, then we embed all polytopes from region $l \in L$ as blocking states, and make them unreachable.

Given only the purely discrete problem of modifying a quotient to satisfy a formula by taking a subset of its transitions, our approach is guaranteed to terminate, finding a solution when one exists, as it is exhaustive and follows a tree of size limited by the total number of transitions in the initial quotient. In the combined problem of transition and parameter removal, computation will still terminate but a potential solution might be missed due to the approximations. If a solution is found, however, it is guaranteed to be correct.

Going back to the tree construction from Section 5.1, in general, our algorithm will produce more than one solution (each leaf corresponds to a satisfying transition system). Selecting the "best" solution is a non-trivial problem, and might depend on the application. For example, it is possible to introduce additional constraints (such as requiring that a particular transition is present in the solution) or compare total number of transitions of the solutions, since more reachable states from the initial one with more transitions result in a richer language. In the case study presented at the end of this paper, we chose the latter.

Our solution to Problem 1 is summarized in Algorithm 1.. In order to prevent unnecessary computation, we first check the system from each initial state. If there exists an initial state from which the negation of the formula is satisfied, then there are no satisfying trajectories originating there, so a solution will not be found by refining the transitions (and corresponding parameters). As stated earlier, the algorithm is guaranteed to terminate, as its execution follows at tree of finite size.

Algorithm 1. Obtain subsets of parameters for a PWA system Σ_{in} such that an LTL formula ϕ is satisfied.

$T_{sat} = \emptyset$;
Construct $\overline{T_e/_\sim}$ from the initial PWA system Σ_{in};
for each $X \in Q_{0e}/_\sim$ **do**
  if $\overline{T_e/_\sim}(X) \models \neg\phi$ **then**
    return $\emptyset$;
  end if
end for
$T_{all} = \{(\Sigma_{in}, \overline{T_e/_\sim})\}$;
while $T_{all} \neq \emptyset$ **do**
  for each pair $(\Sigma, T) \in T_{all}$ **do**
    $T_{all} = T_{all} \setminus (\Sigma, T)$;
    generate the shortest counter-example c for T and formula ϕ;
    if $c = \emptyset$ and $L_T \neq \emptyset$ **then**
      add (Σ, T) to T_{sat};
    else
      for each transition $X \to Y$ of counterexample c **do**
        Find $\mathcal{X}_l$ such that $X \subseteq \mathcal{X}_l$;
        Construct Σ' from Σ by setting $\mathcal{P}'_l = \mathcal{P}_l \cap \underline{P^{X \not\to Y}}$;
        Reconstruct quotient T' from Σ' and ensure no previously removed transitions reappear;
        Make blocking states of T' unreachable
        if initial states in T' are non-blocking **then**
          add (Σ', T') to $\{T_{all}\}$
        end if
      end for
    end if
  end for
end while
return $\{T_{sat}\}$;

Both the number of states and transitions in the embedding $\overline{T_e/_\sim}$ contribute to the complexity of Algorithm 1.. A high dimensional system with many regions of different dynamics and propositions would be embedded with a high number of states. This, together with the complexity of the LTL formula affects the time required to perform model checking on the system. The number of transitions in the original embedding, on the other hand, depends on the dynamics of the system and determines how many times model checking must be performed, since the execution of the algorithm follows a finite tree described in Section 5.1. As a result, Algorithm 1. can perform well even on high dimensional systems, as long as the total number of transitions is low.

6 Construction of Bisimulation Quotients

In this section we show that if the parameters of the PWA system (Equation (5)) are restricted to appropriate subsets, an exact finite bisimulation quotient can be constructed without extensive iterative computation. Subsequently, satisfiability of an LTL formula by the original PWA system can be proven if model checking this quotient with the negation of the formula produces a counterexample. Of course, by limiting the sets of parameters, certain transitions might disappear from the system and, therefore, the richness of its language might be diminished.

Definition 6. *Given two polytopes X and Y in $\mathbb{R}^N$, the set of parameters for which the image of X is completely included in Y is defined as:*

$$P^{X \to Y} = \{p \in \mathbb{R}^{(N^2+N)} \mid A(p)x + b(p) \in Y \text{ for all } x \in X\} \tag{11}$$

Proposition 3. *Let X and Y be polytopes in $\mathbb{R}^N$ given in the V-representation as $X = Conv\{v_1, \dots v_m\}$ and in the H-representation as $Y = \{x \in \mathbb{R}^N \mid c_i^T x + d_i < 0,\ i = 1, \dots, n\}$, respectively. Then*

$$P^{X \to Y} = \{p \in \mathbb{R}^{(N^2+N)} \mid c_i^T(A(p)v_j + b(p)) + d_i < 0,\ i = 1, \dots, n,\ j = 1, \dots, m\}$$

Proof. See `http://iasi.bu.edu/~yordanov/papers/HSCC2008full.pdf`.

In other words, the polyhedral set of parameters $P^{X \to Y}$ can be computed immediately from the V-representation of X and the H-representation of Y.

Proposition 4. *If in each location $l \in L$, the parameters of the PWA system (5), are restricted to $\mathcal{P}_l \cap (\bigcup_{i \in L} P^{\mathcal{X}_l \to \mathcal{X}_i})$, then the propositional equivalence quotient $T_e/_\sim$ is a bisimulation quotient, and it is computable.*

Proof. The proof for bisimulation follows immediately from Definitions 2, 3 and Proposition 3. On the computation of the quotient, the equivalence classes are computed as above, and a transition $(X, Y) \in \to_{e\sim}$ exists if and only if $X \subseteq \mathcal{X}_l$ and $\mathcal{P}_l \cap P^{X \to Y} \neq \emptyset$.

7 Analysis of a Genetic Toggle Switch

We illustrate the proposed method by analyzing the genetic network shown in Figure 1 (A). The system is described by a two dimensional discrete time PWA model, using ramp functions to represent gene regulation. A ramp function is defined by two threshold values, which induce three regions of different dynamics. At low concentrations of repressor (below threshold 1) the regulated gene is fully expressed, while at high repressor concentrations (above threshold 2) expression is only basal. For concentrations between the two thresholds expression is graded. Since there are two repressors, two ramp functions are used and, therefore, the system has a total of nine rectangular invariants. We use $L = \{1, 2, \dots, 9\}$ as a

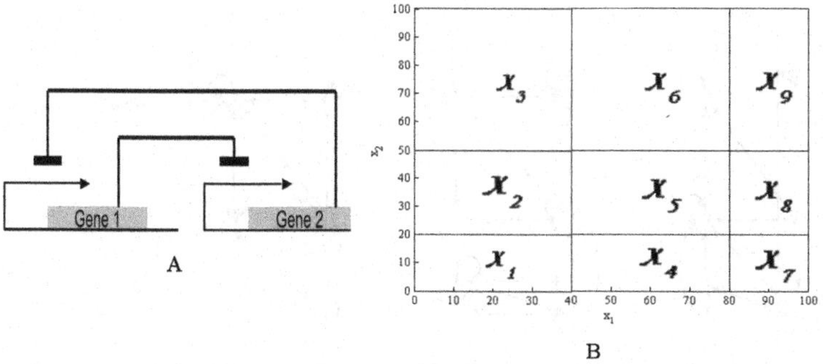

Fig. 1. (A) A genetic switch consisting of two mutual repressors. High levels of one of the products shut down the expression of the other gene. (B) Invariants of the system determined by ramp functions, describing gene regulation.

set of labels and $\{\mathcal{X}_1, \ldots, \mathcal{X}_9\}$ and $\{\mathcal{P}_1, \ldots, \mathcal{P}_9\}$ to denote the invariants (Figure 1 (B)) and parameters of the system, respectively.

We are interested in analyzing the behavior of the system when it is initialized with low concentrations of both genes. To specify this, we introduce two propositions $\Pi = \{\pi_1, \pi_2\}$, where $\pi_1 = \{x_1 - 10 < 0\}$ and $\pi_2 = \{x_2 - 10 < 0\}$ and we set $\mathcal{X}_{in}$ as the region where both predicates are satisfied ($\mathcal{X}_{in} = X_1$ in Figure 2 (A)). We assume hyper-rectangular parameter sets and, by using Proposition 3, we restrict the parameters for each region $l \in L$ to subsets of $P^{\mathcal{X}_l \to \mathcal{X}}$, ensuring that $\mathcal{X}$ is an invariant. The parameter ranges of the system for all regions are available at `http://iasi.bu.edu/~yordanov/papers/HSCC2008full.pdf`.

First, we apply the method outlined in Section 6 in order to modify the parameters of the system and obtain a bisimulation quotient directly. The parameter ranges, computed by the algorithm, are available at `http://iasi.bu.edu/~yordanov/papers/HSCC2008full.pdf` and the resulting bisimulation quotient is shown in Figure 2 (A). As expected, some transitions of the system are lost when parameters are restricted to smaller sets, but a lot of its behavior is captured by the quotient. Due to the language equivalence with the initial PWA system, inherent to the bisimulation quotient, it could provide an useful tool for the analysis of the system.

Next, we apply the approach of Section 5.2 and find subsets of the parameters for each region of the system, such that the property "eventually gene 2 is expressed in high concentrations, while gene 1 is expressed only basally" is always satisfied. For this, we use the same initial PWA model as before. During the execution of Algorithm 1. a number of transitions are removed from the quotient by removing appropriate sets of parameters of the system. The quotient corresponding to a solution, obtained as a leaf node in the computation tree (see Section 5.2) is shown in Figure 2 (B). Regions of parameters for the PWA system obtained as a solution to problem 1 are available at `http://iasi.bu.edu/~yordanov/papers/HSCC2008full.pdf`.

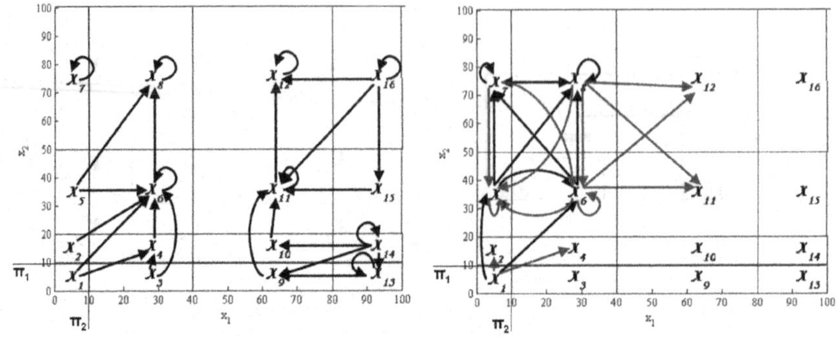

A B

Fig. 2. (A) Graphical representations of the bisimulation quotient obtained from the PWA model. (B) Satisfying simulation quotient. Only transitions for reachable states are shown. Transitions shown in red were eliminated by the algorithm.

8 Conclusion

We showed that an iterative procedure can be used to efficiently obtain subsets of parameters for a PWA system, such that an LTL formula is satisfied. Our method relied on the computation of finite overapproximation simulation quotients and generation of counterexamples. Additionally, we described an approach for the synthesis of parameters, such that a bisimulation quotient can be constructed for the system without extensive computation. We applied our methods to a PWA model of a genetic switch and in the future plan to focus on models of gene networks constructed from experimental data.

References

1. Clarke, E.M., Peled, D., Grumberg, O.: Model checking. MIT Press, Cambridge (1999)
2. Davoren, J., Coulthard, V., Markey, N., Moor, T.: Non-deterministic temporal logics for general flow systems. In: Alur, R., Pappas, G.J. (eds.) HSCC 2004. LNCS, vol. 2993, pp. 280–295. Springer, Heidelberg (2004)
3. Tabuada, P., Pappas, G.: Model checking LTL over controllable linear systems is decidable. In: Maler, O., Pnueli, A. (eds.) HSCC 2003. LNCS, vol. 2623, Springer, Heidelberg (2003)
4. Kloetzer, M., Belta, C.: A fully automated framework for control of linear systems from LTL specifications. In: Hespanha, J.P., Tiwari, A. (eds.) HSCC 2006. LNCS, vol. 3927, pp. 333–347. Springer, Heidelberg (2006)
5. Loizou, S.G., Kyriakopoulos, K.J.: Automatic synthesis of multiagent motion tasks based on LTL specifications. In: 43rd IEEE Conference on Decision and Control (2004)
6. Fainekos, G.E., Kress-Gazit, H., Pappas, G.J.: Hybrid controllers for path planning: a temporal logic approach. In: Proceedings of the 2005 IEEE Conference on Decision and Control (2005)

7. Antoniotti, M., Park, F., Policriti, A., Ugel, N., Mishra, B.: Foundations of a query and simulation system for the modeling of biochemical and biological processes. In: Proceedings of the Pacific Symposium on Biocomputing, pp. 116–127 (2003)
8. Batt, G., Ropers, D., de Jong, H., Geiselmann, J., Mateescu, R., Page, M., Schneider, D.: Validation of qualitative models of genetic regulatory networks by model checking: Analysis of the nutritional stress response in *Escherichia coli*. Bioinformatics 21(Suppl. 1), i19–i28 (2005)
9. Batt, G., Belta, C., Weiss, R.: Model checking genetic regulatory networks with parameter uncertainty. In: Bemporad, A., Bicchi, A., Buttazzo, G. (eds.) HSCC 2007. LNCS, vol. 4416, pp. 61–75. Springer, Heidelberg (2007)
10. Juloski, A.L., Heemels, W., Ferrari-Trecate, G., Vidal, R., Paoletti, S., Niessen, J.: Comparison of four procedures for the identification of hybrid systems. In: Morari, M., Thiele, L. (eds.) HSCC 2005. LNCS, vol. 3414, pp. 354–369. Springer, Heidelberg (2005)
11. Lin, J.N., Unbehauen, R.: Canonical piecewise-linear approximaions. IEEE Transactions on Circuits and Systems - I: Fundamental Theory and Applications 39(8), 697–699 (1992)
12. Heemels, W.P.M.H., Schutter, B.D., Bemporad, A.: Equivalence of hybrid dynamical models. Automatica 37(7), 1085–1091 (2001)
13. Alur, R., Henzinger, T.A., Lafferriere, G., Pappas, G.J.: Discrete abstractions of hybrid systems. Proceedings of the IEEE 88, 971–984 (2000)
14. Pappas, G.J.: Bisimilar linear systems. Automatica 39(12), 2035–2047 (2003)
15. Yordanov, B., Batt, G., Belta, C.: Model checking discrete-time piecewise affine systems: application to gene networks. In: European Control Conference (2007)
16. Clarke, E., Fehnker, A., Han, Z., Krogh, B., Ouaknine, J., Stursberg, O., Theobald, M.: Abstraction and counterexample-guided refinement in model checking of hybrid systems. International Journal of Foundations of Computer Science 14(4), 583–604 (2003)
17. Bernot, G., Comet, J.P., Richard, A., Guespin, J.: Application of formal methods to biological regulatory networks: Extending Thomas' asynchronous logical approach with temporal logic. Journal of Theoretical Biology 229(3), 339–347 (2004)
18. Chabrier-Rivier, N., Chiaverini, M., Danos, V., Fages, F., Schächter, V.: Modeling and querying biomolecular interaction networks. Theoretical Comp. Science 325(1), 25–44 (2004)
19. Eker, S., Knapp, M., Laderoute, K., Lincoln, P., Talcott, C.: Pathway logic: Executable models of biological networks. Electronic Notes in Theoretical Computer Science 71 (2002)
20. Bouajjani, A., Fernandez, J.C., Halbwachs, N.: Minimal model generation. In: Clarke, E., Kurshan, R.P. (eds.) CAV 1990. LNCS, vol. 531, pp. 197–203. Springer, Heidelberg (1991)
21. Kanellakis, P.C., Smolka, S.A.: CCS expressions, finite-state processes, and three problems of equivalence. Inform. Computat. 86, 43–68 (1990)
22. Habets, L.: Personal communication. Eindhoven University of Technology (2007)
23. Barmish, B.R., Sankaran, J.: The propagation of parametric uncertainty via polytopes. IEEE Transactions on automatic control 24, 346–349 (1979)

Necessary Conditions for the Impulsive Time-Optimal Control of Finite-Dimensional Lagrangian Systems

Kerim Yunt

Swiss Federal Institute of Technology, Center of Mechanics
Tannenstr. 3, 8092 Zurich, Switzerland

Abstract. In this work, necessary conditions for the impulsive time-optimal control of finite-dimensional Lagrangian systems are stated. The conditions are obtained by the application sub-differential calculus techniques to extended-valued lower semi-continuous functionals. The considered functional is a generalized Bolza functional that is evaluated on multiple intervals. Contrary to the approach in literature so far, the instant of possibly impulsive transition is considered as an instant of Lebesgue measure zero. This approach is in comparison to other impulsive necessary conditions consistent with different hybrid system modeling methods in which transitions happen instantaneously. The necessary conditions provide necessary criteria for the determination of optimal transition times and locations.

Keywords: Impulsive Optimal Control, Impactive Systems, non-smooth analysis, hybrid, variational inequalities.

1 Introduction

The optimal control of finite-dimensional Lagrangian systems with discontinuous states is a recently investigated area. An impact in mechanics is defined as a discontinuity in the generalized velocities of a Lagrangian system which is induced by impulsive forces, therefore optimal control of such impulsive systems inevitably encompasses optimal control with discontinuous states. In this work, necessary conditions for the impulsive time-optimal control of finite-dimensional scleronomic Lagrangian systems is studied. The relation between time-optimal control and impulsive control is emphasized, because in the philosophy of time-optimal control, it is taken advantage of any excessive control action in order to attain the goal and impulsive control action is the utmost excessive control action that can be applied to a dynamical system, since impulsive control forces can grow to infinity on a single time instant. The underlying Lagrangian structure includes the important class of rigid-body multi-body systems.

An introduction to impacts in rigid-body mechanics can be found in [11], and a literature survey on Lagrangian impactive systems is provided in [3]. The dynamics and modeling of discontinuities in Lagrangian dynamics is extensively

M. Egerstedt and B. Mishra (Eds.): HSCC 2008, LNCS 4981, pp. 556–569, 2008.

treated in [7], [8], [9], [10]. The control of hybrid Lagrangian systems is an active research area and some references include [24], [26], [27], [28], [29], [30], [31] and [32]. In this work, it is assumed that the instant of discontinuity is reduced to an instant with Lebesgue measure zero, instead of taking an interval opening approach, which is the approach considered in literature so far. In the approaches provided in reference such as [1], [13] and [22], the impulsive control problem is transformed into a problem of an ordinary differential inclusion problem, which requires to determine trajectories for the "discontinuous" states during the "impulsive" control action. In [12], impulses arising from unilateral constraints are considered but again in the framework of interval-opening approach and transformation technique. The instantaneous transition approach is in comparison to other impulsive necessary conditions consistent with different common hybrid system modeling methods in which transitions happen instantaneously such as in [2]. The smooth dynamics of a finite-dimensional Lagrangian system is characterized in every interval of motion (an interval being the time period between two transition times) by a different differential equation system, in general; depending on the "free" directions of motion, that is discretely being handled by a structure-varying controller. Another issue therefore is the representation of the Lagrangian dynamics in different modes and is discussed in section (3).

2 Preliminaries

2.1 Internal Boundary Variations and Discontinuous Transversality Conditions

Impulsive optimal control requires to seek extremizing arcs in the space of bounded variation functions $\mathcal{BV}$. Every function $\mathbf{x} : [t_0, t_1] \to \mathbb{R}^n$ of bounded variation is associated with an $\mathbb{R}^n$-valued regular Borel measure $d\mathbf{x}$ on $[t_0, t_1]$. The atoms for $d\mathbf{x}$ occur only at discontinuities of $\mathbf{x}$, of which there are at most countably many. Trajectories of bounded variation in $\mathbb{R}^n$ are defined to be an equivalence class, and the space of all arcs is denoted by $\mathcal{BV}$. The space of absolutely continuous arcs $\mathcal{AC}$ is a subspace of $\mathcal{BV}$. There are uniquely determined functions $\mathbf{x}^+(t)$ and $\mathbf{x}^-(t)$ in $[t_0, t_1] \to \mathbb{R}^n$, right and left continuous respectively, such that $\mathbf{x}^+(t) = \mathbf{x}^-(t) = \mathbf{x}(t)$ at all the non-atomic points, and at the end points $\mathbf{x}^-(t_0) = \mathbf{x}(t_0)$ and $\mathbf{x}^+(t_f) = \mathbf{x}(t_f)$ are valid. Therefore, a further classification of $\mathbf{x} \in \mathcal{BV}$ is to subdivide these functions into left-continuous bounded variation ($\mathcal{LCBV}$) and right-continuous bounded variation ($\mathcal{RCBV}$) functions. The absolutely continuous part of the measure $d\mathbf{x}$ is denoted by $\dot{\mathbf{x}}\,dt$. The singular part of $d\mathbf{x}$, can be represented as $(\frac{d\mathbf{x}}{d\sigma})\,d\sigma$, where $d\sigma$ is some nonnegative singular measure (a regular Borel measure), and $\frac{d\mathbf{x}}{d\sigma}$ is the Radon-Nikodym derivative of $d\mathbf{x}$ with respect to $d\sigma$, which is also denoted as $\mathbf{x}'$. A good overview on the topic of treatment of functions of bounded variation in time is provided in [15].

A transition with a discontinuity in the state can be regarded as an internal boundary in the domain of interest. A time instant of Lebesgue measure zero is considered as a transition time $t_i \in \mathcal{I}_T$ if one of the two events occure together or for itself:

- **Event 1.** Some directions of motion of the system are opened or closed by the control strategy, which entails a change in the degrees of freedom (DOF) of the system.
- **Event 2.** An impulsive control action is exerted on the system, which may be accompanied by a discontinuity of the generalized velocities of the Lagrangian system.

The concurrence of both events where some directions of motion are closed is called "blocking". In the time-optimal control of dynamical systems one has to consider the variations in the end time. In the classical calculus of variations where the final state and final time are free, the variations of the final state are composed of two parts, namely, the part that arises of the variations at a given time and the part arising from variations due to final time. Since the transitions times are assumed to be free, the two-part character of the variations at pre- and post-transition states is considered. The assumptions during a possibly impactive transition are given as follows:

Hypotheses 1

- The transitions may be impactively.
- The generalized position remain unchanged during transition.
- The impulsive control action acts on the system at a time instant t_i which is Lebesgue-negligible.
- At a possibly impactive transition, the pre-transition controller configuration is assumed to be effective.
- There are no transitions at initial time t_0 and final time t_f.

The above stated assumptions are converted into requirements to the variations at the internal boundaries. At the boundaries of the time domain, the pre-transition state variations are considered separately from the post-transition variations. In impact mechanics, the generalized accelerations and velocities are eligible to become discontinuous where as the generalized positions are of absolutely continuous character. The absolute continuity of the generalized positions means that the total variation of the generalized positions at the pre-transition and post-transition instants are equal. The pre-transition and post-transition variations are interrelated by the transition conditions which can be seen as the bases of transversality conditions that join two trajectories discontinuously. The transition conditions are introduced symmetrically with respect to pre-, and post-transition states. The transition conditions are of two types, namely, the impact equations and the constitutive impact laws. The impact equations relate the discontinuity in the impulse of the Lagrangian system to the impulsive forces/controls. The impact law (.i.e. the moreau-newton impact law), however, is a constitutive law which is chosen depending on the modeling approach preferred. As a case study, in reference [27] the blocking of some DOF of an underactuated manipulator by tangential fully-inelastic impact is discussed and the necessary conditions are stated.

2.2 The Generalized Problem of Bolza

By the application of subdifferential calculus techniques to extended-valued lower semi-continuous functionals, necessary conditions are obtained. In publications of R. T. Rockafellar such [18] and [19] a summary of the rules in subdifferential calculus are provided, which is one of the most flourishing branches of mathematics. Consider a problem in Bolza form (GPB), in which the objective is to choose an absolutely continuous arc $\mathbf{x} \in \mathcal{AC}$ in order to minimize

$$J(x) = l(\mathbf{x}(a), \mathbf{x}(b)) + \int_{\mathrm{a}}^{\mathrm{b}} L(t, \mathbf{x}(t), \dot{\mathbf{x}}(t))\, dt \ . \tag{1}$$

where the function $L : [a,b] \times \mathbb{R}^{\mathrm{n}} \times \mathbb{R}^{\mathrm{n}} \to \mathbb{R} \cup \{+\infty\}$ is $\mathcal{L} \times \mathcal{B}$ measurable. Here $\mathcal{L} \times \mathcal{B}$ denotes the σ-algebra of subsets of $[a,b] \times \mathbb{R}^{\mathrm{n}}$ generated by product sets $\mathcal{M} \times \mathcal{N}$, where $\mathcal{M}$ is a Lebesgue measurable subset of $[a,b]$ and $\mathcal{N}$ is a Borel subset of $\mathbb{R}^{2n}$. For each $t \in [a,b]$, the function l and L are lower semi-continuous on $\mathbb{R}^{\mathrm{n}} \times \mathbb{R}^{\mathrm{n}}$, with values in $\mathbb{R} \cup \{+\infty\}$. For each $(t, \mathbf{x})$ in $[a,b] \times \mathbb{R}^{\mathrm{n}}$, the function $L(t, \mathbf{x}, \cdot)$ is convex and l represents the endpoint cost. GPB concerns the minimization of a functional whose form is identical to that in the classical calculus of variations. The endpoint cost l and the integrand L are allowed to take the value $+\infty$, so that a variety of endpoint and differential constraints can be treated. An important class of optimal control problems constrain the derivative of an admissible arc and they can be stated as the following Mayer problem (M):

$$\min\{l(\mathbf{x}(a), \mathbf{x}(b)) : \dot{\mathbf{x}}(t) \in \mathcal{F}(t, \mathbf{x}(t)) \quad \text{a.e.} \quad t \in [a,b]\}. \tag{2}$$

The problem (M) can be seen as minimizing the Bolza functional J over all arc $\mathbf{x}$. To cover the Mayer problem, it suffices to choose:

$$L(t, \mathbf{x}, \mathbf{v}) = \Psi_{\mathcal{F}(t,\mathbf{x})}(\mathbf{v}) = \begin{cases} 0, \ \mathbf{v} \in \mathcal{F}(t, \mathbf{x}) \ , \\ \quad +\infty \ . \end{cases} \tag{3}$$

The function $\Psi_{\mathcal{C}}$ is the indicator function of the set $\mathcal{C}$. It is evident that for any arc $\mathbf{x}$, one has

$$\int_{\mathrm{a}}^{\mathrm{b}} L(t, \mathbf{x}(t), \dot{\mathbf{x}}(t))\, dt = \begin{cases} 0, \ \dot{\mathbf{x}}(t) \in \mathcal{F}(t, \mathbf{x}) \quad \text{a.e.} \quad t \in [a,b], \\ \quad +\infty \ . \end{cases} \tag{4}$$

The Mayer type variational problem can arise from a typical dynamic constraint in controls with a control state-pair $(\boldsymbol{\tau}, \mathbf{x})$ such as

$$\dot{\mathbf{x}}(t) = \mathbf{f}(t, \mathbf{x}(t), \boldsymbol{\tau}(t)), \ \boldsymbol{\tau}(t) \in \mathcal{C}_{\mathcal{T}} \quad \text{a.e.} \quad t \in [a,b] \ . \tag{5}$$

If a control state-pair $(\boldsymbol{\tau}, \mathbf{x})$ satisfies equation (5), then

$$\dot{\mathbf{x}}(t) \in \mathcal{F}(t, \mathbf{x}) := \{\mathbf{v} | \mathbf{v} = f(t, \mathbf{x}(t), \boldsymbol{\tau}(t)) : \boldsymbol{\tau}(t) \in \mathcal{C}_{\mathcal{T}} \quad \text{a.e.} \quad t \in [a,b]\} \tag{6}$$

certainly also does (well-known theorem of Fillipov).

In order to guarantee the well-behaving of $\mathcal{F}$ and l let following hypotheses hold:

Hypotheses 2. An arc $\bar{\mathbf{x}} : [a,b] \to \mathbb{R}^{\mathrm{n}}$ is given. On some relatively open subset $\Omega \subseteq [a,b] \times \mathbb{R}^{\mathrm{n}}$ containing the graph of $\bar{\mathbf{x}}$, the following statements hold:

- The multifunction $\mathcal{F}$ is $\mathcal{L} \times \mathcal{B}$ measurable on Ω. For each $(t, \mathbf{x})$ in Ω, the set $\mathcal{F}(t, \mathbf{x})$ is nonempty, compact and convex.
- There are nonnegative integrable functions $k(t)$ and $\Phi(t)$ on $[a, b]$ such that
  1. $\mathcal{F}(t, \mathbf{x}) \subseteq \Phi(t)\, B$ for all $\mathbf{x}$ in Ω_{t}, almost everywhere, and
  2. $\mathcal{F}(t, \mathbf{x}) \subseteq \mathcal{F}(t, \mathbf{x}) + k(t)|\mathbf{y} - \mathbf{x}| \mathrm{cl}\, \mathbb{B}$ for all $\mathbf{x}, \mathbf{y} \in \Omega_{\mathrm{t}}$, almost everywhere.
- The endpoint cost function l is Lipschitz on $\Omega_a \times \Omega_{\mathrm{b}}$, with Lipschitz constant K_{l}.

where Ω_{t} is given by $\Omega_{\mathrm{t}} = \{\mathbf{x} \in \mathbb{R}^{\mathrm{n}} \mid (t, \mathbf{x}) \in \Omega\}$ for each $t \in [a, b] \backslash \{t_{\mathrm{i}}\} \in \mathcal{I}_{\mathrm{T}}$ and $\mathbb{B}$ is the unit ball. It is assumed that conditions of hypotheses (1) are fulfilled for the Lebesgue-measurable part of the Lagrangian dynamics in the "almost everywhere" sense. By the way Ω_{t} is defined, the instants of the discontinuity are excluded. The symbols $\partial f(\mathbf{x})$ and $\partial f^{\infty}(\mathbf{x})$ stand for the sets of limiting proximal subgradients and singular limiting proximal subgradients associated with an extended-valued function f at a point $\mathbf{x}$ such that $f(\mathbf{x})$ is finite and the epigraph of f is locally closed near $(\mathbf{x}, f(\mathbf{x}))$. Given a closed set $\mathcal{C}$, the set of limiting proximal normals associated with $\mathcal{C}$ at a point $s \in \mathcal{C}$ is denoted by $\mathcal{N}_{\mathcal{C}}(\mathbf{s})$. The indicator function exhibits following property:

$$\mathcal{N}_{\mathcal{C}}(\mathbf{s}) = \partial \Psi_{\mathcal{C}}(\mathbf{s}) = \partial \Psi_{\mathcal{C}}^{\infty}(\mathbf{s}) \ . \tag{7}$$

Having set the stage, the necessary conditions for the impulsive optimal control problem of finite-dimensional Lagrangian systems is formally derived by considering a problem in GPB, in which the objective is to choose an arc $\mathbf{x} \in \mathcal{BV}$ in order to minimize:

$$J(\mathbf{x}) = \sum_{i=1}^{N} l_{\mathrm{i}}(\mathbf{x}(t_{\mathrm{i+1}}^{-}), \mathbf{x}(t_{\mathrm{i}}^{+})) + \int_{t_{\mathrm{i}}^{+}}^{t_{\mathrm{i+1}}^{-}} L_{\mathrm{i}}(s, \mathbf{x}(s), \dot{\mathbf{x}}(s))\; sds \ . \tag{8}$$

Here it is assumed that the control horizon is composed of N different phases, which are separated from eachother by $N-1$ possibly discontinuous transitions. The theory at hand treats optimal solutions as solutions of multipoint boundary value problems (MBVP) with discontinuous transitions in the state. In this setting, the prespecification of the mode sequence and number of intervals must be given in advance.

3 Projected Newton-Euler Equations (PNE) in Impulsive Control Form

The PNE equations are first treated in [7] for uncontrolled rigid-body mechanical systems. The interaction of the mechanical system with the surroundings as well as the control actions imposed on the system necessitates to allow discontinuity events in the velocities and accelerations of the system. The PNE equations have to be supplemented with some force laws that relate the external forces f and controls τ with the system's state $(\mathbf{q}, \mathbf{u})$. The existence of the generalized velocities $\mathbf{u}$ and accelerations $\dot{\mathbf{u}}$ jointly on intervals is limited to the instants where $\mathbf{u}$ and $\boldsymbol{\tau}$ are continuous. Because of the set of discontinuity points $\{t_i\} \in \mathcal{I}_T$ of $\mathbf{u}$ and discontinuities in the controls $\boldsymbol{\tau}$, where $\dot{\mathbf{u}}$ does not exist, the PNE equations are stated in the following form:

$$\mathbf{M}(\mathbf{q})\dot{\mathbf{u}} - \mathbf{h}(\mathbf{q},\mathbf{u}) = \mathbf{f} + \mathbf{B}(\mathbf{q})\,\boldsymbol{\tau}, \quad \text{a.e.} \quad . \tag{9}$$

Here $\mathbf{M}$ is the symmetric and positive definite generalized mass matrix depending smoothly on the generalized positions $\mathbf{q}$, and $\mathbf{h}$ is a smooth function of $\mathbf{q},\mathbf{u}$ containing the gyroscopical, coriolis, centripedal accelerations of the Lagrangian system, as well as all smooth finite forces such as spring and damping forces. The linear operator $\mathbf{B}(\mathbf{q})$ includes the generalized directions of control forces. In order to investigate the discontinuity points of the velocities $\mathbf{u}$ and accelerations $\dot{\mathbf{u}}$ properly, equation (9) is replaced by the corresponding equality of measures in the sense of [16]:

$$\mathbf{M}(\mathbf{q})\,d\mathbf{u} - \mathbf{h}(\mathbf{q},\mathbf{u})\,dt = d\mathbf{R} + \mathbf{B}(\mathbf{q})\,d\boldsymbol{\Gamma}\ , \tag{10}$$

where it has been introduced for uncontrolled rigid-body mechanical systems. This form of representation of the projected Newton-Euler equations has wider range of validity such that it is valid "everywhere" instead of " almost everywhere". For the force measure $d\mathbf{R}$ following decomposition is valid:

$$d\mathbf{R} = \mathbf{f}\,dt + \mathbf{F}'\,d\sigma\ , \tag{11}$$

such that $\mathbf{f}$ and $\mathbf{F}'$ represent Lebesgue-measurable and Borel-measurable forces, respectively. The Radon-Nykodym derivative of $d\mathbf{R}$ with respect to $d\sigma$ is given by $\mathbf{F}'$. Similarly the differential measure of controls is decomposed as:

$$d\boldsymbol{\Gamma} = \boldsymbol{\tau}\,dt + \boldsymbol{\zeta}'\,d\sigma\ . \tag{12}$$

Here $\boldsymbol{\tau}$ and $\boldsymbol{\zeta}'$ represent the Lebesgue-measurable and Borel-measurable controls, respectively. Here, the Radon-Nykodym derivative of $d\boldsymbol{\Gamma}$ with respect to $d\sigma$ is given by $\boldsymbol{\zeta}'$. The substitution of (11) into (10) along with $d\mathbf{u} = \dot{\mathbf{u}}\,dt + \boldsymbol{\pi}'\,d\sigma$ reveals:

$$\mathbf{M}(\mathbf{q})\,\dot{\mathbf{u}}\,dt + \mathbf{M}(\mathbf{q})\,\boldsymbol{\pi}'\,d\sigma - \mathbf{h}(\mathbf{q},\mathbf{u})\,dt = (\mathbf{f} + \mathbf{B}(\mathbf{q})\,\boldsymbol{\tau})\,dt + \left(\mathbf{F}' + \mathbf{B}(\mathbf{q})\,\boldsymbol{\zeta}'\right)\,d\sigma\ . \tag{13}$$

Here $\boldsymbol{\pi}'$ denotes the Radon-Nykodym derivative of the differential measure of generalized velocities w.r.t $d\sigma$. Equation (13) can be split into a Lebesgue and Borel part as given below:

$$\mathbf{M}(\mathbf{q})\,\boldsymbol{\pi}'\,d\sigma = \left(\mathbf{F}' + \mathbf{B}(\mathbf{q})\,\boldsymbol{\zeta}'\right)\,d\sigma\ , \tag{14}$$

$$\mathbf{M}(\mathbf{q})\,\dot{\mathbf{u}}\,dt - \mathbf{h}(\mathbf{q},\mathbf{u})\,dt = (\mathbf{f} + \mathbf{B}(\mathbf{q})\,\boldsymbol{\tau})\,dt\ . \tag{15}$$

By evaluating the Lebesgue-Stieltjes Integral over an atomic time $t_i \in \mathcal{I}_T$ of equation (13) reveals the impact equation:

$$\mathbf{M}(\mathbf{q}(t_i))\,(\boldsymbol{\pi}_i^+ - \boldsymbol{\pi}_i^-) = \mathbf{F}_i^+ - \mathbf{F}_i^- + \mathbf{B}(\mathbf{q}(t_i))\,(\boldsymbol{\zeta}_i^+ - \boldsymbol{\zeta}_i^-)\ , \tag{16}$$

where t_i is an element of discontinuity points of the velocity $\mathbf{u}$. The Lebesgue part which remains unaffected by the points of discontinuity can be expressed in two forms as below:

$$\mathbf{M}(\mathbf{q}^+)\,\dot{\mathbf{u}}^+\,dt - \mathbf{h}(\mathbf{q}^+,\mathbf{u}^+)\,dt = \left(\mathbf{f}^+ + \mathbf{B}(\mathbf{q}^+)\,\boldsymbol{\tau}^+\right)\,dt\,, \tag{17}$$

$$\mathbf{M}(\mathbf{q}^-)\,\dot{\mathbf{u}}^-\,dt - \mathbf{h}(\mathbf{q}^-,\mathbf{u}^-)\,dt = \left(\mathbf{f}^- + \mathbf{B}(\mathbf{q}^-)\,\boldsymbol{\tau}^-\right)\,dt\,. \tag{18}$$

Here $\mathbf{f}^+$ and $\mathbf{f}^-$ are meant to be the right and left limits of $\mathbf{f}$ with respect to time, respectively. As a corollary, the directional Newton-Euler equations can be stated as follows:

$$\mathbf{M}(\mathbf{q}^+)\,\dot{\mathbf{u}}^+ - \mathbf{h}(\mathbf{q}^+,\mathbf{u}^+) = \mathbf{f}^+ + \mathbf{B}(\mathbf{q}^+)\,\boldsymbol{\tau}^+, \quad \text{a.e.}\,, \tag{19}$$

$$\mathbf{M}(\mathbf{q}^-)\,\dot{\mathbf{u}}^- - \mathbf{h}(\mathbf{q}^-,\mathbf{u}^-) = \mathbf{f}^- + \mathbf{B}(\mathbf{q}^-)\,\boldsymbol{\tau}^-, \quad \text{a.e.}\,. \tag{20}$$

3.1 Lagrangian Dynamics in Different Phases of Motion

After the possibly impactive transition the equations of motion on acceleration level may differ from the pre-transition equations of motion based on the closed directions of motion. It is assumed that the interaction of the Lagrangian system with the surroundings (unilateral contacts, etc.) do not interfere during the course of control action ($d\mathbf{R} = \mathbf{0}$). A direction of interest γ, which for example can be the relative velocity at a blockable joint, is expressed as a linear combination of generalized velocities as in equation (21):

$$\gamma_b = \mathbf{w}^T(\mathbf{q})\,\mathbf{u}\,. \tag{21}$$

The directions, which are closed during an interval can be expressed vectorially:

$$\boldsymbol{\gamma}_b = \mathbf{W}_b^T(\mathbf{q})\,\mathbf{u}\,, \tag{22}$$

where $\boldsymbol{\gamma}_b$ is such that $w_i \in \mathrm{col}\{\mathbf{W}_b\}$. Here $\mathrm{col}\{\cdot\}$ denotes the set of column vectors of the relevant linear operator. The generalized acceleration of the finite-dimensional Lagrangian system when some DOF are closed by $\boldsymbol{\tau}_b$, is given by (23):

$$\dot{\mathbf{u}} = \mathbf{M}^{-1}(\mathbf{q})\mathbf{h}(\mathbf{q},\mathbf{u}) + \mathbf{M}^{-1}(\mathbf{q})\mathbf{W}_b(\mathbf{q})\,\boldsymbol{\tau}_b + \mathbf{M}^{-1}(\mathbf{q})\mathbf{B}(\mathbf{q})\,\boldsymbol{\tau}\,. \tag{23}$$

The controls $\boldsymbol{\tau}_b$ represent the forces which are required to constrain the vector field from evolving in certain directions. The linear operator $\mathbf{W}_b$ denotes the generalized force direction of the constraining forces, such that $\mathrm{col}\{\mathbf{W}_b\} \subset \mathrm{col}\{\mathbf{B}\}$. The accelerations in the closed directions must be zero, as a consequence one has:

$$\dot{\boldsymbol{\gamma}}_b = \mathbf{W}_b^T\dot{\mathbf{u}} + \dot{\mathbf{W}}_b^T\mathbf{u} = \mathbf{0}\,. \tag{24}$$

The insertion of equation (23) in equation (24) reveals:

$$\mathbf{W}_b^T\dot{\mathbf{u}} + \dot{\mathbf{W}}_b^T\mathbf{u} = \mathbf{W}_b^T\mathbf{M}^{-1}\mathbf{h} + \mathbf{W}_b^T\mathbf{M}^{-1}\mathbf{W}_b\,\boldsymbol{\tau}_b + \mathbf{W}_b^T\mathbf{M}^{-1}\mathbf{B}\,\boldsymbol{\tau} + \dot{\mathbf{W}}_b^T\mathbf{u} = \mathbf{0}\,. \tag{25}$$

The equation (25) can be solved for the blocking forces/moments as below:

$$\boldsymbol{\tau}_b = -(\mathbf{W}_b^T\mathbf{M}^{-1}\mathbf{W}_b)^{-1}\left(\mathbf{W}_b^T\mathbf{M}^{-1}\mathbf{h} + \mathbf{W}_b^T\mathbf{M}^{-1}\mathbf{B}\,\boldsymbol{\tau} + \dot{\mathbf{W}}_b^T\mathbf{u}\right)\,. \tag{26}$$

Defining the projector $\mathbf{P}_{\parallel}$ as

$$\mathbf{P}_{\parallel} = \mathbf{W}_{\mathrm{b}}(\mathbf{W}_{\mathrm{b}}^{\mathrm{T}}\mathbf{M}^{-1}\mathbf{W}_{\mathrm{b}})^{-1}\mathbf{W}_{\mathrm{b}}^{\mathrm{T}}\mathbf{M}^{-1} \tag{27}$$

and inserting into equation (23) gives the projected dynamics:

$$\mathbf{M}\,\dot{\mathbf{u}} - \mathbf{h} - \mathbf{P}_{\parallel}\,(\mathbf{h} + \mathbf{B}\,\boldsymbol{\tau}) + \mathbf{W}_{\mathrm{b}}(\mathbf{W}_{\mathrm{b}}^{\mathrm{T}}\mathbf{M}^{-1}\mathbf{W}_{\mathrm{b}})^{-1}\dot{\mathbf{W}}_{\mathrm{b}}^{\mathrm{T}}\mathbf{u} - \mathbf{B}\,\boldsymbol{\tau} = \mathbf{0}\,. \tag{28}$$

The equations of motion after the directions $\mathbf{W}_{\mathrm{b}}$ are closed in the generalized coordinates can be rearranged as below:

$$\mathbf{M}\,\dot{\mathbf{u}} - \mathbf{P}_{\perp}\,\mathbf{h} - \mathbf{P}_{\perp}\,\mathbf{B}\,\boldsymbol{\tau} + \mathbf{W}_{\mathrm{b}}(\mathbf{W}_{\mathrm{b}}^{\mathrm{T}}\mathbf{M}^{-1}\mathbf{W}_{\mathrm{b}})^{-1}\dot{\mathbf{W}}_{\mathrm{b}}^{\mathrm{T}}\mathbf{u} = \mathbf{0}\,. \tag{29}$$

The new vector of coriolis and gyroscopical forces as well as the linear operator of generalized control directions can be redefined as:

$$\mathbf{h}_{\mathrm{b}} = \mathbf{P}_{\perp}\,\mathbf{h} - \mathbf{W}_{\mathrm{b}}(\mathbf{W}_{\mathrm{b}}^{\mathrm{T}}\mathbf{M}^{-1}\mathbf{W}_{\mathrm{b}})^{-1}\dot{\mathbf{W}}_{\mathrm{b}}^{\mathrm{T}}\mathbf{u}\,, \tag{30}$$

$$\mathbf{B}_{\mathrm{b}} = \mathbf{P}_{\perp}\,\mathbf{B}\,, \tag{31}$$

to yield

$$\mathbf{M}(\mathbf{q})\,\dot{\mathbf{u}} - \mathbf{h}_{\mathrm{b}}(\mathbf{q},\mathbf{u}) - \mathbf{B}_{\mathrm{b}}(\mathbf{q})\,\boldsymbol{\tau} = \mathbf{0}\,. \tag{32}$$

Here the projector $\mathbf{P}_{\perp}$ is defined by $\mathbf{P}_{\perp} = \mathbf{I} - \mathbf{P}_{\parallel}$ and $\mathbf{I}$ is an identity matrix of appropriate size.

4 Statement of the Optimal Control Problem

The impulsive time-optimal control of finite-dimensional Lagrangian systems is considered, for which the transition times $t_{\mathrm{i}} \in \mathcal{I}_{\mathrm{T}}$, final time t_{f} and transition locations characterized by triplets $\{\mathbf{q}(t_{\mathrm{i}}), \mathbf{u}(t_{\mathrm{i}}^{+}), \mathbf{u}(t_{\mathrm{i}}^{-})\}$ are free. The goal function is to minimize the final time t_{f}. The set of $\{\mathbf{q}(t),\ \mathbf{u}(t),\ \dot{\mathbf{u}}(t),\ \boldsymbol{\tau}(t)\}$ that fulfill the Lebesgue measurable part of the dynamics in every time-interval $(t_{\mathrm{i}}^{+}, t_{\mathrm{i+1}}^{-})$ is denoted by $\mathcal{S}_{\mathrm{i}}$:

$$\mathbf{S}_{\mathrm{i}} = \mathbf{M}_{\mathrm{i}}(\mathbf{q}(t))\dot{\mathbf{u}}(t) - \mathbf{h}_{\mathrm{i}}(\mathbf{q}(t),\mathbf{u}(t)) - \mathbf{B}_{\mathrm{i}}(\mathbf{q}(t))\,\boldsymbol{\tau}(t) = \mathbf{0}\,, \quad t \in (t_{\mathrm{i}}^{+}, t_{\mathrm{i+1}}^{-})\,. \tag{33}$$

The measurable controls $\boldsymbol{\tau}$ is constrained to a bounded closed polytopic convex set $\mathcal{C}_{\boldsymbol{\tau}}$. The set $\mathcal{C}_{\mathrm{I_i}}^{+}$ denotes the set of $\{\mathbf{q}(t_{\mathrm{i}}^{+}),\ \mathbf{u}(t_{\mathrm{i}}^{+}),\ \mathbf{u}(t_{\mathrm{i}}^{-}),\ \boldsymbol{\zeta}_{\mathrm{i}}^{+},\ \boldsymbol{\zeta}_{\mathrm{i}}^{-}\}$ that fulfill the impact equation:

$$\mathbf{M}\left(\mathbf{q}(t_{\mathrm{i}}^{+})\right)\left(\mathbf{u}(t_{\mathrm{i}}^{+}) - \mathbf{u}(t_{\mathrm{i}}^{-})\right) - \mathbf{B}_{\mathrm{i}}\left(\mathbf{q}(t_{\mathrm{i}}^{+})\right)\left(\boldsymbol{\zeta}_{\mathrm{i}}^{+} - \boldsymbol{\zeta}_{\mathrm{i}}^{-}\right) = \mathbf{0}\,, \quad \forall t_{\mathrm{i}} \in \mathcal{I}_{\mathrm{T}}\,. \tag{34}$$

The set $\mathcal{C}_{\mathrm{I_i}}^{-}$ denotes the set of $\{\mathbf{q}(t_{\mathrm{i}}^{-}),\ \mathbf{u}(t_{\mathrm{i}}^{+}),\ \mathbf{q}(t_{\mathrm{i}}^{-}),\ \boldsymbol{\zeta}_{\mathrm{i}}^{+},\ \boldsymbol{\zeta}_{\mathrm{i}}^{-}\}$ that fulfill the impact equation:

$$\mathbf{M}\left(\mathbf{q}(t_{\mathrm{i}}^{-})\right)\left(\mathbf{u}(t_{\mathrm{i}}^{+}) - \mathbf{u}(t_{\mathrm{i}}^{-})\right) - \mathbf{B}_{\mathrm{i}}\left(\mathbf{q}(t_{\mathrm{i}}^{-})\right)\left(\boldsymbol{\zeta}_{\mathrm{i}}^{+} - \boldsymbol{\zeta}_{\mathrm{i}}^{-}\right) = \mathbf{0}\,, \quad \forall t_{\mathrm{i}} \in \mathcal{I}_{\mathrm{T}}\,. \tag{35}$$

The equations (34) and (35) represent smooth manifolds and are smoothly differentiable in their arguments. Further, let $\mathcal{C}_{\mathrm{T_i}}^{+}$ denotes the set defined by the equality $\mathbf{p}^+(\mathbf{q}(t_i^+), \mathbf{u}(t_i^+), \mathbf{u}(t_i^-)) = \mathbf{0}$, that arises from the constitutive impact laws. Analogously, $C^-_{T_i}$ denote the set defined by the equality $\mathbf{p}^-(\mathbf{q}(t_i^-), \mathbf{u}(t_i^+), \mathbf{u}(t_i^-)) = \mathbf{0}$. Both $\mathbf{p}^-$ and $\mathbf{p}^+$ are at least C^2 in their arguments. The end state is to be in a convex set $\mathcal{C}_f(\mathbf{q}(t_f), \mathbf{u}(t_f))$. The necessary conditions are derived by making use of following hypotheses on the general problem:

Hypotheses 3

1. The interior of the intersection of all sets involved in the problem considered is nonempty $\forall t_i \in \mathcal{I}_T$, $\forall t \in \Omega_t$.
2. The dual states $\boldsymbol{\nu}$ is assumed left-continuous locally bounded variation functions ($\mathcal{LCLBV}$), and the generalized velocities $\mathbf{u}$ of the Lagrangian system is assumed right-continuous locally bounded variation functions ($\mathcal{RCLBV}$), whereas the generalized positions are in class $\mathcal{AC}$.
3. The mode sequence and number of intervals for the MBVP constitute a feasible hybrid trajectory.

Under hypotheses (1), (2) and (3) the value function possesses regularity properties which enable the statement of sharp necessary conditions. In its full glory the impulsive optimal control problem is stated as:

$$\min_{\{t_i\}, t_f, \boldsymbol{\tau}, \{\boldsymbol{\zeta}_i^+, \boldsymbol{\zeta}_i^-\}} J \,, \tag{36}$$

where J is given by:

$$J = l_0 + \sum_{(\forall i | t_i \in \mathcal{I}_T)} l_i(\mathbf{q}(t_i), \mathbf{u}(t_i^+), \mathbf{u}(t_i^-)) + \sum_{i=1}^{N} \int_{t_i^+}^{t_{i+1}^-} L_i(\mathbf{q}(s), \mathbf{u}(s), \dot{\mathbf{u}}(s))\, ds \,. \tag{37}$$

The costs associated with boundary terms and the integrand are composed in the following manner:

$$\begin{aligned}
l_i &= \Psi_{\mathcal{C}^+_{T_i} \cup \mathcal{C}^-_{T_i}}(\mathbf{q}(t_i), \mathbf{u}(t_i^+), \mathbf{u}(t_i^-)) + \Psi_{\mathcal{C}^+_{I_i} \cup \mathcal{C}^-_{I_i}}(\mathbf{q}(t_i), \mathbf{u}(t_i^+), \mathbf{u}(t_i^-), \boldsymbol{\zeta}_i^+, \boldsymbol{\zeta}_i^-) \,, \\
l_0 &= \lambda(t) + \Psi_{\mathcal{C}_f}(\mathbf{q}(t_f), \mathbf{u}(t_f)) \,, \\
L_i &= \Psi_{\mathcal{C}_\tau}(\boldsymbol{\tau}) + \Psi_{\mathcal{S}_i^+}(\mathbf{q}(t^+), \mathbf{u}(t^+), \dot{\mathbf{u}}(t^+), \boldsymbol{\tau}(t^+)) \,.
\end{aligned}$$

5 Necessary Conditions

Theorem 1. *Let Hypotheses (1), (2) and (3) be valid for the optimal control problem. If optimal trajectories of generalized positions $\mathbf{q}^*(t^+) \in \mathcal{AC}[\mathbb{R}^n]$, velocities $\mathbf{u}^*(t^+) \in \mathcal{RCLBV}[\mathbb{R}^n]$ provide a minimum for the described optimal control problem, then there exist optimal controls $\boldsymbol{\tau}^*(t)$, optimal transition times $t_i^* \in \mathcal{I}_T$, dual multipliers $\boldsymbol{\xi}_i^{+*}$, $\boldsymbol{\xi}_i^{-*}$, $\boldsymbol{\alpha}_i^{+*}$, $\boldsymbol{\alpha}_i^{-*}$, $\forall t_i^* \in \mathcal{I}_T$, transition location triplets $\{\mathbf{q}^*(t_i), \mathbf{u}^*(t_i^+), \mathbf{u}^*(t_i^-)\}$, dual state $\boldsymbol{\nu}^*(t^-) \in \mathcal{LCLBV}^*[\mathbb{R}^n]$ (where * denote dual space) and a scalar $\lambda(t) \in \{0,1\}$, such that $\lambda(t) + |\boldsymbol{\nu}| > 0$, which fulfill:*

1. *the Lebesgue-measurable dynamics* $\mathbf{S}_\mathrm{i}^+$ *in every interval of motion* $t \in (t_\mathrm{i}^{+*}, t_{\mathrm{i}+1}^{-*})$

$$\mathbf{M}(\mathbf{q}^*(t^+))\dot{\mathbf{u}}^*(t^+) - \mathbf{h}_\mathrm{i}(\mathbf{q}^*(t^+), \mathbf{u}^*(t^+)) - \mathbf{B}_\mathrm{i}(\mathbf{q}^*(t^+))\,\boldsymbol{\tau}^{+*} = \mathbf{0}, \; a.e., \tag{38}$$

2. *the Lebesgue-measurable dual dynamics*

$$\ddot{\boldsymbol{\nu}}^*(t^-)\,\mathbf{D}_\mathrm{i} + \dot{\boldsymbol{\nu}}^*(t^-)\,\mathbf{E}_\mathrm{i} + \boldsymbol{\nu}^*(t^-)\,\mathbf{F}_\mathrm{i} = \mathbf{0}\;, \quad a.e., \quad t \in (t_\mathrm{i}^{+*}, t_{\mathrm{i}+1}^{-*}), \tag{39}$$

where the coefficients in the differential equation above are given by:

$$\begin{aligned}
\mathbf{D}_\mathrm{i} &= \mathbf{M}(\mathbf{q}^*(t^+)),\\
\mathbf{E}_\mathrm{i} &= 2\dot{\mathbf{M}}(\mathbf{q}^*(t^+)) + \nabla_\mathbf{u}\,\mathbf{h}_\mathrm{i}(\mathbf{q}^*(t^+), \mathbf{u}^*(t^+)),\\
\mathbf{F}_\mathrm{i} &= \nabla_\mathbf{q}[\mathbf{M}(\mathbf{q}^*(t^+))\,\dot{\mathbf{u}}^*(t^+) - \mathbf{h}_\mathrm{i}(\mathbf{q}^*(t^+), \mathbf{u}^*(t^+)) - \mathbf{B}_\mathrm{i}(\mathbf{q}^*(t^+))\,\boldsymbol{\tau}] + \ddot{\mathbf{M}}(\mathbf{q}^*(t^+))\\
&\quad + \frac{d}{dt}\left(\nabla_\mathbf{u}[\mathbf{h}_\mathrm{i}(\mathbf{q}^*(t^+), \mathbf{u}(t^+))]\right) \quad ,
\end{aligned}$$

3. *the optimal control law*

$$-\,\boldsymbol{\nu}^*(t^-)\,\nabla_\tau\,\mathbf{S}_\mathrm{i}^+ \in \mathcal{N}_{\mathcal{C}_\tau}(\boldsymbol{\tau}^{+*}), \quad a.e. \quad t \in (t_\mathrm{i}^{+*}, t_{\mathrm{i}+1}^{-*})\;, \tag{40}$$

4. *the condition*

$$\begin{aligned}
&\left(\boldsymbol{\nu}^*(t_\mathrm{i}^-)\left(\nabla_\mathbf{u}\,\mathbf{h}_\mathrm{i}^-\,\mathbf{u}^*(t_\mathrm{i}^-) - \mathbf{M}\dot{\mathbf{u}}^*(t_\mathrm{i}^-)\right) + \left(\dot{\boldsymbol{\nu}}^*(t_\mathrm{i}^-)\,\mathbf{M} + \boldsymbol{\nu}^*(t_\mathrm{i}^-)\,\dot{\mathbf{M}}^-\right)\mathbf{u}^*(t_\mathrm{i}^-)\right)\\
&+\left(\boldsymbol{\nu}^*(t_\mathrm{i}^+)\left(\mathbf{M}\dot{\mathbf{u}}^*(t_\mathrm{i}^+) - \nabla_\mathbf{u}\,\mathbf{h}_{\mathrm{i}+1}^+\mathbf{u}^*(t_\mathrm{i}^+)\right) - \left(\dot{\boldsymbol{\nu}}^*(t_\mathrm{i}^+)\,\mathbf{M} + \boldsymbol{\nu}^*(t_\mathrm{i}^+)\,\dot{\mathbf{M}}^+\right)\mathbf{u}^*(t_\mathrm{i}^+)\right)\\
&= \mathbf{r}_{\mathrm{i}1}\,\mathbf{u}^*(t_\mathrm{i}^-) + \mathbf{r}_{\mathrm{i}2}\,\mathbf{u}^*(t_\mathrm{i}^+) + \mathbf{r}_{\mathrm{i}3}\,\dot{\mathbf{u}}^*(t_\mathrm{i}^-) + \mathbf{r}_{\mathrm{i}4}\,\dot{\mathbf{u}}^*(t_\mathrm{i}^+), \quad \forall t_\mathrm{i}^* \in \mathcal{I}_\mathrm{T}\;,
\end{aligned} \tag{41}$$

where the vectors $\mathbf{r}_{\mathrm{i}1}$, $\mathbf{r}_{\mathrm{i}2}$, $\mathbf{r}_{\mathrm{i}3}$ *and* $\mathbf{r}_{\mathrm{i}4}$ *are given by:*

$$\begin{aligned}
\mathbf{r}_{\mathrm{i}1} &= \boldsymbol{\alpha}_\mathrm{i}^{-*}\,\nabla_\mathbf{q}\,\mathbf{p}^-(\mathbf{q}^*(t_\mathrm{i}^-), \mathbf{u}^*(t_\mathrm{i}^+), \mathbf{u}^*(t_\mathrm{i}^-))\\
&\quad + \boldsymbol{\xi}_\mathrm{i}^{-*}\,\nabla_\mathbf{q}\left[\mathbf{M}\left(\mathbf{q}^*(t_\mathrm{i})\right)\left(\mathbf{u}(t_\mathrm{i}^{+*}) - \mathbf{u}(t_\mathrm{i}^{-*})\right) - \mathbf{B}_\mathrm{i}\left(\mathbf{q}^*(t_\mathrm{i})\right)\left(\boldsymbol{\zeta}_\mathrm{i}^{+*} - \boldsymbol{\zeta}_\mathrm{i}^{-*}\right)\right]\;,\\
\mathbf{r}_{\mathrm{i}2} &= \boldsymbol{\alpha}_\mathrm{i}^{+*}\,\nabla_\mathbf{q}\,\mathbf{p}^+(\mathbf{q}^*(t_\mathrm{i}^+)\mathbf{u}^*(t_\mathrm{i}^+), \mathbf{u}^*(t_\mathrm{i}^-))\\
&\quad + \boldsymbol{\xi}_\mathrm{i}^{+*}\,\nabla_\mathbf{q}\left[\mathbf{M}\left(\mathbf{q}^*(t_\mathrm{i})\right)\left(\mathbf{u}(t_\mathrm{i}^{+*}) - \mathbf{u}(t_\mathrm{i}^{-*})\right) - \mathbf{B}_\mathrm{i}\left(\mathbf{q}^*(t_\mathrm{i})\right)\left(\boldsymbol{\zeta}_\mathrm{i}^{+*} - \boldsymbol{\zeta}_\mathrm{i}^{-*}\right)\right]\;,\\
\mathbf{r}_{\mathrm{i}3} &= \boldsymbol{\alpha}_\mathrm{i}^{-*}\,\nabla_{\mathbf{u}(t_\mathrm{i}^-)}\,\mathbf{p}^-(\mathbf{q}^*(t_\mathrm{i}^-), \mathbf{u}^*(t_\mathrm{i}^+), \mathbf{u}^*(t_\mathrm{i}^-))\\
&\quad - \boldsymbol{\alpha}_\mathrm{i}^{+*}\,\nabla_{\mathbf{u}(t_\mathrm{i}^-)}\,\mathbf{p}^-(\mathbf{q}^*(t_\mathrm{i}^-), \mathbf{u}^*(t_\mathrm{i}^+), \mathbf{u}^*(t_\mathrm{i}^-)) - \boldsymbol{\xi}_\mathrm{i}^{+*}\,\mathbf{M}(\mathbf{q}(t)) - \boldsymbol{\xi}_\mathrm{i}^{-*}\,\mathbf{M}(\mathbf{q}(t))\;,\\
\mathbf{r}_{\mathrm{i}4} &= \boldsymbol{\alpha}_\mathrm{i}^{-*}\,\nabla_{\mathbf{u}(t_\mathrm{i}^+)}\,\mathbf{p}^+(\mathbf{q}^*(t_\mathrm{i}^+), \mathbf{u}^*(t_\mathrm{i}^+), \mathbf{u}^*(t_\mathrm{i}^-))\\
&\quad - \boldsymbol{\alpha}_\mathrm{i}^{+*}\,\nabla_{\mathbf{u}(t_\mathrm{i}^+)}\,\mathbf{p}^+(\mathbf{q}^*(t_\mathrm{i}^+), \mathbf{u}^*(t_\mathrm{i}^+), \mathbf{u}^*(t_\mathrm{i}^-)) + \boldsymbol{\xi}_\mathrm{i}^{+*}\,\mathbf{M}(\mathbf{q}(t)) + \boldsymbol{\xi}_\mathrm{i}^{-*}\,\mathbf{M}(\mathbf{q}(t))\;,
\end{aligned}$$

5. *the impact equation and transition conditions at a transition*

$$\begin{aligned}
\mathcal{C}_{\mathrm{T}_\mathrm{i}}^* &= \mathcal{C}_{\mathrm{T}_\mathrm{i}}^{*+} \cup \mathcal{C}_{\mathrm{T}_\mathrm{i}}^{*-}, \quad \forall t_\mathrm{i}^* \in \mathcal{I}_\mathrm{T}\;,\\
\mathcal{C}_{\mathrm{I}_\mathrm{i}}^* &= \mathcal{C}_{\mathrm{I}_\mathrm{i}}^{*+} \cup \mathcal{C}_{\mathrm{I}_\mathrm{i}}^{*-}, \quad \forall t_\mathrm{i}^* \in \mathcal{I}_\mathrm{T}\;,
\end{aligned}$$

6. *the variational inequalities (VI) that govern the discontinuity conditions of the dual state $\boldsymbol{\nu}$ and of its time-derivative $\dot{\boldsymbol{\nu}}$:*

$$
\begin{aligned}
&(\boldsymbol{\nu}^*(t_\mathrm{i}^+) - \boldsymbol{\nu}^*(t_\mathrm{i}^-))\ \mathbf{M}(\mathbf{q}^*(t)) = \qquad (42)\\
&\boldsymbol{\alpha}_\mathrm{i}^{+*}\,\nabla_{\mathbf{u}(t_\mathrm{i}^+)}\left(\mathbf{p}^+(\mathbf{q}^*(t_\mathrm{i}^+),\mathbf{u}^*(t_\mathrm{i}^+),\mathbf{u}^*(t_\mathrm{i}^-)) + \mathbf{p}^-(\mathbf{q}^*(t_\mathrm{i}^-),\mathbf{u}^*(t_\mathrm{i}^+),\mathbf{u}^*(t_\mathrm{i}^-))\right)\\
&+\boldsymbol{\alpha}_\mathrm{i}^{-*}\,\nabla_{\mathbf{u}(t_\mathrm{i}^-)}\left(\mathbf{p}^+(\mathbf{q}^*(t_\mathrm{i}^+),\mathbf{u}^*(t_\mathrm{i}^+),\mathbf{u}^*(t_\mathrm{i}^-)) + \mathbf{p}^-(\mathbf{q}^*(t_\mathrm{i}^-),\mathbf{u}^*(t_\mathrm{i}^+),\mathbf{u}^*(t_\mathrm{i}^-))\right)\ ,\\
&\forall t_\mathrm{i}^* \in \mathcal{I}_\mathrm{T}\ ,
\end{aligned}
$$

and

$$
\begin{aligned}
&\left((\dot{\boldsymbol{\nu}}^*(t_\mathrm{i}^+)\mathbf{M} + \boldsymbol{\nu}^*(t_\mathrm{i}^+)\dot{\mathbf{M}}^+) + \boldsymbol{\nu}^*(t_\mathrm{i}^+)\nabla_\mathbf{u}\,\mathbf{h}_{\mathrm{i}+1}^+\right) - \qquad (43)\\
&\qquad\left(\dot{\boldsymbol{\nu}}^*(t_\mathrm{i}^-)\mathbf{M} + \boldsymbol{\nu}^*(t_\mathrm{i}^-)\dot{\mathbf{M}}^- + \boldsymbol{\nu}^*(t_\mathrm{i}^-)\nabla_\mathbf{u}\,\mathbf{h}_\mathrm{i}^-\right) =\\
&-\nabla_\mathbf{q}\left[\boldsymbol{\alpha}_\mathrm{i}^{+*}\mathbf{p}^+(\mathbf{q}^*(t_\mathrm{i}^+),\mathbf{u}^*(t_\mathrm{i}^+),\mathbf{u}^*(t_\mathrm{i}^-)) + \boldsymbol{\alpha}_\mathrm{i}^{-*}\,\mathbf{p}^-(\mathbf{q}^*(t_\mathrm{i}^-),\mathbf{u}^*(t_\mathrm{i}^+),\mathbf{u}^*(t_\mathrm{i}^-))\right]\\
&-(\boldsymbol{\xi}_\mathrm{i}^{+*} + \boldsymbol{\xi}_\mathrm{i}^{-*})\ \nabla_\mathbf{q}\left[\mathbf{M}\left(\mathbf{u}^*(t_\mathrm{i}^+) - \mathbf{u}^*(t_\mathrm{i}^-)\right) - \mathbf{B}_\mathrm{i}\left(\boldsymbol{\zeta}_\mathrm{i}^{+*} - \boldsymbol{\zeta}_\mathrm{i}^{-*}\right)\right]\ ,\\
&\forall t_\mathrm{i}^* \in \mathcal{I}_\mathrm{T}\ ,
\end{aligned}
$$

7. *the impulsive optimal control law condition*

$$
\boldsymbol{\xi}_\mathrm{i}^{-*}\,\mathbf{B}_\mathrm{i}(\mathbf{q}^*(t_\mathrm{i})) = 0,\quad \boldsymbol{\xi}_\mathrm{i}^{+*}\,\mathbf{B}_\mathrm{i}(\mathbf{q}^*(t_\mathrm{i})) = 0,\quad \forall t_\mathrm{i}^* \in \mathcal{I}_\mathrm{T}\ , \qquad (44)
$$

8. *the boundary constraints $\mathcal{C}_\mathrm{f}$,*
9. *the variational inequality with respect to the variations at final time $\hat{t}_\mathrm{f}$:*

$$
\left(\boldsymbol{\nu}^*(t_\mathrm{f})\,(\nabla_\mathbf{u}\,\mathbf{h}_{\mathrm{i}+1}\mathbf{u}^*(t_\mathrm{f}) - \mathbf{M}\dot{\mathbf{u}}^*(t_\mathrm{f})) + (\dot{\boldsymbol{\nu}}^*(t_\mathrm{f})\,\mathbf{M} + \boldsymbol{\nu}^*(t_\mathrm{f})\,\dot{\mathbf{M}})\mathbf{u}^*(t_\mathrm{f})\right)\,\hat{t}_\mathrm{f} + \Psi_{\mathcal{C}_\mathrm{f}}^{\uparrow}(\cdot,\hat{t}_\mathrm{f}) \geq 0\ , \qquad (45)
$$

10. *the normal cone inclusion condition at final state:*

$$
-\left(\begin{bmatrix} -(\dot{\boldsymbol{\nu}}^*(t_\mathrm{f})\mathbf{M} + \boldsymbol{\nu}^*(t_\mathrm{f})\dot{\mathbf{M}}) - \boldsymbol{\nu}^*(t_\mathrm{f})\nabla_\mathbf{u}\,\mathbf{h}_\mathrm{i} \\ \boldsymbol{\nu}^*(t_\mathrm{f})\mathbf{M} \end{bmatrix}\right) \in \mathcal{N}_{\mathcal{C}_\mathrm{f}}\left(\mathbf{q}^*(t_\mathrm{f}),\mathbf{u}^*(t_\mathrm{f})\right)\ . \qquad (46)
$$

Since the derivatives and gradients of $\dot{\mathbf{M}}$, $\ddot{\mathbf{M}}$, $\nabla_\mathbf{u}\mathbf{h}$ involve the generalized velocities and accelerations of the system at pre-, and post-transition state, the right supscripted signs denote wether the pre-transition or post-transition values of the relevant entities are meant. The gradients and time derivatives of several tensors in the Einstein notation convention are given as follows:

$$
\begin{aligned}
&\dot{m}_\mathrm{ij} = \nabla_{\mathbf{q}_\mathrm{k}}\,m_\mathrm{ij}\mathbf{u}_\mathrm{k}(t),\ \ddot{m}_\mathrm{ij} = \nabla^2_{\mathbf{q}_\mathrm{k}\,\mathbf{q}_\mathrm{l}}\,m_\mathrm{ij}\mathbf{u}_\mathrm{k}(t)\,\mathbf{u}_\mathrm{l}(t) + \nabla_{\mathbf{q}\mathrm{k}}\,m_\mathrm{ij}\dot{\mathbf{u}}_\mathrm{k}(t),\\
&\frac{d}{dt}[\nabla_{\mathbf{u}_\mathrm{k}}\mathbf{h}_\mathrm{p}] = \nabla^2_{\mathbf{u}_\mathrm{k}\,\mathbf{u}_\mathrm{l}}\mathbf{h}_\mathrm{p}\dot{\mathbf{u}}_\mathrm{l}(t) + \nabla^2_{\mathbf{u}_\mathrm{k}\,\mathbf{q}_\mathrm{l}}\mathbf{h}_\mathrm{p}\mathbf{u}_\mathrm{l}(t)\ ,
\end{aligned}
$$

where a_ij denotes the relevant element of a second-order tensor $\mathbf{A}$.

6 Discussion and Conclusion

In this work, necessary conditions of strong local minimizers for the impulsive optimal control problem of finite-dimensional Lagrangian systems is presented. The necessary conditions provide criteria for the determination of optimal transition times and locations in the presence of discontinuity of generalized velocities. The introduced framework is capable to model and control of hybrid Lagrangian systems with discontinuous state transitions among different system modes. In the proposed setting concurrent discontinuity on an Lebesgue-negligible atomic time instant of the generalized velocities $\mathbf{u}$ and the dual state $\boldsymbol{\nu}$ is handled. This capability is in comparison to other impulsive control necessary conditions far more consistent with different hybrid system modeling approaches in which transitions happen instantaneously. The crux in the derivation of these necessary conditions is to handle joint discontinuity of the state and the dual state in the framework of integration theory which has long been recognized as a problem if state and costate should become concurrently discontinuous as has been addressed in [15] and [20]. The proposed discontinuous transversality conditions and the internal boundary variations by the author are capable, given the assumptions in the statement of the optimal control problem, to handle this problem properly.

The derivation of conditions benefit of the underlying Lagrangian structure. One of the advantages of the Lagrangian dynamics is the fact, that the generalized directions of control, which are the rows of the linear operator $\mathbf{B}$ are only dependent on the generalized positions $\mathbf{q}$. Since the generalized positions are of absolutely continuous character, the generalized directions of impulsive control remain unchanged during a transition. Another fact is that in the framework of finite-dimensional Lagrangian systems, impact equations and constitutive impact laws are provided, that are means to "join" two optimal trajectories discontinuously.

The proposed necessary conditions are for strong local minimizers and are valid in singular intervals. The optimal control law as stated in equation (40) is valid in singular intervals, because the zero vector belongs to normal cone. The discontinuity in the controls of bang-bang type controller are on Lebesgue negligible intervals so the control law is valid in the "almost everywhere" sense.

The bang-bang control law can be affected at a transition due to two effects, which may concur:

- The change in the structure of the Lebesgue-measurable dynamics as discussed in subsection (3.1), may induce a switching of the polarity of a bang-bang controller.
- The discontinuity of the generalized velocities and the dual state may result in a change of the polarity after impulsive control action.

There are two sets of necessary conditions that belong to the considered optimal control problem. The first set of necessary conditions are obtained by taking the generalized positions and velocities as $\mathcal{RCLBV}$ functions and the dual state as a $\mathcal{LCLBV}$ function. The second set of necessary conditions is obtained interchanging the classes of primal states $\mathbf{q}(t), \mathbf{u}(t)$ and dual state $\boldsymbol{\nu}(t)$. In the case of state-continuous transitions, these two sets of necessary conditions would coincide. Indeed, what distinguishes the necessary conditions stated in Theorem 1 from its counterpart if all transitions were state-continuous are the conditions (41), (42) and (43). These conditions are derived by allowing variations in the post-transition and pre-transition states along with impact equations and constitutive impact laws. Impulsive control law in (44) takes this particular form because the impulsive controls are unbounded in this setting.

For the underlying non-convex problem the given conditions can only propose the candidates for minimizers, for the conditions of sufficiency further work needs to conducted.

References

1. Arutyunov, A., Karamzin, D., Pereira, F.: A Nondegenerate Maximum Principle for Impulse Control Problem with State Constraints. SIAM J. Control Optim. 43, 1812–1843 (2005)
2. Branicky, M.S., Borkar, V.S., Mitter, S.M.: A unified framework for hybrid control: Model and optimal theory. IEEE Transactions on Automatic Control 43, 31–45 (1998)
3. Brogliato, B.: Non-smooth Impact Mechanics. Lecture Notes in Control and Information Sciences. Springer, Heidelberg (1996)
4. Brogliato, B., Daniilidis, A., Lemaréchal, C., Acary, V.: On the equivalence between complementarity systems, projected systems and differential inclusions. Systems and Control Letters 55, 45–51 (2006)
5. Clarke, F.H.: Optimization and Nonsmooth Analysis. In: SIAM Classics in Applied Mathematics, Wiley, New York (1983)
6. Cottle, R.W., Pang, J.-S., Stone, R.E.: The Linear Complementarity Problem. Academic Press, Boston (1992)
7. Glocker, C.: Set-Valued Force Laws, Dynamics of Non-Smooth Systems. Lecture Notes in Applied Mechanics, vol. 1. Springer, Berlin (2001)
8. Glocker, C.: On Frictionless Impact Models in Rigid-Body Systems. Phil. Trans. Royal Soc. Lond. A359, 2385–2404 (2001)
9. Glocker, C., Pfeiffer, F.: Multiple Impacts with Friction in Rigid Multibody Systems. Nonlinear Dynamics 7, 471–497 (1995)
10. Glocker, C.: The Geometry of Newtonian Impacts with Global Dissipation Index for Moving Sets. In: Proc. of the Int. Conf. on Nonsmooth/ Nonconvex Mechanics, Thessaloniki, pp. 283–290 (2002)
11. Glocker, C.: An Introduction to Impacts. In: Haslinger, J., Stavroulakis, G. (eds.) Nonsmooth Mechanics and Solids, CISM Courses and Lectures, vol. 485, pp. 45–101. Springer, Heidelberg (2006)
12. Miller, B.M., Bentsman, J.: Optimal Control Problems in Hybrid Systems with Active Singularities. Nonlinear Analysis 65, 999–1017 (2006)
13. Karamzin, D.Y.: Necessary Conditions of the Minimum in an Impulse Optimal Control Problem. Journal of Mathematical Sciences 139 (2006)
14. Loewen, P.D., Rockafellar, R.T.: Bolza Problems with General Time Constraints. SIAM J. Control Optim. 35, 2050–2069 (1997)

15. Moreau, J.J.: Bounded Variations in time. In: Moreau, J.J., Panagiotopoulos, P.D., Strang, G. (eds.) Topics in Non-smooth Mechanics, pp. 1–74. Birkhäuser, Basel (1988)
16. Moreau, J.J.: Unilateral Contact and Dry Friction in Finite Freedom Dynamics. In: Non-smooth Mechanics and Applications, CISM Courses and Lectures, vol. 302, Springer, Wien (1988)
17. Rockafellar, R.T.: Convex Analysis, Princeton Landmarks in Mathematics. Princeton University Press, Princeton (1970)
18. Rockafellar, R.T.: Generalized Directional Derivatives and Subgradients of Nonconvex Functions. Can. J. Math. 32, 257–280 (1980)
19. Rockafellar, R.T.: Directionally Lipschitzian Functions and Subdifferential Calculus. Proc. London Math. Soc. 39, 331–355 (1979)
20. Rockafellar, R.T.: Dual Problems of Lagrange for Arcs of Bounded Variation. In: Russell, D.L. (ed.) Calculus of Variations and Control Theory, pp. 155–192. Academic Press, London (1976)
21. Rockafellar, R.T., Loewen, P.D.: The Adjoint Arc in Nonsmooth Optimization. Trans. Amer. Math. Soc. 325, 39–72 (1991)
22. Silva, G.N., Vinter, R.B.: Necessary Conditions for Optimal Impulsive Control Problems. SIAM J. Control Opim. 35, 1829–1846 (1997)
23. Shahid Shaikh, M., Caines, P.E.: On the optimal control of hybrid systems: Optimization of trajectories, switching times, and location schedules. In: Maler, O., Pnueli, A. (eds.) HSCC 2003. LNCS, vol. 2623, pp. 466–481. Springer, Heidelberg (2003)
24. Yunt, K., Glocker, C.: Trajectory Optimization of Hybrid Mechanical Systems using SUMT. In: IEEE Proc. of Advanced Motion Control Istanbul, pp. 665–671 (2006)
25. Pontryagin, L.S., Boltyanskii, V.S., Gamkralidze, R.V., Mischenko, E.F.: The Mathematical Theory of Optimal Processes. In: Trirogoff, T.K.N., Neustadt, L.W. (eds.), John Wiley, New York (1962)
26. Yunt, K., Glocker, C.: Time-Optimal Trajectories of a Differential-Drive Robot. In: Van Campen, D.H., Lazurko, M.D., van der Oever, W.P.J.M. (eds.) Proceedings of the Fifth Euromech Nonlinear Dynamics Conference, pp. 1589–1596.
27. Yunt, K., Glocker, C.: A Combined Continuation and Penalty Method for the Determination of Optimal Hybrid Mechanical Trajectories. In: Yu, H.Y., Kreuzer, E. (eds.) IUTAM Symposium on Dynamics and Control of Nonlinear Systems with Uncertainty 2006. IUTAM Bookseries, pp. 187–196. Springer, Heidelberg (2007)
28. Yunt, K.: Optimal Trajectory Planning for Structure-Variant Mechanical Systems. In: IEEE Proc. of Int. Workshop on Variable Structure Systems VSS 2006, pp. 298–303 (2006)
29. Yunt, K., Glocker, C.: Modeling and Optimal Control of Hybrid Rigid-Body Mechanical Systems. In: Bemporad, A., Bicchi, A., Buttazzo, G. (eds.) HSCC 2007. LNCS, vol. 4416, pp. 614–627. Springer, Heidelberg (2007)
30. Yunt, K.: Impulsive Time-Optimal Control of Underactuated Manipulators with Impactively Blockable Degrees of Freedom. In: European Control Conference (ECC 2007), pp. 3977–3984 (2007)
31. Yunt, K., Glocker, C.: Trajectory Optimization of Mechanical Hybrid Systems Using SUMT. In: IEEE Proc. of Advanced Motion Control AMC 2005, pp. 665–671 (2005)
32. Yunt, K.: Impulsive Time-Optimal Control of Structure-Variant Rigid-Body Mechanical Systems. In: 3rd International IEEE Scientific Conference on Physics and Control (Physcon 2007) (2007), IPACS Open Library, http://lib.physcon.ru
33. Silva, G.N., Vinter, R.B.: Necessary Conditions for Optimal Impulsive Control Problems. SIAM J. Control Optim. 35/6, 1829–1846 (1997)

Composition of Motion Description Languages

Wenqi Zhang and Herbert G. Tanner

Mechanical Engineering Department,
University of New Mexico, Albuquerque NM 87131

Abstract. We introduce a new formalism to compose interacting heterogeneous systems described by extended motion description languages (MDLes). The novelty lies in producing a composed system whose behavior could be a superset of the union of the behaviors of its generators. In the class of systems modeled using MDLes, the composition operator is closed, and language equivalence can be decidable. Our approach consists of representing MDLes as normed processes, recursively defined as a guarded system of recursion equations in restricted Greibach Normal Form over a basic process algebra. Basic processes have well defined semantics for composition, which we exploit to establish the properties of our composed MDLes.

1 Introduction

Motion Description Languages (MDLs) [1] translate collections of control algorithms into robust and reusable software [2]. MDLes (e standing for "extended") have been criticized for not capturing concurrency and interaction between systems. This paper is an attempt to address at least one of this issues, namely interaction, and set a framework in which MDLes can be composed, verified, and allow automated motion and task planning for collections of heterogeneous robotic systems.

We identify MDLes as recursive systems in some basic process algebra (BPA) written in Greibach Normal Form (Lemma 1). We propose a simple context-free grammar that generates MDLes and use the machinery available for BPAs to formally define a composition operation for MDLes at the level of grammars. The technical core of this paper indicates how appropriately defined MDLe grammars can be composed (Definition 8), and language equivalence (whether two such grammars generate the same finite traces), is decidable up to bisimulation. The main difference of our composition operation is the appearance in the composed system of events (transitions) not enabled in the generators: the composed system can behave in ways its generators cannot. In our approach, one still needs to identify beforehand these events that can be activated after the composition; nonetheless, the proposed definition partially captures the fact that the whole can be more than the sum of its parts.

Are basic process algebras the *right* formalism to map hybrid robotic systems to discrete models of computation? We do not claim it is, but we believe it is an appropriate one: not too complex, yet not oversimplifying. The justification for choosing BPAs comes first from our desire to model robotic systems using MDLes. Section 3 attempts a brief and incomplete introduction to MDLes and BPAs; the interested reader is refered for more information to [3] and [4].

M. Egerstedt and B. Mishra (Eds.): HSCC 2008, LNCS 4981, pp. 570–583, 2008.

Alternative formulations include maneuver automata [5] and petri nets [6]. Maneuver automata are finite automata that produce sequences of predetermined maneuvers for unmanned vehicles. Admissible motion is expressed as the set of traces the automaton accepts. Maneuver automata, however, generate regular languages, and MDLes are not [3]. Thus, maneuver automata appear to have less expressive power than MDLes.

Petri nets, on the other hand, generate context-sensitive languages. They are therefore more expressive than BPAs but this comes at a cost: bisimulation is undecidable for petri nets [7], which poses an obstacle for further analysis and abstraction. MDLes, on the other hand, are context-free [8]. The equality problem for context-free languages and push-down processes being undecidable notwithstanding [9], we show in this paper that the slightly finer semantics given to an MDLe expressed in a BPA framework allow decidability for language equivalence [10, 11]. The tools we use to arrive at this decidability result are the properties of BPAs introduced in [12, 13, 14], and refined in [15].

Other modeling tools may be available; however, we feel that BPAs strike a reasonable balance between complexity and expressiveness when it comes to modeling systems expressed by, and controlled through, MDLes. Showing that under the extended notion of composition we introduce the resulting system is an MDLe (Lemma 3), and that the decidability properties are preserved (Corollary 2), gives us hope that the resulting (big) system can be abstracted to the point that some of the available model checkers [16, 17, 18] can be used to construct admissible motion plans in the form of "counterexamples."

2 MDLe Preliminaries

MDLe, an extension of the early motion description languages [19], is a device-independent programming language for hybrid motion control. It allows one to compose complex, interrupt-driven control laws, from a set of simple primitives and a number of syntactic rules [2, 3]. Every MDLe string consists of a control part, an interruption part, and the special symbols ")", "(", and ",". A robotic system can generically be described as

$$\dot{x} = f(x, u), \quad y = h(x); \quad x \in \mathbb{R}^n,\ u \in \mathbb{R}^m,\ y \in \mathbb{R}^p, \tag{1}$$

where x is the state of the system, u the control input, and y the measurable output. Let U be a finite set of feedback control laws (or quarks [8]) $u : \mathbb{R}^n \times \mathbb{R} \to \mathbb{R}^m$, for (1), and B a finite set of boolean functions $\xi : \mathbb{R}^p \times \mathbb{R} \to \{0, 1\}$ of output y and time $t \leq T \in \mathbb{R}_+$ (the interrupt quarks [8]).

The basic element of an MDLe is the *atom,* denoted (u, ξ), in which ξ is an *interrupt* selected from set B, and u is a control law selected from U. To *evaluate* or *run* an atom (u, ξ), means to apply the input u to (1) until the interrupt function ξ evaluates true ($\xi = 1$). An MDLe *plan* is composed of a sequence of atoms. For example, evaluating the plan $a = ((u_1, \xi_1), (u_2, \xi_2))$ means that the system state x, flows along $\dot{x} = f(x, u_1)$ until $\xi_1 = 1$, and then along $\dot{x} = f(x, u_2)$ until $\xi_2 = 1$. Plans can also be composed to generate higher order strings, as in $b = ((u_3, \xi_3), a, (u_4, \xi_4))$.

3 From MDLes to Basic Process Algebras

The pumping lemma is utilized in [8] to show that an MDLe is not regular language; it is suggested that it is context-free. Context-free languages are generated by context-free grammars (CFGs), which can always be expressed in Chomsky normal form. A variation of the Chomsky normal form, is the Greibach normal form.

Definition 1 ([15]). *A context-free grammar in which every production rule is of the form $A \to a\alpha$, where A is a variable, a is a terminal, and α is a possibly empty string of variables, is said to be in* Greibach normal form (GNF)*. If, moreover, the length of α (in symbols) does not exceed* 2*, we say that the context-free grammar is in restricted Greibach normal form.*

3.1 The Link between BPAs and Push-Down Automata

A BPA is a mathematical structure consisted of set of constants, $A = \{a, b, c, \ldots\}$, called *atomic actions*, a set Σ_{BPA} of two binary operators on these constants (the alternative composition $+$ and the sequential composition $\cdot$), and a set of axioms E_{BPA} that determine the properties of the operations on the atomic actions [15]. The set Σ_{BPA} is sometimes called *signature*, while set E_{BPA} *equation* set (hence the symbols). The theory associated to a BPA is considered to be parameterized by the set A, which is specified according to the particular application.

The symbol $\cdot$ denoting sequential composition is typically omitted, and we usually write xy instead of $x \cdot y$. We assume that $\cdot$ binds stronger than $+$, thus $(xy)+z = xy+z$ (brackets omitted). The set E_{BPA} consists of five axioms (or equations), appearing in Table 1. Composing atomic actions according to Table 1, yields more complex *processes*. Any such process, is an element of some algebra satisfying the axioms of BPA, and all processes produced in this way make up the set P. The axiom system of Table 1 is the core of a variety of more extensive process axiomatizations:

Table 1. The axioms of a BPA

$x + y = y + x$	A1
$(x + y) + z = x + (y + z)$	A2
$x + x = x$	A3
$(x + y)z = xz + yz$	A4
$(xy)z = x(yz)$	A5

– $x \cdot y$ is the process that first executes x, and upon completion of x, process y starts.
– $x + y$ is the process that either executes x, or executes y (but not both).

Just as in the case of finite state machines, processes are identified by the set of action sequences they admit. Some [20] prefer to include a set Atom of atomic processes or *atoms*. The set Proc of *processes* contains all terms in the free algebra over Atom generated by sequential composition and disjunction. A process algebra is defined by a finite set Π of productions of the form $X \xrightarrow{a} P$, where $X \in$ Atom, $a \in A$, and $P \in$ Proc. The semantics of the above production is as follows: atomic process X performs action a and evolves into process P. Let us identify a process with an automaton, in which a transition denotes the execution of an atomic action. The states of this automaton are all the processes derived through the set of production rules. Action relations are presented in Table 2, in which $x \xrightarrow{a} y$, with x and y being processes and a an atomic action, means that process x evolves into process y after the atomic action a is executed.

Table 2. The operational semantics of BPA

$a \xrightarrow{a} \surd$	R1
$a \xrightarrow{a} x' \Rightarrow x + y \xrightarrow{a} x'$ and $y + x \xrightarrow{a} x'$	R2
$x \xrightarrow{a} \surd \Rightarrow x + y \xrightarrow{a} \surd$ and $y + x \xrightarrow{a} \surd$	R3
$x \xrightarrow{a} x' \Rightarrow xy \xrightarrow{a} x'y$	R4
$x \xrightarrow{a} \surd \Rightarrow xy \xrightarrow{a} y$	R5

The symbol $\surd$ stands for successful termination. It is said that a relation is true iff it can be derived from the relations of Table 2. Note the distinction between the relation operator ($\rightarrow$) and sequential composition ($\cdot$): the fact that $x \xrightarrow{a} y$ does not imply that $y = x \cdot a$, since a is an action executed as x runs, not after it is completed. The only thing that can be inferred about action a is that it is an action that process x can execute.

3.2 Recursive and Guarded Processes

Let us focus on a special type of BPAs with finer semantics. The restrictions we imposed enable us to define composition more comfortably, and prove the decidability of language equivalence for the systems produced by means of composition.

Definition 2 **([10]).** *A* recursive equation *over a* BPA *is an equation of the form* $X = s(x)$, *where* X *is a variable that can take values in* P *and* $s(x)$ *is a term over the* BPA *containing* X*, but no other variable.*

A set of recursive equations give rise to a specification:

Definition 3 **([10]).** *A recursive specification* E *over a* BPA *is a set of recursion equations over the* BPA.

We thus have a set of variables $V = \{x_0, \cdots, x_n\}$, and equations of the form $X = s_x(V)$ with $x \in V$, where s_x is a term over the BPA containing variables in V. Set V contains one distinguished variable called the root variable x_0. A variable in V is called guarded in a given term, if it is preceded by an atomic action:

Definition 4 **([10]).** *Let* s *be a term over a* BPA, *containing variable* X.

- *An occurrence of* X *in* s *is said to be* guarded, *if* s *has a sub term of the form* $a \cdot t$, *where* a *is an atomic action, and* t *a term containing this occurrence of* X; *otherwise this occurrence of* X *in* s *is said to be* unguarded.
- *A term* s *is* completely guarded *if all occurrences of all variables in* s *are guarded. A recursive specification* E *is completely guarded if all right hand sides of all equations of* E *are completely guarded terms.*

Equations over a BPA can also be written in Greibach normal form.

Definition 5 **([10]).** *If a system* E *of recursion equations is guarded and without brackets, then each recursion equation is of the form* $X_i = \sum_j a_j \cdot \alpha_j$, *where* α_j *is a possibly empty product (sequential composition) of atoms and variables. Now if, in addition,* α_j *is exclusively a product of variables,* E *is said to be in* Greibach normal form, *analogous to the same definition for context-free grammars. If each* α_j *in* E *has length not exceeding 2,* E *is in* restricted *Greibach normal form.*

3.3 Composition of BPAs

BPAs can be equipped with a merge operator, $\|$. Process $x\|y$ is the process that executes process x and y in parallel. The left merge operator, $\llfloor$, describes two processes that occur in parallel, in a way similar to $\|$, but with the restriction that the first step must come from the process on the left of the expression. With the new operators, the BPA axioms and action relations are expanded as shown in Tables 3 and 4, respectively.

Table 3. The BPA axioms, expanded with the introduction of merge ($\|$) and left merge ($\llfloor$) operators

$x+y=y+x$	A1
$(x+y)+z=x+(y+z)$	A2
$x+x=x$	A3
$(x+y)z=xz+yz$	A4
$(xy)z=x(yz)$	A5
$x\|y=x\llfloor y+y\llfloor x$	M1
$a\llfloor x=ax$	M2
$ax\llfloor y=a(x\|y)$	M3
$(x+y)\llfloor z=x\llfloor z+y\llfloor z$	M4

Table 4. The action relations of BPA, expanded using the composition operators

$a\xrightarrow{a}\surd$	R1
$a\xrightarrow{a}x'\Rightarrow x+y\xrightarrow{a}x'$ and $y+x\xrightarrow{a}x'$	R2
$x\xrightarrow{a}\surd\Rightarrow x+y\xrightarrow{a}\surd$ and $y+x\xrightarrow{a}\surd$	R3
$x\xrightarrow{a}x'\Rightarrow xy\xrightarrow{a}x'y$	R4
$x\xrightarrow{a}\surd\Rightarrow xy\xrightarrow{a}y$	R5
$x\xrightarrow{a}x'\Rightarrow x\|y\xrightarrow{a}x'\|y$ and $y\|x\xrightarrow{a}y\|x'$	R6
$x\xrightarrow{a}\surd\Rightarrow x\|y\xrightarrow{a}y$ and $y\|x\xrightarrow{a}y$	R7
$x\xrightarrow{a}x'\Rightarrow x\llfloor y\xrightarrow{a}x'\|y$	R8
$x\xrightarrow{a}\surd\Rightarrow x\llfloor y\xrightarrow{a}y$	R9

Two BPA processes p_1 and p_2 are *bisimilar*, if whenever p_1 performs a certain action, p_2 can perform the same action, and *vise versa*. The following definition of bisimulation equivalence for processes is quoted from [11], and is chosen only because of its conceptual association to similar definitions of bisimulation for transition systems, that have appeared in the controls literature [21].

Definition 6 ([11]). *A binary relation $\approx$ on the set of processes* Proc *is a bisimulation, if the following conditions are satisfied:*

- *for all p, q, and p' in* Proc*, and $a\in A$ such that $p\approx q$ and $p\xrightarrow{a}p'$, there exists $q'\in$* Proc *such that $q\xrightarrow{a}q'$ and $p'\approx q'$.*
- *for all p, q, and q' in* Proc*, and $a\in A$ such that $p\approx q$ and $q\xrightarrow{a}q'$, there exists $p'\in$* Proc *such that $p\xrightarrow{a}p'$ and $q'\approx p'$.*

4 Main Results

4.1 MDLes Are a Special Class of BPAs

The representation of an MDLe as a BPA requires an intermediate step, which is the expression of the former as a context-free grammar. We define a context-free grammar $G=(V,\eta,R,S)$ which generates MDLe $L=\{(u,\zeta):u\in U,\zeta\in B\}$ as follows:

- $V=\{u_1,u_2,u_3,\ldots,u_n\}$ is the finite set of *variables*, one for each $u_i\in U$;

- $\eta = \{\nu_1, \nu_2, \dots \nu_n\}$ is the finite set of terminals, which are the atoms of L, $\nu = (u_i, \zeta_j)$ with $u_i \in V$, and $\zeta_j \in B$;
- S is the start symbol in V;
- R is the rules by which we create the strings of L:

$$S \to U \qquad U \to UU \qquad U \to \nu \qquad U \to \emptyset\ , \tag{2}$$

where U can be any element of V, and ν an arbitrary element of η.

We define below the push-down automaton that is equivalent to the context-free grammar described above, according to [22]. Definition 7 allows us to conveniently switch between representations.

Definition 7. *Consider a context-free grammar G defined in* (2). *The push-down automaton $P = (V, \eta, \Sigma, \Gamma, \delta, S, Z_0)$ where*

- $V = \{u_1, u_2, u_3, \dots, u_n\}$ *is the set of* states, *identified with the* variables *in G;*
- $\eta = \{\nu_1, \nu_2, \dots \nu_n\}$ *is the set of* enabled events, *identified as the terminals in G and associated with possible transitions in P;*
- $\Sigma = V \cup \eta$ *is the stack alphabet;*
- $\Gamma : V \to \Gamma(V)$ *is the event activation function that determines which enabled events can generate transitions at each state;*
- $\delta : V \times \eta \to V$ *is the transition function such that* $\delta(x, \nu) \mapsto R(x, \nu) = y \in V$*;*
- $S \in V$ *is the start state in G;*
- Z_0 *is the start symbol in stack;*

The range of Γ defines all active events, the ones that correspond to transitions the automaton can autonomously take. Note the distinction between η and $\Gamma(V)$: this is what enables us to capture actions the system cannot execute autonomously, but potentially can in collaboration with another system. We allow $\Gamma(V) \not\subseteq \eta$, but the transitions which the automaton can autonomously take are in $\Gamma(V) \cap \eta$. Informally, we think of the transitions associated with events in η as ones that the system has the "potential" of taking (but may not know how), and the transitions associated with events in $\Gamma(V)$ as jumps that the system "knows" how to perform but may or may not have the capability of making. The next Lemma confines MDLes to set of languages generated by a special class of context-free grammars (CFGs).

Lemma 1. *An* MDLe *is produced by a* CFG *in Greibach normal form.*

Proof. We rewrite (2) in Chomsky normal form, an intermediate stage before we arriving at the Greibach normal form. Let us first combine rules (2) into a single one, using the disjunction operator $|$, and arrange them on the left hand side of (3).

$$\begin{array}{ll} S_0 \to S|\emptyset & S_0 \to \emptyset \\ S \to U & S_0 \to UU|\nu \\ U \to UU|\nu & U \to UU|\nu \end{array} \tag{3}$$

The right hand side of (3) is obtained first by defining a new start symbol S_0 to replace S, then remove $\emptyset$ from the set of rules that involve U, and finally eliminating the new start symbol S_0.

Then we translate (3) into Greibach normal form, by first eliminating left-recursion. We first add a new rule $B \to V|VB$ to eliminate the left-recursion $V \to VV$ from the right hand side of (3). Finally, we use the rule $V \to \nu|\nu B$ to make all the other rules start with a terminal, and thus transform the right hand side of (3) as follows.

$$\begin{array}{ll} S_0 \to \emptyset & S_0 \to \nu U|\nu BU|\nu|\emptyset \\ S_0 \to UU|\nu & U \to \nu|\nu B \\ U \to UU|\nu & B \to \nu B|\nu BB|\nu \end{array} \tag{4}$$

The rule set (4) is now in Greibach normal form. □

The next Lemma states that an MDLe can be translated into a BPA in GNF [10].

Lemma 2. *The terms of an* MDLe *are a finite trace set of a normed process p, recursively defined by means of a guarded system of recursion equations in restricted Greibach normal form over a* BPA.

Proof. Lemma 1 allows us to express an MDLe as a CFG in Greibach normal form, which in addition satisfies the conditions of Notation 4.5 of [10]. We apply Notation 4.5 in conjunction with Proposition 5.2 of [10] to write the CFG of (4) as a BPA as follows. According to [10], if E is the system represented as a CFG in Greibach normal form, let us use E' to denote the system represented in BPA by replacing $|$ by $+$, and $\to$ by $=$. Now let E' be in restricted Greibach normal form over the BPA, with unique solution p. Then $\text{ftr}(p)$ (the set of finite traces of p) is just the context-free language generated by E. Applying the change of notation suggested,

$$\begin{array}{ll} & S_0 = \emptyset \\ S_0 \to \nu U|\nu BU|\nu|\emptyset & S_0 = \nu U + \nu BU + \nu \\ U \to \nu|\nu B & U = \nu + \nu B \\ B \to \nu B|\nu BB|\nu & B = \nu B + \nu BB + \nu \end{array} \tag{5}$$

and thus we have a BPA in restricted Greibach normal form. Note that according to Definition 5, each variable string in the right hand side of (5) has length of at most two. By applying Proposition 5.2 of [10], to remove the parts of the system that do not contribute to the generation of the finite traces, we conclude that the BPA of (5) generates the strings of the original MDLe. □

4.2 Composition of MDLes

In the preceding section we distinguished between events associated to transitions a push-down automaton representing an MDLe can take autonomously, and events that cannot initiate transitions. Among the latter, there can be events that when *synchronized* with some of another push-down automaton, become active and do initiate transitions. Given two push-down automata P_1 and P_2 defined according to Definition 7, let $H \subseteq \eta_1 \cup \eta_2$ be the collection of events on which P_1 and P_2 should be synchronized. It includes events that become active due to the composition and is has three components:

1. $(\Gamma_2 \cup \eta_1) \setminus (\Gamma_2 \cup \eta_2) \setminus (\Gamma_1 \cup \eta_1)$, (part I in Figure 1), which contains enabled events of P_1 that P_1 can now activate because of P_2;

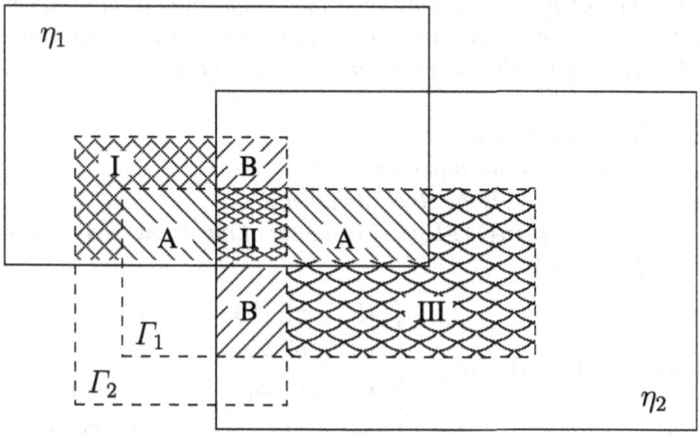

Fig. 1. Enabled, active and common events. Set A includes private active events of P_1; set B contains private active events of P_2; sets I, II, and III represent the common active events of the composed system, the ones that make up H.

2. $(\Gamma_1 \cup \eta_2) \setminus (\Gamma_2 \cup \eta_2) \setminus (\Gamma_1 \cup \eta_1)$, (part III in Figure1), which contains enabled events of P_2 that now become active because of P_1; and
3. $(\Gamma_1 \cup \eta_2) \cap (\Gamma_2 \cup \eta_1)$, (part II in Figure 1), which includes common active events in both systems.

The components of H in 1 and 2 do not appear in the set of (active) events of the composed system under the conventional definition of composition [23]. Our definition of composition is stated as follows.

Definition 8. *Consider two* MDLes, *expressed as context-free grammars* $G_1 = (V_1, \eta_1, R, S_{01})$ *and* $G_2 = (V_2, \eta_2, R, S_{02})$, *both with rule sets* R *of the form* (2). *Let* E_1 *and* E_2 *be their corresponding representations as a system of guarded recursive equations, in restricted Greibach normal form over a* BPA. *The composition of* G_1 *and* G_2 *is defined as the context-free grammar* $G = (V, \eta, R, S_0)$, *where (with reference to Figure 1)*

- $V := V_1 \times V_2$;
- $\eta := \eta_1 \cup \eta_2$, *is the set of enabled events (also denoted* $\eta_{(1\|2)}$*)*;
- $S_0 := S_{01} \times S_{02}$;
- $R(V \times \eta) = R((V_1, V_2) \times \eta) := \begin{cases} (R(V_1, \eta), R(V_2, \eta)) & \textit{if } \eta \in H, \\ (R(V_1, \eta), V_2) & \textit{if } \eta \in A, \\ (V_1, R(V_2, \eta)) & \textit{if } \eta \in B \\ \textit{undefined}, & \textit{otherwise}. \end{cases}$

The transitions of the composed system still respect the grammar rules (2), however, the composition restricts the domain of R. The push-down automaton representing the composed system can be defined as follows:

Definition 9. *The automaton resulting from the composition of push-down automata* P_1 *and* P_2 *that accept the strings of two different* MDLes *is the automaton* $P_1 \| P_2 = (V, \eta_{(1\|2)}, \Sigma, \Gamma_{(1\|2)}, \delta, V_0, Z_0)$, *where (with reference to Figure 1)*

- $V = V_1 \times V_2$ *is the set of states;*
- $\eta = \eta_{(1\|2)} = \eta_1 \cup \eta_2$ *is the input alphabet;*
- $\Sigma = (V_1 \times V_2) \cup \eta_{(1\|2)}$ *is the stack alphabet;*
- $\Gamma_{(1\|2)}((u_1, u_2)) = \Gamma_1(u_1) \cup \Gamma_2(u_2)$ *is the set of inputs that may generate transitions at state* (u_1, u_2),
- $\delta(V \times \eta) = R((V_1, V_2) \times \eta) := \begin{cases} (R(V_1,\eta), R(V_2,\eta)) & \text{if } \eta \in H, \\ (R(V_1,\eta), V_2) & \text{if } \eta \in A, \\ (V_1, R(V_2,\eta)) & \text{if } \eta \in B \\ \text{undefined}, & \text{otherwise} \end{cases}$
- $V_0 = (V_{01} \times V_{02})$ *is the set of initial (start) states;*
- $Z_0 = (Z_{01} \times Z_{02})$ *is the start symbol of the stack.*

The next section ensures that the composition of variables and terminals of systems in (guarded) Greibach normal form over a BPA, conforms to the same rules.

4.3 MDLes Are Closed Under Composition

Lemma 3. *An* MDLe *written as a system of guarded recursive equations in restricted Greibach normal form is closed under the left merge* $\lfloor\!\lfloor$ *operator.*

Proof. Assume that G is written as a system of guarded recursive equations in restricted Greibach form, according to (4). According to Table 3,

$$\begin{aligned}
U \lfloor\!\lfloor B &\overset{M4,M2}{=} \nu B + (\nu B) \lfloor\!\lfloor B \overset{M3}{=} \nu B + \nu(B \| B) \overset{A3,M1}{=} \nu B + \nu(B \lfloor\!\lfloor B) \\
U \lfloor\!\lfloor S_0 &\overset{M4,M2}{=} \nu S_0 + (\nu B) \lfloor\!\lfloor S_0 \overset{M3,M1}{=} \nu S_0 + \nu(B \lfloor\!\lfloor S_0 + S_0 \lfloor\!\lfloor B) \\
B \lfloor\!\lfloor S_0 &\overset{M4,M2}{=} \nu S_0 + (\nu B) \lfloor\!\lfloor S_0 + (\nu BB) \lfloor\!\lfloor S_0 \\
&\overset{M3,A5}{=} \nu S_0 + \nu(B \lfloor\!\lfloor S_0 + S_0 \lfloor\!\lfloor B) + \nu(BB \lfloor\!\lfloor S_0 + S_0 \lfloor\!\lfloor BB)
\end{aligned}$$

Note that reversing the order of variables in the above merge operations yields the same type of expressions encountered above:

$$\begin{aligned}
B \lfloor\!\lfloor U &= (\nu B + \nu BB + \nu) \lfloor\!\lfloor U = \nu U + \nu(BB \lfloor\!\lfloor U + U \lfloor\!\lfloor BB) + \nu(B \lfloor\!\lfloor U + U \lfloor\!\lfloor B) \\
S_0 \lfloor\!\lfloor U &= (\nu U + \nu BU + \nu) \lfloor\!\lfloor U = \nu U + \nu(U \lfloor\!\lfloor U) + \nu(BU \lfloor\!\lfloor U + U \lfloor\!\lfloor BU) \\
S_0 \lfloor\!\lfloor B &= (\nu U + \nu BU + \nu) \lfloor\!\lfloor B = \nu B + \nu(U \lfloor\!\lfloor B + B \lfloor\!\lfloor U) + \nu(BU \lfloor\!\lfloor B + B \lfloor\!\lfloor BU) \quad \square
\end{aligned}$$

Since the left-merge operation $\lfloor\!\lfloor$ is closed, it is easy to show using Lemma 3 and M1 of Table 3 that $\|$ is closed too.

4.4 MDLe Equivalence Is Decidable

Systems of guarded recursive equations enjoy nice properties in the sense that verifying the bisimulation equivalence is decidable [10].

Theorem 1 ([10]). *Let E_1, E_2 be normed systems of guarded recursion equations (over basic process algebras) in restricted Greibach normal form. Then the bisimulation relation $\approx$, that is whether $E_1 \approx E_1$, is decidable.*

Corollary 1. *If* MDLe*s are written in the form of a system of guarded recursive equations in Greibach normal form over a* BPA*, the bisimulation relation is decidable.*

Proof. (Sketch) Using Lemma 1, each MDLe is written as a context-free language in Greibach Normal Form. Lemma 2 translates this representation into a system of guarded recursive equations in restricted Greibach normal form over a BPA. By Theorem 1 of [10], language equivalence for systems in (guarded) restricted Greibach normal form such as the MDLes translated using Lemma 2, is decidable up to bisimilarity. □

4.5 MDLe Composition Preserves Bisimilarity

Proposition 1. *The composition operator $\|$ preserves bisimilarity. That is, if $P \approx Q$, then $P\|R \approx Q\|R$.*

Proof. Consider a relation $\mathcal{R}$ over the set of processes, such that $P\|R$ and $Q\|R$ belong to $\mathcal{R}$ whenever $P \approx Q$. We show that $\mathcal{R}$ is a bisimulation.

Case 1. Process P (or Q) executes action a. If $P \approx Q$, then $(P\|R, Q\|R) \in \mathcal{R}$. Assume that $P \xrightarrow{a} P'$. Then by action relation R6 in Table 4, we have $P \xrightarrow{a} P' \Rightarrow P\|R \xrightarrow{a} P'\|R$. Since $P \approx Q$, there exists Q' such that $Q \xrightarrow{a} Q'$, and $P' \approx Q'$. By definition, $(P'\|R, Q'\|R) \in \mathcal{R}$. Similarly, it can be shown that if $Q \xrightarrow{a} Q'$, then there exists a P', with $P' \approx Q'$ and $(P'\|R, Q'\|R) \in \mathcal{R}$.

Case 2. Process R executes action a. Since bisimulation is reflexive, this case reduces to the previous one, and $(P\|R, P\|R) \in \mathcal{R}$.

Case 3. Process P terminates after executing action a ($P \xrightarrow{a} \surd$). Relation R7 of Table 4 implies that $P \xrightarrow{a} \surd \Rightarrow P\|R \xrightarrow{a} R$. Since $P \approx Q$, we need to have $Q \xrightarrow{a} \surd$. Thus, by R7 of Table 4, $Q\|R \xrightarrow{a} R$. By definition, $R \approx R$ and thus the processes derived with the a-transition belong $\mathcal{R}$. The case where Q terminates after executing a is identical.

Case 4. Process R terminates after executing a ($R \xrightarrow{a} \surd$). By R7 of Table 4, $R \xrightarrow{a} \surd \Rightarrow P\|R \xrightarrow{a} P$. Similarly, $R \xrightarrow{a} \surd \Rightarrow Q\|R \xrightarrow{a} Q$. Given that $P \approx Q$, the processes derived from $P\|R$ and $Q\|R$ when R executes a, belong to $\mathcal{R}$.

Case 5. Processes P and R are synchronously execute action a. In this case, we resort to axiom M1 of Table 3, and treat the transitions of P and R separately according to cases 1 and 2 above. The case where Q executes a synchronously with R is identical.

Case 6. Processes P and R terminate synchronously by executing action a. Axiom M1 of Table 3 allows us to treat the synchronous transition to termination as an asynchronous one. In this case, we proceed according to cases 3 and 4.

Thus, for all combinations of possible transitions for $P\|R$ and $Q\|R$, we have that $P\|R \approx Q\|R$ if $P \approx Q$. The conditions of Definition 6 are satisfied and therefore $\mathcal{R}$ is a bisimulation relation. □

From Proposition 1 it follows that

Corollary 2. *The composition of* MDLe*s is decidable up to bisimulation equivalence.*

Proof. The operation $'\|'$ is closed (Lemma 3) and also preserve bisimilarity (Proposition 1), which means the composition of MDLes can also be written as a system of guarded recursive equations in restricted Greibach normal form over a BPA. By Theorem 1, this composition is decidable. □

5 A Case Study: The Sliding Block Puzzle

Representing an instance of the sliding block puzzle as a multi-robot hybrid system serves as a reality check, to ensure that our formulation captures the possible interaction between heterogeneous robot systems. It has been shown that in general, sliding-block puzzles are PSPACE-complete [24,25]. However, under certain simplifying assumptions and for cases of such puzzles like the one we consider here (Figure 2), a polynomial algorithm can be constructed to move a single block from any initial position to any final position [25].

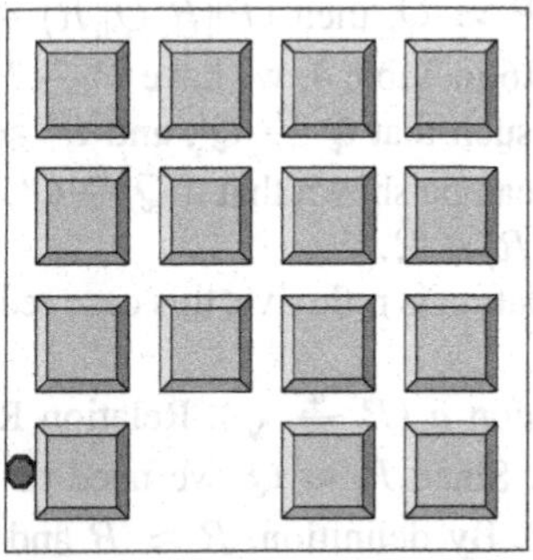

Fig. 2. Realization of a sliding block puzzle. Square blocks (tiles) cover all but one cell of a 4 × 4 grid. A robot (round object) is moving along the rows and columns of the grid reconfiguring the blocks. Blocks and robot are modeled as agents moving according to their own MDLe.

Fig. 3. Enumeration of agent positions for the agents in the sliding block puzzle. Positions 1 through 16 can be occupied by blocks. (In Figure 2, position 2 is not occupied.) Positions 17 through 81 represent possible positions for the robot agent.

In the simple instance of the sliding block puzzle depicted in Figure 2, the goal is for the robot (initially at position 26) to move the block at position 1 to location 6. Robot and blocks are thought to be autonomous agents, each with its own MDLe. A block can do nothing by itself; any transitions within the block's MDLe may only be activated after composition with the robot agent, which can *push* a block to a different location. However, these potential transitions in the block's configuration need to be encoded in its enabled event set η.

We model the state of the block as a triplet, consisting of the state of motion (the analogous of the controller in a robotic system), its position, and the availability of an empty location in the immediate neighborhood. The block automaton is $B = (V_b, \eta_b, V_b \cup \eta_b, \Gamma_b, \delta_b, V_{0b}, Z_{0b})$, where

1. $V_b := \{V_{b1}, V_{b2}, V_{b3}\}$ is the set of states, where
   - $V_{b1} \in \{u_1, \ldots, u_5\}$ is a motion state: u_1 (be pushed east), u_2 (be pushed west), u_3 (be pushed north), u_4 (be pushed south), u_5 (stay at location);
   - $V_{b2} \in \{1, \ldots, 16\}$ is the position of the block; and
   - $V_{b3} \in \{b_1, \ldots, b_5\}$ are possible empty nearby locations: b_1 (east), b_2 (west), b_3 (north), b_4 (south), b_5 (none);
2. $\eta_b = \{\nu_b \mid \nu_b = ((u_i, j, b_k), \xi)\}$, with i and k in $\{1, \ldots 5\}$, and j in $\{1, \ldots, 16\}$, includes all events (MDLe atoms; ξ_b is the block's interrupt function) ;
3. $\Gamma_b : V_b \to 2^{\eta_b}$ is the event activation function (initially mapping to $\emptyset$);
4. $\delta_b : V_b \times \eta_b \to V_b$ is the transition function, also mapping to $\emptyset$ since the range of Γ_b is empty, suggesting that the block automaton can make no transitions on its own (except for the case of u_5).

Symbols V_{0b} and Z_{0b} correspond to the initial state and stack symbol, respectively.

For the robot, an atom consists of the state of motion (controller running) and its position. The robot can move along the rows and columns of the grid, and push against a block in order to move it. The automaton for the robot is a tuple $R = (V_r, \eta_r, V_r \cup \eta_r, \Gamma_r, \delta_r, V_{0r}, Z_{0r})$, where

1. $V_r = \{(V_{r1}, V_{r2})\}$ is the set of states, where
   - $V_{r1} \in \{w_1, \ldots, w_9\}$ are the available controllers for the robot: w_1 (push east) w_2 (push west), w_3 (push north), w_4 (push south), w_5 (stay at location), w_6 (move east), w_7 (move west), w_8 (move north), w_9 (move south); and
   - $V_{r2} \in \{17, \ldots, 81\}$ are the possible positions for the robot;
2. $\eta_r = \{\nu_r \mid \nu_r = ((w_i, j), \xi_r)\}$, where i is in $\{1, \ldots, 9\}$, j in $\{17, \ldots, 81\}$, and ξ_r is the robot's interrupt function, includes all the events associated with possible robot transitions;
3. $\Gamma_r : V_r \to 2^{\eta_r}$ is the activation function determining which events are active at each robot state; and
4. $\delta_r : V_r \times \eta_r \to V_r$ is the transition function.

Similarly, V_{0r} and Z_{0r} are the initial state and the start stack symbol for the robot automaton, respectively.

The system expressing all possible transitions in the sliding block puzzle is generated by composing the robot with the fifteen blocks. Note that traditional notions of (parallel) composition [23] produce a system where nothing can happen (the puzzle configuration cannot change). However, by identifying "pushing" events in both systems as common: $u_i = w_i$, for $i = 1, \ldots, 5$ and including them in $H = \{u_1, \ldots, u_5\}$, the composed system can take synchronised transitions on these events. Therefore, to move a block from position 1 to position 6, starting from the configuration shown in Figure 2 we give the composed system the following input string:

((5,27,1,1,1,1,26),2)((8,27,5,2,2,5,27),1)((8,32,2,2,2,8,27),1)((8,41,2,2,2,8,32),1)((8,46,2,2,2,8,41),1)
((5,46,2,2,2,8,46),1)((7,46,2,2,2,5,46),1)((7,50,2,2,2,7,46),1)((5,50,2,2,2,7,50),1)((8,50,2,2,2,5,50),1)
((4,50,4,5,4,5,50),2)((5,36,4,5,4,4,50),1)((6,36,5,1,3,5,36),1)((6,32,3,1,3,6,36),1)((6,37,3,1,3,6,32),1)
((6,33,3,1,3,6,37),1)((5,33,3,1,3,6,33),1)((8,33,3,1,3,5,33),1)((8,42,3,1,3,8,33),1)((5,42,3,1,3,8,42),2)
((7,42,3,1,3,5,42),1)((2,42,2,6,2,5,42),1)((5,41,2,6,2,2,42),1)((9,41,5,5,1,5,41),2)((9,32,1,5,1,9,41),1)
((9,27,1,5,1,9,32),1)((9,18,1,5,1,9,27),1)((5,18,1,5,1,9,18),1)((6,18,1,5,1,5,18),1)((6,23,1,5,1,6,18),1)
((5,23,1,5,1,6,23),1)((8,23,1,5,1,6,23),1)((3,23,3,2,3,5,23),2) ((5,37,3,2,3,3,23),1)((8,37,5,6,4,5,37),1)

where due to space restrictions, we have abbreviated the composed atoms, and included only the components corresponding to the block (distinguished by its position) that physically interacts with the robot.

6 Conclusion

Our approach to composition of MDLes and cooperative behavior between heterogeneous systems is based on allowing systems to have additional cooperative transitions, that become active only when the systems are composed with appropriate others. We engineered the mechanics of this interaction by identifying these related, or interdependent, transitions between systems and placing them in a set H that affects how the transitions of the composed system are synchronized. By mapping MDLes to a specific type of basic process algebras we obtained well defined semantics to such compositions, and established computability properties (at least when it comes to language equivalence) for these processes and their compositions. Further steps include the construction of a bisimulation algorithm to allow us to abstract the discrete (but big) systems resulting from such compositions, and the subsequent use of available model checkers for motion and task planning by negating reachability predicates and using counterexamples.

Acknowledgement. This work is supported by NSF IIS grant # 0447898.

References

1. Brockett, R.: Formal languages for motion description and map making. In: Bailleul, J., Brockett, R., Donald, B. (eds.) Robotics, vol. 41, pp. 181–193. ACM, New York (1990)
2. Manikonda, V., Krishnaprasad, P., Hendler, J.: Languages, behaviors, hybrid architectures and motion control. In: Baillieul, J., Willems, J.C. (eds.) Mathematical Control Theory, pp. 200–226. Springer, Heidelberg (1998)
3. Hristu, D., Krishnaprasad, P., Anderson, S., Zhang, F., D'Anna, L., Sodre, P.: The MDLe engine: A software tool for hybrid motion control. Technical Report 2000-54, Institute for Systems Research, University of Maryland (2000)

4. Baeten, J.: A brief history of process algebra. Technical Report CSR 04-02, Vakgroep Informatica, Technische Universiteit Eindhoven (2004)
5. Frazzoli, E., Dahleh, M.A., Feron, E.: Maneuver-based motion planning for nonlinear systems with symmetries. IEEE Trans. on Robotics 21, 1077–1091 (2005)
6. Murata, T.: Petri nets: Properties, analysis and applications. Proceedings of the IEEE 77, 541–580 (1989)
7. Jancar, P.: Undecidability of bisimilarity for petri nets and some related problems. Theoretical Computer Science 148, 281–301 (1995)
8. Hristu-Varsakelis, D., Egerstedt, M., Krishnaparsad, P.: On the structural complexity of the motion description language MDLe. In: Proceedings of the 42nd IEEE Conference on Descision and Control, pp. 3360–3365 (2003)
9. Burkart, O., Steffen, B.: Composition, decomposition and model checking of pushdown processes. Nordic Journal of Computing 158, 89–125 (1995)
10. Baeten, J., Bergstra, J., Klop, J.W.: Decidability of bisimulation equivalence for process generating context-free languages. Journal of the ACM 40, 653–683 (1993)
11. Hirshfeld, Y., Jerrum, M., Moller, F.: A polynomial-time algorithm for deciding bisimulation equivalence of normed basic parallel process. Theoretical Computer Science 158, 143–159 (1996)
12. Milner, R.: A Calculus of Communicating Systems. LNCS, vol. 92. Springer, Heidelberg (1980)
13. Milner, R.: Communication and Concurrency. Prentice-Hall, Englewood Cliffs (1989)
14. Hoare, C.: Communicating Sequential Processes. Lecture Notes in Computer Sciences. Prentice-Hall, Englewood Cliffs (1985)
15. Baeten, J.C.M., Weijland, W.P.: Process Algebra. Cambridge Tracts in Theoretical Computer Science, vol. 18. Cambridge University Press, Cambridge (1991)
16. Bengtsson, J., Larsen, K., Larsson, F., Pettersson, P., Yi, W.: UPPAAL - a tool suite for automatic verification of real-time systems. In: DIMACS Workshop on Verification and Control of Hybrid Systems, Springer, Heidelberg (1995)
17. Henzinger, T., Ho, P.H., Wong-Toi, H.: A user guide to HYTECH. In: Brinksma, E., Steffen, B., Cleaveland, W.R., Larsen, K.G., Margaria, T. (eds.) TACAS 1995. LNCS, vol. 1019, pp. 41–71. Springer, Heidelberg (1995)
18. Daws, C., Olivero, A., Tripakis, S., Yovine, S.: The tool KRONOS. In: Alur, R., Sontag, E.D., Henzinger, T.A. (eds.) HS 1995. LNCS, vol. 1066, pp. 208–219. Springer, Heidelberg (1996)
19. Brockett, R.W.: On the computer control of movement. In: Proceedings of the IEEE International Conference on Robotics and Automation, pp. 534–540 (1988)
20. Hirshfeld, Y., Jerrum, M.: Bisimulation equivalence is decidable for normed process algebra. Technical Report ECS-LFCS-98-386, School of Informatics at the University of Edinburgh (1998)
21. Pappas, G.J.: Bisimilar linear systems. Automatica 39, 2035–2047 (2003)
22. Sipser, M.: Introduction to the Theory of Computation. PWS Publishing Company (1997)
23. Cassandras, C.G., Lafortune, S.: Introduction to Discrete Event Systems. Kluwer Academic Publishers, Dordrecht (2001)
24. Hopcroft, J., Schwarz, J., Sharir., M.: On the complexity of motion planning for multiple independent objects:pspace-hardness of the 'warehouseman's problem. International Journal of Robotics Tesearch 3, 76–88 (1984)
25. Robert, A., Hearn, E.D.D.: Pspace-completeness of sliding-block puzzles and other problems through the nondeterministic constraint logic model of computation. Theoretical Computer Science 343, 72–96 (2005)

On Optimal Quadratic Regulation for Discrete-Time Switched Linear Systems*

Wei Zhang and Jianghai Hu

School of Electrical and Computer Engineering,
Purdue University, West Lafayette, IN 47907, USA
{zhang70,jianghai@purdue.edu}

Abstract. This paper studies the discrete-time linear quadratic regulation problem for switched linear systems (DLQRS) based on dynamic programming approach. The unique contribution of this paper is the analytical characterizations of both the value function and the optimal control strategies for the DLQRS problem. Based on the particular structures of these analytical expressions, an efficient algorithm suitable for solving an arbitrary DLQRS problem is proposed. Simulation results indicate that the proposed algorithm can solve randomly generated DLQRS problems with very low computational complexity. The theoretical analysis in this paper can significantly simplify the computation of the optimal strategy, making an NP hard problem numerically tractable.

1 Introduction

A switched system usually consists of a family of subsystems described by differential or difference equations and a logical rule that orchestrates the switching among them. Such systems arise in many engineering fields, such as power electronics [1,2], embedded systems [3,4], manufacturing [5], and communication networks [6], etc. In the last decade or so, the stability and stabilizability of switched systems have been extensively studied [7,8,9]. Many theoretical and numerical tools have been developed for the stability analysis of various switched systems. These stability results have also led to some controller synthesis algorithms which stabilize certain simple switched systems [10]. However, for many engineering applications, ensuring the stability is only the first step rather than an ultimate design goal. How to design a control strategy that not only stabilizes a given switched system, but also optimizes certain design criteria is an even more meaningful yet challenging research problem.

The focus of this paper is on the optimal discrete-time linear quadratic regulation problem for switched linear systems, hereby referred to as the DLQRS problem. The goal is to develop a computationally appealing algorithm to construct an optimal control law that minimizes the given quadratic cost function. The problem is of fundamental importance in both theory and practice and has

* This work was partially supported by the National Science Foundation under Grant CNS-0643805.

M. Egerstedt and B. Mishra (Eds.): HSCC 2008, LNCS 4981, pp. 584–597, 2008.

challenged researchers for many years. The bottleneck is mostly on the determination of the optimal switching strategy. Many methods have been proposed to tackle this problem, most of which are in a divide-and-conquer manner. Algorithms for optimizing the switching instants with a fixed mode sequence have been derived for general switched systems in [11] and for autonomous switched systems in [12]. Although an algorithm for updating the switching sequence is discussed in [12], finding the best switching sequence is still an NP-hard problem, even for switched linear systems.

This paper studies the DLQRS problem from the dynamic programming (DP) perspective. The last few years have seen increasing interest in using DP to solve various optimal control problems of switched systems. In [13], DP is used to derive a search algorithm to find the optimal switching instants for fixed switching sequences. In [14,15,16], DP-based numerical methods are proposed to compute the optimal switching regions. More recently, Lincoln and Rantzer [17] develop an iterative algorithm to approximate the true value functions with guaranteed accuracy. The algorithm is also used to study switched systems in [18,19]. Compared with previous studies, the contributions of this paper are the following. First, we characterize analytically the value function and the optimal control strategy for general DLQRS problems. More specifically, we show that the value function at each time step of any DLQRS problem is the pointwise minimum of a finite number of quadratic functions, and that the optimal state-feedback gain is of a Kalman-type form with a state-dependent positive semi-definite matrix. Although other researchers have also suggested a piecewise affine structure for the optimal feedback control [14,15,16], few of them derive explicitly the optimal feedback gains and identify their connections with the Kalman gain and Riccati recursion of the traditional LQR problem as we do in this paper. Secondly, we prove that under certain conditions of the subsystems, the value function converges exponentially fast as the control horizon increases. Finally, based on the particular structure of the value function and its convergence property, an efficient algorithm is proposed to solve general DLQRS problems. Simulation results indicate that the proposed algorithm can compute the optimal switching strategy and the optimal control input simultaneously with very low computational complexity for randomly generated DLQRS problems. It is worth mentioning that in [17], Lincoln *et al.* proposes a similar structure of the value function when they apply their general theory of relaxed dynamic programming to switched linear systems. The approach adopted in this paper follows naturally from the traditional LQR problem and is substantially different from the one used in [17]. Moreover, different from [17], we allow nonzero terminal cost in the objective function, which is especially important when the time horizon is finite. More comparisons of our result with [17] can be found in Remark 4.

This paper is organized as follows. In Section 2, the DLQRS problem is formulated. The value function of the DLQRS problem is derived in a simple analytical form in Section 3. An algorithm is developed in Sections 4 and 5 to compute the value function in an efficient way. Numerical simulations are performed in Section 6 to demonstrate the algorithm. Finally, some concluding remarks are given in Section 7.

2 Problem Formulation

Consider the discrete-time switched linear system defined as:

$$x(t+1) = A_{v(t)}x(t) + B_{v(t)}u(t),\ t = 0, \ldots, N-1, \tag{1}$$

where $x(t) \in \mathbb{R}^n$ is the continuous state, $v(t) \in \mathbb{M} \triangleq \{1, \ldots, M\}$ is the discrete control or switching strategy, and $u(t) \in \mathbb{R}^p$ is the continuous control. For each $i \in \mathbb{M}$, A_i and B_i are constant matrices of appropriate dimension, and the pair (A_i, B_i) is called a subsystem of (1). This switched linear system is time invariant in the sense that the set of available subsystems $\{(A_i, B_i)\}_{i=1}^M$ is independent of time t. We assume that there is no internal forced switchings, i.e., the system can stay at or switch to any mode at any time instant. In this paper, the terminal cost function $\psi(x)$ and the running cost function $L(x, u, v)$ are assumed to be in the following quadratic forms:

$$\psi(x) = x^T Q_f x, \quad L(x, u, v) = x^T Q_v x + u^T R_v u,$$

where $Q_f = Q_f^T \succeq 0$ is the terminal state weight, and $Q_v = Q_v^T \succeq 0$ and $R_v = R_v^T \succ 0$ are the running weights for the state and the control for subsystem $v \in \mathbb{M}$, respectively. The overall objective function to be minimized over the time horizon $[0, N]$ can thus be defined as

$$J(u, v) = \psi(x(N)) + \sum_{j=0}^{N-1} L(x(j), u(j), v(j))). \tag{2}$$

The goal of this paper is to solve the following discrete-time LQR problem for the switched linear system (1) (referred to as DLQRS problem hereby).

Problem 1 (DLQRS problem). Find the u and v that minimize $J(u, v)$ subject to the dynamic equation (1).

3 The Value Function of the DLQRS Problem

Following the idea of dynamic programming, for each time $t \in \{0, 1, \ldots, N\}$, we define the value function $V_{t,N} : \mathbb{R}^n \to \mathbb{R}$ as:

$$V_{t,N}(z) = \min_{\substack{v(j)\in\mathbb{M},u(j),\\ t\leq j\leq N-1}} \Big\{ \psi(x(N)) + \sum_{j=t}^{N-1} L(x(j), u(j), v(j)) \Big| \text{ subject to eq. (1) with } x(t) = z \Big\}. \tag{3}$$

The $V_{t,N}(z)$ so defined is the minimum cost-to-go starting from state z at time t. The minimum cost for the DLQRS problem with a given initial condition $x(0) = x_0$ is simply $V_{0,N}(x_0)$. Due to the time-invariant nature of the switched system (1), its value function depends only on the number of remaining time steps, i.e.,

$$V_{t,N}(z) = V_{t+m,N+m}(z),$$

for all $z \in \mathbb{R}^n$ and all integers $m \geq -t$. In the rest of this paper, when no ambiguity arises, we will denote by $V_k(z)$ the value function at time $t = N - k$ when there are k time steps left, i.e., $V_k(z) \triangleq V_{N-k,N}(z)$.

In the special case when $M = 1$, the switched system consists of only one subsystem, say, (A, B). Thus, the DLQRS problem degenerates into the classical LQR problem. Denote by Q and R the state and control weighting matrices in this degenerate case. Then, according to the LQR theory, the value function defined in (3) is of the following quadratic form:

$$V_k(z) = z^T P_k z, \quad k = 0, \ldots, N, \tag{4}$$

where $\{P_k\}_{k=0}^N$ is a sequence of positive semi-definite matrices satisfying the Difference Riccati Equation (DRE)

$$P_{k+1} = Q + A^T P_k A - A^T P_k B(R + B^T P_k B)^{-1} B^T P_k A, \tag{5}$$

with initial condition $P_0 = Q_f$. Some important facts about the matrices P_k's are summarized in the following lemma.

Lemma 1 ([20,21]). *Let $\mathcal{A}$ be the set of all positive semi-definite (p.s.d.) matrices, then*

1. *If $P_k \in \mathcal{A}$, then $P_{k+1} \in \mathcal{A}$.*
2. *If (A, B) is stabilizable, then the sequence $\{||P_k||_2\}_{k=0}^\infty$ is uniformly bounded.*
3. *Let C be a matrix such that $Q = C^T C$. If (A, B) is stabilizable and (A, C) is detectable, then $\lim_{k\to\infty} P_k = P^*$, where P^* is the unique stabilizing solution to the Algebraic Riccati Equation (ARE)*

$$P = Q + A^T P A - A^T P B(R + B^T P B)^{-1} B^T P A.$$

In general, when $M \geq 2$, the value function $V_k(z)$ is no longer a simple quadratic form as in (4). To derive the value function for the general switched linear system (1), define the Riccati mapping $\rho_i : \mathcal{A} \to \mathcal{A}$ for each subsystem (A_i, B_i), $i \in \mathbb{M}$:

$$\rho_i(P) = Q_i + A_i^T P A_i - A_i^T P B_i(R_i + B_i^T P B_i)^{-1} B_i^T P A_i. \tag{6}$$

Let $\mathcal{H}_0 = \{Q_f\}$ be a set consisting of only one matrix Q_f. Define the set $\mathcal{H}_k$ for $k \geq 0$ iteratively as

$$\mathcal{H}_{k+1} = \rho_{\mathbb{M}}(\mathcal{H}_k) \triangleq \{P \in \mathcal{A} : P = \rho_i(P_k), \text{for some } i \in \mathbb{M} \text{ and } P_k \in \mathcal{H}_k\}. \tag{7}$$

In other words, each matrix in $\rho_{\mathbb{M}}(\mathcal{H}_k)$ is obtained by taking the Riccati mapping for some matrix in $\mathcal{H}_k$ through some subsystem i. Denote by $|\mathcal{H}_k|$ the number of distinct matrices in $\mathcal{H}_k$. Then it can be easily seen that $|\mathcal{H}_0| = 1$ and $|\mathcal{H}_k| \leq M^k$ for any $k \geq 0$.

Theorem 1. *The value function for the DLQRS problem at time $N-k$, i.e., with k time steps left, is*

$$V_k(z) = \min_{P \in \mathcal{H}_k} z^T P z. \tag{8}$$

Furthermore, for $k \geq 0$, if we define

$$(P_k^*(z), i_k^*(z)) = \arg\min_{(P \in \mathcal{H}_k, i \in \mathbf{M})} z^T \rho_i(P) z, \tag{9}$$

then the optimal mode (discrete control) and the optimal continuous control at state z and time $N-(k+1)$ are $v^*(N-(k+1)) = i_k^*(z)$ and $u^*(N-(k+1)) = -K_{i_k^*(z)}(P_k^*(z))z$, respectively, where $K_i(P)$ is the Kalman gain for subsystem i with matrix P, i.e.,

$$K_i(P) \triangleq (R_i + B_i^T P B_i)^{-1} B_i^T P A_i. \tag{10}$$

.

Proof. The theorem can be proved through induction. It is obvious that for $k=0$ the value function is $V_k(z) = z^T Q_f z$, satisfying (8). Now suppose equation (8) holds for a general integer k, i.e., $V_k(z) = \min_{P \in \mathcal{H}_k} z^T P z$, we shall show that it is also true for $k+1$. By the principle of dynamic programming and noting that $V_k(\cdot)$ represents the value function at time $N-k$, the value function at time $N-(k+1)$ can be recursively computed as

$$\begin{aligned}
V_{k+1}(z) &= \min_{i \in \mathbf{M}, u} \left[z^T Q_i z + u^T R_i u + V_k(A_i z + B_i u) \right] \\
&= \min_{i \in \mathbf{M}, u} \left[z^T Q_i z + u^T R_i u + \min_{P \in \mathcal{H}_k} \left((A_i z + B_i u)^T P (A_i z + B_i u) \right) \right] \\
&= \min_{i \in \mathbf{M}, P \in \mathcal{H}_k, u} \left[z^T Q_i z + u^T R_i u + (A_i z + B_i u)^T P (A_i z + B_i u) \right] \\
&= \min_{i \in \mathbf{M}, P \in \mathcal{H}_k, u} \left[z^T (Q_i + A_i^T P A_i) z + u^T (R_i + B_i^T P B_i) u + 2 z^T A_i^T P B_i u \right] \\
&\triangleq \min_{i \in \mathbf{M}, P \in \mathcal{H}_k, u} f(i, P, u).
\end{aligned} \tag{11}$$

With a symmetric matrix P, it can be easily computed that

$$\frac{\partial f(i,P,u)}{\partial u} = 2(R_i + B_i^T P B_i) u + 2 B_i^T P A_i z.$$

Since u is unconstrained, its optimal value u^* must satisfy $\frac{\partial f(i,P,u^*)}{\partial u} = 0$, i.e.,

$$u^* = -(R_i + B_i^T P B_i)^{-1} B_i^T P A_i z = -K_i(P) z, \tag{12}$$

where $K_i(P)$ is the matrix defined in (10). Substitute u^* into (11), we obtain

$$\begin{aligned}
V_{k+1}(z) &= \min_{i \in \mathbf{M}, P \in \mathcal{H}_k} f(i, P, u^*) \\
&= \min_{i \in \mathbf{M}, P \in \mathcal{H}_k} \left[z^T \left(Q_i + A_i^T P A_i - A_i^T P B_i K_i(P) \right) z \right] \\
&= \min_{i \in \mathbf{M}, P \in \mathcal{H}_k} z^T \rho_i(P) z.
\end{aligned}$$

Let $P_k^*(z)$ and $i_k^*(z)$ be the matrix and the index that minimize $z^T\rho_i(P)z$, i.e., they are defined as in (9). Then the optimal continuous control and discrete control at time $N-(k+1)$ and state z are $u^*(N-(k+1)) = -K_{i_k^*(z)}(P_k^*(z))z$ and $v^*(N-(k+1)) = i_k^*(z)$, respectively. Furthermore, observing that $\{\rho_i(P) : i \in \mathbb{M}, P \in \mathcal{H}_k\} = \rho_{\mathbb{M}}(\mathcal{H}_k) = \mathcal{H}_{k+1}$, we have $V_{k+1}(z) = \min_{P\in\mathcal{H}_{k+1}} z^T Pz$.

According to Theorem 1, comparing to the discrete-time LQR case, the value function of the DLQRS problem is no longer a single quadratic function; it actually becomes the pointwise minimum of a finite number of quadratic functions. In addition, at each time step, instead of having a single Kalman gain for the entire state space, the optimal state feedback gain becomes state dependent. Furthermore, the minimizer $(P_k^*(z), i_k^*(z))$ of equation (9) is radially invariant, indicating that at each time step all the states along the same radial direction have the same optimal mode and optimal feedback gain.

4 Equivalent Subset of p.s.d. Matrices

According to Theorem 1, the value function $V_k(\cdot)$ is completely characterized by the set $\mathcal{H}_k$, which can be obtained iteratively by (7). Since the size of the set $\mathcal{H}_k$ grows exponentially fast, it becomes unfeasible to compute $\mathcal{H}_k$ when k gets large. However, in terms of computing the value function, we only need to keep the matrices in $\mathcal{H}_k$ that give rise to the minimum of (8) for at least one $z \in \mathbb{R}^n$. To remove the redundant matrices in $\mathcal{H}_k$ and simplify the compuation, the following definitions are introduced.

Definition 1 (Equivalent Sets of p.s.d Matrices). *Let $\mathcal{H}$ and $\hat{\mathcal{H}}$ be two sets of p.s.d matrices. The set $\mathcal{H}$ is called* equivalent *to $\hat{\mathcal{H}}$, denoted by $\mathcal{H} \sim \hat{\mathcal{H}}$, if $\min_{P\in\mathcal{H}} z^T Pz = \min_{\hat{P}\in\hat{\mathcal{H}}} z^T \hat{P}z$, $\forall z \in \mathbb{R}^n$.*

Therefore, any equivalent sets of p.s.d. matrices will define the same value function of the DLQRS problem. To ease the computation, we are more interested in finding the smallest equivalent subset of $\mathcal{H}_k$.

Definition 2 (Minimum Equivalent Subset (MES)). *Let $\mathcal{H}$ and $\hat{\mathcal{H}}$ be two sets of symmetric p.s.d matrices. $\hat{\mathcal{H}}$ is called an* equivalent subset *of $\mathcal{H}$ if $\hat{\mathcal{H}} \subseteq \mathcal{H}$ and $\hat{\mathcal{H}} \sim \mathcal{H}$. Furthermore, $\hat{\mathcal{H}}$ is called a* minimum equivalent subset *(MES) of $\mathcal{H}$ if it is the equivalent subset of $\mathcal{H}$ with the fewest elements. Note that the MES of $\mathcal{H}$ may not be unique. Denote by $\Gamma(\mathcal{H})$ one of the MES's of $\mathcal{H}$.*

Remark 1. It is also worth mentioning that due to its special structure, the value function is homogeneous, namely, $V_k(\lambda z) = \lambda^2 V_k(z)$, for all $z \in \mathbb{R}^n$ and $\lambda \in \mathbb{R}^1$. Therefore, it suffices to consider only the points z on the unit sphere in checking the conditions in the above two definitions.

The following lemma provides a test for the equivalent subsets of $\mathcal{H}_k$.

Lemma 2. *$\hat{\mathcal{H}}$ is an equivalent subset of $\mathcal{H}$ if and only if*

1. $\hat{\mathcal{H}} \subseteq \mathcal{H}$
2. $\forall P \in \mathcal{H}$ *and* $\forall z \in \mathbb{R}^n$, *there exists a* $\hat{P} \in \hat{\mathcal{H}}$ *such that* $z^T \hat{P} z \leq z^T P z$.

Proof. (a) (sufficiency): We need to prove $\min_{P \in \mathcal{H}} z^T P z = \min_{\hat{P} \in \hat{\mathcal{H}}} z^T \hat{P} z, \forall z \in \mathbb{R}^n$. Obviously $\min_{P \in \mathcal{H}} z^T P z \leq \min_{\hat{P} \in \hat{\mathcal{H}}} z^T \hat{P} z, \forall z \in \mathbb{R}^n$ because $\hat{\mathcal{H}} \subseteq \mathcal{H}$. On the other hand, by the second condition, for each $z \in \mathbb{R}^n$ and $P \in \mathcal{H}$, there exist a $\hat{P}$ such that $z^T \hat{P} z \leq z^T P z$. Thus, $\min_{\hat{P} \in \hat{\mathcal{H}}} z^T \hat{P} z \leq \min_{P \in \mathcal{H}} z^T P z$. (b) (necessity): straightforward by a standard contradiction argument.

Remark 2. Lemma 2 can be used as an alternative definition of the equivalent subset. Although the original definition is conceptually simpler, the conditions given in this lemma provide a more explicit characterization of the equivalent subset, which proves to be more beneficial in the subsequent discussions.

All the equivalent subsets of $\mathcal{H}_k$ define the same value function $V_k(z)$. Thus, in terms of computing the value function, all the matrices in $\mathcal{H}_k \setminus \Gamma(\mathcal{H}_k)$ are redundent. More rigorously, $\hat{P} \in \mathcal{H}_k$ is called *redundent* with respect to $\mathcal{H}_k$ if for all $z \in \mathbb{R}^n$, there exists a $P \in \mathcal{H}_k \setminus \{\hat{P}\}$ such that $z^T \hat{P} z \geq z^T P z$. Thus, to simplify the computation, we shall prune away as many as possible redundant matrices and obtain an equivalent subset of $\mathcal{H}_k$ as close as possible to $\Gamma(\mathcal{H}_k)$. However, testing whether a matrix is redundant or not is itself a challenging problem. Geometrically, any p.s.d. matrix defines uniquely an ellipsoid in $\mathbb{R}^n$. It can be easily verified that $\hat{P} \in \mathcal{H}_k$ is redundant if and only if its corresponding ellipsoid is completely contained in the union of all the ellipsoids corresponding to the matrices in $\mathcal{H}_k \setminus \{\hat{P}\}$. Since the union of ellipsoids are not convex in general, there is in general no efficient way to verify this geometric condition or equivalently the original mathematical condition of redundancy. Nevertheless, a sufficient condition for a matrix to be redundant can be easily obtained and is given in the following lemma.

Lemma 3. $\hat{P}$ *is redundant with respect to* $\mathcal{H}_k$ *if there exist nonnegative constants* $\alpha_1, \ldots, \alpha_{|\mathcal{H}_k|-1}$ *such that* $\sum_{i=1}^{|\mathcal{H}_k|-1} \alpha_i = 1$ *and* $\hat{P} \succeq \sum_{i=1}^{|\mathcal{H}_k|-1} \alpha_i P^{(i)}$, *where* $\{P^{(j)}\}_{j=1}^{|\mathcal{H}_k|-1}$ *is an enumeration of* $\mathcal{H}_k \setminus \{\hat{P}\}$.

Proof. Straightforward.

For given $\hat{P}$ and $\mathcal{H}_k$, the condition in Lemma 3 can be easily verified using various existing convex optimization algorithms [22]. Lemma 3 can not guarantee to identify all the redundent matrices, however, it usually can help to eliminate a large portion of the redundant matrices in $\mathcal{H}_k$. During the value iteration, each matrix in $\mathcal{H}_k$ will be tested according to Lemma 3. If the condition in Lemma 3 is met, then the matrix under consideration will be discarded; otherwise, the matrix will be kept and used to generate the set $\mathcal{H}_{k+1}$. A detailed description of this process is given in Algorithm 1. The returned set $\mathcal{H}_k^{(|\mathcal{H}_k|)}$ by Algorithm 1 is an equivalent subset of $\mathcal{H}_k$ with usually a much smaller size.

Algorithm 1

1. Denote by $P^{(j)}$ the $j^{(th)}$ matrix in $\mathcal{H}_k$. Set $\mathcal{H}_k^{(1)} = \{P^{(1)}\}$.
2. For each $j = 2, \ldots, |\mathcal{H}_k|$, if $P^{(j)}$ satisfies the condition in Lemma 2 with respect to $\mathcal{H}_k$, then $\mathcal{H}_k^{(j)} = \mathcal{H}_k^{(j-1)}$, otherwise $\mathcal{H}_k^{(j)} = \mathcal{H}_k^{(j-1)} \cup \{P^{(j)}\}$.
3. Return $\mathcal{H}_k^{(|\mathcal{H}_k|)}$.

5 Computation of the Value Function

In this section, we use the equivalent-subset concept to simplify the computation of the value function of the DLQRS problem. For each $k \leq N$, let $\hat{\mathcal{H}}_k$ be an arbitrary equivalent subset of $\mathcal{H}_k$. The following corollary follows immediately from Definition 2.

Corollary 1. *The result in Theorem 1 still holds if every $\mathcal{H}_k$ is replaced by $\hat{\mathcal{H}}_k$.*

Corrollary 1 says that to compute the value function and the optimal control strategy, it suffices to use an equivalent subset of $\mathcal{H}_k$ for each k. In the last section, we have developed an algorithm to prune the redundant matrices in $\mathcal{H}_k$. However, the complexity of the algorithm still depends on $|\mathcal{H}_k|$, which grows exponentially fast as k increases. To overcome this difficulty, the following lemma is introduced.

Lemma 4 (Self Iteration). *Let the sequence of sets $\{\hat{\mathcal{H}}_k\}_{k=0}^N$ be generated by*

$$\hat{\mathcal{H}}_0 = \mathcal{H}_0, \text{ and } \hat{\mathcal{H}}_{k+1} = Algo(\rho_{\mathbb{M}}(\hat{\mathcal{H}}_k)) \text{ for } 0 \leq k \leq N-1, \tag{13}$$

where $Algo(\mathcal{H})$ denotes the equivalent subset of $\mathcal{H}$ returned by Algorithm 1. Then $\hat{\mathcal{H}}_k \sim Algo(\mathcal{H}_k)$.

Proof. The interested readers are refered to [23] for the proof of this lemma.

According to Lemma 4, $Algo(\mathcal{H}_k)$ is equivalent to $Algo(\rho_{\mathbb{M}}(\hat{\mathcal{H}}_{k-1}))$. Thus, to compute the desired equivalent subset of $\mathcal{H}_k$, one can apply Algorithm 1 to $\rho_{\mathbb{M}}(\hat{\mathcal{H}}_{k-1})$ instead of the original set $\mathcal{H}_k$. Denoted by $|\hat{\mathcal{H}}_k|$ the size of $\hat{\mathcal{H}}_k$. The set $\rho_{\mathbb{M}}(\hat{\mathcal{H}}_{k-1})$ contains at most $M \cdot |\hat{\mathcal{H}}_k|$ matrices which is usually much smaller than $|\mathcal{H}_k| = M^k$. Therefore, Lemma 2 could significantly simplify the computation of $Algo(\mathcal{H}_k)$. Although $|\hat{\mathcal{H}}_k|$ grows reasonably slow, it is still possible to become out of hand if the control horizon N is large. The following theorem allows us to terminate the computation with guaranteed accuracy on the optimal cost at some early stage for large time horizon N.

Theorem 2. *Suppose that (i) $Q_f \succ 0$ and $Q_i \succ 0$ for each $i \in \mathbb{M}$; (ii) at least one subsystem is stabilizable. Then $V_k(z)$ converges exponentially fast to $V_\infty(z)$ for each $z \in \mathbb{R}^n$ as $k \to \infty$. Furthermore, the convergence is uniform on the unit* *sphere in* $\mathbb{R}^n$ *and the difference between the value functions at time step* $N - k_1$ *and* $N - k_2$ *is bounded above by*

$$|V_{k_1}(z) - V_{k_2}(z)| \leq (\beta + \lambda_f^+)\alpha\gamma^{k_2}\|z\|^2, \tag{14}$$

where β, λ_f^+, α *and* γ *are all parameters depending only on the subsystem matrices.*

Remark 3. Note that the first condition in the above theorem is not restrictive because a randomly selected p.s.d. matrix is almost surely nonsingular. The proof of this theorem is quite involved and is beyond the scope of this paper. The interested readers are referred to [23] for a complete proof.

Remark 4. Compared with the convergence result in [17], Theorem 2 has several distinctive features. Firstly, it allows nonzero terminal cost, which is especially important for finite-horizon DLQRS problem. Secondly, its conditions are much easier to verify as they are expressed in terms of the system matrices instead of the infinite-horizon value functions as is the case in [17]. Finally, by inequality (14), the convergence rate can be approximated using the system matrices. Thus, for a given tolerance on the optimal cost, an upper bound of the required number of iterations can be simply computed before the actual computation starts. This provides an efficient means to stop the value iterations.

The exponential convergence result is crucial for the efficient computation of the value function. Given a reasonable tolerance on the accuracy, the value function usually converges in only a few steps. This greatly simplifies the value function computation, especially for the case with large time horizon N. In practice the convergence is usually tested only on a finite set of sampling points on the unit sphere. These sampling points should be chosen dense enough to capture the behaviors of all the value functions on the entire unit sphere. The existence of such sampling points is guaranteed by the following corollary of Theorem 2.

Corollary 2. *Under the same conditions as in Theorem 2, the sequence of value functions* $\{V_k(z)\}_{k=0}^{\infty}$ *is equicontinuous on the unit sphere.*

Proof. Denote by B_u the unit sphere in $\mathbb{R}^n$. Obviously, each value function $V_k(z)$ is continuous on B_u. By theorem 2, $V_k(\cdot)$ converges uniformly on B_u. Since B_u is a compact set, the desired result follows directly from Theorem 7.24 in [24].

With all the results developed so far, a general procedure for solving the DLQRS problem is summarized in Algorithm 2.

Table 1. $|\hat{\mathcal{H}}_k|$ for Ex1

k	1	2	3	4	5	6
$\lvert\hat{\mathcal{H}}_k\rvert$	2	4	5	5	5	5

Algorithm 2

1. Set $\hat{\mathcal{H}}_0 = Q_f$ and specify a tolerance ϵ for the minimum cost. Choose a finite set of sampling points on the unit sphere of R^n and denote it by $\mathbb{S}$.
2. For each step $k \geq 1$, compute $\hat{\mathcal{H}}_k = Algo(\rho_{\mathbb{M}}(\hat{\mathcal{H}}_{k-1}))$ where $Algo(\cdot)$ represents Algorithm 1.
3. Compute the value function $V_k(z)$ for each $z \in \mathbb{S}$ using $\hat{\mathcal{H}}_k$.
4. If $|V_k(z) - V_{k-1}(z)| > \epsilon$ for some $z \in \mathbb{S}$, then let $k = k + 1$ and go back to step 2. Otherwise let $k_\epsilon = k$ and continue to step 5.
5. Define $\hat{\mathcal{H}}_k = \hat{\mathcal{H}}_{k_\epsilon}$ for $k_\epsilon \leq k \leq N$.
6. The optimal trajectory can now be obtained by

$$x(t+1) = A_{v^*(t)}x(t) + B_{v^*(t)}u^*(t), \text{ with } x(0) = x_0,$$

where $v^*(t)$ and $u^*(t)$ are determined using Corollary 1 based on the set $\hat{\mathcal{H}}_{N-(t+1)}$.

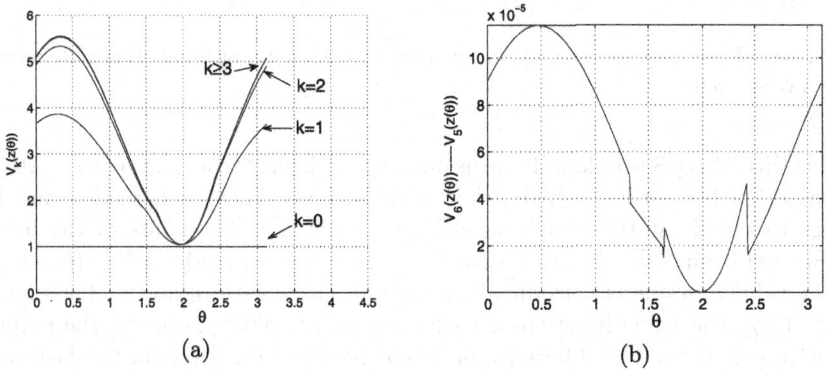

Fig. 1. Convergence results for Ex1. (a) Convergence of the Value function. (b) Difference between the last two iterations.

6 Examples

6.1 Example 1

First consider a simple DLQRS problem, referred to as Ex1, with control horizon $N = 100$ and two second-order subsystems:

$$A_1 = \begin{bmatrix} 2 & 1 \\ 0 & 1 \end{bmatrix}, \quad B_1 = \begin{bmatrix} 1 \\ 1 \end{bmatrix}, \quad A_2 = \begin{bmatrix} 2 & 1 \\ 0 & 0.5 \end{bmatrix}, \quad B_2 = \begin{bmatrix} 1 \\ 2 \end{bmatrix}.$$

Suppose that state and control weights are $Q_1 = Q_2 = I_{2\times 2}$ and $R_1 = R_2 = 1$, respectively. Both subsystems are unstable but controllable. Algorithm 2 is applied

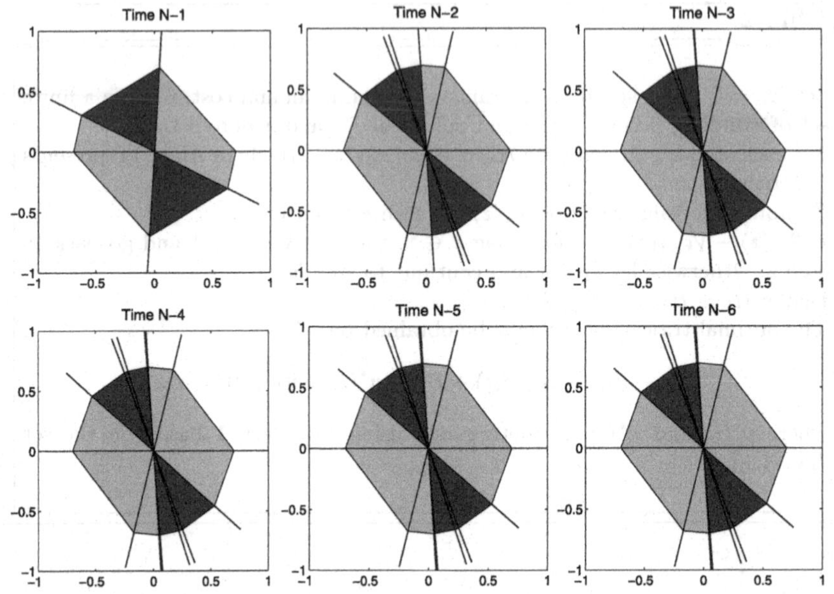

Fig. 2. Switching Regions for Ex1: Gray Region – mode 1is optimal; Black Region – mode 2 is optimal

to solve this DLQRS problem. It turns out that with the error tolerance $\epsilon = 10^{-3}$ the value function of Ex1 converges in 6 steps. Since $V_k(z)$ is homogeneous, it suffices to plot it at the points on the unit circle, i.e. the points of the form $z(\theta) = [\cos(\theta), \sin(\theta)]^T$. It can be easily verified that $V_k(z(\theta)) = V_k(z(\theta + \pi))$, i.e., the value function is periodic along the unit circle with period π. Therefore, in Fig. 1-(a), the value function at each time step is plotted only at the points $z(\theta)$ with $\theta \in [0, \pi]$. The difference between the value functions in the last two iterations are shown in Fig. 1-(b). The number of elements in $\hat{\mathcal{H}}_k$ at each step is listed in Table 1. It can be seen that $|\hat{\mathcal{H}}_k|$ is indeed very small, and will stay at the maximum value 5 as opposed to growing exponentially as k increases.

Furthermore, the optimal switching strategy is illustrated in Fig. 2. At each time step, the whole state space is divided into several conic regions. The regions with the same gray scale have the same optimal mode. However, the points with the same optimal mode may correspond to different optimal feedback gains. The radial lines in Fig 2 further divide the optimal-mode regions into smaller conic regions each with a different optimal-feedback gain. In this way, the proposed approach actually characterizes the optimal control strategies for the entire state space.

6.2 Example 2

Consider a more complex DLQRS example, referred to as Ex2, with 4 subsystems. The first two subsystems are the same as in Ex1 and the other two are

Table 2. $|\hat{\mathcal{H}}_k|$ for Ex2

k	1	2	3	4	5
$\lvert\hat{\mathcal{H}}_k\rvert$	3	9	15	15	15

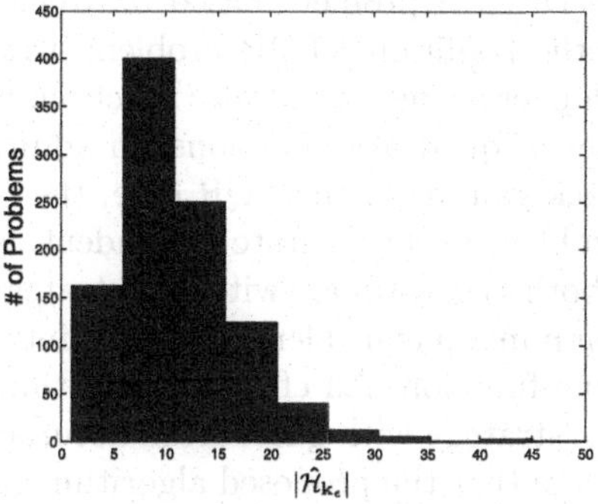

Fig. 3. Distribution of $|\hat{\mathcal{H}}_{k_\epsilon}|$ for randomly generated problems

defined as:

$$A_3 = \begin{bmatrix} 3 & 1 \\ 0 & 0.2 \end{bmatrix}, \quad A_4 = \begin{bmatrix} 1 & 1 \\ 0 & 0.8 \end{bmatrix}, \quad B_3 = B_1, \quad \text{and} \quad B_4 = B_2.$$

With the same tolerance, the value function of Ex2 converges in 5 steps. This indicates that under the same tolerance, the speed of the convergence of the value function may not necessarily increase with the number of subsystems. However, with more subsystems, $|\hat{\mathcal{H}}_k|$ grows more rapidly as shown in Table 2. It is worth mentioning that the maximum $|\hat{\mathcal{H}}_k|$ for this example is only 15 (as opposed to the nominal size of $\mathcal{H}_N$, $|\mathcal{H}_N| = 4^{100}$). Therefore, the proposed method has dramatically simplified the problem, making an NP hard problem numerically tractable.

6.3 Random Examples

This subsection is devoted to demonstrating the generic solvability of a general second-order DLQRS problem using the proposed algorithm. Our goal here is not to present a formal proof but rather to illustrate through simulations some important observations. In this set of simulations, the proposed algorithm is tested on 1000 randomly generated second-order DLQRS problems with a fairly large number of subsystems ($M = 10$). The control horizon is the same as in the last two examples, i.e., $N = 100$. All of these problems are successfully solved and the distribution of $|\hat{\mathcal{H}}_{k_\epsilon}|$, namely, the maximum number of matrices kept before convergence, is plotted in Fig. 3. It can be seen from the figure that the number $|\hat{\mathcal{H}}_{k_\epsilon}|$ in all of these 1000 problems are smaller than 50, and for a majority of the problems, $|\hat{\mathcal{H}}_{k_\epsilon}|$ is smaller than 15. Therefore, most second-order DLQRS problems may be efficiently solved using the proposed algorithm. Formally proving the generic solvability is a focus of our future research.

7 Conclusion

This paper studies the DLQRS problem based on dynamic programming approach. Different from the traditional LQR problem, the value function of the DLQRS problem is no longer a single quadratic function; it is the pointwise minimum of a finite number of quadratic functions. In addition, instead of having a single Kalman feedback gain as in the LQR case, the optimal state-feedback gain in the DLQRS problem becomes state dependent. Analytical expressions have been derived for both the optimal switching strategy and optimal control inputs. The concept of minimum equivalent subsets is introduced to simplify the computation of the value function. An efficient algorithm is developed to compute the optimal control strategy with guaranteed accuracy on the optimal cost. Simulation results indicate that the proposed algorithm can efficiently solve any randomly generated second-order DLQRS problems. Future research will focus on how to compute the exact MES of $\mathcal{H}_k$ in a general-dimensional state space and on proving the generic solvability of general DLQRS problems.

References

1. Geyer, T., Papafotiou, G., Morari, M.: Model Predictive Control in Power Electronics: A Hybrid Systems Approach. In: IEEE Conference on Decision and Control, Seville, Spain (December 2005)
2. Beccuti, A.G., Papafotiou, G., Morari, M.: Optimal Control of the Boost dc-dc Converter. In: IEEE Conference on Decision and Control, Seville, Spain (December 2005)
3. Zhang, W., Hu, J., Lu, Y.-H.: Optimal Power Modes Scheduling Using Hybrid Systems. In: Proceedings of the American Control Conference, New York City, NY (July 2007)
4. Zhang, W., Hu, J.: Optimal Buffer Management Using Hybrid Systems. In: IEEE Conference on Decision and Control, New Orleans, LA (December 2007)
5. Cassandras, C.G., Pepyne, D.L., Wardi, Y.: Optimal control of a class of hybrid systems. IEEE Transactions on Automatic Control 46(3), 398–415 (2001)
6. Hespanha, J., Bohacek, S., Obraczka, K., Lee, J.: Hybrid modeling of TCP congestion control. In: Di Benedetto, M.D., Sangiovanni-Vincentelli, A.L. (eds.) HSCC 2001. LNCS, vol. 2034, pp. 291–304. Springer, Heidelberg (2001)
7. Liberzon, D., Morse, A.S.: Basic problems in stability and design of switched systems. IEEE Control Systems Magazine 19(5), 59–70 (1999)
8. Liberzon, D., Hespanha, J.P., Morse, A.S.: Stability of switched systems: A lie-algebraic condition. Systems and Control Letters 37(3), 117–122 (1999)
9. DeCarlo, R., Branicky, M., Pettersson, S., Lennartson, B.: Perspectives and results on the stability and stabilizability of hybrid systems. Proceedings of IEEE, Special Issue on Hybrid Systems 88(7), 1069–1082 (2000)
10. Pettersson, S.: Synthesis of switched linear systems. In: IEEE Conference on Decision and Control, Maui, HI, pp. 5283–5288 (December 2003)

11. Xu, X., Antsaklis, P.J.: Optimal control of switched systems based on parameterization of the switching instants. IEEE Transactions on Automatic Control 49(1), 2–16 (2004)
12. Egerstedt, M., Wardi, Y., Delmotte, F.: Optimal control of switching times in switched dynamical systems. IEEE Transactions on Automatic Control 51(1), 110–115 (2006)
13. Xu, X., Antsaklis, P.: A dynamic programming approach for optimal control of switched systems. In: Proceedings of the IEEE Conference on Decision and Control, Sydney, Australia, pp. 1822–1827 (December 2000)
14. Bemporad, A., Giua, A., Seatzu, C.: Synthesis of state-feedback optimal controllers for continuous-time switched linear systems. In: Proceedings of the IEEE Conference on Decision and Control, pp. 3182–3187 (2002)
15. Borrelli, F., Baotic, M., Bemporad, A., Morari, M.: Dynamic programming for constrained optimal control of discrete-time linear hybrid systems. Automatica 41, 1709–1721 (2005)
16. Seatzu, C., Corona, D., Giua, A., Bemporad, A.: Optimal control of continuous-time switched affine systems. IEEE Transactions on Automatic Control 51, 726–741 (2006)
17. Lincoln, B., Rantzer, A.: Relaxing dynamic programming. IEEE Transactions on Automatic Control 51(8), 1249–1260 (2006)
18. Rantzer, A.: Relaxed dynamic programming in switching systems. IEE Proceedings - Control Theory & Applications 153(5), 567–574 (2006)
19. Rinehart, M., Dahleh, M., Kolmanovsky, I.: Optimal control of switched homogeneous systems. In: Proceedings of the American Control Conference, New York City, NY, pp. 1377–1382 (July 2007)
20. Caines, P.E., Mayne, D.Q.: On the discrete time matrix riccati equation of optimal control. Internation Journal of Control 12(5), 785–794 (1970)
21. Chan, S., Goodwin, Sin, G.K.: Convergence properties of the riccati difference equation in optimal filtering of nonstabilizable systems. IEEE Transactions on Automatic Control 29(2), 110–118 (1984)
22. Boyd, S., Vandenberghe, L.: Convex Optimization. Cambridge University Press, New York (2004)
23. Zhang, W., Hu, J.: Optimal quadratic regulation for linear switched systems (to be submitted for journal publication, available upon request)
24. Walter, R.: Principles of Mathematical Analysis. International Series in Pure and Applied Mathematics. McGraw-Hill, New York (1976)

Approximation of General Stochastic Hybrid Systems by Switching Diffusions with Random Hybrid Jumps

Alessandro Abate[1], Maria Prandini[2], John Lygeros[3], and Shankar Sastry[1]

[1] University of California, Berkeley - Berkeley, USA
{aabate,sastry}@eecs.berkeley.edu
[2] Politecnico di Milano - Milano, Italy
prandini@elet.polimi.it
[3] ETH Zurich - Zurich, Switzerland
lygeros@control.ee.ethz.ch

Abstract. In this work we propose an approximation scheme to transform a general stochastic hybrid system (SHS) into a SHS without forced transitions due to spatial guards. Such switching mechanisms are replaced by spontaneous transitions with state-dependent transition intensities (jump rates). The resulting switching diffusion process with random hybrid jumps is shown to converge in distribution to the original stochastic hybrid system execution. The obtained approximation can be useful for various purposes such as, on the computational side, simulation and reachability analysis, as well as for the theoretical investigation of the model. More generally, it is suggested that SHS which are endowed exclusively with random jumping events are *simpler* than those that present spatial forcing transitions.

In the opening of this work, the general SHS model is presented, a few of its basic properties are discussed, and the concept of generator is introduced. The second part of the paper describes the approximation procedure, introduces the new SHS model, and proves, under some assumptions, its weak convergence to the original system.

We describe the general stochastic hybrid system model introduced in [1].

Definition 1 (General Stochastic Hybrid System). *A* General Stochastic Hybrid System *(GSHS) is a collection* $\mathcal{S}_g = (\mathcal{Q}, n, A, B, \Gamma, R^\Gamma, \Lambda, R^\Lambda, \pi)$, *where*

- $\mathcal{Q} = \{q_1, q_2, \dots, q_m\}, m \in \mathbb{N}$, *is a countable set of discrete modes;*
- $n : \mathcal{Q} \to \mathbb{N}$ *is a map such that, for* $q \in \mathcal{Q}$, *the continuous state space is the Euclidean space* $\mathbb{R}^{n(q)}$. *The hybrid state space is then* $\mathcal{S} = \cup_{q \in \mathcal{Q}} \{q\} \times \mathbb{R}^{n(q)}$;
- $A = \{a(q,\cdot) : \mathbb{R}^{n(q)} \to \mathbb{R}^{n(q)}, q \in \mathcal{Q}\}$ *is a collection of drift terms;*
- $B = \{b(q,\cdot) : \mathbb{R}^{n(q)} \to \mathbb{R}^{n(q) \times n(q)}, q \in \mathcal{Q}\}$ *is a collection of diffusion terms;*
- $\Gamma = \cup_{q \in \mathcal{Q}} \{q\} \times \Gamma_q \subset \mathcal{S}$, *where* $\Gamma_q = \cup_{q' \neq q \in \mathcal{Q}} \gamma_{qq'}$ *is a closed set composed of* $m-1$ *disjoint guard sets* $\gamma_{qq'}$ *causing forced transitions from* q *to* $q' \neq q$;
- $R^\Gamma : \mathcal{B}(\mathbb{R}^{n(\cdot)}) \times \mathcal{Q} \times \Gamma \to [0,1]$ *is the reset stochastic kernel associated with* Γ. *Specifically,* $R^\Gamma(\cdot | q', (q,x))$ *is a probability measure concentrated on* $\mathbb{R}^{n(q')} \setminus \Gamma_{q'}$, *which describes the probabilistic reset of the continuous state when a jump from mode* q *to* q' *occurs from* $x \in \gamma_{qq'}$;

M. Egerstedt and B. Mishra (Eds.): HSCC 2008, LNCS 4981, pp. 598–601, 2008.

- $\Lambda : \mathcal{S} \backslash \Gamma \times \mathcal{Q} \rightarrow \mathbb{R}^+$ *is the transition intensity function governing spontaneous transitions. Specifically, for any* $q \neq q' \in \mathcal{Q}$, $\lambda_{qq'}(x) := \Lambda((q,x),q')$ *is the jump rate from mode* q *to mode* q' *when* $x \in \mathbb{R}^{n(q)} \setminus \Gamma_q$;
- $R^\Lambda : \mathcal{B}(\mathbb{R}^{n(\cdot)}) \times \mathcal{Q} \times \mathcal{S} \setminus \Gamma \rightarrow [0,1]$ *is the reset stochastic kernel associated with* Λ. *In particular,* $R^\Lambda(\cdot|q',(q,x))$ *is a probability measure concentrated on* $\mathbb{R}^{n(q')} \setminus \Gamma_{q'}$ *that describes the probabilistic reset of the continuous state when a jump from mode* q *to* q' *occurs from* $x \in \mathbb{R}^{n(q)} \setminus \Gamma_q$;
- $\pi : \mathcal{B}(\mathcal{S}) \rightarrow [0,1]$ *is a measure on* $\mathcal{S} \backslash \Gamma$ *describing the initial distribution.* □

In the definition above, $\mathcal{B}(\mathcal{S})$ denotes the σ-field on $\mathcal{S}$.

Assumption 1 (on the system dynamics).

1. *The drift and diffusion terms* $a(q,\cdot)$ *and* $b(q,\cdot), q \in \mathcal{Q}$, *are bounded and uniformly Lipschitz continuous.*
2. *The jump rate function* $\Lambda : \mathcal{S} \backslash \Gamma \times \mathcal{Q} \rightarrow \mathbb{R}^+$ *satisfies the following conditions:*
   - *it is measurable and bounded;*
   - *for any* $q, q' \in \mathcal{Q}, q \neq q'$, *and any sample path* $\omega^{(q,x)}(t)$, $t \geq 0$, *of the process solving the SDE in* q, *initialized at* $x \in \mathbb{R}^{n(q)} \setminus \Gamma_q$, *there exists* $\epsilon_{qq'}(x) > 0$ *such that* $\lambda_{qq'}(\omega^{(q,x)}(t))$ *is integrable over* $[0, \epsilon_{qq'}(x))$.
3. *For all* $C \in \mathcal{B}(\mathbb{R}^{n(\cdot)})$, $R^\Gamma(C|\cdot)$ *and* $R^\Lambda(C'|\cdot)$ *are measurable.*
4. *For any execution associated with* $\pi = \delta_s$, $s \in \mathcal{S} \backslash \Gamma$, *the expected value of the number of jumps within the time interval* $[0,t]$ *is bounded for all* $t \geq 0$. □

Intuitively, Assumption 1.1 guarantees the existence and uniqueness of the $n(q)$-dimensional solution to the SDE associated with $q \in \mathcal{Q}$, $d\mathbf{v}(t) = a(q,\mathbf{v}(t))dt + b(q,\mathbf{v}(t))d\mathbf{w}_q(t)$, where $\mathbf{w}_q$ is a $n(q)$-dimensional standard Wiener process.

The semantic definition of the GSHS $\mathcal{S}_g$, given via the notion of *execution* (a stochastic process $\{\mathbf{s}(t) = (\mathbf{q}(t), \mathbf{x}(t)),\ t \geq 0\}$, with values in $\mathcal{S}$, solution of $\mathcal{S}_g$), can be done as in [1]. Note that a sample-path of a GSHS execution is a right-continuous, $\mathcal{S}$-valued function on $[0,\infty)$, with left-limits on $(0,\infty)$ (*càdlàg*). Furthermore, the following property holds.

Proposition 1. *Consider a GSHS* $\mathcal{S}_g$. *Under assumptions 1.1-1.2-1.3-1.4, the execution* $\mathbf{s}(t), t \geq 0$, *of* $\mathcal{S}_g$ *is a càdlàg strong Markov process.* □

It is interesting to associate to the set of real-valued functions f, acting on Markov processes defined on a Borel space, a *strong generator* $\mathcal{L}$, and a weaker, yet more general, *extended generator* [2]. Denote with $C_b^2(\mathcal{S})$ the class of real-valued, twice continuously differentiable and bounded functions on $\mathcal{S}$. Let $\frac{\partial f(q,x)}{\partial x} a(q,x) = \sum_{i=1}^{n(q)} \frac{\partial f(q,x)}{\partial x_i} a_i(q,x)$ be the Lie derivative of $f(q,\cdot)$ along $a(q,\cdot)$, and $H_f(q,x) = \left[\frac{\partial^2 f(q,x)}{\partial x_i \partial x_j}\right]_{i,j=1,2,\ldots,n(q)}$ be the Hessian of $f(q,\cdot)$.

Proposition 2 (Extended Generator of $\mathcal{S}_g$). *The extended generator* $\mathcal{L}_g : \mathcal{D}(\mathcal{L}_g) \rightarrow \mathcal{B}_b(\mathcal{S})$ *associated with the executions of* $\mathcal{S}_g$ *is, for* $s = (q,x) \in \mathcal{S} \setminus \Gamma$:

$$\mathcal{L}_g f(s) = \mathcal{L}_g^d f(s) + I_{\mathcal{S}\backslash\Gamma}(s) \sum_{q' \in \mathcal{Q}, q' \neq q} \lambda_{qq'}(x) \int_{\mathbb{R}^{n(q')}} (f((q',z)) - f(s)) R^\Lambda(dz|q',s),$$

where $\mathcal{L}_g^d f(s) = \sum_{q\in\mathcal{Q}} \frac{\partial f(q,x)}{\partial x} a(q,x) + \frac{1}{2} Tr\big(b(q,x)b(q,x)^T H_f(q,x)\big)$.

The domain $\mathcal{D}(\mathcal{L}_g)$ *of* $\mathcal{L}_g$ *is the set of functions* $f \in C_b^2(\mathcal{S})$ *satisfying the condition:* $f(s) = \sum_{q'\in\mathcal{Q}, q'\neq q} \int_{\mathbb{R}^{n(q')}} f((q',z)) R^{\Gamma}(dz|q',s), \quad s \in \Gamma.$ □

Consider the GSHS system $\mathcal{S}_g$ in Definition 1. The guard set of $\mathcal{S}_g$ within mode $q \in \mathcal{Q}$ is made up of $\gamma_{qq'} \subset \mathbb{R}^{n(q)}$, $q' \in \mathcal{Q}$, $q' \neq q$. Assume that each set $\gamma_{qq'}$ can be expressed as a zero sub-level set of a continuous function $h_{qq'} : \mathbb{R}^{n(q)} \to \mathbb{R}$:

$$\gamma_{qq'} = \{x \in \mathbb{R}^{n(q)} : h_{qq'}(x) \leq 0\}.$$

Pick a small enough $\delta > 0$, and by the continuity of $h_{qq'}$, introduce the sets

$$\gamma_{qq'}^{-\delta} = \{x \in \mathbb{R}^{n(q)} : h_{qq'}(x) \leq -\delta\} \subseteq \gamma_{qq'} \subseteq \gamma_{qq'}^{\delta} = \{x \in \mathbb{R}^{n(q)} : h_{qq'}(x) \leq \delta\}.$$

For any $q \in \mathcal{Q}$, define the set of functions $\lambda_{qq'}^{\delta} : \mathbb{R}^{n(q)} \to \mathbb{R}^+$, $q' \in \mathcal{Q}$, $q' \neq q$,

$$\lambda_{qq'}^{\delta}(x) = \begin{cases} \left(\dfrac{1}{d(x,\gamma_{qq'}^{-\delta})} - \dfrac{1}{\sup\limits_{y:h_{qq'}(y)=\delta} d(y,\gamma_{qq'}^{-\delta})} \right) \wedge \left(\dfrac{1}{\sup\limits_{y:h_{qq'}(y)=0} d(y,\gamma_{qq'}^{-\delta})} \right), & x \in \gamma_{qq'}^{\delta} \\ 0, & x \in \mathbb{R}^{n(q)} \setminus \gamma_{qq'}^{\delta} \end{cases}$$

where $a \wedge b = \min\{a,b\}$, whereas $d(z,A) = \inf_{y\in A} ||z-y||, z \in \mathbb{R}^{n(q)}, A \subset \mathbb{R}^{n(q)}$.

We associate to $\mathcal{S}_g$ a new stochastic hybrid system $\mathcal{S}_\delta$, which is made up of the elements of $\mathcal{S}_g$, except for the following:

- The spatial guards set is empty, $\Gamma = \emptyset$;
- The transition intensity function Λ, whose domain of definition is $\mathcal{S} \setminus \Gamma \times \mathcal{Q}$, is replaced by $\Lambda^\delta : \mathcal{S} \times \mathcal{Q} \to \mathbb{R}^+$ given by $\Lambda^\delta((q,x),q') := \lambda_{qq'}^{\delta}(x) + \lambda_{qq'}(x)$ where for any $q' \neq q \in \mathcal{Q}$, the original jump rate $\lambda_{qq'}(\cdot)$ is extended to $\mathbb{R}^{n(q)}$ by setting it to zero over Γ_q;
- The stochastic reset kernel $R^{\Lambda^\delta} : \mathcal{B}(\mathbb{R}^{n(\cdot)}) \times \mathcal{Q} \times \mathcal{S} \to [0,1]$ associated with Λ^δ is given by $R^{\Lambda^\delta}(C_{q'}|q',(q,x)) = R^{\Lambda}(C_{q'}|q',(q,x)) + R^{\Gamma}(C_{q'}|q',(q,x))$, for any Borel set $C_{q'}$ of $\mathbb{R}^{n(q')}$, where the original stochastic reset kernels $R^{\Lambda}(C_{q'}|q',\cdot)$ and $R^{\Lambda}(C_{q'}|q',\cdot)$ are extended to $\mathcal{S}$ by setting them to zero outside their original domain of definition.

Notice that the conclusions in Proposition 1 hold true also for the SHS $\mathcal{S}_\delta$. The extended generator $\mathcal{L}_\delta$ of $\mathcal{S}_\delta$ can be derived in a similar way as for that for $\mathcal{S}_g$, but has no condition on the points of the guard set. Its domain $\mathcal{D}(\mathcal{L}_\delta)$ is the set of functions $f \in C_b^2(\mathcal{S})$. This implies that $\mathcal{D}(\mathcal{L}_g) \subseteq \mathcal{D}(\mathcal{L}_\delta)$, for $\delta > 0$.

Let us formally show that, as $\delta \to 0$, the sequence of stochastic processes $\{\mathbf{s}_\delta(t)\}_{\delta>0}$ converges, in some sense, to $\mathbf{s}(t)$, for any $t \geq 0$. The forthcoming notions are found in [3].The concept of extended generator can be useful in showing that a sequence of Markov processes converges to a given Markov process. Qualitatively, given a sequence of $\mathcal{S}$-valued processes $\{\mathbf{X}_n\}_{n\geq 1}$ and a process $\mathbf{X}$, with extended generators $(A_n, \mathcal{D}(A_n))$ and $(A, \mathcal{D}(A))$ respectively, to prove that

$\mathbf{X}_n \Rightarrow \mathbf{X}$ (convergence in the weak sense), it is sufficient to show that for all functions $f \in \mathcal{D}(\mathcal{A})$, there exist $f_n \in \mathcal{D}(\mathcal{A}_n)$, such that $f_n \to f$ and $A_n f_n \to Af$. The following fact, needed in Theorem 2, is verified:

Theorem 1 (Compact Containment Condition). *Consider the GSHS $\mathcal{S}_g$, the SHS $\mathcal{S}_\delta$, and their corresponding unique global solutions $\mathbf{s}(t)$ and $\mathbf{s}_\delta(t), t \geq 0$. The stochastic processes $\mathbf{s}_\delta(t)$ are such that, for any $\epsilon > 0, N > 0$, there exists a compact set $K_{\epsilon,N} \subset \mathcal{S}$ such that*

$$\liminf_{\delta \downarrow 0} \mathcal{P}\left[\mathbf{s}_\delta(t) \in K_{\epsilon,N}, \forall 0 \leq t \leq N\right] \geq 1 - \epsilon.$$

Similarly for the stochastic process $\mathbf{s}(t)$. □

Given a sequence of entities $\{c_n\}_{n \geq 1}$ and a scalar c, let us denote as $\lim_n^\star c_n = c$ the conditions $\lim_{n\to\infty} c_n = c$ and $(\vee_n \|c_n\|) \vee \|c\| < \infty$, where $\|\cdot\|$ is the sup norm. Similarly if the indexing parameter tends to zero ($\delta = 1/n$). A process $\mathbf{X}$ is said to be a solution of the local martingale problem for a linear operator (A, π) if $\mathcal{P} \circ \mathbf{X}(0)^{-1} = \pi$, and for each $f \in \mathcal{D}(A)$, $f(\mathbf{X}(t)) - f(\mathbf{X}(0)) - \int_0^t Af(\mathbf{X}(s))ds$ is a local martingale, $\forall t \geq 0$. In order to complete the proof of the following Theorem 2, it is necessary to raise the following

Assumption 2. *1. Given a GSHS, as in Definition 1, assume that the probabilistic reset kernels $R^\Gamma(\cdot|q', (q, x))$ are continuous in x, for any $q' \neq q \in \mathcal{Q}$.*
2. The local martingale problem for $(\mathcal{L}_g, \mathcal{D}(\mathcal{L}_g))$ is well posed, that is, it admits a unique *solution.* □

The following theorem is based on results from [4, Theorem 4.4].

Theorem 2 (Weak Convergence of $\mathcal{S}_\delta$ to $\mathcal{S}_g$). *Consider the SHS model $\mathcal{S}_\delta$, the GSHS model $\mathcal{S}_g$ under Assumption 2.1, and their associated $\mathcal{S}$-valued unique solution processes $\mathbf{s}_\delta(t)$ and $\mathbf{s}(t), t \geq 0$, where $\mathbf{s}_\delta(0) = \mathbf{s}(0) = (q_0, x_0) \in \mathcal{S}$. Consider further their extended generators $(\mathcal{L}_\delta, \mathcal{D}(\mathcal{L}_\delta))$ and $(\mathcal{L}_g, \mathcal{D}(\mathcal{L}_g))$, and conjecture that Assumption 2.2 is valid. It holds that*

- $\mathcal{L}_g \subset C_b^0(\mathcal{S}) \times C^0(\mathcal{S})$;
- *For all $f \in \mathcal{D}(\mathcal{L}_g), \exists f_\delta \in \mathcal{D}(\mathcal{L}_\delta)$, such that $\lim_\delta^\star f_\delta = f, \lim_\delta \mathcal{L}_\delta f_\delta = \mathcal{L}f$;*
- *$\mathcal{D}(\mathcal{L})$ is dense in $C_b^0(\mathcal{S})$ with respect to $\lim^\star$.*

By Theorem 1, as the approximation step $\delta \downarrow 0$, the solution of the SHS $\mathcal{S}_\delta$ weakly converges to that of the GSHS $\mathcal{S}_g$: $\mathbf{s}_\delta(t) \Rightarrow \mathbf{s}(t), \forall t \geq 0$. □

References

1. Bujorianu, M.L., Lygeros, J.: Toward a general theory of stochastic hybrid systems. In: Blom, H.A.P., Lygeros, J. (eds.) Stochastic Hybrid Systems. LNCIS, vol. 337, pp. 3–30. Springer, Heidelberg (2006)
2. Davis, M.H.A.: Markov Models and Optimization. Chapman & Hall/CRC Press, London (1993)
3. Ethier, S.N., Kurtz, T.G.: Markov processes: Characterization and convergence. John Wiley & Sons, Chichester (1986)
4. Xia, A.: Weak convergence of markov processes with extended generators. The Annals of Probability 22, 2183–2202 (1994)

On Stability of Switched Linear Hyperbolic Conservation Laws with Reflecting Boundaries

Saurabh Amin[1], Falk M. Hante[2], and Alexandre M. Bayen[1]

[1] University of California, at Berkeley - Berkeley, CA, USA
{amins,bayen}@berkeley.edu
[2] Universität Erlangen-Nürnberg, 91058 Erlangen, Germany
hante@am.uni-erlangen.de

Abstract. We consider stability of an infinite dimensional switching system, posed as a system of linear hyperbolic partial differential equations (PDEs) with reflecting boundaries, where the system parameters and the boundary conditions switch in time. Asymptotic stability of the solution for arbitrary switching is proved under commutativity of the advective velocity matrices and a joint spectral radius condition involving the boundary data.

Problem Formulation. Motivated by applications [2], we consider hybrid dynamics governed by linear hyperbolic PDE systems and a discrete set of modes:

$$\begin{matrix} \partial_t u(t,s) + A^j \partial_s u(t,s) = 0 \\ C_L^j u(t,a) = 0,\ C_R^j u(t,b) = 0 \end{matrix}, \quad j \in \mathcal{Q} \simeq \{1,\dots,N\}, \tag{1}$$

where the matrices $A^j \in \mathbb{R}^{n\times n}$ specify the advective velocities and the matrices $C_L^j \in \mathbb{R}^{(n-m_j)\times n}$ and $C_R^j \in \mathbb{R}^{m_j\times n}$ specify the boundary data for the unknown vector function $u(t,s) = (u^1(t,s),\dots,u^n(t,s))^\top$ on the space-time strip $\Omega([t_1,t_2]) := \{(t,s)\,|\,t\in[t_1,t_2], s\in[a,b]\}$. We assume that

(H)$_1$ the subsystems for fixed j are strictly hyperbolic, i. e. A^j has m_j negative and $(n-m_j)$ positive eigenvalues λ_i^j with n corresponding linearly independent left (right) eigenvectors l_i^j (r_i^j);

(H)$_2$ the switching signals in time $\mathcal{T} = \{t \geq 0\}$ are piecewise constant functions $\sigma(\cdot)\colon \mathcal{T} \to \mathcal{Q}$ with switching times τ_k ($k\in\mathbb{N}$) such that there are only finitely many switches $j \curvearrowright j'$ in each finite time interval of $\mathcal{T}$.

We consider the switched system in the space of piecewise continuously differentiable functions, denoted as $\mathcal{PC}^1 = \mathcal{PC}^1([a,b],\mathbb{R}^n)$, setting $\mathbf{u}(t) := u(t,\cdot)$, and say that for an initial condition $\bar{u}(\cdot) \in \mathcal{PC}^1$, the function $\mathbf{u}(\cdot)\colon \mathcal{T} \to \mathcal{PC}^1$ is a solution of the switched system (1) if

$$\mathbf{u}|_{t=0} = \bar{u} \quad \wedge \quad \begin{cases} \mathbf{u}|_{\tau_k+} := \mathbf{u}|_{\tau_k-} \text{ for all switching times } \tau_k \text{ of } \sigma(\cdot), \\ \mathbf{u}|_{(\tau_k+,\tau_{k+1}-)} \text{ solves (1) with } j=\sigma(t)=\text{const.} \end{cases} \tag{2}$$

Under the above assumptions, it is easy to see that the system is well-posed, if and only if it is well-posed in each mode, i. e., following [1]:

$$\operatorname{rank}\big[(C_L^j)^\top \big| l_1^j \big| \cdots \big| l_{m_j}^j\big] = \operatorname{rank}\big[(C_R^j)^\top \big| l_{m_j+1}^j \big| \cdots \big| l_n^j\big] = n \quad \text{for all } j\in\mathcal{Q}. \tag{3}$$

M. Egerstedt and B. Mishra (Eds.): HSCC 2008, LNCS 4981, pp. 602–605, 2008.

For a fixed $j \in \mathcal{Q}$, it is convenient to consider system (1) in an equivalent diagonal form. Using the transformation $S_j A^j S_j^{-1}$, where $S_j := \left[l_1^j | \cdots | l_n^j\right]^\top$, the system (1) can be written in *characteristic coordinates* $\xi := S_j u$

$$\begin{aligned} \partial_t \xi(t,s) + \operatorname{diag}(\Lambda_I^j, \Lambda_{II}^j)\partial_s \xi(t,s) = 0 \\ \xi_{II}(t,a) = G_L^j \xi_I(t,a), \quad \xi_I(t,b) = G_R^j \xi_I(t,b) \end{aligned} \tag{4}$$

where, $\xi_I = (\xi^1, \ldots, \xi^m)^\top$, $\xi_{II} = (\xi^{m+1}, \ldots, \xi^n)^\top$, $\Lambda_I^j = \operatorname{diag}(\lambda_1^j, \ldots, \lambda_{m_j}^j)$, $\Lambda_{II}^j = \operatorname{diag}(\lambda_{m_j+1}^j, \ldots, \lambda_n^j)$ and

$$\begin{aligned} G_R^j &= -\left(\left[c_{n-m_j+1}^j | \cdots | c_n^j\right]^\top \left[r_1^j | \cdots | r_{m_j}^j\right]\right)^{-1} \left[c_{n-m_j+1}^j | \cdots | c_n^j\right]^\top \left[r_{m_j+1}^j | \cdots | r_n^j\right] \\ G_L^j &= -\left(\left[c_1^j | \cdots | c_{n-m_j}^j\right]^\top \left[r_{m_j+1}^j | \cdots | r_n^j\right]\right)^{-1} \left[c_1^j | \cdots | c_{n-m_j}^j\right]^\top \left[r_1^j | \cdots | r_{m_j}^j\right]. \end{aligned} \tag{5}$$

Thus, the solution (2) of the switched system (1) can equivalently be written as $\mathbf{u}(\cdot) = S_{\sigma(\cdot)}^{-1} \boldsymbol{\xi}(\cdot)$, where $\boldsymbol{\xi}(\cdot)$ satisfies

$$\boldsymbol{\xi}|_{t=0} = S_{\sigma(0)} \bar{u} \quad \wedge \quad \begin{cases} \boldsymbol{\xi}|_{\tau_k+} = S_{\sigma(\tau_k+)} S_{\sigma(\tau_k-)}^{-1} \boldsymbol{\xi}|_{\tau_k-} \text{ for all } \tau_k, \\ \boldsymbol{\xi}|_{(\tau_k+, \tau_{k+1}-)} \text{ solves (4) with } j = \sigma(t) = \text{const}. \end{cases} \tag{6}$$

Note that if all the subsystems are simultaneously diagonalisable, i. e. $S_{j'} = S_j$ for all $j, j' \in \mathcal{Q}$, then (6) shows that the solution of system (1) is constant along its *characteristic paths* that change their slope at switching times.

Main Result. We consider stability of the above switching system, motivated by a simple PDE counterpart to the well known ODE observation [3] that asymptotic stability of all subsystems is *not* sufficient, even for all subsystems in diagonal form (4).

Example 1. $\mathcal{Q} = \{1,2\}$, $A^j = \operatorname{diag}(-1,+1)$, $[a,b] = [0,1]$, $G_L^j = 1.5(j-1)$, $G_R^j = 1.5(2-j)$. For $\bar{u}(\cdot) \equiv 1$, the solution of the subsystems is 0 for all $t > 2$, but alternating $\sigma(\cdot)$ at $t = 0.5, 1.5, 2.5, \ldots$ leads to $\lim_{t\to\infty} \|\mathbf{u}(t)\|_\infty = \infty$. □

Indeed, the non-diagonal system (1) can be shown to blow up under switching of the advective velocity matrices, although its boundaries are un-switched *and* are "dissipative" in the sense of [4]; i. e., the following spectral radius condition holds:

$$\|G(G_L, G_R)\|_{\min} := \inf_{\gamma=\operatorname{diag}\{\gamma_i\}, \gamma_i>0 (i=1,\ldots,n)} \left\| \begin{pmatrix} 0 & |G_R| \\ |G_L| & 0 \end{pmatrix} \right\|_\infty < 1. \tag{7}$$

Moreover, it is easy to see that a switched system in diagonal form even satisfying (7) in each mode can blow up just by alternately changing m_j.

Our goal here is thus to impose sufficient conditions for the switched system to be asymptotically stable under arbitrary switching. For $\mathbf{u}(\cdot) \in \mathcal{PC}^1$, we use the norm $\|\mathbf{u}(\cdot)\| := \max_{i=1,\ldots,n;\ s\in[a,b]} |\mathbf{u}^i(s)|$ and, w. l. o. g., we consider $\mathbf{u}(\cdot) \equiv 0$ as the only equilibrium state of the switched system. We say that the switched system is asymptotically stable under arbitrary switching, if for all $\varepsilon > 0$ sufficiently small, there exists a $\delta(\varepsilon) > 0$ such that if $\|\bar{u}(\cdot)\| \le \delta$, then $\|\mathbf{u}(\cdot)\| \le \varepsilon$ for all $t \ge 0$ and $\lim_{t\to\infty} \|\mathbf{u}(\cdot)\| = 0$, independently of the switching signal $\sigma(\cdot)$. Our main result is the following.

Theorem 1. *Consider a system* (1) *under hypotheses* $(H)_{1,2}$ *being well-posed in the sense of* (3) *and suppose that the following conditions hold for all* $j, j' \in \mathcal{Q}$

$$(a)\ m_j = m_{j'} \qquad (b)\ A^j A^{j'} = A^{j'} A^j \qquad (c)\ \|G(G_L^j, G_R^{j'})\|_{\min} < 1 \tag{8}$$

where G_L^j, G_R^j *are given as in* (5) *and* $\|G(\cdot,\cdot)\|_{\min}$ *is defined as in* (7). *Then the system is asymptotically stable under arbitrary switching.*

Proof. Under condition $(8)_b$, the system (1) can be simultaneously diagonalized for all modes to (4) with $S_{j'} = S_j$ for all $j, j' \in \mathcal{Q}$ and we can consider its solution $\boldsymbol{\xi}(\cdot)$ along its characteristic paths, see (6). Then we follow arguments of Li [4] Lemma 2.1, concluding that condition $(8)_c$ implies

$$\begin{aligned}\theta &:= \max_{j,j'\in\mathcal{Q}} \{\||G_L^j||G_R^{j'}|\|_\infty, \||G_R^{j'}||G_L^j|\|_\infty\} \\ &= \max_{\substack{r=1,\dots,m\\ l=m+1,\dots,n\\ j,j'\in\mathcal{Q}}} \left\{ \sum_{p=1}^{m} \sum_{k=m+1}^{n} |g_{rk}^{R,j'}||g_{kp}^{L,j}|,\ \sum_{k=m+1}^{n} \sum_{p=1}^{m} |g_{lp}^{L,j}||g_{pk}^{R,j'}| \right\} < 1,\end{aligned} \tag{9}$$

where $G_L^j = (g_{pq}^{L,j})$ and $G_R^{j'} = (g_{pq}^{R,j'})$. It suffices to show that for any fixed $\varepsilon > 0$, there exists $\delta(\varepsilon) > 0$ such that

$$|\xi(t,s)| := \max_{i=1,\dots,n} |\xi^i(t,s)| \le \varepsilon \tag{10}$$

for all $0 \le t < \infty$, $a \le s \le b$. Let $T_{\min} := \left(\max_{i=1,\dots,n;j=1,\dots,N} |\lambda_i^j|\right)^{-1}$. By boundedness of $\bar{u}$ and thus $\bar{\xi} := S_{\sigma(0)}\bar{u}$, by continuity of the solution along the characteristic path and by linearity of the boundary conditions for fixed $j \in \mathcal{Q}$, there exists a $\delta(\varepsilon) \le \varepsilon$ such that

$$|\xi(t,s)| \le \alpha\varepsilon \quad \text{for all } (t,s) \in \Omega([0,T^\circ)) \tag{11}$$

for some $T^\circ > 0$ sufficiently small (i. e. smaller than $\tau_1 > 0$) and for some $\alpha \le 1$ to be specified later. Thus, to show (10), it suffices to prove that for any fixed $T > 0$, if (10) holds on $\Omega([0,T])$, then it still holds on domain $\Omega([0, T + T_{\min}])$. So assume (10) holds on $\Omega([0,T])$ and fix some $(t^*, s^*) \in \Omega([T, T + T_{\min}])$. Due to $(8)_a$, let z_r denote the r-th characteristic path passing through (t^*, s^*) $(r = 1, \dots, m)$. Backwards in time, z_r either intersects $t = 0$ before hitting any boundary (case 1) or it intersects the line $s = b$ (case 2). See Figure 1 for an illustration with an example switching configuration. For case 1: Using (2), $\xi^r(t^*, s^*) = \xi^r(0, \tilde{s}_1)$ for some $a \le \tilde{s}_1 \le b$. So, $|\xi^r(t^*, s^*)| \le \delta \le \varepsilon$ by assumption. For case 2: Again by (2), $\xi^r(t^*, s^*) = \xi^r(t_r, b)$, where $0 \le t_r \le t^*$ is the time

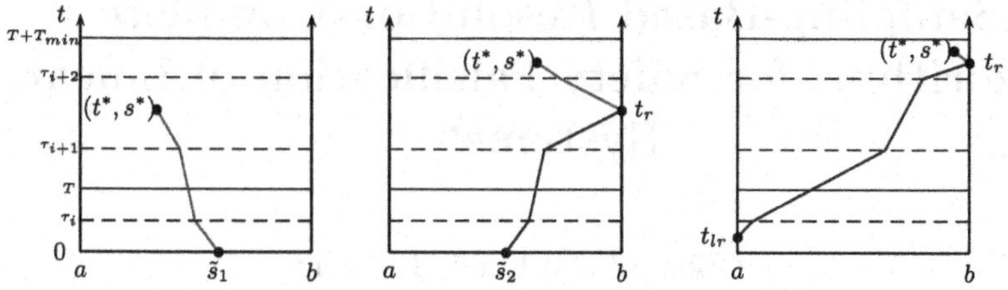

Fig. 1. (a) Case 1, (b) Case 2 (i), (c) Case 2 (ii)

when the r-th characteristic path hits $s = b$. Thus,

$$|\xi^r(t^*, s^*)| = |\sum_{l=m+1}^{n} g_{rl}^{R,j} \xi^l(t_r, b)| \le \sum_{l=m+1}^{n} |g_{rl}^{R,j}||\xi^l(t_r, b)| \tag{12}$$

with $j = \sigma(t_r)$. Now, let z_l denote the l-th characteristic path passing though (t_r, b) $(l = m+1, \ldots, n)$. Then, either z_l intersects the line $t = 0$ before hitting the line $s = a$ (case 2(i)) or it hits $s = a$ (case 2(ii)). For case 2(i), we have $|\xi^l(t_r, b)| = |\xi_l(0, \tilde{s}_2)| \le \delta \le \alpha\varepsilon$ for some $a \le \tilde{s}_2 \le b$ by assumption. Substituting this in (12), we get $|\xi^r(t^*, s^*)| \le K_1^j \alpha\varepsilon$ with $K_1^j := \sum_{l=m+1}^{n} |g_{rl}^{R,j}|$. For case 2($ii$), we have $|\xi^l(t_r, b)| = |\xi^l(t_{rl}, a)| = |\sum_{p=1}^{m} g_{lp}^{L,j'} \xi^p(t_{rl}, a)| \le |\sum_{p=1}^{m} g_{lp}^{L,j'}||\xi^p(t_{rl}, a)|$ with $0 \le t_{rl} \le T_{min}$ is the time when the characteristic path z_l hits $s = a$ and $j' = \sigma(t_{rl})$. Substituting this in (12), we get by assumption and using (9) $|\xi^r(t^*, s^*)| \le \sum_{l=m+1}^{n} \sum_{p=1}^{m} |g_{rl}^{R,j}||g_{lp}^{L,j'}||\xi^p(t_{rl}, a)| \le \theta\varepsilon \le \varepsilon$.

Similar estimates can be obtained for $\xi^l(t, s)$ $(l = m+1, \ldots, n)$ with constants $K_2^j := \sum_{p=1}^{m} |g_{lp}^{L,j}|$. Define $K := \max_{j \in \mathcal{Q}}\{K_1^j, K_2^j\}$. Choosing δ in (11) with $\alpha = \max\{1, \frac{1}{K}\}$ we conclude (10) for all $t \ge 0$ by induction. Essentially the same arguments applied to $\hat{\boldsymbol{\xi}}(t) := \exp(\beta t)\boldsymbol{\xi}(t)$, show that $\|\boldsymbol{\xi}(t)\| \le \varepsilon \exp(-\beta t)$ for $\beta > 0$ sufficiently small, (see [4], page 185). The system is thus asymptotically stable. □

Acknowledgments. This work is supported by the NSF awards #CCR–0225610, #CNS–0615299 and the Elite Network of Bavaria (#K-NW-2004-143).

References

1. Frid, H.: Initial-boundary value problems for conservation laws. Journal of Differential Equations 128, 1–45 (1996)
2. Leugering, G., Schmidt, J.P.G.: On the modeling and stabilisation of flows in networks of open canals. SIAM Journal of Control and Optimization 41(1), 164–180 (2002)
3. Liberzon, D.: Switching in Systems and Control. In series Systems and Control: Foundations and Applications. Birkhauser (2003)
4. Li, T.-T.: Global classical solutions for quasilinear hyperbolic systems. In: Research in Applied Mathematics, Masson and Wiley, Paris, Milan, Barcelona (1994)

Sampling-Based Resolution-Complete Algorithms for Safety Falsification of Linear Systems*

Amit Bhatia[1] and Emilio Frazzoli[2]

[1] University of California at Los Angeles, Los Angeles, CA 90095
abhatia@ucla.edu
[2] Massachusetts Institute of Technology, Cambridge, MA 02139
frazzoli@mit.edu

Abstract. In this paper, we describe a novel approach for checking safety specifications of a dynamical system with exogenous inputs over infinite time horizon. We introduce the notion of resolution completeness for analysis of safety falsification algorithms and present sampling-based resolution-complete algorithms for safety falsification of discrete-time linear time-invariant systems. Given a target resolution of inputs, the algorithms terminate either with a reachable state that violates the safety specification, or prove that the system does not violate the specification at the given resolution of inputs.

1 Introduction

The problem of finding the set of all states a system can reach (called as the reachable set) based on its dynamics and initial conditions, is known as the *reachability problem* in the literature. For continuous and hybrid systems, this problem is in general known to be undecidable [1]. For analyzing safety specifications of dynamical systems, a wide variety of methods have been proposed (for references, see [2]). However, most of these methods attempt to verify safety of a given system by over approximating the actual reachable set over a finite time horizon. As a result, they are liable to generate infeasible counterexamples to safety and cannot analyze safety over infinite time horizon. Moreover, they fail to guarantee that the procedure of refining the simulation parameters (to conclusively certify that the system is safe) will ever terminate [3].

2 Sampling-Based Safety Falsification

To complement verification-based approaches, falsification methods using sampling-based incremental-search algorithms have been proposed recently

* The research leading to this work was supported by the National Science Foundation (grants number 0715025 and 0325716).

M. Egerstedt and B. Mishra (Eds.): HSCC 2008, LNCS 4981, pp. 606–609, 2008.

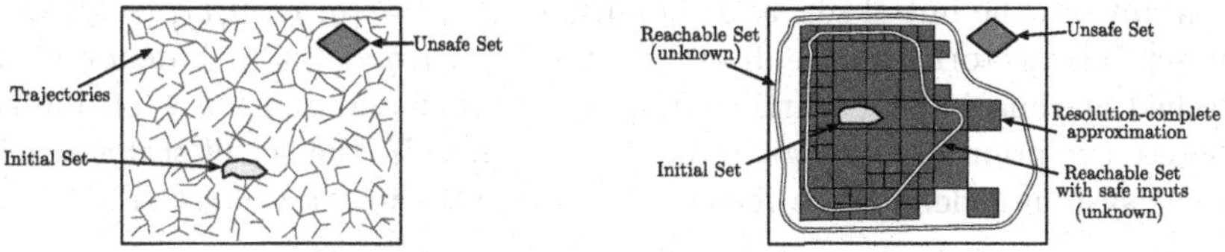

Fig. 1. Probabilistic vs resolution completeness

(e.g., [4,5]). The algorithms try to falsify safety of the system quickly by incremental construction of trajectories (e.g., Fig. 1, left). However, they are only *probabilistically complete*, meaning that the probability of finding a feasible counterexample (if one exists) goes to 1 as the number of samples goes to infinity. As a result, if no counterexample is found in finite number of iterations, then the algorithms become inconclusive. To obtain stronger completeness guarantees for the falsification problem, we have recently introduced the notion of *resolution completeness* for safety falsification of dynamical systems with exogenous inputs in [6,7]. This notion of completeness is defined on the space of exogenous inputs and considers safety over infinite time horizon. A safety falsification algorithm is called resolution-complete if for any given resolution of inputs, it is guaranteed to terminate in finite time with either a feasible counterexample or else a proof of system safety at given input resolution (e.g., Fig. 1, right).

Relation to other approaches: The proposed approach differs from other complete approaches (e.g., [8,9]) in the following ways. The notion of resolution completeness is defined on the space of exogenous inputs; the requirements on discretization of state space do *not* depend on time length of trajectories and the space of inputs is *not* discretized to obtain completeness guarantees. Furthermore, the proposed approach makes no assumption on the distance of unsafe set to the reachable set or the number of discrete mode switches that can occur.

3 Preliminaries

Definition 1 (Hybrid System). *A discrete-time LTI hybrid system H is denoted as a tuple, $H = (\mathcal{Q}, \mathcal{X}, \mathcal{U}, \Phi, \Delta, \mathcal{I}, \mathcal{S}, \mathcal{T})$.*

$\mathcal{Q}$ is the discrete state space and $\mathcal{X} \subseteq \mathbb{R}^n$ is the continuous state space. $\mathcal{U}$ is a family of admissible inputs. Each input $u \in \mathcal{U}$ is a function $u : [0, t_f] \to U$, where $t_f \in \mathbb{N}$ and U is a compact subset of $\mathbb{R}^m$. $\Phi : \mathcal{Q} \times \mathcal{X} \times \mathcal{U} \to \mathcal{X}$ is a function describing the evolution of the system on continuous space, governed by a difference equation of the form $x(i+1) = \Phi(q, x, u) = A_q x(i) + B_q u(i), i \in \mathbb{N}$. The matrices A_q, B_q are real matrices of size $n \times n, n \times m$ respectively. $\phi^k(q, x, u)$ denotes continuous evolution over k time steps. $\Delta \subset (\mathcal{Q} \times \mathcal{X}) \times (\mathcal{Q} \times \mathcal{X})$, is a relation describing discrete transitions in the hybrid states. Discrete transitions can occur on location-specific subsets $\mathcal{G}(q, q') \subseteq \mathcal{X}$, called guards, and result in jump relations of the form $(q, x) \mapsto (q', x)$. $\mathcal{I}, \mathcal{S}, \mathcal{T} \subseteq \mathcal{Q} \times \mathcal{X}$ are, respectively, the invariant set, the initial set, and the unsafe set. $\Omega = \{\bar{q}, \bar{q} : [0, t_f] \to Q\}$ denotes the set of trajectories on the discrete space. $\psi(z, u, \bar{q}, i) \in \mathcal{Q} \times \mathcal{X}$ denotes a point reached at time $i \leq t_f$, starting from $z \in \mathcal{Q} \times \mathcal{X}$ and using $u \in \mathcal{U}$, under the discrete evolution $\bar{q}$. For a given family of inputs $\mathcal{U}$, the set of states reachable by the system is denoted as $\mathcal{R}(\mathcal{U})$. A° denotes the interior of set A.

Definition 2 (Resolution completeness). *An algorithm is resolution-complete for safety falsification of a system H, if there exists a sequence of family of inputs, $\{\mathcal{U}_j\}_{j=1}^{\infty}$, satisfying $\mathcal{U}_j \subset \mathcal{U}_{j+1}, \forall j$, and $\lim_{j\to\infty} \mathcal{U}_j = \mathcal{U}$, such that, for any given $j \geq 1$, the algorithm terminates in finite time, producing, either a counterexample $\psi(z_0, u, \bar{q}, t) \in \mathcal{T}$, using an input $u \in \mathcal{U}, z_0 \in \mathcal{S}, \bar{q} \in \Omega, t \geq 0$, or a guarantee that, $\mathcal{R}^\circ(\mathcal{U}_j) \cap \mathcal{T} = \emptyset$.*

4 Main Ideas

To achieve completeness, we construct an approximation $\mathcal{R}_j$ (while searching for counterexamples at resolution j) that satisfies the set inclusion $\mathcal{R}^\circ(\mathcal{U}_j) \subseteq \mathcal{R}_j \subseteq \mathcal{R}(\mathcal{U})$. The inclusion $\mathcal{R}_j \subseteq \mathcal{R}(\mathcal{U})$ guarantees feasibility of counterexamples and the inclusion $\mathcal{R}^\circ(\mathcal{U}_j) \subseteq \mathcal{R}_j$ guarantees safety with respect to inputs belonging to $\mathcal{U}_j$ (if no counterexample is found). The approximation $\mathcal{R}_j$ is constructed using multi-resolution grids. For a discrete location $q \in \mathcal{Q}$, $G(q)$ denotes the multi-resolution grid for location q that over-approximates $\mathcal{R}(\mathcal{U}) \cap \mathcal{I}(q, \cdot)$. The algorithms keep a record of the portion of $G(q)$ that is found to be reachable (denoted as $G_f(q)$), either *a priori* or during an execution of the algorithm. $G_u(q)$ denotes the rest of $G(q)$, i.e., $G_u(q) = G(q) \setminus G_f(q)$.

State Space Discretization: The conditions for state-space discretization relate the grid resolution $\varepsilon_j(q)$ to the resolution of inputs being used, i.e., $\mathcal{U}_j$. More precisely, $\varepsilon_j(q)$ is chosen such that finding one feasible point $\phi^k(q, x_0, u)$ in a grid region $\xi(\varepsilon_j(q))$ of size $\varepsilon_j(q)$, with $x_0 \in G_f(q), u \in \mathcal{U}_j, k > 0$, is enough to claim that for every point $x \in \xi$, there exists $u' \in \mathcal{U}$ such that $x = \phi^k(q, x_0, u')$ (see [2]).

Algorithms: We now informally explain the main steps of our resolution-complete algorithms for the case when card $(\mathcal{Q}) = 1$ (Fig. 2) and for details refer the reader to [2,7]. The search for counterexample begins at input resolution of j and stops at $j+1$. After initialization, the algorithm samples a grid region ξ_{sample} from G_u and checks if $\exists x_1 \in \xi_{\text{sample}}$, such that $x_1 = \phi^k(q, x_0, u)$, for some $x_0 \in G_f, u \in \mathcal{U}_j$ and a fixed $k > 0$. If the answer is yes, then $G_f \to G_f \cup \xi_{\text{sample}}$. If $G_f \cap \mathcal{T} \neq \emptyset$, the algorithm declares the system to be unsafe and terminates. Otherwise, the search is continued by sampling a new grid region. As no counterexample is found at resolution j in this example, the search is continued at resolution level $j+1$. Since no counterexample to safety is found at resolution $j+1$ either, the system is certified to be safe $\forall u \in \mathcal{U}_{j+1}$.

Termination guarantees and heuristics: Under the assumption of boundedness of the grids in each discrete mode (using system stability or some other arguments), the algorithms are guaranteed to terminate in finite time. To find the

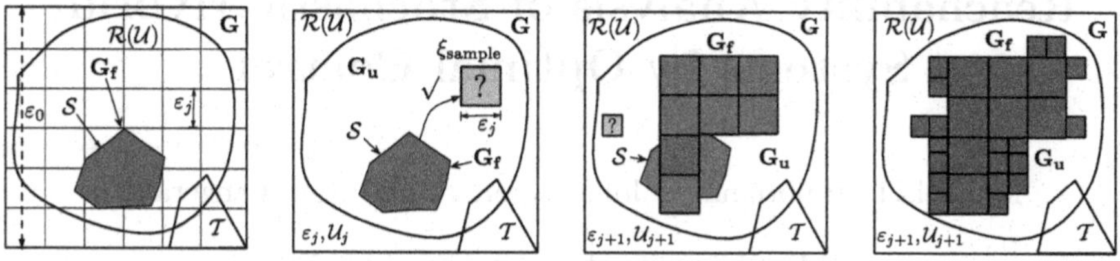

(a) Initialization (b) Sampling at j (c) Sampling at $j+1$ (d) Termination

Fig. 2. Execution of a resolution-complete algorithm for card $(\mathcal{Q}) = 1$

counterexamples quickly (when they exist), heuristics like breadth-first search, branch and bound, and incremental grid sampling are used (see [2]).

5 Conclusions

In this paper, we have proposed a novel approach for checking safety specifications of a dynamical system with exogenous inputs over infinite time horizon. We have presented sampling-based resolution-complete algorithms for safety falsification of linear systems. The algorithms terminate either with a feasible counterexample violating the specification, or prove that the system does not violate the specification at the given input resolution. We plan to investigate extensions of the algorithms for nonlinear systems in the future.

References

1. Kesten, Y., Pnueli, A., Sifakis, J., Yovine, S.: Integration graphs: A class of decidable hybrid systems. In: Grossman, R.L., Ravn, A.P., Rischel, H., Nerode, A. (eds.) HS 1991 and HS 1992. LNCS, vol. 736, pp. 179–208. Springer, Heidelberg (1993)
2. Bhatia, A., Frazzoli, E.: Sampling-based resolution-complete algorithms for safety falsification of linear systems (January 2008), `http://arxiv.org/abs/0801.0570`
3. Silva, B.I., Stursberg, O., Krogh, B.H., Engell, S.: An assessment of the current status of algorithmic approaches to the verification of hybrid systems. In: Conference on Decision and Control (2001)
4. Bhatia, A., Frazzoli, E.: Incremental search methods for reachability analysis of continuous and hybrid systems. In: Alur, R., Pappas, G.J. (eds.) HSCC 2004. LNCS, vol. 2993, pp. 142–156. Springer, Heidelberg (2004)
5. Kim, J., Esposito, J.M., Kumar, V.: An rrt-based algorithm for testing and validating multi-robot controllers. In: Robotics: Science and Systems, pp. 249–256 (2005)
6. Bhatia, A., Frazzoli, E.: Resolution complete safety falsification of continuous time systems. In: Conference on Decision and Control (2006)
7. Bhatia, A., Frazzoli, E.: Sampling-based resolution-complete safety falsification of linear hybrid systems. In: Conference on Decision and Control (2007)
8. Cheng, P., Kumar, V.: Sampling-based falsification and verification of controllers for continuous dynamic systems. In: WAFR (2006)
9. Girard, A.: Approximately bisimilar finite abstractions of stable linear systems. In: Bemporad, A., Bicchi, A., Buttazzo, G. (eds.) HSCC 2007. LNCS, vol. 4416, pp. 231–244. Springer, Heidelberg (2007)

Reachability Analysis of Stochastic Hybrid Systems by Optimal Control

Manuela L. Bujorianu[1,3], John Lygeros[2], and Rom Langerak[1]

[1] EWI, University of Twente, Enschede NL
{l.m.bujorianu,langerak}@cs.utwente.nl
[2] Automatic Control Laboratory, ETH Zurich, CH
[3] CICADA, University of Manchester, UK

Abstract. For stochastic hybrid systems, the reachability analysis is an important and difficult problem. In this paper, we prove that, under natural assumptions, reachability analysis can be characterised as an optimal stopping problem. In this way, one can apply numerical methods from optimal control to solve the reachability verification problems.

Keywords: Stochastic hybrid systems, Markov processes, reachability problem, optimal stopping.

1 Introduction

The paper addresses the reachability problem for stochastic hybrid systems, which are a class of non-linear stochastic continuous time/space hybrid dynamical systems. For a stochastic hybrid system, we show that the reach set probabilities coincide with the value functions of some particular optimal stopping problems corresponding to the indicator functions of the target sets. These optimal stopping problems are formulated in the language of the Markov process that describes the realizations of the given hybrid system. Our method is based on the (Riesz) representation of the value function for the optimal stopping problem and it was successfully used for some particular classes of Markov processes [7]. The application of this method is sketched for stochastic hybrid systems.

2 Stochastic Hybrid Systems

Stochastic Hybrid Systems can be described as an interleaving between a finite or countable family of diffusion processes and a Markov chain. We adopt the General Stochastic Hybrid System model presented in [2]. Let Q be a set of discrete states. For each $q \in Q$, we consider the Euclidean space $\mathbb{R}^{d(q)}$ with dimension $d(q)$ and we define an *invariant* as an open subset X^q of $\mathbb{R}^{d(q)}$. The hybrid state space is the set $X(Q,d,\mathcal{X}) = \bigcup_{i\in Q}\{i\} \times X^i$. The closure of $X(Q,d,\mathcal{X})$ will be $\overline{X} = X \cup \partial X$, where $\partial X = \bigcup_{i\in Q}\{i\} \times \partial X^i$. $(X, \mathcal{B}(X))$ is

M. Egerstedt and B. Mishra (Eds.): HSCC 2008, LNCS 4981, pp. 610–613, 2008.

a Borel space, where $\mathcal{B}(X)$ is the Borel σ-algebra of X. Let $\mathbf{B}(X)$ be the Banach space of bounded positive measurable functions on X with the norm given by the supremum. A (General) Stochastic Hybrid System (SHS) is a collection $H = ((Q, d, \mathcal{X}), b, \sigma, Init, \lambda, R)$, where the full meaning of the constituents can be find in [2]. The realization of an SHS is built as a *Markov string* H [2]. This string is a Markov process. Denote by $M = (\Omega, \mathcal{F}, \mathcal{F}_t, x_t, P_x)$ this Markov process. Let $\mathcal{P} = (P_t)_{t>0}$ denote the *semigroup of operators* associated to M, which maps $\mathbf{B}(X)$ into itself given by $P_t f(x) = E_x f(x_t), \forall x \in X$, where E_x is the expectation w.r.t. P_x. A nonnegative function $f \in \mathbf{B}(X)$ is called (α-)*excessive* ($\alpha \geq 0$) if $(e^{-\alpha t})P_t f \leq f$ for all $t \geq 0$ and $(e^{-\alpha t})P_t f \nearrow f$ as $t \searrow 0$. Let $\mathcal{E}_M$ be the *cone of excessive functions.* Suppose that M is *transient*[1], i.e. there is a strictly positive measurable function q such that $Uq \leq 1$. The infinitesimal generator $\mathcal{L}$ is the derivative of P_t at $t = 0$. Under the standard assumptions the realization M of an SHS is a Borel right process with cadlag property and the infinitesimal generator of an SHS is an integro-differential operator [2].

3 Stochastic Reachability as an Optimal Stopping Problem

In this section, in the framework of SHS, we prove that the stochastic reachability problem is equivalent with an optimal stopping problem.

Let us consider $M = (\Omega, \mathcal{F}, \mathcal{F}_t, x_t, P_x)$ a (strong right) Markov process, being the realization of an SHS. For this Markov process we address the *stochastic reachability problem* as follows. Given a target set, the objective of the reachability problem is to compute the probability that the system trajectories from an arbitrary initial state will reach the target set. Formally, given a set $A \in \mathcal{B}(X)$ and a time horizon $T \in [0, \zeta]$ (where ζ is the life time of M), define $Reach_T(A) := \{\omega \in \Omega \mid \exists t \geq 0 : x_t(\omega) \in A\}$. The reachability problem consists of determining the probabilities of such a set, i.e. $P(T_A < T)$, where T_A is the first hitting time of A (i.e. $T_A = \inf\{t > 0 | x_t \in A\}$) and $(\Omega, \mathcal{F}, P)$ is the underlying probability space of M. P can be chosen to be P_x, if we want to consider the trajectories that start in x.

For any $f : X \to \mathbb{R}_+$, we denote *he réduite of* f by Rf, i.e $Rf := \inf\{u \in \mathcal{E}_M | u \geq f\}$. Rf differs from f only on a negligible set. For any $A \subset X$ and $v \in \mathcal{E}_M$, the function $R_A v = R(1_A v)$ is called *the réduite*[2] *of* v *on* A. The *balayage of the excessive function* v *on* A denoted by $B_A v$, is the $\mathcal{U}$-excessive regularization of $R_A v$ [3]. For any $x \in X$ and $A \in \mathcal{B}(X)$, we have $P_x[Reach_\infty(A)] = B_A 1(x) = P_x[T_A < \zeta]$ [3]. Since $R_A v = B_A v$ on $X \backslash A$ (see [3]), when the process starts in $x \notin A$, finding the reach set probability $P_x[Reach_\infty(A)]$ is equivalent to finding the reduite $R(1_A)(x)$. The existence of the réduite for $g \in \mathbf{B}(X)$ is based on the following equality: $Rg(x) = \sup\{E_x[g(x_S) 1_{\{S<\zeta\}}];\ S \text{ stopping time}\}$. The right hand side of the above equality is related with the so-called *optimal stopping problem* (OSP) associated with a Markov process. For different classes of

[1] The transience hypothesis guarantees that the cone $\mathcal{E}_M$ is rich enough to be used.
[2] We use the convention $0 \cdot (+\infty) = (+\infty) \cdot 0 = 0$.

stochastic processes[3], the fact that the optimal value function coincides with the smaller excessive majorant of the exercise payoff is a well known result. This result has been extended for right processes in [4].

Proposition 1. *If $A \in \mathcal{B}(X)$ then the reachability function $w_A : X \to [0,1]$ associated to A, defined as $w_A(x) := P_x[Reach_\infty(A)]$, coincides with the value function of the reward process $y_t = 1_A(x_t)$, i.e. $w_A(x) = \sup\{P_x(x_\tau \in A)|\tau$ stopping time$\}$, $\forall x \in X$.*

4 From Optimal Stopping to Stochastic Reachability

The realizations of SHS are (Borel) right processes, and therefore the general theory of optimal stopping developed for right processes [1] can be applied. For the OSP associated to (Borel) right processes, we propose a method based on representations of excessive functions. This method consists in establishing first an integral representation for excessive (super-harmonic) functions and then deriving information about final behaviour of paths. We show that finding the solution of such a problem is equivalent to finding the representation of the value function of the OSP in terms of the Green kernel. The support of the measure that appears in this representation is the *stopping region* for the problem.

Dealing with Optimal Stopping. For the a Markov process M and the optimal stopping problem, one can introduce: *continuation set* $C = \{x \in X|v(x) > g(x)\}$; and the *stopping set* $D = \{x \in X|v(x) = g(x)\}$.

Using the operator semigroup $\mathcal{P}$, one can define the *kernel operator* U by $Uf(x) = \int_0^\infty P_t f(x)dt$, $f \in \mathbf{B}(X)$. Uf is the solution of the equation $-\mathcal{L}\phi = f$. If in expression of U, f ranges over the indicator functions of measurable sets, we can write U as a stochastic kernel $U(x, A) = \int_0^\infty P_x(x_t \in A)dt$. For the scope of this section, we suppose that the assumptions from [6] are in force. The main assumption is related to the absolute continuity of the kernel operator U w.r.t. a σ-finite excessive measure m on $(X, \mathcal{B})$, called *reference measure*.

Assumption 1. *There exists a $\mathcal{B} \times \mathcal{B}$ measurable function $u \geq 0$ such that $U(x, dy) = u(x, y)m(dy)$, $x \in X$; and $x \longmapsto u(x, y)$ is excessive, $y \in X$.*

The *potential density* $u(x, y)$ is used to define the potential of a measure μ by setting $U\mu(x) := \int_X u(x, y)\mu(dy)$. For Borel right processes, h is harmonic iff $P^-_{K^c}h = h$, $m - a.e.$[4], for every compact K (with the complement $K^c = X\backslash K$) in an appropriate compactification of X, where $P^-_{K^c}$ is the hitting operator associated to K^c[5].

Theorem 1 (Riesz Decomposition). *[6] Let $f \in \mathcal{E}_M$. Then there exists a measure μ on $(X, \mathcal{B})$ and an harmonic function h such that $f = U\mu + h$, $m - a.e.$Moreover, μ is unique and h is unique $m - a.e.$*

[3] diffusions, Feller/Hunt/standard processes.

[4] $m - a.e.$ (m almost everywhere), i.e. outside of a set with m-measure zero.

[5] i.e. $P^-_{K^c}h = E_x[h(x_{T^-_{K^c}})]$, $T^-_{K^c} = \inf\{t|0 < t < \zeta;\ x_{t-} \in K^c\}$.

Using Ass.1 and the characterization of $U\mu$, in the decomposition of Th.1, if there exists a compact set K such that the representing measure μ *does not charge* K^c, then f is harmonic on K^c, i.e. $\mu(K^c) = 0 \Longrightarrow f$ is harmonic on K^c. Then the problem of finding the maximal payoff function is equivalent to the problem of finding the representing measure μ_v of v. The continuation region C is the biggest set *not charged* by the representing measure μ_v of v, i.e. $\mu_v(C) = 0$. So, the value function v is harmonic on C.

Proposition 2. *The* measure μ_v gives the value function v, *and the support of the representation measure gives the stopping region* D, *i.e.* $D = supp(\mu_v)$.

Reach Set Probability Computation. Suppose that the target set A is an open set of the state space X. Define $F := X \backslash A$. Suppose that last exit time from F is finite almost surely (the process is transient), i.e. $S_F = \sup\{t \geq 0 | x_t \in F\} < \infty$. Then the reachability problem turns in an *exit time problem*, and then computing the reach set probabilities is equivalent with the computation of a dual probability $P_x[x_{S_F} \in F | S_F > 0]$.

Proposition 3. *[5] For all positive* $f \in \mathbf{B}(X)$, *we have* $P_x[(1_F f)(x_{S_F}) | S_F > 0] = \int u(x,y)(1_F f)(y)\mu(dy)$, *where* μ *is a measure on* X.

Therefore, for $f \equiv 1$, the reach set probabilities are $P_x[x_{S_F} \in F | S_F > 0] = \int_F u(x,y)\mu_F(dy)$, where μ_F is the *equilibrium measure* of F.

5 Conclusions

In this paper, we have characterised the reachability problem of stochastic hybrid systems as an optimal stopping problem with a discontinuous reward function. To deal with the stochastic reachability, we consider that the method based on representations of the value function of the equivalent optimal stopping problem suits best in this context.

References

1. Bismut, J.-M., Skalli, B.: Temps d'arrêt Optimal, Théorie Générale des Processus et Processus de Markov. Prob. Th. Rel. Fields 36(4), 301–313 (1977)
2. Bujorianu, M.L., Lygeros, J.: Towards Modelling of General Stochastic Hybrid Systems. LNCIS, vol. 337, pp. 3–30 (2006)
3. Bujorianu, M.L., Lygeros, J.: New Insights on Stochastic Reachability. In: Proc. 46th Conference in Decision and Control (2007)
4. El Karoui, N., Lepeltier, J.-P., Millet, A.: A Probabilistic Approach to the Reduite in Optimal Stopping. Probab. Math. Statist. 13(1), 97–121 (1992)
5. Glover, J.: Representing last exit potentials as potentials of measures. Z. Wahrsch. Verw. Gebiete 61(1), 17–30 (1982)
6. Graversen, S.E.: A Riesz Decomposition Theorem. Nagoya Math. J. 114, 123–133 (1989)
7. Mordecki, E., Salminen, P.: Optimal stopping of Hunt and Lévy processes. Stochastics 79(3-4), 233–251 (2007)

An Integrated Approach to Parametric and Discrete Fault Diagnosis in Hybrid Systems

Matthew Daigle, Xenofon Koutsoukos, and Gautam Biswas

EECS Department/ISIS, Vanderbilt University
Nashville, TN 37235, USA
{matthew.j.daigle,xenofon.koutsoukos,gautam.biswas}@vanderbilt.edu

1 Fault Diagnosis of Electrical Power Systems

Fault diagnosis is crucial for ensuring the safe operation of complex engineering systems. Faults and degradations need to be quickly identified so that corrective actions can avoid catastrophic situations. Most real-world, embedded systems are hybrid in nature. In such systems, hybrid models have to be employed for correct tracking and diagnosis. The majority of hybrid systems diagnosis work, however, has focused on either discrete or parametric fault diagnosis. In contrast, we present an integrated model-based approach to diagnosing both parametric and discrete faults in hybrid systems. This extends our previous work in diagnosis of parametric faults in hybrid systems [1,2] by including discrete faults, resulting in a unified hybrid diagnosis methodology. We demonstrate our approach using experimental results performed on a complex electrical power system.

The Advanced Diagnostics and Prognostics Testbed (ADAPT) [3], deployed at NASA Ames Research Center, is functionally representative of a spacecraft's electrical power system. Over fifty relays and circuit breakers configure the system into different modes of operation. Therefore, the system behavior is naturally hybrid. Parametric faults, such as changes in resistance and inductance values, can occur in the components. Discrete faults, such as relays becoming stuck, may also occur. We consider a subset of ADAPT that involves a battery discharging to two parallel DC loads, as shown in Fig. 1, which includes two relays (Sw_1 and Sw_2) and one circuit breaker (CB). The selected sensors measure the battery voltage, $V_B(t)$, the currents through the loads, $I_{L1}(t)$ and $I_{L2}(t)$, and the on/off position of the circuit breaker, $P_{CB}(t)$.

Hybrid System Modeling. We develop component-based models of hybrid physical systems using hybrid bond graphs (HBGs) [4]. Bond graphs define an energy-based, multi-domain, topological modeling scheme for dynamic systems. HBGs extend bond graphs by allowing switching behavior of components, defined through a *control specification* (CSPEC), modeled as a finite automaton [4,2]. The state transitions may be attributed to controlled or autonomous events, and the output of the CSPEC determines the component state.

We focus on the diagnosis of single, abrupt, persistent faults in hybrid systems, and classify these faults as either (*i*) *parametric faults*, or (*ii*) *discrete*

M. Egerstedt and B. Mishra (Eds.): HSCC 2008, LNCS 4981, pp. 614–617, 2008.

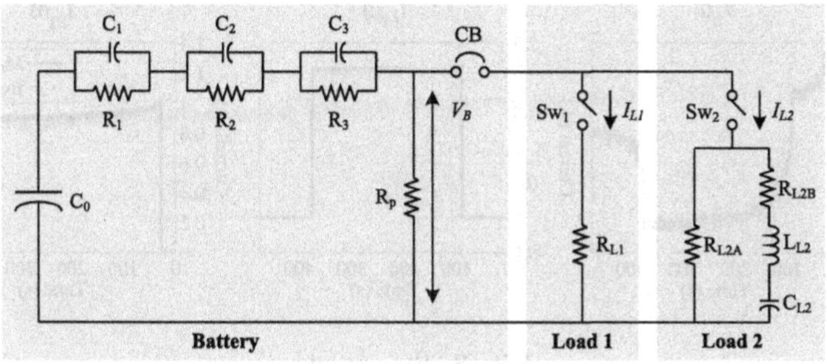

Fig. 1. Electric circuit equivalent for the battery system

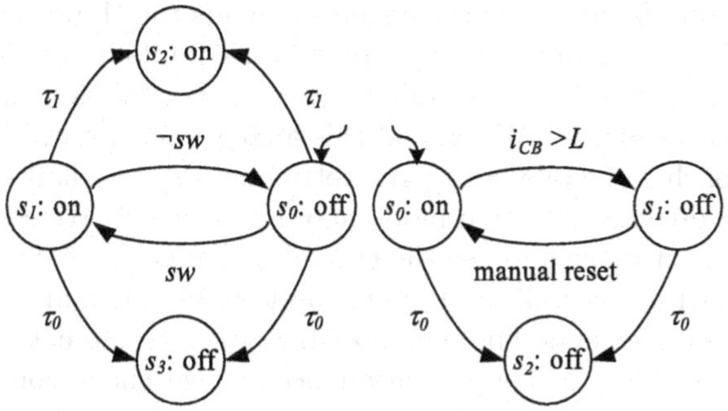

Fig. 2. Relay (left) and circuit breaker (right) CSPECs for ADAPT

faults. Parametric faults cover partial failures or degradations in system components, and are modeled as an unexpected change in the value of a system parameter in the model. For example, the load resistance R_{L1} may increase or decrease. Discrete faults are modeled as a discrepancy between the actual and expected mode of a switching element. Discrete faults in ADAPT include switch malfunctions. For example, a switch may be commanded to close, but remain stuck open. Also, it may unexpectedly open or close without a command. Because the switching behavior in HBGs is captured by CSPECs, we model discrete faults as unobservable fault events in the CSPEC.

Example CSPECs for ADAPT are given in Fig. 2, with the state outputs shown. The relay CSPEC (Fig. 2, left) includes fault events τ_0 and τ_1. Event τ_1, corresponding to the relay being stuck on, causes a transition to the stuck on state, s_2. If the relay was previously off, then this fault manifests in the measurements immediately, because it switches off by itself. Otherwise, it will only manifest when sw becomes true, i.e., it becomes stuck on. The case is similar for the τ_1 event. For the circuit breaker CSPEC (Fig. 2, right), only the stuck off fault, τ_0, is appropriate, and the behavior is similar. The circuit breaker may switch off due to its current, i_{CB} exceeding the limit L, which is nominal behavior, or may switch off due to a fault.

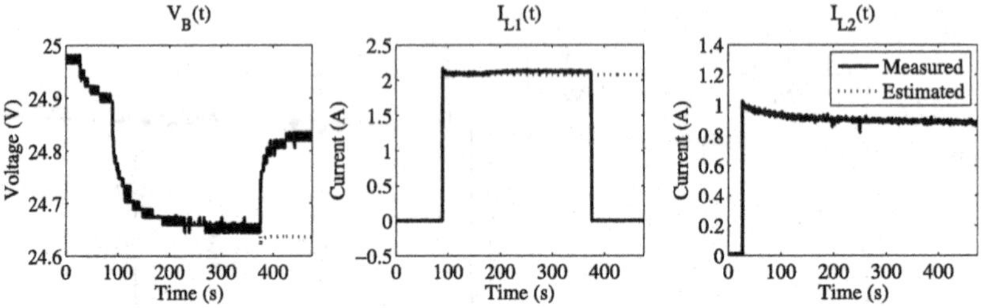

Fig. 3. Sw_1 opens

Hybrid Diagnosis Approach. Our method for integrated diagnosis of parametric and discrete faults in hybrid systems extends the Hybrid TRANSCEND [2] approach for diagnosing single, abrupt, parametric faults in hybrid systems. The diagnosis is based on analysis of fault transients to establish the fault and the mode in which it occurs [1]. We extend this analysis to discrete faults, and augment the approach to handle both parametric and discrete faults. When a fault is detected, the estimated system mode may be incorrect. We compute possible modes of fault occurrence and use the extended diagnosis model to hypothesize parameter deviations as well as discrete fault events that are consistent with the observed measurements. For each possible fault, we predict future measurement deviations. When a new deviation occurs, we check consistency of the fault candidates. Because mode changes may change the predictions, we update our candidates to the possible true system modes. Inconsistent candidates are dropped, and consistent candidates are retained. Details may be found in [5].

Experimental Results. We demonstrate our algorithms on discrete faults injected into the actual system. Our set of possible faults includes parametric faults in the battery and loads (C_0^-, R_1^+, R_{L1}^+, R_{L1}^-, R_{L2A}^+, R_{L2A}^-), sensor faults (V_B^+, V_B^-, I_{L1}^+, I_{L1}^-, I_{L2}^+, I_{L2}^-, P_{CB}^+, P_{CB}^-), and discrete faults in the switches ($Sw_1.off$, $Sw_1.on$, $Sw_2.off$, $Sw_2.on$, $CB.off$). We denote the system mode by q_{ijk} where i is the mode of Sw_1, j is the mode of Sw_2, and k is the mode of CB. We first consider an unexpected switch fault. Within the first 100 s, both loads are brought online. At 375.5 s, Sw_1 switches off by itself. Fig. 3 shows the measured and estimated outputs. As a result, $I_{L1}(t)$ goes immediately to zero, and $V_B(t)$ increases. The fault is detected at 376.0 s, and the symbol generator reports a decrease in $I_{L1}(t)$. Because P_{CB} does not immediately change, the only possible mode of fault occurrence is q_{111}, so the initial fault set is $\{(I_{L1}^-, q_{111}), (R_1^+, q_{111})), (R_{L1}^+, q_{111})), (R_{L2A}^+, q_{111})), (R_{L2A}^-, q_{111})), (Sw_1.off, , q_{011})\}$. At 376.5 s, the symbol generator reports an increase in $V_B(t)$, thus eliminating the sensor fault as a candidate. At 378.5 s, the symbol generator reports that I_{L1} went to zero. Since only $Sw_1.off$ may cause this behavior, it is correctly isolated.

Next, we consider a stuck switch fault. At 414.0 s, Sw_1 is commanded off but remains on. Fig. 4 shows the outputs. The estimated system mode is q_{011}, but the actual system mode is q_{111}, and $\hat{I}_{L1}(t)$ goes to zero, while $I_{L1}(t)$ remains

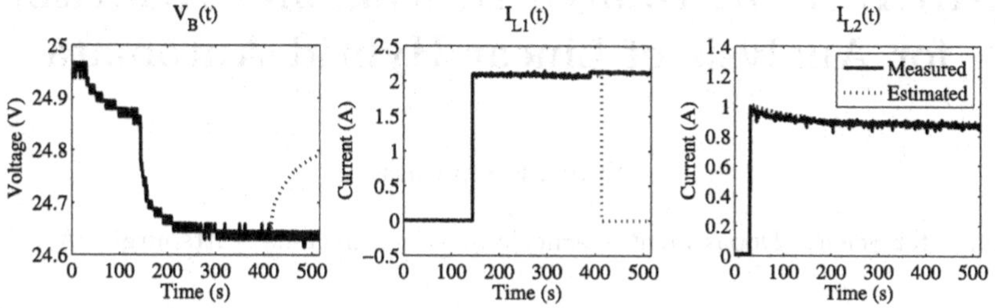

Fig. 4. Sw_1 gets stuck closed

nonzero. The fault is detected at 416.0 s, and the symbol generator reports that $I_{L1}(t)$ has increased. Because the expected mode is q_{011}, the only reason for the current to deviate is due to a discrete fault or a sensor fault, so the initial hypothesis set is $\{(I_{L1}^-, q_{011}), (Sw_1.on, q_{111})\}$. At 418.5 s, the symbol generator reports that $I_{L1}(t)$ became nonzero when expected to be zero. Because sensor faults are also allowed to cause discrete behavior, both faults are retained. At 419.5 s, we observe a decrease in $V_B(t)$, and since I_{L1}^- cannot cause this, $Sw_1.on$ is isolated as the true fault. Additional experiments have shown correct fault isolation, with ambiguities resulting only for certain types of sensor faults [5].

Acknowledgments

This work was supported in part by grants NSF-NASA USRA 08020-013, NASA NRA NNX07AD12A, NSF CNS-0615214, and NSF CNS-0347440.

References

1. Mosterman, P., Biswas, G.: Diagnosis of continuous valued systems in transient operating regions. IEEE Transactions on Systems, Man and Cybernetics, Part A 29(6), 554–565 (1999)
2. Narasimhan, S., Biswas, G.: Model-based diagnosis of hybrid systems. IEEE Transactions on Systems, Man and Cybernetics, Part A 37(3), 348–361 (2007)
3. Poll, S., Patterson-Hine, A., Camisa, J., Nishikawa, D., Spirkovska, L., Garcia, D., Hall, D., Neukom, C., Sweet, A., Yentus, S., Lee, C., Ossenfort, J., Roychoudhury, I., Daigle, M., Biswas, G., Koutsoukos, X., Lutz, R.: Evaluation, selection, and application of model-based diagnosis tools and approaches. In: AIAA Infotech@Aerospace 2007 Conference Proceedings (2007)
4. Mosterman, P.J., Biswas, G.: A theory of discontinuities in physical system models. Journal of the Franklin Institute 335B(3), 401–439 (1998)
5. Daigle, M., Koutsoukos, X., Biswas, G.: An integrated approach to parametric and discrete fault diagnosis in hybrid systems. Technical Report ISIS-07-815, Institute for Software Integrated Systems, Vanderbilt University, Nashville, TN, USA (2007)

d-IRA: A Distributed Reachability Algorithm for Analysis of Linear Hybrid Automata

Sumit Kumar Jha

Computer Science Department, Carnegie Mellon University, Pittsburgh PA 15213

Abstract. This paper presents the design of a novel distributed algorithm d-IRA for the reachability analysis of linear hybrid automata. Recent work on *iterative relaxation abstraction* (IRA) is leveraged to distribute the reachability problem among multiple computational nodes in a non-redundant manner by performing careful infeasibility analysis of linear programs corresponding to spurious counterexamples. The d-IRA algorithm is resistant to failure of multiple computational nodes. The experimental results provide promising evidence for the possible successful application of this technique.

1 Introduction

The verification of linear hybrid automata is a computationally expensive procedure and is efficient only for systems with few continuous variables. Linear hybrid automata (LHA) are an important class of hybrid systems which can approximate nonlinear hybrid systems in an asymptotically complete fashion [3]. We extend our earlier work [5] on applying counterexample guided abstraction refinement (CEGAR) based model checking algorithms [1] to the analysis of linear hybrid automata and present a distributed algorithm for their reachability analysis.

This paper makes the following three novel contributions:

1. We present the first fault-tolerant distributed algorithm for the reachability analysis of linear hybrid automata.
2. On the theoretical side, we establish a partial-order among counterexamples and relaxations of linear hybrid automata. We find counterexamples not related by the partial order and build relaxations to refute each of them in a distributed manner.
3. The global state which needs to be preserved for failure-tolerance of the distributed system is only a discrete finite state machine. We also illustrate the potential for efficient online back-ups of the global state.

2 The Distributed Algorithm (d-IRA)

The distributed algorithm assumes one master computation node and (N-1) other computational (slave) nodes. Initially, the master node initialises a counter i to zero, chooses the empty set as an initial set of variables $\mathcal{I}_0$ and learns the deterministic finite automata corresponding to Σ^* (where Σ is the alphabet of the

M. Egerstedt and B. Mishra (Eds.): HSCC 2008, LNCS 4981, pp. 618–621, 2008.

linear hybrid automata) as the initial discrete over-approximate *global abstraction* of the language of the LHA H. Now, we explain the distributed algorithm.

1. During the ith iteration, the jth computational node constructs its own relaxation H_i^j of the linear hybrid automata H using the set of variables I_i^j. This step could involve invoking the Fourier-Motzkin elimination routine. Each computational node then constructs a discrete abstraction $Temp^j$ corresponding to the relaxed linear hybrid automata H_i^j. This step involves making calls to the underlying reachability engine like PHAVer [2]. Both the above steps are identical to the corresponding steps in the IRA algorithm [5] and are not discussed here for brevity.
2. Each computational node sends to the master the discrete abstraction $Temp^j$ which it learnt from the relaxed linear hybrid automata H_i^j. The master node updates the discrete *global abstraction* A_{CE}^{i+1} by taking the intersection of the previous discrete *global abstraction* A_{CE}^i with all the newly learnt discrete abstractions $Temp^j$.
3. Then, the master uses partial order relation among the counter-examples A_{CE}^{i+1} to pick a set CE of N *non-redundant* counterexamples. The construction of partial order relation is detailed in Section 3.
4. The master node checks if the set of counterexamples CE is empty. If A_{CE}^{i+1} has no counterexamples, then no bad states are reachable in the system [5] and hence, it is declared to be safe. Otherwise, the master computational node forms a set of linear programs $\mathcal{C}$, where each linear program corresponds to one of the counterexamples in CE_{i+1}. This step is similar to the corresponding step in the IRA algorithm [5] and is discussed in [6].
5. The master node checks if any of the linear programs in $\mathcal{C}$ is feasible. In any of them, say C, is feasible, it stops and reports that the bad state is reachable [6] and reports the corresponding counterexample. If none of the linear programs is feasible, the master node finds the *irreducible infeasible subsets* (IIS) for each of the linear programs. The master node uses the support of the IIS as the choice for the next set of variables $\mathcal{I}_{i+1}$ which will be used to construct the relaxations. The master node communicates the set I_{i+1}^j to the jth client.

3 A Partial Order for Counterexamples and Relaxations

In order to make the distributed computation effective, it is essential that the various computational nodes do not solve equivalent reachability sub-problems. In particular, we want to make sure that the relaxed linear hybrid automata for the ith iteration H_i^j and H_i^k are different. We achieve this goal by making a suitable choice of counterexamples from the global abstraction A_{CE}^{i+1}. Before we present our algorithmic methods, we define some related notions. Our definitions of linear hybrid automata, relaxations and counterexamples are identical to those in literature [3,5]. Given a path ρ in a linear hybrid automata H, we can derive a set of corresponding linear constraints $Constraints(H, \rho)$ which is feasible if and only if the path is feasible. This construction [5,6] is omitted here.

Definition 1. Minimal Explanation for Infeasible Counterexamples : *Given a counterexample path ρ which is infeasible in a linear hybrid automata H but* *feasible in a relaxation H' of H, (i.e. $H' \sqsubseteq H$), a set of linear constraints $IIS(\rho)$ is said to be an irreducible infeasible subset (IIS) for ρ if and only if:*

- *$IIS(\rho) \subseteq Constraints(H, \rho)$ and $IIS(\rho)$ is not feasible.*
- *for any set S s.t. $S \subset IIS(\rho)$, S is feasible.*

The special basis [5] Var of the IIS of ρ is called a minimal explanation for the infeasible counterexample *and we write it as $Var(\rho, IIS(\rho))$.*

In the following, we assume that there exists a function $\mathcal{IIS}$ which maps each counterexample to a unique IIS.

Definition 2. Dominance of Counterexamples : *A counterexample ce is said to dominate a counterexample ce′ if and only if $Var(ce, \mathcal{IIS}(ce)) \subseteq Var(ce', \mathcal{IIS}(ce'))$. We write $ce \succeq ce'$.*

Definition 3. *Two counterexamples ce and ce′ are said to be equivalent iff $Var(ce, \mathcal{IIS}(ce)) = Var(ce', \mathcal{IIS}(ce'))$. Then, we say $ce \approx ce'$.*

The relaxations of hybrid automata form a partial order. We summarize our results based on this key observation in the following theorems. The proofs are presented in [4].

Theorem 1. *The dominance relation $\succeq$ among counterexamples is a partial order relation.*

Theorem 2. *Let H_{ce} be the relaxation of H w.r.t. $Var(ce, \mathcal{IIS}(ce))$ and $H_{ce'}$ be the relaxation of H w.r.t. $Var(ce', \mathcal{IIS}(ce'))$. If the counterexample ce dominates the counterexample ce′ i.e. $ce \succeq ce'$, then H_{ce} is a relaxation of $H_{ce'}$ i.e. $H_{ce} \sqsubseteq H_{ce'}$.*

The algorithm *Select_CE* presented below for selecting N counterexamples is based on the above results.

Algorithm *Select_CE*
Input: Global Abstraction Automata A^i_{CE}, LHA H, a timer TIMEOUT.
Output: N counterexamples: $CE = \{ce_1, \ldots ce_N\}$
1. Initialize CE to be the empty set.
2. Pick a set of m ($> N$) distinct counterexamples $C = \{ce_1, ce_2 \ldots ce_m\}$ from A^i_{CE}.
3. Build a set of linear programs $\{lp_1, lp_2 \ldots lp_m\}$ corresponding to each of $\{ce_1, ce_2 \ldots ce_m\}$
4. For each (infeasible) linear program lp_i, obtain an IIS and remember it as $\mathcal{IIS}(lp_i)$
5. For each counterexample $ce_i \in C$,
   a. Check whether there exists a counterexample $ce_j \in C$ such that $ce_j \succeq ce_i$ $(i \neq j)$.
   b. If no such counterexample ce_j exists, add ce_i to CE.
   c. Remove ce_i from C.
6. If ($|CE| < N$ *and* $!TIMEOUT$) , $m = m \times 2$; goto step 2.
7. RETURN the first N members of CE as a set.

Table 1. Distributed IRA vs IRA

Example	♯-Variables	Time for d-IRA [s]	Time for IRA [s]	Speedup
ACC-4	4	11	15	1.36
ACC-8	8	100	192	1.92
ACC-16	16	1057	3839	3.63
ACC-19	19	2438	9752	**4.0**

4 Failure Tolerance of d-IRA

Resistance to Failures and Restarts of Slave Nodes: This is possible because the slave nodes do not store any global state information during the distributed computation and hence, the overall distributed reachability computation is robust to failure of slave nodes. If the ith slave node fails during the jth iteration, then the d-IRA algorithm can still proceed by making the assumption that $L(Temp_i) = \Sigma^*$.

Tolerance to Failure of Master Node: The current state of the distributed computation is really captured completely by the global abstraction A^i_{CE} after the ith iteration. It is hence desirable to back-up the global abstraction to a group of *shadow masters* during periods of low communication activity.

5 Experimental Results and Conclusion

We implemented a version of our distributed algorithm using the IRA infrastructure which parallelized only the relaxation step. We found up to a 4-X improvement runtime on our four processor machine[1] with this implementation on a set of parameterized adaptive cruise control examples [5]. .

References

1. Clarke, J.E.M., Grumberg, O., Peled, D.A.: Model Checking. MIT Press, Cambridge, MA, USA (1999)
2. Frehse, G.: PHAVer: Algorithmic Verification of Hybrid Systems Past HyTech. In: Morari, M., Thiele, L. (eds.) HSCC 2005. LNCS, vol. 3414, pp. 258–273. Springer, Heidelberg (2005)
3. Ho, P.-H.: Automatic Analysis of Hybrid Systems, Ph.D. thesis, technical report CSD-TR95-1536, Cornell University, pages 188 (August 1995)
4. Jha, S.K.: Design of a distributed reachability algorithm for analysis of linear hybrid automata. CoRR, abs/0710.3764 (2007)
5. Jha, S.K., Krogh, B.H., Weimer, J.E., Clarke, E.M.: Reachability for linear hybrid automata using iterative relaxation abstraction. In: Bemporad, A., Bicchi, A., Buttazzo, G. (eds.) HSCC 2007. LNCS, vol. 4416, pp. 287–300. Springer, Heidelberg (2007)
6. Li, X., Jha, S.K., Bu, L.: Towards an Efficient Path-Oriented Tool for Bounded Reachability analysis of Linear Hybrid Systems using Linear Programming. In: BMC (2006)

[1] We ran our experiments on a four processor 64-bit AMD Opteron(tm) 844 SMP machine running Red Hat Linux version 2.6.19.1-001-K8.

Sufficient Conditions for Zeno Behavior in Lagrangian Hybrid Systems

Andrew Lamperski and Aaron D. Ames

Control and Dynamical Systems
California Institute of Technology, Pasadena, CA 91125
{andyl,ames}@cds.caltech.edu

Abstract. This paper presents easily verifiable sufficient conditions for the existence of Zeno behavior in Lagrangian hybrid systems, i.e., hybrid systems modeling mechanical systems undergoing impacts.

1 Introduction

This paper is motivated by the lack of analytic tools for proving the existence of Zeno behavior in nontrivial hybrid systems. In particular, mechanical systems undgergoing impacts, modeled by Lagrangian hybrid systems [3], provide a large class of systems that often appear to display Zeno behavior. While Zeno behavior is often intuitively clear and supported with simulation results [2], formal proofs of Zeno behavior have been limited to very simple systems, e.g., the bouncing ball.

To study Zeno behavior, we consider *Zeno equilibria*—subsets of the continuous domains of a hybrid system that are fixed points of the discrete dynamics but not the continuous dynamics—which are defined in analogy to equilibria of dynamical systems. Given the success of studying isolated equilibria in dynamical systems, a natural starting point to the study of Zeno behavior is a detailed analysis of *isolated Zeno equilibria*—those Zeno equilibria with no other nearby Zeno equilibria. Recently, however, it was observed that Lagrangian hybrid systems with isolated Zeno equilibria must have one dimensional configuration manifolds [6]. Most Lagrangian hybrid systems of interest, however, have higher dimension configuration manifolds. Thus a large set of systems believed to show Zeno behavior cannot be adequately studied with attention restricted to isolated Zeno equilibria.

These observations motivate the main result of this paper: sufficient conditions for Zeno behavior in Lagrangian hybrid systems with configuration spaces of arbitrary dimension. These conditions for Lagrangian hybrid systems generalize those in [6], but remain remarkably simple. When applied to examples, such as a ball bouncing on a sinusoidal surface or a pendulum on a cart, the conditions for Zeno behavior are easily verifiable and intuitively appealing.

This work complements other work on Zeno, including [7], [4] and [5].

M. Egerstedt and B. Mishra (Eds.): HSCC 2008, LNCS 4981, pp. 622–625, 2008.

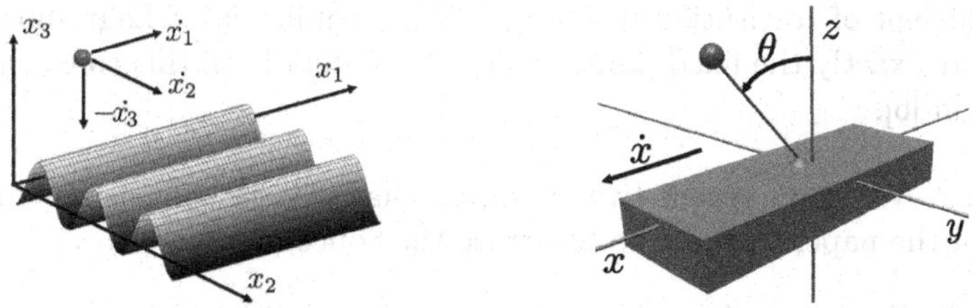

Fig. 1. Ball bouncing on a sinusoidal surface (left). Pendulum on a cart (right).

2 Simple Hybrid Mechanical Systems

Mechanical systems undergoing impacts are naturally modeled as hybrid systems. In this section, we will consider hybrid systems of this form and recall how one obtains such systems from hybrid Lagrangians, which are the hybrid analogue of Lagrangians. For more on hybrid Lagrangians and Lagrangian hybrid systems, see [1].

Due to space constraints, we are unable to formally define hybrid systems, executions and Zeno equilibria. We will use the definitions and notation from [6] unchanged to avoid any confusion.

Hybrid Lagrangians and Lagrangian Hybrid Systems. In the context of smooth mechanical systems, one begins with a Lagrangian $L : T\Theta \to \mathbb{R}$ on a configuration space Θ and associates to this Lagrangian a dynamical system:

$$M(\theta)\ddot{\theta} + C(\theta, \dot{\theta})\dot{\theta} + N(\theta) = 0,$$

through the Euler-Lagrange equations. Similarly, in the context of mechanical systems undergoing impacts, one begins with a *hybrid Lagrangian* and associates to this a *Lagrangian hybrid system*. In particular, consider the following:

Definition 1. *A hybrid Lagrangian is a tuple* $\mathbf{L} = (\Theta, L, h)$, *where* $\Theta \subset \mathbb{R}^n$ *is the configuration space,* $L : T\Theta \to \mathbb{R}$ *is a Lagrangian, and* $h : \Theta \to \mathbb{R}$ *is a unilateral constraint function. We assume that* 0 *is a regular value of* h.

Given a hybrid Lagrangian $\mathbf{L} = (\Theta, L, h)$, the *Lagrangian hybrid system associated to* $\mathbf{L}$ is the hybrid system

$$\mathscr{H}_{\mathbf{L}} = (\Gamma = (\{q\}, \{(q, q)\}), D_{\mathbf{L}}, G_{\mathbf{L}}, R_{\mathbf{L}}, F_{\mathbf{L}}),$$

where Γ is a graph with one node and one edge, $D_{\mathbf{L}} = \{D_h\}$ and $G_{\mathbf{L}} = \{G_h\}$ are given by

$$D_h = \{(\theta, \dot{\theta}) \in T\Theta : h(\theta) \geq 0\}, \quad G_h = \{(\theta, \dot{\theta}) \in D_h : h(\theta) = 0,\ dh(\theta)\dot{\theta} \leq 0\},$$

$F_{\mathbf{L}} = \{f_L\}$ is the vector field obtained from the Lagrangian L, and $R_{\mathbf{L}} = \{R_h\}$ with $R_h(\theta, \dot{\theta}) = (\theta, P(\theta, \dot{\theta}))$, where

$$P(\theta, \dot{\theta}) = \dot{\theta} - (1 + e)\frac{dh(\theta)\dot{\theta}}{dh(\theta)M(\theta)^{-1}dh(\theta)^T} M(\theta)^{-1} dh(\theta)^T, \tag{1}$$

with coefficient of restitution $0 \leq e \leq 1$. Zeno equilibria of Lagrangian hybrid systems are exactly the fixed points of R_h. More details on this construction can be found in [6].

Examples. We now present two examples that will be considered throughout the rest of the paper in order to illustrate the concepts involved.

Example 1 (Ball). Our first running example is a ball bouncing on a sinusoidal surface (cf. Fig. 1). In this case $\mathbf{B} = (\Theta_{\mathbf{B}}, L_{\mathbf{B}}, h_{\mathbf{B}})$, where $\Theta_{\mathbf{B}} = \mathbb{R}^3$, and for $x = (x_1, x_2, x_3)$,

$$L_{\mathbf{B}}(x, \dot{x}) = \frac{1}{2} m \|\dot{x}\|^2 - mgx_3, \qquad h_{\mathbf{B}}(x_1, x_2, x_3) = x_3 - \sin(x_2).$$

From this hybrid Lagrangian, one obtains a Lagrangian hybrid system $\mathscr{H}_{\mathbf{B}}$.

Example 2 (Cart). Our second running example is a constrained pendulum on a cart (cf. Fig. 1); this is a variation on the classical pendulum on a cart, where the pendulum is not allowed to "pass through" the cart. In this case $\mathbf{C} = (\Theta_{\mathbf{C}}, L_{\mathbf{C}}, h_{\mathbf{C}})$, where $\Theta_{\mathbf{C}} = \mathbb{S}^1 \times \mathbb{R}$, $q = (\theta, x)$, and

$$L_{\mathbf{C}}(\theta, \dot{\theta}, x, \dot{x}) = \frac{1}{2} \begin{pmatrix} \dot{\theta} & \dot{x} \end{pmatrix} \begin{pmatrix} mR^2 & mR\cos(\theta) \\ mR\cos(\theta) & M + m \end{pmatrix} \begin{pmatrix} \dot{\theta} \\ \dot{x} \end{pmatrix} - mgR\cos(\theta).$$

where m is the mass of the pendulum, M is the mass of the cart and R is the length of the pendulum. Finally, the constraint $h_{\mathbf{C}}(\theta, x) = \cos(\theta)$ ensures that the pendulum cannot pass through the cart. One obtains a Lagrangian hybrid system $\mathscr{H}_{\mathbf{C}}$ from the hybrid Lagrangian $\mathbf{C}$.

3 Sufficient Conditions for Zeno Behavior in Lagrangian Hybrid Systems

In this section, we present sufficient conditions for the existence of Zeno behavior in Lagrangian hybrid systems. Before presenting this conditions, we characterize Zeno equilibria in systems of this form.

Zeno equilibria in Lagrangian hybrid systems. If $\mathscr{H}_{\mathbf{L}}$ is a Lagrangian hybrid system, then due to the special form of these systems we find that the point $z = \{(\theta^*, \dot{\theta}^*)\}$ is a Zeno equilibria iff $\dot{\theta}^* = P(\theta, \dot{\theta}^*)$, with P given in (1). In particular, the special form of P implies that this holds iff $dh(\theta^*)\dot{\theta}^* = 0$. Therefore the set of all Zeno equilibria for a Lagrangian hybrid system is given by the hypersurfaces in G_h:

$$Z = \{(\theta, \dot{\theta}) \in G_h : dh(\theta)\dot{\theta} = 0\}.$$

Note that if $\dim(\Theta) > 1$, the Zeno equilibria in Lagrangian hybrid systems are always non-isolated (see [6])—this motivates the study of such equilibria.

Theorem 1. *Let $\mathscr{H}_{\mathbf{L}}$ be a Lagrangian hybrid system and Let $z = \{(\theta^*, \dot{\theta}^*)\}$ be a Zeno equilibria of $\mathscr{H}_{\mathbf{L}}$. If $0 < e < 1$ and*

$$\ddot{h}(\theta^*, \dot{\theta}^*) = (\dot{\theta}^*)^T H(h(\theta^*))\dot{\theta}^* + dh(\theta^*)M(\theta^*)^{-1}(-C(\theta^*, \dot{\theta}^*)\dot{\theta}^* - N(\theta^*)) < 0,$$

where $H(h(\theta^*))$ is the Hessian of h at θ^*, then there is a neighborhood $W \subset D_h$ of $(\theta^*, \dot{\theta}^*)$ such that for every $(\theta, \dot{\theta}) \in W$, there is a unique Zeno execution χ of $\mathscr{H}_{\mathbf{L}}$ with $c_0(\tau_0) = (\theta, \dot{\theta})$.

Example 3 (Ball). We first demonstrate that the hybrid system $\mathscr{H}_{\mathbf{B}}$ modeling a ball bouncing on a sinusoidal surface is Zeno. First, the Zeno equilibria of this system are given by the set

$$Z = \{(x, \dot{x}) \in G_{h_{\mathbf{B}}} : \dot{x}_3 - \dot{x}_2 \cos(x_2) = 0\}.$$

Now, one can easily verify that for $(x^*, \dot{x}^*) \in Z$

$$\ddot{h}_{\mathbf{B}}(x^*, \dot{x}^*) = \sin(x_2)\dot{x}_2^2 - g.$$

Therefore, there are clearly Zeno equilibria satisfying the conditions of Theorem 1, namely when $\dot{x}_2$ is small, and thus $\mathscr{H}_{\mathbf{B}}$ is Zeno.

Example 4 (Cart). We now demonstrate that the hybrid system modeling a pendulum on a cart, $\mathscr{H}_{\mathbf{C}}$, is Zeno. First, note that the Zeno equilibria are given by the set:

$$Z = \{(\theta, x, \dot{\theta}, \dot{x}) \in G_{h_{\mathbf{C}}} : \sin(\theta)\dot{\theta} = 0\},$$

and for $(\theta^*, x^*, \dot{\theta}^*, \dot{x}^*) \in Z$,

$$\ddot{h}_{\mathbf{C}}(\theta^*, x^*, \dot{\theta}^*, \dot{x}^*) = -\frac{g}{R} < 0.$$

Therefore, for every Zeno equilibria of the pendulum on a cart there a neighborhood of the Zeno equilibria such that every execution with an initial condition in that neighborhood is Zeno.

References

1. Ames, A.D.: A Categorical Theory of Hybrid Systems. PhD thesis, University of California, Berkeley (2006)
2. Ames, A.D., Zheng, H., Gregg, R.D., Sastry, S.: Is there life after Zeno? Taking executions past the breaking (Zeno) point. In: 25th American Control Conference, Minneapolis, MN (2006)
3. Brogliato, B.: Nonsmooth Mechanics. Springer, Heidelberg (1999)
4. Camlibel, M.K., Schumacher, J.M.: On the Zeno behavior of linear complementarity systems. In: 40th IEEE Conference on Decision and Control (2001)
5. Heymann, M., Lin, F., Meyer, G., Resmerita, S.: Analysis of Zeno behaviors in a class of hybrid systems. IEEE Transactions on Automatic Control 50(3), 376–384 (2005)
6. Lamperski, A., Ames, A.D.: Lyapunov-like conditions for the existence of Zeno behavior in hybrid and Lagrangian hybrid systems. In: IEEE Conference on Decision and Control (2007)
7. Zhang, J., Johansson, K.H., Lygeros, J., Sastry, S.: Zeno hybrid systems. Int. J. Robust and Nonlinear Control 11(2), 435–451 (2001)

Separation in Stability Analysis of Piecewise Linear Systems in Discrete Time

Ji-Woong Lee

Department of Electrical Engineering
Pennsylvania State University
University Park, PA 16802
jiwoong@psu.edu

Abstract. Stability analysis of piecewise linear systems, without affine terms, consists of the problem of finding maximal stabilizing sets of switching paths among possible system coefficients and that of obtaining a sequence of state-space partitions in the order of increasing refinement. Exploiting the fact that these two problems can be solved separately, one can find subsets of the state space such that the piecewise linear system restricted to these sets is uniformly exponentially stable.

1 Introduction

Successful analysis of the stability of a piecewise linear system hinges on one's ability to construct an appropriate Lyapunov function. Common approaches involve piecewise quadratic Lyapunov functions [1,2,3,4] and piecewise higher-order polynomial Lyapunov functions [5,6]. However, these approaches are conservative because only a subset of all asymptotically stable piecewise linear systems admits these types of Lyapunov functions.

We focus on discrete-time piecewise linear systems under a polyhedral partition of the state space but without affine terms, and propose that the problem of determining the asymptotic stability of such a system be divided into two separate problems. The first problem draws on the recent characterization of all uniformly stabilizing sets of switching sequences [7]. To obtain stabilizing switching sequences, it suffices to obtain so-called maximal admissible sets of switching paths of length L over $L = 0, 1, \ldots$. These sets are independent of the switching structure imposed by the underlying state-dependent switching among different system coefficients, and associated with each of them is a switching-path-dependent quadratic Lyapunov function. On the other hand, the second problem is to obtain all admissible polyhedral partitions of depth L over $L = 0, 1, \ldots$. The task here is to explore the underlying switching structure of the system by obtaining an increasing family of state-space partitions. This task can be done regardless of how each state-space partition affects the form of the Lyapunov function. Combining these two problems leads to a novel stability analysis method for piecewise linear systems.

M. Egerstedt and B. Mishra (Eds.): HSCC 2008, LNCS 4981, pp. 626–629, 2008.

2 Problem Formulation

Let $\mathcal{A} = \{\mathbf{A}_1, \ldots, \mathbf{A}_N\}$ with $\mathbf{A}_1, \ldots, \mathbf{A}_N \in \mathbb{R}^{n\times n}$. Let $\mathcal{D} = \{D_1, \ldots, D_N\}$ be a partition of $\mathbb{R}^n$ (i.e., $\bigcup_{i=1}^{N} D_i = \mathbb{R}^n$ and $D_i \cap D_j = \varnothing$ whenever $i \neq j$). Then the pair $(\mathcal{A}, \mathcal{D})$ defines the discrete-time piecewise linear system represented by

$$\mathbf{x}(t+1) = \mathbf{A}_{\theta(t)}\mathbf{x}(t) \tag{1}$$

with $\theta(t) = \{i\colon \mathbf{x}(t) \in D_i\}$ for $t = 0, 1, \ldots$.

Definition 1. *Let $C \subset \mathbb{R}^n$. The pair $(\mathcal{A}, \mathcal{D})$ is said to be C-*uniformly exponentially stable *if there exist $c \geq 1$ and $\lambda \in (0,1)$ such that*

$$\|\mathbf{x}(t)\| \leq c\lambda^{t-t_0}\|\mathbf{x}(t_0)\| \tag{2}$$

for all t_0, $t \in \{0, 1, \ldots\}$ with $t \geq t_0$ and for all $\mathbf{x}(t_0) \in C$.

Given a pair $(\mathcal{A}, \mathcal{D})$, our stability analysis problem is *to determine a (maximal) set $C \subset \mathbb{R}^n$ such that the pair $(\mathcal{A}, \mathcal{D})$ is C-uniformly exponentially stable.*

3 Two Separate Problems

The first problem is to find maximal admissible sets of switching paths. Let $\Theta \subset \{1, \ldots, N\}^\infty$ be nonempty. The pair $(\mathcal{A}, \Theta)$ defines the discrete-time switched linear system represented by (1) over all $(\theta(0), \theta(1), \ldots) \in \Theta$. Searching for all Θ such that the pair $(\mathcal{A}, \Theta)$ is uniformly exponentially stable amounts to finding (the countable family of) all $\mathcal{A}$-maximal sets [7]. We shall write $\mathbf{X} < \mathbf{0}$ to mean that $\mathbf{X}$ is symmetric and negative definite. To simplify notation, set $(i_j, \ldots, i_k) = 0$ if $j > k$, and set $\{1, \ldots, N\}^0 = \{0\}$.

Definition 2. *The pair $(\mathcal{A}, \Theta)$ is said to be* uniformly exponentially stable *if there exist $c \geq 1$ and $\lambda \in (0,1)$ such that (2) holds for all t_0, $t \in \{0, 1, \ldots\}$ with $t \geq t_0$, for all $\mathbf{x}(t_0) \in \mathbb{R}^n$, and for all $(\theta(0), \theta(1), \ldots) \in \Theta$.*

Definition 3. *Let L be a nonnegative integer. Elements of $\{1, \ldots, N\}^{L+1}$ are called L-*paths*. A nonempty set $\mathcal{N}$ of L-paths is said to be $\mathcal{A}$-*admissible *if, for each $(i_0, \ldots, i_L) \in \mathcal{N}$, there exist an integer $M > L$ and a $(i_{L+1}, \ldots, i_M) \in \{1, \ldots, N\}^{M-L}$ such that $(i_{M-L}, \ldots, i_M) = (i_0, \ldots, i_L)$ and $(i_t, \ldots, i_{t+L}) \in \mathcal{N}$ for $0 \leq t \leq M-L$, and if there exist matrices $\mathbf{X}_{(j_1, \ldots, j_L)} > \mathbf{0}$ such that*

$$\mathbf{A}_{i_L}^{\mathrm{T}}\mathbf{X}_{(i_1, \ldots, i_L)}\mathbf{A}_{i_L} - \mathbf{X}_{(i_0, \ldots, i_{L-1})} < \mathbf{0} \tag{3}$$

*for all L-paths $(i_0, \ldots, i_L) \in \mathcal{N}$. Moreover, if the only $\mathcal{A}$-admissible $\widetilde{\mathcal{N}}$ with $\widetilde{\mathcal{N}} \subset \mathcal{N}$ (resp. $\mathcal{N} \subset \widetilde{\mathcal{N}}$) is $\mathcal{N}$ itself, then $\mathcal{N}$ is called $\mathcal{A}$-*minimal *(resp. $\mathcal{A}$-*maximal*).*

Lemma 4. [7] *There exists a nonempty $\Theta \subset \Omega$ such that the pair $(\mathcal{A}, \Theta)$ is uniformly exponentially stable if and only if there exist an integer $L \geq 0$ and an $\mathcal{A}$-admissible $\mathcal{N} \subset \{1, \ldots, N\}^{L+1}$. Associated with each $\mathcal{A}$-minimal $\mathcal{N}$ is a periodic $\theta = (\theta(0), \theta(1), \ldots)$ such that $(\mathcal{A}, \{\theta\})$ is uniformly exponentially stable.*

The second problem is to generate a countable family of partitions of the state space in the order of increasing refinement. Each of these partitions are made according to the switching structure that the underlying state-dependence of the switching sequence dictates. Define sets $D_{(i_0,\dots,i_L)} \subset \mathbb{R}^n$ recursively by

$$D_{(i_0,\dots,i_{L+1})} = \{\mathbf{x} \in D_{(i_0,\dots,i_L)} \colon \mathbf{A}_{i_0}\mathbf{x} \in D_{(i_1,\dots,i_{L+1})}\}$$

for $L = 0, 1, \dots$ and for $(i_0, \dots, i_L) \in \{1, \dots, N\}^{L+1}$. Then, for each L, the indexed family $\{D_{(i_0,\dots,i_L)} \colon (i_0, \dots, i_L) \in \{1, \dots, N\}^{L+1}\}$ defines a partition of $\mathbb{R}^n$, which we shall call an *L-path partition* of $\mathbb{R}^n$.

4 Proposed Algorithm for Stability Analysis

We propose that the stability analysis formulated in Section 2 be tackled by combining the two decoupled problems described in Section 3. Suppose we have solved the two problems described above. Let us fix a nonnegative integer L, and suppose that $\mathcal{D}_L$ and $\mathcal{D}_{L+1}$ are the L-path partition and $(L+1)$-path partition of the state space. Partition $\mathcal{D}_{L+1}$ is finer than $\mathcal{D}_L$ and enables one to construct a switching sequence as follows: given a nonempty $D_{(i_0,\dots,i_L)} \in \mathcal{D}_L$, let $\theta(0) = i_0$, $\dots$, $\theta(L) = i_L$; if there exists a nonempty $D_{(i_0,\dots,i_L,i_{L+1})} \in \mathcal{D}_{L+1}$, then let $\theta(L+1) = i_{L+1}$; if there exists a nonempty $D_{(i_1,\dots,i_{L+1},i_{L+2})} \in \mathcal{D}_{L+1}$, then let $\theta(L+2) = i_{L+2}$; and so on. Any switching sequence that can be constructed this way generates an infinite chain of L-paths, which we shall call a *chain of L-paths generated by $D_{(i_0,\dots,i_L)}$ and $\mathcal{D}_{L+1}$*. The following is immediate by construction:

Lemma 5. *Let $D_{(i_0,\dots,i_L)} \in \mathcal{D}_L$. If each chain of L-paths generated by $D_{(i_0,\dots,i_L)}$ and $\mathcal{D}_{L+1}$ has a limit set that is contained in an $\mathcal{A}$-maximal set of L-paths, then the piecewise linear system $(\mathcal{A}, \mathcal{D})$ is $D_{(i_0,\dots,i_L)}$-uniformly exponentially stable.*

This lemma suggests an algorithm to generate a nested sequence $C_0 \subset C_1 \subset \cdots$ such that the pair $(\mathcal{A}, \mathcal{D})$ is C_i-uniformly exponentially stable for each i:

Step 0. Set $C_{-1} = \varnothing$; set $L = 0$.
Step 1. Obtain the partition $\mathcal{D}_{L+1}$ of the state space.
Step 2. Obtain $\mathcal{A}$-maximal sets of L-paths.
Step 3. Let C_L be the union of C_{L-1} and all $D_{(i_0,\dots,i_L)}$ such that each chain of L-paths generated by $D_{(i_0,\dots,i_L)}$ and $\mathcal{D}_{L+1}$ has a limit set that is contained in an $\mathcal{A}$-maximal set of L-paths.
Step 4. Increment L to $L + 1$; go to Step 1.

For example, if $N = 2$ and if $\mathcal{A}$ and $\mathcal{D}$ have

$$\mathbf{A}_1 = \begin{bmatrix} 0 & 0 \\ -1/2 & 3/2 \end{bmatrix}, \quad \mathbf{A}_2 = \begin{bmatrix} 1/2 & 1 \\ -1 & 1/2 \end{bmatrix}; \quad \begin{cases} \mathbf{D}_1 = \{[x_1\ x_2]^{\mathrm{T}} \in \mathbb{R}^2 \colon x_1 \geq x_2\}, \\ \mathbf{D}_2 = \{[x_1\ x_2]^{\mathrm{T}} \in \mathbb{R}^2 \colon x_1 < x_2\}, \end{cases}$$

then the algorithm gives us $C_0 = C_1 = C_2 = \varnothing$, $C_3 = D_{1212} \cup D_{2121} \cup D_{2212}$, and $C_4 = C_5 = \cdots = D_{1212} \cup D_{2121} \cup D_{2212} \cup D_{22212}$. In this particular example, the

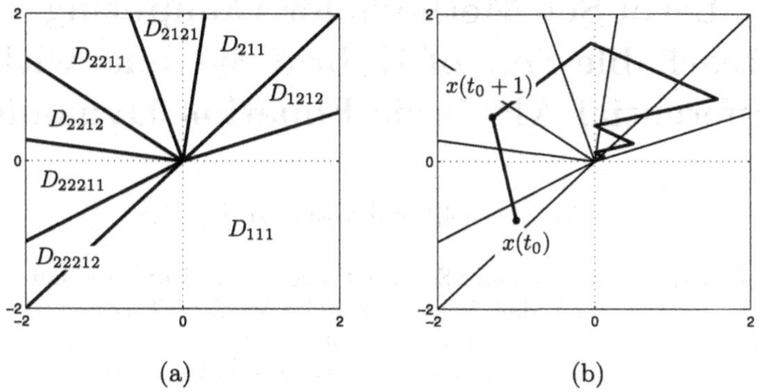

Fig. 1. Illustrative example. (a) the four-path partition of the state space. (b) a typical state trajectory converging to the origin.

process of iteratively partitioning the state space terminates at the path length of $L = 4$ since none of the states in $\mathbb{R}^2 \setminus C_4$ converges to the origin. The stability of the pair $(\mathcal{A}, \mathcal{D})$ can be completely assessed using the four-path partition given by Fig. 1(a); a typical state trajectory that starts in C_4 is depicted in Fig. 1(b).

5 Conclusion

A novel stability analysis method was proposed based on the fact that the task of characterizing all stabilizing sets of switching sequences can be done independently of that of successively refining the partition of the state space. Questions to be answered regarding the algorithm presented in Section 4 are as follows: (a) Is $C_\infty = \lim_{i\to\infty} C_i$ maximal? (b) Under what condition, do we have $C_\infty = \mathbb{R}^n$? (c) Under what condition, do we have $C_\infty = C_L$ for some finite L?

References

1. Hassibi, A., Boyd, S.: Quadratic stabilization and control of piecewise-linear systems. In: Proc. IEEE Amer. Contr. Conf (1998)
2. Johansson, M., Rantzer, A.: Computation of piecewise quadratic Lyapunov functions for hybrid systems. IEEE Trans. Automat. Control 43(4), 555–559 (1998)
3. Feng, G.: Stability analysis of piecewise discrete-time linear systems. IEEE Trans. Automat. Control 47(7), 1108–1112 (2002)
4. Ferrari-Trecate, G., Cuzzola, F.A., Mignone, D., Morari, M.: Analysis of discrete-time piecewise affine and hybrid systems. Automatica 38(12), 2139–2146 (2002)
5. Prajna, S., Papachristodoulou, A.: Analysis of switched and hybrid systems—beyond piecewise quadratic methods. In: Proc. IEEE Amer. Contr. Conf. (2003)
6. Biswas, P., Grieder, P., Löfberg, J., Morari, M.: A survey on stability analysis of discrete-time piecewise affine systems. In: Proc. 16th IFAC World Congress (2005)
7. Lee, J.W., Dullerud, G.E.: Uniformly stabilizing sets of switching sequences for switched linear systems. IEEE Trans. Automat. Control 52(5), 868–874 (2007)

Level Set Methods for Computing Reachable Sets of Hybrid Systems with Differential Algebraic Equation Dynamics

Ian M. Mitchell[1] and Yoshihiko Susuki[2]

[1] Department of Computer Science, University of British Columbia,
2366 Main Mall, Vancouver, BC, Canada V6T 1Z4
mitchell@cs.ubc.ca
http://www.cs.ubc.ca/~mitchell

[2] Department of Electrical Engineering, Kyoto University,
Katsura, Nishikyo, Kyoto, Japan 615–8510
susuki@dove.kuee.kyoto-u.ac.jp
http://www-lab23.kuee.kyoto-u.ac.jp/susuki

Abstract. In previous work we demonstrated that reachability algorithms using level set methods and based on the Hamilton-Jacobi PDE can be adapted to systems whose dynamics are described by differential algebraic equations. Here we extend those results to hybrid systems. The only significant addition required is a mechanism for handling the state reset that occurs during discrete jumps between modes. We demonstrate the technique on a nonlinear power system voltage safety problem.

1 Introduction

The reachable set or tube is an effective tool for verification, but it can rarely be determined exactly for hybrid or continuous systems. Many approximate reachability algorithms have been proposed, and we refer to [1] and the citations within for further discussion of such algorithms. A central assumption of virtually all algorithms has been that the continuous dynamics of the system are modeled by ordinary differential equations (ODEs). The differential algebraic equation (DAE) is a generalization of the ODE, and in previous work [2] we described how to adapt reachability algorithms based on level set methods and the Hamilton-Jacobi (HJ) partial differential equation (PDE) to approximate the backwards reachable tube for continuous systems modeled by DAEs. Here we demonstrate how to extend the algorithm to hybrid systems in which DAEs drive the continuous dynamics through a hybrid version of the nonlinear power system voltage safety scenario. We do not have room in this brief paper to provide all of the details, but code containing those details and recreating the results below can be found at [3].

Given a system state space $\mathbb{S}$ and a set of known unsafe states $T \subset \mathbb{S}$, we seek to approximate the backwards reachable tube

$$B(T, [0,t]) \triangleq \{x_0 \in \mathbb{S} \mid \exists \hat{x} \in T, \exists s \in [0,t], x(s) = \hat{x}\},$$

M. Egerstedt and B. Mishra (Eds.): HSCC 2008, LNCS 4981, pp. 630–633, 2008.

where $x(\cdot)$ is a trajectory of the system starting at $x(0) = x_0$. For systems whose continuous trajectories are specified by ODEs, we described in [4] how the reachable tube for some fixed t can be implicitly defined as $B(T, [0, t]) = \{x \in \mathbb{S} \mid \phi(x) \leq 0\}$, where $\phi : \mathbb{S} \to \mathbb{R}$ is the viscosity solution of an HJ PDE (if t may vary, ϕ will depend on t). The method is extended to continuous systems specified by index one DAEs in [2].

We will not address here the theoretical questions that arise when substituting DAEs for ODEs in a hybrid automata (HA) model, and therefore avoid a formal HA definition. The primary computational challenge of extending the procedure from [2] to a hybrid setting is the implicitly defined jump that occurs in the continuous state when a discrete mode switch causes a change in the governing DAE. We describe below how to convert this implicit jump into an explicit reset map, and then how to map the implicit surface representation of the reach tube ϕ through this reset.

2 Mapping the Reachable Tube across Mode Jumps

In a DAE model the standard ODE $\dot{x}(s) = f(x(s))$ is replaced by a coupled set of differential and algebraic equations. We focus on index one DAEs which can be written in semi-explicit form as

$$\dot{y}(s) = f_{\mathbb{D}}(y(s), z(s); p) \tag{1}$$

$$0 = g(y(s), z(s); p) \tag{2}$$

where the state $x = (y, z)$ is divided into differential variables y and algebraic variables z, and p are some known parameters. In a hybrid system with modes denoted by variable q, the parameters will depend on the mode $p = p(q)$. Under appropriate conditions, such DAEs can be understood as the ODE (1) evolving on the constraint manifold $C(p) = \{(y, z) \mid g(y, z; p) = 0\}$. We described two procedures for approximating the reachable tube of a continuous system modeled by (1)–(2) in [2]. In the hybrid system extension, either procedure may be used for the continuous evolution of the reachable tube.

Consider now the effect of a discrete jump in the HA from a mode q^- with parameters $p^- = p(q^-)$ to a mode q^+ with parameters $p^+ = p(q^+)$. As we are working with backwards reachability, we assume that an implicit representation of the backwards reachable tube is available for mode q^+ in the form $\phi^+(x)$, and we wish to find a representation for mode q^- in the form $\phi^-(x)$ (after which continuous evolution in mode q^- will begin). We seek a reset mapping $x^+ = \rho(x^-, p^-, p^+)$ so that we can construct $\phi^-(x) = \phi^+(\rho(x, p^-, p^+))$.

In a standard HA this reset mapping ρ is given explicitly [4], but in the DAE model it is implicit. To determine ρ we assume that the constraint (2) arises in the limit $\epsilon \to 0$ from some "fast" dynamics given by the ODE $\epsilon \dot{z} = g(y, z; p)$. When a discrete mode switch causes a change in parameters such that $g(y^-, z^-; p^+) \neq 0$, we fix $y^+ = y^-$ (since y governed by (1) cannot react fast enough) and solve the ODE $\dot{z} = g(y^+, z; p^+)$ with initial condition $z(0) = z^-$ in auxiliary "fast" time to a fixpoint $\lim_{t \to \infty} z(t) = z^+$.

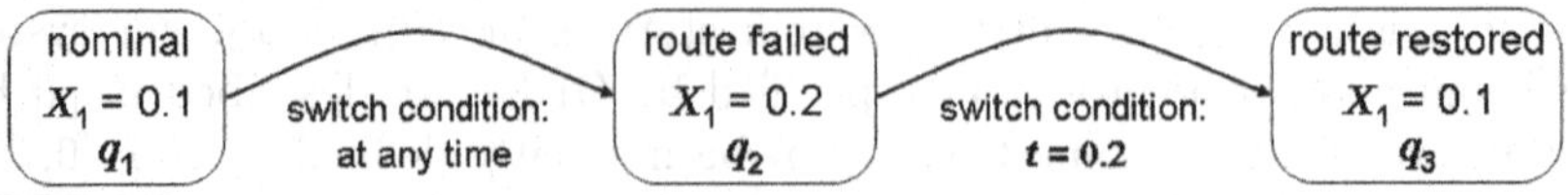

Fig. 1. Hybrid automaton for the example

3 Single Machine-Load Bus Example

We now demonstrate our reset mapping procedure on a concrete example. For the continuous dynamics, we use a three dimensional DAE model of a single machine-load bus from [5]. For lack of space we are forced to omit all of the details of the continuous model; the discussion that follows may not make much sense without first reading those details in [2]. All three state variables (E', E_f, E) are voltages. The state variables E' and E_f appear in the differential component of the DAE (they correspond to differential variable y), while the algebraic constraint relates E and E' (so E corresponds to algebraic variable z) in a manner dependent on a parameter $p = X_1$. Note that the prime is not a derivative—E' is a separate variable from E. The discrete component of the HA for the system is shown in figure 1; it and the safety analysis problem are adapted from [6], where interested readers can also find further discussion of related work on power system models.

In words, the HA in figure 1 describes a scenario in which the system starts in its nominal operating mode q_1 with two transmission routes and parameter $X_1 = 0.1$. An uncontrollable event may cause one route to fail at any time, and the system jumps into a single route mode q_2 with $X_1 = 0.2$. The failure is detected after a brief period (12 cycles at 60 Hertz is 0.2 seconds) and relays switch in a backup route to restore the system to its nominal parameter $X_1 = 0.1$ in mode q_3. The unsafe behaviour of the system is that the load bus voltage E may drop below a defined minimum value $E_c = 0.7$. The failure may occur due to continuous oscillations in the voltages and/or due to discrete voltage jumps when the number of transmission routes change.

Figure 2(a) shows samples of the reset mapping ρ for the q_1 to q_2 switch, as well as the constraint surfaces for the two values of X_1. The plot is in the E vs E' plane because the constraint does not depend on E_f. When working with level set methods, ϕ is stored on a discrete grid. Consequently, we only need to determine $\rho(x, p^-, p^+)$ where x is a node of the grid—a finite number of samples. We then use interpolation on ϕ^+ to construct a value for ϕ^-, since $\rho(x, p^-, p^+)$ will not generally be a node in the grid even if x is.

In [2] we approximated the set of states leading to continuous failure in the nominal operating mode q_1 without any switches (although we used a different value of parameter Q_0 in those calculations). Two algorithms were proposed: one that works on the constraint manifold and one that works in the full dimensional state space. We show only the former here, although the reset mapping procedure is easily extended to the latter. For our coordinate system on the constraint manifold we choose E and E_f, so the reachable tubes shown are essentially projections of the full dimensional reachable tubes onto these two variables. Figure 2(b) shows the results of the reachability analysis on the manifold.

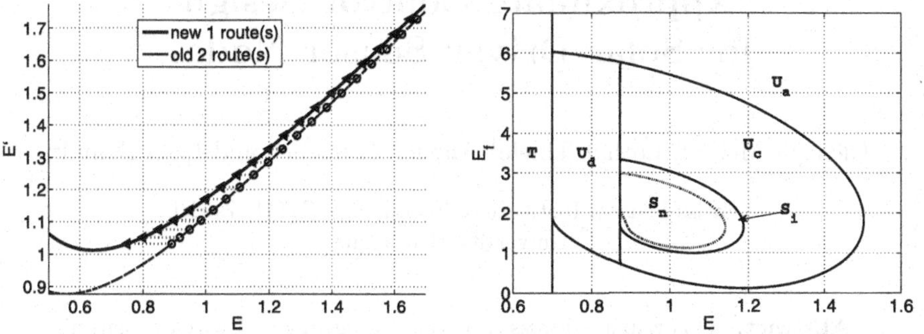

(a) The constraint surfaces $C(X_1)$ and samples of the reset mapping ρ. The reset mapping goes from states labeled by circles to states labeled by triangles.

(b) The reachability results for the example with parameter $Q_0 = 0.25P_m$ (if $Q_0 = 0.5P_m$ from [2] were used, there would be no safe states).

Fig. 2. Results for the example. Note that the vertical axes are different variables in the two plots. The sets labeled in the right subplot are: known unsafe target set T, states unsafe in the nominal mode with no discrete switching U_a, states that become unsafe during discrete switches U_d, states which become unsafe due to a combination of discrete and continuous evolution $U_c \cup S_i$, and safe states S_n for mode q_1 of the HA from figure 1. If there was no 12 cycle delay in detecting the route failure, the safe states would be $S_n \cup S_i$. If there was never a route failure (the situation examined in [2]), the safe states would be $S_n \cup S_i \cup U_c \cup U_d$.

References

1. Mitchell, I.M.: Comparing forward and backward reachability as tools for safety analysis. In: Bemporad, A., Bicchi, A., Buttazzo, G. (eds.) HSCC 2007. LNCS, vol. 4416, pp. 428–443. Springer, Heidelberg (2007)
2. Cross, E.A., Mitchell, I.M.: Level set methods for computing reachable sets of systems with differential algebraic equation dynamics. In: Proceedings of the American Control Conference, Seattle, WA (2008), `http://www.cs.ubc.ca/~mitchell/Papers/submittedReachDAE.pdf`
3. [Online], `http://www.cs.ubc.ca/~mitchell/ToolboxLS`
4. Tomlin, C., Mitchell, I., Bayen, A., Oishi, M.: Computational techniques for the verification of hybrid systems. Proceedings of the IEEE 91(7), 986–1001 (2003)
5. Venkatasubramanian, V., Schättler, H., Zaborszky, J.: Voltage dynamics: Study of a generator with voltage control, transmission, and matched MW load. IEEE Transactions on Automatic Control 37(11), 1717–1733 (1992)
6. Susuki, Y., Hikihara, T.: Predicting voltage instability of power system via hybrid system reachability analysis. In: Proceedings of the American Control Conference, New York, NY, pp. 4166–4171 (2007)

Approximate Control Design for Solar Driven Sensor Nodes

Clemens Moser[1], Lothar Thiele[1], Davide Brunelli[2], and Luca Benini[2]

[1] Swiss Federal Institute of Technology (ETH) Zurich
[2] University of Bologna

Abstract. This paper addresses power management of wireless sensor nodes which receive their energy from solar cells. In an outdoor environment, the future available energy is estimated and used as input to a receding horizon controller. We want to maximize the utility of the sensor application given the time-varying amount of solar energy. In order to avoid real-time optimization, we precompute off-line an explicit state feedback solution. However, it is a well-known problem of the optimal feedback solution that the computational complexity grows very quickly, which is particularly unfavourable for sensor nodes. A new method to derive approximate solutions to a multiparametric linear programming problem is presented. The resulting control laws substantially reduce the on-line complexity in terms of computational and storage demand. We show that a sensor node's performance is not necessary decreased due to suboptimality of the control design.

1 Introduction

Wireless sensor networks (WSN) have opened up an exciting field of research that is increasingly becoming popular nowadays. A WSN can be seen as a system of self-powered, wireless sensors which are able to detect and transmit events to a base station. Above all, sensor nodes are anticipated to be small and inexpensive devices which can be unobtrusively embedded in their environment. Thus, a sensor node's hardware is stringently limited in terms of computation, memory, communication as well as storable energy. These resource constraints limit the complexity of the software executed on a sensor node.

Recently, techniques to harvest energy via photovoltaic cells have received increasing attention in the sensor network community. A general approach to optimize the utilization of solar energy has been presented in [1]. The authors apply multiparametric linear programming to obtain a piecewise linear state feedback over a polyhedral partition of the state space. The optimization problem is basically solved off-line and look-up tables are stored and evaluated in the on-line case. For state explosions, which occur already for problems of moderate complexity, the limited storage capabilities of sensor nodes are quickly exceeded. Furthermore, the evaluation of the numerous states will cost considerable time as well as energy. In this paper, a new algorithm for approximate multiparametric linear programming is presented which generates much simpler look-up tables then the optimal solution. Another approximation method has been proposed, e.g., in [2].

M. Egerstedt and B. Mishra (Eds.): HSCC 2008, LNCS 4981, pp. 634–637, 2008.

2 System Model

We restrict ourselves to the discussion of an example application which is modeled by the hierarchical control model illustrated in Fig. 1. The same control model has been used in [3]. It is introduced here since it significantly improves the robustness compared to a system with only one estimation and one control unit. The linear programs underlying subcontroller 1 and 2 have to be solved repeatedly, yielding a receding horizon control (RHC) strategy. For a specification of the linear programs and a detailed description of the system dynamics, the reader is referred to [4]. Note that the capability to bypass the storage device is a typical feature of latest prototypes. It offers the opportunity to save substantial energy by using the solar energy directly when available.

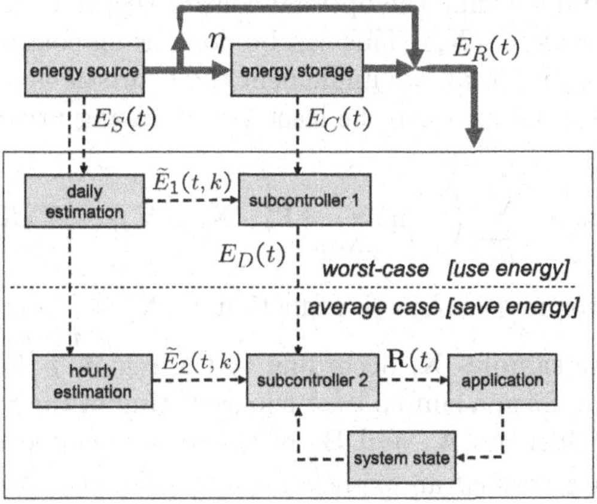

Fig. 1. Illustration of the hierarchical control model

3 Approximate Multiparametric Linear Programming

At first, we define a state vector $\mathbf{X}$ consisting of the actual system state, the level of the energy storage as well as the estimation of the incoming energy over the finite prediction horizon (cp. Fig.1). For subcontroller 1, e.g., the state vector $\mathbf{X}$ can be written as

$$\mathbf{X}(t) = \left(E_C(t)\,,\, \widetilde{E}_1(t,0)\,,\ldots,\widetilde{E}_1(t,N-1)\right)^T \tag{1}$$

where $\widetilde{E}_1(t,0)\,,\ldots,\widetilde{E}_1(t,N-1)$ denote the energy predictions for N time intervals. Furthermore, let us define the vector of optimal control inputs $\mathbf{U}^*(\mathbf{X})$, i.e., the vector of optimal rates $\mathbf{R}$ for the N prediction intervals.

In the following, we present a new algorithm for approximative multiparametric linear programming. The basic idea is

- to take a large number of samples $\mathbf{X}_i$ of the state space of $\mathbf{X}$,
- to solve a linear program for each sample $\mathbf{X}_i$ to get the optimal control $\mathbf{U}_i^*$,

- to find a (preferably simple) fitting function $\hat{\mathbf{U}}^*(\mathbf{X})$ for the multidimensional data $(\mathbf{X}_i, \mathbf{U}_i^*)$,
- and finally to use $\hat{\mathbf{U}}^*(\mathbf{X})$ (which has been calculated off-line) as approximation for $\mathbf{U}^*(\mathbf{X})$ in the on-line case.

At first, a random number generator is used to generate the samples $\mathbf{X}_i$, $1 \leq i \leq N_S$, where N_S denotes the total number of samples. We used independent, uniformly distributed random values as samples for the single elements of $\mathbf{X}$. As fitting algorithm, we opted for the algorithm proposed in [5]. This algorithm attempts to fit data samples to a set of convex, piece-wise linear candidate functions. The optimal control rates $\mathbf{U}^*(\mathbf{X})$ are not necessary convex over the state space $\mathbf{X}$. However, it has been shown that the optimal objective value $J^*(\mathbf{X})$ exhibits the wished convexity property. For each sample $\mathbf{X}_i$, we now solve a linear program and determine the optimal control vector $\mathbf{U}^*(\mathbf{X}_i)$ as well as the optimal objective value $J^*(\mathbf{X}_i)$. This can be done using common simplex-based or interior-point solvers. Next, we implement the heuristic algorithm in [5] to fit the objective $J^*(\mathbf{X}_\mathrm{i})$, i.e. to solve the least square fitting problem

$$\text{minimize} \quad \sum_{i=1}^{N_S} \left(\max_{j=1,\ldots,\hat{N}_{CR}} (\hat{\mathbf{T}}_j^T \cdot \mathbf{X}_i + \hat{\mathbf{V}}_j) - J^*(\mathbf{X}_i) \right)^2 \tag{2}$$

We obtain the approximated objective function $\hat{J}^*(\mathbf{X}) = \max_{j=1,\ldots,\hat{N}_{CR}} \{\hat{\mathbf{T}}_j^T \cdot \mathbf{X} + \hat{\mathbf{V}}_j\}$ Next, we group the samples $\mathbf{X}_i$ according to the region j they belong to. For each region j, we perform a simple least square fitting of the respective samples to compute the coefficients $\hat{\mathbf{A}}_j$ and $\hat{\mathbf{B}}_j$ of the approximated control rates $\hat{\mathbf{U}}^*$. As a result, we have derived an explicit form for the control rates $\hat{\mathbf{U}}^*(\mathbf{X})$ as a function of the current state $\mathbf{X}$:

$$\hat{\mathbf{U}}^*(\mathbf{X}) = \hat{\mathbf{A}}_j \mathbf{X} + \hat{\mathbf{B}}_j \quad \text{if } \hat{\mathbf{H}}_j \mathbf{X} \leq \hat{\mathbf{K}}_j, j = 1, \ldots, \hat{N}_{CR} \tag{3}$$

Everything done so far has to be done off-line. The approximated control law in (3) can now be used in an on-line controller instead of the exact solution.

4 Simulation Results

Table 1 displays the evaluation of an approximate control law with $\hat{N}_{CR} = 4$ regions for both subcontroller 1 and subcontroller 2. In comparison, the optimal solution exhibits 30 and 161 critical regions, respectively. The primary optimization objective of regulating the sensing rate $\hat{r}_1$ is met almost as well as for the exact solution. We define the average efficiency η_{avg} of the energy utilisation as a metric to quantify the performance of the sensor node. Obviously, the approximated algorithm manages to save even slightly more energy then its exact counterpart. The stored energy $\hat{E}_C$ is varying up to 11.57% from E_C. However, the peak of $\hat{E}_C$ is just 4.03% above the one of E_C. That is, the capacity of the energy storage is required to be approximately 5% higher if the system is controlled by an approximated algorithm. Showing a comparable performance during runtime, the

Table 1. Comparison of multiparametric and approximate-mp control design, sc = subcontroller, storage in real numbers, ops in the worst case

control design	$\max_t \left\lvert \frac{\hat{r}_1(t)}{r_1(t)} - 1 \right\rvert$	$\max_t \left\lvert \frac{\hat{E}_C(t)}{E_C(t)} - 1 \right\rvert$	η_{avg}	N_{CR} (or $\hat{N}_{CR}$)	storage	ops
optimal, sc1	0%	0%	93.00%	30	1920	3689
sc2				161	2898	4829
approximate, sc1	1.52%	11.57%	93.75%	4	256	308
sc2				4	108	69
approximate, sc1	0.82%	5.47%	92.97%	4	256	308
sc2				9	243	173

main advantage of the approximation becomes obvious considering the complexity of the control laws. According to Table 1, the storage demand is significantly reduced by 92.44% compared to the optimal solution. In terms of worst case computation demand, the reduction even amounts 95.57%. Here, worst case refers to the situation where the currently active region is the last region to be tested. Table 1 also outlines the results for a second low-complexity approximation.

Acknowledgements

The work presented in this paper was partially supported by the National Competence Center in Research on Mobile Information and Communication Systems (NCCR-MICS), a center supported by the Swiss National Science Foundation under grant number 5005-67322. In addition, this research has been founded by the European Network of Excellence ARTIST2.

References

1. Moser, C., Thiele, L., Brunelli, D., Benini, L.: Adaptive power management in energy harvesting systems. In: DATE 2007: Proceedings of the Conference on Design, Automation and Test in Europe, pp. 773–778. ACM Press, New York (2007)
2. Filippi, C.: An algorithm for approximate multiparametric linear programming. Journal of Optimization Theory and Applications 120(1) (23), 73–95 (2004)
3. Moser, C., Thiele, L., Brunelli, D., Benini, L.: Robust and Low Complexity Rate Control for Solar Powered Sensors. In: Design, Automation and Test in Europe (DATE 2008), March 10-14, 2008, Munich, Germany (2008)
4. Moser, C., Thiele, L., Brunelli, D., Benini, L.: Approximate Control Design for Solar Driven Sensor Nodes. TIK-Report 279, Computer Engineering and Networks Laboratory, ETH Zurich (January 2008)
5. Magnani, A., Boyd, S.: Convex piecewise-linear fitting. In: Optimization and Engineering (submitted) (April 2006), `http://www.stanford.edu/~boyd/reports/cvx_pwl_fit.pdf`

Modular Development of Hybrid Systems for Verification in *Coq*

Milad Niqui* and Olga Tveretina**

Institute for Computing and Information Sciences,
Radboud University Nijmegen, The Netherlands
{M.Niqui,O.Tveretina}@cs.ru.nl

Abstract. In this paper we present a formalization of the theory of hybrid automata and algorithms for building trajectory trees using module types and functors in the *Coq* proof assistant.

1 Preliminaries

Hybrid systems are systems in which there is a significant interaction between the continuous and discrete parts. Many of the applications of hybrid systems are *safety critical* and require the guarantee of a safe operation. The problem of safety verification seeks an answer to the *reachability* problem: is there a potentially unsafe state reachable from an initial state?

The notion of a hybrid automaton was introduced in order to extend verification methods towards the systems with continuous and discrete dynamics [1]. A Hybrid automaton can be defined as a tuple $\mathcal{H} = (\mathcal{DS}, n, \mathcal{S}_0, \mathcal{I}, \phi, \mathcal{G}, \mathcal{R})$ with the following components: $\mathcal{DS}$ is a finite set of discrete locations; $n \geq 0$ is the dimension of $\mathcal{H}$. The state space of $\mathcal{H}$ is $\mathcal{S} := \mathcal{DS} \times \mathbb{R}^n$. Each state has thus the form (l, x), where $l \in \mathcal{DS}$ and $x \in \mathbb{R}^n$. $\mathcal{S}_0 \subseteq \mathcal{S}$ is a set of initial states. $\mathcal{I} : \mathcal{DS} \to \mathcal{P}(\mathbb{R}^n)$ assigns to each location l an invariant set $\mathcal{I}(l) \subseteq \mathbb{R}^n$. $\phi : (\mathcal{DS} \times \mathbb{R} \times \mathbb{R}_{\geq 0})^n \to \mathbb{R}^n$ defines the flow of a system in a discrete location with an initial condition $\phi(l, x_0, 0) = x_0$. ϕ is a vector of n functions $f_i : \mathcal{DS} \times \mathbb{R} \times \mathbb{R}_{\geq 0} \to \mathbb{R}_{\geq 0}$ such that for each i exists $g_i : \mathcal{DS} \times \mathbb{R} \times \mathbb{R} \to \mathbb{R}_{\geq 0}$ such that for all $d \in \mathcal{DS}$, $x, y \in \mathbb{R}$, $t \in \mathbb{R}_{\geq 0}$ if $f_i(d, x, t) = y$ then $g_i(d, x, y) = t$. $\mathcal{G} : \mathcal{DS} \times \mathcal{DS} \to \mathbb{R}^n$ describes a guard condition. $\mathcal{R} : \mathcal{DS} \times \mathcal{DS} \times \mathbb{R}^n \to \mathbb{R}^n$ is a reset function. The semantics of a hybrid automaton is given by the transition system [2].

Our method is based on decomposing the continuous state space according to an n-dimensional rectangular grid. We denote by χ an abstract state, by S^a the set of all abstract states, and by S_0^a the set of initial abstract states.

Definition 1 (Strict Abstract Transition System – *SATS*). *A hybrid automaton* $\mathcal{H} = (\mathcal{DS}, n, \mathcal{S}_0, \mathcal{I}, \phi, \mathcal{G}, \mathcal{R})$ *and an abstract state space* S^a *generate the* strict abstract transition system $\mathcal{T}^{sats} = \{\mathcal{S}^a, \leadsto_c, \leadsto_d, S_0^a\}$ *with*

* Research supported by the Netherlands Organisation for Scientific Research (NWO).
** Research supported by the BRICKS/FOCUS project 642.000.501.

M. Egerstedt and B. Mishra (Eds.): HSCC 2008, LNCS 4981, pp. 638–641, 2008.

- *the set of initial abstract states* $\mathcal{S}_0^a$*: an abstract state* $(l,\chi) \in \mathcal{S}_0^a$ *if there is* $(l,x) \in \mathcal{S}_0$ *such that* $x \in \chi$;
- $$(l,\chi) \rightsquigarrow_c (l,\chi') \Leftrightarrow \exists t \geq 0, x \in \chi, x' \in \chi', l' \in \mathcal{DS},\ f_i(l,x_i,t) = x'_i \wedge (f_i(l,x_1,t),\ldots,f_i(l,x_n,t)) \in \mathcal{G}(l,l') \wedge (\forall \bar{t} \in [0,t]\ ,(f_i(l,x_1,\bar{t}),\ldots,f_i(l,x_n,\bar{t})) \in \mathcal{I}(l))\ ,\ \textit{where}\ x = (x_1,\ldots,x_n), x' = (x'_1,\ldots,x'_n)\ ;$$
  $$(l,\chi) \rightsquigarrow_d (l',\chi') \Leftrightarrow \exists x \in \chi, x' \in \chi', (l,x) \in \mathcal{G}(l,l') \wedge x' = \mathcal{R}(l,l',x)\ .$$

2 Formalization of Hybrid Automaton in *Coq*

Coq [3] is an interactive theorem prover based on constructive type theory. Among the many ingredients of *Coq*, what is of interest in the present work is the ability to axiomatize theories as *modules*. In short we have *module types*, that we will use for formalizing the general theory of hybrid automata; and the *module implementations* that are basically concrete hybrid automata. Implementing a module then means that we should provide parameters and *prove* that they satisfy the axioms.

Another characteristic aspect of *Coq* that is relevant for our work is the presence of *dependent types*. Central in our work is the dependent type of vectors to model the n-dimensional space of continuous states.

In our formalization of $\mathcal{H}$ we need some basic data-types that are used in this project. Most of these (eg. natural and real numbers, booleans) are defined in the standard library of *Coq* [3] in a straightforward way. Some use inductive types — a generalization of more familiar algebraic types— which are the main building blocks of *Coq* and its logic *Calculus of Inductive Constructions.* We use the inductive type of `List` of polymorphic finite lists and `Vector` of representing the n-dimensional vectors of elements of a set A, (i.e. elements of A^n).

```
Inductive Vector (A:Set): ℕ → Type :=
   | ∅̆ : Vector A 0
   | ⁙ : ∀ (a:A) (n:ℕ), Vector A n → Vector A n+1.
```

Thus, a 0-dimensional vector is $\breve{\varnothing}$ (the empty vector), and an n-dimensional vector $a ⁙ v$ is obtained by "pairing" an element $a \in A$ with an $n-1$-dimensional vector v. One can consider vectors as lists of length n where n is coded in their type. The type of a vector is dependent on its dimension.

The theory of hybrid automata in *Coq* will be an abstract data-type defined as the following *module type*.

```
Module Type 𝓗.
 Parameter 𝓓𝓢: FiniteSetOfNaturals.
 Parameter dim: ℕ.
 Definition ℝ^dim:= Vector ℝ dim.
 Definition 𝓢 := 𝓓𝓢×ℝ^dim.
```

```
 Parameter 𝒮₀ : 𝒮 → Prop.
 Parameter ℐ: 𝒟𝒮 → ℝ^dim → Prop.
 Parameter ϕ: Vector (𝒟𝒮 → ℝ → ℝ≥0 → ℝ) dim.
 Parameter 𝒢: 𝒟𝒮 → 𝒟𝒮 → ℝ^dim → Prop.
 Parameter ℛ: 𝒟𝒮 → 𝒟𝒮 → ℝ^dim → ℝ^dim.
 Axiom ϕ_invertible:is_true_∀_coord _ _ ϕ
                           (λf∃g, ∀d x r t, f d x t = r → g d x r = t).
End ℋ.
```

The Parameters in this definition correspond to those of hybrid automaton, while the sole axiom corresponds to the property that the flow (which is the vector of solutions to differential equations) should contain only invertible functions. In above FiniteSetOfNaturals, a type for finite subsets of ℕ, is defined using a combination of module types and dependent types. The type Prop, the universe of propositions, is used to formalize subsets as predicates on a set.

The function is_true_∀_coord in this axiom is the function that given a vector of elements of some set A (in this case ϕ) and a property P of elements of A checks whether P holds for all coordinates of the vector (underscore (_) denotes the automatically inferable arguments of functions). In our case P is a property of the functions $\mathcal{DS} \to \mathbb{R} \to \mathbb{R}_{\geq 0} \to \mathbb{R}$ and states that

$$P(f) \text{ iff } \exists g \forall dxrt, ((f(d))(x))(t) = r \implies ((g(d))(x))(r) = t \ .$$

The above code lays the basis of the theory of hybrid automata and it can be extended to provide the abstract data types for various transition systems. An $SATS$ is definable as a module type with four parameters that extends the above module:

```
Declare Module H: ℋ.
 Parameter Grid: Vector Partition H.dim.
 Parameter Grid_initial : List Label.
 Parameter ⇝c : Abstract_State → Abstract_State → bool.
 Parameter ⇝d : Abstract_State → Abstract_State → bool.
```

Here Partition is a list of elements of ℝ that denote the grid in each dimension. Moreover, H.*dim* means that the dimension *dim* should be inherited from the parent theory $\mathcal{H}$ which is declared as H. For Label we first define what a *hyperinterval* is. This is formalized as a record containing a hypercube (vector of intervals) and a property that checks whether the edges of this hypercube correspond to *consecutive* intervals in the Partition. A Label is then a pair of a discrete state and a List of hyperintervals. Finally Abstract_State is a pair containing a discrete state and a hyperinterval in that discrete state.

After defining the module type extension for $SATS$ we can develop a theory by defining functions and proving the lemmas that hold for *every* instance of $SATS$. In particular we can formalize an algorithm BuildTreeOATPS that builds the tree of trajectories in each $SATS$:

```
Definition BuildTreeOATPS (d0:Label): MTree Label :=
  gist_BuildHistoryTreeOATPS
   (BuildHistoryTreeOATPS
     (Build_Label_ext (fst d0) (snd d0)
                      (λd:H.DS, if d=(fst d0) then snd d0
                                                else ∅)
                      false MAX)
    ).
```

Next we can instantiate the theory with the thermostat in [2].

```
Module Thermostat_as_H <: H.
 Definition DS:= { 1, 2, 3}.
 Definition Heat:=1.
 Definition Cool:=2.
 Definition Check:=3.
 Definition dim:=2.
 Definition clock (v:ℝ^dim) : ℝ := Vhead _ 1 v.
 Definition temperature (v:ℝ^dim) : ℝ := Vhead _ 0 (Vtail _ 1 v).
 Definition coordinates (v:ℝ^dim) :=(clock v,temperature v).
 Definition S0 (s:S) : Prop :=
   let (d,v):=s in d = Heat ∧ clock v=0 ∧ 5≤temperature v≤10.
 Definition I (d:DS) (v:ℝ^dim):Prop:=
   d=Heat∧ (clock v ≤ 3) ∧ (temperature v ≤ 10) ⋁
   d=Cool∧ (5 ≤ temperature v) ⋁
   d=Check ∧ (clock v ≤ 1).
   ⋮
 Lemma ϕ_invertible:is_true_∀_coord _ _ ϕ
                     (λf∃g, ∀d x r t, f d x t = r → g d x r = t).
End Thermostat_as_H.
```

Note that this time instead of an axiom we have to prove a lemma. The proof in this case is easy and boils down to proving simple properties of `exp` and `ln` functions.

References

1. Alur, R., Courcoubetis, C., Halbwachs, N., Henzinger, T.A., Ho, P.-H., Nicollin, X., Olivero, A., Sifakis, J., Yovine, S.: The algorithmic analysis of hybrid systems. Theoretical Computer Science 138(1), 3–34 (1995)
2. Alur, R., Dang, T., Ivančić, F.: Predicate abstraction for reachability analysis of hybrid systems. ACM transactions on embedded computing systems (TECS) 5(1), 152–199 (2006)
3. The Coq Development Team. *The Coq Proof Assistant Reference Manual, Version 8.1.* LogiCal Project (December 2007) [cited 8 Jan. 2008], http://coq.inria.fr/V8.1pl3/refman/index.html

Steering a Leader-Follower Team Via Linear Consensus

Fabio Pasqualetti, Simone Martini, and Antonio Bicchi

Università di Pisa, Interdipartimental Research Center "E. Piaggio", Italy,
Facoltà di Ingegneria, Università di Pisa, via Diotisalvi, 2
56126 Pisa, Italy
fabiopass@gmail.com, s.martini@ingegneria.pisa.it, bicchi@ing.unipi.it
www.piaggio.ccii.unipi.it

Abstract. The paper considers the problem of driving a formation of autonomous mobile agents. The group of mobile devices is represented by a leader-follower network, where the followers update their position using a simple local consensus procedure, while the leaders, whose positions represent the control inputs of the network, are free to move. We characterize the transient behavior of the network, and we solve the containment problem without relying on auxiliary sensors.

1 Introduction

In an increasing number of applications in robotics, surveying, industrial automation, etc., the use of large teams of networked mobile agent systems is being proposed to achieve effectiveness and robustness to failures of single agents. In these schemes, teams (also referred to as formations, or flocks, etc.) coordinate their motion based on local interactions between neighbors, without referring to a centralized authority. An important class of decentralized motion control strategies is that of *consensus algorithms* (see e.g. [1,2]), for which a rather well established theory is available that enables a thorough analysis of convergence properties. In this paper we consider the steering problem, i.e. that of leading a team of autonomous agents using only local interactions and communications, in the accomplishment of a task where some degree of global information (e.g. on the environment) is necessary. To this purpose, we refer to a leader-follower structure, whereby a (small) subset of agents is assumed to have access to global information, and to lead through local consensus interactions the remaining agents. We adopt the team structure proposed in [3], which is particularly suitable when the goal is to steer a group of agents while maintaining certain geometric properties. For instance, if the agents transport some dangerous materials, it is important to keep them inside a proper area, not to contaminate the outer region. In [3], authors investigate properties such as controllability, containment and optimal control of leader - follower consensus structure for steering a group of mobile agents. Containment techniques rely on

M. Egerstedt and B. Mishra (Eds.): HSCC 2008, LNCS 4981, pp. 642–645, 2008.

the use of sensors to detect the movements of the driven agents, and to trigger hybrid control actions by the team leaders. Several interesting problems remain open in leader-follower networks, including e.g. a characterization of the equilibrium manifold for a team with a given connectivity graph, and the minimal number of leaders necessary to achieve a specified task. The contribution of this short paper consists of solving the containment problem by characterizing the convergence speed of the consensus law implemented by the followers, and hence allows to use a containment technique without recurring to additional sensors to test the presence of the agents in the desired region.

2 Leader - Follower Consensus Networks

Consider a set $V = \{1, \ldots, n\}$ of mobile agents, communicating as described by a directed graph G_r. The digraph is defined by the triple $(V, \mathcal{E}, H)$, being $\mathcal{E}$ a set of edges, and H an $n \times n$ weighted adjacency matrix whose entries satisfy $h_{kj} > 0$ if the pair $(j, k) \in \mathcal{E}$. The agents V are partitioned into an m dimensional leader set L, and a follower set F, so that $L \cap F = \emptyset$, and $L \cup F = V$. Leaders and followers differ in their motion law. Indeed, the former arbitrarily update their positions while the latter use a linear consensus law described by the $n - m \times n$ stochastic matrix $[A \;\; B]$. The equation describing the motion along the X axis of the followers is $x_F(t+1) = Ax_F(t) + Bx_L(t)$, where x_F and x_L collect respectively the followers and the leaders positions. Since analogous considerations can be made for the motion along the Y axis, in the rest of the paper we only focus on the X dimension. Note that, if G_r is connected, the matrix A is stable, so that, when x_L is constant, the system reaches an equilibrium configuration described by $\bar{x}_F = (I - A)^{-1} Bx_L$.

3 The Containment Problem

We define the containment problem as the problem of driving a collection of autonomous mobile agents (followers) to a given target location, while guaranteeing that their motion remains confined in the smallest rectangle R_L containing the positions of the leaders. It has already been shown ([3]) that, in the equilibrium, the followers are contained in the convex hull defined by the positions of the leaders, and hence in R_L. However, if the motion of the leaders is not properly controlled, some followers could exit the region R_L during the process. For simplicity, but without loss of generality, we assume that the leaders coordinate their motion in a way that the sequence of vertexes defining the convex hull remains the same during the maneuver.

Let $x = (x_F, \; x_L)^T$, and $\delta(t) = x(t+1) - x(t)$. The vector $\delta(0)$ contains the initial movements of the agents, which are 0 for the followers, and δ_0 for the leaders, where δ_0 is the maximum leaders velocity that ensures containment. The evolution of δ is $\delta(t+1) = \begin{bmatrix} A & B \\ \mathbf{0} & I \end{bmatrix} \delta(t)$. When t grows, we have

$$\lim_{t\to\infty} \delta(t) = \lim_{t\to\infty} \begin{bmatrix} A & B \\ \mathbf{0} & I \end{bmatrix}^t \delta(0) = \begin{bmatrix} 0 & (I-A)^{-1}B \\ 0 & I \end{bmatrix} \delta(0) = \delta_0 \mathbf{1},$$

where the last passage holds because $[A\ B]$ is stochastic. It follows that, when the leaders move at constant velocity, the group of agents behaves asymptotically as a flock, where all the agents move at the same speed. The convergence speed of the variable δ is dictated by the matrix A. Define ρ as the spectral radius of A, and consider the consensus error of the follower i as $\varepsilon_i(t) = \delta_0 - \delta_i(t)$. Since ε_i converges exponentially fast, it can be upper bounded by $\rho^t \delta_0$. Consequently, it must be $\sum_{t=0}^{\infty} \delta_0 - \delta_i(t) < d$, where d is the minimum among the distances between the followers and the leaders. We obtain $\sum_{t=0}^{\infty} \rho^t \delta_0 \leq d$. Because of the stability of A, we have $\sum_{t=0}^{\infty} \rho^t = (1-\rho)^{-1}$, and finally

$$\delta_0 \leq \frac{d}{(1-\rho)^{-1}}. \tag{1}$$

Condition (1) characterize the maximum constant velocity of the leaders that guarantees the containment property. We might also be interested in ensuring that the connectivity in the network is maintained during the motion. In that case, let r be the communication range, then

$$\delta_0 \leq \frac{\min(d, d_r)}{(1-\rho)^{-1}}, \quad d_r = r - d. \tag{2}$$

For completeness, we describe an upper bound for ρ.

Theorem 1 (Leader - Follower Convergence Rate). *Let G be a Leader - Follower consensus network with matrices A and B, then $\rho < (1 - w_{min}^l)^{1/l}$, where ρ is the spectral radius of A, and w_{min}, l are respectively the minimum weight of the edges in the network and the diameter of the communication graph.*

Proof. We use the same procedure as in [4]. Note that it takes at most l steps to reach a leader state from a follower state with probability not less than $w_{\min}^l$. Since $\rho \leq \left|\left|A^k\right|\right|^{1/k}, \forall\ k \in \mathbb{Z}_{>0}$, then $\rho \leq \left|\left|A^k\right|\right|_{\infty}^{1/k} < (1 - w_{\min}^l)^{1/l}$.

4 A Simulation Study

As an example consider a swarm of helicopters consisting of 20 agents. For some strategic reasons, the optimal disposition of the followers is a double-layer pentagon, as in Fig. 1(c). The leaders have to maintain such structure while moving among obstacles toward a target location. Moreover, they know the trajectory to follow, and they adjust the size of their steps in order to guarantee the containment and the connectivity properties as in (2). In Fig. 4 some steps of the steering process are reported. Starting from the initial situation of Fig. 1(b), leaders create the desired followers formation, and steer the swarm. Because of the presence of some obstacles, the formation is shaped as in Fig. 1(e), and eventually recovered (Fig. 1(f)).

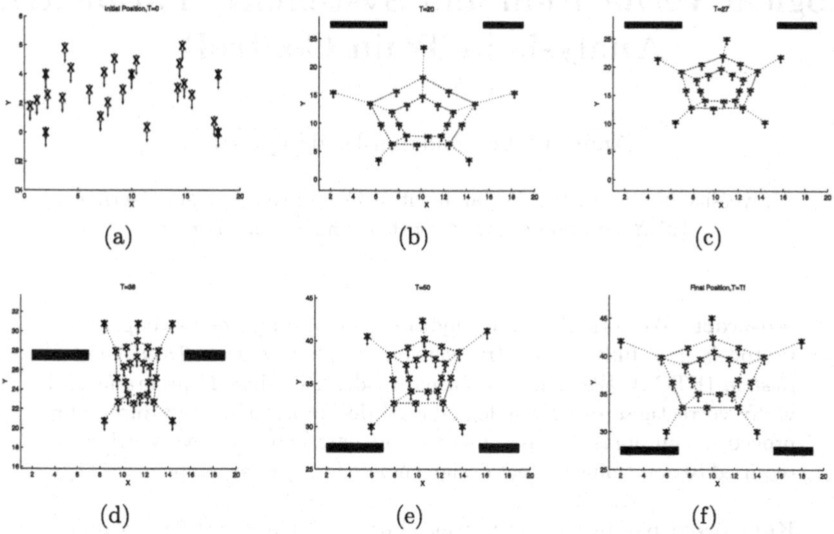

Fig. 1. Safe steering of a group of vehicles

5 Conclusions and Future Work

In this short paper, we have shown that the requirement of using sensors to detect transitions of follower agents outside a guarded region in a leader-follower containment problem can be removed, provided that leaders choose their velocity according to bounds that depend on the consensus network convergence properties. Future work will address the investigation of other properties of such systems, including a characterization of the geometry of the steerable manifold for a general leader-follower network, and the study of the minimal number of leaders required to achieve given geometric properties.

References

1. Fax, J.A., Murray, R.M.: Information flow and cooperative control of vehicle formations. IEEE Transactions on Automatic Control 49(9), 1465–1476 (2004)
2. Olfati-Saber, R., Fax, J.A., Murray, R.M.: Consensus and cooperation in networked multi-agent systems. IEEE Proceedings 95(1), 215–233 (2007)
3. Ferrari-Trecate, G., Egerstedt, M., Buffa, A., Ji, M.: Laplacian sheep: A hybrid, stop-go policy for leader-based containment control. In: Hespanha, J.P., Tiwari, A. (eds.) HSCC 2006. LNCS, vol. 3927, Springer, Heidelberg (2006)
4. Pasqualetti, F., Bicchi, A., Bullo, F.: Distributed intrusion detection for secure consensus computations. IEEE Conf. on Decision and Control (2007)

Logical Verification and Systematic Parametric Analysis in Train Control*

André Platzer and Jan-David Quesel

University of Oldenburg, Department of Computing Science, Germany
{platzer,quesel}@informatik.uni-oldenburg.de

Abstract. We formally verify hybrid safety properties of cooperation protocols in a fully parametric version of the *European Train Control System* (ETCS). We present a formal model using hybrid programs and verify correctness using our logic-based decomposition procedure. This procedure supports free parameters and parameter discovery, which is required to determine correct design choices for free parameters of ETCS.

Keywords: parametric verification, logic for hybrid systems, symbolic decomposition.

1 Introduction

Most hybrid systems contain substantial degrees of freedom including how specific parameters are instantiated or adjusted [1,2]. Yet, virtually any hybrid system is only safe under certain constraints on these parameters. For instance, the *European Train Control System* (ETCS) [3] has a wide range of different possible configurations of trains, track layouts, and different driving circumstances. Still, it only is safe under certain conditions on external parameters, e.g., when the speed of each train does not exceed its specific braking power given the remaining distance to the next train. Similarly, internal control design parameters for speed control and braking triggers need to be adjusted in accordance with the train dynamics. Moreover, parameters must be constrained such that the system remains correct when passing from instant reaction continuous models to *sampled data discrete time controllers* of hardware implementations. Yet, determining the range of external parameters and choice of internal design parameters for which ETCS is safe, is not possible just by looking at the model.

Likewise, it is difficult to read off the parameter constraints that are required for correctness from a failed verification attempt of model checkers [4], as these often exploit non-structural heuristic splits of the state space, which can lead to nonuniform parameter requirements for different states. Model checkers for hybrid systems, e.g. HyTech [5] and PHAVer [4], verify by exploring the state space of the system. For these model checkers concrete numbers for most of the parameters are necessary. To discover constraints on free parameters, we use a

* This research was partly supported by the German Research Council (DFG) of the Transregional Collaborative Research Center (SFB/TR 14 AVACS).

M. Egerstedt and B. Mishra (Eds.): HSCC 2008, LNCS 4981, pp. 646–649, 2008.

logic based approach and verify safety properties of the parametric ETCS case study with significant automation in our new verification tool KeYmaera.

Batt et al. [2] give heuristics for splitting regions by linear constraints that can be used to determine parameter constraints. This approach is not applicable in ETCS, which requires nonlinear parameter constraints for correctness.

2 Differential Dynamic Logic

The logic $d\mathcal{L}$ [6,7] is a first-order logic with built-in correctness statements about hybrid systems. It is designed such that parametric verification analysis can be carried out in $d\mathcal{L}$. Generalizing the principle of dynamic logic [8] to the hybrid case, $d\mathcal{L}$ combines hybrid system operations and correctness statements about system states within a single specification and verification language. For hybrid system α, $d\mathcal{L}$ provides correctness statements like $[\alpha]\phi$, that expresses that all traces of system α lead to states in which condition ϕ holds. Further, $d\mathcal{L}$ provides conditional correctness statements like $\phi \rightarrow [\alpha]\psi$, saying that α satisfies ψ if condition ϕ holds at the initial state.

As a uniform operational model, $d\mathcal{L}$ provides *hybrid programs* (HP) as a program notation for hybrid systems that is amenable to deductive structural decomposition in $d\mathcal{L}$ [6,7]. HP of $d\mathcal{L}$ can represent hybrid automata [5], unlike other logics [9]. Hybrid programs are regular combinations of basic actions: the assertion that ϕ holds is written as $?\phi$, $x := \theta$ to assign the value of θ to the variable x, random real numbers can be assigned using $x := *$, and $\dot{x} = \theta$ is used to express continuous evolutions along differential equations. The regular combination operators are $\alpha;\ \beta$ for sequential composition, $\alpha \cup \beta$ for non-deterministic choice and α^* to represent the repetition of hybrid automata transitions.

3 Fully Parametric European Train Control System

The European Train Control System (ETCS) [3,10] is a standard to assure safe operation of trains and high throughput of high speed trains. ETCS level 3 follows the *moving block principle*, i.e., movement authorities are not known beforehand but determined based on the current track situation by a *Radio Block Controller* (RBC). Trains are only allowed to move within their current movement authority block (denoted by m), which can be updated by the RBC using wireless communication. Hence the train controller needs to regulate the movement of a train locally such that it always remains within m. The automatic train protection unit (*atp*) determines a safety envelope around the train, within which it considers driving safe, and adjusts the train acceleration a accordingly. Figure 1 illustrates the dynamic assignment of movement authorities. When approaching the end of its movement authority the train switches from *far* mode (where speed can be regulated freely) to negotiation (*neg*), which, at the latest, happens at the point indicated by ST (*start talking*). During negotiation the RBC grants or denies m-extensions. Instead, the RBC can announce emergencies, which force train controllers to switch to the recovery mode applying full

$$
\begin{array}{lll}
\text{ETCS} & : & (\text{train} \cup \text{rbc})^* \\
\text{train} & : & \text{spd};\ \text{atp};\ \text{move} \\
\text{spd} & : & (?v \le r;\ a := *;\ ?-b \le a \le A) \\
 & & \cup(?v \ge r;\ a := *;\ ?0 > a \ge -b) \\
\text{atp} & : & (?(m - p \le SB \vee msg = stop);\ a := -b) \\
 & & \cup(?m - p \ge SB \wedge msg \ne stop) \\
\text{move} & : & t := 0;\ (\dot{p} = v, \dot{v} = a, \dot{t} = 1 \,\&\, v \ge 0 \wedge t \le \varepsilon) \\
\text{rbc} & : & (msg := stop) \\
 & & \cup\ (m := *;\ ?v^2 \le 2b(m - p);\ r := *;\ r > 0)
\end{array}
$$

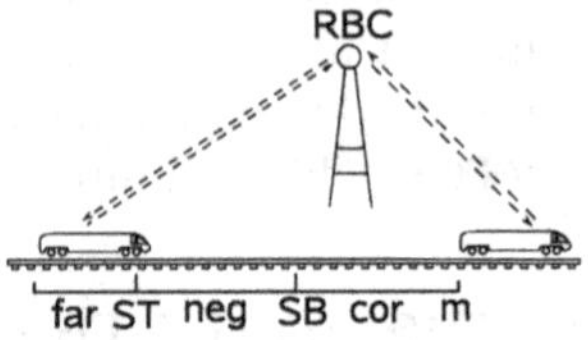

Fig. 1. ETCS train coordination protocol

emergency brakes. After the train has come to a full stop, the controller switches to a failsafe state and awaits manual clearance. If the RBC does not grant m-extension in time or messages are lost, the train starts immediate recovery after passing the point SB (*start braking*).

4 Parametric Verification of the ETCS System

After determing a correctness constraint $SB \ge \frac{v^2}{2b} + (\frac{A}{b} + 1)(\frac{A}{2}\varepsilon^2 + \varepsilon\, v)$ on the free parameters [7] we prove the following safety property of ETCS:

Proposition 1 (Safety). *Assuming the train starts in a controllable state, the following global and unbounded-horizon safety formula about the system in Fig. 1* $[\text{ETCS}]\ p \le m$ *holds.*

As system invariant we choose $inv \equiv v^2 \le 2b(m - p) \wedge \varepsilon > 0 \wedge v \ge 0$, which expresses that it is possible to completely stop the train within the distance left to the end of the movement authority. This constraint describes a controllable state of the train and therefore we choose inv as initial configuration of our system.

As an example to illustrate the proof structure for the verification of Proposition 1 in KeYmaera by automatic decomposition, consider the sketch in Fig. 2. By convention, such proofs start with the conjecture at the bottom and proceed by decomposition to the leafs. We need to prove that the assumption that the train is in a controllable state expressed by inv entails $p \le m$. As the system consists of a global loop, we need to prove that inv is an invariant of this loop. Using KeYmaera it can be shown easily that the invariant is initially valid and implies the post condition. As usual, proving that the invariant is preserved by the loop-body is the most challenging part of the proof (lower middle branch). On the left branch we have to show that the RBC

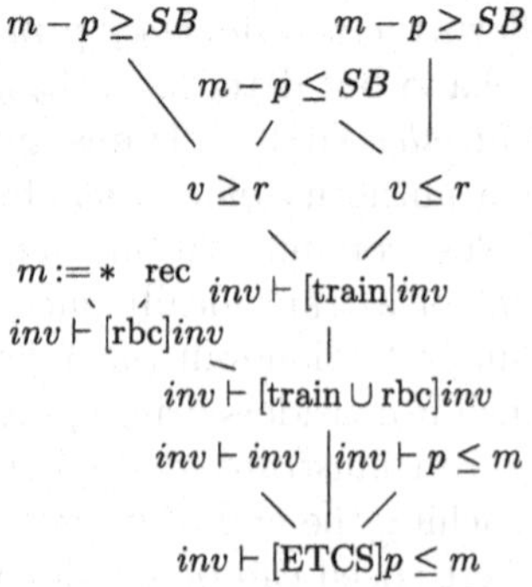

Fig. 2. Proof graph

preserves the invariant. On the right branch we have to show that the train controller also preserves the invariant. The proof splits due to the choice in the *spd* component depending on the relation of the current speed to the recommended speed. The next split on both of these branches depends on the value of SB. If the train has passed the point SB, the train applies maximal brakes and the goal can be closed as consequence from *inv*. The outer branches, where the train has not passed SB, can be closed as train behavior befor SB is not safety critical.

All correctness properties and parameter constraints of ETCS can be verified with 95.6% to 100% automation in our deductive verification tool KeYmaera, see Tab. 1 for experimental results.

Table 1. Experimental results for ETCS in the verification tool KeYmaera

Case study	Proof steps	Interactions	Time	Symbolic variables
Safety	190	1	4303s	15
Safety (simplified)	160	1	85s	15
Controllability	18	0	0.5s	5
RBC controllability	45	0	1.1s	13
Reactivity	150	0	8.8h	10
Liveness	112	5	21s	10
Reactivity corollary	344	14	289s	15

References

1. Damm, W., Hungar, H., Olderog, E.-R.: Verification of cooperating travel agents. International Journal of Control 79(5), 395–421 (2006)
2. Batt, G., Belta, C., Weiss, R.: Model checking genetic regulatory networks with parameter uncertainty. In: Bemporad, A., Bicchi, A., Buttazzo, G. (eds.) HSCC 2007. LNCS, vol. 4416, Springer, Heidelberg (2007)
3. ERTMS User Group, UNISIG: ERTMS/ETCS System requirements specification. Version 2.2.2 (2002), `http://www.aeif.org/ccm/default.asp`
4. Frehse, G.: PHAVer: Algorithmic verification of hybrid systems past HyTech. In: Morari, M., Thiele, L. (eds.) HSCC 2005. LNCS, vol. 3414, pp. 258–273. Springer, Heidelberg (2005)
5. Alur, R., Henzinger, T.A., Ho, P.-H.: Automatic symbolic verification of embedded systems. IEEE Trans. Software Eng. 22(3), 181–201 (1996)
6. Platzer, A.: Differential dynamic logic for verifying parametric hybrid systems. In: Olivetti, N. (ed.) TABLEAUX 2007. LNCS (LNAI), vol. 4548, pp. 216–232. Springer, Heidelberg (2007)
7. Platzer, A.: Differential dynamic logic for hybrid systems. J. Autom. Reasoning (to appear, 2008)
8. Harel, D., Kozen, D., Tiuryn, J.: Dynamic logic. MIT Press, Cambridge (2000)
9. Davoren, J.M., Nerode, A.: Logics for hybrid systems. Proceedings of the IEEE 88(7), 985–1010 (2000)
10. Faber, J., Meyer, R.: Model checking data-dependent real-time properties of the European Train Control System. In: FMCAD, pp. 76–77. IEEE Computer, Los Alamitos (2006)

Information Theoretical Approach to Identification of Hybrid Systems

Li Pu, Jinchun Hu, and Badong Chen

Tsinghua University, Beijing 100084, China
State Key Laboratory of Intelligent Technology and Systems
{pl06,chenbd04}@mails.tsinghua.edu.cn, hujinchun@tsinghua.edu.cn

Abstract. In this paper, we present a noisy version of the algebraic geometric approach of identifying parameters of discrete-time linear hybrid system. Two approximate ways of estimating hybrid parameters are considered: one is using MSE criteria, while the other is based on the information divergence that measures the distance between the error probability density function (PDF) of the identified model and the desired error PDF. A stochastic information divergence gradient algorithm is derived for the identification problem of non-gaussian system.

1 Introduction

Switched Auto-Regressive system with eXogenous inputs (SARX) is widely studied in recent years. It consists of several discrete ARX models and a switching mechanism that determines which ARX model takes effect in each period. We will focus on the parameter identification problem of SARX system. The method presented in this paper is a noisy version of algebraic geometric approach [1,2,3] - an ingenious method that is able to handle the identification problem of SARX system with all possible switching mechanism.

Definition 1. *The* noisy SARX system *consists of a SARX system* $x(k) = \sum_{j=1}^{n_a} a_j^{\lambda(k)} x(k-j) + \sum_{i=1}^{n_c} c_i^{\lambda(k)} u(k-i)$, *and noisy measurements* $y(k) = x(k) + m(k)$, *where the switching mechanism is formulated as the* mode function $\lambda(k) : \mathbb{Z} \to \{1, 2, \cdots, n\}$ *which assigns each sample to one of the ARX models (n is the number of ARX models, and assumed known in this paper).* $a_j^{\lambda(k)}$ *and* $c_i^{\lambda(k)}$ *are the parameters of each ARX model.* $y(k)$ *and* $u(k)$ *are the output and input of the system respectively.* $m(k)$ *is the i.i.d. measurement noise with PDF* $f_m(m)$.

We have the following assumptions: 1) all the ARX models are *minimal*, which means the numerator and denominator of the transfer functions are coprime polynomials; 2) the mode function $\lambda(k)$ is unknown but deterministic.

The sampling data set $S = \{y(k), u(k)\}, (k = 1, 2, \cdots, N)$ and the ARX parameters can be reformed as $\boldsymbol{x} = [u(k-n_c), \ldots, u(k-1), y(k-n_a), \ldots, y(k-1), -y(k)]^T \in \mathbb{R}^K$, $\boldsymbol{m} = [m(k-n_a), \ldots, m(k-1), m(k)]^T \in \mathbb{R}^{n_a+1}$, $\boldsymbol{b}_i = [c_{n_c}^i, \ldots, c_1^i, a_{n_a}^i, \ldots, a_1^i, 1]^T \in \mathbb{R}^K$, $\boldsymbol{a}_i = [-a_{n_a}^i, \ldots, -a_1^i, 1]^T \in \mathbb{R}^{n_a+1}$, where $K = n_a + n_c + 1$. The noisy SARX system is rewritten as $\boldsymbol{b}_{\lambda(k)}^T \boldsymbol{x} + \boldsymbol{a}_{\lambda(k)}^T \boldsymbol{m} = 0$.

M. Egerstedt and B. Mishra (Eds.): HSCC 2008, LNCS 4981, pp. 650–653, 2008.

2 Noisy SARX System Identification

Let $w_{\lambda(k)} = \boldsymbol{a}_{\lambda(k)}^T \boldsymbol{m}$ be the colored noise with PDF $f_w(w)$ that can be determined from $f_m(m)$ at every instant k. Inspired by the hybrid decoupling polynomial in noiseless algebraic geometric approach (AGA) [2], we have the following *noisy hybrid polynomial* (NHP) and its expanded form by applying $\boldsymbol{b}_{\lambda(k)}\boldsymbol{x}+w_{\lambda(k)} = 0$,

$$\prod_{i=1}^{n}(\boldsymbol{b}_i^T\boldsymbol{x} + w_{\lambda(k)}) = \prod_{i=1}^{n}(\boldsymbol{b}_i^T\boldsymbol{x}) + w_{\lambda(k)} \prod_{j\neq\lambda(k)} \boldsymbol{b}_j^T\boldsymbol{x} = 0 \tag{1}$$

The first component of (1) is in fact a homogeneous polynomial of degree n in K variables [2], $p_n(\boldsymbol{x}) = \prod_{i=1}^{n}(\boldsymbol{b}_i^T\boldsymbol{x}) = \sum h_{n_1,\ldots,n_K} x_1^{n_1}\cdots x_K^{n_K} = \boldsymbol{h}^T v_n(\boldsymbol{x})$, where $v_n : \mathbb{R}^K \to \mathbb{R}^{M_n(K)}$ is the Veronese map of degree n. $\boldsymbol{h} \in \mathbb{R}^{M_n(K)}$ is the hybrid parameter vector that represents the hybrid system, where $M_n(K) = C_{n+K-1}^{K-1}$.

Theorem 1 (Noisy Hybrid Polynomial Equation). *For any instant k, let x_K be the last element of $\boldsymbol{x}$ such that,*

$$p_n(\boldsymbol{x}) + \sum_{d=1}^{n}\left(\frac{w_{\lambda(k)}^d}{d!}\frac{\partial^d p_n(\boldsymbol{x})}{\partial x_K^d}\right) = \boldsymbol{h}^T \sum_{d=0}^{n}\left(\frac{w_{\lambda(k)}^d}{d!}\frac{\partial^d v_n(\boldsymbol{x})}{\partial x_K^d}\right) = 0 \tag{2}$$

Theorem 2 (Noisy Hybrid Parameter Decomposition, NHPD). *For any instant k, the parameter vector $\boldsymbol{b}_{\lambda(k)}$ of ARX model can be obtained by,*

$$\boldsymbol{b}_{\lambda(k)} = C\left(\boldsymbol{h}^T \sum_{d=0}^{n-1}\left(\frac{w_{\lambda(k)}^{d-n+1}}{d!}\frac{\partial^{d+1} v_n(\boldsymbol{x})}{\partial \boldsymbol{x}\partial x_K^d}\right)\right)^T \tag{3}$$

The proper value of $w_{\lambda(k)}$ may be determined among n roots of (2) by utilizing prior knowledge, e.g. choosing the nearest real root to the mean of $w_{\lambda(k)}$. The coefficient C in (3) is insignificant here because we can recover $\boldsymbol{b}_{\lambda(k)}$ by scaling its last element to 1. By dropping the higher-order partial derivatives in (3), the method used in [2] of estimating $\boldsymbol{b}_{\lambda(k)}$ is obtained.

It is difficult to recover $\boldsymbol{h}$ from the nonlinear equation (2), so we have to resort to some approximate methods. A straightforward approach is to ignore the higher-order components of $w_{\lambda(k)}$ (first-order approximation, FOA). If measurement noise is small and $w_{\lambda(k)}$ is zero-mean, we obtain the approximate system $\frac{\boldsymbol{h}^T v_n(\boldsymbol{x})}{\boldsymbol{h}^T D_1(\boldsymbol{x})} + w_{\lambda(k)} \approx 0$, where $D_1(\boldsymbol{x}) = \frac{\partial p_n(\boldsymbol{x})}{\partial x_K}$. Thus, the nonlinear identification model is $\frac{\boldsymbol{h}^T v_n(\boldsymbol{x})}{\boldsymbol{h}^T D_1(\boldsymbol{x})}$; it is similar to the normalizing approach in [1]. The difference between the output of system (always equals 0 in this case) and the output of identification model is called *(identification) model error* with notation e.

If $m(k)$ is zero-mean gaussian, $w_{\lambda(k)}$ is zero-mean gaussian too, but with different variances in different modes. So it is practical to adopt LMS algorithm (FOA-LMS); the recursive identifier of $\boldsymbol{h}$ is $\hat{\boldsymbol{h}}(k+1) = \hat{\boldsymbol{h}}(k) - \eta \frac{2\alpha(k)}{(\beta(k))^3}[\beta(k)v_n(\boldsymbol{x}(k)) - \alpha(k)D_1(\boldsymbol{x}(k))]$, where η is the step size adjusted by users, $\alpha(k) = \hat{\boldsymbol{h}}(k)^T v_n(\boldsymbol{x}(k))$, $\beta(k) = \hat{\boldsymbol{h}}(k)^T D_1(\boldsymbol{x}(k))$. However, if $m(k)$ is not zero-mean gaussian, the LMS identifier usually fails to provide ideal results. In this case, we resort to information theoretic criteria based identification algorithm.

3 Stochastic Information Divergence Gradient Algorithm

Recently, to more accurately depict higher-order statistics of signals, some information theoretic criteria have been studied [4]. Here we use the symmetric information divergence (SID) to compare the model error PDF and the true PDF. In FOA, true PDF is the PDF of $w_{\lambda(k)}$, which can be acquired by prior knowledge. The SID is defined as $D(f,g) = KL(f||g) + KL(g||f)$, where $KL(.||.)$ is KL-divergence and f and g are two PDFs. In order to deal with non-gaussian noise, we adopt the *Parzen window* method with gaussian kernel to approximate the PDFs. The 1-dimensional Parzen window PDF estimator is defined as $\hat{f}(s) = \frac{1}{|S_f|\sigma_f} \sum_{s_k \in S_f} K\left(\frac{1}{\sigma_f}(s - s_k)\right)$, where S_f denotes the sample set drawn from PDF $f(s)$, $K(s) = (2\pi)^{-1/2} e^{(-s^2/2)}$ is the kernel function, and σ_f denotes the kernel width. Thus, the estimator of $D(f,g)$ is $\hat{D}(f,g) = D(\hat{f},\hat{g}) = KL(\hat{f}||\hat{g}) + KL(\hat{g}||\hat{f})$. It can be proven that $\hat{D}(f,g) \geq 0$ with equality i.f.f. $\hat{f}(s) = \hat{g}(s)$. By assuming $\hat{D}(f,g) = 0$, $f(s)$ and $g(s)$ are close enough when $\min\{|S_f|,|S_g|\} \to \infty$. So the estimated information divergence could be used as an approximate measure of the distance between the actual PDFs. Then we use gradient algorithm to minimize the SID between PDFs of e and e^d, where e^d is the *desired error* whose PDF approximates to the true PDF. By dropping the expectation operators of KL-divergence in $\hat{D}(f,g)$, the instantaneous value of SID at instant k is,

$$\hat{D}\left(p_e, p_e^d, k\right) = \log \frac{\hat{p}_e\left(e(k)\right)}{\hat{p}_e^d\left(e(k)\right)} + \log \frac{\hat{p}_e^d\left(e^d(k)\right)}{\hat{p}_e\left(e^d(k)\right)} \tag{4}$$

Let $S_e(k) = \{e(k-1), e(k-2), \ldots, e(k-L_1)\}$ and $S_e^d = \{\bar{e}^d(1), \bar{e}^d(2), \ldots, \bar{e}^d(L_2)\}$ be the Parzen window sequence of e and e^d respectively. S_e^d and σ_2 are designed by users to approximate the true PDF; $e^d(k) = E(w_{\lambda(k)})$ (mean of $w_{\lambda(k)}$) such that $\hat{p}_e(e(k)) = \frac{1}{L_1\sigma_1} \sum_{i=k-1}^{k-L_1} K\left(\frac{e(k)-e(i)}{\sigma_1}\right)$, $\hat{p}_e^d(e^d(k)) = \frac{1}{L_2\sigma_2} \sum_{i=1}^{L_2} K\left(\frac{e^d(k)-\bar{e}^d(i)}{\sigma_2}\right)$. Then we obtain the SID gradient algorithm (SIDG) with respect to the hybrid parameter vector $\hat{\boldsymbol{h}}(k+1) = \hat{\boldsymbol{h}}(k) - \eta \frac{\partial \hat{D}(p_e, p_e^d, k)}{\partial \hat{\boldsymbol{h}}}$, where η is the step-size.

4 Experiments

We use the system in [5], where the authors made detailed studies of effects of noise for four different identification methods, including the similar approach as

FOA. The system is as following, where $r(k) \sim \mathcal{N}(0, 0.01)$ denotes the normally distributed additive noise. The sequence $x(k)$ is generated with $x(0) = -10$, uniformly distributed $u(k) \sim \mathcal{U}([10, 11])$, and $m(k)$ with PDF $f_m(m)$.

$$\begin{cases} x(k+1) = 2x(k) + u(k) + r(k), & x(k) \leq 0 \\ x(k+1) = -1.5x(k) + u(k) + r(k), & x(k) > 0 \\ y(k) = x(k) + m(k) \end{cases} \quad (5)$$

We also use the following formula to measure the accuracy of the identified parameters as in [5]: $\Delta = \max_{1 \leq i \leq n} (\min_{1 \leq j \leq n} (||\hat{\boldsymbol{b}}_i - \boldsymbol{b}_j||_2 / ||\boldsymbol{b}_j||_2))$. Figure 1 shows Δ for zero-mean normally distributed $m(k) \sim \mathcal{N}(0, \sigma_m^2)$ with different σ_m^2. We can see that the performances of FOA-LMS and FOA-SIDG are almost the same, and better than AGA when σ_m^2 increases; the value of Δ also matches the case in [5]. Then we change the following parameters: $r(k) = 0$, $m(k) \sim \mathcal{U}([-1, -0.5] \cup [0.5, 1])$, $S_e^d = \{-2, -1.6, -1.6, -0.3, -0.3, -0.3, 0.3, 0.3, 2, 2.2\}$, and $\sigma_2 = 0.5$. The involved error PDFs are shown in Fig. 2; true PDF is generated by $\boldsymbol{h}$; designed PDF is the Parzen window approximation using S_e^d and σ_2; FOA-SIDG and FOA-LMS produced PDFs are also depicted, which show SIDG has better PDF matching performance.

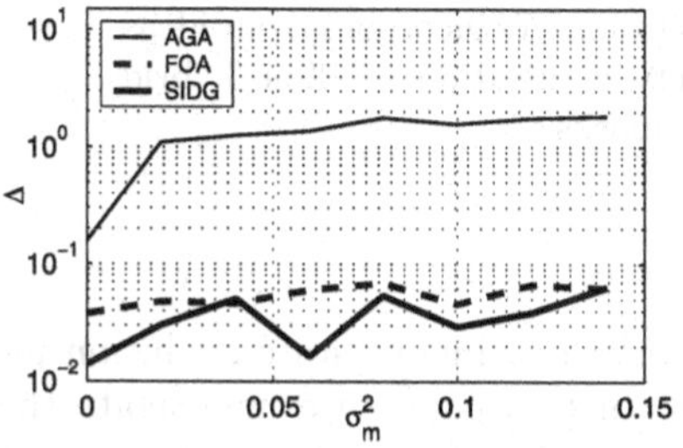

Fig. 1. Δ for different σ_m^2

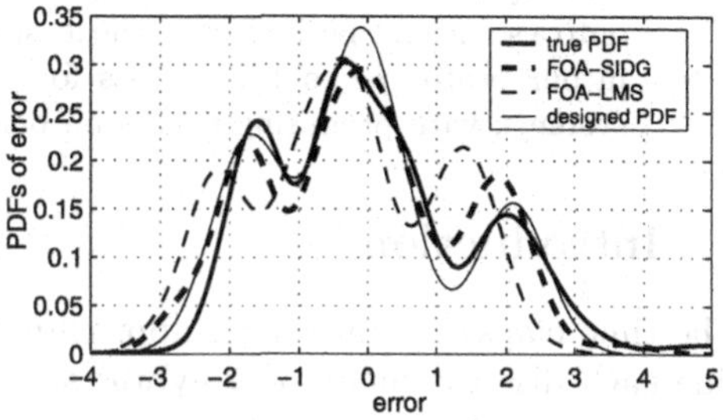

Fig. 2. Error PDFs

References

1. Vidal, R.: Generalized Principal Component Analysis (GPCA): an Algebraic Geometric Approach to Subspace Clustering and Motion Segmentation. PhD thesis, University of California (2003)
2. Vidal, R., Anderson, B.: Recursive identification of switched ARX hybrid models: exponential convergence and persistence of excitation. In: 43rd CDC conference (2004)
3. Hashambhoy, Y., Vidal, R.: Recursive Identification of Switched ARX Models with Unknown Number of Models and Unknown Orders. In: 44th CDC conference (2005)
4. Erdogmus, D., Principe, J.C.: Generalized information potential criterion for adaptive system training. IEEE Transactions on Neural Networks 13(5), 1035–1044 (2002)
5. Juloski, A., Heemels, W., Ferrari-Trecate, G., Vidal, R., Paoletti, S., Niessen, J.: Comparison of four procedures for the identification of hybrid systems. In: Morari, M., Thiele, L. (eds.) HSCC 2005. LNCS, vol. 3414, pp. 354–369. Springer, Heidelberg (2005)

A Policy Iteration Technique for Time Elapse over Template Polyhedra
(Extended Abstract)

Sriram Sankaranarayanan[1], Thao Dang[2], and Franjo Ivančić[1]

[1] NEC Laboratories America, Princeton, NJ, USA
[2] Verimag, Grenoble, France
{srirams,ivancic}@nec-labs.com, thao.dang@imag.fr

Abstract. We present a technique to compute over-approximations of the time trajectories of an affine hybrid system using template polyhedra. Such polyhedra are obtained by conjoining a set of inequality templates with varying constant coefficients. Given a set of template expressions, we show the existence of a smallest template polyhedron that is a positive invariant w.r.t to the dynamics of the continuous variables, and hence, an over-approximation of the time trajectories. However, the least invariant is hard to compute efficiently. Therefore, we propose a policy iteration technique that iterates over the space of invariant certificates to converge onto a solution that is close to the least solution. We incorporate our ideas in our prototype tool TimePass for safety verification of affine hybrid systems, with promising results on benchmarks.

1 Introduction

The time elapse operator over-approximates the continuous state evolution inside each discrete mode of a hybrid system. In this paper, we investigate the computation of the time elapse over *template polyhedra.* A *template* is a set $H = \{h_1(\boldsymbol{x}), \ldots, h_m(\boldsymbol{x})\}$ of linear expressions over $\boldsymbol{x}$, represented as an $m \times n$ matrix H. Given a template, a family of template polyhedra is obtained by considering conjunctions of the form $\bigwedge_i h_i(\boldsymbol{x}) \leq c_i$.

Definition 1 (Template Polyhedron). *A* template polyhedron *over a template H is a polyhedron of the form $H\boldsymbol{x} \leq \mathbf{c}$, wherein $\mathbf{c} \in \mathcal{R}_+^m$. Such a polyhedron will be represented as $\langle H, \mathbf{c}\rangle$. Further properties of template polyhedra are presented in our previous work [4].*

An instance of the *time elapse* problem consists of an initial region $\langle H, \mathbf{c}_0\rangle$, a location invariant $\langle H, \mathsf{inv}\rangle$, and the vector field $\mathbf{D} : \dot{\boldsymbol{x}}_i = f_i(\boldsymbol{x})$ specifying the dynamics of each state variable $\boldsymbol{x}_i$. We assume that $\mathbf{D}$ is an affine vector field. The Lie derivative $\mathcal{L}_{\mathbf{D}}(f)$ for any affine function $f : \boldsymbol{c}^T\boldsymbol{x} + d$ is also affine.

If $\mathbf{c}_1 \leq \mathbf{c}_2$ (the $\leq$ relation is applied entry-wise) then $\langle H, \mathbf{c}_1\rangle \subseteq \langle H, \mathbf{c}_2\rangle$. Given a template H, operations such as join, intersection, post-condition, emptiness and containment checks can all be carried out efficiently.

Positive Invariant Sets. Informally, a closed region C is a positive invariant iff at every point on its surface, the vector field "points" back inside the region [1].

M. Egerstedt and B. Mishra (Eds.): HSCC 2008, LNCS 4981, pp. 654–657, 2008.

The polyhedron $\langle H, \boldsymbol{d}\rangle$ s.t. $\boldsymbol{c}_0 \leq \boldsymbol{d} \leq \mathsf{inv}$, is a *positive invariant* w.r.t $\langle H, \mathsf{inv}\rangle$ iff for each row i, either (a) $\langle H, \boldsymbol{d}\rangle \wedge H_i\boldsymbol{x} = \boldsymbol{d}_i \models \mathcal{L}_{\mathbf{D}}(H_i\boldsymbol{x}) > 0$, or (b) $\boldsymbol{d}_i = \mathsf{inv}_i$. The notion of positive invariance can be relaxed using *Lagrangian relaxation.* $\langle H, \boldsymbol{d}\rangle$ is a *relaxed invariant* w.r.t a *scale factor* $\mu \in \mathcal{R}$, iff $\boldsymbol{c}_0 \leq \boldsymbol{d} \leq \mathsf{inv}$, and

$$\forall\, i \in [1, m],\ \text{if}\ \ \boldsymbol{d}_i < \mathsf{inv}_i\ \text{then}\ \ \langle H, \boldsymbol{d}\rangle \models\ \mathcal{L}_{\mathbf{D}}(H_i\boldsymbol{x} - \boldsymbol{d}_i) + \mu(H_i\boldsymbol{x} - \boldsymbol{d}_i) \leq 0\,.$$

Theorem 1. *If $\langle H, \boldsymbol{d}\rangle$ is a relaxed invariant w.r.t some scale factor μ, then it is a positive invariant.*

2 Policy Iteration

We now sketch the salient aspects of our *policy iteration* technique to compute relaxed invariants[1]. The technique presented here extends earlier work by Gaubert et al. to continuous systems [2]. Consider the instance $\langle H, \boldsymbol{c}_0, \mathsf{inv}, \mathbf{D}\rangle$ along with a fixed value for the scale factor μ. Policy iteration starts from an initial relaxed invariant $\boldsymbol{\alpha}(0) = \mathsf{inv}$, and computes a sequence of invariants: $\mathsf{inv} = \boldsymbol{\alpha}(0) > \boldsymbol{\alpha}(1) > \cdots > \boldsymbol{\alpha}(N) = \boldsymbol{\alpha}(N+1) \geq \boldsymbol{c}_0$, eventually converging to a relaxed invariant $\boldsymbol{\alpha}(N)$. For simplicity, we assume that the initial conditions and the invariants are *non-empty* and *bounded.*

Dual Certificate. Let $\langle H, \boldsymbol{\alpha}\rangle$ be a relaxed invariant w.r.t a scale factor μ. We define a *certificate* to verify this fact. The key requirement to be checked is that for each row $j \in [1, m]$, if $\boldsymbol{\alpha}_j < \mathsf{inv}_j$, then $\langle H, \boldsymbol{\alpha}\rangle \models \mu(H_j\boldsymbol{x} - \boldsymbol{\alpha}_j) + \mathcal{L}(H_j\boldsymbol{x}) \leq 0$. This condition is checked by verifying that the linear program L_j has a non-positive solution:

$$L_j :\ \max\ \mu(H_j\boldsymbol{x} - \boldsymbol{\alpha}_j) + \mathcal{L}(H_j\boldsymbol{x} - \boldsymbol{\alpha}_j)\ \text{s.t.}\ \langle H, \boldsymbol{\alpha}\rangle\,, \tag{1}$$

Note that since $\langle H, \boldsymbol{\alpha}\rangle$ is feasible and bounded (because $\boldsymbol{c}_0 \leq \boldsymbol{\alpha} \leq \mathsf{inv}$), the optimal solution to L_j exists and is bounded. A row j for which $\boldsymbol{\alpha}_j \geq \mathsf{inv}$ is termed a *frozen row.* The value of $\boldsymbol{\alpha}_j$ is justified by the invariant for such a row. Let $H_j'\boldsymbol{x} + h_j$ denote the Lie derivative of $H_j\boldsymbol{x}$. Dualizing Eqn. 1, we obtain

$$D_j :\ \min\ \boldsymbol{\alpha}^T\boldsymbol{\lambda} - \mu\boldsymbol{\alpha}_j + h_j\ \text{s.t.}\ \ H^T\boldsymbol{\lambda} = (\mu(H_j) + H_j')^T\ \wedge \boldsymbol{\lambda} \geq 0 \tag{2}$$

The solution to D_j certifies the validity of Eqn. 1 if its optimal value is non-negative: $\boldsymbol{\alpha}^T\boldsymbol{\lambda} - \mu\boldsymbol{\alpha}_j + h_j \leq 0$. The dual solutions can certify a relaxed invariant.

Definition 2 (Invariant Certificate). *An* invariant certificate *is a tuple $\langle F, \Lambda\rangle$ wherein $F \subseteq \{1, \ldots, m\}$ is a set of* frozen *row indices, while Λ is a $m \times m$ matrix with non-negative entries; s.t. for each index $j \in [1, m] - F$, $H^T\Lambda_j = (\mu(H_j) + H_j')^T \wedge \Lambda_j \geq 0$ (Eqn. 2), and for each index $j \in F$, $\Lambda_j = \mathbf{0}$.*

An invariant $\langle H, \boldsymbol{\alpha}\rangle$ is certified by $\langle F, \Lambda\rangle$ iff for each $j \in F$, $\boldsymbol{\alpha}_j = \mathsf{inv}_j$ and for each $j \in [1, m] - F$, $\boldsymbol{\alpha}^T\Lambda_j - \mu\boldsymbol{\alpha}_j + h_j \leq 0$. Given an invariant $\boldsymbol{\alpha}$, we can extract its certificate as follows: First, we solve the LP D_j for each row j. Following

[1] A detailed version of this paper may be obtained by requesting the authors.

L_j, it always has an optimum. If the optimal value is positive, then $j \in F$ and $\Lambda_j = 0$. Otherwise, Λ_j is set to the optimal solution for D_j. The certificates obtained using this procedure will be called *vertex certificates.* Therefore, every relaxed invariant $\langle H, \boldsymbol{\alpha} \rangle$ is certified by some vertex certificate π.

On the flip side, given certificate $\pi : \langle F, \Lambda \rangle$, the relaxed invariants that are certified by it are obtained using the following constraints:

$$L_\pi : \boldsymbol{c}_0 \leq \boldsymbol{y} \leq \mathsf{inv} \wedge \bigwedge_{j \in F} \boldsymbol{y}_j = \mathsf{inv}_j \wedge \bigwedge_{j \in [1,m]-F} \Lambda_j^T \boldsymbol{y} - \mu \boldsymbol{y}_j + h_j \leq 0 \quad (3)$$

A certificate π is *feasible* iff the constraint L_π is feasible; i.e, it certifies at least one relaxed invariant.

Lemma 1. *If certificate π is feasible, then it has a* minimal solution. *I.e., $\exists\, \mathbf{c} \in [\![L_\pi]\!]$, s.t. $\forall \boldsymbol{d} \in [\![L_\pi]\!]$, $\mathbf{c} \leq \boldsymbol{d}$.*

The minimal solution can be found by solving the LP: $\mathsf{min.} \sum_j \boldsymbol{y}_j$ s.t. L_π. The following result forms the basis of our technique:

Theorem 2. *There are finitely many ($O(2^{|H|} \cdot |H|^{2^{|H|}})$) vertex certificates.*

Let $P = \{\pi_1, \ldots, \pi_M\}$ be the set of all feasible vertex certificates, and $C = \{\mathbf{c}_i | \mathbf{c}_i \text{ is the least solution to } L_{\pi_i}\}$ be the corresponding least relaxed invariants.

Lemma 2. *For every relaxed invariant $\mathbf{c}$, there exists a relaxed invariant $\mathbf{c}_j \in C$, s.t. $\mathbf{c}_j \leq \mathbf{c}$.*

Applying Lemma 2 repeatedly, we show that C has a minimum element. As a result, the least relaxed invariant exists and can be computed algorithmically by enumerating all the elements of the set C, in turn obtained by enumerating P. However, the naive procedure is doubly exponential in the size of the template.

Therefore, we use a *policy iteration* algorithm to converge to a relaxed invariant while exploring a tiny fraction of the set C in practice. However, this solution is not always guaranteed to be the least solution. Starting from $\boldsymbol{\alpha}(0) = \mathsf{inv}$, we repeat the policy improvement steps (shown below) until $\boldsymbol{\alpha}(j+1) = \boldsymbol{\alpha}(j)$.

1. Compute the certificate $\pi(j)$ for $\boldsymbol{\alpha}(j)$ by solving D_j (Eqn. 2).
2. Compute $\boldsymbol{\alpha}(j+1)$ by solving the LP $L_{\pi(j)}$ in Eqn. 3.

Theorem 3. *The policy iteration eventually converges to a relaxed invariant.*

3 Implementation and Experiments

Our prototype tool TIMEPASS implements the techniques described in this paper using template polyhedra for the safety analysis of affine hybrid systems. TIMEPASS primarily uses a flowpipe construction technique for template polyhedra described in an earlier work [4]. The policy iteration algorithm is used to restrict the invariant region for the flowpipe construction. The resulting flowpipe construction is more precise. Surprisingly, the policy iteration technique also leads to fewer flowpipe segment and therefore a non-trivial speedup.

Table 1. Performance of our tool on hybrid systems benchmarks. All timings are in seconds and memory in MBs. Note, **H**: Template size, **T**:Time, **Mem:** memory, **Prf?**: Property proved.

Name	Description	Bench Size				Policy Iter.			FPipe		Comb.	
		#Var	#Loc	#Trs	$\|H\|$	T	Mem	Prf?	T	Prf?	T	Prf?
nav01	Benchmark [3]	4	8	18	64	10	30	Y	260	Y	22	Y
nav02	-	4	8	18	64	12	25	Y	362	Y	23	Y
nav03	-	4	8	18	64	8	24	Y	390	Y	20	Y
nav04	-	4	8	18	64	2	12	N	1147	Y	18	Y
nav05	-	4	8	18	64	2	10	N	7	N	513	Y
nav06	-	4	8	18	64	5	15	N	45	N	1420	N
nav07	-	4	15	39	64	14	31	Y	1300	N	572	Y
nav08	-	4	15	39	64	12	27	N	139	N	572	Y

Experiments. Table 1 shows the performance of our tool on some hybrid systems benchmarks consisting of small but complex systems, designed to test the accuracy of the flowpipe construction and its propagation. A detailed description is available elsewhere [3]. We compare the performance of three ways for computing the time elapse: (A) policy iteration, (B) flowpipe construction and (C) their combination. Note that policy iteration alone is unable to prove many of the properties. Furthermore, the strengths of the two approaches seem complementary. Together, they can prove properties beyond the reach of either. Our timings are competitive with those reported by tools such as PHaVer, HSolver and a previous version of our tool using full convex polyhedra. Furthermore, we are able to prove more systems using our techniques than previously reported elsewhere.

References

1. Blanchini, F.: Set invariance in control. Automatica 35 11, 1747–1889 (1999)
2. Gaubert, S., Goubault, E., Taly, A., Zennou, S.: Static analysis by policy iteration on relational domains. In: De Nicola, R. (ed.) ESOP 2007. LNCS, vol. 4421, pp. 237–252. Springer, Heidelberg (2007)
3. Fehnker, A., Ivančić, F.: Benchmarks for hybrid systems verification. In: Alur, R., Pappas, G.J. (eds.) HSCC 2004. LNCS, vol. 2993, pp. 326–341. Springer, Heidelberg (2004)
4. Sankaranarayanan, S., Dang, T., Ivančić, F.: Symbolic model checking of hybrid systems using template polyhedra. In: Ramakrishnan, C.R., Rehof, J. (eds.) TACAS 2008. LNCS, vol. 4963, pp. 188–202. Springer, Heidelberg (2008)

Generating Box Invariants*

Ashish Tiwari

SRI International, 333 Ravenswood Ave, Menlo Park, CA, U.S.A
Tel/Fax:+1.650.859.4774/2844
tiwari@csl.sri.coma

Abstract. Box invariant sets are box-shaped positively invariant sets. We show that box invariants are computable for a large class of nonlinear and hybrid systems. The technique for computing these invariants is based on nonlinear constraint solving. This paper also shows that the class of multiaffine systems, which has been used successfully for modeling and analyzing regulatory and biochemical reaction networks, can be generalized to the class of *monotone* and *quasi-monotone* systems without losing any of its nice properties.

A *positively invariant* set is a subset of the state space of a dynamical system with the property that, if the system state is in this set at some time, then it will stay in this set in the future [1].[1] A rectangular box, $Box(\boldsymbol{l}, \boldsymbol{u})$, specified using two diagonally opposite points $\boldsymbol{l}$ and $\boldsymbol{u}$ in $\Re^n$, where $\boldsymbol{l} < \boldsymbol{u}$ (interpreted componentwise), and its vertices and faces, are defined as follows.

$$\begin{aligned}
Box(\boldsymbol{l}, \boldsymbol{u}) &= \{\boldsymbol{x} \in \Re^n \mid \boldsymbol{l}_i \leq \boldsymbol{x}_i \leq \boldsymbol{u}_i, \text{ for all } i\} \\
Vert(\boldsymbol{l}, \boldsymbol{u}) &= \{\boldsymbol{x} \in \Re^n \mid \boldsymbol{x}_i = \boldsymbol{l}_i \text{ or } \boldsymbol{x}_i = \boldsymbol{u}_i, \text{ for all } i\} \\
Faces(\boldsymbol{l}, \boldsymbol{u}) &= \bigcup_{j=1}^{n} (L^j(\boldsymbol{l}, \boldsymbol{u}) \cup U^j(\boldsymbol{l}, \boldsymbol{u})) \\
L^j(\boldsymbol{l}, \boldsymbol{u}) &= \{\boldsymbol{x} \in Box(\boldsymbol{l}, \boldsymbol{u}) \mid \boldsymbol{x}_j = \boldsymbol{l}_j\} \\
U^j(\boldsymbol{l}, \boldsymbol{u}) &= \{\boldsymbol{x} \in Box(\boldsymbol{l}, \boldsymbol{u}) \mid \boldsymbol{x}_j = \boldsymbol{u}_j\}
\end{aligned}$$

We are interested in the case when $Box(\boldsymbol{l}, \boldsymbol{u})$ is a positively invariant set [2,3]. We say a hybrid system is box invariant if there exists a box that is also a positively invariant set. This is formally defined below.

Definition 1. *A hybrid system is said to be box invariant if there exists a finite rectangular box, $Box(\boldsymbol{l}, \boldsymbol{u})$, such that*

(a) for each mode q with continuous dynamics $\dot{\boldsymbol{x}} = \boldsymbol{p}^q(\boldsymbol{x})$ and invariant $Inv(q)$, for any point $\boldsymbol{y} \in Faces(\boldsymbol{l}, \boldsymbol{u})$, it is the case that, for all j, $\boldsymbol{p}^q_j(\boldsymbol{y}) \geq 0$ whenever $\boldsymbol{y} \in L^j(\boldsymbol{l}, \boldsymbol{u}) \cap Inv(q)$ and $\boldsymbol{p}^q_j(\boldsymbol{y}) \leq 0$ whenever $\boldsymbol{y} \in U^j(\boldsymbol{l}, \boldsymbol{u}) \cap Inv(q)$, and

* Research supported in part by the National Science Foundation under grant CNS-0720721 and by NASA under grant NNX08AB95A.

[1] A positively invariant set, as defined above, is called an *inductive* property in computer science terminology. An invariant, in computer science, is a subset of the state space that is a superset of the set of all reachable states.

M. Egerstedt and B. Mishra (Eds.): HSCC 2008, LNCS 4981, pp. 658–661, 2008.

(b) for each discrete transition from mode q to q' — with guard $G(q,q') \subseteq \Re^n$ and a reset map R that resets state $\boldsymbol{y}$ to some state in $R(q,q',\boldsymbol{y}) \subseteq \Re^n$ — and for each point $\boldsymbol{y}$ in $Box(\boldsymbol{l},\boldsymbol{y})$ that satisfies the invariant, $\boldsymbol{y} \in Inv(q)$, and the guard, $\boldsymbol{y} \in G(q,q')$, if $\boldsymbol{y'} \in R(q,q',\boldsymbol{y})$ then $\boldsymbol{y'} \in Box(\boldsymbol{l},\boldsymbol{u})$.

Note that we are interested in a *single global* box such that each of the constituent continuous dynamical system in the hybrid system is box invariant with respect to it. The above definition can be extended to systems with inputs $\boldsymbol{u}$ by treating $\boldsymbol{u}$ as state variables whose derivative is 0. It is easy to see that a box invariant set, as defined above, is indeed a positively invariant set for the hybrid system. This paper only considers hybrid systems with identity reset maps, whence Condition (b) of Definition 1 becomes trivial.

Related Work. Box invariance of linear systems [3] and nonlinear and hybrid systems [2] was introduced recently. This paper identifies the classes of monotone, quasi-monotone, and uniformly quasi-monotone systems on which box invariants computation can be reduced to constraint solving. Sankaranarayanan et. al. [4] used constraint solving to search for invariants of a given *form*. Inductive invariants for linear systems [5,6], nonlinear systems [7], and hybrid systems [8,9], have been previously considered. In contrast, the work here is focused on a very simple form of invariant and computing it for special classes of polynomial systems. Specialized forms of the notion of box invariance have been studied previously in the form of componentwise asymptotic stability [10] and Lyapunov stability under the infinity vector norms [11], but this paper differs by considering *computational* aspects of box invariance for *nonlinear* systems.

Polynomial Hybrid Systems. In polynomial hybrid systems, the dynamics are specified using polynomials over the state variables and the guards, invariants, and resets are specified using semi-algebraic sets. For such systems, Condition (a) of Definition 1 can be written as a formula in the first-order theory of reals

$$\exists \boldsymbol{l},\boldsymbol{u}. \bigwedge_{q\in Q} (\forall \boldsymbol{x}. \textstyle\bigwedge_{1\le j\le n} ((\boldsymbol{x} \in L^j \wedge \boldsymbol{x} \in Inv(q) \Rightarrow \boldsymbol{p}^q_j(\boldsymbol{x}) \ge 0) \wedge$$
$$(\boldsymbol{x} \in U^j \wedge \boldsymbol{x} \in Inv(q) \Rightarrow \boldsymbol{p}^q_j(\boldsymbol{x}) \le 0))), \qquad (1)$$

where $\boldsymbol{p}^q$ specifies the dynamics in mode $q \in Q$. If resets are not identity maps, we need additional formulas to express Condition (b). This is also expressible in the first-order theory of reals for polynomial hybrid systems. Since the first-order theory of reals is decidable [12], the following result follows.

Theorem 1. *Box invariance of polynomial hybrid systems is decidable.* □

This theoretical result is not very attractive due to the high complexity of the decision procedure for real-closed fields. We specialize the above result to some subclasses of polynomial systems.

Monotone Systems. A function $f : \Re \mapsto \Re$ is *monotonically increasing* if $f(x) \le f(x')$ whenever $x < x'$, and $f(x)$ is *monotonically decreasing* if

$f(x) \geq f(x')$ whenever $x < x'$. A function $f(x_1, \ldots, x_n)$ is said to be *monotonic with respect to* x_i if for every choice $c_1, \ldots, c_n$ of values for the variables, the function $f(c_1, \ldots, c_{i-1}, x_i, c_{i+1}, \ldots, c_n)$ is either monotonically increasing or monotonically decreasing. For example, the function $x_1x_3 - x_2x_3$ is monotonic with respect to x_3 since if we fix the values c_1, c_2 (for x_1, x_2 respectively), the function $c_1x_3 - c_2x_3$ will always be either monotonically increasing (if $c_1 - c_2 \geq 0$) or monotonically decreasing (if $c_1 - c_2 \leq 0$).

A system $\dot{\boldsymbol{x}} = \boldsymbol{p}(\boldsymbol{x})$ is *monotone* if each function $\boldsymbol{p}_i$ is monotonic with respect to each variable x_j. Every multiaffine system [13] is monotone. The converse is not true; for example, the system $\dot{x_1} = x_1^3 + x_1$ is monotone but not multiaffine. Monotone systems not only generalize multiaffine systems, but also inherit some of their nice properties, such as the following variant of Corollary 1 from [14].

Proposition 1. *If $f : \Re^n \mapsto \Re$ is a function that is monotonic (with respect to all of its argument variables), then for any point $\mathbf{c} \in Box(\boldsymbol{l}, \boldsymbol{u})$, we have*

$$\min(\{f(\boldsymbol{x}) \mid \boldsymbol{x} \in Vert(\boldsymbol{l}, \boldsymbol{u})\}) \leq f(\mathbf{c}) \leq \max(\{f(\boldsymbol{x}) \mid \boldsymbol{x} \in Vert(\boldsymbol{l}, \boldsymbol{u})\}).$$

Consequently, $f(\boldsymbol{x}) \sim 0$ everywhere in $Box(\boldsymbol{l}, \boldsymbol{u})$ if and only if $f(\boldsymbol{x}) \sim 0$ for all vertices $\boldsymbol{x} \in Vert(\boldsymbol{l}, \boldsymbol{u})$, where $\sim \in \{=, \leq, \geq\}$. □

Quasi-Monotone Systems. We generalize the class of monotone systems and call a system $\dot{\boldsymbol{x}} = \boldsymbol{p}(\boldsymbol{x})$ *quasi monotone* if each function $\boldsymbol{p}_i$ is monotonic with respect to variable x_j *for all $j \neq i$*. A *quasi-monotone hybrid* system is a hybrid system in which each constituent mode is quasi monotone. Every monotone system is naturally also quasi monotone. The system over variable x_1 defined by $\dot{x_1} = 1 - x_1^2$ is quasi monotone but it is not monotone (and not multiaffine).

Proposition 2. *A quasi-monotone hybrid system with identity resets is box invariant iff the following formula is valid*

$$\exists \boldsymbol{l}, \boldsymbol{u} \in \Re^n. \bigwedge_{q \in Q, \mathbf{c} \in Vert(\boldsymbol{l}, \boldsymbol{u}), 1 \leq j \leq n} (\mathbf{c} \in Inv(q) \Rightarrow \alpha_j(\mathbf{c})\boldsymbol{p}_j^q(\mathbf{c}) \geq 0), \qquad (2)$$

where $\alpha_j(\mathbf{c}) = 1$ if $c_j = l_j$ and $\alpha_j(\mathbf{c}) = -1$ if $c_j = u_j$. □

Formula 1 had both existential and universal quantifiers. Quasi monotonicity has allowed us to eliminate the universal quantifier and obtain simply a conjunction of $n2^n|Q|$ (existentially quantified) constraints shown in Formula 2. Any constraint solving engine that can handle nonlinear constraints can now be used (and we do not necessarily need a quantifier elimination procedure).

Uniformly Quasi-Monotone Systems. Proposition 2 still requires checking satisfiability of an *exponential* number of (nonlinear) constraints. However, for a very useful subclass of uniformly quasi-monotone systems, we can reduce the number of constraints in each mode (from $n2^n$) to $2n$. A function $f : \mathbb{R}^n \mapsto \mathbb{R}$ is *uniformly monotonic with respect to a variable x_j in domain Inv* if for all points $\boldsymbol{x} \in Inv$ and $\boldsymbol{x}' \in Inv$ that differ only in the j-th component, $f(\boldsymbol{x}) \leq f(\boldsymbol{x}')$ (or $f(\boldsymbol{x}) \geq f(\boldsymbol{x}')$) whenever $\boldsymbol{x}_j < \boldsymbol{x}'_j$; that is,

$$\forall \boldsymbol{x}, \boldsymbol{x}' \in Inv.(\bigwedge_{i \neq j} \boldsymbol{x}_i = \boldsymbol{x}'_i \wedge \boldsymbol{x}_j \leq \boldsymbol{x}'_j \Rightarrow f(\boldsymbol{x}) \leq f(\boldsymbol{x}')), \text{ or,}$$

$$\forall \boldsymbol{x}, \boldsymbol{x}' \in Inv.(\bigwedge_{i \neq j} \boldsymbol{x}_i = \boldsymbol{x}'_i \wedge \boldsymbol{x}_j \leq \boldsymbol{x}'_j \Rightarrow f(\boldsymbol{x}) \geq f(\boldsymbol{x}')).$$

For example, $x_1x_3 - x_2x_3$ is not uniformly monotonic with respect to x_3, whereas it is monotonic with respect to x_3. However, $x_1x_3 - x_2x_3$ is uniformly monotonic with respect to x_1 in the domain $Inv := \{x_1 \geq 0, x_2 \geq 0, x_3 \geq 0\}$. A system $\dot{\boldsymbol{x}} = \boldsymbol{p}(\boldsymbol{x})$ is said to be a *uniformly quasi-monotone system* in the domain *Inv* if, for each i, $\boldsymbol{p}_i$ is uniformly monotonic with respect to x_j in the domain *Inv* for each $j \neq i$.

Proposition 3. *Let $\dot{\boldsymbol{x}} = \boldsymbol{p}(\boldsymbol{x})$ be a uniformly quasi-monotonic system in the domain Inv such that $Box(\boldsymbol{l}, \boldsymbol{u}) \subseteq Inv$. Then, the $n2^n$ constraints for each mode in Formula 2 of Proposition 2 are equivalent to a subset of $2n$ constraints.* □

References

1. Blanchini, F.: Set invariance in control. Automatica 35, 1747–1767 (1999)
2. Abate, A., Tiwari, A.: Box invariance of hybrid and switched systems. In: 2nd IFAC Conf. on Analysis and Design of Hybrid Systems, ADHS, pp. 359–364 (2006)
3. Abate, A., Tiwari, A., Sastry, S.: Box invariance for biologically-inspired dynamical systems. In: CDC (2007)
4. Sankaranarayanan, S., Sipma, H., Manna, Z.: Constructing invariants for hybrid systems. In: Alur, R., Pappas, G.J. (eds.) HSCC 2004. LNCS, vol. 2993, pp. 539–554. Springer, Heidelberg (2004)
5. Tiwari, A.: Approximate reachability for linear systems. In: Maler, O., Pnueli, A. (eds.) HSCC 2003. LNCS, vol. 2623, pp. 514–525. Springer, Heidelberg (2003)
6. Yazarel, H., Pappas, G.J.: Geometric programming relaxations for linear system reachability. In: Proc. 2004 American Control Conference (2004)
7. Tiwari, A., Khanna, G.: Nonlinear Systems: Approximating reach sets. In: Alur, R., Pappas, G.J. (eds.) HSCC 2004. LNCS, vol. 2993, pp. 600–614. Springer, Heidelberg (2004)
8. Rodriguez-Carbonell, E., Tiwari, A.: Generating polynomial invariants for hybrid systems. In: Morari, M., Thiele, L. (eds.) HSCC 2005. LNCS, vol. 3414, pp. 590–605. Springer, Heidelberg (2005)
9. Prajna, S., Jadbabaie, A.: Safety verification of hybrid systems using barrier certificates. In: Alur, R., Pappas, G.J. (eds.) HSCC 2004. LNCS, vol. 2993, pp. 477–492. Springer, Heidelberg (2004)
10. Pastravanu, O., Voicu, M.: Necessary and sufficient conditions for componentwise stability of interval matrix systems. IEEE Tran. Aut. Con. 49(6) (June 2004)
11. Kiendl, H., Adamy, J., Stelzner, P.: Vector norms as Lyapunov functions for linear systems. IEEE Transactions on Automatic Control 37(6) (June 1992)
12. Tarski, A.: A Decision Method for Elementary Algebra and Geometry, 2nd edn. University of California Press (1948)
13. Belta, C., Habets, L., Kumar, V.: Control of multi-affine systems on rectangles with applications to hybrid biomolecular networks. In: CDC, pp. 534–539 (2002)
14. Kloetzer, M., Belta, C.: A fully automated framework for control of linear systems from ltl specifications. In: Hespanha, J.P., Tiwari, A. (eds.) HSCC 2006. LNCS, vol. 3927, pp. 333–347. Springer, Heidelberg (2006)

Qualitative Stability Patterns for Lotka-Volterra Systems on Rectangles

Laurent Tournier and Jean-Luc Gouzé

INRIA Sophia-Antipolis, COMORE team, France
{laurent.tournier,jean-luc.gouze}@sophia.inria.fr

Abstract. We present an analysis of the Lotka-Volterra differential equation within rectangles that are transverse with respect to the flow. In a similar way to existing works on affine systems (and positively invariant rectangles), we consider nonlinear LV equations, in rectangles with any kind of tranverse patterns. Notably, we give conditions for the existence of such rectangles. We also analyze the dynamical behavior inside a rectangle. This work is a first step towards a qualitative abstraction and simulation of Lotka-Volterra systems.

1 Introduction

The work presented here may be viewed within the context of hybrid analysis of nonlinear smooth dynamical systems. In classical hybrid approaches, piecewise *linear* or *affine* systems are used in simplexes, rectangles or more general polytopes (see for instance [4] or [6]). More recently, [8] proposed a more general *multi-affine* framework. We focus here on the Lotka-Volterra (LV) differential system, which is a slightly different class of dynamical systems that arises in many biological applications [7]. Our results constitute a first step towards a *qualitative abstraction* of LV systems. This concept consists in describing sets of continuous trajectories by giving a sequence of transitions between rectangular regions. Besides the algorithmic power of such an abstraction approach (see [4] in a different framework), qualitative abstraction has two major advantages. First, it is particularly robust with respect to the parameters (in many applications, the values of certain parameters are indeed only loosely known, as for instance in [4]). Secondly, it gives a discrete approximation (see [9]) that can be used in different tasks, for instance in the design of a discrete controller of a continuous system. Here we propose theoretical results (mainly Proposition 1 and Theorem 2) describing the dynamics of the nonlinear LV system on rectangles, that are transverse with respect to the flow. Details and proofs of the following results can be found in [10].

2 LV Systems and Transverse Rectangles

We consider the non-degenerate LV n-dimensional differential system (see [7]):

$$\dot{x} = x \otimes A(x - x^*) =: f^{\mathrm{lv}}(x) \,, \qquad x \in (\mathbb{R}_+^*)^n \tag{1}$$

M. Egerstedt and B. Mishra (Eds.): HSCC 2008, LNCS 4981, pp. 662–665, 2008.

where A is a $n \times n$ invertible real matrix, x^* is a n-dimensional real vector and $\otimes$ designates the componentwise product of real vectors. It is well known that the hyperplanes $x_i = 0$ are invariant, and so is each orthant, delimited by these hyperplanes. For clarity, we will suppose that the equilibrium $x^* \gg 0$ (*ie* all its coordinates are positive), and we will study this system in the positive orthant. We will also refer to the associate affine system:

$$\dot{x} = A(x - x^*) =: f^{\text{lin}}(x) , \qquad x \in (\mathbb{R}_+^*)^n \tag{2}$$

Throughout this paper, we are interested in the dynamical behavior of (1) in full-dimensional rectangles, comprised in the positive orthant, defined by: $R = [m, M] = \{x \in \mathbb{R}^n \mid \quad m \leq x \leq M\}$, where $0 \ll m \ll M$. The $(n-1)$-dimensional faces of such a rectangle are denoted $\mathcal{F}_i+$ and $\mathcal{F}_i^-$ $(i \in \{1, \dots, n\})$, where:

$$\begin{aligned} \mathcal{F}_i^+ &= \textstyle\prod_{j=1}^{i-1} [m_j, M_j] \times \{M_i\} \times \prod_{j=i+1}^{n} [m_j, M_j] \\ \mathcal{F}_i^- &= \textstyle\prod_{j=1}^{i-1} [m_j, M_j] \times \{m_i\} \times \prod_{j=i+1}^{n} [m_j, M_j] \end{aligned}$$

If, for all $x \in \mathcal{F}_i^\varepsilon$, the vector field coordinate $f_i^{\text{lv}}(x)$ does not vanish (it then keeps a constant sign $s \in \{+, -\}$), the face $\mathcal{F}_i^\varepsilon$ is said *transverse* (the flow of (1) crosses the face in a fixed direction: it is incoming if $s \neq \varepsilon$ and outgoing if $s = \varepsilon$). It is easy to see that this property is equivalent for the LV system (1) and the affine system (2). It is also straightforward that this property can be checked by looking only at the sign of the f_i^{lin} at the vertices of the face (see [10] for more details). A rectangle R with all its faces transverse is also said *transverse*. If for all $i \in \{1, \dots, n\}$, $\mathcal{F}_i^+$ and $\mathcal{F}_i^-$ are both incoming or both outgoing, the transverse pattern of R is said to be *symmetrical*. We first give the following result:

Proposition 1. *Let $0 \ll m \ll M$ and $R = [m, M]$, f designates the affine or LV vector field. Then,*

(i) Suppose that R is transverse. Then, $x^* \in R$ if and only if the pattern of R is symmetrical (and then x^* belongs necessarily to the interior of R).
(ii) Suppose $x^* \notin R$. Then, given any initial condition $x^0 \in R$, the solution $t \mapsto x(t, x^0)$ of $\dot{x} = f(x)$ leaves R in finite time.

A proof of this proposition can be found in [10]. We deduce from it that any rectangle R that does not contain the equilibrium is *transient* (in the sense that any trajectory starting in R eventually leaves R), regardless of the fact that it is transverse. However, transversality is important in order to describe the dynamics inside the rectangle containing the equilibrium. We therefore start by giving some conditions to ensure that this particular rectangle is transverse.

3 Necessary and Sufficient Conditions for the Existence of a Transverse Rectangle, with Symmetrical Pattern

The question addressed here is to link the existence of a transverse rectangle, with a symmetrical pattern, with the particular structure of matrix A, for the n-dimensional nonlinear LV system (1). This problem has already been investigated in the linear framework, notably in [1] (see also [3,5] results in the case of general polytopes). Theorem 1 given below generalizes the result of [1] in two directions: on the one hand, it considers the nonlinear LV system (1) instead of the affine system (2), and on the other hand, it gives conditions for the existence of a transverse rectangle with any symmetrical pattern and not only a positively invariant rectangle.

The proof of this theorem can be found in [10], and essentially relies on the theory of nonnegative matrices, in particular of the special class of *M-matrices* (defined for instance in the book of Berman and Plemmons [2]).

Theorem 1. *Consider the dynamical system (1) with A invertible. Let $m, M \in (\mathbb{R}_+^*)^n$, $0 \ll m \ll M$, and let R designate the n-dimensional rectangle $[m, M]$. Suppose there exists $p \in \{0, \ldots, n\}$ such that the p pairs of faces $\mathcal{F}_i^\pm$ of R ($i \in \{1, \ldots, p\}$) are outgoing and the $n-p$ pairs of faces $\mathcal{F}_i^\pm$, for $i \in \{p+1, \ldots, n\}$ are incoming. Then the two following properties hold:*

- $(\mathbf{P_1})$ *The comparison matrix $\mathcal{C}(A)$ of A is a non-singular M-matrix.*
- $(\mathbf{P_2})$ *Diagonal entries of A satisfy:*

$$\begin{array}{ll} \forall i \in \{1, \ldots, p\}\,, & a_{ii} > 0 \\ \forall i \in \{p+1, \ldots, n\}\,, & a_{ii} < 0 \end{array}$$

We recall here the classical definition of a *comparison matrix*: if A is an $n \times n$ real matrix, the comparison matrix $\mathcal{C}(A)$ of A is the matrix $(c_{ij})_{i,j=1\ldots n}$, where, for $i \in \{1, \ldots, n\}$, $c_{ii} = |a_{ii}|$ and for $j \neq i$, $c_{ij} = -|a_{ij}|$. A theorem (see [2, p 134]) provides several characterizations of M-matrices (*e.g*, one can easily show that $\mathcal{C}(A)$ is an M-matrix by checking that all its principal minors are positive).

Theorem 1 gives explicit necessary conditions on matrix A to ensure the existence of a transverse rectangle around the equilibrium. In addition to this, we also developed the converse of Theorem 1: provided that A satisfies properties $(\mathbf{P_1})$ and $(\mathbf{P_2})$, we give a constructive way to build transverse rectangles around the equilibrium. The interested reader can refer to [10] for a statement and a proof of this converse theorem.

4 Dynamical Behavior within Transverse Rectangles

If the matrix A satisfies Theorem 1 (*ie* properties $(\mathbf{P_1})$ and $(\mathbf{P_2})$), then we can deduce the signs of the real parts of the eigenvalues of A (see [10]). We can then deduce the stability of equilibrium x^* for the affine system (2) and for the LV system (1). In the affine case, this is sufficient to determine the behavior of (2) within rectangle R. It is however not sufficient in the LV case, as the LV equation is nonlinear. The following theorem allows us to generalize the results to the LV framework:

Theorem 2. *Consider dynamical system (1) and $m, M \in (\mathbb{R}_+^*)^n$ such that $m \ll M$ and such that the rectangle $R = [m, M]$ has $p \in \{0, \ldots, n\}$ pairs of outgoing faces $\mathcal{F}_i^\pm$, $i = 1, \ldots, p$ and $n-p$ pairs of incoming faces $\mathcal{F}_i^\pm$, $i = p+1, \ldots, n$. Then,*

- *if* $p = 0$, *any trajectory starting in* R *converges towards the equilibrium* x^*.
- *if* $p = n$, *any trajectory starting in* R *(except the equilibrium itself) leaves* R *in finite time.*
- *If* $1 \leq p \leq n-1$, *then for almost every initial condition* $x^0 \in R$, *the solution* $x(t; x^0)$, $t \geq 0$ *of (1) leaves* R *in finite time.*

The proof of this theorem, based on Lyapunov stability and instability theorems, can be found in [10].

5 Conclusion

Theoretical results presented here set up a first step towards a qualitative abstraction of Lotka-Volterra dynamical systems. Proposition 1 and Theorem 2 classify the different dynamical behaviors of a LV system within rectangles that either contain the equilibrium or not. If A does not satisfy property $(\mathbf{P_1})$, we have proved that it is impossible to build a transverse rectangle around the equilibrium. A next step is to study the qualitative behavior of a LV system on a rectangular mesh, using discrete abstraction. We should then focus on the design of a discrete controller (see [9]) of the system on rectangles (in order for instance to steer the trajectories to a designated face). As an example, the linear feedback approach presented in [6] can be extended in the LV framework. Another extension is the study of a general Lotka-Volterra hybrid system, with different LV systems in each rectangle; as in [4], the vector field then becomes discontinuous, and we have to face complex issues such as sliding motions and Filippov solutions on the boundaries.

References

1. Abate, A., Tiwari, A.: Box invariance of hybrid and switched systems. In: 2nd IFAC Conf. on Analysis and Design of Hybrid Systems, pp. 359–364 (2006)
2. Berman, A., Plemmons, R.J.: Nonnegative matrices in the mathematical sciences. In: Classics in Applied Mathematics, SIAM Press, Philadelphia (1994)
3. Castelan, E.B., Hennet, J.C.: IEEE Trans. Auto. Cont. 38(11), 1680–1685 (1993)
4. de Jong, H., Gouzé, J.-L., Hernandez, C., Page, M., Sari, T., Geiselmann, J.: Bull. Math. Biol., 66, 301–340 (2005)
5. Farina, L., Benvenuti, L.: IMA J. Math. Cont. Info. 15, 233–240 (1998)
6. Habets, L.C.G.J.M., van Schuppen, J.H.: Automatica. 40, 21–35 (2004)
7. Hofbauer, J., Sigmund, K.: Evolutionary games and population dynamics. Cambridge University Press, Cambridge (1998)
8. Kloetzer, M., Belta, C.: Reachability analysis of multi-affine systems. In: Hespanha, J.P., Tiwari, A. (eds.) HSCC 2006. LNCS, vol. 3927, Springer, Heidelberg (2006)
9. Lunze, J., Raisch, J.: Discrete models for hybrid system. In: Modelling, Analysis, and Design of Hybrid Systems. LNCIS, pp. 67–82. Springer, Heidelberg (2002)
10. Tournier, L., Gouzé, J.-L.: Research Report 6346, INRIA (2007), `http://hal.inria.fr/inria-00186247`

Sampled-Data Event Control of Hybrid Systems for Control Specifications Given by Predicates

Yoshiyuki Tsuchie and Toshimitsu Ushio

Graduate school of Engineering Science,
Osaka University, Toyonaka,
Osaka 560-8531, Japan
yoshiyuki@hopf.sys.es.osaka-u.ac.jp, ushio@sys.es.osaka-u.ac.jp

Abstract. We consider a hybrid system controlled by a sampled-data controller whose action is periodically time-driven, that is, the control inputs can change only at the particular time instants. We introduce a transition system as semantics of the controlled hybrid system and consider a control specification given by a predicate. First, we derive a necessary and sufficient condition for the predicate to be control-invariant and show that there always exists the supremal control-invariant subpredicate for any predicate. Finally, we propose a procedure to compute it.

1 Introduction

In a direct method for a design of a sampled-data controller, a sampled-data controlled system is described as a model with continuous-time variables (a plant) and discrete-time variables (a digital controller). So a hybrid system is a suitable continuous-time model for the direct method [1].

Silva and Krogh proposed an extension of a hybrid automaton with time-driven events to model explicitly discrete transitions that are based on time-driven sampling of the continuous state and define a transition system as semantics to verify its dynamics[2, 3]. Tsuchie and Ushio discussed the state feedback control of a hybrid automaton with time-driven events. However, the controller is designed in continuous-time setting. In this paper, we discuss a sampled-data event controller and consider a control specification given by a predicate on the state set of the controlled hybrid system, where the sampled-data event controller assigns a set of control-enabled events, called a control pattern, based on the state of the hybrid system and updates it at each sampling time so that all reachable states of the closed-loop system satisfy the predicate.

We use a labeled transition system $T = (Q, Act, \mathscr{T}, Q_0)$ in order to define semantics of controlled hybrid systems, where Q is a states set, Act is a label set, $\mathscr{T} \subseteq Q \times Act \times Q$ is a state transition relation, and $Q_0 \subseteq Q$ is the initial state set. Let $\mathscr{P}(Q)$ be the set of all predicates on Q. A partial order "$\leqslant$" for $\mathscr{P}(Q)$ is defined as follows: for $P_1, P_2 \in \mathscr{P}(Q)$, $P_1 \leqslant P_2 \Leftrightarrow P_1(q) \leq P_2(q) \forall q \in Q$. For each $a \in Act$, we define two predicates as follows[4]:

M. Egerstedt and B. Mishra (Eds.): HSCC 2008, LNCS 4981, pp. 666–669, 2008.

$$D_a(\mathscr{T})(q) = \begin{cases} 1 & \text{if } a \in \{\tilde{a} \in Act | \exists q' \in Q \text{ s.t. } (q, \tilde{a}, q') \in \mathscr{T}\}, \\ 0 & \text{otherwise,} \end{cases} \tag{1}$$

$$wlp_a(P, \mathscr{T})(q) = \begin{cases} 1 & \text{if } P(q') = 1 \forall q' \in \{\tilde{q}' \in Q | (q, a, \tilde{q}') \in \mathscr{T}\}, \\ 0 & \text{otherwise.} \end{cases} \tag{2}$$

For a subset $A \subseteq Act$, we define $wp_A(P, \mathscr{T}) = \bigvee_{a \in A} wp_a(P, \mathscr{T})$.

2 Controlled Hybrid Automaton

We consider a plant modeled by a hybrid automaton $H{=}(V, E, \Sigma, inv, init, flow, jump)$, where V and Σ are the set of nodes and events, $E \subseteq V \times \Sigma \times V$ is the set of edges, that is, $e(v, \sigma, v') \in E$ is an edge e from v to v' labeled by σ and corresponds to a discrete transition by the occurrence of σ, $inv(v) \subseteq \Re^n$ is the set of values which the continuous state can take in v, $flow(v) \subseteq \Re^n \times \Re^n$ is a set of values which $(x, \dot{x})$ can take in v, $init(v)$ is the set of all possible initial continuous states in v, for each $e(v, \sigma, v') \in E$, $jump(e) \subseteq 2^{\Re^n \times \Re^n}$ is the jump relation, that is, $(x, x') \in jump(e)$ means that the continuous state $x \in inv(v)$ jumps to $x' \in inv(v')$ when $\sigma \in \Sigma$ occurs[1].

We assume that H has forcible events which can be forced to occur by external control actions and are controllable. Let Σ_f be the set of forcible events. Then, note that $\Sigma_c \cap \Sigma_u = \emptyset$, $\Sigma = \Sigma_c \cup \Sigma_u$, and $\Sigma_f \subseteq \Sigma_c$. The state set Q_H of H is given by $Q_H = \{(v, x) | v \in V, x \in inv(v)\}$. Let $guard(e)$ be an occurrence condition of the discrete transition by $e(v, \sigma, v') \in E$, that is, $guard(e) = \{x \in inv(v) | \exists x' \in inv(v') \text{ s.t. } (x, x') \in jump(e)\}$. We assume that $guard(e)$ is a closed set for any $e(v, \sigma, v') \in E$ and $\sigma \in \Sigma_f$.

Let $\mathscr{F}(P, \delta, v, x, x')$ be a set of functions $F : [0, \delta] \to \Re^n$ with $F(0) = x$, $F(\delta) = x'$, $F(\epsilon) \in inv(v)$ and $(F(\epsilon), \dot{F}(\epsilon)) \in flow(v)$ for any $\epsilon \in (0, \delta)$, and $P(v, F(\epsilon_i)) = P(v, F(\epsilon_j))$ for any $\epsilon_i, \epsilon_j \in (0, \delta)$. Moreover, $\mathscr{F}(P, \delta, v, x, *) = \bigcup_{x' \in inv(v)} \mathscr{F}(P, \delta, v, x, x')$.

Let $f : Q_H \to 2^{\Sigma} \times 2^{\Sigma_f}$ be an event controller denoted by $f = (f_1, f_2)$, where f_1 and f_2 give a set of control-enabled events and forced events by the controller, respectively. Note that, for any $q \in Q_H$, $f_2(q) \subseteq f_1(q) \cap \Sigma_f$ and $\Sigma_u \subseteq f_1(q)$. Let T be a sampling period. Then, the control input signal is denoted by, for each time t, $f((v(nT), x(nT)))$, where $(v(t), x(t))$ is a state trajectory at the time t and $n = \lfloor t/T \rfloor$. Denoted by H^f is H controlled by the sampled-data event controller f.

We define transition systems to be used as semantics for the hybrid automaton H.

(I) A sampled-data time-abstract transition system is defined by $\mathcal{S}^a(P) = (Q_s, Act_{sa}, \mathscr{T}_{sa}(P), Q_{s0})$, where $Q_s = Q_H \times \Gamma_1 \times \Gamma_2 \times [0, T]$ is the set of states, $Q_{s0} = \{(q_0, \gamma_1, \gamma_2, 0) \in Q_s | q_0 \in Q_{H0}\}$ is the initial state set, $Act_{sa} = \Sigma \cup \{\tau_u, \tau_c\}$ is the set of events, and $\mathscr{T}_{sa}(P)$ is the set of transition relations. Intuitive meaning of each element of a state $(q, \gamma_1, \gamma_2, \omega) \in Q_s$ is as follows: q indicates a state of H, ω is an elapsed time from the latest sampling time, $\gamma_1 \in \Gamma_1$ and $\gamma_2 \in \Gamma_2$

are control patterns assigned at the latest sampling time, and $\mathscr{T}_{sa}(P)$ is defined as follows: Consider $q_s = ((v,x),\gamma_1,\gamma_2,\omega)$ and $q_s' = ((v',x'),\gamma_1',\gamma_2',\omega') \in Q_s$. Then, **(A)**for $\sigma \in \Sigma$, $(q_s,\sigma,q_s') \in \mathscr{T}_{st}(P)$ iff $\sigma \in \gamma_1$, $\gamma_1 = \gamma_1'$, $\gamma_2 = \gamma_2'$, $\omega = \omega'$, and $\exists e(v,\sigma,v') \in E$ s.t. $(x,x') \in jump(e)$, **(B)** $(q_s,\tau_c,q_s') \in \mathscr{T}_{sa}(P)$ iff $q = q'$, $\omega = T$, and $\omega' = 0$, and **(C)** $(q_s,\tau_u,q_s') \in \mathscr{T}_{sa}(P)$ iff $v = v', \omega < \omega'$, and $\exists F \in \mathscr{F}(P,\omega'-\omega,v,x,*)$ such that $F(\omega'-\omega) = x'$, $\gamma_1 = \gamma_1'$, $\gamma_2 = \gamma_2'$, and $\hat{\sigma} \notin \gamma_2 \forall t \in [0,\omega'-\omega)$ and $e(v,\hat{\sigma},\hat{v}) \in E$ with $F(t) \in guard(e)$.

The transition relation labeled by τ_u means the uncontrollable time elapse which cannot be interrupted by any controller.

Next, we define a transition system as semantics of the controlled hybrid automaton H^f.

(II) A sampled-data time-abstract transition system controlled by f is defined by $\mathcal{S}^a(H^f,P) = (Q_s, Act_{sa}, \mathscr{T}_{sa}^f(P), Q_{s0}^f)$, where the state set Q_s is the same state set as that of $\mathcal{S}^a(P)$ and $Q_{s0}^f = \{(q_0,\gamma_1,\gamma_2,0) \in Q_s | q_0 \in Q_{H0}, f(q_0) = (\gamma_1,\gamma_2)\}$. $Act_{sa} = \Sigma \cup \{\tau_u,\tau_c\}$. $\mathscr{T}_{sa}^f(P) \subseteq Q_s \times Act_{sa} \times Q_s$ is defined as follows: **(A)** for each $a \in Act_{sa} \backslash \{\tau_c\}$, $(q_s,a,q_s') \in \mathscr{T}_{sa}^f(P)$ iff $(q_s,a,q_s') \in \mathscr{T}_{sa}(P)$ and **(B)** $(q_s,\tau_c,q_s') \in \mathscr{T}_{sa}^f(P)$ iff $(q_s,\tau_c,q_s') \in \mathscr{T}_{sa}(P)$, $f(q) = (\gamma_1',\gamma_2')$, $\omega = T$, and $\omega' = 0$.

We extend a predicate $P_H : Q_H \to \{0,1\}$ on Q_H to a predicate $P_s \in \mathscr{P}(Q_s)$ on Q_s as follows: $P_s(q,\gamma_1,\gamma_2,\omega) = P_H(q)$ for any $(q,\gamma_1,\gamma_2,\omega) \in Q_s$.

3 Control-Invariance

We extend a concept of the control-invariance to a hybrid system with sampled-data state feedback control.

Definition 1. *Let H and $P \in \mathscr{P}(Q_s)$ be a hybrid automaton and a predicate. A predicate P is said to be control-invariant if there exists a controller f such that satisfies $P \leqslant wlp_a(P, \mathscr{T}_{sa}^f(P)) \forall a \in \Sigma \cup \{\tau_u,\tau_c\}$. We call the controller f a permissive controller.*

We introduce a necessary and sufficient condition for the control-invariance.

Theorem 1. *$P \in \mathscr{P}(Q_s)$ is control-invariant iff the following conditions hold:*

$$P \leqslant wlp_a(P, \mathscr{T}_{sa}(P)) \text{ for any } a \in \Sigma \cup \{\tau_u\}, \text{ and} \tag{3}$$

$$\bigvee_{(\gamma_1,\gamma_2)\in\Gamma_1\times\Gamma_2} P(q,\gamma_1,\gamma_2,T) \leq \bigvee_{(\tilde{\gamma}_1,\tilde{\gamma}_2)\in\Gamma_1\times\Gamma_2} P(q,\tilde{\gamma}_1,\tilde{\gamma}_2,0) \text{ for any } q \in Q_H. \tag{4}$$

Theorem 1 shows that we can restrict our interest in behavior on the time interval $[0,T]$ in order to verify the control-invariance of the hybrid automaton with an event controller. Then, if $P \in \mathscr{P}(Q_s)$ is control-invariant, one of permissive controllers f is defined as follows: $f(q) = (\gamma_1,\gamma_2)$ with $P(q,\gamma_1,\gamma_2,T) \leq P(q,f(q),0)$.

In general, a given predicate $P \in \mathscr{P}(Q_s)$ is not necessarily control-invariant. We propose a procedure for the computation of the supremal control-invariant subpredicates of P. Let $\mathscr{C}I(P) \in 2^{\mathscr{P}(Q_s)}$ and $\mathbf{0} \in \mathscr{P}(Q_s)$ be the set of all control-invariant subpredicates of $P \in \mathscr{P}(Q_s)$ and the predicate with $\mathbf{0}(q_s) = 0$

for each $q_s \in Q_s$. Note that $\mathscr{C}I(P) \neq \emptyset$ since $\mathbf{0} \in \mathscr{C}I(P)$. We call $P^\uparrow \in \mathscr{C}I(P)$ a supremal control-invariant subpredicate of P if $P' \leqslant P^\uparrow$ for each $P' \in \mathscr{C}I(Q_s)$. The following theorem shows that there exists $P^\uparrow$ for any predicate $P \in \mathscr{P}(Q_s)$.

Theorem 2. *Let I be any index set. If $P_i \in \mathscr{P}(Q_s)$ is control-invariant for each $i \in I$, then $P_I = \bigvee_{i \in I} P_i$ is control-invariant.*

We consider the following iterative scheme: $P_0 = P$ and, for $k = 0, 1, 2, \ldots$,

$$P_{k+1} = P_k \wedge \left(\bigwedge_{a \in \Sigma \cup \{\tau_u\}} wlp_a(P_k, \mathscr{T}_{sa}(P_k)) \right) \wedge mlp_{\tau_c}(P, \mathscr{T}_{sa}(P_k)), \text{ where} \quad (5)$$

$$mlp_{\tau_c}(P, \mathscr{T}_{sa}(P))(q_s) = \begin{cases} 1 & \text{if } \neg D_{\tau_c}(\mathscr{T}^f_{sa}(P)) \text{ or,} \\ & \exists q'_s \in Post(q_s, \tau_c, \mathscr{T}_{sa}(P)) \text{ s.t. } P(q'_s) = 1, \\ 0 & \text{otherwise.} \end{cases} \quad (6)$$

Theorem 3. *If $P_k = P_{k+1}$ for some $k \geq 0$, then $P^\uparrow = P_k$.*

Practically, the iterative computation in Theorem 3 is implemented by using a bisimulation relation, and its termination is closely related to the existence of a finite bisimulation.

4 Conclusion

This paper considered the sampled-data event control of a hybrid automaton with forcible events as a model of computer-controlled systems where control specifications are given by predicates. We introduced transition systems as semantics and showed a necessary and sufficient condition for the control specification to be control-invariant. Finally, we proved that there always exists the supremal control-invariant subpredicate for any predicate and proposed an iterative scheme to compute it.

The procedure for computation of the supremal control-invariant subpredicate is not decidable in general. So it is future work to investigate a condition under which the procedure is decidable.

References

[1] Henzinger, T.A.: The theory of hybrid automata. In: Proceedings of the 11th Symposium on Logic in Computer Science, pp. 278–292 (1996)
[2] Silva, B.I., Krogh, B.H.: Modeling and verification of sampled-data hybrid systems. In: ADPM 2000, pp. 237–242 (2000)
[3] Silva, B.I., Krogh, B.H.: Modeling and verification of hybrid systems with clocked and unclocked events. In: Proc. 40th IEEE CDC, pp. 762–767 (2001)
[4] Ramadge, P.J., Wonham, W.M.: Modular feedback logic for discrete event systems. SIAM Journal on Control and Optimization 25(5), 1202–1218 (1987)

On the Timing of Discrete Events in Event-Driven Control Systems

Manel Velasco, Pau Martí, and Camilo Lozoya

Automatic Control Department, Technical University of Catalonia,
Pau Gargallo 5, 08028 Barcelona, Spain
manel.velasco@upc.edu

Abstract. This paper presents an analysis method to determine offline at what intervals have to be taken the samples for various types of event-driven control systems.

1 Introduction

For certain type of event-driven controllers and for time-driven controllers this paper shows that the distance covered by the system trajectory is proportional to the norm of the state. This property permits to determine the variations in the sampling times generated by discrete-events as a function of the state direction. For second order systems a geometric approach is proposed.

2 Event-Driven Control Systems Model

We consider the control system

$$\begin{aligned} \dot{x} &= Ax + Bu \\ y &= Cx \end{aligned} \tag{1}$$

with $x \in \mathbb{R}^{n\times 1}$, $A \in \mathbb{R}^{n\times n}$, $B \in \mathbb{R}^{n\times m}$, $u \in \mathbb{R}^{1\times m}$, and $C \in \mathbb{R}^{1\times n}$. Let

$$u_k = Lx_k \tag{2}$$

be the control updates given by a linear feedback controller designed in the continuous-time domain but using only samples of the state at discrete instants $t_0, t_1, \ldots, t_k, \ldots$. Between control updates, $u(t) = u_k$ in $t \in [t_k, t_{k+1}[$.

3 Analysis of Various Event Conditions

In event-driven control systems, event conditions are the controller execution rules. We analyze event conditions where samples are taken when some function of the system state exceeds a threshold, as in e.g. [1] or [2]. Let

$$e(t) = x(t) - x_k \tag{3}$$

M. Egerstedt and B. Mishra (Eds.): HSCC 2008, LNCS 4981, pp. 670–673, 2008.

be the error evolution between consecutive samples with $t \in [t_k, t_{k+1}[$. In the approach presented in [1] the event condition is defined as

$$\gamma_k : |e(t)| = \eta |x(t)| \tag{4}$$

where $0 < \eta \leq 1$. And in the scheme of [2], the event condition can be stated as

$$\gamma_k : e_k^T M e_k = \eta x_k^T M x_k \tag{5}$$

where $0 < \eta \leq 1$ and $M \in \mathbb{R}^{n \times n}$.

In general, for some event-driven schemes, event conditions can be defined as

$$\gamma_k : g(e(t), x_k, \eta) = 0 \tag{6}$$

where $g(\cdot) \in \mathbb{R}$, and η is a set of given parameters. We study whether time-driven control systems can be similarly specified. Let

$$\begin{aligned} x_{k+1} &= \Phi(t) x_k + \Gamma(t) u_k \\ y_k &= C x_k \end{aligned} \tag{7}$$

be the discrete-time system obtained by sampling (1) with period $t = h$, where

$$\Phi(t) = e^{At} \quad \text{and} \quad \Gamma(t) = \int_0^t e^{As} ds B.$$

From (3), (7), and (2) we observe that the event condition

$$\gamma_k : e_k = (\Phi(h) + \Gamma(h)L - I)\, x_k \tag{8}$$

triggers control updates at equidistant points in time, given by h.

For notation convenience, a vector v_k will be denoted as

$$v_k = r_k^v \begin{bmatrix} \cos\theta_k^v \\ \sin\theta_k^v \end{bmatrix} \tag{9}$$

where r_k^v and θ_k^v are the modulus and angle of v_k.

Proposition 1. *For two-dimensional systems described by (1)-(2), if control updates are triggered by event conditions (4), (5) or (8), it holds that*

$$\|e_k\| = \alpha \|x_k\| f(\theta_k^x, t) \tag{10}$$

with $\alpha \in \mathbb{R}$, $f : [0, 2\pi[\to \mathbb{R}$, *and* e_k *given by (3).*

Proof. Event condition (4) can be rewritten as

$$e_k^T e_k = \eta^2 x_k^T P(t) x_k \tag{11}$$

where $P(t) = (\Phi(t) + \Gamma(t)L)^T (\Phi(t) + \Gamma(t)L)$. Eq. (11) in terms of (9) is

$$(r_k^e)^2 \begin{bmatrix} \cos\theta_k^e & \sin\theta_k^e \end{bmatrix} \begin{bmatrix} \cos\theta_k^e \\ \sin\theta_k^e \end{bmatrix} = \eta^2 (r_k^x)^2 \begin{bmatrix} \cos\theta_k^x & \sin\theta_k^x \end{bmatrix} P(t) \begin{bmatrix} \cos\theta_k^x \\ \sin\theta_k^x \end{bmatrix} \tag{12}$$

which simplifies to

$$r_k^e = \eta r_k^x \sqrt{\left[\cos\theta_k^x \; \sin\theta_k^x\right] P(t) \begin{bmatrix}\cos\theta_k^x \\ \sin\theta_k^x\end{bmatrix}}. \tag{13}$$

From (8) with $t = h$, it follows that

$$e_k^T e_k = x_k^T Q(t) x_k \tag{14}$$

where $Q(t) = (\Phi(t) + \Gamma(t)L - I)^T(\Phi(t) + \Gamma(t)L - I)$. Then Eq. (14) simplifies to

$$r_k^e = r_k^x \sqrt{\left[\cos\theta_k^x \; \sin\theta_k^x\right] Q(t) \begin{bmatrix}\cos\theta_k^x \\ \sin\theta_k^x\end{bmatrix}}. \tag{15}$$

Similarly, condition (5) can be written as

$$(r_k^e)^2 \left[\cos\theta_k^e \; \sin\theta_k^e\right] M \begin{bmatrix}\cos\theta_k^e \\ \sin\theta_k^e\end{bmatrix} = \eta (r_k^x)^2 \left[\cos\theta_k^x \; \sin\theta_k^x\right] M \begin{bmatrix}\cos\theta_k^x \\ \sin\theta_k^x\end{bmatrix} \tag{16}$$

which reduces to

$$r_k^e = \sqrt{\eta} r_k^x \frac{\left[\cos\theta_k^x \; \sin\theta_k^x\right] M \begin{bmatrix}\cos\theta_k^x \\ \sin\theta_k^x\end{bmatrix}}{\left[\cos\theta_k^e \; \sin\theta_k^e\right] M \begin{bmatrix}\cos\theta_k^e \\ \sin\theta_k^e\end{bmatrix}} = \sqrt{\eta} r_k^x g(\theta_k^x, t) \tag{17}$$

The last equality, considering $R(t) = (\Phi(t) + \Gamma(t)L)$, holds because

$$\theta_k^e = \arctan\left(\frac{y^e}{x^e}\right) = \arctan\left(\frac{r_k^x \left[0\,1\right] R(t) \begin{bmatrix}\cos\theta_k^x \\ \sin\theta_k^x\end{bmatrix}}{r_k^x \left[1\,0\right] R(t) \begin{bmatrix}\cos\theta_k^x \\ \sin\theta_k^x\end{bmatrix}}\right) \tag{18}$$

□

Remark 1. Equations (13), (15), and (17) specify invariant boundaries for $|e_k|$ when for example a spheric parametrization of the unitary vector of the system state is used. These boundaries provide information about all possible covered distances by the system trajectory after the occurrence of an event.

4 Geometric Approach

Since the derived boundaries scale on the norm of the system state, we can compare systems by geometrically mapping boundaries. Note that boundary (15) has constant period h. Therefore, solving (13) and (15) for t, or (17) and (15), we can determine the variations in sampling times generated by event conditions (4), (5), or any event-driven scheme whose event condition fulfills proposition 1. The mapping consists in plotting a time grid composed by boundaries generated by

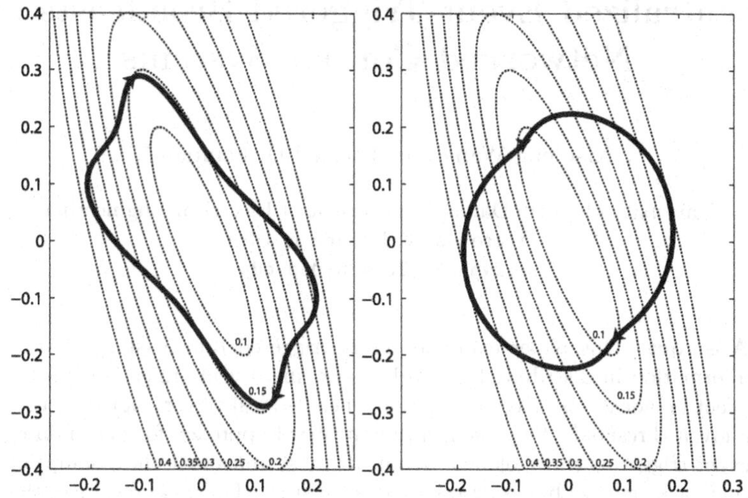

Fig. 1. Mapping of (17) (left) and (13) (right) on top of a time grid generated by (15)

(15) with different periods. And on top of them, we plot the boundary generated by (13) or (17). Then by inspecting the superposition, we can directly assert the character of time between sampling instants that (4) or (5) generates.

As an example, consider that the double integrator system is controlled by (2) with $L = [1.0001\ 1.7322]$, which can be obtained from eq. (1)-(6) of [2]. It is easy to verify that L stabilizes the system when applied with event conditions (4), (5), or (8) ($\eta = 0.5$). In Figure 1 we plot the mapping for (17) (left) and (13) (right). The time grid has been generated using (15) for periods $h = 0.1$ to 0.4. For example, by looking to the left sub-figure, we deduce that the maximum and minimum sampling interval are approximately 0.38s and 0.15s, respectively.

5 Conclusions and Future Work

This paper has presented an analysis method that permits to study timing properties for various types of event-driven schemes. Future work will focus on finding the analytical solutions for the graphical method and it extension to an n-dimensional space. In additional, for schedulability of event-driven controllers and regulation of CPU load, it will be of interest to apply non-lineal techniques to study the nature of periods' dynamics.

References

1. Tabuada, P.: Event-triggered real-time scheduling of stabilizing control tasks. IEEE Transactions on Automatic Control 52(9), 1680–1685 (2007)
2. Wang, X., Lemmon, M.: Self-triggered Feedback Control Systems with Finite-Gain L2 Stability. IEEE Transactions on Automatic Control (Submitted, 2007)

Decentralized Event-Triggered Broadcasts over Networked Control Systems

Xiaofeng Wang and Michael D. Lemmon*

University of Notre Dame, Department of Electrical Engineering,
Notre Dame, IN, 46556, USA
{xwang13,lemmon}@nd.edu

Abstract. This paper examines event-triggered broadcasting of state information in distributed networked systems. Event-triggering has the agent broadcast its state information when its local "error" signal exceeds a given threshold. We present a decentralized approach for determining event-triggering thresholds for nonlinear subsystems with the assumption that each agent only has access to its local state. The main results of this paper show that our decentralized event triggering scheme guarantees the asymptotic stability of the entire networked control system.

1 Introduction

A networked control system (NCS) is a collection of control systems where individual subsystems exchange information over some communication network. The networking of control effort can be advantageous in terms of lower system costs due to streamlined installation and maintenance costs. Meanwhile, such distributed systems may be more reliable since the failure of a single subcomponent will not bring down the entire system.

Communication capacity is important in NCSs. Early work focused on one packet transmission problem [1], where a supervisor summarizes all subsystem data into this single packet. As a result such schemes may be impractical for large-scale systems. Asynchronous broadcasts were considered in [2], [3]. These works derived bounds on the maximum admissible transfer interval that a message can be delayed while still maintaining closed loop system stability. However, all of the previous work confined its attention to control area network (CAN) buses where centralized computers are used to schedule communication.

In recent years there has been considerable interest in developing distributed controllers over ad hoc wireless networks [4]. The problem faced in using wireless networks is that their throughput capacity is limited [5]. As network density increases, the throughput seen by an individual agent asymptotically approach zero. There is, therefore, great interest in being able to develop networked control systems which are extremely frugal in their use of network bandwidth.

This paper addresses this problem through a decentralized event-triggering scheme, which reduces the communication frequency so that the bandwidth

* The authors gratefully acknowledge the partial financial support of the National Science Foundation (NSF CNS-0720457).

M. Egerstedt and B. Mishra (Eds.): HSCC 2008, LNCS 4981, pp. 674–677, 2008.

requirements can be reduced. Event-triggering has the agent broadcast its state information when its local "error" signal exceeds a given threshold . We present an approach for selecting event-triggering thresholds that assures the asymptotic stability of the group. Our analysis applies to nonlinear subsystems. The novelty of our paper is its consideration of completely "decentralized" design over distributed systems other than single processor real-time systems [6], [7]. By "decentralized", it means a controller's broadcast decisions are made using its local state and the last received state information from its neighbors and the designer's selection of the threshold also only requires information about an individual subsystem and its immediate neighbors.

The paper is organized as the following: section 2 formulates the problem; the event-triggering scheme is presented in section 3; final conclusions are found in section 4.

2 Problem Formulation

Notation: For a nonlinear system containing N agents, $\{\mathbf{P}_i\}_{i=1}^N$, let $\mathcal{N} = \{1, 2, \cdots, N\}$. $Z_i \subset \mathcal{N}$ denotes the set of agents whose state $\mathbf{P}_i$ can access. $D_i \subset \mathcal{N}$ denotes the set of agents that directly drive $\mathbf{P}_i$'s dynamics. $U_i \subset \mathcal{N}$ denotes the set of agents that can receive $\mathbf{P}_i$'s broadcasts. $S_i \subset \mathcal{N}$ denotes the set of agents who are directly driven by $\mathbf{P}_i$. Let $x_i : \mathbb{R} \to \mathbb{R}^{n_i}$, $u_i \in \mathbb{R}^{m_i}$, $x_{i0} \in \mathbb{R}^{n_i}$ be the ith agent's state trajectory, control variable, initial state, respectively. $x = (x_1^T, \cdots, x_N^T)^T$ is the overall system state. Let $\bar{n} = \Sigma_{j\in\mathcal{N}} n_j$ and $T_i = D_i \cup Z_i$. For a set $S \subseteq \mathcal{N}$ and a vector $x \in \mathbb{R}^{\bar{n}}$, let $n_S = \sum_{j\in S} n_j$ and $x_S = \{x_j\}_{j\in S} \in \mathbb{R}^{n_S}$.

Consider a sampled-data distributed system, where each agent broadcasts its state information to its neighbors in an aperiodic manner. $\mathbf{P}_i$'s broadcasts are characterized by a monotone increasing sequence of time instants, $\{b_k^i\}_{k=1}^\infty$, where b_k^i denotes the time instant when $\mathbf{P}_i$ broadcasts for the kth time. b_k^i is also $\mathbf{P}_i$'s sampling time since we assume there is no delay between sampling and broadcasts. Let $\hat{x}(t) \in \mathbb{R}^{\bar{n}}$ be the latest broadcasted states at time t. The system dynamics of $\mathbf{P}_i$ are defined as the following:

$$\begin{aligned} \dot{x}_i(t) &= f_i(x_{D_i}, u_i) \\ u_i &= \gamma_i(\hat{x}_{Z_i}(t_k)), \quad x_i(0) = x_{i0} \end{aligned} \tag{1}$$

for $t \in [t_k, t_{k+1})$, $k = 1, \ldots, \infty$, where t_k represents the kth broadcast time instant among all broadcasts, $\gamma_i : \mathbb{R}^{n_{Z_i}} \to \mathbb{R}^{m_i}$ is the given feedback strategy of $\mathbf{P}_i$ satisfying $\gamma_i(0) = 0$, and $f_i : \mathbb{R}^{n_{D_i}} \times \mathbb{R}^{m_i} \to \mathbb{R}^{n_i}$ is a given function satisfying $f_i(0,0) = 0$. Notice that the sequence of $\{t_k\}_{k=1}^\infty$ is the increasing sorted sequence of the elements in $\{b_k^j \mid \forall k \in \mathbb{N}, \forall j \in \mathcal{N}\}$. In particular we assume there exists a smooth, proper, positive-definite function $V : \mathbb{R}^{\bar{n}} \to \mathbb{R}$, such that for any $x \in \mathbb{R}^{\bar{n}}$

$$\sum_{i\in\mathcal{N}} \frac{\partial V}{\partial x_i} f_i(x_{D_i}, \gamma_i(x_{Z_i})) \leq 0 \tag{2}$$

and the equality holds if and only if $x = 0$.

The main objective of this paper is to find a locally constructed "decentralized" event for $\mathbf{P}_i$ to trigger its broadcasts, such that $\{b_k^i\}_{i=1}^{\infty}$ is well-characterized to ensure the asymptotic stability of the entire NCS. By "decentralized", we mean each agent can only detect its own state.

3 Decentralized Broadcast-Triggering Events Design

This section derives a threshold condition for event-triggering having the agent broadcast its state information to its neighbors. We're interested in determining condition under which such event-triggering preserves the system's asymptotic stability. We use $|S| \in \mathbb{N}$ to denote the number of the elements in a given set S, $\|\cdot\|_2$ to denote 2-norm of a vector, and $\|\cdot\|$ to denote the matrix norm.

Theorem 1. *For system 1, assume that there exist a smooth, proper, positive-definite function $V : \mathbb{R}^{\bar{n}} \to \mathbb{R}$, continuous functions $\eta_i : \mathbb{R}^{n_i} \to \mathbb{R}^{l_i}$, and continuous, positive definite functions $\phi_i \in \mathbb{R}^{n_i} \to \mathbb{R}$, $\psi_i \in \mathbb{R}^{l_i} \to \mathbb{R}$, $i = 1, \cdots, N$, such that the following inequality*

$$\sum_{i\in\mathcal{N}} \frac{\partial V}{\partial x_i} f_i(x_{D_i}, \gamma_i(y_{Z_i})) \leq \sum_{i\in\mathcal{N}} -\phi_i(x_i) + \sum_{i\in\mathcal{N}} \psi_i(\eta_i(x_i) - \eta_i(y_i)) \tag{3}$$

holds for all $x, y \in \mathbb{R}^{\bar{n}}$. If for every $i \in \mathcal{N}$, there exists a constant $\rho_i \in (0,1)$ such that the broadcast sequence $\{b_k^i\}_{k=1}^{\infty}$ satisfies

$$-\rho_i\phi_i(x_i(t)) + \psi_i(\eta_i(x_i(t)) - \eta_i(x_i(b_k^i))) \leq 0 \tag{4}$$

for all $t \in [b_k^i, b_{k+1}^i)$, then system 1 is asymptotically stable.

Proof. By equation 3, $\dot{V} \leq \sum_{i\in\mathcal{N}} \left[-\phi_i(x_i(t)) + \psi_i(\eta_i(x_i(t)) - \eta_i(x_i(b_k^i)))\right]$ holds for all $t \in [t_k, t_{k+1})$. Combining this inequality and equation 4, $\dot{V} \leq -\sum_{i\in\mathcal{N}}(1-\rho_i)\phi_i(x_i(t))$ holds for all $t \in [t_k, t_{k+1})$, $k = 1, \cdots, \infty$, which means $\dot{V}(t) < 0$ when $x \neq 0$ and $\dot{V}(t) = 0$ if and only if $x = 0$ since $\phi_i(x_i)$ is positive definite and $\rho_i < 1$. This is sufficient to show that system 1 is asymptotically stable. □

Theorem 1 says that under the structural conditions in equations 3, the threshold condition implicit in equation 4 can be used to assure the overall system's asymptotic stability. Here the "error" signal is $\eta_i(x_i(t)) - \eta_i(x_i(b_k^i))$. The following theorem presents a decentralized design scheme by which each agent constructs its threshold condition.

Theorem 2. *For system 1, assume that there exist continuous functions $\eta_i : \mathbb{R}^{n_i} \to \mathbb{R}^{l_i}$, $L_i : \mathbb{R}^{n_{T_i}} \to \mathbb{R}^+$, $i = 1, \cdots, N$, such that for all $x, y \in \mathbb{R}^{\bar{n}}$, $i \in \mathcal{N}$,*

$$\|f_i(x_{D_i}, \gamma_i(x_{Z_i})) - f_i(x_{D_i}, \gamma_i(y_{Z_i}))\|_2 \leq L_i(x_{T_i})\|\eta_{Z_i}(x_{Z_i}) - \eta_{Z_i}(y_{Z_i})\|_2, \tag{5}$$

where $\eta_{Z_i}(x_{Z_i}) = \{\eta_j(x_j)\}_{j\in Z_i}$. Given a constant $\delta \in \mathbb{R}^+$ and continuous functions $\beta_i(x_i)$, $i = 1, \cdots, N$, if there exist smooth, proper, positive definite functions $V_i : \mathbb{R}^{n_i} \to \mathbb{R}$ and continuous functions $\alpha_i : \mathbb{R}^{n_i} \to \mathbb{R}$, $i = 1, \cdots, N$, such that for all $x \in \mathbb{R}^{\bar{n}}$ and $i \in \mathcal{N}$,

$$-\alpha_i(x_i) + (|S_i \cup U_i| - 1)\beta_i(x_i) \text{ is negative definite, and} \tag{6}$$

$$\frac{\partial V_i}{\partial x_i} f_i(x_{D_i}, \gamma_i(x_{Z_i})) + \frac{1}{2\delta} L_i^2(x_{T_i}) \left\| \frac{\partial V_i}{\partial x_i} \right\|_2^2 \leq -\alpha_i(x_i) + \Sigma_{j \neq i, j \in T_i} \beta_j(x_j), \tag{7}$$

then $\phi_i : \mathbb{R}^{n_i} \to \mathbb{R}$ *and* $\psi_i : \mathbb{R}^{l_i} \to \mathbb{R}$, $i = 1, \cdots, N$, *defined by*
$\phi_i(x_i) = \alpha_i(x_i) - (|S_i \cup U_i| - 1)\beta_i(x_i)$ *and* $\psi_i(z_i) = \frac{|U_i|\delta}{2} \|z_i\|_2^2$,
satisfy equation 3 in theorem 1 with $V(x) = \sum_{i \in \mathcal{N}} V_i(x_i)$.

Proof. By completing square and applying equation 5, 7, we have
$\sum_{i \in \mathcal{N}} \frac{\partial V_i}{\partial x_i} f_i(x_{D_i}, \gamma_i(y_{Z_i})) \leq \sum_{i \in \mathcal{N}} \left[-\phi_i(x_i) + \frac{|U_i|\delta}{2} \|\eta_i(y_i) - \eta_i(x_i)\|_2^2 \right]$.

Since $-\phi_i(x_i)$ is negative definite according to equation 6, this inequality implies the satisfaction of equation 3 in theorem 1. □

In the design, δ, $\{\beta_j\}_{j \in \mathcal{N}}$, and $\{\eta_j\}_{j \in \mathcal{N}}$ are determined ahead of time. $\mathbf{P}_i$'s local problem is to construct V_i and α_i such that equation 6 and 7 hold. By equation 4 with any $\rho_i \in (0, 1)$, b_{k+1}^i is triggered by the violation of the inequality $-\rho_i \alpha_i(x_i) + \rho_i(|S_i \cup U_i| - 1)\beta_i(x_i) + \frac{|U_i|\delta}{2} \|\eta_i(x_i(b_k^i)) - \eta_i(x_i)\|_2^2 < 0$. The asymptotic stability of the overall system is guaranteed by theorem 1.

The existence of the solutions to equation 7 cannot be guaranteed in general. However, for linear systems, the solutions always exist and the decentralized event-design scheme for each agent can be posed as a local LMI problem. Due to space limitations, we will not present these results in this paper.

4 Conclusion

This paper examines event-triggered broadcasting of state information in nonlinear distributed networked control systems. We provided a decentralized design scheme for agents to construct event-triggering thresholds that preserve asymptotic stability while only requiring "local" information to make their decisions.

References

1. Krtolica, R., Ozguner, U.: Stability of linear feedback systems with random communication delays. In: Proceedings of American Control Conference (1991)
2. Walsh, G., Ye, H., Bushnell, L.: Stability analysis of networked control systems. IEEE Transactions on Control Systems Technology 10(3), 438–446 (2002)
3. Nesic, D., Teel, A.: Input-output stability properties of networked control systems. IEEE Transactions on Automatic Control 49, 1650–1667 (2004)
4. Sinopoli, B., Sharp, C., Schenato, L., Schaffert, S., Sastry, S.: Distributed control applications within sensor networks. Proceedings of the IEEE 91(8), 1235–1246 (2003)
5. Gupta, P., Kumar, P.: The capacity of wireless networks. IEEE Transactions on Information Theory 46(2), 388–404 (2000)
6. Tabuada, P., Wang, X.: Preliminary results on state-triggered scheduling of stabilizing control tasks. IEEE Conference on Decision and Control (2006)
7. Hristu-Varsakelis, D., Kumar, P.: Interrupt-based feedback control over a shared communication medium. In: IEEE Conference on Decision and Control (2002)

Author Index

Abate, Alessandro 1, 598
Agha, Gul 316
Al-Hammouri, Ahmad T. 16
Ames, Aaron D. 622
Amin, Saurabh 602
Åström, Karl 358
Attia, Sid Ahmed 30
Azhmyakov, Vadim 30

Bako, Laurent 43
Bartocci, E. 229
Bayen, Alexandre M. 101, 602
Belta, Calin 287, 542
Bemporad, A. 130, 144
Benini, Luca 634
Benvenuti, L. 58
Bhatia, Amit 606
Bicchi, Antonio 158, 642
Biswas, Gautam 614
Bloch, Gérard 330
Branicky, Michael S. 16
Brogliato, B. 259
Brunelli, Davide 634
Bujorianu, Manuela L. 610

Camlibel, M.K. 259
Candau, Yves 415
Caveney, Derek 301
Chatterjee, Krishnendu 72, 87
Chen, Badong 650
Clarke, Edmund M. 344
Claudel, Christian G. 101
Collins, Pieter 486
Corradini, F. 229
Cuijpers, P.J.L. 116

D'Innocenzo, Alessandro 1
Daigle, Matthew 614
Dang, Thao 654
Di Benedetto, Maria D. 1
Di Cairano, S. 130, 144
Dullerud, Geir E. 401

Entcheva, E. 229

Feron, Eric 443
Ferrari, A. 58
Fontanelli, Daniele 158
Fränzle, Martin 172
Frazzoli, Emilio 443, 457, 606
Frehse, Goran 187

Girard, Antoine 201, 215
Gouzé, Jean-Luc 662
Greco, Luca 158
Grosu, R. 229

Han, Tingting 244
Hante, Falk M. 602
Heemels, W.P.M.H. 130, 259
Henzinger, Thomas A. 72, 87
Hermanns, Holger 172
Hespanha, João P. 358
Hu, Jianghai 584
Hu, Jinchun 650

Imura, Jun-ichi 514
Ivančić, Franjo 654

Jha, Sumit Kumar 187, 618
Johansson, K.H. 144
Jokic, A. 273

Kapinski, James 344
Katoen, Joost-Pieter 244
Kloetzer, Marius 287
Koutsoukos, Xenofon 429, 614
Kowshik, Hemant 301
Krogh, Bruce H. 187, 344
Kumar, P.R. 301
Kwon, YoungMin 316

Lamperski, Andrew 622
Langerak, Rom 610
Lauer, Fabien 330
Lazar, M. 130, 273
Le Guernic, Colas 215
Lee, Ji-Woong 626
Lemmon, Michael D. 674
Lerda, Flavio 344

Liberatore, Vincenzo 16
Liberzon, Daniel 500
Lozoya, Camilo 670
Lunze, Jan 471
Lygeros, John 598, 610

Majumdar, Rupak 72
Martí, Pau 670
Martini, Simone 642
Mazzi, E. 58
Megretski, Alexandre 443
Mereacre, Alexandru 244
Meslem, Nacim 415
Mesquita, Alexandre R. 358
Mitchell, Ian M. 630
Moser, Clemens 634
Murray, R.M. 144

Nakura, Gou 372
Niqui, Milad 638

Pasqualetti, Fabio 642
Petreczky, Mihály 386
Platzer, André 646
Pola, Giordano 201
Prabhakar, Pavithra 401
Prabhu, Vinayak S. 87
Prandini, Maria 598
Pu, Li 650

Quesel, Jan-David 646

Raisch, Jörg 30
Ramírez, Antonio 528
Ramdani, Nacim 415
Recalde, Laura 528
Reniers, M.A. 116
Riley, Derek 429
Riley, Kasandra 429
Roozbehani, Mardavij 443

Sanfelice, Ricardo G. 457
Sankaranarayanan, Sriram 654
Sastry, Shankar S. 1, 598
Schild, Axel 471
Schumacher, J.M. 259
Sella, Lorenzo 486
Sharon, Yoav 500
Silva, Manuel 528
Smolka, S.A. 229
Susuki, Yoshihiko 630

Tabuada, Paulo 201
Tanner, Herbert G. 570
Tazaki, Yuichi 514
Teige, Tino 172
Thiele, Lothar 634
Tiwari, Ashish 658
Tournier, Laurent 662
Tsuchie, Yoshiyuki 666
Tveretina, Olga 638

Ushio, Toshimitsu 666

van den Bosch, P.P.J. 273
Vázquez, C. Renato 528
Velasco, Manel 670
Vidal, René 43, 386
Vincentelli, A.L. Sangiovanni 58
Viswanathan, Mahesh 401
Vladimerou, Vladimeros 401

Wang, Xiaofeng 674
Wasilewska, A. 229

Yordanov, Boyan 542
Yunt, Kerim 556

Zhang, Wei 584
Zhang, Wenqi 570

Lecture Notes in Computer Science

Sublibrary 1: Theoretical Computer Science and General Issues

For information about Vols. 1–4661
please contact your bookseller or Springer

Vol. 4988: R. Berghammer, B. Möller, G. Struth (Eds.), Relations and Kleene Algebra in Computer Science. X, 397 pages. 2008.

Vol. 4981: M. Egerstedt, B. Mishra Eds.), Hybrid Systems: Computation and Control. XV, 680 pages. 2008.

Vol. 4974: M. Giacobini, A. Brabazon, S. Cagnoni, G.A. Di Caro, R. Drechsler, A. Ekárt, A.I. Esparcia-Alcázar, M. Farooq, A. Fink, J. McCormack, M. O'Neill, J. Romero, F. Rothlauf, G. Squillero, A.Ş. Uyar, S. Yang (Eds.), Applications of Evolutionary Computing. XXV, 701 pages. 2008.

Vol. 4973: E. Marchiori, J.H. Moore (Eds.), Evolutionary Computation, Machine Learning and Data Mining in Bioinformatics. X, 213 pages. 2008.

Vol. 4972: J. van Hemert, C. Cotta (Eds.), Evolutionary Computation in Combinatorial Optimization. XII, 289 pages. 2008.

Vol. 4971: M. O'Neill, L. Vanneschi, S. Gustafson, A.I. Esparcia Alcázar, I. De Falco, A. Della Cioppa, E. Tarantino (Eds.), Genetic Programming. XI, 375 pages. 2008.

Vol. 4963: C.R. Ramakrishnan, J. Rehof (Eds.), Tools and Algorithms for the Construction and Analysis of Systems. XVI, 518 pages. 2008.

Vol. 4962: R. Amadio (Ed.), Foundations of Software Science and Computational Structures. XV, 505 pages. 2008.

Vol. 4961: J.L. Fiadeiro, P. Inverardi (Eds.), Fundamental Approaches to Software Engineering. XIII, 430 pages. 2008.

Vol. 4960: S. Drossopoulou (Ed.), Programming Languages and Systems. XIII, 399 pages. 2008.

Vol. 4959: L. Hendren (Ed.), Compiler Construction. XII, 307 pages. 2008.

Vol. 4957: E.S. Laber, C. Bornstein, L.T. Nogueira, L. Faria (Eds.), LATIN 2008: Theoretical Informatics. XVII, 794 pages. 2008.

Vol. 4943: R. Woods, K. Compton, C. Bouganis, P.C. Diniz (Eds.), Reconfigurable Computing: Architectures, Tools and Applications. XIV, 344 pages. 2008.

Vol. 4934: U. Brinkschulte, T. Ungerer, C. Hochberger, R.G. Spallek (Eds.), Architecture of Computing Systems – ARCS 2008. XI, 287 pages. 2008.

Vol. 4927: C. Kaklamanis, M. Skutella (Eds.), Approximation and Online Algorithms. X, 289 pages. 2008.

Vol. 4921: S.-i. Nakano, M.. S. Rahman (Eds.), WALCOM: Algorithms and Computation. XII, 241 pages. 2008.

Vol. 4919: A. Gelbukh (Ed.), Computational Linguistics and Intelligent Text Processing. XVIII, 666 pages. 2008.

Vol. 4917: P. Stenström, M. Dubois, M. Katevenis, R. Gupta, T. Ungerer (Eds.), High Performance Embedded Architectures and Compilers. XIII, 400 pages. 2008.

Vol. 4915: A. King (Ed.), Logic-Based Program Synthesis and Transformation. X, 219 pages. 2008.

Vol. 4912: G. Barthe, C. Fournet (Eds.), Trustworthy Global Computing. XI, 401 pages. 2008.

Vol. 4910: V. Geffert, J. Karhumäki, A. Bertoni, B. Preneel, P. Návrat, M. Bieliková (Eds.), SOFSEM 2008: Theory and Practice of Computer Science. XV, 792 pages. 2008.

Vol. 4905: F. Logozzo, D.A. Peled, L.D. Zuck (Eds.), Verification, Model Checking, and Abstract Interpretation. X, 325 pages. 2008.

Vol. 4904: S. Rao, M. Chatterjee, P. Jayanti, C.S.R. Murthy, S.K. Saha (Eds.), Distributed Computing and Networking. XVIII, 588 pages. 2007.

Vol. 4878: E. Tovar, P. Tsigas, H. Fouchal (Eds.), Principles of Distributed Systems. XIII, 457 pages. 2007.

Vol. 4875: S.-H. Hong, T. Nishizeki, W. Quan (Eds.), Graph Drawing. XIII, 402 pages. 2008.

Vol. 4873: S. Aluru, M. Parashar, R. Badrinath, V.K. Prasanna (Eds.), High Performance Computing – HiPC 2007. XXIV, 663 pages. 2007.

Vol. 4863: A. Bonato, F.R.K. Chung (Eds.), Algorithms and Models for the Web-Graph. X, 217 pages. 2007.

Vol. 4860: G. Eleftherakis, P. Kefalas, G. Păun, G. Rozenberg, A. Salomaa (Eds.), Membrane Computing. IX, 453 pages. 2007.

Vol. 4855: V. Arvind, S. Prasad (Eds.), FSTTCS 2007: Foundations of Software Technology and Theoretical Computer Science. XIV, 558 pages. 2007.

Vol. 4854: L. Bougé, M. Forsell, J.L. Träff, A. Streit, W. Ziegler, M. Alexander, S. Childs (Eds.), Euro-Par 2007 Workshops: Parallel Processing. XVII, 236 pages. 2008.

Vol. 4851: S. Boztaş, H.-F.(F.) Lu (Eds.), Applied Algebra, Algebraic Algorithms and Error-Correcting Codes. XII, 368 pages. 2007.

Vol. 4848: M.H. Garzon, H. Yan (Eds.), DNA Computing. XI, 292 pages. 2008.

Vol. 4847: M. Xu, Y. Zhan, J. Cao, Y. Liu (Eds.), Advanced Parallel Processing Technologies. XIX, 767 pages. 2007.

Vol. 4846: I. Cervesato (Ed.), Advances in Computer Science – ASIAN 2007. XI, 313 pages. 2007.

Vol. 4838: T. Masuzawa, S. Tixeuil (Eds.), Stabilization, Safety, and Security of Distributed Systems. XIII, 409 pages. 2007.

Vol. 4835: T. Tokuyama (Ed.), Algorithms and Computation. XVII, 929 pages. 2007.

Vol. 4818: I. Lirkov, S. Margenov, J. Waśniewski (Eds.), Large-Scale Scientific Computing. XIV, 755 pages. 2008.

Vol. 4800: A. Avron, N. Dershowitz, A. Rabinovich (Eds.), Pillars of Computer Science. XXI, 683 pages. 2008.

Vol. 4783: J. Holub, J. Žďárek (Eds.), Implementation and Application of Automata. XIII, 324 pages. 2007.

Vol. 4782: R. Perrott, B.M. Chapman, J. Subhlok, R.F. de Mello, L.T. Yang (Eds.), High Performance Computing and Communications. XIX, 823 pages. 2007.

Vol. 4771: T. Bartz-Beielstein, M.J. Blesa Aguilera, C. Blum, B. Naujoks, A. Roli, G. Rudolph, M. Sampels (Eds.), Hybrid Metaheuristics. X, 202 pages. 2007.

Vol. 4770: V.G. Ganzha, E.W. Mayr, E.V. Vorozhtsov (Eds.), Computer Algebra in Scientific Computing. XIII, 460 pages. 2007.

Vol. 4769: A. Brandstädt, D. Kratsch, H. Müller (Eds.), Graph-Theoretic Concepts in Computer Science. XIII, 341 pages. 2007.

Vol. 4763: J.-F. Raskin, P.S. Thiagarajan (Eds.), Formal Modeling and Analysis of Timed Systems. X, 369 pages. 2007.

Vol. 4759: J. Labarta, K. Joe, T. Sato (Eds.), High-Performance Computing. XV, 524 pages. 2008.

Vol. 4746: A. Bondavalli, F. Brasileiro, S. Rajsbaum (Eds.), Dependable Computing. XV, 239 pages. 2007.

Vol. 4743: P. Thulasiraman, X. He, T.L. Xu, M.K. Denko, R.K. Thulasiram, L.T. Yang (Eds.), Frontiers of High Performance Computing and Networking ISPA 2007 Workshops. XXIX, 536 pages. 2007.

Vol. 4742: I. Stojmenovic, R.K. Thulasiram, L.T. Yang, W. Jia, M. Guo, R.F. de Mello (Eds.), Parallel and Distributed Processing and Applications. XX, 995 pages. 2007.

Vol. 4739: R. Moreno Díaz, F. Pichler, A. Quesada Arencibia (Eds.), Computer Aided Systems Theory – EUROCAST 2007. XIX, 1233 pages. 2007.

Vol. 4736: S. Winter, M. Duckham, L. Kulik, B. Kuipers (Eds.), Spatial Information Theory. XV, 455 pages. 2007.

Vol. 4732: K. Schneider, J. Brandt (Eds.), Theorem Proving in Higher Order Logics. IX, 401 pages. 2007.

Vol. 4731: A. Pelc (Ed.), Distributed Computing. XVI, 510 pages. 2007.

Vol. 4728: S. Bozapalidis, G. Rahonis (Eds.), Algebraic Informatics. VIII, 291 pages. 2007.

Vol. 4726: N. Ziviani, R. Baeza-Yates (Eds.), String Processing and Information Retrieval. XII, 311 pages. 2007.

Vol. 4719: R. Backhouse, J. Gibbons, R. Hinze, J. Jeuring (Eds.), Datatype-Generic Programming. XI, 369 pages. 2007.

Vol. 4711: C.B. Jones, Z. Liu, J. Woodcock (Eds.), Theoretical Aspects of Computing – ICTAC 2007. XI, 483 pages. 2007.

Vol. 4710: C.W. George, Z. Liu, J. Woodcock (Eds.), Domain Modeling and the Duration Calculus. XI, 237 pages. 2007.

Vol. 4708: L. Kučera, A. Kučera (Eds.), Mathematical Foundations of Computer Science 2007. XVIII, 764 pages. 2007.

Vol. 4707: O. Gervasi, M.L. Gavrilova (Eds.), Computational Science and Its Applications – ICCSA 2007, Part III. XXIV, 1205 pages. 2007.

Vol. 4706: O. Gervasi, M.L. Gavrilova (Eds.), Computational Science and Its Applications – ICCSA 2007, Part II. XXIII, 1129 pages. 2007.

Vol. 4705: O. Gervasi, M.L. Gavrilova (Eds.), Computational Science and Its Applications – ICCSA 2007, Part I. XLIV, 1169 pages. 2007.

Vol. 4703: L. Caires, V.T. Vasconcelos (Eds.), CONCUR 2007 – Concurrency Theory. XIII, 507 pages. 2007.

Vol. 4700: C.B. Jones, Z. Liu, J. Woodcock (Eds.), Formal Methods and Hybrid Real-Time Systems. XVI, 539 pages. 2007.

Vol. 4699: B. Kågström, E. Elmroth, J. Dongarra, J. Waśniewski (Eds.), Applied Parallel Computing. XXIX, 1192 pages. 2007.

Vol. 4698: L. Arge, M. Hoffmann, E. Welzl (Eds.), Algorithms – ESA 2007. XV, 769 pages. 2007.

Vol. 4697: L. Choi, Y. Paek, S. Cho (Eds.), Advances in Computer Systems Architecture. XIII, 400 pages. 2007.

Vol. 4688: K. Li, M. Fei, G.W. Irwin, S. Ma (Eds.), Bio-Inspired Computational Intelligence and Applications. XIX, 805 pages. 2007.

Vol. 4684: L. Kang, Y. Liu, S. Zeng (Eds.), Evolvable Systems: From Biology to Hardware. XIV, 446 pages. 2007.

Vol. 4683: L. Kang, Y. Liu, S. Zeng (Eds.), Advances in Computation and Intelligence. XVII, 663 pages. 2007.

Vol. 4681: D.-S. Huang, L. Heutte, M. Loog (Eds.), Advanced Intelligent Computing Theories and Applications. XXVI, 1379 pages. 2007.

Vol. 4672: K. Li, C. Jesshope, H. Jin, J.-L. Gaudiot (Eds.), Network and Parallel Computing. XVIII, 558 pages. 2007.

Vol. 4671: V.E. Malyshkin (Ed.), Parallel Computing Technologies. XIV, 635 pages. 2007.

Vol. 4669: J.M. de Sá, L.A. Alexandre, W. Duch, D.P. Mandic (Eds.), Artificial Neural Networks – ICANN 2007, Part II. XXXI, 990 pages. 2007.

Vol. 4668: J.M. de Sá, L.A. Alexandre, W. Duch, D.P. Mandic (Eds.), Artificial Neural Networks – ICANN 2007, Part I. XXXI, 978 pages. 2007.

Vol. 4666: M.E. Davies, C.J. James, S.A. Abdallah, M.D. Plumbley (Eds.), Independent Component Analysis and Signal Separation. XIX, 847 pages. 2007.

Vol. 4665: J. Hromkovič, R. Královič, M. Nunkesser, P. Widmayer (Eds.), Stochastic Algorithms: Foundations and Applications. X, 167 pages. 2007.

Vol. 4664: J. Durand-Lose, M. Margenstern (Eds.), Machines, Computations, and Universality. X, 325 pages. 2007.